Pro Oracle Database 10*g* RAC on Linux

Installation, Administration, and Performance

Julian Dyke and Steve Shaw

Apress®

Pro Oracle Database 10*g* RAC on Linux: Installation, Administration, and Performance

Copyright © 2006 by Julian Dyke and Steve Shaw

Softcover reprint of the hardcover 1st edition 2006

ISBN-13 (pbk): 978-1-4842-2089-4
ISBN 978-1-4302-0214-1 (eBook)
DOI 10.1007/978-1-4302-0214-1

Lead Editors: Matthew Moodie, Tony Davis
Technical Reviewers: Kevin Closson, Wallis R. Pereira, Brett A. Collingwood
Editorial Board: Steve Anglin, Ewan Buckingham, Gary Cornell, Jason Gilmore, Jonathan Gennick,
    Jonathan Hassell, James Huddleston, Chris Mills, Matthew Moodie, Dominic Shakeshaft, Jim Sumser,
    Keir Thomas, Matt Wade
Project Managers: Elizabeth Seymour, Beckie Brand
Copy Edit Manager: Nicole LeClerc
Copy Editors: Heather Lang, Nicole LeClerc, Jennifer Whipple
Assistant Production Director: Kari Brooks-Copony
Production Editor: Kelly Winquist
Compositor: Kinetic Publishing Services, LLC
Proofreaders: Lori Bring, Linda Seifert
Indexer: Broccoli Information Management
Artist: Kinetic Publishing Services, LLC
Cover Designer: Kurt Krames
Manufacturing Director: Tom Debolski

For information on translations, please contact Apress directly at 2560 Ninth Street, Suite 219, Berkeley, CA 94710. Phone 510-549-5930, fax 510-549-5939, e-mail info@apress.com, or visit http://www.apress.com.

The source code for this book is available to readers at http://www.apress.com in the Source Code section.

Contents at a Glance

About the Authors xxi

About the Technical Reviewers xxii

Acknowledgments xxiii

Introduction. xxv

CHAPTER 1	Introduction to RAC 1
CHAPTER 2	Introduction to Linux 21
CHAPTER 3	RAC Concepts 31
CHAPTER 4	RAC Design. 59
CHAPTER 5	Benchmarking Concepts 83
CHAPTER 6	Hardware 99
CHAPTER 7	Storage 125
CHAPTER 8	Oracle Cluster File System (OCFS). 171
CHAPTER 9	Automatic Storage Management (ASM). 201
CHAPTER 10	Installing Linux 235
CHAPTER 11	Configuring and Verifying Linux 259
CHAPTER 12	Installing and Configuring Oracle Software 301
CHAPTER 13	Creating and Configuring Databases 327
CHAPTER 14	Installing and Configuring Enterprise Manager 363
CHAPTER 15	Linux Administration 385
CHAPTER 16	Oracle Clusterware. 401
CHAPTER 17	Application Development 425
CHAPTER 18	Using Administrative Tools. 465
CHAPTER 19	Workload Management. 493
CHAPTER 20	Adding and Deleting Nodes and Instances 521
CHAPTER 21	Trace and Diagnostics. 553
CHAPTER 22	RAC Internals 575
CHAPTER 23	Benchmarking Tools: Hammerora and Swingbench. 607

CHAPTER 24   Performance Monitoring. 649

CHAPTER 25   Backup and Recovery 683

CHAPTER 26   Disaster Recovery 717

APPENDIX   Third-Party Clustering Solutions 743

INDEX 753

Contents

About the Authors xxi

About the Technical Reviewers xxii

Acknowledgments xxiii

Introduction xxv

CHAPTER 1   Introduction to RAC 1

What Is Real Application Clusters? 1

Clustered Database Concepts 2

    Cluster Terminology 2

    High Availability 4

    Scalability 5

    Disaster Recovery 7

Why Deploy RAC? 7

    Cost of Ownership Advantages and Benefits 8

    High Availability Advantages and Disadvantages 10

    Scalability Advantages and Disadvantages 12

    Manageability Advantages and Disadvantages 14

    Transparency Advantages and Disadvantages 15

Alternatives to RAC 15

    Single Instance Databases 16

    Data Guard 16

    Third-Party Clustering Solutions 16

Differences Between Single-Instance and RAC Databases 16

Differences Between Oracle 9*i* and Oracle 10*g* 17

History of Real Application Clusters 19

Summary 20

CHAPTER 2   Introduction to Linux 21

History of Linux 21

    UNIX 21

    Free Software 22

    Linux 23

    Open Source 24

Oracle, Open Source, and Linux 25
    Unbreakable Linux 25
    Red Hat Enterprise Linux 26
    SUSE Linux Enterprise Server 27
    Asianux 29
Summary 29

■CHAPTER 3   **RAC Concepts** 31

Oracle Clusterware 31
    Oracle Cluster Registry 32
    Voting Disk 33
Node Applications 33
    Listener 33
    Oracle Notification Service (ONS) 33
    Virtual IP (VIP) 34
    Global Services Daemon (GSD) 34
Database Structure 34
    Datafiles 34
    Control Files 35
    Online Redo Log Files 35
    Undo Tablespaces 36
    Archived Logs 36
    Recovery Area 36
Instances 36
    Global Cache Service (GCS) 37
    Global Enqueue Service (GES) 37
Parameters 37
    Initialization Parameter File (PFILE) 38
    Server Parameter File (SPFILE) 39
    Global Parameters 40
    Instance-Specific Parameters 40
    RAC-Specific Parameters 40
Background Processes 42
    RDBMS Instance Background Processes 42
    ASM Instance Background Processes 47
Workload Management 48
    Services 48
    Connection Load Balancing 49
    Transparent Application Failover (TAF) 49
Administration 50
    Enterprise Manager 50
    Server Control Utility (SRVCTL) 51
    SQL*Plus 51
    CRSCTL 51

Monitoring. 51

　　Operating System Utilities. 51

　　Enterprise Manager 52

　　Automatic Workload Repository (AWR) 52

　　Automatic Database Diagnostic Monitor (ADDM). 52

　　Active Session History (ASH). 52

　　Dynamic Performance Views 52

　　Statistics 53

Tools and Utilities 53

　　Cluster Verification Utility 53

　　Oracle Universal Installer (OUI) 53

　　Virtual IP Configuration Assistant (VIPCA) 54

　　Database Creation Assistant (DBCA) 54

　　Database Upgrade Assistant (DBUA) 54

　　Network Configuration Assistant (NETCA) 54

　　Oracle Interface Configuration Tool (OIFCFG) 54

　　OCR Configuration Tool (OCRCONFIG) 55

Backup and Recovery 55

　　Recovery Manager (RMAN). 55

　　Storage-Based Backup and Recovery 55

Disaster Recovery 55

　　Data Guard 56

　　Stretch Clusters 57

　　Hardware Disaster Recovery Solutions 57

Summary 57

CHAPTER 4   **RAC Design** 59

Business Requirements. 59

　　Technical Requirements 59

　　Business Constraints. 60

　　Upgrade Policy 61

Architecture 62

　　Development and Test Systems 62

　　Disaster Recovery 62

　　Stretch Clusters 63

　　Reporting Systems. 64

　　Spare Servers. 65

Storage Requirements. 65

　　ASM and Cluster File Systems 65

　　Shared Oracle Homes vs. Local Oracle Homes. 66

　　Backup and Recovery 66

　　Archived Redo Logs. 68

Hardware Requirements 70

Application Design 70
    Bind Variables 70
    Sequences 70
Database Design 72
    Cursor Sharing 72
    Optimizer Statistics 72
    Histograms 73
    Dynamic Sampling 73
    System Statistics 73
    Locally Managed Tablespaces 74
    Automatic Segment Space Management (ASSM) 74
    Reverse Key Indexes 75
    Partitioning 76
Summary 81

■CHAPTER 5   **Benchmarking Concepts** 83

Load Testing and Benchmarks 83
TPC Benchmarks 86
    The TPC-C Benchmark 86
    The TPC-H Benchmark 91
Summary 98

■CHAPTER 6   **Hardware** 99

Oracle Availability 100
Server Architecture 101
    Processors 101
    Memory 112
    Additional Platform Features 115
Network and Private Interconnect 117
    Network I/O 118
    Private Interconnect Selection 119
    Fully Redundant Ethernet Interconnects 121
Summary 124

■CHAPTER 7   **Storage** 125

RAC I/O Characteristics 125
    Read Activity 125
    Write Activity 126
    Forced Reads and Writes 128
    Asynchronous I/O 128
    Direct I/O 129

Storage Fundamentals 130
    Disk Drive Performance 130
    RAID.. 131
    RAID 0 Striping... 131
    RAID 1 Mirroring 132
    RAID 10 Striped Mirrors 133
    RAID 0+1 Mirrored Stripes 133
    RAID 5... 134
    Storage Cache 135
    RAID Summary... 136
    Intelligent Storage 136
Storage Protocols for Linux....................................... 138
    SCSI... 139
    Fibre Channel 140
    iSCSI 141
    S-ATA.. 142
    Using Block-Based Storage 143
    Linux I/O Scheduling 143
    NAS 144
    SAN and NAS Compared....................................... 144
SAN Storage Example 146
    PowerPath 147
    HBA and Driver Configuration............................... 149
    Fibre Channel Switch Configuration......................... 151
    EMC CLARiiON Configuration 152
NFS and iSCSI Storage Example 158
    NetApp Filer RAID Configurations........................... 158
    Aggregates and Volumes 159
    NFS 160
    Snapshot Backup and Recovery............................... 164
    iSCSI 166
Summary 170

CHAPTER 8   Oracle Cluster File System (OCFS) 171

Cluster File Systems and OCFS 171
OCFS Version 1.. 172
    OCFS Design Considerations 173
    Installation and Configuration............................. 175
    Tools and Utilities.. 179
    Debugging and Tracing OCFS................................. 186
    Operating System Utilities................................. 188

OCFS Version 2 (OCFS2) 188
    Installation and Configuration 188
    Tools and Utilities 197
Summary 200

■CHAPTER 9   **Automatic Storage Management (ASM)** 201

Introducing ASM 201
ASM Installation 202
    configure 203
    start 204
    stop 204
    status 204
    createdisk 205
    scandisks 205
    listdisks 205
    querydisk 205
    deletedisk 205
ASM Instance Configuration 206
    Adding an ASM Instance Using DBCA 206
    Adding an ASM Instance Manually 210
    Deleting an ASM Instance Using DBCA 211
    Deleting an ASM Instance Manually 211
    Re-Creating the ASM Instance 212
    Using Files Instead of Devices 212
ASM Components 212
    ASM Instance 213
    ASM Files 217
ASM Administration 220
    ASM Administration Using DBCA 221
    ASM Administration Using SQL*Plus 221
    ASM Administration Using SRVCTL 221
    ASM Administration Using Enterprise Manager 222
    ASM Administration Using FTP 223
    ASM Administration Using ASMCMD 224
Monitoring ASM 231
    Dynamic Performance Views 231
    Fixed Views 231
Summary 233

■CHAPTER 10   **Installing Linux** 235

Linux Software Selection 235
Hardware Requirements 236
Networking Requirements 236

Installing Red Hat Enterprise Linux 4 AS 237
    Starting the Installation 237
    Installation Media Check 238
    Anaconda Installation 238
    Language Selection 238
    Keyboard Configuration 238
    Upgrade Examine 238
    Disk Partitioning 239
    Boot Loader Configuration 243
    Network Configuration 243
    Firewall Configuration 244
    Additional Language Support 244
    Time Zone Selection 244
    Root Password Configuration 245
    Package Installation Defaults 245
    Package Group Selection 245
    Start Installation 247
    Installing Packages 247
    Installation Complete 247
    Welcome 247
    License Agreement 247
    Date and Time 248
    Display 248
    Red Hat Login 249
    Why Register? 249
    System User 249
    Additional CDs 249
    Finish Setup 249
    Manual Package Installation 249
Installing SUSE Linux Enterprise Server 250
    Starting the Installation 250
    License Agreement 251
    Select Your Language 251
    Previous Installation 251
    Installation Settings 251
    Suggested Partitioning 251
    Preparing Hard Disk 251
    Expert Partitioner 253
    Software Selection 253
    Time Zone 255
    Warning 256
    Root Password 256
    Network Configuration 256
    Test Internet Connection 257

Service Configuration 257
User Authentication Method 257
Add a New Local User 257
Release Notes 258
Summary 258

▓CHAPTER 11 **Configuring and Verifying Linux** 259

Operating System and RPM Package Checks. 259
Hostnames and Name Resolution 260
NTP 261
Hangcheck-Timer. 263
Kernel Parameters 264
Shared Memory 265
Semaphores. 268
Network 269
Open Files. 271
Kernel Parameter Example 271
Oracle User Configuration 272
Creating the dba and oinstall Groups. 272
Creating the oracle User 272
Setting the Password for the oracle User 273
Setting Environment Variables 273
Creating the Oracle Software Directories 278
Setting Security Limits 278
Secure Shell Configuration 279
Shared Storage Configuration. 281
Partitioning 281
Preparing the Oracle Clusterware Partitions 285
Channel Bonding 287
Cluster Verification 290
Java Runtime Environment. 291
Syntax. 292
Stage Checks 292
Component Checks 295
Summary 299

▓CHAPTER 12 **Installing and Configuring Oracle Software** 301

Preparing to Install. 301
Installation Media. 302
Oracle Clusterware 303
Preinstallation Tasks 303
Verifying the Configuration 304

Running the Installer 305

Verifying the Oracle Clusterware Installation 314

Oracle Database Software Installation. 315

Verifying the Configuration 315

Running the Installer 317

Troubleshooting 320

Cluster Verification Utility 321

Common Problems 321

Other Information Sources 322

Configuration Files 323

Inventory 323

OCR 324

/etc/inittab 324

Deinstallation 324

Summary 325

CHAPTER 13   Creating and Configuring Databases 327

Using DBCA As a GUI Tool 327

Configuring ASM 329

Creating a Database 332

Deleting a Database 345

Creating a Template 345

Managing Instances 349

Managing Services 349

Using DBCA at the Command Line 350

Creating a Database Using Scripts. 351

Primary node 352

Secondary Nodes 360

Running the Scripts 361

Summary 362

CHAPTER 14   Installing and Configuring Enterprise Manager 363

Manageability Infrastructure 364

Database Control 365

Grid Control 366

Planning 367

Preparation 371

Management Service Installation and Configuration 372

Starting and Stopping the Management Service 380

Management Agent Installation 381

Summary 384

■CHAPTER 15   **Linux Administration** 385

Run Levels 385
Services 387
Terminal Sessions 388
Manual Pages. 388
Bash Shell. 389
            Commands 392
Packages. 393
Kernel Parameters 394
Swap Space and File Systems 395
            Swap Space 395
            General File Systems. 396
            NFS 397
Booting the System 398
            Bootloaders. 398
            Initial Ramdisk Image 399
Log Files, Tracing, and Debugging 399
            Log Files 400
            Tracing 400
            Debugging 400
Summary 400

■CHAPTER 16   **Oracle Clusterware** 401

Oracle Clusterware Components 401
            Cluster Synchronization Services (CSS) 402
            Cluster Ready Services (CRS). 402
            Event Manager (EVM) 402
Oracle Clusterware Files 402
            Oracle Cluster Registry (OCR). 402
            Voting Disk 403
Oracle Clusterware High Availability Framework 403
Oracle Clusterware Installation and Configuration 404
            Virtual Internet Protocol Configuration Assistant (VIPCA). 404
            OIFCFG 407
Administering Oracle Clusterware 408
            CRSCTL. 408
            CRS_STAT 413
            OCRCONFIG 416
            OCRCHECK 421
            OCRDUMP. 422
Administering Voting Disks 422

Oracle Clusterware Logging 423
Summary 423

CHAPTER 17   Application Development 425

RAC-Specific Development Considerations. 425
    Instances and Database Services 425
    Multiple SGAs. 426
    Local and Shared Storage. 427
    Node Affinity. 428
Transparent Application Failover 430
Fast Application Notification 437
    Oracle Notification Service 439
    Server-Side Callouts 441
    Fast Connection Failover. 442
Oracle Clusterware High Availability Framework 446
    Example Application 447
    Implementing the HA Framework. 452
    HA Framework Commands. 454
Summary 463

CHAPTER 18   Using Administrative Tools 465

Using EM. 465
    Starting and Stopping Databases and Instances 467
    Setting Parameters 470
    Performance Options. 471
    Administrative Options 472
    Maintenance Options. 474
Using SRVCTL. 475
    SRVCTL Syntax. 476
    Administering Databases 477
    Administering Instances 480
    Administering Node Applications 483
    Administering the Listener 486
Using SQL*Plus. 487
    Setting the SQL*Plus Prompt 487
    Connecting to a RAC Instance Using SQL*Plus. 487
    Starting an Instance. 488
    Stopping an Instance. 488
    Setting Parameters in an Initialization Parameter File (PFILE). 489
    Setting Parameters in a Server Parameter File (SPFILE) 490
Summary 492

CHAPTER 19   **Workload Management** 493

Workload Distribution 493
    Client-Side Connection Balancing 494
    Server-Side Connection Balancing. 494
Database Services. 497
    Implementing Database Services. 499
    Administering Database Services 501
    Monitoring Services. 511
Summary 519

CHAPTER 20   **Adding and Deleting Nodes and Instances** 521

Running GUI Tools 521
Adding a Node 522
    Plan the Installation 522
    Install and Configure the New Hardware. 523
    Configure the Network 523
    Install the Operating System. 523
    Configure the Storage 524
    Install Oracle Clusterware 525
    Install Oracle Database Software 528
    Configure the Listener. 530
Adding an Instance 535
Deleting an Instance 540
Deleting a Node 544
    Delete ASM Instance 544
    Delete the Listener Process 544
    Delete the Oracle Database Software 547
    Update Inventories on Remaining Hosts 548
    Remove Node-Specific Interface Configuration 548
    Disable Oracle Clusterware Applications. 549
    Delete the Node from the OCR 550
    Delete the Oracle Clusterware Software 550
    Update the Inventories on the Remaining Hosts. 551
    Verify Node Deletion Using CLUVFY 552
Summary 552

CHAPTER 21   **Trace and Diagnostics** 553

Trace File Locations. 553
    Alert Log 553
    Trace Files. 554

DBMS_MONITOR 555

Tracing Applications. 556

Tracing Multitier Applications 557

DBA_ENABLED_TRACES. 558

ORADEBUG 559

LKDEBUG 563

Events 572

Summary 574

CHAPTER 22   **RAC Internals** 575

Global Enqueue Services. 576

Background Processes 576

Resources and Enqueues 576

Lock Types 577

Library Cache Locks 577

Row Cache Locks 580

Tracing GES Activity. 581

Optimizing Global Enqueues. 581

Global Cache Services. 581

Global Resource Directory (GRD) 582

Cache Coherency. 584

Cache Fusion 584

Cache Fusion Examples 586

Disk Writes 599

System Change Numbers (SCNs). 603

Optimizing the Global Cache. 604

Instance Recovery 604

Summary 605

CHAPTER 23   **Benchmarking Tools: Hammerora and Swingbench** 607

Hammerora. 607

Installation 608

Bespoke Application Load Tests. 610

TPC-C Simulation. 622

Swingbench 633

Installation and Configuration. 633

Calling Circle 635

Developing Swingbench Benchmarks. 644

Summary 647

▉CHAPTER 24 **Performance Monitoring** 649

Oracle Performance Monitoring 649
   Performance Monitoring with Enterprise Manager 649
   AWR Reports 652
   Active Session History 660
   Automatic Database Diagnostic Monitor 661
   Performance Monitoring Using SQL*Plus 662
   GV$ Views 663
   System Statistics 663
   Segment Statistics 663
   Global Cache Services 664
   Global Enqueue Service 669
   Library Cache 669
   Dictionary Cache 670
   Lock Conversions 671
Linux Performance Monitoring 672
   ps 672
   free 673
   top 675
   vmstat 676
Summary 681

▉CHAPTER 25 **Backup and Recovery** 683

Backup and Recovery Strategy 683
Recovery Manager (RMAN) 685
   RMAN Utility 686
   RMAN Repository 689
   Backup Sets 692
   Tags 693
   Parameters 693
   Flashback Recovery Area 698
   Performing Backups 700
   Image Copies 703
   Incremental Backups 705
   Block Change Tracking 706
   Incrementally Updated Backups 707
   Housekeeping 707
   Performing a Restore 710
   Performing Recovery 712
RAC Considerations 714
   Archived Redo Logs 715
Summary 716

■CHAPTER 26   **Disaster Recovery** 717

Oracle Data Guard 718
Data Protection Modes 719
   Maximum Performance Mode 719
   Maximum Availability Mode 719
   Maximum Protection Mode 719
   Setting the Data Protection Mode 720
Redo Transport Services 720
   ARCn Background Process 721
   LGWR Background Process 721
   Asynchronous Network I/O (ASYNC) 721
   Synchronous Network I/O (SYNC) 722
Standby Redo Logs 722
   Log Apply Services 723
Role Management 723
   Read-Only Mode 723
   Switchover 723
   Failover 724
RAC and Physical Standby 724
RMAN 725
NOLOGGING Attribute 725
Archive Log Gaps 726
Initialization Parameters 726
   LOG_ARCHIVE_DEST_n 726
   LOG_ARCHIVE_DEST_STATE_n 727
   LOG_ARCHIVE_START 727
   LOG_ARCHIVE_FORMAT 727
   DB_UNIQUE_NAME 728
   LOG_ARCHIVE_CONFIG 728
   REMOTE_ARCHIVE_ENABLE 728
   STANDBY_ARCHIVE_DEST 728
   STANDBY_FILE_MANAGEMENT 729
   FAL_CLIENT 729
   FAL_SERVER 729
Creating a Physical Standby Database 729
   Enable Archiving on the Primary Database 730
   Create Password Files on Primary Nodes 731
   Force Logging on the Primary Database 732
   Back Up the Primary Database 732
   Set Parameters on the Primary Database 733
   Create Directories on Standby Nodes 733
   Create Password Files on Standby Nodes 734
   Create Server Parameter File for Standby Database 734

Create Initialization Parameter Files on Standby Nodes 734

Copy the RMAN Backup from Primary to Standby 735

Update /etc/oratab on Standby Nodes. 735

Add the Standby Database to the OCR 735

Update the Listener Configuration Files on Standby Nodes 735

Update Oracle Net Configuration Files on All Nodes. 736

Set Parameters on the Standby Database. 737

Create Standby Database 737

Enable Managed Recovery on the Standby Database 738

Check the Standby Configuration. 738

Verify Log Transportation 738

Role Management 739

Read-Only Mode 739

Switchover 739

Failover 740

Summary 741

▮APPENDIX **Third-Party Clustering Solutions** 743

Clusterware 743

Third-Party Certification Programs. 745

PolyServe Matrix Server 745

Central Cluster Management Console. 747

SAN Management Layer 747

Sophisticated Fencing. 747

Dynamic Volume Manager 748

CFS 748

Matrix Server ODM 748

Summary 751

▮INDEX 753

About the Authors

 **JULIAN DYKE** is an independent consultant specializing in Oracle Database technology. He has over 20 years of database experience, including more than 15 years as an Oracle DBA, developer, and consultant. He is chair of the UK Oracle User Group Real Application Clusters Special Interest Group (UKOUG RAC SIG) and a member of the Oak Table Network. He regularly presents at conferences, seminars, and user-group meetings in the UK, Europe, and the US. He also maintains www.juliandyke.com, which specializes in Oracle diagnostics, optimization, and internals. He is an Oracle Certified Professional and holds a bachelor of science degree in computation from the University of Manchester Institute of Science and Technology (UMIST), UK.

 **STEVE SHAW** is the lead Oracle technologist for Intel Corporation in EMEA (Europe, the Middle East, and Africa). Steve has over 12 years of commercial IT experience with 8 years dedicated to working with the Oracle Database, including a period of time with Oracle Corporation. Steve is the author of Hammerora, the open source Oracle load-test tool, and an expert on Oracle benchmarks and performance. Steve has contributed articles to many Oracle publications and web sites and presents regularly at Oracle seminars, conferences, and special-interest group meetings. He is an Oracle Certified Professional and holds a master of science degree in computing from the University of Bradford, UK.

About the Technical Reviewers

KEVIN CLOSSON is a chief software architect at PolyServe, Inc. His 18-year career has included engineering, technical marketing, and support positions specializing in Oracle and clustered platforms. Kevin's positions within PolyServe, IBM, Sequent, and Veritas focused on the scalability and availability of the Oracle server on high-end SMP and clustered systems. Kevin holds patents for SMP locking algorithms and database caching methods. He is a frequent speaker at Oracle user groups and a member of the Oracle Oak Table Network. In addition to book collaborations, Kevin's written work has appeared in *Oracle Magazine, Oracle Internals Magazine*, IBM Redbooks, and *SELECT*.

In a previous life, **WALLY PEREIRA** was a hippie, a surfer, and a mountaineer. During this period, he graduated from University Without Walls in Berkeley, California (one of those experimental colleges of the late 1960s), became a high school teacher, and obtained a master of arts degree in education and an master of business administration degree from California State University, Dominguez Hills. He decided to get serious and started working on microcomputers in 1979 and hasn't looked back. He began working with Oracle in 1988 and developed his own expertise though working with some of the best Oracle experts, including the authors of this book and his fellow reviewers.

Wally credits his sanity to his lovely wife Lois and is immensely proud of his four children: Layla, Irena, Ben, and Sam. He still loves the surf and the mountains. When Wally isn't out walking the seaside bluffs near his home or refereeing teenage soccer games, he is a senior consultant with Intel Solution Services.

BRETT A. COLLINGWOOD has been using Oracle products for over 18 years. Brett started his IT career as an application developer using Oracle version 5. He has used Oracle on almost every general-purpose computer and operating system, including PCs, proprietary midrange systems, large SMPs, open systems, and mainframes. Along the way, Brett became frustrated with the perceived problems that his co-workers and customers were having with their databases. In many situations, problems were caused by a poorly architected system, botched implementation, or ignored warning signs presented by the database, operating system, or peripheral devices.

Since that time, Brett has focused his efforts on architecting databases, operating systems, and applications in a manner where expectations are correctly set while at the same time making an efficient use of the computer platform. Brett can usually be found implementing large clustered systems and complex applications, extending the infrastructure, and occasionally reengineering sites that have poorly architected systems, botched implementations, ignored warning signals, and so forth.

Acknowledgments

We would like to thank all of those people who assisted in the writing of this book, including our customers, managers, colleagues, and contacts.

We would like to thank the Apress production team, including our technical editors, Matthew Moodie and Tony Davis; our project managers, Elizabeth Seymour and Beckie Brand; our technical reviewers, Kevin Closson, Wally Pereira, and Brett Collingwood; and our copy editors, Heather Lang, Nicole LeClerc, and Jennifer Whipple.

We would also like to thank Phil Davies, Joel Goodman, Dominic Giles, John Nangle, Dave Storey, Bruce Carter, Phil Newlan, Erik Petersen, Paul Schuster, Paul Nothard, Stuart Pass, Fiona Godley, Jeff Browning, and Chris Gale for their assistance with the research and development of this book.

Julian Dyke and Steve Shaw

I would like to thank a few people who have helped me throughout my career, contributing either directly or indirectly to this book.

Most important, thank you to my wife, Isabel, and my children, Emma and Roberto, for their patience, tolerance, and support over the past 18 months.

I would also like to thank Steve Adams, James Anthony, Christian Antognini, Mike Bedford, Stephan Bendall, Lee Cashmore, Nigel Chapman, Carel-Jan Engel, Dave Ensor, Michael Erwin, Lex de Haan, Justin Hudd, Jeff Hunter, Howard Jones, Anjo Kolk, David Kurtz, Tom Kyte, Jonathan Lewis, Niall Litchfield, Richard Miller, Cary Millsap, Michael Möller, Dave Moore, James Morle, Graham Murray, Mogens Nørgaard, Tanel Põder, Rob Philpotts, David Phizacklea, Jože Senegačnik, John Skarin, Kevin Smith, Billy Taylor, Clive Taylor, Raies Uddin, Murali Vallath, Tim Waterton, and Plamen Zyumbyulev.

Finally, thank you to members of the Oak Table Network and the UKOUG RAC SIG for your assistance and inspiration over the years.

Julian Dyke

Above all, I owe an immeasurable debt of gratitude to my wife, Angela, my daughter, Evey, and my son, Lucas, for their boundless enthusiasm, motivation, and support for my writing of this book.

I would also like to thank Peter MacNamara, Neil Blecherman, Keith Shea, Alastair McKeeman, Eias Daka, Nigel Wayman, and Martinus JC Marx.

Finally, I would like to thank Todd Helfter, Jeff Hobbs, Zoran Vasiljevic, Donal Fellows, John LoVerso, Csaba Nemethi, Steve Cassidy, Brett Bercich, Bob Vance, Andy Duncan, Geoff Ingram, and everyone who has contributed time and skills to the development of Hammerora and Oracle on open source and Linux.

Steve Shaw

Introduction

This book is about deploying Oracle Real Application Clusters (RAC) databases on the Linux operating system. RAC enables multiple Oracle instances running on separate servers to access a single database located on shared storage. RAC technology ensures that all instances can physically modify any block in the database while maintaining a single logical copy of the data.

RAC was introduced as part of Oracle 9*i* in 2001 and has been improved significantly in each subsequent major release. In Oracle 10*g* Release 2, RAC has become a highly stable production environment on all platforms, particularly on Linux.

Linux has been available as an open source operating system for many years. However, robust, fully supported, enterprise-level versions from Red Hat and Novell SUSE have only been available since around 2001. Linux offers almost all of the features included in proprietary UNIX offerings; it also offers additional functionality in many areas.

The number of Oracle customers implementing RAC databases has grown exponentially over the last couple of years. The cost of deploying RAC has decreased because of its use of industry-standard hardware.

RAC has four main objectives:

- Increased availability
- Increased scalability
- Improved manageability
- Reduced total cost of ownership

Achieving at least one of the aforementioned objectives is essential for a successful Oracle RAC deployment, and a few customers may achieve two or even three. It is very rare to encounter a customer who achieves all four goals, as to some extent, the objectives conflict with each other. In this book, we describe how to achieve each objective and we outline some of the pitfalls.

Oracle RAC may not be the optimum choice as a high-availability solution for all users. While we have met hundreds of Oracle customers who have successfully deployed Oracle RAC, we also know a handful for whom RAC has not been appropriate. Before you design an Oracle RAC architecture, you should investigate other options that might be available, including Oracle features such as Data Guard and Streams, and third-party solutions such as active/passive clusters, third-party cluster file systems, and SAN-level replication. Any high-availability solution should be considered within the context of your business needs, not the sales targets of your Oracle account manager.

Oracle documentation has greatly improved over the last few releases. Taken together with MetaLink web site notes and other information available on the Internet, there is plenty of information in the public domain for new Oracle RAC users. We have tried to consolidate as much information as possible into this book. Where we describe procedures such as installation, configuration, and adding and deleting nodes, we illustrate these with screenshots when possible to help you visualize the required steps.

We also venture into many areas that are not always covered by Oracle RAC books, including hardware and storage configuration, Enterprise Manager Grid Control, backup and recovery using RMAN, and disaster recovery using Data Guard. We also include a chapter on application development describing some of the latest RAC technologies.

Coverage and Audience

The book is intended for an audience of DBAs, developers, managers, and consultants—in short, anybody concerned with the installation, configuration, administration, or tuning of RAC databases on the Linux operating system. A basic knowledge of Linux or a background in other Unix variants would be useful but is not essential.

We concentrate on the two main Linux platforms on which the Oracle Database 10g RAC option is supported, namely Red Hat Enterprise Linux (http://www.redhat.com) and SUSE Linux Enterprise Server (http://www.novell.com). We cover both Oracle 10g Release 1 and Release 2 running on Red Hat 4 and SUSE 9. However, some material does cover earlier releases of both Oracle RAC and the Linux operating system.

Of course, other high-availability products and solutions are available. One such product is PolyServe Matrix Server, about which one of our technical reviewers, Kevin Closson, has written an appendix. We hope this appendix will give you insight into the PolyServe solution and demonstrate that in some cases third-party high-availability architectures might address your business needs more appropriately.

Standards and Conventions

We adopt a number of standards and conventions throughout this book. We generally avoid using the Oracle marketing names for releases and versions and use the numeric version numbers instead. The major releases discussed in this book are listed in Table 1.

Table 1. *Oracle Version Numbers*

Version Name	Version Number
Oracle 9*i* Release 1	Oracle 9.0.1
Oracle 9*i* Release 2	Oracle 9.2.0
Oracle 10*g* Release 1	Oracle 10.1
Oracle 10*g* Release 2	Oracle 10.2

We also use a standard configuration for all the examples in the book. As we are both based in the UK, we invented an environment in which our primary site is in London and our disaster-recovery site is in Reading, which is around 40 miles (60 kilometers) west of the capital. Our primary nodes, therefore, are called london1, london2, london3, and so on, and our standby nodes are called reading1, reading2, and so on.

We also attempt to use standard prompts throughout the book. Most are self-explanatory, but we deviate from our standards on a couple of occasions and abbreviate the prompts to avoid commands overflowing onto subsequent lines. All operating system–level commands in this book are run by the root user, for which we occasionally use the # prompt, or the oracle user, for which we use the $ prompt.

Errata and Additional Material

Despite our best endeavors, there may be errors and omissions throughout the book. While we can only apologize for these in advance, we will try to maintain up-to-date errata on the Apress web site and on our own sites. Errata for this book can be found on the Apress web site (http://www.apress.com). Additional material can be found on our personal web sites, which are http://www.juliandyke.com for Julian Dyke and http://www.sourceora.com for Steve Shaw.

■ ■ ■

## CHAPTER 1

Introduction to RAC

The Oracle Real Application Clusters (RAC) option was first released in a blaze of publicity as part of Oracle 9.0.1 in the summer of 2001. It is considered by many within the Oracle community to be the most significant feature introduced in Oracle 9*i*.

Although RAC has been marketed as an entirely new feature, much of the technology was inherited from Oracle Parallel Server (OPS), which was introduced in Oracle 6.0 and developed steadily over the next decade.

This chapter contains a general introduction to the features of RAC and discusses the potential costs and benefits of deploying a RAC cluster.

What Is Real Application Clusters?

A cluster consists of multiple interconnected servers that appear to end users and applications as if they are one single server. A RAC database allows multiple instances residing on different servers in the cluster to access a common database residing on shared storage. The combined processing power of the multiple servers in the cluster can provide greater throughput and scalability than is available from a single server. A basic RAC setup is depicted in Figure 1-1.

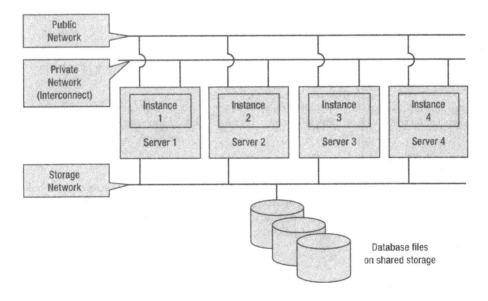

Figure 1-1. *A four-node RAC cluster*

Oracle defines the database as being the structures that reside in files permanently on disk, including the datafiles, the control files, and the online redo logs. In the case of a RAC cluster, the database must be located on shared physical disk storage that all servers in the cluster must be able to access equally. The servers communicate with the shared storage via a storage network.

The instance is defined as the structures that are created in memory within the operating system running on a server, including the Shared Global Area (SGA) and the associated background processes. An instance must be started before a database can be created. All persistent data is stored in the database files and will remain on disk when the instance or the operating system is shut down.

An instance can only mount and open a single database. In a single instance environment, as the name suggests, there is a one-to-one mapping between an instance and a database. A database, however, may be mounted by one or more instances on separate servers. The database may be accessed as long as at least one instance is started and has mounted it.

The servers in the cluster are bound together using cluster management software called Oracle Clusterware, which enables the servers to appear as though they are a single server. Servers in the cluster communicate with each other using a dedicated private network known as the *cluster interconnect*.

In a RAC cluster, each instance can execute transactions concurrently because database access is coordinated to ensure data consistency and integrity. Instances exchange messages with each other across the interconnect to manage the state of individual Oracle data blocks and locks.

Each server is also connected to a public network that allows the cluster to communicate with the outside world, including clients and application servers.

Note In Real Application Clusters terminology, the terms *server* and *node* are used interchangeably.

RAC databases offer a number of advantages over single-instance databases. These include

- **Availability**: In the event of a node failure, other nodes in the cluster can continue to operate and the availability of the database will be unaffected.

- **Scalability**: Multiple nodes allow clustered databases to scale beyond the limits imposed by single-node databases.

- **Manageability**: Multiple legacy databases can be consolidated into a single RAC database reducing management complexity and introducing economies of scale.

- **Cost of Ownership**: RAC can be deployed on industry-standard, nonproprietary hardware, reducing costs of purchase, maintenance, and support.

Many existing applications can be deployed on RAC clusters without modification. The general rule is that if an application scales well on a single-instance database, it should also scale on a RAC database.

Clustered Database Concepts

Before considering why you should deploy RAC we will introduce some of the concepts of clustered databases and the areas to consider in terms of deploying clustered architectures. We will take into account the cluster terminologies in use today and the importance of high availability in cluster configurations. We will also introduce the concepts of achieving scalability in a clustered database environment.

Cluster Terminology

Multiple conflicting terminologies that relate to the database clustering are in use by both hardware and software vendors. Here we will introduce the most common terms in order to clarify the terminology used in Oracle RAC environments.

Active/Active and Active/Passive Cluster Configurations

There are two basic methods of cluster operation: active/passive and active/active.

Active/Passive

An active/passive cluster generally contains two identical nodes. At any time, one of the nodes is active, and the other is passive. Oracle single-instance database software is installed on both nodes, but the database is located on shared storage. During normal operation, the Oracle database instance runs only on the active node. In the event of a failure of the currently active primary system, clustering software will transfer control of the disk subsystem to the secondary system, a process known as *failover*. As part of the failover process, the Oracle instance on the secondary node is started, thereby recovering and resuming the service of the Oracle database. All connections to the instance on the primary system at the time of failure are terminated and must be reestablished with the new instance on the secondary system. On resolution of the issue, the Oracle instance is cleanly shut down on the secondary system, control of the disk subsystem is transferred back to the primary system, and the Oracle instance is started to resume normal operations.

A number of third-party products are available to implement active/passive clustering on Linux. For the Microsoft Windows platform Oracle supports Oracle Fail Safe, which is integrated with Microsoft Cluster Server to implement active/passive functionality. Earlier releases of Oracle RAC also allowed an active/passive configuration. Although this functionality appears to be supported still, it has definitely been deemphasized in recent releases.

Active/Active

An active/active cluster has an identical hardware infrastructure to an active/passive one. However, Oracle instances run concurrently on both servers and access the same database, which is located on shared storage. The instances must communicate with each other to negotiate access to shared data in the database. In the event of a server failure, the remaining server can continue processing the workload and, optionally, failed sessions can be reconnected. The benefit of an active/active cluster over an active/passive cluster is that, during normal processing, the workload can be shared across both servers in the cluster.

Oracle RAC is designed to run in an active/active environment.

Shared-All and Shared-Nothing Cluster Configurations

Depending on the disk configuration, clusters can also be shared-all or shared-nothing.

Shared-Nothing

A *shared-nothing* database cluster is configured as a number of nodes in a cluster where each node has its own private, individual storage that is inaccessible to others in the cluster. The database is vertically partitioned between the nodes; result sets of queries are returned as the unioned result sets from the individual nodes. The loss of a single node results in the inability to access the data managed by the failed node, and therefore, a shared-nothing cluster is often implemented as a number of individual active/passive or active/active clusters to increase availability.

Shared-All

Oracle RAC is a *shared-all* cluster. As you have seen, all of the nodes in the cluster access the same data simultaneously, as the Oracle instances on each node of the cluster mount the same database located on the same set of shared disks.

With RAC, in the event of a node failure, no loss of any portion of the database dataset occurs (although, note that any data held on private storage, such as external tables or archived redo logs, would still be lost unless clustered independently of RAC). The remaining Oracle instances in the cluster recover any incomplete transactions from the failed instance and continue to provide the database service. Sessions connected to the failed instance may be automatically transferred to a surviving instance for some classes of user operations. Sessions terminated at the time of failure may reconnect to another instance. When the cause of failure has been resolved, the failed Oracle instance can be restarted and resume its role in the cluster.

High Availability

Clusters are constructed with a view to eliminating any single point of failure (SPOF) and this is generally achieved by introducing redundant components. There must also be some technology capable of monitoring for component failures and of switching the workload across to another component if necessary. This is failover should, where possible, be transparent to any processes that were executing on the component at the time of failure.

An SPOF describes any component within a system where the failure of that individual component will cause the failure of the entire system. One of the main aims of high availability architecture is to eliminate all possible single points of failure; therefore, an important concept within high availability systems is that of redundancy. Redundant components of a system protect it from failure by acting as a backup in the event of the failure of a primary component. A system has full redundancy if all components are backed up by secondary resources.

Providing redundancy for components such as power supplies is trivial and therefore common in most industry-standard servers. Redundancy can be built into the storage level in many forms, including the mirroring of files and disks and the use of RAID technology to ensure against individual disk failures. Redundancy for components such as system memory is more complex and therefore available in some but not all architectures.

The highest level of complexity is present in the system processor itself, where redundancy is provided by all processors being paired with a second processor and operating in lockstep mode. In *lockstep* mode, two processors execute exactly the same instructions at the same time, and in the event of the failure of one processor, the system will continue to operate uninterrupted.

Linux systems are available in fully redundant configurations; however, the level of complexity of providing redundancy for all components is reflected in the significant additional cost of the entire system.

As discussed previously, a RAC system comprises two or more physical nodes. It is possible for a single node within a RAC cluster to fail without compromising the availability of the cluster as a whole. Therefore, a significant benefit of RAC is the ability to implement a highly available clustered configuration without all of the individual components of the nodes in the cluster being fully redundant. Redundancy is provided at the level of cluster, as opposed to the level of the individual nodes themselves. Consequently, the cost of the server components may be significantly lower than that for fully redundant single-system configurations.

Oracle offers a number of technologies that are associated with making failovers appear seamless to the end user. For example, Transparent Application Failover (TAF) enables an application to fail over connections in the event of node or instance failure. Existing sessions can be automatically reconnected to a different node in the database if their connection fails.

In Oracle 10.1 and above the Oracle Notification Service (ONS) provides an out-of-band messaging service that provides information to interested parties such as listeners and application servers about the availability of each node in the cluster. ONS provides the foundation for other services, such as Fast Application Notification and Fast Connection Failover.

In Oracle 10.2 and above, the Clusterware High Availability Framework allows the Oracle Clusterware software to manage external applications in addition to database instances. In the event of a node failure, the external application can be restarted or failed over to another node in the cluster.

While the main benefits of redundancy are normally regarded as protection from unplanned hardware failures, the existence of redundant nodes also allows individual nodes to be removed from the cluster in order to perform planned hardware or software upgrades and maintenance. It is therefore possible to perform a like-for-like exchange of any server component while the database continues to be available to all other nodes. It is sometimes possible to upgrade individual components without stopping the entire database. This is dependent on the nature of the component, the drivers required for that component, and any operating system, database software, or application software dependencies.

It should be noted that it is never possible to eliminate all single points of failure in an Oracle database environment, whether a single instance or a RAC configuration. A corruption of the data itself can be caused by a number of factors. For example, any of the following might compromise the integrity of the data in the database:

- Hardware errors such as memory or storage errors

- Application software errors or bugs

- Database software errors or bugs

- Human errors

Even though there might be multiple physical, redundant copies of the data operated upon by multiple instances, there can only be one logical copy of the database. Therefore, while redundant hardware may guarantee that data is never physically lost, it cannot guarantee that the same data will not be logically corrupted, either by a failure of a single hardware component, or an errant application or human error. It should therefore be clear that the approach to disaster recovery should be afforded the same level of diligence in a RAC environment as would be required in a single-instance environment.

Scalability

Scalability measures the ability of a system to deliver consistent performance while the workload increases. Scalability is generally calculated by measuring the effect on throughput of increasing the workload.

A successful RAC implementation requires optimal scalability on at least five levels:

- Hardware scalability

- Storage scalability

- Operating system scalability

- Database scalability

- Application scalability

Hardware scalability is determined by key hardware resources such as the server processors and memory and configuration of the cluster interconnect. We discuss the importance of these attributes in Chapter 6.

Storage scalability is dependent on factors such as disk configurations, redundancy, and the performance of the paths between the server and the storage devices. Storage configuration is considered in Chapter 7.

Operating system scalability depends on the ability of the operating system to handle multiple resource requests simultaneously. Configuring the operating system correctly is important to achieving scalability and we detail the installation and configuration of Linux in Chapters 10 and 11.

Database scalability depends on the ability of the database to perform tasks in parallel without causing internal contention. Application scalability requires applications to be designed so that no bottlenecks occur in a system in which every instance is attempting to update the same data most of the time. You will find that database and application scalability is a recurrent theme throughout this book—for example, from RAC design in Chapter 4 to performance tuning in Chapter 24.

There are two basic concepts in scalable processing: scale-up and scale-out.

Scale-Up

If you can achieve greater throughput over a fixed period of time by increasing the amount of parallelism, it is known as *scale-up*. Scale-up is achieved by increasing the amount of hardware resources, such as processors and memory, available within a single system image.

Scale-Out

In a clustered environment it is possible to add hardware resources by adding another node. This is known as *scale-out*.

In some instances, scale-up on existing hardware can be more efficient than scale-out. This is because the overheads associated with maintaining cache coherency and database locks between the different instances divert some of the available resources away from application processing. However, the levels of processing power available in industry-standard servers at two- and four-processor configurations make a scale-out solution with RAC extremely competitive, with the maximum number of nodes in Oracle 10g Release 2 being around 1,023.

It is important to understand that while a correctly configured RAC database is guaranteed to give higher availability than similar hardware in a single-instance configuration, it cannot be guaranteed that the application will also scale.

Clusters are designed so that the workload can be divided between all available servers. The level of scalability of a system reflects the increase in overall throughput that system can achieve with additional hardware.

All systems attempt to achieve linear scalability. For example, if the number of servers is doubled, the number of transactions that can be processed in a specified period will also double. In reality, linear scalability is often difficult to achieve because of the processing overheads of the cluster and often because of limitations within the application.

Alternatively, scalability can be considered in terms of response times. We consider these measurements of scalability in depth in Chapter 5.

Consider an OLTP (online transaction processing) application where response time is the critical metric. If the number of users is doubled and the amount of hardware is doubled there are three possibilities: the response time may increase, decrease, or not change. The most likely outcome is that response time increases. In a RAC system, this is generally caused by an increase in interinstance messaging and the interinstance contention for limited resources. In a very well designed application, the response time may be unchanged, in which case the application is displaying linear scalability where the workload supported grows in proportion with the resources available. In very rare cases, the response time might actually decrease. This might occur if it is possible to partition the data so that each node works with a separate subset. As the number of nodes grows, each node will be able to hold a higher proportion of its own data in the buffer cache, thereby reducing overall response times. Appropriate partitioning of data may also decrease the amount of interinstance messaging traffic.

The scalability achieved by Oracle RAC clusters varies according to the application and database design. While linear scalability can be achieved for some applications, it is more common to see scalability in the 80% to 90% range. This is because of the overhead incurred in maintaining cache coherency and managing locks. Scalability may also be affected by contention for scarce resources and serialization of processing.

Disaster Recovery

RAC is primarily a single-site, high availability solution. Nodes in a RAC cluster generally exist within the same location. Therefore, disaster planning is essential. A number of disaster recovery (DR) solutions are available. DR solutions generally ensure that all changes made to the database at the primary site are propagated to one or more standby databases, at least some of which will be in physically different locations. If the system is mission-critical, then a DR solution such as Oracle Data Guard is necessary to ensure continued availability in the event of a disaster at the primary site.

As with all databases, backup and recovery plays an important part in assuring recoverability in the event of catastrophic failure or data corruption.

Additional options for disaster recovery are available in an Oracle environment with further refinements available for a RAC database. As we have seen, the availability features of RAC provide a significant amount of recoverability in the event of hardware failure. However, these features alone do not provide protection against disasters such as total loss of the data center.

In order to provide protection in the event of such a disaster, data must be replicated to one or more remote sites. A number of possible solutions exist in the Oracle RAC environment:

- Storage-level replication
- Database replication
- Logical standby
- Physical standby
- Stretch clusters

Storage-level replication mirrors changes to data in the storage subsystem across a wide area network (WAN). Database replication can be achieved using features such as Oracle Advanced Replication and Oracle Streams, which was introduced in Oracle 9.2. Logical standby databases were also introduced in Oracle 9.2. To maintain a logical standby database, statements executed on a local database are reexecuted on one or more remote databases. Physical standby databases have been available since Oracle 7.3. To maintain a physical standby database, changes performed on the local database are reapplied on one or more remote databases. Oracle Corporation bundles logical and physical standby databases into Oracle Data Guard, which includes additional disaster recovery functionality along with command-line and GUI utilities to simplify administration. Applied changes to standby database configurations may also be delayed in order to detect and correct errors of data corruption before they have been applied to the standby site.

A stretch cluster does not involve any replication of data; instead, the nodes and storage belonging to a single cluster are distributed across physical locations. This may protect against site failure; however, there still remains only a single logical copy of the database.

Another option is to maintain parallel copies of the database in separate locations. This works well for databases where input and output is performed by a single component—for example, an application server or another database server. It may also be appropriate for data warehouses.

Why Deploy RAC?

RAC can be a complex and costly technology to implement. It requires higher levels of skill and experience to architect, install, configure, tune, and support. The licenses may cost significantly more than comparable single-instance systems. So why are so many users interested in implementing RAC?

Most users implement RAC to achieve either higher availability, greater scalability, or a combination of these. Other users implement RAC to simplify database management or to reduce the cost of ownership of their database systems. This section discusses the advantages and disadvantages of each of the perceived benefits of RAC.

Cost of Ownership Advantages and Benefits

Many users adopt RAC in order to reduce their overall IT cost structure. If there is sufficient scope for consolidation, thereby producing economies of scale in hardware, licensing, and administration costs, this can be a very compelling argument. RAC systems are generally implemented on industry hardware, which is of a lower cost than the proprietary hardware required to create equivalent single-server systems. Hardware maintenance contracts for RAC systems are usually less expensive. However, for many users, there are a lot of additional costs involved in deploying RAC, varying from licensing costs for Oracle, the operating system and other components, and increased staff costs.

RAC vs. SMP

Much of the marketing around RAC has concentrated on the cost of ownership. It is undeniable that the cost of hardware for a cluster based on Intel Architecture is much lower than that of proprietary hardware such as RISC-based systems. For example, the hardware required to implement a 4-node RAC system with 4 processors in each node will be much less expensive than an equivalent 16-node symmetric multiprocessing (SMP) system. As the size of the system increases, the cost savings are magnified. Other components, such as memory, internal disks, network cards, and host bus adapters are also less expensive for industry-standard hardware.

In addition, RAC on Linux systems can be constructed from industry-standard servers that are used throughout the data center. Similar hardware may be used for many purposes, including database servers, file servers, application servers, and web servers running on both the Linux and Microsoft Windows operating systems. Not only is the cost of industry-standard hardware much lower, but economies of scale can be achieved in purchasing systems and spares, and maintenance and support of this hardware. There is more flexibility, as hardware can be deployed to different applications during its lifetime.

In a RAC system, servers can be added or dropped at any time, without necessarily stopping the database. Therefore, it is possible for a new cluster to start with a minimum number of servers and for new ones to be added as the workload increases. In other words, the cluster can grow with the business.

SLAs

Many database systems require 24-7 availability. In order to achieve this, the user must have an equivalent support contract for the hardware so that any failure can be resolved as quickly as possible to maintain any service level agreement (SLA). Such premium support can be extremely expensive. A RAC environment, however, is tolerant of hardware failures and therefore a 24-hour support contract may not be necessary. Many RAC users elect to allocate one or more spare servers that can be quickly provisioned in the event of a hardware failure.

In large environments with many servers, it is not even necessary to carry dedicated spare servers for specific clusters. The spares can be pooled and provisioned to different databases or other applications dependent on need. This forms one of the cornerstones of the Grid technology central to Oracle 10g.

Management

As discussed previously, economies of scale can be achieved by consolidating many databases into one or more clustered databases. This can result in reduced management costs. For example, instead of many databases with each having a separate backup, there may be a consolidated backup that is much simpler to monitor, verify, and test. In addition, it may be cost-effective to implement a disaster recovery solution for the RAC database, where before it may have been too labor-intensive to administer for a number of smaller databases.

Additional Cluster Capacity

In order to provide continuing availability following a node failure, it is necessary for the cluster to have excess capacity. This extra capacity can be utilized to support normal operations while the full complement of servers is available. However, in the event of a node failure, it will be necessary for the remaining servers to support the workload. Note that it may be possible to disable certain activities during the period of restricted availability, such as index creation, statistics generation, purging, and so on. It may also be possible to restrict the number of users accessing the system.

If none of the aforementioned options are possible, then it will be necessary to include one additional server to the cluster for each node failure that the cluster is designed to accommodate. In most clusters this will be a single system, as the probability of two nodes failing at the same time is relatively low.

Additional Hardware Costs

The cost of server hardware represents only a fraction of the total cost of a RAC cluster. There are significant additional costs, which may differ from comparable single-instance scale-up configurations:

- A data center environment, including power, air-conditioning, and security.

- A storage subsystem. This must be configured to provide some form of redundancy.

- A storage infrastructure. In many environments this involves providing switches and other devices to implement redundant paths in a storage area network (SAN).

- Host bus adapters. These are effectively network cards that allow the servers to communicate with the SAN.

- Multipathing software. This supports multiple routes through the storage network to the storage devices.

- A network infrastructure. RAC systems require a minimum of two separate networks. Redundant paths are normally provided for networks using network interface card (NIC) teaming. Additional networks are provided at some sites for backup traffic and monitoring software.

- Management and monitoring software. This is often licensed on a per-server or per-CPU basis.

- Backup software. Prior to the introduction of Oracle Backup, additional third-party software was needed to manage tape media.

- Operating system software and support.

Many large sites have certified product stacks. This is a configuration including hardware, operating systems, drivers, and even databases. A typical stack might contain between 12 and 15 different layers. Each stack costs time and resources to validate, so most users attempt to minimize the number of stacks that are supported. A decision to implement a RAC cluster in such an environment will almost inevitably lead to the development of a new product stack.

Staff and Training Costs

You should also consider staff costs. Existing staff will need to be trained to work with both clusters and Oracle RAC databases. Clustering skills are still at a premium and, therefore, it will be more expensive both to retain existing staff and to attract replacements.

When a RAC environment is introduced, it is also necessary to implement and test new database maintenance procedures, including backup and recovery procedures. Any disaster-recovery solution must also be reviewed and retested.

In addition, you will need to upgrade any test or quality assurance to use RAC databases. If availability is the main justification for using RAC in your environment, it is unlikely that you will wish to apply any upgrade or a patch to your production systems without testing them on a development cluster first.

License Costs

A significant cost for most users will be the cost of the Oracle database licenses. The current price list can be obtained from Oracle Corporation through the Oracle web site. At the time of this writing, Oracle was offering two standard licensing models: processor licensing and named-user licensing. In the processor licensing model, Oracle Enterprise Edition is licensed per CPU with the RAC option incurring an additional license fee per CPU. The Partitioning option, which is frequently used with RAC, is also licensable. With Oracle Standard Edition, users with a maximum of four CPUs can use the RAC option at no additional cost, provided that the database is implemented using Automatic Storage Management (ASM). We discuss ASM in Chapter 9. At the time of this writing, for processing licensing on Linux systems the license for an AMD or Intel dual-core processor (we discuss dual-core processors in Chapter 6) was effectively the same as the license for a single-core processor.

In the named-user licensing model, Oracle is licensed per individual named users. For Standard Edition, the minimum number of named users per processor is 5; for Enterprise Edition, the minimum number of named users per processor is 25. The processor license costs are equivalent to the cost of 50 named users per CPU. Therefore, if you have less than 50 named users per CPU, you should investigate named-user licensing.

You can download and use Oracle free of charge in a development environment. For test, quality assurance, and production environments you must have a full license.

In addition to the Oracle licensing costs, there may be other license costs. For the Linux operating system the software is open source. However, it is mandatory to maintain a subscription to support services from a certified Linux software vendor. We introduce Linux in more depth in Chapter 2.

High Availability Advantages and Disadvantages

The Oracle 8*i* message told us that "the Internet changes everything." Over the past few years this has been demonstrated to be true. Many businesses now operate external and internal web sites requiring 24-7 availability. Other businesses have consolidated their database operations to a single global location that serves customers and employees around the world. These environments do not enjoy the luxury of regular maintenance windows. Applications and databases must be available at all times. RAC databases require a considerable additional investment in hardware, licenses, and management. Therefore, most sites only consider RAC for applications that must be highly available.

Many customers initially considering purchasing the RAC option are interested in the increased scalability potentially offered by the option (covered in the next section). However, in our experience, most customers actually justify the deployment of a RAC database on increased availability.

Node Failure

While RAC does not offer 100% uptime, it does allow a more proactive approach to database management in which nodes can be added and removed from the cluster at any time. In addition, the cluster should be capable of handling node failures. In a correctly configured RAC cluster, it should be possible for any node to fail without impacting the overall availability of the database. In other words, sufficient redundancy is designed into the system architecture to guarantee that if any component fails, processing will continue on the remaining components.

The Oracle RAC option protects the database against the failure of an individual server or any of its related components. While component failures are relatively rare, when there are a large number of servers, the overall mean time to failure may be quite low. The RAC option guarantees that on a correctly sized system, processing will continue in the event of a server failure. In Oracle 10.1 and above it is possible to dynamically add nodes while the cluster is running.

For a RAC cluster to be highly available, it must be possible for any node to fail without affecting the overall workload of the cluster. This means that in the event of a node failure there must be sufficient spare capacity among the remaining nodes to continue processing the workload. This concept has a number of implications.

When designing an N-node system, you must ensure that the same workload can be run on an N-1 node system. In other words the last node must be completely redundant.

Online Maintenance

The RAC option allows you to perform limited maintenance while the database is still running. It is possible to shut down individual nodes and perform upgrades without impacting the availability of the database.

High Availability Testing

To date, most customers implementing RAC on Linux clusters have been cautious of both the technology and the marketing. As such, they generally wish to validate the technology themselves before deployment. This normally involves porting their existing application from the legacy platform to Oracle RAC on Linux and then performing tests to explore the scalability and availability.

Availability tests invariably go without a hitch. This is for a number of reasons. First and foremost, the Oracle high availability software works very well. It usually does exactly what it is supposed to do, though not always as quickly as the customer might expect. It may take a few attempts to find the optimal settings for the hardware, database, and application software involved. But once these have been established, the failover process becomes relatively deterministic, giving the potential customer confidence in the technology. Therefore, most customers justify their purchase of the RAC option on the basis of increased availability.

High Availability Targets

When designing a high availability architecture, it is essential to have a target level of availability. It is important to set such a target in order to verify that the solution meets the expected level of availability. However, it is also important that the target is not exceeded to the point where the cost of the solution becomes excessive. The target level of availability is often reflected in the SLA between the IT department and the internal or external customer.

The target level of availability is often expressed as a percentage of the total time the system could be available—for example, 99.99%. This is not entirely intuitive; so for 24-7 systems, the percentage is often converted into the total amount of time the system can be down during one year.

Table 1-1 shows the relationship between the target level of availability and the total downtime per annum.

Table 1-1. *Total Downtime for Different Levels of Availability*

Level of Availability	Total Downtimes
99%	3.6 days
99.9%	8.76 hours
99.99%	52 minutes
99.999%	5 minutes
99.9999%	30 seconds
99.99999%	3 seconds

For a standalone Oracle RAC cluster, a 99% level of availability is probably the highest attainable target. A target closer to 98% is probably more reasonable. In fact, it is highly likely that the level of availability achieved for a clustered database will be less than that achieved for a single-instance database, because there are more components in the product stack for a clustered database. This means that there are potentially more drivers to be patched or updated. In addition, all components in the stack must be compatible. It is therefore often necessary to patch more than one level in order to maintain dependencies.

However, the target level of availability does not differentiate between planned and unplanned downtime. While there will inevitably be more planned downtime on a clustered database, there should, in theory, be less unplanned downtime. For many customers, this is entirely sufficient. For example, most financial institutions trade five days a week at most. Even for firms with a global presence, there is a period during the weekend when all global markets are closed. Customers running ERP (enterprise resource planning) or CRM (customer relationship management) systems also usually have quiet periods when maintenance can be performed. However, customers whose databases support external-facing customer systems may require 24-7 availability, in which case no maintenance window will be available. For these customers, the only option will be to invest in Data Guard (standby) technology to guarantee availability.

If your target level of availability is 98% or more, you probably should be considering adding one or more standby databases. However, as explained previously, standby databases require additional hardware, operating systems, and Oracle licenses. They also require monitoring and maintenance, thus increasing the administrative burden on the IT department. Applications also need to be aware of when a failover to the standby database has occurred so that in-flight transactions are not lost.

When predicting the amount of time required for planned outages, remember that the process of upgrading software or drivers can be quite lengthy. For example, consider an upgrade to the Oracle software. It is good practice to perform a database backup immediately before applying the changes. It is then necessary to stop the instances on all of the nodes and possibly to stop the Oracle Clusterware. The upgrade or patch can then be applied. Depending on the patch, it may be necessary to reboot the node. You may want to start one instance and perform some testing on the upgrade or patch to verify that it has been correctly installed. You may also need to run scripts to update objects in the database or to run one-off programs to upgrade application data. Finally, depending on the nature of the change, you may wish to perform another backup before the system is released back to the users.

Scalability Advantages and Disadvantages

As businesses consolidate their applications into larger and larger systems, a need has arisen for environments that can handle increasingly large databases and increasingly high workloads. Developments in storage technology, together with the introduction of new features such as the Partitioning option, guarantee that Oracle databases can grow in size almost without restriction. While the size of the database itself can grow almost infinitely, the size of the workload is still restricted by the server on which the instance that is accessing the database is running. The RAC option removes this restriction by allowing more than one instance to access the same database concurrently.

Scalability Testing

As discussed in the previous section, many users are initially attracted to RAC by the promise of increased scalability, but finally justify their purchase on the basis of increased availability. Given the right application, Oracle RAC systems can be highly scalable. However, given the wrong application, scalability may be poor.

During availability and scalability testing it is often possible to achieve significant improvements in both performance and scalability by making minor changes to the application. However, this leads to the perception that developers need to understand the nature of the clustered database in order to realize its full potential. So, while RAC potentially offers increased scalability, the benefits are much harder to quantify and, therefore, are less likely to impact the purchasing decision.

Scalability Options

The Oracle RAC option potentially offers greatly increased scalability. In a correctly designed RAC cluster, additional hardware resources should yield increases in overall throughput. In other words, if you add another server to the cluster, it will either be able to handle an increased workload, or response times will be reduced. In addition, many large tasks can be divided into subtasks and executed concurrently on multiple nodes.

A RAC cluster offers opportunities for both speed-up and scale-out. For batch jobs and long-running queries, the RAC option can achieve speed-up using features such as partitioning and parallel execution. For OLTP workloads, the RAC option offers Cache Fusion, which effectively allows the buffer cache to be shared between multiple instances. This allows transactions to be processed on multiple servers, thus increasing overall transaction throughput of the system.

For hybrid workloads, which consist of a mixture of OLTP and batch jobs, the RAC option offers database services that can be used to control which instances are used for a specific job, effectively allowing the workload to be partitioned between instances.

Oracle offers a number of other features that offer improvements in scalability for RAC clusters. These include sequences, partitioning, locally managed tablespaces, Automatic Segment Space Management (ASSM), and reverse indexes. These features can often be implemented by the DBA without access to the source code. Although many changes should be transparent to a well-written application, you should verify that the vendor will continue to support the application before making them.

While Cache Fusion clearly offers significant benefits in scalability over any preceding technology, it does not come without significant cost. The cache must be consistent at all times. This means that only one instance can modify a block at a time, and that following modification, all other instances can see the changes. In order to guarantee that the cache is consistent across all instances, Oracle RAC implements a number of mechanisms to maintain a Global Resource Directory (GRD) including Global Cache Service (GCS) and Global Enqueue Service (GES). These mechanisms communicate by exchanging messages over the interconnect. They are managed by a set of additional Oracle background processes for each instance and represent an increased workload on each server.

Cache Fusion also affects server (foreground) processes. Whenever a block is read from disk or modified, the server process must first check and possibly update the current state of the block in the GRD. Responsibility for the maintenance of the GRD is shared equally between all instances in the cluster, so it may be necessary to send a message to another instance to perform the actions. Therefore, for any block read or update operation, there is a longer code path in a RAC database than in a single-instance database.

In a RAC database, Cache Fusion usually represents both the most significant benefit and the most significant cost. The benefit is that Cache Fusion theoretically allows scale-up, potentially achieving near-linear scalability. However, the additional workload imposed by Cache Fusion can be in the range of 10% to 20%. While significant scale-up can still be achieved, this often falls short of user expectations.

Global locks also have a significant impact on cluster throughput. This impact can usually be alleviated by modification of the application code. For example, the amount of parsing performed by an application may be significantly reduced if literal values in SQL statements are replaced by bind variables. If you do not have access to the source, then you may reduce the overall amount of lock activity by implementing cursor sharing. Creating and deleting tables requires a significant amount of lock activity, which can be reduced by using global temporary tables.

Scalability Limitations

The level of scalability of a RAC solution is dependent on a number of factors. In theory, all systems should be capable of linear scalability. In reality, constraints imposed by hardware, operating system, database, and application software limit the level of scalability that can be achieved in any system. In this section, we will discuss some of these constraints.

In most systems, the main factor limiting scalability is the design of the application. The success of a RAC implementation is often dictated by the user's access to the source code of the application, whether directly or through the software vendor. We have repeatedly found that very small changes to applications can yield huge improvements in scalability.

Most of the limitations imposed on scalability by applications are related to contention for resources. Applications may, for example, contend for row-level locks for both data and indexes, block-level locks for block updates, segment header locks, dictionary locks, or application locks. Many points of contention can be eliminated either by modifying the application code or by changing the physical structure of the database.

Manageability Advantages and Disadvantages

In many organizations, the number of databases supported by the IT department has grown exponentially over the past few years. It is not unknown for larger organizations to have in excess of 10,000 databases. Each database requires administrative tasks such as space monitoring and backup. RAC clusters allow many smaller databases to be consolidated into one or more larger databases. While such databases present security issues, they greatly simplify management and reduce administrative costs.

RAC databases are much more complex to manage than their single-instance equivalents. Support of a RAC database requires additional skills for the DBA, the system administrator, the storage engineer, and the network engineer.

Economies of scale in manageability can only be achieved if multiple single-instance databases can be consolidated into one or more RAC clusters.

In an environment containing many small single-instance databases, a consolidated RAC database may be a viable option, providing increased availability and recoverability. It will almost certainly be more efficient to back up a single RAC cluster than to attempt to back up multiple smaller databases. Hardware economies of scale can be achieved while at the same time potentially increasing the level of availability of all the constituent databases.

In a large consolidated RAC database, it is also possible to partition applications onto groups of nodes. Additional nodes can be allocated to specific applications during periods of peak resource usage. Database services have been available for several releases, but their full potential was released in Oracle 10.1 and above. In these releases, the overall workload of the system can be assigned to a set of database services. For each database service, it is possible to define a group of preferred instances on which the database services should normally run and, optionally, to define a group of backup instances onto which the database services should fail over in the event that the preferred instances are unavailable. It is possible to assign resources to individual database services so that throughput and response time are maximized without a framework of appropriate workload priorities.

Transparency Advantages and Disadvantages

When RAC was initially launched, it was claimed that any application could run on it without modification. Early adopters soon discovered that this claim was not entirely accurate, as there was no guarantee that the application would scale. The claim was subsequently refined, and it is now claimed that any application that scales well on a single-instance database should scale well on a RAC database.

The concept of transparency implies that a RAC environment is functionally equivalent to a single-instance Oracle database environment. In other words, it is not necessary to make code changes in order to deploy an application on a RAC database if the application runs efficiently in a single-instance Oracle environment.

While it can be argued that core Oracle functionality does port transparently to a RAC environment, there are many examples of peripheral features that may require coding changes. These are usually features that manipulate local memory or files on each node. For example, the DBMS_ALERT and DBMS_SIGNAL packages cannot be used in a symmetric RAC environment. Similarly, instance-specific code implemented as external C procedures and instance-specific Java code may need amendment before it can run successfully in a clustered database.

Although most applications that run efficiently on single-instance Oracle databases do scale reasonably well in RAC environments, poor scalability is frequently seen in newly ported applications. RAC introduces a number of additional overheads that are not seen in single-instance databases. These particularly affect reading and writing of blocks and use of database locks. In both cases, the work can be distributed across two or more instances, requiring additional CPU resource on each node and also generating additional traffic on the interconnect network.

Another marketing claim is that features such as Cache Fusion simplify the administration of RAC environments and eliminate the need to perform capacity planning. Efficient resource usage at both the application and system levels means that you do not need to perform time-consuming resource configurations by examining data access patterns, as RAC does this automatically. These claims can only be justified if the hardware resources available significantly exceed the actual workload. If resources are limited in any way or you anticipate that the workload will grow in the future, then you will need to perform some capacity planning. Although in Oracle 10g, RAC can be configured to make a reasonable attempt at balancing the workload between nodes, it does not necessarily optimize statements any better than a single-instance Oracle database. Therefore, an inefficient SQL statement can be just as destructive in a RAC environment, affecting all nodes in the cluster, not just the node on which it is executing.

Alternatives to RAC

Before you commit to implementing a RAC system, we recommend that you carefully consider the alternatives.

When you are evaluating your options, remember that hardware is developing all the time. If your business needs do not require you to be at the cutting edge, then we recommend you talk to other users, consultants, and industry experts to establish which solutions might be viable for your environment. Do not be tempted to jump on the latest technology bandwagon until you have seen evidence that it works.

Also, remember that while the number of RAC sites is comfortably in the thousands, the number of single-instance Oracle databases is in the millions. While RAC technology is now proven in several configurations, there is safety in numbers. So we recommend that you follow recognized and, if possible, certified architectures.

Single Instance Databases

If you are considering RAC for greater scalability, remember that it may be more cost-effective to use a single larger server. For example, if you are considering two 32-bit servers, you may achieve similar throughput with a single 64-bit server. This will eliminate any RAC overheads and also reduce management and administrative complexity.

Similarly, as dual-core and multicore servers become available, it may be more cost-effective to upgrade servers to use newer processors than to migrate to RAC. You should bear in mind that the cost of a new server can be significantly less than the cost of the RAC license. Also, as Oracle can be licensed by CPU, it makes commercial sense to use the fastest CPUs available to minimize the number required. However, a single-instance database will not provide the same failover capabilities as a RAC cluster.

Data Guard

If you are considering RAC only for availability, then Oracle Data Guard (standby databases) may be more appropriate. Most RAC clusters exist on a single site. This gives a high level of availability in the event of the failure of a single component. It does not, however, protect against failure of the entire site through fire, natural disaster, terrorist activity, or human error. Therefore, many Oracle sites implement a standby database at a secondary location. Changes applied to the primary database are transported and applied to the standby database. In the event of a disaster at the primary site, the database can be failed over to the standby database. For many customers requiring high availability in the form of disaster recovery capabilities but not requiring high levels of scalability, a standby database may represent a more cost-effective solution than a RAC cluster.

Third-Party Clustering Solutions

There are also a number of third-party high availability offerings from vendors such as PolyServe, Red Hat, and Veritas. PolyServe offers its Matrix Server product on both Novell SUSE and Red Hat distributions, whereas Red Hat Cluster Suite and Veritas Cluster Server are offerings only available on Red Hat. These solutions are generally more expensive than RAC, but do offer greater functionality when deployed appropriately. These solutions vary in price based upon what the suite consists of. Some consist of a cluster file system, others just a high availability engine that performs database probes and responds to node failure with database failover. Failover times vary by product, but generally occur on the order of 30 seconds.

Differences Between Single-Instance and RAC Databases

If you have never encountered a RAC database before, you might think that there are many differences between RAC and non-RAC databases. However, RAC and non-RAC instances share the same code base with only minor differences. Many RAC features are visible in non-RAC systems and, in fact, many of the more confusing features of non-RAC systems become much clearer when viewed within a RAC environment.

Each RAC instance has the same set of background processes found in a single-instance environment, including SMON, PMON, DBWn, LGWn, ARCn, and CKPT. Each instance also has a handful of RAC-specific background processes, including LMON, LMSn, LMDn, and DIAG, which are discussed in more detail in Chapter 3.

Each RAC instance also has its own System Global Area (SGA), which is an area of memory that is shared between all Oracle processes running on the node and connecting to the instance. The

SGA contains a number of shared memory structures, including the buffer, the cache, the shared pool, the library cache, the dictionary cache, the large pool, the Java pool, and, in Oracle 10.1 and above, the streams pool.

Each RAC instance also has its own set of online redo logs. Redo log files are grouped together into threads. There is one redo log thread for each instance.

If Automatic Undo Management is configured, then each RAC instance will also have its own undo tablespace.

All clusters require special software often referred to as clusterware that monitors and coordinates membership of nodes in the cluster. RAC clusters are no exception. In Oracle 10.2, cluster management services are provided by Oracle Clusterware, which was known as Cluster Ready Services (CRS) when it was introduced in Oracle 10.1. Oracle Clusterware stores configuration information in the Oracle Cluster Repository (OCR), which must be located on shared storage available to all nodes. Membership of the cluster is determined using a quorum file known as the voting disk, which must also be available to all nodes. While it is still possible to use third-party clusterware on proprietary platforms, it is neither recommended nor necessary on the Linux platform.

Oracle Clusterware comprises a set of daemons including the Event Manager Daemon (emvd), the Oracle Cluster Synchronization Services Daemon (ocssd), and Cluster Ready Services Daemon (crsd). These processes maintain the cluster configuration in the OCR, which resides on shared storage and has replaced the server management file.

Other Unix ports have an additional Oracle Clusterware daemon called the Process Monitor Daemon (oprocd). It is responsible for monitoring the cluster and providing I/O fencing. The Process Monitor Daemon is responsible for detecting that a node has hung, and rebooting the node to prevent I/O corruption. This daemon is not required on Linux platforms where the same functionality is provided by the hangcheck-timer, which is implemented as a kernel module in both Red Hat and SUSE.

Single-instance databases can be administered using Enterprise Manager or using the SQL*Plus command line. These tools can also be used with RAC databases. In addition, you can also administer RAC databases with the SRVCTL utility, which allows you to start and stop the database and individual instances and to control services.

Differences Between Oracle 9*i* and Oracle 10*g*

This section summarizes some of the features affecting RAC that have been introduced or significantly enhanced in Oracle 10*g*.

Oracle Clusterware

Oracle Clusterware is the Oracle cluster management software. It replaces the oracm cluster management software, which was only supported for the Linux platform in Oracle 9*i*. In Oracle 10.1, it was renamed to Oracle Cluster Ready Services, and in Oracle 10.2 it has been renamed again to Oracle Clusterware.

Oracle Clusterware supports high availability by automatically restarting stopped components. In Oracle 10.2 and above, an application programming interface (API) is also provided to enable you to control non-Oracle processes using Oracle Clusterware.

Virtual IP

In Oracle 9*i*, tuning TCP/IP connections to correctly handle node failures was challenging. The default timeout values were invariably too long and led to clients hanging if they attempted to communicate with a failed node. In Oracle 10.1 and above, each node has a virtual IP address that differs from the node's public address. Clients communicate directly with the VIP address. In the event of a node failure, the VIP address is transferred to another node, allowing the client to continue communicating with the database.

Automatic Storage Management (ASM)

Introduced in Oracle 10.1, ASM provides an alternative to proprietary volume managers. ASM file systems can provide double or triple mirroring for database files and an attractive alternative to raw devices if you do not wish to use Oracle Cluster File System (OCFS). However, they are only capable of storing Oracle database files and associated files, such as archived redo logs and the Flash Recovery Area, which stores and manages recovery files. Therefore, an alternative cluster file system will be required if you want to create a shared $ORACLE_HOME directory.

Automatic Workload Repository (AWR)

The AWR, which was introduced in Oracle 10.1, allows you to record an extended set of database usage statistics in the database for subsequent analysis and performance tuning. AWR is an evolution of the STATSPACK tool, and the statistics recorded in the repository are similar to those previously included in a STATSPACK snapshot.

Automatic Database Diagnostic Monitor (ADDM)

The ADDM, which was introduced in Oracle 10.1, provides similar reporting functionality to the STATSPACK reports in previous releases. In addition to detecting problems, ADDM provides advice on possible resolutions.

Active Session History (ASH)

ASH, which was introduced in Oracle 10.1, records wait events for each session. This information is initially stored in the SGA (Oracle System Global Area) and is subsequently summarized and flushed to persistent storage in the database providing historical trend data for time-based performance tuning.

Fast Application Notification (FAN)

FAN, which was introduced in Oracle 10.1, allows databases, listeners, application servers, and clients to receive rapid notification of database events, such as the starting and stopping of the database, instances, or services. This allows the application to respond in a timely fashion to the event. It may be possible for a well-written application to reconnect to another instance without the end user ever being aware that the event has occurred.

Enterprise Manager

The Oracle Enterprise Manager, which was formerly written in Java, has been rewritten as an HTML application; and its functionality has been greatly extended. It is available in two versions: Data Control, which allows a single RAC database cluster to be managed; and Grid Control, which allows enterprise-level management of multiple servers, databases, and other resources.

Database Services

In Oracle 10.1 and above, the concept of database services, which were introduced in Oracle 8i, has been enhanced. A database service is a logical grouping of user sessions. Each database service can be assigned to a set of preferred instances that will be used if possible, and a set of backup instances that are used if the preferred instances are not available.

Database Scheduler

The Database Scheduler, which was introduced in Oracle 10.1, is a replacement for the DBMS_JOB package, which was originally released in Oracle7 and was never completely satisfactory. The Database Scheduler is much more flexible, allowing jobs to be grouped together in classes, job chains, and windows to be created, and external jobs such as shell scripts to be executed. Unlike the DBMS_JOB package, the Database Scheduler is also RAC-aware.

Cluster Verification Utility

The Cluster Verification Utility was introduced in Oracle 10.2 and provides a method of verifying each stage of the installation process. It can also be used to verify the installation of individual components. Although it is only supplied with Oracle 10.2 and above, it can be separately downloaded and can also be used to verify Oracle 10.1 configurations.

History of Real Application Clusters

In the final section of this chapter, we will examine the history and development of RAC.

The code that forms the basis for RAC has a long history. It was originally known as Oracle Parallel Server (OPS) and introduced in Oracle 6.0.35 (subsequently known as Oracle 6.2). Initially it was only available on Digital VAX/VMS clusters, using a distributed lock manager (DLM) developed by Oracle. The OPS code matured through Oracle7, Oracle8, and Oracle 8i. In Oracle 9.0.1, OPS was relaunched as the RAC option. It has continued to mature in Oracle 9.2 and Oracle 10.

Oracle has been available on Linux platforms for several years. However, it was not until the launch of enterprise-level editions of Linux by Red Hat and SUSE, with associated road maps and support, that the Linux operating system became stable enough to justify the significant investment that it sees today from Oracle Corporation. These operating systems began to emerge as enterprise-quality platforms around 2001. Running on industry-standard hardware, the Linux-based platforms offered new cost models to Oracle OPS and RAC users.

At the time the name was changed from OPS to RAC, the marketing material implied that RAC was an entirely new product. However, this was not entirely correct, since much of the code in RAC is derived directly from its OPS predecessor. In view of the reticence within much of the Oracle user community to implement the first release of any new feature, the claim that RAC was a completely new product may have proved to be an own goal, since many users decided to postpone investigation of RAC until a future release.

Technically, however, there was a significant difference between OPS and RAC in the area of cache coherency. In order to update a database block, an instance must first obtain the current version of the block. There can only be one current version of the block in the cluster. Therefore, if more than one instance needs to update the block, it must be passed from one instance to another. Blocks that have been updated are referred to as *dirty blocks* until the version of the block in the buffer cache has been written to disk.

In OPS, block coordination between instances was handled by a mechanism called Parallel Cache Management (PCM). If instance A required the current version block that was being held by instance B, then instance B would have to write the dirty block back to storage and then signal instance A to read the current version of the block from storage. This operation is known as a *disk ping*. Disk pings are resource-intensive operations that should be avoided if at all possible.

The introduction of Cache Fusion Phase I in Oracle 8i saw the elimination of disk pings for consistent reads or read-only traffic. In this release, consistent read blocks can be transferred between instances across the interconnect network. However, it was still necessary for instances to transfer blocks by disk for current reads, which are required for blocks to be updated.

In Oracle 9i, Cache Fusion Phase II was introduced, which eliminated all disk pings. In this release, both consistent read blocks and current read blocks are transferred between instances across the interconnect. In the previous example, if instance A requires the current version of a block being held by instance B, then instance B will transmit the dirty block directly to instance A across the interconnect. This is a much faster operation than a disk ping.

Although a significant amount of OPS code was included in RAC, existing OPS users were required to buy new RAC licenses. The cost of the new RAC licenses provided a disincentive for existing OPS users to upgrade. This in turn meant that there were relatively few early RAC adopters with experience in running clustered databases.

The RAC option is supported on a number of platforms, including Sun Solaris, Hewlett-Packard HP-UX and Tru64, IBM AIX, Microsoft Windows, and Linux. However, earlier versions of Linux lacked two features that are essential in a clustered environment: a cluster manager, and a clustered file system. Oracle addressed both of these weaknesses in Oracle 9*i*. A cluster manager called oracm was shipped with Linux versions of Oracle 9*i*, providing node membership and high availability functionality. Cluster configuration information was stored in the server management file, which was located on central storage and shared by all nodes. Membership of the cluster was determined using a Quorum disk, which was also located on shared storage.

Oracle also initiated the OCFS open source project. The first version of OCFS allowed Oracle database files to be located on shared storage and appears as a standard Unix file system within the Linux operating system. The main weakness of OCFS was that it did not support storage of the Oracle executables. Therefore, it was not possible to create a shared Oracle home directory on OCFS.

In 2003, Oracle 10.1 was released with significant improvements in RAC manageability. The oracm cluster manager was replaced by CRS, which is available on all supported platforms. The server management file was replaced by the Oracle Cluster Repository, and the Quorum disk is now known as the voting disk. This version also saw the release of ASM, which is a logical volume manager that can also be used as a cluster file system for Oracle databases and associated files.

In 2005, OCFS2 was released. This contains the same functionality as OCFS, but is now a POSIX-compliant cluster file system, which supports all types of files including the Oracle binaries. At the time of this writing, OCFS2 was only supported on a limited number of 32-bit Linux platforms.

Since RAC was introduced, the nature of the server market has changed from the larger enterprise servers to smaller industry-standard servers generally based on Intel Architecture. During the same period, the Linux operating system became more accepted as an operating system within many enterprises. The combination of Linux with industry-standard servers delivers significant hardware cost reductions. As the total cost of ownership has been reduced, RAC has become a viable option for more and more Oracle users.

Summary

In this chapter we discussed some of the features of Oracle Real Application Clusters and the costs and benefits associated with deploying a RAC cluster. We have examined the advantages and disadvantages in terms of cost of ownership, availability, scalability, manageability, and transparency.

In many ways, this chapter is the most important in the book, because here we must stress that RAC is not appropriate for all users. If you deploy RAC for the wrong reasons, your project may fail and will certainly not be judged in a positive light. Consider all the options before deploying RAC. For example, what are your availability requirements? Does your system need to scale? If so, can RAC deliver the desired scalability? Would a Data Guard physical standby be more appropriate? Or a third-party product such as PolyServe? What are the real costs of ownership, including power, data centers, storage, networking, licenses, training, and support? While RAC is currently a great addition to your CV, will your current employers lose or gain from its deployment? We have examined many of these questions in this chapter, but we urge you to keep these in mind as you read the remainder of this book, and when you interact with the Oracle RAC community thereafter.

In the next chapter we will discuss some of the underlying concepts behind open source software in general and the benefits of choosing RAC on the Linux operating system in particular.

■ ■ ■

## CHAPTER 2

Introduction to Linux

Linux is an enterprise-class operating system at the forefront of the development and support of the Oracle database. Linux is available and deployed on a wide range of industry-standard hardware platforms, from notebooks and desktops to the largest and most demanding mission-critical multi-processor environments. In this chapter, we discuss the background of Linux and Oracle's relationship with Linux, including the Oracle Unbreakable Linux initiative.

History of Linux

A considerable advantage of choosing Oracle over many alternative commercial database environments has always been the wide availability of Oracle on different hardware and operating system environments. This freedom of choice has enabled Oracle's customers to maintain their competitive advantage by selecting the best technology available at any single point in time. No other operating system exemplifies this advantage more than Linux. Linux has proven to be a revolutionary operating system, and Oracle has been at the forefront of the revolution with the first commercial database available on the platform.

Linux has broken the trend of running Oracle on proprietary operating systems only available on hardware at significant expense from a single vendor. Similarly clustered Oracle solutions were beyond the reach of many Oracle customers due to the requirement to purchase hardware interconnect technology and clustering software from the same vendors.

Linux offers a higher standard and a greater level of choice to Oracle customers when selecting the best overall environment for their needs. At the time of this writing, the wide adoption of this new standard is illustrated by the fact that one-third of all deployments of Oracle Database 10*g* are on Linux—more than any other operating system.

The openness of Linux also means that for the first time, affordable clustered Oracle database solutions eliminate the requirement for third-party clustering software and hardware interconnects. By removing these barriers to entry for clustered database solutions, the increasing popularity of RAC has been closely related to the adoption of Linux as the platform of choice for Oracle customers.

When you choose to run Oracle on Linux, examining the origins of the operating system and its historical context in terms of its relationship to commercial UNIX operating systems is useful. Possessing a level of knowledge about the nature of the GNU General Public License and open source development is also beneficial to establish the license models under which Linux and related software is available. We cover these topics in the sections that follow.

UNIX

To truly understand Linux, you need to start by looking at the background of the Unix operating system. Unix was created in 1969 by Ken Thompson, a researcher at Bell Laboratories (a division of AT&T), and it was designed to be an operating system with multitasking and multiuser capabilities.

In 1973, Unix was rewritten in the new C programming language from Dennis Ritchie in order to be a portable operating system easily modified to run on hardware from different vendors. Further development proceeded in academic institutions to which AT&T had made Unix available for a nominal fee.

AT&T took this course of action, as opposed to developing Unix as a commercial operating system, because since 1956, AT&T was bound by a consent decree instigated from a complaint made by Western Electric in 1949. This decree prevented AT&T, as a regulated monopoly in the telephony industry, from engaging in commercial activity in other nontelephony markets such as computing. The consent decree is often attributed with being a significant milestone in the birth of the open source movement, enabling the wide and rapid dissemination of Unix technology. For example, one of the most important derivatives of Unix, Berkeley Software Distribution (BSD), was developed at the University of California, Berkeley, as a result.

The judgment on which the consent decree was based was vacated in 1982 when Bell was removed from AT&T, and AT&T developed and sold UNIX System III as a commercial product for the first time. In addition, all Unix derivatives also now required a license to be paid to AT&T. AT&T combined features from the multiple versions of Unix in distribution, such as BSD, into a unified release of UNIX called System V Release 1, which was released in 1983. Subsequent commercial versions of UNIX were developed under a license from this System V code base, with improvements from releases incorporated into System V, eventually resulting in the seminal release of System V Release 4 (SVR4) in 1989. Commercial variants of Unix licensed from AT&T source code were distinguished by the capitalization of the word UNIX, and examples of UNIX included Hewlett Packard's HP-UX, IBM's AIX, and Sun Microsystems's Solaris.

In 1991, AT&T formed the company UNIX System Laboratories (USL), which held the rights and source code to UNIX, as a separate business entity. AT&T retained majority ownership until Novell acquired USL in 1993. A year later, the rights to the UNIX trademark and specification, now known as the *Single UNIX Specification*, were transferred by Novell to the X/Open Company, and the UNIX source code and UnixWare operating system were acquired by SCO, marking a point at which the UNIX trademark was separated from the source code. In 1996, the X/Open Company merged with the Open Software Foundation (OSF) to form The Open Group. At the time of this writing, The Open Group owns the trademark UNIX in trust and has also acquired the UnixWare operating system from SCO, which retains the UNIX source code.

As the UNIX source code is separate from the UNIX trademark, there can be and are multiple implementations of UNIX. For an operating system to be defined as UNIX, it must adhere to the standards dictated by The Open Group's Single UNIX Specification and also license the rights from The Open Group to use the UNIX trademark. You can view a list of compliant UNIX operating systems on The Open Group's web site (http://www.opengroup.org).

Free Software

At the same time AT&T began developing Unix commercially, Richard Stallman, a programmer at MIT, initiated a project to construct a Unix-like operating system for which the source code was to be freely available. Stallman's system was named the *GNU Project*, with the recursive acronym standing for "GNU's Not Unix." To guarantee the freedom of the software, Stallman created the Free Software Foundation (FSF), the definition of "free" in this case being related to the concept of liberty (i.e., freedom) as opposed to lack of revenue.

This concept of freedom for software is encapsulated in the GNU General Public License (GPL), which incorporates a modified form of copyright known as *copyleft*. The GNU GPL, which has become the most popular license for free software, grants its recipients the following rights:

- The freedom to run the program for any purpose

- The freedom to study how the program works and modify it (implying that the source code must be made freely available)

- The freedom to redistribute copies
- The freedom to improve the program and release the improvements to the public

GNU GPL–licensed software is always released in conjunction with the source code, and as the recipient you are free to modify and distribute the software as you wish; however, you must subsequently grant the same rights for your version of the software as you received from the original. You therefore may not, for example, take GNU GPL software and modify it, copyright it, and subsequently sell executable-only versions.

The first major output of the GNU Project was the GNU C Compiler (GCC), whose release was followed by numerous other tools and utilities required for a fully functional Unix operating system. The Hurd project was also underway to create the kernel of this free Unix operating system; however, it was still far from completion when Linux originated.

Linux

In 1991, Linus Torvalds, then a student at the University of Helsinki, bought a PC with an Intel 80386 processor and installed a commercially available operating system called Minix (miniature Unix), developed by Andrew Tanenbaum, to fully exploit the potential of the system. Torvalds began to rewrite parts of the software to introduce desired operating system features, and in August 1991 version 0.01 of the Linux kernel was released. Version 0.01 actually still ran wholly under the Minix operating system, and version 0.02 enabled a small number of GNU utilities, such as the bash shell, to be run. The first stable version of the Linux kernel, version 1.0, was released in 1994. *Kernel* refers to the low-level system software that provides a hardware abstraction layer, disk and file system control, multitasking, load balancing, networking, and security enforcement. Torvalds continues to this day to oversee the development of the Linux kernel. Since the initial Linux version, thousands of developers around the world have contributed to the Linux kernel and operating system.

Linux is written almost entirely in C, with a small amount of assembly language. The Linux kernel is released under the GNU GPL and is therefore free software.

Major releases of the Linux kernel in recent years have included Linux 2.4.0 in January 2001 and 2.6.0 in December 2003. Linux kernel version numbers have the following format:

```
<kernel_version>.<major version>.<minor_version>.<patch>
```

For example, recent versions have been numbered 2.4.13 and 2.6.12.3. Until recently, only the kernel and major and minor version numbers were used. The patch number was added during version 2.6.

Within the Linux kernel version format, the kernel version number is changed least frequently— only when major changes in the code or conceptual changes occur. It has been changed twice in the history of the kernel: in 1994 (version 1.0) and in 1996 (version 2.0).

The second number denotes the major revision of the kernel. Even numbers indicate a stable release (i.e., one deemed fit for production use, such as 2.4 or 2.6); odd numbers indicate development releases (such as 2.5) and are intended for testing new features and drivers until they become sufficiently stable to be included in a production release.

The third number indicates the minor revision of the kernel. Prior to version 2.6.8, this was changed when security patches, bug fixes, new features, or drivers were implemented in the kernel. In version 2.6.8 and above, however, this number is changed only when new drivers or features are introduced; minor fixes are indicated by the fourth number.

The fourth number, or patch number, first occurred when a fatal error, which required immediate fixing, was encountered in the NFS code in version 2.6.8. However, there were not enough other changes to justify the release of a new minor revision (which would have been 2.6.9). So, version 2.6.8.1 was released, with the only change being the fix of that error. With version 2.6.11, the addition of the patch number was adopted as the new official versioning policy. Bug fixes and security patches are now managed by this fourth number, and bigger changes are implemented only in minor revision changes (the third number).

Our emphasis here has been on the Linux kernel, but it is important to note that a Linux operating system should more correctly be viewed as a GNU/Linux operating system—without the GNU tools and utilities, Linux would not be the fully featured Unix operating system on which Oracle RAC installations can and do provide all the features and more to make it comparable to commercial operating systems.

Clarifying the distinction between Linux and commercial UNIX is also worthwhile. Because the Linux community has not licensed the use of the UNIX trademark and is not fully compliant in all aspects with the Single UNIX Specification, it is by definition not a UNIX operating system. Later versions of glibc (the GNU Project's C standard library), however, do include levels of functionality as defined by the Single UNIX Specification, and the close relationship and common heritage between Linux and UNIX are apparent. It is therefore normal to see Linux referred to as a "Unix" or "Unix family" operating system, where the use of initial capitalization is intended to draw the distinction between the registered trademark UNIX held by The Open Group and the historical concepts and origins of the Unix operating system from which Linux emerged.

Open Source

Partly based on the growing popularity of free software development inspired by the success of Linux, the term "open source" was coined in 1998 to clarify and expand on the definition of what had previously been described as "free" software. *Open source* is defined by the following nine rules:

- **Free redistribution**: Open source software cannot prevent someone from using the software in a larger aggregated software bundle, such as a Linux distribution that is subsequently sold or given away.

- **Source code**: The source code for any open source software must be available either bundled with the executable form of the software or with the executable form easily accessible. The source code must remain in a form that would be preferential to the author for modification and cannot be deliberately obfuscated.

- **Derived works**: This stipulation of open source is directly inherited from free software and ensures that redistribution of modified forms of the software is permitted under the same license as the original.

- **Integrity of the author's source code**: This condition enables a greater level of restriction than that of free software by ensuring that it is possible to prevent the redistribution of modified source as long as modifications are permitted in the form of patch files. The license may also prevent redistribution of modified software with the same name or version number as the original.

- **No discrimination against persons or groups**: Open source licenses cannot discriminate against individuals or groups in terms of to whom the software is available. Open source software is available to all.

- **No discrimination against fields of endeavor**: Open source licenses cannot place limitations on whether software can be used in business or commercial ventures.

- **Distribution of license**: The license applied to open source software must be applicable as soon as the software is obtained and prohibits the requirement for additional intermediary licensing.

- **License must not be specific to a product**: The license that applies to the open source software must apply directly to the software itself and cannot be applied selectively only when that software is released as part of a wider software distribution.

- **License must not restrict other software**: The license cannot place requirements on the licensing conditions of other independent software that is distributed along with the open source software. It cannot, for example, insist that all other software distributed alongside it must also be open source.

For software to be correctly described as open source, it must adhere to each and every one of the preceding criteria. In some cases, software is described as open source to simply mean that the source code has been made available along with the executable version of the software. However, this form of open source is often accompanied by restrictions relating to what can be done with the source code once it has been obtained, especially in terms of modification and redistribution. Only through compliance with the preceding rules can software be termed "open source"; the software included in distributions of the Linux operating system are genuinely defined as open source.

Oracle, Open Source, and Linux

In 1998, the Oracle database became the first established commercial database to be available on Linux. Oracle Corporation's commitment to Linux has continued with all Oracle products being made available on the operating system.

At the time of this writing, Oracle RAC is supported on the following Linux releases: Red Hat Enterprise Linux, Novell's SUSE Linux Enterprise Server, and Asianux. For users based in the Americas, Europe, Middle East, and Africa, the choice is between Red Hat Enterprise Linux and Novell's SUSE Linux Enterprise Server. Asianux, on other hand, is supported in the Asia Pacific region only. We do not advocate any of these distributions over the others—all are ideal Linux platforms for running Oracle.

Note If you wish to know whether a particular Linux distribution is certified by Oracle and therefore qualifies for support, the definitive source of information is the Certify – Oracle's Certification Matrices web site (http:// www.oracle.com/technology/support/metalink/index.html).

Although the Oracle database on Linux remains a commercial product that requires the purchase of a license for production installations in exactly the same way as the Oracle database on other commercial operating systems, Oracle maintains a deep relationship with Linux. Within Oracle Corporation is a Linux Projects development group, whose aim is to produce enhancements and improvements to Linux in order to improve the performance, reliability, and manageability of the operating system for running Oracle products. Oracle works closely with Red Hat and Novell to create software to be incorporated into Red Hat Enterprise Linux and SUSE Linux Enterprise Server, and the open source nature of the development work ensures that the improvements can benefit all Linux distributions. Oracle also releases a number of products under open source licenses, such as Oracle Cluster File System (OCFS).

Unbreakable Linux

Unique among platforms supported by Oracle, the Linux operating system is backed by Oracle's Unbreakable Linux initiative, which provides Oracle worldwide support for the selected Linux distributions we have highlighted: Red Hat Enterprise Linux, Novell's SUSE Linux Enterprise Server, and Asianux. Unbreakable Linux establishes a high level of confidence in the commitment of Oracle to the Linux platform and support available for enterprise-class deployments of Oracle.

The Unbreakable Linux initiative is delivered at no extra charge from Oracle. However, to participate in the Unbreakable Linux initiative, you must have a support contract with Oracle for

Oracle products and a standard support subscription contract for the operating system with Red Hat or Novell (or an Asianux alliance member in the Asia Pacific region). As support for all components must be purchased, there are no direct cost savings as such. The main distinguishable benefit of the Unbreakable Linux format is that you can deal directly with Oracle support for both the Oracle database and Linux operating system, ensuring that any issues that impact the running of the Oracle database in the Linux environment are managed and resolved directly by Oracle Corporation itself.

The Unbreakable Linux program imposes a number of compliance restrictions on customers, including disqualification of Oracle support for the Linux operating system when using a proprietary kernel module or recompiled kernel. These cases usually occur when a third-party vendor provides a binary module that is loaded into the kernel, and in some circumstances a module may be open source but not published under the GNU GPL. If an installed module is not published under the GNU GPL, it results in what is termed a *tainted kernel*. In this event, Oracle will continue to support the Oracle software products, but not the Linux operating system, and the customer must go directly to the Linux vendor for support.

We suggest that you adhere to the Unbreakable Linux format wherever possible. Using the supported Linux distributions in a standard form ensures that you are taking an established and widely used platform already successfully deployed in multiple mission-critical environments. The single Oracle support contact is also able to provide a streamlined support service, and as Oracle is also actively engaged in contributing to the Linux kernel by collaborating with Red Hat and Novell, users of these distributions are likely to benefit from enhancements sooner. Overall, we believe that adhering to Unbreakable Linux will give you a greater level of confidence when deploying Oracle RAC in any environment.

Under the Oracle Unbreakable Linux initiative, Oracle provides operating system support on key hardware that is certified with Red Hat Linux, SUSE Linux, and Asianux. You should therefore verify that your hardware vendor has subscribed to the Unbreakable Linux program. If the vendor has not, you will still be able to receive support from Oracle for the Oracle software but not for the Linux operating system itself. Detailed information on what hardware is supported by the Linux vendors is available online for example through the Red Hat Hardware Catalog (`http://bugzilla.redhat.com/hwcert`) and the Novell YES CERTIFIED Program web site (`http://developer.novell.com/devnet/yes`).

Oracle products will install and run on a number of Linux distributions not classified under the Unbreakable Linux initiative. These Linux distributions are termed *Generic Linux* releases by Oracle. Generic Linux releases may be certified by Oracle, such as Linux on IBM. For these certified releases, Oracle will support the Oracle software but not the Linux operating system. Other Generic Linux releases may be uncertified, and in these cases Oracle support may provide basic levels of information; however, for product fixes or extended support, evidence of the issues for which support is required must be presented on certified Linux releases. Uncertified Linux distributions should not be used in production environments.

In this book, our emphasis is on the versions of Linux and hardware platforms supported by Oracle under the Unbreakable Linux initiative in order to focus on the environments applicable to the widest number of Oracle RAC on Linux deployments. To this end, in the sections that follow we discuss Red Hat Enterprise Linux, SUSE Linux Enterprise Server, and Asianux.

Red Hat Enterprise Linux

In 1994, Marc Ewing released his own distribution of Linux, which he called Red Hat Linux. The following year, ACC Corporation, a company formed by Bob Young in 1993, merged with Ewing's business and the resulting company became Red Hat Software.

Red Hat grew steadily over the next few years, expanding into Europe and Japan, and introducing support, training, and the Red Hat Certified Engineer (RHCE) program.

In July 1998, Oracle announced support for Red Hat Linux. However, at the time, Linux was perceived by some as a complex platform to work with due to the rapid pace of development and number of releases available at any one time. The open source mantra of "release early, release often" presented difficulties for enterprise environments used to the slower, more genteel development cycles of commercial operating systems.

In March 2002, Red Hat announced its first enterprise-class Linux operating system, Red Hat Linux Advanced Server. Oracle, along with the hardware vendors Dell, IBM, and Hewlett-Packard, announced support of the platform. A policy was put in place to stabilize releases on this version for 18 months in order to allow partners such as Oracle to port, test, and deploy their applications. This policy has largely been successful, although Red Hat's quarterly updates still often contain significant changes. Red Hat has also undertaken to support each release of Red Hat Enterprise Linux for seven years from initial release.

In March 2003, the Red Hat Enterprise Linux family of operating system products was launched. Red Hat Linux Advanced Server, which was aimed at larger systems, was rebranded Red Hat Enterprise Linux AS (Advanced Server). In addition, two more variants were added: Red Hat Enterprise Linux ES (Edge Server or Entry-level Server) for medium-sized systems and Red Hat Enterprise Linux WS (Workstation) for single-user clients.

Since 2003, Red Hat has focused on the business market and Red Hat Enterprise Linux. Red Hat Linux 9 was the final consumer release and was replaced by the Fedora Project.

In Red Hat Enterprise Linux 3, Red Hat backported many of the features from the Linux 2.5 development kernel to the version of the Linux 2.4 kernel on which the release was based. Red Hat Enterprise Linux 3 was superseded in February 2005 by Red Hat Enterprise Linux 4, which is based on the Linux 2.6 kernel.

Table 2-1 summarizes the major Red Hat Enterprise Linux releases to date.

Table 2-1. *Red Hat Enterprise Linux Releases*

Version	Release Date
2.1 AS (Pensacola)	March 2002
2.1 ES (Panama)	May 2003
3 (Taroon)	October 2003
4 (Nahant)	February 2005

By early 2005, Red Hat had sold around 300,000 enterprise version support subscriptions and had approximately 70% of the market for the support of enterprise Linux server operating systems. Red Hat subscription pricing is dependent on processor type and the level of support provided. At the time of this writing, three support packages are offered: Basic, Standard, and Premium editions for both Red Hat Enterprise Linux AS and Red Hat Enterprise Linux ES. Subscriptions are charged on a per-system annual basis.

CentOS, Scientific Linux, and White Box Enterprise Linux offer clones of Red Hat Enterprise Linux that aim to be compatible with Red Hat Enterprise Linux versions.

SUSE Linux Enterprise Server

SuSE was originally a German company founded in 1992 as a UNIX consulting group by Hubert Mantel, Burchard Steinbild, Roland Dyroff, and Thomas Fehr. *SuSE* is a German acronym that stands for "Software und System Entwicklung," which translates in English as "software and system development."

The company started by distributing a German version of Slackware Linux but eventually decided to release its own distribution. The Jurix distribution developed by Florian LaRoche was used as a basis for the first SuSE distribution, released in 1996 as SuSE Linux 4.2.

May 2002 saw the formation of the United Linux consortium, in which SuSE played a prominent role. United Linux was a collaboration among a number of Linux distributors with the goal of creating a single Linux enterprise standard to unify their distributions in terms of development, marketing, and support. The members of United Linux were SuSE, Turbolinux, Conectiva, and the SCO Group. The initial version (1.0) of United Linux was based on the 2.4.18 kernel; however, various factors resulted in United Linux ultimately being unsuccessful in its aims of unification despite support for the Oracle database being available on this release.

During this period, SuSE continued to release its own distributions of Linux. SuSE Enterprise Linux 8.0 (SLES8), based on the 2.4 kernel, was released in May 2002. This release provided a solid foundation on which to run Oracle9i.

In October 2003, SuSE released SLES9, based on the 2.6 kernel. SLES9 includes support for the Native POSIX Thread Library, a key feature of Linux 2.6 releases that significantly boosts the performance of multithreaded Linux applications.

The termination of the United Linux consortium was announced in January 2004 and coincided with the completion of Novell's acquisition of SuSE. Around this time, SuSE was renamed as *SUSE*.

Table 2-2 summarizes the major SUSE Linux Enterprise Server releases.

Table 2-2. *SUSE Linux Enterprise Server Releases*

Version	Release Date
8.0	April 2002
9.0	October 2003

At the time of this writing, SLES9 subscription pricing is dependent on the number and type of processors installed in a server. Subscriptions can be purchased for two-way servers, for four- to sixteen-way servers, and for systems with more than sixteen processors in eight-processor increments. Maintenance support costs after the first year are equivalent to the initial subscription prices.

ENTERPRISE LINUX AND OPEN SOURCE

It is important to be aware that the software included in an enterprise Linux distribution remains open source and the Linux kernel is free software. Therefore, when you purchase a license for an enterprise edition of Linux, you are purchasing the prepackaged distribution of that software and, most important, a subscription to the vendor's Linux support services. You are not purchasing or licensing the Linux software in a manner similar to which you purchase an Oracle software license, for example. Enterprise Linux versions may or may not be available for download from the Linux vendors in an installable form; however, they are always available as stipulated by the conditions of open source as source code and remain freely distributable.

It is especially important to note, however, that if you are running the Oracle database on Linux, you must have purchased a subscription to the enterprise Linux operating system of choice on each and every server in your RAC cluster. Without a subscription for support of your enterprise Linux distribution, you will not receive support services from either Oracle Corporation or the Linux vendor for the Oracle software or Linux distribution.

Asianux

Asianux, as its name suggests, is a Linux operating system available in the Asia Pacific region, and it is supported by Oracle under the Unbreakable Linux initiative. Asianux is the result of an alliance among three of Asia's leading Linux distributors to produce an enterprise Linux standard in the region. The distributors are China's Red Flag Software, Japan's Miracle Linux, and Korea's Haansoft, with support for RAC at a minimum release of Red Flag DC Server 4.1, Miracle Linux 3.0, and Haansoft 1.0.

It is interesting to note that the level of involvement of Oracle with Linux is higher in the Asia Pacific than any other global region. For example, Oracle cofounded Miracle Linux with NEC Corporation in June 2000. Oracle currently owns over 50% of Miracle Linux, and the majority of the executive positions in the company are held by Oracle Corporation Japan.

As our focus in this book is on the Linux distributions with the widest global Unbreakable Linux support provided by Oracle, we do not cover Asianux in subsequent chapters. However, even if you do not plan to use Asianux, we recommend that you keep up to date with developments of RAC on Linux in the Asia Pacific region. Many pioneering initiatives in terms of the latest hardware and software trends originate from this area, the knowledge of which may prove beneficial in your own RAC environment.

Summary

In this chapter, we examined the history of and concepts behind the Linux operating system, with a focus on understanding the features of the Linux platform that distinguish it from the alternative proprietary operating systems on which Oracle RAC is available. In particular, the aim of this chapter was to clarify the meaning of the terms "free software" and "open source," and the relationship of Oracle to open source. In addition, we introduced the versions of Linux on which you may consider deploying your Oracle RAC environment.

CHAPTER 3

■■■

RAC Concepts

Within this chapter we introduce the concepts that underlie the successful implementation of a RAC on a Linux environment. This chapter details the most important components and terminologies you will experience when using RAC and provides the foundation for subsequent chapters where we investigate these technologies in depth.

We will introduce the software and applications implemented at the Oracle Clusterware level. We will then take a closer look at the RAC database itself, in terms of its structure and instances, parameters, and processes. Subsequently, we will consider some of the tools and utilities available for managing the workload and the monitoring and administration of a RAC environment. Finally, we will introduce some of the options available for backup and recovery and disaster recovery in a RAC environment.

Oracle Clusterware

Clusterware is software installed on a group of nodes running in the same physical cluster. It manages the association of the nodes in the cluster in terms of the status of node membership and provides a single database service at a cluster level. As discussed in Chapter 1, high availability configurations have redundant components that allow operational continuity by eliminating single points of failure. In the event of a component failure, Oracle Clusterware is responsible for relocating that component's processing to a backup component. Oracle Clusterware coordinates the remastering of resources, the recovery of partial or failed transactions, and the reallocation of services to the remaining nodes.

Prior to Oracle 10.1, Clusterware was platform-dependent. On most platforms, Clusterware was provided by the hardware vendor. On Linux and Windows, however, the Clusterware was provided by Oracle. In Oracle 9.0.1 and 9.2 on Linux this was known as the Oracle Cluster Manager (oracm). In Oracle 10.1, Oracle supplies a complete, integrated Clusterware facility called Cluster Ready Services (CRS) on all platforms. CRS provides all the features required to manage the cluster database, including node membership, group services, global resource management, and high availability functionality. In Oracle 10.2, CRS has been renamed to Oracle Clusterware and is mandatory in Linux RAC environments, since third-party Clusterware is not supported by Oracle on the Linux platform.

Oracle Clusterware is installed as part of the RAC installation process. Many Oracle database features provide their capabilities using the underlying Clusterware mechanisms. In addition, in Oracle 10.2 and above, Oracle Clusterware provides a High Availability Framework that can support third-party applications running in a clustered environment, enabling them to be maintained in a running state at all times.

In a RAC environment it is necessary to install and configure Oracle Clusterware before installing the Oracle database software. A separate ORACLE_HOME directory must be created for Oracle Clusterware. This directory continues to be referred to as CRS_HOME in the Oracle 10.1 CRS terminology.

Oracle Clusterware consists of the following components:

- Cluster Synchronization Services (CSS): manages cluster node membership
- Cluster Ready Services (CRS): performs management operations and high availability recovery
- Event Manager (EVM): manages event notifications and callouts

You only need to install one copy of Oracle Clusterware on each node. This installation can handle any number of instances running on the same node. On Linux platforms, Oracle Clusterware is implemented as three daemons: evmd, ocssd and crsd.

■**Caution** We recommend that you check very carefully that all preinstallation activities have been performed successfully before installing CRS.

In Oracle 10.1, the installation of CRS is usually the most difficult aspect of an Oracle 10*g* RAC installation. CRS must be successfully installed on each node before Oracle database software can be installed on any node. This means that all prerequisites must be met before installation of CRS commences, including installation of the operating system; configuration of networking, including the secure shell (ssh); configuration of local storage; creation of users, groups, and directories; and the setting of environment variables. If any of the prerequisites are not met, the installation of CRS will fail. In this case, it is necessary to back out the installation manually on all nodes.

In Oracle 10.2, the installation of Oracle Clusterware has been significantly improved, mainly by the inclusion of the Cluster Verification Utility (CLUVFY), which can be used to check that each stage of the process has been successfully completed. The CLUVFY utility can also be used to verify Oracle 10.1 RAC installations. While it is not included in the 10.1 Cluster Ready Services software distribution, it can be downloaded directly from the Oracle technology web site.

When Oracle Clusterware is installed, entries are added to the /etc/inittab file, and the init process spawns the EVMD, OCSSD, and CRSD processes when the node is rebooted. In Oracle 10.1, the only supported way to start CRS is to restart (reboot) the node. In Oracle 10.2 and above, Oracle Clusterware can be started and stopped using the CRSCTL (Cluster Ready Services Control) command.

Oracle Clusterware uses two additional files that must be accessible to all nodes. These are the Oracle Cluster Registry (OCR) and the voting disk.

Oracle Cluster Registry

In Oracle 10.1 and above, shared storage must also be available for the OCR in which Oracle stores details of the cluster configuration, including the names and current status of the database, associated instances, services, and node applications, such as the listener process. The OCR is used by Oracle Clusterware and is managed by a number of tools, including the Database Configuration Assistant (DBCA), Enterprise Manager (EM), and the Server Control (SRVCTL) command-line utility.

The OCR can be stored on a raw device or on a cluster file system. It cannot, however, be stored on an Automatic Storage Management (ASM) file system.

In Oracle 10.2 and above, the OCR can be mirrored, eliminating the potential for it to become a single point of failure. A maximum of two copies can be maintained by Oracle Clusterware.

Voting Disk

Shared storage is also required for a voting (or quorum) disk, which is used to determine the nodes that are currently available within the cluster. The voting disk is used by the OCSSD to detect when nodes join and leave the cluster and is therefore also known as the Cluster Synchronization Services (CSS) voting disk.

The voting disk has similar storage characteristics to the OCR. It can be stored on a raw device or on a cluster file system. It cannot be stored on an ASM file system.

In Oracle 10.2 and above, the voting disk can be mirrored, eliminating the potential for it to become a single point of failure. By default, three copies of the voting disk will be created. Oracle recommends that an odd number of voting disk copies is maintained.

Node Applications

A number of node applications are automatically configured on each RAC instance. These are described in the following sections. If the node applications are enabled they will be automatically started when the node is booted. They can also be started and stopped using the SRVCTL utility.

Listener

The listener process runs on each node and listens for incoming connection requests from clients that are then redirected to an appropriate instance. The listener process is responsible for managing connections for both dedicated and shared servers. It also behaves as an intermediary in the workload-balancing mechanism.

In a single-instance environment, the listener process runs as a daemon process and is usually started using the LSNRCTL utility. In a RAC environment, the listener process is configured to run as a node application within the OCR. While the listener can still be started, stopped, and refreshed using the LSNRCTL utility, it is normally managed with the other node applications using the SRVCTL utility.

Oracle Notification Service (ONS)

Oracle Notification Service (ONS) is used by Oracle Clusterware to propagate messages both within the RAC cluster and to clients and application-tier systems. ONS uses a publish-and-subscribe method to generate and deliver event messages to both local and remote consumers.

ONS is automatically installed as a node application on each node in the cluster. In Oracle 10.1 and above, it is configured as part of the Oracle Clusterware installation process. ONS daemons run locally, sending and receiving messages from ONS daemons on other nodes in the cluster. The daemons are started automatically by Oracle Clusterware during the reboot process.

ONS provides the foundation for Fast Application Notification (FAN), which in turn provides the basis for Fast Connection Failover (FCF).

Fast Application Notification (FAN)

FAN is a mechanism by which RAC notifies other processes about changes in configuration and service level. FAN is also used to notify applications about service status changes, such as the starting and stopping of instances or services.

Whenever the cluster configuration changes, the RAC High Availability Framework immediately publishes a FAN event. Applications can react immediately after they receive the FAN event. This is more efficient than allowing the applications to poll the database to detect any problem.

FAN also publishes load-balancing advisory events. Applications can take advantage of these events to direct work requests to the instance in the cluster that is providing the best level of service.

Fast Connection Failover (FCF)

Fast Connection Failover (FCF) was introduced in Oracle 10.1 and relies on the ONS infrastructure. It works with integrated connection pools in application servers and clients and is used to prevent new connections being directed to failed nodes or instances. When a failure occurs, the application is immediately notified of the change in cluster configuration by ONS, and the connection pool can react by directing new connections to surviving instances. This behavior is performed internally by the connection pool and is transparent to both the developer and the application.

Oracle clients that provide FCF include Java Database Connectivity (JDBC), Oracle Call Interface (OCI), and the ODP.NET CLI.

Virtual IP (VIP)

In Oracle 10.1 and above, a RAC database instance can be accessed through a virtual IP address (VIP) address, which is an alternate public address that client connections use instead of the standard public IP address. The VIP address is a spare IP address for each node that belongs to the same subnet as the public network. Clients should always specify the VIP address, as opposed to the real IP address, when attempting to connect to an instance.

If a node fails, then the node's VIP address fails over to another node. Clients attempting to connect to the VIP will be redirected to another node. This eliminates some of the issues with TCP timeouts, which were prevalent in Oracle 9*i* RAC and caused long delays when clients attempted to connect to failed nodes.

VIP runs as a node application that is configured in the OCR and can be started and stopped with the other node applications using SRVCTL. VIP can be configured using the Virtual IP Configuration Assistant (VIPCA) utility.

Global Services Daemon (GSD)

In Oracle 9*i* each node runs a Global Services Daemon (GSD). The GSD allows clients including the SRVCTL utility, the EM, and the DBCA to execute administrative commands such as instance start-up and shutdown.

In Oracle 9*i*, the GSD is implemented as a Java program. It is not an Oracle instance background process. It is managed independently using the Global Services Daemon Control utility (GSDCTL). In Oracle 10.1 and above the GSD is implemented as a node application and can only be managed using Oracle Clusterware or the SRVCTL utility.

Database Structure

The physical structure of a RAC database contains a superset of the components found in a single-instance database, namely, one or more control files, datafiles, online redo logs, and—if archiving is enabled—archive log files. In addition, there may be a server parameter file (SPFILE) that allows all global and instance-specific parameter settings to be stored in one location. There will also be one client-side parameter file (PFILE) on each node and, depending on the configuration, a password file per node.

As a minimum, the control files, datafiles, online redo logs, and server parameter file must reside on shared storage. There are two RAC-specific files, the OCR and the voting disk, which must also be located on shared storage. The remaining files may be located on local disks for each node. However, it is advisable, if not mandatory, to locate any archive log directories on shared storage.

Datafiles

Datafiles contain all the data belonging to the database, including tables, indexes, the data dictionary, and compiled PL/SQL code. In a RAC database there is only one copy of each datafile, which is located on shared storage and can be accessed by all instances. The datafiles are identical to those found in a single-instance database.

Datafiles are not mirrored by Oracle. Most users choose to implement redundancy at storage level to prevent loss of datafiles. In Oracle 10.1 and above this can also be achieved using ASM.

Control Files

Oracle uses control files to store information about the datafiles and redo logs belonging to the database. Since the introduction of the Recovery Manager (RMAN) in Oracle 8.0, the control file has also been used to store the RMAN catalog.

In both single-instance and RAC environments it is recommended that multiple copies of the control file are created and maintained. Oracle automatically synchronizes the contents of all files specified by the CONTROL_FILES parameter. Each copy should be identical and can be updated by any instance. The control file copies should all be located on shared storage.

While it is good practice to maintain a minimum of two copies of the control file, take care not to create too many copies, since in a RAC environment in particular, the control file is subject to regular updates and can become a cause of contention if too many identical copies must be maintained. If the shared storage is correctly configured, then the control file should be protected against physical corruption. If Oracle is configured to maintain two or more copies, then the control file should also be protected against most human errors, such as accidental deletion.

Online Redo Log Files

Oracle writes every change applied to the database to an online redo log before it can apply the same change to the undo segment or the data block. In RAC, each instance writes to its own set of online redo log groups. The redo managed by an individual instance is called a *redo log thread*, and each thread must contain at least two redo log groups. Each online redo log group is associated with a particular thread number. While there is a one-to-one mapping between the instance and the redo log thread (i.e., each instance maintains its own redo log thread), it is not necessarily the case that the instance number is the same as the thread number. When the online redo log file is archived, the thread number should be included in the name of the archive log file. This number is also used if it becomes necessary to recover the thread from the archived redo logs.

Each redo log group may contain one or more identical redo log files or members. If more than one member is configured, Oracle will software mirror, or multiplex the redo log file to each separate file. This eliminates a potential single point of failure in environments where hardware mirroring is either unavailable or undesirable.

For systems with high redo rates, we have found that it is necessary to create between three and five redo log groups per thread in order to eliminate waits for the archiver process, particularly if the process is writing to remote locations.

Only the owning instance of a redo log thread ever performs write operations on the members of the redo log thread. However, in the event of an instance failure, another instance may open the redo log thread of the failed instance and read the contents in order to perform instance recovery on behalf of the failed instance. This includes rolling forward the changes recorded in the redo log and then rolling back any uncommitted changes. This ensures that the cluster can continue to function without loss of data or data integrity in the event of instance failure.

In many systems, the redo log's performance is critical to overall database performance. Every time redo is flushed to the redo log file, the log writer process must wait for acknowledgement from the storage device that redo has been written to disk before it can continue processing. Therefore, redo logs are often located on the fastest disks.

Undo Tablespaces

Automatic Undo Management (AUM) was introduced in Oracle 9.0.1 and is recommended for RAC databases. If AUM is implemented, then one undo tablespace is required for each instance. If you decide to implement manual undo management using rollback segments, then a single rollback segment tablespace can be used for the entire database.

Archived Logs

Archived logs are copies of online redo logs. The archived redo logs plus the current online redo logs constitute a complete history of all changes that have been made to the database. When an online redo log becomes full, the archiver process is signaled to make a copy of the online redo log in a separate location. When the copy is complete, the online redo log becomes available for reuse. The archived redo logs should be backed up, usually to tape, before they are deleted. They may, optionally, be retained on disk for an arbitrary time period in order to improve recovery times in the event of a database restore being required.

Unlike all other Oracle database files, archived redo logs cannot be located on raw devices; they must be written to a file system.

In a RAC environment, each instance maintains its own set of archived redo logs. These may either be located on local file systems on each node or in a shared file system that can be accessed by all nodes. While space considerations may dictate that archived redo logs be stored on local file systems, we recommend that you attempt to locate these files on a shared file system. That is because it may be necessary to restore these files and a remote node may be performing the restore.

If your architecture or budget forces you to use local file systems, we recommend that you employ a completely symmetrical configuration and ensure that all nodes can access each archived redo log location over NFS or a similar protocol.

Recovery Area

In Oracle 10.1 and above, you can optionally configure a recovery area on shared storage. This area of storage is managed directly by Oracle and contains most of the files required for backup and recovery, including archived redo logs, file copies, flashback database logs, and change tracking logs.

Instances

A RAC database normally consists of two or more instances. Each instance generally resides on a different node and consists of a superset of the shared memory structures and background processes used to support single-instance databases.

It is possible for RAC to run on one instance. This is essential to provide database availability in the event of a node or instance failure in a two-node cluster. It is also an integral part of the database start-up process. Some sites implement RAC test systems using one instance, as this contains much of the standard RAC functionality without requiring expensive shared storage or interconnect hardware.

However, the vast majority of RAC production databases consist of two or more instances. Each instance has an area of shared memory called the System Global Area (SGA). All processes attaching to the instance can access data in the SGA. Oracle prevents multiple processes from updating the same area of memory by using mechanisms such as latches and locks. A latch is a lightweight mechanism that is used for very fast accesses. Processes do not queue for latches; if a latch is not immediately available a process will spin (loop repeatedly) for a limited period and then sleep, waking up at regular intervals to check if the latch has become available. On the other hand, locks are obtained for longer periods. Access to locks is managed by structures called enqueues, which maintain queues of processes requiring access to the locks.

The largest area of memory within the SGA on each instance is usually the buffer cache. This is a set of buffers that is used to hold blocks that have been read from the database. When blocks are modified, the changes are immediately written to the redo buffer and are flushed to the redo log when the transaction commits. The changes are applied to the block in the buffer cache where it remains until it is subsequently written back to disk by the database writer process.

In order to maintain consistency between the instances in the database, RAC maintains a virtual structure called the Global Resource Directory (GRD), which is distributed across the SGAs of all active instances and contains information about all blocks and locks held by instances and processes across the cluster. The information in the GRD is maintained by two internal services known as the Global Cache Service (GCS) and the Global Enqueue Service (GES). These services are implemented using background processes on each instance and communicate with the equivalent processes on the other instances across the interconnect.

Global Cache Service (GCS)

In a RAC database each instance has its own database buffer cache, which is located in the SGA on the local node. However, all instances share the same set of datafiles. It is therefore possible that one or more instances might attempt to read and/or update the same block at the same time. So access to the data blocks across the cluster must be managed in order to guarantee only one instance can modify the block at a time. In addition, any changes must be made visible to all other instances immediately once the transaction is committed. This is managed by the GCS, which coordinates requests for data access between the instances of the cluster.

Global Enqueue Service (GES)

In a RAC database, the GES is responsible for interinstance resource coordination. The GES manages all non-Cache Fusion intra-instance resource operations. It tracks the status of all Oracle enqueue mechanisms for resources that are accessed by more than one instance. Oracle uses GES to manage concurrency for resources operating on transactions, tables, and other structures within a RAC environment.

Parameters

Parameters are used to configure and control the behavior of the Oracle database. It is generally only necessary to modify a small set of parameters on most systems; the default values are sufficient in most cases.

There are two main types of parameters—supported and unsupported:

- Supported parameters are documented by Oracle. Users are free to change these within the specified ranges indicated in the documentation. For example, the SHARED_POOL_SIZE parameter defines the initial size of the shared pool in the SGA.

- Unsupported parameters start with an underscore. They should only be changed from their default values after consultation with Oracle Support. For example, by default, only members of the dba group can read trace files. Setting the _TRACE_FILES_PUBLIC parameter to TRUE changes the permissions on trace files so that all users can read them.

In Oracle 10.1 and above, a new type of parameter appeared. These are parameters that are maintained directly by the database and consequently can only be used with server parameter files. They are prefixed by two underscore characters. In the initial release they were used to support automatic memory management. For example, the _DB_CACHE_SIZE parameter is used to store the current optimum size of the buffer cache as calculated by automatic memory management.

Almost all parameters have default values. Some default values are constants; others are derived from the values of other parameters when the instance is started. In addition, the majority of parameters can be updated dynamically while the database is running. However, there are still a number of parameters that require a restart of the database in order for modifications to take effect.

Traditionally, on single-instance databases, parameter values were stored in a text file called the *initialization parameter file* (PFILE). In an OPS environment, one PFILE was required for each instance. The PFILE is usually modified using a text editor.

In Oracle 9.0.1 and above, it is also possible to use an SPFILE with both single-instance and RAC databases. The SPFILE is a binary file that can be updated using ALTER SYSTEM statements. In a RAC environment, an SPFILE can be located on shared storage and, consequently, instance parameters can be managed centrally.

In an SPFILE it is possible to specify both global and instance-specific parameters. It is also possible to specify global and instance-specific parameters in a PFILE; however, there is no guarantee that any global parameters will be consistent between the different instances.

Initialization Parameter File (PFILE)

The PFILE is often referred to as an init.ora file, as it usually has the name init<SID>.ora, where SID is the instance identifier. By default, the PFILE is located in the $ORACLE_HOME/dbs directory on each node. The PFILE is only read when the instance is started. Subsequent changes to the PFILE will not be read until the next update.

The initialization parameter file contains a series of name-value pairs, and in a RAC environment, parameters can be global, in which case they apply to all instances. It is necessary to specify instance-specific values for the parameters INSTANCE_NAME, INSTANCE_NUMBER, and THREAD. If automatic undo management is configured, it is also necessary to specify instance-specific values for the UNDO_TABLESPACE parameter.

It is possible to specify instance-specific values for many other parameters. This may be desirable where there is an asymmetric workload; however, it should be remembered that one of the main benefits of RAC is availability and this could be compromised if instance-specific parameters are modified in such a way that instance-failover functionality is affected.

PFILEs have a number of disadvantages in production environments:

- PFILEs are stored on file systems, and DBAs therefore need access to the file system in order to update the parameter files using a text editor. This may not be desirable due to the security requirements of many environments.

- PFILEs are difficult to manage because global changes must be made to the PFILE on every node in the cluster. Maintaining four or more PFILEs can be tedious and prone to human error.

- Dynamic changes are not written to PFILEs. Such modifications therefore need to be applied twice—once using the ALTER SYSTEM command, and once by editing the initialization parameter file. This means that autotuning features cannot make parameter changes persistent when the instance is restarted.

- RMAN is not aware of PFILEs, and therefore alternative arrangements must be made to back them up.

While we recommend using server parameter files as discussed in the next section, it is still necessary to know how to use initialization parameter files in a couple of situations.

- If you create a database manually using scripts (as opposed to using the DBCA) you will need to create a PFILE, which is required to start the instance prior to running the CREATE DATABASE statement. It is not possible to use an SPFILE for this purpose.

- It is possible to make conflicting updates to the server parameter file. If changes are deferred until the instance is restarted, it is sometimes not possible to restart the instance. This affects both supported and unsupported parameters. For example, it is easy to inadvertently modify the supported parameters for a database running with a physical standby in MAXIMUM PROTECTION mode such that the instance cannot subsequently be restarted. In this case, the only solution is to convert the server parameter file back to an initialization parameter file, update the parameters using a text editor, and then recreate the server parameter file.

Server Parameter File (SPFILE)

In Oracle 9.0.1 and above, it is possible to store parameters in an SPFILE. This is a binary file that can only be modified using SQL statements. The SPFILE is shared between all instances and should therefore be located in shared storage.

The server parameter file can either be updated using EM or the ALTER SYSTEM statement. If the instance is using a server parameter file, then the ALTER SYSTEM statement allows you to specify whether the value of the parameter should be changed in memory only, in the server parameter file or in both.

An SPFILE can contain both global and instance-specific parameters. Global parameters are identified by an asterisk (*) while instance-specific parameters are identified by their Oracle system identifier (SID). Most parameters can have different values on different instances. These parameters have a default value that is the same for all instances. You can change the value on one or more specific instances using the SID clause of the ALTER SYSTEM statement.

We recommend using a server parameter file in a RAC environment. Server parameter files have a number of advantages over initialization parameter files:

- A single server parameter file can be shared by all instances. Global parameters can be defined centrally while it is still possible to define instance-specific parameters within the same file.

- It is easier to keep parameters consistent across all instances in an SPFILE, as they are only set in one place.

- The server parameter file can be administered using the SQL statements instead of using an operating system text editor.

- It is not necessary to have access to the file system in order to update the server parameter file, as all changes can be performed using SQL statements.

- Changes to parameter values can be applied to both the current instance and the server parameter file by the same statement.

- RMAN is aware of server parameter files and can back them up.

- Oracle can automatically update the server parameter file with values derived from workload analysis.

Global Parameters

A number of parameters must have the same value for every instance in the database. These are known as global parameters:

- ACTIVE_INSTANCE_COUNT
- ARCHIVE_LAG_TARGET
- CLUSTER_DATABASE
- CLUSTER_DATABASE_INSTANCES
- CONTROL_FILES
- DB_BLOCK_SIZE
- DB_DOMAIN
- DB_FILES
- DB_NAME
- DB_RECOVERY_FILE_DEST
- DB_RECOVERY_FILE_DEST_SIZE
- MAX_COMMIT_PROPAGATION_DELAY
- TRACE_ENABLED
- UNDO_MANAGEMENT

In addition, if Data Manipulation Language (DML) locks are disabled by setting the DML_LOCKS parameter to zero, then this parameter must have the same value on every instance.

Instance-Specific Parameters

The following parameters should have different values on every instance in the database:

- INSTANCE_NAME
- INSTANCE_NUMBER
- THREAD
- UNDO_TABLESPACE

On each individual instance, the INSTANCE_NUMBER and THREAD parameters usually have the same values. This simplifies administration. In addition, if you use the ROLLBACK_SEGMENTS parameter, Oracle recommends that this should have a unique value for each instance.

RAC-Specific Parameters

The following parameters are used to control the instances operating in a RAC environment. This ranges from signifying to the instance whether it is operating in a cluster, to parameters notifying the instance of the specific resources that are allocated to them in particular.

CLUSTER_DATABASE: This global parameter specifies that the database should be started in cluster mode. This parameter should be set to TRUE on all instances. Occasionally it is necessary to stop all instances and change this parameter to FALSE on a single instance in order to make administrative changes—for example, to enable archiving or to change the standby protection mode.

CLUSTER_DATABASE_INSTANCES: This global parameter specifies the number of instances in the cluster. This parameter should be set to the maximum number of instances you plan to have running concurrently before the next database restart. This parameter affects the amount of memory reserved in the SGA for each and every new instance. If you overestimate the value of this parameter you will reserve memory that might be more efficiently used by other components of the SGA.

CLUSTER_INTERCONNECTS: This parameter specifies the cluster interconnect in the event that there is more than one interconnect in the cluster. It is not normally necessary to set this parameter on a Linux cluster. It should not be set if there is only one cluster interconnect or if the default cluster interconnect meets the bandwidth requirements of the RAC database.

If you specify more than one interconnect with this parameter, Oracle will attempt to distribute interconnect traffic between the different network interfaces. If a single interconnect cannot satisfy your bandwidth requirements, consider using this parameter.

For example, if you have one database with high bandwidth requirements you can specify multiple interconnects using

```
CLUSTER_INTERCONNECTS = ic1:ic2
```

In this example, Oracle will use both the specified interconnects and attempt to balance the load between them while they remain operational. Note that if you specify multiple interconnects and one of them fails you will receive an application error; Oracle will not automatically fail over to another interconnect.

Alternatively, if you have two databases sharing the same set of servers, you can specify a different interconnect for each database using this parameter. For example, for database 1 use

```
CLUSTER_INTERCONNECTS = ic1
```

For database 2 use

```
CLUSTER_INTECONNECTS = ic2
```

DB_NAME: This parameter specifies the name of the database. This parameter must have the same value for all instances.

INSTANCE_NAME: This parameter is used to distinguish between the different instances. It is usually the same as the ORACLE_SID environment variable for the node that comprises the database name and the instance number, for example, RAC1. This parameter should have a different value for each instance.

INSTANCE_NUMBER: This parameter is used to distinguish between the different instances. Instances are usually numbered consecutively starting at 1. In many RAC clusters, the instance number is the same as the thread number. This parameter should have a different value for each instance.

MAX_COMMIT_PROPAGATION_DELAY: This global RAC-specific parameter specifies the maximum amount of time allowed before the system change number (SCN) held in the SGA of each instance is refreshed by the log writer process (LGWR). This parameter affects how quickly remote instances can see changes on the local instance. In Oracle 10.1, the default value is seven seconds, which means that block changes made by the local instance will not be visible on remote instances for up to seven seconds after they are committed. This may be an issue for some applications, in which case the value of this parameter should be reduced to zero if possible.

In Oracle 9.2 reducing this parameter below the default value increases the amount of interinstance messaging. As the value approaches zero, performance may be seriously affected. The algorithm appears to have been improved in Oracle 10.1, and MAX_COMMIT_PROPAGATION_DELAY can be set to zero without serious performance degradation. In Oracle 10.2 and above, the algorithm has been further improved; the default value of this parameter is zero, and in most cases this parameter can be safely ignored.

SPFILE: This parameter specifies the location of a server parameter file. If you choose to use a server parameter file, this parameter must be specified in the PFILE for each instance. If this parameter is specified, all other parameters in the PFILE will be ignored.

THREAD: This parameter specifies the redo thread number to be used by the instance. It should be unique for each instance.

UNDO_TABLESPACE: If Automatic Undo Management is enabled, the UNDO_TABLESPACE parameter should specify a different undo tablespace for each instance.

Background Processes

Each RAC instance has a number of background processes that exist for the lifetime of the instance. On UNIX platforms, including Linux, each Oracle background process runs in its own operating system process; on Windows platforms, the instance runs in a single operating system process, and each background process runs in a separate operating system thread. The number of background processes is determined by the database version and the features configured.

In Oracle 10.1 and above, there are two types of instances: RDBMS and ASM. The quantity, name, and purpose of background processes vary according to the instance type.

RDBMS Instance Background Processes

Every instance of the Oracle database server software or Relational Database Management System (RDBMS) has a number of background processes described in the following sections.

Mandatory Background Processes

An Oracle 10g instance includes a number of mandatory background processes. The background processes detailed in this section will exist for all Oracle 10g database instances, whether they are single-instance or RAC configurations.

SMON

There is one system monitor background process (SMON) per instance. It is responsible for performing recovery at instance start-up and cleaning up temporary segments that are no longer in use. It also coalesces contiguous free extents in dictionary-managed tablespaces.

In Oracle 9.0.1 and above, SMON also maintains a table called SMON_SCN_TIME that correlates the current time with the SCN. This table is used to convert time into SCNs for flashback recovery.

In a RAC environment, the SMON process of one instance can perform instance recovery in the event of the failure of another server or instance.

If the SMON process crashes for any reason, the entire instance halts immediately. For this reason we often test instance failover by manually aborting the SMON process using the operating system kill command.

PMON

There is one process monitor (PMON) background process per instance. In the event of a user process failing, PMON is responsible for cleaning up the memory structures such as locks on resources and for freeing any database buffers that the user was holding.

The PMON background process is also responsible for registering information about the instance and dispatcher processes with the listener process. In a RAC environment, this information can optionally be used for connection balancing.

LGWR

There is one LGWR process per instance. Every change made to the database must be rewritten to the redo log before it can be written back to the database. The LGWR process is responsible for reading changes from the log buffer and writing them to the current online redo log.

The redo log buffer is a circular buffer. Server processes copy redo entries into the redo log buffer. The LGWR then writes these redo entries to disk. All redo entries created since the last time the LGWR process was invoked are written together. As the online redo logs are written sequentially, the LGWR process normally writes fast enough to ensure there is space available in the redo buffer for new entries.

In a RAC environment, there is one LGWR process per instance and this process can only write to the current online redo log. This effectively serializes the output of redo information. In our experience, the LGWR process is often the limiting factor for scalability. When ramping up loads on a well-tuned database, writes to the redo log are frequently the bottleneck. There are several possible solutions including

- Reduce the amount of redo generated.
- Use faster disk technology.
- Add more instances to the cluster.

The LGWR background process can be configured to maintain more than one redo log destination; for example, in a physical standby configuration LGWR may be responsible for updating both the local and the remote redo log destinations. It is possible to specify whether a destination is mandatory— in which case the update must be performed before processing can continue—or optional, in which case the update may fail because of some external reason, such as a network timeout.

DBW*n*

The database writer (DBW*n*) process writes dirty blocks from the buffer cache back to the data files. Dirty blocks, which are blocks that have been updated by one of the foreground processes, cannot be written to disk until the changes have been written to the current online redo log. However, once the changes have been written to the redo log, it is not necessary for the database writer processes to write blocks back to disk immediately. Therefore, the blocks are written back asynchronously either when additional space is required in the buffer cache or in a RAC instance when a write is requested by the block master.

The buffer cache is maintained using a modified LRU (least recently used) algorithm. The DBW*n* processes attempt to delay writing dirty blocks back to disk as long as possible. This is because there is a high probability that the same blocks will be updated again while they are in the buffer cache.

There can be one or more DBW*n* processes per instance. The number of DBW*n* background processes is specified by the DB_WRITER_PROCESSES initialization parameter. The default value is based on the number of CPUs.

In Oracle 9.0.1 there can be up to 10 DBW*n* processes (DBW0 to DBW9). In Oracle 9.2 and above there can be up to 20 DBW*n* processes (DBW0 to DBW9, DBWa to DBWj).

CKPT

The checkpoint is the position in the redo log thread from which an instance recovery should begin. This position is determined by the oldest dirty buffer in the buffer cache. Performing a checkpoint involves updating the headers of each of the database files. This was originally done by the DBWn process, but for databases with a number of datafiles, this could lead to significant pauses in processing while the headers were updated.

The CKPT background process was introduced in Oracle 7.0 where it could be optionally enabled by setting the CHECKPOINT_PROCESS parameter. In Oracle 8.0 and above, it has been a mandatory background process and is no longer configurable. The purpose of the CKPT process is to update the database file headers; dirty buffers are still written back to disk by the DBWn background processes. There is one checkpoint background process per instance.

MMAN

In Oracle 10.1 and above, SGA memory can be managed automatically. An overall memory size is specified using the SGA_TARGET initialization parameter. Oracle will then determine how much memory to allocate to each of the pools within the SGA. If a server parameter file is configured, current sizes of each pool are stored in it when the instance shuts down, and then it is reloaded when the instance is restarted.

The MMAN background process is responsible for the Automatic Shared Memory Management feature. There is one MMAN process per instance.

MMON

In Oracle 10.1 and above, the MMON background process performs manageability-related tasks, including capturing statistics values for SQL objects that have been recently modified and issuing alerts when metrics exceed their threshold values. MMON also takes database snapshots by spawning additional slave processes.

MMNL

In Oracle 10.1 and above, the MMNL background process performs manageability-related tasks such as session history capture and metrics computation.

Optional Background Processes

An instance may also include optional background processes. The processes that are started in a particular environment are related to the optional features, such as archiving and ASM.

ARCn

The Oracle database can optionally be configured to ARCn background processes to copy completed online redo log files to a separate area of disk, following each log switch. The archiver process is only started if the LOG_ARCHIVE_START parameter is set to TRUE. In addition, the database must be running in ARCHIVELOG mode with automatic archiving enabled.

In Oracle 9.0.1 and above, there can be up to 10 ARCn background processes numbered ARC0 to ARC9. In Oracle 10.2 and above, there can be up to 30 archiver processes numbered ARC0 to ARC9, ARCa to ARCt. The LGWR background process will automatically start a new ARCn process if the current number of ARCn processes is insufficient to handle the workload. The maximum number of archiver processes can be specified by the initialization parameter LOG_ARCHIVE_MAX_PROCESSES.

It is important to maintain the disk area allocated to archived redo logs. If this area becomes full, then archiving will be suspended. This will result in the database hanging, as no further changes can be logged.

In a RAC environment we recommend that archived log files be written to shared storage, and in Oracle 10.1 and above, to the Flash Recovery Area.

RECO

The RECO background process was introduced in Oracle 7.0 and is used in distributed database configurations to automatically resolve failures in distributed transactions. The RECO background process connects to other databases involved in an in-doubt distributed transaction.

Distributed database configurations enable transactions to be performed on multiple databases. This is not the same as RAC, where transactions are performed by different instances against the same database.

CJQ0

Job queue background processes are used to run batch jobs within the Oracle database. Jobs can be scheduled to run at a specified date and time or at regular intervals.

There is one CJQ0 process per instance. This manages the jobs that need to be run and allocates the job queue slave processes. There can be up to 1,000 job queue slave processes in an instance (J000 to J999). Each slave process runs one job at a time.

The maximum number of job queue processes that can be run concurrently on an instance is specified by the JOB_QUEUE_PROCESSES initialization parameter. Like other dynamic background processes, job queue slave processes can fail without causing the instance to fail.

QMNn

Queue monitor (QMNn) processes are optional background processes that monitor the message queues for Oracle Advanced Queuing.

In Oracle 9.0.1 and 9.2, up to ten queue monitor processes can be configured per instance (QMN0 to QMN9) using the AQ_TM_PROCESSES initialization parameter.

In Oracle 10.1, a queue monitor coordinator (QMNC) process is automatically created if either Advanced Queuing or Streams is configured. The QMNC process dynamically spawns queue monitor slaves (q000 to q009). The number of slave processes is determined automatically so it is no longer necessary to set AQ_TM_PROCESSES.

ASMB

The ASMB background process runs in the RDBMS instance and connects to the foreground processes in the ASM instance.

RBAL

The RBAL background process in the RDBMS instance performs global opens to the disks in the disk groups in the database instance. Note that there is also an RBAL background process in the ASM instance that has a completely different purpose.

RAC-Specific Background Processes

There are a number of RAC-specific background processes. These background processes implement the Global Cache and Global Enqueue services and manage the diagnostic information related to node failures.

LMS*n*

The Global Cache Service background processes (LMS*n*) manage requests for data access between the nodes of the cluster. Each block is assigned to a specific instance using the same hash algorithm that is used for global resources. The instance managing the block is known as the resource master. When an instance requires access to a specific block, a request is sent to an LMS process on the resource master requesting access to the block. The LMS process can build a read-consistent image of the block and return it to the requesting instance, or it can forward the request to the instance currently holding the block.

The LMS processes coordinate block updates, allowing only one instance at a time to make changes to a block and ensuring that those changes are made to the most recent version of the block. The LMS process on the resource master is responsible for maintaining a record of the current status of the block, including whether it has been updated.

In Oracle 9.0.1 and Oracle 9.2 there can be up to 10 LMS*n* background processes (LMS0 to LMS9) per instance; in Oracle 10.1 there can be up to 20 LMS*n* background processes (LMS0 to LMS9, LMSa to LMSj) per instance; in Oracle 10.2 there can be up to 36 LMS*n* background processes (LMS0 to LMS9, LMSa to LMSz). The number of required LMS*n* processes varies depending on the amount of messaging between the nodes in the cluster.

LMON

In a single-instance database, access to database resources is controlled using enqueues that ensure that only one session has access to a resource at a time and that other sessions wait on a first in, first out (FIFO) queue until the resource becomes free. In a single-instance database, all locks are local to the instance. In a RAC database there are global resources, including locks and enqueues that need to be visible to all instances. For example, the database mount lock that is used to control which instances can concurrently mount the database is a global enqueue, as are library cache locks, which are used to signal changes in object definitions that might invalidate objects currently in the library cache.

The Global Enqueue Service Monitor (LMON) background process is responsible for managing global enqueues and resources. It also manages the Global Enqueue Service Daemon (LMD) processes and their associated memory areas. LMON is similar to PMON in that it also manages instance and process expirations and performs recovery processing on global enqueues.

In Oracle 10.1 and below there is only one lock monitor background process.

LMD*n*

The current status of each global enqueue is maintained in a memory structure in the SGA of one of the instances. For each global resource, three lists of locks are held, indicating which instances are granted, converting, and waiting for the lock.

The LMD background process is responsible for managing requests for global enqueues and updating the status of the enqueues as requests are granted. Each global resource is assigned to a specific instance using a hash algorithm. When an instance requests a lock, the LMD process of the local instance sends a request to the LMD process of the remote instance managing the resource. If the resource is available, then the remote LMD process updates the enqueue status and notifies the local LMD process. If the enqueue is currently in use by another instance, the remote LMD process will queue the request until the resource becomes available. It will then update the enqueue status and inform the local LMD process that the lock is available.

The LMD processes also detect and resolve deadlocks that may occur if two or more instances attempt to access the two or more enqueues concurrently.

In Oracle 10.1 and below there is only one lock monitor daemon background process named LMD0.

LCK0

The instance enqueue background process (LCK0) is part of GES. It manages requests for resources other than data blocks—for example, library and row cache objects. LCK processes handle all resource transfers not requiring Cache Fusion. It also handles cross-instance call operations.

In Oracle 9.0.1 there could be up to ten LCK processes (LCK0 to LCK9). In Oracle 9.2 and Oracle 10.1 and 10.2 there is only one LCK process (LCK0).

DIAG

The DIAG background process captures diagnostic information when either a process or the entire instance fails. This information is written to a subdirectory within the directory specified by the BACKGROUND_DUMP_DEST initialization parameter. The files generated by this process can be forwarded to Oracle Support for further analysis.

There is one DIAG background process per instance. It should not be disabled or removed. In the event that the DIAG background process itself fails, it can be automatically restarted by other background processes.

Data Guard–Specific Background Processes

There are a number of additional background processes supporting Data Guard operations:

- DMON: Data Guard Broker monitor process
- INSV: Data Guard Broker instance slave process
- NSV0: Data Guard Broker NetSlave process
- DSM*n*: Data Guard Broker Resource Guard process
- MRP0: Managed Standby Recovery process
- LSP0: Logical standby
- LSP1: Dictionary build process for logical standby
- LSP2: Set Guard Standby Information for logical standby
- LNS*n*: Network server

The requirements and functionality of implementing Data Guard with RAC is discussed in detail in Chapter 26, which addresses background processes specific to Data Guard environments.

ASM Instance Background Processes

ASM instances, in similarity to RDBMS instances, have both mandatory background processes and RAC-specific background processes. In addition to these, ASM instances have background processes specific to storage management functionality.

Mandatory Background Processes

Each ASM instance has a separate set of background processes. Many of these background processes are similar to those found in an RDBMS RAC instance:

- SMON
- PMON
- LGWR
- DBW*n*

- CKPT
- MMAN

RAC-Specific Background Processes

In a RAC environment, it is necessary for ASM instances to communicate with each other to coordinate access to the file systems and to manage interinstance locking. Therefore, each ASM instance will have a set of RAC-specific background processes:

- LMS*n*
- LMON
- LMD*n*
- LCK0
- DIAG

ASM-Specific Background Processes

Finally, each ASM instance has a handful of ASM-specific background processes:

RBAL: The ASM rebalance master process controls all ASM rebalancing operations, allocating work to the ASM rebalance slaves, which actually perform the rebalancing.

ARB*n*: The ASM rebalance slaves perform rebalancing of data extents across the ASM file systems. In Oracle 10.2 there are up to ten rebalance slaves named ARB0 to ARB9.

GMON: The disk group monitor process, which was introduced in Oracle 10.2, monitors the ASM disk groups.

PSP0: The process spawner background process is responsible for starting and stopping ASM rebalance slaves. This reduces the workload of the RBAL background process.

Workload Management

Workload management enables you to manage workloads to optimize use of resources for users and applications. Workload management is based on the concept of *database services*, which are used to specify the set of instances that should be used for a group of connections, and *connection load balancing*, which determines the instance within the set of preferred instances that is selected for a specific connection. We will also outline Transparent Application Failover (TAF), which defines the behavior of a connection in the event of the failure of the node or instance to which it is connected.

Services

In Oracle 10.1 and above, database services can be used to logically group sessions together based on their workload characteristics. There are two default database services: one that represents the background processes, and one that represents the user's sessions. These can be extended with user-defined database services. These allow a complex database workload to be divided into a few database services, each of which can be managed independently, thereby reducing the need to manage individual users or sessions.

Each database service can be assigned to a set of preferred instances depending on its resource requirements. If these instances are available, then the workload will be distributed across them. It is also possible to assign a set of alternate or "available" instances to each database service. These will be used in the event that one or more of the preferred instances is not available.

Database services provide a powerful mechanism by which resource usage can be distributed across instances. They provide the basis for grid architectures in which many applications run on a single RAC cluster. Each application can be configured to run as one or more database service and can be allocated to a specific set of primary and backup servers. Statistics can be monitored by services, and trace can also be enabled at database service level, or within a database service, for individual modules and/or actions. Database services can be mapped to Resource Manager consumer groups to control resource usage—for example, to limit the total amount of CPU consumed by a database service. Many other Oracle features, including the Job Scheduler, Parallel Execution, and Advanced Queuing, are aware of database service and can use them to manage their workload.

Services can be administered using the EM, the DBCA, or the SRVCTL utility. In Oracle 10.1, services administration functionality is restricted to starting and stopping services in EM. However, in Oracle 10.2 and above, EM can perform all services administration tasks.

Connection Load Balancing

Oracle provides the ability to balance client connections across the instances in a RAC cluster. This enables the workload to be distributed across nodes in order to maximize throughput or to minimize response times. There are two types of load balancing: client-side and server-side load balancing.

With client-side load balancing, the client distributes connection requests randomly to all available listener processes. With server-side load balancing the listener process attempts to direct connections to the best instance, using load information provided by the instances. In Oracle 10.2, this information is presented in the form of a load balancing advisory, which provides information to applications about the current service levels being provided by each instance. The load balancing advisory provides recommendations to applications describing where to direct requests to obtain the best service, based on the defined policy.

The load balancing advisory generates advice based on the specified connection load balancing goal for each service, which can either be long or short:

- **Long**: Used for applications that have long-lived connections, such as connection pools and SQL*Forms sessions.

- **Short**: Used for applications that have short-lived connections, such as stateless web applications that do not connect using a connection pool.

Transparent Application Failover (TAF)

In the event of an instance failure, TAF allows TAF-enabled applications to automatically reconnect to another instance. The new connection will be identical to the original. However, any uncommitted transactions existing at the time of failure will be rolled back.

TAF can be configured to perform two types of failover: session and select. With both types of failover, any uncommitted transactions will be rolled back and the session will be connected to another instance. In addition, with select failover only, if a SELECT statement is executing at the time of failure, it will be reexecuted by the new session—using the same system change number—and fetched rows will be discarded up to the point that the original query failed. The SELECT statement will then continue to return the remaining rows to the client. The select option adds a negligible overhead on the client side to the CPU cost of each fetch operation.

In addition, it is possible to specify a connection method. This defines when connections are made to the failover instance. Basic connections are performed at the time of failover. However, creating a new connection is a very resource-intensive process in Oracle and, consequently, for instances with a large number of concurrent users, establishing new connections at failover time can cause long delays. Therefore, it is also possible to specify that connections should preconnect to the failover instance. In this case, a session will have two concurrent connections. However, it will only activate the connection to the failover instance in the event that the original instance fails. While preconnection is less resource-intensive at failover time, it obviously consumes additional resources during normal operations.

Administration

Oracle provides a number of tools that can be used to administer RAC databases, including those described in the following sections.

Enterprise Manager

EM is the recommended GUI-based Oracle database management tool. Prior to Oracle 10g, many DBAs avoided Oracle Enterprise Manager (OEM), which was originally written in C and was later rewritten in Java. However, neither the C nor Java versions offered the full range of functionality offered by SQL commands, so many DBAs preferred to continue using command-line tools such as SQL*Plus or third-party GUI tools as their administration tool of choice.

In addition, prior to Oracle 10g the infrastructure surrounding OEM was both complex and unreliable. Every host managed by OEM required an OEM agent. This is an operating system process that executed SQL queries against the database and returned results to the OEM front end. Even in releases as recent as Oracle 9.2, the OEM agent was difficult to configure and notoriously unreliable.

In Oracle 10g OEM was rewritten as an HTML-based three-tier application and is now known as *Enterprise Manager* (EM). The HTML version is much more flexible than its C and Java forerunners. The result of the increased flexibility is that a much higher percentage of functionality offered by SQL commands is now available in the HTML interface. In addition, Oracle 10g offers a significant amount of new functionality, much of which is managed using complex SQL statements and PL/SQL subroutine calls. It is much easier to execute these commands through the EM interface than to attempt to enter them at the command-line prompt. An agent on each node is still required to communicate information to the management server. However, the agent has been improved and the configuration process has been streamlined.

EM contains RAC-specific functionality that allows you to start and stop nodes and also to create, delete, start, and stop services.

There are two versions of EM, Database Control and Grid Control, which are described in the following sections.

Database Control

Database Control is installed by default when you create a database using the Database Configuration Assistant. A Database Control session can be started from a browser window immediately after installation has completed. The Database Control allows you to administer all targets related to a single RAC database, including instances, listeners, hosts, and the cluster. It provides sufficient functionality to start and stop the database; back up and restore data; administer users, tablespaces, datafiles, and objects; set parameters; and address performance issues.

Grid Control

Grid Control is a more complex version of the Database Control that can administer multiple cluster databases, cluster database instances, and their hosts. If you wish to use EM to configure Oracle Data Guard to manage standby databases, you must use Grid Control.

Grid Control enables the monitoring and administration of the entire Oracle environment from a single network location. It can manage hosts, databases, listeners, application servers, HTTP servers, and web applications.

Sites that have used OEM with a management server in previous versions of Oracle will probably upgrade to use Grid Control. However, if you do not have multiple databases or do not intend to use Data Guard, you may wish to avoid using Grid Control. This is because Grid Control uses a separate database to store management information. If you do not take adequate precautions, the Grid Control database could become a single point of failure within your database. Therefore, you should consider carefully whether the added functionality provided by Grid Control justifies the additional cost and administrative overhead of maintaining another database.

Server Control Utility (SRVCTL)

SRVCTL is a powerful command-line utility that allows you to control many aspects of database operation. These include starting and stopping the database and individual instances, adding, removing, and relocating services, and controlling node applications that include VIP, GSD, the Oracle Net listener process, and the ONS daemon. SRVCTL is fully integrated with the OCR and is therefore the preferred method for administering RAC databases at the command line.

SQL*Plus

It is still possible to administer RAC databases using the SQL*Plus command-line utility. Unlike EM and SRVCTL, SQL*Plus can only connect to one instance at a time. Therefore, to start or stop a database using SQL*Plus it is necessary to connect to each instance individually.

Unlike EM and SRVCTL, however, SQL*Plus is not integrated with the OCR. Therefore, administrative operations performed in SQL*Plus may not be fully reflected in the OCR. While this can sometimes be inconvenient, we have found that the tools are much better integrated in Oracle 10.1 and above than they were in Oracle 9.2, and it is possible, for example, to work with both SRVCTL and SQL*Plus during the same administrative session.

CRSCTL

The CRSCTL utility is a command-line tool that can be used to manage Oracle Clusterware. In Oracle 10.1 this tool has limited functionality; in Oracle 10.2 and above it can be used to start and stop Oracle Clusterware.

Monitoring

A number of utilities are provided at both the operating system level and within Oracle to monitor performance.

Operating System Utilities

Linux includes versions of all the standard operating system utilities. These include ps, free, top, vmstat, netstat, iostat, mpstat, and sar.

However, these utilities are not always part of the standard installation, and it is sometimes necessary to install additional packages from the software distribution or to download them from the Internet.

Linux also provides a wealth of other open source operating system tools and utilities, some of which are Linux-specific and others which have been ported from legacy UNIX platforms. These include strace, which is similar to truss, which is found on a number of other UNIX platforms and traces system call executions.

Enterprise Manager

In Oracle 10.1 and above, EM provides increasing amounts of monitoring information. In particular, in Oracle 10.2 several pages have been redesigned to provide additional information, and the cache coherency statistics have been enhanced.

Automatic Workload Repository (AWR)

In Oracle 10.1 and above it is possible to create an Automatic Workload Repository (AWR) in the Oracle database. The AWR, which is created automatically if the database is built using the DBCA, contains snapshots of database statistics and workload information.

The AWR forms the basis for much of the self-management functionality in Oracle 10.1 and above. It retains historical information allowing comparisons to be made with the current performance and trends to be identified.

By default, snapshots are performed by the MMON background process every 60 minutes and are retained in the workload repository which is located in the SYSAUX tablespace for seven days, after which time they are automatically purged.

Automatic Database Diagnostic Monitor (ADDM)

Automatic Database Diagnostic Monitor (ADDM) was introduced in Oracle 10.1. It uses data captured in the AWR to diagnose database performance, identify any problems, and suggest potential solutions. ADDM is built directly into the kernel, minimizing any performance overhead.

ADDM analyzes database performance holistically. In other words it considers all activity across the database before making recommendations about specific areas of the workload. It runs automatically after each AWR snapshot and the results are saved in the database. If ADDM detects any issues, alerts are generated that can be inspected in the EM tools. ADDM reports can also be run manually.

Active Session History (ASH)

Active Session History (ASH) was introduced in Oracle 10.1. It is a component of the AWR. ASH samples all sessions once a second and records information about those that are currently waiting. This information is used by ADDM to classify any problems that have been identified.

ASH acquires information directly by sampling the session state objects. This information acquired by ASH is stored in a circular buffer in the SGA. The circular buffer occupies a fixed amount of memory that is allocated at database start-up. The default size of the circular buffer is derived from the number of CPUs and the size of the shared pool.

ASH only records information about active sessions. It does not include information about recursive sessions or sessions waiting for idle events. This means that sessions waiting for "SQL*Net message from client" will not be included. By default, ASH also excludes background processes waiting for their normal timer events, or parallel slaves waiting for idle events. However, you can optionally force ASH to record information about all sessions

The information collected by ASH is flushed to disk periodically. By default, only one sample every ten seconds is flushed from the ASH buffer to disk and is written to the workload repository, which is in the SYSAUX tablespace. Flushing of data to disk can be optionally disabled if necessary.

Dynamic Performance Views

Oracle includes a large number of RAC-specific dynamic performance views. These will be installed automatically if you create your database using the DBCA.

As with single-instance databases, each instance maintains local dynamic performance views that have a V$ prefix, such as V$BH, which describes the contents of the buffer cache. The underlying X$ fixed tables can be aggregated from each instance into a single global view which has a GV$ prefix, for example, GV$BH.

Statistics

Oracle includes a number of RAC-specific statistics that describe the amount of traffic over the interconnect. These statistics are interpreted by various tools, including EM, the ADDM, and STATSPACK.

Statistics are available in dynamic performance views at instance level, database service level, and session level. They can also be optionally enabled at module and/or action level.

Tools and Utilities

A number of tools and utilities are provided to support RAC database installation and configuration. These are described in the following sections.

Cluster Verification Utility

In Oracle 10.2 and above, Oracle provides the Cluster Verification Utility, which allows you to verify the configuration of your cluster at any stage during the installation process and also when the database is in production. The CLUVFY utility only reads information, it never updates configuration files and, consequently, it can safely be run at any time.

CLUVFY can either be used to verify the state of a cluster at a particular stage of the installation process, or, alternatively, it can be used to verify the state of any individual component.

It is also possible to use CLUVFY with Oracle 10.1 where it may provide some useful diagnostics.

Oracle Universal Installer (OUI)

Oracle Universal Installer (OUI) is a Java-based installation utility that is now used for all Oracle installations of software and patch sets. It is a GUI-based tool and therefore in Linux must be invoked from an X Window environment.

Before running the OUI you must configure a cluster file system that is shared by all nodes in the cluster or, alternatively, has created raw devices on shared storage that are accessible to all nodes.

By default, the OUI will install the RAC option if it recognizes that the installation is being performed on a cluster. When installing Oracle Clusterware or Oracle database software you will be asked to specify on which nodes the software will be installed. The OUI will then install the specified software on the local node and copy it using the secure shell copy to all other nodes.

During each OUI installation you must specify an Oracle Home directory, which is the top-level directory into which the software will be installed. If you are installing on multiple nodes, the Oracle Home directory will be the same for any specific component. Oracle recommends that you create a separate Oracle Home directory for Oracle Clusterware, ASM, and the Oracle database software. This is intended to simplify future upgrades by reducing the dependencies between the components.

To install a RAC database it is necessary to run the OUI at least twice, possibly three times or more. Oracle Clusterware must be installed first. If you have chosen to use a separate Oracle Home for ASM, then this should be installed next. Finally, the Oracle database software can be installed. Following the installation of the Oracle database software, the OUI can optionally invoke the DBCA to create a new database and the Network Configuration Assistant (NETCA) to configure the network for the RAC environment.

Virtual IP Configuration Assistant (VIPCA)

In Oracle 10.1 and above, virtual IP addresses are created for each instance. In the event of a node failure, Oracle fails over the VIP address to a surviving node.

The Virtual IP Configuration Assistant (VIPCA) is used to create the initial VIP configuration. In Oracle 10.1 it is invoked during the Oracle database software installation process; in Oracle 10.2 it is invoked silently during Oracle Clusterware installation. VIPCA can also be run as a stand-alone program, although this should not be necessary during normal operation.

Database Creation Assistant (DBCA)

The DBCA has become a sophisticated wizard that allows you to rapidly create databases in various configurations. Over the past few versions of Oracle, this utility has undergone significant enhancement.

In Oracle 10.1, the DBCA will create an ASM instance on each node during the database creation process; in Oracle 10.2 this process has been streamlined and it is now possible to create an ASM instance separately.

In Oracle 10.2 and above, the DBCA contains functionality to add and delete instances from the cluster. It also allows you to create clone copies of the database structure optionally including the data.

The DBCA enables the database for use by the EM utilities. It also allows you to specify a set of database services for the database. You can allocate different types of workloads to different database services and then use the Resource Manager to control the resources allocated to each workload. This allows you to establish workload priorities and resource limits within the cluster.

It is also still possible to create the database using scripts. However, we would only recommend that you use scripts if this is essential. For example, your change control procedures may require all changes to be performed using scripts that have been tested on a nonproduction database. In particular, if you intend to use ASM, then we strongly recommend that you use the DBCA to create the ASM instances on each node.

Database Upgrade Assistant (DBUA)

The Database Upgrade Assistant (DBUA) is a GUI tool that guides you through the various steps in the upgrade process and configures the database for the target release. In Oracle 10.1 and above the DBUA also makes recommendations for configuration options such as tablespaces and redo logs. For example, it recommends sizing information for the SYSAUX tablespace introduced in Oracle 10.1.

The DBUA performs a number of preupgrade checks. The upgrade will not be attempted until all of the preupgrade steps have been completed.

DBUA is fully RAC-aware. In a RAC environment, the DBUA upgrades all database and configuration files on all nodes in the cluster.

Network Configuration Assistant (NETCA)

NETCA has been available for several years and is executed automatically at the end of the install process. It is a Java-based utility that creates initial configurations for Oracle Net files, including listener.ora, sqlnet.ora, and tnsnames.ora. In Oracle 10.1 and above, the initial configuration is satisfactory for most clustered databases, and you may find that you never need to modify the files manually.

Oracle Interface Configuration Tool (OIFCFG)

The OIFCFG is a command-line tool that can be used to allocate and deallocate network interfaces to or from components. It can also be used to direct components to use specific network interfaces and to display configuration information.

OCR Configuration Tool (OCRCONFIG)

OCRCONFIG is a command-line tool used for administration of the OCR, including configuration of backups and mirrored copies. Other OCR-related tools include the OCRCHECK, which checks the consistency of the repository, and the OCRDUMP, which dumps the contents of the OCR to a text file.

Backup and Recovery

A number of tools are available for backup and recovery of RAC databases, but in reality the vast majority of RAC users either use the RMAN or a storage-based backup and recovery solution. These are described in the following sections.

Recovery Manager (RMAN)

The RMAN tool provides backup, restore, and recovery capabilities. RMAN was introduced in Oracle 8.0 and initially had a bad reputation because of the complexity of its command language and limited functionality. However, RMAN has evolved rapidly over the years and is implemented by the vast majority of RAC users.

RMAN backs up, restores, and recovers datafiles, control files, online redo logs, server parameter files, and archived redo logs. It can either back up files to disk or it can be integrated with a media manager to back up files to external storage, which is usually tape. At the time of this writing Oracle had announced its own media management product called Oracle Secure Backup, which can be used in place of third-party media managers.

RMAN can be managed by either using the EM or a command-line utility. In a RAC environment it can perform both backups and recovery in parallel. In addition, RMAN channels can be dynamically allocated across several RAC instances. In the event of a node failure, channels can fail over to another node to complete their operation.

In an optimal RAC environment, RMAN is configured so that all instances can access all archived log threads throughout the cluster. In the event of a media failure, a single instance will initiate the recovery process which is simplified if that instance can access a local copy of the archived redo logs from all instances in the database.

Storage-Based Backup and Recovery

As an alternative to using RMAN for backup and recovery, some sites use snapshot or triple mirroring technology at storage area network (SAN) or network-attached storage (NAS) level. These backups ensure that the impact on the database is minimized while the backup is taken. Typically, only a few seconds are required to take the snapshot or to break one of the mirrors. The database can then continue processing while the backup is written to tape and, in the case of triple-mirroring, the third disk is resilvered. Oracle includes a number of commands to suspend database updates and to ensure the consistency of the database when such backups are performed.

Disaster Recovery

Oracle RAC provides protection against individual node or instance failures. It does not, however, provide protection against site failures such as those caused by power cuts, natural disasters, or terrorism. In order to provide protection against site failures, it is necessary to ensure that a disaster recovery solution is implemented. These can be achieved by either using Oracle technology or within hardware.

Data Guard

Oracle Data Guard uses standby databases to protect data against errors, failures, and corruptions. Data Guard maintains a transactionally consistent copy of the Oracle database at a remote location, which can be used to recover from the loss of or damage to the production database. The two types of Data Guard database, physical standby and logical standby, are described in the following sections.

Physical Standby

A physical standby is initially created from a backup of the primary database. Thereafter, the physical standby database is updated by applying all the redo changes that have been applied to the production database. Redo changes are propagated from the primary database to the standby database by either the LGWR or the ARCH background process at time intervals determined by the level of protection required. Protection levels include

- **Maximum protection**: No data loss is permitted. Therefore, redo is propagated to the standby database by the LGWR process immediately at the point in time that it is committed on the primary database. If the standby database is shut down, the primary database will also be shut down. This ensures that every transaction is recorded in both locations.

- **Maximum availability**: Some data loss is possible. Redo is propagated to the standby database by the LGWR process immediately when it is committed on the primary database. However, if the standby database fails, the primary database will continue generating redo. This ensures that processing can continue, although there is a possibility of data loss in the event of the failure of both databases simultaneously.

- **Maximum performance**: Data loss is probable in the event of a failure. Redo is propagated from the primary to the standby database by either the LGWR process using an asynchronous copy, or by the ARCH process when a log file switch occurs. In either case there is a delay before the redo is transferred to the standby database, and if the primary site fails there is a probability that redo will be lost.

Physical standby databases can be opened in read-only mode for limited reporting purposes.

It is possible to perform a switchover between the primary and standby database. Processing is transferred to the standby database. This is useful if, for example, it is necessary to shut down the primary database for site maintenance. When the primary site is available again, it is possible to switch back between the standby site and the primary site. Neither operation involves any data loss or requires rebuilding of the database.

It is also possible to perform a failover operation between the primary and standby database. This is the real reason for maintaining a standby database, but, fortunately, failovers are a rare occurrence. All processing will be moved to the standby database. Prior to Oracle 10.2 it was necessary to rebuild the primary database following a failover, making it an expensive operation. In Oracle 10.2 and above it is possible to avoid rebuilding the primary database if the flashback database feature was enabled prior to the failure.

Physical standby databases have been available since Oracle 7.3 and have become very popular in the Oracle user community.

Logical Standby

A logical standby is initially created from a backup of the primary database. However, a logical standby is maintained by replicating SQL statements that have been executed on the primary database. It is possible to select which objects are maintained by the logical standby, and these can have different physical structures on the logical standby to the primary database. For example, they can have different indexes or a different partitioning key. The logical standby database can be opened with read-write access, although objects in recovery can only be opened as read-only. Therefore a logical standby database can provide a flexible alternative in demanding reporting environments.

Logical standby databases were introduced in Oracle 9.2 but are still relatively rarely deployed in the Oracle community.

Stretch Clusters

Over the past couple of years, interest has grown in the implementation of stretch clusters. These are RAC databases where one set of nodes is in one location and the other set of nodes is in another physically separate location. The instances must all communicate via the same interconnect which must offer low latency for performance to be acceptable. Storage must also be replicated between the two sites while a third site must be used to implement an independent quorum disk to prevent split brain syndrome in the event of the failure of the interconnect.

Stretch clusters are complex and expensive to build. They do, however, maximize investment in server hardware and also in RAC licenses. They also potentially eliminate the need to maintain standby databases.

Hardware Disaster Recovery Solutions

Some sites choose to implement hardware-based disaster recovery solutions, often because economies of scale can be achieved by using a single solution for a multivendor database estate. For example, the EMC Symmetrix Remote Data Facility (SRDF) and HP Storage Works Continuous Access both ensure that all block changes on a storage array at one location are replicated at another location.

Summary

Within this chapter we introduced the concepts underlying RAC. We paid particular attention to Oracle Clusterware and the areas where RAC differs from a single-instance Oracle configuration. We also introduced a number of tools and utilities that you will want to consider using in a RAC environment. The information presented in this chapter provides the grounding for the installation and configuration of a RAC on Linux environment and also provides a reference for understanding the technology components you will encounter when building RAC on Linux systems.

CHAPTER 4

■■■

RAC Design

When designing a RAC cluster, you should fully define and identify your business requirements. Once you have defined your business requirements, your next step is to identify your architectural decisions, which will, in turn, allow you to specify storage and hardware requirements. Your architectural decisions will be reflected in the logical and physical design of the application. The logical design of your application will result in the physical design, and hence will be reflected in the RAC implementation.

In this chapter, we will examine some of the design decisions you need to consider before implementing a RAC cluster.

Business Requirements

The first things to consider are the business needs of your application. The business requirements will be reflected in resource requirements, which may change over time. By thoroughly understanding the business requirements of your application, you will be able to do a good job designing and sizing your RAC implementation.

Oracle documentation commonly makes a distinction between OLTP applications and DSS, also known as data warehouses, but in our experience, almost all RAC applications fall somewhere between these two extremes.

Obviously, the RAC cluster must be sized correctly to handle the required workload. Therefore, you need to accurately estimate the number of users, the number of database connections, and the physical workload, including peaks and seasonal variations. Pay particular attention to projected growth in the workload over the lifetime of the cluster.

Technical Requirements

For RAC users, many of whom develop their own applications and deploy bespoke systems, it is important to establish how many and which types of resources the application will require and when. Resource consumption is generally measured in terms of CPU usage, memory consumption, and disk I/O. In the last case, distinguishing between read and write operations is important, as these have significantly different effects at storage level.

While it is possible, in the light of experience, to make an educated guess at the performance of a planned RAC system, it is impossible to guarantee that performance without actually testing the application with a representative user load. Even minor changes to application code can have a major impact on scalability.

If you are using a commercially available package, verify that the vendor has tested and certified the application for RAC. Many Oracle applications may not have been designed for a RAC environment. The application vendor should preferably have had access to an in-house RAC system for development and testing. Also, check whether any of their other customers are using RAC.

If you are using an existing package, seek advice on hardware requirements from the vendor. You may also be able to find other customers running the same package on RAC.

By far, the best way to evaluate the impact of running your application is to subject it to load testing specific to your environment for the number of users and projected workload. Testing the application in this manner will highlight any weaknesses in your application or environment that need to be addressed before it can be put into production on a RAC cluster.

Most of the larger hardware vendors, such as Dell, HP, and Intel, have porting and testing centers where you can test your application on various hardware configurations. This exercise can also reduce the learning curve, as you will receive assistance and instruction in RAC best-practices from their employees, who do this kind of work on a regular basis for their customers. In recent years, Oracle has also invested heavily in assisting users to deploy their application on RAC.

If the application is in production in your environment, then you should be able to measure the amount of physical I/O that it currently requires. Remember that when the application is ported from a single-instance database to a multinode RAC database, from one platform to another, or from one Oracle version to another, the I/O characteristics will most likely differ in the initialization parameters, cache sizes, and enhancements to the cost-based optimizer (CBO). CPU utilization may also be affected by these factors and by other improvements, such as optimizations in the PL/SQL compiler, Parallel Execution, new background processes, and so on.

Do not automatically assume that you will see performance improvements when moving to a newer version of Oracle. Many recent enhancements have been introduced on the basis that they should improve performance for the majority of systems. The most important thing that you can do is test an upgrade before you actually upgrade your production systems. Testing will allow you to proactively measure the potential performance gains.

One of the main benefits of a RAC cluster is that the database continues to be available in the event of a node failure. It is essential that the remaining nodes are capable of handling the required workload following a failure. You may decide all users do not need access to the cluster or that you are willing to run in a degraded performance mode until the node is repaired. You may even choose to restrict certain classes of users while one or more nodes are unavailable. In Oracle 10g, this can easily be implemented using database services.

However, following a node failure, the remaining nodes must have sufficient capacity to handle the essential workload to preserve the prefailure performance expectation of the users. Depending on the performance of your application, the user's expectations might lead you to implement a cluster consisting of four two-CPU nodes, as opposed to two four-CPU nodes. In the event of a failure, the former configuration would have six CPUs remaining, whereas the latter configuration would have four CPUs. In the unlikely event of a second node failure, the former configuration would still have four CPUs, but the latter configuration would have suffered a complete failure, and the database would be inaccessible.

Business Constraints

You will also need to identify the constraints under which your application must run. At one extreme, it may need to run 24-7, 365 days a year; at the other, it may only need to be available during normal working hours. The reality for most users is somewhere between these two extremes.

Your design will be affected by the level of availability required for the production platform. If a high level of availability is required on the production system, you will almost certainly need a separate test system, on which you can explore performance issues and test patches and other changes.

Check any SLAs that may exist in your organization. In addition, question any existing practices to ensure that they are still relevant for Oracle 10g. For example, if the previous system was implemented using Oracle 7, it may still be halted once a week for a cold backup, requiring a time window of several hours. Systems of this age, which still use dictionary managed tablespaces, are often defragmented on a regular basis. While always questionable in prior versions, this exercise has been unnecessary since the introduction of locally managed tablespaces in Oracle 8.1.5. However, convincing operational staff, DBAs, or senior management that tasks such as these are no longer necessary is often quite difficult, though, particularly if they perceive that these tasks' elimination constitutes a risk to the business.

It is important to identify how much downtime will be available; acceptable levels of downtime should be clearly identified in your business requirements. In our experience, most sites can survive a short amount of downtime on a scheduled, fairly regular basis. One of the advantages of RAC is that downtime can be planned with reasonable certainty. You may also need to restrict access while patches are applied to the data dictionary and other persistent structures. In general, the less maintenance time that is available, the more expensive the system will become to support.

Remember to identify any seasonal peaks or variations in workload. Many systems are implemented during quiet periods, such as the summer or holiday weekends, when demand for the system is lower. However, testing should reflect the maximum load that you anticipate. For example, mobile telecommunication operators' annual peak is reached between 12:00 a.m. and 1:00 a.m. on January 1, and their systems must be able to handle the traffic generated at this time.

Keep an open mind when examining business constraints and question why particular rules, practices, and procedures exist. These are often embedded in the corporate culture and, on closer examination, apply only to legacy systems. The introduction of a new system presents an excellent opportunity to eliminate these unnecessary business constraints.

Check and eliminate tasks that serve no useful purpose in current versions of Oracle, such as defragmentation or frequent computation of statistics for very large tables. In particular, look for tasks currently performed serially that could be parallelized, which can be achieved three ways in a RAC database. The most obvious way is to identify tasks that can be performed at the same time. For example, if you are using RMAN to back up your RAC database, you may be able to execute some reports or run some batch jobs concurrently. While there may be some contention between the backup and the processing for resources, the overall times for the jobs may still be reduced, because these processes tend to run in the off hours, away from general online users.

The second way is to use the parallelization features built into Oracle, including parallel execution (parallel query and parallel DML). Over the past ten years, support for parallelization has improved significantly and has also been extended to various tools and utilities. Many of these operations are designed into the database and are automatically turned on and off without your knowledge. For example, in Oracle 10.1 and above, you can export and import data using the Data Pump utilities. The original imp utility operates serially, whereas the Data Pump import utility loads data in parallel.

The third way to implement parallelization is to use RAC itself. You can direct workloads with different characteristics to specific nodes or instances. For example, the backup might run on one node while the batch jobs run on another, optimizing the use of the SGA in each instance and minimizing the amount of interconnect traffic. Database services provide an excellent way of allocating tasks to different instances, with the assurance that if the instance fails, processing can be resumed on another instance.

Upgrade Policy

Another consideration when designing your cluster is your upgrade policy. Some sites implement the latest version of Oracle and then update the patches at every opportunity, which can be justified if your application makes use of recently introduced features. However, you should remember that each patch set introduces a certain amount of risk, so there should be a definable benefit to your business in performing the upgrade.

At the other end of the scale, many sites wait until an Oracle release is completely stable before implementing it. At the time of this writing, Oracle 10g has been available for over two years, but many sites are still implementing new systems on Oracle 9.2. While this delay in switching to Oracle 10g may be prudent in a single-instance environment, it is not advisable in a RAC environment, where the pace of development is much faster, and the benefits of using newer releases are much more tangible. For RAC on Linux in particular, we strongly recommend that you consider Oracle 10.2 as a platform for initial deployment.

Many users implement new systems and plan never to upgrade them once they go live. If adequate testing has been performed prior to going into production, this can be a good option, as project teams often disperse as their members seek new challenges once a project has gone live. However, these users are often in a minority. For many users, the realities of their businesses mean that their IT systems continually change as events arise, such as mergers, acquisitions, growth, downsizing, consolidation, and so on. For these users, the demands on their database estate are dynamic and must be addressed on a continuing basis.

Architecture

Having established your business requirements, you are now in a position to design the architecture. Most users have finite budgets, and consequently, their optimal architectures are not usually obtainable. Therefore, your architectural design will probably be a compromise between your business requirements and your budget.

For example, your optimal architecture might include a four-node primary RAC cluster, a four-node RAC standby cluster at a separate location, and similar systems for development and quality assurance. However, you may be able to afford only a two-node primary cluster, with a single-instance standby database and a single-instance test database.

We recommend that you start by designing your optimal architecture for your business requirements and then iteratively eliminating the least essential components until your system is within budget. You should then recheck your cluster's capability of meeting your business requirements. If it's not capable, you should revisit either the business requirements or your budget to correctly set the expectations of your management and user community. Implementing a system that does not fulfill its business needs is a guaranteed recipe for failure.

Development and Test Systems

In addition to the production RAC cluster, you may need one or more additional RAC clusters to support the production cluster, depending largely on the nature of your application and the level of availability required. If the application is a purchased package, then you will need a RAC test system to validate patches and updates before applying them to the production system. If the application is developed in-house, you may also need to support RAC development or QA systems that are equivalent to the production system. We advise on some of the fundamentals of testing strategies in Chapter 5. We do not recommend that you ever use your production hardware as a test platform.

Disaster Recovery

Disaster recovery capabilities can be implemented at the storage or database level. If you opt for the latter in a RAC environment, you will probably use Oracle Data Guard to create a physical or logical standby database in a separate location. Ideally, the hardware and storage at the standby location should be as close as possible in specification to the production site. Identical hardware and storage are not always economical or feasible, and consequently, customers frequently lower the specification of the hardware on their standby site accepting a potential throughput reduction in return for cost savings. However, the main consideration when implementing a standby strategy is to accurately determine whether the business will be able to continue to operate in the event of the total loss of the primary site.

Figure 4-1 shows an Oracle Data Guard configuration for a two-node RAC primary database located in London and a two-node RAC standby database located in Reading. A public network is required between the two locations to transmit the redo log shipping traffic. In reality, this network would probably be dedicated to prevent interference from other competing network traffic. The interconnect or storage network does not need to span the locations, although that can be another alternative. This architecture would be identical for either a physical or a logical standby database.

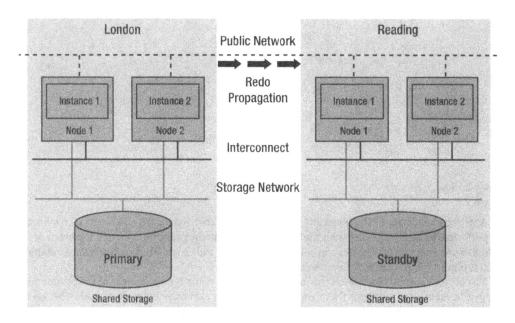

Figure 4-1. *Oracle Data Guard configuration*

You can configure a RAC primary database with either a RAC standby database or a single-instance database. It is common to see a single-instance database being used for the standby, which significantly reduces hardware and software licensing costs.

Stretch Clusters

The *stretch cluster* is an apparently attractive architecture that maximizes the utilization of cluster resources across two or more locations. For example, for a four-node stretch cluster, you might locate two nodes of the cluster at one site and the other two nodes of the cluster at a second site.

Figure 4-2 shows a stretch cluster where two nodes are located in London and the other two are in Reading. The diagram shows that three different network connections are required between the sites: the public network, a private network for the interconnect, and a storage network for block replication between the storage devices at each location.

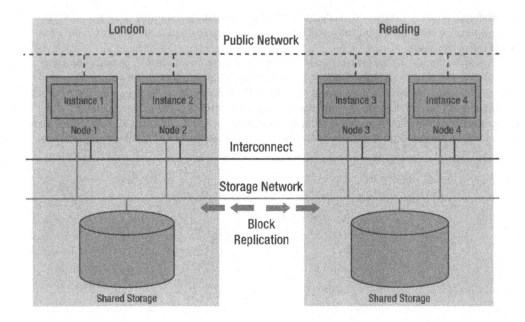

Figure 4-2. *Stretch clusters*

A stretch cluster can be deployed as a disaster recovery solution if each site has its own storage that performs the replication between the sites. This deployment guarantees that, in the event of the loss of one site, remaining sites can continue to operate and the database will remain available, which is important for many 24-7 systems.

The obvious benefit of a stretch cluster is that all nodes contribute resources to the production system. The main disadvantage is that a very fast and possibly expensive network must exist between the sites, as the cluster nodes require a fast interconnect network, and the data storage must be replicated between nodes. While node affinity is vastly improved in Oracle 10.2, nodes will still need to communicate with each other to synchronize access to resources using global enqueues.

From a network point of view, storage-level replication is much less efficient than Data Guard. Consider a transaction that updates a single row. Data Guard will only transmit the redo for the transaction, which consists of the changes made to the row, plus the undo required to reverse the changes. In the case of a small change, this transmission will not amount to more than 200 bytes. However, if replication is performed at the storage level, all affected blocks will be replicated, including blocks from the online redo log, datafiles, undo segment headers, undo blocks, and the archived redo log. Thus, a minimum of five block changes will be transmitted across to storage at the remote site.

Consequently, in a stretch cluster the latency of the network between the sites is the vital limiting factor. Despite increasing interest in new technologies, such as InfiniBand, at the time of this writing, it is still extremely rare to encounter stretch clusters in production.

Reporting Systems

Many sites implement reporting systems that are physically separated from the production database. While not strictly necessary in a RAC environment, a reporting system can act as a useful validation tool to test the backup and recovery procedure if it is built from a backup copy of the database. Alternatively, the reporting system can be built as a physical or logical standby database, thereby validating the disaster recovery capability when this function is tested on a regular basis.

Spare Servers

Compared to the cost of other RAC components, including the storage and the RAC licenses, server hardware is relatively inexpensive. This comparison changes the cost models that systems tradition- ally operate under. When you are designing your RAC cluster, you should consider whether to carry a stock of spare servers, which can be quickly swapped into the cluster in event of a node failure.

We recommend that you obtain quotes for hardware maintenance contracts at different service levels and compare these to the costs of purchasing hot spares. If you purchase a maintenance contract, remember that it may not be possible for a component in a failed server to be replaced immediately. A replacement server supplied by the maintenance company will need to be built, either with a standard operating system image or manually, before it can be added to the cluster. On the other hand, if you have a spare server in stock, it can be prepared in advance. Having a prebuilt spare on hand will save critical time during an outage, since it can be provisioned much more quickly than a system built from scratch.

If you do carry a spare server, ensure that it contains all the correct components, including CPU, memory, and network and fiber cards. If you need to borrow components from the spare server for the live cluster, ensure that these are replaced and retested as soon as possible. If you follow good change control policies, you will ensure that the spare server is quickly restocked for parts and ready to be provisioned on short notice in case of a failure of the production system.

Storage Requirements

In this section, we will discuss some of the design issues you will encounter when planning storage for your cluster.

You may decide which storage type to use based on your current production environment, but you should ideally decide based on your business uptime and performance requirements. For exam- ple, if you already have a SAN, then you will probably wish to utilize this technology for the new cluster. Similarly, if you already have existing NAS, then you will probably wish to use this type of storage for your RAC cluster. We cover in detail the storage options available to you in Chapter 7.

If you do not have an existing storage platform, then you should consider a number of issues when designing your storage configurations for a RAC cluster.

ASM and Cluster File Systems

In this book we describe how to configure your shared storage to using OCFS and ASM, which are both Oracle products. We cover the configuration of OCFS in Chapter 8 and ASM in Chapter 9. Alternatively, a number of third-party cluster file systems are commercially available, including Red Hat Global File System (GFS), PolyServe Matrix Server, or NFS, which is certified for specific NAS configurations.

At the time of this writing, a significant proportion of RAC users still implement raw devices instead of a cluster file system. However, we believe that many of these users are running Oracle 9i or earlier and deployed their systems before OCFS became sufficiently stable to be a viable option. We do not advise new RAC users to implement systems on raw devices, as the manageability of the alternatives, such as ASM, is significantly higher.

You should test the performance of the cluster file system. In test systems, we have seen a per- formance degradation of up to 15% in both OCFS and ASM over their native equivalents. Clustered file systems provide more flexibility and ease of use from a DBA perspective, and in many cases, this ease of use more than makes up for the decrease in performance of the file system.

If you are using ASM with RAID-protected storage, ensure that you specify external protection when creating the ASM disk group. In theory, providing redundancy at storage level is better than within ASM, because storage-level protection will be managed within the storage device, which is optimized for I/O at the device level, whereas ASM is managed by the operating system and uses local CPU and I/O resources to implement redundancy and disk balancing.

Shared Oracle Homes vs. Local Oracle Homes

Prior to Oracle 10g, most RAC users implemented separate physical Oracle homes tied to individual applications. In other words, they installed multiple copies of the Oracle binaries and supporting software on the local disks of each of the nodes in the cluster. In Oracle 10.1 and above, you can create a shared Oracle home where a single copy of the Oracle binaries is located on shared storage. Each approach has advantages and disadvantages.

The advantage of using a shared Oracle home is that you have only one set of binaries to support. Patching is simplified, as only one location has to be updated. However, this can turn into a disadvantage if the system needs to be available 24-7, as it will be difficult to apply the patches. In this scenario, depending on the severity and composition of the patch, the instances may have to be shut down, preventing user access to the application.

The advantage of using local Oracle homes is that patches can be applied to a subset of servers. The database can then be stopped and any updates can be applied to the database before it is restarted with the newly patched servers. The remaining servers can then be patched and restarted sequentially, minimizing the overall downtime for the cluster.

Backup and Recovery

If you do not have an existing storage platform or SAN, then you will need to think carefully about your current and future requirements. When identifying your storage requirements, you should factor in your backup and recovery strategy and any disaster recovery objectives, namely data replication, Recovery Point Objective (RPO), and mean time to recovery (MTTR). These requirements will drive the design of your storage subsystem and will ultimately determine what database architectures are viable for your environment.

For example, there are several methods for performing backups on a SAN or on NAS. These include triple mirroring and point-in-time snapshots, both of which allow a disk backup to be taken of the database in a matter of seconds, minimizing disruption to users. In addition, both SAN and NAS storage can be replicated over relatively long distances using synchronous and asynchronous methods, thereby providing disaster recovery capabilities.

If your budget and infrastructure are sufficient to support storage-based backup, recovery, and replication, then you should give these methods serious consideration as they are more generic, and often more reliable, than database-based methods. Another consideration of the storage system-based backup and recovery method is the working relationship between the storage and database administrators. Using a storage-based backup strategy will involve significantly more assistance from the storage administrator, which will require a lot of trust and goodwill between the storage and database administration teams to successfully implement this strategy. Storage-based backup solutions are frequently used at sites that maintain large, heterogeneous database estates.

If you wish to use database-based backup and recovery for RAC databases, we recommend that you investigate the RMAN utility, which has become the standard backup tool among the vast majority of RAC customers. RMAN functionality is implemented generically within Oracle using custom libraries linked to the database. These libraries are provided by storage vendors who imbed hardware knowledge about the tape or disk devices that they provide with their products. Other backup tools also exist, but we recommend using these only if you have a pre-existing relationship with the vendor. If you choose to use third-party tools, ensure that they fully support hot and cold backup, restore, and recovery methods for RAC databases. Also, check for any limitations in the database architectures that they support.

Having selected a suitable backup tool, you need to make a number of design decisions about the nature and location of the backups. Writing the backup files to a central location is preferable for ease of manageability. In the event of a node failure, the central location enables any remaining node to perform the recovery by looking for required files in a centralized, well-known location. If backup files are written to the local disk of one server, then a single point of failure has been introduced if that server is damaged or offline.

RMAN backups can be written either to disk or to tape. If you have sufficient space available, we recommend that you write the backup to disk initially and then copy it onto tape subsequently; this strategy is commonly called the *disk-to-disk-to-tape method* of backup and restore. Restores generally occur much faster when the database image is available online, so that a backup of the database is always available on disk. It is invariably faster to restore from a disk backup than a tape backup. The downside to this scenario is that additional disk space is required to implement a backup-to-disk strategy.

In Oracle 10g and above, you can optionally configure a Flashback Recovery Area, that is, an area of disk used for all backup and recovery files, including datafile copies and archived redo logs. You only need to specify a pathname and a maximum size for the Flashback Recovery Area when it is created. Oracle will manage the files contained in the Flashback Recovery Area and purge those that are no longer needed. If there is insufficient space, then Oracle will delete files starting with the oldest ones that have been backed up.

DBAs who learned their trade with Oracle 6.0 and early versions of Oracle 7 often still like to perform regular full exports of the database. While not strictly necessary, having an export file available on disk can be comforting, as it provides some level of reassurance that the database can be recovered in the event of an administrative disaster. Exporting the database by user will allow individual copies of applications to be taken independently of the entire database, which can be handy for recovering individual application components. Performing an export also provides additional validation of the blocks in the database used to store table information, since they are physically checked in the export phase.

Database blocks can become corrupted and remain unidentified until they are accessed on the live system. By performing regular exports of the database, these problems can be identified in advance of their appearance on the production system. Unlike tables where all rows are written to the export file, only the definitions of indexes are included in the export. Unfortunately, the export does not perform any validation of blocks in index segments, and therefore, index corruption is difficult to detect.

If you are performing RMAN backups, there is little value in performing additional exports. However, if you have sufficient resources, then exporting the database once a week can do no harm. Remember, however, that the export file will occupy a significant amount of space on disk. It can, of course, be compressed as it is written out to disk, thereby reducing the amount of space required. If space is at a premium, then in our opinion, make RMAN backup copies of the database rather than using the same disk space for an export.

Your backup and recovery strategy will also be limited by the availability and speed of tape devices. The optimum solution is to have separate networked tape devices that can be shared by many systems. Some users install additional network cards in each server, so that the backup can be written directly to the tape device over a dedicated network to prevent the backup interfering with other network traffic. Whether you use networked tape devices or directly attached tape devices, you should have a minimum of two to eliminate another potential single point of failure, as well as to increase the overall speed of the backup.

Archived Redo Logs

Another area for consideration is the location of the archived redo log files. We strongly recommend placing these in a central location on shared storage in a symmetrical data structure. This structure is straightforward to back up and makes recovery from any node much simpler, because the redo logs are located in a centralized location. By locating the redo log files on a shared storage system, you can take advantage of the safety, reliability, and increased performance of these storage devices.

Figure 4-3 shows the recommended configuration: a four-node RAC database where all archived redo log directories are written to shared storage.

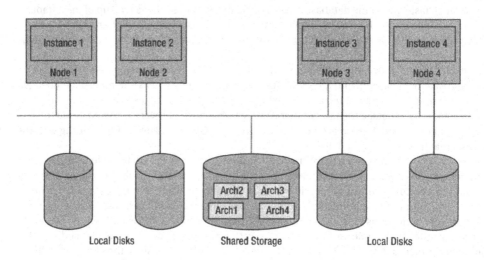

Figure 4-3. *Archived redo log storage*

If you do not have a cluster file system or ASM, then your options are more limited. One acceptable option is to use NFS for archived redo logs. Configure multiple log archive destinations to allow each server to copy its archived redo logs to two or more NFS locations on central servers. Alternatively, some users choose to locate their archived redo logs on the local disk of each server.

Figure 4-4 shows a four-node RAC cluster in which the archived redo logs are written to local disks. This configuration introduces a potential single point of failure in the event that the server dies. To circumvent this problem, some users configure a second log archive destination parameter to write the archived redo logs to the local disks of a second server. The second server eliminates the single point of failure, but it still makes recovery unnecessarily difficult. Another disadvantage of this configuration is the overhead of making duplicate I/Os for each redo log entry. This duplication places additional CPU cycles on the servers that could be better used servicing data requests.

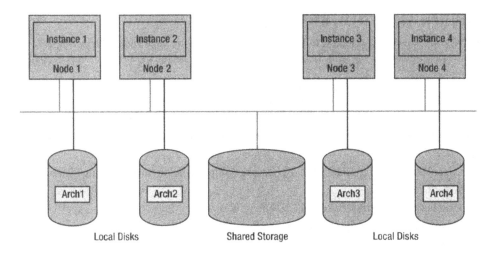

Figure 4-4. *Local archived redo log storage*

Figure 4-5 shows a four-node RAC database with a revised archived redo log configuration, in which each archived redo log is written to one local disk and one remote disk. Remote disks are mounted using NFS.

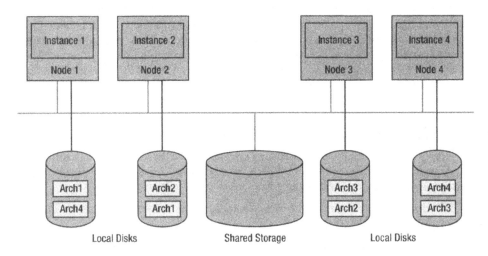

Figure 4-5. *Local and remote archived redo log storage*

Hardware Requirements

In this section, we provide an overview to some of the considerations to be given to selecting the server hardware when designing your RAC configuration. We discuss the hardware options available in Chapter 6.

While RAC will run on almost any industry-standard system configuration, these servers do not need to be of an identical configuration; however, they are much simpler to maintain if they are. Bear in mind that it is almost impossible to source identical servers, as most manufacturers change the specifications of the components on a regular basis. However, using similar hardware has several benefits:

- Initial faults are easier to isolate and fix, because components can be interchanged between servers.

- Support is simpler, and staff training costs are minimized.

- Low-level drivers, patches, and upgrades can be tested on an identically configured server, while the rest of cluster is running for subsequent rollout.

If you expect your cluster to grow over time, then it makes sense to have reliable guarantees that you will be able to source additional compatible servers.

When you are designing your cluster, make sure you understand any SLAs that are in place with your vendors, which may affect your hardware purchase. For example, in a mission-critical application, you may decide to have additional nodes available on a permanent basis in case of a node failure. For less important applications, the additional nodes may be built, but kept as hot spares, and possibly disabled to avoid paying the license fees. If you are building a grid architecture, then the additional nodes might also be deployed on other databases or used in non-mission-critical applications within the grid and redeployed when necessary. Alternatively, you might use database services to configure a node to have a primary purpose, for example, as a report server, when the cluster is running normally and a secondary purpose, such as an additional OLTP server, in the event of the failure of another OLTP node.

Application Design

If you have access to the source code of an existing system or have the advantage of writing an application from scratch, then you should consider a few application design issues, such as the use of bind variables and sequences. These issues are described in the following sections.

Bind Variables

If your application is likely to use shared SQL statements, then you should check that all statements use bind variables. Using bind variables increases the probability that individual SQL statements will reside in the library cache. Cached SQL statements can be shared and reused, consequently reducing the amount of hard parsing and reloading. It is very important that SQL statements are written identically, including the case (lower or upper), to ensure that they remain in the SQL cache for as long as possible.

Sequences

The most widely reported scalability issue in Oracle RAC is caused by sequences implemented within application tables. *Sequences* are sequential numbers generated within the database and are normally used as keys for database rows. The use of sequential numbers is a common feature in application packages that have been designed to be portable across several database platforms, as not all operating systems provide support for sequences. Managing unique sequential numbers is a performance-intensive operation for the database. Minimizing the use of sequences and/or using the caching feature will help prevent or reduce single points of contention with the database.

Use of sequential numbers can be a highly sensitive subject within organizations. This sensitivity is often a legacy of previous systems and is usually imposed from outside the IT department. Before designing a solution to a sequence numbering problem, it is always worth examining why the sequence is required in the first place. Sometimes it is needed for legal or auditing reasons and cannot be avoided. Many other systems, however, implement sequences simply for convenience, and seeking alternative solutions may be prudent.

Sequential number generation can present a number of performance issues in both single-instance and RAC environments.

In many applications, the maximum value of a sequential number is stored in a database table. When a new value is required, the application reads the current value from the database table, increments it, and then writes the new value back to the database table. Though this approach works well in a single-user database, it does not scale well in a multinode configuration, because the current session must make a row-level lock on the row containing the current sequence number. While this lock is being held, no other sessions can update the sequence until the current session has committed or rolled back.

In Oracle 8.1.5 and above, a PL/SQL autonomous transaction can be used to generate the next sequential number. Using a PL/SQL transaction reduces the amount of time that the transaction will lock the database table but may still cause contention if a large number of sessions are attempting to update the sequence concurrently.

RAC amplifies the impact on performance of sequences implemented using database tables. When a new sequence number is acquired, the session must first perform a consistent read on the database block containing the current sequence number. If the sequence number was last updated by another instance, then a read-consistent image of the database block will need to be obtained from that instance. The sequence number can then be incremented and written back to the database block, requiring the current version of the database block, which must also be obtained from the other instance. It may be necessary to wait until any row-level lock currently being held by a session on the other instance is released. Therefore, sequential number generation implemented using database tables can cause severe contention in a RAC environment.

For many years, Oracle has provided a solution to this problem in the form of Oracle sequences, which are a type of database object. For example, an Oracle sequence can be created as follows:

```
CREATE SEQUENCE seq1;
```

The next value of a sequence can be obtained in a single operation using the NEXTVAL pseudo-column as follows:

```
SELECT seq1.NEXTVAL FROM dual;
```

The highest value allocated by a sequence is recorded in the SEQ$ data dictionary table. To avoid updating this table every time a new value is selected from the sequence, by default sequences cache twenty values. The number of values that should be cached can be specified using the CACHE clause. In a RAC environment, each instance maintains its own separate cache of values.

It is often a requirement that sequentially generated numbers should not include gaps. However, gaps are very difficult to avoid because of database shutdowns or application errors. If a transaction rolls back instead of committing, it does not release any sequence values that it may have generated. In addition, if caching is enabled, then the unused sequence values may be lost when the database is stopped and restarted.

As with many forms of database tuning, the best way to solve a performance problem is by not introducing performance problems into the application design. For example, you may wish to review your requirements to determine whether sequence gaps may be acceptable. Sequences are often used to generate meaningless numbers that guarantee the uniqueness of primary keys. Occasionally, sequences will also be used to generate order numbers, invoice numbers, serial numbers, and so on, in which case they may be reflected in external systems. However, gaps in these sequences may still be acceptable as long as the individual numbers can be guaranteed to be unique, and the key relationships between database rows are preserved.

In many situations, therefore, sequence gaps do not represent a major problem. However, there may be external constraints, such as legal or accounting rules. Completely eliminating sequence gaps using Oracle sequences is not possible, as values are not reused if a transaction rolls back. However, you can limit the number of sequence gaps at the expense of performance and scalability.

In a single-instance environment, the number of unused sequence values that are lost can be minimized by specifying the following NOCACHE clause:

```
CREATE SEQUENCE seq1 NOCACHE;
```

However, if the NOCACHE clause is specified, then the SEQ$ data dictionary table will be updated every time a new sequence value is generated, which may cause high levels of contention for blocks in the SEQ$ table, particularly in RAC environments. Therefore, we do not recommend using NOCACHE for busy sequences.

In a RAC environment, each instance maintains its own cache of sequence values. Therefore, sequence values may not be allocated in ascending order across the cluster. If ascending order is a requirement, then you can to specify the ORDER clause for a sequence as follows:

```
CREATE SEQUENCE seq1 ORDER;
```

The ORDER clause guarantees that the values returned by the sequence are in ascending order. However, you should be aware that specifying the ORDER clause will effectively serialize the sequence across all nodes in the cluster. If the sequence is accessed frequently, this may cause contention, and hence possible performance problems between nodes that request the sequence.

Database Design

If you do not have access to the source code, then it may not be possible to modify the application. Even sites with access to the source code may regard changes to the application as being a high-risk activity if, for example, the developers have moved on to other roles. In this section, we will describe some of the ways the DBA can positively influence the resource consumption of a RAC application without access to the source code.

Cursor Sharing

You should ensure that your application uses bind variables to increase the number of SQL statements that can be shared. If it is not possible to modify your application, then you might consider using *cursor sharing*, which replaces literal values in SQL statements with temporary bind variables prior to parsing.

In a RAC environment, statement parsing is significantly more expensive because of the need to lock resources using GES, the locking mechanism that spans the nodes that belong to the RAC cluster. Cursor sharing reduces the amount of hard parsing that is necessary within the instance. It also potentially reduces the amount of memory required to store the cursor in the library cache.

Optimizer Statistics

Maintaining optimizer statistics is important, so that the CBO has sufficient information to base its decisions on when generating execution plans.

However, the statistics do not need to be completely accurate or up-to-date. In Oracle 10.1 and above, the sampling algorithm has improved to the extent that estimated statistics can satisfy the optimizer's needs. For very large tables, even statistics based on a 1% estimate can be sufficient; for smaller tables, estimates in the range of 10%–30% are common.

If tables do not change on a regular basis, then gathering the statistics for them is not necessary. Therefore, you may wish to customize your statistics gathering jobs to concentrate on volatile and growing tables.

We recommend that you use the DBMS_STATS package, as opposed to the ANALYZE statement. While the latter is still supported, it is deprecated, meaning that it will eventually go away. There are a couple of good reasons for using DBMS_STATS:

- Statistics can be gathered in parallel.
- Statistics are calculated correctly for partitioned tables and indexes.

Histograms

Where data is skewed, make sure that you are maintaining histograms for affected columns to allow the optimizer to make better decisions about the execution plans it is generating.

In Oracle 9.0.1 and above, if a statement includes bind variables, then the optimizer bases its decisions on the values of the bind variables supplied the first time the statement is executed, which is known as *bind variable peeking*.

In general, bind variable peeking is beneficial. However, it can lead to very inefficient execution plans in the event that the first value is atypical. If this appears to be a consistent problem, then you may need to consider creating a stored outline for the statement in question.

Dynamic Sampling

The CBO makes assumptions about the selectivity of data in joins that can lead to inefficient execution plans.

By default, dynamic sampling is enabled in Oracle 10.1 and above. When a statement is parsed, if insufficient information is available about the selectivity of columns in a join, then Oracle will scan a sample of the rows in the joined tables to calculate more accurate sample selectivity.

System Statistics

By default, the CBO generates execution plans based on the predicted number of logical I/Os that will be required. Basing execution plans on logical I/O is not entirely realistic, as some execution plans require much more CPU than others, particularly statements including built-in functions, PL/SQL subroutines, Java methods, and embedded regular expressions.

In Oracle 8.1.5 and above, you can optionally enable the gathering of system statistics over an interval of a few hours or more. The kernel records information about the relative costs of CPU and I/O operations in a table called AUX_STAT$ in the SYS schema. This data is used to adjust the costs of operations when the CBO is optimizing SQL statements and may result in the generation of different execution plans. This method of generating execution plans is known as the *CPU cost model*.

We recommend that you experiment with system statistics. For most users, they have a positive effect. However, we suggest that you take a backup of the AUX_STAT$ table prior to gathering statistics in case you decide to revert to the I/O cost model.

Locally Managed Tablespaces

Locally managed tablespaces, which were introduced in Oracle 8.1.5, use a bitmap to manage space within the tablespace. Locally managed tablespaces replaced dictionary managed tablespaces, which contained tables of used and free extents in the data dictionary. While both types update the data dictionary, locally managed tablespaces perform less work while the dictionary is locked and, consequently, are more efficient.

Locally managed tablespaces are also a prerequisite for ASSM, described in the following section. If your existing database still contains dictionary managed tablespaces, we recommend that you convert them to locally managed tablespaces during the migration process.

Automatic Segment Space Management (ASSM)

Following the hugely successful introduction of locally managed tablespaces, which use bitmaps to manage extent allocation and deallocation, the next logical step was to use bitmaps to manage free space within blocks.

Prior to Oracle 10.1, Oracle always used freelist segment space management. A *freelist* is basically a chain of block pointers that links together all the blocks with free space. When updates or deletions reduce the amount of a data below a threshold specified by the PCTUSED attribute, the block is returned to the freelist, which is a single linked list whose head and tail are held on the segment header. The block remains on the list until the amount of data in the block reaches the threshold specified by the PCTFREE attribute, at which point it is removed from the freelist. Removing the block requires a further update of the segment header.

Unsurprisingly, on volatile systems, freelist segment space management caused significant contention for the segment header. In order to reduce this contention, multiple freelists were introduced. While these allowed multiple sessions to scan for free space concurrently, they did not address the fundamental issue of segment header contention, so Oracle introduced *freelist groups*, in which each freelist header is allocated to a separate block. In a RAC environment, the number of freelist groups will usually be equivalent to the maximum number of instances in the cluster. Within each freelist group, it is still possible to have multiple freelists, thus allowing sessions to search for free space concurrently.

The introduction of freelist groups significantly reduced the amount of contention experienced for segment headers in RAC environments. However, the space allocation algorithm could still lead to hot spots in the datafiles where multiple sessions were attempting to perform inserts, updates, and deletes against the same range of blocks.

Therefore, Oracle 9.0.1 saw the introduction of ASSM. As the name suggests, the intention of this feature is to reduce the amount of work required by the DBA to configure and maintain the freelists in a tablespace. ASSM is optimized to allow transactions from different instances to concurrently insert data into the same table without contention to locate space for new records. It is used to manage space for transactions in both table and index segments. ASSM must be specified when a tablespace is created as follows:

```
CREATE TABLESPACE ts1
DATAFILE '/dddd' SIZE 10000M
EXTENT MANAGEMENT LOCAL
SEGMENT SPACE MANAGEMENT AUTO;
```

ASSM can only be specified for locally managed tablespaces. It must be specified when the tablespace is created and cannot be subsequently amended.

ASSM uses a hierarchy of bitmap blocks to manage free space. This hierarchy can be up to three levels deep. However, two levels are sufficient for all but the largest segments. Within the level 1 bitmap block, groups of bits are used to represent the amount of remaining free space on each block.

You can still specify a value for the PCTFREE attribute for ASSM tablespaces. While you also can still specify a value for PCTUSED, this value is ignored. Any values specified for FREELISTS and/or FREELIST GROUPS are also ignored.

ASSM has been designed specifically for a RAC environment. The bitmap hierarchy is structured so that each instance can use a different first level bitmap block to allocate and deallocate space within blocks, thus reducing contention. In addition, each instance will also insert new rows into a different range of blocks, also reducing contention for blocks.

While ASSM is effective for insertions, performance cannot be guaranteed for update and delete statements. For example, instance A may be inserting rows into a contiguous set of blocks, but once these rows have been committed, nothing stops instance B from updating the same rows and updating the amount of space required to store these rows. Instance A and instance B, therefore, may be contending for the same ASSM bitmap block. In addition, ASSM cannot guarantee to eliminate contention for inserts, updates, or deletes against indexes. Situations such as those described previously can only be prevented by effective application design, effective physical storage design, or, of course, luck.

Table and index scans behave differently for segments created in ASSM tablespaces. In a freelist-managed tablespace, each segment has a high water mark (HWM). The segment header contains a pointer to the last initialized block in the object. If the last block is full, then the next five blocks are initialized, and the HWM pointer is updated in the segment header. The HWM can only be reset by truncating the table. Even if all rows are deleted from the segment, the HWM will be unaffected, so a table or index potentially contains a large number of empty blocks. When the segment is scanned, each block is read sequentially from the segment header to the HWM. Therefore, even if the segment is empty, a table or index scan can result in a large number of logical I/Os.

In an ASSM tablespace, there are two HWMs, the low high water mark (LHWM) and the high high water mark (HHWM). The LHWM is equivalent to the HWM in a freelist-managed tablespace. Blocks between the LHWM and HHWM may or may not have been initialized, so their existence cannot be guaranteed. Therefore, in an ASSM tablespace, it is not possible to scan all blocks in a segment up to the HHWM. Instead, all blocks are scanned up to the LHWM. Thereafter, the bitmap blocks are used to identify blocks that have been initialized between the LHWM and HHWM, and these blocks are read individually.

In Oracle 10.1 and above, ASSM should be your default method for segment space management. You may still wish to experiment with manual space management for databases experiencing extremely high levels of concurrent insert activity; however, we recommend ASSM for most applications.

Reverse Key Indexes

ASSM can reduce the impact of hot blocks when insertion is performed by multiple instances on the same segment, by eliminating the segment header as a point of contention and by ensuring that each instance has a separate set of blocks. Eliminating this point of contention works well for unsorted or heap data. However, data often needs to be stored in an index to guarantee uniqueness or to support sort operations. In this case, the location of each entry is determined by the sort order, so techniques such as hashing cannot be used to distribute updates across multiple blocks.

Therefore, in Oracle 8.0 and above, you can create reverse key indexes, in which the data in each index column is stored in reverse order, which has the effect of distributing consecutive keys across different leaf blocks in the index. The data in the table columns is unaffected. Reverse key indexes can be created with single columns:

```
CREATE INDEX i1 ON t1 (c1) REVERSE;
```

Single column reverse key indexes are useful in situations where the key value is being generated using a sequence. You can also create a reverse key index with multiple columns, as in the following example:

```
CREATE INDEX i2 ON t2 (c1,c2) REVERSE;
```

The data in each column is reversed separately, so, in the preceding example, if column c1 in table t2 contains ABC and column c2 contains DEF, then the index key will be stored as CBAFED.

You can specify the REVERSE clause for both nonpartitioned and partitioned indexes. You can also specify it for compressed indexes. However, you cannot use the REVERSE clause with an Index-Organized Table (IOT), nor can you specify it with an IOT Secondary Index.

While reverse key indexes are an excellent way of reducing contention for index blocks, they impose some limitations in the execution plans that can be generated using the index. Reverse key indexes work optimally with queries that include equality predicates on the leading edge of the index key columns. They do not perform well if the execution plan uses range scan operations, such as INDEX (RANGE SCAN), against them. Therefore, the following queries might perform well against table t2:

```
SELECT * FROM t2 WHERE c1 = 33;
SELECT * FROM t2 WHERE c1 = 33 AND c2 = 42;
SELECT * FROM t2 WHERE c1 = 33 AND c2 > 42;
```

However, the following queries almost certainly will not perform well if the reverse key index is used:

```
SELECT * FROM t2 WHERE c1 < 33;
SELECT * FROM t2 WHERE c1 >= 33;
```

It is difficult to assess the effect of reversing an index in an existing application that might use the existing index in many different statements. Although you can create NOSEGMENT indexes in Oracle 8.1.5 and above to evaluate the impact of adding a new index on execution plans, this technique is does not particularly help you in assessing the effect of reversing an existing index. As with so many other RAC features, there is no substitute for testing reverse key indexes in an environment that mirrors your production database as closely as possible.

Partitioning

In Oracle 8.0, the *partitioning* option was introduced. Initially designed to address some of the problems posed by very large databases (VLDBs), partitioning offers a highly flexible solution to a number of administrative and performance problems.

Over the years, partitioning technology has evolved, but the basic principles have remained unchanged. A *nonpartitioned object* contains only one data segment; a *partitioned object* can potentially contain many data segments.

Both tables and indexes can be partitioned. Various methods of partitioning exist, including range, hash, and list partitioning. In addition, partitioned objects can be further divided into subpartitions. All partitions in the partitioned object share the same logical structure, which is defined in the data dictionary.

Partitioned objects present a number of administrative advantages. Large tables and indexes can be divided into a number of smaller segments, which can be managed independently. Individual partitions can be added, dropped, truncated, merged, and split. Data can also be exchanged between a single partition and a nonpartitioned table with the same logical structure.

Every partitioned object has a partition key that consists of one or more columns. The partition key determines the partition (or segment) that each row will be stored in. The partition key does not necessarily need to be the same as the primary key, nor does it need to be unique.

In Oracle 8.0, the only type of partitioning available was *range partitioning*, in which the partitioning key represents a range of values for each partition. Range partitioning is often used to represent data ranges and is still the most common form of partitioning in use today. An example follows:

```
CREATE TABLE orders
(
        orderkey NUMBER,
        orderdate DATE,
        custkey NUMBER,
        quantity NUMBER,
        value NUMBER
)
PARTITION BY orderdate
(
        PARTITION 200605
                VALUES LESS THAN (TO_DATE ('31-MAY-2006','DD-MON-YYYY' ));
        PARTITION 200606
                VALUES LESS THAN (TO_DATE ('30-JUN-2006','DD-MON-YYYY' ));
        PARTITION 200607
                VALUES LESS THAN (TO_DATE ('31-JUL-2006','DD-MON-YYYY' ))
);
```

In the preceding example, the partition key is the ORDERDATE column. For each partition, an upper bound is defined for the partition key. All values before 31-MAY-2006 will be stored in the first partition, all values less than 30-JUN-2006 will be stored in the second partition, and all remaining values will be stored in the final partition.

An attempt to insert data into a partition that is out of range—for example, 01-SEP-2006—will result in the following error:

```
ORA-14400: inserted partition key does not map to any partition
```

Most sites using time-based range partitions similar to the one illustrated previously manually create additional partitions as part of their maintenance procedures to ensure that a partition will always exist for the newly inserted data. For the table shown previously, for example, the next partition might be added at the end of July to ensure that space exists for the rows created during August:

```
ALTER TABLE orders
ADD PARTITION 200608
VALUES LESS THAN (TO_DATE ('31-AUG-2006','DD-MON-YYYY' ));
```

Alternatively, you can create an unbounded partition that accepts any data value above the last explicitly defined partition range. This is not particularly meaningful for time-based range partitions, but it can be appropriate for other tables with numeric values such as the following example:

```
CREATE TABLE t1
(
        c1 NUMBER,
        c2 NUMBER
)
PARTITION BY c1
(
        PARTITION p1 VALUES LESS THAN (100),
        PARTITION p2 VALUES LESS THAN (200),
        PARTITION p3 VALUES LESS THAN (MAXVALUE)
);
```

In the preceding example, all rows with a partition key greater than 200 will be stored in partition p3.

By default, you can update the partition key as long as the row remains in the same partition. Updates to the partition key that would cause the row to be moved to another partition will result in the following error:

```
ORA-14402: updating partition key column would cause a partition change
```

In Oracle 8.1.5 and above, you can enable movement of updated rows between partitions using the ENABLE ROW MOVEMENT clause:

```
ALTER TABLE t1 ENABLE ROW MOVEMENT;
```

From a performance point of view, partitioned tables perform well for queries where the partition key is known. Consider a range-partitioned table containing one partition for each month over the last five years. If there are no suitable indexes, then a query will have to perform a full table scan of all rows in each of the 60 partitions. However, if the query knows the partition key, it can use this information to eliminate unnecessary partitions and scan only a single partition. Similarly, if part of the partition key is known, then a smaller range of partitions might be scanned. Therefore, partitions have the potential to minimize the amount of I/O performed by the database.

You can create indexes against partitioned tables. These indexes may be either nonpartitioned or partitioned. If the index is partitioned, then it may be either local or global. Locally partitioned indexes have the same number of partitions as the table that they index. The columns of a locally partitioned index key must include all the columns in the partition key for the table. When a new partition is added to the table, a corresponding partition will also be added to the local index.

From a performance point of view, local indexes can be highly efficient or highly inefficient, depending on how they are accessed. In a partitioned local index, each partition contains a separate B-tree.

If, for example, the index contains one partition for each month in the last five years, there would be 60 partitions and 60 separate B-trees. When the locally partitioned index is accessed, if the partition key is known, Oracle can identify the partition directly and scan a single B-tree index. It is highly likely that the depth of each partitioned B-tree would be lower than the B-tree depth of an equivalent nonpartitioned index; therefore, using the locally partitioned index would be more efficient.

However, if the partition key is not known when the locally partitioned index is accessed, then Oracle will need to scan all 60 B-trees for the relevant partition. Depending on the number of rows in each partition, the optimizer may still decide to use this index in an execution plan, as it may still be more efficient than performing a full-table scan. It will, however, be significantly less efficient than using the equivalent nonpartitioned index.

Maintenance of local indexes is highly efficient. For example, if you drop a table partition, the corresponding local index partition will also be dropped. The remaining partitions of the local index will be unaffected and will continue to be available.

Sometimes, however, a locally partitioned index is not sufficient. For example, a table may have a secondary key that must have a unique value throughout the entire table. The secondary key cannot be efficiently enforced using locally partitioned indexes, as it would be necessary for the constraint to check every partition each time a DML statement updated any of the key columns. In this case, a globally partitioned index is more appropriate.

A *globally partitioned index* can be partitioned using a different partition key to the table that it indexes. The number of partitions can also vary. The only restriction is that a range-partitioned global index must include a default partition that is declared using the VALUES LESS THAN (MAXVALUE) clause. The columns of a globally partitioned index must contain the columns of the partition key.

Globally partitioned indexes can be highly efficient for index lookups. To continue the previous example, you might create a globally partitioned index with 32 partitions. Each of these partitions will contain a B-tree index. If you know the partition key when you use this index to access the table, you can perform partition elimination and access only the partition containing the relevant index entry.

However, globally partitioned indexes can cause significant problems with maintenance. As the one-to-one mapping between index and table has been lost, it is not possible to guarantee the consistency of the index when partition operations, such as DROP or TRUNCATE, are performed on the table. Therefore, when DDL is performed against the table, all global indexes on that table are marked INVALID and need to be rebuilt, which may affect performance for queries that are unable to use the global index to perform lookups and performance in terms of I/O needed to rebuild the index.

In Oracle 9.0.1 and above, the UPDATE GLOBAL INDEXES clause can be specified for DDL statements on partitioned tables:

```
ALTER TABLE t1
DROP PARTITION p1
UPDATE GLOBAL INDEXES;
```

The UPDATE GLOBAL INDEXES clause can be used with the ADD, COALESCE, DROP, EXCHANGE, MERGE, MOVE, SPLIT, and TRUNCATE partition operations. When this clause is specified, Oracle will update all global indexes whenever DDL operations are performed against that table instead of invalidating them. For example, if you need to drop a partition, each row that is dropped from the table also will be dropped from the global index.

Clearly, the UPDATE GLOBAL INDEXES clause is most effective if you are making a small number of changes to a large table. On the other hand, if you are making a significant number of changes to the table, it may still be more efficient to drop the global indexes before the operation and then re-create them afterward.

The range partitioning introduced in Oracle 8.0 was a great leap forward in terms of both administration and performance for very large tables. Many applications, particularly those written by in-house development teams, center on a single table, which can often represent more than 80% of the total data in the database. These tables are typically range partitioned by date and introduce a new performance issue. For example, if the table is partitioned by month, most updates will typically affect one partition, potentially resulting in block contention. While this block contention can be serious in a single-instance environment, it can cause severe problems in a RAC environment, where blocks must be exchanged between instances.

Therefore, in Oracle 8.1.5 and above, two new forms of partitioning were introduced: hash partitioning and range-hash partitioning. When a table is *hash partitioned*, the partition key is mapped to the appropriate partition using an Oracle internal hash algorithm. This algorithm is slightly limited in behavior, so Oracle recommends that the number of partitions in the table is a power of two, that is, 2, 4, 8, 16, 32, and so on.

Like other forms of hashing, hash clustering is only effective if you know the partition key for every access. If you do not always know the partition key and no suitable indexes exist, then Oracle will resort to a full table scan of every partition. Although there is a hash partition range scan operation, it is rarely invoked by the optimizer.

From a performance point of view, hash partitions represent a good way of distributing rows between a number of partitions, thereby reducing or eliminating potential contention. However, only a limited number of access paths are available for a hash partition, so they may not be suitable for all applications.

In Oracle 8.1.5 and above, you can also use *range-hash composite partitioned tables.* The table is initially partitioned by range, and then subpartitioned by hash keys. This partitioning presents the best of both worlds as the table is logically divided into range partitions, enabling more efficient administration, and then it is physically divided into a small number of hash partitions (usually eight or fewer), reducing contention.

In a *composite partitioned table*, a segment exists for each of the subpartitions. Data is only stored at the subpartition level. At the partition level, no segment exists, and no data is stored.

The partition key can be different at partition level to the subpartition level, meaning that if the partition key is known, but the subpartition key is not, partitions can still be eliminated, and the worst case is that each of the hash subpartitions within that partition must be scanned.

In the example of the orders table, you might create the following four subpartitions for each partition:

```
CREATE TABLE orders
(
      orderkey NUMBER,
      orderdate DATE,
      custkey NUMBER,
      quantity NUMBER,
      value NUMBER
)
PARTITION BY RANGE (orderdate)
SUBPARTITION BY HASH (custkey)
(
      PARTITION 200605
      VALUES LESS THAN (TO_DATE ('31-MAY-2006','DD-MON-YYYY' ))
      (
            SUBPARTITION 200605_1,
            SUBPARTITION 200605_2,
            SUBPARTITION 200605_3,
            SUBPARTITION 200605_4
      ),
      PARTITION 200606
      VALUES LESS THAN (TO_DATE ('30-JUN-2006','DD-MON-YYYY' ))
      (
            SUBPARTITION 200606_1,
            SUBPARTITION 200606_2,
            SUBPARTITION 200606_3,
            SUBPARTITION 200606_4
      ),
      PARTITION 200607
      VALUES LESS THAN (TO_DATE ('31-JUL-2006','DD-MON-YYYY' ))
      (
            SUBPARTITION 200607_1,
            SUBPARTITION 200607_2,
            SUBPARTITION 200607_3,
            SUBPARTITION 200607_4
      )
);
```

In Oracle 8.1.5 and above, you can also create partitioned IOTs. These have all the advantages of nonpartitioned IOTs and offer the administrative advantages of partitioned tables.

Oracle 9.0.1 saw the introduction of *list partitions*. These are useful for tables for which neither range nor hash partitioning is appropriate. For each partition, a list or set of partition keys is specified. This list of keys is useful to create partitions based on logical entities or groups of entities.

In Oracle 9.2 and above, list partitioned tables can contain hash subpartitions. The behavior of list-hash partitioned tables is similar to that of range-hash partitioned tables.

Partitioned tables offer the same administrative and performance benefits in a RAC environment as they do in single-instance databases. In an optimal configuration, each partition in a table would have an affinity with a specific instance to guarantee that blocks from a specific partition will only appear in a single buffer cache, to minimize interinstance block traffic, and to maximize the effectiveness of the buffer cache.

Prior to Oracle 10.1, if you wanted to achieve affinity between the partitions of a table and specific instances, then the simplest way was to modify the application to connect to the appropriate instance. If the required instance was not known before the connection was made, then you needed to maintain a connection to each instance. However, in the event of a node failure, you would need to manually handle the redistribution of connections to other instances with the application. Manually redistributing connections requires a fair amount of intelligence within the application, and the resultant code can still be quite inefficient following a node failure.

In Oracle 10.1 and above, the mechanism just described has been formalized by Oracle into database services. You may still need to maintain multiple connections to each instance, but you can now define a database service for each instance and specify a backup instance in the event of the failure of the primary instance.

Therefore, in Oracle 10.1 and above, you can spread large partitioned tables evenly across all available instances. Node failures can be handled by Oracle Services rather than by application-specific code, which leads to the most efficient use of the buffer cache as blocks subject to update within the partitioned table will normally only appear in the buffer cache of one instance.

Summary

In this chapter, we reviewed the factors that should influence the design stage of your RAC implementation. We considered the business requirements and architectural decisions that you should take into account and some of the design decisions to make for storage and hardware selection. Finally, we looked at the areas to note when designing your application and database for RAC.

CHAPTER 5

■ ■ ■

Benchmarking Concepts

Andrew Holdsworth, Director of Real World Performance for Oracle Corporation, identifies three factors that often contribute to problems in building large Oracle systems:[1]

- Getting the application design wrong
- Not understanding the technology
- Insufficient or irrelevant testing

In this chapter, we look at the concepts behind the third of these identified factors; specifically, we will examine how to test a RAC configuration and make the testing count by stressing the right components in the stack. We will first introduce benchmarking and load testing, and establish the goals that load tests should set out to achieve. Second, we will look at interpreting the RAC benchmarks officially published by Oracle in conjunction with its hardware partners to see what we can infer about achieving the best levels of RAC performance. Oracle and its partners invest significant time and resources in conducting and publishing benchmarks, and make a wealth of information available in the published data. Knowing how to interpret these results can give an essential insight into how Oracle delivers performance and scalability with RAC and a head start in building and optimizing your own RAC configurations and constructing relevant test scenarios to verify their validity.

Load Testing and Benchmarks

Load testing describes the means by which you systematically expose an application to simulated usage conditions in a controlled environment to analyze and predict application performance and behavior up to and beyond expected usage levels. When focusing on the quality of service of an application in this way, we are interested in measuring the following three aspects:

- **Performance**: The throughput measured as the number of transactions or queries processed in a defined unit of time, coupled with the response times experienced by the users of the application
- **Scalability**: The potential to increase (or decrease) performance by adding (or removing) system resources in direct proportion to the performance desired
- **Reliability**: The availability and functional integrity of an application and its infrastructure before it is deployed

---

1. Ensor, Dave, Tim Gorman, Kyle Hailey, Anjo Kolk, Jonathan Lewis, Connor McDonald, Cary Millsap, James Morle, Morgens Nørgarrd, David Ruthven, and Gaja Krishna Vaidyanatha. *Oracle Insights: Tales of the Oak Table* (Berkeley: Apress, 2004).

Our interest in benchmarking here means that we are focusing on the first two areas of testing, termed *performance testing* and *scalability testing*, as opposed to reliability testing. Reliability, however, is arguably the most crucial component, and at the most basic level, this testing can be applied in the form of a soak, or endurance, test, whereby application simulations are run for extended periods of time at differing levels of intensity to observe the long-term behavior of the system. In a RAC environment, conducting this testing in conjunction with simulations of component failure, such as a node, SAN, or interconnect, is also essential. This testing ensures that the DBA is prepared to maintain data integrity and cluster availability in the event of failures occurring once the application has been deployed.

In terms of performance and scalability, as you will see later in this chapter, successfully applied benchmarks tend to take throughput as the key metric, while also ensuring individual response times are maintained within predetermined limits. The performance measurements taken can then be used to draw a comparison between different hardware and software configurations, such as RAC and non-RAC installations.

One area extremely important to load testing is the criteria used to define performance. Criteria are usually separated into two distinct areas: those for judging the performance of online transaction processing (OLTP) systems and those for the performance of query-based data warehouse systems.

When judging the performance of transactional systems, confusion arises from the question, "What is a transaction?" The primary reason for this confusion is that the term "transaction" defines both computer and business functions that can be applied similarly to database processing.

From a computing-based perspective, Oracle uses transactions to guarantee data integrity. According to this definition, a *transaction* is a discrete series of SQL statements used to achieve a task that is either committed or rolled back as a unit. The task itself is the transaction from a business perspective and typically reflects a change in the environment about which the database system is storing information, such as an exchange of goods or services. The confusion often derives from the fact that a one-to-one relationship does not necessarily exist between the Oracle and business transactions.

In Oracle, a transaction is initiated implicitly with the first executable SQL statement. In simple terms, every executable DML statement is part of a transaction that is completed when the modifications are either committed or rolled back. When this transaction ends, another one begins with the next unit of work. The statistics of these transactions are recorded within the database and exposed within the V$SYSSTAT view as the VALUE column, corresponding to the entries of user commits and user rollbacks in the NAME column. These values can therefore be taken as indications of performance when measured over a predetermined amount of time. However, these values are only applicable when comparing the performance of an application with an implementation of exactly the same application. The frequency of commits depends entirely on the application developer, and with Oracle, artificially increasing the commit rate of an application is highly unlikely to increase performance. Therefore, when using Oracle transactions to compare application performance, only use these figures comparatively, and not in terms of achieving the highest statistical value possible.

A more useful indication of performance is the *business transaction*. Business transactions are defined in terms of the logical tasks that the application is designed to achieve. For example, in an order processing system the number of orders processed in a period of time can be used as the measurement of performance. This measurement also has the advantage that it can be used as comparative indication of performance of the same application among database platforms, irrespective of the number of commits and rollbacks that occur in processing these transactions. At this point, you should clearly see that all-encompassing statements such as "a system with the ability to process 100,000 transactions a minute" are meaningless when made out of the context of a particular application for either Oracle or business transaction measurements.

In a nontransactional system, such as a data warehouse or decision support system, the system could possibly be under heavy load from read-intensive processing despite a minimal transactional rate. Therefore, using an alternative measure of performance is necessary. The most direct method is to measure the number of queries that can be completed over a defined time period; again, the measurement can only be taken in the context of a particular application and its own queries and dataset.

Of particular importance to measuring query-based performance, but also relevant to measuring transactional performance, is the response time of the queries or transactions. The response time is the most important variable in terms of user experience, and therefore an essential criterion to capture as an indication of the level of system load.

Once the performance standards are defined, a critical phase in any load test environment is to clearly define the success criteria of the testing exercise, and to plan the testing required to determine when the performance criteria have been met. Another essential requirement is the performance of a thorough pretest phase, where the tests themselves are rigorously examined to ensure accuracy and repeatability. Testing performed ad hoc with an undefined goal or an incorrectly configured environment can result in a level of unwarranted confidence in an application.

For the ideal scenario, to completely and accurately judge database performance, you must re-create a concurrent load and stress test on a database of the same size as the production database on exactly the same hardware and in the same software environment. For example, if the application is to run in production with Oracle Data Guard running in synchronous mode, then this constraint should also be applied to the test configuration. Changing only one variable at a time during testing is also important to be certain of the impact that the changes have.

A common error is to assume that an application will deliver the same performance on a small subset of data with a single user when scaled up to a multiuser environment. A small subset of data is unlikely to give the same performance as a larger one for every hardware and software environment, as different systems offer different levels of sustainability in performance as the workload increases. We discuss some of these different characteristics of scalability of the hardware platform for RAC in Chapter 6.

The only accurate method to determine scalability is to conduct a number of tests at differing levels of intensity up to the maximum capabilities of the target environment. The results of these tests can then be used as the expected target setting for capacity planning of the life cycle of the system when put into production. For RAC, as with any clustered database solution, always test the application in a single instance environment as well as a RAC environment to establish the baseline of the level of scalability that can be expected.

In practice, time and budgetary constraints mean that a fully replicated system is difficult to achieve for testing. These constraints can be from legal or space requirements for replicating data, the time it requires the DBA to install the duplicate testing environments, or the complexity of an installation where multiple and varied application tiers make it impractical to simulate the entire configuration. In light of these constraints, generic load and stress test applications can prove useful in shortening the testing cycle by enabling the rapid deployment of a repeatable workload. The results of the generic testing can then be used over time to give initial indications of hardware and software performance and to narrow the scope for the testing of the production application itself. Genuine confidence in any particular application, however, can never be fully established without testing that application in particular.

In terms of constructing your own test scenarios, Chapter 23 presents an example of Oracle load testing tools adhering to the criteria that they are freely available and run on the Linux platform. However, the most useful place to start in terms of understanding how benchmarks should be constructed lies with the independently audited benchmark specifications of the Transaction Processing Performance Council (TPC).

TPC Benchmarks

The TPC is an independent, nonprofit corporation. It defines database benchmarks and oversees the dissemination of transaction processing performance data in a form that can be used to draw comparisons between different database and hardware environments. Like all major database vendors, Oracle is a member of the TPC and publishes the results of TPC-audited benchmarks in conjunction with a test sponsor; the test sponsor usually being the vendor of the hardware upon which Oracle is run.

The TPC publishes a number of benchmark specifications, of which TPC-C and TPC-H are of the most interest to database professionals. TPC-C and TPC-H relate to different types of workload. TPC-C defines an OLTP benchmark with multiple transaction types and is measured in transactions per minute (tpmC), whereas TPC-H defines a decision support system (DSS) benchmark with a number of ad hoc queries and concurrent data modifications and is measured in terms of the Composite Query-per-Hour Performance Metric (QphH@Size). Therefore, ensuring that the results from one benchmark are not confused with the results from the other is crucial. Also, no direct inference can be drawn regarding the applicability of a particular platform for a transaction-based application from TPC-H results or for a data warehouse–type application from TPC-C results. Whether you focus on TPC-C or TPC-H depends on the application for which you want to determine relevant performance data.

An advantage to Oracle specialists researching and comparing Oracle environments is that the results of TPC benchmarks are independently audited and approved, and include the complete, published evidence in the form of an extensive full disclosure report. Used in conjunction with the TPC specifications, the full disclosure reports can provide a great deal of information about how Oracle implements a performance benchmark and, of particular interest to us, the configuration of an Oracle RAC on Linux clustered benchmark. We can use the information from the full disclosure report and specification to gain a great deal of insight into how Oracle configures RAC to achieve the best levels of performance.

The full disclosure report for a TCP benchmark is available for anyone to download and review at no charge. Therefore, we advise that any Oracle specialist looking to obtain Oracle performance data should have more than a passing familiarity with the TPC benchmarks. This information can then be leveraged to ensure that custom benchmarks and tests for individual applications are appropriate and relevant.

The TPC-C Benchmark

The TPC-C benchmark is the best known database benchmark for OLTP and is fully defined in a specification. The specification gives both a detailed textual description and sample implementations of the requirements that must be met to ensure any submitted benchmarks comply with the standards.

The TPC-C benchmark implements an application that simulates an order entry system for a wholesale supplier and was introduced in 1992, after two years of development by the TPC. The intention is to define a real-world system as closely as possible, as opposed to using an artificial benchmark, and to this end, the specification includes full definitions for the user interface, menu response times, transaction response times, and keying and thinking times.

The TPC-C schema takes the form shown in Figure 5-1, defining nine tables and the relationships among them.

Some immediate observations can be made about the basic TPC-C schema. The most important of these is that, apart from the ITEM table, all of the tables in the schema are of an unfixed size. The overall schema size is factored according to the number of warehouses configured and has been designed so that the number of users and warehouses must scale out linearly for throughput by multiplying the number of warehouses and users by ten per home warehouse. All tables are populated with nonuniform, randomly generated data of variable length, and all horizontal and vertical data partitioning must be entirely transparent to the application code.

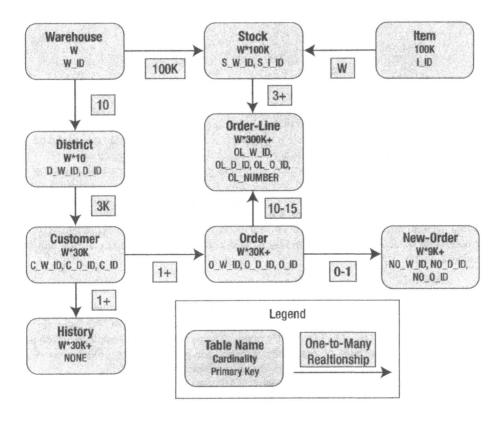

Figure 5-1. *TPC-C schema*

As a transactional benchmark, five transactions are observed to generate the expected OLTP activity of selects, updates, inserts, and deletes. These transactions are shown in Table 5-1, along with their definitions and the percentage that each individual transaction occupies in the overall database workload.

Table 5-1. *TPC-C Transaction Mix*

Transaction	Definition	% of Total
New-Order	Receive a new order from a customer	45%
Payment	Update the customer's balance to record a payment	43%
Delivery	Deliver orders asynchronously	4%
Order-status	Retrieve the status of customer's most recent order	4%
Stock-level	Return the status of the warehouse's inventory	4%

Note that the officially reported tpmC figure is the recorded number of new orders processed per minute, while the system is also processing the additional transactions measured over a 7,200-second (two-hour) measurement period. Therefore, when interpreting a TPC-C benchmark result, the overall system load and Oracle transaction rate will be considerably greater than the tpmC figure measured.

When implementing these transactions, the TPC-C specification dictates that user keying and thinking time are to be applied, and therefore, achieving high-levels of transaction rates demands a large number of users. With the defined ten users per warehouse, achieving a high transaction rate will also be reflected in the overall size of the schema created, as users operate with most of their activity located on the home warehouse, to ensure an even distribution of the workload across the database. The exceptions are that, in the Payment transaction, 15% of CUSTOMER table records and, in the New-Order transaction, 1% of STOCK table records are nonlocal to the home warehouse.

A simple conclusion to draw would be that you could, relatively straightforwardly, implement a benchmark to achieve high transaction rates by constructing a cluster with an extremely high number of nodes supporting a large number of warehouses and users. As a result, although each individual user and warehouse transaction rate would be low, the overall transaction rate would be high. The TPC-C specification prevents this from occurring by defining an overscaling rule.

When viewing whether a system is overscaled, considering the theoretical transaction limits of an infinitely fast system is important. Because the specification defines the user keying and thinking time that must occur between transactions, if a target database was infinitely fast, a null response time would result from a transaction. In other words, the target system would perform at such a level that if a transaction were submitted, the response would be received instantly, and the transaction level would be defined by the minimum keying and thinking times only. In this case, the transaction level would be as follows:

$$\text{Null transaction response time} + \text{Minimum keying and think times} = 1.286 \text{ tpmC/user}$$

Because the specification determines ten users per warehouse, an infinitely fast system can do a maximum of 12.86 tpmC per warehouse and no more. To prevent overscaling, the TPC-C specification defines that throughput must be at least 70% of the 12.86 tpmC per warehouse level, which is 9 tpmC. Therefore, a benchmark with an oversized cluster and a large number of warehouses would be disqualified if the transaction rate was not more than 9 tpmC per warehouse.

Consider the following real RAC-based example: to achieve over 1 million tpmC in 2003, Oracle based the configuration on 128,016 warehouses, which could deliver a theoretical maximum of tpmC of 1,646,286. At this level, the overscaling rule defines the minimum allowable tpmC for this number of warehouses to be 1,152,144 (70% of 1,646,286). The actual tpmC achieved of 1,184,893, therefore, satisfied the overscaling rule.

You can see that sizing the environment to submit a TPC-C is not a trivial task, and balance needs to be achieved by creating the optimal number of warehouses to realize the best returns of scalability. This example also serves to highlight the fact that achieving a higher transaction rate within the TPC-C benchmark will always mean that the benchmark has been run on a larger dataset. For example, in comparison to the 1,184,893 tpmC recorded on Oracle 10g RAC with Linux on 128,016 warehouses, Oracle9i RAC with Linux recorded a 138,362 tpmC result in October 2002 implemented on 11,520 warehouses, a dataset less than 1/10 the size. The size of the dataset should always be noted when comparing different tpmC results.

The tpmC results for a system should also be considered in conjunction with the ratio of price to the number of transactions (Price/tpmC) to evaluate the cost of the performance. The cost is not only the cost of the main database server, but also the total cost of ownership of the entire system used to submit the results over three years, including all hardware, software, and maintenance costs for three years. This total cost of ownership (TCO) is then divided by the tpmC value to derive the Price/tpmC, as follows:

$$\text{Three-year TCO of } \$6,541,770/1,184,893 = \text{Price/tmpC of } \$5.52$$

A low Price/tpmC value is desirable and can be achieved by reducing the overall system cost and/or increasing the tpmC rate. The Price/tpmC value also enables the comparison of the cost of ownership of a Linux RAC-based system with an alternative UNIX SMP-based configuration.

The RAC-based example of creating a TPC-C schema with 128,016 warehouses requires the number of users to be a multiple of ten, which gives 1.28 million users to be simulated to generate the required transactions. For the Oracle-based benchmarks, these users interact with a Pro*C application through a web browser via the Apache HTTP Server. The application formats the menus, input forms, and data output using HTML and communicates by TCP/IP with the client. Between the application and the database sits BEA Tuxedo transaction processing software to process client requests. BEA Tuxedo serves two functions: first, for the delivery transaction, it provides the queuing mechanism to enable asynchronous completion; and second, routing tables are configured to route requests to the different Oracle cluster nodes dependent on the warehouse ID to accurately distribute the load. With our understanding of the way that the TPC-C benchmark has been designed for scalability, we can conclude that the Cache Fusion traffic for interinstance communication will be minimized by pairing clients with their home warehouses on corresponding cluster nodes through the transaction processing medium. Note, therefore, that the configuration of this dependent request routing is a critical component for the performance and scalability of RAC in this form of transactional benchmark environment.

The storage requirements for 128,016 warehouses at approximately 100MB per warehouse would be between 12TB and 13TB (terabytes) at minimum. In practice, however, the storage provision for such a schema is approximately five times this amount for several reasons. First, the additional disk capacity enables destroking for improved performance at the disk level (we discuss desktroking in more depth in Chapter 7). Second, a wide distribution of data blocks across a greater number of disks reduces contention at an Oracle level, and finally, the disk capacity provides a level of storage for 60 days' activity as defined by the specification. Unlike a standard production environment, the disks are configured as raw devices in a Redundant Array of Independent Disks 0 (RAID 0) configuration with a distinct storage allocation between data and redo logs. Storage caching is set 100% to cache write-based data, with the role of read-based caching assigned to the buffer cache on the Oracle nodes themselves. You can see that this storage configuration compromises the reliability and manageability usually needed in a production database environment in order to achieve the best I/O performance available. However, with Price/tpmC always an important factor, the cost of the storage may ultimately have some bearing on the ability to utilize the highest performing disk configuration available.

Also note that the interconnect for an Oracle RAC on Linux TPC-C benchmark is invariably a standard Gigabit Ethernet–based interconnect. Although this interconnect needs to be considered against the minimization of the interinstance traffic, because processing is based on home warehouses, it indicates that a Gigabit Ethernet–based interconnect can offer a level of performance sufficient for the most demanding of applications when coupled with the right level of server processing capability.

In terms of the RAC-based schema configuration itself, you might be interested to note that eight of the nine TPC-C tables are single table hash clusters or table constructs introduced with 10g: sorted hash clusters. When performance is the key driver, with lower priority for factors such as efficient space utilization or manageability, hash clusters can deliver optimal results; the reasons for this are best understood in context of the hardware deployed and are discussed in Chapter 6.

Although hash clusters are also used in single instance–based benchmarks in the RAC environment for some of the tables with the highest potential for contention, the hash clusters are often sized so that the AVG_BLOCKS_PER_KEY value in USER_CLUSTERS is 1. This sizing gives the indication that for some of the tables, the rows are deliberately distributed to assign one row per hash cluster key value, which, in turn, is sized to one data block. Because Cache Fusion operates at the data block level, you can conclude that, in some circumstances with RAC, enabling rows where interinstance contention is expected to be stored within a single block can be advantageous.

The sorted hash clusters feature introduced with Oracle Database 10g is used for storing the TPC-C new order data in a first in, first out (FIFO) manner. This feature is used instead of the partitioned Index-Organized Table (IOT) used in previous RAC benchmarks. The advantages of the hash cluster feature are that new orders are physically organized on disk in lists of rows sorted by the new order ID and any subsequent select statement on the hash key columns has a default return order in the sort key order, without any requirement to specify an ORDER BY clause. When correctly implemented, the in-table sorting of hash clusters eliminates the sorting required at the session level, increasing the overall processing efficiency.

When looking for sizing information regarding a RAC benchmarking system, the full disclosure report offers a great deal of insight by including the full range of system parameters applied to the nodes in the cluster. For example, in terms of memory of the 10g 16-node Linux cluster, you can observe from the cache sizes that each node has a 45GB SGA size, making collectively 720GB of SGA across the cluster. Multiple block sizes and caches are used to segregate data, of which the STOCK table alone has a 35GB cache per node, illustrating that, within RAC, caching as much data locally as is possible is advantageous. In addition, you can see that for a RAC TPC-C benchmark where sorted hash clusters are used, the SORT_AREA_SIZE or PGA_AGGREGATE_TARGET parameter, indicating a minimal level of user sorting activity, is not set, and no Java pool, large pool, or streams pool exists, showing that these pools should only be defined in cases where they are needed.

Other interesting Oracle system parameter settings are the following: the STATISTICS_LEVEL set to BASIC and the TIMED_STATISTICS set to FALSE. These settings mean that the instrumentation available is significantly reduced. This reduction is desirable in a benchmarking setting but demonstrates the trade-off between achieving the highest levels of performance and the monitoring that is required in a production environment. A similar trade-off is observed with the parameters DB_BLOCK_CHECKING and DB_BLOCK_CHECKSUM set to FALSE. By default, these parameters will utilize system CPU but provide ongoing background checking for block corruption. Setting these values to FALSE would not be advised in a production environment; however, the impact of block corruption is acceptable when performance is the only consideration of the application. That a considerable number of underscore parameters would explicitly not be set in a production environment is also worth noting.

Arguably, the most significant parameter setting to observe in a RAC TPC-C benchmark is the parameter GC_FILES_TO_LOCKS. Setting this parameter to any value other than the default disables Cache Fusion processing and replaces it with a manual specification, and therefore, observing that this parameter is indeed set within RAC benchmarks is significant. As you are already aware, a limited percentage of transactions exist outside of the users' home warehouse, and the application is scaled in very much a parallel manner. The schema design can, therefore, dictate whether Cache Fusion may be disabled in favor of a manual specification approach; however, note that where Cache Fusion has been disabled, you cannot make observations around the performance and scalability of Cache Fusion in RAC from such a benchmark.

Additional areas of interest about which general RAC performance information can be gained from the TPC-C benchmarks are the redo and undo configurations. The redo logs are invariably large, for example, 24.5GB each in the 10g RAC configuration with two redo logs per instance. No archiving is performed with the logs sized to such an extent that all of the redo information generated during a benchmark run is held within the online logs. No log switches cause checkpoints; instead, the LOG_CHECKPOINT_TIMEOUT parameter is set to 1740, meaning that a block could remain dirty in the buffer cache for up to 29 minutes. The conclusion to draw from the redo configuration is that recoverability provides a trade-off situation with performance, and the minimal requirements are implemented to ensure that the system is recoverable for the testing period only. A production RAC environment would not be able to employ the same techniques.

In terms of undo configuration, you can see that automatic undo is used, as is the parameter TRANSACTIONS_PER_ROLLBACK_SEGMENT set to 1, to reduce contention and to bring online the maximum number of rollback segments at start-up. The UNDO_RETENTION parameter is set to the relatively low value of 5, as the benchmark has no long-running transactions and therefore minimal undo retention is required.

In summary, this brief review of an official TPC-C benchmark conducted in a RAC environment highlights a number of key areas. First, the sizes of the applications required to conduct an official benchmark are significant and likely to be greater than the vast majority of production applications. In addition, the configuration highlights the areas in which performance is a trade-off with features that are essential in a production environment, such as recoverability and manageability. To gain familiarity with TPC-C, we present an example of conducting an open source simulation based on the TPC-C specification in Chapter 23.

The TPC-H Benchmark

The TPC-H benchmark measures the performance of a complex decision support workload. The benchmark was introduced in 1999 as the result of five years of development by the TPC. TPC-H models a data warehouse environment containing information about customers' orders for the purchase of parts from a number of suppliers distributed across a number of international locations. The tables in the TPC-H schema form a data warehouse constellation schema, where LINEITEM and PARTSUPP are the fact tables, and SUPPLIER, PART, and ORDERS are the dimension tables. The addresses for customers and suppliers are stored in separate dimension tables for the national and world regions as illustrated in Figure 5-2.

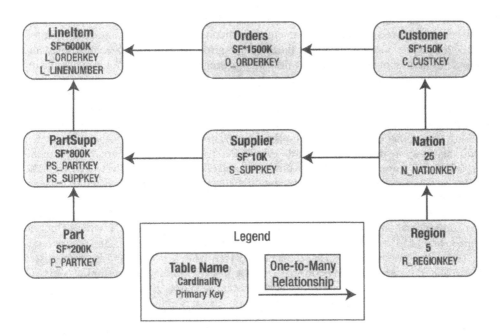

Figure 5-2. *TPC-H schema*

As shown in Figure 5-2, the schema can be sized according to a scale factor, resulting in a size ranging from 1GB to 10TB. These scale factors are shown in Table 5-2 and are for the base data only, not including indexes and temporary tables, which can significantly increase the capacity required. Only results within an individual schema size are comparable—they cannot be compared to the results determined by any other scale factor.

Table 5-2. *Schema Scale Factors*

Scale Factor (SF)	Size
100,000	100,000GB
30,000	30,000GB
10,000	10,000GB
3,000	3,000GB
1,000	1,000GB
300	300GB
100	100GB
30	30GB
10	10GB
1	1GB

The workload for the TPC-H benchmark consists of 22 business-oriented query templates (Q1 to Q22) that vary in complexity and two concurrent data refresh functions (RF1 and RF2). The 22 queries provide templates for a query workload within which substitution variables are replaced with applicable random values, ensuring that each individual query executed is as close as possible to being ad hoc. A *query set* is defined as the sequential execution of each and every one of the queries Q1 to Q22. Queries cannot be modified from the templates given, with the variables substituted into the actual ad hoc queries to be used for the workload by a program called qgen. You can download qgen along with the program dbgen, which is used to generate the schema data, from the TPC web site (http://www.tcp.org), and we describe building these executables on Linux later in this chapter.

Also, dbgen generates refresh datasets for the refresh functions such that datasets are generated for inserting and deleting 0.1% of new rows with primary key values unused in the standard dbgen datasets. The refresh functions can then be implemented by the test sponsor in the following manner: for RF1, new rows are inserted into the ORDERS and LINEITEM tables equivalent to the 0.1% of the table size, and for RF2, rows are deleted from the ORDERS and LINEITEM tables equivalent to the 0.1% of the table size. This implementation ensures that the schema size remains consistent between benchmark tests.

The metrics for the TPC-H benchmark contain a greater degree of complexity than those for the TPC-C benchmark. First, the database build time, although not a primary metric, is always reported for the time to build and load the database, including the time to create the associated indexes and statistics. The primary metrics for the TPC-H benchmarks are the values for composite queries per hour (QphH) and the ratio of price to performance ($/QphH). The combined parts for the composite figures are from two distinct benchmark tests: the power test and the throughput test. The power test has no concurrency; queries are submitted in a single stream running the RF1 refresh stream, followed by query set 0, and finally the RF2 refresh stream. This results in the measurement of the geometric queries-per-hour value according to the scale factor size. The throughput test must follow immediately after a power test. For the throughput test, the measurement is taken for multiple concurrent query streams where the number of streams is determined by the scale factor as illustrated in Table 5-3.

Table 5-3. *Number of Query Streams*

Scale Factor (SF)	Streams (S)
100,000	11
30,000	10
10,000	9
3,000	8
1,000	7
300	6
100	5
30	4
10	3
1	2

The query streams are executed in parallel with a single refresh stream. Therefore, the query streams execute their own individual query sets of Q1 to Q22 serially, while the refresh stream executes RF1, followed by RF2, until all query sets are complete. The throughput metric reports the linear queries per hour according to the scale factor. During the benchmark run, a client or presentation layer such as required by the TPC-C benchmark is optional, and the streams are permitted to execute their refresh functions and query sets directly on the database servers themselves.

When the throughput metric has been determined, the power and throughput metrics are then combined to deliver the Composite Query-per-Hour rating (QphH@Size) as follows:

$$QphH@Size = \sqrt{Power @ Size \times Throughput @ Size}$$

An example Oracle 10*g* RAC on Linux TPC-H metric is 11,743 QphH@300GB, achieved by a cluster of two nodes of four CPUs each. Similar to the methodology for deriving the TPC-C price performance values, the total cost of ownership of the system divided by the Composite Query-per-Hour rating gives a value in this case of US$21.84 per QphH@300GB.

The implementation of a TPC-H benchmark derived from a full disclosure report can enable us to gain important information in terms of configuring Oracle 10*g* RAC on Linux for a data warehousing environment.

For the storage configuration in this example, 14 logical unit numbers (LUNs), each containing 12 physical disk drivers, are all configured in a RAID 1+0 configuration. This configuration draws the distinction with the RAID 0 configurations preferred for OLTP-based benchmarks—the predominantly read-based nature of the TPC-H benchmark favors the use of mirrored volumes to satisfy the read requests from both sides of the mirror. The write impact is not as significant as it would be in a transactional environment. Each LUN is divided into two partitions: one partition is configured with a standard Linux Second Extended File System (Ext2 fs) to be mounted on only one node in the cluster, and another partition is configured as a raw device for the Oracle database files. The flat file partitions are designated for the loading files, and the raw partitions are consequently configured into Automatic Storage Management (ASM) disk groups, with ASM managing the placement of the database datafiles and log files across the storage system. This configuration serves to highlight that, in a data warehouse environment, ASM can deliver on the requirements for performance in a RAC environment balancing the I/O load across the LUNs presented.

For the schema configuration in TPC-H, the most significant point to note is the use of hash partitioning or range partitioning for all tables and indexes except for the nation and region tables. Each partitioned table has 16 partitions, mostly partitioned by a hash value on the primary key.

Where range partitioning is used, the values are initially partitioned by date values before being subpartitioned by hash. Each table or index specifies the parallel clause to enable parallel processing to be active on it. The use of partitioning in conjunction with parallel query processing is a technique that makes RAC especially applicable to data warehousing environments, enabling the division of the workload equally between the nodes.

Also note that the interconnect in this particular benchmark uses a low-cost crossover cable, which is ordinarily unsupported in an Oracle production environment. Similar to the TPC-C benchmark, this interconnect illustrates that standard Gigabit Ethernet networking is also used for the TPC-H benchmark, with the emphasis placed on the division of the workload to achieve performance, as opposed to the use of a high-speed remote direct memory access (RDMA) interconnect, primarily because of the number of nodes involved. We review the merits of both approaches in Chapter 6.

The data load of the flat files generated by the dbgen program and the inserts of the refresh function RF1 are realized using externally organized tables of the type ORACLE_LOADER. The data delete functions of RF2 also occur by reference to the data in the externally organized table. Externally organized tables, therefore, present one of the most efficient methods for inserting and deleting data in a data warehouse with reference to data from external sources presented as flat files.

In terms of the initialization parameters for parallelism, the values set for each instance are as follows: PARALLEL_ADAPTIVE_MULTI_USER set to TRUE, PARALLEL_MIN_SERVERS to 64, PARALLEL_MAX_SERVERS to 128, and PARALLEL_EXECUTION_MESSAGE_SIZE to 16384. Other significant values of note to data warehouses are the large-block size setting, DB_BLOCK_SIZE, set to 16384 in conjunction with a large multiblock read count value, DB_FILE_MULTIBLOCK_READ_COUNT, set to 128. These block settings enable efficient processing when the environment requires the reading of large amounts of data sequentially, and with these block settings in particular, the data will be fetched in batches of 2MB. The most notable difference with a transactional environment is the fact that the SGA_TARGET size, of which the DB_CACHE_SIZE is a component, is set to a modest 2GB; however, the PGA_AGGREGATE_TARGET value is set 12GB per instance for this TCP-H benchmark, whereas as you have seen it is usually set to 0 for a TPC-C benchmark. For processing complex business queries, the availability of sufficient capacity for in-memory sorting is crucial to performance.

In summary, you can draw some general conclusions in terms of configuring Oracle 10g RAC for a data warehousing environment. First, configuring storage as RAID 1+0 using raw devices with ASM is the method to achieve good performance for a read-based workload. In addition, the correct configuration of partitioning and parallelism enables the division of the workload between the nodes. Finally, the sizing of the PGA_AGGREGATE_TARGET to enable sorting in memory, as opposed to on disk, is essential for performance when processing complex queries.

Building a TPC-H Schema

The most productive method for gaining familiarity with the TPC-H benchmark is to build and load the schema, and generate and run the queries in a RAC on a Linux environment using the dbgen and qgen programs. From the default TPC-H page on the TPC web site, you can download the C source code for the dbgen and qgen software. Using this software and standard Oracle utilities, you can build and populate TPC-H schema in your environment and generate the queries to simulate your own TPC-H workload.

To build this software, first download either the .zip file or .tar.gz format file from the link on the TPC-H web page, such as tpch_20051026.tar.z, and extract this file to a directory such as /home/oracle/tpch on your Linux system using the following command:

```
[oracle@london1 oracle]$ tar zxvf tpch_20051026.tar.z
```

There is a Makefile within the top-level directory that requires some modification before being suitable for an Oracle on Linux environment. Rename the file makefile.suite to Makefile as follows:

```
[oracle@london1 dbgen]$ mv makefile.suite Makefile
```

By default, the Makefile does not support an Oracle configuration, and therefore, you will need to create the configuration. Although the Makefile does not explicitly mention Linux as a machine type, Linux is actually supported and defined within the file config.h. Edit the Makefile, and set a value of gcc for the parameter CC. Set the value of DATABASE to ORACLE, the value of MACHINE to LINUX, and WORKLOAD to TPCH. This section of the Makefile will resemble the following:

```
################
## CHANGE NAME OF ANSI COMPILER HERE
################
CC      = gcc
# Current values for DATABASE are:   INFORMIX, DB2, TDAT (Teradata)
#                                     SQLSERVER, SYBASE
# Current values for MACHINE are:     ATT, DOS, HP, IBM, ICL, MVS,
#                                     SGI, SUN, U2200, VMS
# Current values for WORKLOAD are:    TPCH, TPCR
DATABASE = ORACLE
MACHINE = LINUX
WORKLOAD = TPCH
#
```

Edit the file tpcd.h, and add default definitions corresponding to the ORACLE database setting you have just created in the Makefile to the end of the file as follows:

```
#ifdef ORACLE
#define GEN_QUERY_PLAN ""
#define START_TRAN ""
#define END_TRAN ""
#define SET_OUTPUT ""
#define SET_ROWCOUNT ""
#define SET_DBASE ""
#endif
```

With these changes in place, use the make command to compile the software as follows:

```
[oracle@london1 tpch]$ make
gcc -g -DDBNAME=\"dss\" -DLINUX -DORACLE -DTPCH   -c -o build.o build.c
gcc -g -DDBNAME=\"dss\" -DLINUX -DORACLE -DTPCH   -c -o driver.o driver.c
gcc -g -DDBNAME=\"dss\" -DLINUX -DORACLE -DTPCH   -c -o bm_utils.o bm_utils.c
```

The compilation will have generated two executables of interest: dbgen and qgen. The data with which to populate the TPC-H schema is generated using dbgen. Before generating the data, create a schema owner such as tpch, and as this user within SQL*Plus, create the TPC-H tables. For example, create the LINEITEM table as follows:

```
SQL> create table lineitem (
  l_orderkey integer not null,
  l_partkey integer not null,
  l_suppkey integer not null,
  l_linenumber integer not null,
  l_quantity decimal(15,2) not null,
  l_extendedprice decimal (15,2) not null,
  l_discount decimal(15,2) not null,
  l_tax decimal(15,2) not null,
  l_returnflag char(1) not null,
  l_linestatus char(1) not null,
  l_shipdate date not null,
  l_commitdate date not null,
  l_receiptdate date not null,
  l_shipinstruct char(25) not null,
```

```
 l_shipmode char(10) not null,
 l_comment varchar(44) not null);
Table created.
```

At the operating system command prompt, use the dbgen executable to create the datafiles corresponding to the tables. Without any options at the command prompt, dbgen generates eight datafiles, one for each table by default of the scale factor 1. The -h option displays a usage summary of the command line options available. To generate datafiles for the individual tables, dbgen takes two arguments: -s for the scale factor of the schema and -T for the table type. For example, to generate a scale factor 1 datafile for the LINEITEM table, use the following command:

```
[oracle@london1 tpch]$ ./dbgen -s 1 -T L
TPC-H Population Generator (Version 2.3.0 )
Copyright Transaction Processing Performance Council 1994 - 2005
```

This produces a datafile named after the table it is created for, in the same directory, with contents in a text-based form as follows:

```
[oracle@london1 tpch]$ more lineitem.tbl
1|155190|7706|1|17|21168.23|0.04|0.02|N|O|1996-03-13|1996-02-12|
1996-03-22|DELIVER IN PERSON|TRUCK|blithely regular ideas caj|
1|67310|7311|2|36|45983.16|0.09|0.06|N|O|1996-04-12|1996-02-28|
1996-04-20|TAKE BACK RETURN|MAIL|slyly bold pinto beans detect s|
1|63700|3701|3|8|13309.60|0.10|0.02|N|O|1996-01-29|1996-03-05|
1996-01-31|TAKE BACK RETURN|REG AIR|deposits wake furiously dogged,|
```

This data can then be inserted into the applicable precreated schema table with the SQL*Loader utility or the datafiles defined as externally organized tables of type ORACLE_LOADER. To use SQL*Loader, create a control file describing the correct fields. The control file for the LINEITEM table takes the following form:

```
[oracle@london1 tpch]$ more load_lineitem.ctl
LOAD DATA
INFILE 'lineitem.tbl'
INTO TABLE lineitem
FIELDS TERMINATED BY '|'
(l_orderkey,l_partkey,l_suppkey,l_linenumber,l_quantity,
l_extendedprice,l_discount,l_tax,l_returnflag,l_linestatus, l_shipdate
"to_date(:l_shipdate,'YYYY/MM/DD')", l_commitdate
"to_date(:l_commitdate,'YYYY/MM/DD')", l_receiptdate
"to_date(:l_receiptdate,'YYYY/MM/DD')",l_shipinstruct,l_shipmode,l_comment)
```

You can then use SQL*Loader and the control file to insert the data created as follows:

```
[oracle@london1 tpch]$ sqlldr tpch control=load_lineitem.ctl DIRECT=TRUE
Password:
SQL*Loader: Release 10.2.0.1.0 - Production on Fri Aug 26 10:39:51 2005
Copyright (c) 1982, 2005, Oracle.  All rights reserved.
Load completed - logical record count 6001215.
```

Review the log file, in this case load_lineitem.log, to ensure that the load occurred successfully. With the data in place, ensure that the correct indexes are created, such as i_l_orderkey on the LINEITEM table as in the following code:

```
SQL> create index i_l_orderkey on lineitem(l_orderkey);
```

Also, ensure that statistics are gathered on the fully populated tables and indexes that have been created.

When called with the -U argument, dbgen is also used to create the datasets for the refresh functions. For example, to create a single update set at the default scale size, use the following command:

```
[oracle@london1 tpch]$ ./dbgen -U 1
TPC-H Population Generator (Version 2.3.0 )
Copyright Transaction Processing Performance Council 1994 - 2005
```

This command generates three files: two datafiles for the update refresh function orders.tbl.u1 and lineitem.tbl.u1, and delete.1, containing the primary key range for the delete refresh function. The -O d option generates the SQL for the delete function, as opposed to just the key range.

With the schema created, you can generate the appropriate queries using the qgen executable. There are 22 query templates in the queries directory. Copy these files to the same directory as qgen as follows:

```
[oracle@london1 tpch]$ cp queries/* .
```

Then qgen can be used to produce the queries specified by the TPC-H benchmark. Similar to dbgen, qgen has a number of command line options with -h displaying a usage summary. If called without command line options, qgen will generate a file containing a query set of all of the available queries; specifying the argument of the value 1 to 22 dictates the query template to use. For example, the following command:

```
[oracle@london1 tpch]$ ./qgen 1 > query1.sql
```

produces the following query that acts against the LINEITEM table:

```
[oracle@london1 tpch]$ more query1.sql
-- using 1906318034 as a seed to the RNG

select
        l_returnflag,
        l_linestatus,
        sum(l_quantity) as sum_qty,
        sum(l_extendedprice) as sum_base_price,
        sum(l_extendedprice * (1 - l_discount)) as sum_disc_price,
        sum(l_extendedprice * (1 - l_discount) * (1 + l_tax)) as sum_charge,
        avg(l_quantity) as avg_qty,
        avg(l_extendedprice) as avg_price,
        avg(l_discount) as avg_disc,
        count(*) as count_order
from
        lineitem
where
        l_shipdate <= date '1998-12-01' - interval '102' day (3)
group by
        l_returnflag,
        l_linestatus
order by
        l_returnflag,
        l_linestatus;
```

Using qgen, you can generate the query sets used for simulating a TPC-H benchmark. You can then use a load generation tools such as Hammerora or Swingbench, detailed in Chapter 23, to generate a multiuser load with these queries and the refresh functions against the TPC-H schema to conduct a data warehousing simulation in a test environment.

Summary

In this chapter, we introduced the concepts behind load testing and benchmarking with a view to being able to understand the approaches to prepare to construct your own test scenarios of RAC configurations. Toward this aim, we discussed some of the techniques that Oracle employs in conducting benchmarks published by the Transaction Processing Performance Council (TCP) in order to identify which of these techniques are applicable to real-world RAC implementations.

CHAPTER 6

■ ■ ■

Hardware

In this chapter, we will consider the technology decisions to be made in terms of the hardware required for a RAC cluster. The question of hardware is often neglected by DBAs; however, for a well-tuned application, the potential performance improvements offered by the latest hardware running Linux can often be orders of magnitude greater than those achievable by upgrades or software tuning in an existing environment.

To compare systems, we can use the independently audited results of TPC-C benchmarks, the fundamentals of which have already been discussed in Chapter 5. At the time of this writing, the highest-ranking TPC-C result, submitted with Oracle 10*g* RAC on Linux in August 2003, was 1,184,893 tpmC with a price of US$5.52/tpmC. This benchmark was performed on a 64-processor configuration. Another sample 64-processor configuration submitted four years earlier, in June 1999, on an Oracle 8 single-instance configuration had results of 93,901 tpmC and a price of US$131.67/tpmC. In just four years, these results show a twelve-fold performance increase and a twenty-four-fold price performance increase. This price performance value also highlights the pitfall of considering the costs of hardware alone while not accounting for the significant potential savings also offered in software licensing when migrating to a Linux-based platform.

In a RAC environment, this knowledge is even more important as, with a requirement for increased capacity, you are often presented with a decision between adding another node to an existing cluster and replacing the cluster in its entirety with updated hardware. You also have the choice between a great number of small nodes and a small number of large nodes in the cluster. Knowing the hardware building blocks of your cluster is fundamental to making the correct choice; it can also assist in understanding the underlying reasons of how to configure the Linux operating system to achieve optimal Oracle RAC performance for installing, configuring, and verifying Linux (see Chapters 10 and 11).

Considering hardware presents a challenge in that, given the extraordinary pace of development in computing technology, reviewing the snapshot of any particular cluster configuration, in time, will soon be made obsolete by the next generation of systems. So rather than focus on any individual configuration, instead we will review the general areas to consider when purchasing hardware for RAC that should remain relevant over time. With this intent, we will also refrain from directly considering different form factors, such as blade or rack-mounted servers, and instead consider the lower-level technology that often lies behind a form factor decision.

The aim of this chapter is to provide a grounding to build a checklist when selecting a hardware platform for RAC on Linux to enable you to make an optimal choice. However, one factor that should be abundantly clear before proceeding is that this chapter will not tell you precisely what server, processor, or network interconnect to purchase. No two Oracle environments are the same, and therefore, a different configuration may be entirely applicable to each circumstance.

Oracle Availability

Before beginning the selection of a hardware platform to run Oracle RAC on Linux, your first port of call should be Oracle itself, to identify the architectures on which Oracle releases the Oracle database for Linux with the RAC option.

At the time of this writing, the following four architectures using Oracle terminology have production releases of Oracle on Linux:

- **x86**: A standard 32-bit Intel compatible x86 processor

- **x86-64**: A 64-bit extended x86 processor (i.e., Intel EM64T, AMD64)

- **Itanium**: The Intel Itanium processor

- **z/LINUX**: An IBM mainframe

In this chapter, our focus is on the first three architectures, because of their support under the Oracle Unbreakable Linux campaign as discussed in Chapter 2.

In addition to simply reviewing the software availability, also view the technology matrix on the Certify – Oracle's Certification Matrices page of Oracle's web site to identify platform-specific information for running Oracle RAC in a particular environment.

To do this on the certification site (http://www.oracle.com/technology/support/metalink/index.html), click the Certify tab, followed by View Certifications by Platform. Scroll down the list of architectures to the Linux section with the following three options listed:

- Linux (Itanium)

- Linux (x86)

- Linux x86-64 (AMD64/EM64T)

Highlight the platform of interest, and click Submit. Then, under the Product Group Selection, click Real Application Clusters, and click Submit. This brings up the Product Group Selection page, which, if platform-specific information is available, will include a link to a RAC Technologies Compatibility Matrix (RTCM) for Linux Clusters. These are classified into the following four areas:

- Server/Processor Architecture

- Storage

- Network Interconnect

- Cluster Software

Selecting the correct storage for RAC is a wide-ranging subject, which will be covered in detail in Chapter 7. Ahead of that chapter, however, the importance of the storage compatibility matrix published by the storage vendors you are evaluating is worth stressing. Many storage vendors perform comprehensive testing of server architectures running against their technology, often including Oracle RAC as a specific certification area. To ensure compatibility and support for all of your chosen RAC components, the servers should not be selected completely independently of the storage, and vice versa, for an optimal solution.

An additional subject for compatible technology for RAC is cluster software, which, as a software component, is covered in detail in Chapters 12 and 16, as a closely integrated component of Oracle RAC for installing and configuring the Oracle Database 10g software and Clusterware.

In this chapter, we will concentrate on the remaining hardware components and consider the selections of the most applicable server/processor architecture and network interconnect for your requirements.

Server Architecture

The core components of any Linux RAC configuration are the servers themselves that act as the cluster nodes. These servers all provide the same service in running the Linux operating system but do so with differing technologies. We will review the basic building blocks common to all platforms beginning with the processor itself, which provides the reference point for the rest of the architecture.

Processors

As you have previously seen, selecting a processor on which to run Linux and Oracle presents you with three choices. Table 6-1 shows the information gleaned from the choices' textual descriptions in the Oracle technology matrix.

Table 6-1. *Processor Architecture Information*

Server/Processor Architecture	Processor Architecture Details
Linux x86	Support on Intel and AMD processors that adhere to the 32-bit x86 architecture.
Linux x86-64	Support on Intel and AMD processors that adhere to the 64-bit x86-64 architecture. 32-bit Oracle on x86-64 with a 64-bit operating system is not supported. 32-bit Oracle on x86-64 with a 32-bit operating system is supported.
Itanium	Support on Intel Itanium processors that adhere to the 64-bit EPIC architecture. 32-bit Oracle on Itanium is not supported.

From these processor architecture details, you can clearly see that one of the first questions that DBAs must ask is whether they would benefit from running Oracle RAC on Linux on a 32-bit or on a 64-bit CPU platform, and we will consider this question from an Oracle perspective before looking in more depth at the processors' architectures.

32-Bit or 64-Bit

Two fundamental differences exist between 32- and 64-bit computing. The most significant is in the area of memory addressability. In theory, a 32-bit system can address memory up to the value of 2 to the power of 32, making a maximum of 4GB of addressable memory. A 64-bit system can address up to the value of 2 to the power of 64, making a maximum of 16 exabytes, or 16 billion GB, of addressable memory—vastly greater than the amount that could be physically installed into any RAC cluster available today.

In addition to memory addressability, a benefit is the move to 64-bit registers within the processors themselves. A *register* can be viewed as an immediate holding area for data before and after calculations. With 64-bit registers, the processor can manipulate high-precision data more quickly by processing more bits in each operation.

Given the differences between 32-bit and 64-bit computing, you can identify the following two areas of applications that benefit most from 64-bit computing:

- **Enterprise-class applications**: These applications spend a significant amount of time reading data from disk-based storage compared to the processing of the data itself. They benefit primarily from the increased memory addressability afforded by 64-bit computing and are, therefore, a category into which the Oracle database is most likely to fall.

- **High Performance Computing (HPC) applications**: These scientific/technical computing applications spend most of their time processing vast amounts of data with high-precision floating-point operations. Building these systems in clusters containing thousands of CPUs is not uncommon, and more detailed information about them and the applications they run can be found at the TOP500 Supercomputer Sites web site (http://www.top500.org).

Do not confuse the benefits of 64-bit computing for these two distinct areas. In particular, the LINPACK Benchmark, used to determine the TOP500 Supercomputers ranking, measures the overall ability of system to solve a dense system of linear equations and bears little relevance to the suitability of a platform on which to run the Oracle database server. The single most important factor for the move to 64-bit computing for Oracle is the potential for memory addressability and, hence, the size of the SGA for a particular Oracle instance. A brief overview of the components of the SGA is useful to put this Oracle addressability in a hardware context.

The SGA is shared memory that Oracle allocates consisting of a fixed and variable area unique to each instance in the cluster. The variable area is sized either manually by the DBA by setting Oracle parameters or automatically by the MMAN process according to requirements within the bounds defined by the SGA_TARGET and SGA_MAX_SIZE parameters.

The variable values can be summarized as follows:

- **Database buffer cache** (DB_CACHE_SIZE **parameter**): Memory that Oracle allocates for caching data blocks.

- **Shared pool** (SHARED_POOL_SIZE **parameter**): Memory allocated for uses such as parsed SQL and PL/SQL statements, query plans, packages, object information, and parallel execution buffers.

- **Large pool** (LARGE_POOL_SIZE **parameter**): Memory allocated when using features such as shared server, RMAN, or Advanced Queuing (AQ). This parameter can be set to zero if these features are not used.

- **Java pool** (JAVA_POOL_SIZE **parameter**): Memory allocated for Java in the database. This parameter can be zero if Java is not used within the database itself.

- **Redo log** (LOG_BUFFER **parameter**): The redo log buffer is always sized manually; however, a log buffer of 1MB–5MB, depending on the application, is usually recommended.

The most significant contributor to the SGA size, and therefore the drive to 64-bit computing, is usually the caching of the data blocks themselves. With cached data, you reduce the number of physical reads and improve overall performance by fetching the data blocks from memory instead of from disk. Also note that when moving to a 64-bit platform, Oracle recommends doubling the size of the other memory regions, such as the shared pool and large pool, to accommodate the same applications. This recommendation is as a direct result of increasing the word size from 32 to 64 bits.

Note also that some additional memory is required within the SGA for increasing the number of user connections and will be allocated within the fixed SGA on start-up based on the PROCESSES parameter. However, in terms of the memory allocated to each individual user, the PGA is private memory for the server process related to each user session. This work area is allocated for operations, such as sorting, and is, therefore, usually required to be larger in a data warehouse environment. Setting the parameter PGA_AGGREGATE_TARGET determines the maximum amount of memory in total that Oracle will allow for all of the user processes on the system. As the PGA is private memory, more users indirectly affect the SGA requirements in demand, for example, by the volume of data but not in allocating memory for the user sessions themselves. The number of users in itself does not directly impact whether a system should be 32- or 64-bit. However, a significantly large number of users also depend on the memory handling of the underlying Linux operating system for all of the individual processes, which may itself benefit from 64-bit memory addressability.

As you have seen, the theoretical limit for memory addressability on a 32-bit system is 4GB, and if this 4GB limit is enforced as a singular limit across the entire operating system, any Oracle database system will soon be memory constrained. Fortunately, the Linux releases of interest to us and the 32-bit x86 architecture support the concepts of virtual memory and physical memory, which we discuss in the context of memory later in this chapter. With a standard Linux SMP kernel on a 32-bit system and the maximum 4GB of virtual memory available to the Oracle instance, you have a potential allocation that adheres to the divisions presented in Table 6-2.

Table 6-2. *Standard Oracle Memory Allocation on Linux*

Memory	Allocation
1.0GB	Oracle code and shared libraries
1.7GB	SGA
0.3GB	Stack
1.0GB	Kernel

In this environment, you can lower the default memory address where Oracle is loaded in the system with the following command run in the $ORACLE_HOME/rdbms/lib directory:

```
[oracle@london1 lib]$ genksms -s 0x15000000 > ksms.s
```

Reviewing ksms.s shows that the new SGA beginning base address has now been set as follows:

```
[oracle@london1 lib]$ more ksms.s
      .set    sgabeg,0X15000000
      .globl  ksmsgf_
      .set    ksmsgf_,sgabeg+0
```

This address can then be compiled and relinked into Oracle as follows:

```
[oracle@london1 lib]$ make -f ins_rdbms.mk ksms.o
```

```
[oracle@london1 lib]$ make -f ins_rdbms.mk ioracle
```

The Oracle RDBMS executables and libraries are then loaded at a lower mapped base, enabling a potential SGA size of up to 2.7GB on a 32-bit system.

Within the confines of the 32-bit processor and the Linux SMP kernel, 2.7GB would be the maximum size to which you would be able to increase the SGA. However, a standard x86 system, in fact, has 36-bit physical memory addressability behind the 32-bit virtual memory addressability. This 36-bit physical implementation now gives us a potential of 64GB of memory to use with a feature called Page Addressing Extensions (PAE) to translate the 32-bit virtual addresses to 36-bit physical addresses. The Linux kernel needs to be able to implement PAE to use any memory over 4GB, and depending on the version of Linux, this is the distinguishing feature of the enterprise kernel. On a 32-bit enterprise kernel, you can mount a shared memory-based file system (shmfs) of more than 4GB with a command such as the following:

```
[root@london1 root]# mount -t shm shmfs -o size=12g /dev/shm
```

To ensure that the file system is mounted at boot time, you need to also put an entry within the file /etc/fstab. To use this file system for the Oracle buffer cache, the Oracle parameter USE_INDIRECT_DATA_BUFFERS is required to be set to the value TRUE. This setting enables an SGA of up to 62GB on a 32-bit system.

However, a practical consideration in implementing PAE is that you need to use a significant amount of memory to build the page table entries for the virtual to physical translations. As you are limiting the kernel memory to 1GB, depending on the page size, the 1GB of kernel memory could be exhausted before the potential of the physical addressability could be used. For this reason, on earlier versions of Linux the practical limitation of very large memory (VLM) was more likely to be 16GB than 64GB.

In Red Hat Linux, the hugemem kernel was developed to allocate 4GB to the kernel and 4GB to the user process with the terminology *4GB/4GB split*. The 4GB/4GB split enabled the hugemem memory allocation in Table 6-3.

Table 6-3. *Hugemem Oracle Memory Allocation*

Memory	Allocation
1.0GB	Oracle code and shared libraries
2.7GB	SGA
0.3GB	Stack
4.0GB	Kernel

This allocation now gives a default SGA size of 2.7GB with the possibility to increase it to 3.7GB with a lower mapped memory base, as described previously, or to implement a memory resident file system for the buffer cache up to the full potential of 62GB. Also remember that, with RAC, you are using multiple instances, thus increasing the amount of SGA memory available across the entire cluster.

Understanding of the advantages of 64-bit versus 32-bit technology, you can see that the main reason for Oracle to be on a 64-bit platform is that performance on a 32-bit system may be restricted by a buffer cache that is limited in size. This limit causes Oracle to fetch data from the SAN or NAS storage more often than would be needed if a larger buffer cache were configurable.

Fortunately, Oracle can quantify whether this is the case for us in the view V$DB_CACHE_ADVICE, the statistics of which are also included within an Automatic Workload Repository (AWR) report, the generation of which we discuss in Chapter 24. The V$DB_CACHE_ADVICE view illustrates the estimated activity for 20 potential buffer cache sizes from 10% of the current size up to 200% of the current size. Every potential cache size has a row in the view with the corresponding estimated physical reads for that particular cache size. If the estimated physical reads are reduced by increasing the size of the buffer cache, then performance will increase by spending less time reading from disk when compared to the faster access from memory. This view, therefore, enables you to judge individually for every instance in the cluster whether you would benefit from the native large SGA sizes of a 64-bit system.

If you are in the position of migrating from a 32-bit Linux platform to any 64-bit Linux platform supported under the Unbreakable Linux program, be aware that the structures of the Oracle database files themselves remain completely unaltered. In addition, all client programs can connect to the 64-bit Oracle database without requiring any modifications. Once the 64-bit hardware, operating system, and Oracle are installed and connected to the storage on which the database is resident, you only need to re-create the control files, start up the instances in the cluster, and recompile the PL/SQL packages. These steps can also be done using the Database Upgrade Assistant.

Architecture Overview

From the discussion of 32- or 64-bit computing, you can determine that memory addressability and a large SGA are the key reasons for Oracle on Linux to be based on 64-bit technology. Remember, however, that whether a large SGA is or is not required, the architectural features of a CPU will be of much greater importance for performance than simply its addressability, and moving forward 64-bit computing will become the standard as all of the software required in a 64-bit Linux environment gradually becomes available.

Reviewing the processors available for Oracle on Linux, you have three architectural choices: standard 32-bit x86 architecture processors, extended 64-bit x86 architecture processors, and Itanium 64-bit Explicitly Parallel Instruction Computing (EPIC) architecture processors. Before looking at the individual architectures, you will find a very high-level overview of the attributes of a processor useful as a background to the benefits they will provide you in terms of running Oracle.

First, the clock speed is often erroneously used as a singular comparative measure of processor performance. The *clock speed*, or *clock rate*, is usually measured in gigahertz, where 1GHz represents 1 billion cycles per second, and it determines the speed at which the processor executes instructions. However, the CPU architecture is absolutely critical to the overall level of performance, and no reasonable comparison can be made based on clock speed alone.

For a CPU to process information, it needs to first load and store the instructions and data it requires for execution. The fastest mode of access to data is to the processor's registers, which can occur within a single clock cycle. A general-purpose register can be used for arithmetic and logical operations, indexing, shifting, input, output, and general data storage before the data is operated upon. All of the CPUs listed have additional registers for floating-point operations and other architecture-specific features. As the registers store the data and instructions for processing, the more registers a CPU has, the more likely that it will operate efficiently by having more data ready to process on every clock cycle, resulting in comparatively higher performance. Taking a 2GHz CPU as an example, retrieving the data in its registers will take one clock cycle of 1/2 a billionth of a second. Fewer registers means more clock cycles to accomplish the same workload.

Although a large number of registers in a processor is desirable, registers store a small fraction of the data required for Oracle, and all of the data will ultimately reside on disk-based storage. Assuming that your disks have an access time of ten milliseconds, if the example 2GHz CPU were required to wait for a single disk access, it would wait for a period of time equivalent to 20 million CPU clock cycles. Fortunately, the Oracle SGA acts as an intermediary resident in Random Access Memory (RAM) on each node in the cluster. Memory access times can vary, and we discuss the performance potential of each type of memory later in this chapter. However, with the type of random access to memory typically associated with Oracle, the wait will take approximately 60 nanoseconds, which is one single memory access in a 60-millionth of a second. The time delay represents 120 clock cycles for which the example 2GHz CPU must wait to retrieve data from main memory.

As you now have comparative statistics for accessing data from memory and disk, in an Oracle RAC environment, the most important question to ask is, "How does Cache Fusion compare to local memory and disk access speeds?" A good average receive time for a consistent read or current block for Cache Fusion will be approximately two to four milliseconds with a gigabit-based interconnect, the equivalent of 4 to 5 million clock cycles for remote Oracle cache access, compared to 120 clock cycles for local Oracle cache access. Accessing data from a remote SGA through Cache Fusion, therefore, gives you a dramatic improvement over accessing data from disk, although it also shows that you can greatly improve performance by having an optimal buffer cache configured on each and every node in the cluster to minimize both disk and Cache Fusion traffic wherever possible.

x86 and x86-64

The x86 architecture is a complex instruction set computer (CISC) architecture and has been in existence since 1978, when Intel Corporation introduced the 16-bit 8086 CPU. The de facto standard for Linux systems is x86, as it is the architecture on which Linux evolved from a desktop-based Unix implementation to one of the leading enterprise-class operating systems. Today's x86 architecture processors deliver high performance with features such as being superscalar, being pipelined, and possessing out-of-order execution; and understanding some of the basics of these features can help in designing an optimal x86-based Oracle RAC environment.

In common with all processors, an x86 CPU sends instructions on a path termed the *pipeline* through the processor on which a number of hardware components act on the instruction until it is executed and written back to memory. At the most basic level, these instructions can be classified into the following four stages:

- **Fetch**: The next instruction of the executing program is loaded from memory. In reality, the instructions will already have been preloaded in larger blocks into the instruction cache, and we discuss the importance of cache later in this chapter.

- **Decode**: x86 instructions themselves are not executed directly, but are instead translated into microinstructions. Decoding the complex instruction set into these microinstructions may take a number of clock cycles to complete.

- **Execute**: The microinstructions are executed by dedicated execution units depending on the type of operation. For example, floating-point operations are handled by dedicated floating-point execution units.

- **Write-back**: The results from the execution are written back to an internal register or system memory via the cache.

This simple processor model executes the program by passing instructions through these four stages, one per clock cycle. However, performance potentially improves if the processor does not need to wait for one instruction to complete write-back before fetching another, and a significant amount of improvement has been accomplished through pipelining. Pipelining enables the processor to be at different stages with multiple instructions at the same time, and since the clock speed will be limited by the time needed to complete the longest of its stages, breaking the pipeline into shorter ones enables the processor to run at a higher frequency. For this reason, current x86 enterprise processors often have large 20 to 30 stage pipelines termed *hyper* or *super pipelines* that provide increased throughput. Although each instruction will take more clock cycles to pass through the pipeline, and only one instruction will actually complete on each clock cycle, the higher frequency increases the overall throughput, and this frequency scaling is a crucial aspect of performance for x86 deep pipelined designs.

One of the most important aspects of performance to current x86 processors is out-of-order execution, which adds the following two stages to your simple example pipeline around the execution stage:

- **Issue/schedule**: The decoded microinstructions are issued to an instruction pool where they are scheduled onto available execution units and executed independently. Maintaining this pool of instructions increases the likelihood that an instruction and its input will be available to process on every clock cycle, thereby increasing throughput.

- **Retire**: As the instructions are executed out of order, they are written to the reorder buffer (ROB) and retired by being put back into the correct order intended by the original x86 instructions before write-back occurs.

Further advancements have also been made in instruction-level parallelism (ILP) with superscalar architectures. ILP introduces multiple parallel pipelines to execute a number of instructions in a single clock cycle, and current x86 architectures support a peak execution rate of at least three instructions per cycle.

In terms of Oracle RAC, a transactional profile features a large number of concurrent users with small random data operations. A high degree of complexity translates into large instruction and data sets and inevitably results in stalls for both instructions and data where the processor is required to wait while the required information is retrieved from memory, Cache Fusion, or disk, with the length of the stall dependent on where the information is retrieved. The role of a large CPU cache in multiprocessor environments, as we discuss later in this chapter, is crucial in reducing the likelihood of these stalls.

For 64-bit Linux x86-64 architecture, CPUs implement the familiar x86 CISC architecture while extending the number and width of the registers and address space. Note that these CPUs actually have a physical addressability of 40 bits and a virtual addressability of 48 bits, enabling a potential addressability of up to 1TB.

One advantage of x86-64 for general-purpose applications is that the processors can operate in three different modes: 32-bit mode, compatibility mode, or 64-bit mode. The mode is selected at boot time and cannot be changed without restarting the system with a different operating system. In 32-bit mode, the processor operates in exactly the same way as standard x86, utilizing the standard eight of the general-purpose registers. In compatibility mode, a 64-bit operating system is installed, but 32-bit x86 applications can run on the 64-bit operating system. Compatibility mode has the advantage of affording the full 4GB addressability to each 32-bit application. Finally, the processor can operate in 64-bit mode, realizing the full range of its potential for 64-bit applications.

This compatibility is indispensable when running a large number of 32-bit applications developed on the widely available x86 platform mixed with a smaller number of 64-bit applications; however, remember from Oracle's published certification information that, on the x86-64 architecture, 32-bit Oracle is not supported on a 64-bit version of Linux. The architecture may be used for 32-bit Linux with 32-bit Oracle or for 64-bit Linux with 64-bit Oracle. The different version cannot be mixed, though, and compatibility mode may not be used. To take advantage of 64-bit capabilities, full 64-bit mode must be used with a 64-bit Linux operating system, associated device drivers, and 64-bit Oracle, all certified specifically for the x86-64 platform.

IA64 EPIC

The alternative to x86-based or x86-64–based systems for Oracle on Linux is the Itanium processor based on the 64-bit IA64 EPIC architecture; Itanium-based systems have been commercially available since 2001. As the name suggests, the fundamental principles of EPIC are built around *parallelization*, the breaking up and simultaneous handling of instructions and data, with less focus on a sequential pipelined approach.

With EPIC, the hardware usage logic for extracting parallelism lies primarily with the compiler for precise scheduling of interdependent instructions dictating what parts of the CPU should be used for processing, enabled by an enhanced instruction set.

For Oracle, this crucial role that the compiler plays takes place when Oracle development compiles the Oracle RDBMS server software, and within this approach lies the belief that, because the compiler can view and analyze the entire code base, it is in the position to determine an efficient strategy for achieving ILP, as opposed to other architectures that determine code parallelism and assign instructions to the execution units at runtime. When operating in a multiuser, multithreaded environment, such as Oracle, EPIC has the potential for greater efficiency with the CPU spending its time executing the plan determined by the compiler in parallel, as opposed to both determining and executing the plan.

In realizing EPIC, a predetermined instruction length makes decoding considerably less complex than with x86; this, in turn, reduces the pipeline to eight stages on an Itanium 2 processor, decreasing one of the primary requirements for high clock frequencies. Also, in contrast to x86's out-of-order execution, EPIC employs in-order execution in conjunction with speculative precomputation (SP) for prefetching of data and a large number of registers to reduce the impact of memory latency.

Finally, the parallelism enabled by the EPIC architecture executes instructions in what are termed *instruction bundles*. These instruction bundles consist of three instructions, of which two are scheduled every clock cycle to allow the processor to execute a maximum of six instructions in a single clock cycle.

CPU Cache

For both x86 and EPIC architectures, if memory, Cache Fusion, or disk access speeds were the maximum at which the CPU could fetch the data and instructions it requires, it would spend much of its clock cycles stalling, waiting for them to be retrieved. Therefore, crucial components of the processor for Oracle workloads are the faster units of memory on the processor itself called the cache.

The CPU cache stores the most commonly accessed areas of main memory in terms of data, executable code, and the page table entries in the transaction look-aside buffer (TLB). For Oracle 10g on Linux, the RDBMS kernel executable size ranges from 70MB on an x86 system to over 200MB on Itanium, and you will therefore gain immediate benefit from a large cache size to store as much of this executable as possible, while also providing rapid access to data.

Cache is usually (although not always) implemented in a hierarchy with the different levels feeding each other. Typically Level 1, or L1, cache can be accessed in a single clock cycle, L2 cache can be accessed in 5–7 clock cycles, and L3 cache in 12–15 clock cycles. Therefore, even data stored in L3 cache can be accessed up to ten times faster than data stored in main memory, providing a considerable performance improvement. Also, as with registers, the more cache within the CPU, the more likely it will perform efficiently by having data available to process within its clock cycles. The data in cache is ultimately populated with the data from main memory, and when a requested byte is copied from memory with its adjacent bytes as a memory block, it is stored in the cache as a *cache line*. A *cache hit* occurs when this data is requested again, and instead of going to memory, the request is satisfied from the cache. By implementing a hierarchical system, the need to store the most-requested data close to the processor illustrates one of the reasons why maintaining an optimal Oracle indexing strategy is essential. Unnecessary full-table scans on large tables within the database are guaranteed to challenge even the most advanced caching implementations.

Of course, this view of caching provides an oversimplification for the implementation of a multiprocessor system (and uniprocessor systems using direct memory access [DMA] for I/O) as every read from a memory address must always provide the most up-to-date memory from that address, without fail. When multiple processors all share the same memory, they may all may have their own copies of a particular memory block held in cache, and if these are updated, some mechanism must be employed to guarantee consistency between main memory and the cache lines held on each and every single processor. The more processors that are added, the greater the workload required for ensuring consistency, and this process for ensuring consistency is termed *cache coherency*. Cache coherency is one of the reasons, for example, why features such as hash clusters, where Oracle stores the rows for multiple tables in the same data blocks, or Index-Organized Tables (IOTs), where the data is stored in the same blocks as the index, can bring significant performance benefits to transactional systems.

At the most basic level, CPU caches operate in one of two modes: write-through or write-back mode. In write-through mode, when the processor modifies a line in the cache, it also writes that date immediately to the main memory. For performance, the processor usually maintains a valid bit to determine whether the cache line is valid at any one time. This valid bit is the simplest method to maintain coherency. In write-back mode, the cache does not necessarily write the value back to another level of the cache hierarchy or memory immediately. This delay minimizes the performance impact but requires a more complex protocol to ensure that all values are consistent across all processors. When processors employ different levels of cache, they do not necessarily employ the same mode or protocol for each level of cache.

All of the architectures of interest implement what is termed a *snooping protocol*, where the processor monitors the system bus for signals associated with cache reads and writes. If an individual processor observes activity relating to a cache line that it has loaded and is currently in a valid state, then some form of action must take place to ensure coherency. If a particular cache line is loaded on another processor but not modified (e.g., if multiple users select the same rows from the Oracle database), the cache line will be valid, but some action must be taken to ensure that each processor is aware that it is not the only one with that particular piece of data. In addition, if a cache line is in a modified state on another processor, then that particular line will need to be either written back to main memory to be reread by the requesting processor or transferred directly between caches. In terms of RAC, the performance potential for cache-to-cache transfers is an important reason that favors fewer cluster nodes with more processors, as opposed to more nodes with fewer processors.

The most basic form of the snooping protocol to implement cache coherency is the Modified Shared Invalid (MSI) protocol. This protocol is applied to each and every line loaded in cache on all of the processors in the system, and the corresponding data located in main memory. A cache line can be in a modified state on one processor and one processor only. When it is in this state, the same data in cache on another processor and main memory must always be in an invalid state. The modified state must be maintained until the main memory is updated (or the modified state is transferred to another processor) to reflect the change and make it available to the other processors. In the shared state, one or more caches have the same cache line, all of which are in the valid state, along with the same data in memory. While a cache line is in a shared state, no other cache can have the data in a modified state. If a processor wishes to modify the cache line, then it must change the state to modified and render all of the corresponding cache lines as invalid. When a cache line is in a shared state, the processor is not required to notify the other processors when it is replaced by other data. The shared state guarantees that it has not been modified. The invalid state determines that the cache line cannot be used and does not provide any information about the state of the corresponding data in main memory.

Table 6-4 illustrates the permitted states available for an example cache line within two caches. Note that more than a passing similarity exists between the way that cache coherency is maintained at the processor level and the way that Cache Fusion operates between the Oracle RAC nodes. This comparison gives you the view that, in a RAC environment, you are, in fact, operating in an environment implementing multiple levels of coherency at both the individual system and cluster levels.

Table 6-4. *MSI Cache States*

	INVALID	SHARED	MODIFIED
INVALID	Invalid	Shared	Modified
SHARED	Shared	Shared	Not Permitted
MODIFIED	Modified	Not Permitted	Not Permitted

Although theoretically simple to implement, the MSI protocol would require all state changes to be atomic actions and, therefore, would prove impractical to implement on a real system running software such as Oracle. Instead, additional exclusive and owner states are added for the architectures of interest to realize the Modified Exclusive Shared Invalid (MESI) protocol and the Modified Owned Exclusive Shared Invalid (MOESI) protocol. The exclusive state is similar to the shared state, except that the cache line is guaranteed to be present in one cache only. This limitation enables the processor to then change the state of the cache line, for example, from an Oracle UPDATE statement to modified, if required, without having to notify the other processors across the system bus. The addition of the exclusive state is illustrated in Table 6-5.

Table 6-5. *MESI Cache States*

	INVALID	SHARED	EXCLUSIVE	MODIFIED
INVALID	Invalid	Shared	Exclusive	Modified
SHARED	Shared	Shared	Not Permitted	Not Permitted
EXCLUSIVE	Exclusive	Not Permitted	Not Permitted	Not Permitted
MODIFIED	Modified	Not Permitted	Not Permitted	Not Permitted

The owner state signifies that the processor holding a particular cache line is responsible for responding to all requests for that particular cache line, with the data in main memory or other processors being invalid. This state is similar to the modified state; however, the additional state is a necessity when an architecture implements the concept of individual CPUs being privately responsible for a particular section of main memory.

Multicore Processors

A *multicore processor* is one that contains two or more independent execution cores in the same physical processor that enable higher performance and greater power efficiency in the same profile platform than a single core processor. A dual-core processor, for example, can execute two processes completely independently and simultaneously without contending for resources, such as registers. Advantages may also be leveraged from sharing some resources between the cores, such as the CPU cache. The trend toward multicore processors is also seen in reducing the emphasis on processor performance away from increasing clock frequency and toward implementing more parallelism through a number of shorter pipelines than earlier processor architectures. Multicore processors complement RAC architectures by enabling a greater level of processing power in increasingly lower profile platforms. The availability of high performance parallel processing capabilities in dual-processor servers increases the flexibility of architecting a grid solution based on RAC with a finer granularity available for deploying the resources contained in an individual server.

Hyper-Threading (HT) is a feature distinct from multicore processing that appears on some processors. HT makes a single execution core appear to the operating system as two processors. Therefore, a single core CPU with HT will appear as two processors, a dual-core HT processor will appear as four processors, and so on. This appearance is a logical representation, and the number of physical processors remains the same. HT enables more efficient usage of a single processor core by scheduling two threads onto the processor at the same time. This usage means that, in a multi-process environment, the processor is most likely to process two simultaneous threads more rapidly than in the total time taken to complete the two threads consecutively.

Users of Red Hat Enterprise Linux 4 with multicore or HT processors should be aware that some of the earlier x86 and x86-64 releases of the operating system only enabled the configuration of eight CPUs by default, whereas, for example, a system with eight dual-core, or four dual-core, and four HT processors would present sixteen CPUs. On earlier versions of Red Hat Enterprise Linux 4, a kernel patch is required from Red Hat to resolve the issue; although on the x86 release, the boot parameter apic=bigsmp may also be used as a workaround. The issue is resolved in the update 3 release for both the x86 and x86-64 platforms, and the correct number of physical and logical CPUs presented to the operating system can be viewed in /proc/cpuinfo. The following extract shows some of the information for the first CPU, processor 0, on a system:

```
[root@london1 root]# cat /proc/cpuinfo
processor : 0
vendor_id : GenuineIntel
cpu family : 15
model : 4
model name : Intel(R) Xeon(TM) CPU 3.60GHz
stepping : 3
cpu MHz : 3591.749
cache size : 2048 KB
```

Each processor on the system has a separate entry, and totaling the entries or reviewing the highest processor number will show the number of physical and logical CPUs presented. This value will be adopted for the Oracle CPU_COUNT parameter, on which the potential for performing parallel operations will be based, and this parameter should not be modified under any circumstances.

The performance gains from multicore processing, in particular, places a great deal of emphasis on the optimal utilization of Oracle parallel operations, and the multicore RAC environment should be seen as providing the potential for multiple degrees of parallel operations at both the instance and cluster level and is especially relevant in data warehousing environments.

Parallelism can be realized for resource-intensive operations, such as Parallel Queries; full-table scan SELECT statements; INSERT, UPDATE and DELETE statements; Parallel DML, such as CREATE TABLE or CREATE INDEX; and Parallel Data Pump operations. Some of these operations, such as Parallel DML, can only be performed on partitioned objects and serve to highlight the extent that an awareness of the attributes of the hardware platform translates into the requirements for schema design for realizing the best levels of Oracle performance.

With Oracle 10g, the potential for parallelism is set automatically, and no requirement exists for setting specific Oracle parameters to enable parallelism, such as PARALLEL_AUTOMATIC_TUNING, which is a deprecated parameter at the Oracle 10g release. You may, however, wish to set some parameters to tune parallel operations in the RAC environment. First, PARALLEL_THREADS_PER_CPU is used as a factor in determining the number of threads to create for parallel operations, most important, without any requirement to modify the CPU_COUNT parameter. Both of these parameters are used as input values for setting the default value of PARALLEL_MAX_SERVERS to define the maximum number of parallel execution servers that can be created, and conversely, PARALLEL_MIN_SERVERS, which is by default 0, sets the minimum number. These parameters may also be set manually to specific user-defined limits. In a RAC environment, the INSTANCE_GROUPS parameter may also be defined in order to assign instances to individual groups. The PARALLEL_INSTANCE_GROUP parameter may then be specified with an ALTER SESSION command to allocate the instances within the cluster that a Parallel Query operation may run against in an individual session.

The number of parallel execution servers created for an individual operation is the degree of parallelism (DOP) and can be set in order of precedence with a PARALLEL hint for a particular statement, with the ALTER SESSION FORCE PARALLEL command for an individual session or a PARALLEL value specified within a table or index definition. Depending on the DOP defined, the parallel execution servers are then initiated equally across all of the instances within the cluster.

Statistics related to parallel operations can be monitored in the V$PQ_SYSSTAT and V$PQ_SESSTAT tables for system and session levels, respectively.

If no DOP is specified, all operations will be executed in a single-threaded mode by default, and on a multicore processor, they will utilize the resources of a single core only to execute the thread. In an OLTP RAC environment with a high number of concurrent users, this type of utilization may be the desired outcome with multiple users fully utilizing all server resources; however, in data warehouses, where single users are issuing large, full-table scans, parallel operations in multicore RAC environments are essential.

Processor Summary

Ultimately, processor architecture plays a major role in determining the potential scalability of an Oracle solution, and applying this equally to RAC, as well as large single-instance SMP configurations, is important, especially where transactional workloads are undertaken. We recommend considering x86-based Linux RAC clusters of up to 32 processor deployments and IA64 EPIC environments of up to 512 processor configurations.

No matter which processor architecture you select, you can determine processor activity within the context of an individual Oracle10g instance from the V$OSSTAT performance view. Within this view, contrasting the columns AVG_BUSY_TICKS and AVG_IDLE_TICKS can determine the relative intensity at which the system is working, and examining the columns AVG_IN_BYTES and AVG_OUT_BYTES shows the levels of performance that the processors are delivering to Oracle. The columns with the AVG prefix reflect the values averaged across all of the processors installed in the server; therefore, V$OSSTAT can be used in conjunction with the Linux performance monitoring tools detailed in Chapter 24 to ascertain whether a system is performing to the levels anticipated for Oracle on every node in the cluster.

Memory

As we have progressed through the server architecture, you should clearly see that, in an Oracle RAC context, one of the most important components on each node is the RAM. Memory is where your SGA resides and is the place where Cache Fusion of data blocks between the instances in the cluster takes place. Understanding how this memory is realized in hardware is essential to understanding the potentials of cluster performance.

Virtual Memory

When a process is initially created, the Linux kernel creates a set of page tables as virtual addresses that do not necessarily bear any relation to the physical memory addresses. Linux maintains the directory of page table entries for the process directly in physical memory to map the virtual memory addresses to the physical ones. This translation between virtual and physical memory addresses means that, for example, on a 32-bit system, each Linux process has its own 4GB address space, rather than the entire operating system being limited to 4GB.

This directory of page table entries has a number of levels, which means that when a virtual memory access is made, translating the virtual address can result in a number of physical memory accesses to eventually reach the actual page of memory required. To reduce this impact on performance within the Memory Management Unit (MMU) located on the CPU, a table exists with its own private memory—the TLB. Every request for data goes to the MMU, where the TLB maps the virtual memory addresses to the physical memory addresses based on the tables set up in the TLB. These tables are populated by the kernel according to the most recent memory locations accessed. If the page table entries are not located in the TLB, then the information must still be fetched from the page tables in main memory. Therefore, ensuring that as many memory references as possible can be satisfied from the TLB is advantageous.

As the TLB capacity is usually small and the standard page size on an x86 Linux system is 4KB, given the large amount of memory required by Oracle, most accesses will not be satisfied from the TLB, resulting in lower-than-optimal performance. As Oracle uses a large amount of contiguous memory, the references to this memory could more efficiently managed by mapping a smaller number of larger pages. For this reason, on Linux systems implementing the 2.6 kernel, Oracle 10*g* can take advantage of a huge TLB pool, and the configuration of these huge pages, which we strongly recommend, is described in Chapter 11. When correctly implemented, huge pages increase the likelihood that an Oracle memory access will be satisfied from the TLB, as opposed to traversing a number of physical memory locations to discover the desired memory address. It also saves CPU cycles that would otherwise be spent managing a large number of small pages and saves on physical memory to provide the address mappings in the first place.

Understanding the TLB and memory addressability can assist you in understanding why sizing the SGA too large for requirements can be detrimental, especially in a RAC environment. Sizing the SGA too large means that you could have a large number of address mappings that you do not need, increasing the likelihood that accessing the memory location that you do require will take longer by requiring that you traverse the ones you do not. For RAC, an oversized SGA has an additional impact of requiring an increased number of blocks to be mastered unnecessarily across the entire cluster. The SGA on each node in the cluster should be sized optimally, ensuring that it is not too small, but also not too large.

Physical Memory

Many different physical types of memory that can vary significantly in terms of performance and capacity may be installed in computer systems. Most non-enterprise-based computer systems use single data rate RAM (SDRAM); however, enterprise class–based systems normally use double data rate RAM (DDR), which has been generally available since 2002. This technology has advanced to DDR-2, available since 2004, with DDR-3 scheduled as the next revision.

Memory speed is measured in terms of memory clock performance. Memory clock performance, in fact, governs the speed of the memory I/O buffers and the rate at which data is prefetched, so the clock performance does not necessarily correspond directly with the speed of the memory itself, called the *core frequency*. DDR is technologically extremely similar to SDRAM; however, unlike SDRAM, DDR reads data on both the rising and falling edges of the memory clock signal, so it can transfer data at twice the rate.

When reviewing a hardware specification for memory, the definition will resemble the following:

```
RAM Type -- PC2100 ECC registered DDR266A SDRAM
```

This definition enables you to determine the bandwidth of the memory specified. As most memory buses are 64 bits wide (which equals to 8 bytes), you can multiply the bus speed by 8 bytes (or 64 bits) to determine the bandwidth. Therefore, if you have a bus speed of 266MHz (which is, in fact, 2 of 133MHz), you can calculate that the following example is named PC2100:

$$2 \times 133\text{MHz} \times 8 \text{ bytes } (64 \text{ bits}) = 2100\text{MB/s (or 2.1GB/s)}$$

Similarly, the following memory type is named PC2700:

$$2 \times 166\text{MHz} \times 8 \text{ bytes } (64 \text{ bits}) = 2700\text{MB/s (or 2.7GB/s)}$$

Increased performance with DDR2 means that the clock frequency is increased, and data is transferred at four times the core frequency of the memory itself. The calculations are the same as those just presented, but the multiplier is a factor of four when using the core frequency or two when using the clock frequency. Table 6-6 summarizes the bandwidths available from some common memory types.

Table 6-6. *Common Memory Bandwidths*

Bandwidth	Core Frequency	Clock Frequency	Name	Memory Type
1.6GB/s	100MHz	100MHz	PC1600	DDR200
2.1GB/s	133MHz	133MHz	PC2100	DDR266
2.7GB/s	166MHz	166MHz	PC2700	DDR333
3.2GB/s	200MHz	200MHz	PC3200	DDR400
3.2GB/s	100MHz	200MHz	PC2-3200	DDR2-400
4.3GB/s	133MHz	266MHz	PC2-4300	DDR2-533
5.3GB/s	166MHz	333MHz	PC2-5300	DDR2-667
6.4GB/s	200MHz	400MHz	PC2-6400	DDR2-800

From the table, you can see that at the clock frequency of 200MHz, the throughput of 3.2GB/s is the same for both DDR and DDR2, but the core frequency is lower for DDR2, offering more scope to increase frequencies and bandwidth for DDR2. The lower core frequency also means that the power consumption is lower, with a voltage for DDR2 at 1.8V compared to 2.5V for DDR. The trade-off, however, is that with a lower memory core frequency, latency times may be longer for the time taken to set up any individual data transfer.

Many DBAs would conclude for their RAC system that they simply want the highest level of throughput possible. However, within the selection criteria, you can have an additional trade-off between throughput and capacity. Because of the architecture of the memory itself, defined as a stub-bus or multi-drop-bus architecture, the signal degrades as speed and density are increased. This degradation often results in the choice of a lower amount of the higher throughput memory per system or a greater amount of lower throughput memory.

The RAC DBA should consider that, generally speaking, a system will support only one type of memory, and the server architecture could additionally limit the type, bandwidth, and capacity of memory available. These limitations should be considered against the throughput and latency of the cluster, the private interconnect, and the level of interconnect traffic expected. The RAC DBA can then use the memory configurations available as a factor in deciding whether a large number of small nodes with less, but faster, memory are more beneficial than fewer large nodes with more, but slower, memory.

No matter which memory type is selected, the theoretical limits of 64-bit computing are not troubled by the current physical memory implementations. Technological advancements, such as Fully-Buffered Dual Inline Memory Modules (FB-DIMMs), offer a significant step forward in replacing the stub-bus architecture with a point-to-point serial architecture incorporating an Advanced Memory Buffer (AMB). The AMB enables the repeating of the memory signal between DIMMs, reducing the degradation while increasing both memory capacity and bandwidth.

In addition to selecting the correct memory type and bandwidth, you also need to transfer the data to the CPU itself, and this transfer will depend upon the qualities of the system bus that connects the memory via the Memory Controller to the CPU itself, termed the *Front Side Bus* (*FSB*), and is similar to memory implementations, the FSB runs at different frequencies. (Throughout the different implementations of FSB technologies, from system shared to dual independent to direct interconnect, the fundamentals remain the same.)

Data transfers are also made by the FSB in clock cycle multiples, and therefore, common terminologies regarding the FSB are dual-pumped and quad-pumped. *Dual-pumped* signifies that one transfer is on the rising edge and one transfer on the falling edge of a clock cycle, while *quad-pumped* means four bus transfers with two on each edge. In addition, the FSB can have different widths, and therefore, comparisons cannot be made on frequency alone. As in the following example, a 128-bit double-pumped 200MHz bus would deliver this:

$$400\text{MHz} \,(200\text{MHz} \times 2) \times 16\,\text{bytes} \,(128\,\text{bits}) = 6400\text{MB/s} \,(\text{or}\,6.4\text{GB/s})$$

A 64-bit-wide quad-pumped 200MHz bus also arrives at the same result, as follows:

$$800\text{MHz} \,(200\text{MHz} \times 2 \times 2) \times 8\,\text{bytes} \,(64\,\text{bits}) = 6400\text{MB/s} \,(\text{or}\,6.4\text{GB/s})$$

These figures should always be cross-referenced against the memory specification and the number of channels of memory available. The number of channels will depend on the Memory Controller, as opposed to the memory itself, and in a two- to four-CPU–based server configuration, could be dual- or quad-channel. Therefore, in the preceding example, two channels of PC2-3200 DDR2 would ensure that the memory itself could match the transfer rates of the FSB, and slower memory would not match the potential bandwidth afforded by the FSB.

Do not confuse the role of the Memory Controller with the MMU discussed earlier in the context of virtual memory. In the architectures we are discussing, the Memory Controller may be located on the FSB, between the CPU and main memory, or on the CPU itself. The Memory Controller provides a similar translation function to the MMU, but one of its roles is to map the physical addresses to the real memory addresses of the associated memory modules. In addition to the translation role, it provides the counting of read and write references to the real memory pages, averages the access gap for each memory bank, and manages the power states of each individual memory module. Depending on its level of sophistication, the Memory Controller will also provide a degree of error checking and memory RAID.

Memory RAID

In the era of 64-bit Linux computing and gigabytes of data held in buffer cache, the DBA should be fully aware of the technologies and limitations of memory available in enterprise-based servers, especially in a RAC environment using multiple SGAs and holding much of the database in memory at the same time. If there is a memory failure on one of the nodes, depending on the frequency of checkpointing, you risk a considerable reduction in service while one of the remaining nodes recovers from the redo logs of the failed instance. As SGAs increase in size, the potential for the time to recover increases. On Oracle 10g, the checkpointing process is self-tuning and does not require the setting of any specific parameters; however, if parameters such as FAST_START_MTTR_TARGET are not set, you have less direct control over the possible recovery time.

To mitigate the possibility of a memory error halting the cluster for a significant period of time, all systems will include a degree of memory error detection and correction. Initially, parity-based checking afforded the detection and correction of single-bit memory errors; however, the common standard for memory is now Error Correction Code (ECC) to detect and correct multiple-bit errors and even offline failing memory modules. However, with the demand for 64-bit computing and large SGA sizes, simply detecting and correcting single- or multiple-bit errors is not sufficient to prevent downtime when failures of entire DIMMs occur. For this reason, considering RAID, mirrored and spare memory in their systems is of great importance to the Oracle RAC DBA. RAID terminology will be further discussed with the storage concepts in Chapter 7, and you will apply exactly the same principles to ensure that the database remains available in the event of memory errors enabling failed memory modules to be replaced online.

Additional Platform Features

In addition to the server attributes we have already discussed are a number of platform features, the sophistication of which is becoming increasingly important to maintaining the highest levels of cluster availability.

The following sections describe a number of the features that may be available, depending on the platform chosen and their applicability to deploying a successful RAC environment.

Power Management

As processors and other server components reach greater clock frequencies, power management can present two challenges: using increased amounts of power and generating increased levels of heat. First, power always comes at a cost, and the levels of power that can be supported in any particular data center environment will always have a finite limit. Second, all of the heat generated requires dissipating to keep all of the computing components within recommended operating temperatures.

Therefore, reviewing the server technologies considered for any advanced power management features available is beneficial. For example, recall that DDR2-based memory offers a lower level of power consumption than DDR-based memory.

In terms of power management of the CPU itself, you can employ technology termed *demand-based switching* (*DBS*), which steps processor voltage and frequency up and down in increments in response to the demands for processing power. If this feature is available on a platform, it can be determined within the CPU information of the basic input/output system (BIOS) with an entry such as Demand-Based Power Management. If set to ENABLED, once the Linux operating system has booted, the output of the dmesg command should display information regarding the CPU frequency such as cpufreq: CPU0 - ACPI performance management activated, followed by the frequency steps available for the processors in question. Once enabled, the frequency can be monitored and set by the cpuspeed daemon and controlled by the corresponding cpuspeed command according to temperature and external power supplies of CPU idle thresholds. The processor frequency can also be controlled manually by sending signals to the cpuspeed daemon with the kill command. The current active frequency setting for a particular processor can be viewed from the CPU MHz entry of /proc/cpuinfo.

Note that issues were reported in using cpuspeed on some earlier versions of Red Hat Enterprise Linux 4 and SUSE Linux Enterprise Server 9 for both x86 and x86-64 releases. If necessary, this feature can be disabled by using the `chkconfig` command, which we describe in Chapter 11, to disable the `cpuspeed` daemon on Red Hat Linux. On SUSE Linux, you need to edit the file `/etc/sysconfig/powersave/common` and set the entry `POWERSAVE_CPUFREQD_MODULE` to off. These issues are reported to have been resolved in update 2 of Red Hat Enterprise Linux 4 and service pack 2 of SUSE Linux Enterprise Server 9.

Onboard RAID Storage

Chapter 7 contains a detailed discussion of RAID storage; note that the value of a server equipped with an onboard RAID storage system is resiliency. By far, the most common fault occurring within a server will be failure of the hard disk. In a RAC environment, the failure of an unprotected drive containing the operating system or Oracle binaries will cause the ejection of the node from the cluster and a lengthy reconfiguration once the drive is replaced. Wherever possible, all internal disk drives should be protected by an onboard RAID storage system. (Booting from a protected SAN or hosting the Oracle Home directories on a SAN or NAS are also viable options.) If an onboard RAID storage system is not available, then software mirroring within the Linux operating system of disk drives should be adopted.

Machine Check Architectures

A *Machine Check Architecture* (MCA) is an internal architecture subsystem that exists to some extent on all x86- and x86-64–based systems, with Enhanced MCA on Itanium-based systems. MCA exists to provide detection and resolution of hardware-based errors. However, not all hardware errors—for example, the failing of a disk—will be reported through the MCA system.

All MCA events fall within the following two categories:

- **CPU errors**: Errors detected within the components of the CPU such as the following:
  - External bus logic
  - Cache
  - Data TLB
  - Instruction fetch unit
- **Platform errors**: Errors delivered to the CPU regarding non-CPU errors, and events such as memory errors.

Depending on the severity of the error detected, the following three resolutions are possible, depending on the level of MCA available:

- **Continue**: Resolves an error detected and corrected by the CPU or the server firmware that is transparent to the operating system. Examples of these errors are single- or multiple-bit memory error corrections or cache parity errors. Corrected machine check (CMC) is used to describe an error corrected by the CPU. A corrected platform error (CPE) is an error detected and corrected by the platform hardware.

- **Recover**: A process has read corrupted data, termed *poisoned data*, when this resolution is used. Poisoned data is detected by the firmware and forwarded to the operating system, which, through MCA support, terminates the process. However, the operating system remains available.

- **Contain**: The resolution used when serious errors, such as system bus address parity errors, are detected, and the server is taken offline to contain them. These *noncorrected*, or *fatal*, errors can also be termed MCA, in this case meaning *Machine Check Abort*.

Overstating the importance of MCA features within a RAC environment would be difficult. Within RAC, detecting errors as soon as possible is important, as is either correcting them or isolating the node. The worst possible outcome is for a failing node to corrupt the data stored on disk within the database, which is the only copy of the data in the entire cluster.

The RAC DBA must be fully aware of what level of MCA is available within a platform and supported by the Linux operating system. Gaining familiarity with error checking systems at the time that errors are suspected is never advisable.

Remote Server Management

In any enterprise-level RAC environment, remote server management is an essential feature to meet with the level of responsiveness required to manage clustered systems. A method must be available to access the system remotely in terms, diagnostics, or system management board functions and to administer the system from any location regardless of the current state.

In a standard environment without remote server management, if the operating system has not started successfully, accessing the system will not be possible. In a RAC environment, being fully in control of all systems that have write access to the disks on the external storage where the database is located is especially important. Unless the DBA is always in a physical location near the RAC cluster, then remote management is a necessity.

Virtualization

Virtualization is a method that enables installing and running multiple operating systems and their applications on a single hardware platform. This form of abstraction enables the consolidation of diverse environments while allocating the hardware resources as desired between the virtual machines hosting the guest operating systems.

Virtualization can be realized with software solutions from VMware, Microsoft, or the open source alternative Xen, with all alternatives supporting the installation of Linux operating systems. Some server platforms also offer enhancements to software-based virtualization by providing features such as hardware-based memory protection, hardware-based transition between virtual machines and operating systems, and differing levels of privilege over hardware resources.

A commonly associated use of virtualization for RAC is the ability to install multiple nodes of the same cluster into virtual machines on the same hardware platform, thereby realizing a cluster configuration on a single server. Virtualized images can also enable the rapid provisioning of RAC environments. Virtualization is of increasing importance to RAC and worth the time invested keeping up to date in developments of the technology.

At the time of this writing, Oracle does provide support for single-instance environments running under VMware, and unfortunately, Oracle does not support RAC running under VMware or provide Unbreakable Linux support to an Oracle system in a virtualized environment. Therefore, we recommend monitoring the status of support for virtualization in order to leverage its advantages in the event of it becoming a fully supported configuration.

Network and Private Interconnect

The private interconnect is an essential component of a RAC installation enabling high-speed communication between the nodes in the cluster for Cache Fusion traffic. Within this section we will review the hardware availability for implementing the interconnect from the I/O implementation on the server to the available protocols and their related implementations supported on the Linux operating system.

Network I/O

Previously in this chapter, we walked through the components of server architecture relevant to Oracle from the processor to the system memory. Beyond local memory, you can access your data blocks through Cache Fusion, and before taking into account the available interconnect technologies external to the server, we will consider the fundamentals of the system bus on the server itself, through which all network communication takes place. These input/output (I/O) attributes of the server are also relevant in connecting to the SAN or NAS subsystem, which we discuss further in Chapter 7.

PCI

For nearly all of the architectures available to run Linux, server I/O will be based on the Peripheral Component Interconnect (PCI). PCI provides a bus-based interconnection with expansion slots to attach additional devices such as Network Interface Cards (NIC) or Fibre Channel host bus adapters (HBAs). For Oracle RAC in an enterprise environment, common requirements include the following: one external network interface, one backup network interface, two teamed network interconnect interfaces, and two teamed storage-based interfaces, either network- or Fibre Channel–based. Of the six connections required, some may be satisfied by dual or quad cards, and in some environments, such as a blade-based system, the connections are shared between servers. The expansion slots within a particular server may also have different specifications. Therefore, DBAs need to know whether the connections and bandwidth available from a particular environment will meet their requirements. Also note whether the PCI slots available are *hot pluggable*, meaning that a failed card may be replaced without requiring server downtime.

The original implementation of PCI offered a 32-bit bus running at frequency of 33MHz. The following calculation shows that this presents 133MB/s of bandwidth:

$$33 \times 4 \text{ bytes (32 bits)} = 133\text{MB/s}$$

PCI-X

The bandwidth shown for PCI is shared between all of the devices on the system bus, and in a RAC environment, the PCI bus would be saturated by a single Gigabit Ethernet connection. For this reason, the original 32-bit, 33MHz PCI bus has been extended to 64 bits at 266MHz. However, the 64-bit bus has also been extended to 100MHz and 133MHz and is referred to as *PCI-X*. The configurations of PCI are summarized in Table 6-7.

Table 6-7. *PCI Configurations*

Bus	Frequency	32-bit Bandwidth	64-bit Bandwidth
PCI	33MHz	133MB/s	266MB/s
PCI	66MHz	266MB/s	532MB/s
PCI-X	100MHz	Not applicable	800MB/s
PCI-X	133MHz	Not applicable	1GB/s

PCI-X has sufficient capability to sustain a RAC node with gigabit-based networking and 1Gb- or 2Gb-based storage links. However, like PCI, PCI-X is a shared bus implementation, and when Ethernet and Fibre Channel standards move to 10Gb-based implementations, sufficient bandwidth is likely to be unavailable for all of the connections that an Oracle RAC node requires.

PCI-Express

The consideration of 10Gb connections should be made in conjunction with selecting a platform that supports the generation of PCI called *PCI-Express*. PCI-Express should not be confused with PCI-X, and as opposed to a shared bus, it implements a high-speed point-to-point serial I/O bus.

In contrast to PCI, a PCI-Express link consists of dual channels, implemented as a transmit pair and a receive pair, to enable bidirectional transmission simultaneously. The bandwidth of a PCI-Express link can be scaled by adding additional signal pairs for multiple paths between the two devices. These pairs are defined as supports x1, x4, x8, and x16 according to the number of pairs, and the original implementations offer the bandwidth shown in Table 6-8.

Table 6-8. *PCI-Express Configurations*

PCI-Express Implementation	Encoded Data Rate	Unencoded Bandwidth
x1	5Gb/s	500MB/s
x4	20Gb/s	2GB/s
x8	40Gb/s	4GB/s
x16	80Gb/s	8GB/s

The unencoded bandwidth is approximately 80% of the encoded data rate, as PCI-Express uses a form of encoding that utilizes the remaining 20%. The encoding enables better synchronization, error detection, and error resolution.

Being based on a point-to-point architecture, PCI-Express will support the 10Gb links to the interconnect and storage without sharing bandwidth. PCI-Express adapters also natively support features that are usually managed at the system-board level with PCI and PCI-X, such as hot plug, hot swap, and advanced power management.

When reviewing a server's I/O capacity, bear in mind that in a transactional environment the multiple instances in a RAC cluster will mean multiple threads of redo; therefore, the I/O capabilities of the sum of the nodes may also offer the potential for increased throughput.

Private Interconnect Selection

Building on the I/O capabilities of the server platform, you can implement the cluster interconnect with a number of different technologies, of which we will take into account Ethernet and remote direct memory access (RDMA).

Ethernet

The most popular choice for an Oracle RAC cluster interconnect is a Gigabit Ethernet switched network. Gigabit Ethernet run in full duplex mode with a nonblocking, data center class switch should be the minimum interconnect standard applied.

■**Note** A simple network crossover cable may at first appear to be a low-cost alternative to connect a two-node cluster to create a directly linked network between two cluster nodes. However, this alternative is not supported as an interconnect with RAC on Linux. Without the electrical isolation provided by a switch, NIC hardware errors on one of the servers could also cause hardware errors on the other server, rendering the entire cluster unavailable. This configuration also eliminates the option of a redundant networking configuration and prevents the addition of more than two nodes to the cluster.

Gigabit Ethernet supports transfer rates of 1,000Mb/s and latencies of approximately 60 to 100 microseconds for shorter packet sizes. A clear difference exists between this latency and the two to four milliseconds we previously specified for the average receive time for a consistent read or current block for Cache Fusion. In addition to the Oracle workload, processing the network stack at the Linux operating system level is a major contributory factor to the latency of Cache Fusion communication.

For standard TCP/IP networking, reading from or writing to a network socket causes a context switch, where the data is copied from user to kernel buffers and processed by the kernel through the TCP/IP stack and Ethernet driver appropriate to the NIC installed. Each stage in this workload requires a degree of CPU processing, and tuning kernel network parameters, such as described in Chapter 11, can play a role in increasing network throughput. Even with optimal tuning in place, the level of CPU utilization can remain considerable. An approximate guideline is that each bit per second of TCP/IP bandwidth equates to 1Hz of the CPU capacity of an x86 processor, and therefore, a Gigabit Ethernet interconnect will consume 1GHz of processing power on the system.

To minimize the overhead of network processing, the default protocol for Oracle 10g RAC on Linux is User Datagram Protocol (UDP) as opposed to Transmission Control Protocol (TCP). UDP as a non-connection-oriented protocol has no guarantee of data ordering and places the responsibility of verification of data transmitted with the application, in this case Oracle, thereby reducing the kernel networking requirements.

Even with the UDP protocol, network CPU utilization will have some level of impact in a Gigabit Ethernet environment and the implications are clear for sustaining the 10Gb transfer rates supported at the server platform level with PCI-Express. Therefore, technologies for reducing the workload of network processing on the CPU are likely to gain in popularity in RAC environments.

One option for increased network throughput is the use of TCP/IP Offload Engines (TOEs) requiring a dedicated NIC and software to offload networking for processing directly in hardware. However, when this approach is adopted, consider that some implementations may have a bearing on the level of Unbreakable Linux support available for the platform in bypassing a major component of the kernel.

Some systems offer an alternative with the inclusion of I/O acceleration technologies directly at the server platform level. This method offloads some of the I/O-based tasks from the CPU, while maintaining the standard Linux networking implementation, where the technology is enabled directly in releases of Oracle supported Unbreakable Linux platforms.

RDMA

RDMA is a high-speed interconnect commonly associated with high-performance computing (HPC) environments. RDMA enables parallel, direct, memory-to-memory transfers between the nodes in the cluster and requires dedicated RDMA adapters, switches, and software, while avoiding the CPU processing and context switching overheads associated with Ethernet-based implementations.

One of the most popular RDMA solutions is InfiniBand, which has no requirement for TCP/IP networking; instead, the direct access programming library (DAPL) is used in conjunction with the Sockets Direct Protocol (SDP) for communication between the nodes in the cluster.

RDMA solutions have the performance advantage of offering bandwidths of 10Gb in conjunction with latencies of approximately ten microseconds; however, some disadvantages, when compared to Ethernet, include the relatively higher cost and nonstandard Linux implementations.

Private Interconnect Selection Summary

We recommend, in the absence of compelling statistical evidence for a higher performance interconnect, selecting the default UDP protocol running over Ethernet at a minimum of a gigabit rating for a default installation of an Oracle RAC cluster. Gigabit Ethernet offers a simpler, more cost-effective method, and where cost is a decisive factor, implementing RDMA should be compared against the alternative of Gigabit Ethernet, coupled with high-performance server processors and the memory to provide an adequate buffer cache on all server nodes, rather than focusing on the interconnect entirely in isolation. Gigabit Ethernet also offers greater potential for building redundancy into the interconnect configuration as detailed in the sections that follow.

The exception, where an RDMA interconnect may prove a valuable investment, is when implementing large data warehousing environments to realize high levels of interinstance parallel processing capabilities.

Fully Redundant Ethernet Interconnects

In a standard environment with a two-node cluster and no resiliency, each node connects to a single interconnect with a single NIC in addition to the public network and any additional networks, such as the backup network. Figure 6-1 shows the interconnect network for simplicity.

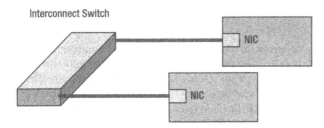

Figure 6-1. *Nonredundant interconnect*

If a single interconnect NIC fails, the Oracle Clusterware will attempt reconnection for a user-defined period of time (by default 60 seconds) before taking action to remove the node from the cluster. When this happens, the master node directs the Oracle database Global Cache Service to initiate recovery of the failed instance. However, if the interconnect network fails because, for example, the network switch itself fails, a scenario will result equivalent to the failure of every single node in the cluster except for the designated master node. The master node will then proceed to recover all of the failed instances in the cluster before providing a service from a single node. This will occur irrespective of the number of nodes in the cluster.

Clearly, since the master node must first recover all instances, it will result in a significant reduction in the level of service available, and therefore, we recommend the implementation of a fully redundant interconnect network configuration. A common consideration is to implement the Oracle CLUSTER_INTERCONNECTS parameter. This parameter requires the specification of one or more IP addresses, separated by a colon, to define the network interfaces that will be used for the interconnect. This network infrastructure is configured as shown in Figure 6-2.

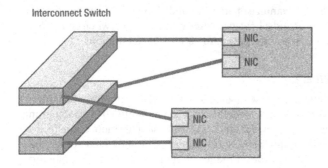

Figure 6-2. *Clustered interconnects*

This use of the CLUSTER_INTERCONNECTS parameter, however, is available to distribute the network traffic across one or more interfaces to increase the bandwidth available for interconnect traffic. The parameter explicitly does not implement failover functionality; therefore, the failure of an interconnect switch will continue to result in the failure of the interconnect network and a reduced level of service.

Before any setting of CLUSTER_INTERCONNECTS is required, once Oracle has been installed, verifying which network Oracle is using for its interconnect traffic is straightforward. In Oracle 10g, the network address is held within the Oracle Cluster Repository (OCR) and can be determined with the oifcfg command, for example:

```
[root@london1 root]# oifcfg getif
eth0  147.43.1.0  global  public
eth1  192.168.0.0  global  cluster_interconnect
```

The interconnect address can also be deleted with the oifcfg delif command and added with oifcfg setif. Note, however, that if the CLUSTER_INTERCONNECTS parameter is used, it will override the default setting in the OCR. The precise value used by the Oracle instance can be determined by querying the table X$KSXPIA. This table displays the interface and its corresponding address under the columns NAME_KSXPIA and IP_KSXPIA, respectively. If the PICK column contains OSD, this illustrates that the setting was configured from the OCR. If, however, it contains the entry CI, the NAME_KSXPIA column will be empty, and the setting is determined by the CLUSTER_INTERCONNECTS parameter.

When using Gigabit Ethernet, you can also verify that Oracle is correctly using the UDP protocol by connecting to Oracle with a SYSDBA connection and issuing the following commands:

```
SQL>oradebug setmypid
SQL>oradebug ipc
```

This generates a trace file in the USER_DUMP_DEST directory. The trace file contains a section identified as "info for network 0" with the IP address and protocol that Oracle is using for the interconnect traffic. You can see in the following example that the IP address used for the private interconnect is 192.168.0.1, and the protocol is confirmed as UDP:

```
info for network 0
socket no 9      IP 192.168.0.1 UDP 43307
sflags SSKGXPT_WRITESSKGXPT_UP
info for network 1
socket no 0      IP 0.0.0.0 UDP 0
sflags SSKGXPT_DOWN
```

If for any reason the protocol is incorrect, it can be modified with the command `make -f ins_rdbms.mk ipc_udp ioracle` run in the `/rdbms/lib` directory of the Oracle software.

When using Gigabit Ethernet with UDP, modifying the Maximum Transmission Unit (MTU) size of the interconnect interface to use a feature called Jumbo Frames is often recommended. This can be done on a temporary basis with `ifconfig` command, for example:

```
[root@london1 root]# ifconfig eth1 mtu 9000 up
```

The setting can also be made permanent by setting `MTU=9000` in the file corresponding to the interface in question, such as `etc/sysconfig/network-scripts/ifcfg-eth1`. We do, however, urge caution, and this feature should always be tested for the benefits to interconnect performance with the NIC in question before being modified from the default value. In some instances, the maximum MTU should be set to a slightly lower value than the default 9000, such as 8998 or 8960.

To implement a fully redundant interconnect configuration requires the implementation of software termed *NIC teaming software* at the operating system level. This software operates at the network driver level to provide two physical network interfaces to operate underneath a single IP address. In the simplest usage, the software provides failover functionality, where one card is used to route traffic for the interface and the other remains idle until the primary card fails. When a failure occurs, the interconnect traffic is routed through this secondary card. This occurs transparently to Oracle without interruption, the IP address remains the same, and the software driver also remaps the hardware or MAC address of the card so that failover is instantaneous. The failover is usually only detectable within Oracle by a minimal IPC time-out wait event. It is also possible in some configurations to provide increased bandwidth. This would deliver a similar solution to the `CLUSTER_INTERCONNECTS` parameter, with the additional protection of redundancy.

When implementing a teaming solution, understanding the implications of NIC failure, as opposed to failure of the switch itself, is important. Consider the physical implementation shown in Figure 6-2 of two nodes connected separately to two switches. In this scenario, if a primary NIC fails on either of the nodes, that node will switch over to use its secondary NIC. However, this secondary NIC is now operating on a completely independent network from the primary card that still remains operational on the fully functional node. Communication will be lost, and the Oracle Clusterware will initiate cluster reconfiguration to eject the nonmaster node from the cluster.

For this type of redundancy to operate successfully, it requires *switch spanning*, where one or more links are provided between the switches themselves, as shown in Figure 6-3. To use switch spanning, the network infrastructure must support the Spanning Tree Protocol (STP). Switches must also support `802.3ad` `DYNAMIC` mode to enable failover between teams. When this is implemented with the previous scenario and a NIC fails, the network traffic is routed through the secondary interface. This secondary interface continues to communicate with the primary interface on the remaining node across the interswitch link. In a failover mode when no failures have occurred, only the primary switch is providing a service. After a failure, both switches are active and routing traffic between them.

Interconnect Switch

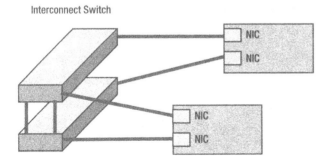

Figure 6-3. *Fully redundant clustered interconnects*

Crucially, this failover scenario also guards against the failure of a switch itself. While operational, if the secondary switch fails, the network traffic remains with the primary interconnect, and no failover operations are required. However, if the primary switch fails, exactly the same action is taken by the driver software as if all of the primary NICs on all of the nodes in the cluster failed at exactly the same time. All of the NICs simultaneously switch from their primary to their secondary interface, so communication continues with all of the network traffic now operating across the secondary switch for all nodes. This implements a solution with no single point of failure in that either a single NIC, network cable, switch, or interswitch link can fail without impacting the availability of the cluster. If these components are hot-swappable, they can be replaced and the fully redundant configuration can be restored without impacting the availability of the clustered database.

This form of teaming requires interaction with the network driver of the NICs used for teaming and, therefore, is best implemented with channel bonding as described in Chapter 11.

Summary

Within this chapter, we have looked at the RAC Technologies Compatibility Matrix (RTCM) and investigated the hardware components available to you for building for RAC clusters on Linux. This chapter should give you as an Oracle DBA the knowledge to intelligently interpret hardware specifications and drill down into the features that are required in a successful RAC environment. It should also enable you to balance all of the components from processor and memory to the network interconnect and determine their relative advantages and limitations within a RAC environment to select the optimal configuration of hardware to achieve the desired performance, scalability, and reliability.

CHAPTER 7

■ ■ ■

Storage

In this chapter, we cover the aspects of storage input/output (I/O) relating to RAC. In the context of RAC, I/O relates to the reads and writes performed on a disk subsystem irrespective of the protocols used. The term *storage* encompasses all aspects relating to this I/O that enable communication of the server serving as the RAC node with nonvolatile disk. In Chapter 6, we discussed the implementation of I/O on the server itself in the context of networking, and this chapter presents the fundamentals of connecting the server to disk, along with example implementations of some of the most popular storage options available.

As we introduced in Chapter 1, an important basic concept is that the storage required for a professional RAC implementation will be presented from a dedicated storage array separate from any of the individual nodes in the cluster. Before considering the storage options available, we will provide a brief background in the I/O characteristics of RAC that will occur on this storage.

RAC I/O Characteristics

The I/O characteristics of an Oracle database, including a RAC-based one, can be classified into four groups: random reads, random writes, sequential reads, and sequential writes. The prominence of each is dependent on the profile of the application; however, some generalizations can be made.

In a transactional environment, a number of random writes will be associated with the database writer (DBWRn) process (we use DBWRn to represent all of the database writer processes), in addition to the sequential writes associated with the redo logs and the log writer (LGWR) process. A level of random reads would also be expected from index-based queries and undo tablespace operations. Sequential read performance from full-table scans and parallel queries is normally more prominent in data warehouse environments, with less emphasis on write activity except during batch loads.

As a foundation for a discussion of storage, we will now focus on the read and write behavior that an Oracle cluster is expected to exhibit.

Read Activity

In this chapter, we have used the terms "random reads" and "sequential reads" from a storage perspective. However, the Oracle wait event usually associated with a sequential read realized on the storage is db file scattered read, whereas the Oracle wait event usually associated with a random read on the storage is db file sequential read. Therefore, clarifying the differing terminology seems worthwhile.

Within Oracle, the reading of data blocks is issued from the shadow process for a user's session. A *scattered read* is a mutliblock read for full-table scan operations where the blocks, if physically read from the disk storage, are normally accessed contiguously. The operations required to read the blocks into the buffer cache are passed to the operating system where the number of blocks to fetch in a single call is determined by the Oracle initialization parameter DB_FILE_MULTIBLOCK_READ_COUNT. The long-standing methodology for UNIX multiple buffer operations is termed *scatter/gather*, and with Linux, for example, the SCSI generic (sg) packet device driver introduced scatter/gather I/O in the 2.2 kernel. For Oracle on Linux, a similar methodology is employed where scattered reads are issued with the pread() system call to read or write multiple buffers from a file descriptor at a given offset into the user session's program global area (PGA) and subsequently written into noncontiguous buffers in the buffer cache in the SGA. The key concept to note is that the data may be retrieved from the disk in a contiguous manner, but it is distributed into noncontiguous, or scattered, areas of the SGA.

A db file sequential read event, on the other hand, is associated with index-based reads and often retrieves a single block or a small number of blocks that are then stored contiguously within the SGA. A single block read, by definition, is stored in contiguous memory, and therefore this form of I/O is termed sequential if physically read from the disk storage, despite the fact that the file locations for these blocks are accessed randomly.

Whichever method you employ, as you saw in Chapter 6, the important aspect to note in terms of read storage activity for RAC is that accessing data blocks through Cache Fusion from other nodes in the cluster is preferable to accessing them from disk. However, the buffer cache should always be sufficiently sized on each node to minimize both Cache Fusion and physical disk reads and to ensure that as much read I/O as possible is satisfied logically from the local buffer cache.

Write Activity

In a transactional environment, the most important aspect of storage performance for RAC in an optimally configured system will most likely be the sequential writes of the redo logs. The online redo logs will never be read as part of normal database operations, with a couple of exceptions.

■**Note** The fact that Oracle redo logs are only ever written in a sequential manner may not be true where the redo logs are based on a file system where direct I/O has not been implemented. In this case, the operating system may need to read the operating system block before providing it to Oracle to write the redo information, and subsequently write the entire block back to the storage. Therefore, on a file system, a degree of read activity may be associated with disks where the redo logs are located when observed from Linux operating system utilities.

These exceptions are as follows: when one node in the cluster has failed, so the online redo logs are being read and recovered by another instance; and when the archiver (ARCn) process is reading an online redo log to generate the archive log. These activities, however, will not take place on the current active online redo log for an instance.

To understand why these sequential writes take prominence in a transactional environment, looking at the role of the LGWR process is important. The LGWR process writes the changes present in the memory resident redo log buffer to the online redo logs located on disk. LGWR does not wait until a commit is issued before flushing the contents of the log buffer to the online logs; instead, by default, it will write when the log buffer is 1/3 full, when it contains 1MB of data, or every three seconds—whichever occurs first.

Note two important aspects from this activity in terms of storage utilization. First, little benefit will be derived from sizing the log buffer to greater than a few megabytes, and therefore, in a high-performance OLTP environment, storage performance for redo logs is crucial to overall database throughput. Second, issuing a rollback instead of a commit does not interrupt the sequential write activity of the LGWR process to the online redo logs. The rollback operation is completed instead from the information stored in the undo tablespace, and because these undo segments are also stored in the database buffer cache, the rollback operation will also generate redo, resulting in further sequential writes to the online redo logs.

When an Oracle client process ends a transaction and issues a commit, the transaction will not be recoverable until all of the redo information in the log buffer associated with the transaction and the transaction's system change number (SCN) have been written to the online redo log. The client will not initiate any subsequent work until this write has been confirmed; instead, it will wait on a log file sync event until all of its redo information is written.

Given sufficient activity, LGWR may complete a log file sync write for more than one transaction at a time. When this write is complete, the transaction is complete, and any locks held on rows and tables are released.

Note that the modified blocks stored in the database buffer will not necessarily have been written to the storage at this point and, in any event, will always lag behind the redo information to some degree. The redo information is sufficient for database recovery; however, the key factor is the time taken to recover the database in the event of a failure. The more that the SCN in the online redo logs and archive logs is ahead of the SCN in the database datafiles, the longer the time that will be taken to recover.

In terms of RAC, Oracle has multiple redo log threads—one for each instance. Each instance manages its own redo generation and will not read the log buffer or online redo logs of another instance while that instance is operating normally. The redo log threads, therefore, operate in parallel, and in some circumstances, the presence of these multiple threads can increase the throughput of the overall system in comparison to a single instance configuration.

For RAC, all of the redo log threads should be placed on storage with the same profile to maintain equilibrium of performance across the cluster. The focus for redo should also be placed on the ability of the storage to support the desired number of I/O operations per second (IOPS) and the latency time for a single operation to complete, with less emphasis placed on the bandwidth available.

In addition to the sequential write performance associated with the redo log threads, other important storage aspects for transactional systems are the random reads and writes associated with the buffer cache and the writes of the DBWR*n* process. Similarly to the LGWR process, DBWR*n* also has a three-second time-out when idle, and when active, it may write dirty or modified blocks to disk. This may happen before or after the transaction that modified the block commits. This background activity will not have a direct impact on the overall database performance. However, when a redo log switch occurs or the limits set by the LOG_CHECKPOINT_TIMEOUT or LOG_CHECKPOINT_INTERVAL parameter are reached, a checkpoint occurs, and every dirty or modified block in the buffer cache will be written to the datafiles located on the storage. As an alternative, setting the parameter FAST_START_MTTR_TARGET to a time value calculates the correct checkpoint interval based on the desired recovery time. The operation is complete when the checkpoint (CKPT) process writes the most recent SCN to the datafile headers and the control files. Note that with Oracle 10*g*, the CKPT process is self-tuning, so the setting of checkpoint-related parameters is not mandatory. The DBWR*n* process will also be active in writing dirty buffers to disk, if reading more data into the buffer cache is required and no space is available.

The differing profiles of the LGWR and DBWR*n* processes on the nodes of the cluster will dictate the activity observed on the storage with a greater deal of emphasis to be made on LGWR activity in a transactional, as opposed to a data warehouse, environment. Some of the balance in activity between LGWR and DBWR*n* processes lies in the mean time to recover, but given redo logs of a sufficient size, a checkpoint on each node will most likely occur at the time of a log switch. This checkpoint will allow sufficient time for DBWR*n* to flush all of the dirty buffers to disk. If this flushing does not complete, then the Checkpoint Not Complete message will be seen in the alert.log of the corresponding instance as follows:

```
Private_strands 0 at log switch
Thread 2 advanced to log sequence 59
  Current log# 5 seq# 59 mem# 0:
+DG01/rac/onlinelog/group_5.268.3
Thread 2 cannot allocate new log, sequence 60
```

```
Checkpoint not complete
Current log# 5 seq# 59 mem# 0:
+DG01/rac/onlinelog/group_5.268.3
```

When this error occurs, throughput will stall until the DBWR*n* has completed its activity and enabled the LGWR to allocate the next log file in the sequence.

In summary, the most important distinction to make in terms of storage performance requirements is that the presence of a correctly sized buffer cache on each node in the cluster means that the data block write activity should not require the same immediacy of response as the redo log activity.

Forced Reads and Writes

An important question for RAC for both read and write activity arises in how Oracle maintains coherency between instances when a data block has been modified on only one instance, though clearly checkpoints can and do occur on different instances at different times. Chapter 22 discusses the process through which this consistency is achieved in detail, but we will provide a brief summary here in the context of storage activity.

When a second instance requires the data block already in use, that data block is shipped via the interconnect through Cache Fusion to the requesting instance while the original instance maintains a copy of the original block called a *past image*. The past image must be held until its block master signals whether it can be written to disk or discarded.

When a checkpoint occurs on one node and a data block is written to disk, the past images of that block on other nodes now contain invalid images of that block. However, the overhead of immediately notifying all of the other nodes to discard that image would result in an undue level of activity across the cluster. Thus, only when a process attempts to utilize a past image held in its own buffer cache and is notified by the block master that this particular image has been invalidated will the block be discarded and then reread from disk. This activity can be viewed in the FORCED_READS column in the data dictionary view GV$CACHE_TRANSFER. The corresponding FORCED_WRITES column entry records when a block has been written to disk, so that a process on another instance can subsequently gain exclusive access to that block. This statistic corresponds to the block ping in Oracle Parallel Server (OPS) that has been eliminated by Cache Fusion in RAC and, therefore, should always have a value of zero. The importance of these activities illustrates the level of additional disk-related activity required of a RAC environment and the utility of Cache Fusion in eliminating the overhead of forced writes.

Asynchronous I/O

Without asynchronous I/O, every I/O request that Oracle makes to the operating system is completed singly and sequentially for a particular process. Once asynchronous I/O has been enabled, multiple I/O requests can be made in parallel within a single system call without waiting for the requests to complete, potentially increasing efficiency and throughput for both DBWR*n* and LGWR processes.

In an Oracle RAC on Linux environment, I/O processing is likely to benefit from enabling asynchronous I/O. However, we recommend that you always test to compare the performance of synchronous and asynchronous I/O in any particular environment.

On Linux, to utilize asynchronous I/O for Oracle, you need to ensure that RPM packages libaio and libaio-devel have been installed, according to the process described in Chapter 10. Asynchronous I/O can be enabled directly on raw devices, and we describe the configuration of raw devices in the context of preparing raw devices for the Oracle Clusterware partitions in Chapter 11. Asynchronous I/O can also be enabled on file systems that support it, such as the OCFS, and it is enabled by default on Automatic Storage Management (ASM) instances, which we discuss in Chapters 8 and 9, respectively. At the time of this writing, asynchronous I/O is not supported on NFS file systems.

By default, asynchronous I/O is enabled in an Oracle 10*g* Release 2 database installation on Linux but not in Oracle 10*g* Release 1. To ensure that asynchronous I/O is enabled on Oracle 10*g* Release 1, you need to take action to link in the asynchronous I/O libraries on each node in the cluster while any Oracle instances are stopped. Care should be taken to ensure that the asynchronous I/O libraries are specified explicitly as follows:

```
[oracle@london1 lib]$ cd $ORACLE_HOME/rdbms/lib
[oracle@london1 lib]$ make PL_ORALIBS=-laio -f ins_rdbms.mk async_on
[oracle@london1 lib]$ make PL_ORALIBS=-laio -f ins_rdbms.mk ioracle
```

Similarly, asynchronous I/O can also be disabled on 10*g* Release 1 by specifying the async_off option. Once asynchronous I/O has been enabled, by default the initialization parameter DISK_ASYNC_IO is set to TRUE, and it will, therefore, be used on raw devices when the instance is started.

If using asynchronous I/O on a supporting file system such as OCFS, however, you also need to set the parameter FILESYSTEMIO_OPTIONS, which by default is set to NONE.

This parameter should be set to the value ASYNCH by executing the following commands on one instance in the cluster:

```
[oracle@london1 lib]$ srvctl stop database -d RAC
SQL> startup nomount;

SQL> alter system set filesystemio_options=asynch scope=spfile;

SQL> shutdown immediate;

[oracle@london1 lib]$ srvctl start database -d RAC
```

Once asynchronous I/O is enabled, to ascertain whether it is being used, review /proc/slabinfo as follows:

```
[root@london1 root]# cat /proc/slabinfo | grep kio
kioctx          0     0   256   0    0   1 : 4284 1071
kiocb           0     0   256   0    0   1 : 4284 1071
kiobuf       4305  4305   128  35   35   1 : 4284 1071
```

These values will illustrate buffers being allocated if asynchronous I/O is being used. The watch command, described in Chapter 24, is useful here for automatically refreshing the display.

The size of the asynchronous I/O operations can be modified with the kernel parameter fs.aio-max-size. By default, this size is set to 131072, which is sufficient for transactional systems. However, for data warehouse environments, setting this parameter to 1MB may be preferable.

Direct I/O

Asynchronous I/O should not be confused with direct I/O. Direct I/O is an Oracle parameter set to avoid file system buffering on compatible file systems, and depending on the file system in question, it may be used either independently or in conjunction with asynchronous I/O.

Direct I/O can be enabled in the initialization parameter file by setting the parameter FILESYSTEMIO_OPTIONS to DIRECTIO. If enabling both asynchronous I/O and direct I/O is desired, then this parameter can alternatively be set to the value of SETALL, for example:

```
SQL> alter system set filesystemio_options=directIO scope=spfile;
```

or

```
SQL> alter system set filesystemio_options=setall scope=spfile;
```

A combination of the parameters DISK_ASYNCH_IO and FILESYSTEMIO_OPTIONS, therefore, can be used to fine-tune the I/O activity for the RAC cluster. Supportability should always be referenced against the operating system version and storage. For example, in Oracle 10g, RAC asynchronous I/O is available on raw datafiles and OCFS, but not on NFS, and direct I/O is available on OCFS and NFS. If using a combination of raw devices and file systems, such as raw redo logs and file system–based datafiles, for example, you can set asynchronous I/O for use against the raw devices with DISK_ASYNC_IO set to TRUE in conjunction with FILESYSTEMIO_OPTIONS set to DIRECTIO to use only direct I/O against the file system. Similarly, setting the FILESYSTEMIO_OPTIONS parameter to ASYNCH will use only asynchronous I/O, but not direct I/O, and SETALL will enable both.

Where direct I/O is available and asynchronous I/O is not, such as with NFS, another good practice is to increase the number of database writer processes with the DB_WRITER_PROCESSES parameter for increased write throughput in a parallel manner.

Direct I/O would not normally be used on raw datafiles, as the setting would bear little relevance to a non-file-system implementation. However, as we will discuss further in Chapter 11, with the 2.6 Linux kernel, the use of character special raw devices has been deprecated in favor of using direct I/O, and using a raw device, in fact, opens the underlying device using the O_DIRECT flag to provide backward compatibility. Setting direct I/O explicitly within Oracle for raw devices is therefore not required, although it can be done if desired in order to explicitly avoid configuring raw devices for the database datafiles. We recommend avoiding setting direct I/O explicitly, however, because of the possibility of the required parameters becoming unset at some point in the future.

Although asynchronous I/O is enabled by default on ASM, the parameters should be set according to the configuration of the underlying disks. These disks will usually be raw devices, meaning that asynchronous I/O is the most applicable parameter.

Storage Fundamentals

The previous synopsis of RAC I/O characteristics activity illustrates that the most important aspects of I/O are ensuring that all committed data is absolutely guaranteed to be written to the storage and that the database is always recoverable in a timely and predictable manner in the event of a node, cluster, or even site failure. In terms of the permanent storage, it is able to recover when the data is actually written to the disks themselves.

In this section, we will consider the fundamental aspects of storage important to both resilience and performance common to all vendor and protocol implementations from the disk drives themselves to RAID, storage cache, and intelligent storage implementations.

Disk Drive Performance

Disk drives tend to offer dramatically increased capacity and a degree of improved performance as newer models are introduced; however, the basic technology has remained the same since hard disks were introduced by IBM in the 1950s.

Within each drive, a single actuator with multiple heads reads and writes the data on the rotating platters. The overall performance of the drive is determined by two factors: seek time and latency. *Seek time* is the time the heads take to move into the desired position to read or write the data. Disks in enterprise storage tend to be available in configurations of up to 10,000 or 15,000 rotations per minute (rpm), with the 15,000 rpm disks utilizing smaller diameter platters. The shorter distance traveled by the heads results in a lower seek time. *Latency* is the time taken for the platter to rotate to the correct position once the head is in position to read or write the correct sector of data. A full rotation on a 15,000 rpm drive takes approximately four milliseconds and on a 10,000 rpm drive, it takes six milliseconds; therefore, with these full rotations resulting in the longest latency possible, the average latency will be approximately half this amount for all reads and writes. Once the head and platter are in the correct position, the time taken to actually transfer the data is negligible compared to the seek and latency times.

An additional important concept to achieving the maximum performance from a drive is that of *destroking*. Destroking is storing data only on the outer sectors of the disk, leaving the inner sectors unused. The outer sectors store more, and therefore enable the reading and writing of more data without repositioning the heads, thus improving overall access time.

A single 15,000 rpm drive will transfer data at a maximum sustained throughput of 60MB/s and with an average formatted transfer rate of approximately half this amount.

This level of performance would clearly be a limiting factor for access by multiple nodes in a RAC cluster. The desire for increased disk drive performance across the cluster and to mitigate the risks of drive failure causing data loss clarifies the importance of using a RAID configuration for RAC storage.

RAID

RAID was defined in 1988 as a Redundant Array of Inexpensive Disks by David A. Patterson, Garth Gibson, and Randy H. Katz at the University California, Berkeley. Later use often sees the "Inexpensive" replaced with "Independent"; the two terms are interchangeable without affecting the concepts.

The original RAID levels defined are 1, 2, 3, 4, and 5 (and 0), with additional terminology added at later points in time, such as RAID 0+1, RAID 10, and RAID-50.

In general, the term *RAID* is applied to two or more disks working in parallel but presented as a logical single disk to the user to provide enhanced performance and/or resilience from the storage. RAID can be implemented in one of three ways:

- Just a Bunch of Disks (JBOD) is presented to volume management software running on the server that implements RAID on these devices and presents logical volumes of disks to the database. RAID processing takes place using the server CPU.

- A JBOD is presented to the server, but the RAID processing is done by a dedicated RAID host bus adapter (HBA) or incorporated onto the motherboard of the server itself, that is, RAID on motherboard (ROMB). RAID processing is, therefore, done on the server but not by the server CPU.

- The server is connected to an external RAID array with its own internal RAID controller and disks and is presented a configurable logical view of disks. RAID processing is done completely independently from the server.

In terms of RAC, the RAID implementation must be cluster-aware of multiple hosts accessing the same disks at the same time. This implementation restriction rules out the second RAID option and limits the choice in the first category to third-party solutions (from companies such as PolyServe and Symantec) that may be overlaid with cluster file systems and Oracle ASM, which we describe in Chapter 9. A more common RAID solution for RAC is the third option, that is, using an external dedicated storage array.

Whichever implementation is used, RAID is based on the same concepts and is closely related to the Oracle stripe-and-mirror-everything (SAME) methodology for laying out a database on storage for optimal performance and resilience. Therefore, in the following sections we will look at the most popular and practical implementations of RAID.

RAID 0 Striping

RAID 0 implements striping across a number of disks by allocating the data blocks across the drives in sequential order as illustrated in Table 7-1. This table shows a stripe set of eight disks. The blocks from A to X represent not Oracle blocks but logical blocks of contiguous disk sectors, for example, 128KB. We have one stripe against eight disks, which makes our total stripe size 1MB (8×128KB).

Table 7-1. *RAID 0*

DISK 1	DISK 2	DISK 3	DISK 4
BLOCK-A	BLOCK-B	BLOCK-C	BLOCK-D
BLOCK-I	BLOCK-J	BLOCK-K	BLOCK-L
BLOCK-Q	BLOCK-R	BLOCK-S	BLOCK-T
DISK 5	**DISK 6**	**DISK 7**	**DISK 8**
BLOCK-E	BLOCK-F	BLOCK-G	BLOCK-H
BLOCK-M	BLOCK-N	BLOCK-O	BLOCK-P
BLOCK-U	BLOCK-V	BLOCK-W	BLOCK-X

This implementation does not cater to redundancy, and therefore, by the strictest definition, is not RAID. The loss of a single drive within the set results in the loss of the entire RAID group, so, on one hand, this implementation offers a lower level of protection in comparison to the presentation of individual drives.

What it does offer, on the other hand, is improved performance in terms of operations per second and throughput over the use of individual drives for both read and write operations. The example in the table would in theory offer eight times the number of operations per second of an individual drive and seven times the average throughput. (The throughput is marginally lower due to the increased latency to retrieve all of the blocks in a stripe set as the heads must move in parallel on all drives to a stripe.)

For RAC, this implementation of RAID delivers the highest-performing solution; however, the lack of resilience makes it unsuitable for any production implementation. RAID 0 is heavily utilized mainly for commercial database benchmarks. The combination of RAID 0 and destroking is ideal for an environment where data loss or the cost of unused disk space is not a significant consideration.

RAID 1 Mirroring

In RAID 1 all data is duplicated from one disk or set of disks to another, resulting in a mirrored, real-time copy of the data (see Table 7-2).

Table 7-2. *RAID 1*

DISK 1		DISK 2	DISK 3		DISK 4
BLOCK-A	=	BLOCK-A	BLOCK-D	=	BLOCK-D
BLOCK-B	=	BLOCK-B	BLOCK-E	=	BLOCK-E
BLOCK-C	=	BLOCK-C	BLOCK-F	=	BLOCK-F
DISK 5		**DISK 6**	**DISK 7**		**DISK 8**
BLOCK-G	=	BLOCK-G	BLOCK-J	=	BLOCK-J
BLOCK-H	=	BLOCK-H	BLOCK-K	=	BLOCK-K
BLOCK-I	=	BLOCK-I	BLOCK-L	=	BLOCK-L

RAID 1 offers a minor performance improvement over the use of single drives, because read requests can be satisfied from both sides of the mirror. However, write requests are written to both drives simultaneously, offering no performance gains. The main benefits of this form of RAID are that, in the event of a single drive failure or possibly multiple drive failures, the mirror is broken, but data availability is not impacted, so performance is only marginally impaired, if at all, until the drive is replaced. At this point, however, performance is impacted by the resilvering process of copying the entire contents of the good drive to the replacement, a lengthy and intensive I/O operation.

When implemented in software using a volume manager, the CPU load from mirroring is the lowest of any form of RAID, although the server I/O traffic is doubled, which should be a consideration in comparing software- to hardware-based RAID solutions.

The most significant cost of this form of RAID comes in using exactly double the amount of storage as that which is available to the database.

RAID 10 Striped Mirrors

RAID 10 offers the advantages and disadvantages of both RAID 0 and RAID 1 by first mirroring all of the disks onto a secondary set and then striping across these mirrored sets. Table 7-3 shows this configuration.

Table 7-3. *RAID 10*

DISK 1		DISK 2	DISK 3		DISK 4
BLOCK-A	=	BLOCK-A	BLOCK-B	=	BLOCK-B
BLOCK-E	=	BLOCK-E	BLOCK-F	=	BLOCK-F
BLOCK-I	=	BLOCK-I	BLOCK-J	=	BLOCK-J
DISK 5		**DISK 6**	**DISK 7**		**DISK 8**
BLOCK-C	=	BLOCK-C	BLOCK-D	=	BLOCK-D
BLOCK-G	=	BLOCK-G	BLOCK-H	=	BLOCK-H
BLOCK-K	=	BLOCK-K	BLOCK-L	=	BLOCK-L

This form of RAID is usually only available with hardware-based RAID controllers. It achieves the same I/O rates that are gained by striping and can sustain multiple simultaneous drive failures in which the failures are not experienced on both sides of a mirror. In this example, four of the drives could possibly fail with all of the data, and therefore the database, remaining available. RAID 10 is very much the implementation of SAME that Oracle extols; however, like RAID 1, it comes at the significant overhead of an additional 100% requirement in storage capacity above and beyond the database.

RAID 0+1 Mirrored Stripes

RAID 0+1 is a two-dimensional construct that implements the reverse of RAID 10 by striping across the disks and then mirroring the resulting stripes. Table 7-4 shows the implementation of RAID 0 across disks 1, 2, 5, and 6 mirrored against disks 3, 4, 7, and 8.

Table 7-4. *RAID 0+1*

DISK 1	DISK 2		DISK 3	DISK 4
BLOCK-A	BLOCK-B	=	BLOCK-A	BLOCK-B
BLOCK-E	BLOCK-F	=	BLOCK-E	BLOCK-F
BLOCK-I	BLOCK-J	=	BLOCK-I	BLOCK-J
DISK 5	**DISK 6**		**DISK 7**	**DISK 8**
BLOCK-C	BLOCK-D	=	BLOCK-C	BLOCK-D
BLOCK-G	BLOCK-H	=	BLOCK-G	BLOCK-H
BLOCK-K	BLOCK-L	=	BLOCK-K	BLOCK-L

RAID 0+1 offers identical performance characteristics to RAID 10 and has exactly the same storage capacity requirements. The most significant difference occurs in the event of a drive failure. In this RAID 0+1 configuration, if a single drive fails—for example, disk 1—then you lose access to the entire stripe set on disks 1, 2, 5, and 6. At this point, you only have to lose another disk on the stripe set on the other side of the mirror to lose access to all of the data and, thus, the database it resides on.

Therefore, you might reasonably question where a RAID 0+1 configuration would be used instead of RAID 10. If implementing RAID in hardware on a dedicated storage array, the answer would be "never"; RAID 10 should always be used. However, if using software RAID, such as with Oracle ASM, in combination with any number of low-cost modular storage arrays, a RAID 0+1 configuration can be used to stripe the disks at storage level for performance and then mirrored by software between multiple arrays for resilience.

RAID 5

RAID 5 introduces the concept of parity. In Table 7-5, you can see the eight disks striped similarly to RAID 0, except you have a parity block at the end of each stripe. This parity block is the same size as the data blocks and contains the results of the exclusive OR (XOR) operation on all of the bits in every block in the stripe. This example shows the first three stripes, and if it were to continue across all of the disks, you would have seven disks of data and one disk of parity.

Table 7-5. *RAID 5*

DISK 1	DISK 2	DISK 3	DISK 4
BLOCK-A	BLOCK-B	BLOCK-C	BLOCK-D
BLOCK-I	BLOCK-J	BLOCK-K	BLOCK-L
BLOCK-Q	BLOCK-R	BLOCK-S	BLOCK-T
DISK 5	**DISK 6**	**DISK 7**	**DISK 8**
BLOCK-E	BLOCK-F	BLOCK-G	PARITY
BLOCK-M	BLOCK-N	PARITY	BLOCK-H
BLOCK-U	PARITY	BLOCK-O	BLOCK-P

In this RAID configuration, the data can be read directly in the same way as RAID 0. However, changing a data block requires writing the data block, and reading, recalculating, and subsequently rewriting the parity block. This additional overhead for writes on RAID 5 is termed the *write penalty*. Note that from the properties of the XOR operation for a write operation, touching the data block and the parity block is only necessary for a write operation; the parity can be calculated without it being required to access all of the other blocks in the stripe. When implemented on a hardware-based RAID controller, the impact of the parity calculation is negligible compared to the additional read and write operations, and the write penalty will range from 10% to 30%, depending on the storage array used. RAID 5 is less effective when implemented as a software solution, because of the requirement to read all of the data, including the parity information, back to the server, calculate the new values, and then write all of the information back to the storage, with the write penalty being approximately 50%.

Recalling our discussion of storage fundamentals for RAC, this RAID configuration may appear completely unsuited to LGWR activity from a redo thread presenting the system with a large number of sequential writes and no reads. From a theoretical standpoint, this unsuitability is true. However, good RAID 5 storage systems can take this sequential stream of writes and calculate the parity block without first needing to read the parity block from disk. All of the blocks and the parity block are written to disk in one action, similar to RAID 0, and hence, in the example shown, eight write operations are required to commit blocks A to G to disk, compared to the fourteen required for RAID 10, though these can be completed in parallel.

The primary attraction of RAID 5 is that, in the event of a disk failure, the parity block means that the missing data for a read request can be reconstructed using the XOR operation on the parity information and the data from the other drives. Therefore, to implement resiliency, the 100% overhead of RAID 10 has been significantly reduced to the lower overhead of the parity disk. Unlike RAID 10, however, the loss of another drive will lead to a total data loss. The loss of the single drive also leads to the RAID 5 group operating in a degraded mode, with the additional load of reading all of the blocks and parity in the stripe to calculate the data in the failed block increasing the workload significantly. Similarly, when all of the drives are replaced, all of the blocks and the parity need to be read to regenerate the block to be written to the replaced drive.

In terms of parity-based RAID, an important area to note is the impact of significantly larger disk media introduced since the original RAID concepts were defined. Despite the increase in disk size, the likelihood of a disk failure remains approximately the same, and therefore, for a RAID 5 configuration of a given capacity, the chances of operating in degraded mode or even losing data are comparatively higher. This risk has led to the emergence of RAID 50–based systems with mirrored RAID 5 configurations. However, RAID 50 offers further challenges in terms of the impact on performance for RAC.

Storage Cache

In using the term "cache," we are referring to the RAM set aside to optimize the transfer of the Oracle data from the storage and are primarily concerned with the storage array controller cache. In terms of data access, other levels of cache exist at the hardware level through which the Oracle data will pass, for example, the CPU cache on the processor (discussed in Chapter 6) and the buffer cache on the hard drive itself, both usually measured in a small number of megabytes.

As we have seen previously in this chapter, for a transactional system the storage will experience a number of random reads and writes along with a continual stream of shorter sequential writes. Data warehouse activity will buffer much of the data in the SGA with minimal write and redo log activity outside of data loading times. You can, therefore, conclude that storage cache will have a marginal benefit in terms of your RAC read operations, with the vast majority of reads ideally being satisfied by the database buffer cache. If the block is not in cache, the next port of call will be to retrieve the block by Cache Fusion from another instance, and finally only if this fails, the read request will be sent to the storage.

For write operations, the effect of cache on the storage controller can be significant to a point. If operating as a write-back cache, the write request is confirmed as complete as soon as the data is in cache, before it has been written to disk. For Oracle, this cache should always be mirrored in RAM and supplied with a backup battery power supply. In the event of failure, this backup enables the data within cache to be written to disk before the storage array shuts down, reducing the likelihood of database corruption. Write cache is also significant in RAID 5 systems, because it enables the calculation of parity for entire stripes in cache and stores frequently used parity blocks in cache, reducing the read operations required.

This benefit from write cache, however, is valuable only to a certain extent in coping with peaks in throughput. In the event of sustained throughput, the data will be written to cache faster than the cached data can be written to disk. Inevitably, the cache will fill and throughput will operate at disk speed. Storage write cache should be seen as an essential buffer to enable the efficient writing of data back to disk. Allocating a large amount of cache, however, will never be a panacea for a slow disk layout or subsystem.

RAID Summary

Of the generally available RAID configurations discussed, a popular choice is RAID 5. The reasons are straightforward: RAID 0 is not practical in terms of redundancy, and RAID 1 is not suitable for performance. Although RAID 10 and RAID 0+1 offer the best performance and reliability, they have the significant cost of requiring a 100% overhead in storage compared to usable capacity. In theory, RAID 5 offers the middle ground, sacrificing a degree of performance for resilience while maintaining most of the storage capacity as usable.

In practice, the costs and benefits are not as well defined. The case tends to be that with RAID 1, RAID 0, and combinations of these levels throughput calculations tend to be straightforward, whereas with RAID 5, benchmarking and tests are required to clearly establish the performance thresholds. The reason for these testing requirements is that the advantages for RAID 5 tend to be stated from the viewpoint of a single sequential write stream combined with random reads where performance is predictable. In practice, hosting more than one database environment on a storage system is highly likely, and adding RAC into the equation with multiple redo log streams, the I/O activity tends to be less identifiable than the theory dictates.

For example, as the RAID 5 system increases in activity, you are less likely to be taking direct advantage of storing and calculating your stripes in cache and writing them together to disk in one action. Multiple, single-logical-block updates will take at least four I/O operations for the parity updates, and the increased number of I/O operations will be compounded in the event of *stripe crossing*, that is, where the cluster file system or ASM stripe is misaligned with the storage stripe. Stripe crossing will result in more than one parity operation per write compounding the effect on throughput still further.

As more systems and activity are added to the RAID 5 storage, the impact becomes less predictable, meaning that RAID 10 is more forgiving of the practice of allocating storage ad hoc, rather than laying it out in an optimal manner. This difference between the theory and practice of RAID 5 and RAID 10 tends to lead to polarity between Oracle DBAs and storage administrators between the merits of RAID 5 and RAID 10. Both are, in fact, correct from their viewpoints.

In summary, when determining a RAID specification for RAC, RAID 10 with hardware is the optimal choice for fault tolerance, read performance, and write performance. Where RAID 5 is used, the careful planning, layout, and testing of the database across the storage can deliver a cost-effective solution, especially where the workload is predominantly read-only, such as a data warehouse. For a transactional system, RAID 10 for the redo log threads and RAID 5 for the datafiles can provide a practical compromise.

Intelligent Storage

In a similar way that RAID functionality can be realized in software or hardware, there is also a choice in the level at which to implement additional key resiliency features, namely snapshots and remote mirroring. When implementing these features at a hardware level, it can be an important factor in selecting a storage subsystem for RAC.

Before selecting a vendor for specialized storage technologies, view the certified platforms under the Oracle Storage Compatibility Program (OSCP). Under this program Oracle lays down a strict set of guidelines to validate functionality against the Oracle database ensuring a fully supportable solution.

Oracle currently tests the following technologies:

- Network-attached file server technologies
- Snapshot technologies
- Remote mirroring technologies

Network-attached file server technologies are a significantly greater subject area than the other technologies and will be covered at length later in this chapter.

Snapshot Technologies

Snapshot copies can be done in a number of ways for a RAC cluster and can be implemented at both hardware and software levels.

The common type of snapshot is a metadata-based copy using functionality termed *copy-on-write*. A metadata copy is made almost instantaneously, initially involving the copying of pointers from the primary storage area to a secondary area without copying the data. Subsequently, the metadata is tracked, and before data blocks are changed in the original storage area, a copy is written to the secondary storage area. This copy ensures that the original data can be restored by replacing only the modified blocks with the original blocks in the secondary area. This functionality enables the rapid restoration of data to a point in time without requiring a complete copy of the data. It does not, however, provide any guarantee against disk failure, and database backups must still be done as normal, albeit from the snapshot image. Snapshots also have some impact on write performance from the impact of the required copy before the write is permitted, and the backup will still require scanning the original data source.

Snapshot images of the database can be done either at the storage array level or using the Oracle 10*g* Flashback database functionality. Using the software-based approach requires the creation of flashback logs and a flashback recovery area within the storage visible to the database.

Alternative snapshot functionality can be implemented simply by configuring RAID 1 mirroring and maintaining the mirror up to the point where the snapshot is taken. At this point, the mirror is split, resulting in the original database and a complete copy of the database at that point in time. This method has the advantage of resulting in a complete copy of the database without requiring the original disk to construct the image, but it has a 100% overhead in storage capacity to implement.

Remote Mirroring Technologies

Snapshot technologies are useful in providing backup functionality to recover from user or application errors and point-in-time images from which to run backups. Remote mirroring technologies, though, are a business continuity solution to replicate the primary data source to a secondary remote geographical location in anticipation of a catastrophic failure at the primary site.

Similar to snapshot technologies, Oracle also implements a software-based disaster-recovery solution in its Data Guard product; however, several other vendors offer storage array–based solutions validated under the OSCP.

For RAC in particular, if a remote mirroring solution is required, then the hardware-based solution has an advantage over Data Guard in being transparent to the operation of the database. This eliminates the bottleneck of a single standby node applying the redo from all of the primary nodes and, therefore, is likely to be the higher performing solution for active transactional systems.

To implement remote mirroring, an idle RAC configuration is installed in a standby site. The storage in the standby site is connected to the primary site with a mirror copy of the data and redo logs. As changes are applied to the primary storage, they are replicated across to the standby site. In the event of a failure at the primary site, the standby RAC configuration is started on this mirrored storage and continues to provide the database service, but from the remote geographical location.

The key technical challenge is one of the latency in the connection between the primary and secondary sites because of distance, and similarly to a Data Guard solution, this latency results in a decision between utilizing synchronous or asynchronous mirroring.

Synchronous remote mirroring means that when a write request is received at the primary site, the primary site will write the data to its own disk subsystem while transmitting the data to the remote site. Upon receiving the data, the remote site will write it to disk and transmit a confirmation back to the primary storage. At this point, the primary storage will confirm the write operation as complete back to the host system, and hence the Oracle database. This confirmation has the effect of being an extremely secure solution but will manifest itself in terms of lower performance at the primary site during normal operations. Conversely, with *asynchronous mirroring*, the primary site will write the data to disk and confirm the write operation before it has transmitted the data to the remote site. Asynchronous mirroring results in higher performance during normal operations; however, it risks a certain degree of data loss when the standby site is activated. The chosen solution will primarily be a factor of the distance between the primary and secondary sites, the latency incurred, and the business requirements for the solution.

Storage Protocols for Linux

DBAs are presented with a multitude of terminologies and techniques for selecting and configuring storage for RAC. Although the key determining characteristic is the requirement for simultaneous access to the storage from all of the nodes in the cluster, options to satisfy this requirement on Linux, from a practical standpoint, include technologies such as FireWire, Small Computer System Interface (SCSI), Fibre Channel Storage Area Network (SAN), Internet Protocol (IP) SAN, and Network Area Storage (NAS).

The correct decision depends on a number of factors, and as no two environments are identical, the factors are likely to differ case by case. It is also important not to consider storage entirely in isolation. As seen previously, crucial functionalities, such as RAID and intelligent storage features, can be implemented at either at the hardware or software level, and the level implemented should be determined before a purchasing decision is made.

An important point to note is that the storage protocol decision is not necessarily a decision between storage vendors. Leading storage vendors offer the same products with compatibility to support many different protocols according to circumstance.

Though our prime consideration up to this point has been storage performance for RAC, additional equally important decision criteria include cost, resilience, manageability, and supportability of the entire database stack from storage to server hardware and software. For example, ruling out any particular storage protocol due to the CPU overhead on the cluster nodes is counterintuitive without taking into account the predicted workload and CPU capacity available on the nodes.

Although, as we have stated, from a practical point of view, a RAC cluster can be built on low-cost storage with a medium such as FireWire, this configuration is not worthy of consideration in a production environment in terms of both performance and supportability. In reality, the storage and storage infrastructure will most likely be the most costly hardware components of the entire solution.

Despite the number of options available for the configuration of storage for RAC, you have, in fact, two major approaches to implementing I/O for RAC on Linux: *block I/O* and *file I/O*. Although these often are categorized as SAN and NAS, respectively, implementations such as Internet small computer system interface (iSCSI) mean that the distinctions are not necessarily clearly defined, and therefore, we will look at the protocols available, beginning with the primary foundation of block I/O, the SCSI protocol.

SCSI

Some of the confusion regarding I/O in Linux stems from the fact that SCSI defines both a medium—that is, the physical attachment of the server to the storage—and the protocol for communicating across that medium. To clarify, here we refer to the SCSI protocol operating over a standard copper SCSI cable.

The SCSI protocol is used to define the method by which to send data from the host operating system to peripherals, usually disk drives. This data is sent in chunks of bits, hence the term "block I/O," in parallel over the physical medium of a copper SCSI cable. Because this SCSI data is transmitted in parallel, all bits must arrive in unison.

The original implementation of SCSI in 1986 utilized an 8-bit data path at speeds of up to 5MB/s and enabled up to eight devices (including the host adapter itself) connected to a single host adapter. Because of the signal strength and the deviation from the original source being transmitted, called *jitter*, the maximum distance a SCSI device could be from the host system using a high voltage differential was effectively limited to under 25 m.

SCSI has subsequently been revised and updated to speeds of 320MB/s with 16 devices, although at a lower bus length of 12 m using a low-voltage differential.

Each SCSI device has an associated target ID, and this target can be further divided into subdevices identified by LUNs. Because a server can have several host adapters and each one may control one or more SCSI buses, to uniquely identify a SCSI device an operating system must account for the controller ID, the channel (or bus) ID, the SCSI ID, and the LUN. This hierarchy is precisely the one implemented in Linux for addressing SCSI devices and can be viewed with the following command:

```
[root@london1 root]# cat /proc/scsi/scsi
Attached devices:
Host: scsi1 Channel: 00 Id: 00 Lun: 00
  Vendor: SEAGATE  Model: ST336607LC       Rev: 0007
  Type:   Direct-Access                    ANSI SCSI
revision: 03
Host: scsi1 Channel: 00 Id: 06 Lun: 00
  Vendor: ESG-SHV  Model: SCA HSBP M24      Rev: 1.0A
  Type:   Processor                        ANSI SCSI
revision: 02
```

From this truncated output, you can see a SCSI device on SCSI ID 6 and a drive on SCSI ID 0 and the adapter scsi1.

Existing devices may be added or removed by echoing the command scsi remove-single-device or scsi add-single-device to /proc/scsi/scsi with the controller ID, the channel ID, SCSI ID, and LUN; however, all other devices on the bus should be inactive if these commands are attempted, and we do not recommend doing so in a shared storage environment such as in RAC.

The names of the actual SCSI devices, once attached, can be found in the /dev directory. Unlike some UNIX operating systems that identify devices by their SCSI bus address, Linux SCSI devices are identified by their major and minor device numbers; there are eight major block numbers for SCSI disks: 8, 65, 66, 67, 68, 69, 70, and 71. Each major block number has 256 minor numbers, of which some are used to identify the disks themselves and some the partitions of the disks. Up to 15 partitions are permitted per disk, and they are named with the prefix sd and a combination of letters for the disks and numbers for the partitions.

Taking major number 8 as an example, the first SCSI disk with minor number 0 will be /dev/sd0, and minor number 1 will be the first partition /dev/sda1. The last device will be minor number 255 corresponding to /dev/sdp15. This letter and number naming convention continues with /dev/sdq for major number 65 and minor number 0, and after /dev/sdz15 at major number 65 and minor number 159, continues with /dev/sdaa at major number 65 and minor number 160. The final SCSI disk device available to allocate at 71,255 is /dev/sddx15, meaning that a total of 128 possible disks exist, each with 15 partitions. In a RAC cluster, no strict technical requirement insists that the disks to be allocated with exactly the same device names on all of the hosts in the cluster, but from a manageability point of view, every effort should be made to do so.

SCSI, by itself, as a protocol and medium, is not generally associated with the term "SAN." First, the number of devices that can be connected to a single SCSI bus is clearly limited and a strict SCSI implementation restricts the access to the bus to one server at a time, making it unsuitable for RAC. Second, although using link extenders to increase the length of SCSI buses is possible, doing so is impractical in a data-center environment compared to alternative technologies.

These disadvantages have led to advancements in SCSI, most notably the development of Serial Attached SCSI (SAS) to overcome the limitations of the parallel transmission architecture and to include the support of I/O requests from more than one controller at a time. However, these developments need to be balanced against overcoming the disadvantages of the SCSI medium with alternative technologies such as Fibre Channel (FC).

Despite these disadvantages, the SCSI protocol itself remains the cornerstone of block-based storage for Linux. Its maturity and robustness have meant that additional technologies and protocols used to realize SANs are implemented at a lower level than the SCSI protocol, and therefore, even though SCSI cabling will rarely be used, the device naming and presentation will remain identical as far as the operating system and Oracle are concerned.

Fibre Channel

FC was devised as a technology to implement networks and overcome the limitations in the standard at the time, that is, Fast Ethernet running at 100Mb/s. Although FC is used to a certain extent for networks, these ambitions were never fully realized because of the advent of Gigabit Ethernet. However, the development of FC for networks made it compatible with the requirements for overcoming the limitations of SCSI-based storage as follows: transmission over long distances with a low latency and error rate, and the implementation of a protocol at a hardware level to reduce the complexities and CPU overheads of implementing a protocol at the operating system level.

These features enabled the connection of multiple storage devices within the same network, hence the terminology "Storage Area Network." Note that although FC and SAN are often used interchangeably, they are not synonymous—a SAN can be implemented without FC, and FC utilized for other reasons apart from SANs. Also, similarly to SCSI, with FC distinguishing between the medium and the protocol is important. Despite the name, FC can be realized over copper or fiber-optic cabling, and the name "Fibre Channel" is correctly used to refer to the protocol for communication over either.

The FC protocol has five levels: FC-0 to FC-4. Levels FC-0 to FC-3 define the protocol from a physical standpoint of connectivity through to communication. FC-4 details how the Upper Layer Protocols (ULPs) interact with the FC network with, for example, the FC Protocol (FCP) implementing the SCSI protocol understood by the operating system with the FCP functionality delivered by a specific device driver. Similarly, IPFC implements the Internet Protocol (IP) over FC. There are also three separate topologies for FC: fabric, arbitrated loop, and point-to-point. By far, the most common of these topologies for RAC is the fabric topology, defining a switch-based network enabling all of the nodes in the cluster to communicate with the storage at full bandwidth.

Optical cabling for FC uses two unidirectional fiber-optic cables per connection, with one for transmitting and the other for receiving. On this infrastructure, the SCSI protocol is transmitted serially, meaning distances of up to 10 km are supported at high transfer rates. As well as supporting greater distances, fiber-optic cabling is also insensitive to electromagnetic interference, increasing the integrity and reliability of the link. The server itself must be equipped with an FC HBA that implements the FC connectivity and presents the disk devices to the host as SCSI disks.

At the time of this writing, FC products supporting transfer rates of 400MB/s are available, with standards for 800MB/s recently ratified. However, these available rates must always be considered in conjunction with the underlying disk performance. For example, you must have a minimum of five drives in the underlying storage to outperform SCSI alone.

When implementing a SAN environment in a fabric topology, a method must be in place to distinguish between the servers to present the storage to. RAC is delete the perfect example to illustrate that no restriction exists in the number of hosts that are presented an identical view of the same storage. To realize this lack of restriction, all devices connected to a fabric are identified by a globally unique 64-bit identifier called a World Wide Name (WWN). When the WWN logs into a fabric, it is assigned a 24-bit identifier representing the device's position within the topology, and zoning is configured at the switch layer to ensure that only the designated hosts have a view of their assigned storage. This explanation is, to some extent, an oversimplification, as resilience systems can be equipped with multiple HBAs and connected to the same storage by different paths through separate switches to guard against hardware failure. This configuration is realized at the host level by multipathing software unifying the multiple paths into a single disk image view, and we will review an example of this later in this chapter.

With these advantages of performance and connectivity over SCSI, FC has become the dominant protocol for SAN. However, it does also have some distinct disadvantages in realizing these benefits. One of the most significant of these is cost. The components for FC—the server HBA, optical cabling, and infrastructure—are significantly more expensive than their copper equivalents. Concerns have also been voiced about the lack of security implemented within the FC protocol, and the supported distances of up to 10 km are still a significant constraint in some environments.

In addition, arguably the most problematic area for Fibre Channel SAN, especially for RAC, is that of interoperability and support. To Oracle and the operating system, FC is interacting with SCSI devices, possibly with a clustered file system layered on top, and could be using asynchronous and/or direct I/O. The device driver for the server HBA implements the SCSI interaction with the storage using FCP and could be running multipathing software across multiple HBAs. The storage is also likely to be dealing with requests from multiple servers and operating systems at the same time. Coupled with RAC, all of the servers in the cluster are now interacting simultaneously with the same disks. For example, one node in the cluster recovering after a failure could be scanning the storage for available disks while the other nodes are intensively writing redo log information. You can see an exponential increase in the possible combinations and configurations. For this reason, FC storage vendors issue their own compatibility matrices of tested combinations, of which clustering—Oracle RAC, in particular—is often an included category detailing information such as the Oracle and Linux versions, number of nodes in the cluster, multipathing software support, and HBA firmware and driver versions. In reality, this certification often lies behind the curve in Oracle versions, patches, and features; in Linux releases and support; in server architectures; and in many other factors, making the planning and architecting of the entire stack for compatibility a crucial process when working on FC SAN-based systems. Storage vendors should always be consulted with respect to support at the planning stage of an FC-based RAC solution on Linux.

iSCSI

There are, in fact, three competing protocols for transporting block-based storage over an IP-based network: Internet Small Computer Systems Interface (iSCSI), Internet FC Protocol (iFCP), and FC over TCP/IP (FCIP).

FCIP supports tunneling of FC over an IP network, while iFCP supports FCP level 4 implemented over the network. Whereas these protocols are often implemented in environments looking to interconnect or interoperate with existing FC-based SANs, the emerging leader is iSCSI; it makes no attempt to implement FC, and instead defines a protocol to realize block-based storage by encapsulating SCSI into the Transmission Control Protocol (TCP) to be transmitted over a standard IP network. This native use of TCP/IP means that an existing Gigabit Ethernet infrastructure can be used for storage, unifying the hardware requirements for both storage and networking. The major benefits that stem from this unification are the reduced cost of implementation, ease of administration of the entire network, increased distance capabilities through the existing LAN or WAN, and well-understood IP-based security practices.

In iSCSI terminology, the client systems, which in this case are the RAC cluster nodes, require an iSCSI initiator to connect the storage target. Initiators can be realized in either software or hardware. The software initiator is, in effect, a driver that pairs the SCSI drivers with the network drivers to translate the requests into a form that can be transferred. This translation can be then be used with a standard Ethernet network interface card (NIC) connected to the storage by Category-5 cabling.

Like FC, once successfully implemented, Oracle and Linux view and interact with the disks at a SCSI protocol level, and therefore, Oracle needs to be based on raw devices or a cluster file system on the storage presented. iSCSI software drivers for Linux can be found on the open source Source-Forge web site at the Linux iSCSI project (http://linux-iscsi.sourceforge.net).

An alternative for iSCSI is the use of specialized iSCSI HBAs to integrate the entire iSCSI protocol stack of Ethernet, TCP/IP, and iSCSI onto the HBA, removing all of I/O protocol processing from the server. At the time of this writing, these HBAs are available at gigabit speeds over standard Category-5 cabling. Products supporting 10Gb speeds are available with fiber-optic cabling or the copper-based 10GBase-CX4 cable associated with InfiniBand. However, costs approach those of the better-established FC despite improved performance infrastructure.

In terms of Oracle, iSCSI is a technology that can be implemented for RAC on Linux today, backed by support from the major storage vendors. The most significant contributory factor for future adoption will be the standardization of products supporting 10Gb Ethernet over Category-5 cable. Products have been demonstrated with this technology, and therefore, greater adoption will be driven by the available bandwidth at a considerable cost difference to FC.

S-ATA

Serial Advanced Technology Attachment (S-ATA) has received a degree of attention as a means of providing resilient low-cost storage. The reason that S-ATA is being considered is the comparatively high cost of SCSI- and FC-based disks. This lower cost for S-ATA, however, comes with some significant disadvantages. S-ATA is based on a point-to-point architecture in which disk requests cannot be queued, therefore the maximum throughput is significantly lower compared to its higher-cost rivals, especially for random I/O. Rotational speeds are also lower, and hence latency tends to be higher for S-ATA.

In addition, the maximum cable length for S-ATA is 1 m, introducing some physical limitations that mean, in practice, S-ATA–based arrays need to be connected to the target host systems by existing SAN or NAS technologies.

The most significant disadvantage cited for S-ATA, however, is that the mean time between failures (MTBF) is up to three times that of SCSI- or FC-based disks. As you have seen previously, the failure rate is crucial when selecting a RAID strategy, as the impact on performance of failed devices is significantly higher for RAID 5 than RAID 10. Coupled with the larger disk media associated with S-ATA and, therefore, the greater tendency to failure for a given total storage capacity, S-ATA tends to demand a striped and mirrored configuration for performance and resilience. However, the maximum practical limit is 12 to 16 devices per controller. Realizing database storage using this type of disk technology requires the management of multiple storage arrays from the target host level, hence the applicability of volume management software such as ASM. As we noted earlier in our discussion of RAID 0 and RAID 1, using multiple storage arrays to achieve satisfactory levels of performance dictates that RAID 0+1 be used to mirror arrays at a host level of disks striped at the array level. Coupled with increased disk failure rates, this approach is not being targeted for high-level OLTP-based environments and is instead being aimed at the following uses:

- Online disk backup and recovery
- Development and testing databases
- Reporting databases

- Disaster recovery databases
- Data warehouses

Within these areas, the intention is to build a low-cost S-ATA environment and overcome the performance and reliability restrictions of the technology by building a database storage grid of multiple arrays managed at the server level.

Using Block-Based Storage

Once the block storage is available on all of the hosts in the cluster and visible in /proc/scsi/scsi, you have a choice about how to configure the devices in a form for use by Oracle on more than one system simultaneously. Standard file systems such as ext2 or ext3 are often used for single-instance environments. However, these file systems are not applicable for use in clustered environments where data may be cached and blocks modified on multiple nodes without synchronization between them, resulting in corruption of the data.

From a protocol standpoint, the simplest approach is for Oracle to use the devices directly as raw character devices, and the process to configure raw devices is described in Chapter 11. Raw devices can be used not only for the Oracle Clusterware partitions (see Chapter 11), but also for database files, redo log files, control files, and SPFILEs. However, an Oracle file and the underlying raw device can only have a one-to-one mapping between them. Raw devices may also be used for configuring the storage underlying Oracle ASM as discussed in Chapter 9.

The alternative to using the raw character device is to use the corresponding block-based device with a file system designed specifically for operating in a clustered environment, and we look at the configuration of the OCFS in Chapter 8.

Linux I/O Scheduling

I/O scheduling is how the order of processing disk I/O requests is determined. In Linux, I/O scheduling is determined by the Linux kernel, and with 2.6 Linux kernel releases, four different I/O schedulers are available. Selecting the most appropriate scheduler may have an influence on the performance of your block-based storage. The schedulers available are as follows:

- Completely Fair Queuing (CFQ)
- Deadline
- NOOP
- Anticipatory

The scheduler can be selected by specifying the elevator option of the Linux boot loader. For example, if you are using GRUB, the following options would be added to the /boot/grub/grub.conf file: CFQ uses elevator=cfq, Deadline uses elevator=deadline, NOOP uses elevator=noop, and Anticipatory uses elevator=as.

CFQ is the default scheduler for both Red Hat and SUSE Enterprise Linux releases and balances I/O resources across all available resources. The Deadline scheduler attempts to minimize the latency of I/O requests with a round robin–based algorithm for real-time performance. The Deadline scheduler is often considered more applicable in a data warehouse environment where the I/O profile is biased toward sequential reads. The NOOP scheduler minimizes host CPU utilization by implementing a FIFO queue and can be used where I/O performance is optimized at the block device level. Finally, the Anticipatory scheduler is used for aggregating I/O requests where the external storage is known to be slow, but at the cost of latency for individual I/O requests.

CFQ is usually expected to deliver the optimal level of performance to the widest number of configurations and is tunable with the nr_requests parameter in /proc/sys/scsi according to the bandwidth capacity of your storage. Therefore, we recommend using the CFQ scheduler unless evidence from your own benchmarking shows another scheduler delivers better I/O performance in your environment. We do, however, recommend testing your RAC storage configuration and chosen I/O scheduler using the benchmarking tools described in Chapter 23 wherever possible. In particular, independent testing has indicated that in some cases that the Deadline scheduler may outperform CFQ even for write-intensive applications.

If, after testing, you conclude that you would benefit from using a nondefault I/O scheduler, ensure that you are using the same scheduler on each and every node in the cluster.

NAS

We have seen the realization of block-based storage for Oracle RAC and the technology underlying the implementation of SANs. In contrast to SAN, there is NAS, which takes another approach in providing storage for RAC. Like snapshot and remote mirroring technologies, any NAS solution selected should be carefully verified for support against the OSCP.

Although the approach is different, many storage vendors support both a SAN and/or NAS implementation from the same hardware. By definition, iSCSI is both SAN and NAS. To draw the distinction, we will use NAS to define storage presented over a network but provided as a file-based system, as opposed to a block-based one. In terms of Linux and RAC, the only file system with which you need to be concerned is the Network File System (NFS) developed by Sun Microsystems.

As we have seen with block-level storage, Oracle RAC can either use the block devices directly or, for greater manageability, layer a file system such as OCFS on top of the block devices at the operating system level. The challenge for such a clustered file system is the managed synchronization of access between the nodes to prevent corruption of the underlying storage when a node is ejected from the cluster. Therefore, such an approach requires a degree of communication between the nodes. With a NAS approach, however, the file system itself is presented by the storage device and mounted by the RAC nodes across the network, meaning that file system synchronization is reconciled at the storage level. NAS storage also enables further file system features such as journaling, file-based snapshots (not to be confused with general snapshot technologies discussed earlier), and volume management implemented and managed at the storage level for greater efficiency.

At the hardware level, NAS is realized by a file server, and the RAC nodes communicate with the file server through standard Ethernet connectivity. We want to stress that, in terms of a RAC cluster, this storage network should be an absolutely private, dedicated network with strictly no other non-storage-related network traffic. The RAC cluster should not be connected simply by the local LAN, with NAS configuration requiring the same respect accorded to FC. Because file servers were originally designed for file sharing, their functionality is compatible with the RAC shared-all database approach, and as file servers are designed for this one function only, they tend to be highly optimized and efficient compared to a generic operating system in this role. A RAC cluster should not be based on an NFS file system served by anything but specialized hardware designed for the purpose and supported under the OSCP.

SAN and NAS Compared

First, let's stress that a comparison between NAS and SAN for RAC can never be entirely conclusive. The offerings on the market vary significantly, and therefore, some SAN solutions may outperform some NAS solutions and vice versa. In addition, advances in technology mean that the criteria change over time, such as with iSCSI. Additionally, many storage systems also support both SAN and NAS, sometimes simultaneously from the same hardware. Despite these complications, we will attempt to make some generic observations.

If disk performance is the one and only consideration for a RAC cluster, then the choice is straightforward. For the best throughput, the Oracle instances on the cluster nodes should have an SGA carefully configured for the maximum efficient caching of data. Redo logs should be sized in order that frequent checkpointing does not incur a significant overhead. The storage should be connected by FC to a number of storage arrays dedicated to their own individual roles, such as data files and redo logs, with the storage cache set to enable the maximum write cache available. The disks should be configured as RAID 0 with destroking in effect to utilize only the external portion of the drives. The disks should be presented and used by the database as raw volumes accessed with asynchronous I/O.

Clearly, although configuring the storage of a RAC cluster for maximum performance is straight-forward, the system just described will be suitable for one activity only: benchmarking. The real challenge is presented in configuring a solution to satisfactorily meet the requirements of not just performance, but also manageability, supportability, resilience, and cost. All of these requirements are unique to a particular environment, and therefore, selecting either SAN, NAS, or both can be entirely the right choice depending on circumstance.

In evaluating performance alone, the results from similarly equipped SAN and NAS environments will generally favor SAN, and NAS presents some additional points to consider. First, whenever a file is accessed, the data must be read from the disks into the main memory of the file server operating system and then transmitted from memory out across the network. Therefore, each file request will traverse the system bus of the file server twice, assuming that the data is not cached. Also, as discussed for iSCSI, generally available Ethernet technology currently operates at gigabit speeds below that of the available bandwidth for FC. A commonly quoted restriction is that the data is transferred from the nodes via TCP/IP, which is implemented by the server CPU, and the communication between the CPU and the NIC results in a higher number of CPU interrupts. As you saw in Chapter 6, however, the introduction of server-based network acceleration technologies can negate some of this impact, but overall the additional overhead will reduce the level of performance available to Oracle when compared to a SAN implementation on the same storage.

In practice, as you saw previously in this chapter, a great deal of SAN performance depends on the RAID configuration and, when coupled with the abstraction of either OCFS or ASM block-based storage, requires a great deal of time and expertise to ensure an optimal layout to reduce the impact of stripe crossing, making NAS a more forgiving solution in this respect.

Another important consideration for RAC is that of the shared access to the Oracle data files. As we have discussed, NFS has been in existence since 1984 and is a mature technology for sharing files realized on the storage itself, thereby enabling the performance of the storage array to be optimized for the file system. Adding storage can be done without downtime required on the cluster.

For block-based storage, the first option is to use the raw devices directly. Although an excellent option for performance, using raw devices is a challenge in terms of cost and manageability. Raw devices tend to be more expensive, as all of a raw device is allocated to a particular data file up front, and unlike deployment on a shared file system, allocating multiple files to auto-extend into shared available disk is not possible. With raw devices, you also need to ensure that all devices are presented in the same order to all hosts, and when adding new disks, you have no guarantee that these disks will be presented to the Oracle nodes after the existing ones. In practice, adding new devices may require a reconfiguration of /etc/sysconfig/rawdevices, unless persistent binding is supported and has been configured on the HBA to bind a system SCSI target ID to a specific FC device, even though the device's ID may change. In all cases when adding new SCSI disks, a reboot is advised.

The alternative for block-based storage is to configure the storage with a clustered file system (such as Oracle OCFS) or volume management (such as ASM), and on balance, when using block based storage, the manageability advantages of a clustered file system or volume management often tend to outweigh the performance advantages of raw devices directly.

One area of note is the storage and maintenance of the Oracle software itself, as opposed to the Oracle database datafiles. With block-based storage using either raw devices, OCFS version 1, or ASM support for this central storage is available for the database files only. This availability limitation means that the Oracle software must be installed locally and maintained on each and every node. When using NFS, the Oracle software is supported for installation on the NFS-based storage. This support has its advantages in that nodes can be added or subtracted from the cluster without requiring additional

Oracle software installations. Patching and upgrades are also straightforward, requiring action on only one set of Oracle software, and limiting the possibility of the software becoming out of synchronization on the nodes in the cluster. The disadvantage is that with this approach, rolling upgrades are not possible, and therefore, downtime will be required for maintenance.

Note that with most vendors supporting both NAS and SAN, implementing a dual SAN and NAS approach with a central binary installation on NFS and datafiles on block-based storage, if desired, is entirely feasible.

When selecting any storage solution for Oracle RAC, we have previously noted that vendor-based support is crucial. For SAN-based storage, this support will begin with the vendor compatibility matrix, and for NAS, with the OSCP. As you have seen with SAN, this matrix will often mean adherence to a strict software stack, including a particular Linux release and kernel version. Adherence can present a challenge when aligning all of the required software components within a particular environment. With NAS, once storage support is certified under the OSCP, the requirement on the host is for standard Ethernet drivers, giving NAS an advantage in the area of software stack supportability and the adoption of advanced Linux operating system releases. A NAS-based infrastructure also has a cost advantage: the HBA, cabling, switches, and the storage array itself tend to be of a lower cost than the equivalent SAN installation, in addition to being easier for support personnel to understand and keep secure.

Ultimately in each environment, the factors advocating SAN or NAS will be attributed different weightings according to the goals of the RAC implementation, and to this point, we have considered these factors mostly from a theoretical standpoint.

The optimal way to understand the nuances of each approach is through hands-on examples; therefore, in the remaining sections of this chapter, we present an example of building a SAN-based system and a NAS-based system for RAC. The aim is not necessarily to provide a detailed step-by-step guide to each, but to use the examples of configuring some of the most popular SAN- and NAS-based solutions to illustrate how the RAC I/O characteristics, storage fundamentals, and storage protocols we have discussed previously in this chapter are put into practice.

SAN Storage Example

As an example of configuring an FC SAN-based solution for Oracle 10g RAC, we will use an EMC CLARiiON CX500.

The CX500 can provide simultaneous access for up to 128 hosts in SAN, NAS, and iSCSI environments, but it will support only one of these environments at any one time. The EMC CLARiiON can be configured with all of the RAID levels described in the preceding section: RAID 0 available on 3 to 16 drives, RAID 1 on a mirrored pair of drives, RAID 10 data mirrored and striped across 4 to 16 drives, and RAID 5 on 3 to 16 disks. Any combination of RAID levels can be created on a single system with a stripe depth configurable as 4, 16, 64, 128, or 256 sectors per disk, offering a great deal of flexibility to an Oracle RAC configuration. The EMC CLARiiON is architected with two storage processors, each with two 2Gb optical front-end FC ports and two 2Gb back-end FC ports to guard against a single point of failure. The CX500 supports up to 120 disk drives across two redundant loops.

Both storage processors, called SPA and SPB, can access all of the disks in the system; however, when each individual LUN is configured, it is assigned to and accessed by the Oracle cluster nodes directly through one storage processor only. In the event of a storage processor failure, the LUNs on the failed processor will trespass over to the remaining storage processor with all access occurring directly through the remaining path. Therefore, enabling zoning at the FC switch layer of the infrastructure is crucial, so that all of the nodes in the cluster have access to the storage through both storage processors. In a high-availability environment, enabling dual-pathing at the node level with a dual-HBA installation coupled with EMC PowerPath software is also important. Dual-pathing ensures that, in the event of LUN trespassing, rebooting the hosts is not necessary to re-enable access to the LUNs through a different path.

When configuring an Oracle RAC cluster using EMC CLARiiON storage, the first reference should always be the EMC interoperability matrix. Within this matrix, EMC tests and certifies detailed Oracle RAC configurations, and therefore, the cluster configuration, including the operating system and Oracle versions, should always adhere to this matrix to ensure a supportable configuration.

If you are planning to use snapshot and mirroring technologies, both EMC SnapView and EMC MirrorView have been validated under the OSCP, and reference should be made to the OSCP regarding these technologies.

SnapView snapshot technology is based on the copy-on-first-write approach; therefore, maintaining SnapView images can impact performance with approximately a 10% overhead. Alternatively, the performance overhead can be reduced with SnapView Business Continuance Volumes (BCVs) utilizing a mirrored-write approach to maintain mirrored copies in real time; however, this approach incurs the expense of using double the amount of storage as required for storing the database. Using either method, the SnapView images can then be used for database backups independent of the production data.

MirrorView is the EMC method to provide a disaster-recovery solution through synchronous or asynchronous mirroring between EMC CLARiiON arrays. MirrorView can be considered as an alternative technology to deploying a Data Guard–based solution, the difference being that MirrorView operates entirely at the array level maintaining a byte-level copy and is therefore transparent to the Oracle RAC cluster itself.

When configuring the EMC CLARiiON for Oracle RAC, addressing the LUNs on the host translates directly to addressing on the storage itself; therefore, planning and designing the database before configuring the storage is important to enable optimal performance corresponding to our RAC storage fundamentals. A general guideline has often been to distribute datafiles that are accessed simultaneously with different access patterns on different physical drives. These datafiles are usually classified into tables, indexes, temporary tablespaces, undo tablespaces, and redo logs. This traditional approach, however, almost always presents practical limitations given the increased capacity of disk drives, and separating the objects would result in an unacceptable overhead in unused space. We therefore recommend that, wherever possible, as a practical compromise divide the physical disk drives between the redo logs and all other database datafiles. Also consider the database performance profile when selecting RAID types for the LUNs and RAID groups. The default choice within an OLTP environment, without given limits upon disk capacity, are for all LUNs to be configured as RAID 10 devices. In data warehouse environments or where RAID 10 is not practical for cost considerations, RAID 5 may be considered for all datafiles with the exception of the redo logs. Every effort should be made, for performance reasons, to ensure that the redo logs are configured on RAID 10 devices.

An important concept to be aware of before configuring the LUNs on an EMC CLARiiON is the distinction between a metaLUN and standard LUN—or FLARE LUN (FLU) given its correct terminology, with FLARE being the name of the operating system of the CLARiiON itself. The FLU is simply a logical partition of a RAID group; it can be used directly for storage and is traditionally the representative of the storage to the host systems associated with the EMC CLARiiON storage. The disadvantage of using this type of LUN directly is that the LUN itself cannot be dynamically increased or decreased in size without its being unbound and re-created, impacting the flexibility of the storage. A metaLUN, though, presents a dynamic LUN consisting of two or more FLUs. These components of a metaLUN can be either concatenated or restriped and offer both improved flexibility in sizing the LUNs presented to the host and improved performance by enabling a greater number of physical disks to be utilized for each metaLUN.

PowerPath

As we have seen in an EMC CLARiiON environment, the host has access to its storage through a path to either storage processor A or storage processor B at any one point in time. In the most straightforward implementation, for functionality the host will be connected to the storage through a single HBA either directly to the storage itself or through a single FC switch. In the event of the fail-ure of one of the components in the I/O path, the host will lose access to the storage. In the event of the failure of an EMC CLARiiON storage processor, given the correct configuration of the infrastruc-ture between the host and the storage, only a host reboot (or driver module reconfiguration) is required to re-enable access to the storage through the remaining storage processor. However, given the fail-ure of the HBA itself the host will lose access to the storage until the failed component is physically replaced. In the event of a single FC switch failure, all hosts will lose access to the storage in its entirety until the switch is replaced. In a production RAC environment, eliminating the prospect of a single point of failure within the I/O path is desirable. The solution for this within an EMC CLARiiON envi-ronment is EMC PowerPath software.

EMC PowerPath can be summarized as offering the following features:

- **Multiple path support**: Access to the storage through multiple channels increases per-formance and availability.

- **Path failover**: Automatic redirection of data from a failed path to an alternate channel offers increased resiliency.

- **Dynamic load balancing**: Improves performance by automatically distributing data across all of the channels available according to the workload.

- **Online recovery**: Automatically detects and recovers when failed paths are re-established without interruption.

In an EMC CLARiiON RAC environment, PowerPath software is installed at the Linux operating system level on every node within the cluster. Every node must have at least two HBAs with inde-pendent paths through to the same storage on the CLARiiON itself through both storage processor A (SPA) and storage processor B (SPB). Once PowerPath is installed and configured, the software creates a power driver on the host immediately above the HBA driver layer. PowerPath then creates virtual power or pseudodevices to the storage itself as shown in Figure 7-1.

Within a standard Linux-based configuration, these power devices have pseudonames that follow the naming convention /dev/emcpowera, /dev/emcpowerb, /dev/emcpowerb, and so on. The mappings to the underlying devices are stored in the file /etc/opt/emcpower/emcpower.conf. In a RAC environment, ensuring that the mappings within this file are consistent across all of the nodes in the cluster is important. The multipath support is accessed by the operating system, allo-cating one pseudodevice for every LUN presented by the storage; however, standard devices also remain available for each physical path to the LUN. Once PowerPath is installed, the pseudodevices should always be used instead of the standard devices and can be accessed in exactly the same way as the standard devices, such as /dev/sda and /dev/sdb. For example, they can be partitioned using fdisk with the partitions appearing in /proc/partitions as standard. The power devices also sup-port Oracle usage through overlying file systems, such as OCFS, and can be used with ASM and raw devices. The functionality of PowerPath is transparent to the functionality of the Oracle cluster or database server software.

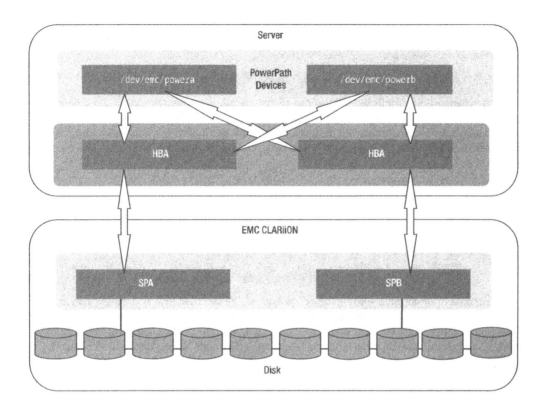

Figure 7-1. *EMC PowerPath*

Usage of PowerPath requires additional verification with the EMC compatibility matrix to ensure that the HBA and driver are compatible with the Linux release of the operating system and the EMC PowerPath driver. With the correct HBA driver previously installed, PowerPath is installed as an RPM package as in the following example:

```
[root@london1 root]# rpm -Uvh EMCpower.LINUX.*.rpm
```

PowerPath is then run as a service as follows:

```
[root@london1 root]# service PowerPath start
```

and is configured using the powermt utility. This configuration must be done on all nodes to ensure a consistent configuration across the cluster.

HBA and Driver Configuration

The host-level component of the SAN infrastructure is the HBA. The most commonly supported HBAs in an EMC CLARiiON environment are from the vendors QLogic and Emulex, and the compatibility matrix should be observed to ensure full system support for the card chosen. The HBA itself carries a significant level of the processing intelligence for the protocols it implements, as opposed to these consuming resources from the host CPU. The HBA determines the bandwidth supported by the host for communication with the storage and, therefore, must be considered in terms of the bandwidth supported by the switched fabric infrastructure and storage itself to ensure compatibility at the performance levels attainable. Some HBAs have the ability to auto-negotiate the speed at which they operate with the storage.

With the HBA physically installed on the PCI bus of the server, the command lspci can be used to confirm that is has been correctly seated. The following truncated output from lspci illustrates that this host has a single Emulex LP9802 FC HBA:

```
10:01.0 Fibre Channel: Emulex Corporation LP9802 Fibre Channel Adapter (rev 01)
```

If the adapter is physically established before the operating system installation takes place, then the most appropriate driver will usually be installed for the HBA at this time as a kernel module. This driver can be confirmed with the lsmod command. The following truncated output shows that the Emulex lpfc driver is loaded and operational along with additional SCSI- and disk-based modules:

```
[root@london1 root]# lsmod
Module              Size  Used by    Tainted: GF
lpfc              471712  25
mptscsih           94488  3
mptbase            97480  3  [mptscsih]
diskdumplib         7192  0  [mptscsih mptbase]
sd_mod             32896  56
scsi_mod          236416  4  [sg lpfc mptscsih sd_mod]
```

Additional information regarding the driver may also be recorded in /var/log/messages at driver load time or within the directory structure /proc/scsi. For example, the following output taken from within /proc/scsi/lpfc shows the configuration of the Emulex HBA, and the fact the link is up and ready shows that the HBA is correctly cabled through to the switch infrastructure:

```
[root@london1 lpfc]# cat 2
Emulex LightPulse FC SCSI 7.0.3
Emulex LightPulse LP9802 2 Gigabit PCI Fibre Channel Adapter
 on PCI bus 10 device 08 irq 58
SerialNum: BG35232345
Firmware Version: 1.81A1 (H2D1.81A1)
Hdw: 2003806d
VendorId: 0xf98010df
Portname: 10:00:00:00:c9:3a:83:3a   Nodename: 20:00:00:00:c9:3a:83:3a

Link Up - Ready:
   PortID 0x10201
   Public Loop
   Current speed 2G
lpfc0t00 DID 010000 WWPN 50:06:01:68:30:20:3d:23 WWNN 50:06:01:60:b0:20:3d:23
```

Ensuring that this driver corresponds to the EMC supported and certified software is necessary. If the driver is not installed or is at the incorrect version, then the supported version of the driver should be acquired from EMC or the vendor and installed manually according to the vendor-specific instructions. The installation may be from an RPM package or compiled from the source code. Whichever method you choose, we recommend installing the driver as a kernel module wherever possible for the most flexible approach. When this is done, ensure that the driver is installed on boot after any existing SCSI drivers already present on the system for the internal drivers, for example. Ensure the driver is installed correctly by configuring the /etc/modprobe.conf file. As shown in the following output, the driver lpfc is set to install after the driver mptscsih, by assigning the alias scsi_hostadapter2, this alias maintains the consistency of device naming every time the system is booted. The /etc/modprobe.conf file is also the location to specify module-specific configurations to be set at load time with the options parameter.

```
[root@london1 root]# cat /etc/modprobe.conf
alias eth0 e1000
alias scsi_hostadapter mptbase
alias scsi_hostadapter1 mptscsih
alias usb-controller usb-uhci
alias usb-controller1 ehci-hcd
alias eth1 e1000
alias scsi_hostadapter2 lpfc
options scsi_mod max_scsi_luns=255 scsi_allow_ghost_devices=1
options lpfc lpfc_lun_skip=1 lpfc_topology=0x04
```

The /etc/modprobe.conf file also details the configuration for when the mkinitrd command is run, building the initial RAM disk image to preload the SCSI devices at boot time. Only SCSI host adapters and their options included in this file will be loaded at boot. Without rebuilding the appropriate RAM disk image, you will always need to manually load the module using the modprobe command after the system has booted. This technique is not suitable as it means that files such as the cluster voting disk (required by Oracle Clusterware) are not available when the Clusterware itself starts.

Fibre Channel Switch Configuration

With the host configured, driver-functional, and cabled to the switch infrastructure, you need to configure the FC switch itself to enable communication between the host and its designated storage through zoning. This example shows configuration of the Brocade Silkworm switch using its Java-based administrative applet. The home switch explorer page is shown by connecting to the IP address or hostname of the switch itself. From the Switch Explorer page, click zone admin in the icon tray at the bottom left of the window.

The View menu of the Zone Administration has the following options: mixed zoning, port zoning, World Wide Name (WWN) zoning, and AL_PA zoning. The traditional view of zoning has commonly been in terms of hard zoning based on the port and soft zoning based on the WWN what is unique to every FC interface. AL_PA zoning is used in an arbitrated loop environment. Modern switch implementations blur the distinction between hard and soft zoning as depending on the vendor and product; zoning on the port and WWN can be implemented as securely as desired without unauthorized access occurring in either. In some cases, implementing more than one form of zoning at the same time on the same switch is possible, such as with the mixed zoning supported by Brocade. Further investigation into zoning is encouraged for complex strategies. For this RAC environment that has a dedicated switch infrastructure, port-based zoning will be shown.

To configure a zone under the Zone tab, click Create and enter a zone name in the dialog box. Within this zone, you can add the ports themselves and the devices. If the port is used, whichever device is connected to that port will belong to the zone. If a device is selected, the device itself will belong to the zone irrespective of the port to which it is connected.

For port-based zoning under the Ports and Devices list, highlight the ports required and click the Add Member button to add the selected port to the relevant zone. Figure 7-2 shows Zone 0 with ports 1,0 and 1,2 configured.

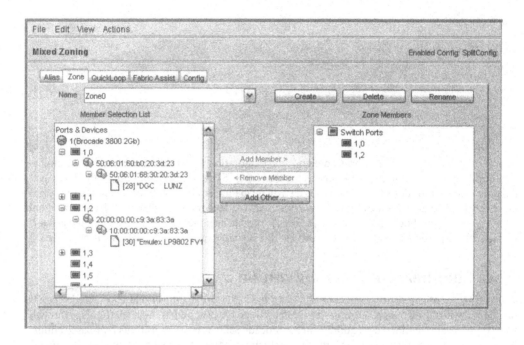

Figure 7-2. *Zone administration*

Drilling down the menus of the ports to the devices shows that you have an EMC CLARiiON initiator on port 1,0 and your host, with the Emulex device, on 1,2. Use the Add Member button to add the desired ports into the Zone Members window. This zone associates the two ports and, once enabled, permits traffic between the devices connected to each. Although this configuration with a single switch and single HBA per host is relatively simple, even in this scenario multiple zones should be configured in order that the host has a distinct path to both storage processor A and storage processor B of the EMC CLARiiON. Without this configuration, a system could lose access to its LUNs, if those LUNs are trespassed between storage processors on the CLARiiON.

When all of the required zones have been created, they can be grouped into a particular configuration that is activated either by the key combination Ctrl+E or by selecting to enable the specified configuration from the Actions menu. In this example, the configuration is termed SplitConfig and contains Zones 0 and 1 corresponding to Oracle cluster nodes london1 and london2. With the zones active, the hosts have a view corresponding to the storage in order that once the storage is configured, the LUNs will be presented back to them.

EMC CLARiiON Configuration

The CLARiiON CX storage series is also configured from a Java-based application accessed through a web browser. Although some of the processes can be automated by the host-based Navisphere agent, this automation is not essential for full functionality, so we will illustrate the basic manual steps required in a configuration of the EMC CLARiiON for a RAC cluster.

Connect to the IP address or hostname of the EMC CLARiiON to initiate the Navisphere administrative applet and display the Enterprise Storage window.

The first action required is to ensure that the hosts are correctly connected and the switch zones configured. To do this, right-click the icon for the storage array itself and select the menu option to display the connectivity status.

If a Navisphere agent is installed on the host and operating correctly, registration can proceed automatically. If an agent is not present under the registration tab for each unregistered host, complete the details for registration. When selected, the Show Storage System Initiators check box will show information about the EMC CLARiiON connectivity itself and is not required for registering hosts. After registration is complete, click OK on the Connectivity Status window. The hosts can now be observed as having been manually registered and associated with the storage in the top-level Enterprise Storage window.

Before configuring the RAID groups and LUNs to present the storage to the host systems, an important stage is to verify the settings of the CLARiiON cache accessed by right-clicking the storage and selecting the Properties menu option to display the screen shown in Figure 7-3.

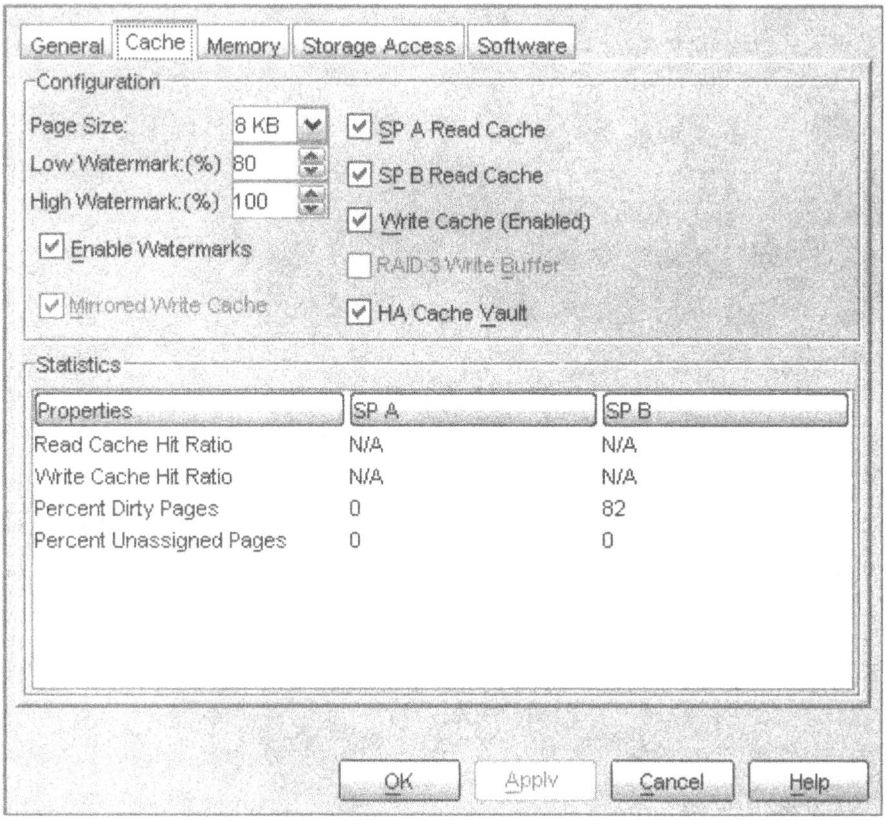

Figure 7-3. *Cache configuration*

The most important setting here is the cache page size, which should be set to correspond to the Oracle block size. If multiple block sizes are used, we recommend 8KB as a standard default value. Both write and read caching should be enabled. In addition the customizable options accessible from the Memory tab on the System Properties window should show the majority of the cache dedicated to write activity. Dedicating the cache thusly is beneficial, because a significant amount of read caching will be done on the hosts themselves, and therefore the storage cache should be biased more heavily toward write activity. Read caching should be left enabled to some degree, however, to take advantage of intelligent read-ahead algorithms for improving read performance through prefetching. The low and high watermark values refer to the bounds between which the write cache begins actively flushing the contents to disk. In an Oracle environment, the values 80% and 100% are applicable for the low and high values, respectively.

With the communication successfully established between the hosts, and the storage and general cache settings assessed, the next step is to create a RAID group from all or a subset of the disks available within the storage. To do this, right-click the storage itself and select the option Create RAID Group to access the dialog box shown in Figure 7-4.

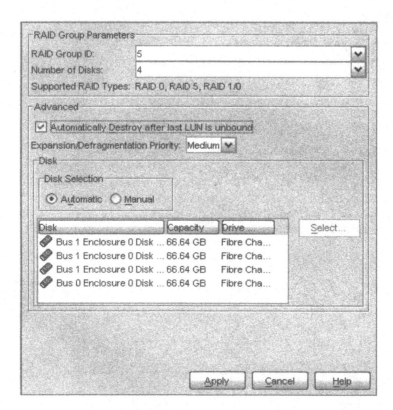

Figure 7-4. *RAID group creation*

Select a RAID Group ID and the number of disks to include in the RAID group. The number of disks selected will determine the options available in selecting a RAID type when the first LUN is bound upon the RAID group. You should also remember that the number and type of disks in the RAID group will have an impact on the level of performance attainable. Click Apply to display the confirmation dialog. Click Yes to confirm the RAID group creation operation. The operation completes almost immediately, irrespective of the size of the RAID group created. Click OK to confirm the success of the RAID group creation. The RAID group appears under the RAID Groups menu as unbound.

Before the configured RAID group can be accessed, you need to bind LUNs of the required size on the RAID group. To bind the LUNs, right-click the newly created RAID Group and select the option to bind a LUN. Alternatively bring up the same dialog by right-clicking the storage itself and selecting the same option as shown in Figure 7-5.

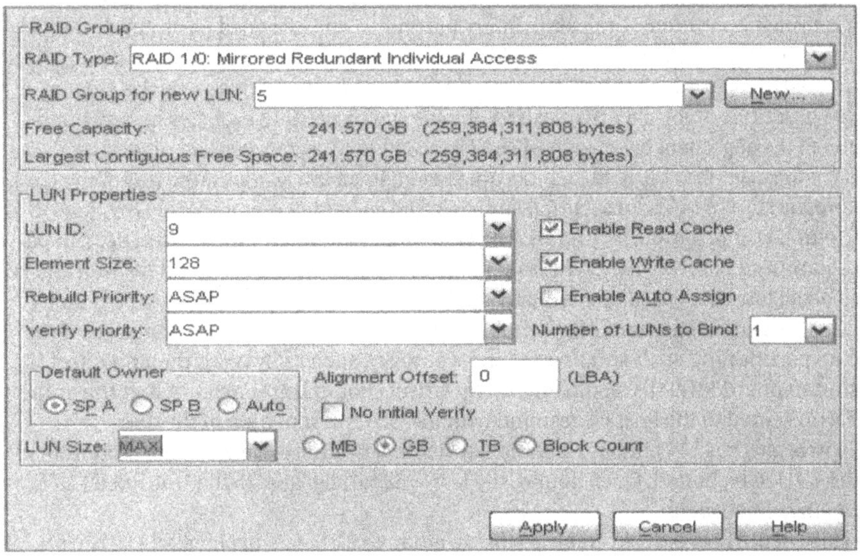

Figure 7-5. *LUN binding*

The difference between the selection options is that selecting from the RAID group automatically selects itself as the RAID group from which to configure a LUN, otherwise you need to select the RAID group to use on the Bind LUN window. On the first LUN binding operation, select the RAID Type to use. Depending on the number of disks within the RAID group the options are as follows:

- **RAID 0**: Nonredundant individual access
- **RAID 1**: Mirrored pair
- **RAID 1/0**: RAID-mirrored redundant individual access
- **RAID 5**: Redundant individual access (high throughput)
- **Disk**: Individual disk
- **Hot Spare**: Hot spare replacement

If, for example, the RAID type "RAID 5" is selected, then future Bind LUN operations will only permit RAID 5 to be selected for this particular RAID group, and therefore, this first bind operation is especially important in defining the RAID group usage. For Oracle RAC–based systems, we recommend RAID 10 (termed "RAID 1/0" by CLARiiON) wherever possible. We also recommend maintaining the caching values and LUN properties to their default values, especially maintaining the Element Size at 128 unless explicitly advised to modify the value by EMC support. If desired, however, the Enable Read Cache and Enable Write Cache check boxes offer the possibility to select whether to enable caching for that LUN in particular. This may be desirable, for example, where it is known that a LUN will only support read-only tablespaces, and therefore, write caching may be disabled for this LUN. The default owner specifies whether the LUN will be presented to the host through storage processor A or storage processor B or allocated to a storage processor by the EMC CLARiiON itself. We recommend manually maintaining an even balance of distribution of LUNs between the storage processors. You can select a particular size for the LUN to BIND or to select MAX, which allocates all of the remaining space.

An important value to be set according to the usage of the LUN is the Alignment Offset value. This value needs to be modified according to the partitioning scheme planned for usage upon the LUN. On Linux, this partitioning scheme will usually be one of two forms, and we discuss the partitioning options further in Chapter 10. On a default Linux master boot record (MBR) disk, you can create up to four primary partitions; or three primary partitions, one extended partition, and unlimited logical drives within this extended partition. The maximum volume size is 2TB. On a Globally Unique Identifier (GUID) partition table (GPT) disk, up to 128 primary partitions can be created, and no extended partitions or logical drives exist. Volumes can be up to 18 exabytes in size. Importantly, in relation to the alignment offset with MBR disks, 63 hidden sectors contain platform-critical data at the start of the disk. This MBR, in fact, occupies a single sector; however, the rest of the track is reserved before the start of the boot sector, resulting in the 63 hidden sectors. With GPT disks, this data is located within visible partitions, and GPT disks contain redundant primary and backup partition tables for improved data integrity. Wherever possible, GPT partitioning should be used and is fully supported on all Itanium-based systems and some x86-based systems with the parted utility. When using a GPT disk, the alignment offset should always be left at the value 0. Similarly, if the disk is to have no partitioning at all and be used in its entirety, such as by ASM, then no offset is required. If using standard MBR disks, the Alignment Offset should be set to 63 so that the stripe sizes of the LUN presented to the host correspond with the OS representation of the disk.

Click Apply to begin the LUN binding operation, which will take an amount of time proportional to the size of the LUN to be bound. Once bound, the LUN will be allocated to the Unowned LUNs section of the main storage menu.

The final stage of the process is to create a storage group to associate the created LUNs with one or more hosts. Right-click the storage itself and select the Create Storage Group menu option. Change the name of the storage group if desired, and click OK. Storage Group 1 now appears under the Storage Groups menu. Right-click the storage group and select the Connect Hosts option to access the dialog box shown in Figure 7-6.

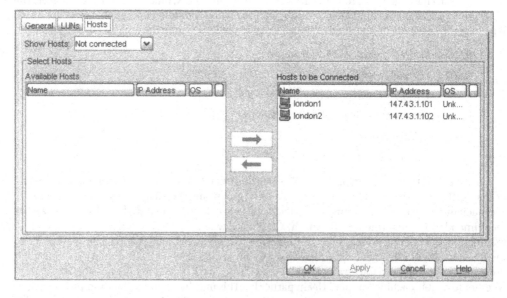

Figure 7-6. *Storage Group Properties, Hosts tab*

Highlight the hosts, use the directional arrows to select them, and click OK to add all of the Oracle RAC nodes to the storage group. By default, the presented LUNs will be shareable between all of the hosts within the storage group. To select the LUNs for the storage group, click the LUNs tab on the Storage Group Properties page as shown in Figure 7-7.

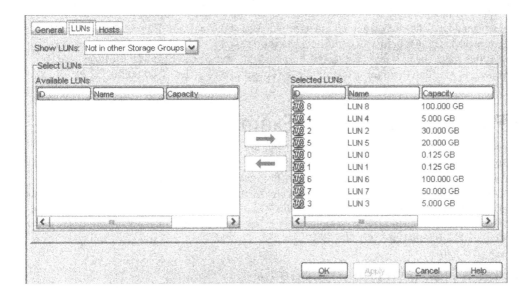

Figure 7-7. *Storage Group Properties, LUNs tab*

Highlight the LUNs and use the directional arrows to move them between the Available LUNs and Selected LUNs panes. Click OK. The selected LUNs will now be presented to the hosts in the storage group, and the tasks required through Navisphere are complete.

On the hosts, the LUNs can be added as SCSI devices dynamically by echoing the command scsi add-single-device to /proc/scsi/scsi with the correct arguments or by removing and reinserting the FC driver module. If the operation is successful, the disks will appear within /proc/scsi/scsi, as shown by the following truncated output:

```
[root@london1 root]# cat /proc/scsi/scsi
Attached devices:
Host: scsi2 Channel: 00 Id: 00 Lun: 00
  Vendor: DGC     Model: RAID 10         Rev: 0207
  Type:   Direct-Access                  ANSI SCSI revision: 04
```

Despite the ability to add SCSI devices dynamically, we always recommend rebooting the system to ensure that the FC driver is successfully loaded and all of the disks discovered consistently at boot time. The information regarding the driver and disk discovered will be reported in /var/log/messages such as the following:

```
[root@london1 root]# cat /var/log/messages
May  4 10:52:52 london1 kernel: Emulex LightPulse FC SCSI 7.0.3
May  4 10:52:52 london1 kernel: PCI: Found IRQ 58 for device 10:01.0
May  4 10:52:52 london1 kernel: lpfc0:1303:LKe:Link Up Event x1 received
Data: x1 x1 x8 x2
May  4 10:52:52 london1 kernel: scsi2 : Emulex LightPulse LP9802 2 Gigabit
PCI Fibre Channel Adapter on PCI bus 10 device 08 irq 58
May  4 10:52:52 london1 kernel:    Vendor: DGC       Model: RAID 10
```

```
Rev: 0207
May  4 10:52:52 london1 kernel:    Type:    Direct-Access
ANSI SCSI revision: 04
May  4 10:52:52 london1 kernel: blk: queue e00000007f3305b0, I/O limit
17592186044415Mb (mask 0xffffffffffffffff)
```

Reviewing this output is worthwhile after the first reboot in conjunction with the disk information reported from the fdisk command to ensure that all of the disks are discovered consistently with the same device names across all of the nodes in the cluster.

At this stage, the SAN disks are successfully configured and presented with the hosts, and you now need to partition them using the utilities fdisk and parted as described in Chapter 11.

NFS and iSCSI Storage Example

For NAS, we will present a configuration based on the Network Appliance (NetApp) Filer model FAS920c. Although we are focusing on NAS and iSCSI in this section, noting that this filer supports several access modes, including block and file access from the same machine, is important. The support for FC SAN, iSCSI SAN, and NAS, among other access methods, means that, for example, you can locate the Oracle binaries on NFS with the Oracle data on FC or iSCSI on the same filer at the same time. This FAS920c can support up to 12TB or 336 spindles in a clustered environment internally connected in the form of an FC arbitrated loop (FC-AL).

NetApp Filer RAID Configurations

Taking a more in-depth look at the RAID and internal file system configuration that takes a significant departure from the usual RAID configurations introduced in the storage fundamentals section would be useful here. NetApp filers utilize RAID 4 for all data stored in the disk subsystem. At a basic level, RAID 4 can be understood in the same manner as RAID 5, except instead of the parity information being interleaved across all of the drives in the RAID group all of the parity information is held on a single drive. In its standard form, RAID 4 is not as common as RAID 5, because this dedicated parity disk is a limiting factor, especially for random write performance. However, in their basic forms both RAID 4 and RAID 5 are not considered in terms of file system structure and activity. Therefore, the writing of the parity data is inconsistent with the layout of the data specified by the file system.

The NetApp RAID 4 implementation, though, is tightly integrated with the Write Anywhere File Layout (WAFL) file system, which, unlike a standard file system, enables file system metadata and data to be written anywhere on disk. In addition, the filer collects multiple write requests in a non-volatile transaction log, confirming the requests back to Oracle when committed to the log. The log is then flushed to disk at regular intervals. This flushing reduces the impact of the RAID write penalty by always issuing multiple writes to RAID stripes located close together along with the parity information at the same time, minimizing the number of disk seeks required and eliminating the stripe crossing often seen with nonintegrated file systems. Also, because the RAID 4 design does not interleave the parity information like RAID 5, the file system can still be rapidly expanded without being rebuilt. Because WAFL enables file system metadata to be written anywhere on the disk, reading or writing of all metadata or data must take place through the file-system inode with pointers to the 4KB data blocks. The initial inode pointers address up to 16 4KB data blocks, so an I/O operation of greater than 64KB is referenced through indirection. The DBA should, therefore, be aware that, as with all file systems, fragmentation can reduce the efficiency of the ability to coalesce multiple writes into a single operation, thereby increasing the RAID penalty and impacting performance. Managing file systems well and allowing sufficient capacity for both the metadata and data are essential in ensuring optimal Oracle performance.

Another notable difference enabled by the WAFL file system is in terms of the snapshot technologies discussed earlier in the section on intelligent storage. Traditionally, as we have discussed, snapshots are associated with copy-on-write functionality, where the original block is read and written to the snapshot area before it is overwritten, resulting in two writes when snapshots are enabled. With the WAFL approach of metadata being stored along with the data, snapshots are still virtually instantaneous, but once a snapshot is taken new blocks can be written to a separate area without the impact on performance usually associated with this technology. Once taken, the snapshot is static and read-only and is therefore suitable for Oracle backups. Snapshots can also provide the basis for asynchronous remote mirroring between sites transparent to Oracle, again without an impact on performance.

Similar to the drawbacks of a traditional RAID-with-parity environment, the filer will operate in a degraded mode in the event of single disk failing, and as seen with the emergence of RAID 50, the tendency toward ever-increasing disk media increases the likelihood of a single disk failure occurring for a given capacity of disk storage and, therefore, demands an alternative approach. In the filer environment, this approach is the migration from RAID 4 to RAID with Double Parity (RAID-DP). RAID-DP adds a second diagonal parity stripe and an additional, fixed parity disk to the existing horizontal stripe and parity disk to duplicate the parity protection. These additions provide protection against two disk failures: either both parity disks, a parity disk and data disk, or two data disks. Resiliency is increased by a factor of 4,000 compared to a single parity disk against the cost of approximately a 2–3% reduction in performance because of the additional parity.

In terms of the physical setup of this example configuration, the FAS920c implements a clustered solution. There are two filers connected by an InfiniBand-based interconnect, with each taking primary responsibility for servicing a subsection of the disks. The filers maintain mirrored copies of the pages of each other's nonvolatile RAM (NVRAM).

In the event of a hardware failure on one of the filers, the other filer initiates an automatic failover and boots a virtual machine image of the failed filer, taking control of all of the disks in the cluster, the Media Access Control (MAC) address, and all outbound connections, making the failure transparent to Oracle RAC. Coupled with RAC, this automatic failover presents a highly available solution throughout the architecture with no single point of failure.

This example of a configured solution is presented to the RAC cluster with standard networking infrastructure. The servers in the cluster are equipped with standard Gigabit Ethernet cards on the same private storage network in order that the servers can communicate with the filers over standard TCP/IP communication, providing the basis for both NFS and iSCSI simultaneously.

Aggregates and Volumes

The filer cluster can be configured from the command line through a telnet or ssh connection or from the na_admin graphical interface using a Java-enabled web browser by accessing the IP address of the filer. The command line can also be accessed through this graphical interface. Selecting FilerView from the menu presents a number of options available in the left pane of the window alongside the current status of the system. This system status displays information about the filer identity disks and whether the system is operating normally.

The first consideration in terms of configuring the system is the aggregate, which can be selected from the main menu. Figure 7-8 shows an aggregate with the default name of aggr0 and 27 disks as RAID-DP.

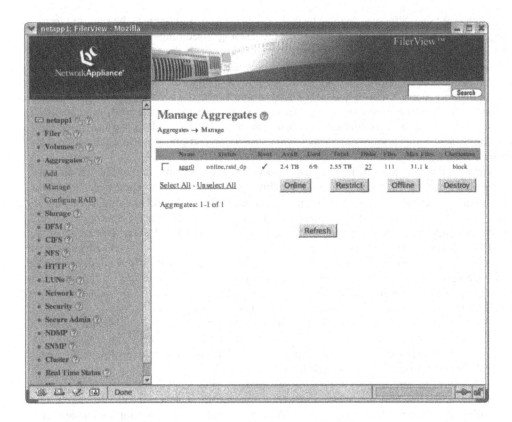

Figure 7-8. *Manage Aggregates*

The aggregate is the bottom-level structure defining the container of a pool disks. Flexible volumes can then be created from this aggregate. Up to 100 flexible volumes can be created within an individual aggregate. The flexible volume enabled by the aggregate is distinct from traditional volume associated with a standard RAID group. A traditional volume limits the smallest granularity of a volume to the size of an available individual disk with a minimum size of at least one disk per volume. These volumes can also be increased in size by adding additional disks, but cannot be decreased. A significant disadvantage of a traditional volume, however, is that performance may be limited by binding volumes to a smaller number of disks than is available to the entire system. The flexible volume, on the other hand, can be created within the aggregate from a 50MB minimum volume up to the maximum size of the entire aggregate without being bound to particular disks. Flexible volumes can thus be increased or decreased in size within the physical bounds of the aggregate. Higher performance is enabled by ensuring that volumes are not bound to traditional smaller collections of disks per volume. RAID-DP is applied by default at the entire aggregate level.

NFS

The following section describes the process required to configure the volumes and NFS exports required for an Oracle RAC installation.

To create a volume, use the Volume Wizard available from the Volume Add menu option. In this example, we have previously created the dbhome volume allocated for the shared ORACLE_HOME between the instances and the oradata volume for the Oracle data, and we will create a third volume for the redo log area. Note that in this example the segregation of logs and data is for manageability; as you have seen, both volumes will reside on the same aggregate, and therefore the same physical disks, offer no performance difference from placing them in the same volume.

Before creating a volume, note that where "command access" is referred to it can be accessed from the main menu under the Filer - Use Command Line option. After starting the Volume Wizard, click Next to advance to the Volume Type Selection page shown in Figure 7-9.

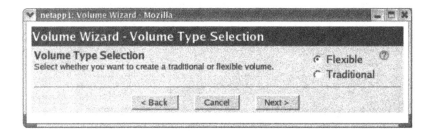

Figure 7-9. *Volume Type Selection*

Select Flexible and click Next to create a volume within the preconfigured aggregate displayed in Figure 7-10. Creating a traditional volume requires separate disks available external to the aggregate.

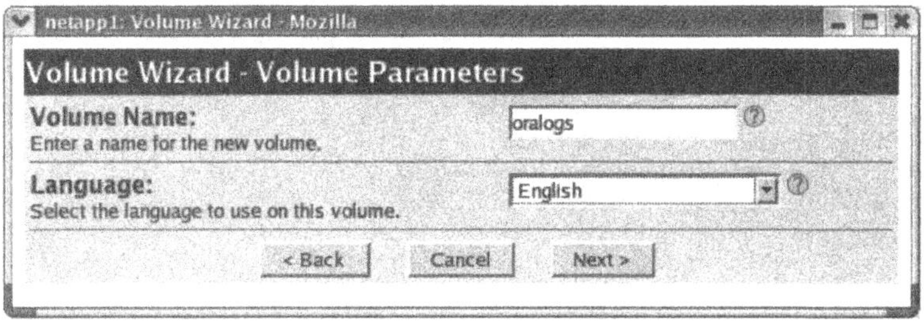

Figure 7-10. *Volume Parameters*

Enter the name of the volume and the language to use on the volume and click Next to advance to the configuration of Flexible Volume Parameters shown in Figure 7-11.

Figure 7-11. *Flexible Volume Parameters*

Select the underlying aggregate, in this example aggr0, and the desired volume size and click Next. Review the summary and click Commit. The volume creation is almost instantaneous. Click

Close to end the Volume Wizard. A summary of the created volumes is available from the Manage Volumes page accessed from the main menu. Figure 7-12 shows an example.

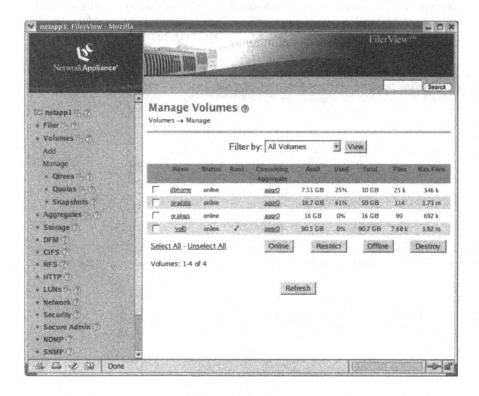

Figure 7-12. *Manage Volumes*

To make this created volume available as an NFS export, from the main menu, select the NFS Heading and Add an NFS Export to initiate the NFS Export Wizard shown in Figure 7-13.

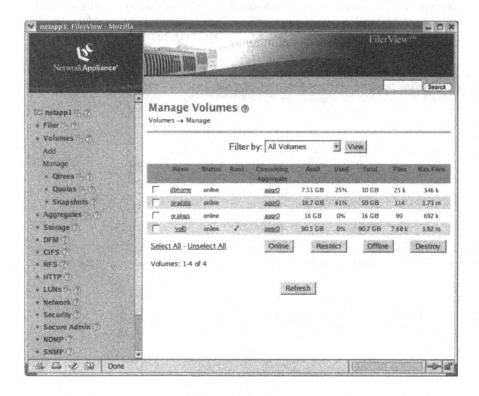

Figure 7-13. *NFS Export Wizard*

Select the Read-Write Access, Root Access, and Security check boxes and click Next to proceed to the Path page shown in Figure 7-14.

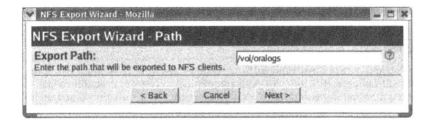

Figure 7-14. *Path*

On the Path page, enter the name of the volume to export and click Next to advance to the Read-Write Access page. Enter the hosts that are to have read and write access. In this example, All Hosts has been selected to enable any host within the network to be able to mount the exported NFS file system. Click Next. On the root access page, enter the name of at least one host to have root access to the exported volume—for example, host london1. Click OK and then Next to advance to the Security page shown in Figure 7-15.

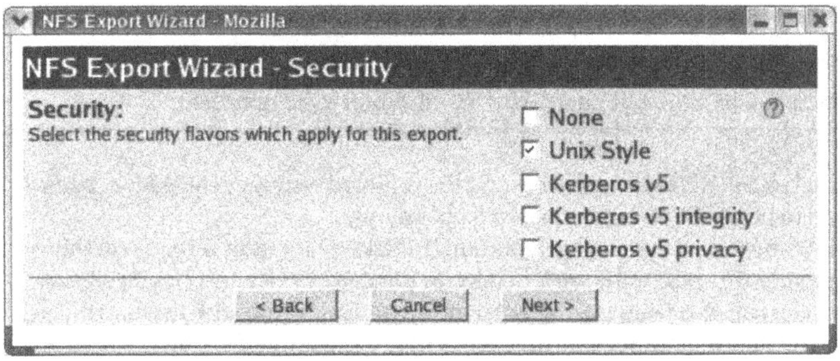

Figure 7-15. *Security*

On the Security page, select Unix Style security and click Next. On the Commit page, confirm the selection and click Commit. The created volume is now available to be mounted as an NFS volume by the RAC cluster nodes.

The storage is now configured and ready to be mounted on the RAC cluster.

On each node in the cluster, as the root user, edit the /etc/fstab file and add entries such as the following to ensure that the exported NFS volumes are mounted at boot time:

```
[root@london1 root]# cat /etc/fstab
netapp1:/vol/dbhome      /u01                    nfs
rsize=32768,wsize=32768,hard,nointr,rw,bg,vers=3,tcp,actimeo=0
netapp1:/vol/oradata     /u02                    nfs
rsize=32768,wsize=32768,hard,nointr,rw,bg,vers=3,tcp,actimeo=0
netapp1:/vol/oralogs     /u03                    nfs
rsize=32768,wsize=32768,hard,nointr,rw,bg,vers=3,tcp,actimeo=0
```

This example illustrates three volumes exported by the filer netapp1 to be mounted on the directories /u01, /u02, and /u03 with the file system type given as NFS. The additional options given specify the parameters listed in Table 7-6.

Table 7-6. *NFS Parameters*

Parameter	Setting
rsize/wsize	NFS client network read and write sizes. The rsize and wsize parameters have default values of 4KB, but 32KB is recommended by NetApp to enable reads and writes of this greater size to occur in one single transmission when used in conjunction with the tcp option.
hard	A default mount option for NFS but strongly recommended to be explicitly included to prevent any possibility of data corruption from the soft option being specified.
nointr	An additional mandatory option, nointr prevents the NFS client software from being interrupted and possibly returning an unexpected error when communicating with the server.
rw	Enables read and write access to the directory and its contents.
bg	Sets the NFS mount command to retry in the background if it does not complete immediately. All file systems should be available before the Oracle Clusterware processes are started, and if this availability presents a difficulty, then the fg option may be specified, but bg should be sufficient in most cases.
vers	Specifies the version of NFS to use and should be set to version 3.
tcp	Uses the TCP protocol instead of UDP for NFS traffic.
actimeo	Increase the time-out interval for file attributes to be refreshed.

No additional kernel parameters above and beyond the standard settings detailed for Oracle installation are required to be modified for optimal NFS operations.

We recommend investigating a teamed NIC solution if a failover solution is required; this solution should be approached in exactly the same manner as a teamed interconnect configuration, described in Chapter 6. You can also team interfaces for increased bandwidth with the caveat that a single session cannot use more bandwidth than is available from a single interface. Before pursuing this approach, however, monitoring the bandwidth requirements of the application is important. The Filer At a Glance performance monitor is started from the top-level menu at the na_admin screen. This screen displays the data input being received and transmitted by the filer in KB/s and is, therefore, useful in determining whether increased bandwidth will be of benefit in a particular scenario.

Snapshot Backup and Recovery

One of the unique aspects of running an Oracle RAC cluster in a NetApp Filer environment is the ease with which you can create and use snapshots with no impact on performance, thereby enabling rapid backup and recovery capabilities to recover from scenarios such as user error. Reiterating that these capabilities are in addition to regular full backups to recover from scenarios such as hardware failure or database corruption is worthwhile. For either case, the database must be running in archive log mode.

Before configuring snapshots for Oracle backups, set the Scheduled Snapshots to zero so no hourly and nightly snapshots occur, as illustrated in Figure 7-16.

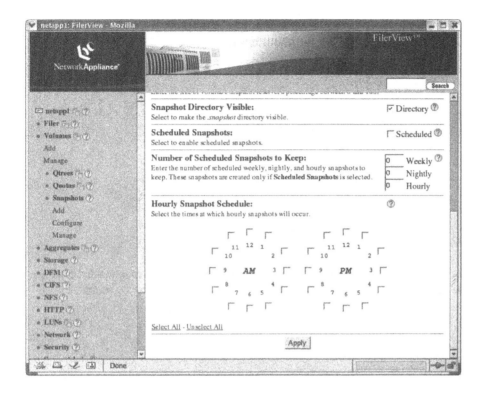

Figure 7-16. *Scheduled Snapshots*

To ensure a useable backup, place all of the Oracle tablespaces in hot backup mode, take a snapshot on the filer, and end the hot backup mode. To use these snapshots for hot backups, the best practice is to put the Oracle datafiles in a volume or a number of volumes, separate from control files and redo logs, to enable the snapshot to track the changes to the data files only. The following example assumes this case with the data files in the volume `oradata`:

```
#!/bin/bash
SNAPNAME=${ORACLE_SID}-`date +%Y%m%d%H%M%S`
sqlplus /nolog <<END1
CONNECT sys/oracle as sysdba
ALTER DATABASE BEGIN BACKUP;
EXIT
END1
rsh -l root netapp1 snap create oradata $SNAPNAME
sqlplus /nolog <<END2
CONNECT sys/oracle as sysdba
ALTER DATABASE END BACKUP;
EXIT
END2
```

Running this script presents the following output:

```
[oracle@london1 scripts]$ ./hotbackup.bash
SQL*Plus: Release 10.1.0.3.0 - Production on Wed Mar 2 13:24:38 2005
Copyright (c) 1982, 2004, Oracle.  All rights reserved.
SQL> Connected.
SQL>
```

```
Database altered.
SQL> Disconnected from Oracle Database 10g Enterprise Edition
 Release 10.1.0.3.0 - 64bit Production
With the Partitioning, Real Application Clusters, OLAP and Data Mining options
creating snapshot...
SQL*Plus: Release 10.1.0.3.0 - Production on Wed Mar 2 13:24:40 2005
Copyright (c) 1982, 2004, Oracle.  All rights reserved.
SQL> Connected.
SQL>
Database altered.
```

The created snapshot can now be viewed on the filer as follows:

```
[oracle@london1 scripts]$ rsh -l root netapp1 snap list oradata
Volume oradata
working...
  %/used       %/total  date          name
---------- ---------- ------------- --------
  0% ( 0%)    0% ( 0%)  Mar 02 13:28  RAC1-20050302132437
```

In the event of recovery being required, we recommend doing this process manually; however, for illustrative purposes, the commands required are summarized in the following script:

```bash
#!/bin/bash
srvctl stop database -d RAC
rsh -l root netapp1 snap list oradata
echo Enter snapshot to restore:
read SNAPNAME
echo $SNAPNAME
rsh -l root netapp1 snap restore -f -t vol -s $SNAPNAME oradata
srvctl start instance -i RAC1 -d RAC -o mount
sqlplus /nolog <<END
connect / as sysdba
set autorecovery on;
recover database;
exit
END
srvctl stop instance -i RAC1 -d RAC
srvctl start database -d RAC
```

From the script, you can see that to action the recovery you need to shut down the entire cluster and restore the snapshot on the filer. One instance is then started in mount mode and the database recovered. Then restarting the cluster is possible.

iSCSI

Before detailing iSCSI configuration on the filer, re-emphasizing the capability of the NetApp range to support multiple protocols simultaneously on the same filer is important. As we have discussed, NFS is a supported platform for a shared ORACLE_HOME and the Oracle Clusterware devices. We therefore recommend, if you're planning to use iSCSI with an Oracle RAC installation, that you take advantage of this ability and create iSCSI LUNs for use with raw devices, OCFS, or ASM, while maintaining the NFS ORACLE_HOME for the Oracle binaries.

Also note that, at the implementation level, iSCSI LUNs are, in fact, files resident within the WAFL file system on the filer. Therefore, taking an Oracle data file located on NFS and converting it into a LUN (so that it can subsequently be accessed by Oracle as a raw device bound to an iSCSI device) is entirely possible.

The following procedures detail the requirements to suitably configure iSCSI on the filer and Oracle nodes for an Oracle configuration. Although dedicated iSCSI HBAs are available and offer improved levels of performance, we cover the most widely used implementation: software-based iSCSI initiator. This software-based iSCSI initiator requires exactly the same hardware and operating system configurations listed for the NFS installation and requires no modification for the two protocols to coexist.

Before commencing with configuration, ensure that iSCSI is licensed on the NetApp Filer with the following command:

```
netapp1> license
            iscsi site GVCJHSI
```

At the time of this writing, the iSCSI license was available at no additional charge. Next, check the status of the iSCSI service.

```
netapp1> iscsi status
iSCSI service is not running
```

If the iSCSI service is not running, start it with the command `iscsi start`:

```
netapp1> iscsi start
iSCSI service started
Wed Mar  2 14:44:05 GMT [netapp1: iscsi.adapter.online:notice]:
ISCSI: iswta, Adapter brought online.
Wed Mar  2 14:44:05 GMT [netapp1: iscsi.service.startup:info]:
iSCSI service startup
```

Using the command `iscsi nodename` on the filer, list the iSCSI target of the filer to be input into the configuration files of the Oracle cluster nodes.

```
netapp1> iscsi nodename
iSCSI target nodename: iqn.1992-08.com.netapp:sn.50409193
```

At this point, create a volume using exactly the same process you used for creating a volume for NFS, but do not proceed with configuring an NFS export. For this example, we have precreated a volume called `oracleiscsi` of 20GB in size.

On the Oracle RAC nodes, iSCSI functionality is provided by the iSCSI Software Initiator (`iscsi_sfnet` driver module), and the `iscsi-initiator-utils` RPM package and is included on Red Hat and SUSE Enterprise Linux Releases. This RPM package provides the server daemon for the iSCSI protocol, as well as the utility programs needed to manage it. The Linux iSCSI Initiator implementation is the open source version of the Cisco closed source driver available for alternative platforms; booting from iSCSI disks is not supported with Cisco's software.

On the nodes are two files important to iSCSI configuration: `/etc/inititiatorname.iscsi` and `/etc/iscsi.conf`.

On every node in the cluster, `/etc/inititiatorname.iscsi` must be unique. Before configuration, the file will have the following contents:

```
[root@london1 root]# cat /etc/initiatorname.iscsi
GenerateName=yes
```

This ensures that when the iSCSI service is first started, it will generate a unique initiator name and should therefore be left unmodified.

Enter the following details into the file `/etc/iscsi.conf`. The following example shows the file configured for two target filers. Note that the `TargetName` string is entered from the output of the `iscsi nodename` run on the filer and that the `DiscoveryAddress` is a resolvable hostname, for example, entered into the `/etc/hosts` file:

```
[root@london1 root]# cat /etc/iscsi.conf
# =====================================================================
# iSCSI Configuration File Sample - see iscsi.conf(5)
# =====================================================================
Continuous=no
HeaderDigest=never
DataDigest=never
ImmediateData=yes
MaxDiskTimeOut=180
ConnFailTimeout=180
DiscoveryAddress=netapp1
DiscoveryAddress=netapp2
TargetName=iqn.1992-08.com.netapp.sn.50409193
TargetName=iqn.1992-08.com.netapp:sn.50409347
```

Start the iSCSI service with the following command:

```
[root@london1 root]# service iscsi start
```

This command starts the service and populates the file /etc/initiatorname.iscsi with
a unique initiator name. Note the initiator name for use in creating initiator groups on the filer.

```
[root@london1 root]# cat /etc/initiatorname.iscsi
## DO NOT EDIT OR REMOVE THIS FILE!
## If you remove this file, the iSCSI daemon will not start.
## If you change the InitiatorName, existing access control lists
## may reject this initiator.  The InitiatorName must be unique
## for each iSCSI initiator.  Do NOT duplicate iSCSI InitiatorNames.
InitiatorName=iqn.1987-05.com.cisco:01.28120eefe74
```

The most straightforward method of creating a LUN and the associated initiator group is with
the LUN Wizard started from the main menu. On the LUN Wizard welcome screen, click Next.

On the Specify LUN Parameters page, shown in Figure 7-17, enter the name of a LUN in an
existing volume.

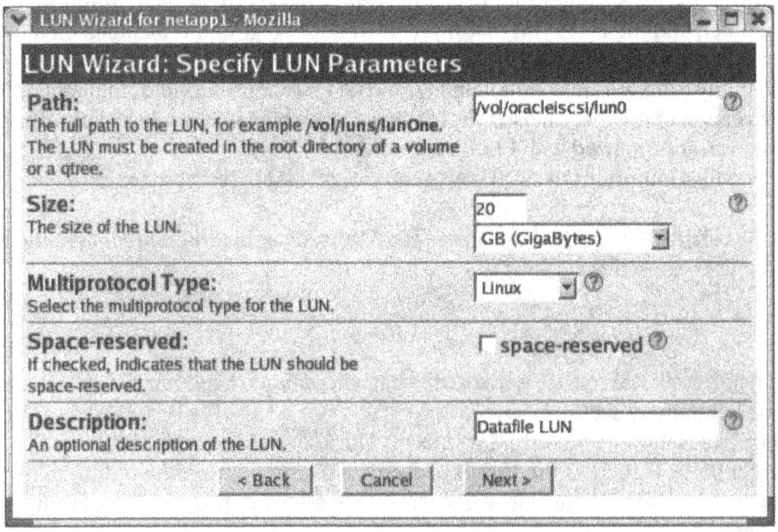

Figure 7-17. *Specify LUN Parameters*

Here you are creating lun0 to use all of the space in the precreated volume oracleiscsi. Select the protocol type Linux and deselect space-reserved. If space-reserved is enabled, you will reserve exactly double the size of the LUN in order that enough space will be available for snapshots. Enter a description for the LUN and click Next to proceed to the Add Initiator Groups page. The LUN Wizard prompts that no initiator groups have been added. Click Add Group to specify new group parameters, as shown in Figure 7-18.

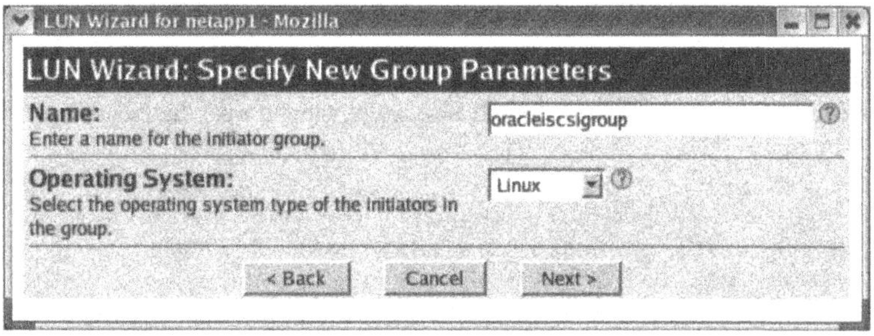

Figure 7-18. *Specify New Group Parameters*

Enter a name for the new initiator group, select Linux for the operating system, and click Next. The wizard prompts that no initiators have been added to the group. Select Add Initiator. Enter the initiator name as given in the file /etc/inititiatorname.isci on the first node in the RAC cluster and click Next. Repeat the process until all of the nodes have been added, as shown in Figure 7-19.

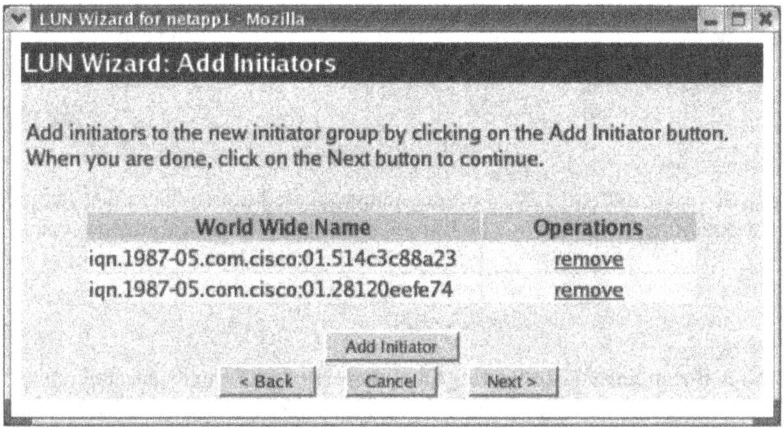

Figure 7-19. *Add Initiators*

When all of the nodes in the cluster have been added, click Next on the Add Initiators page, and click Next on the Add Initiator Groups page, which now shows the name of the new initiator group, to advance to the Specify LUN Mappings page. Enter a LUN ID or accept the default lowest ID and click Next. On the Commit Changes page, click Commit, and on the Success page, click Close Window.

The LUN has now been created and made available to the Oracle RAC nodes specified in the initiator group.

At the filer command line, the command show initiator will detail the connected initiators.

```
netapp1> iscsi show initiator
Initiators connected on adapter iswta:
  Tgt_PG  iSCSI Initiator Name / ISID
     4      iqn.1987-05.com.cisco:01.28120eefe74 / 00:02:3d:00:00:01
     4      iqn.1987-05.com.cisco.01.514c3c88a23 / 00:02:3d:00:00:01
Adapter iswtb operates on behalf of the partner host.
Use the partner command to view this adapter when in takeover mode.
```

Note that when creating subsequent LUNs, you can add these to the existing initiator group to present them to the same cluster.

On commit, the iSCSI LUN will be presented to the hosts and available for use, without needing to reboot the nodes or restart the iSCSI service. These LUNs can be viewed with the following iscsi-ls command:

```
root@london1 root]# iscsi-ls
*************************************************************************
        SFNet iSCSI Driver Version ... 3.6.2 (27-Sep-2004 )
*************************************************************************
TARGET NAME              : iqn.1992-08.com.netapp:sn.50409193
TARGET ALIAS             :
HOST NO                  : 4
BUS NO                   : 0
TARGET ID                : 0
TARGET ADDRESS           : 10.240.85.81:3260
SESSION STATUS           : ESTABLISHED AT Fri Mar  4 11:22:53 2005
NO. OF PORTALS           : 1
PORTAL ADDRESS 1         : 10.240.85.81:3260,4
SESSION ID               : ISID 00023d000001 TSID d2c
```

The LUNs will also now be viewable as standard SCSI disks and can be used in the same way as any SCSI device initially to be partitioned using the utilities fdisk and parted as described in Chapter 11.

```
[root@london1 etc]# cat /proc/scsi/scsi
Host: scsi3 Channel: 00 Id: 00 Lun: 00
  Vendor: NETAPP   Model: LUN            Rev: 0.2
Type:   Direct-Access                    ANSI SCSI revision: 04
```

Within the Filer at a Glance window, the iSCSI traffic is differentiated from NFS traffic by being shown in yellow, thereby enabling the monitoring of resources utilized by iSCSI within the system.

Summary

In this chapter, we reviewed the options for configuring the storage required for an Oracle RAC environment. We examined the characteristics of the I/O profile of RAC and looked at the fundamentals of storage common to all storage solutions available. We then reviewed the storage protocols available to us on Linux and the considerations to be made for both SAN and NAS solutions. Finally, we used a hands-on example to work through the stages of configuring both a popular SAN-based and a popular NAS-based solution to illustrate how these are put into practice in presenting storage to RAC.

CHAPTER 8

■■■

Oracle Cluster File System (OCFS)

In this chapter, we discuss the Oracle Cluster File System (OCFS), which is an open source cluster file system provided by Oracle for use with Linux, Windows, and, most recently, Solaris. In the following chapter, we will discuss ASM, which provides similar functionality, but also includes volume management capabilities, such as disk balancing and redundancy.

If you are using the Oracle Database 10*g* Standard Edition with the RAC option, then you are contractually obligated to use ASM for datafile storage. However, you may still wish to use OCFS version 2 to store shared Oracle home directories or other nondatabase files, as ASM cannot be used for this purpose.

Cluster File Systems and OCFS

A cluster file system allows all nodes in a cluster to concurrently access a storage device via a standard file system interface, which simplifies management of applications needing to run across the cluster at the expense of a slight decrease in performance.

Prior to the introduction of OCFS, shared storage for Oracle RAC databases was commonly implemented using raw devices, which remain the best-performing storage solution. Many sites still implement raw devices, particularly for single-instance databases. However, in an Oracle RAC database environment, raw devices have some limitations.

First, each datafile, online redo log, and control file must have a separate raw device. The maximum number of raw devices that can be configured is limited to 255 by the Linux operating system. The limitation on the number of raw devices restricts the physical number of datafiles that a database can contain and, consequently, limits the maximum physical size of a database.

Second, raw devices cannot be used for archived redo logs. Therefore, it is not possible to locate archived redo logs on shared storage. Instead, archived redo logs must be written to local disks and copied to other nodes on the network to guarantee recoverability.

Finally, Oracle databases implemented on raw devices can be inflexible and difficult for system administrators to manage. In a shared disk system using raw volumes, the administrator will see device names for individual volumes, but will not be able to see the actual datafiles and their attributes using standard file system tools such as df and mv. Some of this inflexibility can be overcome by using a good volume management tool, which can make the manipulation of the disk subsystem significantly easier and, in some cases, can allow disk maintenance to be performed on a live system without having to shut down the database.

In order to address these issues and encourage the deployment of RAC on Linux, Oracle initiated the OCFS open source project. OCFS is a shared disk cluster file system that is specifically designed to support Oracle RAC databases. It presents a consistent file system image across all nodes in the cluster.

OCFS has a number of advantages over raw devices. It has the look and feel of a regular file system, while simplifying administration by eliminating the need to manage raw devices directly. You do not need to create a raw partition for every file in the database and the upper limit of 255 raw devices does not apply.

OCFS can run on top of raw devices, Logical Volume Managers (LVMs), and logical partitions (LUNs) presented by storage area networks (SANs). However, OCFS cannot run on NFS file systems.

OCFS is also available for Windows. However, the internal implementation of OCFS on Windows is not compatible with the Linux implementation, and therefore, Linux and Windows nodes can never mount the same OCFS partition.

The first version of OCFS was released in December 2002 and allowed RAC users to run clustered databases without having to directly manage raw devices. The file system was designed to store database related files, such as datafiles, control files, redo logs, and archive logs. In addition, in Oracle 10.1 and above, OCFS version 1 could be used for both the OCR and the voting disk. However, OCFS version 1 did not support storage of Oracle binaries or configuration files and, consequently, could not be used for a shared Oracle home.

OCFS2 was released in September 2005 and was designed to be a general-purpose cluster file system. In addition to the database-related files, it can store Oracle binaries and configuration files, which allows the creation of a shared Oracle home, thus simplifying management of RAC clusters with a large number of nodes.

OCFS2 supports Context Dependent Symbolic Links (CDSLs). CDSLs allow a file or directory name to be shared by all nodes, but also allow the contents to differ for each node. This functionality is useful in a shared Oracle home environment, where the vast majority of files are identical for all nodes, but a handful, such as a customized listener.ora file, might vary between the nodes.

When comparing OCFS performance with other file system types, such as ext3, remember than OCFS uses direct I/O for all reads and writes, bypassing the operating system cache. In an ext3 file system, reads may be satisfied from the operating system cache, which is very efficient for cache hits. However, for cache misses, blocks have to be read from disk, and the block will be copied into both the operating system cache and the Oracle buffer cache, which requires more CPU and memory resources.

Unlike most Oracle software, OCFS is released under the GNU General Public License (GPL). OCFS support is provided to customers with an Oracle support license. Oracle will only support OCFS if it has been installed using binary RPMs compiled by Oracle for Red Hat and SUSE. You can download the source code, but you will not be supported by Oracle if you compile the sources locally, nor will OCFS be supported on platforms where the kernel has been recompiled.

OCFS Version 1

Version 1 of OCFS is designed to support the creation, deletion, movement, and backup of Oracle database files only. Supported file types include datafiles, control files, online redo logs, archived redo logs, the Oracle Cluster Registry (OCR), and the CSS voting disk. OCFS does not support some Oracle software, such as binary files or scripts, nor does it support non-Oracle files of any description.

OCFS is not intended to be a POSIX-compliant file system. Therefore, you cannot guarantee that the behavior of OCFS will be similar to that of other file systems, even on the same platform. The recommended backup and recovery tool for OCFS is RMAN. You can also use operating system utilities such as cp, dd, mv, and tar. However, in order to be able to access files on the OCFS partitions while the database is open, these utilities must support direct I/O. You can download upgraded versions of these utilities from Oracle's Open Source Support web site (http://oss.oracle.com).

You can use most other standard Linux operating system commands with OCFS, such as ls, cd, mkdir, rmdir, chown, chgrp, chmod, and pwd. You can also use I/O performance monitoring tools, such as sar, vmstat, and iostat.

OCFS only runs on the Linux 2.4 kernel and, at the time of this writing, is supported on Red Hat 2.1 AS, Red Hat EL 3.0, and SUSE SLES8. It is also supported on two Asian Unix variants: Red Flag DC Server 4.1 and Miracle Linux v3.0. On most Linux variants, OCFS is supported on three architectures: 32-bit (i686), 32-bit extensions (x86-64), and 64-bit (ia64).

From a performance point of view, OCFS without asynchronous I/O is not as efficient as raw devices. If you configure asynchronous I/O, which is available with OCFS versions 1.0.14 and above, then OCFS performance can be roughly equivalent to, or even slightly better than, raw devices.

OCFS Design Considerations

If you wish to optimize your use of OCFS, then you will be subject to a number of design constraints. Many of these are reminiscent of the best practices employed by DBAs in Oracle 6 and Oracle 7 to minimize disk fragmentation, because OCFS is primarily designed to support large continuous files. When a file is created in OCFS, it must occupy contiguous blocks in the file system. If the file is subsequently extended, then the new extent must also be contiguous, but need not necessarily adjoin the initial extent.

OCFS partitions are divided into equally sized blocks. Valid block sizes are 4KB, 8KB, 16KB, 32KB, 64KB, 128KB, 256KB, 512KB, and 1MB. For each OCFS partition, you need to calculate the optimum block size. As the block size increases, the maximum number of files that can be stored on an OCFS file system decreases. Overall performance increases, because more data is stored within each block, hence fewer disk seeks are required to read the same physical amount of data. Therefore, you are faced with a trade-off between a larger block size and the total number of files required. Typically, a larger block size can be used for applications, such as data warehouses, which perform a significant number of full table scans, whereas for an OLTP application, a smaller block size should be used.

Remember that your block size should be an even multiple of the block size of your disk subsystem to optimize the amount of I/O and minimize the amount of disk head movement from your storage devices.

Also, note that you cannot modify the block size after you have created the file system. If you wish to change the block size, you will need to delete and re-create the file system.

To determine the optimum block size, you need to understand the characteristics of the types of files you will be storing on each partition. In an OCFS partition, every file occupies one or more blocks. Even a file containing a single byte would occupy an entire block. However, this detail is not particularly important, as OCFS is designed to specifically support Oracle database files. With the possible exception of control files and server parameter files, most database files, including datafiles, online redo logs, and archived redo logs, will be larger than the 1MB maximum block size.

Storing all database files in a single OCFS partition is not a good idea, because each partition has a space allocation bitmap that must be locked every time a file is created or deleted. Manipulating a large number of locks in a file system, with a large number of files, means a lot of extra overhead in an individual file system, which, in turn, decreases I/O and overall performance. By adding multiple nodes accessing the same physical file system, you may cause unnecessary contention for the partition locks between nodes. The maximum number of OCFS partitions in a cluster is limited by the number of raw devices available on each node. However, each OCFS partition requires a dedicated daemon process on each node in the cluster, and consequently, most sites restrict the number of OCFS partitions to 10–20 to limit this overhead.

Storing archived redo logs in separate directories for each node is recommended. Using separate directories avoids contention for the space allocation bitmap in the OCFS file system if multiple nodes attempt to create archived logs simultaneously. While only one node should ever write archived redo logs to each OCFS file system, you may find that archived redo logs from more than one node appear in the same OCFS file system, because Oracle permits other nodes to archive redo for nodes that have been unavailable for extended periods. This functionality is required to ensure that any outstanding redo created by a failed node is archived in a timely fashion. It is particularly important if the node does not subsequently rejoin the cluster because of hardware failure or redeployment.

If your application generates large amounts of redo, and consequently, you anticipate I/O bottlenecks on the redo log disks, you might consider moving the online redo logs to OCFS partitions on dedicated or faster storage. You should avoid placing the online redo logs on the same OCFS partitions as the archived redo logs.

Placing online redo logs and the redo log archive point on the same physical file system causes contention. Every time a disk block is read from the online redo log, it must be physically rewritten to the same physical disk in the archive log file. In many poorly implemented databases, it is very apparent that performance drops when the archive log is written to the same file system that holds the online log. If the archiver process gets too far behind when writing archive redo logs, the performance of the database will be affected. We recommend that you pay close attention to your database design prior to implementation and that you carefully monitor disk read/write and I/O performance when the system is in production.

Oracle also recommends storing datafiles for tables and indexes in different OCFS file systems. Using separate file systems allows you to rebuild your indexes without affecting file systems containing tables.

The default block size of 128KB should be satisfactory for most OLTP systems, where each I/O typically involves a single Oracle block. In data warehousing environments, you may achieve performance improvements by increasing the file system block size in line with the underlying disk subsystem block size up to a limit of 1MB. In all cases, you should attempt to ensure that the Oracle extent sizes within the datafiles are aligned on a block boundary to minimize the number of physical I/Os required to read each block.

You can calculate the maximum number of files per partition using the following formula:

$$(< partition\_size > - 8MB) / < block\_size > = < max\_files >$$

For example, for a 200MB partition using the default 128KB block size, the maximum number of files is as follows:

$$(209{,}715{,}200 - 8{,}388{,}608) / 131{,}072 = 1{,}536 \text{ files}$$

This block size could be appropriate for archived redo logs. With the 128KB block size, files can vary in size from 128KB to 1TB.

For a similar partition, using the maximum 1MB block size, the maximum number of files is

$$(209{,}715{,}200 - 8{,}388{,}608) / 1{,}048{,}576 = 192$$

This block size should be appropriate for datafiles but might not be satisfactory for archived logs. The theoretical maximum size of an OCFS file is 8TB. In practice, however, this size is further limited by the Linux operating system to a maximum of 1TB. Therefore, with a 1MB block size, files can vary from 1MB to 1TB in size.

Conversely, the minimum partition size can be calculated using the following formula:

$$< block\_size > \times < max\_files > + < overhead > = < minimum\ partition\ size >$$

where the overhead is 8MB. Therefore, with a block size of 1,048,576 and a maximum of 192 files, the minimum partition size will be

$$1{,}048{,}576 \times 192 + 8{,}388{,}608 = 200MB$$

Installation and Configuration

Installation of OCFS does not require any additional kernel parameters over and above those required for the installation of the Oracle database.

OCFS can be downloaded from http://oss.oracle.com/projects/ocfs. Make sure you download the correct packages for your distribution and architecture. The following three packages are required:

- ocfs-support
- ocfs
- ocfs-tools

These can be installed using the RPM package, as shown in the following example:

```
london1 # rpm -Uvh ocfs-support-1.0.10-1.i386.rpm
london1 # rpm -Uvh ocfs-2.4.21EL-1.0.14-1.i686.rpm
london1 # rpm -Uvh ocfs-tools-1.0.10-1.i386.rpm
```

Alternatively, you can use the following command, which resolves any dependencies between the individual packages and installs them in the correct order:

```
london1 # rpm -Uvh ocfs*.rpm
```

The ocfs_support RPM installs the OCFS service, which should be started at levels 3, 4, and 5. The start and stop actions for the OCFS service are defined in the /etc/init.d/ocfs script. After installation, you can verify that the service has been correctly installed using

```
london1 # chkconfig --list ocfs
```

which should return

```
ocfs    0:off    1:off    2:off    3:on    4:on    5:on    6:off
```

Configuring OCFS

The OCFS service is configured using the /etc/ocfs.conf configuration file, which contains node-specific data and must be generated on each node in the cluster. It can be generated automatically using a GUI utility called ocfstool or created manually using a text editor and a command line utility called ocfs_uid_gen.

The parameters of /etc/ocfs.conf include the following:

- **node_name**: Specifies the server hostname.
- **ip_address**: Specifies the IP address to be used by OCFS. It must be possible to communicate with all nodes in this cluster via this IP address.
- **ip_port**: Specifies the IP port to be used by OCFS to communicate with other nodes in the cluster. This value must be the same on all nodes in the cluster. The default value is 7000.
- **comm_voting**: Specifies the voting method used by OCFS. If the value is 0, which is the default, then OCFS will use disk voting; if the value is 1, then OCFS will use network voting. We recommend you enable network voting, as it will improve the performance of various operating system commands. If OCFS is configured to use network voting, and the network becomes unavailable, then OCFS will fall back transparently to disk voting.
- **guid**: Specifies a 32-character hexadecimal string that must be generated on each node using ocfstool or ocfs_uid_gen. This string is required to uniquely identify the NIC on each host. It should never be updated manually.

To configure /etc/ocfs.conf manually, on each node create /etc/ocfs.conf:

```
#
# ocfs config
# Ensure this file exists in /etc
#
        node_name = london1-priv
        ip_address = 192.168.1.1
        ip_port = 7000
        comm_voting = 1
```

The ocfs_uid_gen shell script generates a GUID that is a 128-bit value that uniquely identifies the node to OCFS. The first 80 bits are generated using the /dev/urandom pseudodevice and should, in theory, be unique for each node. The remaining 48 bits are the MAC address of the NIC used by the interconnect. The script takes the following parameters:

```
Usage:          ocfs_uid_gen -c [ -f ]
                ocfs_uid_gen -r

-c      Create a new GUID for a new node before it enters the cluster
-f      Force - overwrite any existing GUID in the configuration file
-r      Recover the GUID, inserting the new MAC address. This operation is only for
        existing nodes whose MAC address has been changed
```

To generate a GUID for a manually created /etc/ocfs.conf use the following command:

```
london1 # ocfs_uid_gen -c -f
```

This command will append a GUID to /etc/ocfs.conf:

```
#
# ocfs config
# Ensure this file exists in /etc
#
        node_name = london1-priv
        ip_address = 192.168.1.1
        ip_port = 7000
        comm_voting = 1
        guid = E000F0A38E7144223D7B0040F4BB2E4C
```

If you subsequently need to reconfigure or replace the NIC, then you will need to regenerate the MAC address portion of the guid using

```
london1 # ocfs_uid_gen -r
```

Starting the OCFS Service

The first time you start OCFS after installation, you can use the following script:

```
london1 # /sbin/load_ocfs
```

The following script calls the insmod command to load the ocfs module into the kernel specifying the appropriate parameters:

```
Mar 21 21:37:40 london1 load_ocfs: /sbin/insmod ocfs node_name=london1-priv
ip_address=192.168.1.1 cs=1808 guid=E000F0A38E7144223D7B0040F4BB2E4C
comm_voting=1 ip_port=7000
```

Once you have fully configured OCFS, the recommended way to start the OCFS service is to run the /etc/init.d/ocfs script with the start option. You can run this script either directly or using the following command:

```
london1 # service ocfs start
```

If any OCFS file systems are defined in /etc/fstab, the service will load the ocfs module into the kernel and then mount the configured OCFS file systems.

Note that /etc/init.d/ocfs takes a number of parameters including start, link, status, stop, force_reload, and restart. The status option reports whether the OCFS service is currently loaded:

```
london1 # service ocfs status
Checking if OCFS is loaded:                                    [ OK ]
```

The link option will attempt to load the ocfs module into the kernel, if it is not already loaded. The stop, force_reload, and restart options are all dummy options that have no effect.

The OCFS module creates a daemon process called ocfslsnr on each node. In addition, it creates one daemon process for each OCFS file system. These daemon processes are named ocfsnm-0, ocfsnm-1, ocfsnm-2, and so on and are owned by the root user.

Formatting an OCFS Partition

The /sbin/mkfs.ocfs utility builds an OCFS file system on a device or partition. It must be executed by the root user. To avoid overwriting data, mkfs.ocfs will not format a partition that is currently mounted by any node.

The disk must be formatted on one node only. Once the disk has been formatted, it is available for use and can be mounted by any number of nodes in the cluster.

Before running the utility, you must create the logical partition either on a disk or on shared storage. The partition must be a minimum of 200MB in size.

To display the help message for mkfs.ocfs, use

```
london1 # mkfs.ocfs -h
```

This displays the following message:

```
usage: mkfs.ocfs -b block_size [-C] [-F] [-g gid] [-h] -L volume-label -m mount-path
[-n] [-p permissions] [-q] [-u uid] [-V] device
        -b Block size in kilobytes
        -C Clear all data blocks
        -F Force format existing OCFS volume
        -g GID for the root directory
        -h Help
        -L Volume label
        -m Path where this device will be mounted
        -n Query only
        -p Permissions for the root directory
        -q Quiet execution
        -u UID for the root directory
        -V Print version and exit
```

The -C option forces mkfs.ocfs to format all blocks in the partition. Depending on the size of the partition, this process can take a long time.

The -F option forces reformatting of a partition that has previously been formatted for OCFS.

The -b option specifies the block size in kilobytes. If you do not specify this option, then the default value of 128KB will be used. Remember that the disk subsystem block size, OCFS block size, and database block size should all be even multiples of each other to avoid inducing performance problems in the database.

For example, the following is a typical mount command that forces the formatting of an OCFS volume on device /dev/sda1 with a block size of 128KB; the volume is then mounted on directory /u02 with an owner of oracle, group of dba, and permissions of rwxrwxr-x:

```
london1 # mkfs.ocfs -F -b 128 -g dba -u oracle -m /u02 -p 775 /dev/sda1
```

Mounting OCFS File Systems

OCFS file systems can be mounted manually using the mount command or automatically when the system is booted by configuring /etc/fstab. To mount a file system manually, use the mount command specifying the device and mount directory:

```
london1 # mount -t ocfs /dev/sda1 /u02
```

The mount point, in this case /u02, must be precreated as in the following example:

```
london1 # mkdir /u02
```

To mount the OCFS file system automatically, add the following entry to /etc/fstab:

```
/dev/sda1     /u02    ocfs    netdev   0   0
```

The partition can then be mounted using the command

```
london1 # mount /u02
```

In addition, the OCFS file system will be automatically mounted when the system is rebooted.

For OCFS file systems, the mount options field in /etc/fstab should contain the value _netdev, which specifies that the device requires network access and prevents the system from mounting the file system during a reboot until networking has been enabled.

If you are using a SAN, you may experience problems with device names when LUNs are added or dropped from the SAN, for example, when disks are added to the array. When the LUN assignment is changed, the device IDs can appear to be different to the host, which is known as *device name slippage*. If the LUN assignment changes without a corresponding change on each host, the operating system will not be able to identify and prepare the mount points for Oracle. Device name slippage can lead to a failure to restart the database or, in the event that the devices are mounted with the incorrect LUN assignments, corruption of the database files.

In the previous example, if a new LUN is added to the SAN, the device name /dev/sda1, which is currently used by the OCFS file system, may be reassigned by the new LUN, and the OCFS file system may be relocated to a different device name, such as /dev/sdb1.

To avoid device name slippage, you can specify a volume label when you create the file system and then mount the OCFS file system using that label. The volume label is independent of the device name. When the OS boots and the mount process begins, the disk label is checked against the list of names in /etc/fstab. The mount process will only mount file systems that it recognizes. If you have scripts that automatically start the database upon reboot, the database will fail to start, because the file systems it needs will not be mounted.

You can specify a volume label when you format the OCFS file system with the mkfs.ocfs command:

```
london1 # mkfs.ocfs -F -b 128 -g dba -u oracle -L u02 -m /u02 -g 775 /dev/sda1
```

In the previous example, we created an OCFS file system on device /dev/sda1 that will be mounted on directory /u02. In this example, we used the label u02. Specifying the same name for the label and the mount point is normal administrative practice.

The OCFS file system can now be mounted manually by specifying the mount point and the volume label as follows:

```
london1 # mount -t ocfs -L uO2 /uO2
```

To mount the OCFS file system automatically using the volume label, add the following entry to /etc/fstab:

```
LABEL=uO2    /uO2    ocfs    netdev    0    0
```

The OCFS file system can then be mounted by specifying the command

```
london1 # mount /uO2
```

Alternatively, you can mount the OCFS file system by specifying the following label:

```
london1 # mount -L uO2
```

In addition, the OCFS file system will be automatically mounted when the system is rebooted. Note that /etc/fstab and the mount command are now completely independent of the device name (/dev/sda1).

Backup and Recovery

The recommended backup and recovery tool for systems using OCFS is RMAN. However, you should be aware that if you need to use RMAN to restore a file after a media failure, RMAN will search for a contiguous space in the OCFS file system. If there is not a large enough contiguous space to restore the data, because of file fragmentation, the restore operation will fail. OCFS currently has no defragmentation tool. In the worst-case scenario, you may have to defragment a partition before you restore. If so, you may need to copy all the files (or the individual file, if you know it) to another file system using either RMAN or operating system utilities.

Tools and Utilities

OCFS is supported by a number of tools and utilities that are supplied in the ocfs-tools and ocfs-support packages. These tools and utilities are described in the following sections.

ocfstool

The ocfstool is a GUI configuration utility for managing OCFS file systems. It can generate the OCFS configuration file, format file systems, mount and unmount volumes, and display information about file systems and individual files.

In order to execute ocfstool, you must be logged on as the root user in an X Windows–based GUI environment. The DISPLAY environment variable must be correctly set to point you to the machine where you plan to execute ocfstool. The default value of :0.0 is satisfactory if you are executing ocfstool on a local system.

When you start ocfstool, two panes are displayed (Figure 8-1).

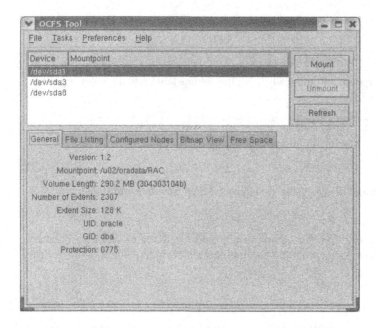

Figure 8-1. *The OCFS Tool General tab*

The upper pane lists all known OCFS-formatted partitions and allows you to mount and unmount them.

The lower pane includes the following five tabs that display information about the OCFS file system currently selected in the upper window:

- General
- File Listing
- Configured Nodes
- Bitmap View
- Free Space

The General tab shows the version, mount point, volume size, number of extents, block size, and ownership information.

You can edit this information by selecting Preferences from the top menu and Advanced from the submenu to display an Edit button. This button allows you to update the information on the General tab.

The File Listing tab, shown in Figure 8-2, displays a tree listing of all directories and files in the selected file system. For each file, it displays the node currently mastering the file, the actual size of the file, the amount of space the file occupies in the file system, file permissions, and a list of the nodes that have opened the file.

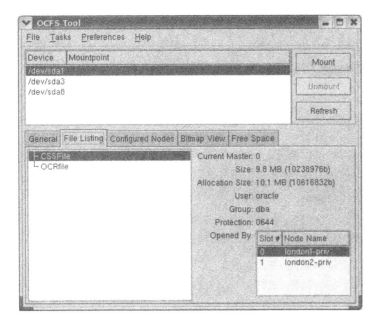

Figure 8-2. *The OCFS Tool File Listing tab*

The Configured Nodes tab (Figure 8-3) lists all nodes that are currently using the file system.

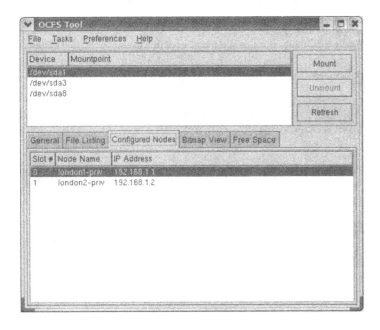

Figure 8-3. *The OCFS Tool Configured Nodes tab*

The Bitmap View tab (Figure 8-4) displays the extents that are currently used and free in the file system; used extents are colored blue (i.e., darker gray in Figure 8-4).

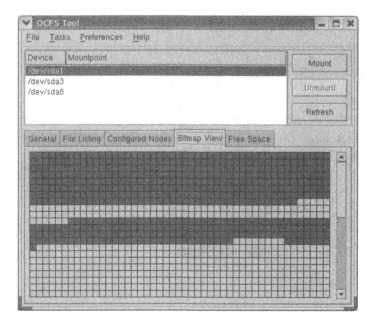

Figure 8-4. *The OCFS Tool Bitmap View tab*

The information in this view is derived from the bitmap allocation table. The Bitmap View gives you a visual representation of the level of extent fragmentation in the file system. Knowing the level of fragmentation in an OCFS file system is important, as contiguous space must be available to create or extend files; otherwise the operation will fail.

Finally, the Free Space tab (Figure 8-5) shows the size and location of free extents in the file system.

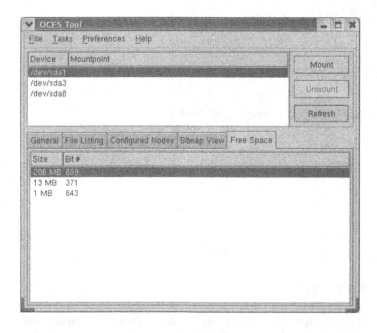

Figure 8-5. *The OCFS Tool Free Space tab*

You can use ocfstool to generate the OCFS configuration file (/etc/ocfs.conf). To generate an initial configuration, select Tasks ➤ Generate Config. This will display the OCFS Generate Config dialog box (Figure 8-6).

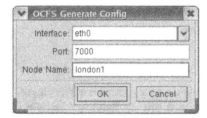

Figure 8-6. *The OCFS Tool Generate Config dialog box*

The Generate Config dialog box prompts for the name of the network interface, the port number, and the node name. Note that the network interface, which is not stored in the configuration file, is used to derive the IP address, which is stored in the configuration file. All nodes should be accessible from the specified network interface.

You can select any unused IP port number for OCFS. However, all nodes should use the same port number.

The ocfstool will automatically generate a new GUID and append it to /etc/ocfs.conf. However, ocfstool will not allow a new configuration file to be generated if one already exists. You can also create the OCFS configuration file using a text editor and then update the GUID with the ocfs_uid_gen utility.

You can also format OCFS file systems using ocfstool. To format a new file system, select Tasks ➤ Format. The OCFS format dialog box (Figure 8-7) will be displayed.

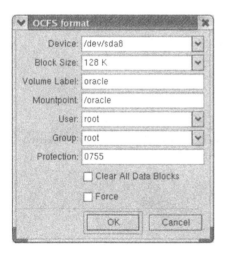

Figure 8-7. *The OCFS Tool format dialog box*

The OCFS format dialog box prompts for device name, block size, volume label, mount point, and file permissions.

If you check the Clear All Data Blocks box, all blocks will be reinitialized during the formatting process. Selecting this option will make the process significantly slower for larger OCFS file systems, since every block must be written back to disk.

If you have previously formatted the partition as an OCFS file system, you should check the Force box to ensure that any existing data blocks and metadata are reinitialized.

■**Note** You can also use the mkfs.ocfs utility to format OCFS file systems.

You can resize an OCFS file system using ocfstool. By default, the resize option is not displayed, so you must manually enable it by selecting Preferences ➤ Advanced. You can then select Tasks ➤ Resize.

The OCFS Resize dialog box (Figure 8-8) allows you to specify an existing OCFS file system to resize. We recommend that you use the resizeocfs or the synonymous tuneocfs command line utility to resize OCFS file systems, as these allow you to specify the volume size. By default, the tool will use all of the available disk on the volume.

Figure 8-8. *The OCFS Tool Resize dialog box*

fsck.ocfs

The fsck.ocfs utility can be used to check an OCFS file system on a specified partition. The syntax of fsck.ocfs is as follows:

```
usage: fsck.ocfs [options] device
         -n       No heartbeat check
         -w       Writeable
         -V       Version
         -v       verbose
         -q       Quiet
```

By default, fsck.ocfs will perform a read-only check. If you wish fsck.ocfs to fix any errors that it encounters, you must specify the following -w option:

```
london1 # fsck.ocfs -w /dev/sda8
```

To specify the -w option, the OCFS file system must be unmounted by all nodes.

mounted.ocfs

You can use mounted.ocfs to check which nodes are currently mounting a specific device:

```
london1 # /sbin/mounted.ocfs /dev/sda1
Device:  /dev/sda1
Label:/u02/oradata/RAC
Id:BA77B9A6587A17722D288F6B198F7D0C
Nodes:london1-priv, london2-priv
```

resizeocfs

The resizeocfs utility is a symbolic link to the tuneocfs utility. See the following section for further details.

tuneocfs

Use tuneocfs to accomplish the following:

- Change filesystem metadata, such as file permissions.
- Resize existing OCFS volumes.
- List and clear node configuration slots.

The syntax of tuneocfs is

```
usage:  tuneocfs [-F] [-g gid] [-h] [-l] [-n] [-N nodenum] [-p permissions] [-q]
[-S size] [-u uid] [-V] device
        -F       Force resize existing OCFS volume
        -g       Group ID for the root directory to gid
        -h       Help
        -l       List all the node configuration slots
        -n       Query only
        -N       Specifies node configuration slot to be cleared
        -p       Change permissions for the root directory
        -q       Quiet execution
        -S       Set volume size for root directory
                 e.g. 50G (M for mega, G for giga, T for tera)
        -u       Change user ID for the root directory
        -V       Print version and exit
```

As stated earlier, you can use tuneocfs to resize an OCFS file system. The file system must be unmounted on all nodes before it can be resized, meaning that the database must be shut down or that all tablespaces and/or datafiles using the file system must be offline.

We recommend that you create a full backup of all files in the OCFS file system before you perform a resize operation.

Use the following to increase the size of a file system:

```
london1 # tuneocfs -S 210M /dev/sda8
Increasing volume size from 209715200 bytes to 220200960 bytes
Increasing number of blocks from 1585 to 1665
Proceed (y/N): y
Changes written to disk
```

If you do not specify a size, then the size of the file system will be increased to include all blocks on the logical partition. You can also decrease the size of a file system as follows:

```
london1 # tuneocfs -S 200M /dev/sda8
Decreasing volume size from 222050304 bytes to 209715200 bytes
```

```
Decreasing number of blocks from 1679 to 1585
Proceed (y/N): y
Changes written to disk
```

Each node that accesses a file system reserves a node configuration slot. If you subsequently delete the node or assign it to another cluster, the node configuration slot will remain occupied. Therefore, manually clearing all OCFS node configuration slots whenever you delete or reassign a node is good practice.

To list the existing node configuration slots use the following:

```
london1 # tuneocfs -l /dev/sda1
# Name          IP Address    IP Port  Node GUID
=============   ===========   ======   ==================================
0 london1-priv  192.168.1.1    7000    E000F0A38E7144223D7B0040F4BB2E4C
1 london2-priv  192.168.1.2    7000    CCA341DE7627878F25930040F4BB2E50
```

You can also clear a specific node configuration slot. The following example clears slot number 2:

```
london1 # tuneocfs -N 2 /dev/sda1
```

ocfsextfinder

To print a list of unused extents, use `ocfsextfinder`. This information can also be found for the specified device in the Free Space tab in `ocfstool`.

Debugging and Tracing OCFS

OCFS Version 1 is a relatively new product, but it has become quite stable and reliable since its release. Encountering bugs in OCFS itself is rare. However, in our experience, OCFS does not always detect or report errors in lower layers of the storage infrastructure, for example, incorrect configuration of the network fabric, which can lead to subsequent, apparently unexplained media failures. If you intend to use OCFS on a SAN then, in our opinion, understanding and monitoring the current condition of that SAN is essential. In particular, monitor for failed disks, fiber cards, network cards, and switches. Do not rely on OCFS to report back underlying problems, as it does not necessarily have sufficient functionality to interpret them.

A couple of useful tools are provided to allow you to debug and trace OCFS. These may help in diagnosing any underlying problems with a particular file system.

Debugging OCFS

The `debugocfs` tool can be used to diagnose problems. It allows you to extract metadata information from OCFS partitions.

The `debugocfs` tool takes the following options:

```
usage: debugocfs [-?] [-h] [-g] [-l] [-v range] [-p range]
[-d /dir/name] [-f /file/name [-s /path/to/file]] [-a range] [-A range]
[-b range] [-B range] [-r range] [-c range] [-L range] [-M range]
[-n nodenum] /dev/name
        -h:     volume header
        -g:     global bitmap
        -l:     full listing of all file entries
        -v:     vote sector
        -2:     print 8-byte number as 2 4-byte numbers
        -p:     publish sector
        -d:     first ocfs_dir_node structure for a given path
```

```
-D:     all ocfs_dir_node structures for a given path
-f:     ocfs_file_entry structure for a given file
-F:     ocfs_file_entry and ocfs_extent_group structures for a given file
-s:     suck file out to a given location
-a:     file allocation system file
-A:     dir allocation system file
-b:     file allocation bitmap system file
-B:     dir allocation bitmap system file
-r:     recover log file system file
-c:     cleanup log system file
-L:     vol metadata log system file
-M:     vol metadata system file
-n:     perform action as node number given
/dev/name:  readable device
range:  node numbers to inspect (0-31)
            commas and dashes ok e.g. 0-3,5,14-17
```

To display the usage message, use

```
london1 # debugocfs -help
```

The following example dumps the volume header for the OCFS file system on device
/dev/sda1:

```
london1 # debugocfs -h /dev/sda1
```

Dump the voting sector using the following command:

```
london1 # debugocfs -v /dev/sda1
```

and dump a list of all files using

```
london1 # debugocfs -l /dev/sda1
```

To dump the file entry structure for a specific file, use

```
london1 # debugocfs -f <pathname> <device>
```

For example, the following command dumps the file entry structure for the file /oradata/RAC/
ts01.dbf on device /dev/sda1:

```
london1 # debugocfs -f /oradata/RAC/ts01.dbf' /dev/sda1
```

Note that the pathname is relative to the mount point of the OCFS file system, not to the root
directory of the node. In the previous example, the mount point of the OCFS file system is /u03 and,
consequently, the full pathname of the specified file is /u03/oradata/RAC/ts01.dbf.

Tracing OCFS

You can also enable tracing for OCFS. Trace messages will be written to /var/log/messages. OCFS
tracing must be enabled by the root user. To enable OCFS tracing, use

```
london1 # echo -1 > /proc/sys/kernel/ocfs/debug_level
london1 # echo -1 > /proc/sys/kernel/ocfs/debug_context
```

To disable OCFS tracing again, use

```
london1 # echo 0 > /proc/sys/kernel/ocfs/debug_level
london1 # echo 0 > /proc/sys/kernel/ocfs/debug_context
```

Note that OCFS tracing writes a significant amount of data to /var/log/messages and can easily fill up the destination file system over time, causing additional problems. Therefore, we recommend that you do not enable OCFS tracing permanently in /etc/sysctl.conf.

Operating System Utilities

OCFS uses direct I/O. Any utility that performs I/O on an OCFS file system must use direct I/O to read and write data blocks. RMAN automatically uses direct I/O on OCFS file systems. However, other utilities, including cp, dd, mv, and tar, do not use direct I/O by default. If you wish to use these utilities against an OCFS file system, you must download the following updated versions of these commands from the Oracle coreutils project, which can be found at http://oss.oracle.com/projects/coreutils:

- **coreutils**: Includes cp, dd, mv, and a number of other core utilities
- **tar**: Includes only the tar executable

Make sure that you download the correct packages for your distribution and architecture. Install them using the RPM utility, as in the following example:

```
london1 # rpm -Uvh coreutils-4.5.3-41.386.rpm
london1 # rpm -Uvh tar-1.13.25-16.i386.rpm
```

When using the updated commands (cp, dd, mv, and tar), you must specify the direct I/O option whenever you use these utilities to read or write blocks from datafiles that reside in the OCFS file system. The basic syntax for these commands is as follows:

```
cp --o_direct <source> <destination>
dd --o_direct  if=<source> of=<destination>
mv --o_direct <source> <destination>
tar --o_direct -cfv <archive> <source_files>
```

Early versions of the dd utility used direct=yes instead of the --o_direct option that is now standardized across all utilities.

OCFS Version 2 (OCFS2)

OCFS2 is an extent-based, POSIX-compliant cluster file system. OCFS2 is an all-purpose file system that can be used for shared Oracle home installations, simplifying management of a RAC cluster.

OCFS2 has a number of new features including context dependent symbolic links; file system journaling; improved performance of file metadata operations, such as space allocation; improved data caching; and locking for files, such as the Oracle binaries and libraries.

Installation and Configuration

Installation of OCFS2 does not require the addition or modification of any kernel parameters beyond those required for the installation of the Oracle database, as described in Chapter 11.

OCFS2 only runs on the Linux 2.6 kernel. If you are running SUSE Linux Enterprise Server 9 (SLES9) Update 2 or above, OCFS2 will be bundled into the software distribution. If you are running an earlier version of SLES9, then you will need to upgrade to Update 2 and install the ocfs2-tools and ocfsconsole packages.

If you are running Red Hat Enterprise Linux 4 (RHEL4), then OCFS2 will not be bundled. You will have to download the appropriate packages from the Oracle web site (http://oss.oracle.com/projects/ocfs2). Make sure you download the correct packages for your operating system distribution and hardware architecture. The following three packages are required:

- ocfs2
- ocfs2-tools
- ocfs2console

The ocfs2-tools package contains the command line tools, which are mandatory in this version of OCFS. The ocfs2console package contains a GUI front end for the tools. Installation of the latter package is optional, but recommended for ease of use. These can be installed using the RPM package, as follows:

```
london1 # rpm -Uvh ocfs2-2.6.9-22.0.1.ELsmp-1.0.8-1.i686.rpm
london1 # rpm -Uvh ocfs2-tools-1.0.2-1.i386.rpm
london1 # rpm -Uvh ocfs2console-1.0.2-1.i386.rpm
```

Alternatively, you can use the following command, which resolves any dependencies between the packages and then installs them in the correct order:

```
london1 # rpm -Uvh ocfs2*.rpm
```

The ocfs2 RPM installs the o2cb service, which starts the OCFS2 daemon processes and is defined by the /etc/init.d/o2cb script. This service should be started at levels 2, 3, 4, and 5. You can verify that the service has been correctly installed using

```
london1 # chkconfig --list o2cb
```

which should return the following output:

```
o2cb    0:off   1:off   2:on    3:on    4:on    5:on    6:off
```

Configuring OCFS 2

The OCFS service is configured using the /etc/ocfs2/cluster.conf configuration file. This file should be the same on each node and contain details of every node in the cluster. New nodes can be added to the cluster dynamically, but any other change, such as a new node name or IP address, requires a restart of the entire cluster in order to update information that has been cached on each node.

Oracle recommends that you use the ocfs2console GUI utility to create the cluster configuration in /etc/ocfs2/cluster.conf and then propagate the configuration to all other nodes in the cluster. The utility uses ssh to propagate the files; therefore, ssh must be set up in advance, so that the keys to each node are authorized without prompting for a password.

To run the utility, start an X Window session and log in as root:

```
london1 # ocfs2console
```

The window shown in Figure 8-9 will be displayed.

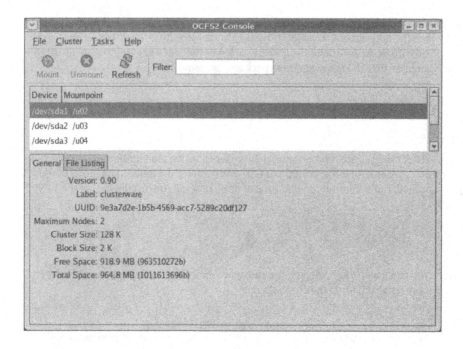

Figure 8-9. *The OCFS2 Console General tab*

Select Cluster ➤ Configure Nodes. If a cluster configuration file does not already exist, then a new file called /etc/ocfs2/cluster.conf will be created with a default cluster name of ocfs2.

To add nodes to the cluster, click the Add button in the Node Configuration dialog box (Figure 8-10), and the Add Node dialog box will be displayed (Figure 8-11).

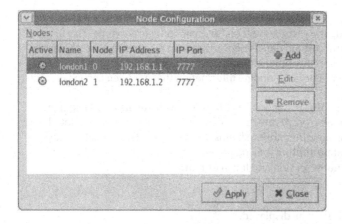

Figure 8-10. *The OCFS2 Console Node Configuration dialog box*

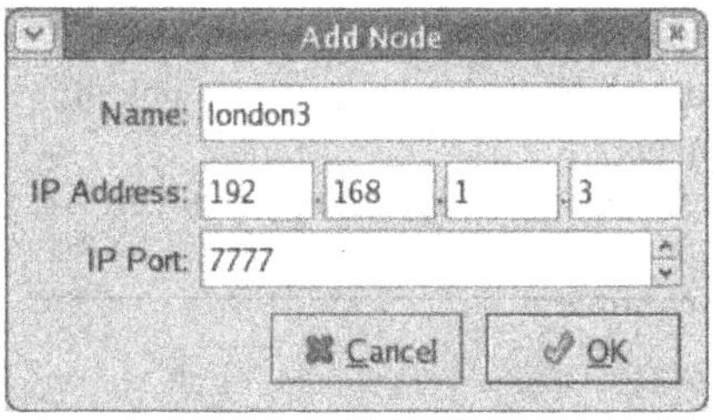

Figure 8-11. *The OCFS2 Console Add Node dialog box*

For each node, enter the node name, IP address, and IP port number (the default port number is 7777). There can be a maximum of 255 nodes in the cluster.

When you have added all the nodes, you can propagate the configuration to the other nodes by selecting Cluster ➤ Propagate Configuration from the submenu. Alternatively, you can copy the configuration file to the other nodes manually.

For example, a two-node cluster the /etc/ocfs2/cluster.conf configuration file might contain the following entries:

```
node:
        ip_port = 7777
        ip_address = 192.168.1.1
        number = 0
        name = london1
        cluster = ocfs2

node:
        ip_port = 7777
        ip_address = 192.168.1.2
        number = 1
        name = london2
        cluster = ocfs2

cluster:
        node_count = 2
        name = ocfs2
```

The /etc/ocfs2/cluster.conf file contains the following two sections:

- The cluster section includes

    - **node_count**: Specifies the maximum number of nodes in the cluster.

    - **name**: Defaults to ocfs2.

- The node section includes

    - **ip_port**: The IP port to be used by OCFS to communicate with other nodes in the cluster. This value must be identical on every node in the cluster. The default value is 7777.

    - **ip_address**: The IP address to be used by OCFS. The network must be configured in advance of the installation to communicate with all nodes in this cluster via this IP address.

    - **number**: The node number, which is assigned sequentially from 0 to 254.

    - **name**: The server hostname.

    - **cluster**: The name of cluster.

The o2cb Service

OCFS2 has its own cluster stack called o2cb. This stack includes a number of components including a node manager, heartbeat service, and distributed lock manager.

The /etc/init/o2cb script performs most OCFS2 management operations, many of which require the cluster to be online.

You can manually configure OCFS2 using the following command:

```
london1 # /etc/init/o2cb configure
Configuring the O2CB driver.

This will configure the on-boot properties of the O2CB driver.
The following questions will determine whether the driver is loaded on
boot. The current values will be shown in brackets ('[]'), Hitting
<ENTER> without typing an answer will keep that current value. Ctrl-C
will abort.

Load O2CB driver on boot (y/n) [n] :y
Cluster to start on boot (Enter "none" to clear) [ocfs2]:
Writing O2CB configuration: OK
Loading module "configfs": OK
Creating directory '/config': OK
Mounting configfs filesystem at /config: OK
Loading module "ocfs2_nodemanager" : OK
Loading module "ocfs2_dlm": OK
Loading module "ocfs2_dlmfs": OK
Creating directory '/dlm': OK
Mounting ocfs2_dlmfs filesystem at /dlm: OK
Starting cluster ocfs2: OK
```

If the cluster is online before you load the O2CB driver, the following messages will be displayed:

```
Load O2CB driver on boot (y/n) [n] :y
Cluster to start on boot (Enter "none" to clear) [ocfs2]:
Writing O2CB configuration: OK
Cluster ocfs2 already online
```

To use the OCFS2 file system, the o2cb modules must be loaded. If you have not configured the modules to load automatically upon system start-up, you can load them manually using the following command:

```
london1 # /etc/init.d/o2cb load
Loading module "configfs": OK
Mounting configfs filesystem at /config: OK
Loading module "ocfs2_nodemanager": OK
Loading module "ocfs2_dlm": OK
Loading module "ocfs2_dlmfs": OK
Mounting ocfs2_dlmfs filesystem at /dlm: OK
```

If you need to manually unload the modules, you can use the following command:

```
london1 # /etc/init.d/o2cb unload
Unmounting ocfs2_dlmfs filesystem: OK
Unloading module "ocfs2_dlmfs": OK
Unmounting configfs filesystem: OK
Unloading module "configfs": OK
```

You can bring the cluster service online and take it offline again. To bring the cluster file system online, use the following command:

```
london1 # /etc/init.d/o2cb online [cluster_name]
```

To bring cluster ocfs2 online, use

```
london1 # /etc/init.d/o2cb online ocfs2
Starting cluster ocfs2: OK
```

Use the following command to take the cluster file system offline:

```
/etc/init.d/o2cb offline [cluster_name]
```

For example, to take the cluster ocfs2 offline again, use

```
/etc/init.d/o2cb offline ocfs2
Cleaning headerbeat on ocfs2: OK
Stopping cluster ocfs2: OK
```

You can manually start the OCFS2 service using the following command:

```
london1 # /etc/init.d/o2cb start [cluster_name]
```

For example, to restart the cluster, use

```
london1 # /etc/init.d/o2cb start ocfs2
Loading module "configfs": OK
Mounting configfs filesystem at /config: OK
Loading module "ocfs2_nodemanager": OK
Loading module "ocfs2_dlm": OK
Loading module "ocfs2_dlmfs": OK
Mounting ocfs2_dlmfs filesystem at /dlm: OK
Starting cluster ocfs2: OK
```

The o2cb start command loads the modules and then brings the cluster file system online. To stop the OCFS2 service, use

```
london1 # /etc/init.d/o2cb stop [cluster_name]
```

For example, to stop a cluster called ocfs2, use

```
london1 # /etc/init.d/o2cb stop ocfs2
Checking heartbeat on ocfs2: OK
Stopping cluster ocfs2: OK
Unmounting ocfs2_dlmfs filesystem: OK
Unloading module "ocfs2_dlmfs": OK
Unmounting configfs filesystem: OK
Unloading module "configfs": OK
```

The o2cb command takes the cluster file system offline and unloads the modules. To check the current status of a RAC cluster, you can use the following command:

```
london1 # /etc/init.d/o2cb status
Module "configfs": Loaded
Filesystem "configfs": Mounted
Module "ocfs2_nodemanager": Loaded
Module "ocfs2_dlm": Loaded
Module "ocfs2_dlmfs": Loaded
Filesystem "ocfs2_dlmfs": Mounted
Checking cluster ocfs2: Online
Checking heartbeat: Not active
```

Formatting an OCFS2 Partition

The o2cb service must be running to format a partition. The o2cb service checks and verifies that the volume is not currently mounted before the format will be allowed to execute. Volumes can be formatted using either the ocfs2console tool or the mkfs.ocfs2 command line tool.

The disk must be formatted on one node only. Before formatting the disk, you must create the logical partition on a disk or shared storage system and provision it in such a way that every node in the cluster has read/write access to the shared disk. Once the disk is formatted, it can be mounted by any number of nodes.

To format a volume using ocfs2module, select Tasks ➤ Format on the main menu. The dialog box in Figure 8-12 will be displayed.

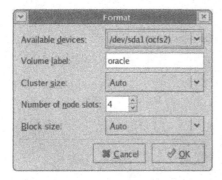

Figure 8-12. *The OCFS Console Format dialog box*

The dialog box contains the following options:

- **Available devices**: This option allows you to select a device to format from the drop-down list of available devices.

- **Volume label**: This label can be changed to describe your configuration.

- **Cluster size**: This size can range in value between 4KB and 1MB. If omitted, this value will be derived from the size of the logical partition. For volumes that will store database files, a cluster size of 128KB or more is recommended. For other volumes, use 16KB to 64KB.

- **Number of node slots**: This option determines the number of nodes that can mount the volume concurrently, each node requiring one slot. The default value is 4.

- **Block size:** Valid sizes range between 512 bytes and 4KB. Oracle recommends a block size of 1KB, 2KB, or 4KB.

You can also use the mkfs.ocfs2 command to format a volume. This command has the following syntax:

```
mkfs.ocfs2 [ -b block-size ] [ -C cluster-size ] [ -L volume-label ]
[ -N number-of-nodes ] [ -J journal-options ] [ -F ] [ -q ] [ -v ] [ -V ] device
```

The options in the syntax have the following meanings:

- **-b block-size**: Valid values are 512 bytes, 1KB, 2KB, or 4KB. If omitted, this value will be determined from the logical partition size.

- **-c cluster-size**: Valid values are 4KB, 8KB, 16KB, 32KB, 64KB, 128KB, 256KB, 512KB, and 1MB. If omitted, this value will also be determined from the logical partition size.

- **-L volume-label**: Useful for mounting by label.
- **-N number-of-node-slots**: Specifies the maximum number of nodes that can mount the partition. Valid values range from 1 to 255.
- **-J journal-options**: Currently specifies only the journal size, for example, -J size=4M.
- **-F force**: The volume will be formatted, even if it is currently mounted by other nodes.
- **-q**: Quiet mode.
- **-v**: Verbose mode.
- **-V**: Print version and exit.

For example, the following command creates an ocfs2 file system on device /dev/sda1 with the label "u02":

```
london1 # mkfs.ocfs2 -L "u02" /dev/sda1
```

This command is equivalent to the following:

```
london1 # mkfs.ocfs2 -b 4k -C 32K -L "u02" -N 4 / dev/sda1
```

Mounting OCFS2 File Systems

OCFS file systems can be mounted manually using the mount command or mounted automatically when the system is booted by configuring /etc/fstab.

You can also mount a file system manually using the ocfs2console tool. To do so, select Device from the upper pane of the window shown in Figure 8-13, and then click the Mount icon.

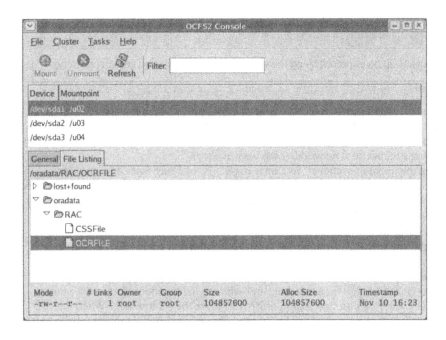

Figure 8-13. *The OCFS2 Console File Listing tab*

Specify the mount point and any options in the mount dialog box, shown in Figure 8-14.

Figure 8-14. *The OCFS2 mount dialog box*

You can also use the mount command, specifying the device and mount directory, as in the following example:

```
london1 # mount -t ocfs2 /dev/sda1 /u02
```

Remember that you must create the directory for the mount point before you attempt to mount the file system on that node. The mount point, /u02 in this example, can be created using the following command:

```
london1 # mkdir /u02
```

If the volume contains the Oracle Cluster Registry (OCR), voting disk file, datafiles, redo logs, archive logs, or control files, then it must be mounted with the -o datavolume mount option to ensure that the files are opened with the o_direct flag, which specifies direct I/O:

```
london1 # mount -t ocfs2 -o datavolume /dev/sda1 /u02
```

To mount the OCFS2 file system automatically, add the following entry to /etc/fstab:

```
/dev/sda1  /u02   ocfs2   datavolume,netdev  0    0
```

The partition can then be mounted using the standard operating system mount command:

```
london1 # mount /u02
```

In addition, the OCFS2 file system will be automatically mounted when the system is rebooted.

For OCFS2 file systems, the mount options field in /etc/fstab should contain the value _netdev. This value specifies that the device requires network access and prevents the system from mounting the file system during a reboot until networking has been enabled.

As described in the previous section, if you are using a SAN, you may experience problems with device name slippage when LUNs are added or removed from the SAN. For example, if a new LUN is added to the SAN, the device name /dev/sda1, which is currently used by the OCFS2 file system, may be reused by the new LUN, and the OCFS2 file system may be relocated to a different device name, such as /dev/sdb1, when the node is rebooted. The operating system may not be able to correctly identify or mount the volume, and corruption of the database files may result when the instance is restarted.

Again, to avoid this situation, you can specify a volume label when you create the file system and then mount the OCFS2 file system using that label, which is independent of the device name. The operating system scans the partition attempting to recognize the volume label. When it recognizes a volume label, the mount command will be successfully executed. With a volume labeling and mount strategy using a label, subsequent mount operations will be unaffected by changes of device names.

You can specify a volume label when you format the OCFS2 file system using the mkfs.ocfs command, as in the following example:

```
london1 # mkfs.ocfs2 -b 4k -C 32K -L "u02" -N 4 / dev/sda1
```

This example creates an OCFS2 file system on device /dev/sda1 with a label of "u02". Note that we have specified a volume label of u02. Using the same name for the volume label and mount point is a good administrative practice.

The OCFS2 file system can now be mounted manually by specifying the mount point and the volume label:

```
london1 # mount -t ocfs2 -L u02 /u02
```

To mount the OCFS2 file system automatically using the volume label, add an entry to /etc/fstab as in the following example:

```
LABEL=u02    /u02    ocfs2    datavolume,_netdev    0    0
```

The OCFS2 file system can then be mounted using the following command:

```
london1 # mount /u02
```

Alternatively, you can mount the OCFS2 file system using the label

```
london1 # mount -L u02
```

By specifying a label, the OCFS2 file system can be automatically mounted when the system is rebooted. In addition, the /etc/fstab file and the mount command are now completely independent of the physical device name (/dev/sda1).

Tuning an OCFS2 Partition

You can perform a number of tuning operations on existing partitions using the ocfs2console tool or the tunefs.ocfs2 command line utility. You can use the tuning tools to increase the number of node slots, change the volume label, and increase the size of the journal file. The o2cb cluster service must be running to perform these operations.

You can increase the number of node slots using the tunefs.ocfs2 tool. The volume must be unmounted on all nodes to perform this operation. For example, to increase the number of node slots to eight for the volume assigned to device /dev/sda2, use the following command:

```
london1 # tunefs.ocfs2 -N 8 /dev/sda2
Changing number of node slots from 4 to 8
```

This command creates one journal for each additional node. As in the following example, you can also change the volume label using the tunefs.ocfs2 tool:

```
london1 # tunefs.ocfs2 -L newlabel /dev/sda2
Changing volume label from ora_crs_home to newlabel
```

You can also change the journal size using the tunefs.ocfs2 tool. You can extend the journal for each of the assigned node slots as follows:

```
london1 # tunefs.ocfs2 -J size=64M /dev/sda2
```

Tools and Utilities

OCFS2 is supported by a number of tools and utilities that are supplied in the ocfs2-tools package. These are described in the following sections.

fsck.ocfs2

The fsck.ocfs2 tool can be used to check the health of an OCFS2 file system on an individual partition. The syntax follows:

```
Usage: fsck.ocfs2 [ -fGnuvVy ] [ -b superblock block ] [-B block size ]device

Critical flags for emergency repair:
 -n              Check, but don't' change the file system
 -y              Answer 'yes' to all repair questions
 -f              Force checking even if file system is clean
 -F              Ignore cluster locking (dangerous!)

Less critical flags
 -b superblock  Treat given block as the super block
 -B blocksize   Force the given block size
 -G             Ask to fix mismatched inode generations
 -V             Print version number
 -v             Verbose mode
```

You can use fsck.ocfs2 to check a file system as follows:

```
london1 # fsck.ocfs2 -n /dev/sda1
Checking OCFS2 filesystem in /dev/sda1:
  label:             clusterware
  uuid:              9e 3a 7d 2e 1b 5b 45 69 ac c7 52 89 c2 0d f1 27
  number of blocks:  493952
  bytes per block:   2048
  number of clusters: 7718
  bytes per cluster: 131072
  max slots:         2

/dev/sda1 is clean. It will be checked after 20 additional mounts
```

If errors are found, they can be automatically repaired using the -y option of fsck.ocfs:

```
london1 # fsck.ocfs -y /dev/sda1
```

mounted.ocfs2

Use mounted.ocfs2 to check the nodes currently mounting a specific device. Options include -d, which performs a quick detect, and -f (the default), which performs a full detect. For example, by default the mounted.ocfs2 command returns a list of nodes:

```
london1 # /sbin/mounted.ocfs2 /dev/sda1
Device:        FS     Nodes
/dev/sda1      ocfs2 london1, london2
```

Context Dependent Symbolic Links

Context dependent symbolic links (CDSLs) allow your instances to share a file with the same name on a cluster file system but allow each node to see a different version of that file. The advantage of using CDSLs is that generic directory names can be used on each node, and files that must be unique to a given node, for example, Oracle Clusterware files, can be separated. This feature will become increasingly useful as Oracle moves toward using a shared Oracle home. For example, each node requires a unique version of the $TNS_ADMIN/listener.ora file. At present, these files must be stored in separate directories. Using CDSLs, each node can address a different version of the same file, uniquely tied to a node, using the identical pathnames.

CDSL uses soft links to associate file or directory names to their contents. The ocfs2cdsl command is used to create the link.

Consider the following example. On node london1, create a hostname-dependent CDSL in a shared directory:

```
london1 # ocfs2cdsl /u03/test
```

On node london1, update the file:

```
london1 # echo "This is london1" >> /u03/test
london1 # cat /u03/test
This is london1
```

On node london2, create the following hostname-dependent CDSL with the same file name in the same shared directory:

```
london1 # ocfs2cdsl /u03/test
```

On node london2, update the file:

```
london1 # echo "This is london2" >> /u03/test
london1 # cat /u03/test
This is london2
```

On node london1, you can still see the original contents of the file:

```
london1 # cat /u03/test
This is london1
```

Each node can now access a different copy of the file test on shared storage using the same file name. Any changes made to the file on one node will not be visible to the other node.

You can also convert an existing file into a CDSL file as follows:

```
london1 # ocfs2csdl -c sqlnet.ora
```

The simplest way to understand how CDSL files are implemented is to examine the soft links that are created to support them, as in the following example from node london1:

```
london1 # ls -l test
  lrwxrwxrwx  1 root root 33 Nov 10 19.26 test -> .cluster/hostname/{hostname}/test
```

By default, ocfs2cdsl assumes that the type is a hostname. You can use the -t option to specify a machine name (mach), operating system (os), node number (nodenum), system (sys), user ID (uid), or group ID (gid).

You also can edit a file that belongs to another node. For example, on node london1, you can update a file owned by london2:

```
london1 # echo "Overwritten by london1" >> /u03/.cluster/hostname/london2/test
```

On node london2, you can see the changes made to the file on london1:

```
london1 # cat /u03/test
Overwritten by london1
```

Finally, to delete a CDSL file, use the rm command as usual:

```
london1 # rm /u03/test
```

However, you should note that this command only deletes the local copy of the file.

Summary

In this chapter, we have discussed the Oracle Clustered File System (OCFS). At the time of this writing, OCFS1 is in production at many sites on Oracle 9.2, 10.1, and 10.2. However, it only supports the 2.4 kernel; therefore, it has a limited lifespan, as both SUSE9 and Red Hat 4 implement the 2.6 kernel. OCFS2 supports the 2.6 kernel, but at the time of this writing, it is only supported on Red Hat 4 32-bit platforms, and its future is very much in the balance. We anticipate that greatest number of new RAC deployments will be on x86-64 platforms, so the long-term prospects for OCFS2 will continue to be in doubt until it is certified on x86-64, at a minimum. At the current time, it is not certified on SUSE distributions or Itanium platforms.

Therefore, if you wish to take advantage of the newer Linux distributions, you may need to look elsewhere for a cluster file system. In the next chapter, we will discuss Automatic Storage Management (ASM), which offers an alternative storage management option to OCFS.

CHAPTER 9

■ ■ ■

Automatic Storage Management (ASM)

In this chapter, we will describe ASM, which was introduced in Oracle 10.1 and is intended to simplify storage administration by automating disk and file management tasks to reduce management overhead and deployment costs.

ASM is a generic alternative to OCFS that works on all platforms. ASM provides similar functionality to OCFS but includes volume management capabilities, such as disk balancing and redundancy. If you are using the Oracle Database 10g Standard Edition with the free RAC option, you must use ASM for datafile storage.

In our experience, with the introduction of Oracle 10.2, ASM has become the most popular choice for storage management on new deployments and has reached relative maturity in a remarkably short period of time. Because of uncertainty over the future of OCFS, many customers are opting for ASM, which has the benefit of being a fully integrated core Oracle product.

We will begin this chapter with an introduction to ASM. Then we'll discuss ASM installation, instance configuration, components, administration, and monitoring.

Introducing ASM

ASM builds on technology introduced in Oracle 9.0.1 by the Oracle Managed Files (OMF) feature, which automates the creation and deletion of database files, including datafiles, control files, and online redo logs. Under OMF, tablespaces can be managed without reference to file names. ASM can be used with both single-instance and RAC databases.

ASM can manage many types of database files including datafiles, tempfiles, control files, online redo logs, archive logs, and RMAN backup sets. It can also manage some of the file types introduced in more recent releases, such as server parameter files, change tracking files, and flashback logs.

ASM reduces management overhead. It is designed to allow an Oracle DBA to perform most disk management tasks. For some sites, ASM can potentially replace a Logical Volume Manager (LVM) or RAID system. However, for many larger sites, ASM will offer fewer benefits as the complexity of storage management and related network infrastructure will still require specialist knowledge. The complexity of managing large numbers of disks is reduced by assigning each disk to a group of disks with similar characteristics that can be managed together.

ASM can perform some of the tasks, including striping and mirroring, that previously required third-party storage management products, potentially providing increased reliability and performance. By default, ASM implements two-way mirroring to maintain a redundant copy of data to provide fault tolerance but, for particularly important data, can also implement three-way mirroring.

If mirroring capabilities are already provided in the storage layer, then ASM can utilize these instead. ASM performs mirroring at the file level, as opposed to disk level, theoretically giving you more control over placement.

ASM also stripes data across multiple disks, providing increased read and write performance. The stripe size is determined by the class of database file.

ASM performs a limited amount of load balancing of files between disks. Rebalancing operations to uniformly distribute file extents across all disks are automatically performed whenever disks are added or removed from a disk group. This automatic rebalancing prevents hot spots and optimizes performance, so in theory, it is not necessary to perform manual disk fragmentation or data relocation.

ASM is compatible with both single-instance and RAC databases. Many Oracle storage concepts, such as tablespaces, segments, and extents, are identical under ASM. You can combine operating system files, OMFs, and ASM files in the same database, which can be useful during testing and migration to ASM.

We recommend that you investigate the capabilities of ASM before procuring additional storage technology. ASM does not always perform as well as other storage solutions, particularly those provided by third parties. Early versions of ASM inevitably suffered from the usual issues experienced by most new features but, at the time of this writing, many of the original issues have been resolved, and the Oracle 10.2 version is surprisingly solid for such a young product. ASM, like RMAN, is provided free of charge within your Oracle license agreement and may therefore bring significant cost savings when deployed in appropriate environments.

In Oracle 10.1, ASM only supports Oracle 10.1 databases. If the patch sets differ—for example, if the database instance is 10.1.0.2 and the ASM instance is 10.1.0.3—then the ASM instance will revert to the earlier functionality. If the ASM instance is 10.1.0.2 and the database instance is 10.1.0.3, the ASM instance will continue to use the 10.1.0.2 functionality.

However, in Oracle 10.2 and above, ASM supports multiple database versions. Oracle 10.2 ASM instances support Oracle 10.1 database instances without loss of functionality. Oracle Corporation has stated its intention to maintain both forward and backward compatibility for as long as possible with future releases.

ASM Installation

In Oracle 10.2 and above, Oracle recommends that you install the ASM binaries in a separate Oracle home directory. We think this recommendation is reasonable, as it improves your flexibility to perform patching and upgrades.

Oracle recommends, unless you have extreme availability requirements, that you install the ASM binaries for production systems on shared storage, which has several benefits. The amount of disk space occupied by the binaries is reduced, though shared storage is generally more expensive per gigabyte than equivalent locally attached storage. Installation and upgrade times are also reduced, as only one copy of the binaries needs to be written to disk. On the debit side, shared Oracle homes are less flexible during upgrades, as it is necessary to upgrade all nodes at once.

We are aware of several users who have experienced problems with shared Oracle homes in Oracle 10g, and therefore, we recommend that you create a separate Oracle home directory on each node for the ASM binaries, if possible.

For development and test systems, it is not necessary to install a separate Oracle home directory for the ASM binaries. ASM can use the same Oracle executables as the database instances.

On Linux, ASM requires a number of additional RPM packages, which can be downloaded from http://oss.oracle.com. These include the following:

- oracleasm-support
- oracleasm
- oracleasmlib

Download these RPMs, and install them as follows:

```
rpm -Uvh oracle-support-1.0.3-1.i386.rpm
rpm -Uvh oracleasm-2.4.21-EL-1.0.3-1.i686.rpm
rpm -Uvh oracleasmlib-1.0.0-1.i386.rpm
```

The exact version numbers will change on a fairly regular basis as the packages are fixed and enhanced. On installation, a device is created for ASM called /dev/oracleasm. The ASM packages install a service called oracleasm that takes a number of options. You can run this script in the following two ways:

```
[root@london1 root] # /etc/init.d/oracleasm <options>
[root@london1 root] # service oracleasm <options>
```

You must be logged on as the root user to run the oracleasm script. The script calls a number of library functions which are declared in /usr/lib/oracleasm/oracleasm.init.functions. The /etc/init.d/oracleasm script takes the following options:

- **configure**: Configure ASM.
- **start**: Start the ASM service.
- **stop**: Stop the ASM service.
- **status**: Print the status of ASM service.
- **createdisk**: Create an ASM disk.
- **scandisks**: Search for ASM disks.
- **listdisks**: List ASM disks.
- **querydisk**: Query the current status of an ASM disk.
- **deletedisk**: Delete an ASM disk.
- **restart**: Restart the ASM service.
- **link**: Load the oracleasm module.
- **enable**: Enable the ASM service.
- **disable**: Disable the ASM service.

Several of these options are described in more detail in the following sections.

configure

ASM is initially configured on each host using /etc/init.d/oracleasm configure:

```
[root@london1 root] # /etc/init.d/oracleasm configure
This will configure the on-boot properties of the Oracle ASM library \
driver. The following questions will determine whether the driver is
loaded on boot and what permissions it will have. The current values
will be shown in brackets ('[ ]'). Hitting <ENTER> without typing an
answer will keep that current value. Ctrl-C will abort.
Default user to own the driver interface [ ]: oracle
Default group to own the driver interface [ ]: dba
Start Oracle ASM library driver on boot (y/n) [n]: y
Fix permissions of Oracle ASM disks on boot (y/n) [y]: y
Writing Oracle ASM library driver configuration          [ OK ]
Creating /dev/oracleasm mount point                      [ OK ]
Mounting ASMlib driver filesystem                        [ OK ]
Scanning system for ASM disks                            [ OK ]
```

The basic ASM configuration is stored in the file /etc/sysconfig/oracleasm, as shown in the following example:

```
# This is a configuration file for automatic loading of the Oracle
# Automatic Storage Management library kernel driver. It is generated
# by running /etc/init.d/oracleasm configure. Please use that method
# to modify this file
#ORACLEASM_ENABLED: true means to load the driver on boot
ORACLEASM_ENABLED=true
#ORACLEASM_UID: Default user owning the /dev/oracleasm mount point
ORACLEASM_UID=oracle
#ORACLEASM_GID: Default group owning the /dev/oracleasm mountpoint
ORACLEASM_GID=dba
#ORACLEASM_SCANBOOT: true means fix disk permissions on boot
ORACLEASM_SCANBOOT=true
# ORACLEASM_CLEARBOOT: true means clean old disk permissions on boot
ORACLEASM_CLEARBOOT=true
#ORACLEASM_SCANORDER: Matching patterns to order disk scanning
ORACLEASMSCANORDER=
#ORACLEASM_SCANEXCLUDE: Matching patterns to exclude disks from scan
ORACLEASM_SCANEXCLUDE=
```

start

ASM is implemented using a loadable kernel module, also called oracleasm. The ASM service can be started and the module can be loaded using the following:

```
[root@london1 root] # /etc/init.d/oracleasm start
```

stop

The ASM service can be stopped and the oracleasm module unloaded using

```
[root@london1 root] # /etc/init.d/oracleasm stop
```

status

You can check the status of the ASM service as follows:

```
[root@london1 root] # /etc/init.d/oracleasm status
```

You should get the following results:

```
Checking if ASM is loaded:                    [ OK ]
Checking if /dev/oracleasm is mounted:        [ OK ]
```

createdisk

You can create ASM disks on logical partitions using the createdisk option. Before creating ASM disks, you must create suitable disks or logical partitions at the operating system level. In a RAC environment, these disks should be created on shared storage. You can specify either raw devices or logical partition names when adding disks to ASM. If you intend to use raw devices, ensure that the definitions are identical on every node. In the following example, we have used logical partition names:

```
[root@london1 root] # /etc/init.d/oracleasm createdisk VOL1 /dev/sdb1
Marking disk "/dev/sdb1" as an ASM disk             [ OK ]
[root@london1 root] # /etc/init.d/oracleasm createdisk VOL2 /dev/sdc1
Marking disk "/dev/sdc1" as an ASM disk             [ OK ]
[root@london1 root] # /etc/init.d/oracleasm createdisk VOL3 /dev/sdd1
Marking disk "/dev/sdd1" as an ASM disk             [ OK ]
```

scandisks

You need to create ASM disks on only one node. On the second and subsequent nodes, you can scan for existing ASM disks using the following command:

```
[root@london1 root] # /etc/init.d/oracleasm scandisks
Scanning system for ASM disks                       [ OK ]
```

listdisks

You can verify that the disks have been created on any host using /etc/init.d/oracleasm listdisks:

```
[root@london1 root] # /etc/init.d/oracleasm listdisks
VOL1
VOL2
VOL3
```

querydisk

You can query the status of an existing disk using the querydisk option, as in the following example:

```
[root@london1 root] # /etc/init.d/oracleasm querydisk VOL1
Disk "VOL1" is a valid ASM disk
```

deletedisk

You can delete an existing disk using the deletedisk option, as follows:

```
[root@london1 root] # /etc/init.d/oracleasm deletedisk VOL1
Removing ASM disk "VOL1"
```

ASM Instance Configuration

If you intend to create a database using ASM, the ASM instance must be created before you can create the database. You can create the ASM instance using the Database Configuration Assistant (DBCA), or you can create it manually. If you intend to use DBCA to create your database instance, then we recommend using it to create the ASM instance as well. If you intend to create your database instance manually, then you can use either DBCA or manual scripts to create the ASM instance.

Adding an ASM Instance Using DBCA

We recommend that you use DBCA to install ASM. In Oracle 10.1, DBCA will create an ASM instance when the first database is installed on the cluster; in Oracle 10.2 and above, DBCA has been enhanced to create an ASM instance independently. In the next two sections, we will discuss the processes for adding an ASM instance, first in Oracle 10.2 and above and then in Oracle 10.1.

Oracle 10.2 and Above

In Oracle 10.2 and above, when you start DBCA, you will be asked whether you wish to create a RAC database or a single-instance database. Select the RAC database option, and click Next to continue.

You will then be presented with the list of available operations shown in Figure 9-1.

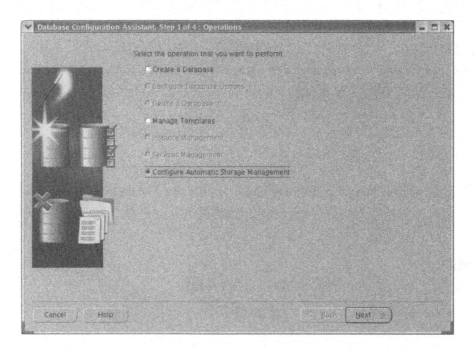

Figure 9-1. *The DBCA Operations page*

If this is a new installation, some of the operations will be unavailable. In Oracle 10.2 and above, select Configure Automatic Storage Management; in Oracle 10.1, select Create a Database. In Oracle 10.2 and above, click Next to continue to the Node Selection page (Figure 9-2).

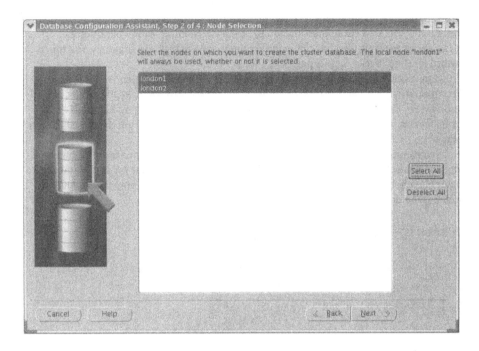

Figure 9-2. *The DBCA Node Selection page*

On the Node Selection page, select the nodes in the cluster on which you wish to install ASM by clicking their names. Alternatively, click Select All to install ASM on all nodes. Click Next to continue to the Create ASM Instance page, shown in Figure 9-3.

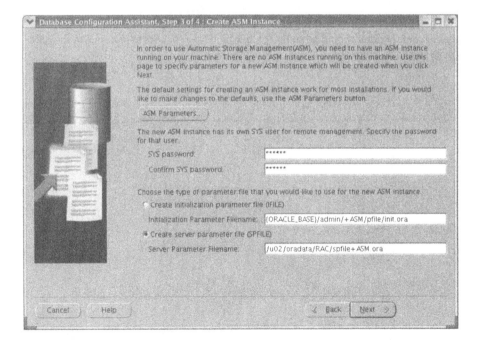

Figure 9-3. *The DBCA Create ASM Instance page*

The Create ASM Instance page allows you to specify configuration and security information for the ASM instance. Click the ASM Parameters button to modify ASM initialization parameters.

The ASM instance has a SYS user that can be used to manage the instance remotely. You must specify a password for the SYS user on this page.

The ASM instance also has an initialization parameter file. This file can either be a text parameter file (PFILE) or a server parameter file (SPFILE). You can choose which you wish to use and also specify a location on the Create ASM Instance page. Note that, if you are not using a shared Oracle home, the default location for the SPFILE will be incorrect, and you will need to modify it to a location on shared storage.

Click Next to continue. DBCA will then create and start the ASM instance. Once the ASM instance has been started, you can create ASM disk groups, which can be used as storage for your databases.

If you do not already have a listener process configured on each instance, you may receive a message similar to the one shown in Figure 9-4.

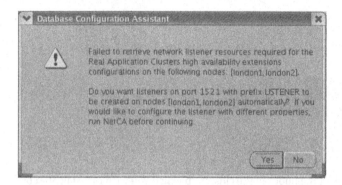

Figure 9-4. *The DBCA listener creation message*

If you wish to customize your listener processes, you will need to run the Network Configuration Assistant (NETCA) before you can continue with ASM installation. However, for most RAC installations, the default listener configuration should be sufficient, in which case click Yes to continue to the ASM Disk Groups page shown in Figure 9-5.

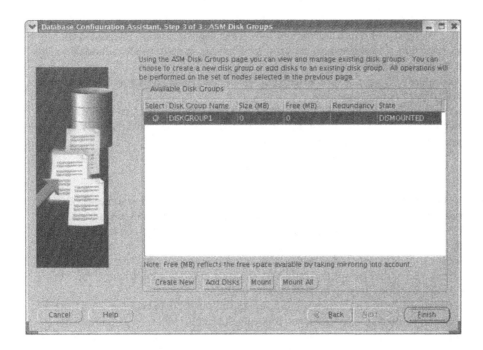

Figure 9-5. *The DBCA ASM Disk Groups management page*

On the ASM Disk Groups page, you can select the disk groups you wish to use in the ASM instance. You can also use this page to manage existing disk groups. For example, select a disk group from the list, and then click Create New to display the Create Disk Group page shown in Figure 9-6.

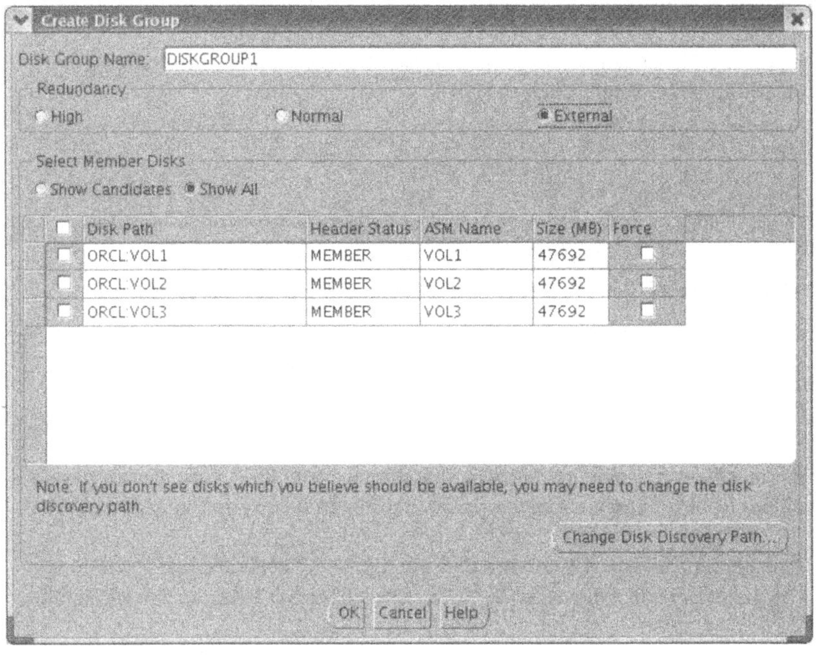

Disk Path	Header Status	ASM Name	Size (MB)	Force
ORCL:VOL1	MEMBER	VOL1	47692	
ORCL:VOL2	MEMBER	VOL2	47692	
ORCL:VOL3	MEMBER	VOL3	47692	

Figure 9-6. *The Create Disk Group page*

On the Create Disk Group page, you can select the redundancy level for the disk group: High (triple mirroring), Normal (mirrored), or External. The default value is Normal. You should choose External redundancy only if you are using a SAN that implements an appropriate redundancy algorithm, such as RAID 1+0 or RAID 5.

You can also specify the volumes you wish to add to the disk group. These volumes must have been precreated using the oracleasm utility.

When you have configured the Disk Group, click OK to return to the ASM Disk Groups page.

When you have configured any remaining disk groups, you have completed the installation of the ASM instance and can click Finish to exit DBCA.

Oracle 10.1

If you are using Oracle 10.1, you cannot explicitly create an ASM instance. When you select the Create Database operation, DBCA offers three storage options: file systems, raw devices, and ASM. If you select ASM as your storage option, DBCA will automatically create an ASM instance on each node, if one does not already exist. DBCA will prompt you for a password for the SYS user on the ASM instance. This password does not need to be the same as the SYS user's on any database instances. DBCA will also show a list of disk groups that have been discovered by the ASM instance. You can select appropriate disk groups for your database from this list.

If you are running ASM in a RAC environment, you must remember to create an ASM instance on each node that you add to an existing cluster. You will not be able to create a database instance on the new node until you have created and started an ASM instance. Similarly, if you intend to reuse a node that you have removed from your cluster without reinstalling the operating system, then you should delete the ASM instance after you have deleted any database instances.

Adding an ASM Instance Manually

You can also install ASM manually. A number of additional steps are required to install ASM in a RAC environment. This section provides an example of the manual addition of an ASM instance. In the following procedure, we will follow the Oracle convention of naming the ASM instances +ASM1 and +ASM2.

As the Oracle user, create the administration directories. These can be located either on the local file system or on a shared file system, such as NFS.

```
[oracle@london1 oracle] $ mkdir -p $ORACLE_BASE/admin/+ASM
[oracle@london1 oracle] $ mkdir $ORACLE_BASE/admin/+ASM/bdump
[oracle@london1 oracle] $ mkdir $ORACLE_BASE/admin/+ASM/cdump
[oracle@london1 oracle] $ mkdir $ORACLE_BASE/admin/+ASM/hdump
[oracle@london1 oracle] $ mkdir $ORACLE_BASE/admin/+ASM/udump
```

On each node, create a password file in the $ORACLE_HOME/dbs directory using this:

```
[oracle@london1 oracle] $ orapwd password=oracle file=$ORACLE_HOME/dbs/orapw<SID>
```

For example, to create a password for the +ASM1 instance, you would use the following:

```
[oracle@london1 oracle] $ orapwd password=oracle file=$ORACLE_HOME/dbs/orapw+ASM1
```

On one node, create a file containing initialization parameters. Initially, creating a text parameter is simpler. You will not be able to create a server parameter file until you have created the ASM instance.

In this example, on each node, you will create a file called $ORACLE_HOME/dbs/init<sid>.ora. For example, on the first node, create a file called $ORACLE_HOME/dbs/init+ASM1.ora containing the following entries:

```
cluster_database=TRUE
instance_type=ASM
large_pool_size=12M
remote_login_passwordfile=exclusive

background_dump_dest=/u01/app/oracle/admin/+ASM/bdump
core_dump_dest=/u01/app/oracle/admin/+ASM/cdump
user_dump_dest=/u01/app/oracle/admin/+ASM/udump

asm_diskgroups = 'DISKGROUP1'

+ASM1.instance_number=1
+ASM2.instance_number=2
```

Copy the initialization parameter file to $ORACLE_HOME/dbs/init+ASM2.ora on the second node. On each host, add an entry to /etc/oratab for the new instance. For example, on the first node add

```
+ASM1:/u01/app/oracle/product/10.1.0/db:N
```

To create an entry for each ASM instance in the OCR, use the following code:

```
london1 $ srvctl add asm -n london1 -i +ASM1 -o $ORACLE_HOME
london1 $ srvctl add asm -n london2 -i +ASM2 -o $ORACLE_HOME
```

Start the ASM instance on each node as follows:

```
london1 $ srvctl start asm -n london1
london1 $ srvctl start asm -n london2
```

Alternately, you can start the ASM instance manually on each node using SQL*Plus. When the instance is running, you can create disk groups, as in the following example:

```
[oracle@london1 oracle] $ export ORACLE_SID=+ASM1
[oracle@london1 oracle] $ sqlplus /nolog
SQL> CONNECT / AS SYSDBA
SQL> CREATE DISKGROUP diskgroup1
> EXTERNAL REDUNDANCY DISK
> 'ORCL:VOL1',
> 'ORCL:VOL2',
> 'ORCL:VOL3';
```

Deleting an ASM Instance Using DBCA

Although you can create an ASM instance using DBCA, you cannot delete an ASM instance using DBCA. Instead you must follow the manual procedure described in the following section.

Deleting an ASM Instance Manually

To delete an ASM instance manually, first stop all databases currently accessing the instance. Then stop the ASM instance using SQL*Plus or SRVCTL.

Next, delete the ASM instance from the OCR:

```
london1 $ srvctl remove asm -n london1 -i +ASM1
london1 $ srvctl remove asm -n london2 -i +ASM2
```

You do not need to specify the ASM instance using the -i option in the previous command if there is only one ASM instance on each node.

On each node, delete the ASM instance from /etc/oratab. Then, on each node, delete the parameter file, as in the following example:

```
[oracle@london1 oracle] $ rm $ORACLE_HOME/dbs/init+ASM.ora
```

Finally, on each node, delete the password file:

```
[oracle@london1 oracle] $ rm $ORACLE_HOME/dbs/orapw+ASM1
```

Re-Creating the ASM Instance

The ASM metadata area is re-created at the start of each ASM file and contains details of all the extents contained in the file.

If you need to re-create the ASM instance on disks that have previously been used for ASM, then you will need to reinitialize the ASM metadata area using the dd utility. For example, you might use the following commands to initialize the disks:

```
[root@london1 root] # dd if=/dev/zero of=/dev/sda5 bs=8192 count=12800
[root@london1 root] # dd if=/dev/zero of=/dev/sda6 bs=8192 count=12800
[root@london1 root] # dd if=/dev/zero of=/dev/sda7 bs=8192 count=12800
```

Using Files Instead of Devices

You can create an ASM file system based on operating system files instead of devices on Linux. You should not attempt this configuration on a production system, but it can be useful for testing or educational reasons. The following steps have been successfully tested on a RAC database but have limited applicability, as only one instance has access to the ASM disks that are created on the local disks of one node.

Create a directory to contain the ASM files:

```
[root@london1 root] # mkdir /asm
```

Create the files using the dd command:

```
[root@london1 root] # dd if=/dev/zero of=/asm/vol4 bs=1M count=1000
```

As the root user, associate a loop device with each file using the losetup command:

```
[root@london1 root] # losetup /dev/loop1 /asm/vol4
```

You can check that the loop devices have been created correctly as follows:

```
[root@london1 root] # losetup /dev/loop1
/dev/loop1: [0302]:2326846 (/asm/vol4) offset 0, no encryption
```

Use the createdisk of the oracleasm service script to create ASM disks using the loop devices:

```
[root@london1 root] # /etc/init.d/oracleasm createdisk VOL4 /dev/loop1
```

You can then create an ASM disk group in SQL*Plus using the new ASM disks, as in the following example:

```
SQL> CREATE DISKGROUP diskgroup2 EXTERNAL REDUNDANCY DISK 'ORCL:VOL4';
```

ASM Components

ASM has three main components: the ASM instance, ASM disk groups, and ASM files. These components are discussed in further detail in the following sections.

ASM Instance

In a single-instance environment, ASM requires the creation of an additional instance that is separate from any database instances that might be running on the node. The ASM instance must be started before other database instances can access files located in ASM storage. If the ASM instance is terminated, all client database instances will also be terminated.

The ASM instance handles management of the storage configuration. For example, the ASM instance rebalances datafiles across physical disks in order to eliminate hot spots.

The database instance communicates with the ASM instance to obtain information about ASM datafiles. However, the ASM instance does not perform I/O directly for applications. Application I/O is still performed by the server processes and background processes associated with the database instances.

The ASM instance is a stripped-down version of a standard instance, which is now referred to as an RDBMS instance. The instance type is defined in the INSTANCE_TYPE parameter, which can take the value RDBMS (which is the default value) or ASM.

In a RAC environment, an ASM instance must be created on each node. The ASM files should be located on shared storage accessible by all nodes in the cluster. By default, database instances on each node will connect to the local ASM instance for storage management services.

Unlike a database instance, the ASM instance does not mount any datafiles. It does not have any associated control files, online redo logs, or datafiles. Consequently, it does not have a data dictionary or any of the associated views. However, the ASM instance does include a complete set of dynamic performance views and fixed views that are hard-coded into the database kernel.

You must connect to the ASM instance as an administrator with either the SYSDBA or SYSOPER privilege. Either the SYSOPER or SYSDBA privilege is required to start up and shut down the ASM instance; mount, dismount, check, and offline disk groups; and access the ASM dynamic performance views. The SYSDBA privilege is required to create disk groups and to add or drop disks.

All disk group management commands must be issued from within the ASM instance. The database has no direct connection to the disk groups.

Instance Names

Every ASM instance has an instance name. If you use DBCA to create an ASM instance for a nonclustered database, the default instance name will be +ASM. If you use DBCA to create ASM instances on a clustered database, the default instance names will be +ASM1, +ASM2, and so on. While these instance names are not mandatory, we recommend that you follow these naming conventions if you create your ASM instances manually.

SGA

The ASM instance maintains a separate SGA. The size of a nonclustered instance is normally around 64MB. ASM also requires additional disk space to maintain configuration files and log files, including an ASM instance–specific alert log. Oracle recommends allowing 100MB of disk space for each ASM instance.

Background Processes

In a single-instance environment, an ASM instance has a number of background processes, including PMON, SMON, DBW0, LGWR CKPT, and MMAN. In a RAC environment, additional background processes support clustering, including LMON, LMD0, LMS0, LCK0, and DIAG.

In addition, each ASM instance has two new background processes: the ASM rebalance master background process (RBAL), which coordinates disk rebalancing activity, and the ASM rebalancing slave processes (ARB0, ARB1, etc.), which perform the actual rebalancing by moving data extents between disks.

Every Oracle database that connects to the ASM instance also has the following two new background processes:

- RBAL: Performs global opens of the disks in ASM disk groups. Note that the functionality of RBAL on a database instance is different from that of RBAL on an ASM instance.

- ASMB: Acts as a link between the ASM and database instances. It connects as a foreground process to the ASM instance to communicate information, such as datafile creation and deletion.

Parameters

Each ASM instance has a parameter file. This can be either a text parameter file (PFILE) or a server parameter file (SPFILE). You should ensure that this file is included in your backup procedure.

Only a handful of parameter values need to be specified in order to create an ASM instance. For example, you might specify the following parameters:

```
CLUSTER_DATABASE = TRUE
INSTANCE_TYPE = ASM
DB_UNIQUE_NAME = +ASM
ASM_POWER_LIMIT = 1
ASM_DISKSTRING = '/dev/sda*, /dev/sdb*, /dev/sdc*, /dev/sdd*'
ASM_DISKGROUPS = 'DISKGROUP1, DISKGROUP2'
LARGE_POOL_SIZE = 16M
```

CLUSTER_DATABASE

This parameter indicates that the ASM instance is a member of a cluster. Additional background processes will be created to support cluster functionality.

INSTANCE_TYPE

This parameter must be set to ASM for ASM instances. The default value for this parameter is RDBMS, which indicates that the instance is a normal database instance.

DB_UNIQUE_NAME

This parameter can be used to uniquely identify the ASM instance. The default value is +ASM. You should change this parameter if more than one ASM instance is running on the same node.

ASM_POWER_LIMIT

When disks are added to or removed from disk groups, ASM moves file extents between disks to balance I/O equally between all disks in the group. The ASM_POWER_LIMIT parameter determines how aggressively the rebalancing operation is performed. The parameter takes a numeric value ranging from 1 (slowest) to 11 (fastest). The default value is 1.

ASM_DISKSTRING

This parameter specifies a set of disk locations used by Oracle during disk discovery. When a new disk is added to a disk group, the ASM instance discovers the new disk by searching in the directories specified by this parameter. The default value is NULL. In the following example, the disk string has been set to include three SCSI devices:

```
ASM_DISKSTRING = '/dev/sdb*, /dev/sdc*, /dev/sdd*'
```

If the default value is not overwritten, then Oracle assumes a value of ORCL:*, which is equivalent to all of the ASM disks created using the oracleasm createdisk option.

ASM_DISKGROUPS

An ASM disk group is a set of ASM disks containing ASM files. The underlying disks are managed indirectly by managing the disk group. A single ASM disk group can contain files from multiple databases. All access to ASM files is performed via the ASM disk group.

ASM allocates space in extents called allocation units. By default, each allocation unit is 1MB in size.

To specify a list of disk groups that will be mounted automatically when the ASM instance is started, use the ASM_DISKGROUPS parameter. The default value is NULL. If you use a text parameter file (PFILE), you will need to set the values for this parameter manually; if you use a server parameter file (SPFILE), then the ASM instance will automatically update the SPFILE whenever disk groups are created or dropped. In the following example, there are two ASM disk groups called DISKGROUP1 and DISKGROUP2:

```
ASM_DISKGROUPS = 'DISKGROUP1, DISKGROUP2'
```

LARGE_POOL_SIZE

In an ASM instance, the large pool should be a minimum of 12MB.

Striping

ASM implements striping of files across the disks within a disk group to optimize I/O performance. Therefore, every disk within the group should have the same type and performance characteristics. Two types of striping—coarse and fine—are implemented depending on the database file type.

Coarse striping is used for most file types, including datafiles, tempfiles, archived redo logs, parameter files, transportable tablespaces, backup sets, dump sets, autobackup control files, change tracking files, and Data Guard configuration files. The default stripe size is 1MB.

By default, *fine striping* is only used for control files, online redo logs, and flashback logs. The stripe size is 128MB. Also by default, eight stripes are created for each file; therefore, the optimum number of disks in a disk group is a multiple of eight.

Mirroring

ASM uses mirroring to provide data redundancy. ASM mirrors extents at the file level. This differs from most operating system mirroring, which is performed at disk level. If a redundant disk is lost, the mirrored disk can continue operations without data loss or interruption to service. In the event of a disk failure, ASM can reconstruct the failed disk using the mirrored extents from other disks in the same group. The use of striping means that the I/O required to reconstruct the new disk is spread evenly across the remaining disks in the group.

Failure Groups

If a disk controller fails, then all disks that are connected to it will be inaccessible. ASM defines *failure groups*, which are groups of disks that are dependent on a single point of failure, such as a controller. To ensure redundancy, each mirror should be located on a different failure group. In the event of a controller failure, ASM can, therefore, guarantee that it can reconstruct the failed disk group from mirrored copies of extents in remaining disk groups.

Redundancy

ASM supports three types of redundancy: external, normal, and high.

External redundancy does not involve any mirroring. It uses existing operating system or storage array protection, such as RAID or LVMs. Note, however, that if you select external redundancy, it is your responsibility to ensure that the underlying storage is correctly configured; ASM cannot guarantee recoverability in the event of a failure. You do not need to define any failure groups if you are using external redundancy.

Normal redundancy, which is the default, implements two-way mirroring, in which each file extent will be written to two disk groups using one primary extent and one mirrored extent. To guarantee redundancy, you must define at least two failure groups.

High redundancy implements three-way mirroring, in which each file extent will be written to three disk groups using one primary extent and two mirrored extents. To guarantee redundancy, you must define at least three failure groups.

Creating a Disk Group

Disk groups can be created when a database is created using DBCA or using Enterprise Manager. Disk groups can also be created manually using the CREATE DISKGROUP command in SQL*Plus when connected to the ASM instance, as in the following example:

```
SQL> CREATE DISKGROUP diskgroup1
> NORMAL REDUNDANCY
> FAILGROUP failgroup1 DISK
>   '/dev/sda1',
>   '/dev/sdb1',
>   '/dev/sdc1',
>   '/dev/sdd1'
> FAILGROUP failgroup2 DISK
>   '/dev/sde1',
>   '/dev/sdf1',
>   '/dev/sdg1',
>   '/dev/sdh1';
```

If no FAILGROUP clause is specified, then each disk will be in its own failure group. ASM will automatically mount the newly created disk group. If you are using a server parameter file (SPFILE) for the ASM instance, then the disk group name will be added automatically to the ASM_DISKGROUPS parameter. If you are using a text parameter file (PFILE), then you will have to add the name of the disk group to the ASM_DISKGROUPS parameter manually, so that the group is mounted automatically whenever the ASM instance is restarted.

Modifying a Disk Group

Once you have created a disk group, you cannot modify the redundancy level. You can, however, add and drop disks.

To add a disk to an existing disk group, use the ALTER DISKGROUP statement when connected to the ASM instance, as follows:

```
SQL> ALTER DISKGROUP diskgroup1 ADD DISK '/dev/sdi1';
```

If you do not include a FAILGROUP clause, then a new failure group will be created for the new disk. You can specify a failure group for the new disk using the following:

```
SQL> ALTER DISKGROUP diskgroup1 FAILGROUP failgroup1 DISK '/dev/sdi1';
```

You cannot change the failure group for an existing disk. Instead, you must drop the disk and then add it back to specify the new failure group.

To drop a disk, use the following ALTER DISKGROUP statement:

```
SQL> ALTER DISKGROUP diskgroup1 DROP DISK '/dev/sdi1';
```

You can also use the ALTER DISKGROUP statement to manually initiate a rebalancing operation on a disk group:

```
SQL> ALTER DISKGROUP diskgroup1 REBALANCE POWER 8;
```

The POWER clause specifies the level of parallelization for the rebalancing operation, which determines the speed of the operation and the impact on other processes. If you do not specify a POWER clause, then the current value of the ASM_POWER_LIMIT parameter will be used. It should not be necessary to use this statement very frequently, as ASM automatically rebalances extents across the disk group whenever a disk is added or dropped.

The ALTER DISKGROUP statement supports a number of other operations including rebalancing the disk group, checking all disks in the disk group, checking all disks in a specific failure group, and checking all disks used by a specific file. You can also use this statement to specify new sizes for existing disks.

Dropping a Disk Group

To drop a disk group, use the DROP DISKGROUP statement, as follows:

```
SQL> DROP DISKGROUP diskgroup1;
```

By default, the DROP DISKGROUP statement will return an error if the disk group currently contains any files. To drop a nonempty disk group, specify the INCLUDING CONTENTS clause:

```
SQL> DROP DISKGROUP diskgroup1 INCLUDING CONTENTS;
```

ASM Files

Within ASM, all data is stored in ASM files. Each ASM file can belong to only one disk group. By default, a file will be striped across up to eight disks in a disk group. The size of the stripe is dependent on the class of database file. Recall that, by default, the stripe size is 128KB for control files, online redo logs, and flashback logs; for all other files, including datafiles, the default stripe size is 1MB.

ASM can only be used to store database files. There is a one-to-one mapping between database files and ASM files, which cannot be used to store operating system files, such as binaries, configuration files, trace files, alert logs, audit files, or core files. You cannot see ASM files at the operating system level, as they exist only within their disk groups.

ASM files cannot be backed up directly using operating system utilities. Instead, we recommend that you use RMAN to create image copies and backupsets of ASM database files.

The redundancy policy and striping level of a disk group are defined by the disk group to which it belongs.

File Names

ASM automatically generates file names for every file. In addition, you may specify file name aliases with more user-friendly names.

Within the database instance, ASM file names are stored in the control file and in the recovery catalog. They are also externalized in dynamic performance views, including V$DATAFILE, V$TEMPFILE, and V$LOGFILE.

The four ASM file naming conventions are as follows:

- Fully qualified file names
- Numeric file names
- Alias file names
- Incomplete file names

If you are creating a new file, you must use an alias file name or an incomplete file name. You can optionally specify a template that describes various attributes of the new file. If you are creating multiple files, you must use an incomplete file name, with or without a template.

If you are referencing existing files, then you can use fully qualified ASM file names, numeric ASM file names, or alias ASM file names (without a template).

The different naming conventions are discussed further in the following sections.

Fully Qualified File Names

Fully qualified ASM file names can only be used for referencing existing ASM files. The fully qualified file name is always generated by ASM when the file is created. It cannot be modified and is sometimes known as the *system alias*. The syntax is as follows:

```
+DiskGroup/DatabaseName/FileType/Tag/File.Incarnation
```

The FileType is the ASM file type, for example, datafile, online log, or control file. The Tag contains type-specific information about the file. For datafiles, the tag is the tablespace name, for example, SYSTEM or SYSAUX; for online redo logs, the tag is the group name, for example, group_2; and for current control files, the tag is Current.

The following is an example of a fully qualified ASM file name:

```
+diskgroup1/RAC/datafile/SYSTEM.256.1
```

Numeric File Names

Numeric ASM file names can be used only for referencing existing ASM files. The numeric file name is also generated by ASM when the file is created. Here is the syntax:

```
+DiskGroup/File.Incarnation
```

The following example is of a numeric file name:

```
+diskgroup1/256.1
```

Alias File Names

Oracle automatically generates fully qualified names for all ASM files. As you have seen, fully qualified file names can be a little unwieldy. You can also create user-friendly ASM file name aliases for system-generated file names. Alias file names can be added at any time after file name creation.

Alias ASM file names can be used with or without templates to reference existing ASM files. They can also be used with templates to create new ASM files, as in the following example:

```
+diskgroup1/RAC/system.dbf
+diskgroup1/RAC/sysaux.dbf
+diskgroup1/RAC/redo1.log
```

You can create a directory hierarchy for alias file names. For example, if you wish to create a file called file1 within a directory called directory1, you must first create the directory using an ALTER DISKGROUP statement:

```
SQL> ALTER DISKGROUP diskgroup1
> ADD DIRECTORY '+diskgroup1/directory1';
```

The directory must exist before you can create any files within it.

Alias file names are also created using the ALTER DISKGROUP statement. You can create new file names by specifying the ADD ALIAS clause or rename an existing alias file name using the following RENAME alias clause:

```
SQL> ALTER DISKGROUP diskgroup1
> ADD ALIAS '+diskgroup1/directory1/file1'
> FOR '+diskgroup1/RAC/datafile/TS99.280.1';
```

Alias file names can be dropped using the ALTER DISKGROUP statement as follows:

```
SQL> ALTER DISKGROUP diskgroup1
> DROP ALIAS '+diskgroup1/directory1/file1'
```

If you drop an alias, ASM will not automatically delete the referenced file. If you wish to delete the file as well, you will need to specify either the fully qualified or numeric ASM file name. For example, this statement will drop the file and any associated alias:

```
SQL> ALTER DISKGROUP diskgroup1
> DROP FILE '+diskgroup1/RAC/datafile/TS99.280.1';
```

Incomplete File Names

Incomplete ASM file names can only be used when creating ASM files. They can be used with or without templates. An incomplete ASM file name consists of a disk group name only:

```
+diskgroup1
```

Templates

ASM file attributes include the redundancy level (external, normal, or high) and the striping format (coarse or fine).

Templates can be used to determine which attributes will be applied to the file when it is created. They can be applied to individual files or assigned within a disk group. Once you have created a file, you cannot change its attributes directly. Instead, you must use RMAN to build a copy of the file with the new attributes.

You can specify a template during file creation using an incomplete file name or an alias file name. Using an incomplete file name, the syntax is

```
+diskgroup(template)
```

For example, the following statement creates a tablespace called TS1 in DISKGROUP1 with an OMF-generated file name:

```
SQL> CREATE TABLESPACE ts1 DATAFILE '+diskgroup1(datafile)';
```

Using an alias file name, this is the syntax:

```
+diskgroup(template)/alias
```

The following statement now creates a tablespace called TS1 in DISKGROUP1 with a single datafile called ts1.dbf:

```
SQL> CREATE TABLESPACE ts1 DATAFILE '+diskgroup1(datafile)/ts1.dbf';
```

A number of default templates are associated with a disk group when it is created; these are known as *system templates*. The system templates in Table 9-1 are created by default. In addition, you can create your own custom templates.

Table 9-1. *ASM System Templates*

Template Name	Description	Stripe
PARAMETERFILE	Parameter file	Coarse
DUMPSET	Dump set	Coarse
CONTROLFILE	Control file	Fine
ARCHIVELOG	Archived redo log	Coarse
ONLINELOG	Online redo log	Fine
DATAFILE	Datafile	Coarse
TEMPFILE	Tempfile	Coarse
BACKUPSET	Backupset	Coarse
AUTOBACKUP	Autobackup control file	Coarse
XTRANSPORT	Transportable tablespace	Coarse
CHANGETRACKING	Change tracking file	Coarse
FLASHBACK	Flashback log	Fine
DATAGUARDCONFIG	Data Guard configuration	Coarse

You can add your own templates to a disk group, as in the following example:

```
SQL> ALTER DISKGROUP diskgroup1
> ADD TEMPLATE template1 ATTRIBUTES (MIRROR, FINE);
```

The ATTRIBUTES clause specifies the redundancy level (MIRROR or UNPROTECTED) and the stripe granularity (FINE or COARSE). If the MIRROR keyword is specified, then either two- or three-way mirroring will be used, depending on the redundancy level for the file group.

The template can subsequently be altered as follows:

```
SQL> ALTER DISKGROUP diskgroup1
> ALTER TEMPLATE template1 ATTRIBUTES (COARSE);
```

You can also use this statement to alter system templates. You can drop the template again using the following statement:

```
SQL> ALTER DISKGROUP diskgroup1
> DROP TEMPLATE template1;
```

You can only drop user-defined templates; you cannot drop system templates.

ASM Administration

The ASM instance can be administered using SQL*Plus, the Server Control Utility (SRVCTL), DBCA, or Enterprise Manager.

In Oracle 10.2 and above, you can access the ASM file systems using FTP. Using FTP provides capabilities to list the contents of directories and transfer files in and out of the file system. You can also perform limited administrative tasks with the new ASM Command Line (ASMCMD) utility.

ASM Administration Using DBCA

In Oracle 10.2, you can administer ASM using DBCA. When you start DBCA, on the Operations page, specify Configure Automatic Storage Management. If the ASM instance already exists, you will be taken to the ASM Disk Groups page, which allows you to create, alter, and drop disk groups.

ASM Administration Using SQL*Plus

You can administer ASM using SQL*Plus. The CREATE, ALTER, and DROP DISKGROUP commands allow you to create and manage ASM disk groups and their contents. A number of ASM-specific dynamic performance views are available and populated in the ASM instance.

In addition, you can start and stop ASM using SQL*Plus, although in a RAC environment, SRVCTL is the preferred command line utility. In order to use SQL*Plus, you must set your ORACLE_SID environment variable as follows:

```
london1 $ export ORACLE_SID=+ASM1
```

To start the ASM instance, run SQL*Plus and issue the following STARTUP command:

```
london1 $ sqlplus /nolog
SQL> CONNECT / AS SYSDBA
SQL> STARTUP
```

By default, the instance will be started and mounted. You can optionally specify the MOUNT, NOMOUNT, FORCE, or RESTRICT option for the STARTUP command. However, specifying the OPEN option is not meaningful, as the ASM instance does not open any database files. The options have the following effects:

- **STARTUP MOUNT**: Starts the instance and mounts the disk groups specified by the ASM_DISKGROUPS parameter
- **STARTUP NOMOUNT**: Starts the instance but does not mount any disks
- **STARTUP FORCE**: Issues a SHUTDOWN ABORT followed by a STARTUP MOUNT
- **STARTUP RESTRICT**: Prevents any database instances from connecting to the ASM instance

To shut down an ASM instance, run SQL*Plus and issue the SHUTDOWN command. You can specify any of the SHUTDOWN options, including NORMAL, IMMEDIATE, TRANSACTIONAL, and ABORT. The SHUTDOWN command will be forwarded, together with any specified options, to all database instances currently connected to the ASM instance. Therefore, all database instances will be shut down when the ASM instance is shut down or fails. However, if any database instance fails, the ASM instance and any other database instances on the same node will be unaffected.

ASM Administration Using SRVCTL

The commands in this section can be issued by the Server Control Utility (SRVCTL) in Oracle 10.1 and above.

You can add and remove an ASM instance using SRVCTL. To add an ASM instance to the OCR, use the following:

```
$ srvctl add asm -n <node_name> -i <asm_instance_name> -o <oracle_home>
```

To remove the ASM instance, use

```
$ srvctl remove asm -n <node_name> [ -i <asm_instance_name> ]
```

You can start, stop, and check the current status of an ASM instance using SRVCTL. To start an ASM instance, use

```
$ srvctl start asm -n <node_name> [ -i <asm_instance_name> ][ -o <start_options> ]
```

To stop an ASM instance, use

```
$ srvctl stop asm -n <node_name> [ -i <asm_instance_name> ] [ -o <start_options> ]
```

To check the current status of an ASM instance, use

```
$ srvctl status asm -n <node_name>
```

The following example checks the status of the ASM instances on nodes london1 and london2:

```
[oracle@london1 oracle] $ srvctl status asm -n london1
ASM instance +ASM1 is running on node london1
[oracle@london1 oracle] $ srvctl status asm -n london2
ASM instance +ASM1 is not running on node london2
```

To check the current configuration of an ASM instance, use

```
$ srvctl config asm -n <node_name>
```

The following example checks the current configuration on nodes london1 and london2:

```
[oracle@london1 oracle] $ srvctl config asm -n london1
+ASM1 /u01/app/oracle/product/10.2.0/db_1
[oracle@london1 oracle] $ srvctl config asm -n london2
+ASM2 /u01/app/oracle/product/10.2.0/db_1
```

You can also use SRVCTL to enable and disable an existing ASM instance. To enable an existing ASM instance, use

```
$ srvctl enable asm -n <node_name> [ -i <asm_instance_name> ]
```

To disable an ASM instance, use

```
$ srvctl disable asm -n <node_name> [ -i <asm_instance_name> ]
```

ASM Administration Using Enterprise Manager

You can also administer ASM disk groups using Enterprise Manager (EM). Each ASM instance is administered separately.

From the Cluster Database Summary page, select a database instance name from the Instances table to display the Cluster Database Instance page for the selected instance. In the General area of the Cluster Database Instance page, click the ASM link to display the Automatic Storage Management Instance page.

Automatic Storage Management Instance Page

The Automatic Storage Management Instance page describes the ASM instance and contains the following four tabs:

- Home
- Performance
- Administration
- Configuration

The Home tab contains general information and a pie chart showing current disk usage by each client database together with internal ASM overhead and free space. This tab also lists current client databases and any alerts.

The Performance tab contains graphs describing Disk Group I/O Response Time, Disk Group I/O Operations Per Second, and Disk Group Throughput. It also contains a table showing cumulative I/O statistics for the ASM instance and individual I/O statistics for each disk group. You can click the name of any disk group to display the Disk Group page for that group.

The Administration tab contains a list of disk groups. You can click the name of any disk group to display the Disk Group page for that group.

The Configuration tab allows you to set a number of parameters, including the disk discovery path (ASM_DISKSTRING), automounted disk groups (ASM_DISKGROUPS), and the default rebalance power (ASM_POWER_LIMIT).

Disk Group Page

The Disk Group page describes an individual disk group and contains these four tabs:

- General
- Performance
- Templates
- Files

The General tab includes a pie chart showing a breakdown of space usage for the disk group. The chart includes a segment for each client database, internal ASM overhead, and free space. This tab also contains a graph showing usage history for the disk group, as well as a table showing all member disks. You can click the ASM disk name for any disk to display the Member Disk page for that disk.

The Performance tab contains a set of graphs equivalent to the ASM instance Performance tab, including Disk Group I/O Response Time, Disk Group I/O Operations Per Second, and Disk Group throughput. It also contains a table showing cumulative I/O statistics for the disk group and individual I/O statistics for each disk. You can click the name of any disk to display the Member Disk page for that disk.

The Templates tab contains a table of the current system and user-defined templates for the disk group. You can click the name of any template to edit the redundancy and striping attributes.

The Files tab contains a tree that can be expanded to show all files in each database using the disk group. You can expand each directory to show the individual file names and click the file names to show the properties page for that file. Properties include name, type, redundancy level, stripe size, and size in blocks.

Member Disk Page

The Member Disk Page shows performance statistics for an individual disk. It includes graphs for Disk I/O Response Time, Disk I/O Operations Per Second, and Disk Throughput. It also includes various Disk I/O statistics and general information about the disk found in V$ASM_FILE, such as the name, path, failure group, total space, and free space remaining.

ASM Administration Using FTP

When ASM was introduced in Oracle 10.1, there was no supported way of viewing or modifying the contents of the file system. In Oracle 10.2, you can use FTP to access the ASM file system.

In order to use FTP, you must have installed XML DB, which is included in the default DBCA installation. You must manually configure port numbers for FTP and HTTP/WebDAV. These can be configured using either the Enterprise Manager XDB Configuration page or SQL*Plus. We recommend the latter.

To configure the port numbers using SQL*Plus, first assign spare port numbers for each service. In our example, we will use 7777 for FTP and 8888 for HTTP/WebDAV. Make sure that any ports you allocate are not in use by any other services. The ports are configured using the script $ORACLE_HOME/rdbms/admin/catxdbdbca.sql, which should be run by a user with SYSDBA privileges. The script takes the FTP port as its first parameter and the HTTP/WebDAV port as its second parameter:

```
SQL> @$ORACLE_HOME/rdbms/admin/catxdbdbca.sql 7777 8888
```

When the port numbers have been assigned, the FTP service is available for immediate use.

By default, the FTP client will attempt to use Kerberos authentication when connecting to the FTP server. To suppress this specify the -u option when running ftp:

```
london1 $ ftp -u
```

The FTP prompt should be displayed. You can then open the host. For example, if you are running the FTP session on the same server, you might specify the following host and port number:

```
ftp> open localhost 7777
```

You will then be prompted for a username and password. Note that this should be an Oracle username, rather than an operating system username:

```
ftp> user system
331 pass required for SYSTEM
Password: oracle
230 SYSTEM logged in
```

If an ASM instance exists, then the ASM file system will be located under the /sys/asm directory. Each disk group will have its own subdirectory. You can use most of the standard FTP functionality, as in the following example:

```
ftp> cd /sys/asm/DISKGROUP1/RAC/CONTROLFILE
ftp> ls
-rw-r--r-- 1 SYS    oracle  7258112   SEP 08 18:30 Current.305.566832105
ftp> bin
ftp> get Current.305.566832105
ftp> bye
```

The preceding session navigates to the TEST/CONTROLFILE directory in DISKGROUP1 and copies the current control file to the local working directory. You can also use the put command to write files back to the ASM file system. If you are transferring binary files using FTP, make sure you first change the default file type to binary using the bin command. Note that the FTP wildcard commands mget and mput do not appear to work, so you will need to copy each file individually.

We recommend exercising some caution when using FTP to write files to the ASM file system, as it is possible to corrupt the database if you overwrite an existing file.

ASM Administration Using ASMCMD

In Oracle 10.2 and above, the ASMCMD utility allows you to inspect the files within the file system and to make very limited modifications. ASMCMD is not as flexible or functional as FTP. It does, however, provide an alternative in environments where FTP is not supported or available.

In order to use ASMCMD, you must first set your ORACLE_SID environment variable to the ASM instance name as follows:

```
export ORACLE_SID=+ASM1
```

Then, ASMCMD establishes a bequeath connection to the instance specified by $ORACLE_SID. The user must be a member of the SYSDBA group, as this privilege is set implicitly by ASMCMD during connection to the instance. When the ASMCMD utility starts successfully, it will display the ASMCMD> prompt.

The syntax of the ASMCMD utility is

```
asmcmd [-p] command
```

If you specify the -p option, the current directory will be displayed in the command prompt:

```
ASMCMD [+DATAFILE/ORCL/CONTROLFILE] >
```

In Oracle 10.2, ASMCMD supports the following commands:

- cd
- du
- find
- help
- ls
- lsct
- lsdg
- mkalias
- mkdir
- pwd
- rm
- rmalias

We describe these commands in the following sections.

cd

The cd command, which is similar to the Unix equivalent, allows you to change your current working directory within the ASMCMD session. The command has the following syntax:

```
cd <dir>
```

To change your current working directory within the ASMCMD session, you can specify a disk group as follows:

```
ASMCMD> cd +DISKGROUP1
```

You can also specify a relative directory:

```
ASMCMD> cd RAC
```

You can append multiple directory names using the following:

```
ASMCMD> cd +DISKGROUP1/RAC/ONLINELOG
```

To go back one level, use

```
ASMCMD> cd ..
```

To return to the root, use

```
ASMCMD> cd +
```

Unlike with Unix, however, the following command does not have any effect:

```
ASMCMD> cd /
```

du

The du command, which is similar to the Unix du -s command, displays the total amount of space for files located recursively under a specified directory. It has the following syntax:

```
du [-H] [dir]
```

If no directory is specified, the current directory is used as the default.

The du command returns two values: the amount of space used before mirroring and the amount of space used including mirrored copies. For example, if normal redundancy is used, the following will be displayed:

```
ASMCMD> du +DISKGROUP1/RAC/ONLINELOG
  Used_MB        Mirror_used_MB
      288                   576
```

You can suppress column headers from the output by specifying the -H option.

find

The find command allows you to search for files in the file system. You can specify a starting directory, which may include wildcards, and a file name pattern, which also may include wildcards. The command has the following syntax:

```
find [-t <type>] <dir> <pattern>
```

where <type> is a valid ASM file type. Common file types include the following:

```
CONTROLFILE
DATAFILE
ONLINELOG
PARAMETERFILE
TEMPFILE
```

For example, to search for all online logs, which in our example database were located in +DISKGROUP1/RAC/ONLINELOG, use the following:

```
ASMCMD > find +DISKGROUP1/RAC group*
+DISKGROUP1/RAC/ONLINELOG/group_1.274.563802389
+DISKGROUP1/RAC/ONLINELOG/group_2.275.563802389
+DISKGROUP1/RAC/ONLINELOG/group_3.278.563802389
+DISKGROUP1/RAC/ONLINELOG/group_4.279.563802389
```

Alternatively, you could perform the search by file type. For example, the following command searches for files of type ONLINELOG:

```
ASMCMD> find -t ONLINELOG +DISKGROUP1/RAC *
```

help

You can display a summary of the commands available in this tool using the following:

```
ASMCMD> help
```

You can also display detailed help for a specific command using help [command], as shown here:

```
ASMCMD> help cd
cd <dir>

Change the current directory to <dir>
```

ls

The ls command lists some or all files and their attributes. The syntax is as follows:

```
ls [-lsdrtLaH] [name]
```

If you do not specify a name, then all files in the current directory are listed. If you do not specify any options, ls returns a list of file names like the following:

```
ASMCMD> cd +DISKGROUP1/RAC/DATAFILE
ASMCMD> ls
SYSAUX.270.563802213
SYSTEM.269.563802213
UNDOTBS1.271.563802217
UNDOTBS2.277.563802499
USERS.272.563802217
```

This information is also available in V$ASM_ALIAS.NAME. You can include the wildcard character * in the name to list a set of files, as the following example shows:

```
ASMCMD> ls U*
UNDOTBS1.271.563802217
UNDOTBS2.277.563802499
USERS.272.563802217
```

You can modify the information returned using the -l option:

```
ASMCMD> ls -l
Type      Redund  Striped Time           Sys  Name
DATAFILE  UNPROT  COARSE  AUG 09 10:0:00  Y    SYSAUX.270.563802213
DATAFILE  UNPROT  COARSE  AUG 09 10:0:00  Y    SYSTEM.269.563802213
DATAFILE  UNPROT  COARSE  AUG 09 10:0.00  Y    UNDOTBS1.271.563802217
DATAFILE  UNPROT  COARSE  AUG 09 10:0:00  Y    UNDOTBS2.277.563802499
DATAFILE  UNPROT  COARSE  AUG 09 10:0:00  Y    USERS.272.563802217
```

This information is also available in V$ASM_FILE and V$ASM_ALIAS.
You can include sizing information using the following -s option:

```
ASMCMD> ls -s
Block_Size  Blocks      Bytes      Space  Name
      8192   42241  346038272  348127232  SYSAUX.270.563802213
      8192   61441  503324672  505413632  SYSTEM.269.563802213
      8192    9601   78651392   80740352  UNDOTBS1.271.563802217
      8192    3201   26222592   27262676  UNDOTBS2.277.563802499
      8192   27201  222830592  224395264  USERS.272.563802217
```

This information is taken from V$ASM_FILE.BLOCK_SIZE, V$ASM_FILE.BLOCKS, V$ASM_FILE.BYTES, V$ASM_FILE.SPACE, and V$ASM_ALIAS.NAME.

If you specify a directory as an argument, then by default the ls command will list the contents. You can display the name of the directory only using the following -d option:

```
ASMCMD> cd +DISKGROUP1/RAC
ASMCMD> ls D*
SYSAUX.270.563802213
SYSTEM.269.563802213
UNDOTBS1.271.563802217
UNDOTBS2.277.563802499
USERS.272.563802217
ASMCMD> ls -d D*
DATAFILE/
```

You can sort by time stamp using the -t option. This lists the latest file first. You can reverse the sort order by specifying the -r option. Combining the -r and -t options will list the most recent file last, which can be useful if you have a large number of files, as the ASMCMD utility does not yet have a page filter.

The information displayed depends on whether the name is a system-created file name or a user-defined alias.

For example, assume that a user-defined alias of USERS exists for the system-generated file USERS.272.563802217. By default, the following information will be displayed about the alias:

```
ASMCMD> ls -l USERS
Type      Redund  Striped Time          Sys Name
                                        N   USERS=> +DISKGROUP1/RAC/DATAFILE/
                                                    USERS.272.563802217
```

You can include information about the aliased file by including the -L option:

```
ASMCMD> ls -lL USERS
Type      Redund  Striped Time          Sys Name
DATAFILE  UNPROT  COARSE  AUG 09 10:0:00 Y   USERS=> +DISKGROUP1/RAC/DATAFILE/
                                                    USERS.272.563802217
```

You can use the -a option to obtain information about any user-defined alias for a system-created file name. Continuing the preceding example, by default, information about the system-created file name will be displayed using the following command:

```
ASMCMD> ls -l USERS.272..563802217
Type      Redund  Striped Time          Sys Name
DATAFILE  UNPROT  COARSE  AUG 09 10:0:00 Y   USERS=> +DISKGROUP1/RAC/DATAFILE/➡
USERS.272.563802217
```

You can include information about the alias by including the -a option:

```
Type      Redund  Striped Time          Sys Name
DATAFILE  UNPROT  COARSE  AUG 09 10:0:00 Y   +DISKGROUP1/RAC/DATAFILE/USERS➡
=> USERS.272.563802217
```

You can suppress column headers from the output by specifying the -H option.

lsct

The lsct command lists all clients and their attributes. This is a subset of the information returned by V$ASM_CLIENT. The syntax is as follows:

```
lsct [-H] [group]
```

for example,

```
ASMCMD> lsct
DB_Name  Status     Software_Version  Compatible_version  Instance_Name
RAC      CONNECTED       10.2.0.1.0         10.2.0.1.0     RAC1
```

You can suppress column headers from the output by specifying the -H option. According to the help message for this option, you can optionally specify a group. However, we were unable to get this syntax to work correctly on Oracle 10.2.0.1.

lsdg

The lsdg command lists all disk groups and their attributes and is a subset of the information returned by V$ASM_DISKGROUP. The following syntax applies:

```
lsdg [-H] [group]
```

This command produces output in the following format:

```
ASMCMD> lsdg
State     Type    Rebal  Unbal  Sector  Block        AU  Total_MB  Free MB
MOUNTED   EXTERN  N      N         512   4096   1048576    143076   140497

Req_mirror_free_MB Usable_file_MB  Offline disks  Name
                 0         140497                0  DISKGROUP1/
```

We have modified the output for readability. You can suppress column headers from the output by specifying the -H option here as well. The command will also show if a rebalance operation is currently in progress. You can optionally specify a disk group, as in the following example:

```
ASMCMD> lsdg DISKGROUP1
```

mkalias

The mkalias command allows you to create a user-defined alias for a file. The alias must be created in the same disk group as the system-created file. Aliases are analogous to hard links in Unix file systems. However, unlike Unix hard links, you can create only one user-defined alias for each file, using the following syntax:

```
mkalias <filename> <alias>
```

For example, the following command creates an ASM alias of USERS for the ASM file USERS.272.563802217:

```
ASMCMD> mkalias USERS.272.563802217
```

The mkalias command is equivalent to the following SQL command:

```
SQL> ALTER DISKGROUP <datagroup_name> ADD ALIAS <alias>;
```

mkdir

The mkdir command allows you to create a directory within the ASM file system. The command has the following syntax:

```
mkdir <dir1 dir2 ... >
```

As shown here, the directory can be specified using either an absolute or a relative pathname:

```
ASMCMD> mkdir +DISKGROUP1/RAC/ONLINELOG2
ASMCMD> cd +DISKGROUP1/RAC
ASMCMD> mkdir ONLINELOG3
```

You cannot create a directory within the root (+) directory.

The `mkdir` command is equivalent to the following SQL command:

```
SQL> ALTER DISKGROUP <diskgroup_name> ADD DIRECTORY <dir1, dir2, ...>
```

pwd

The following `pwd` command, similar to its Unix equivalent, prints the current working directory within the ASMCMD session:

```
ASMCMD> pwd
+DISKGROUP1/RAC/ONLINELOG
```

At the root level, this command will print the following:

```
ASMCMD> pwd
+
```

rm

The `rm` command deletes aliases, files, and directories from the file system. It uses the following syntax:

```
rm [-rf] <name1 name2 ...>
```

and is equivalent to the following SQL command:

```
SQL> ALTER DISKGROUP <diskgroup_name> DROP FILE <name1, name2 ...>;
```

Take extreme care to understand the semantics of this command. If a file name or alias is specified, then the `rm` command deletes both the system-created file and the user-defined alias. This is not analogous to hard links in Unix file systems, where the file will remain after an alias is deleted. If you wish to delete just the alias, then use the `rmalias` command instead.

If a directory name is specified, then the `rm` command will only delete it if it is user-defined and empty. The `rm` command will not delete system-created or nonempty directories.

You can optionally specify the `-r` option to delete files and directories recursively. If you specify either the `-r` option or a wildcard in the name, you will be prompted for confirmation before each file is deleted. You can force deletion by specifying the `-f` option.

rmalias

The `rmalias` command allows you to delete a user-defined alias for a file. It does not, however, delete the file or its system-created file name. The syntax is as follows:

```
rmalias [r] <alias1 dir1 alias2 dir2>
```

For example, the following command deletes the user-defined alias USERS:

```
ASMCMD> rmalias USERS
```

The following SQL command is equivalent to `rmalias`:

```
SQL> ALTER DISKGROUP <datagroup_name> DROP ALIAS <alias>;
```

If you specify the `-r` option, then `rmalias` will recursively delete user-defined directories and user-defined aliases. It will not, however, delete system-created directories and system-created file names.

Specifying `rmalias` with the `-r` option is equivalent to the SQL command:

```
SQL> ALTER DISKGROUP <datagroup_name> DROP DIRECTORY <dir> FORCE;
```

Monitoring ASM

In this section, we will describe some of the dynamic performance views (V$) and fixed views (X$) that have been introduced to support ASM. All views are compiled into the Oracle kernel and are, therefore, available in both the ASM and RDBMS instances. However, they do not necessarily contain the same information in each instance type.

Dynamic Performance Views

A number of new dynamic performance views have been introduced to support ASM. These views contain different information, depending on whether they are accessed from the ASM instance or the RDBMS instance only. The dynamic performance views are as follows:

- **V$ASM_ALIAS**: In the ASM instance, this view lists all aliases in all currently mounted disk groups. It is not used in the database instance.

- **V$ASM_CLIENT**: In the ASM instance, V$ASM_CLIENT lists all client databases currently accessing disk groups. In the database instance, it contains one row for the ASM instance, if the database has any currently open ASM files.

- **V$ASM_DISK**: In the ASM instance, V$ASM_DISK lists all disks discovered by the ASM instance. In the database instance, it contains one row for each disk in disk groups currently in use by the database instance.

- **V$ASM_DISKGROUP**: In the ASM instance, this view lists all disk groups discovered by the instance. In the database instance, it lists all disk groups currently in use by the instance.

- **V$ASM_FILE**: In the ASM instance, all ASM files belonging to disk groups mounted by the ASM instance are listed by this view. It is not used in the database instance.

- **V$ASM_OPERATION**: In the ASM instance, this view shows information about any long-running operations, such as rebalancing, and it is not used in the database instance.

- **V$ASM_TEMPLATE**: In the ASM instance, V$AM_TEMPLATE shows all templates for all disk groups currently mounted by the instance. In the database instance, it lists all templates for disk groups currently in use by the instance.

Oracle 10.2 or above also includes the two following additional dynamic performance views:

- **V$ASM_DISKGROUP_STAT**: In the ASM instance, this view provides the same information as V$ASM_DISKGROUP, but it does not discover new disk groups.

- **V$ASM_DISK_STAT**: This view provides the same information as V$ASM_DISK in the ASM instance, but it does not discover new disks.

These two views are less resource intensive than their counterparts from the previous list, but they will not include information about disks or disk groups that have been added since the ASM instance was started.

Fixed Views

A number of new fixed views have been introduced to support ASM (see Table 9-2). Most of these are used by the new dynamic performance views discussed in the previous section.

Table 9-2. *ASM Fixed Views*

View Name	Description
X$KFALS	ASM aliases
X$KFDSK	ASM disks
X$KFFIL	ASM files
X$KFGRP	ASM disk groups
X$KFGMG	ASM operations
X$KFKID	ASM disk performance
X$KFNCL	ASM clients
X$KFMTA	ASM templates

There are two additional fixed views called X$KFFXP and X$KFDAT. In the ASM instance, these views externalize the mappings between ASM disk extents and database file extents. There are no equivalent dynamic performance views for these fixed views in either Oracle 10.1 or Oracle 10.2.

X$KFFXP

This view contains one row for every extent that is currently in use in each ASM disk. Useful columns in this view include those listed in Table 9-3.

Table 9-3. *X$KFFXP Columns*

Column Name	Description
GROUP_KFFXP	Disk group number
NUMBER_KFFXP	ASM file number
INCARN_KFFXP	ASM file incarnation number
XNUM_KFFXP	ASM file extent number
DISK_KFFXP	ASM disk number
AU_KFFXP	ASM disk allocation unit number

The view describes the mapping between each extent in the ASM file (GROUP_KFFXP, NUMBER_KFFXP, INCARN_KFFXP, and XNUM_KFFXP) and each allocation unit in the ASM disk group (GROUP_KFFXP, DISK_KFFXP, and AU_KFFXP).

The X$KFFXP view is useful for determining how well balanced individual disks are within a disk group. You can use the following code to check:

```
SQL> SELECT group_kffxp, disk_kffxp, COUNT(*)
FROM x$kffxp
GROUP BY group_kffxp, disk_kffxp;
```

X$KFDAT

This view contains one row for every extent in each ASM disk, and useful columns in this view include those listed in Table 9-4.

Table 9-4. *X$KFDAT Columns*

Column Name	Description
GROUP_KFDAT	Disk group number
NUMBER_KFDAT	ASM disk number
AUNUM_KFDAT	ASM disk allocation unit number
FNUM_KFDAT	ASM file number
XNUM_KFDAT	ASM file extent number

The view describes the mapping between each allocation unit in the ASM disk group (GROUP_KFDAT, NUMBER_KFDAT, and AUNUM_KFDAT) and each extent in the ASM file (GROUP_KFDAT, FNUM_KFDAT, and XNUM_KFDAT).

Summary

In this chapter, we examined ASM in detail. At the time of this writing, ASM has not completely fulfilled its promise in terms of performance and manageability. However, Oracle Corporation has dedicated a considerable amount of resources to resolving the underlying issues, and ASM is clearly a priority. Therefore, we can reasonably assume that ASM will continue to evolve and improve over subsequent releases.

ASM is unlikely to compete, in terms of performance, with third-party storage solutions. However, many Oracle customers implement RAC for reasons of availability rather than performance, and ASM may be sufficient for such purposes.

For some users, ASM may also represent a reduction in management costs. However, for most sites, we think this argument is dubious. If you already have a consolidated storage policy, a dedicated storage team, and non-Oracle databases or legacy Oracle databases (prior to Oracle 10.1), then the complexities of changing your working practices to accommodate ASM may significantly outweigh any manageability benefits.

Ultimately, however, we anticipate that ASM will entirely replace OCFS for RAC clusters. Therefore, if you are deploying RAC, we recommend that you investigate ASM before committing to OCFS or a third-party storage solution.

CHAPTER 10

■ ■ ■

Installing Linux

This chapter describes the steps required to install the Linux software operating system for the Oracle Database 10g RAC. The emphasis is placed on the Red Hat and SUSE Linux releases supported by Oracle under the Unbreakable Linux Partner Initiative and therefore you should review Chapter 2 to ensure that the benefits and restrictions of deciding to use an Unbreakable Linux platform are fully understood. The installation process is covered for the standard hardware platforms supported by Oracle under Unbreakable Linux, namely x86, x86-64, and Intel Itanium. The installation steps described in this chapter should be performed identically on each node in the cluster.

Linux Software Selection

One of the major choices in selecting between the versions of a particular Linux flavor is dependent on the Linux kernel on which the release is based. Oracle 10.1 and 10.2 span a major Linux kernel revision from the 2.4 to the 2.6 kernel and run on releases based on both kernel versions. In terms of the Red Hat and SUSE versions of Linux, at the time of this writing, the supported releases available for the Oracle Database 10g based on a 2.4 kernel are Red Hat 2.1, Red Hat 3, and SUSE 8. The 2.6 kernel–based versions are Red Hat 4 and SUSE 9. It should be noted that Red Hat 3 is somewhat an exception because, although it is 2.4 kernel–based, it contains a number of features backported from the 2.6 kernel. In addition, Red Hat 2.1 is only supported for Oracle 10.1. Bearing this in mind, it is useful to understand the benefits of a 2.6 kernel–based release.

In terms of Oracle, some of the advantages of a 2.6-based kernel are related to I/O configuration and performance. In particular, there is no limitation of the 256 disk devices imposed on the 2.4-based releases, and individual partitions can be sized in excess of 2TB. There is also support for asynchronous I/O and direct I/O within the kernel, as opposed to patch-based support at 2.4. The main benefits here are improved performance and a reduction in CPU utilization for I/O purposes. There are also significant improvements within the virtual memory implementation, meaning that thousands of users can be handled reliably and larger amounts of memory can be supported. On a 32-bit system this means memory can be used beyond the 2.4 kernel practical limitation of 16GB, up to the 64GB installable maximum on the 2.6 kernel–based releases of Red Hat and SUSE Linux.

■**Note** The maximum memory of 64GB applies to 32-bit x86 releases of Linux only. On x86-64, the certified maximum memory is 128GB with a theoretical maximum of 1TB. On Intel Itanium, the certified maximum memory is 256GB with a theoretical maximum of 1024TB.

Huge TLB–based features implemented in the 2.6 kernel also deliver improved performance, (the importance of the TLB is discussed in Chapter 6). The virtual memory improvements are also conducive to the scalability improvements in the kernel, such as Non-Uniform Memory Access (NUMA) support. In addition, whereas the 2.4 kernel ran optimally on systems with up to 4 CPUs, the 2.6 kernel efficiently supports systems with 32 CPUs and beyond, making Linux-based RAC clusters with nodes of greater than 4 CPUs a practicable alternative, a factor that is also of importance in multicore CPU environments.

The stability and benefits of the 2.6 kernel lead us to recommend the use of a minimum release level of Red Hat Enterprise Linux 4 AS or SUSE Linux Enterprise Server 9 wherever possible, and for the reasons detailed we focus on these releases for the Linux installations in this chapter.

Hardware Requirements

Oracle publishes a minimal set of hardware requirements for each server. These are shown in Table 10-1. The minimum requirements are needed to install and configure a working Oracle database; production environments should adhere to at least the recommended values. We strongly recommend that every node of the cluster has an identical hardware configuration, although this is not strictly mandatory.

Table 10-1. *Minimum and Recommended Server Requirements*

Hardware	Minimum	Recommended
CPU	1 CPU per node	2 or more CPUs per node
Interconnect network	1Gb	2 teamed Gb
External network	100Mb	1Gb
Backup network	100Mb	1Gb
HBA or NIC for SAN, iSCSI, or NAS	1Gb HBA	Dual-pathed storage vendor certified HBA
Memory	512MB per node	1GB to 2GB per CPU
Oracle server software disk space	1.5GB	3GB
Companion software disk space	1GB	2GB
Temporary disk space	400MB	1GB

Networking Requirements

An important step to be taken before installation is to specify the network configuration for each node in the cluster. This involves allocating server hostnames and private interconnect names, public IP addresses, VIP addresses, and private IP addresses. In addition, you will need to establish subnet names, subnet masks, and domain names. In more sophisticated networks you may also need to consider routers, Domain Name System (DNS) servers, Network Information Service (NIS) servers, and Lightweight Directory Access Protocol (LDAP) servers. Discuss these requirements with your system and network administrators.

We suggest that you follow a logical naming convention that is easy to remember. There is nothing to stop you from configuring a host named *server1*, with private interconnect *server2-priv*, and a VIP of *server3-vip*. However, doing so increases the probability of human errors occurring. In addition, if you anticipate adding nodes to the cluster in the future, remember to allow for these nodes in your naming scheme.

Ensure that all public IP addresses and VIP addresses are unique within the network and located on the same subnet, and, if required, have been added to your DNS configuration. Table 10-2 shows a sample network configuration checklist for a two-node cluster.

Table 10-2. *Sample Network Configuration*

Network Configuration	Example
Node names	london1, london2
VIP names	london1-vip, london2-vip
Interconnect names	london1-priv, london2-priv
External IP addresses	147.43.1.101, 147,43,1,102
VIP addresses	147.43.1.201, 147.43.1.202
Private interconnect IP addresses	192.168.1.1, 192.168.1.2
Gateway	147.43.1.254
External subnet mask	255.255.0.0
Private interconnect subnet mask	255.255.255.0
DNS domain name	sourceora.com
DNS server	147.43.1.251

Installing Red Hat Enterprise Linux 4 AS

This section describes installation of Red Hat Enterprise Linux version 4. It is applicable to x86, x86-64, and Itanium architecture–based systems and to Advanced Server (AS) and Enterprise Server (ES) versions. Where we use AS we also mean ES; the main difference is that the ES version only supports up to two processors and 16GB of RAM.

The operating system software can be supplied by a number of methods, including CD-ROM, NFS, FTP, and HTTP. We will concentrate on the most commonly used method, which is a direct install from CD-ROM.

Note You may need to download the installation media from the Internet. Both Red Hat and SUSE Linux are supplied as a series of ISO files. These should be burned to CD-ROM using a CD-writing utility that is capable of writing ISO files. If your CD writer is attached to a Linux system, you can use the cdrecord utility; if your CD writer is attached to a Windows system, you can download cdburn.exe, which is part of the Windows Resource Kit.

Starting the Installation

The precise method used to start the CD-ROM–based installation depends on the architecture of the server, whether it is x86, x86-64, or Itanium.

Installation on x86 or x86-64

To start a CD-ROM–based install on an x86 architecture server with a standard BIOS layer, boot the server with the first CD-ROM of the install set. It may be necessary to configure the BIOS to select the Boot from CD-ROM option. The BIOS can usually be accessed when booting the server by pressing a key combination dependent on the BIOS vendor.

Upon a successful boot from CD-ROM, the following prompt should be displayed:

```
To install or upgrade Red Hat enterprise Linux in graphical mode,
Press the <ENTER> key.
```

Press the Enter key to run the Red Hat Anaconda installer.

Installation on Itanium

Instead of the BIOS layer, Itanium-based systems (and potentially x86 systems) use the Extensible Firmware Interface (EFI) as the interface between the operating system and the platform firmware. EFI resides permanently in NVRAM, enabling access to the boot interface without any additional external software.

An installation on an EFI-based system can be initiated by booting the server with the first CD-ROM of the install media in the CD-ROM drive. An install session can also be started from the boot manager menu on a booted EFI-based server by selecting the CD-ROM drive and pressing the Enter key as follows:

```
Please select a boot option
CD/DVD ROM/Pci (1F|1) /Ata(Primary,Master)
ELILO boot:
```

Lastly, the installer can be started on a prebooted Itanium-based system by navigating to the device corresponding to the CD-ROM drive. The EFI map command lists the mapping of devices; for example, if fs0 corresponds to the CD-ROM device, type fs0: at the prompt.

```
Shell> fs0:
```

Remember to append the colon after the device name. The ELILO Linux bootloader can then be started manually using this command:

```
Fs0:\> elilo.efi
ELILO boot:
```

Installation Media Check

Before a Red Hat Enterprise Linux CD-ROM–based install session you are prompted with the option to verify the installation media. We recommend that you test the media before using it for the first time to avoid unnecessary failures later in the installation process.

Test each individual CD-ROM from the install set by selecting OK. Alternatively, if the media has already been verified, choose Skip to start the Red Hat Linux Anaconda installer.

Anaconda Installation

The welcome page gives details of installation instructions and an opportunity to review the release notes. When you are ready, click Next to continue.

Language Selection

Choose the language to use for the installation process and click Next. The language specified here is used during the installation process; a different language can be specified when the operating system is installed onto the system.

Keyboard Configuration

Choose an appropriate keyboard and click Next. This selection can be modified once the system is operational through the System Settings menu.

Upgrade Examine

The installer searches for the existence of any previous installations of Red Hat Enterprise Linux. If there has been an installation of Red Hat Linux on the system, such as version 3, the installer detects the installation and displays on the Upgrade Examine page the option to upgrade. We recommend always doing a fresh install to achieve the most consistent installation base across all of the nodes in the cluster. Choose Install Red Hat Enterprise Linux AS and click Next. If there is no previous installation detected, or the Linux operating system is not a Red Hat release, this page will not be displayed and the installation will proceed to the Disk Partitioning Setup page.

Disk Partitioning

To install a Red Hat Enterprise Linux system suitable for Oracle Database 10g RAC, we recommend creating a customized partitioning scheme. To do this, select the Manually Partition with Disk Druid option and click Next.

The Disk Setup page will be displayed showing the options for partitioning. The top pane displays the drives available and their corresponding sizes; the bottom pane shows any existing partitions. If the drives are not currently partitioned, all the devices will be shown as *Free*.

Note We recommend that your server disk drives are protected by a form of onboard RAID storage as detailed in Chapter 6. If onboard RAID is not available, you should consider the options for configuring a Logical Volume Manager during the disk partitioning stage, in addition to the partitioning recommendations given here.

If you are using a SAN configuration and your HBA is correctly installed and configured with LUNs presented to the system, you will also see these external LUNs presented as disks for configuration. Do not install the operating system on these external drives unless you are intending to use a boot-from-SAN configuration.

There are a number of options in partitioning the devices suitable for a node of Oracle Database 10g RAC. If the Oracle software is to be installed locally on each node then it is necessary to remember that at least 1.5GB of disk space will need to be available for this installation. If you have decided to use a shared directory for the Oracle binaries, it is not necessary to allocate space locally for them.

The choice of partitioning formats is dependent on whether the interface between the hardware and operating system is BIOS- or EFI-based. With BIOS-based systems the most commonly used partitioning format, typically on x86 and x86-64 systems, is the MS-DOS–based master boot record (MBR) format. With the MBR format, up to 4 primary partitions can be created on each disk. One of these primary partitions can be extended and subdivided into logical partitions. The logical partitions are chained together, so, theoretically, the maximum number of logical partitions is unlimited. However, for SCSI disks, Linux limits the total number of partitions to 15. Typically, the most common support for SCSI disks within Linux is based on 32-bit block addresses limiting any single partition to 2TB in size. This limit is also enforced within the MBR formatting scheme and the 2.4 kernel. Therefore, using either 32-bit SCSI addressing hardware, MBR formatting, or a 2.4 kernel will mean the maximum partition size is 2TB. The MBR format stores one copy of the partition table and also stores some system data in hidden or unpartitioned sectors, which is an important factor when ensuring that disk partitions are correctly aligned with external storage arrays as discussed in Chapter 7.

EFI-based systems also support MBR formatting; however, we recommend using the GUID partition table (GPT) format for the advantages that this scheme brings. Firstly, GPT partitions are not limited to the primary and logical partitioning of the MBR and, instead, support up to 128 partitions per disk. Subject to using 64-bit SCSI addressing and a 2.6 kernel–based system, GPT partitions can be up to 18 exabytes in size, as opposed to the 2TB limit. In addition, the GPT partitioning format uses primary and backup partition tables and checksum fields for redundancy and integrity to protect against partition table corruption. GPT partition tables also do not store any data in hidden sectors making alignment offsets for external storage arrays unnecessary with this scheme. Up to and including Red Hat 4 the Red Hat Anaconda installer only supports GPT partition tables on

Itanium-based systems, and therefore only Itanium platforms support creating devices of larger than 2TB during and after installation. The / (root device) and /boot directories must always be configured on devices of 2TB in size or less, irrespective of the partitioning format.

Many system administrators prefer to partition the system with a number of partitions for distinct / (root device), swap, /boot, /home, /var, /usr /home, ORACLE_BASE, and other site-dependent configurations. One of the main historical factors for adopting this schema was the risk of corruption and the time taken to complete file system checks in the event of a system restart when using a nonjournaled file system. For Linux-based Oracle Database 10g RAC nodes, when the 2TB limit of the / (root device) is not a limiting factor and journaled file systems such as ext3 are available, we have found that simplicity gives the most flexible approach. Therefore, we recommend a minimal configuration. For Red Hat Enterprise Linux on x86 and x86-64 based systems this must include at least two partitions: a root partition (/) and a swap partition (swap). For Itanium systems, it must include at least three partitions: a root partition (/), a boot partition (/boot/efi)—of which both must be type VFAT—and a swap partition (swap). The additional EFI system partition is only required on one disk in the system and partly maintains some of the functional equivalence of the hidden data within the MBR formatting scheme. The database software is usually located within a directory tree below the ORACLE_BASE directory. Under the Optimal Flexible Architecture the mount point is the /u01 directory. If only one physical disk is available, an additional primary partition can be created for the /u01 mount point. Alternatively, the /u01 can be created in the root partition. If more than one physical disk is available, we recommend using the second disk for the /u01 directory.

Taking an example 160GB device, the chosen partitioning scheme could be 100MB for the boot partition (/boot on x86 and x86-64, and /boot/efi on Itanium) and 6GB for the swap partition (swap), and the remaining disk space divided between the root partition (/) and the ORACLE_BASE partition (/u01).

The space required for the boot device is dependent on the number of kernels compiled and configured for booting. Oracle Database 10g RAC nodes only require the standard precompiled kernel and, therefore, space utilization rarely exceeds 30MB. The actual space used is dependent on the hardware architecture.

In terms of swap space, Oracle recommends that a system must have at least 1GB. For systems with more than 2GB of RAM, the swap space should be between one and two times the size of RAM. Red Hat recommends a swap partition equal to twice the amount of RAM you have on the system, up to 2GB of RAM, and then an equal amount of swap to RAM for any RAM available above 2GB. There is no limit on the maximum size of an individual swap partition on any architecture, including 32-bit x86 systems. The only restrictions are that no more than 64GB of swap can be configured in total within 32 individual swap partitions or swap files per system.

Swap space can be regarded as a disk-based component of virtual memory. In Linux, unlike some other UNIX operating systems, virtual memory is the sum total of RAM plus swap space. The requirements for swap being one or two times the size of RAM are often based on the requirements of traditional UNIX operating systems. This swap configuration was required because an executable program had been loaded into both swap space and RAM at the same time. Oracle's guidelines on swap allocation tend to reflect these traditional requirements. Linux on the other hand maintains swap space for demand paging. When an executable is loaded on Linux it is likely that a portion of it will not be required—for example, much of the error-handling code. For efficiency, Linux only loads virtual memory pages when they are used. If RAM is fully utilized and one process requires loading a page into RAM, Linux will write out the page to swap space from another process, according to a Least Recently Used (LRU) algorithm.

As the performance of disk-based storage is orders of magnitude slower than memory you should plan to never be in the position of having pages written to swap because of demand for RAM from competing processes. Oracle should always run in RAM without exception. As a basic rule, for Oracle on Linux you do not need a significant amount of swap if there is enough memory installed. Every rule has an exception, however, and Linux tends to be reasonably aggressive in managing swap space, maintaining as much RAM to be free as possible. It does this by writing out memory pages to swap that have not been recently used, even if there is no current demand for the memory at the time. This approach is designed to prevent a greater impact on performance than doing all of the maintenance work when the space is required. And it frees up RAM for potential other uses such as the disk buffer.

With this information we can intelligently size swap for Oracle. For the basic operating environment, swap should not be utilized by the Oracle SGA and core processes during normal operations. Therefore, with enough memory, even a single 2GB swap partition will often suffice with no impact on performance. The exception is the case where many Oracle user processes are created and intersperse active periods with idle time. In this scenario it is necessary to allocate swap for when these processes are temporarily paged out of memory. The swap space needed will depend upon application requirements. However, it is also likely from this application profile that an Oracle shared server configuration will be more efficient.

Taking as an example a system with 4GB of RAM and sufficient disk capacity for swap, we recommend using the Red Hat guidelines and configuring 6GB of swap, 4GB to represent double the first 2GB of RAM, and an additional one-to-one mapping of RAM to swap for the remaining 2GB. In this scenario, we should have enough swap capacity for any eventuality within an Oracle environment. If additional swap space is required at a later point in time, it can also be added when the system is operational using the mkswap command.

To begin partitioning the disk, highlight the free space available in the bottom pane of the Disk Setup page and click New. This brings up the Add Partition dialog box shown in Figure 10-1.

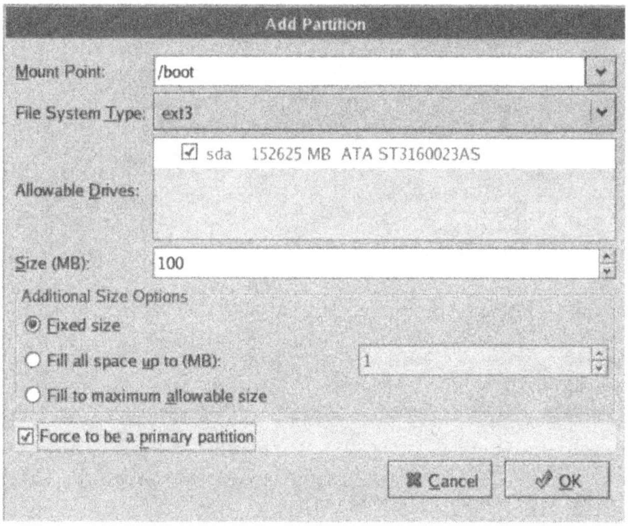

Figure 10-1. *Add Partition dialog box*

From the Mount Point drop-down list, select /boot on x86 and x86-64, or /boot/efi on Itanium. For the File System Type select ext3 for x86 and x86-64, or VFAT for Itanium. If more than one disk drive is available, all of the drives will be selected by default as Allowable Drives. Uncheck any external drives to prevent the operating system from being installed onto them. Leave the default 100 for Size (MB), and ensure Fixed Size is selected in Additional Size Options. On x86 and x86-64 systems, select Force to Be a Primary Partition. On Itanium systems, the GPT partitioning scheme is used by default and there is no requirement for primary or extended partitions. The Force to Be a Primary Partition check box is therefore not included within the Add Partition dialog. Click OK to save this partition configuration information.

With the remaining free space on the device highlighted, click New again to bring up the Add Partition dialog box. For File System Type select Swap, and the Mount Point drop-down will change to <Not Applicable>. Enter the size of the required swap partition and ensure that Fixed Size is selected in Additional Size Options. Do not select Force to Be a Primary Partition. Since swap will not be heavily used during normal operations, it can be placed toward the less efficient end portion of the disk without overdue concern. Do not modify any other options before clicking OK. In particular, do not select Fill to Maximum Allowable Size when sizing swap, since the installer will incorrectly limit the swap partition size to 2GB.

Highlight the remaining free space and click New to bring up the Add Partition dialog box for the third time. Select a Mount Point of / and a File System Type of ext3, and select Force to Be a Primary Partition. If you're not creating the ORACLE_BASE directory as a separate mount point do not modify the Size (MB) option. Instead, select Fill to Maximum Allowable Size in the Additional Size Options and click OK. If creating an additional partition on the same disk for the ORACLE_BASE directory limit the / partition to a fixed size of approximately half the remaining disk space, and create an additional /u01 partition using the same process to fill to the maximum allowable size.

The partitioning pane will then display the configured formatted scheme as shown in Figure 10-2.

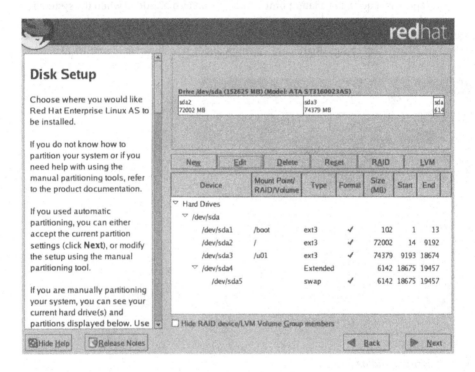

Figure 10-2. *Partitioning pane*

You can see that when precisely four partitions are created on x86 or x86-64 systems the installer creates an extended partition, even though its use is not strictly necessary, since four primary partitions would suffice. On an Itanium-based system the GPT partitioning scheme means that there will not be an extended partition created by the installer in any circumstance. Click Next to save the partitioning map and advance to the Boot Loader Configuration page on x86 and x86-64 systems. The disks will not be physically partitioned at this point. This will only occur once all of the installation information has been collected and before the installation of packages has commenced.

Boot Loader Configuration

The Boot Loader Configuration page is displayed on x86 and x86-64 systems. Accept all of the default GRUB bootloader options. Click Next to continue to the Network Configuration page. On an Itanium system the configuration is done through EFI and the associated Linux bootloader ELILO and therefore this page is not displayed.

Network Configuration

An Oracle Database 10g RAC node needs at least two network devices, one for the external interface and one for the private interconnect network. These network devices should already have been cabled and configured to their respective networks by a network administrator. Assuming Ethernet is used, these will be displayed as devices with names eth0, eth1, eth2, and so on. If you are planning to use NIC teaming for interconnect resilience as discussed in Chapter 6, the Network Configuration page will display more than the required number of devices. As teaming cannot be configured until after installation is complete, only configure primary devices leaving the Active on Boot check box unchecked against the planned secondary devices. The primary device configuration created at this stage will be useful when migrating to the teamed configuration.

Whether using single network devices or a teamed configuration it is important to ensure that all nodes have the same interface name for the external device. For example if eth0 is configured as the public interface on the first node then eth0 should also be selected as the public interface on all of the other nodes. This is a requirement for the correct operation of the VIP addresses configured during the Oracle Clusterware software installation.

On the Network Configuration page, highlight the primary external devices—for example, eth0—and click Edit. This brings up the Edit Interface dialog box for eth0. We strongly recommend that you use fixed IP addresses for all Oracle servers; therefore, uncheck the Configure Using DHCP check box. Ensure that the Activate on Boot check box is selected. Complete the IP Address and Netmask as supplied by your network administrator and click OK. Complete the information for the private interconnect device using an IP address from Table 10-3. These IP addresses have been reserved for use in private networks. For most clusters with less than 254 nodes, a class-C network address with a nonsegmented subnet mask (255.255.255.0) should be sufficient.

Table 10-3. *IP Addresses for Private Networks*

Class	Networks	Subnet Mask
A	10.0.0.0 through 10.255.255.255	255.0.0.0
B	172.16.0.0 through 172.31.0.0	255.255.0.0
C	192.168.0.0 through 192.168.255.0	255.255.255.0

Manually set the hostname and any gateway or DNS server addresses to appropriate values as advised by your network administrator.

Your naming conventions should allow for additional nodes and also for any standby databases that may be added in the future. If planning to use an Oracle Data Guard standby configuration we recommend using a geographically based naming convention where the first node in the cluster would be london1, the second node london2, a third node would be london3, and so on, tailored to your location. Figure 10-3 shows a configuration for host london1 with an external network configuration on eth0 and an interconnect configuration on eth1.

When you have finished updating the network settings, click Next to continue to the Firewall Configuration page.

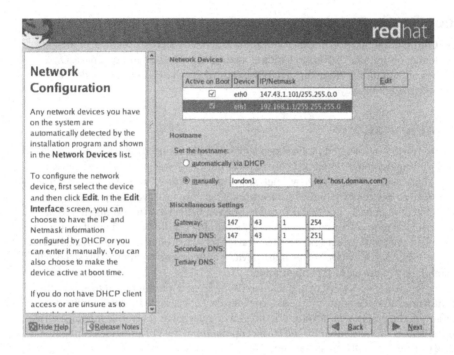

Figure 10-3. *Network Configuration page*

Firewall Configuration

Red Hat Enterprise Linux enables varying degrees of network security to be configured. However, for an Oracle Database 10g RAC node, enabling a firewall configuration can inhibit the correct functioning of Oracle services. For the Oracle Database 10g RAC, we suggest you implement a dedicated firewall infrastructure on the network, but do not configure a firewall on any of the Oracle nodes themselves. On the Firewall page, therefore, choose No Firewall and click Next to continue. There is an additional warning dialog box to confirm that no firewall has been configured; click Proceed to advance to the Additional Language Support page.

Additional Language Support

The Additional Language Support page is somewhat inappropriately titled and is often mistaken for languages in addition to the language selected on the Language Selection page. Instead, on this page the default language for the system is the language that will be used once the system is operational. The additional languages provide alternatives should you choose to switch languages at a later point. For an Oracle Database 10g RAC node it should not be necessary to change languages once operational and, therefore, a single default language should be sufficient. The default chosen will always be highlighted in the Additional Languages pane, and at least one language must be selected. Therefore, if you wish to deselect the default language of English (USA), you must select your other language first. Click Next to continue to the Time Zone Selection page.

Time Zone Selection

The time zone required will be determined by the geographical location of your cluster. All nodes within a cluster should have the same time zone configuration. You can select the nearest location on the interactive map or from the drop-down list below the map.

Red Hat Enterprise Linux allows you to specify whether the hardware clock should be set to UTC/GMT time or local time. We recommend setting the system clock to UTC by checking System Clock Uses UTC. This enables automatic adjustment for regional daylight saving time. Setting the hardware clock to local time is useful only for systems that are configured to dual boot with other operating systems that require a local time setting. It is unlikely that you will want to configure dual booting for a production Oracle Database 10g RAC node.

After selecting the correct system time zone, click Next to continue to the Root Password Configuration page.

Root Password Configuration

The password for the root user account must be at least six characters in length. Enter and confirm a suitable password, and click Next to continue to the Package Installation Defaults page.

Package Installation Defaults

The Package Installation Defaults page gives the option to accept a default set of packages for the Linux installation or to customize the set of packages available. For an Oracle Database 10g RAC node the default installation omits some essential packages and includes some that are not required. Choose the Customize the Set of Packages to Be Installed option and click Next to continue to the Package Group Selection page.

Package Group Selection

The Package Group Selection page shown in Figure 10-4 allows you to select groups of packages using the associated check boxes and to select individual packages by clicking Details.

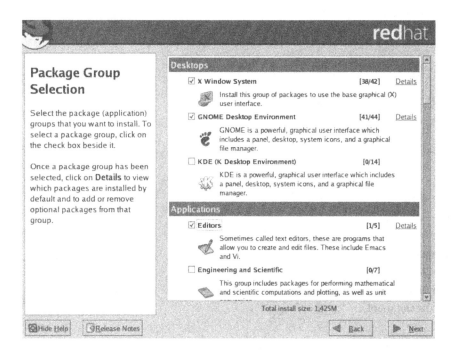

Figure 10-4. *Package Group Selection page*

Table 10-4 illustrates the minimal set of package groups required to support an Oracle Database 10*g* RAC installation. The options include an X Window desktop environment and graphical administration tools. You may wish to install additional packages specific to your environment, however, do not omit any packages selected here.

Table 10-4. *Package Group Selection*

Package	Recommended Selection
Desktops	
X Window System	✓
GNOME desktop environment	✓
KDE (K Desktop Environment)	✗
Applications	
Editors	✓
Engineering and scientific	✗
Graphical Internet	✓
Text-based Internet	✗
Office/productivity	✗
Sound and video	✗
Authoring and publishing	✗
Graphics	✗
Games and entertainment	✗
Servers	
Server configuration tools	✗
Web server	✗
Mail server	✗
Windows file server	✗
DNS name server	✗
FTP server	✗
PostgreSQL database	✗
MySQL database	✗
News server	✗
Network servers	✗
Legacy network server	✗
Development	
Development tools	✓
X software development	✗
GNOME software development	✗
KDE software development	✗
Legacy software development	✗

Package	Recommended Selection
System	
Administration tools	✓
System tools	✗
Printing support	✗
Miscellaneous	
Everything	✗
Minimal	✗

The administration tools are only required if you intend to administer the server using GUI tools. If you are comfortable using the command line for operating system administration you do not need to install these packages. When you have selected all of the recommended packages, click Next to continue to the About to Install page.

Start Installation

Click Next to proceed with the installation from the About to Install page. The Required Media dialog box is displayed detailing the CDs that will be needed, depending on the packages selected. Click Continue to initiate the installation process.

Installing Packages

The Installing Packages page shows the packages currently being installed and gives an estimate of the time remaining to complete the installation. Change the CD-ROM when prompted by the installer.

Installation Complete

Following package installation, remove any remaining CD-ROMs and click Reboot.

Welcome

The first time that the system boots after installation it calls the /etc/rc.d/init.d/firstboot script, enabling final configuration before the installation process completes. After the first occasion that this has been run, the process creates the file /etc/sysconfig/firstboot with an entry RUN_FIRSTBOOT=NO. To rerun firstboot on any subsequent reboots, it is necessary to remove this file and ensure the firstboot script is called during the boot process by executing the command chkconfig -level 5 firstboot on. When firstboot runs, the Welcome screen is displayed with the stages required for the firstboot process listed in the left-hand pane. Click Next to advance to the first of these, the License Agreement page.

License Agreement

Browse the license agreement to be aware of the conditions and select Yes, I Agree to the License Agreement. There is no alternative except to agree to complete the firstboot process. Click Next to continue to the Date and Time configuration page.

Date and Time

The Date and Time page displays the information received from the internal system clock as shown in Figure 10-5.

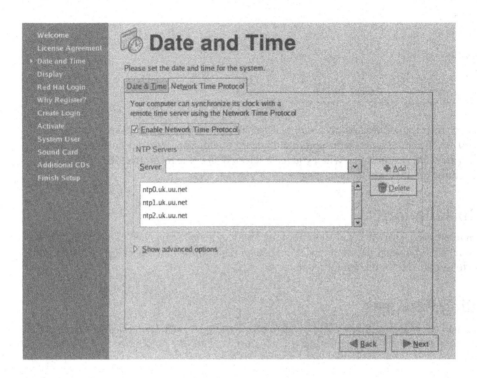

Figure 10-5. *Date and Time configuration page*

Before installing Oracle Database 10*g* RAC, it is essential that all of the nodes within the cluster are configured with exactly the same time settings. You can do this by selecting the Network Time Protocol tab. If you are setting the Network Time Protocol here, select the Enable Network Time Protocol check box. If you do not have specific NTP servers available, there are public NTP servers given by default at the addresses 0.pol.ntp.org, 1.pol.ntp.org, and 2.pol.ntp.org. You can either use these public servers or delete these from the Server list box and add the names of NTP servers you have permission to use. Click Next and the system will contact the NTP servers specified before proceeding to the Display page.

Display

If a monitor is directly connected to the server it should have been successfully probed automatically and should show the correct values. However, in an Oracle Database 10*g* RAC environment it is likely that a KVM (keyboard, video, mouse) switch will have been deployed. A KVM switch is a hardware device that enables a single keyboard, video monitor, and mouse to control more than one server. In this environment you may need to manually select a monitor from the manufacturer's list by clicking Configure. Select a color depth and screen resolution compatible with your video card and monitor. When you have finished configuring the display, click Next to advance to the Red Hat Login page.

Red Hat Login

All versions of the Linux operating system are based upon open source software, the majority of which is licensed under the GPL. This means you are free to distribute all Linux operating systems, including enterprise versions, without incurring license fees or agreements. However, all production standard operating systems have a basic requirement for technical support and maintenance and security updates. On Red Hat Enterprise Linux this is provided through a subscription model, and Oracle will only provide support for Red Hat customers with standard or premium subscription agreements as discussed in Chapter 2.

The Red Hat Login page provides the means to either use an existing login or create a new one with the details you received when you purchased your subscription. This activation process requires access to Red Hat systems via the Internet and, once enabled, connects the system to the Red Hat Network. In a clustered environment we do not recommend connecting any of the nodes to the Red Hat Network. Instead, we advise managing registrations and updates manually from a system such as a management workstation, not from the cluster nodes themselves. Select Tell Me Why I Need to Register and Provide a Red Hat Login and click Next.

Why Register?

You will probably wish to defer registration of the operating system until you have completed the installation of all servers in the cluster. On the Why Register? page, you can select "I Cannot Complete Registration at This Time. Remind Me Later." Click Next to bypass registration and proceed to the System User page.

System User

Red Hat recommends creating a system user in addition to the standard root user on the system. More specific details than are available here are required, in terms of the Oracle user and groups. Therefore, click Next, followed by Continue on the warning dialog box to skip creating any additional users at this point. A subsequent page will be displayed if a sound card is detected on the system. But it is unlikely that on a server dedicated to Oracle that a sound card will be present. However, if one is detected, click Next on the displayed page to test the configuration. Click Next to continue to the Additional CDs page.

Additional CDs

The Additional CDs page gives the opportunity to install applications additional to the standard Red Hat Enterprise Linux software. No additional software is required to be installed at this stage for an Oracle configuration. Click Next to continue to the Finish Setup page.

Finish Setup

The Finish Setup page summarizes the status of the installation and the activation of the Red Hat software subscription. Click Next to end the firstboot process and complete the installation.

Manual Package Installation

By following the process, you will have installed all packages required for an Oracle Database 10*g* RAC node. However, depending on the particular update version of Red Hat Enterprise Linux 4 that you have, you may find that the mandatory asynchronous I/O libraries for the Oracle Database 10*g* RAC have not been installed. To verify their presence on your system, login as the root user and run this command:

```
[root@london1 /]# rpm -q libaio
package libaio is not installed
```

If this command returns the name of the libaio packages, then they have been successfully installed. If it does not, then it is necessary to install the packages from CD #3 of the Red Hat Enterprise Linux software. Insert CD #3 into the CD drive. The CD will mount automatically. Change directory to the RPMs directory on the CD, and install the libaio packages with the rpm command.

```
[root@london1 RPMS]# cd /media/cdrom/RedHat/RPMS

[root@london1 RPMS]# rpm -ivh libaio*
warning: libaio-0.3.102-1.i386.rpm: V3 DSA signature:
NOKEY, key ID db42a60e
Preparing...
######################################## [100%]
   1:libaio
######################################## [ 50%]
   2:libaio-devel
######################################## [100%]
```

Use the rpm -q command to verify that the asynchronous I/O libraries are installed and the Red Hat Linux Enterprise installation is complete.

```
[root@london1 RPMS]# rpm -q libaio
libaio-0.3.102-1
[root@london1 RPMS]# rpm -q libaio-devel
libaio-devel-0.3.102-1
```

Installing SUSE Linux Enterprise Server

This section describes the installation of SUSE Linux Enterprise Server version 9 (SLES9) applicable to x86, x86-64, and Itanium architecture-based systems.

We will again assume a method of direct install by CD-ROM. Before installing SUSE Linux Enterprise Server we recommend reviewing the "Installing Red Hat Enterprise Linux 4 AS" section earlier in this chapter. Many of the fundamentals of installation are the same; however, the installation process with SUSE Linux is managed with the Yet Another Setup Tool (YaST). To prevent undue repetition, we have only covered non-release-specific information such as partitioning guidelines and networking within the Red Hat Enterprise Linux section.

When installing SUSE Linux Enterprise Server with a local console on an Itanium-based system we have found that the installer may fail to initialize the display. This is reported with a message beginning "Your computer does not fulfill all requirements for a graphical installation." If this occurs, you are guided through a text-based installation where all of the actions and requirements are identical to the graphical-based details described in this section. Continue installing the operating system in text mode, including configuration of items such as the network, after the system reboots for the first time. At the end of configuration you will be presented with a graphical console login and the same operating system configuration you would normally expect after a standard graphical mode installation.

Starting the Installation

When the system successfully boots from the CD, it presents a menu of installation choices and a section within which to manually enter boot options. The format of the menu can vary between different hardware architectures. On all systems, select the Installation option from the menu to continue.

License Agreement

The installer displays a License Agreement dialog box. Review the license agreement and click I Agree to proceed with the installation.

Select Your Language

On the Welcome to YaST2 page, select the language to use for interaction during the installation. This language will also be the default installed language for the system during normal operations. Click Accept, and the installation continues by scanning the system for previous Linux operating system installs.

Previous Installation

If a previous installation of Linux is detected, the installer displays a number of options to repair or update the existing installation. This will be displayed for both SUSE and non-SUSE installs. Select New Installation and click OK to continue. If there is no existing Linux operating system detected, then this dialog is not shown.

Installation Settings

In contrast to the sequential step approach taken by the Red Hat Anaconda installer, the SUSE YaST installer presents the overview Installation Settings page within which there are a number of headings presented as hyperlinks. These can be individually selected without requiring that they be approached in any predetermined order. All of these options have default settings of which many are sufficient. However, some require modification for the operating system to be suitable for an Oracle Database 10g RAC node. To implement the first of these modifications click the Partitioning link to advance to the Suggested Partitioning page.

Suggested Partitioning

The Suggested Partitioning page recommends a minimal automatic partitioning layout based on the disks installed in your system. The option is available, however, to configure a more applicable layout for an Oracle Database 10g RAC node. Select Create Custom Partition Setup and click Next.

Preparing Hard Disk

On the Preparing Hard Disk page, choose Custom Partitioning for Experts and click Next to display the Expert Partitioner page. On this page, highlight the existing / (root) partition and press Delete. Click Yes to confirm that you want to delete the partition. Also, delete the recommended swap partition to leave the entire unpartitioned device remaining in the Expert Partitioner window. Alternatively, all of the partitions can be deleted by highlighting the disk device itself before pressing Delete. When presented with an unpartitioned disk, click Create and then click What Type of Partition Do You Want to Create? Leave Primary Partition selected on x86 and x86-64 based systems and click OK. This dialog is not shown on Itanium-based systems where the GPT partitioning scheme is used and, therefore, there is no dependency upon primary and extended partitions. Figure 10-6 shows the Create a Primary Partition on /dev/sda window displayed with the precise device name according to the type of disks that you have.

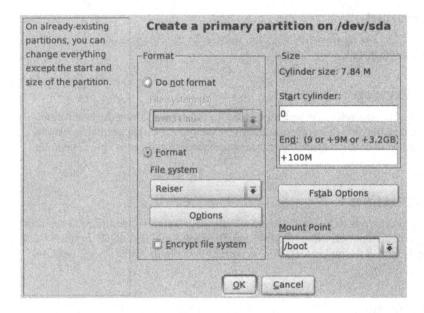

Figure 10-6. *Create a primary partition window*

In the Mount Point drop-down list, select /boot and in the End: box enter either 100M or +100M to specify the size of the /boot partition. Leave all other options unmodified with the exception of the File System type on Itanium systems, which must be set to FAT, and click OK.

When returned to the Expert Partitioner window, shown in Figure 10-7, highlight the disk device, click Create, and choose a primary partition. Follow the process used to create the /boot partition to create the / (root) partition. If desired, create a separate /u01 partition for your Oracle software installation. We recommend using the default Reiser file system on SUSE Linux–based installs. It is worth noting that in terms of installing Oracle software, Oracle certifies to the operating system and not to individual file systems; therefore, you have the choice of using any file system available on a supported Linux operating system release. Create a swap partition in relation to your installed memory size based upon the guidelines described for the Red Hat Enterprise Linux installation. When configuring the swap partition, select Swap as the file system type from the drop-down list.

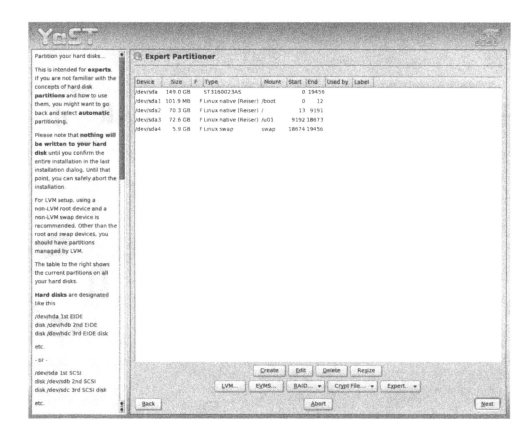

Figure 10-7. *Expert Partitioner window*

Expert Partitioner

When the creation of the individual partitions is complete the Expert Partitioner window displays
a summary of the formatting scheme. It is of note that with the YaST installer on x86 and x86-64
systems, because you are presented with the option of selecting primary or extended partitions, you
can select a configuration with four primary partitions without utilizing any extended or subsequent
logical partitions. Click Next to return to the Installation Settings page, and click the Software link to
proceed to the Software Selection page.

Software Selection

When the Software Selection screen is displayed, click Detailed Selections to display the Selections
page. As shown in Figure 10-8, the left-hand pane shows a list of software that can be selected or
deselected through associated check boxes.

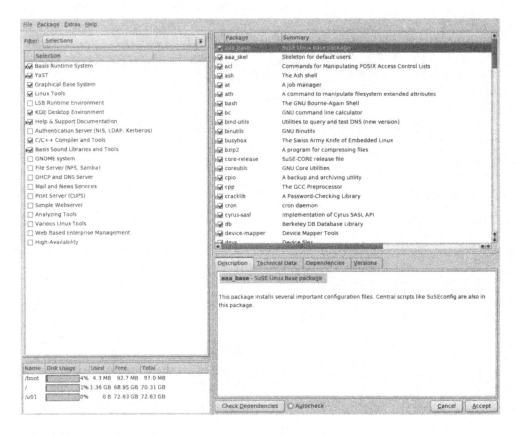

Figure 10-8. *Selections page*

Table 10-5 details the software choices that should be selected.

Table 10-5. *Detailed Software Selection*

Detailed Selection	
Basic runtime system	✓
YaST	✓
Graphical base system	✓
Linux tools	✓
LSB runtime environment	✗
KDE	✓
Help & support documentation	✓
Authentication server (NIS, LDAP, Kerberos)	✗
C/C++ compiler and tools	✓
Basis sound libraries and tools	✓
GNOME system	✗
File server (NFS, Samba)	✗
DHCP and DNS server	✗
Mail and news services	✗

Detailed Selection	
Print server (CUPS)	✗
Simple Webserver	✗
Analyzing tools	✗
Various Linux tools	✗
Web-based enterprise management	✗
High-Availability	✗

Click Accept to confirm the choice of software packages and return to the Installation Settings page. On the x86-64 architecture the installer may display a dialog box indicating additional packages have been selected to resolve dependencies. If this is the case, click Continue to accept the additional package recommendations.

Time Zone

Scroll down on the Installation Settings page shown in Figure 10-9, and click the Time Zone link to display the Clock and Time Zone Configuration page. Set the time zone according to your geographical location and ensure that the hardware clock is set to UTC. The Change Time or Date button gives the option to make manual settings. Click Accept to return once more to the Installation Settings page.

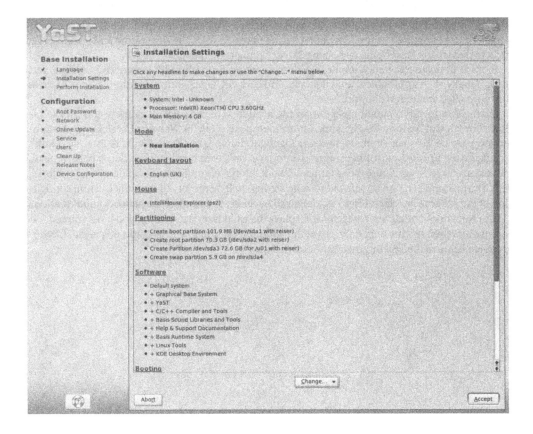

Figure 10-9. *Installation Settings page*

The Installation Settings page now displays all of the modified options required to proceed with package installation. Click Accept.

Warning

The Warning dialog box is displayed. Click Yes, Install to proceed with the installation. Insert the specified CDs when prompted by the installer. Once package installation is complete, the system will automatically reboot and proceed to the system configuration stage.

Root Password

The first screen displayed for system configuration is the Password for Root page. Enter and confirm your chosen password and click Next to proceed to the Network Configuration page.

Network Configuration

On the Network Configuration page the suggested default configuration is for a single interface to be configured with the Dynamic Host Configuration Protocol (DHCP) protocol. DHCP is not suitable for Oracle Database 10*g* RAC nodes and therefore the network interfaces should be configured with static IP addresses. To modify the network configuration click the Network Interfaces link.

On the Network Cards Configuration page, click Change on the Already Configured Devices pane to change the settings of your first network device; this will be a device with a name such as eth0.

On the Network Cards Configuration overview page click Edit to modify the network configuration as shown in Figure 10-10.

Select Static Address Setup on the Network Address Setup page and enter the IP address and associated subnet mask to be used for your external network. Click the Host Name and Name Server button to display the Host Name and Name Server Configuration page.

Enter your hostname and, if applicable, domain name. Enter the addresses of your DNS servers and, optionally, their applicable search domains and click OK. Once returned to the Network Address Setup page click the Routing button.

On the Routing Configuration page enter the IP address of your default gateway and click OK, followed by clicking Next on the Network Address Setup page. On the Network Cards Configuration overview page click Finish. From the Network Configuration page click the Network Interfaces link to configure the private interconnect network interface. On the Network Address Setup page, repeating the steps taken to configure the external network interface, configure the section Static Address Setup. The hostname, name server, and routing settings will be preserved from the existing configuration of the external interface. Click Next followed by Finish to complete the network configuration.

The Network Configuration page now displays the valid interface settings you have entered. There are no requirements to modify any of the additional settings from the links displayed. Click Next to continue to the Test Internet Connection page.

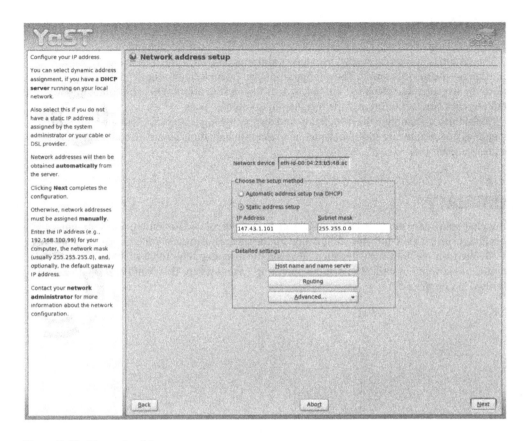

Figure 10-10. *Network address setup page*

Test Internet Connection

It is usually not desirable to configure an Internet connection for any server in a RAC cluster. There-fore you will probably wish to skip this test, and click Next to continue.

Service Configuration

Similarly, on the Service Configuration page there is also no requirement to configure CA manage-ment or OpenLDAP server. Select Skip Configuration, and click Next to continue.

User Authentication Method

For the User Authentication Method page select Local (/etc/passwd) and click Next to continue.

Add a New Local User

As we will add the custom Oracle user configuration manually after installation, click Next to skip the Add a New Local User page without modifying any settings. Click Yes in the Empty user login dialog box to confirm that you do not want to create a user at this point. The installer proceeds to a Writing the System Configuration page that requires no user interaction. Once complete, the Release Notes page is displayed.

Release Notes

Review the release notes and click Next to advance to the Hardware Configuration page.

The system is probed for hardware graphics and sound settings and displays a suggested configuration for the devices found. The configuration can be modified for both graphics card and monitor by selecting the Graphics Card link to activate the SaX2 utility. When the configuration is complete, click Next to continue to the Installation Completed page.

Click Finish to complete the installation and display the login page. SUSE Linux Enterprise Server does not require any additional manual package installations before installing the Oracle Database 10g software.

Summary

In this chapter we have described the step-by-step installation of Red Hat Enterprise Linux and SUSE Linux Enterprise Server to provide a foundation for the successful installation of Oracle Database 10g RAC. Before running the Oracle installer, however, the next step required is to make a number of essential preparatory modifications to the operating system setup. This configuration process is described in Chapter 11.

CHAPTER 11

■ ■ ■

Configuring and Verifying Linux

This chapter describes the steps required to configure the Linux operating system in preparation for an Oracle 10*g* RAC installation. The emphasis is placed on an Unbreakable Linux configuration of Red Hat Enterprise Linux 4.0 or SUSE Linux Enterprise Server 9 on x86, x86-64, and Itanium architecture systems. Our aim is also not to simply list the configuration changes required, but to explain the reasons for them and their effects, enabling the intelligent optimization of each individual environment.

Unless stated otherwise, each configuration step should be performed by the root user on every node in the cluster. We recommend that you fully install all nodes in the cluster and confirm that the network is operational before attempting to configure the secure shell and shared storage.

In this chapter, we concentrate on changes that are either essential or of great benefit for installing and operating Oracle RAC. We suggest you try to avoid unnecessary or complex custom configurations, as the benefits of these can be questionable. In particular, we recommend that, if possible, you do not recompile the kernel directly or use third-party software that modifies the Linux kernel. Doing so means that Oracle will continue to support the Oracle software but will not support the operating system under the Unbreakable Linux initiative.

We will discuss the following configuration and verification topics: operating system and RPM package checks, hostnames and name resolution, Network Time Protocol (NTP), the hangcheck-timer, kernel parameter settings, Oracle user configuration, secure shell, shared storage, channel bonding, and cluster verification. All of the configuration changes described in this chapter can be made to the standard Linux installation without invalidating Unbreakable Linux support. This chapter is intended to assist you in making the requiring settings for a successful Oracle 10*g* RAC installation, and also in understanding why these settings are required to make decisions to achieve an optimal configuration.

Operating System and RPM Package Checks

The first system check that you should make is to determine the kernel release level of the Linux operating system that you have installed. Oracle will support Oracle 10*g* on any 2.6 kernel included with the base release of Red Hat 4.0 or SUSE 9 and subsequent update releases and service packs. Some support exists for Oracle 10*g* on earlier 2.4-based releases of Red Hat and SUSE. Noting the kernel release is useful, however, in referencing the level of certain features and parameters on your operating system and can be done with the command uname -r:

```
[root@london1 root]# uname -r
2.6.9-5.EL
```

It is also useful to verify that you have correctly installed the necessary RPM packages required for a successful Oracle installation—namely make, binutils, gcc, libaio, and glibc. You can verify installation with the rpm command as follows; the precise versions of the packages reported will vary according to your operating system release.

```
[root@london1 root]# rpm -q make binutils gcc libaio glibc
make-3.80-5
binutils-2.15.92.0.2-10.EL4
gcc-3.4.3-9.EL4
libaio-0.3.102-1
glibc-2.3.4-2
```

If any of the packages are reported as not installed, then you need to install them manually before installing Oracle 10g. If any of these packages are not present, a warning is given by the Oracle Installer during the installation process. An additional package check is performed for Oracle 10.1, so the preinstallation system check may report that package openmotif-2.1.30-11 was not found. This package is only required if the server is to be used for compiling Oracle Forms and Reports. If the server is to be used only as a standard Oracle database server, then ignoring this warning is safe for 10.1; the package can be installed at a later date if required. The check is not performed for Oracle 10.2.

On SUSE Linux systems, you may want to consider downloading and running the orarun RPM package from the Novell web site to automatically accomplish some of the configuration tasks in the following sections. This RPM package will not, however, complete all of the stages required for an Oracle RAC installation; therefore, if you choose to use orarun, we advise consulting the accompanying documentation to determine the configuration tasks remaining for completion.

Hostnames and Name Resolution

After installation, the hostname of the system is set in the file /etc/HOSTNAME on SUSE-based systems and /etc/sysconfig/network on Red Hat systems. On Red Hat, the file will also contain additional content for enabling networking and defining the gateway.

If you need to change the system hostname for any reason, then the recommended method to do this is through the graphical user interface. On SUSE, under YaST2, select Network Services, followed by DNS and Host Name. Then you can change the hostname and domain name on this page. On Red Hat systems, select Network from the System Settings menu, and the hostname can be modified under the DNS tab of this utility. On any Oracle 10g RAC system, neither the hostname nor the domain name should be modified after Oracle Clusterware has been installed.

Whether or not you are using DNS for name resolution, we recommend that the /etc/hosts file be kept updated with the primary, virtual, and private interconnect addresses of all the nodes in the cluster. Keeping the file updated ensures no break in operations during any temporary failure of the DNS service. Once again, the preferred method is to modify the settings using the graphical user interface. For SUSE systems, under YaST2, select Network Services, followed by Host Names. On Red Hat, navigate to the same utility used to set the hostname and select the Hosts tab. Both utilities give the option to add, edit, or delete the address, hostname, and aliases of hosts relevant to the cluster. On Red Hat–based systems, the default hostnames should also be modified to remove the configured hostname from the 127.0.0.1 loopback address to prevent potential name resolution errors in the Oracle software. These errors can occur, for example, when using the srvctl utility. Only the local hostname should be associated with this loopback address. It is particularly important that you do not remove this loopback address completely; removing it will result in errors within Oracle network components, such as the listener. On SUSE systems, you should also remove or comment out all of the special IPv6 addresses. Some Oracle software components may fail if the IPv6 localhost line is present.

As an example, the following /etc/hosts file is for a two-node cluster:

```
# Do not remove the following line, or various programs
# that require network functionality will fail.
127.0.0.1              localhost
147.43.1.101           london1
147.43.1.102           london2
147.43.1.201           london1-vip
147.43.1.202           london2-vip
192.168.1.1            london1-priv
192.168.1.2            london2-priv
```

The external IP address and the virtual IP address (denoted by the -vip suffix) should be registered with the DNS service. The virtual IP address will only be usable after Oracle is installed and the Oracle VIPCA utility has been run to configure the interface.

If DNS is used for resolving hostnames, we recommend that the fully qualified hostname, including the domain name extension, be included as an alias within the host file for both external and virtual IP addresses. In addition, the following entries should be added to the /etc/resolv.conf file to prevent DNS failures causing subsequent interruptions to the Oracle Net service:

```
options attempts:5
options timeout:15
```

NTP

All nodes in an Oracle cluster must have exactly the same system time settings. If the system clocks are not synchronized, you may experience unpredictable behavior in the cluster, for example, failure to successfully register or evict a node when required. Also, manually adjusting the clock on a node by a time factor of minutes could cause unplanned node evictions. Therefore, we strongly advise that you synchronize all systems to the same time and make no major adjustments during operation. ("Major adjustments" do not include local time adjustments, such as regional changes for daylight saving time.)

Within Linux, the most common method to configure time synchronization is to use the Network Time Protocol (NTP). This protocol allows your server to synchronize its system clock with a central server. Your preferred time servers will be available from your Internet service provider. Alternatively, if these are not available, there are a number of open access public time servers that you can use.

A good practice within a network environment is to configure a single local dedicated time server to synchronize with an external source and set all internal servers to synchronize with this local time server. If this method is employed, use the configuration detailed shortly to set the local time server to be the preferred server, with additional external time servers configured in case of the failure of the local one.

Setting the Oracle server to use NTP on Red Hat Enterprise Linux systems can be done from the graphical user interface by right-clicking the Date and Time tab displayed on your main panel and selecting Adjust Date & Time. Select the second tab on this page and add your NTP servers using the process in Chapter 10. NTP can also be configured manually by modifying the /etc/ntp.conf and /etc/ntp/step-tickers files and using the chkconfig and service commands.

To do this, first you should ensure that the NTP service has been installed on the system by using the chkconfig command:

```
[root@london1 root]# chkconfig --list ntpd
ntpd    0:off   1:off   2:off   3:off   4:off   5:off   6:off
```

Manually edit the /etc/ntp.conf file and add lines specifying your own time servers, as in the following examples:

```
server ntp0.uk.uu.net
server ntp1.uk.uu.net
server ntp2.uk.uu.net
```

If you have a preferred time server, add the keyword `prefer` to ensure synchronization with this system, if available:

```
server ntp0.uk.uu.net prefer
```

To use open access time servers, enter the following:

```
server 0.pool.ntp.org
server 1.pool.ntp.org
server 2.pool.ntp.org
```

Although you will also have a default `restrict` line at the head of your configuration file, another good practice is to include server-specific security information for each server that prevents that particular NTP server from modifying or querying the time on the system, such as the following:

```
restrict ntp0.uk.uu.net mask 255.255.255.255 nomodify notrap noquery
```

Modify your `/etc/ntp/step-tickers` step-tickers and add the same servers listed in your `/etc/ntp.conf` file:

```
server ntp0.uk.uu.net
server ntp1.uk.uu.net
server ntp2.uk.uu.net
```

Make sure that the NTP daemon will always start at boot time at run levels 3 and 5 using the `chkconfig` command:

```
[root@london1 root]# chkconfig --level 35 ntpd on
```

Verify the configuration using `chkconfig --list`:

```
root@london1 root]# chkconfig --list ntpd
ntpd  0:off  1:off  2:off  3:on  4:off  5:on  6:off
```

The start-up options for the NTP daemon are detailed in the `/etc/sysconfig/ntpd` file. In normal circumstances, the default options should be sufficient. You can then start the service to synchronize the time using the following command:

```
[root@london1 root]# service ntpd start
```

Then, the `date` command can be used to query the system time to ensure that the time has been set correctly. The NTP daemon will not synchronize your system clock with the time server if they differ significantly. If they do differ too much, the NTP daemon will refer to the systems in the `/etc/ntp/step-tickers` files to set the time correctly. Alternatively, the time can be set manually using the `ntpdate` command:

```
[root@london1 root]# ntpdate -u -b -s ntp0.uk.uu.net
```

On SUSE Linux Enterprise systems, the NTP settings can be modified by starting YaST2 and navigating to the NTP Client on the Network Services page. Within this page, add your NTP Servers and ensure that the default option is set to automatically start the daemon when booting the system. NTP on SUSE Linux can also be set manually using a process similar to the one described for Red Hat systems to edit the `/etc/ntp.conf` file. The main differences are that the `xntpd` daemon is used, and therefore, `chkconfig` should be used to enable `xntpd` at run levels 3 and 5, and the service is started with the following command:

```
[root@london1 root]# /etc/init.d/xntpd start
```

Hangcheck-Timer

In a RAC environment, Oracle needs to rapidly detect and isolate any occurrence of node failure within the cluster. It is particularly important to ensure that, once a node has entered an uncertain state, it is evicted from the cluster to prevent possible disk corruption caused by access that is not controlled by the database or cluster software. On Linux, this eviction is ensured by the hangcheck-timer kernel module.

The hangcheck-timer module uses the internal Time Stamp Counter (TSC) register of the CPU on the x86 and x86-64 systems and the Interval Time Counter (ITC) register on Itanium systems. The module sets a timer that periodically checks for a delay during the last interval. Utilizing the CPU, the timer is extremely accurate under normal circumstances, so a delay indicates a system *hang state*. The timer has a configurable margin of error, which, if exceeded, will result in the hangcheck-timer module causing a system reboot. If the hangcheck-timer itself fails, the Oracle Clusterware will reset the node.

For the hangcheck-timer module to operate optimally, it must be correctly configured for the system. The module takes two parameters: the hangcheck_tick parameter is the timer duration in seconds, with a default value of 60 seconds, and the hangcheck_margin parameter is the margin of error in seconds, with a default value of 180 seconds. By default, every 60 seconds the hangcheck-timer module checks the timer's wait time. If this amount of time exceeds the hangcheck_margin, the machine is restarted. Therefore, there is a period of time, depending on when the timer runs, that means, by default, that a system hang of between the minimum hangcheck_margin of 180 seconds and the hangcheck_margin + hangcheck_tick of 240 seconds may not be sufficient to be detected. These values should be adjusted to reduce the maximum hang time permitted on a system. Also note that for the system to be rebooted, it must hang and then recover to a sufficient operational state for the hangcheck-timer module to run. A permanent hang will not be detected, and the system must be rebooted manually.

Any adjustment to the hangcheck_margin and hangcheck_tick values should be made with reference to the Oracle Clusterware misscount value. This configurable value is set when the root.sh script is run as part of the Clusterware installation. By default, the value is set to one minute in the following line:

```
CLSCFG_MISCNT="-misscount 60"
```

To summarize, the hangcheck-timer acts on the node that is experiencing the failure, whereas Oracle Clusterware acts on the surviving nodes to evict a failed node with which they are unable to communicate.

In most circumstances, if the hangcheck-timer is not operational and a failed node recovers after it has been evicted from the cluster, the instance on this node will still be terminated based on information received from the surviving nodes. The failed node, however, will not be rebooted.

On the other hand, if the failed node recovers once eviction has started but before it has been completed, then a *split-brain* scenario may result—that is, a scenario in which more than one node is attempting to reconfigure the cluster at the same time. The split-brain scenario will result in one or more nodes rebooting to remove themselves from the cluster. The hangcheck-timer is vital in this circumstance to reboot the failed node itself to prevent any interruption in cluster reconfiguration once eviction has commenced, and therefore, the hangcheck_tick + hangcheck_margin must always be less than the misscount. With a default misscount of 60 seconds, we recommend a hangcheck_tick of 10 seconds and a hangcheck_margin of 30 seconds. However, these values may be modified according to your system capacity, the misscount value, and the expected system load. If the system load grows to such an extent that the margin is missed, then the following error message is reported and the system rebooted:

```
Aug 10 15:43:23 london1 kernel: Hangcheck: hangcheck value past margin!
```

The hangcheck-timer kernel module must be loaded into the kernel before the Oracle instance is started. This insertion is accomplished with the modprobe command with a successful action returning to the command line without output:

```
[root@london1 root]# modprobe hangcheck-timer
```

The hangcheck-timer should be configured to load automatically when the system boots. To configure this, edit /etc/rc.d/rc.local on Red Hat systems and /etc/rc.d/boot.local on SUSE systems, and add the following line to insert the module during start-up:

```
modprobe hangcheck-timer
```

Whether loading the module manually or automatically at boot time, you can specify its required parameters at the command line, but we recommend setting the parameters within the modprobe.conf file. The changes should be made in /etc/modprobe.conf on Red Hat systems and /etc/modprobe.conf.local on SUSE systems by adding the following line:

```
options hangcheck-timer hangcheck_tick=10 hangcheck_margin=30
```

Whenever the hangcheck-timer module is inserted, it will use these parameters. Information from the module is reported to /var/log/messages, confirming the correct application of the parameters as follows:

```
Aug 10 14:15:19 london1 kernel: Hangcheck: starting hangcheck timer
0.5.0 (tick is 10 seconds, margin is 30 seconds).
```

TESTING THE HANGCHECK TIMER

The hangcheck-timer can be tested using the related hangcheck-delay module, which induces a suitable delay. Running the following command will hang the system for a default period of 30 seconds:

```
[root@london1 root]# modprobe hangcheck-delay
```

You can also specify a custom delay period at the command line:

```
[root@london1 root]# modprobe hangcheck-delay hangcheck_delay=10
```

The hangcheck-delay module can be especially useful in a development environment for understanding and fine-tuning system failure detection parameters. The hangcheck-delay module should never be used once a production system is operational.

Kernel Parameters

For the successful operation of the Oracle 10*g* database software on Linux-based systems, Oracle recommends the customization of the kernel parameters shown in Table 11-1.

Table 11-1. *Kernel Parameter Recommended Values*

Kernel Parameter	Recommended Value
kernel.sem (semmsl)	250
kernel.sem (semmns)	32000
kernel.sem (semopm)	100
kernel.sem (semmni)	128
kernel.shmall	2097152
kernel.shmmax	Half the size of physical memory
kernel.shmmni	4096
fs.file-max	65536
net.core.rmem_default	262144
net.core.rmem_max	262144
net.core.wmem_default	262144
net.core.wmem_max	262144
net.ipv4.ip_local_port_range	1024 to 65000

We recommend that you set all kernel parameters in the /etc/sysctl.conf parameter file to ensure that the modified values persist across reboots. Kernel parameters can also be changed dynamically, as described in Chapter 15.

On SUSE installations, two additional steps are necessary before making the parameter changes: first, in creating the /etc/sysctl.conf file, and second, in ensuring that the file is read and that the parameters are applied when the system boots by issuing the command

```
[root@london1 root]# chkconfig boot.sysctl on
```

The values in /etc/sysctl.conf will now be automatically applied when the system boots.

The recommended Linux kernel parameter settings are very much general guidelines, and understanding these parameters and how applicable they are to your particular system is essential. These parameters can be loosely grouped into four classifications: shared memory, semaphores, network settings, and open files. We will examine each of these in turn.

Shared Memory

When an Oracle instance starts, it allocates shared memory segments for the SGA. This allocation applies to RAC instances in exactly the same way as a single instance. The SGA has fixed and variable areas. The fixed area size cannot be changed, but the variable area, as the name implies, will vary according to the Oracle database parameters set in the SPFILE or init.ora file.

Failure to set the shared memory kernel parameters correctly could result in the Oracle instance failing to start successfully if the system call shmget() (issued by Oracle to allocate the SGA) fails.

The two most significant Oracle parameters to be aware of are SGA_TARGET and SGA_MAX_SIZE. Setting these parameters enables Oracle to use automatic shared memory management and prevents having to size these components individually. However, the values encompassed within SGA_TARGET can be set as its individual components if desired, and these individual components are discussed in Chapter 6.

As you have also seen in Chapter 6, in addition to the automatically sized components, additional components can be manually sized. When SGA_TARGET is set, these manual components are given priority for the allocated shared memory, with the balance of the memory subsequently allocated to the automatically sized components. These manual components are the redo log buffer, streams pool, and nondefault database caches, such as the keep, recycle, and no default block size caches. Session-level memory set with the PGA_AGGREGATE_TARGET parameter is not allocated from this shared memory.

For example, if you wish to set the following Oracle parameters:

```
SGA_MAX_SIZE = 10G
SGA_TARGET = 8G
```

then the kernel settings should be modified to reflect these requirements, such as in the following:

```
kernel.shmall = 2097152
kernel.shmmax = 10737418240
kernel.shmmni = 4096
```

The shared memory parameters have the meanings as discussed in the next few sections. You can view the allocated shared memory segments using the command

```
ipcs -lm
```

kernel.shmmax

The shmmax parameter sets the maximum size, in bytes, for a shared memory segment allowed on the system. By default, it is set to 33554432 on all Enterprise Linux releases and hardware architectures, and it is the single most important shared memory–related kernel parameter. It limits the maximum permissible size of a single Oracle SGA and must be set to exceed the value of SGA_MAX_SIZE, which must itself be greater than SGA_TARGET. Setting shmmax as follows will limit a single Oracle SGA size to 2GB:

```
kernel.shmmax = 2147483648
```

However, setting this value in excess of your desired SGA_MAX_SIZE enables Oracle to manage its own memory effectively. With the example shown previously, assuming a system with 16GB of RAM available, an SGA_MAX_SIZE of 10GB, and an SGA_TARGET of 8GB, setting

```
kernel.shmmax = 10737418240
```

enables a maximum shared memory segment of just over 10GB, which is above that required by the Oracle parameters.

■**Note** By default, on 32-bit x86 systems, the maximum Oracle SGA size is 1.7GB. The reasons for this limit are explained in Chapter 6.

---

kernel.shmmni

The shmmni parameter specifies the maximum number of shared memory segments permissible on the entire system. For an Oracle system, this parameter reflects the maximum number of Oracle instances that you wish to start on a single server. Therefore, the default value of 4096 should be retained, although in an operational environment, the number of shared memory segments is highly unlikely to ever approach this value.

kernel.shmall

Use shmall to define the maximum number of shared memory pages in total that can be allocated at any one time on the system; its default value is 524288 on Itanium systems and 2097152 on x86-based architectures. This value is given in system pages, not in bytes, and should be set to at least the value of shmmax/system page size to ensure sufficient memory pages to allocate a single required SGA. This value should be increased if you are running more than one Oracle instance on the same server.

The recommended value of

```
kernel.shmall = 2097152
```

on an x86 system with a default 4KB page size would permit a maximum shared memory allocation of 8GB. On an Itanium-based system, the default page size is 16KB, so the default setting of 524288 would also translate to an 8GB maximum for shared memory. Therefore, if your required SGA is less than 8GB, then the default setting for shmall should be sufficient; otherwise, the shmall setting should be increased sufficiently to accommodate the SGA required.

vm.nr_hugepages

Although not detailed as an Oracle recommended parameter, an additional virtual memory parameter available on 2.6 kernel–based systems is vm.nr_hugepages, which configures hugetlb settings. Setting this value with sysctl configures the number of huge pages available for the system, and the default value is 0. The size of an individual huge page is dependent on the Linux operating system installed and the hardware architecture. The huge page size on your system can be viewed at the end of /proc/meminfo. The following example for a SUSE Linux x86 system shows a huge page size of 2MB:

```
[root@london1 root]# cat /proc/meminfo
...
HugePages Total:   0
HugePages Free:    0
Hugepagesize:      2048kB
```

On Red Hat Linux x86 systems, the huge page size is 4,096KB. However, on both Red Hat and SUSE Itanium systems, it is 262,144KB. This page size value, therefore, should always be known before setting the vm.nr_hugepages value.

■**Note** On Red Hat Enterprise Linux 3.0–based systems, huge pages are configured with the parameter vm.hugetlb_pool. Setting this value using sysctl configures the number of huge pages available for the system in megabytes, with the default value of 0. Therefore, this parameter does not need to be sized according to the particular huge page size on the system.

Huge pages are allocated as much larger contiguous memory pages than the standard system pages and improve performance at the Translation Lookaside Buffer (TLB) level. As discussed in greater detail in Chapter 6, the larger page size enables a large range of memory addresses to be stored closer to the CPU level, increasing the speed of Oracle SGA access. Access speed increases by improving the likelihood that the virtual memory address of the pages that Oracle requires is already cached. The vm.nr_hugepages can be set at runtime. However, the pages are required to be contiguous, and therefore we advise setting the required number in /etc/sysctl.conf, which is applied at boot time. Once allocated, huge pages are not pageable and, therefore, guarantee that an Oracle SGA using them will always remain resident in main memory.

The vm.nr_hugepages parameter must be set to a multiple of the huge page size to reach a value greater than the required Oracle SGA size. In addition, the Oracle user must have permission to use huge pages, which is granted by additional kernel parameters, depending on the release of your kernel, and identified through the command uname -r. For kernels prior to release 2.6.7, the parameter is vm.disable_cap_mlock and should be set to the value of 1. This enables all nonroot users to use memory allocated in huge pages. For kernel releases after 2.6.7, the parameter vm.hugetlb_shm_group offers a finer granularity of security. This parameter should be set to the value of a user group to which the Oracle user belongs. This user group can be either a dedicated huge page users group or, if only the oracle user is to use huge pages, simply the dba or oinstall groups. You do not need to set any further huge page–related kernel parameters for Oracle's use.

For testing purposes, the huge page allocation can be mounted as file system of type hugetlbfs, and memory can be utilized from it using mmap. For Oracle using shmget, however, there is no requirement for the hugetlbfs file system to be mounted during normal operations. When the Oracle 10g instance starts, the shmget() call to allocate the shared memory for the SGA includes the SHM_HUGETLB flag to use huge pages, if available. If the SGA required is greater than the huge pages available, then Oracle will not use any huge pages at all and instead will use standard memory pages. However, the huge pages will still remain allocated to their pool, reducing the overall amount of available memory on the system that can be used. The shmmax parameter is still applicable when using huge pages and still must be sized greater than the desired Oracle SGA size.

The values in the file /proc/meminfo can be viewed again to monitor the successful use of huge pages. After an Oracle instance is started, viewing /proc/meminfo will show the following:

```
Huge_Pages_Total: 20
Huge_Pages_Free:  16
Hugepagesize:      262144KB
```

This output shows that 5GB of 20 huge pages (262,144KB each), were created, and the Oracle instance took 4GB of this allocation for its SGA. If the instance has been started and the total remains the same as the free value, then Oracle has failed to use huge pages, and the SGA has been allocated from the standard pages. Note also that huge pages cannot be used with very large memory settings applicable to x86 systems. Setting the Oracle parameter use_indirect_data_buffers=true will result in the following error on attempting to start the instance:

```
ORA-00385: cannot enable Very Large Memory with new buffer cache parameters.
```

In respect to setting the shmall parameter, the huge pages are expressed in terms of standard system memory pages, and one single huge page taken as shared memory will be translated into the equivalent number of standard system pages when allocated from the available shmall total. The shmall value needs to account for all of the huge pages used, not just the finite Oracle SGA size. For example, on an Itanium system, a database requiring a 1.87GB SGA would occupy seven huge pages and would require shmall to be set to 114772 to start. Setting shmall to 100, for example, would result in the following Oracle error when starting the instance:

```
ORA-27102: out of memory
```

Instead, the minimum required shmall value of 114772, divided by the standard 16KB system page size, arrives at the seven huge pages used.

Semaphores

Semaphores are used by Oracle for resource management as a post/wait mechanism by enqueues and writers for events, such as free buffer waits. Semaphores are used extensively by Oracle and are allocated to Oracle at instance start-up in sets by the Linux kernel. Processes use semaphores from the moment they attach to an Oracle instance waiting on semop() system calls. Semaphores are set within one line of the `sysctl` command or the `/etc/sysctl.conf` file, which differs from other Unix operating systems, where the different values are often allocated individually.

kernel.sem

The default value of `kernel.sem` is

```
kernel.sem = 250 32000 32 128
```

We recommend the following setting:

```
kernel.sem = 250 32000 100 128
```

This setting allocates values for the `semmsl`, `semmns`, `semopm`, and `semmni` parameters respectively. Semaphores can be viewed with the following operating system command:

```
ipcs -ls
```

The `semmsl` parameter defines the total number of semaphores in a semaphore set. This should be set to the minimum value of 100 or to the required number of Oracle user processes plus ten, whichever is lower. Setting `semmsl` should always be considered in terms of `semmns`, as both parameters impact the same system resources.

The `semmns` parameter sets the total number of semaphores permitted in the Linux system, and 32000 is the recommended default high-range value. Because the previously discussed value `semmsl` sets the maximum number of semaphores per set, and `semmni` sets the maximum number of semaphore sets, the overall number of semaphores that can be allocated will be the minimum of `semmns` or `semmsl` multiplied by the value of `semmni`. A default value of 32000 for `semmns` ensures that this value is used by the system for its total semaphore limit.

The `semopm` parameter defines the maximum number of semaphore operations that can be performed by the `semop()` system call. In Linux, `semop()` can set multiple semaphores within a single system call. The recommended setting for this value is 100.

The `semmni` parameter sets the maximum number of total semaphore sets defined and should have a minimum setting of 100, though it is often overridden by `semmns`.

Unless an extremely large number of Oracle user connections are required on each node, the recommended semaphore settings should be sufficient.

Network

The correct setting of network parameters is especially important in a RAC environment because of the reliance on a local high-performance network interconnect between the Oracle instances.

The Oracle guidelines for Linux network settings are restricted to increasing the local port range for outgoing connections; however, for a number of other values, customized values can be beneficial. The key values to modify are the default and maximum send buffer sizes and the default and maximum receive buffer sizes; modifying these can prevent network overflow of Cache Fusion traffic. In addition, there are recommended TCP settings for the optimal use of Transparent Application Failover (TAF).

net.ipv4.ip_local_port_range

The `net.ipv4.ip_local_port_range` parameter sets the range of local ports for outgoing connections, by default 32768 to 61000. Changing the lower port value to 1024 and the upper port to 65000 is recommended.

net.ipv4.ip_forward

The net.ipv4.ip_forward parameter should be set to 0 to disable packet forwarding for security purposes.

net.ipv4.conf.default.rp_filter

The net.ipv4.conf.default.rp_filter parameter should be set to 1 to enable packet filtering for security purposes. Setting this parameter is only necessary on x86 systems, as the default value is 1 on Itanium systems.

net.ipv4.tcp_rmem, net.ipv4.tcp_wmem

In Linux releases based on the 2.6 kernel, the values of the network settings are designed to auto-tune. You only need to modify the values of tcp_rmem and tcp_wmem, which specify the following minimum, default, and maximum values of the socket send and receive buffers:

```
net.ipv4.tcp_rmem = 4096 87380 174760
net.ipv4.tcp_wmem = 4096 16384 131072
```

These settings benefit from being increased to these values:

```
net.ipv4.tcp_rmem = 4096 262144 524288
net.ipv4.tcp_wmem = 4096 262144 524288
```

net.core.rmem_default, net.core.wmem_default, net.core.rmem_max, and net.core.wmem_max

In Linux versions based on the 2.6 kernel, you no longer strictly need to set the values of the kernel parameters net.core.rmem_default, net.core.wmem_default, net.core.rmem_max, and net.core.wmem_max. These values are the default setting, in bytes, of the socket receive and send buffers and their maximum sizes. The default values are 65536 for the default parameters and 131071 for the maximum parameters on all architectures. Oracle, however, recommends modifying both of these values to 262144, and failing to do so results in warnings during the installation of the Oracle software. Setting both these values and the auto-tune parameters has a different effect for both the default and maximum parameters. In terms of the default parameters, the auto-tune values take precedence, so you must set them to achieve Oracle's recommended setting of 262144. For the maximum values, however, the static settings take precedence, overriding the auto-tune parameters. You will, therefore, need to increase these maximum values to 524288 after installation, if you prefer the system to find the optimal buffer sizes.

net.ipv4.tcp_syn_retries and net.ipv4.tcp_retries2

When using Oracle TAF, you need to ensure that the Linux system responds in a timely manner to record the failure of a network connection. The number of times a network connection is retried is significant here. The tcp_syn_retries parameter specifies the maximum number of times that SYN packets will be sent for an active TCP connection. The default value for this parameter is 5 (approximately 3 minutes). Reducing this value to 2 is recommended. Once a connection is established, the tcp_retries2 parameter specifies the maximum number of times a TCP packet is retransmitted before giving up on the connection. The default value is 15 (approximately 15 to 30 minutes), so reducing this value to 3 is recommended.

Consider these values in terms of the functionality provided by the virtual IP addresses configured as part of the Oracle Clusterware software installation. In the event of a node failure, the virtual IP address associated with that node in the cluster is reassociated with one of the other nodes in the cluster. The Clusterware software uses the Address Resolution Protocol (ARP) to ensure that all network packets are immediately sent to the new node and existing client connections to the failed node receiving the error ORA-03113: End-of-file on Communication Channel. This feature ensures that, in terms of node failure, less emphasis is placed on these kernel parameters used to enforce TCP time-outs, as client network errors are returned immediately. These values are still useful, however, in preventing lengthy client connection delays because of errors that cause TCP time-outs but are not serious enough to result in the migration of the virtual IP address.

net.ipv4.tcp_keepalive_time, net.ipv4.tcp_keepalive_probes, and net.ipv4.tcp_keepalive_intvl

These network-related parameters govern the length of time to keep network connections alive once they have been detected as being idle, preventing a large number of inactive connections to the server from consuming valuable resources. Each connection has a timer, and if the connection is idle for the time specified by the `tcp_keepalive_time` parameter, which defaults to 7200 seconds, the designated maximum number of `tcp_keepalive_probes` (default 9) at intervals of seconds specified in `tcp_keepalive_intvl` (default 75 seconds) are sent to keep the connection alive. If the maximum value of `tcp_keepalive_time` or `tcp_keepalive_probes` is reached without response, the connection is dropped. We recommend setting `tcp_keepalive_time` to 30 seconds, setting `tcp_keepalive_intvl` to 60 seconds, and leaving `tcp_keepalive_probes` at the default value of 9.

Open Files

Two parameters that affect the number of open files are `fs.file-max` and `fs.aio-max.size`.

The `fs.file-max` parameter is used to set the maximum limit of open files that a single process can have within the system, but there is little benefit in setting it. Although setting this maximum to a very large value, such as 65536, ensures Oracle will not receive a Too Many Open Files error when opening the database, even this large value is likely to be lower than the default value, which ranges between 445644 and 836601 depending on the kernel and system architecture.

Similarly, setting `fs.aio-max-size` to 131072 is often recommended. However, this is also the default value for the parameter, so setting the parameter explicitly to this value has no direct benefit. You may, however, wish to increase the value of this parameter for data warehouse environments, as discussed in Chapter 7.

Kernel Parameter Example

We have observed the Linux kernel parameter settings that Oracle recommends and, more important, the meaning behind these parameters, to enable you to modify them to optimal values.

The following example is an `/etc/sysctl.conf` file suitable for an SGA of 1.6GB on an x86 system. It sets the huge pages to 1.6GB within 800 2,048KB pages. The shared memory maximum is set to 2GB. The `semopm` semaphore has been increased from 32 to 100, and network settings have been applied.

```
vm.nr_hugepages=800
vm.disable_cap_mlock=1
kernel.shmmax = 2147483648
kernel.shmall = 2097152
kernel.sem = 250 32000 100 128
net.ipv4.tcp_rmem = 4096 262144 524288
net.ipv4.tcp_wmem = 4096 262144 524288
net.core.rmem_default = 262144
net.core.rmem_max = 262144
net.core.wmem_default = 262144
net.core.wmem_max = 262144
```

```
net.ipv4.tcp_syn_retries = 2
net.ipv4.tcp_retries2 = 3
net.ipv4.tcp_keepalive_time = 30
net.ipv4.tcp_keepalive_intvl = 60
net.ipv4.ip_forward = 0
net.ipv4.conf.default.rp_filter = 1
net.ipv4.ip_local_port_range = 1024 65000
```

When the /etc/sysctl.conf file has been saved, the settings can be applied using the following command:

```
[root@london1 root]# sysctl -p
```

Oracle User Configuration

The Oracle software should be installed under its own unique operating system user identity, typically the oracle user. This user should belong to a group that classifies the users who administer the database. The installation of Oracle software also requires the account nobody, which is assigned to users or processes that should not have any special permissions or privileges. You can add users and groups on Red Hat Linux systems using the User Manager utility by selecting System Settings followed by Users & Groups. From Users & Groups, select Add User or Add Group and complete the fields presented. On SUSE Linux, similar functionality can be accessed under YaST2 with the Security and Users utility. When using the graphical tools, the oracle user and the oinstall and dba groups should be created according to the guidelines detailed here for the command line–based alternatives.

Creating the dba and oinstall Groups

In some environments, one group of users will install and maintain Oracle software while a separate group of users will utilize the Oracle software to maintain the database. Maintaining separate groups requires the creation of user groups to draw a distinction between permissions to install Oracle software, which requires access to the Oracle Universal Installer (OUI) and oraInventory, and permissions for these general database administration tasks. These two groups are typically named oinstall and dba.

In most RAC environments, the DBA installs, maintains, and uses the Oracle software, and in this case, the oinstall group may appear superfluous. However, the Oracle inventory group is included within some preinstallation system checks; therefore, using this group for Oracle software installation is a good practice.

To create the dba group for the oracle user, use the following command:

```
[root@london1 root] # groupadd -g 500 dba
```

The dba group will have been appended to the /etc/group file.

Similarly, create the oinstall group with the next available group ID. You should explicitly state the group ID using the -g option for the groupadd command. Any group ID may be used, but the same group ID should be used for the dba and oinstall groups on all nodes in the cluster.

Creating the oracle User

To create the oracle user as a member of the dba and oinstall groups, run the following command:

```
[root@london1 root] # useradd -u 500 -g dba -G oinstall oracle
```

The oracle user will be appended the /etc/passwd file with the group ID of the dba group and added to the dba and oinstall groups in the /etc/group file.

Here, with no further arguments supplied to the creation command, the oracle user has been created with the default home directory of /home/oracle as a directory with the login name in the default home area. The home directory can be specified by using the useradd command with the -d option and can be in any location, but keeping it distinct from the ORACLE_HOME directory where the Oracle software is to be installed is good practice. The user has also been created with the default bash shell, which can be modified using the useradd command with the -s option.

As with the group ID, you should explicitly state the user ID using the -u option for the useradd command and any user ID may be used. The same user ID should be used for the oracle user on all nodes in the cluster.

You can verify that the oracle user and dba group have been correctly configured using the id command as in this example:

```
[root@london1 root] # id oracle
uid=500(oracle) gid=500(dba) groups=500(dba),501(oinstall)
```

Setting the Password for the oracle User

After account creation, you must set the password for the oracle user with the passwd command:

```
[root@london1 root]# passwd oracle
Changing password for user oracle
New password:
Retype new password:
passwd: all authentication tokens updated successfully.
```

Setting Environment Variables

With the user created and the password supplied, it is possible to log in with the newly created oracle user account. If using the default bash shell, the oracle user account will be configured with a default ~/.bash_profile in the oracle user's home directory, which, if unmodified, will resemble the following:

```
[oracle@london1 oracle]$ cat ~/.bash_profile
# .bash_profile

# Get the aliases and functions
if [ -f ~/.bashrc ]; then
        . ~/.bashrc
fi

# User specific environment and startup programs

PATH=$PATH:$HOME/bin

export PATH
unset USERNAME
```

You need to update the ~/.bash_profile file with the environment variables required for installing the Oracle software. In addition, Oracle recommends including the following stty command to suppress stty errors that may occur during the Oracle Clusterware installation:

```
if [ -t 0 ]; then
stty intr ^C
fi
```

You should also have within the ~/.bash_profile the following entry to set the value of umask to 022:

```
umask 022
```

The umask command applies a default mask to the permissions on newly created files and directories. The value 022 ensures that these are created with permissions of 644, preventing other users from writing to the files created by the Oracle software owner.

■**Note** The ~/.bashrc file is primarily for setting user-defined aliases and functions with environment variables being added directly to the ~/.bash_profile file. Oracle does not require any additional aliases and functions, so there is no need to modify this file.

There is conflicting advice within the Oracle documentation itself regarding which environment variables should be set for Oracle software installation. In some areas, unsetting the ORACLE_SID, ORACLE_HOME, and ORACLE_BASE environment variables before installing the Oracle software is recommended, but other areas specify that the ORACLE_BASE environment variable must be set. We recommend that, at a minimum, the oracle user should set one environment variable, ORACLE_BASE, for the successful installation of the Oracle Clusterware and RAC software, and may set a number of optional variables for a customized configuration. After installation, at least the PATH, ORACLE_SID, ORACLE_HOME, CRS_HOME, and ORACLE_BASE environment variables should be set. Environment variables must be configured identically on all nodes except for ORACLE_SID, which is instance, and therefore node, specific. The following sections detail the purpose of the most relevant environment variables applicable to an oracle user installing and administering 10g RAC on Linux.

ORACLE_BASE

Setting the ORACLE_BASE environment variable defines the root of the Oracle directory tree. If the ORACLE_BASE environment variable is not set explicitly, it will default to the value of the oracle user's home directory. All Oracle software installed on the system is located below the directory specified by ORACLE_BASE, such as /u01/app/oracle, if you're using an OFA-compliant directory structure. The oracle user must have been granted read, write, and execute privileges on this directory. If installing Oracle 10g RAC software on an OCFS2 file system on SAN or NAS storage presented as an NFS file system, then the ORACLE_BASE and the directories below it can be located on this shared storage with a single directory and software installation shared between all of the nodes in the cluster.

ORACLE_SID

The ORACLE_SID environment variable defines the Oracle system identifier (SID) of the database instance on an individual node. In a standard, single-instance Oracle environment, the ORACLE_SID is the same as the global database name. In a RAC environment, each node has an instance accessing the same database, and therefore, each instance should have a different ORACLE_SID. We recommend that these should take the form of the global database name, which begins with an alphabetic character, can be up to eight characters in length, and has a suffix for which the default is the instance number. For example, a database with a global database name of RAC might have the corresponding ORACLE_SID values of RAC1, RAC2, RAC3, and RAC4 on the different nodes.

ORACLE_HOME

The ORACLE_HOME environment variable specifies where the Oracle Database Server software is installed. This location must not be the same as CRS_HOME. An example location would be $ORACLE_BASE/product/ 10.2.0/db_1. If the ORACLE_HOME environment variable is not set, then a default location will be determined by the OUI.

CRS_HOME

The CRS_HOME environment variable specifies a directory located below the ORACLE_BASE directory where the Oracle Clusterware software is installed, for example, $ORACLE_BASE/product/10.2.0/crs. Depending on the particular release of Oracle 10*g*, this environment variable may not used directly by the OUI, and instead, the ORACLE_HOME must temporarily be set to this value for installing the Clusterware to a particular user-specified directory. Once operational, however, this environment variable provides a distinct value for identifying the directory where the Clusterware software is installed.

NLS_LANG

The NLS_LANG environment variable specifies the client-side character set in order that, if necessary, Oracle can perform automatic conversion between the client and database character sets. The default value is AMERICAN-AMERICA.UTF8.

ORA_NLS10

The environment variable ORA_NLS10 should be set to the path $ORACLE_HOME/nls/data to create a database with any character set other than US7ASCII, which is given within the CREATE DATABASE statement.

TNS_ADMIN

The environment variable TNS_ADMIN specifies the path of a directory containing the Oracle network configuration files, such as tnsnames.ora. If TNS_ADMIN is not set, the default location for the network configuration files is used, that is, $ORACLE_HOME/network/admin.

PATH

The PATH environment variable defines the executable search path and should include both the $ORACLE_HOME/bin directory and the $CRS_HOME/bin directory.

LD_LIBRARY_PATH

The LD_LIBRARY_PATH environment variable specifies a list of directories which the runtime shared library loader searches for shared libraries. It is important to be aware, for security purposes, that shared libraries found within this list take priority over default and compiled loader paths; therefore, only trusted libraries should be included in this list. Programs with the set-uid privilege always ignore the settings of LD_LIBRARY_PATH. Systemwide custom runtime library paths can also be set in the file /etc/ld.so.conf by running the command ldconfig. For Oracle, the LD_LIBRARY_PATH environment variable is not required for the standard server software, though it may be needed for additional Oracle or third-party products that use shared libraries and, if so, should be set to include the $ORACLE_HOME/lib directory.

CLASSPATH

The CLASSPATH environment variable specifies a list of directories and class libraries to be searched by the Java loader. This environment variable is only required when using Java utilities, such as jdbc or sqlj.

SQLPATH

The environment variable SQLPATH is set to a directory name containing the location of a directory that SQL*Plus searches for SQL scripts. If this environment variable is not set, then no default value is enabled. The most useful script found in this location is login.sql, enabling the customization of the SQL*Plus profile for the oracle user.

LD_ASSUME_KERNEL

The LD_ASSUME_KERNEL environment variable specifies which glibc shared library to use at runtime. This variable should not be set when running Oracle RAC, as performance may be impacted. This environment variable should be temporarily set only on a case-by-case basis when encountering errors in running Oracle Java utilities. Oracle Support may offer advice to set this environment variable to resolve these errors by using a different set of shared libraries for a particular application. This environment variable is often set implicitly within these utilities, depending on the system architecture, for example, in the VIPCA utility. You should only set this environment variable when required manually at the command line and never within the .bash_profile file.

DISPLAY

The DISPLAY environment variable specifies an X Window display to which graphics should be displayed. This environment variable should be set to a server name followed by a colon, an X server number followed by a period, and a screen number. In most cases, when displaying directly onto the default X display of a system, the server number and screen number will both be zero. An example setting would be london1:0.0. The most common exception is when running multiple instances of software, such as Virtual Network Computing (VNC) for displaying graphics across the Internet.

TEMP and TMPDIR

By default, the directory used for the storage of temporary files on Linux is usually the /tmp directory. In this directory, Oracle will create files, such as installation log files, and utilities will create files to track values, such as process identifiers. It should not be confused with the intended location of the Oracle TEMP tablespace, which must reside in a permanent storage area and not in /tmp. If it is desired for Oracle to use a directory other than /tmp for temporary storage, both TEMP and TMPDIR should be set to the path of this directory.

DISABLE_HUGETLBFS

An incorrect configuration of huge pages may result in the Oracle error ORA-27125: Unable to Create Shared Memory Segment when trying to create an Oracle instance. To ensure that Oracle will not attempt to use huge pages on start-up, even if correctly configured, the environment variable DISABLE_HUGETLBFS can be set to the value 1.

DBCA_RAW_CONFIG

When using raw devices for database storage, you can create a mapping file to predetermine the relationship between the raw devices and database files. This file is used by DBCA instead of requiring all of the entries to be entered manually into the utility. The environment variable DBCA_RAW_CONFIG should be set to the full path of the location of the mapping file.

CV_JDKHOME, SRVM_TRACE, CV_DESTLOC, and CVUQDISK_GRP

The CV_JDKHOME, SRVM_TRACE, CV_DESTLOC, and CVUQDISK_GRP environment variables are all related to the operation of the Cluster Verification Utility. CV_JDKHOME specifies the directory location of a Java Development Kit (JDK) version 1.4.2 on the system required for running the utility. Setting SRVM_TRACE to TRUE enables tracing the utility to a log file. CV_DESTLOC specifies the utility's work directory for creating temporary files for its operation. If this environment variable is not set, the directory /tmp will be used. Finally, CVUQDISK_GRP is set to an operating system group that owns the software for the package CVUQDISK. If this environment variable is not set, the default value is oinstall. The software itself is installable from the RPM package cvuqdisk-1.0.1-1.rpm and enables the utility to carry out discovery work on the shared storage configuration.

Example Settings

An example ~/.bash_profile file for a fully operational, postinstallation Oracle 10*g* RAC node with a configuration of environment variables and settings as described follows. Note that the export command is used on each environment variable line to both set the value of the variable and ensure that this value is passed to all child processes created within the environment.

```
[oracle@london1 oracle]$ cat ~/.bash_profile
# .bash_profile

if [ -t 0 ]; then
stty intr ^C
fi

# Get the aliases and functions
if [ -f ~/.bashrc ]; then
        . ~/.bashrc
fi

# User specific environment and startup programs
umask 022
export ORACLE_BASE=/u01/app/oracle
export CRS_HOME=$ORACLE_BASE/product/10.2.0/crs
export ORACLE_HOME=$ORACLE_BASE/product/10.2.0/db_1
export ORACLE_SID=RAC1
export PATH=$ORACLE_HOME/bin:$CRS_HOME/bin:$PATH
export LD_LIBRARY_PATH=$ORACLE_HOME/lib
export ORA_NLS10=$ORACLE_HOME/nls/data
```

These environment variables would be set automatically on login or directly with the following command:

```
[oracle@london1 oracle]$ source .bash_profile
```

Creating the Oracle Software Directories

Before installing the Oracle software, you need to create the directories to install the Oracle 10*g* software corresponding to the environment variables set. The minimum required for OFA compliance is the existence of the ORACLE_BASE directory, and the OUI will create the ORACLE_HOME and CRS_HOME to default specifications.

For this minimum requirement, issue the following commands as root:

```
[root@london1 root]# mkdir -p /u01/app/oracle
[root@london1 root]# chown -R oracle:dba /u01/app/oracle
[root@london1 root]# chmod -R 775 /u01/app/oracle
```

Using mkdir, the directories specified by CRS_HOME and ORACLE_HOME can also be precreated to use the preferred directory instead of the default value from the OUI:

```
[root@london1 root]# mkdir -p /u01/app/oracle/product/10.2.0/crs
[root@london1 root]# mkdir -p /u01/app/oracle/product/10.2.0/db_1
```

You should also ensure that these directories are owned by the oracle user using the chown command.

Setting Security Limits

To complete the Oracle environment configuration, some modifications must be made to the file /etc/security/limits.conf to enable the oracle user to use the number of file descriptors set in the fs.file-max kernel parameter and the number of processes the oracle user would be allowed to open on the system. These values can be viewed and changed with the ulimit -u and ulimit -n commands, respectively, where the command shows the soft limit set on the user. The *soft limit* specifies the default value, and the *hard limit* specifies the value up to which users can change their settings.

To set these limits, edit the file /etc/security/limits.conf and add the following lines:

```
oracle          soft    nproc    2047
oracle          hard    nproc    16384
oracle          soft    nofile   1024
oracle          hard    nofile   65536
```

To modify the values at login outside this file, you can edit the file /etc/profile on Red Hat Linux systems and /etc/profile.local on SUSE Linux to set the ulimit values for the oracle user anywhere up to the hard limits specified in /etc/security/limits.conf. The following statement should be added to the end of the file:

```
if [ $USER = "oracle" ]; then
ulimit -u 16384 -n 65536
fi
```

If these are known values, however, simply raising the soft values to a higher level may be a more preferable alternative. Whichever method is chosen, changing the ulimit values, either within /etc/profile at login or at the command line with the ulimit command, may result in the following error depending on the current security configuration:

```
[root@london1 root]# su - oracle
-bash: ulimit: max user processes: cannot modify limit: Operation not permitted
```

If you receive this error message, ensure that the following line exists in the files relating to the security settings for the methods that you use to log in as the oracle user, such as /etc/pam.d/login, /etc/pam.d/su, and /etc/pam.d/sshd:

```
session required /pam_limits.so
```

After you log in as the oracle user, the ulimit command confirms that the new values have been successfully applied as follows:

```
[oracle@london1 oracle]$ ulimit -u
16384
[oracle@london1 oracle]$ ulimit -n
65536
```

Secure Shell Configuration

Before installing any Oracle 10*g* RAC software, install and configure secure shell (ssh) so that the node on which the installer is initiated can run commands and copy files to the remote nodes. The secure shell must be configured, so no prompts or warnings are received when connecting between hosts. This step should be performed after all of the nodes have been installed and configured with the operating system and the public and private networks are fully operational.

To configure secure shell on the cluster nodes, first run the following commands as the oracle user to create a hidden directory called ~/.ssh, if the directory does not already exist (we use the standard tilde character [~] here to represent the location of the oracle user's home directory):

```
[oracle@london1 oracle]$ mkdir ~/.ssh
[oracle@london1 oracle]$ chmod 755 ~/.ssh
```

Create private and public keys using the ssh-keygen command. Accept the default file locations and enter an optional passphrase, if desired:

```
[oracle@london1 oracle]$ /usr/bin/ssh-keygen -t rsa
Generating public/private rsa key pair.
Enter file in which to save the key (/home/oracle/.ssh/id_rsa):
Enter passphrase (empty for no passphrase):
Enter same passphrase again:
Your identification has been saved in /home/oracle/.ssh/id_rsa.
Your public key has been saved in /home/oracle/.ssh/id_rsa.pub.
The key fingerprint is:
d9:8d:ea:83:46:b4:d6:3e:e1:5c:b6:e0:47:7f:9a:d7 oracle@london1
```

Now, create the DSA version:

```
[oracle@london1 oracle]$ /usr/bin/ssh-keygen -t dsa
Generating public/private dsa key pair.
Enter file in which to save the key (/home/oracle/.ssh/id_dsa):
Enter passphrase (empty for no passphrase):
Enter same passphrase again:
Your identification has been saved in /home/oracle/.ssh/id_dsa.
Your public key has been saved in /home/oracle/.ssh/id_dsa.pub.
The key fingerprint is:
e8:10:74:6f:66:08:c2:2f:5e:b3:4a:c3:b3:24:4e:06 oracle@london1
```

These commands will create four files in ~/.ssh called id_rsa, id_rsa.pub, id_dsa, and id_dsa.pub containing the RSA and DSA private and public keys.

In the .ssh directory, copy the contents of the id_rsa.pub and id_dsa.pub files to a temporary file. This file will be copied to all other nodes, so you use the hostname to differentiate the copies:

```
[oracle@london1 oracle]$ cat id_rsa.pub id_dsa.pub > london1.pub
```

Repeat this procedure for each host in the cluster. Copy the public key file to all other hosts in the cluster, as in the following example:

```
[oracle@london1 oracle] scp london1.pub london2:/home/oracle/.ssh
```

On each host in the cluster, concatenate all the public key files into /ssh/authorized_keys:

```
cat london1.pub london2.pub > authorized_keys
```

Finally, set the permissions of the authorized keys file on all nodes:

```
[oracle@london1 oracle]$ chmod 644 authorized_keys
```

On some systems, the file authorized_keys2 may have been created previously. However, authorized_keys2 relates to earlier versions of the secure shell software and modification should only be made to the authorized_keys file.

If no passphrase was specified, ssh and scp will now be able to connect across all nodes. If a passphrase was used, then these two additional commands should be run in every new bash shell session to prevent a prompt being received for the passphrase for every connection:

```
[oracle@london1 oracle]$ ssh-agent $SHELL
[oracle@london1 oracle]$ ssh-add
```

Enter the passphrase, and the identity will be added to the private key files. Test the ssh and scp commands by connecting to all node combinations, remembering to check the connection back to the same node you are working upon. Connections should be tested across both public and private networks.

```
[oracle@london1 oracle]$ ssh london1
[oracle@london1 oracle]$ ssh london2
[oracle@london1 oracle]$ ssh london1-priv
[oracle@london1 oracle]$ ssh london2-priv
```

All combinations should be tested. On the first attempted connection, the following warning will be received, and the default of answer yes should be entered to add the node to the list of known hosts to prevent this prompt from stalling the Oracle installation:

```
The authenticity of host 'london1 (10.240.85.21)' can't be established.
RSA key fingerprint is c3:6b:95:d3:d7:7f:67:53:dd:f3:7c:48:06:6a:b6:16.
Are you sure you want to continue connecting (yes/no)? yes
Warning: Permanently added 'london1' (RSA) to the list of known hosts.
```

If the ssh or scp command is run by the oracle user on a system running an X Window–based desktop from another user, then, unless X authority information is available for the display, the session will receive the following warning:

```
Warning: No xauth data; using fake authentication data for X11 forwarding.
```

This warning is received because by default, ssh is configured to do X11 forwarding, and there is no corresponding entry for the display in the ~/.Xauthority file in the home directory of the oracle user on the system where the command was run. To prevent this warning from occurring during the Oracle software installation, edit the file /etc/ssh/ssh_config and change the line ForwardX11 yes to ForwardX11 no.

Restart the sshd service on SUSE Linux using the sshd script in /etc/init.d or on Red Hat systems as follows:

```
[root@london1 root]# servce sshd restart
```

X11 forwarding will now be disabled, and the warning should not be received for ssh or scp connections. Alternatively, X11 forwarding can be disabled at a user level by creating a file called config in the .ssh directory of only the oracle user with the following entries:

```
[oracle@london1 .ssh]$ cat config
Host *
ForwardX11 no
```

If X11 forwarding is disabled at the system or user level, you can still request to forward X Window display information manually by the ssh or scp command with the -X option, for example:

```
[oracle@london1 oracle]$ ssh -X london2
```

If X11 forwarding is re-enabled after installation, then using ssh with the -x option specifies that X information is not forwarded manually:

```
[oracle@london1 oracle]$ ssh -x london2
```

Shared Storage Configuration

Before installing Oracle 10*g* RAC, it is necessary, at minimum, for shared storage to be available for the Oracle Cluster Registry (OCR) and the Clusterware Cluster Synchronization Services (CSS) voting disk. Further shared storage will also be required for the database files before database creation, although an Oracle software-only installation may be done with a database creation at a later point in time.

This storage must present the same disk images to all of the nodes in the cluster for shared access and be configured with this shared access in mind. For example, a file system type, such as ext3, can be used with a single mount point only and is, therefore, not suitable for formatting the shared disk storage used within a clustered environment.

Successful storage configuration is a vital foundation for RAC, and we have covered storage options, in general, in Chapter 7. OCFS is discussed in Chapter 8, and ASM in Chapter 9. Reviewing these chapters in advance of configuring your Linux operating system will provide significant detail in selecting the storage solution for a particular environment.

Whichever option you select, in the context of configuring Linux, the distinction should be clearly understood between the storage used for installing the Oracle Clusterware and database server software and the storage used for holding the Oracle database files. The Oracle software may be installed on locally created file systems on every node of the cluster or on a shared installation among all of the nodes in the cluster as NFS on a certified NAS storage device or an OCFS version 2 file system. OCFS version 1, ASM, and raw devices are not supported for software installations. Oracle database files may be installed on ASM, OCFS file systems versions 1 and 2 (note that, as discussed in Chapter 8, version 1 of OCFS is supported on 2.4 kernel–based Linux, and version 2 on 2.6 kernel–based installations), or using raw devices. The recovery area, however, cannot be created on raw devices, and none of the Oracle database files can be created on locally configured storage for RAC.

If using a NAS-based solution, no further storage configuration steps are required beyond correctly presenting the NFS file systems to the nodes in the cluster, so the Oracle software installation can proceed. For SAN-based installations (we include iSCSI NAS in this description), further steps are required to partition the LUNs presented by the SAN storage.

Partitioning

As you learned in Chapter 7, SAN disks are presented to a Linux system as SCSI disks, and the disks attached can be viewed in the file /proc/scsi/scsi, such as in the following excerpt showing a single device:

```
Host: scsi2 Channel: 00 Id: 00 Lun: 00
  Vendor: HITACHI  Model: OPEN-L*2       Rev: 2106
  Type:   Direct-Access                  ANSI SCSI
revision: 02
```

If using OCFS or raw devices for the Oracle database files, you need to first create partitions on the disks. ASM can use a disk in its entirety without the need for partitioning. The command used to create partitions on these disks is `fdisk` on x86-based and x86-64–based systems, and `parted` on Itanium systems.

The command `fdisk -l` displays all of the disks available to partition. The output for this command should be the same for all of the nodes in the cluster. The `fdisk` command should be run on one node only, however, to actually partition the disks. All other nodes will read the same partition information, though we recommend rebooting these nodes for the partition information to be fully updated and displayed correctly.

The following example shows the corresponding disk for the device detailed previously. In this example, `/dev/sda` is the internal drive on which the operating system is installed, and `/dev/sdb` is the first external disk to be partitioned.

```
[root@london1 root]# fdisk -l /dev/sdb
Disk /dev/sdb: 72.9 GB, 72900771840 bytes
255 heads, 63 sectors/track, 8863 cylinders
Units = cylinders of 16065 * 512 = 8225280 bytes
```

To partition the drives, use `fdisk` with the argument of the disk device to partition:

```
[root@london1 root]# fdisk /dev/sdb
```

As an example, the shared device `/dev/sdb` has been selected as the disk where the OCR and Clusterware CSS voting disk will reside, and we will create the two required partitions for configuration as raw devices and a single larger partition for general use. The minimum sizes for the OCR and CSS partitions are 100MB and 20MB, respectively; however, these sizes are minimums, and in creating partitions, there is no guarantee that all of the space requested will be usable. In this example, the partitions will be created as 200MB and 50MB partitions to ensure there are no space constraints once operational.

■**Note** The creation of separate partitions for the OCR and CSS voting disk, as shown in the following example, is only required when using raw devices. If using a cluster file system, the OCR and CSS voting disk may simply be created as multiple files within the cluster file system created on a single disk partition.

At the `fdisk` prompt, enter option n to add a new partition, p to make it a primary partition, and the number of the next available primary partition. Accept the default value for the first cylinder and enter the size of the partition in the form +200M for a 200MB partition. For these selections the `fdisk` dialogue will resemble the following:

```
[root@london1 root]# fdisk /dev/sdb
The number of cylinders for this disk is set to 8863.
There is nothing wrong with that, but this is larger than 1024,
and could in certain setups cause problems with:
1) software that runs at boot time (e.g., old versions of LILO)
2) booting and partitioning software from other OSs
   (e.g., DOS FDISK, OS/2 FDISK)

Command (m for help): n
Command action
   e   extended
   p   primary partition (1-4)
p
Partition number (1-4): 1
First cylinder (1-8863, default 1):
Using default value 1
Last cylinder or +size or +sizeM or +sizeK (1-8863,default 8863): +200M
```

Repeat the process to add the second partition of 50MB and accept the default cylinder value to create a third general use partition using the rest of the disk:

```
Command (m for help): n
Command action
   e   extended
   p   primary partition (1-4)
p
Partition number (1-4): 2
First cylinder (26-8863, default 26):
Using default value 26
Last cylinder or +size or +sizeM or +sizeK (26-8863,default 8863): +50M

Command (m for help): n
Command action
   e   extended
   p   primary partition (1-4)
p
Partition number (1-4): 3
First cylinder (33-8863, default 33):
Using default value 33
Last cylinder or +size or +sizeM or +sizeK (33-8863,default 8863):
Using default value 8863
```

At this point, the partition table created will not have been written to the disk. Enter option w to write the partition table to disk:

```
Command (m for help): w
The partition table has been altered!

Calling ioctl() to re-read partition table.
Syncing disks.
```

The newly created partition can now be displayed as follows:

```
[root@london1 root]# fdisk -l /dev/sdb
Disk /dev/sdb: 72.9 GB, 72900771840 bytes
255 heads, 63 sectors/track, 8863 cylinders
Units = cylinders of 16065 * 512 = 8225280 bytes

   Device Boot    Start      End    Blocks    Id System
/dev/sdb1              1       25    200781    83 Linux
/dev/sdb2             26       32     56227+   83 Linux
/dev/sdb3             33     8863  70935007+   83 Linux
```

Reboot the remaining nodes in the cluster and use fdisk -l to verify that all of the nodes can view the partition tables written to the disk.

On an Itanium system, fdisk can still be used to format disks with the MBR formatting scheme, but parted must be used to take advantage of GPT partitioning. Similar to fdisk, parted is invoked with the argument of the disk to partition. On starting, it prints the version of the software and licensing information to the screen and presents the (parted) prompt:

```
[root@london1 root]# parted /dev/sdb
...
Using /dev/sdb
(parted)
```

If the disk label type is not already specified as gpt (the default), then use the mklabel command to specify the new disk label type:

```
(parted) mklabel
New disk label type? [gpt]?
```

The print command is used to display the partition table. In this example, as we have just created the partition table, it shows that the disk label type is gpt and no partitions have yet been created:

```
(parted) print
Disk geometry for /dev/sdb: 0.000-35003.599 megabytes
Disk label type: gpt
Minor Start End Filesystem Name Flags
(parted)
```

To create a partition, use the mkpart command. At the prompts, accept the default values for partition type and file system type. Though mkpart can be used for creating a local file system at the same as the partition, it does not support any clustered file systems shareable between nodes. For the partition sizes, enter the starting value for the partition in megabytes. The first value will be 0, and the ending value will be in megabytes. In the following example, as we illustrated previously with fdisk, we will create a 200MB partition:

```
(parted) mkpart
Partition type? [primary]?
File system type? [ext2]?
Start? 0
End? 200
(parted)
```

Use mkpart to create the subsequent partitions. Accept the default values for partition type and file system type. Enter the ending point of the previous partition for the starting point of the new one, and the ending point, in megabytes, of the starting point plus the desired partition size. For the final partition size, enter the value of the disk size detailed in the disk geometry section. Printing the partition table now displays the created partition. You do not need to call an additional write command, and the partition table will remain on exiting the parted application:

```
(parted) print
Disk geometry for /dev/sdb: 0.000-35003.599 megabytes
Disk label type: gpt
Minor    Start      End         Filesystem Name    Flags
1         0.017    200.000         fat16
2       200.000    250.000
3       250.000  35003.583
(parted)
```

Using fdisk to display the device serves to illustrate that the created GPT partitions are not visible within this command:

```
[root@london1 root]# fdisk -l /dev/sdb
Disk /dev/sdb: 36.7 GB, 36703934464 bytes
255 heads, 63 sectors/track, 4462 cylinders
Units = cylinders of 16065 * 512 = 8225280 bytes
Device       Boot      Start     End      Blocks     Id  System
/dev/sdb1                1       463    35843685+    ee  EFI GPT
```

However, viewing /proc/partitions shows that the partitions have been successfully created and are available for use:

```
[root@london1 root]# cat /proc/partitions
major minor  #blocks  name
...
   8    16   35843686  sdb
```

```
8    17    204783    sdb1
8    18    51200     sdb2
8    19    35587669  sdb3
```

Preparing the Oracle Clusterware Partitions

During installation, the Oracle Clusterware software itself will reside on either local disk file systems or a cluster file system that supports the installation of the Oracle software shared between the nodes, such as OCFS version 2 or NFS. Irrespective of the method selected for the Clusterware software installation, during the process, it creates both the OCR and the CSS voting disk. These require available disk space of 100MB and 20MB, respectively, and can be created on a supported cluster file system, NFS, or raw devices.

Cluster File System

If using a file system method, the Clusterware installation will create the OCR and CSS voting disk as files during the installation process. The only requirement, therefore, is to format the disk partitions you created previously with a suitable cluster file system, such as OCFS, as discussed in Chapter 8. You may then specify file names, such as /u02/oradata/RAC/OCRFile1 and /u02/oradata/RAC/CSSFile1, to be created at the time of the Clusterware installation process. Clusterware installation is detailed in Chapter 12.

Raw Devices

If using SAN storage, you may alternatively locate the OCR and the CSS voting disk devices on raw disk storage, which requires the configuration in advance of the Clusterware installation of raw disk devices.

From Oracle 10. 2, the creation of multiple copies of the OCR and CSS disks is supported, and if these copies are to be configured on raw devices, a device must exist for every copy required. If using multiple copies, two OCR disks are sufficient to provide a mirrored registry. For the CSS disks, at least three copies are required. However, you can still proceed with one copy of each if installed on storage that provides a redundant disk configuration to protect against failure.

On most existing Unix operating systems, raw access is supported by accessing the disk through an existing character special device. On Linux systems based on the 2.4 kernel, this form of access is enabled through specifically binding raw devices to the block-based devices of interest. These raw devices are character devices with a control interface in the device /dev/rawctl. Once these raw devices are bound, they can be used to perform raw I/O directly to the underlying block devices, bypassing the Linux kernel's block buffer cache completely.

On Linux 2.6 kernel–based systems, this use of raw devices is deprecated in favor of using the O_DIRECT flag when opening the device. Using the O_DIRECT flag enables improved administration and security without requiring root access for the setup and maintenance of special bindings for raw devices. The disadvantage of this approach, however, is that the use of the O_DIRECT flag is entirely within the domain of the software developer, meaning that if access is not available to modify the source code, then it is not possible to direct the software to use the O_DIRECT flag.

To correct this situation within 2.6 kernel–based Linux Enterprise implementations, the raw device bindings have been reinstated with administration occurring in exactly the same way as earlier systems. However, the functionality of these bindings is now different, with the raw device driver enabling the use of O_DIRECT for reads and writes to the specified block device, even if not directly requested, ensuring continuity between the different Linux versions. In terms of Oracle, the use of O_DIRECT is supported when using Oracle 10.2 with a 2.6 kernel–based Linux, and therefore, the creation of specific raw devices is not required. For other combinations of Oracle and Linux, the raw device bindings are necessary. If you are in doubt of the functionality available, a default choice is to create the raw device bindings in all configurations. As we have seen, this choice guarantees that access will occur automatically in the correct way supported by a particular environment.

Raw devices are configured by specifying bindings in the file /etc/sysconfig/rawdevices on Red Hat systems and in /etc/raw on SUSE. Putting the bindings in the configuration files ensures that they are persistent across reboots. As an example, for the partitions created in the previous section /dev/sdb1 and /dev/sdb2, you need to add the following entries to the configuration file on Red Hat Linux:

```
/dev/raw/raw1 /dev/sdb1
/dev/raw/raw2 /dev/sdb2
```

and these entries on SUSE Linux:

```
raw1:sdb1
raw2:sdb2
```

The ownership of these devices should be made to the root user with the oinstall group, as follows, to ensure that the oracle user has the required permissions to access them:

```
[root@london1 root]# chown root:oinstall /dev/raw/raw[12]
[root@london1 root]# chmod 660 /dev/raw/raw[12]
```

Note that on Red Hat Enterprise Linux 4.0, the ownership and permissions are not preserved across system reboots, but you may specify all of the chown and chmod commands you used in the /etc/rc.d/rc.local file to ensure that the permissions are modified when the system starts. Alternatively, to change the default behavior of permissions, you can modify the file /etc/udev/permissions.d/50-udev.permissions and alter the default ownership of raw devices from the root user to oracle.

With these entries in place, restart the raw devices service. On Red Hat Systems, restart with the script /etc/init.d/rawdevices or the command service rawdevices with the argument restart. On SUSE Linux, the script /etc/init.d/raw is used, and you need to use the chkconfig command to ensure that the raw devices service is started at run levels 3 and 5. This is already done by default on Red Hat systems. When the service restarts, it displays the raw bindings configured:

```
[root@london1 root]# service rawdevices restart
Assigning devices:
          /dev/raw/raw1  -->    /dev/sdb1
/dev/raw/raw1:  bound to major 8, minor 17
          /dev/raw/raw2  -->    /dev/sdb2
/dev/raw/raw2:  bound to major 8, minor 18
done
```

The raw command with the -qa option shows the currently bound raw devices:

```
[root@london1 root]# raw -qa
/dev/raw/raw1:  bound to major 8, minor 17
/dev/raw/raw2:  bound to major 8, minor 18
```

Copying the rawdevices file, changing the permissions on all nodes in the cluster, and starting the raw devices service ensure that all systems will be able to access the specified disks as raw devices.

The raw device partitions to be used for the OCR and CSS files should be initialized before installing the Clusterware. On one node only, use the dd command to initialize the partitions. We recommend you run this command as the oracle user to confirm that it has sufficient privileges on the partitions for the subsequent Oracle software installation:

```
[oracle@london1 oracle]$ dd if=/dev/zero of=/dev/raw/raw1 bs=1M count=100
100+0 records in
100+0 records out
```

```
[oracle@london1 oracle]$ dd if=/dev/zero of=/dev/raw/raw2 bs=1M count=20
20+0 records in
20+0 records out
```

When you have configured raw devices for your OCR and CSS voting disk, you may simply specify the raw device binding, such as /dev/raw/raw1, directly during the installation process. Alternatively, you may wish to create a symbolic link from a more meaningful name to the raw device using the ln -s command. You may then use the meaningful names specified by the links, such as /u02/oradata/RAC/OCRFile1 and /u02/oradata/RAC/CSSFile1, during the installation process.

You can also use the devlabel command to manage symbolic links to the raw devices, where the raw binding is configured automatically. The devlabel command is designed to maintain the binding when the underlying device name changes. In the following example, the entries added are stored in the /etc/sysconfig/devlabel file. This file, once generated on one node, can be copied to the other nodes to apply the same changes:

```
[root@london1 root]# devlabel add -s /dev/raw/raw1 -d /dev/sdb1
--uid `id -u oracle` --gid `id -g oracle`
RAW: /dev/raw/raw1 -> /dev/sdb1
Added /dev/raw/raw1 to /etc/sysconfig/devlabel

[root@london1 root]# raw -qa
/dev/raw/raw1:  bound to major 8, minor 17.
```

Channel Bonding

For the reasons described in Chapter 6, we recommend a teamed network interface configuration to be implemented on the private interconnect network to prevent the risk of the interconnect switch itself being a single point of failure for the entire cluster. As detailed in Chapter 6, to implement teaming, you will need two available network interfaces per node in addition to the external network interface. You will also need two network switches connected to each other with an interswitch link, with the switches supporting this form of topology. If this is the case, after installing the Linux operating system according to the guidelines detailed in Chapter 10, you will have an active external interface, an active private interconnect interface, and an additional, currently inactive private network interface.

We will assume that the interfaces' device names are eth0, eth1, and eth2, respectively. You may also have additional interfaces, for example, for a backup network; however, for simplicity, we will consider only the three devices listed here. To optimally implement bonding, all of the interfaces that are intended to communicate on the private interconnect should be configured in this fully redundant way with bonding as well. Care should also be taken to ensure that all of the servers are connected to the active and backup switches with the same corresponding interfaces. In other words, if eth1 on london1 is connected to the active switch, then eth1 on all other nodes should also be connected to this same switch.

Implementing NIC teaming functionality without tainting the kernel requires the configuration and use of the channel bonding kernel module, which is included with both Red Hat and SUSE Enterprise Linux distributions. Alternative teaming drivers that are closely integrated with the network drivers themselves are produced by network card vendors such as Intel's Advanced Networking Services (ANS) for Linux and Broadcom's Broadcom Advanced Server Program. Before investigating these vendor-based solutions, be aware that the modules may not be licensed under the GPL license agreement, will taint the kernel, and will invalidate Unbreakable Linux support. Therefore, we recommend using the channel bonding module.

As bonding is implemented through a loadable kernel module similar to the hangcheck-timer module, you need to set configuration options in the file /etc/modprobe.conf on Red Hat systems or /etc/modprobe.conf.local on SUSE systems. You also need to explicitly load and set the bonding module options when you initiate the private network interface. Creating an alias for the interface name, in this case bond0, enables parameters to be assigned to the bonding module.

```
alias bond0 bonding
options bond0 miimon=100 mode=1
```

Two options are of particular interest. First, either miimon or arp_interval and arp_ip_target must be specified. We recommend setting miimon, as this is the most applicable solution for ensuring high availability and determines how often Media Independent Interface (MII) link monitoring occurs, in milliseconds. In the previous example, the value is set to 100. In addition, all modern NICs should support MII link monitoring, making it an applicable default option.

The second parameter of mode is also absolutely crucial and must be set to the value of 1 or its text equivalent active-backup. This parameter configures the bonding driver to function such that, during normal operations, only a single primary interface will be used. In the event of a single NIC or cable failure, that node only will switch to its backup NIC communicating with the remaining nodes on their active interfaces through the interswitch link. If the switch itself fails, all of the interfaces will switch to their backups, thereby ensuring the continuity of operations. This form of active/backup configuration is optimal for delivering the most reliable form of redundancy that you aim to achieve to prevent the private interconnect being a single point of failure.

To configure the network devices to use the bonding module, you need to modify the file located in the directory /etc/sysconfig/network-scripts on Red Hat systems or /etc/sysconfig/network on SUSE systems. These files require modifications in different ways. On Red Hat systems, assuming the use of devices eth1 and eth2 for the interconnect, copy the file corresponding to the currently configured private interconnect interface, such as ifcfg-eth1, to a new file named ifcfg-bond0. Edit the device name within this file to reflect the alias name detailed in /etc/modprobe.conf. Then ifcfg-bond0 will contain entries similar to the following:

```
DEVICE=bond0
BOOTPROTO=none
ONBOOT=yes
TYPE=Ethernet
USERCTL=no
IPADDR=192.168.1.1
NETMASK=255.255.255.0
```

Modify the files ifcfg-eth1 and ifcfg-eth2 to configure the devices as slaves for the master device configured in ifcfg-bond0 with entries such as those that follow. The files will be identical except for the line specifying the device name to which the configuration file relates:

```
DEVICE=eth1
BOOTPROTO=none
ONBOOT=yes
MASTER=bond0
SLAVE=yes
USERCTL=no
```

On SUSE Enterprise Linux systems, use the command lspci to determine the PCI information of the Ethernet cards installed on your system to use for the private interconnect, as in the following example:

```
0000:03:04.0 Ethernet controller: Intel Corp. 82546GB Gigabit Ethernet Controller
(rev 03)
0000:03:04.1 Ethernet controller: Intel Corp. 82546GB Gigabit Ethernet Controller
(rev 03)
```

Information in the existing unmodified configuration files detailing which device names relate to the PCI information can be determined with an entry such as the following:

```
_nm_name='bus-pci-0000:03:04.0'
```

Similarly to your action for Red Hat, rename or copy the configuration file corresponding to the private interconnect interface to the name associated with the bonded device specified in /etc/modprobe.conf.local:

```
[root@london1 root]# mv ifcfg-eth-id-00:04:23:b5:48:ac ifcfg-bond0
```

The hardware address identifying the file to copy corresponds to the MAC address of the card viewable within the first line of output from the command ifconfig:

```
[root@london1 root]# ifconfig eth1
eth1 Link encap:Ethernet  HWaddr00:04:23:B5:48:AC
```

Edit the file to specify the device as a bonding master, including the PCI bus addresses of the relevant slave devices detailed in the first field of the output of lspci. The file will contain details such as the following:

```
IP_ADDRESS=192.168.1.1
NETMASK=255.255.255.0
STARTMODE='onboot'
BONDING_MASTER=yes
BONDING_SLAVE0='bus-pci-0000:03:04.0'
BONDING_SLAVE1='bus-pci-0000:03:04.1'
```

Delete any existing ifcfg files remaining for the slave devices. For testing purposes, you can restart the network services from the start-up script /etc/init.d/network with the command restart. On Red Hat Linux systems, the command service network or, on SUSE systems, rcnetwork will also call this script. We do, however, recommend rebooting the system as part of the testing process to ensure that the bonding module is loaded during the boot process.

With the bonded network interface activated, the following output from the ifconfig command shows that the private interconnect network is active with its master and slave devices:

```
[root@london1 root]# ifconfig -a
bond0     Link encap:Ethernet  HWaddr 00:04:23:B7:A0:43
          inet addr:192.168.1.1  Bcast:192.168.1.255  Mask:255.255.255.0
          UP BROADCAST RUNNING MASTER MULTICAST  MTU:1500  Metric:1
          RX packets:2612 errors:0 dropped:0 overruns:0 frame:0
          TX packets:725 errors:0 dropped:0 overruns:0 carrier:0
          collisions:0 txqueuelen:0
          RX bytes:392730 (383.5 Kb)  TX bytes:540469 (527.8 Kb)

eth1      Link encap:Ethernet  HWaddr 00:04:23:B7:A0:43
          inet addr:192.168.1.1  Bcast:192.168.1.255  Mask:255.255.255.0
          UP BROADCAST RUNNING SLAVE MULTICAST  MTU:1500  Metric:1
          RX packets:1283 errors:0 dropped:0 overruns:0 frame:0
          TX packets:365 errors:0 dropped:0 overruns:0 carrier:0
          collisions:0 txqueuelen:1000
          RX bytes:194927 (190.3 Kb)  TX bytes:272034 (265.6 Kb)
          Base address:0xdc00 Memory:fcfe0000-fd000000

eth2      Link encap:Ethernet  HWaddr 00:04:23:B7:A0:43
          inet addr:192.168.1.1  Bcast:192.168.1.255  Mask:255.255.255.0
          UP BROADCAST RUNNING NOARP SLAVE MULTICAST  MTU:1500 Metric:1
          RX packets:1329 errors:0 dropped:0 overruns:0 frame:0
          TX packets:360 errors:0 dropped:0 overruns:0 carrier:0
          collisions:0 txqueuelen:1000
          RX bytes:197803 (193.1 Kb)  TX bytes:268435 (262.1 Kb)
```

```
Base address:0xd880 Memory:fcfa0000-fcfc0000
```

Details related to the configuration of the network are also reported in the system log, viewable in /var/log/messages or with the command dmesg. This output should be checked to ensure that the secondary device is configured as a backup and not as an active interface. The following output illustrates that the options set in /etc/modprobe.conf were successfully detected:

```
bonding: bond0: enslaving eth1 as a backup interface with a down link.
e1000: eth1: e1000_watchdog: NIC Link is Up 1000 Mbps Full Duplex
bonding: bond0: link status definitely up for interface eth1.
bonding: bond0: making interface eth1 the new active one.
bonding: bond0: enslaving eth2 as a backup interface with a down link.
e1000: eth2: e1000_watchdog: NIC Link is Up 1000 Mbps Full Duplex
bonding: bond0: link status definitely up for interface eth2.
```

The system log also records the following information showing that, when the link on the primary interface fails, the secondary interface is correctly activated:

```
e1000: eth1: e1000_watchdog: NIC Link is Down
bonding: bond0: link status definitely down for interface eth1, disabling it
bonding: bond0: making interface eth2 the new active one.
```

We recommend that, after the bonding devices are configured on the private interconnect for all of the nodes in cluster, the setup should be thoroughly tested for responses to failures at a NIC, cable, and switch level. Different networking hardware will exhibit different attributes, and you should be completely familiar with the characteristics of your particular environment before installing the Oracle software.

Once bonding has been configured and is active on all of the nodes in the cluster, the interface, in this case bond0, represents the private interconnect interface to use for the Oracle software during installation. The slave device names should not be used directly in any of the configuration steps required.

Cluster Verification

The Cluster Verification Utility (CVU or CLUVFY) was introduced in Oracle 10.2. It is designed to allow you to verify that the cluster has been correctly configured before you attempt to install Oracle Clusterware or the Oracle Database software. Verifying the cluster beforehand reduces the likelihood that the installation will fail because of a configuration oversight. In our experience, CLUVFY is not yet perfect, and you may still experience installation failures. However, it is a significant improvement over some of its predecessors, and we recommend that you use it as a sanity check for all manual installations.

CLUVFY is distributed with Oracle 10.2, but you can also use it to check the configuration of Oracle 10.1 RAC clusters. Note that it is necessary to specify the -r 10gR1 option for some CLUVFY options for the 10.1 checks to function correctly. If you are installing 10.1, we recommend that you consider downloading the Oracle 10.2 Clusterware and running the CLUVFY utility. In our experience, it detects a large number of common configuration errors and may eliminate a significant amount of time-consuming troubleshooting.

CLUVFY performs a read-only check and advises you of any issues it encounters. You can choose whether or not to follow each recommendation. However, you should be aware that if you fail to implement a recommendation, there is a strong possibility that the subsequent installation procedure will fail.

We have also observed that, at least in early production versions, the recommended minimum values required by CLUVFY do not always match those required by the OUI. This inconsistency can also lead to installation failures.

Java Runtime Environment

The CLUVFY utility is written in Java and therefore requires a Java Runtime Environment (JRE). If you do not have an existing JRE, one is supplied on the Oracle Clusterware installation CD-ROM as a .zip file, which is decompressed and temporarily installed every time you run CLUVFY.

Alternatively, you may wish to download and install a permanent JRE. At the time of this writing, the current JRE version is 1.4.2-08 and can be downloaded from http://www.javasoft.com. On the web site, this is described as the J2SE (Core/Desktop), the Java 2 Platform, Standard Edition version 1.4.2 (J2SE 1.4.2). At minimum, you need to download the J2SE JRE, which allows you to run Java applications. Alternatively, you can download the Software Development Kit (SDK), if you wish to develop and build your own Java applications. The SDK includes the components of the JRE.

You can choose to download the JRE as a self-extracting file or as an RPM in a self-extracting file. Both are around 13MB. We normally choose the latter, as we generally store all RPMs used to build our servers on a central FTP server for future use.

When you have downloaded the executable, you will need to change the permissions and execute it to create the RPM, as in the following example:

```
[root@london1 root]# chmod 744 j2re-1_4_2_08-linux-i586-rpm.bin
[root@london1 root]# ./j2re-1_4_2_08-linux-i586-rpm.bin
[root@london1 root]# rpm -Uvh j2re-1_4_2_08-linux-i586-rpm
```

When you execute the binary, you will be asked to accept the Java license agreement. The RPM utility will write the JRE files to the directory /usr/java/j2re1.4.2_08. In order for CLUVFY to use the JRE, you will need to set the following environment variable:

```
[oracle@london1 oracle]$ export CV_JDKHOME=/usr/java/j2re1.4.2_08
```

This can be set either on the command prompt or in .bash_profile.

The CLUVFY utility can be run directly from the installation CD-ROM. Alternatively, if you have downloaded the Oracle executables, then you can unzip the downloaded file and run CLUVFY from disk. In the following discussion, we will follow the Oracle convention and describe the path to the CD-ROM or disk as /mountpoint/.

cvuqdisk Package

If you wish to use the full capabilities of CLUVFY on Red Hat, you will need to install the cvuqdisk package. You can check whether the package has already been installed by using the following:

```
[root@london1 root]# rpm -qa | grep cvuqdisk
```

which should return

```
cvuqdisk-1.0.1-1
```

If the package has not been installed, then you can find it on the Clusterware CD-ROM in the directory /mountpoint/clusterware/rpm. The package can be installed using

```
[root@london1 root]# rpm -Uvh cvuqdisk-1.0.1-1.rpm
```

This installation creates the executable /usr/sbin/cvuqdisk, which is used by CVUVFY to perform various disk checks.

Alternatively, you can prevent the raw disk checks from being performed by setting the following environment variable:

```
[oracle@london1 oracle]$ export CV_RAW_CHECK_ENABLED=FALSE
```

CLUVFY can be executed by the oracle user. On Linux, CLUVFY should be executed using the runcluvfy.sh script, which can be found in /mountpoint/clusterware/cluvfy. This shell script sets up the appropriate environment variables and unzips the Java libraries prior to execution.

You can use CLUVFY in two modes: stage and component. In stage mode, CLUVFY performs all checks required for the specified stage of the installation process. In component mode, CLUVFY performs all checks required for a specified component. Each stage consists of one or more components.

Syntax

CLUVFY contains useful help information that also provides some orientation during initial use. At the top level, you can display a summary of the syntax as follows:

```
[oracle@london1 cluvfy]$ sh runcluvfy.sh -help
USAGE:
cluvfy [ -help]
cluvfy stage {-list | -help}
cluvfy stage {-pre|-post} <stage-name> <stage-specific-options> [-verbose]
cluvfy comp {-list | -help}
cluvfy comp <component-name> <component-specific-options> [-verbose]
```

Using the guidelines from the help output, you can list all the stages and components and their purpose and syntax in order to navigate your way through the usage of CLUVFY.

Stage Checks

In Oracle 10.2, CLUVFY can be used at the following seven possible stages to check the current configuration:

- After hardware/operating system configuration
- Before cluster file system setup
- After cluster file system setup
- Before Oracle Clusterware (CRS) installation
- After Oracle Clusterware (CRS) installation
- Before Oracle Database installation
- Before Oracle Database configuration

These stages are described in the following sections.

After Hardware/Operating System Configuration

In general, we recommend performing a check at the end of each installation stage to confirm that the configuration is correct before proceeding to the next stage.

To check that all hardware and operating system configuration steps have been performed, use

```
sh runcluvfy.sh stage -post hwos -n <node_list>
```

as in the following example:

```
[oracle@london1 cluvfy]$ sh runcluvfy.sh stage -post hwos -n london1,london2
```

Note that you must not include any spaces between hostnames in the node list.
This option checks

- Node reachability
- User equivalence
- Node connectivity
- Shared storage accessibility

If CLUVFY returns an error, you can obtain more information for most of the stages and components using the -verbose option as follows:

```
[oracle@london1 cluvfy]$ sh runcluvfy.sh stage -post hwos -n london1,london2
-verbose
```

Before Cluster File System Setup

You can check that all configuration steps have been performed prior to setting up the cluster file system, as in the following example:

```
[oracle@london1 cluvfy]$ sh runcluvfy.sh stage -pre cfs -n london1,london2
-s /dev/sda
```

where /dev/sda is a SCSI device created on shared storage. Note that the -s option is mandatory for this check. This option also checks the following:

- Node reachability
- User equivalence
- Node connectivity
- Shared storage accessibility

After Cluster File System Setup

Using the following code, where /u02 is the cluster file system, you can check that the system has been correctly configured:

```
[oracle@london1 cluvfy]$ sh runcluvfy.sh stage -post cfs -n london1,london2 -f /u02
```

Note that the -f option is mandatory for this check. The cluster file system setup check verifies

- Node reachability
- User equivalence
- Cluster file system integrity
- Shared storage accessibility

Before Oracle Clusterware Installation

You can also verify that all installation steps have been completed before installation of Oracle Clusterware:

```
[oracle@london1 cluvfy]$ sh runcluvfy.sh stage -pre crsinst -n london1,london2
```

By default, this command will perform Oracle 10.2 checks. If you are verifying an Oracle 10.1 system, then you should include the -r 10gR1 option. This option checks

- Node reachability
- User equivalence
- Administrative privileges
- Node connectivity
- Shared storage accessibility

After Oracle Clusterware Installation

Check that all Oracle Clusterware has been successfully installed using

```
[oracle@london1 cluvfy]$ sh runcluvfy.sh stage -post crsinst -n london1,london2
```

which checks the following:

- Node reachability
- User equivalence
- Cluster manager integrity
- Cluster integrity
- OCR integrity
- CRS integrity
- Node application existence

Before Database Software Installation

Before the installation of Oracle database software, you can check that all installation steps have been completed:

```
[oracle@london1 cluvfy]$ sh runcluvfy.sh stage -pre dbinst -n london1,london2
```

By default, this command also will perform Oracle 10.2 checks. If you are verifying an Oracle 10.1 system, then you should again include the -r 10gR1 option. This option checks

- Node reachability
- User equivalence
- Administrative privileges
- Node connectivity
- System requirements for database
- CRS integrity
- Node application existence

Before Database Configuration

Before running the Database Configuration Assistant to create a database, you can check that all installation steps have been completed using the following:

```
[oracle@london1 cluvfy]$ sh runcluvfy.sh stage -pre dbcfg -n london1,london2
-d $ORACLE_HOME
```

This option determines

- Node reachability
- User equivalence
- Administrative privileges
- Node connectivity
- CRS integrity

Component Checks

The topics in this section detail the component checks that are performed by the CLUVFY utility, including node reachability, connectivity, and minimum system requirements. Some of these checks, such as the minimum system requirements, are also performed during the installation of the Oracle software; therefore, it is worth validating the components with CLUVFY before proceeding with the Oracle software installation.

Node Reachability

Node reachability checks that the entire network configuration is correct and that all nodes can be reached via the network:

```
sh runcluvfy.sh comp nodereach -n <nodelist>
```

as in the following example:

```
[oracle@london1 cluvfy]$ sh runcluvfy.sh comp nodereach -n london1,london2
```

If you do not specify a source node, then CLUVFY will use the node on which the command was issued as the source. You can also check reachability using another node as the source:

```
[oracle@london1 cluvfy]$ sh runcluvfy.sh comp nodereach -n london1,london2
-srcnode london2
```

The nodereach check only verifies that nodes are reachable over the network.

Node Connectivity

The following command checks that the network configuration is correct, that is, that you have configured sufficient network interfaces and included acceptable IP hostnames and addresses in /etc/hosts:

```
[oracle@london1 cluvfy]$ sh runcluvfy.sh comp nodecon -n london1,london2
```

Node connectivity for the public and private subnets is checked. It also checks that suitable VIP addresses have been configured on the public subnet.

Cluster File System Integrity

To verify the integrity of a cluster file system, use

```
[oracle@london1 cluvfy]$ sh runcluvfy.sh comp cfs -n london1,london2 -f /u02
```

If the cluster file system is OCFS, then this command checks the following:

- Existence of the /etc/ocfs.conf file
- Host GUID uniqueness
- Run level configuration for OCFS

The file system integrity check also invokes the shared storage accessibility check described in the next section.

Shared Storage Accessibility

Use the following check that shared storage is accessible:

```
[oracle@london1 cluvfy]$ sh runcluvfy.sh comp ssa -n london1,london2
```

This command will verify OCFS and shared SCSI disks. You can also check individual SCSI disks, as in the following example:

```
[oracle@london1 cluvfy]$ sh runcluvfy.sh comp ssa -n london1,london2 -s /dev/sda
```

Note that if the cvuqdisk package has not been installed, then this command will fail with the following message:

```
WARNING:
Package cvuqdisk not installed
```

Space Availability

The following option can be used to verify that minimum space requirements are met. For example, to meet the default requirements for temporary space in Oracle 10.2.0.1, run

```
[oracle@london1 cluvfy]$ sh runcluvfy.sh comp space -n london1,london2 -l /tmp➥
-z 400M
```

Note that, contrary to the usage message, this command will fail if you leave a space between the number representing the disk space (e.g., 400) and the letter representing the magnitude (e.g., M).

Minimum System Requirements

To verify that minimum system requirements are met for Oracle Clusterware installation, use the following:

```
[oracle@london1 cluvfy]$ sh runcluvfy.sh comp sys -n london1,london2 -p crs
```

You can also use this option to verify that minimum system requirements are met for Oracle Database software installation:

```
[oracle@london1 cluvfy]$ sh runcluvfy.sh comp sys -n london1,london2 -p database
```

On the version we tested, both the crs and database options performed the following checks:

- Total memory on each node of 512MB or larger
- Free space in /tmp directory of 400MB or more
- Swap space of 1GB or more
- System architecture of i686 (on a 32-bit system)
- Kernel version 2.4.21-15EL or above (on Red Hat EL3.0 Update 4)

On Red Hat Linux, both the crs and database options check the minimum version for the following packages:

- make-3.79.1-17
- binutils-2.14.90.0.4-35
- gcc-3.2.3-47
- glibc-2.3.2-95.30
- compat-db-4.0.14-5.1
- compat-gcc-7.3-2.96.128
- compat-gcc-c++-7.3-2.96.128
- compat-libstdc++-7.3-2.96.128
- compat-libstdc++-devel-7.3-2.96.128
- openmotif-2.2.3-3.RHEL3
- setarch-1.3-1

Both the crs and databases options check the existence of the following administrative privileges:

- dba group
- oinstall group
- nobody user

In addition, the database option checks the following kernel parameters at these levels or higher:

- semmsl of 250
- semmns of 32,000
- semopm of 100
- semmni of 128
- shmall of 2,097,152
- shmmni of 4096
- file-max of 65,536
- rmem_default of 262,144
- rmem_max of 262,144
- wmem_default of 262,144
- wmem_max of 262,144

By default, these minimum system verification commands will perform Oracle 10.2 checks. If you are verifying an Oracle 10.1 system, then you should include the -r 10gR1 option here too.

Cluster Integrity

Check the integrity of the cluster with the following:

```
[oracle@london1 cluvfy]$ sh runcluvfy.sh comp clu -n london1,london2
```

Cluster Manager Integrity

The integrity of the cluster manager can be checked by running

```
[oracle@london1 cluvfy]$ sh runcluvfy.sh comp clumgr -n london1,london2
```

This command checks that the CSS component is correctly configured and is running on all nodes.

OCR Integrity

The OCR is checked by

```
[oracle@london1 cluvfy]$ sh runcluvfy.sh comp ocr -n london1,london2
```

This command verifies that the OCR is not configured on nonclustered storage on any node. It also checks that the correct version of the OCR exists (version 2 in Oracle 10.2). Finally, it performs a data integrity check on the OCR.

CRS Integrity

The following option checks the integrity of Oracle Clusterware (CRS):

```
[oracle@london1 cluvfy]$ sh runcluvfy.sh comp crs -n london1,london2
```

This command checks for the existence of the CRS, CSS, and EVM components on each node.

Node Applications

This option checks the existence of node applications by checking that the VIP, ONS, and GSD node applications exist on each node:

```
[oracle@london1 cluvfy]$ sh runcluvfy.sh comp nodeapp -n london1,london2
```

Administrative Privileges

You can also check that administrative privileges have been correctly granted. To check for user equivalence across all nodes in the cluster, use

```
[oracle@london1 cluvfy]$ sh runcluvfy.sh comp admprv -n london1,london2➥
-o user_equiv
```

which checks for the existence of the oracle user on each node in the cluster.

To verify that correct administrative privileges have been granted for the Oracle Clusterware installation, use the following code to check that the oinstall group is the primary group of the oracle user:

```
[oracle@london1 cluvfy]$ sh runcluvfy.sh comp admprv -n london1,london2 -o crs_inst
```

To check that correct administrative privileges have been granted for Oracle Database software installation, use

```
[oracle@london1 cluvfy]$ sh runcluvfy.sh comp admprv -n london1,london2 -o db_inst
```

This command confirms that the oinstall group is the primary group of the oracle user. It also checks that the oracle user belongs to the dba group.

Use the following to check that correct administrative privileges have been granted for Oracle Database software installation:

```
[oracle@london1 cluvfy]$ sh runcluvfy.sh comp admprv -n london1,london2 ➥
-o db_config -d $ORACLE_HOME
```

The -d option is mandatory here. This command performs the same checks as the db_inst option.

Peer Comparison

Peer comparison allows you to compare the current configuration of a node with one or more others. To compare a set of nodes with each other, use

```
[oracle@london1 cluvfy]$ sh runcluvfy.sh comp peer -n london1,london2
```

In this example, the configurations of nodes london1 and london2 will be compared and any differences will be reported.

Use the following to compare a set of nodes with a reference node:

```
[oracle@london1 cluvfy]$ sh runcluvfy.sh comp peer -refnode london1➥
-n london2,london3,london4
```

In this example, the configurations of nodes london2, london3, and london4 will be compared to the reference node london1 and any differences will be reported. The configuration of the reference node is assumed to be correct.

The peer comparison checks the following on each node:

- Total memory
- Amount of swap space
- Kernel version
- System architecture
- Mandatory packages
- Existence and group ID of oinstall group
- Existence and group ID of dba group
- Existence of nobody user

By default, this command will perform Oracle 10.2 checks. As with the other commands, if you are comparing Oracle 10.1 systems, then you should include the -r 10gR1 option.

Summary

In this chapter, we detailed the actions required to configure and verify the Linux operating system before installing the Oracle Clusterware and 10g RAC Database Server software. We focused on explaining all of the available configuration options and the meanings behind the configuration decisions, in order to provide you with the foundation for successful Oracle software installations. We also described the Cluster Verification Utility (CLUVFY), which allows you to check the configuration of all nodes in the cluster at various stages in the installation process.

CHAPTER 12

■■■

Installing and Configuring Oracle Software

In Chapters 10 and 11, you learned how to install, configure, and verify your chosen Linux operating system in preparation for installing the Oracle Database 10g RAC software. This chapter describes the typical installation and configuration procedures of the software required for your RAC environment, the Oracle Clusterware, and the Oracle Database 10g software. We also look at some common troubleshooting techniques and deinstallation.

Preparing to Install

The Oracle Universal Installer (OUI), which is a GUI tool, can be used for the installation and deinstallation of both Oracle Clusterware and the Oracle Database Server. It can also be used to subsequently add software components and options and to apply patch sets.

The Oracle RAC installation process has three steps:

1. Install Oracle Clusterware.

2. Optionally, install Oracle Database Server software for the ASM home directory.

3. Install Oracle Database Server software for the RDBMS home directory.

In Oracle 10.2 and above, Oracle Corporation recommends that ASM have a separate Home directory to the database. Separate Oracle Home directories simplify future upgrades and patches by eliminating any dependencies between the ASM and RDBMS software.

Following the installation of the Oracle Database Server software, you can install any optional software components and companion products.

The OUI should be run by the oracle user from an X Window terminal, and it only needs to be run on one node. All changes will be automatically propagated to the other nodes in the cluster. We recommend using the same node for the installation of all products. If possible, this node should also be used for any deinstallations.

The OUI will occasionally pause and prompt for certain shell scripts to be performed with root user privileges. Sometimes, these scripts are only required on the installation node; at other times, they need to be executed on every node in the cluster. Read the prompts carefully to determine whether the scripts should be run on only the installation node or on all nodes in the cluster.

In Oracle 10.2, Oracle Clusterware must be installed on local disks on each node in the cluster. At the time of this writing, most sites also elect to deploy the ASM and RDBMS software on local disks on each node.

You can install the ASM and RDBMS Oracle Homes on shared storage using NFS, OCFS2, or third-party cluster file systems. However, in our experience, the vast majority of sites still prefer to use local directories for all Oracle Homes.

Using local disks does increase the amount of maintenance required to upgrade or patch releases, as files must be copied to each node. However, it also increases flexibility, particularly for sites that do not have a test cluster. The instance on one node can be stopped, and the patch application can be tested, without affecting the remaining nodes. If successful, the patch can be applied to the remaining nodes. On the other hand, if a shared Oracle Home was used, then you would need to stop all nodes in order to safely apply the patch. The decision of whether to use local or shared storage for Oracle software is, therefore, likely to be driven by a combination of the availability requirements for the cluster and budgetary considerations.

You can install Oracle 10g on a cluster with an existing Oracle 9i software installation. Prior to installation, however, we recommend that you shut down and back up both the Oracle 9i database and the Oracle 9i software.

Installation Media

Prior to Oracle 10.2, Oracle software was supplied to licensed customers on CD-ROM. The software is currently delivered on four disks:

- Oracle Database Server (Standard or Enterprise)
- Oracle Companion Disk
- Oracle Clusterware
- Oracle Client

Oracle 10.2 is the first release for which Oracle software has been supplied on DVD-ROM. Therefore, if you are purchasing new hardware, you should consider specifying DVD readers.

Alternatively, Oracle software is available for download from the Oracle Technology Network web site. The downloaded software is supplied in the following zipped cpio archives:

```
10201_database_linux32.zip
10201_companion_linux32.zip
10201_clusterware_linux32.zip
10201_client_linux32.zip
```

You will generally not require the client download for database servers. It may, however, be required for any middle-tier servers that will be connecting to the database.

Make sure that you download the correct files for your architecture. Available media for Unbreakable Linux platforms have the following file extensions:

- linux32
- linux_x86_64
- linuxitanium

When you have downloaded these files, you should use the sum command to generate a checksum for each file, which should be compared to the value displayed on the Oracle technology download page to verify the integrity of each downloaded file.

It is only necessary to extract the software from the zipped files on one node in the cluster. In previous versions of Oracle, software was extracted into a series of directories called Disk1, Disk2, Disk3, and so on. In Oracle 10.2, files are extracted into subdirectories called clusterware, database, and so on.

We recommend that you create a series of staging directories where the download files can be unzipped and uncompressed. For example, if your Oracle home directory is /u01/app/oracle, then you might create the following directories:

```
[oracle@london1 oracle]$ mkdir /u01/app/oracle/stage
[oracle@london1 oracle]$ mkdir /u01/app/oracle/stage/crs
[oracle@london1 oracle]$ mkdir /u01/app/oracle/stage/db
[oracle@london1 oracle]$ mkdir /u01/app/oracle/stage/ccd
```

After you have downloaded the .zip files into the appropriate directories, use the unzip command to extract and uncompress the files from the archives:

```
[oracle@london1 crs]$ unzip 10201_clusterware_linux32.zip
```

Repeat this command for the remaining download files.

Oracle Clusterware

In Oracle 10g, you must install Oracle Clusterware software in a different location (CRS_HOME) than the Oracle Database Server software (ORACLE_HOME). Both directories can be located in the same directory tree below ORACLE_BASE. However, this location must be the same on every node.

■**Note** There is some ambiguity about the name of the environment variable for the Oracle Cluster Ready Services directory. In this book, we have chosen to use $CRS_HOME. In other documentation, it is also frequently referred to as $ORA_CRS_HOME.

Preinstallation Tasks

Before installing the Oracle Clusterware, make sure that your operating system is correctly configured using the steps in Chapters 10 and 11. You should complete the following actions before installing the Oracle software:

- Install RPMs.
- Install patches.
- Set kernel parameters.
- Create the dba and oinstall groups.
- Create the oracle user and its home directory.
- Configure NIC teaming, if required.
- Configure the public network.
- Configure the private network.
- Add public hostnames, private hostnames, and VIP hostnames for all nodes to /etc/hosts or DNS.
- Configure storage multipathing, if required.
- Configure storage.
- Configure the cluster file system, ASM volumes, or shared raw devices.

The last point is particularly important. Prior to installing the Oracle Clusterware, you should create logical partitions on shared storage and configure raw devices or cluster file systems. If you are planning to use the new mirroring functionality for the OCR and voting disk in Oracle 10.2 and above, you will need a minimum of three OCFS file systems.

If you intend to use ASM, you should also install the ASM RPMs, create the ASM volumes using the createdisk procedure in /etc/init.d/oracleasm, and ensure that these are presented on all nodes in the cluster using the scandisks procedure in /etc/init.d/oracleasm.

Verifying the Configuration

Before installing Oracle Clusterware, verify that the configuration is correct using the CLUVFY utility introduced in Chapter 11:

```
[oracle@london1 cluvfy]$ sh runcluvfy.sh stage -pre crsinst -n london1,london2
Performing pre-checks for cluster services setup

Checking node reachability...
Node reachability check passed from node "london1".

Checking user equivalence...
User equivalence check passed for user "oracle".

Checking administrative privileges...
User existence check passed for "oracle".
Group existence check passed for "oinstall".
Membership check for user "oracle" in group "oinstall" [as Primary] passed.

Administrative privileges check passed.

Checking node connectivity...

Node connectivity check passed for subnet "147.43.0.0" with node(s) london2,london1.
Node connectivity check passed for subnet "192.168.2.0" with node(s) ➡
london2,london1.

Suitable interfaces for VIP on subnet "147.43.0.0":
london2 eth0:147.43.1.104
london1 eth0:147.43.1.103

Suitable interfaces for the private interconnect on subnet "192.168.2.0":
london2 eth1:192.168.2.104
london1 eth1:192.168.2.103

Node connectivity check passed.

Checking system requirements for 'crs'...
Total memory check passed.
Free disk space check passed.
Swap space check passed.
System architecture check passed.
Kernel version check passed.
Package existence check passed for "make-3.79".
Package existence check passed for "binutils-2.14".
Package existence check passed for "gcc-3.2".
Package existence check passed for "glibc-2.3.2-95.27".
Package existence check passed for "compat-db-4.0.14-5".
Package existence check passed for "compat-gcc-7.3-2.96.128".
Package existence check passed for "compat-gcc-c++-7.3-2.96.128".
Package existence check passed for "compat-libstdc++-7.3-2.96.128".
```

```
Package existence check passed for "compat-libstdc++-devel-7.3-2.96.128".
Package existence check passed for "openmotif-2.2.3".
Package existence check passed for "setarch-1.3-1".
Group existence check passed for "dba".
Group existence check passed for "oinstall".
User existence check passed for "nobody".

System requirement passed for 'crs'

Pre-check for cluster services setup was successful.
```

Running the Installer

The OUI must be started from an X Window terminal. If X Window is not currently running on your system, then run the command

```
[root@london1 root]# startx
```

As the oracle user, run the ssh-agent and ssh-add commands to ensure that no passphrase is required when running ssh under this session:

```
[oracle@london1 oracle]$ ssh-agent $SHELL
[oracle@london1 oracle]$ ssh-add
Enter passphrase for /u01/app/oracle/.ssh/id_rsa:
Enter passphrase for /u01/app/oracle/.ssh/id_dsa:
Identity added: /home/oracle/.ssh/id_rsa (/u01/app/oracle/.ssh/id_rsa)
Identity added: /home/oracle/.ssh/id_dsa (/u01/app/oracle/.ssh/id_dsa)
```

Verify that the DISPLAY environment variable is correctly set to the location where the installer is to be run. The default value is the display on the local system, for example:

```
[oracle@london1 oracle]$ echo $DISPLAY
:0.0
```

Before starting the OUI, verify the values of the ORACLE_BASE, CRS_HOME, and ORACLE_HOME environment variables, as in the following example:

```
[oracle@london1 oracle]$ echo $ORACLE_BASE
/u01/app/oracle
[oracle@london1 oracle]$ echo $CRS_HOME
/u01/app/oracle/product/10.2.0/crs
[oracle@london1 oracle]$ echo $ORACLE_HOME
/u01/app/oracle/product/10.2.0/db_1
```

For the purpose of the Oracle Clusterware installation, set the value of the ORACLE_HOME environment variable to that of the CRS_HOME:

```
[oracle@london1 oracle]$ export ORACLE_HOME=$CRS_HOME
[oracle@london1 oracle]$ echo $ORACLE_HOME
/u01/app/oracle/product/10.2.0/crs
```

If you are installing the Oracle software from CD-ROM, insert the relevant CD-ROM in the drive to make the software available to the operating system. If your system is not configured to automount the CD-ROM, then, as the oracle user, issue the following command:

```
[oracle@london1 oracle]$ mount /mnt/cdrom
```

The installer can then be run using the command

```
[oracle@london1 oracle]$ /mnt/cdrom/runInstaller
```

If you need to eject the CD-ROM for any reason, use

```
[oracle@london1 oracle]$ eject
```

This command will fail if your current working directory is the /mnt/cdrom directory or a subdirectory of it.

If you are installing the Oracle software from a staging area on disk, change to the clusterware subdirectory and run the installer:

```
[oracle@london1 oracle]$ cd /u01/app/oracle/stage/crs/clusterware
[oracle@london1 clusterware]$ ./runInstaller
Starting Oracle Universal Installer...

Checking installer requirements...

Checking operating system version: must be redhat-3. SuSE-9,➡
rehat-4, UnitedLinux-1.0, asianux-1 or asianux-2
                                    Passed

All installer requirements met.

Preparing to launch Oracle Universal Installer from /tmp/OraInstall2005-12-20_06
-38-05PM. Please wait ...
Oracle Universal Installer, Version 10.1.0.3.0 Production
Copyright (C) 1999, 2005, Oracle. All rights reserved.
```

The OUI performs a series of checks on prerequisites before installing Oracle Clusterware. You should ensure that all nodes in your production cluster meet these prerequisites, although most should already have been checked by the CLUVFY utility.

However, if you are installing Oracle Clusterware on test hardware, you may be able to complete the installation without the nodes necessarily meeting all of the prerequisites, if, for example, you are using a new version of the operation system or your nodes do not have much physical memory. If you are prepared to accept the risk of a failed installation, then you can specify that the OUI should perform prerequisite checks but ignore the results using the following command:

```
[oracle@london1 clusterware]$ ./runInstaller -ignoresysprereqs
```

If the OUI starts successfully, it displays the Welcome page. The Welcome page allows you to display a list of products currently recorded in the inventory by clicking Installed Products. You can also remove existing products by clicking Deinstall Products. Click Next to continue to the Specify Inventory directory and credentials page, as shown in Figure 12-1.

The first time that the OUI runs on a node, it needs to create and configure an inventory directory. This page will not be displayed for subsequent installations. The default location for the inventory directory is $ORACLE_BASE/oraInventory. The pathname of the inventory directory should be the same on every node. If the ORACLE_BASE environment variable is not set, the default location is the home directory of the oracle user.

The Specify Operating System group name field is set to the group name of the user with permission for to install Oracle software. We suggest that you follow Oracle's recommendation to use the oinstall group.

Click Next to continue to the Specify Home Details page shown in Figure 12-2.

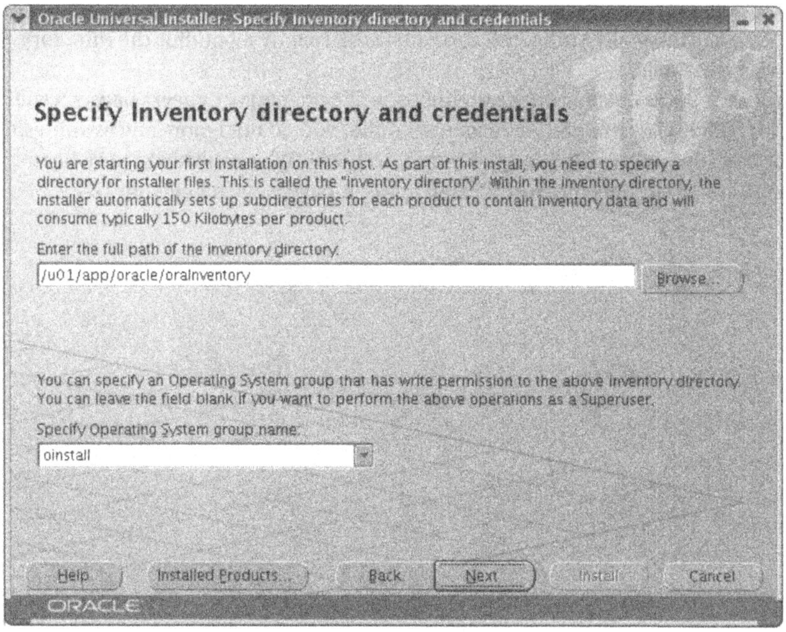

Figure 12-1. *The Specify Inventory directory and credentials page*

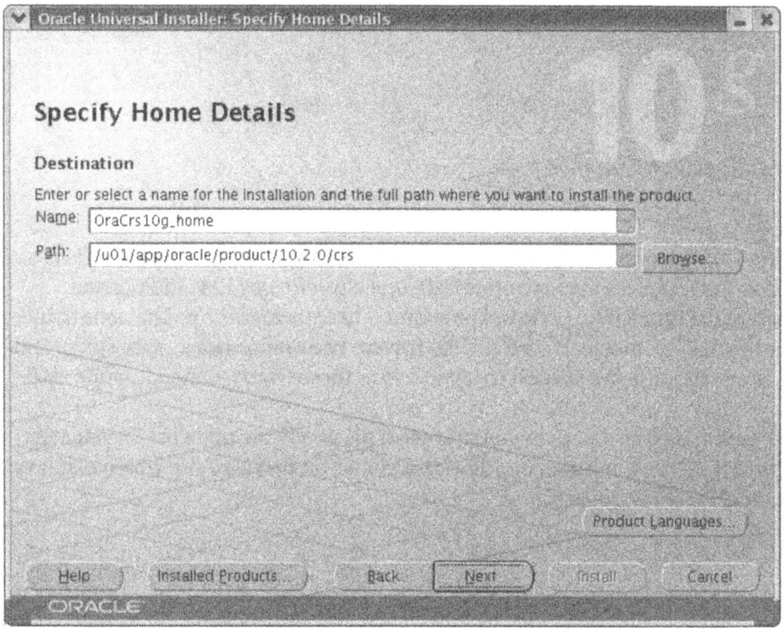

Figure 12-2. *The Specify Home Details page*

On the Specify Home Details page, you can optionally specify a name for the Oracle Clusterware home directory. The default is normally sufficient. You must also specify a path for the directory, below which the files will be installed.

Click Next to execute the checks detailed on the product-specific prerequisite checks page; several checks are performed for Oracle Clusterware. We recommend that you do not ignore any warnings, and if necessary, rectify any configuration issues and retry the checks. When all checks have been passed, click Next to continue to the Specify Cluster Configuration page, shown in Figure 12-3.

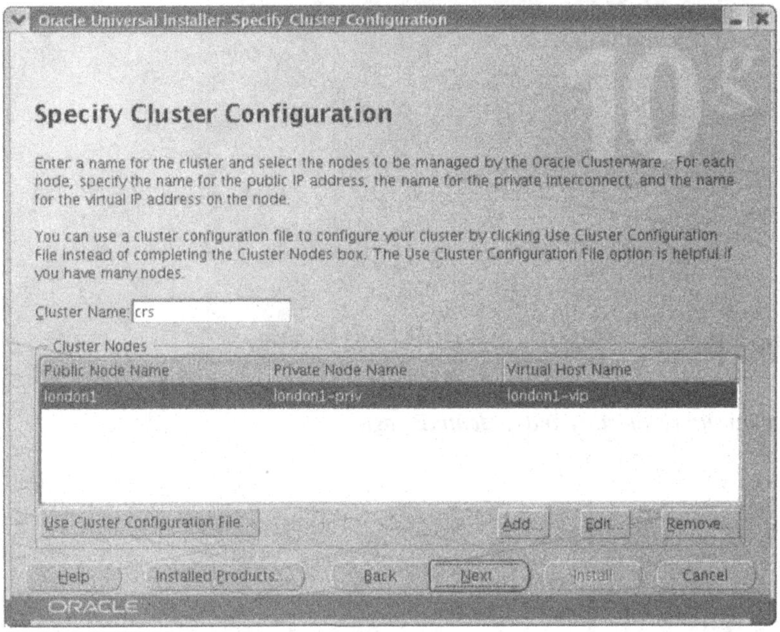

Figure 12-3. *The Specify Cluster Configuration page*

The Specify Cluster Configuration page displays the name of the cluster. The default is crs, which is sufficient unless you intend to manage more than one cluster using EM Grid Control.

Initially, only details of the installation node will be shown. These include the public node name, private node name, and virtual hostname. By default, the private node name has a -priv suffix, and the virtual host name as a -vip suffix. We suggest that you follow these Oracle-defined standards if possible.

If you have a large number of nodes, then you may wish to specify the node list in a cluster configuration file. Alternatively, you can specify additional nodes by clicking Add, which displays the Add a new node dialog box shown in Figure 12-4.

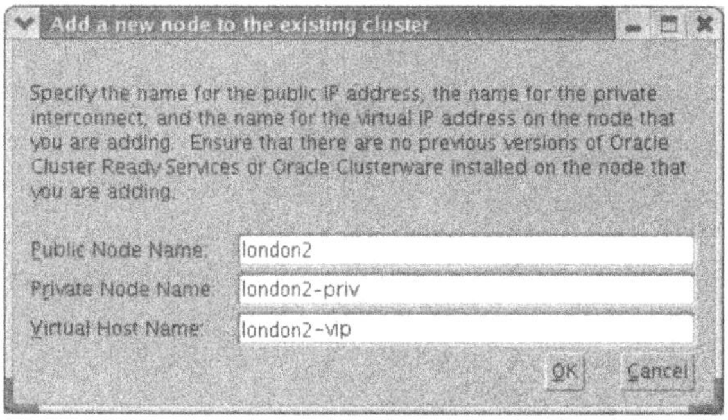

Figure 12-4. *The Add a new node dialog box*

After you have specified a public node name, private node name, and virtual hostname for the new node, click OK to return to the Specify Cluster Configuration page, which now displays the list of nodes in your cluster, as illustrated in Figure 12-5.

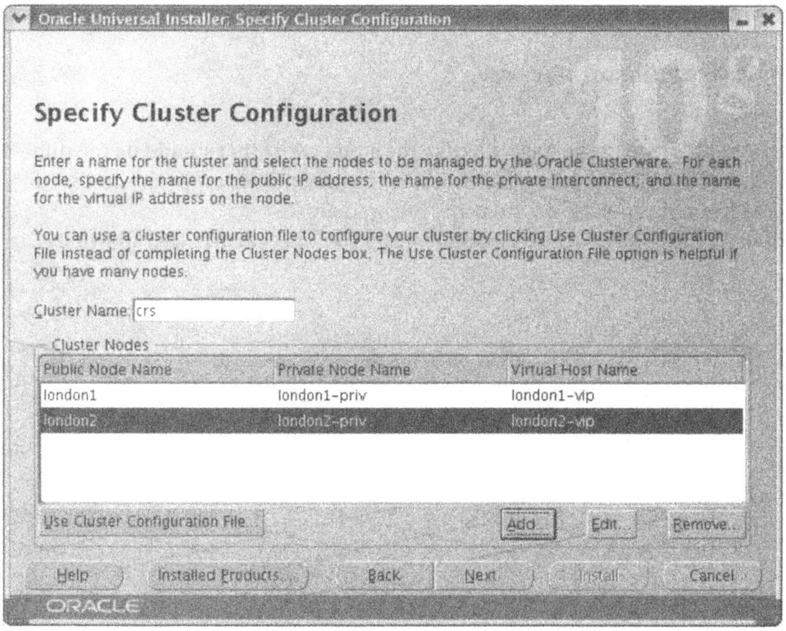

Figure 12-5. *The completed Specify Cluster Configuration page*

When you have added all nodes in the cluster, click Next to continue to the Specify Network Interface Usage page, shown in Figure 12-6.

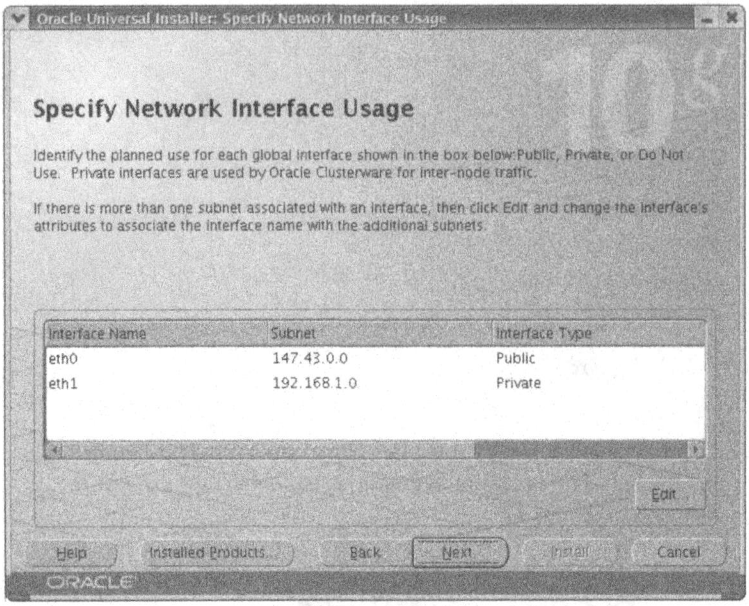

Figure 12-6. *The Specify Network Interface Usage page*

On the Specify Network Interface Usage page, identify the subnetwork that should be the public network and the one that should be the private network. In the previous example, the correct values have been detected from the operating system and are predefined.

Click Next to continue to the Specify Oracle Cluster Registry (OCR) Location page, shown in Figure 12-7.

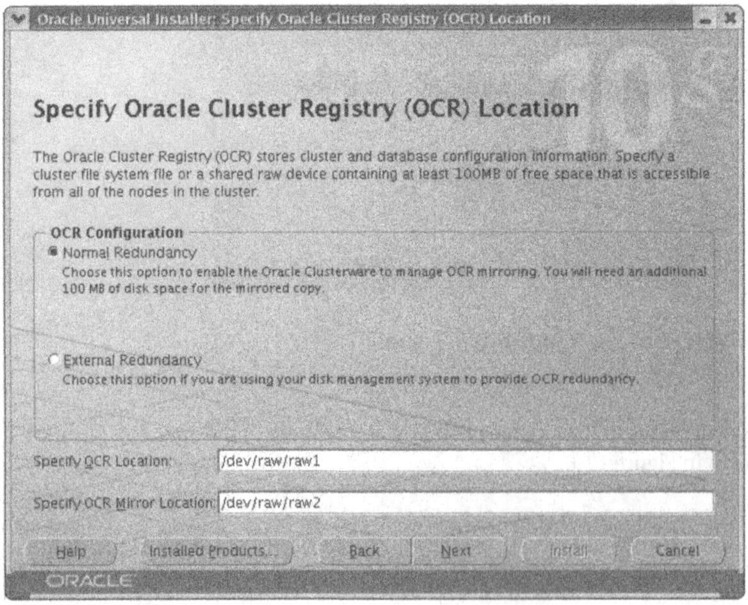

Figure 12-7. *The Specify Oracle Cluster Registry (OCR) Location page*

On the Specify Oracle Cluster Registry (OCR) Location page, you can specify the location of the OCR. In Oracle 10.2, the OCR can be located on either a cluster file system, such as OCFS, or a shared raw device. In either case, there must be at least 100MB of free disk space, and the location must be accessible from all nodes in the cluster using the same path.

In Oracle 10.2 and above, you can also specify a redundancy level for the OCR. If you specify Normal Redundancy, Oracle Clusterware will manage an *OCR mirror file*, which is an exact copy of the OCR in a separate location on the cluster file system or on a separate shared raw device. Alternatively, you can specify External Redundancy, in which case mirroring will be provided by the storage subsystem. We recommend that you specify Normal Redundancy and allow Oracle to manage the OCR mirror, as this reduces the possibility of an operator error resulting in the deletion of the OCR.

Click Next to continue to the Specify Voting Disk Location page shown in Figure 12-8.

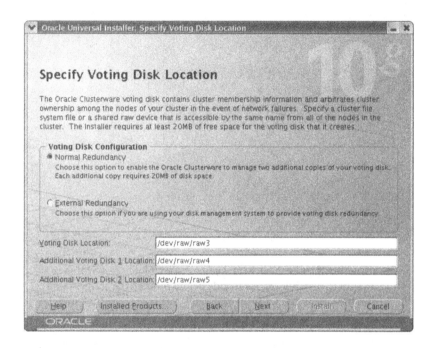

Figure 12-8. *The Specify Voting Disk Location page*

On the Specify Voting Disk Location page, you can specify the location of the voting disk on a cluster file system or on a shared raw device as well. In either case, there must be at least 20MB of free disk space, and the location must be accessible from all nodes in the cluster using the same path.

In Oracle 10.2 and above, you can also specify a redundancy level for the voting disk. If you specify Normal Redundancy, Oracle Clusterware will manage two additional copies of the voting disk. Each is an exact copy of the voting disk in a separate location on the cluster file system or on a separate shared raw device. There must always be an odd number of voting disks. As with the OCR location, you can specify External Redundancy, in which case mirroring will be provided by the storage subsystem. Again, we recommend that you specify Normal Redundancy and allow Oracle to manage the voting disk copies to reduce the possibility of an operator error resulting in the deletion of the voting disk.

Click Next to display the Summary page, and then click Install to proceed with the Clusterware installation. The Install page displays the current progress of the installation. This page also displays the location of the log file for the install session. Log files are located within the logs directory of the inventory.

When installation of the Clusterware software is complete, you will be prompted to execute configuration scripts as the root user on each of the nodes in the cluster by the dialog box shown in Figure 12-9.

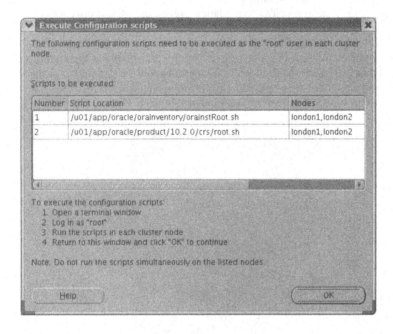

Figure 12-9. *The Execute Configuration scripts dialog box*

The scripts must be run sequentially on each node, and you must wait for each script to complete and for the Clusterware to start successfully on each node before running the script on the next node. The first script creates the Oracle inventory on each node, as in the following example:

```
[root@london1 root]# /u01/app/oracle/oraInventory/orainstRoot.sh
Changing permissions of /u01/app/oracle/oraInventory to 770.
Changing groupname of /u01/app/oracle/oraInventory to oinstall.
The execution of the script is complete
```

The second script installs, configures, and starts Oracle Clusterware and its daemons on each node. On the first node, the script initializes the OCR and voting disk:

```
[root@london1 root]# /u01/app/oracle/product/10.2.0/crs/root.sh
Checking to see if Oracle CRS stack is already configured
/etc/oracle does not exist. Creating it now.

Setting the permissions on OCR backup directory
Setting up NS directories
Oracle Cluster Registry configuration upgraded successfully
assigning default hostname london1 for node 1.
assigning default hostname london2 for node 2.
Successfully accumulated necessary OCR keys.
Using ports: CSS=49895 CRS=49896 EVMC=49898 and EVMR=49897.
node <nodenumber>: <nodename> <private interconnect name> <hostname>
node 1: london1 london1-priv london1
node 2: london2 london2-priv london2
```

```
Creating OCR keys for user 'root', privgrp 'root'..
Operation successful.
Now formatting voting device: /dev/raw/raw3
Now formatting voting device: /dev/raw/raw4
Now formatting voting device: /dev/raw/raw5
Format of 3 voting devices complete.
Startup will be queued to init within 90 seconds.
Adding daemons to inittab
Expecting the CRS daemons to be up within 600 seconds.
CSS is active on these nodes.
        london1
CSS is inactive on these nodes.
        london2
Local node checking complete.
Run root.sh on remaining nodes to start CRS daemons.
```

On the second and subsequent nodes, the root.sh script detects that the OCR and voting disk have already been configured and skips the initialization procedure. On the final node, the root.sh script initializes the virtual IP addresses by calling the Virtual IP Configuration Assistant (VIPCA) in silent mode. In Oracle 10.1, this assistant was executed during database software installation; in Oracle 10.2, it has been moved to Oracle Clusterware installation. On a two-node installation, the output from root.sh on the second node should be similar to the following:

```
[root@london2 root]# /u01/app/oracle/product/10.2.0/crs/root.sh
Checking to see if Oracle CRS stack is already configured
/etc/oracle does not exist. Creating it now.

Setting the permissions on OCR backup directory
Setting up NS directories
Oracle Cluster Registry configuration upgraded successfully
clscfg: EXISTING configuration version 3 detected.
clscfg: version 3 is 10G Release 2.
assigning default hostname london1 for node 1.
assigning default hostname london2 for node 2.
Successfully accumulated necessary OCR keys.
Using ports: CSS=49895 CRS=49896 EVMC=49898 and EVMR=49897.
node <nodenumber>: <nodename> <private interconnect name> <hostname>
node 1: london1 london1-priv london1
node 2: london2 london2-priv london2
clscfg: Arguments check out successfully.

NO KEYS WERE WRITTEN. Supply -force parameter to override.
-force is destructive and will destroy any previous cluster
configuration.
Oracle Cluster Registry for cluster has already been initialized
Startup will be queued to init within 90 seconds.
Adding daemons to inittab
Expecting the CRS daemons to be up within 600 seconds.
CSS is active on these nodes.
        london1
        london2
CSS is active on all nodes.
Waiting for the Oracle CRSD and EVMD to start
Oracle CRS stack installed and running under init(1M)
Running vipca(silent) for configuring nodeapps
```

```
Creating VIP application resource on (2) nodes...
Creating GSD application resource on (2) nodes...
Creating ONS application resource on (2) nodes...
Starting VIP application resource on (2) nodes...
Starting GSD application resource on (2) nodes...
Starting ONS application resource on (2) nodes...
```

When all scripts have been successfully executed, click OK to launch the configuration assistants. Most OUI sessions launch one or more configuration assistants. In the case of the Oracle Clusterware installation, these include the following:

- Oracle Notification Server Configuration Assistant
- Oracle Private Interconnect Configuration Assistant
- Oracle Cluster Verification Utility (CLUVFY)

The commands to be executed by the configuration assistants are logged in the $CRS_HOME/cfgtoollogs/configToolAllCommands script. You can run the configuration assistants again, outside of the OUI, using this script; however, doing so is not supported by Oracle.

When the Configuration Assistant tools have been run, the End of Installation page will be displayed. Click Exit to terminate the OUI session.

Verifying the Oracle Clusterware Installation

You can verify that Oracle Clusterware has been successfully installed by running the CLUVFY utility:

```
[oracle@london1 cluvfy]$ sh runcluvfy.sh stage -post crsinst -n london1,london2
Performing post-checks for cluster services setup

Checking node reachability...
Node reachability check passed from node "london1".

Checking user equivalence...
User equivalence check passed for user "oracle".

Checking Cluster manager integrity...

Checking CSS daemon...
Daemon status check passed for "CSS daemon".

Cluster manager integrity check passed.

Checking cluster integrity...
Cluster integrity check passed

Checking OCR integrity...

Checking the absence of a non-clustered configuration...
All nodes free of non-clustered, local-only configurations.

Uniqueness check for OCR device passed.

Checking the version of OCR...
OCR of correct Version "2" exists.

Checking data integrity of OCR...
Data integrity check for OCR passed.
```

```
OCR integrity check passed.

Checking CRS integrity...

Checking daemon liveness...
Liveness check passed for "CRS daemon".

Checking daemon liveness...
Liveness check passed for "CSS daemon".

Checking daemon liveness...
Liveness check passed for "EVM daemon".

Checking CRS health...
CRS health check passed.

CRS integrity check passed.

Checking node application existence...

Checking existence of VIP node application (required)
Check passed.

Checking existence of ONS node application (optional)
Check passed.

Checking existence of GSD node application (optional)
Check passed.
Post-check for cluster services setup was successful.
```

You can also use the `olsnodes` command in the `$CRS_HOME/bin` to verify that the installation has completed successfully. This command displays all of the active nodes in the cluster:

```
[oracle@london1 bin]$ ./olsnodes
london1
london2
```

In this example, the `olsnodes` command shows that Oracle Clusterware has been successfully installed and is running on nodes `london1` and `london2` in the cluster.

Oracle Database Software Installation

With the Clusterware successfully installed and running on all nodes, the next step is to install the Oracle Database software. The same software is currently used for both RDBMS and ASM instances. However, in Oracle 10.2 and above, Oracle recommends that you create a separate Oracle Home directory for ASM instances.

The Oracle Database software is installed using the OUI. It must be installed from an X Window session, which can be the same session in which Oracle Clusterware was installed.

Verifying the Configuration

Before installing Oracle Database software, verify that the configuration is correct using the CLUVFY utility:

```
[oracle@london1 cluvfy]$ sh runcluvfy.sh #stage -pre dbinst -n london1,london2
Performing pre-checks for database installation
```

```
Checking node reachability...
Node reachability check passed from node "london1".

Checking user equivalence...
User equivalence check passed for user "oracle".

Checking administrative privileges...
User existence check passed for "oracle".
Group existence check passed for "oinstall".
Membership check for user "oracle" in group "oinstall" [as Primary] passed.
Group existence check passed for "dba".
Membership check for user "oracle" in group "dba" passed.

Administrative privileges check passed.

Checking node connectivity...

Node connectivity check passed for subnet "147.43.0.0" with node(s) london2,london1.
Node connectivity check passed for subnet "192.168.2.0" with node(s)➡
london2,london1.

Suitable interfaces for VIP on subnet "147.43.0.0":
london2 eth0:147.43.1.104 eth0:147.43.1.204
london1 eth0:147.43.1.103 eth0:147.43.1.203

Suitable interfaces for the private interconnect on subnet "192.168.2.0":
london2 eth1:192.168.2.104
london1 eth1:192.168.2.103

Node connectivity check passed.

Checking system requirements for 'database'...
Total memory check passed.
Free disk space check passed.
Swap space check passed.
System architecture check passed.
Kernel version check passed.
Package existence check passed for "make-3.79".
Package existence check passed for "binutils-2.14".
Package existence check passed for "gcc-3.2".
Package existence check passed for "compat-db-4.0.14-5".
Package existence check passed for "compat-gcc-7.3-2.96.128".
Package existence check passed for "compat-gcc-c++-7.3-2.96.128".
Package existence check passed for "compat-libstdc++-7.3-2.96.128".
Package existence check passed for "compat-libstdc++-devel-7.3-2.96.128".
Package existence check passed for "glibc-2.3.2-95.27".
Package existence check passed for "openmotif-2.2.3".
Package existence check passed for "setarch-1.3-1".
Kernel parameter check passed for "semmsl".
Kernel parameter check passed for "semmns".
Kernel parameter check passed for "semopm".
Kernel parameter check passed for "semmni".
Kernel parameter check passed for "shmall".
Kernel parameter check passed for "shmmni".
Kernel parameter check passed for "file-max".
Kernel parameter check passed for "rmem_default".
```

```
Kernel parameter check passed for "rmem_max".
Kernel parameter check passed for "wmem_default".
Kernel parameter check passed for "wmem_max".
Group existence check passed for "dba".
User existence check passed for "nobody".

System requirement passed for 'database'

Checking CRS integrity...

Checking daemon liveness...
Liveness check passed for "CRS daemon".

Checking daemon liveness...
Liveness check passed for "CSS daemon".

Checking daemon liveness...
Liveness check passed for "EVM daemon".

Checking CRS health...
CRS health check passed.

CRS integrity check passed.

Checking node application existence...

Checking existence of VIP node application (required)
Check passed.

Checking existence of ONS node application (optional)
Check passed.

Checking existence of GSD node application (optional)
Check passed.

Pre-check for database installation was successful.
```

Running the Installer

If you need to start a new session, ensure that the root user has enabled access for all X clients by issuing the command

```
[root@london1 root]# xhost +
```

Run the following commands as the oracle user to ensure that the OUI can copy files to and execute commands on other nodes:

```
[oracle@london1 oracle]$ ssh-agent $SHELL
[oracle@london1 oracle]$ ssh-add
```

Check that the ORACLE_HOME environment variable has the correct value and is not set to the $CRS_HOME directory:

```
[oracle@london1 oracle]$ echo $ORACLE_HOME
/u01/app/oracle/product/10.2.0/db_1
```

If you are installing from CD-ROM, mount the CD-ROM using

```
[oracle@london1 oracle]$ mount /mnt/cdrom
```

The installer can then be run using the following command:

```
[oracle@london1 oracle]$ /mnt/cdrom/runInstaller
```

If you are installing from a staging area, run the installer from the database subdirectory, as in the following example:

```
[oracle@london1 oracle]$ /u01/app/oracle/stage/db/database/runInstaller
```

to display the Welcome page. Click Next to continue to the Select Installation Type page, shown in Figure 12-10.

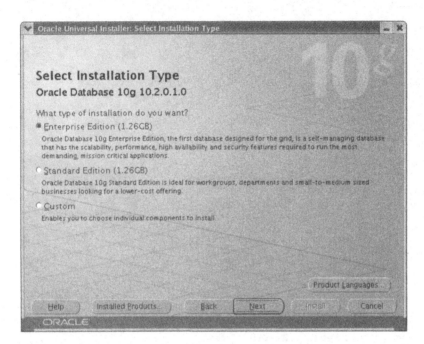

Figure 12-10. *The Select Installation Type page*

On the Select Installation Type page, select Enterprise Edition, Standard Edition, or Custom installation. Your choice will be affected by your Oracle license. If you choose the Custom option, you can include or exclude individual Oracle components. In this example, we will perform an Enterprise Edition installation. Click Next to continue to the Specify Home Details page.

The Specify Home Details page is identical to the one shown for the Clusterware installation, but you should ensure that the default values for the name and path of the directory have been set to values appropriate to the Oracle Database software. You must ensure that the name and path values do not continue to show the name and path of the Clusterware installation. If necessary, you may choose to modify the values before clicking Next to continue to the Specify Hardware Cluster Installation Mode page shown in Figure 12-11.

On the Specify Hardware Cluster Installation Mode page, select the nodes on which you wish to install the Oracle database software. Normally, you will want to install the software on all nodes in the cluster. Click Next to continue to the Product-Specific Prerequisite Checks page.

The Product-Specific Prerequisite Checks page is similar to the one shown in the Oracle Clusterware installation, and again, we recommend that you do not ignore any warnings raised on this page. When all checks have been successfully completed, click Next to continue to the Select Configuration Option page shown in Figure 12-12.

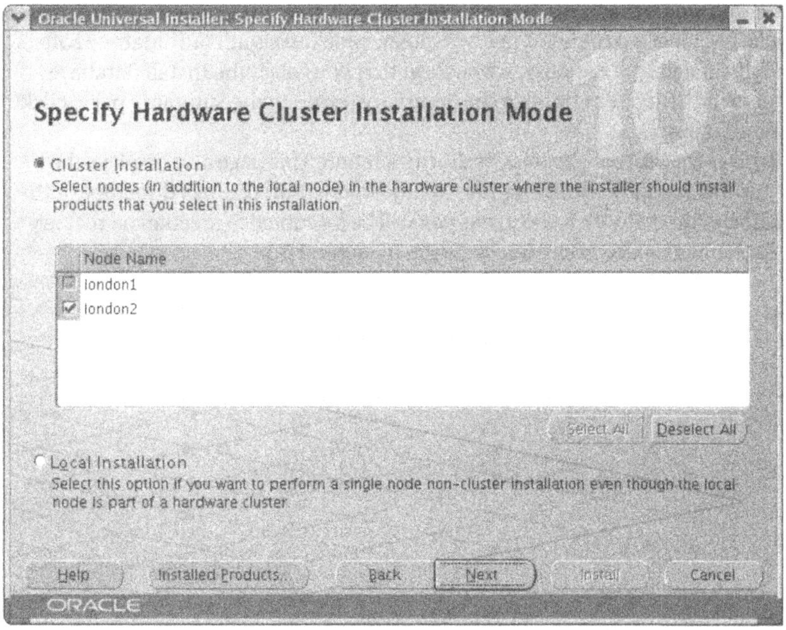

Figure 12-11. *The Specify Hardware Cluster Installation Mode page*

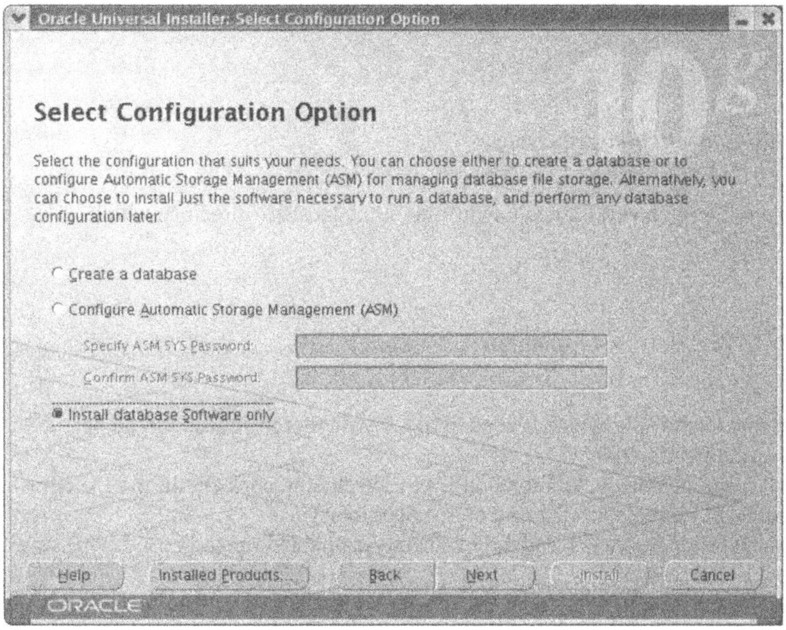

Figure 12-12. *The Select Configuration Option page*

On the Select Configuration Option page, you may choose to create a database or configure ASM; both options invoke DBCA. We recommend that you defer these tasks until the database software has been successfully installed. Therefore, we suggest that you select the Install database Software only option and click Next to continue to the Summary page. On the Summary page, click Install to start the installation process.

The Install page displays the current progress of the installation. This page also displays the location of the log file for the install session. Log files are located within the logs directory of the inventory. When installation of the software is complete, you will be prompted to execute the root.sh script as the root user on each node in the cluster, as shown in Figure 12-13.

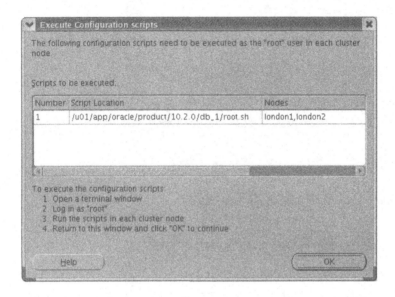

Figure 12-13. *The Execute Configuration scripts page*

By default, the root.sh script creates the following files in the local bin directory, which defaults to /usr/local/bin:

- dbhome

- oraenv

- coraenv

It also creates the /etc/oratab file, which is used to specify whether instances should be automatically started after a node is rebooted.

When the root.sh script has been run on all nodes in the cluster, click OK on the Execute Configuration scripts dialog box to display the End of Installation page.

Make a note of the URLs for iSQL*Plus, which is the browser-enabled version of SQL*Plus, and click Exit to terminate the OUI session.

Troubleshooting

The Oracle Clusterware installation is usually the most problematic part of a RAC database build procedure, because it is the first time that all of the components are tested together. Yet, given a successful Oracle Clusterware installation, the Oracle Database Server software installation rarely fails, as it uses the same components.

Cluster Verification Utility

The most useful troubleshooting tool is undoubtedly the Cluster Verification Utility (CLUVFY). Although CLUVFY was only introduced in Oracle 10.2, it has rapidly established itself as the most comprehensive and reliable utility available. Consequently, in this chapter, we show examples of its use together with output from successful runs. We recommend that you use this tool at every opportunity, as it is extremely good at detecting typos and omissions in the configuration.

You can also use CLUVFY to check Oracle 10.1 configurations, in which case you should specify the -10gR1 option. We have, however, noticed that in early versions of Oracle 10.2, CLUVFY was incompatible with the newly introduced OCFS2 software. It is easy to envisage this situation arising again in future releases where CLUVFY lags behind new technologies.

Common Problems

Over the years, we have encountered a handful of problems that cause installations to fail. Though CLUVFY detects most of these, we have chosen to highlight them in this section.

User IDs

The user ID (uid) for the oracle user must be identical on all nodes. You can verify the uid by logging on as the oracle user and issuing the id command:

```
[oracle@london1 oracle]$ $id
uid=500(oracle) gid=501(oinstall) groups=501(oinstall),500(dba)
```

The uid is stored in the /etc/passwd file. However, you should not update this directly. Instead, we recommend using the usermod command. For example, to change the uid for the oracle user to 600, log in as root, and use the following:

```
[root@london1 root]# usermod -u 600 oracle
```

Remember that if you change the uid for a user, you must also update the ownership of any files belonging to that user using the chmod command.

Group IDs

The group ID (gid) for both the dba group and the oinstall group must also be identical on all nodes. You can verify the gid by logging on as the oracle user and issuing the id command.

The gid is stored in the /etc/group file. You should not update this file directly either; instead, use the groupmod command. For example, to change the gid for the dba group to 700, log in as root and use

```
[root@london1 root]# groupmod -g 700 dba
```

Each user has an initial group ID, which is stored in the /etc/passwd file. Throughout the Oracle installation process, the initial group ID for the oracle user should be the gid of the oinstall group. To modify the gid, use the usermod command. For example, to change the initial group to oinstall for the oracle user, log in as root, and issue the following command:

```
[root@london1 root]# usermod -g oinstall oracle
```

Network Connectivity

In a RAC cluster, every host should be able to communicate with all other hosts in the cluster via both the public network and the private network (interconnect). You can test this connectivity using the ping utility, which performs a handshake between the local and remote hosts. For example, to verify the network connectivity on our example two-node cluster, log in to each host and issue the following commands:

```
[oracle@london1 oracle]$ ping london1
[oracle@london1 oracle]$ ping london1-priv
[oracle@london1 oracle]$ ping london2
[oracle@london1 oracle]$ ping london2-priv
```

The Linux version of ping does not terminate automatically, so you need to press Ctrl+C to stop it. You can also use the -c option to specify the maximum number of packets to send. For example, to continually send packets, use the following:

```
[oracle@london1 oracle]$ ping -c 4 london2
PING london2 (147.43.1.104) 56(84) bytes of data.
64 bytes from london2 (147.43.1.104): icmp_seq=0 ttl=64 time=0.245 ms
64 bytes from london2 (147.43.1.104): icmp_seq=1 ttl=64 time=0.192 ms
64 bytes from london2 (147.43.1.104): icmp_seq=2 ttl=64 time=0.385 ms
64 bytes from london2 (147.43.1.104): icmp_seq=3 ttl=64 time=0.226 ms

--- london2 ping statistics ---
4 packets transmitted, 4 received, 0% packet loss, time 3017ms
rtt min/avg/max/mdev = 0.192/0.262/0.385/0.073 ms, pipe 2
```

Secure Shell

The OUI uses the secure shell scp utility to copy files to other nodes and the ssh utility to execute commands on remote nodes. Therefore, these utilities must work from the installation node to all other nodes for the oracle user.

We recommend that you test secure shell connectivity from the oracle user, using the ssh command to each remote node in turn. The date command is usually a good test. For example, issue the following commands:

```
[oracle@london1 oracle]$ ssh london1 date
Wed Dec 21 11:27:04 GMT 2005
[oracle@london1 oracle]$ ssh london2 date
Wed Dec 21 11:27:04 GMT 2005
```

The first time that you execute these commands from one host to another, a message similar to the following will be displayed:

```
The authenticity of host 'london2 (147.43.1.102)' can't be established.
RSA key fingerprint is 00:99:8c:2a:29:90:ad:87:a0:09:a5:27:3b:35:28:6c.
Are you sure you want to continue connecting (yes/no)? yes
Warning: Permanently added 'london2' (RSA) to the list of known hosts.
```

Secure shell connections must be tested manually, because the first connection requires confirmation.

Other Information Sources

Obviously, including a comprehensive troubleshooting section in a book of this nature would be very difficult, as the information tends to change rapidly. In the past, bugs and other issues have been introduced in one patch set and resolved in the next. Therefore, in this section, we discuss some general troubleshooting techniques for common problems that we have seen frequently at customer sites.

However, the best source for troubleshooting information is the Oracle documentation set, which has become increasingly useful and relevant in recent releases. For Oracle 10.2, consult the following manuals:

- *Oracle Clusterware and Oracle Real Application Clusters Installation Guide for Linux*
- *Oracle Clusterware and Oracle Real Application Clusters Administration and Deployment Guide*

Other information sources include MetaLink and other Internet resources, such as web sites and forums. There is a fair chance that somebody else will have encountered and solved any problem you encounter. If you decide to post a question to an Internet forum, make sure that you have read the documentation first.

Configuration Files

The installation process updates several configuration files across each node. Knowing the location of these files and understanding their purpose is useful when attempting to troubleshoot installation issues.

Inventory

By default, the inventory is created in $ORACLE_BASE/oraInventory. The location of the inventory is specified in the file /etc/oraInst.loc. For the installation described in this chapter, this file contains the following entries:

```
inventory_loc=/u01/app/oracle/oraInventory
inst_group=oinstall
```

The file $ORACLE_BASE/oraInventory/ContentsXML/inventory.xml contains details of the Oracle Home directories that have been created. For example, for the installation described in this chapter, this file contains the following:

```
<?xml version="1.0" standalone="yes" ?>
<!-- Copyright (c) 2005 Oracle Corporation. All rights Reserved -->
<!-- Do not modify the contents of this file by hand. -->
<INVENTORY>
<VERSION_INFO>
   <SAVED_WITH>10.2.0.1.0</SAVED_WITH>
   <MINIMUM_VER>2.1.0.6.0</MINIMUM_VER>
</VERSION_INFO>
<HOME_LIST>
<HOME NAME="OraCrs10g_home" LOC="/u01/app/oracle/product/10.2.0/crs" TYPE="0➥
" IDX="1" CRS="true">
   <NODE_LIST>
      <NODE NAME="london1"/>
      <NODE NAME="london2"/>
   </NODE_LIST>
</HOME>
<HOME NAME="OraDb10g_home1" LOC="/u01/app/oracle/product/10.2.0/db_1" TYPE="0"➥
IDX="2">
   <NODE_LIST>
      <NODE NAME="london1"/>
      <NODE NAME="london2"/>
   </NODE_LIST>
</HOME>
```

OCR

The location of the OCR is specified in the file /etc/oracle/ocr.loc. For the installation described in this chapter, this file contains the following:

```
ocrconfig_loc=/dev/raw/raw1
ocrmirrorconfig_loc=/dev/raw/raw2
local_only=FALSE
```

/etc/inittab

The Oracle Clusterware installation adds the following three lines to /etc/inittab:

```
h1:35:respawn:/etc/init.d/init.evmd run >/dev/null 2>&1 </dev/null
h2:35:respawn:/etc/init.d/init.cssd fatal >/dev/null 2>&1 </dev/null
h3:35:respawn:/etc/init.d/init.crsd run >/dev/null 2>&1 </dev/null
```

The original /etc/inittab is backed up to both /etc/inittab.orig and /etc/inittab.no_crs. The new version of /etc/inittab is also backed up to /etc/inittab.crs.

Deinstallation

Deinstallation of the Oracle Database 10g software and Oracle Clusterware should be performed using the OUI. Before deinstalling the software, all instances, databases, and daemons must be stopped. We also recommend that you take an operating system backup before proceeding.

Ensure that all databases and instances have been stopped. For example, run the following as the oracle user:

```
[oracle@london1 oracle]$ srvctl stop database -d RAC
```

On each node, again as the oracle user, stop any ASM instances that are currently running, for example:

```
[oracle@london1 oracle]$ srvctl stop asm -n london1
[oracle@london1 oracle]$ srvctl stop asm -n london2
```

As the oracle user, also stop the listener process on each node:

```
[oracle@london1 oracle]$ lsnrctl stop
```

On each node as the root user, stop the Oracle Clusterware, using the service command or calling the script directly from /etc/init.d:

```
[root@london1 root]# #service init.crs stop
```

The procedure for starting the installer is similar to the one that is used for installation. To deinstall Oracle database software, run the installer using

```
[oracle@london1 oracle]$ $ORACLE_HOME/oui/bin/runInstaller
```

On the Welcome page, click Deinstall Products to continue. You should deinstall the Oracle Database software before attempting to delete Oracle Clusterware.

To deinstall Oracle Clusterware, run the installer as follows:

```
[oracle@london1 oracle]$ export ORACLE_HOME=$CRS_HOME
[oracle@london1 oracle]$ $ORACLE_HOME/oui/bin/runInstaller
```

Again, on the Welcome page, click Deinstall Products to continue. You may need to deinstall the software manually if, for example, you have inadvertently deleted part of the software already.

Delete the contents of the Oracle Home directory. For example, as the root user, run the following command:

```
[root@london1 root]# rm -rf /u01/app/oracle/product/10.2.0/db_1
```

If you have created a separate Oracle Home for ASM, delete it:

```
[root@london1 root]# rm -rf /u01/app/oracle/product/10.2.0/asm_1
```

Delete the contents of the Oracle Clusterware Home directory as well:

```
[root@london1 root]# rm -rf /u01/app/oracle/product/10.2.0/crs
```

Remove the Oracle Clusterware entries from /etc/inittab, either using a text editor or by copying back the original file:

```
[root@london1 root]# cp /etc/inittab.orig /etc/inittab
```

You should, of course, check that /etc/inittab has not been subsequently modified before overwriting it. Inform the init daemon that the /etc/inittab file has been updated as follows:

```
[root@london1 root]# init q
```

Remove the Oracle Clusterware start-up scripts from the /etc/init.d directory:

```
[root@london1 init.d]# rm init.crs
[root@london1 init.d]# init.crsd
[root@london1 init.d]# init.cssd
[root@london1 init.d]# init.evmd
```

You may also wish to reboot the nodes at this point to ensure that all Oracle daemons have stopped. Next, remove the /etc/oracle directory:

```
[root@london1 root]# rm -rf /etc/oracle
```

Remove the other files created in /etc by the installation process:

```
[root@london1 root]# rm /etc/oratab
[root@london1 root]# rm /etc/oraInst.loc
[root@london1 root]# rm /etc/inittab.no_crs
[root@london1 root]# rm /etc/inittab.crs
```

Delete the OCR and voting disk, along with any mirrors if they are located on a cluster file system, for example:

```
[root@london1 root]# rm /u02/oradata/RAC/OCRFile1
[root@london1 root]# rm /u03/oradata/RAC/OCRFile2
[root@london1 root]# rm /u02/oradata/RAC/CSSFile1
[root@london1 root]# rm /u02/oradata/RAC/CSSFile2
[root@london1 root]# rm /u02/oradata/RAC/CSSFile3
```

If the OCR and voting disk are located on raw devices, you should consider reinitializing them using the dd command before attempting a reinstallation.

Summary

In this chapter, we detailed the procedures required to successfully install the Oracle Clusterware and Database software in your Linux RAC environment step by step. We also reviewed some common troubleshooting procedures to employ when the installation does not proceed as expected and summarized the methods required to deinstall the Oracle software from your system.

CHAPTER 13

∎ ∎ ∎

Creating and Configuring Databases

This chapter describes how to create and configure databases using the Database Configuration Assistant (DBCA) and discusses how to create a RAC database using SQL*Plus scripts.

DBCA provides a user-friendly interface that allows you to create and configure databases; DBCA can create both single-instance and clustered databases. It also helps you to clone and delete databases, add and remove instances, and manage services.

The first two sections in this chapter describe how to run DBCA as a GUI tool and as a command line tool. The final section of this chapter describes creating a RAC database manually using scripts generated by DBCA.

Using DBCA As a GUI Tool

Before you can run DBCA, you must have configured storage (see Chapter 7) installed and configured the operating system (see Chapters 10 and 11), and installed Oracle Clusterware and the Oracle database software (see Chapter 12).

DBCA is a GUI tool that must be run in an X Windows environment. If X Windows is not currently running on your system, then as the root user, run

```
[oracle@london1 oracle]$ startx
```

Next, enter the following command:

```
# xhost +
```

Switch to the Oracle user:

```
su - oracle
```

Run the ssh-agent and ssh-add commands to ensure that no passphrase is required for running ssh under this session:

```
[oracle@london1 oracle]$ ssh-agent $SHELL
[oracle@london1 oracle]$ ssh-add
Enter passphrase for /home/oracle/.ssh/id_rsa: <Press Newline>
Enter passphrase for /home/oracle/.ssh/id_dsa: <Press Newline>
Identity added: /home/oracle/.ssh/id_rsa (/home/oracle/.ssh/id_rsa)
Identity added: /home/oracle/.ssh/id_dsa (/home/oracle/.ssh/id_dsa)
```

Before starting DBCA verify the values of the ORACLE_BASE, and ORACLE_HOME environment variables, for example:

```
[oracle@london1 oracle]$ echo $ORACLE_BASE
/u01/app/oracle
[oracle@london1 oracle]$ echo $ORACLE_HOME
/u01/app/oracle/product/10.2.0/db_1
```

Verify that the DISPLAY environment variable is set correctly to the location where the installer
is to be run. The default value is the display on the local system, as in the following example:

```
[oracle@london1 oracle]$ echo $DISPLAY
:0.0
```

Start DBCA from the $ORACLE_HOME/bin directory, which should be included in the list of directories
specified by your $PATH environment variable:

```
[oracle@london1 oracle]$ dbca
```

If DBCA starts successfully, then the Welcome page shown in Figure 13-1 will be displayed.

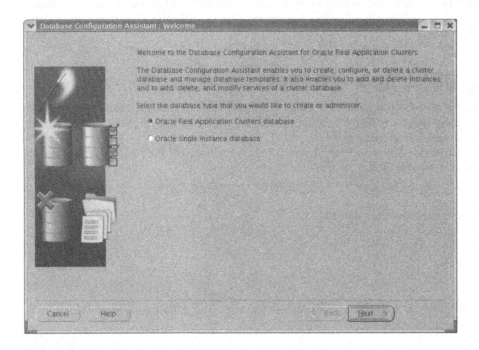

Figure 13-1. *The Welcome page*

You can use DBCA to administer both RAC and single-instance databases. When you start DBCA,
you will be asked to select the database type you wish to create or administer. In Oracle 10.2, RAC
databases and single-instance databases can coexist on the same set of nodes. In most cases, you
will wish to select the Oracle Real Application Clusters database option and click Next to display the
Operations page shown in Figure 13-2.

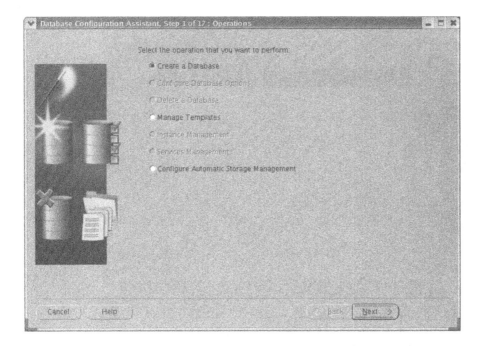

Figure 13-2. *The Operations page*

The Operations page shows DBCA operations that are currently available. In Oracle 10.2, these include the following:

- Create a Database
- Configure Database Options
- Delete a Database
- Manage Templates
- Instance Management
- Services Management
- Configure Automatic Storage Management

As Figure 13-2 shows, when you first run DBCA on a newly installed cluster, you can only create a database, manage templates, or configure ASM. The remaining options become available once you have created a database.

The Configure Automatic Storage Management option is not available on this page in Oracle 10.1. Instead, you may create an ASM instance within the Create a Database option.

These options are described in more detail in the following sections.

Configuring ASM

If you have selected Configure Automatic Storage Management on the Operations page, you must create an ASM instance on each node before you can create the database from the Node Selection page shown in Figure 13-3.

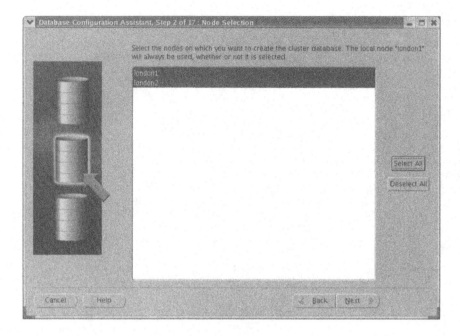

Figure 13-3. *The Node Selection page*

On the Node Selection page, highlight the nodes you wish to use or click Select All. You must install the software on the node from which you are running DBCA, in this case, london1. Click Next to continue to the Create ASM Instance page shown in Figure 13-4.

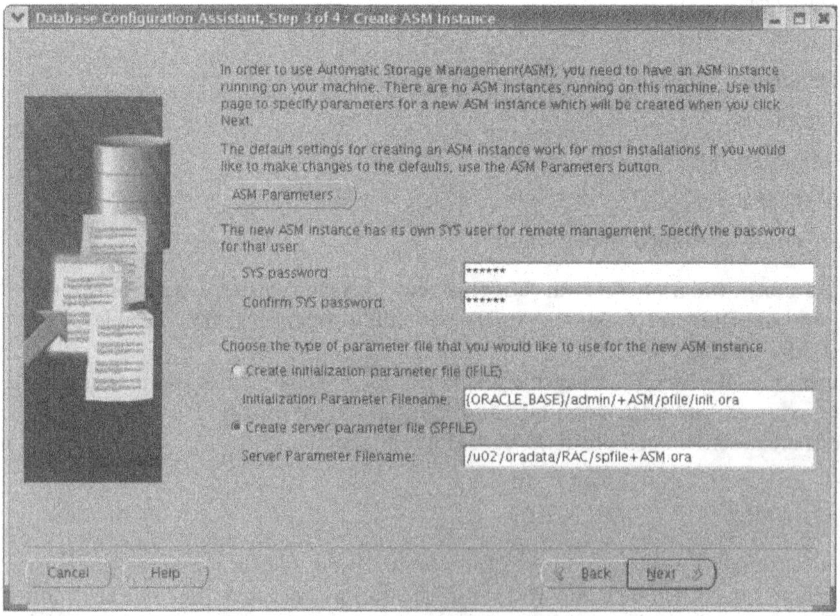

Figure 13-4. *The Create ASM Instance page*

On the Create ASM Instance page, you can set a number of attributes for the ASM instance, including ASM-specific parameters, the password for the SYS user, and the type and location of the parameter file. You can use either an initialization parameter file (PFILE) or a server parameter file (SPFILE). We recommend using an SPFILE if you can locate it on shared storage outside the ASM disk groups, for example, in a cluster file system. Otherwise, we recommend using a PFILE on local file systems.

At this point, DBCA will attempt to create and start the ASM instance. If Oracle Clusterware has been correctly configured, this start-up will only take a few seconds.

If this is the first installation on the nodes, you may receive a message that DBCA cannot detect any listener resources. These are usually configured during database creation and are required by ASM. You will be prompted by DBCA to create listeners on each of the affected nodes with the prefix LISTENER and the port number 1521. If these parameters are acceptable, click Yes; otherwise, run the Network Configuration Agent (NETCA) before continuing.

When the instances can be successfully created, ASM will display a list of available disk groups on the ASM Disk Groups page illustrated in Figure 13-5.

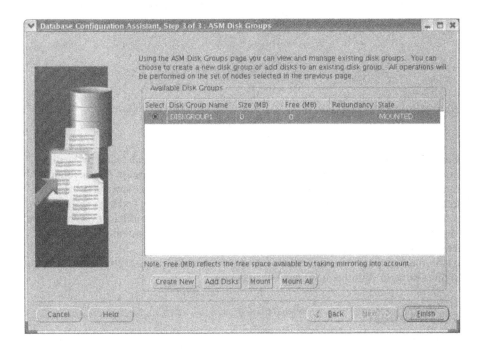

Figure 13-5. *The ASM Disk Groups page*

The existing ASM disk groups will have been configured previously using the /etc/init.d/oracleasm script. On the ASM Disk Groups page, you can create new disk groups or add disks to existing groups. You can also mount and unmount disk groups. To create a disk group, select from the list of available disk groups, and click the Create New button, which will take you to the Create Disk Group page shown in Figure 13-6.

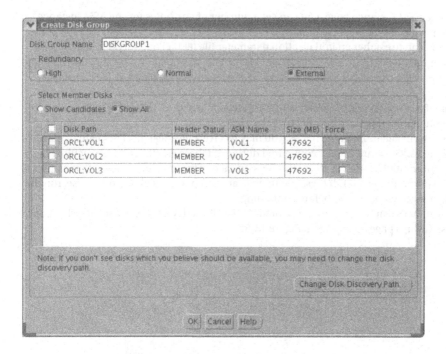

Figure 13-6. *The Create Disk Group page*

On the Create Disk Group page, you can specify the volumes that you wish to use in the disk group. You can also specify the level of redundancy you require for the disk group. You can choose among external redundancy, in which case any mirroring is performed by the storage subsystem; normal redundancy, in which case ASM maintains two copies of each extent; and high redundancy, in which case ASM maintains three copies of each extent. Bear in mind that sufficient volumes must be available and located on physically separate groups of disks in order to guarantee normal and high levels of redundancy.

Following the initial configuration, you can modify your ASM configuration at any time by running DBCA and selecting Configure Automatic Storage Management.

Creating a Database

You can use DBCA to create a database using ASM, OCFS, or shared raw devices. The resulting database can be optionally configured with EM Database Control, Recovery Manager, and a Flashback Recovery Area. The database will be created with Manageability Infrastructure features such as AWR, ADDM, and ASH pre-configured. In a RAC environment, DBCA will create instances on all specified nodes.

You can still create a database using scripts, and you may wish to do so to minimize security risks or for other operational reasons. However, for most users, DBCA represents the most efficient and convenient method of database creation.

When you select Create Database from the menu on the Operations page, the Node Selection page will be displayed again. As previously, select the nodes where you wish to create instances for the database or click Select All. Click Next to continue to the Database Templates page shown in Figure 13-7.

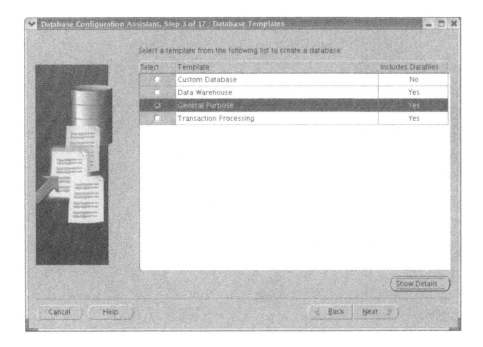

Figure 13-7. *The Database Templates page*

On the Database Templates page, you can select from the following templates:

- Custom Database
- Data Warehouse
- General Purpose
- Transaction Processing

The default database block size is 8192 for all four templates. The only differences among the supplied templates are the values of three initialization parameters, which are summarized in Table 13-1.

Table 13-1. *Database Template Initialization Parameters*

Initialization Parameter	General	Transaction Processing	Data Warehouse
PGA_AGGREGATE_TARGET	24M	16M	32M
DB_FILE_MULTIBLOCK_READ_COUNT	16	8	32
STAR_TRANSFORMATION_ENABLED	FALSE	FALSE	TRUE

You can also select Custom Database from the Database Templates page, which allows you to assign your own parameter values. If you have created any templates of your own, these will also be shown in the select list.

When you have selected a template, click Next to continue to the Database Identification page shown in Figure 13-8.

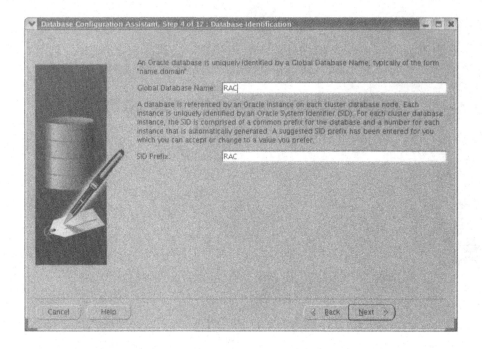

Figure 13-8. *The Database Identification page*

The Database Identification page allows you to enter a global database name that will be used as the default value for the SID and instance name prefixes. In our example, we have used the global database name RAC, for which the instance names are RAC1, RAC2, and so forth.

You may need to review your naming conventions if, like some users, you currently append a number to your global database name, as this may lead to duplicate instance names for very large sites. We have worked around this issue in the past by appending an underscore to the SID prefix.

Click Next to continue to the Management Options page shown in Figure 13-9.

The Management Options page allows you to configure EM and to specify a basic backup strategy. If you choose to configure EM, then you can select between Grid Control and Database Control. If you select Grid Control, you must have an external EM Repository available to manage the database. However, if you select Database Control, then a Repository will be loaded into the local database during the creation process.

You can also specify a mail (SMTP) server for outgoing mail notifications generated by database events.

Finally, on this page you can configure a basic backup, specifying a start time and an operating system username and password, under which the backup should be run.

Click Next to continue to the Database Credentials page shown in Figure 13-10.

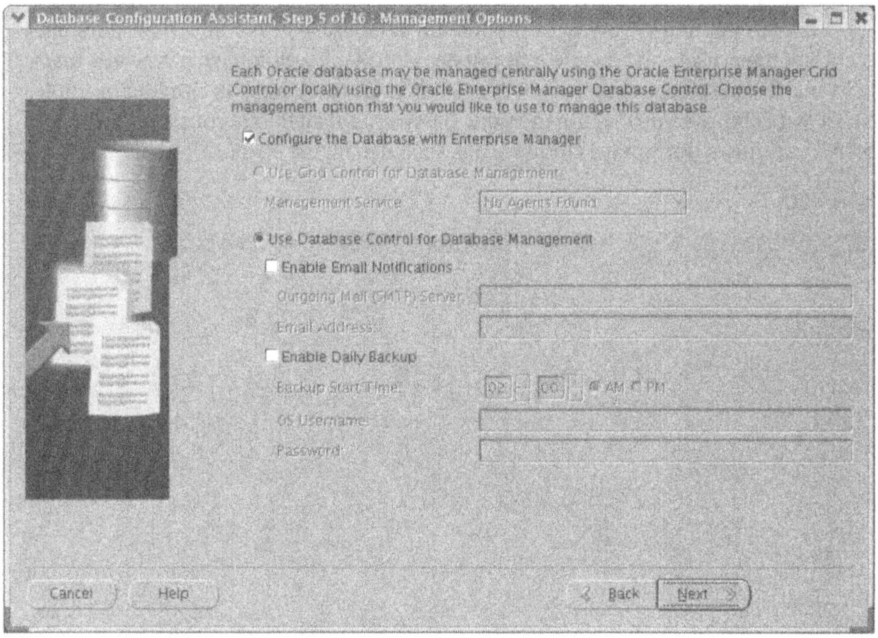

Figure 13-9. *The Management Options page*

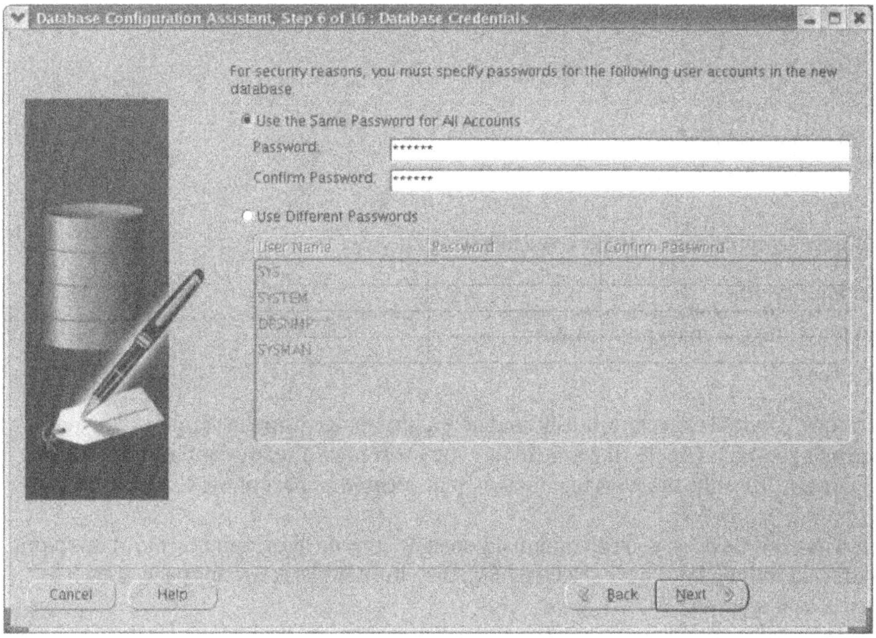

Figure 13-10. *The Database Credentials page*

The Database Credentials page allows you to specify passwords for administrative users including SYS, SYSTEM, DBSNMP, and SYSMAN. On a production database, you should specify different passwords for each of these users and ensure that you do not use the well-known passwords that were the defaults in previous releases, such as CHANGE_ON_INSTALL or MANAGER. If, as in our example, you are building a test database, you can use the same password for all four accounts.

Click Next to continue to the Storage Options page shown in Figure 13-11.

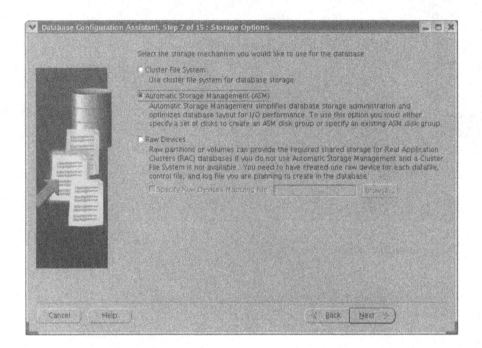

Figure 13-11. *The Storage Options page*

On the Storage Options page, you have the following choices:

- Cluster File System
- Automatic Storage Management (ASM)
- Raw Devices

For all options, you must have previously configured the storage using the appropriate tools.

If you are using ASM in Oracle 10.2 and above, you must have already configured the ASM instances. In Oracle 10.1 only, the ASM instances will be created as part of the Create Database option.

If you are using raw devices, you can optionally specify a raw devices mapping file at this point.

Click Next to continue. If you have selected ASM, then the ASM Disk Groups page, shown in Figure 13-12, will be displayed.

On the ASM Disk Groups page, you can select the disk groups you wish to use for the database files. You can also create new disk groups and add disks to existing disk groups on this page.

Click Next to continue to the Database File Locations page shown in Figure 13-13.

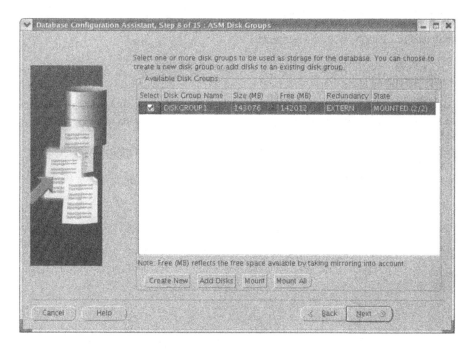

Figure 13-12. *The ASM Disk Groups page*

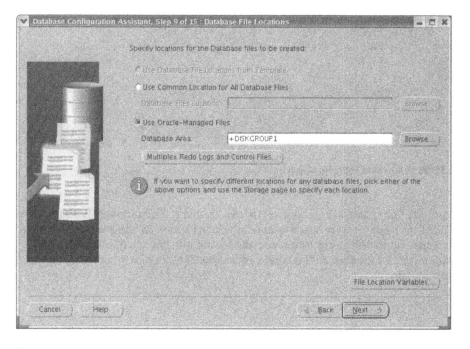

Figure 13-13. *The Database File Locations page*

On the Database File Locations page, you can specify whether DBCA should

- Use database file locations from the template
- Use a single location for all database files
- Use Oracle-Managed Files

On this page, you can also specify whether redo logs and control files should be mirrored. This page establishes default file locations as well; you can customize the locations of individual files later using the Storage page.

The contents and default values of the Database File Location page vary slightly if you are using OCFS instead of ASM.

Click Next to continue to the Recovery Configuration page shown in Figure 13-14.

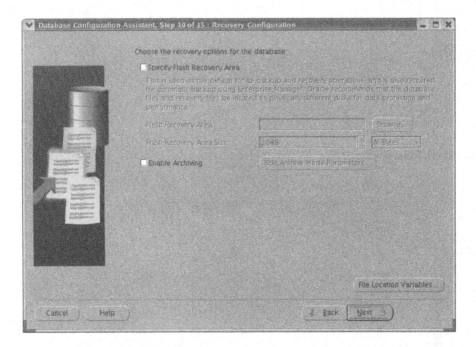

Figure 13-14. *The Recovery Configuration page*

On the Recovery Configuration page, you can specify whether you want to use a Flash Recovery Area. If configured, the Flash Recovery Area is used as the default location for all backup and recovery operations. It is also required if you are using automatic backup with EM. You must specify a location and maximum size for the Flash Recovery area, which should be located on physically separate disks to protect the data.

On this page, you can also specify whether you wish to enable archiving. Prior to Oracle 10.1, database creation generated a large amount of redo; therefore, it was preferable to delay enabling archiving until creation was completed. In Oracle 10.1 and above, if the General template is specified, DBCA builds the database from an RMAN backup. This less redo-intensive process means enabling archiving at creation is acceptable. If you have specified any other template, enabling archiving will slow down the database creation process. You can specify any additional archiving parameters by clicking the Edit Archive Mode Parameters button.

Click Next to continue to the Database Content page shown in Figure 13-15.

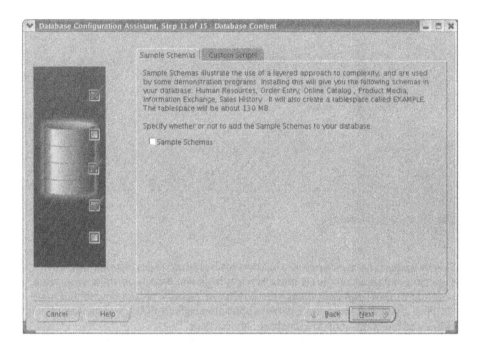

Figure 13-15. *The Database Content page*

On the Database Content page, you can optionally choose to install the Sample Schemas. These were introduced in Oracle 9.0.1 and include Human Resources, Order Entry, Online Catalog, Product Media, Information Exchange, and Sales History. These schemas will be created in a tablespace called EXAMPLE, which is approximately 130MB. The sample schemas are increasingly replacing the use of the SCOTT/TIGER schema in Oracle documentation, MetaLink examples, and demonstration programs.

On this page, you can also select the Custom Scripts tab and specify any scripts you wish to execute after database creation.

Click Next to continue to the Database Services page shown in Figure 13-16.

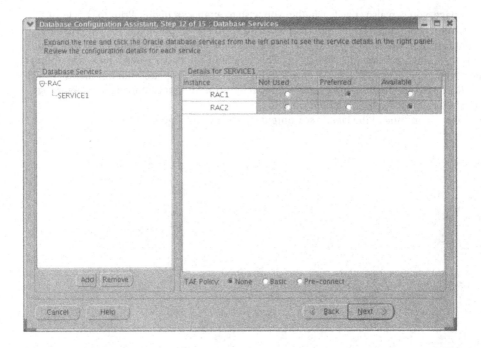

Figure 13-16. *The Database Services page*

You can specify initial databases services to be provided by the database, together with their preferred and available instances, on the Database Services page. You can specify up to 62 services on this page, and you can subsequently change the services using DBCA, EM, or a combination of SRVCTL and SQL*Plus. If you wish to use Transparent Application Failover (TAF), you can also specify a TAF policy of Basic or Pre-connect on the Database Services page.

Click Next to continue to the Initialization Parameters page shown in Figure 13-17.

The four tabs on the Initialization Parameters page are Memory, Sizing, Character Sets, and Connection Mode.

Click the Memory tab to specify the memory management method. For Automatic Memory Management, use the Typical option. If you are running multiple instances on each node, you can set the maximum percentage of memory available for each instance. Alternatively, you can select the Custom option to configure memory manually.

The Sizing tab allows you to specify the database block size, which defaults to 8,192 bytes. You can also specify a value for the PROCESSES parameter, which defines the maximum number of operating system user processes that can connect to the database simultaneously. The default values of a number of other parameters, including the SESSIONS and TRANSACTIONS parameters, are derived from the PROCESSES parameter value, which includes both background and foreground processes.

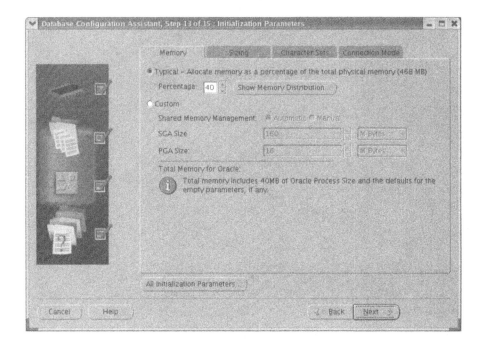

Figure 13-17. *The Initialization Parameters page Memory tab*

On the Character Sets tab, you can specify the Database Character Set, National Character Set, Default Language, and Default Data Format for the database.

You can select whether you want the database to operate in Dedicated Server or Shared Server mode on the Connection Mode tab. In dedicated server mode, for client connection, the database will allocate a resource (process) dedicated to serving only that client. This mode, which is the default, should be used when the total number of client connections is expected to be small or when clients will be making persistent long-running requests to the database. On the other hand, in shared server mode, several client connections share a database-allocated pool of resources. This mode should be used when a large number of users need to connect to the database simultaneously. If you choose shared server mode, you can also specify the number of server processes that you wish to create when an instance starts up.

On the Initialization Parameters page, you can also click the All Initialization Parameters button to modify any other supported initialization parameters that are not available on the tabs.

Click Next to continue to the Database Storage page shown in Figure 13-18.

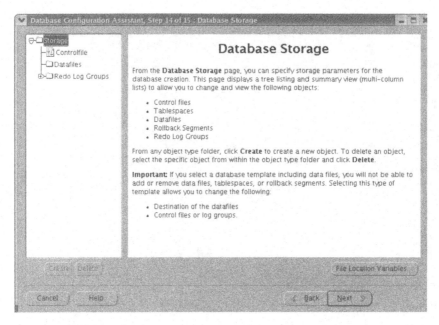

Figure 13-18. *The Database Storage page*

The Database Storage page allows you to specify locations, sizes, and names for control files, tablespaces, datafiles, rollback segments, and online redo log groups. Default values will have been specified on the Database File Locations page.

Click Next to continue to the Creation Options page shown in Figure 13-19.

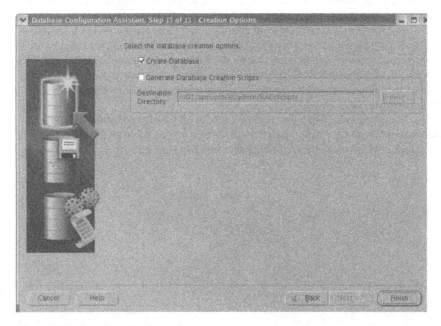

Figure 13-19. *The Creation Options page*

The Creation Options page allows you to specify whether you wish to create the database immediately or generate a set of database creation scripts. The default location for the scripts is `$ORACLE_BASE/admin/<database_name>/scripts`.

If you choose to create the database immediately, click the Finish button. Take extreme care at this point. A summary will be presented showing most of the options that you have selected; you have the option to save this summary as an HTML file. To exit the summary and continue with database creation, click the OK button. You will then be returned to the Creation Options page.

■**Caution** Do NOT click the Finish button more than once on this page or a second concurrent installation will commence.

A progress message will be displayed by DBCA that describes the current operation and the percentage completed. A log file is written to the `$ORACLE_HOME/cfgtoollogs/dbca/<database_name>` directory.

When database creation is completed, a success message will be displayed. This includes information about the database, such as the global database name, SID prefix, and server parameter file name. If you have chosen to configure the EM Database Control, this message also contains the URL, which you should write down for future reference. For the databases created for this book, the URL is `http://london1:1158/em`.

All database accounts except SYS, SYSTEM, DBSNMP, and SYSMAN are locked. You should ensure that these have nondefault passwords if the database is going to be used in a production environment. You can click the Password Management button from this message box.

Click Exit to continue. A final message will be displayed describing the names of cluster database instances and HA services that have been started.

Configuring a Database

Using DBCA, you can configure various database options. In Oracle 10.2, you can configure optional components. You can also switch between dedicated server mode and shared server mode.

Select Configure Database Options from the menu on the Operations page. If you have more than one database, the Database page will be displayed, and you will be asked to select the one you wish to configure. Select a database, and click Next to continue to the Database Content page shown in Figure 13-20.

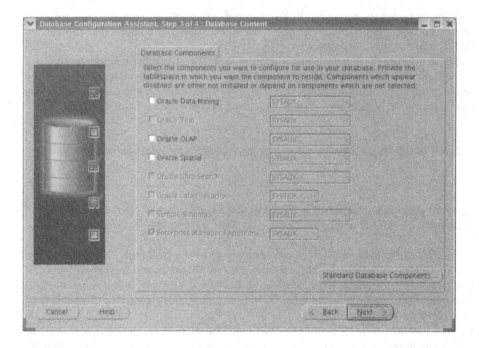

Figure 13-20. *The Database Content page*

On the Database Content page, you can specify the components you wish to configure for your database, which include the following:

- Oracle Data Mining
- Oracle Text
- Oracle OLAP
- Oracle Spatial
- Oracle Ultra Search
- Oracle Label Security
- Sample Schemas
- Enterprise Manager Repository

If an option is grayed out on this page, then it is not installed. You will need to run the OUI to install this component.

Click Next to continue to the Connection Mode page, which allows you to specify whether the database should be running in dedicated or shared server mode. Click Finish to complete the configuration.

Deleting a Database

You can also use DBCA to delete a database. If you have more than one database in your cluster, we recommend that you perform a full backup of all databases before attempting deletion, as DBCA will delete the database and each of the associated instances.

When you select the Delete Database option from the menu on the Operations page, if you have more than one database, then a list of cluster databases will be displayed, as shown in Figure 13-21.

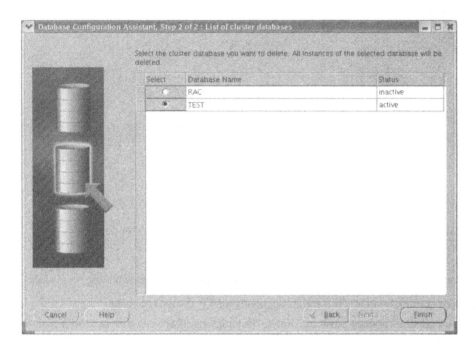

Figure 13-21. *The List of cluster databases page*

Select the database you wish to delete from this list. Before deleting the database, DBCA will ask for confirmation. At the end of the deletion process, a message will be displayed informing you whether the operation was successful.

Creating a Template

You can use DBCA to generate database templates. These are XML files that are stored in the directory $ORACLE_HOME/assistants/dbca/templates. User-defined templates always have a .dbt suffix. For example, if you use DBCA to create Template1, the template will be written to the file $ORACLE_HOME/assistants/dbca/templates/Template1.dbt.

To create a template, select the Manage Templates option from the menu on the Operations page. The Template Management page will be displayed (Figure 13-22).

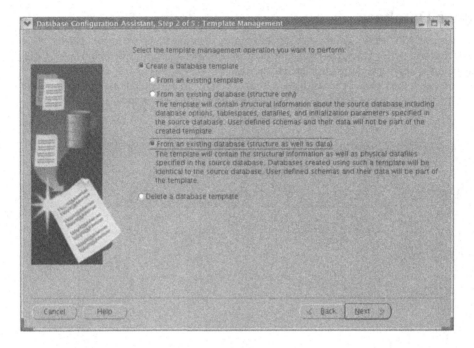

Figure 13-22. *The Template Management page*

The Template Management page allows you to create the template in the following three ways:

- **From an existing template**: You can subsequently modify the new template.

- **From an existing database (structure only)**: The template will contain structural information about the source database, including database options, tablespaces, datafiles, and initialization parameters, as specified in the source database. However, the template will not contain any user-defined schemas, objects, or data.

- **From an existing database (structure as well as data)**: The template will contain the structural information, as well as physical datafiles, specified in the source database. If you create a database using this template, it will be identical to the source database, including all user-defined schemas, objects, and data.

You can also use the Template Management page to delete templates.

Templates from an existing database that include structure and data are generated by creating an RMAN backup of the database. Therefore, you must have sufficient storage available for the template. By default templates are written to the $ORACLE_HOME/assistants/dbca/templates directory.

Click Next to continue to the Source Database page shown in Figure 13-23.

On the Source Database page, select a database from which to create the template from the drop-down list, and click Next to continue to the Template Properties page shown in Figure 13-24.

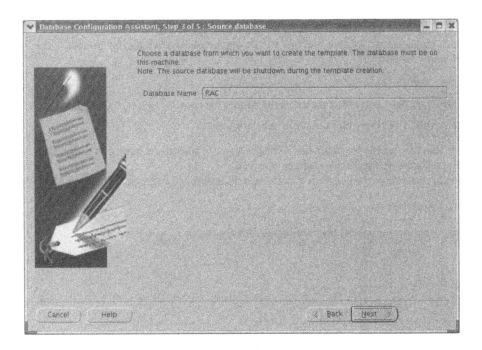

Figure 13-23. *The Source database page*

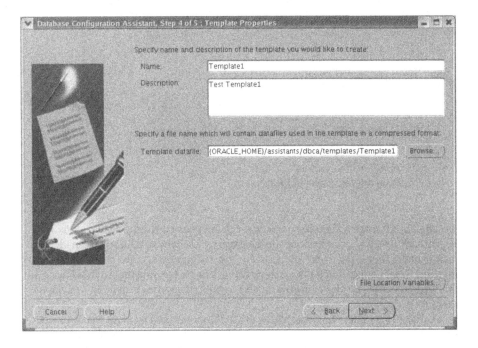

Figure 13-24. *The Template Properties page*

You can enter a name and a description for the template on the Template Properties page. You can also specify a file name that will contain the template and, optionally, the data. If you have opted to include the data, then a number of files will be generated. For example, for Template1, the following files were created:

- Template1.dbt: The XML file containing the template
- Template1.ctl: The binary file containing the control file data
- Template1.dfb: The binary file containing the datafile data

Make sure that the specified location has sufficient space to store the resulting template, as, even for an empty database, the DFB file is larger than 1GB.

Click Next to continue to the Location of database related files page shown in Figure 13-25.

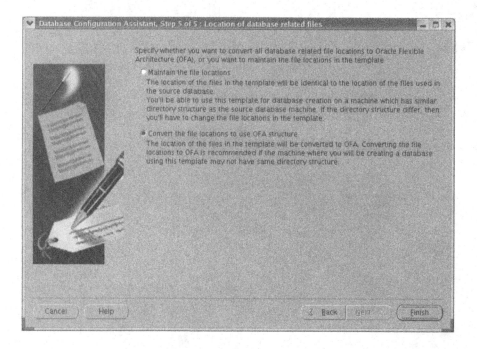

Figure 13-25. *The Location of database related files page*

On the Location of database related files page, you can opt to use the same file locations as in the source database, which allows you to clone the database on a second machine with an identical directory structure to the source database. Alternatively, you can choose to convert the file locations to use an OFA, which is recommended if the machine where you are creating the database has a different directory structure. You can also clone the database within the same cluster. Click Finish to generate the template.

At this point, DBCA prompts for confirmation. Check that the specified location has sufficient space for the template, and click OK to continue. When DBCA has generated the template, a message box will be displayed informing you that the operation was successful.

Managing Instances

You can also use DBCA to add and delete instances. These procedures are described in Chapter 20.

Managing Services

You can use DBCA to manage services, including adding and deleting services, specifying preferred and available instances, and setting a TAF policy.

Select the Services Management option from the menu on the Operations page. If you have more than one database, then you will be asked to select a database from a list. Select a database, and click Next to continue to the Database Services page shown in Figure 13-26.

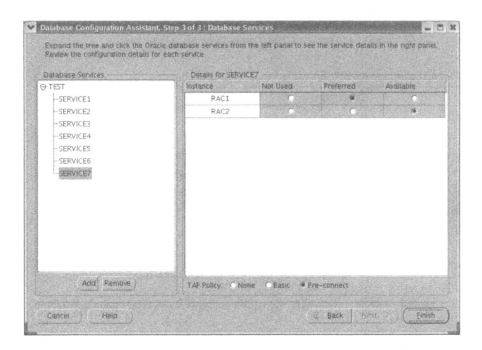

Figure 13-26. *The Database Services page*

The Database Services page is identical to the one displayed during database creation. You can add or remove services on this page. For each service, you can also specify Preferred and Available instances. If you are using TAF, you can specify a TAF policy of Basic or Pre-connect. Click Finish to return to the Operations page.

Using DBCA at the Command Line

The command line version of DBCA contains a significant amount of additional functionality. You can obtain help on the various DBCA commands using the following:

```
[oracle@london1 oracle]$ dbca -help
```

The syntax is as follows:

```
dbca  [-silent | -progressOnly | -customCreate] {<command> <options> } |
{ [<command> [options] ] -responseFile  <response file > }
[-continueOnNonFatalErrors <true | false>]
```

If you do not specify the -silent option, DBCA will attempt to launch a GUI to display progress and error messages. If you do specify the -silent option, progress will be displayed at the command line.

In Oracle 10.2, DBCA allows you to perform the commands listed in Table 13-2.

Table 13-2. *DBCA Command Line Operations*

Command	Description
createDatabase	Create a new database
configureDatabase	Configure an existing database
createTemplateFromDB	Create a template from an existing database
createCloneTemplate	Create a clone template from an existing database
generateScripts	Generate scripts to create a database
deleteDatabase	Delete a database
configureASM	Configure ASM Disk Groups
addInstance	Add an instance
deleteInstance	Delete an instance

Each option has its own syntax. For example, the syntax for the createDatabase option is as follows:

```
dbca -createDatabase
    -templateName <name of an existing template>
    [-cloneTemplate]
    -gdbName <global database name>
    [-sid <database system identifier prefix>]
    [-sysPassword <SYS user password>]
    [-systemPassword <SYSTEM user password>]
    [-emConfiguration <CENTRAL|LOCAL|ALL|NOBACKUP|NOEMAIL|NONE>
        -dbsnmpPassword <DBSNMP user password>
        -sysmanPassword <SYSMAN user password>
        [-hostUserName <Host user name for EM backup job>
        -hostUserPassword <Host user password for EM backup job>
        -backupSchedule <Daily backup schedule in the form of hh:mm>]
        [-smtpServer <Outgoing mail (SMTP) server for email notifications>
        -emailAddress <Email address for email notifications>]
        [-centralAgent <Enterprise Manager central agent home>]]
    [-datafileDestination <destination directory for all database files> |
    -datafileNames
    <text file containing database objects such as controlfiles, tablespaces,
    redo log files and spfile to their corresponding raw device file names
    mappings in name=value format.>]
```

```
[-recoveryAreaDestination <destination directory for all recovery files>]
[-datafileJarLocation
<location of the data file jar, used only for clone database creation>]
[-storageType < CFS | ASM | RAW>
    [-asmSysPassword <SYS password for ASM instance>]
    [-diskString <disk discovery path to be used by ASM>]
    [-diskList <list of disks for the database area disk group>
    -diskGroupName   <database area disk group name>
    -redundancy        <HIGH|NORMAL|EXTERNAL>]
   [-recoveryDiskList <list of disks for the recovery area disk group>
    -recoveryGroupName         <recovery area disk group name>
    -recoveryGroupRedundancy <HIGH|NORMAL|EXTERNAL>]]
[-nodelist <node names separated by comma for the database>]
[-characterSet <character set for the database>]
[-nationalCharacterSet <national character set for the database>]
[-registerWithDirService <true | false>
    -dirServiceUserName     <user name for directory service>
    -dirServicePassword     <password for directory service >
    -walletPassword     <password for database wallet >]
[-listeners  <list of listeners to configure the database with>]
[-variablesFile
   <file name for the variable-value pair for variables in the template>]]
[-variables  <comma seperated list of name=value pairs>]
[-initParams <comma seperated list of name=value pairs>]
[-memoryPercentage <percentage of physical memory for Oracle>]
    [-databaseType <MULTIPURPOSE|DATA_WAREHOUSING|OLTP>]]
```

We recommend that you use the GUI whenever possible, as it is much more user friendly than the command line syntax. If you need to use the command line version for commercial or operational reasons, we recommend that you test your installation using the GUI first and then attempt to repeat it using the command line syntax.

Creating a Database Using Scripts

Prior to Oracle 10.1, most RAC databases were created manually using scripts. In Oracle 10.1 and above, DBCA has become the favored method to create RAC databases. However, many sites still prefer script-based database creation, because scripts can be modified to accommodate database-specific requirements, or because the database creation method must be recorded in a change control system.

In Oracle 9*i*, database creation scripts would have been written from scratch or copied from existing scripts; in Oracle 10.1 and above, starting with a set of scripts generated using DBCA is easier because of the increased level of complexity required during the creation process. These scripts can be customized as necessary.

In this section, we will discuss a series of scripts generated by DBCA from the custom template for a two-node database using ASM storage. By default, DBCA will generate the scripts in $ORACLE_BASE/ admin/<database_name>/scripts, so for a database called RAC, the scripts were stored in $ORACLE_BASE/ admin/RAC/scripts.

Even if you do not plan to use DBCA to generate database creation scripts, studying this output is instructive; it may ensure that you have remembered to include all the necessary steps in scripts that you have prepared independently. As this section is intended to be educational, we have modified the scripts where necessary to improve readability. We have not, however, changed any of the actions defined within the scripts.

DBCA generates scripts on all nodes in the cluster. The scripts on the primary (installation) node should be run first, followed by those on the second and any subsequent nodes.

Primary node

The set of scripts generated by DBCA on the primary (installation) node is described in this section.

RAC1.sh

The name of this shell script is determined by the database name; it contains the following information used to create the database environment at an operating system level:

```
#!/bin/sh

mkdir -p /u01/app/oracle/admin/RAC/adump
mkdir -p /u01/app/oracle/admin/RAC/bdump
mkdir -p /u01/app/oracle/admin/RAC/cdump
mkdir -p /u01/app/oracle/admin/RAC/dpdump
mkdir -p /u01/app/oracle/admin/RAC/hdump
mkdir -p /u01/app/oracle/admin/RAC/pfile
mkdir -p /u01/app/oracle/admin/RAC/udump

mkdir -p /u01/app/oracle/product/10.2.0/db_1/cfgtoollogs/dbca/RAC

ORACLE_SID=RAC1; export ORACLE_SID

echo You should Add this entry in the /etc/oratab:
RAC:/u01/app/oracle/product/10.2.0/db_1:Y

/u01/app/oracle/product/10.2.0/db_1/bin/sqlplus /nolog
@/u01/app/oracle/admin/RAC/scripts/RAC1.sql
```

The preceding script creates the administrative directories in the $ORACLE_BASE/admin/RAC directory. It also creates a log directory to capture output from the remainder of the database creation process. This script also initializes the ORACLE_SID environment variable for the local node. It then runs a SQL*Plus script called RAC1.sql. Note that this script prompts the user to update /etc/oratab with an entry for the new database:

```
echo You should Add this entry in the /etc/oratab:
RAC:/u01/app/oracle/product/10.2.0/db_1:Y
```

Unlike DBCA, which would update /etc/oratab on every configured node, the script-based method relies on the DBA to perform a number of tasks manually on each node. In this case, /etc/oratab must be updated with an entry for the database. Note that in RAC environments the database name (RAC) is used, rather than the database SID (RAC1). Therefore, the same change should be made on all nodes in the cluster.

RAC1.sql

This SQL script, for which the name is also determined by the database name, calls a number of other scripts that perform individual actions within the database creation procedure:

```
set verify off
PROMPT specify a password for sys as parameter 1;
DEFINE sysPassword = &1
PROMPT specify a password for system as parameter 2;
DEFINE systemPassword = &2
PROMPT specify a password for sysman as parameter 3;
DEFINE sysmanPassword = &3
PROMPT specify a password for dbsnmp as parameter 4;
DEFINE dbsnmpPassword = &4
```

```
PROMPT specify ASM SYS user password as parameter 6;
DEFINE asmSysPassword= &6

host /u01/app/oracle/product/10.2.0/db_1/bin/orapwd
file=/u01/app/oracle/product/10.2.0/db_1/dbs/orapwRAC1➡
password=&&sysPassword force=y

@/u01/app/oracle/admin/RAC/scripts/CreateDB.sql
@/u01/app/oracle/admin/RAC/scripts/CreateDBFiles.sql
@/u01/app/oracle/admin/RAC/scripts/CreateDBCatalog.sql
@/u01/app/oracle/admin/RAC/scripts/JServer.sql
@/u01/app/oracle/admin/RAC/scripts/xdb_protocol.sql
@/u01/app/oracle/admin/RAC/scripts/ordinst.sql
@/u01/app/oracle/admin/RAC/scripts/interMedia.sql
@/u01/app/oracle/admin/RAC/scripts/emRepository.sql
@/u01/app/oracle/admin/RAC/scripts/CreateClustDBViews.sql

host echo "SPFILE='+DISKGROUP1/RAC/spfileRAC.ora'" >➡
/u01/app/oracle/product/10.2.0/db_1/dbs/initRAC1.ora

@/u01/app/oracle/admin/RAC/scripts/postDBCreation.sql
```

The script first prompts for passwords for the SYS, SYSTEM, SYSMAN, DBNSM, and the ASM SYS users. Unlike with DBCA, you cannot set all passwords in a single command.

The next step is to run the Oracle password utility with the orapwd command to create a password file in $ORACLE_HOME/dbs/orapwRAC1 using the SYS password entered in the previous step.

The script calls nine more SQL scripts to create the database, install the catalog, configure JServer, XDB, interMedia, and the EM Repository, and finally, run RAC-specific catalog scripts. These scripts are discussed in the following sections.

The next step is to create a PFILE called $ORACLE_HOME/dbs/initRAC1.ora that contains an SPFILE parameter defining the location of the SPFILE in the ASM file system.

The final step is to run the post-database-creation SQL script. This script performs a number of actions, including the creation of redo log threads for the second and subsequent instances, creation of an SPFILE, recompilation of invalid PL/SQL packages, and optionally, configuration of the EM Database Control.

PFILE

The initial PFILE created by DBCA includes a minimal set of default parameters for a RAC environment:

```
# Cache and I/O
db_block_size=8192
db_file_multiblock_read_count=16

# Cluster Database
#cluster_database=true
cluster_database_instances=2
#remote_listener=LISTENERS_RAC

# Cursors and Library Cache
open_cursors=300

# Database Identification
db_domain=""
db_name=RAC
```

```
# Diagnostics and Statistics
background_dump_dest=/u01/app/oracle/admin/RAC/bdump
core_dump_dest=/u01/app/oracle/admin/RAC/cdump
user_dump_dest=/u01/app/oracle/admin/RAC/udump

# File Configuration
db_create_file_dest=+DISKGROUP1

# Job Queues
job_queue_processes=10

# Miscellaneous
compatible=10.2.0.1.0

# Processes and Sessions
processes=150

# SGA Memory
sga_target=272629760

# Security and Auditing
audit_file_dest=/u01/app/oracle/admin/RAC/adump
remote_login_passwordfile=exclusive

# Shared Server
dispatchers="(PROTOCOL=TCP) (SERVICE=RACXDB)"

# Sort, Hash Joins, Bitmap Indexes
pga_aggregate_target=90177536

# System Managed Undo and Rollback Segments
undo_management=AUTO

RAC1.instance_number=1
RAC2.instance_number=2
RAC1.thread=1
RAC2.thread=2
RAC1.undo_tablespace=UNDOTBS1
RAC2.undo_tablespace=UNDOTBS2
```

DBCA will attempt to set reasonable default values for the SGA_TARGET and PGA_AGGREGATE_TARGET parameters. However, appropriate values for these parameters will be affected by the number of instances that you intend to run on each node, so you may wish to manually adjust these parameters.

Note that the values for the CLUSTER_DATABASE and REMOTE_LISTENER parameters are initially commented out. Because the database is not initially created as a clustered database, it must be subsequently manually converted into a clustered database.

CreateDB.sql

The following CreateDB.sql script is called by RAC1.sql and is responsible for executing the CREATE DATABASE statement:

```
connect "SYS"/"&&sysPassword" as SYSDBA
set echo on
spool /u01/app/oracle/admin/RAC/scripts/CreateDB.log

startup nomount pfile="/u01/app/oracle/admin/RAC/scripts/init.ora";
```

```
CREATE DATABASE "RAC"
MAXINSTANCES 32
MAXLOGHISTORY 1
MAXLOGFILES 192
MAXLOGMEMBERS 3
MAXDATAFILES 1024
DATAFILE SIZE 300M
  AUTOEXTEND ON NEXT  10240K MAXSIZE UNLIMITED
  EXTENT MANAGEMENT LOCAL
SYSAUX
  DATAFILE SIZE 120M
  AUTOEXTEND ON NEXT  10240K MAXSIZE UNLIMITED
  SMALLFILE
DEFAULT TEMPORARY TABLESPACE TEMP
  TEMPFILE SIZE 20M
  AUTOEXTEND ON NEXT 640K MAXSIZE UNLIMITED
  SMALLFILE
UNDO TABLESPACE "UNDOTBS1"
  DATAFILE SIZE 200M
  AUTOEXTEND ON NEXT  5120K MAXSIZE UNLIMITED
CHARACTER SET WE8ISO8859P1
NATIONAL CHARACTER SET AL16UTF16
LOGFILE GROUP 1  SIZE 51200K,
GROUP 2  SIZE 51200K
USER SYS IDENTIFIED BY "&&sysPassword"
USER SYSTEM IDENTIFIED BY "&&systemPassword";

set linesize 2048;
column ctl_files NEW_VALUE ctl_files;
select concat('control_files='''', concat(replace(value, ', ', ''',''), ''''))➡
 ctl_files from v$parameter where name ='control_files';
host echo &ctl_files >>/u01/app/oracle/admin/RAC/scripts/init.ora;

spool off
```

The script performs some housekeeping and then starts an instance on the local node using the initialization parameters specified in the supplied PFILE called init.ora.

The next step is to run the CREATE DATABASE statement, which will create a database based on a combination of the specified parameters and the contents of the $ORACLE_HOME/rdbms/admin/sql.bsq file. Note that in Oracle 10.1 and above, the CREATE DATABASE statement includes a mandatory clause for the SYSAUX tablespace. It also creates the SYSTEM tablespace, a default temporary tablespace, and UNDOTBS1, which is the undo tablespace for the initial instance.

The final step in this script updates the CONTROL_FILES parameter in the init.ora file with the default values assigned by the CREATE DATABASE statement.

CreateDBFiles.sql

The CreateDBFiles.sql script creates the remaining tablespaces:

```
connect "SYS"/"&&sysPassword" as SYSDBA
set echo on
spool /u01/app/oracle/admin/RAC/scripts/CreateDBFiles.log

CREATE SMALLFILE UNDO TABLESPACE "UNDOTBS2"
DATAFILE SIZE 200M
AUTOEXTEND ON NEXT  5120K MAXSIZE UNLIMITED;
```

```
CREATE SMALLFILE TABLESPACE "USERS" LOGGING
DATAFILE SIZE 5M
AUTOEXTEND ON NEXT  1280K MAXSIZE UNLIMITED
EXTENT MANAGEMENT LOCAL
SEGMENT SPACE MANAGEMENT  AUTO;

ALTER DATABASE DEFAULT TABLESPACE "USERS";

spool off
```

The first step creates UNDOTBS2, which is the undo tablespace for the second instance. The second step creates a USERS tablespace, which is the default tablespace for the database.

Note that the generated scripts contain a number of redundant clauses. By default, all tablespaces are SMALLFILE tablespaces unless the BIGFILE keyword is explicitly specified. In addition, the default in Oracle 10.2 is for all tablespaces to be locally managed (EXTENT MANAGEMENT LOCAL) and to use ASSM (SEGMENT SPACE MANAGEMENT AUTO).

Note also that, by default, DBCA creates all tablespaces with the AUTOEXTEND parameter enabled. If this is not in accord with your site standards, you may want to remove this clause.

CreateDBCatalog.sql

The CreateDBCatalog.sql script runs the relevant catalog scripts to build the data dictionary and the PL/SQL supplied packages:

```
connect "SYS"/"&&sysPassword" as SYSDBA
set echo on
spool /u01/app/oracle/admin/RAC/scripts/CreateDBCatalog.log

@/u01/app/oracle/product/10.2.0/db_1/rdbms/admin/catalog.sql;
@/u01/app/oracle/product/10.2.0/db_1/rdbms/admin/catblock.sql;
@/u01/app/oracle/product/10.2.0/db_1/rdbms/admin/catproc.sql;
@/u01/app/oracle/product/10.2.0/db_1/rdbms/admin/catoctk.sql;
@/u01/app/oracle/product/10.2.0/db_1/rdbms/admin/owminst.plb;

connect "SYSTEM"/"&&systemPassword"
@/u01/app/oracle/product/10.2.0/db_1/sqlplus/admin/pupbld.sql;

connect "SYSTEM"/"&&systemPassword"
set echo on
spool /u01/app/oracle/admin/RAC/scripts/sqlPlusHelp.log
@/u01/app/oracle/product/10.2.0/db_1/sqlplus/admin/help/hlpbld.sql helpus.sql;
spool off
```

Table 13.3 shows the scripts run by CreateDBCatalog.sql.

Table 13.3. *Scripts Run by CreateDBCatalog.sql*

Script	Description
$ORACLE_HOME/rdbms/admin/catalog.sql	Data dictionary views
$ORACLE_HOME/rdbms/admin/catblock.sql	Lock views
$ORACLE_HOME/rdbms/admin/catproc.sql	PL/SQL-supported packages
$ORACLE_HOME/rdbms/admin/catoctk.sql	Oracle cryptographic tool kit
$ORACLE_HOME/rdbms/admin/owminst.plb	Workspace manager

The next step is to connect as the SYSTEM user to run $ORACLE_HOME/sqlplus/admin/pupbld.sql, which is the SQL*Plus configuration script, and $ORACLE_HOME/sqlplus/admin/help/hldbld.sql, which loads the SQL*Plus help messages, in this case in American English (helpus.sql).

JServer.sql

The following JServer.sql script installs the Java Server engine in the database. This component is optional, but installing it is generally a good idea, as it is a prerequisite for many other components.

```
connect "SYS"/"&&sysPassword" as SYSDBA
set echo on
spool /u01/app/oracle/admin/RAC/scripts/JServer.log

@/u01/app/oracle/product/10.2.0/db_1/javavm/install/initjvm.sql;
@/u01/app/oracle/product/10.2.0/db_1/xdk/admin/initxml.sql;
@/u01/app/oracle/product/10.2.0/db_1/xdk/admin/xmlja.sql;
@/u01/app/oracle/product/10.2.0/db_1/rdbms/admin/catjava.sql;
@/u01/app/oracle/product/10.2.0/db_1/rdbms/admin/catexf.sql;

spool off
```

The scripts described in Table 13.4 are run by JServer.sql.

Table 13.4. *Scripts Run by JServer.sql*

Script	Description
$ORACLE_HOME/javavm/install/initjvm.sql	JVM
$ORACLE_HOME/xdk/admin/initxml.sql	XML development kit (XDK)
$ORACLE_HOME/xdk/admin/xmlja.sql	XML parser
$ORACLE_HOME/rdbms/admin/catjava.sql	Java catalog
$ORACLE_HOME/rdbms/admin/catexf.sql	Expression filter

xdb_protocol.sql

The xdb_protocol.sql script runs the scripts for the optional XDB database:

```
connect "SYS"/"&&sysPassword" as SYSDBA
set echo on
spool /u01/app/oracle/admin/RAC/scripts/xdb_protocol.log
@/u01/app/oracle/product/10.2.0/db_1/rdbms/admin/catqm.sql ➥
change_on_install SYSAUX TEMP;
connect "SYS"/"&&sysPassword" as SYSDBA
@/u01/app/oracle/product/10.2.0/db_1/rdbms/admin/catxdbj.sql;
@/u01/app/oracle/product/10.2.0/db_1/rdbms/admin/catrul.sql;
spool off
```

The scripts run by xdb_protocol.sql are described in Table 13.5.

Table 13.5. *Scripts Run by xsb_protocol.sql*

Script	Description
$ORACLE_HOME/rdbms/admin/catqm.sql	XML catalog
$ORACLE_HOME/rdbms/admin/catxdbj.sql	XDB Java API installation
$ORACLE_HOME/rdbms/admin/catrul.sql	Rules manager

ordinst.sql

The optional `ordinst.sql` script installs the objects that support the interMedia and Spatial options:

```
connect "SYS"/"&&sysPassword" as SYSDBA
set echo on
spool /u01/app/oracle/admin/RAC/scripts/ordinst.log
@/u01/app/oracle/product/10.2.0/db_1/ord/admin/ordinst.sql SYSAUX SYSAUX;
spool off
```

Note that in Oracle 10.1 and above, these objects are created in the SYSAUX tablespace.

interMedia.sql

The optional `interMedia.sql` script installs additional objects for interMedia:

```
connect "SYS"/"&&sysPassword" as SYSDBA
set echo on
spool /u01/app/oracle/admin/RAC/scripts/interMedia.log
@/u01/app/oracle/product/10.2.0/db_1/ord/im/admin/iminst.sql;
spool off
```

emRepository.sql

The optional `emRepository.sql` script installs the EM Repository:

```
connect "SYS"/"&&sysPassword" as SYSDBA
set echo off
spool /u01/app/oracle/admin/RAC/scripts/emRepository.log

@/u01/app/oracle/product/10.2.0/db_1/sysman/admin/emdrep/sql/emreposcre ➥
/u01/app/oracle/product/10.2.0/db_1 SYSMAN &&sysmanPassword TEMP ON;
WHENEVER SQLERROR CONTINUE;

spool off
```

The script runs `$ORACLE_HOME/sysadm/admin/emdrep/sql/emreposcre.sql`, which creates the repository in the local tablespace under the SYSMAN schema.

You only need to run this script if you intend to use EM Database Control to manage your database. If you are planning to use EM Grid Control, the repository should be located in a separate database.

CreateClustDBViews.sql

The `CreateClustDBViews.sql` script runs the RAC-specific catalog scripts:

```
connect "SYS"/"&&sysPassword" as SYSDBA
set echo on
spool /u01/app/oracle/admin/RAC/scripts/CreateClustDBViews.log
@/u01/app/oracle/product/10.2.0/db_1/rdbms/admin/catclust.sql;
spool off
```

In Oracle 10.2, this script runs `$ORACLE_HOME/rdbms/admin/catalog.sql`, which creates a number of synonyms for dynamic performance views; the synonym names were changed from %DLM% to %GES% in Oracle 9.0.1.

postDBCreation.sql

The postDBCreation.sql script is the final database creation script:

```
connect "SYS"/"&&sysPassword" as SYSDBA
set echo on
spool /u01/app/oracle/admin/RAC/scripts/postDBCreation.log

select group# from v$log where group# =3;
select group# from v$log where group# =4;

ALTER DATABASE ADD LOGFILE THREAD 2
  GROUP 3   SIZE 51200K,
  GROUP 4   SIZE 51200K;

ALTER DATABASE ENABLE PUBLIC THREAD 2;

spool off
connect "SYS"/"&&sysPassword" as SYSDBA
set echo on
create spfile='+DISKGROUP1/RAC/spfileRAC.ora'
  FROM pfile='/u01/app/oracle/admin/RAC/scripts/init.ora';

shutdown immediate;
connect "SYS"/"&&sysPassword" as SYSDBA
startup ;

alter user SYSMAN identified by "&&sysmanPassword" account unlock;
alter user DBSNMP identified by "&&dbsnmpPassword" account unlock;

select 'utl_recomp_begin: ' || to_char(sysdate, 'HH:MI:SS') from dual;
execute utl_recomp.recomp_serial();
select 'utl_recomp_end: ' || to_char(sysdate, 'HH:MI:SS') from dual;

host /u01/app/oracle/product/10.2.0/db_1/bin/emca -config dbcontrol db -silent
  -cluster -ASM_USER_ROLE SYSDBA
  -ASM_USER_NAME SYS
  -NODE_LIST server3,server4
  -CLUSTER_NAME crs
  -LOG_FILE /u01/app/oracle/admin/RAC/scripts/emConfig.log
  -DBSNMP_PWD &&dbsnmpPassword
  -SYS_PWD &&sysPassword -ASM_USER_PWD &&asmSysPassword
  -SID RAC -ASM_SID +ASM1
  -DB_UNIQUE_NAME RAC
  -EM_HOME /u01/app/oracle/product/10.2.0/db_1
  -SID_LIST RAC1,RAC2
  -SYSMAN_PWD &&sysmanPassword
  -SERVICE_NAME RAC
  -ASM_PORT 1521
  -PORT 1521
  -LISTENER OH /u01/app/oracle/product/10.2.0/db_1
  -LISTENER LISTENER -ORACLE_HOME /u01/app/oracle/product/10.2.0/db_1
  -HOST server3
  -ASM_OH /u01/app/oracle/product/10.2.0/db_1;

spool /u01/app/oracle/admin/RAC/scripts/postDBCreation.log
exit;
```

The first step creates redo log files for the second instance and enables the second redo log thread. The second step creates the SPFILE in the ASM file system, based on the updated contents of the init.ora file. The third step unlocks the passwords for the EM DBSNMP and SYSMAN users. The next step recompiles any invalid packages. The final step configures EM Database Control using the EM Configuration Assistant ($ORACLE_HOME/bin/emca). This step is only necessary if you intend to manage the database using EM Database Control. It can be removed if you plan to manage the database using EM Grid Control.

Secondary Nodes

Two scripts are created on the second and subsequent nodes.

RAC2.sh

The RAC2.sh script creates the required directory structure on the second node. It also creates a log file directory for DBCA logs, sets the ORACLE_SID environment variable, and executes the RAC2.sql script on the second node:

```
#!/bin/sh

mkdir -p /u01/app/oracle/admin/RAC/adump
mkdir -p /u01/app/oracle/admin/RAC/bdump
mkdir -p /u01/app/oracle/admin/RAC/cdump
mkdir -p /u01/app/oracle/admin/RAC/dpdump
mkdir -p /u01/app/oracle/admin/RAC/hdump
mkdir -p /u01/app/oracle/admin/RAC/pfile
mkdir -p /u01/app/oracle/admin/RAC/udump

mkdir -p /u01/app/oracle/product/10.2.0/db_1/cfgtoollogs/dbca/RAC

ORACLE_SID=RAC2; export ORACLE_SID

echo You should Add this entry in the /etc/oratab:
RAC:/u01/app/oracle/product/10.2.0/db_1:Y

/u01/app/oracle/product/10.2.0/db_1/bin/sqlplus /nolog
@/u01/app/oracle/admin/RAC/scripts/RAC2.sql
```

RAC2.sql

The RAC2.sql script creates the password file on the second node and the PFILE on the second node:

```
set verify off
PROMPT specify a password for sys as parameter 1;
DEFINE sysPassword = &1
PROMPT specify a password for system as parameter 2;
DEFINE systemPassword = &2
PROMPT specify a password for sysman as parameter 3;
DEFINE sysmanPassword = &3
PROMPT specify a password for dbsnmp as parameter 4;
DEFINE dbsnmpPassword = &4
PROMPT specify ASM SYS user password as parameter 6;
DEFINE asmSysPassword= &6
```

```
host /u01/app/oracle/product/10.2.0/db_1/bin/orapwd \
file=/u01/app/oracle/product/10.2.0/db_1/dbs/orapwRAC2 \
  password=&&sysPassword force=y

host echo SPFILE='+DISKGROUP1/RAC/spfileRAC.ora' > ➥
/u01/app/oracle/product/10.2.0/db_1/dbs/initRAC2.ora

host echo Run script "/u01/app/oracle/admin/RAC/scripts/RAC1.sh"
  from node "server3" if you have not already run it.
```

Note that this script contains a number of other calls to SQL scripts that are commented out; we have removed them to improve clarity.

When you run this script, take care to enter the same passwords for each user as you entered on the first node. Alternatively, you can copy the password file from the first node to the subsequent nodes; ensure that you change the instance name component of the file name.

Running the Scripts

When you have finished making any modifications to the scripts generated by DBCA, you are ready to run them. To run the scripts described in this section, log in as the oracle user on the first node, and run RAC1.sh:

```
[oracle@london1 oracle]$ cd $ORACLE_BASE/admin/RAC/scripts
[oracle@london1 oracle]$ sh RAC1.sh
```

Depending on the speed of the server, the scripts may take up to 30 minutes to run.

On the remaining nodes, run the relevant scripts. For example, on the second node, run the RAC2.sh script:

```
[oracle@london2 oracle]$ cd $ORACLE_BASE/admin/RAC/scripts
[oracle@london2 oracle]$ sh RAC2.sh
```

When the scripts have completed on each node, update /etc/oratab with the entry described in RAC1.sh, as in the following example:

```
RAC:/u01/app/oracle/product/10.2.0/db_1:Y
```

On the first node only, add the database to the OCR with the following code:

```
[oracle@london1 oracle]$ srvctl add database -d RAC \
-o $ORACLE_HOME \
-p +DISKGROUP1/RAC/spfileRAC.ora
```

where the -d option specifies the database name, the -o option specifies the Oracle Home, and the -p option specifies the location of the SPFILE.

Again, on the first node only, add the new instances to the OCR as follows:

```
[oracle@london1 oracle]$ srvctl add instance -d RAC -i RAC1 -n london1
[oracle@london1 oracle]$ srvctl add instance -d RAC -i RAC2 -n london2
```

where the -d option again specifies the database name, the -i option specifies the instance name, and the -n option specifies the node name.

Finally, set the CLUSTER_DATABASE parameter to true on the first node:

```
[oracle@london1 oracle]$ export ORACLE_SID=RAC1
[oracle@london1 oracle]$ sqlplus / as sysdba
SQL> STARTUP MOUNT
SQL> ALTER SYSTEM SET cluster_database = true SCOPE = SPFILE;
SQL> SHUTDOWN IMMEDIATE
SQL> EXIT
```

Next, start the database:

```
[oracle@london1 oracle] srvctl start database -d RAC
```

You can verify that all instances have started as follows:

```
[oracle@london1 oracle]$ srvctl status database -d RAC
```

This command should return all currently available instances and their nodes, for example:

```
Instance RAC1 is running on node london1
Instance RAC2 is running on node london2
```

Summary

In this chapter, we described, in detail, the steps for creating a RAC database and the associated ASM configuration using the recommended Database Configuration Assistant (DBCA) tool. We outlined using DBCA as both a GUI and a command line tool. In a RAC environment, DBCA is a particularly powerful tool, as it configures instances on all specified nodes simultaneously.

Also, DBCA has features that allow you to create your own templates and, subsequently, to create databases based on these templates. Its powerful database cloning facilities allow you to make a copy of your database, including the structure and the contents, if you wish. We have also shown how to create a basic RAC database using SQL*Plus scripts generated by DBCA.

Until Oracle 10g, creating databases using manually prepared scripts was usually preferred. However, the manual database creation process is slow, complex, and error-prone. While it is still possible to create databases by hand in Oracle 10g, we strongly recommend that you create all RAC databases using the DBCA, either directly (with the GUI) or indirectly (by generating database creation scripts).

CHAPTER 14

■ ■ ■

Installing and Configuring
Enterprise Manager

Enterprise Manager (EM) is Oracle's graphical user interface (GUI) product for monitoring and administering an Oracle software environment. The first version of the Enterprise Manager family took the form of a Microsoft Windows client-based application installed on the DBA's PC. The second version was implemented as a Java-client application, installable on a number of operating systems, including Linux. Version 2 of EM supported Oracle databases up to release 9.2 and could operate in a stand-alone mode or with a Management Service and a Management Repository database for more advanced installations. However, version 2 could only recognize Oracle9*i* RAC environments when operating with a Management Service and Management Repository configuration. In stand-alone mode, all cluster instances were identified as single-instance installations.

In Oracle 10.1 and above, EM is an HTML-based tool with RAC-specific administration and performance monitoring features. The Enterprise Manager Console provides a GUI-based central point of control for the entire Oracle environment from a web browser, and thus requires no installation of additional client components.

There are two versions of Enterprise Manager 10*g*: Database Control and Grid Control. Database Control allows you to manage a single RAC database and its associated instances, listeners, and nodes; Grid Control allows you to manage multiple RAC databases, as well as instances, listeners, nodes, application servers, HTTP servers, web applications, and even third-party software. It also allows you to create Data Guard standby databases. If you have only a single RAC database and do not plan on using a Data Guard configuration, we recommend that you use Database Control. If you have more than one database, or if you intend to use advanced features such as Data Guard, then we recommend you investigate Grid Control.

If you use the Database Creation Assistant (DBCA) to create your database, the EM Database Control will be automatically configured for your RAC database, and an Enterprise Manager Agent will be installed on each node in the cluster and will perform database and instance discovery. The configuration of Database Control is a default option within DBCA if there is no Grid Control Management Agent already running on the target system. While Database Control is installed automatically by DBCA, Grid Control must be manually installed separately.

EM enables you to start, stop, and monitor databases, instances, and listeners. It also allows you to create and assign resource plans, administer storage (such as undo tablespaces and redo logs), manage archive logging, administer ASM, schedule backup and recovery jobs, modify parameters, and manage the database scheduler, schemas, security, and storage. EM can also be used to display the current host configuration, which includes the memory, CPU, device I/O, network interfaces, and operating system version. It can be used to stage and deploy Oracle patches, provision Linux and Oracle installations, and convert non-RAC databases into RAC.

With Oracle EM 10g, the Java console of version 2 remains available as an option to support features that have not yet migrated to the Grid Control environment. Once all features have been migrated in future product releases, however, the Java console will no longer be included with EM; therefore, we recommend focusing on the HTML-based environment.

Manageability Infrastructure

Understanding how far the EM's capabilities for supporting your RAC environment have advanced with the Oracle Database 10g requires some background in the Oracle 10g Manageability Infrastructure. The Manageability Infrastructure is a collection of database features to realize self-tuning and self-management functionality directly within the Oracle database itself. A performance tool, such as EM, that can leverage these features has significant advantages for managing an Oracle Database 10g RAC environment.

The primary aspect of the Manageability Infrastructure is the automated gathering and processing of base statistics related to database operations, with a key enabling feature of the Manageability Infrastructure being the new background process within the Oracle Database 10g called the Manageability Monitor (MMON). This process performs most of the manageability-related tasks on the database, central to which is the capturing and storing of database statistics. The MMON process captures base statistics every 60 seconds and accesses the SGA directly, thus working efficiently with minimal overhead. Many of the statistics collected will be familiar to users of STATSPACK in previous versions of Oracle; however, there is also a set of time-based statistics termed the Time Model relating to where the database is spending the most time. These statistics are compiled and initially stored in memory to be accessed by dynamic performance views and subsequently flushed to disk in the form of snapshots. Both the in-memory and on-disk collections of statistics are referred to as the AWR, often termed the data warehouse, of the database. A number of performance views with the prefix DBA_HIST_ can be used to access the data; DBA_HIST_SNAPSHOT, for example, shows information regarding all of the snapshots that have been taken.

The MMON process is also assisted by the Manageability Monitor Light (MMNL) process, primarily for performing tasks related to the Active Session History (ASH). The ASH contains session statistics sampled at one-second intervals to record what the sessions are waiting for. The information is stored in memory, where it can be accessed in the view V$ACTIVE_SESSON_HISTORY. The in-memory view is realized as a rolling buffer, and older information is overwritten as newer information is added. Therefore, new information is also written to disk by the MMNL process every 30 minutes. By default, seven days' ASH information is retained on disk and can be seen in the view DBA_HIST_ACTIVE_SESS_HISTORY.

The MMON process also computes and stores metric values based on the statistics themselves, and these can be seen directly in the views V$SYSMETRIC and V$SERVICEMETRIC. For example, V$SYSMETRIC contains information such as the calculated buffer cache hit ratio and user transactions per second. Among the significant uses of the metrics relevant to EM are server-generated alerts, whereby the MMON process checks the metrics it has gathered. Most of these are checked against preconfigured thresholds to determine whether an alert should be raised at a warning or critical level. The alerting system is managed within the target database by the DBMS_SERVER_ALERT package.

When an alert is generated, it is placed on the ALERT_QUE, based on Oracle's AQ infrastructure. The ALERT_QUE, however, is a special, automatically configured queue owned by the SYS user that does not require setting the AQ_TM_PROCESSES parameter to function correctly. If for any reason an alert cannot be added to the queue, a message indicating an inability to raise the alert is written to the database alert log. The unresolved alerts on this queue can be viewed in the DBA_OUTSTANDING_ALERTS view, which includes a suggested action to resolve the condition. Alerts with threshold values are termed *stateful alerts*—if the issue causing the alert is resolved the alert is automatically cleared. An example of a stateful alert is the number of user commits per second. Cleared alerts can be viewed in the DBA_ALERT_HISTORY view. Nonstateful alerts are raised in response to specific database events that occur, such as "snapshot too old"; these alerts are written directly to the DBA_ALERT_HISTORY view.

In an Oracle 10.2 RAC environment with Grid Control, you may find that server-generated alerts on database-related targets, as opposed to instance-level targets, are not initially reported correctly. This incorrect reporting can be rectified simply by saving the configuration for the RAC database at the Grid Control console and restarting the cluster.

Another feature of the Manageability Infrastructure that can be utilized from EM is the Advisory Framework, a number of components providing performance and tuning and advice. At the top level is the ADDM, which will analyze your workload, identify any potential issues, and recommend resolutions to implement for them. As part of its analysis, ADDM may recommend calling other advisories that can also be accessed individually from within the EM interface, such as the SQLTuning Advisor, the SQLAccess Advisor, and the SGA Advisor. Much of the ADDM analysis is based on the new Time Model statistics collected in the AWR, and you can observe these in the views V$SESS_TIME_MODEL and V$SYS_TIME_MODEL, for session and system statistics respectively.

The final component of the Manageability Infrastructure that can be accessed from the EM console is the automation of database tasks based on the DBMS_SCHEDULER package. DBMS_SCHEDULER enables a fine granularity of control over when and how these tasks are run, meaning that the functionality required from EM for creating and managing database-related jobs is simply the configuration of these scheduler tasks.

From this overview of the Manageability Infrastructure, you can see that, within an Oracle Database 10g environment, all of the information required for monitoring and generating alerts, performance tuning, and manageability has already been incorporated directly into the database itself. By accessing the SGA on all of the nodes directly, you minimize the overhead of running external scripts against the database. In a RAC environment, using Manageability Infrastructure components reduces the monitoring overhead across the entire cluster. All of your performance information is also inherently RAC-aware. EM Grid Control does still retain a number of Perl scripts for information gathering; however, with the Oracle Database 10g, these scripts are for collecting nondatabase information, such as host metrics. Any database-related scripts are for maintaining backward compatibility with Oracle versions 8i and 9i and for monitoring external connectivity type events.

When managing a RAC environment, the advantages of using EM 10g are apparent; therefore, we will look at the options available for installing and configuring your Database Control and Grid Control environments.

Database Control

Database Control is supplied and installed with the Oracle Database software, so by definition, it is supported at the same version.

If you are creating a new Oracle 10.1 (or above) database and wish to use Database Control, then we recommend that you install and configure it using DBCA. Provided that no Grid Control Management Agent is previously installed, DBCA will automatically install, configure, and start all of the components you require, including a Management Repository schema owned by the user SYSMAN within the SYSAUX tablespace of the target database, a local Management Service (including an HTTP server), and Management Agents on all nodes. You can ensure that you configure Database Control by explicitly selecting Use Database Control for Database Management within the DBCA on the Management Options page as discussed in Chapter 13. You can then run EM for the RAC database in a browser using the URL returned by DBCA at the end of the database creation procedure.

EM Database Control uses the EM Agents installed on the nodes and associated Management Services to communicate with the database, instances, and other processes. You can check if these are currently running using the following command:

```
$ emctl status dbconsole
```

If the Management Agent is running, this command will return output similar to the following:

```
Oracle Enterprise Manager 10g Database Control Release 10.2.0.1.0
Copyright (c) 1996, 2005 Oracle Corporation. All rights reserved.
http://london1:1158/em/console/aboutApplication
Oracle Enterprise Manager 10g is running.
------------------------------------------------------------------
Logs are generated in directory /u01/app/oracle/product/10.2.0/db_1/london1_RAC1/➥
sysman/log
```

If the Management Agent is not running, then you can start it using

```
$ emctl start dbconsole
```

The Management Agent can be stopped again using

```
$ emctl stop dbconsole
```

By default, DBCA configures Database Control on each node in the cluster, but after installation, the Database Control Console is only started on the node where you ran DBCA. On the remaining nodes, only the Management Agent component is started, and these nodes upload their data to the Database Control Console node.

If you are upgrading an existing Oracle database, have created a database without the use of DBCA, or wish to reconfigure your Database Control, you can do so using the emca utility.

A wide range of configuration options can be performed with emca, and the most straightforward method to install Database Control is to call the command emca, specifying -config dbcontrol db, while also ensuring that you use the -cluster argument.

In common with the way that Database Control is configured with DBCA, you will be running the Database Control Console on the node where you ran emca only. Subsequently calling emctl start dbconsole and emctl stop dbconsole will start and stop the Management Service on this node only. The same commands will start and stop the Management Agent only on the remaining nodes in the cluster.

If the Database Control Console could run on only one node, it would clearly not be a high-availability configuration. Therefore, you can reconfigure the Console to start on a different node, or on more than one if you desire, using the command emca -reconfig dbcontrol -cluster. By default, running this command without additional arguments starts the Console on the node that you ran the command from and directs the Management Agents on all other nodes in the cluster to upload their data to this Console. For further customization, you can directly provide the arguments EM_NODE and EM_SID_LIST to start the Console on the list of nodes specified and instruct the Management Agents listed to upload data to these nodes. You can view the configuration at any time using emca -displayConfig dbcontrol -cluster.

Finally, if you have also added a new node to the cluster, you may use the command emca -addInst db to add it to the database configuration and emca -deleteInst db to remove it, remembering to run the command to remove the instance from a different node in the cluster.

Grid Control

Grid Control is based on a three-tier application environment with three main components: a single Management Repository, one or more Management Services, and a number of Management Agents. In addition, there is the Grid Control console, through which the DBA can access the user interface. Because of the additional complexity of the three-tier configuration, we recommend that you invest additional time in planning and preparation before installing the Grid Control software.

Planning

Before installing and configuring Oracle EM 10*g* Grid Control, we recommend that you consider your planning options to achieve the optimal EM environment. To assist with the planning phase, we will explain the roles of the components that compose the Grid Control architecture and how the Grid Control architecture should be structured to meet your requirements.

Management Service

The Management Service is a J2EE web application installed on the Oracle Application Server. The Management Service communicates with the Management Agents to send and retrieve information, the Management Repository to store information, and the Grid Control Console user interface to render the HTML pages to display. You can configure multiple Management Services within the enterprise, all of which can share a single Management Repository. Detailed configuration of the Management Service is governed by the emoms.properties file in the sysman/config directory of the Management Service Home (OMS Home).

Management Repository

The Management Repository is a schema contained within an Oracle database that contains the configuration of managed targets together with the information collected about these targets. It is generally a dedicated Oracle database, which can optionally be clustered to assure availability.

The schema in question is called SYSMAN and has information stored in two tablespaces: MGMT_TABLESPACE, for storing information gathered by the Management Service, and MGMT_TABLESPACE_ECM_DEPOT_TS, for staging downloaded patch sets. The most active table in the Management Repository is the MGMT_METRICS_RAW table, where all gathered metric data is inserted. Every hour an aggregation process processes the raw data and stores the processed data in the MGMT_METRICS_1HOUR and MGMT_METRICS_1DAY tables.

Management Agent

The Management Agent runs on every managed node. It is a Java-based daemon that monitors all targets on that host and returns the information collected to the Management Service. The Management Agent also contains an HTTP listener process and receives communication from the Management Service, such as jobs to schedule and run. The configuration for the Management Agent is stored in the sysman/config directory of the Management Agent Home (AGENT_HOME) directory within the emd.properties file.

Grid Control Console

The Grid Control Console is rendered as HTML pages across the HTTP protocol; therefore, it only requires the presence of a compatible third-party web browser installed on the client machine. Note that some functionality, such as the topology, is only available with Microsoft Windows–based Internet Explorer browsers. The Management Server can be configured, so that the Grid Control Console will log out if left idle for a preconfigured time. The setting, which is 45 minutes by default, ensures that idle Grid Control sessions are terminated, for both security purposes and resource utilization on the Management Server. The default time period can be modified by setting the maximum active time in the emoms.properties file of the Management Server. For example, set the value to 15 minutes as follows:

```
oracle.sysman.eml.maxInactiveTime=15
```

Communication

Two-way communication is configured between the core components of the Grid Control infrastructure, with the Management Agents both sending and receiving information from the Management Service, and the Management Service sending and receiving information from the Management Repository. The Management Service also logs directly into the managed target hosts and databases for administrative and performance monitoring purposes.

When collecting information from a managed target, the Management Agent collects it directly from the Manageability Infrastructure features and may also action a number of Perl scripts for data gathering. The assembled information is staged in a number of XML files on the target host in the sysman/end/upload directory of the Management Agent Home. At regular intervals, the XML files containing standard metric information are uploaded to the Management Server using the HTTP protocol, directly bypassing the Web Cache on the Management Server. The upload of the XML files is designed to tolerate network outages, and the Management Agent retains the XML files to retry failed transfers until confirmation is given that they have been received, whereupon they are deleted. The connection is not persistent and occurs as and when data is pending transfer, although an upload can be initiated manually from the target host using the emctl upload command. If an alert is detected, however, this information is communicated immediately.

The XML files sent from the Management Agent are temporarily stored in the sysman/recv directory on the Management Server and deleted from the target host. The Management Service parses the XML files and inserts the row data into the database. It maintains a number of threads as persistent connections to the Management Repository using the JDBC protocol. Only after the row data has been committed into the Management Repository and read by the Management Service will the metric and alert information be available to view from the Grid Control Console and the corresponding XML file on the Management Service be deleted. Therefore, one of the most important performance aspects of the Management Repository is the loader backlog, viewed as the total runtime utilization of the thread in the previous hour.

If the backlog increases, the response time for receiving metrics and alerts will be delayed. You can tune the loader capacity by increasing the number of XML loader threads on the Management Server with the em.loader.threadPoolSize parameter of the emoms.properties file in the sysman/config directory of the Management Server home directory. The default number of loader threads is 1, and it can be increased up to 10. The value set should not exceed the number of threads that the CPUs on both the Management and Repository Servers can service at any one time.

You will find that the heading of the XML file identifies the SQL statement into which the data will be inserted. For example,

```
<ROWSET OMS_PROTOCOL_VERSION="10.2.0.0.0" TABLE="MGMT_METRICS_RAW">
```

shows that the data will be inserted into the MGMT_METRICS_RAW table. The loader activity is primarily occupied with inserting metric data. The following extract of a single row from an XML file illustrates metric data to be inserted into the Management Repository:

```
<ROW>
  <TARGET_GUID>7C7C8847BC6CE11CDB80B23FA0EBD5C0</TARGET_GUID>
  <METRIC_GUID>D673D3B2B16DE7F19CCC750C8667FABF</METRIC_GUID>
  <KEY_VALUE />
  <COLLECTION_TIMESTAMP>2005-11-12 12:29:16</COLLECTION_TIMESTAMP>
  <VALUE>66.3521289825439</VALUE>
  </ROW>
<ROW>
```

The row is inserted into the Management Repository with the following SQL statement, where the values are set to the corresponding bind variables:

```
INSERT INTO MGMT_METRICS_RAW(COLLECTION_TIMESTAMP, KEY_VALUE, METRIC_GUID, ➥
STRING_VALUE, TARGET_GUID, VALUE) VALUES ( :1, NVL(:2,' ' ), :3, :4, :5, :6)
```

For an XML file generated by an event or alert, the heading will resemble the following:

```
<ROWSET OMS_PROTOCOL_VERSION="10.2.0.0.0" TABLE=" MGMT_SEVERITY">
```

showing that the data is to be inserted into the MGMT_SEVERITY table. The XML file may contain more than one event or alert, and the row extracted in the following code illustrates a single alert raised on a database waiting an undue amount of time on a high level of transactional activity:

```
<ROW>
  <TARGET_GUID>7C7C8847BC6CE11CDB80B23FA0EBD5C0</TARGET_GUID>
  <METRIC_GUID>C733EA1CFA96377F492528E305462C9D</METRIC_GUID>
  <KEY_VALUE>Commit</KEY_VALUE>
  <COLLECTION_TIMESTAMP>2005-11-12 12:43:55</COLLECTION_TIMESTAMP>
  <SEVERITY_CODE>20</SEVERITY_CODE>
  <MESSAGE>Metrics "Database Time Spent Waiting (%)" is at 75.33789➥
For event class "Commit"</MESSAGE>
  <MESSAGE_NLSID>3503</MESSAGE_NLSID>
  <MESSAGE_PARAMS>
  <![CDATA[ Database Time Spent Waiting (%25)&75.33789&Commit ]]>
  </MESSAGE_PARAMS>
<ACTION_MESSAGE>Run ADDM to get more performance analysis about your system➥
</ACTION_MESSAGE>
  <ACTION_NLSID>3504</ACTION_NLSID>
  <ADVISORY_ID>ADDM</ADVISORY_ID>
  </ROW>
```

The row is inserted into the Management Repository by the Management Service with the following SQL statement; the data from the row once more relates to the bind variables in the statement:

```
INSERT INTO MGMT_SEVERITY(ACTION_MESSAGE, ACTION_NLSID, ADVISORY_ID,
COLLECTION_TIMESTAMP, KEY_VALUE, MESSAGE, MESSAGE_NLSID,
MESSAGE_PARAMS, METRIC_GUID, SEVERITY_CODE, TARGET_GUID) VALUES ( :1, :2, :3,
:4, NVL(:5, ' '), :6, :7, :8, :9, :10, :11)
```

Remember that communication is not a one-way process, and the Management Service also retrieves data from the Management Repository through the persistent JDBC connections for displaying to the Grid Control Console.

Architecture and Design

When installing the Grid Control Management Service, you are presented with a number of configuration options. First, you may install EM 10*g* Grid Control using a new or existing database. You also have the option to install one or more Additional Management Services. The configuration you choose depends on the degree of mission criticality of the EM infrastructure you require.

Your most basic installation choice is the EM 10*g* Grid Control Using a New Database installation, which requires that you have a single server for Grid Control. The installation process will create three Oracle Home directories: one for the Management Service, one for the Management Repository, and one for the Management Agent, which monitors both the Management Service and Repository. The single-instance Management Repository database is created by a call to DBCA during the installation process and does not support the creation of RAC Management Repository configurations. This form of architecture is constrained in terms of scalability and high availability. In particular, if you wish to create an Additional Management Service at some point in the future, you will be starting with an imbalanced configuration.

For a more flexible approach, the EM 10*g* Grid Control Using an Existing Database option installs the Management Service and Management Agent Homes and creates the Management Repository schema within an Oracle database that you have already installed and configured. You can locate the Management Repository in a RAC cluster for high availability.

With an existing database configuration, you also have the option to add Additional Management Services at some point in the future in a balanced manner. These Additional Management Services will connect to the same Management Repository that you have already configured to utilize the same schema. However, note if you do this that although you will have configured the Management Service for some degree of high availability, the Management Agents on the target servers must be configured to connect to an individual Management Service only. Similarly, you must direct your Grid Control console to a specific URL of a Management Server. With this architecture, your Management Agents will be divided equally between Management Servers, but in the event of the failure of one of the Management Servers, there will be no attempt by its associated Agents to connect to the surviving Management Service, unless they are reconfigured and restarted.

To implement a genuine highly available architecture requires the addition of dedicated network load-balancing hardware to provide a layer between the Management Service and the Agents and Console connections. The load-balancing hardware presents a virtual IP address and hostname that distribute the connections across the Management Servers. If adopting this approach, you need to configure the network load-balancing layer before installing Grid Control, in order to use the virtual IP address during the installation process. In addition, the ServerName parameter of the Apache/Apache/conf/httpd.conf file should be modified to present the name and IP address of the load-balanced service back to connections of the Grid Control Console.

In the event of the failure of a Management Server, existing connections to that server would be lost; however, subsequent reconnection, either from the Grid Control Console or the Management Agent for uploads to the virtual hostname, would be directed to the surviving Management Server, ensuring high availability of the entire service.

When implementing load balancing, be aware that the Management Repository is sensitive to having data loaded in chronological order. For example, if a Management Agent uploads data to one Management Service, and that Management Server fails to load the data into the Management Repository, the Management Agent could then connect to an alternative Management Service that succeeds in uploading more recent data points. In this eventuality, when the original Management Service restarts, the earlier data points it holds will be discarded. Missing data may also result in a Management Agent requiring to be manually resynchronized by deleting any XML files pending upload and clearing the status. Failure to do so may result in the affected Management Agent remaining stalled.

To prevent errors occurring because of the order that data is received from multiple Management Services, Grid Control 10.2 has a feature called the Shared Filesystem Loader. In this configuration, the receive directory for all Management Services resides on an NFS-mounted file system from an Oracle-certified NAS device. If a Management Service fails, all XML files can be read from a single location without missing data points. All Management Services to use the shared directory must be made aware of its location using the following command:

```
emctl config oms loader -shared yes -dir ➥
/u01/app/oracle/OracleHomes/oms10g/sysman/recv
```

where the recv directory now resides on an NFS-mounted file system; this directory can be in any location you choose. Once all Management Services have been configured, they should be restarted to use the shared location.

If dedicated network load-balancing hardware is not available, then you can also consider configuring the Oracle Clusterware independently of RAC to protect the Grid Control Management Service in an active/passive cluster configuration. As the Grid Control Management Service runs entirely within the Oracle Application Server, the active/passive configuration can be implemented in exactly the same way as using Oracle Clusterware to protect any standard Oracle Application Server installation.

Preparation

EM is supplied separately from the Oracle database software. It can be downloaded from the Oracle Technology Network (OTN) web site or supplied on an Oracle CD-ROM. The EM distribution contains a copy of the OUI, which is used to install all EM components.

The 10.2 version of EM is supported on SUSE Linux Enterprise Server 9.0, Red Hat Enterprise Linux 3.0, and Red Hat Enterprise Linux 4.0. As with the Oracle Database 10*g*, we recommend installing Grid Control on a Linux 2.6 kernel–based release of either SUSE Linux Enterprise Server 9.0 or Red Hat Enterprise Linux 4.0. If you are using Red Hat Enterprise Linux 3.0, you may need to perform additional preparation tasks, which include ensuring that version 2.96 of the GNU C and C++ compilers are installed and ensuring that Metalink patch 3006854 for the operating system is downloaded and installed. Whichever operating system you choose, it should be installed and configured in the same way required for an Oracle database installation for both the Management Servers and Repository database servers, as discussed in Chapters 10 and 11. For targets of Management Agent installations, which include the Management Servers themselves, you should ensure that the sysstat RPM package is installed to provide operating system performance monitoring tools. If installing the Management Repository database on a RAC installation, you should pay particular attention to ensuring that the NTP settings are correct on all nodes in the cluster. If time settings are incorrect on the Management Repository, errors may occur on the Management Service, resulting in it automatically restarting. However, on the Management Server, you will not be required to configure shared storage or NIC bonding. We recommend configuring the secure shell environment on the Management Servers if you plan to use the mass deployment method of Management Agent installation.

We also recommend using the Oracle 10.2 Management Service, as the 10.1 Management Service does not support the monitoring of a 10.2-based Oracle RAC database.

Before installing EM components, ensure that you have set only the ORACLE_BASE environment variable. Specifically, ensure that ORACLE_SID, ORACLE_HOME, and ORA_NLS10 are not set. If the ORA_NLS10 parameter in particular is set, the opmn service will fail to start during installation, causing a globalInitNLS error resulting in an unsuccessful install.

If you choose to download EM, you will need to unzip the installation files into a staging directory, as described with the Oracle Clusterware and database software in Chapter 12. The OUI runInstaller command is unzipped in the top-level directory.

Before you run the Management Service installation, we recommend that you run the OUI in prerequisite checking mode to ensure that you have configured your Linux operating system correctly. You can do this by changing to the install directory and running the runInstaller executable directly. In some versions, if you run the top-level runInstaller script for the prerequisite checks, it will fail when attempting to pass the deprecated -nowelcome argument. By calling the OUI with arguments such as the following, you can run the prerequisite checks at the command line:

```
./runInstaller
-prereqchecker PREREQ_CONFIG_LOCATION=../rdbms/Disk1/stage/prereq
-entrypoint oracle.sysman.top.oms_Core
-prereqLogLoc /tmp/prereqLogLoc
-silent -waitforcompletion
```

This example runs the prerequisite checks for installing EM Using an Existing Database. To run the checks for an installation using a new database or a Management Agent, change the -entrypoint argument to either oracle.sysman.top.em_seed or oracle.sysman.top.agent, respectively.

If you have installed and configured Linux according to Chapters 10 and 11, the prerequisite checker should report that the system is configured correctly, and you can proceed to installing the Grid Control software.

Management Service Installation and Configuration

EM Grid Control is supplied with a database, and you have the option of using this database to store the Management Repository. Alternatively, you can store the Management Repository in an existing database, which you will need to do if you wish to store the Management Repository in a RAC database.

If you have a sufficiently large Oracle estate to justify using Grid Control, we strongly recommend that you consider locating your Management Repository in a RAC database, as the loss of availability of the Management Repository database will result in the loss of the availability of the entire Grid Control environment.

Even when installing 10.2 Grid Control, the supported database versions for an existing 10*g* database, including RAC, are Oracle 10.1.0.3 and above (and not 10.2). If you have used DBCA to create the database and have installed Database Control, the Management Repository schema will already exist, so it will be necessary to drop the SYSMAN schema and reinstall it. The SYSMAN schema can be reinstalled using the sysman/admin/emdrep/bin/RepManager utility, which can be found in the OMS Home directory. If the schema exists during installation, the installer will also call this utility to drop it first, if you wish. Alternatively, running the following commands manually will also sufficiently remove the schema and associated objects for the Management Repository schema to be reinstalled:

```
drop user SYSMAN cascade;
drop public synonym MGMT_TARGET_BLACKOUTS;
drop public synonym SETEMVIEWUSERCONTEXT;
drop role MGMT_USER;
drop user MGMT_VIEW cascade;
```

Also with a DBCA-created database, before installation, you need to run the DBMS_SHARED_POOL package as the SYS user:

```
SQL> @?/rdbms/admin/dbmspool.sql
Package created.
Grant succeeded.
View created.
Package body created.
SQL> @?/rdbms/admin/prvtpool.plb
View created.
Package body created.
```

A small number of initialization parameters are required for a successful Management Repository schema creation. The SGA_TARGET parameter should be set to a minimum value of 512M, and the PGA_AGGREGATE_TARGET parameter to a minimum of 256M. These values will require adjusting upward according to the number of managed targets in the Grid Control environment. In addition, the SESSION_CACHED_CURSORS parameter must be set to 200 or more, the OPEN_CURSORS parameter to 300 or more, and the JOB_QUEUE processes parameter to 10. You also need to set the AQ_TM_PROCESSES parameter, because if it is not set, the installer will display a warning and terminate. However, once operational, this parameter is not required.

To begin the Management Service install session, run the OUI from the installation media with the runInstaller command. The installer will check the operating system, glibc versions, and the available swap space, and the Specify Installation Type page (Figure 14-1) will be displayed.

If you have already installed and configured your Management Repository database, select Enterprise Manager 10*g* Grid Control Using an Existing Database. Alternatively, if you have decided to create one during the installation process, select Enterprise Manager 10*g* Grid Control Using a New Database, and click Next to continue to the Specify Installation Location page (Figure 14-2).

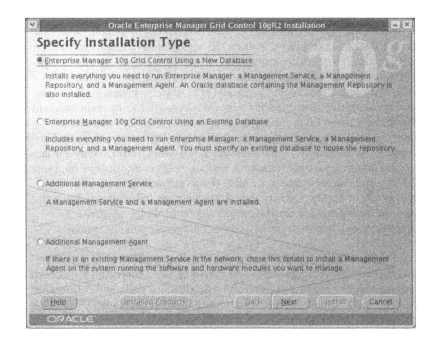

Figure 14-1. *The Specify Installation Type page*

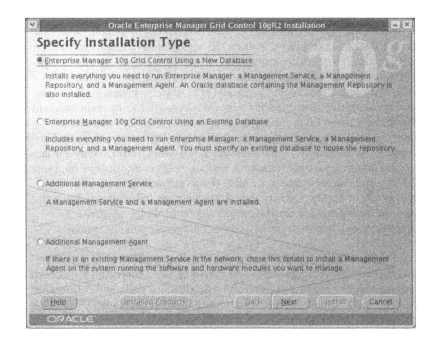

Figure 14-2. *The Specify Installation Location page*

The Specify Installation Location page requires the entry of the directory on the management server, your predefined ORACLE_BASE directory with subdirectory OracleHomes by default. Below this directory lie the product-specific Oracle home directories, such as oms10g for the Management Service. This Oracle Home naming approach marks a departure from 10.1 Grid Control, where the Management Service's ORACLE_HOME and AGENT_HOME were installed in separate locations. The use of the top-level OracleHomes directory makes for a more integrated Grid Control installation that is less prone to errors, for example, an Oracle Home directory being overwritten or incorrect environment variables referring to the wrong location when starting the Grid Control software components.

Click Next to continue. Depending on the languages installed on the operating system, the Language Selection page may be displayed to select the language to run Grid Control. If only one is language installed, or if other languages are not supported, this page will not be displayed, and you may receive a warning dialog. If, as we recommend, no other Oracle software has previously been installed on the host, the Specify Inventory directory and credentials page will be shown. The path of the inventory directory will be displayed as the oraInventory directory under the ORACLE_BASE location. The operating system group name will be a group that the Oracle operating system is a member of, such as oinstall.

Click Next to advance to the Product-Specific Prerequisite Checks page. The checks proceed automatically and ensure that common configuration settings required for a successful install, such as kernel parameter settings, are in place before installation proceeds. Click Next again. For an Enterprise Manager Grid Control Using a New Database installation, the Specify Configuration page (Figure 14-3) will be shown.

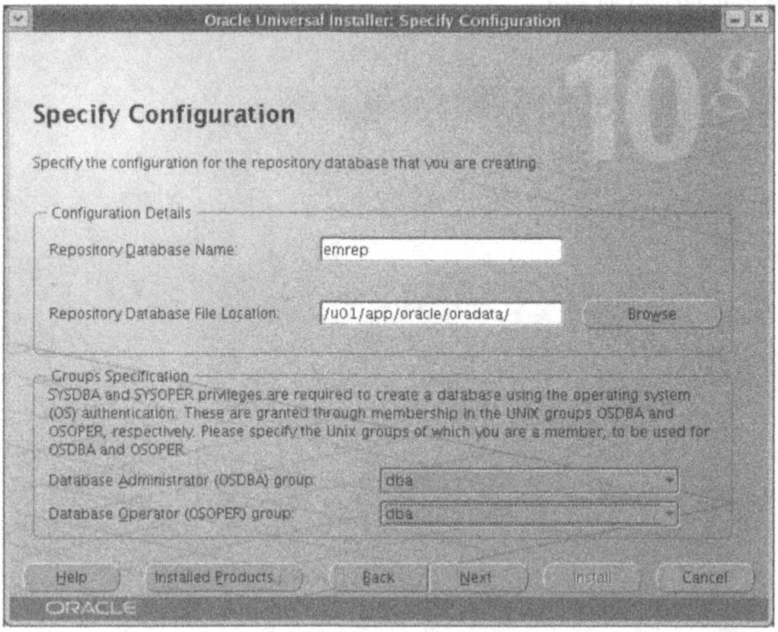

Figure 14-3. *The Specify Configuration page*

Enter the name of the database to be created and the location of the database files. With this install type, the database files must be on the same server as the Management Service installation. Select the operating system groups configured for the oracle user, which are required to specify the correct user credentials when creating the Management Repository database with operating system authentication. Ordinarily, these groups should both be set to the dba operating system group, and not to oinstall.

If Enterprise Manager Grid Control Using an Existing Database is selected, the Specify Repository Database Configuration page (Figure 14-4) will be displayed.

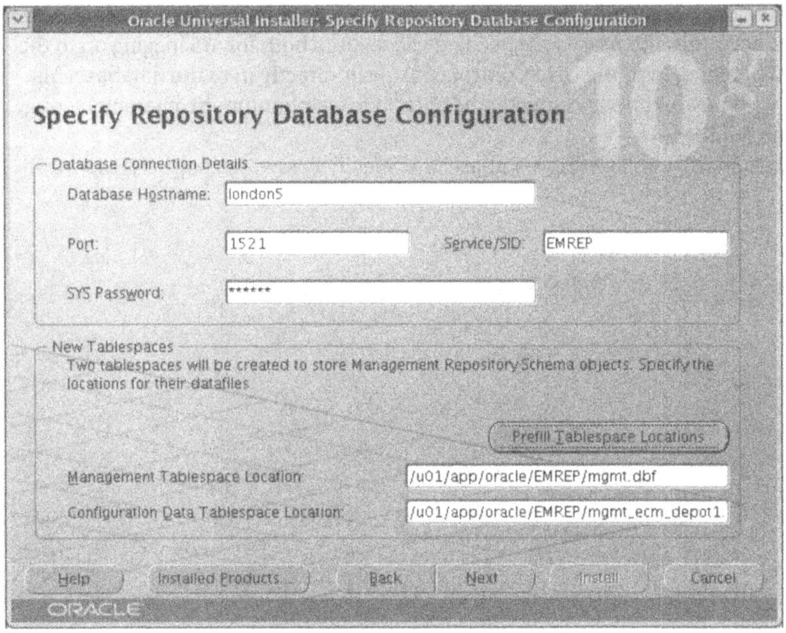

Figure 14-4. *The Specify Repository Database Configuration page*

Enter the hostname listener port, Oracle service name, and SYS user password of the preconfigured target database where the Management Repository schema will be installed. The service name may be the service name for a single instance or a RAC database. Enter the locations on the Management Repository database server where the Management Repository schema tablespaces will be created. The Prefill Tablespace Locations option queries the target databases and completes a location for the tablespaces in the same directory as the SYSAUX tablespace. The management tablespace is initially 20MB and contains the standard metric and alert information gathered by EM. The configuration data tablespace is 100MB and acts as a repository for staging downloaded patch sets to be deployed across the target Oracle install base. After installation, a threshold can be set manually, so that older patch sets will be deleted before newer ones are stored.

Click Next to continue to the Specify Optional Configuration page. On this page, you can optionally set up e-mail notifications for alerts and other messages. If you choose to use e-mail notification, verify that the node that runs the Management Service is able to send messages through any corporate firewall you may have configured. For the MetaLink and Proxy Information, you may optionally enter a MetaLink username and password in order for Grid Control to automatically search and download any new patches from MetaLink to be stored in the configuration data tablespace. If the Management

Service needs to communicate with any of the Management Agents through a firewall, then you can enter the details of the proxy server on this page. All settings can also be modified from the Grid Control console once Grid Control is operational, so the validity of the installation remains unaffected if all of the options are left unchecked at this point.

After clicking Next for an EM Grid Control Using a New Database installation, the Specify Security Options page is shown. Enter the password required for use by all Management Agents when configured to communicate securely. A password is required whether or not the Require Secure Communication for all agents check box is selected. The Management Repository database passwords are the same for a standard Oracle 10g database install and can be used to administer the database once the installation is complete.

The SYSMAN password specifies the Grid Control super administrator password, and if the same password is used for all accounts, the password specified will be used both for SYS logging on to the database and for SYSMAN logging in to the Grid Control console or directly in to the database. All passwords must start with an alphabetic character, be at least five alphanumeric characters long, and contain at least one number.

With EM Grid Control Using an Existing Database, the Specify Passwords page (Figure 14-5) is shown.

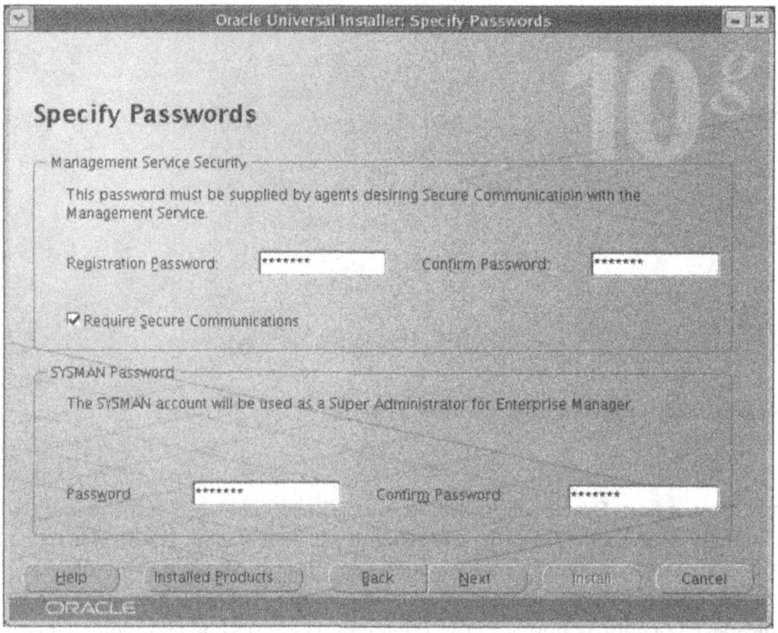

Figure 14-5. *The Specify Passwords page*

For this installation type, on the Specify Passwords page, enter the name of the secure communication password to be used by the Management Agents, and select whether secure communication is to be enabled during the installation. Enter the SYSMAN password to be used for the super administrator on the Grid Control console and Management Repository schema owner. Because the database has already been created, only the SYSMAN password is required on this page. Click Next to show the Summary page (Figure 14-6).

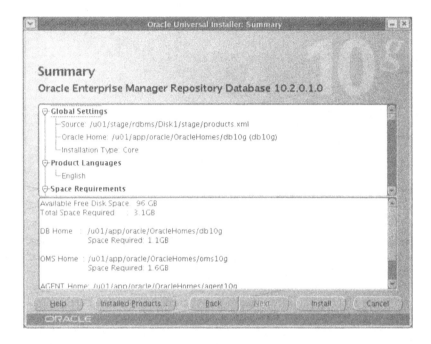

Figure 14-6. *The Summary page*

The Summary page displays the installation options selected. With an EM Grid Control Using a New Database installation, three Oracle Homes will also be created under the parent directory given at the Specify Installation location page: a DB Home for the location of the database software, an OMS Home for the Management Service, and an Agent Home for the central Management Agent to monitor the Grid Control and database software on the Management Server itself. For an EM Grid Control Using an Existing Database installation, the DB Home is not created; therefore, the total disk space required is 2.0GB, not 3.1GB. Click Install to start installation of the Management Service. The Install progress page will be displayed. You will be prompted to run the orainstRoot.sh and allroot.sh scripts for the Management Service as the root user as shown in Figure 14-7.

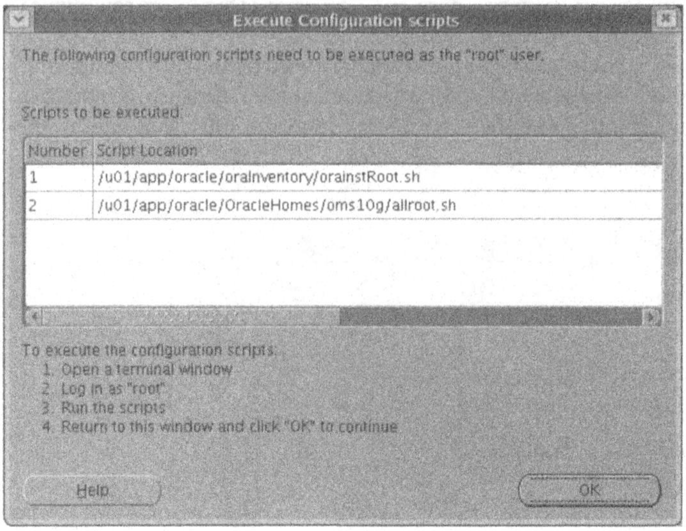

Figure 14-7. *The Execute Configuration scripts page*

Run these scripts in another terminal session. The orainstRoot.sh script sets the permissions and group name of the oraInventory directory. The allroot.sh script executes the root.sh scripts sequentially in the OMS Home, the Management Agent Home, and, if you have elected to create a new database, the DB Home. The first root.sh script to run copies dbhome, oraenv, and coraenv to your local bin directory (usually /usr/local/bin) and performs other configuration tasks requiring root privileges, such as creating the /etc/oratab file and the /etc/oracle directory. When complete, the additional root.sh scripts will be run. Some of the actions run are identical, and you will be prompted as to whether to overwrite the files that already exist in the /usr/local/bin directory. Whether overwritten or not, the files will result in the same contents. When execution of the agent10g/root.sh script is complete, click OK to continue.

When installation of the Management Service is complete, the Configuration Assistants page (Figure 14-8) will be displayed.

If you are using a new database, the configuration assistants will run DBCA to create it at this time. If you are using an existing database, the OMS Configuration stage creates the Management Repository schema in the database you have specified. The configuration assistants may take up to 30 minutes in total to run to completion. Click Next to continue to the end of Installation page; carefully note any information in the window. In particular, make sure that you have a record of the location of the URL that you need to access Grid Control in an entry such as the following:

```
Use the following URL to access the Enterprise Manager Grid Control:
http://london6:4889/em
```

The URL specifies the host, the port number, and the directory of the Grid Control URL. The hostname will be the name of your management server; em will be the name of the directory, and the port will be either 4888, for operation in an unsecured mode, or 4889, when the option for secure communication has been selected. With the information recorded, click Exit to end the installation.

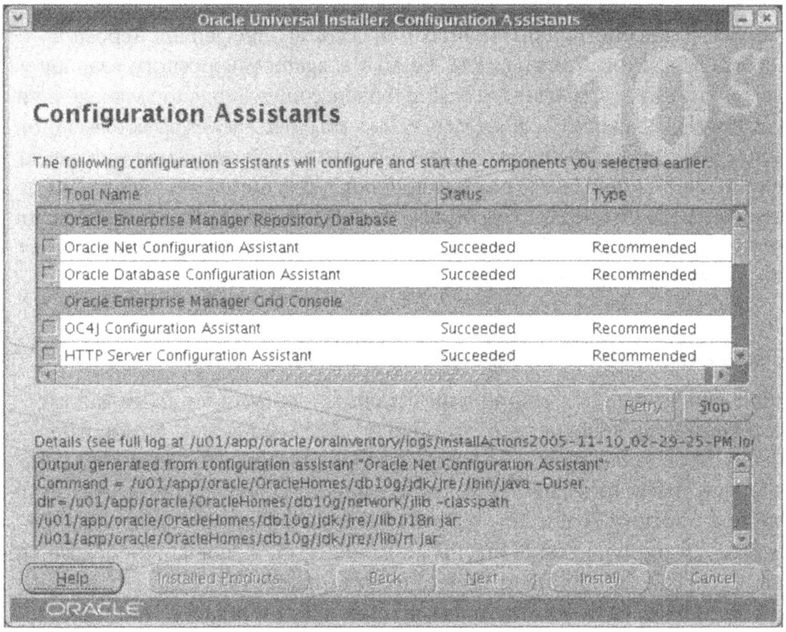

Figure 14-8. *The Configuration Assistants page*

For troubleshooting purposes, you can rerun the configuration scripts manually from the command line using the runConfig.sh command located in the /oui/bin directory of the Management Service:

```
[oracle@london6 OracleHomes]$ ./oms10g/oui/bin/runConfig.sh
ORACLE_HOME=/u01/app/oracle/OracleHomes/oms10g
ACTION=configure MODE=perform RERUN=true
```

You should be aware, however, that using this script is only supported for use in a valid installation in conjunction with a silent install that has previously been run with the -noconfig option.

The installation of another Management Service to use the same Management Repository in the Grid Control environment will proceed in a similar manner to an EM 10*g* Grid Control Using An Existing Database. On starting an install session, at the Specify Installation Type page (shown in Figure 14-1), select Additional Management Service. The most significant difference from the original Management Service installation is that the Specify Repository Database Configuration page no longer prompts for the creation of the Management Repository schema tablespaces, as the schema has already been created. Instead, this page prompts for the hostname, port, service name, and SYSMAN password of the existing Management Repository database, as well as the registration password, if secure communication has been enabled. Because the required passwords are entered on this page, the Specify Passwords page associated with the original Management Service install will also not be displayed. Otherwise, continue the installation as previously, noting that on the Specify Optional Configuration page, there is no entry for Oracle MetaLink information, as this has already been stored in the Management Repository. On completion of the installation, the Additional

Management Service will be able to view all of the information gathered and configured with the original Management Service, as the information is stored in the central Management Repository.

When installation is complete, if you are using a RAC-based Management Repository, you may need to verify the sysman/config/emoms.properties to ensure that the connection to the Management Repository database is correctly load balanced in the oracle.sysman.eml.mntr.emdRepConnectDescriptor field. Note that the presence of the backslash character, although not normally associated with a valid connect descriptor, is required in this field before equality operators. Also, the PREFER_LEAST_LOADED_NODE_LISTENER_NAME parameter in the listener.ora file on all of the nodes in the cluster should be set to the value ON, so LISTENER_NAME is then replaced with the name of the listener. For the configured connect string to take effect, restart the Management Service.

Starting and Stopping the Management Service

You will need to be familiar with starting and stopping the various components for administering the Management Service. The Management Service is configured at EM 10.2 to start or stop when the system boots up or shuts down, respectively. The Management Service locates the script gcstartup in the /etc/init.d directory, which in turn calls the script oms10g/install/unix/scripts/omsstup in the Management Server home directory. That script then calls the command opmnctl, with either the argument startall or stopall. You should ensure that the gcstartup script is added to the chkconfig configuration using the chkconfig -add command, as described in Chapter 11.

The entire Management Service can be also be manually started by running the command emctl start oms from the Management Service ORACLE_HOME directory:

```
[oracle@london6 OracleHomes]$ ./oms10g/bin/emctl start oms
Oracle Enterprise Manager 10g Release 10.2.0.1.0
Copyright (c) 1996, 2005 Oracle Corporation.  All rights reserved.
opmnctl: opmn is already running
Starting HTTP Server ...
Starting Oracle Management Server ...
Checking Oracle Management Server Status ...
Oracle Management Server is Up.
```

Similarly, the commands emctl stop oms and emctl status oms will stop the Management Service components and display whether it is currently operational. The further emctl start iasconsole command may also be used to start the Application Server Control Console to manage the Oracle Application Server directly; however, under normal circumstances, you should not be required to do so.

You may have noticed that the command to start the Management Service did some additional work before starting the Management Server itself. As we have previously seen, the Management Service is a J2EE application deployed within an instance of the Oracle Application Server. More specifically, the Management Service runs as an application in an instance of the Oracle Application Server Container for J2EE (OC4J), where the instance is named OC4J_EM. For this reason, instead of using the emctl command, it is possible to start and stop all of the components required for the Management Service with the opmnctl command for the Oracle Process Management and Notification (OPMN) utility, which is normally used to control applications deployed in the Oracle Application Server. In fact, as the output of the emctl command shows, OPMN is being invoked indirectly only to start the minimum Application Server components required by the Management Service. If you do wish to start and stop all of the components of the Oracle Application Server, you may do so with the commands opmnctl startall and opmnctl stopall, respectively. The OC4J_EM instance is included at start-up; therefore, the EM Management Service is started. The opmnctl command is located in the Management Service ORACLE_HOME opmn/bin directory.

We recommend, under normal circumstances, that you use the emctl commands only to start and stop the Management Services; reserve opmnctl for running the opmnctl status command for troubleshooting any issues that may arise with the individual application server components. The only exception to this recommendation is the optional Application Server Web Cache that may be started with the command `opmnctl startproc ias-component=WebCache` and stopped with the corresponding `startproc` command. Starting the Web Cache may potentially improve the performance and response times to the Grid Control console when accessed through the Web Cache port (usually 7777), for example, `http://london6:7777/em`.

If you have started the Web Cache, the `opmnctl status` command will return output similar to the following, showing that all components are running except for the DSA and LogLoader, which are not required for Grid Control:

```
[oracle@london6 OracleHomes]$ ./oms10g/opmn/bin/opmnctl status
Processes in Instance:
EnterpriseManager0.london6
---------------+--------------+-------+--------
ias-component  | process-type | pid   | status
---------------+--------------+-------+--------
DSA            | DSA          |  N/A  | Down
HTTP_Server    | HTTP_Server  | 31723 | Alive
LogLoader      | logloaderd   |  N/A  | Down
dcm-daemon     | dcm-daemon   | 32649 | Alive
OC4J           | home         | 31724 | Alive
OC4J           | OC4J_EM      | 31725 | Alive
OC4J           | OC4J_EMPROV  | 31726 | Alive
WebCache       | WebCache     | 31746 | Alive
WebCache       | WebCacheAdmin| 31728 | Alive
```

After starting the Management Service, you should also change the directory to the Agent Home on the Management Server and start the Management Agent that monitors the Management Service itself. We will discuss starting and stopping the Management Agent toward the end of the following section on Management Agent installation.

Management Agent Installation

The EM Management Agent must be installed on each node that contains managed targets; therefore, in terms of RAC, each node in the cluster must run its own Management Agent. Similar to the Management Service, the Management Agent should be installed in a separate Oracle Home directory from any existing databases or Oracle Clusterware directories on the nodes. The Management Agent can be installed in a separate process on each node of the cluster individually, or it can be installed with the cluster option on more than one node at the same time.

Because Management Agents are installed in all target environments and are the most frequent Grid Control component installation, a number of methods are available to improve the deployment process. First, the Management Agent can be installed in an interactive manner with the OUI from the same software used to install the Management Service software. We will describe this form of installation later in this section. The OUI can also be run in a silent mode with a response file to automate the process. Second, there is an NFS Mounted Installation option, where the software is deployed on a certified NAS platform for mounting and installation on all hosts; however, note that this method is not supported in a RAC environment. For the third Management Agent installation method, the `agentDownload` script can be run on the target node to retrieve the installation files from a central location, and finally, the `AgentDeploy` application can be run centrally to install the Management Agent on a number of targets.

For all Management Agent installation methods with 10*g* RAC, installations are supported on Oracle Clusterware only. The Management Agent cannot be installed on an OCFS file system, but it can be installed on a local file system or an NFS file system mounted from a NAS-certified storage vendor; this should not be confused with the NFS Mounted Installation option. It is permissible to install the Management Agent for each node on an NFS file system; it is not permissible to use the NFS to deploy the installation.

To perform an interactive installation, from the same software used to install the Management Service software, start an install session of the OUI with the /runInstaller command. The OUI automatically detects that a clustered installation is to be performed and configures the cluster name in the targets.xml file with the name of the cluster used when the Clusterware was installed. You can set the cluster name to a different value in the targets.xml file by setting the CLUSTER_NAME environment variable to the chosen value before running the installer.

When the installer starts the Specify Installation Type page is shown. Select the Additional Management Agent option and click Next to continue to the Specify Installation Location page. Although only the AGENT_HOME will be installed during this session, you still need to specify the parent-level directory, which defaults to OracleHomes, under which the agent10g directory will be installed. Click Next to display the Specify Hardware Cluster Installation Mode page. It is possible to install the Enterprise Manager Agent on more than one node in the same operation. On the Cluster Installation Mode page, check the nodes where you wish to install the Enterprise Manager Agent, or click the Select All button to install on all nodes. Click Next to display the Product-Specific Prerequisite Checks page, and when the checks are complete, click Next to proceed to the Specify Oracle Management Service Location page (Figure 14-9).

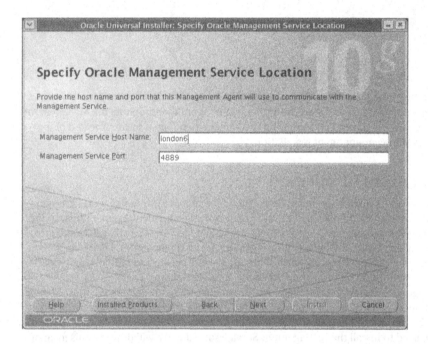

Figure 14-9. *The Specify Oracle Management Service Location page*

On the Specify Oracle Management Service Location page, enter the name of the host and port recorded from the End of Installation page for the Management Service installation and click Next to display the Specify Agent Registration Password page (Figure 14-10).

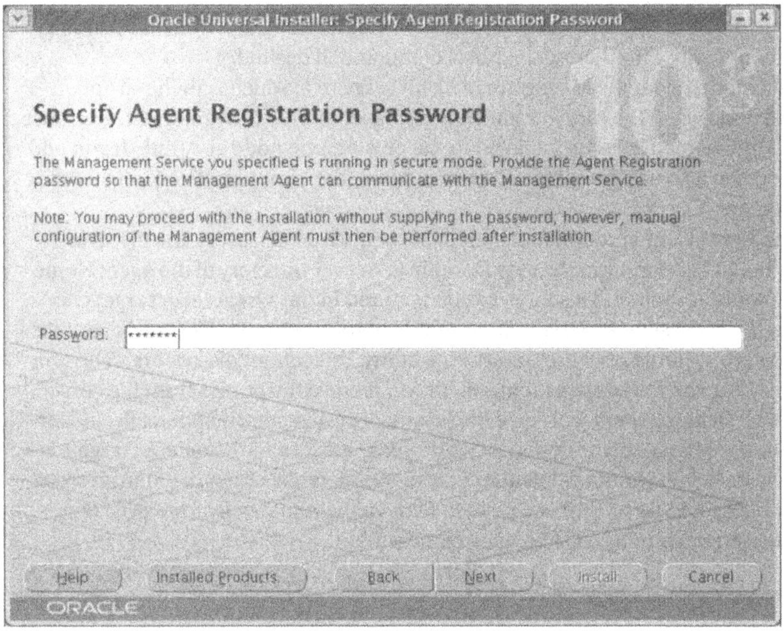

Figure 14-10. *The Specify Agent Registration Password page*

If the Management Service has been installed or subsequently configured to operate in a secure mode, you need to enter the registration password chosen during the Management Service installation. Click Next to display the Summary page, and click Install to begin the installation. The installation will proceed and prompt for the root.sh script to be run as the root user in the AGENT_HOME location in the Execute Configuration Scripts page. The root.sh script performs the same actions as when called by the allroot.sh script during the Management Service installation. The only difference is that, because only one Oracle Home is being installed, the single the root.sh script can be run directly. Click OK to continue, and when installation of the Management Agent is complete, the Configuration Assistants page is shown and the Agent Configuration Assistant is run. When the installation is complete, the End of Installation page is shown, and you can click Exit to end the session.

The Agent Configuration Assistant starts the Management Agent as part of the installation process, and by default, the Management Agent is restarted when the server reboots. Like the Management Server, the start-up action is referenced from the script gcstartup in the /etc/init.d directory to call the script agent10g/install/unix/scripts/agentstup in the AGENT_HOME directory. Also in common with the Management Service, the Management Agent is manually controlled using the emctl command, can be started with emctl start agent, and can be stopped with emctl stop agent called from the Agent Home directory. These commands are indirectly called by gcstartup to control the Management Agent.

Once the Management Agent is operational, the emwd.pl watchdog script also runs as a daemon and ensures that if for any reason the Management Agent fails, it will be restarted. If the Management Agent is up but unable to communicate with the Management Service, it can also be configured to send an e-mail notification directly.

The emctl status agent command is especially useful in returning details regarding the current operation of a particular Management Agent, especially whether there are XML files pending upload that can be sent manually with the emctl upload command, if desired.

Another important command for the Management Agent is agentca, which with the -d option can run rediscovery on a node when the configuration has changed. In a RAC environment, you must run rediscovery on all Management Agents installed in the cluster, one node at a time. If you add a node to the cluster, you can also use the agentca command with the -f option to reconfigure the existing Management Agents.

Whether run by the Agent Configuration Assistant or subsequent rediscovery, the discovery process executes a number of Perl scripts in the sysman/admin/discover directory of the Agent Home to gather information about the system. This information is stored in the sysman/emd/targets.xml file, which is reported to the Management Service. You should not manually edit the targets.xml file. If you wish to add targets, you should only use the agentca utility. You cannot discover targets from the Grid Control console, but you may delete them, which will remove the entries from the corresponding targets.xml file. Deleting them will also remove any historical information collected for the deleted targets from the Management Repository, although a record of the deleted targets is retained. If you remove a host, you should delete the corresponding targets from the Management Agent beforehand. If you forget to do so, you will need to remove them manually from SQL*Plus, logged on as the SYSMAN user, by running the following command:

```
SQL>exec mgmt_admin.cleanup_agent ('host_to_remove port');
```

Summary

In this chapter, we provided an introduction to Oracle Enterprise Manager (EM) and discussed the installation and configuration of Database Control and Grid Control in a RAC environment. EM has a wide range of features to explore for administering your RAC environment, and in Chapter 18, we will give an introduction to navigating the Grid Control Console interface.

CHAPTER 15
■ ■ ■

Linux Administration

In this chapter, we will discuss Linux administration. In Chapter 11, we introduced topics essential to configuring Linux in preparation for installing the Oracle RAC software. In this chapter, we introduce additional useful concepts and commands for ongoing operating system administration that will assist in the day-to-day management of the cluster. The topics covered in this chapter include run levels, services, terminal sessions, manual pages, the bash shell, packages, kernel parameters, swap space, file systems, the process information pseudofile system, booting the system, log files, tracing, and debugging.

Providing an exhaustive list of all Linux commands and features is beyond the scope of this chapter, so we have assumed a basic level of familiarity with Unix commands while focusing on the areas that may arise when managing a RAC environment.

Run Levels

As with most Unix-based operating systems, Linux has seven run levels as described in Table 15-1.

Table 15-1. *System Run Levels*

Run Level	Function
0	System halt
1	Single-user mode (also run level S)
2	Multiuser mode without network functionality
3	Multiuser mode with network functionality
4	Not used
5	Multiuser mode with network functionality and the X Window display manager (xdm)
6	System reboot

Database servers generally run at level 3, if they use the text mode interface, or level 5, if they are using X Window. Occasionally, for administration, using level 1 or the more restrictive level S (single-user mode) is desirable. In practice, however, switching to administrative mode is rarely necessary on a database server, as users can no longer gain access once the instance has been shut down. Levels 2 and 4 are not usually required for Oracle database servers.

The run level can be changed using the init command:

```
[root@london1 root]# init <runlevel>
```

For example, to change to level 3, which is the level at which servers running Oracle databases normally operate, you would use the following command:

```
[root@london1 root]# init 3
```

The init command has a handful of special levels. To shut down the operating system and power off the server, use

```
[root@london1 root]# init 0
```

To shut down and reboot the system, use

```
[root@london1 root]# init 6
```

You can also use the reboot command to shut down and restart the operating system:

```
[root@london1 root]# reboot
```

Use the following code to go into single-user mode:

```
[root@london1 root]# init S
```

You can check the current run level using the who -r command:

```
[root@london1 root]# who -r
         run-level 3 Sep 13 19:41            last=S
```

The preceding result indicates that the system has just been booted from single-user mode to run level 3. You can also use the runlevel command to obtain similar information, including the previous and current run levels. In the following example, the system has just been booted to run level 3:

```
[root@london1 root]# runlevel
N 3
```

When the Linux operating system starts, it creates a process with the ID 1, which runs the init program. This process is the parent of all other processes on the system. These other processes can, in turn, start further processes, resulting in a hierarchy with init at the top. The hierarchy can be viewed with the command pstree. The additional processes that init starts are configurable and are specified in the file /etc/inittab. The contents of /etc/inittab vary between Red Hat and SUSE Enterprise systems; however, the role is the same. In terms of running Oracle, we are particularly interested in the one line of /etc/inittab that sets the default run level; the line will appear after a standard installation as the following entry:

```
id:3:initdefault:
```

In the preceding example, the default run level is 3, which will start a text mode session when the system is rebooted. If you wish to start a graphical mode session when the system is rebooted, change this line to

```
id:5:initdefault:
```

Misconfiguring or corrupting /etc/inittab could result in the system being unable to boot; therefore, exercise caution when modifying this file. The entry within /etc/inittab to define the run level can be one of the seven values defined in Table 15-1.

Services

In Linux, operating system background processes are called *services*. These should not be confused with database services, which are an Oracle-specific concept. A Linux service can consist of one or more daemon processes. When the system is started, Linux services are started by the init process, depending on the contents of an initialization script known as a *service definition file*.

In most versions of Unix, the implementation of service definition files is port specific. In Linux, service definition files are located in the /etc/init.d directory, which contains one definition file for each service. For example, consider the rstatd service, which serves the operating system statistics to interested clients. The service definition file /etc/init.d/rstatd is used to start and stop this service. To start rstatd the service, use the following:

```
[root@london1 root]# service rstatd start
```

To stop the rstatd service, use

```
[root@london1 root]# service rstatd stop
```

Some services provide additional functionality. For example, you can restart the rstatd service using

```
[root@london1 root]# service rstatd restart
```

The best way to discover all available options for a particular service is to inspect its service definition.

The /etc/rc.d directory contains seven subdirectories corresponding to the seven run levels: rc0.d, rc1.d, rc2.d, rc3.d, rc4.d, rc5.d, and rc6.d. Each subdirectory contains symbolic links to the service definition file in /etc/init.d. These can be start scripts, which have an S prefix (e.g., S60rstatd), or stop (kill) scripts, which have a K prefix (e.g., K20rstatd). The number (e.g., 60 or 20) specifies the order in which the scripts will be executed when the run level is entered.

Most Linux distributions, including Red Hat Linux and SUSE, provide a utility to simplify the installation and management of services.

On Red Hat Linux, to customize the services started for run levels, select System Settings from the main system menu. Next select Server Settings and Services to display a graphical utility, where you can check a box to enable or disable a service at a particular run level for the associated service. You can use the Edit Runlevel menu to alter the services at a different run level from the one at which the system is currently operating. You can also start, stop, or restart individual services with this menu.

On SUSE systems, under YaST2, select System followed by Runlevel Editor to display the equivalent utility. Within this tool, Simple mode allows services to be enabled or disabled at the current run level. Expert mode also allows you to set the default run level, as well as modify services at different run levels and start, stop, and refresh services.

Alternatively, in all versions of Linux, you can use the chkconfig command line utility to configure services. It creates symbolic links for each run level and can be controlled either by command line arguments or by formatted comments in the service definition file.

To check the current run levels for rstatd, use

```
[root@london1 root]# chkconfig --list rstatd
```

To configure rstatd to start at run levels 3, 4, and 5, use

```
[root@london1 root]# chkconfig --level 345 rstatd on
```

to create the following links:

```
/etc/rc.d/rc3.d/S60rstatd
/etc/rc.d/rc4.d/S60rstatd
/etc/rc.d/rc5.d/S60rstatd
```

Delete existing links using the following:

```
[root@london1 root]# chkconfig --del rstatd
```

The service definition file can be edited to control chkconfig. For example, for /etc/init.d/ rstatd, the chkconfig line might contain

```
[root@london1 root]# chkconfig: 345 60 20
```

This line specifies that the service will be started for levels 3, 4, and 5; the start priority level will be 60, and the end priority level will be 20. Note that a kill script will be created for every level for which a start script has not been specified.

To add these links, use

```
[root@london1 root]# chkconfig --add rstatd
```

which, for this example, will create the following links:

```
/etc/rc.d/rc0.d/K20rstatd
/etc/rc.d/rc1.d/K20rstatd
/etc/rc.d/rc2.d/K20rstatd
/etc/rc.d/rc3.d/S60rstatd
/etc/rc.d/rc4.d/S60rstatd
/etc/rc.d/rc5.d/S60rstatd
/etc/rc.d/rc6.d/K20rstatd
```

Terminal Sessions

Once the Oracle software is installed and operational, we recommend setting a default run level of 3, so the system will start in text mode. You can alternatively set an initial run level of 5, in which case the system will start in graphical mode.

If you choose to start in text mode, you can also start an X Window graphical user interface by logging on as the root user and typing the command

```
[root@london1 root]# startx
```

By default, seven virtual sessions are available. You can switch between sessions using Ctrl+Alt+Fx, where Fx is a numbered function key between F1 and F7. The first six function keys (Ctrl+Alt+F1 to Ctrl+Alt+F6) correspond to text sessions; Ctrl+Alt+F7 switches to the graphical (X Window) session.

Manual Pages

As in other Unix ports, the Linux man command displays manual pages describing how to run all other commands. By default, the man command can be executed by any user, and its basic syntax is

```
man <command>
```

where command is the manual page that you are interested in. For example, to read the manual page for the ls command, use

```
[oracle@london1 oracle]$ man ls
```

Linux documentation is divided into the sections shown in Table 15-2.

Table 15-2. *Linux Documentation Sections*

Section	Description
1	Commands
2	System calls
3	Library calls
4	Special files
5	File formats and conversions
6	Games
7	Macro packages and conventions
8	System management commands
9	Kernel routines

There may be more than one man page for the same name. For example, section 1 includes a man page for the printf command, and section 3 includes one for the printf library call. The command

```
[oracle@london1 oracle]$ man printf
```

will only display the man page for the printf command in section 1.

You can specify the section using the -S option. For example, to display the man page for the printf library call in section 3, use

```
[oracle@london1 oracle]$ man -S 3 printf
```

You can also display all sections for a specific topic using the -a option:

```
[oracle@london1 oracle]$ man -a printf
```

A whatis database is similar to a help index in Windows. You can create a whatis database using the command /usr/sbin/makewhatis. The whatis database can be searched using the whatis command:

```
[oracle@london1 oracle]$ whatis ls
ls              (1)    - list directory contents
```

This command will display all whatis database entries that match the complete string ls. You can also search the whatis database using the apropos command:

```
[oracle@london1 oracle]$ apropos ls
```

to display all whatis database entries that match the substring ls. The -k option of the man command is equivalent to the apropos command.

Finally, you can obtain further information for many of the manual pages using the info command:

```
[oracle@london1 oracle]$ info ls
```

Bash Shell

Linux includes the following command shells:

- **/bin/bash**: bash shell
- **/bin/ksh**: Korn shell
- **/bin/csh**: C shell
- **/bin/sh**: Bourne shell

Most users install Oracle under either the bash shell or the Korn shell. The choice of shell is a matter of personal preference.

The bash shell is the default command shell and contains a number of additional features to other shells. We recommend using the bash shell to take advantage of the features described in this section. However, some users still prefer the Korn shell, which is supplied in the pdksh package.

Tab Completion

The bash shell features Tab completion of file names. If you enter the prefix of a file or directory name and then press Tab, bash will attempt to complete the name. If the prefix is unique, bash will complete the name; if the prefix is not unique, bash will sound the alarm the first time you hit the Tab key and present a list of valid alternatives if you press the Tab key again.

Command History

The bash shell has a history facility. By default, all command history is written to ~/.bash_history. The command history can be accessed using the up and down arrow keys. The number of commands saved is specified by the $HISTSIZE environment variable, which defaults to 500 or 1000, depending on the version.

The command history can be displayed using

```
[oracle@london1 oracle]$ fc -l
```

Commands can be reexecuted using fc with the -s option and either a prefix or a command number. To reexecute commands by specifying a prefix, use the following code:

```
[oracle@london1 oracle]$ fc -s ls
```

Alternatively, to reexecute them by specifying a command number, use

```
[oracle@london1 oracle]$ fc -s 1004
```

The command number can be obtained from the command history.

Environment Variables

Like all other shells, the bash shell allows you to set environment variables. However, in the bash shell, the syntax is more user-friendly than in other shells. For example, to set an environment variable in the Bourne shell, two commands are required:

```
<environment_variable> = <value>
export $<environment_variable>
```

In the bash shell, an environment variable can be set using a single command:

```
export <environment_variable> = <value>
```

You can use the env command to check the value of all environment variables currently set in the shell:

```
[oracle@london1 oracle]$ env
```

You can also display the current value of an environment variable using the echo command:

```
[oracle@london1 oracle]$ echo $ORACLE_SID
```

The dollar sign ($) prefix indicates to the shell that ORACLE_SID is the name of an environment variable. You can specify initial values for environment variables and execute other commands for all operating system users by adding them to the /etc/profile file. You can specify environment variables for an individual user by adding them to the .bash profile file in the user's home directory. You can execute the commands in a user's .bash_profile script without exiting the current shell using the source command as follows:

```
[oracle@london1 oracle]$ source .bash_profile
```

For Loops

Most Unix shells include a for loop construct, which can be combined with if statements and test expressions to write powerful programs. The basic structure of a for loop follows:

```
for <condition>
do
  <commands>
done
```

You can declare a local environment variable in the condition that is set for each iteration, and the variable can subsequently be referenced within the commands, for example:

```
[oracle@london1 oracle]$ for f in *.txt
> do
>   echo $f
> done
```

This command will print the names of all files with a *.txt prefix and is the equivalent of

```
[oracle@london1 oracle]$ ls -1 *.txt
```

For example, the following script performs a silent case-insensitive search for oracle on each file in the /etc/init.d directory; it copies any files that match to the /tmp directory:

```
[oracle@london1 oracle]$ for f in /etc/init.d/*
> do
>   grep -q -i oracle < $f
>   RES=$f
>   if [ $RES -eq 0 ]
>   then
>      echo "Copying $f to /tmp"
>      cp $f /tmp
>   fi
> done
```

The preceding script might produce the following output:

```
Copying /etc/init.d/init.crs to /tmp
Copying /etc/init.d/init.crsd to /tmp
Copying /etc/init.d/init.cssd to /tmp
Copying /etc/init.d/init.evmd to /tmp
Copying /etc/init.d/ocfs to /tmp
Copying /etc/init.d/oracleasm to /tmp
Copying /etc/init.d/rawdevices to /tmp
```

You can also specify a for loop for a list of files in an existing file. For example, you can create a list of files using the following command:

```
[oracle@london1 oracle]$ ls -1 $ORACLE_HOME/rdbms/admin/*.sql > files.txt
```

You can then edit files.txt to delete those files that do not interest you and execute the following statement on those that remain:

```
[oracle@london1 oracle]$ for f in `cat files.txt`
> do
>    echo $f
>    # more commands here
> done
```

In the bash shell, you can use a for loop enclosed in an additional set of parentheses, a structure similar to that implemented in the C and Java programming languages:

```
[oracle@london1 oracle]$ for (( i = 1 ; i <= 5 ; i++ ))
> do
>    printf "test%03d\n" $i
> done
```

Note that the spaces in the for expression are mandatory. The preceding statement will return the following output:

```
test001
test002
test003
test004
test005
```

Commands

This section outlines some commands that are either specific to Linux or rarely found in older Unix variants that you may be familiar with.

printf

Linux includes a powerful printf command that is similar in many respects to the printf command found in the C programming language. The command takes a variable number of parameters: the first parameter is a format string, and the remaining parameters are the arguments to be formatted.

The format string is less powerful than that found in the standard C library. Table 15-3 describes the valid format string sequences for the printf command.

Table 15-3. *printf Command Format Sequences*

Sequence	Description
\"	Double quote
\\	Backslash
\b	Backspace
\f	Form feed
\n	New line
\r	Carriage return
\t	Tab
%%	Percent sign

A format specification can be given for each argument. Table 15-4 shows possible format specifications.

Table 15-4. *printf Command Format Specifications*

Format Specification	Description
%b	String with \ escapes interpreted
%d	Decimal number
%o	Unsigned octal number
%s	String
%u	Unsigned decimal number
%x	Unsigned hexadecimal number using the characters 0123456789abcdef
%X	Unsigned hexadecimal number using the characters 0123456789ABCDEF

It is also possible to specify a length for each field. For example, to specify the length of ten characters for a string argument, you might use %10s. This format specification will pad the argument with spaces on the left-hand side. To pad the right-hand side of the argument with spaces, use %-10s, for example:

```
[oracle@london1 oracle]$ printf "==%10s==\n" "Oracle"
==    Oracle==
[oracle@london1 oracle]$ printf "==%-10s==\n" "Oracle"
==Oracle    ==
```

You can also specify the length of numeric values. For example to specify a length of eight characters for a hexadecimal argument, you might use %8X, which will pad the argument with spaces on the left-hand side. If you wish to zero-pad the argument, use %08X:

```
[oracle@london1 oracle]$ printf "==%8X==\n" 256
==     100==
[oracle@london1 oracle]$ printf "==%08X==\n" 256
==00000100==
```

less

Linux provides the less command, which is a more powerful version of the more command. The less command has additional functionality; for example, search strings are highlighted. The less command is more efficient than the more command, so we recommend that you use it where possible. In Linux, man pages are automatically piped to less, for example:

```
[oracle@london1 oracle]$ less file1
[oracle@london1 oracle]$ ps -ef | grep -i asm | less
```

Note that the page (pg) command, which provides similar functionality to the more command in most Unix variants, is not available in Linux.

Packages

Linux software is generally supplied in packages that automate installation and configuration of each component. Hundreds of packages are provided with the Linux distribution and additional software, such as drivers, source files, and open source projects, are usually supplied in packages.

The Linux package manager is called RPM. Although this abbreviation stands for *Red Hat Package Manager*, RPM is used in both Red Hat and SUSE. RPM packages are distributed in files that have an rpm suffix and are generally referred to as RPMs. For example, consider pdksh-5.2.14-13.i386.rpm, where pdksh is the name of the package (i.e., the Korn shell), 5.2.4-13 is the version number of the package, and i386 is the architecture.

Most packages are precompiled. When you are downloading precompiled packages, take care to download files with the correct architecture for your cluster. Common architectures include i386 and i686, which are built for 32-bit systems; ia64, which is built for 64-bit Intel Itanium systems, and x86_64, which is built for 64-bit x86 platforms. RPM packages are managed using the rpm utility.

To list all currently installed packages, use

```
[root@london1 root]# rpm -qa
```

Use the following to check whether a package is currently installed:

```
[root@london1 root]# rpm -qa <package_name>
```

List all files in an installed package using

```
[root@london1 root]# rpm -ql <package_name>
```

and all files in an uninstalled package file using

```
[root@london1 root]# rpm -qpl <package_file_name>
```

To identify which package installed a specific file, use

```
[root@london1 root]# rpm -qf <file_name>
```

Use the following command to install a new package:

```
[root@london1 root]# rpm -ivh <package_file_name>
```

To update an existing package, use

```
[root@london1 root]# rpm -Uvh <package_file_name>
```

and to remove an existing package use

```
[root@london1 root]# rpm -e <package_name>
```

RPM packages can have dependencies with other RPM packages. These dependencies must be satisfied before an RPM package can be installed or removed.

Kernel Parameters

There are three ways of setting kernel parameters in Linux: using the /etc/sysctl.conf configuration file, using the sysctl command, and using the cat and echo commands.

In Linux, every kernel parameter has a default value that can be overridden in /etc/sysctl.conf, which is read at boot time. Only nondefault values need be stored in this file, for example:

```
net.core.rmem_default = 262144
net.core.rmem_max = 262144
net.core.wmem_default = 262144
net.core.wmem_max = 262144

kernel.shmmax=2147483648
kernel.sem=250 32000 100 128
fs.file-max=65536
```

After changing this file, you can set the parameters dynamically by issuing the sysctl -p command, which will update the values of all parameters defined in /etc/sysctl.conf. Always verify that the parameter values have been successfully modified using the sysctl -a command. When the system is rebooted, the parameter values in /etc/sysctl.conf will be reapplied.

Many parameters can also be altered dynamically using the `sysctl` command or by writing values directly to pseudofiles in /proc/sys and its subdirectories. You can also use the `sysctl` command to view and set individual kernel parameters:

```
[root@london1 root]# sysctl fs.file-max
fs.file-max = 65536
```

To change the value, you can use `sysctl` with the `-w` option:

```
[root@london1 root]# sysctl -w fs.file-max=131072
```

Parameter values set using `sysctl -w` will not be persistent across reboots.

You can also check the current value of a parameter using the `cat` command. For example, you can check the maximum number of file handles that a running kernel can allocate as follows:

```
[root@london1 root]# cat /proc/sys/fs/file-max
65536
```

To change the value of this parameter, you can run the following command:

```
[root@london1 root]# echo "131072" > /proc/sys/fs/file-max
```

Note You may not always be able to modify parameter files in /proc/sys using the `echo` command. If the files are writable, they can be used to modify the kernel settings; if they are not writable, then the values can be read, but not modified.

Some system administrators set kernel parameters using the `echo` command in the boot scripts. However, we do not recommend this practice, as it is more difficult for others to support.

We also do not recommend using `sysctl` or `echo` to set the values on your production systems, as they will not persist across reboots. These methods are also more prone to errors that could render a system inoperable.

Swap Space and File Systems

In this section, we will discuss swap space and file system administration, including general-purpose file systems, CD-ROM file systems, USB memory file systems, and the Network File System (NFS).

Swap Space

The configuration of swap space during system installation was detailed in Chapter 10, and following those guidelines should ensure that you configure sufficient swap space for your requirements. However, if you do discover that you require additional swap space once the system is operational, you may add it manually. Swap space can be added in one of two ways: by using an empty file in an existing file system or by allocating an existing unused device.

You can obtain a summary of the current allocation of swap space as follows:

```
[root@london1 root]# swapon -s
```

The previous command is equivalent to directly interrogating the swap kernel memory structure using the following:

```
[root@london1 root]# cat /proc/swaps
```

When the system is booted, all swap devices listed in /etc/fstab will be automatically added. To add a new swap file, first create the file. The following command creates a 2MB file called /tmp/swap:

```
[root@london1 root]# dd if=/dev/zero of=/tmp/swap bs=1m count=2048
[root@london1 root]# chmod 600 /tmp/swap
```

Next, create an ext2 file system within the new swap file:

```
[root@london1 root]# mke2fs /tmp/swap
```

You may receive an error message from this command reporting that the new file is not a block special device. You can ignore this message and proceed with the formatting operation.

Set up a Linux swap area within the file:

```
[root@london1 root]# mkswap /tmp/swap
```

Finally, enable use of the new file for paging and swapping:

```
[root@london1 root]# swapon /tmp/swap
```

To add a new device, first create the device using the fdisk utility. Then, follow the steps described previously to format the device and enable use of the device for paging and swapping. In the following example, assume that the device is called /dev/sdc8:

```
[root@london1 root]# mke2fs /dev/sdc8
[root@london1 root]# mkswap /dev/sdc8
[root@london1 root]# swapon /dev/sdc8
```

If you subsequently wish to remove the swap device, you can issue the following command to disable swapping on the specified file:

```
[root@london1 root]# swapoff /dev/sdc8
```

The new swap device will be disabled when the system is rebooted. To make your changes permanent, add the new swap device to /etc/fstab. In the following extract from /etc/fstab, the initial swap device was /dev/hda3, and a second swap device has been added using /dev/sdc8:

```
/dev/hda3    swap      swap      defaults   0   0
/dev/sdc8    swap      swap      defaults   0   0
```

General File Systems

Linux has numerous file system types. However, only a small number of file system types are generally used for local disks in Oracle RAC clusters; these include ext2, ext3, and reiserfs. The file /etc/filesystems lists the file system types supported by the kernel.

To create a file system of default type ext2, use the mkfs command:

```
[root@london1 root]# mkfs /dev/sdb5
```

To mount the file system, use the mount command. For example, use the following to mount the file system on directory /u01:

```
[root@london1 root]# mount /dev/sdb5 /u01
```

The directory /u01 must already exist. If it currently contains any files, these will become inaccessible until the file system is unmounted, but they will not be deleted.

To unmount the file system, use the umount command:

```
[root@london1 root]# umount /u01
```

You can configure file systems to be mounted when the system is rebooted in the file /etc/fstab. If you are using OCFS or NFS, you will probably wish to add entries to this file for these file systems, as in the following example:

```
/dev/sda1      /u02    ocfs    netdev        0    0
LABEL=u03      /u03    ocfs    netdev        0    0
london2:/u01/app/oracle/arch         /london2/arch    nfs    rw    0    0
```

The first entry mounts an OCFS file system using /u02 as the mount point on partition /dev/sda1. The _netdev keyword indicates that the file system should not be mounted until the network has been initialized. The second entry also mounts an OCFS file system using /u03 as the mount point, but specifies the partition by label. We recommend that you mount by label with OCFS, because the underlying device names, such as /dev/sda1, can change if you reconfigure the storage. The third entry illustrates an NFS mount where the mount point is /london2/arch, the remote host is called london2, and the remote directory is /u01/app/oracle/arch. The NFS directory is mounted in read/ write mode.

You can observe the space utilization of a file system using the df command. The -h flag displays the output in a human-readable format. The du command shows a finer level of disk utilization granularity on a file-by-file basis than the df command, with summaries for provided at a directory level.

CD-ROM File Systems

In Linux, the default CD-ROM file system type is ISO9600. To mount the CD-ROM, use the following command:

```
[root@london1 root]# mount /dev/cdrom
```

To unmount the CD-ROM, use

```
[root@london1 root]# umount /dev/cdrom
```

And to unmount and eject the CD-ROM, use

```
[root@london1 root]# eject
```

NFS

This section describes briefly how to set up NFS, which allows one node to mount a remote file system belonging to another node. You may need to use NFS if you cannot, or do not wish to, locate your archived redo logs on shared storage. An NFS file system has an NFS server, on which a local file system is exported, and an NFS client, on which the remote file system is mounted.

In the following example, london2 is the server and london1 is the client. On both nodes, the nfslock and nfs services must be running. On our test system, the nfslock service is configured to run at levels 3, 4, and 5, and the nfs service is not configured to run. To enable the nfs service, run the following command on both nodes:

```
[root@london1 root]# chkconfig --level 345 nfs on
```

To start the nfs services, run the following commands on both nodes:

```
[root@london1 root]# service nfslock start
[root@london1 root]# service nfs start
```

On the server (london2) only, add a list of the file systems to be exported to the file /etc/exports:

```
/u01/app/oracle/arch         london1(rw)
```

In this example, you are only exporting the contents of the directory /u01/app/oracle/arch. The contents will be made available to london1 with read/write permissions. Additional security options can be configured in /etc/exports, /etc/hosts.allow, and /etc/hosts.deny.

The file systems listed in /etc/exports can be exported by running the following command on the NFS server (london2):

```
[root@london1 root]# exportfs -a
```

On the client, you can mount the remote file system using the mount command:

```
[root@london1 root]# mkdir -p /london2/arch
[root@london1 root]# mount server4:/u01/app/oracle/arch /london2/arch
```

To mount the remote file system every time the node is rebooted, add an entry like the following one to /etc/fstab:

```
london2:/u01/app/oracle/arch  /london2/arch   nfs  rw 0 0
```

This command will mount the remote directory called /u01/app/oracle/arch on london2 into the directory /london2/arch on the local server.

Booting the System

You saw in Chapter 11 that the command telinit or init called with the run level of 6 will reboot the operating system. The command reboot will have the same effect:

```
[root@london1 root]# reboot
```

Bootloaders

When a system is booted, it runs a bootloader program. The bootloaders can start Linux and other operating systems. Linux includes several bootloaders, including LILO, ELILO, and GRUB.

GRUB stands for *Grand Unified Bootloader*. GRUB is the default bootloader and is normally installed in the master boot record (MBR) of the primary disk drive. LILO stands for the *Linux Loader* and is an alternative bootloader in these environments. ELILO stands for *Extended Linux Loader* and is the default bootloader on Itanium systems; it is installed on the EFI disk partition formatted with the VFAT file system.

When the system is booted, the bootloader lists the currently configured kernels and waits for the user to select which kernel to boot. If no option is selected before the time-out, which defaults to ten seconds, then the default kernel is booted.

The GRUB configuration file is /boot/grub/grub.conf:

```
# grub.conf generated by anaconda
default=0
timeout=10
splashimage=(hd0,0)/grub/splash.xpm.gz
title Red Hat Linux (2.4.9-e.27smp)
        root (hd0,0)
        kernel /vmlinuz-2.4.9-e.27smp ro root=/dev/sda5
        initrd /initrd-2.4.9-e.27smp.img
title Red Hat Linux Advanced Server (2.4.9-e.17enterprise)
        root (hd0,0)
        kernel /vmlinuz-2.4.9-e.17enterprise ro root=/dev/sda5
        initrd /initrd-2.4.9-e.17enterprise.img
title Red Hat Linux Advanced Server-smp (2.4.9-e.17smp)
        root (hd0,0)
```

```
        kernel /vmlinuz-2.4.9-e.17smp ro root=/dev/sda5
        initrd /initrd-2.4.9-e.17smp.img
```

The preceding code listing shows grub.conf after the kernel was upgraded from 2.4.9-e17 to
2.4.9-e27 using an RPM package.

The default=0 value determines the entry that will be displayed as the default value for the
bootloader and will be used to boot the system if the time-out expires. Note that this default setting
must be altered manually. In the preceding example, the default value was manually changed from
1 to 0 after the kernel was upgraded using the RPM package. Verify that this default parameter is correct, as the boot loader will time out after 30 seconds and boot with the default kernel. If the default
value is incorrect, your system could load an outdated kernel during an unattended boot.

Initial Ramdisk Image

Additional modules may be required in order to boot the system, usually because some of the disk
device drivers are not included in the kernel. Depending on the system configuration, these modules could include IDE, SCSI, RAID, and network drivers. For example, host bus adapters (HBAs)
can be specified in the file /etc/modprobe.conf:

```
alias scsi_hostadapter aix79xx
alias scsi_hostadapter lpfcdd
```

Additional modules required during the boot process must be added to the initial ramdisk
image. A new initial ramdisk image can be created using the mkinitrd command:

```
[root@london1 root]# cd /boot/grub
[root@london1 root]# mkinitrd /boot/initrd-2.4.9-e.27smp.img 2.4.9-e.27smp
```

This command builds a new initial ramdisk image for the 2.4.9-e27smp kernel.

If you are using the GRUB bootloader, the name of the image file should match the initrd entry
in /boot/grub/grub.conf:

```
# grub.conf generated by anaconda
default=0
timeout=10
splashimage=(hd0,0)/grub/splash.xpm.gz
title Red Hat Linux (2.4.9-e.27smp)
        root (hd0,0)
        kernel /vmlinuz-2.4.9-e.27smp ro root=/dev/sda5
        initrd /initrd-2.4.9-e.27smp.img
title Red Hat Linux Advanced Server (2.4.9-e.17enterprise)
        root (hd0,0)
        kernel /vmlinuz-2.4.9-e.17enterprise ro root=/dev/sda5
        initrd /initrd-2.4.9-e.17enterprise.img
title Red Hat Linux Advanced Server-smp (2.4.9-e.17smp)
        root (hd0,0)
        kernel /vmlinuz-2.4.9-e.17smp ro root=/dev/sda5
        initrd /initrd-2.4.9-e.17smp.img
```

In the preceding example, the initrd entry for the newly created ramdisk image is shown in
bold. When the system is booted, GRUB will automatically search the /boot directory for this image.

Log Files, Tracing, and Debugging

When troubleshooting an Oracle RAC system, do not focus exclusively on the Oracle files and diagnostics; also consider the log files and other sources of information on the operating system itself

on all nodes in the cluster. In this section, we detail sources and methods for obtaining this diagnostic information.

Log Files

Linux uses a number of log files. Boot messages are written to the kernel ring buffer and subsequently flushed to the file /var/log/messages. You can examine the contents of this file since the system was last booted using the dmesg command:

```
[root@london1 root]# dmesg
```

Use this command to check that devices and modules have loaded correctly for the current boot. If you need to see messages earlier than the time of the last reboot, you can view /var/log/messages with any text editor.

Tracing

The strace command prints out all system calls and arguments executed by a program. By default, strace output is written to standard error.

You can use strace to execute a new program:

```
[oracle@london1 oracle]$ strace <program> <arguments>
```

or you can use it to attach to an existing program:

```
[oracle@london1 oracle]$ strace -p <pid>
```

A summary of system call usage can be printed as follows:

```
[oracle@london1 oracle]$ strace -c -p <pid>
```

Note that if you use this option, you will need to press Ctrl+C to interrupt collection and print the summary.

You can also use strace to trace Oracle server processes that have been forked or cloned from a foreground process. For example, the following command will trace system calls made by both the foreground and server processes to the file strace.txt:

```
[oracle@london1 oracle]$ strace -f $ORACLE_HOME/bin/sqlplus 2> strace.txt
```

Debugging

The Linux debugger, called gdb, is a powerful debugger that allows you to display the contents of registers, memory addresses, and sections of code; set breakpoints and watch points; and step through the execution of a program.

Summary

In this chapter, we discussed some of the useful features and commands for administering a RAC cluster on Linux. You do not need to know all the commands available within Linux in order to install, configure, and administer Oracle databases. However, if you are not familiar with Unix-based operating systems, we recommend you visit the web site for this book, which contains additional material.

## CHAPTER 16

Oracle Clusterware

Oracle Clusterware is a cluster manager that is integrated into the Oracle database and provides all the features required to manage a cluster database, including node membership, group services, global resource management, and high availability functions.

Oracle Clusterware provides high availability by eliminating single points of failure in environments containing redundant hardware and software. In the event of the failure of a component, the Oracle Clusterware relocates the processing performed by the failed component to a backup component. If the failed component is a node or an instance, the Oracle database will remaster resources and recover partial and failed transactions to enable continued operation on other nodes.

In a RAC environment, all Oracle processes are controlled by Oracle Clusterware. RAC uses Oracle Clusterware to create the infrastructure that enables multiple nodes to operate as if they were a single system. While Oracle does support cluster managers supplied by other vendors, most Linux customers elect to use Oracle Clusterware.

Like many Oracle features, Oracle Clusterware has been known by a number of names as it has evolved through the years. The Linux platform did not initially have suitable clusterware for the Oracle Database, so in Oracle 9.0.1 and 9.2, Oracle Corporation shipped their own Linux cluster manager called Oracle Cluster Management Services (OCMS). A generic cluster manager suitable for all platforms, known as Cluster Ready Services (CRS), was introduced in Oracle 10.1. In Oracle 10.2, CRS has been renamed Oracle Clusterware.

In Oracle 10.2 and above, Oracle Clusterware can also provide cluster management capabilities in a high availability infrastructure.

Oracle Clusterware Components

Oracle Clusterware includes a number of background processes that are implemented in Linux as daemons, including the following:

- Cluster Synchronization Service (CSS)

- Cluster Ready Services (CRS)

- Event Manager (EVM)

These background processes communicate with similar components on other instances in the same database cluster. They also enable communication between Oracle Clusterware and the Oracle database. Under Linux, each daemon can have multiple threads, each of which appears as a separate operating system process.

Cluster Synchronization Services (CSS)

This component manages the cluster configuration by controlling which nodes are members of the cluster. When a node joins or leaves the cluster, CSS notifies the other nodes of the change in configuration. If this process fails, then the cluster will be restarted. Under Linux, CSS is implemented by the ocssd daemon, which runs as the root user.

Cluster Ready Services (CRS)

This component manages high availability operations within the cluster. Objects managed by CRS are known as *resources* and can include databases, instances, services, listeners, virtual IP addresses, and application processes. By default, CRS manages four application process resources: Oracle Net listeners, virtual IP addresses, the Global Services Daemon (GSD), and the Oracle Notification Service (ONS). Configuration information about each resource is stored in the Oracle Cluster Registry (OCR). When the status of a resource changes, CRS generates an event.

CRS monitors resources, such as instances and listeners. In the event of the failure of a resource, CRS will attempt to automatically restart the component. By default, CRS will attempt to restart the resource five times before giving up.

Under Linux, CRS is implemented as the crsd daemon, which runs as the root user. In the event of a failure, this process restarts automatically.

Event Manager (EVM)

The EVM component publishes events created by Oracle Clusterware. Under Linux, EVM is implemented as the evmd daemon, which runs as the root user.

You can specify callout scripts, which will be executed by EVM when a specified event occurs. These callouts are managed by the racgevt process.

In addition to the background processes, Oracle Clusterware also communicates with the Oracle Notification Service (ONS), which is a publish and subscribe service that communicates FAN events to clients.

Oracle Clusterware Files

Oracle Clusterware requires two files that must be located on shared storage: the OCR and the voting disk.

Oracle Cluster Registry (OCR)

The Oracle Cluster Registry (OCR) maintains cluster and database configuration information for RAC and Oracle Clusterware resources, including information about nodes, databases, instances, services, applications, and listeners.

The OCR is similar in many ways to the Windows registry. Information is stored in a hierarchy of key-value pairs within a directory tree structure. The OCR can be updated using EM, the Server Control Utility (SRVCTL), and DBCA.

The OCR must be located on shared storage and must be accessible from all nodes. On each node, the location of the OCR is specified in the file /etc/oracle/ocr.loc:

```
ocrconfig_loc=/u02/oradata/RAC/OCRFile
local_only=FALSE
```

In Oracle 10.2 and above, the OUI can optionally create a mirrored copy of the OCR File. This file should also be located on shared storage. We recommend creating a mirror even if your storage system already implemented external redundancy, as maintaining two copies at the Oracle Clusterware level reduces the chances of inadvertently deleting or overwriting the OCR file.

The following is an example of the contents of /etc/oracle/ocr.loc in Oracle 10.2 with a mirrored OCR:

```
ocrconfig_loc=/u02/oradata/RAC/OCRFile1
ocrmirrorconfig_loc=/u03/oradata/RAC/OCRFile2
local_only=FALSE
```

In addition to mirroring the OCR, you can also replace the OCR if an alert is raised in EM or the Oracle Clusterware alert log. In the event of a configuration error or other OCR error, you can repair the OCR and OCR mirror location so that it is consistent across all nodes in the cluster. You may add an OCR mirror if your configuration did not originally contain one. You can remove the OCR mirror again, if you consider that the mirror is adversely affecting performance, and you have suitable redundant external storage, such as RAID 1+ 0.

Voting Disk

The voting disk, which must reside on shared storage, manages cluster membership information. It is used by RAC to determine instances that are members of the cluster. It is also used to arbitrate cluster ownership between the remaining instances in the event of a network failure.

In Oracle 10.2 and above, you can to create multiple voting disks. Oracle recommends configuring an odd number of voting disks (e.g., three or five). By default in Oracle 10.2, the OUI will create three voting disks, although you can specify a single voting disk if your storage provides mirroring at the hardware level. The voting disk is critical to the operation of Oracle Clusterware and of the database. Therefore, if you choose to define a single voting disk or you are still using Oracle 10.1, you should use external mirroring to provide redundancy.

Oracle Clusterware High Availability Framework

In Oracle 10.2 and above, Oracle Clusterware provides a High Availability Framework that you can use to enable Oracle Clusterware to manage applications or processes running on the cluster. This framework enables you to provide high availability for custom applications in addition to the RAC database.

You can use Oracle Clusterware in conjunction with ASM to create a consolidated pool of storage to support both single-instance and RAC databases running within the cluster. Oracle Clusterware ensures that the ASM file system remains available by eliminating any single points of failure among the ASM instances.

Oracle Clusterware components can detect failures and optionally restart critical user applications and processes. You can either register your applications with the High Availability Framework or extend your applications using the High Availability Framework API. You can also create application profiles that monitor your application and potentially relocate and restart it on another node.

Oracle Clusterware also provides alerts to clients when events occur or configurations change. These alerts allow applications to react immediately to changes in the status of various objects in the cluster.

Oracle Clusterware Installation and Configuration

Oracle Clusterware is distributed on separate installation media as part of the Oracle Database 10g software distribution. It can also be downloaded from the Oracle technology web site.

Oracle Clusterware must be installed before you install the Oracle database software or attempt to create a database. Prior to installing Oracle Clusterware, you must have installed and configured the operating system, created the Oracle user, created the oinstall and dba groups, set kernel parameters and environment variables, and configured shared storage and network interfaces for the public and private networks. You must also have configured the secure shell so that the OUI can copy files to other nodes in the cluster. Note that you will need access to the root user during the installation process to perform various tasks requiring superuser privileges.

While the Oracle Clusterware installation itself is relatively stable, by definition, it will be the first Oracle software that you install on your cluster, so it is susceptible to any configuration errors. In both Oracle 10.1 and 10.2, therefore, we recommend that you use the Cluster Verification Utility (CLUVFY) to check that you have configured your environment correctly. In our experience, using CLUVFY can save a significant amount of time and avoid some unpleasant troubleshooting. CLUVFY is available on the Oracle 10.2 Clusterware installation media. However, it is backward compatible with Oracle 10.1. We recommend that you download and run CLUVFY on all Oracle 10g RAC clusters, even if they are already in production. The utility will not affect existing systems, as it is a read-only utility. It may, however, highlight existing problems that have not been detected in the past. We also recommend that you run the CLUVFY utility on all nodes when adding new nodes and instances.

Prior to installing Oracle Clusterware, you must allocate IP addresses for the public and private networks. You must also allocate a virtual IP address, which is used by the Virtual Internet Protocol Configuration Assistant (VIPCA). In Oracle 10.1, the VIPCA utility is invoked during Oracle Database software installation; in Oracle 10.2, VIPCA is invoked silently during the Oracle Clusterware installation. The Oracle 10.2 approach is more logical, as a single node will normally have only one virtual IP address but may have many database instances.

In Oracle 10.2, both CLUVFY and the silent option of VIPCA make the incorrect assumption that the public network must contain routable IP addresses only. Both utilities signal an error if a non-routable address is encountered. The three ranges of nonroutable addresses follow:

- 10.x.x.x
- 172.16.x.x
- 192.168.x.x

Errors reported by CLUVFY should be ignored. However, errors reported by the silent option of VIPCA cannot be ignored, as the VIP addresses will not be configured within the OUI session and errors will be reported from both VIPCA and a subsequent execution of CLUVFY. These errors are not quite as serious as they may first appear, as VIPCA is the last step in the script executed on the final node by the root user during Oracle Clusterware installation. In the event of a failure, you can execute VIPCA again interactively at the command line, in which case no error will be reported if you specify nonroutable addresses for the private network.

The Oracle Clusterware installation process creates the OCR and the voting disk. It can also optionally create mirrored copies of these files. Creating mirrored copies is recommended, as the redundant copies eliminate a potential single point of failure. Creating redundant copies of these files may also eliminate the need for a third-party storage solution to provide redundancy.

Virtual Internet Protocol Configuration Assistant (VIPCA)

The Virtual Internet Protocol Configuration Assistant (VIPCA) is a GUI utility written in Java that was introduced in Oracle 10.1 to configure the VIP, GSD, and ONS application resources for each cluster node.

In Oracle 10.1, VIPCA is invoked by the OUI during Oracle Database installation. However, virtual IP addresses are configured in the OCR and are shared by all instances on the node. Therefore, in Oracle 10.2 and above, VIPCA is invoked by the Oracle Clusterware installation process. In addition, in Oracle 10.2, sufficient information is available for the virtual IP addresses to be configured automatically. Therefore, on this release, VIPCA is invoked in silent mode when the root.sh script is executed on each node.

For most clusters, you should not need to run VIPCA once Oracle Clusterware has been successfully installed. However, in exceptional circumstances, you may need to execute it again.

Before you can start VIPCA, Oracle Clusterware must be running. You can run VIPCA in both GUI and text (silent) modes. To run VIPCA in GUI mode, run the following command as the root user:

```
[root@london1 root]# $ORA_CRS_HOME/bin/vipca
```

VIPCA initially displays a Welcome page. Click Next to continue to the Network Interfaces page (Figure 16-1).

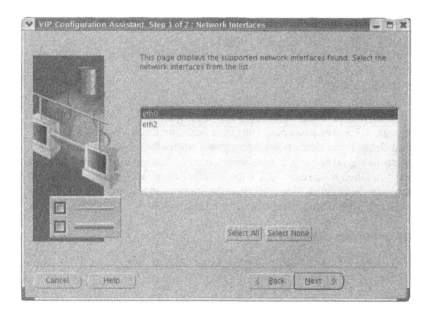

Figure 16-1. *The VIPCA Network Interfaces page*

On the Network Interfaces page, you can select a network interface for the virtual IP address from the list of available interfaces. The virtual IP addresses should be created on the interface created for the public network. In the system shown in Figure 16-1, eth0 was allocated to the public network, while eth2 was allocated to the backup network.

Click Next to continue to the Virtual IPs page (Figure 16-2).

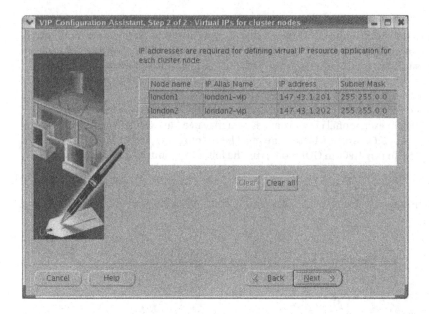

Figure 16-2. *The VIPCA Virtual IPs page*

On the Virtual IPs page, VIPCA will attempt to complete the Node name, IP Alias Name, IP address, and Subnet Mask fields. If you have created appropriate entries for the VIP address in DNS or /etc/hosts, then the defaults should be correct. If not, we recommend that you modify the addresses in DNS and/or /etc/hosts and then reexecute VIPCA. If the supplied values are correct, click Next to continue to the Summary page. Then, click Finish to create the application resources. Remember that, in addition to the VIP application, this utility will also attempt to create GSD and ONS application resources.

The VIPCA utility takes the following parameters:

```
vipca [-silent]
  -nodelist <node1[,...]>
  -nodevips <node-name/ip-name|ip-addr[/netmask[/interface[|interface-i]]][,...]>
  -vipfile <vipFile path>
  -orahome <Oracle home path>
```

If you specify the -silent option, VIPCA will run in text mode; otherwise, it will attempt to start the GUI interface. The nodelist parameter specifies a comma-separated list of nodes to be configured, for example:

```
[root@london1 root]# vipca -nodelist london1,london2
```

For each node, you can supply a nodevips parameter. At minimum, this parameter contains the node name and either the IP address or the DNS name of the VIP address:

```
[root@london1 root]# vipca -nodelist london3 -nodevips london3/147.43.1.203
[root@london1 root]# vipca -nodelist london3 -nodevips london3/london3-vip
```

You can optionally specify a netmask and an interface name:

```
[root@london1 root]# vipca -nodelist london3 \
  -nodevips london3/147.43.1.203/255.255.0.0
[root@london1 root]# vipca -nodelist london3 \
  -nodevips london3/147.43.1.203/255.255.0.0/eth0
```

If you have a large number of nodes in your cluster, you can create a text file containing the required VIP addresses and specify this file using the -vipfile parameter. The input file should specify one per line per node in the following format:

```
<node_name>=<ip-name|ip-addr>/<netmask>/<interface[|interface-i]>
```

OIFCFG

The Oracle Interface Configuration (OIFCFG) utility allows you to define and manage network interfaces for Oracle database components. Although it can be used with single-instance Oracle databases, it is primarily used in RAC environments.

The OIFCFG utility allows you to list and modify the current configuration of each network interface. A network interface is identified using the interface name, subnet mask, and interface type. The supported interface types follow:

- **Public**: Used to communicate externally using components such as Oracle Net and Virtual Internet Protocol (VIP) addresses

- **Private**: Used for interinstance communication across the cluster interconnect

A network interface specification has the following format:

```
<interface_name>/<subnet>:<interface_type>
```

Network interfaces can be stored as global interfaces or node-specific interfaces. An interface is stored as a *global interface* when all nodes in the cluster have the same interface connected to the same subnet. We recommend you use a symmetrical configuration whenever possible. An interface is stored as a *node-specific interface* when other nodes in the cluster have a different set of interfaces and subnets. Using a node-specific interface may be necessary if you have an asymmetrical workload or if you have run out of slots in one or more servers. Node-specific interface definitions override global interface definitions.

You can display the current command syntax for OIFCFG using the following:

```
[oracle@london1 oracle]$ oifcfg -help
```

To display a list of current subnets, use

```
[oracle@london1 oracle]$ oifcfg iflist
eth0    147.43.1.0
eth1    192.168.1.0
```

To include a description of the subnet, specify the -p option:

```
[oracle@london1 oracle]$ oifcfg iflist -p
eth0    147.43.1.0    UNKNOWN
eth1    192.168.1.0    PRIVATE
```

In the version of Oracle 10.2 that we tested, all public interfaces had the description UNKNOWN. To include the subnet mask, append the -n option to the -p option:

```
[oracle@london1 oracle]$ oifcfg iflist -p -n
eth0    147.43.1.0    UNKNOWN    255.255.255.0
eth1    192.168.1.0    PRIVATE    255.255.255.0
```

To display a list of networks, use

```
[oracle@london1 oracle]$ oifcfg getif
eth0    147.43.0.0    global    public
eth1    192.168.2.0   global    cluster_interconnect
```

The preceding command is equivalent to specifying the -global option.

You can also display node-specific configurations by specifying the -node option:

```
[oracle@london1 oracle]$ oifcfg getif -n london1
```

You can display details for a specific interface, for example:

```
[oracle@london1 oracle]$ oifcfg getif -if eth0
eth0    147.43.0.0    global    public
```

Alternatively, you can display details for a specific interface type:

```
[oracle@london1 oracle]$ oifcfg getif -type cluster_interconnect
eth1    192.168.2.0    global    cluster_interconnect
```

You can also create a new interface type. The following example enables the interface on a new set of network cards:

```
[oracle@london1 oracle]$ oifcfg setif -global eth2/147.44.0.0:public
[oracle@london1 oracle]$ oifcfg getif
eth0    147.43.0.0    global    public
eth1    192.168.2.0    global    cluster_interconnect
eth2    147.44.0.0    global    public
```

Note that you must specify a subnet (and not a subnet mask).
To delete the interface again, use the following:

```
[oracle@london1 oracle]$ oifcfg delif -global eth2
[oracle@london1 oracle]$ oifcfg getif
eth0    147.43.0.0    global    public
eth1    192.168.2.0    global    cluster_interconnect
```

Take care not to omit the interface name from the delif option. You can delete all global interfaces using the following command:

```
[oracle@london1 oracle]$ oifcfg delif -global
```

Administering Oracle Clusterware

In this section, we describe a number of administrative tasks that can be performed on the OCR. In Oracle 10.1 and above, the following set of utilities is provided to support OCR administration:

- **CRSCTL**: Performs various administrative operations for Oracle Clusterware
- **CRS_STAT**: Reports the current state of resources configured in the OCR
- **OCRCONFIG**: Performs various administrative operations on the OCR
- **OCRCHECK**: Verifies the integrity of the OCR
- **OCRDUMP**: Dumps the contents of the OCR to a text file

These utilities are further described in the following sections.

CRSCTL

The CRS control (CRSCTL) utility was introduced in Oracle 10.1 and has been significantly enhanced in Oracle 10.2. It is located in $ORA_CRS_HOME/bin and must be executed by the root user. You can list the options available in CRSCTL using

```
[root@london1 root]# crsctl
```

Checking the State of Oracle Clusterware

You can use CRSCTL to check the current state of all Oracle Clusterware daemons as well:

```
[root@london1 root]# crsctl check crs
CSS appears healthy
CRS appears healthy
EVM appears healthy
```

If Oracle Clusterware has been shut down, you should receive messages such as the following:

```
Failure 1 contacting CSS daemon
Cannot communicate with CRS
Cannot communicate with EVM
```

You can also use CRSCTL to check the state of individual Oracle Clusterware daemons:

```
[root@london1 root]# crsctl check cssd
CSS appears healthy
[root@london1 root]# crsctl check crsd
CRS appears healthy
[root@london1 root]# crsctl check evmd
EVM appears healthy
```

Starting and Stopping Oracle Clusterware

In Oracle 10.1, starting Oracle Clusterware by any method other than a reboot of the node was not supported. In Oracle 10.2, you can also start up Oracle Clusterware as follows:

```
[root@london1 root]# crsctl start crs
Attempting to start CRS stack
The CRS stack will be started shortly
```

Note that no further information is displayed. Use crsctl check crs or operating system utilities to verify that Oracle Clusterware has started.

You can shut down Oracle Clusterware using

```
[root@london1 root]# crsctl stop crs
Stopping resources
Successfully stopped CRS resources
Stopping CSSD
Shutting down CSS daemon
Shutdown request successfully issued
```

Enabling and Disabling Oracle Clusterware

You can disable Oracle Clusterware as follows:

```
[root@london1 root]# crsctl disable crs
```

Disabling Oracle Clusterware will prevent it from being restarted the next time the system is rebooted. You can enable Oracle Clusterware again using

```
[root@london1 root]# crsctl enable crs
```

These functions update the file /etc/oracle/scls_scr/<node>/root/crsstart that contains the string enable or disable as appropriate.

Setting CSS Parameters

You can use CRSCTL to get and set CSS parameters. You can discover the names of all CSS parameters by performing an OCRDUMP and examining the output file. To get the current value of the parameter use the following:

```
crsctl get css <parameter>
```

For example, misscount is an integer CSS parameter. In the OCR, it has the key [SYSTEM.css.misscount]. To get the value of this parameter, use the following command:

```
[root@london1 root]# crsctl get css misscount
60
```

Use the following syntax to set a new value for the parameter:

```
crsctl set css <parameter> <value>
```

For example, set the misscount parameter to 120 seconds as follows:

```
[root@london1 root]# crsctl set css misscount 120
Configuration parameter misscount is now set to 120
```

Unset the parameter value as follows:

```
crsctl unset css <parameter>
```

For example, to unset the misscount parameter use

```
[root@london1 root]# crsctl unset css misscount
```

Take extreme care when using the unset option, as it completely deletes the parameter from the OCR.

Managing Voting Disks

You can list the currently configured voting disks:

```
[root@london1 root]# crsctl query css votedisk
0.      0       /u02/oradata/RAC/CSSFile1
1.      1       /u03/oradata/RAC/CSSFile2
2.      2       /u04/oradata/RAC/CSSFile3
```

You should be able to dynamically add and remove voting disks to an existing Oracle Clusterware installation:

```
crsctl add css votedisk <path>
crsctl delete css votedisk <path>
```

However, when we tested these commands on Oracle 10.2.0.1, we received the following errors:

```
Cluster is not in a ready state for online disk addition
Cluster is not in a ready state for online disk removal
```

In Oracle 10.2.0.1, you can, however, force the addition or removal of a disk. You must ensure that Oracle Clusterware has been shut down before using the -force option. This implies that all databases and ASM instances must also have been shut down.

For example, to add a voting disk, use the following:

```
[root@london1 root]# crsctl add css votedisk /u04/oradata/RAC/CSSFile4 -force
Now formatting voting disk: /u04/oradata/RAC/CSSFile4
successful addition of votedisk /u04/oradata/RAC/CSSFile4
```

To remove the voting disk again, use

```
[root@london1 root]# crsctl delete css votedisk /u04/oradata/RAC/CSSFile4 -force
successful deletion of votedisk /u04/oradata/RAC/CSSFile4
```

Listing CRS Versions

You can query the current installed version of Oracle Clusterware:

```
crsctl query crs softwareversion
```

In the initial release of Oracle 10.2, this query returned the following:

```
[root@london1 root]# crsctl query crs softwareversion
CRS software version on node [london1] is [10.2.0.1.0]
```

You can also query the currently running version of CRS:

```
crsctl query crs activeversion
```

which, in the initial release of Oracle 10.2, returned the following:

```
[root@london1 root]# crsctl query crs activeversion
CRS active version on the cluster is [10.2.0.1.0]
```

Debugging

You can list the modules available for debugging in CSS using the following code:

```
[root@london1 root]# crsctl lsmodules css
```

which, in Oracle 10.2, might return

```
CSSD
COMMCRS
COMMNS
```

You can also use the following command to list the modules available for debugging in CRS:

```
[root@london1 root]# crsctl lsmodules crs
```

In Oracle 10.2, this command returns

```
CRSUI
CRSCOMM
CRSRTI
CRSMAIN
CRSPLACE
CRSAPP
CRSRES
CRSOCR
CRSTIMER
CRSEVT
CRSD
CLUCLS
CSSCLNT
COMMCRS
COMMNS
```

You can list the modules available for debugging in EVM as follows:

```
[root@london1 root]# crsctl lsmodules evm
```

In Oracle 10.2 this command might return

```
EVMD
EVMDMAIN
EVMDCOMM
EVMEVT
EVMAPP
EVMAGENT
CRSOCR
CLUCLS
CSSCLNT
COMMCRS
COMMNS
```

You can use CRSCTL to enable tracing of specific modules within CRS components. For each module, a level can be specified. The basic syntax follows:

```
crsctl debug log <component> <module>:<level>{,<module>:<level>]
```

For example, to enable level 2 debugging of the CRSCOMM module of the crsd daemon, use the following command:

```
[root@london1 root]# crsctl debug log crs "CRSCOMM:2"
```

Output will be written to $ORA_CRS_HOME/log/<node>/crsd/crsd.log.
To enable level 1 debugging of the CSSD module in the ocssd daemon, use the following:

```
[root@london1 root]# crsctl debug log css "CSSD:1"
```

Output will be written to $ORA_CRS_HOME/log/<node>/cssd/ocssd.log.
Finally, to enable level 2 debugging of the EVMDCOMM module in the evmd daemon, use

```
[root@london1 root]# crsctl debug log evm "EVMDCOMM:2"
```

Output will be written to $ORA_CRS_HOME/log/<node>/evmd/evmd.log.
Alternatively, you can use environment variables to configure debugging, using the following syntax:

```
ORA_CRSDEBUG_ALL=<level>
```

For example, enable debugging for all CRS modules as follows:

```
[root@london1 root]# export ORA_CRSDEBUG_ALL=1
```

The value specified by the environment variable determines the amount of debugging information that is included.
You can use environment variables to debug individual modules as well using the following syntax:

```
ORA_CRSDEBUG_<module>=<level>
```

For example, to enable level 2 debugging in the CRSCOMM module of crsd, use

```
[root@london1 root]# export ORA_CRSDEBUG_CRSCOMM=2
```

If you wish to use this facility to enable CRS debugging, we suggest you start with level 1 debugging and check the log file to discover the module that is causing the problem. Next, enable additional levels of debugging for that specific module and repeat the test.
You can also enable debugging of resources within the CRSCTL utility using the following basic syntax:

```
crsctl debug log res <resource_name>:<level>
```

State Dumps

You can generate a state dump for each of the Oracle Clusterware components using the following commands. To generate a state dump for the crsd daemon, use the following:

```
[root@london1 root]# crsctl debug statedump crs
```

Output will be written to $ORA_CRS_HOME/log/<node>/crsd/crsd.log.
To generate a state dump for the ocssd daemon, use

```
[root@london1 root]# crsctl debug statedump css
```

Output will be written to $ORA_CRS_HOME/log/<node>/cssd/ocssd.log.
Finally, to generate a state dump for the emvd daemon, use

```
[root@london1 root]# crsctl debug statedump evm
```

Output will be written to $ORA_CRS_HOME/log/<node>/evmd/evmd.log.

CRS_STAT

The CRS_STAT utility reports on the current status of various resources managed by Oracle Clusterware. It is located in the $ORA_CRS_HOME/bin directory.

With no arguments, CRS_STAT lists all resources currently configured:

```
[oracle@london1 bin]$ crs_stat
NAME=ora.RAC.RAC1.inst
TYPE=application
TARGET=ONLINE
STATE=ONLINE on london1

NAME=ora.RAC.SERVICE1.RAC1.srv
TYPE=application
TARGET=OFFLINE
STATE=OFFLINE

NAME=ora.RAC.SERVICE1.cs
TYPE=application
TARGET=OFFLINE
STATE=OFFLINE

NAME=ora.RAC.db
TYPE=application
TARGET=ONLINE
STATE=ONLINE on london1

NAME=ora.london1.ASM1.asm
TYPE=application
TARGET=ONLINE
STATE=ONLINE on london1

NAME=ora.london1.LISTENER_LONDON1.lsnr
TYPE=application
TARGET=ONLINE
STATE=ONLINE on london1
```

```
NAME=ora.london1.gsd
TYPE=application
TARGET=ONLINE
STATE=ONLINE on london1

NAME=ora.london1.ons
TYPE=application
TARGET=ONLINE
STATE=ONLINE on london1

NAME=ora.london1.vip
TYPE=application
TARGET=ONLINE
STATE=ONLINE on london1
```

Note that in the preceding example, we have removed the output for node london2 and instance RAC2. If a node has failed, the STATE field will show the node that the applications have failed over to. You can optionally specify a resource name, which is equivalent to the NAME field in the output, for example:

```
[oracle@london1 bin]$ crs_stat ora.RAC.RAC1.inst
NAME=ora.RAC.RAC1.inst
TYPE=application
TARGET=ONLINE
STATE=ONLINE on london1
```

If you include the -v option, CRS_STAT prints verbose information. If verbose output is enabled, then the following additional information is reported for each resource:

- Number of restart attempts
- Restart count
- Failure threshold
- Failure count

For example, to print verbose information about the ora.RAC.RAC1.inst resource, use the following:

```
[oracle@london1 bin]$ crs_stat -v ora.RAC.RAC1.inst
NAME=ora.RAC.RAC1.inst
TYPE=application
RESTART_ATTEMPTS=5
RESTART_COUNT=0
FAILURE_THRESHOLD=0
FAILURE_COUNT=0
TARGET=ONLINE
STATE=ONLINE on london1
```

The -p option gives more detailed information, for example:

```
[oracle@london1 bin]$ crs_stat -p ora.RAC.RAC1.inst
NAME=ora.RAC.RAC1.inst
TYPE=application
ACTION_SCRIPT=/u01/app/oracle/product/10.1.0/db/bin/racgwrap
ACTIVE_PLACEMENT=0
AUTO_START=1
CHECK_INTERVAL=600
DESCRIPTION=CRS application for Instance
FAILOVER_DELAY=0
```

```
FAILOVER_INTERVAL=0
FAILOVER_THRESHOLD=0
HOSTIMG_MEMBERS=primary1
OPTIONAL_RESOURCES=
PLACEMENT=restricted
REQUIRED_RESOURCES=ora.primary1.vip ora.primary1.ASM1.asm
RESTART_ATTEMPTS=5
SCRIPT_TIMEOUT=600
USR_ORA_ALERT_NAME=
USR_ORA_CHECK_TIMEOUT=0
USR_ORA_CONNECT_STR=/  as sysdba
USR_ORA_DEBUG=0
USR_ORA_DISCONNECT=false
USR_ORA_FLAGS=
USR_ORA_IF=
USR_ORA_INST_NOT_SHUTDOWN=
USR_ORA_LANG=
USR_ORA_NETMASK=
USR_ORA_OPEN_MODE=
USR_ORA_OPI=false
USR_ORA_PFILE=
USR_ORA_PRECONNECT=none
USR_ORA_SRV
USR_ORA_START_TIMEOUT=0
USR_ORA_STOP_MODE=immediate
USR_ORA_STOP_TIMEOUT=0
USR_ORA_VIP=
```

The same fields are reported for all resources. For some resource types, these fields have values; for others, they are null. For example, for a VIP resource type, the following additional fields might be set:

```
USR_ORA_IF=eth0
USR_ORA_NETMASK=255.255.255.0
USR_ORA_VIP=192.168.1.203
```

Finally, the -ls option of CRS_STAT lists the resources with their owners and permissions in a similar layout to the operating system ls -l command:

```
[oracle@london1 bin]$ crs_stat -ls
Name            Owner        Primary PrivGrp      Permission
--------------------------------------------------------------------
ora....C1.inst  oracle       dba                  rwxrwxr--
ora....C2.inst  oracle       dba                  rwxrwxr--
ora....AC1.srv  oracle       dba                  rwxrwxr--
ora....AC2.srv  oracle       dba                  rwxrwxr--
ora....ICE1.cs  oracle       dba                  rwxrwxr--
ora.RAC.db      oracle       dba                  rwxrwxr--
ora....SM1.asm  oracle       dba                  rwxrwxr--
ora....R1.lsnr  oracle       dba                  rwxrwxr--
ora....er1.gsd  oracle       dba                  rwxrwxr--
ora....er1.ons  oracle       dba                  rwxrwxr--
ora....er1.vip  oracle       dba                  rwxrwxr--
ora....SM2.asm  oracle       dba                  rwxrwxr--
ora....R2.lsnr  oracle       dba                  rwxrwxr--
ora....er2.gsd  oracle       dba                  rwxrwxr--
ora....er2.ons  oracle       dba                  rwxrwxr--
ora....er2.vip  oracle       dba                  rwxrwxr--
```

OCRCONFIG

The OCRCONFIG utility allows you to perform various administrative operations on the OCR. It is located in the $ORA_CRS_HOME/bin directory and must be executed by the root user.

You can use the OCRCONFIG utility to show details of automatic physical OCR backups, to restore automatic physical OCR backups, and to export and import the contents of the OCR. In addition, OCRCONFIG is used to upgrade the OCR to the latest version or to downgrade the OCR back to a previous version.

In Oracle 10.1 and above, OCRCONFIG takes the options shown in Table 16-1.

Table 16-1. *OCRCONFIG Options*

Option	Description
-help	Display the help message
-showbackup	Display the node, location, and time stamp for the last three automatic physical backups
-backuploc	Change the OCR physical backup location
-restore	Restore the OCR from an automatic physical backup
-export	Export the contents of the OCR to an operating system file
-import	Import the contents of the OCR from an operating system file
-upgrade	Upgrade the OCR from a previous version
-downgrade	Downgrade the OCR to a previous version

In Oracle 10.2 and above, you can also use the OCRCONFIG utility to create, replace, and remove the OCR file and the OCR mirror file using the options shown in Table 16-2.

Table 16-2. *OCRCONFIG Additional Options in Oracle 10.2 and Above*

Option	Description
-replace	Add, replace, or remove an OCR file or mirror
-overwrite	Overwrite an OCR configuration on disk
-repair	Repair the local OCR configuration

In Oracle 10.1, OCRCONFIG creates a log file called ocrconfig.log in the directory from which it is executed. In Oracle 10.2, OCRCONFIG creates a log file called ocrconfig_<pid>.log in the $ORA_CRS_HOME/log/<node>/client directory.

As this utility must be executed by the root user, you may find it convenient to add $ORA_CRS_HOME/bin to the PATH environment variable in the root profile example:

```
[root@london1 root]# export ORA_CRS_HOME=/u01/app/oracle/product/10.1.0/crs
[root@london1 root]# export PATH=$PATH:$ORA_CRS_HOME/bin
```

During normal operations, you should never need to restore the OCR. In the event of an OCR failure on a production system, we recommend that you contact Oracle Support for the latest advice and assistance.

Backing Up the OCR

In Oracle 10.1 and above, the OCR is backed up automatically every four hours by the crsd daemon on one instance. The previous three backup copies are retained. A backup is also retained for each full day and at the end of each week. The frequency of backups and the number of files retained cannot be modified.

You can check the locations of the backup files using the showbackup option of the OCRCONFIG utility:

```
[root@london1 root]# ocrconfig -showbackup
london1  2005/08/04 11:15:29  /u01/app/oracle/product/10.2.0/crs/cdata/crs
london1  2005/08/03 22:24:32  /u01/app/oracle/product/10.2.0/crs/cdata/crs
london1  2005/08/03 18:24:32  /u01/app/oracle/product/10.2.0/crs/cdata/crs
london1  2005/08/02 18:24:32  /u01/app/oracle/product/10.2.0/crs/cdata/crs
london1  2005/07/31 18:24:32  /u01/app/oracle/product/10.2.0/crs/cdata/crs
```

If you have recently moved your OCR backup directory, this move will be reflected in the path names:

```
[root@london1 root]# ls -l $ORA_CRS_HOME/crs/cdata/crs
-rw-r------  1 root    root    6901760 Aug  4 11:15 backup00.ocr
-rw-r------  1 root    root    6901760 Aug  3 22:24 backup01.ocr
-rw-r------  1 root    root    6901760 Aug  3 18:24 backup02.ocr
-rw-r------  1 root    root    6897664 Aug  2 14:24 day.ocr
-rw-r------  1 root    root    6807552 Jul 31 18:31 week.ocr
```

The backup files are renamed every time a backup is taken so that the most recent backup file is backup00.ocr. In addition, a daily copy (day.ocr) and a weekly copy (week.ocr) are also maintained.

By default, backup files are created in the $ORA_CRS_HOME/crs/cdata/<cluster_name> directory, where cluster_name is the name assigned to the cluster during Oracle Clusterware installation. You can modify this location using the following:

```
ocrconfig -backuploc <directory_name>
```

The directory should preferably be on shared storage, so that all nodes in the cluster can access it.

We recommend that you manually copy the OCR backup files to another device, so you have at least two copies of each file.

Restoring the OCR

Before restoring the OCR, restart any failed applications and run the OCRCHECK utility described later in this chapter, to verify that the OCR file and its mirror have both failed. We recommend that you only attempt to restore the OCR as a last resort.

To restore the OCR from a backup copy, first check that you have a suitable backup:

```
[root@london1 root]# ocrconfig -showbackup
```

Stop Oracle Clusterware on each node:

```
[root@london1 root]# crsctl stop crs
```

Next, identify the most recent backup:

```
[root@london1 root]# ocrconfig -showbackup
```

Then, restore the backup file:

```
[root@london1 root]# ocrconfig -restore <file_name>
```

For example, to restore the most recent backup, use the following:

```
[root@london1 root]# ocrconfig -restore $ORA_CRS_HOME/cdata/crs/backup00.ocr
```

In Oracle 10.2 and above, you can optionally verify the success of the restore operation using the Cluster Verification Utility:

```
[root@london1 root]# cluvfy comp ocr -n all
```

Finally, restart the Oracle Clusterware by rebooting each node in the cluster or in Oracle 10.2 and above:

```
[root@london1 root]# crsctl start crs
```

Note that you cannot use the OCRCONFIG -restore option to restore an OCR backup that was created with the OCRCONFIG -export option. Neither can you use the OCRCONFIG -import option to restore an OCR automatic backup.

Moving the OCR

You may need to move the OCR. For example, you may wish to reconfigure your shared storage to accommodate other applications or users.

To move the OCR, you must restore the registry from a backup copy. Before commencing this procedure, check that you have a suitable backup as follows:

```
[root@london1 root]# ocrconfig -showbackup
```

Stop Oracle Clusterware on each node, for example:

```
[root@london1 root]# crsctl stop crs
```

On each node, edit the /etc/oracle/ocr.loc file, and update the ocrconfig_loc parameter:

```
ocrconfig_loc=/u05/oradata/RAC/OCRFile
local_only=FALSE
```

Move the OCR file to its new location:

```
[root@london1 root]# mv /u02/oradata/RAC/OCRFile /u05/oradata/RAC/OCRFile
```

and restore the backup file:

```
[root@london1 root]# ocrconfig -restore <file_name>
```

For example, to restore the most recent backup, use the following:

```
[root@london1 root]# ocrconfig -restore $ORA_CRS_HOME/cdata/crs/backup00.ocr
```

Check ocrconfig.log for errors:

```
08/14/2005 22:34:59
ocrconfig starts...
Warning!! cluster checking is disabled
Successfully restored OCR and set block 0
```

Note that in Oracle 10.1 the ocrconfig.log file will be created in the directory from which you executed OCRCONFIG. Any error messages will be written to this file.

On each node, run the OCRCHECK utility to verify that the OCR location has been set correctly. Finally, restart the Oracle Clusterware by rebooting each node in the cluster.

Exporting the OCR

You can export the contents of the OCR to an operating system file using the -export option of the OCRCONFIG utility.

Oracle recommends that you export your OCR before making significant configuration changes, for example, adding or deleting a node. First, stop Oracle Clusterware on each node:

```
[root@london1 root]# crsctl stop crs
```

Export the OCR to the operating system file using the following command:

```
[root@london1 root]# ocrconfig -export <pathname>
```

For example, export the contents of the OCR to /tmp/OCRFile:

```
[root@london1 root]# ocrconfig -export /tmp/OCRFile
```

Finally, restart the Oracle Clusterware by rebooting each node in the cluster.
Note that the export file is in a binary format that cannot be edited using a text editor.

Importing the OCR

You can import the contents of the OCR from an operating system file using the -import option of the OCRCONFIG utility. First, stop Oracle Clusterware on each node:

```
[root@london1 root]# crsctl stop crs
```

Next, import the OCR from the operating system file:

```
[root@london1 root]# ocrconfig -import <pathname>
```

For example, import the contents of the OCR from /tmp/OCRFile:

```
[root@london1 root]# ocrconfig -import /tmp/OCRFile
```

Finally, restart the Oracle Clusterware by rebooting each node in the cluster.
In Oracle 10.2 and above, you can optionally run the Cluster Verification Utility (CLUVFY) to check the integrity of the OCR:

```
[root@london1 root]# cluvfy comp ocr -n all
```

You cannot restore your OCR configuration from an automatic physical backup using the -import option of OCRCONFIG. You must use the -restore option instead.

Note that many configuration changes are recorded in the OCR but also affect other files and directories outside the OCR. If you restore the contents of OCR using the -import option, external files and directories will not be affected. Consequently, the contents of the OCR may become inconsistent with the rest of the environment.

Upgrading the OCR

When you install Oracle Clusterware, the OCR is automatically upgraded:

```
[root@london1 root]# ocrconfig -upgrade
```

You should not need to run this command manually unless specifically advised by Oracle Support or as part of a documented procedure.

Downgrading the OCR

When you install Oracle Clusterware, the OCR is automatically downgraded as well:

```
[root@london1 root]# ocrconfig -downgrade
```

As with the upgrade, you should not need to run this command manually unless specifically advised by Oracle support.

Adding an OCR File

In Oracle 10.2 and above, we recommend that you allow Oracle to mirror the OCR file. A maximum of two OCR files are supported: a primary OCR and a secondary OCR. If you have migrated from a previous release or chosen not to create an OCR mirror during installation, you can subsequently use OCRCONFIG to create an OCR file or mirror as follows:

```
[root@london1 root]# ocrconfig -replace ocr <filename>
[root@london1 root]# ocrconfig -replace ocrmirror <filename>
```

When we tested this option in Oracle 10.2.0.1, we found that OCRCONFIG incorrectly calculated the size of the target directory or device and would not allow OCR file creation to continue. We believe this failure is a bug and suggest that you test this procedure on a development system before attempting it in a production environment.

Replacing an OCR File

In Oracle 10.2 and above, if you have mirrored OCR files, you can optionally replace one of the files. The mirrored version of the OCR that you do not intend to replace must be online, and Oracle Clusterware must be running on the local node. The file that you are replacing can be either online or offline.

To replace an existing OCR file, use one of the following commands:

```
[root@london1 root]# ocrconfig -replace ocr <filename>
[root@london1 root]# ocrconfig -replace ocrmirror <filename>
```

These commands replace the existing OCR or OCR mirror file with the file specified by the filename argument.

If any nodes in the cluster are shut down when the -replace command is issued, then you will need to run the -repair option of OCRCONFIG on each of these nodes in order to update the OCR configuration before you can restart Oracle Clusterware successfully.

Deleting an OCR File

In Oracle 10.2 and above, you can use OCRCONFIG to delete the OCR file or the OCR mirror using the following commands:

```
[root@london1 root]# ocrconfig -replace
[root@london1 root]# ocrconfig -replace ocrmirror
```

The remaining OCR file must be online during this operation. You might need to use these commands if, for example, you have moved the OCR to a storage subsystem that implements external redundancy.

If you remove the primary OCR, then the mirrored OCR becomes the new primary OCR.

Repairing the OCR Configuration

In Oracle 10.2 and above, if you use the -replace option of OCRCONFIG to add, replace, or remove an OCR file or mirror, the changes will be applied on all available nodes. However, if some nodes are currently down, the changes will not be propagated. In this case, you must manually apply the changes using the -repair option:

```
[root@london1 root]# ocrconfig -repair ocr <filename>
[root@london1 root]# ocrconfig -repair ocrmirror <filename>
```

This command must be run on each affected node. Oracle Clusterware must be shut down before running this command. If you have deleted one of the OCR files, you can use the following commands to update other nodes:

```
[root@london1 root]# ocrconfig -repair ocr
[root@london1 root]# ocrconfig -repair ocrmirror
```

Overriding OCR Mirroring

In Oracle 10.2 and above, if you have configured mirrored OCR files and one of the available OCR files is lost, Oracle Clusterware is automatically prevented from making further updates to avoid corruption of the surviving OCR file. In addition, Oracle Clusterware will be prevented from starting if the node is rebooted. Alert messages are written to the Oracle Clusterware alert log and are also available in EM.

If you are unable to start any cluster nodes in your environment and you cannot repair the OCR configuration using the -repair option of OCRCONFIG, then you can optionally override the OCR protection mechanism. This override enables you to use the updated OCR file to start your cluster. However, you should be aware that using the override can result in the loss of recent updates to the OCR.

You can force Oracle Clusterware to restart on a node using the following:

```
[root@london1 root]# ocrconfig -overwrite
```

We stress that this command should only be used when all other possibilities have been exhausted.

OCRCHECK

In Oracle 10.1 and above, you can verify the integrity of the OCR using the OCRCHECK utility.

The OCRCHECK utility is located in $ORA_CRS_HOME/bin. It creates a log file called ocrcheck.log in the directory from which it is executed. The following example shows typical output from the OCRCHECK utility:

```
[root@london1 root]# ocrcheck
Status of Oracle Cluster Registry is as follows :
        Version                  :          2
        Total space (kbytes)     :     262144
        Used space (kbytes)      :       7752
        Available space (kbytes) :     254392
        ID                       : 1093363319
        Device/File Name         : /u02/oradata/RAC/OCRFile1
                                   Device/File integrity check succeeded
                                   /u03/oradata/RAC/OCRFile2
                                   Device/File integrity check succeeded
        Cluster registry integrity check succeeded
```

In Oracle 10.1, this utility does not print the ID or device/file name information.

The OCRCHECK utility also creates a log file called ocrcheck.log. In Oracle 10.1, this file will be created in the directory where you run OCRCHECK. In Oracle 10.2, logging information is written to the file ocrcheck_<pid>.log in the $ORA_CRS_HOME/log/<node>/client directory.

The contents of the log file should closely resemble the output of the utility, as in the following example:

```
<timestamp> [OCRCHECK][3076427904]ocrcheck starts...
<timestamp> [OCRCHECK][3076427904]protchcheck: OCR status : total = [262144],
  used = [7752], avail = [254392]
<timestamp> [OCRCHECK][3076427904]Exiting [status=success]...
```

Any error messages will also be written to this file.

OCRDUMP

In Oracle 10.1 and above, you can dump the contents of the OCR using the OCRDUMP utility, which is located in $ORA_CRS_HOME/bin:

```
ocrdump [<dump_file_name>]
```

The contents of the OCR will be written in an ASCII format to the specified file. If the command is executed with no parameters as follows, it will create a file called OCRDUMPFILE in the current working directory:

```
[root@london1 root]# ocrdump
```

Note that you cannot import or restore the contents of the ASCII dump file back into the OCR. You can optionally specify a name for the output file, for example:

```
[root@london1 root]# ocrdump ocr_cluster1
```

This utility has a number of enhancements in Oracle 10.2 and above. For example, you can write output to stdout:

```
[root@london1 root]# ocrdump -stdout
```

You also have the option to restrict the amount of output by specifying a key:

```
[root@london1 root]# ocrdump -stdout SYSTEM
[root@london1 root]# ocrdump -stdout SYSTEM.css
[root@london1 root]# ocrdump -stdout SYSTEM.css.misscount
```

Finally, you can optionally format output in XML:

```
[root@london1 root]# ocrdump -stdout SYSTEM.css.misscount -xml
<OCRDUMP>
<COMMAND>
  $ORA_CRS_HOME/bin/ocrdump.bin -stdout -keyname SYSTEM.css.misscount -xml
</COMMAND>
<KEY>
<NAME>SYSTEM.css.misscount</NAME>
<VALUE_TYPE>UB4 (10)</VALUE_TYPE>
<VALUE><![CDATA[60]]></VALUE>
<USER_PERMISSION>PROCR_ALL_ACCESS</USER_PERMISSION>
<GROUP_PERMISSION>PROCR_READ</GROUP_PERMISSION>
<OTHER_PERMISSION>PROCR_READ</OTHER_PERMISSION>
<USER_NAME>root</USER_NAME>
<GROUP_NAME>root</GROUP_NAME>
</KEY>
</OCRDUMP>
```

In Oracle 10.1, OCRDUMP creates a log file called ocrdump.log in the current working directory; in Oracle 10.2 and above, the log file is called ocrdump_<pid>.log and is created in $ORA_CRS_HOME/log/<node>/client.

Administering Voting Disks

In Oracle 10.2 and above, we recommend that you create multiple voting disks to eliminate a potential single point of failure. However, you should still back up these disks on a regular basis and test recovery procedures. To back up a voting disk, you can use the dd operating system utility:

```
[root@london1 root]# dd if=<voting_disk_name> of=<backup_file_name>
```

You do not need to shut down the database or Oracle Clusterware before backing up the voting disk.

Although the voting disks are, in theory, identical, backing up each configured voting disk is recommended. As voting disk locations are configured in the OCR, modifying them during any recovery process is difficult. Therefore, the most straightforward strategy is to back up all of the voting disks and, if recovery is necessary, restore each copy to its original location.

To recover the voting disks, ensure that all databases and Oracle Clusterware are shut down. You can then restore the voting disks using the dd operating system utility:

```
[root@london1 root]# dd if=<backup_file_name> of=<voting_disk_name>
```

Oracle Clusterware Logging

In Oracle 10.2, Oracle Clusterware log files are created in the $ORA_CRS_HOME/log directory. This directory can be located on shared storage; therefore, it contains a subdirectory for each node (e.g., $ORA_CRS_HOME/log/london1).

The $ORA_CRS_HOME/log/<node> directory contains the Oracle Clusterware alert log (e.g., alertlondon1.log). If you are investigating a problem with Oracle Clusterware, this file should be your first point of reference. The $ORA_CRS_HOME/log/<node> directory also contains of the following subdirectories:

- **client**: Contains log files for various OCR applications, including CLSCFG, CSS, OCRCHECK, OCRCONFIG, OCRDUMP, and OIFCFG
- **crsd**: Contains log files for the crsd daemon, including crsd.log
- **cssd**: Contains log files for ocssd daemon, including ocssd.log
- **evmd**: Contains log files for evmd daemon, including evmd.log
- **racg**: Contains log files for node applications, such as VIP and ONS

The log files in these directories grow quite rapidly, so you may wish to back them up and truncate them periodically. In addition, check for core dumps and delete them when they are no longer required.

In Oracle 10.1, the log files can be found in different locations. There is no equivalent to the client directory; client applications, such as OCRCONFIG and OIFCFG, generally create log files in the current working directory. The remaining daemons create log files in the following directories:

- **crsd**: $ORA_CRS_HOME/crs/log
- **cssd**: $ORA_CRS_HOME/css/log
- **evmd**: $ORA_CRS_HOME/evm/log
- **racg**: $ORA_CRS_HOME/racg/log and $ORA_CRS_HOME/racg/dump

Summary

In this chapter, we discussed Oracle Clusterware, which was introduced in Oracle 10.1 for all RAC platforms. In Oracle 10.1, Clusterware suffers from a number of bugs, and we strongly recommended that you upgrade to Oracle 10.1.0.4 and install all relevant patches if you wish to use Oracle Clusterware in this release.

In Oracle 10.2, Clusterware has been significantly enhanced and has proved to be a solid and stable feature. In our experience, Oracle Clusterware runs adequately for most users in Oracle 10.2.0.1. As Oracle Clusterware is a fundamental part of any RAC database, we recommend that you implement any new systems on Oracle 10.2 in order to benefit from this stability.

CHAPTER 17

■ ■ ■

Application Development

In this chapter, we investigate RAC-specific development concepts. We begin by discussing some RAC-specific development topics, including identifying instances and services, memory and disk considerations, and node affinity. In the second part of the chapter, we examine some advanced RAC pro[(H1F)]gramming techniques and the concepts underlying them, including Transparent Application Failover (TAF), Fast Application Notification (FAN), and the Oracle Clusterware High Availability (HA) Framework.

RAC-Specific Development Considerations

In this section, we discuss some general RAC-related development topics, including the following:

- Instances and database services
- Multiple SGAs
- Local and shared storage
- Node affinity

Instances and Database Services

In a RAC environment, you sometimes need to identify the current instance and database service to which your session is connected. In this section, we describe some methods to determine this information.

Determining the Current Instance

Often, being able to determine the instance to which an application or utility is currently connected is useful. There are a number of ways to do this.

In Oracle 8.1.5 and above, the recommended method is to use the SYS_CONTEXT built-in function, for example:

```
SQL> SELECT SYS_CONTEXT ('USERENV','INSTANCE') FROM dual;
```

This returns the current instance number in the range 1 to N, where N is the maximum number of instances.

Prior to Oracle 8.1.5, the recommended method was to use the USERENV built-in function:

```
SQL> SELECT USERENV ('INSTANCE') FROM dual;
```

This also returns the current instance number in the range 1 to *N*. In Oracle 10*g*, this function is still used in the definitions of many dynamic performance views.

The current instance number can also be obtained from the V$INSTANCE dynamic performance view, as in the following example:

```
SQL> SELECT instance_number FROM v$instance;
```

Finally, the instance number is available in the INST_ID field of every X$ table in the instance. The X$ tables can only be accessed by the SYS user with the SYSDBA privilege, for example:

```
SQL> SELECT inst_id FROM x$ksxpia;
```

Determining the Current Service

You can use the SYS_CONTEXT built-in function to determine the name of the service to which a session is currently connected as follows:

```
SQL> SELECT SYS_CONTEXT ('USERENV','SERVICE_NAME') FROM dual;
```

You may also use the USERENV built-in function to obtain the same information:

```
SQL> SELECT USERENV ('SERVICE_NAME') FROM dual;
```

Multiple SGAs

The majority of applications will run on RAC without modification. However, you should be aware that applications that pass messages between processes in the SGA may work correctly on RAC, including applications using the built-in packages and dynamic performance views discussed in the following sections.

DBMS_ALERT Package

This supplied package allows sessions to register an interest in an alert and to receive a message when another session posts the alert. The memory structures required to support the alert mechanism are stored within the SGA. There is no concept of interinstance messaging for alerts, so both the source and target processes must be connected to the same SGA and, consequently, the same instance in order for the target process to successfully receive the alert.

DBMS_PIPE Package

The DBMS_PIPE supplied package allows sessions to send messages to and receive messages from other sessions. As with the closely related DBMS_ALERT package, memory structures required to support the interprocess communication mechanism are stored in the SGA. Like the alert mechanism, there is no concept of interinstance messaging for pipes, so both the source and destination processes must be connected to the same SGA in order for the destination process to receive the message.

You can resolve the issues arising from use of DBMS_ALERT and DBMS_PIPE by configuring all messages to be exchanged on a single instance. However, this may affect availability. Therefore, you should consider creating a service to allocate a backup instance in the event of failure of the primary instance.

In extreme situations, you may also experience issues with scalability if all messages are exchanged on a single node. If so, we recommend that you investigate modifying your application to use Advanced Queuing (AQ), which can be used to simulate the behavior of the DBMS_ALERT and DBMS_PIPE packages.

Session Variables Package

In addition to interprocess communication issues, if sessions in your application read information that is stored in session-based structures, such as V$SESSION, your application may need modification to work across multiple nodes. Affected fields may include some of those that can be set by the DBMS_APPLICATION_INFO package and returned by either V$SESSION or the built-in SYS_CONTEXT function. These fields include CLIENT_INFO, MODULE, and ACTION. If your application uses these fields to communicate information from one session to another, you may need to modify your application.

Local and Shared Storage

If you are developing a new application or porting an existing application to a RAC environment, you should consider a number of disk-related issues when implementing both Oracle and custom features.

It may be necessary to modify your application if you are using certain Oracle features, including the following:

- Directories
- External tables
- BFILEs
- The UTL_FILE supplied package

Directories

Oracle uses directory objects to support a number of features, including external tables, the Data Pump, and BFILEs. If you are using Oracle directories, you will need to ensure that the directories are located on shared storage. Otherwise, if you have multiple copies of the directories, you will need to ensure that all nodes have access to at least one copy of each directory.

External Tables

If you are using external tables, then you will need to ensure that the files containing the tables are located on shared storage. Otherwise, you will need to ensure that all nodes have access to one or more copies of the external table datafiles.

BFILEs

BFILEs are large object (LOB) structures that exist outside the database, but that are logically part of the database. They can be used to store or reference large files, such as photographs, videos, or sound clips, which may be located on remote servers. Unlike other LOBs such as BLOBs and CLOBs, BFILEs are read-only objects. The files referenced by BFILE objects should be located on shared storage if possible, for ease of maintenance. Alternatively, as they are only accessed for read operations, they can be duplicated on the local storage of each node.

UTL_FILE Package

The UTL_FILE package allows operating system files to be opened, read, and written by Oracle sessions. In previous versions, directories in which UTL_FILE subroutines were permitted to create output files were restricted by the UTL_FILE_DIR initialization parameter. However, this parameter was not system-modifiable and proved to be of limited use.

In Oracle 9.0.1 and above, the UTL_FILE package has been enhanced to include new functionality, which allows you to specify file locations using directory objects. In a RAC environment, ensure that these objects are located, if possible, on shared storage. If locating them on shared storage is not possible, you may be able to store all output files on a single node, but doing so introduces a single point of failure, which may impact availability. If a single point of failure is not acceptable, you may need to modify your application to create one directory on each node.

Custom Features

If your application uses files to store or communicate information, you may need to review your application design.

If you are using shared storage, your application should continue to function as before, though you may need to review any use by your application of implicit file locking functionality.

If you are using local storage, on the other hand, you have a number of choices. You may choose to store all files on a single node, in which case you may adversely affect the availability of your application. If poor application availability is not acceptable, you can create a database service to specify a primary instance and a backup instance for the application. If you specify these, you must ensure that any directory and file structures are replicated on all relevant nodes in the cluster.

Alternatively, you may use OCFS2 or a commercially available cluster file system, such as PolyServe or GFS, to provide additional shared storage for application files.

Finally, you may choose to use NFS, or some other networking protocol, to allow all nodes to access the files. In this case, you should take care not to inadvertently introduce a single point of failure in your application by configuring all clients to rely on the same server.

Node Affinity

As we have seen, developing applications that have affinity for a single node is often preferable. In Oracle 10.1 and above, you can use services to define primary and backup nodes for an application. In Oracle 10.2 and above, these services can also be used within the Oracle Clusterware HA Framework, which is discussed in detail later in this chapter.

In addition, a number of Oracle features can be configured to specify primary and backup nodes, including the following:

- Advanced Queuing
- Scheduler

Advanced Queuing

Advanced Queuing (AQ) was introduced in Oracle 8.0 and allows persistent queue objects to be created in the database. Data can be queued by one session and removed from the queue by one or more other sessions.

Every queue must have a queue table, which is a database object that provides the environment for one or more queue objects. The queue table is created using the CREATE_QUEUE_TABLE procedure of the DBMS_AQADM supplied package. When creating the queue table object, you can specify a primary instance that should normally perform queue monitoring and propagation operations. In addition, you may specify a secondary instance to which queue operations can be relocated in the event of the failure of the primary instance.

In the following example, a queue table called `QUEUE_TABLE1` is created with a primary instance of `RAC1` and a secondary (backup) instance of `RAC2`:

```
SQL> EXECUTE DBMS.AQADM.CREATE_QUEUE_TABLE ( -
queue_table => 'QUEUE_TABLE1', -
queue_payload => 'VARCHAR2', -
primary_instance => 'RAC1', -
secondary_instance => 'RAC2');
```

The default value for both the `primary_instance` and `secondary_instance` parameters is `NULL`, which means that queue monitoring and scheduling will be performed by any available instance. The preferred instances can subsequently be modified using the `ALTER_QUEUE_TABLE` procedure of the `DBMS_AQADM` package, for example:

```
SQ> EXECUTE DBMS.AQADM.ALTER_QUEUE_TABLE ( -
queue_table => 'QUEUE_TABLE1', -
primary_instance => 'RAC3', -
secondary_instance => 'RAC4');
```

Scheduler

The `DBMS_SCHEDULER` package was introduced in Oracle 10.1 to replace the `DBMS_JOB` package. The `DBMS_JOB` package is still available for backward compatibility, but we strongly recommend that you investigate the `DBMS_SCHEDULER` package for any future applications. While `DBMS_JOB` is instance-aware in a RAC environment, it is not capable of performing any load balancing across instances; `DBMS_SCHEDULER` is fully instance-aware and can direct jobs to the least loaded nodes based on current workloads.

In addition to RAC awareness, `DBMS_SCHEDULER` supports schedule windows, detailed logging within the database of job activity, and external operating system calls, and is fully integrated with Resource Manager.

Also, `DBMS_SCHEDULER` supports a number of objects that were not available in the `DBMS_JOB` package. These include the following:

- **Programs**: Define the action that is being performed
- **Schedule**: Specifies when jobs can be executed
- **Jobs**: Combine the program objects and schedule objects and can include user-defined arguments
- **Job Classes**: Group jobs together, allowing priorities to be specified
- **Windows**: Combine time windows with resource profiles
- **Window Groups**: Combine windows together for jobs using windows as a schedule

Jobs are read by a job coordinator process and job slaves are invoked. Job slaves may be internal processes or external programs, and the number of job slaves is controlled by the `MAX_JOB_SLAVE_PROCESSES` parameter.

In a RAC environment, each instance has one job coordinator, as shown in Figure 17-1. The job table is stored in the database; therefore, there is only one job table across the database.

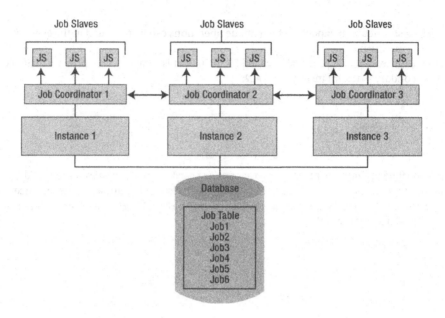

Figure 17-1. *Scheduler architecture*

In addition to controlling the job slaves, the job coordinator processes communicate with each other across the instances to ensure that the workload is balanced across the cluster.

You can optionally indicate what instances should be preferred when executing scheduler jobs by specifying a service name for a job class. Every job executed within that job class will connect using the same database service. The preferred and backup instances are configured within the service.

The service can be optionally specified in the CREATE_JOB_CLASS procedure of the DBMS_SCHEDULER package, for example:

```
SQL> EXECUTE DBMS_SCHEDULER.CREATE_JOB_CLASS ( -
    job_class_name => 'JOB_CLASS1', -
    service => 'SERVICE1');
```

The service can subsequently be altered using the SET ATTRIBUTE procedure of the DBMS_SCHEDULER package as follows:

```
SQL> EXECUTE DBMS_SCHEDULER.SET_ATTRIBUTE ( -
    name => 'JOB_CLASS1', -
    attribute => 'SERVICE' , -
    value => 'SERVICE2');
```

If you do not specify a service name, then the default service will be used. It is also possible to specify a resource consumer group for a job class. However, if one is specified in either the CREATE_JOB_CLASS or SET_ATTRIBUTE procedures, then you cannot specify a service name.

Transparent Application Failover

The Transparent Application Failover (TAF) feature was introduced in Oracle 8.1.5. In the event of an instance failure, TAF allows applications to automatically reconnect to another instance. The new connection will be identical to the original. However, any uncommitted transactions existing at the time of failure will be rolled back.

TAF can be configured to perform two types of failover: session and select. With *session failover*, any uncommitted transactions will be rolled back, and the session will be connected to another instance. With *select failover*, any uncommitted transactions will be rolled back, the session will be connected to another instance, and any SELECT statement that was executing at the time of failure will be reexecuted by the new session using the same SCN and fetched rows will be discarded up to the point that the original query failed. The SELECT statement will then continue to return the remaining rows to the client. The select option adds a small overhead to the CPU cost on the client side of each fetch operation, but for most applications, it should be negligible.

In addition, you can specify a connection method, which determines when connections are made to the failover instance. Basic connections are performed at the time of failover. However, creating a new connection is a very resource-intensive process in Oracle, and consequently, for instances with a large number of concurrent users, establishing new connections at failover time can cause long delays. Therefore, you can also specify that connections should preconnect to the failover instance. In this case, a session will have two concurrent connections. However, it will only activate the connection to the failover instance in the event that the original instance fails. While preconnection is less resource intensive at failover time, it obviously consumes additional resources during normal operations.

A TAF connection must be configured in the tnsnames.ora Oracle Net configuration file. This file is usually located in $ORACLE_HOME/network/admin, unless this location has been overridden by the $TNS_ADMIN environment variable. In Oracle 10.1 and above, the Service Management page of DBCA can generate appropriate TNS entries for TAF, for example:

```
# node1 - preferred
# node2 - preferred
# TAF BASIC
SERVICE1 =
  (DESCRIPTION =
    (ADDRESS = (PROTOCOL = TCP)(HOST = node1-vip)(PORT = 1521))
    (ADDRESS = (PROTOCOL = TCP)(HOST = node2-vip)(PORT = 1521))
    (LOAD_BALANCE = yes)
    (CONNECT_DATA =
      (SERVER = DEDICATED)
      (SERVICE_NAME = SERVICE1)
      (FAILOVER_MODE =
        (TYPE = SELECT)
        (METHOD = BASIC)
        (RETRIES = 180)
        (DELAY = 5)
      )
    )
  )
)
```

In order to configure TAF, the TNS entry must include a FAILOVER MODE clause that defines the properties of the failover as follows:

- The TYPE attribute defines the behavior following a failure. It can take the value SESSION, SELECT, or NONE.

- The METHOD attribute defines when connections are made to the failover instance. It can take the value BASIC or PRECONNECT.

- The RETRIES attribute specifies the number of times that a connection should be attempted before returning an error.

- The DELAY attribute specifies the time in seconds between each connection retry.

- In addition, if the METHOD attribute is PRECONNECT, then you can also specify the BACKUP attribute, which defines the service that should be used for secondary passive connections.

Failing over a large number of connections consumes a significant amount of resources. If the cluster is already busy, then failing over all the connections from a failed node will affect sessions currently connected on the remaining nodes. If impacting existing sessions is not acceptable, then it is possible to preconnect sessions to a failover node. Preconnecting sessions reduces resource consumption at failover time, but clearly requires additional resources, in the form of sessions and processes, to be permanently allocated to the backup nodes.

As mentioned previously, in order to preconnect sessions to a secondary node, you must specify PRECONNECT for the METHOD attribute. In Oracle 10.1 and above, you can also use DBCA to generate TNS entries for TAF preconnection. Two entries will be generated: one for the primary service and another for the preconnect service. For example, the following entries are generated when preconnection is specified for SERVICE2:

```
# node1 - preferred
# node2 - preferred
# TAF- PRECONNECT

SERVICE2 =
    (DESCRIPTION =
        (ADDRESS = (PROTOCOL = TCP)(HOST = node1-vip)(PORT = 1521))
        (ADDRESS = (PROTOCOL = TCP)(HOST = node2-vip)(PORT = 1521))
        (LOAD_BALANCE = yes)
        (CONNECT_DATA =
            (SERVER = DEDICATED)
            (SERVICE_NAME = SERVICE2)
            (FAILOVER_MODE =
                (BACKUP = SERVICE2_PRECONNECT)
                (TYPE = SELECT)
                (METHOD = PRECONNECT)
                (RETRIES = 180)
                (DELAY = 5)
            )
        )
    )

SERVICE2_PRECONNECT =
    (DESCRIPTION =
        (ADDRESS = (PROTOCOL = TCP)(HOST = node1-vip)(PORT = 1521))
        (ADDRESS = (PROTOCOL = TCP)(HOST = node2-vip)(PORT = 1521))
        (LOAD_BALANCE = yes)
        (CONNECT_DATA =
            (SERVER = DEDICATED)
            (SERVICE_NAME = SERVICE2_PRECONNECT)
            (FAILOVER_MODE =
                (BACKUP = SERVICE2)
                (TYPE = SELECT)
                (METHOD = BASIC)
                (RETRIES = 180)
                (DELAY = 5)
            )
        )
    )
```

A primary service and a preconnect service are defined automatically. The primary service defines a FAILOVER_MODE METHOD of PRECONNECT using the SERVICE2_PRECONNECT service. Note, however, that the preconnect service defines a FAILOVER_MODE METHOD of BASIC. The existence of virtual IP addresses in Oracle 10.1 simplifies the configuration of preconnections, as you can specify all nodes in the cluster for each service. Oracle will manage the assignment of sessions to each node.

TAF works with both Java and C applications. In order to use TAF, the client must be using the Oracle Call Interface (OCI) library, so if you are using JDBC, you will need to connect using the OCI thick client.

A special interface called `OracleOCIFailover` defines the constants and callback method that should be used in JDBC TAF programs.

```
public interface OracleOCIFailover
{
        // Failover Types
        public static final int FO_SESSION = 1;
        public static final int FO_SELECT = 2;
        public static final int FO_NONE = 3;

        // Failover Events
        public static final int FO_BEGIN = 1;
        public static final int FO_END = 2;
        public static final int FO_ABORT = 3;
        public static final int FO_REAUTH = 4;
        public static final int FO_ERROR = 5;
        public static final int FO_RETRY = 6;
        public static final int FO_EVENT_UNKNOWN = 7;

        public int callbackFn
                (Connection connection,
                Object ctxt,    // Anything the user wants to save
                int type,       // One of the above possible Failover types
                int event);     // One of the above possible Failover events
}
```

The `OracleOCIFailover` interface defines the following types of failover:

- **FO_SESSION**: The user session will be reauthenticated by the server. Any open cursors in the client must be reexecuted by the application. `FO_SESSION` is equivalent to `FAILOVER_MODE=SESSION` in `tnsnames.ora`.

- **FO_SELECT**: The user session will be reauthenticated by the server. Any cursors open for `SELECT` statements in the client can continue fetching. The client side maintains the fetch state for each open customer. `FO_SELECT` is equivalent to `FAILOVER_MODE=SELECT` in `tnsnames.ora`.

- **FO_NONE**: Disables all failover functionality. The default failover type is `FO_NONE`, and it is equivalent to `FAILOVER_MODE = NONE`. You might wish to specify this value to explicitly prevent failover from occurring.

The `OracleOCIFailover` interface defines the following failover events:

- **FO_BEGIN**: Indicates that failover has detected a lost connection and that failover is starting.

- **FO_END**: Indicates that failover has completed successfully.

- **FO_ABORT**: Indicates that failover has completed unsuccessfully and that there is no possibility of retrying.

- **FO_REAUTH**: Indicates that the user session has been reauthenticated on the failover server.

- **FO_ERROR**: Indicates that failover was unsuccessful. However, this state might only be temporary. The client has the opportunity to sleep for a suitable period and then retry failover.

- **FO_RETRY**: This value is returned by the application if it wishes to retry failover following receipt of an `FO_ERROR` message.

The `callbackFn` method defines the behavior of the application in the event of a failover. Callbacks are registered in case of a failover and are called during the failover to notify the application of the events that are being generated.

The `callbackFn` method is illustrated in the following program, which demonstrates the behavior of TAF. Note that in order to build this program, you will need to add `$ORACLE_HOME/lib` to the `LD_LIBRARY_PATH` environment variable, so that the JRE can find the OCI library.

```java
import java.sql.*;
import oracle.jdbc.OracleConnection;
import oracle.jdbc.OracleOCIFailover;
import oracle.jdbc.pool.OracleDataSource;

public class TAF1
{
  static final String user = "<user>";
  static final String password = "<password>";
  static final String URL = "jdbc:oracle:oci8:@SERVICE1";

  public static void main (String[] args) throws Exception
  {
    CallBack callback = new CallBack ();
    String msg = null;
    Connection connection = null;
    Statement statement = null;
    ResultSet resultSet = null;

    // Create an OracleDataSource instance and set properties
    OracleDataSource ods = new OracleDataSource ();

    ods.setUser (user);
    ods.setPassword (password);
    ods.setURL (URL);

    // Connect to the database
    connection = ods.getConnection ();

    // Register TAF callback function
    ((OracleConnection)connection).registerTAFCallback (callback,msg);

    // Create a statement
    statement = connection.createStatement ();

    // Determine current instance
    resultSet = statement.executeQuery
    ("SELECT SYS_CONTEXT ('USERENV','INSTANCE') FROM dual");
    while (resultSet.next ())
    {
      // Print current instance
      System.out.println ("Instance = " + resultSet.getInt (1));
    }
    resultSet.close ();

    // Print each object id and object name for each row in all_objects
    resultSet = statement.executeQuery
    ("SELECT object_id, object_name FROM all_objects ORDER BY object_id");
    while (resultSet.next ())
```

```
    {
      System.out.println (resultSet.getInt (1) + " " + resultSet.getString (2));

      // Pause for 0.5 seconds
      Thread.sleep (500);
    }

    // Close the resultset
    resultSet.close ();

    // Close the statement
    statement.close ();

    // Close the connection
    connection.close ();
  }
}

class CallBack implements OracleOCIFailover
{
  public int callbackFn
  (Connection connection, Object context, int type, int event)
  {
    String failover_type = null;

    switch (type)
    {
      case FO_SESSION:
        failover_type = "SESSION";
      break;
      case FO_SELECT:
        failover_type = "SELECT";
      break;
      default:
        failover_type = "NONE";
      break;
    }

    switch (event)
    {
      case FO_BEGIN:
        System.out.println (context + ": " + failover_type + " failing over");
      break;
      case FO_END:
        System.out.println (context + ": failover ended");
      break;
      case FO_ABORT:
        System.out.println (context + ": failover aborted");
        // Return FO_ABORT to calling method
        return FO_ABORT;
      break;
      case FO_REAUTH:
        System.out.println (context + ": failover reauthorized");
      break;
      case FO_ERROR:
      {
        System.out.println (context + ": failover error. Sleeping...");
```

```
      try
      {
        Thread.sleep (100);
      }
      catch (InterruptedException e)
      {
        System.out.println ("Failed to sleep");
        System.out.println (e.toString ());
      }
      // Return FO_RETRY to calling method
      return FO_RETRY;
    }
    default:
      System.out.println (context + " invalid failover event");
    break;
  }

  return 0;
  }
}
```

The preceding program assumes that tnsnames.ora contains an entry similar to the one shown previously for SERVICE1 on each node in the cluster. The program performs the following steps:

1. Creates an OracleDataSource object and initializes the values of the user, password, and URL attributes. Remember to substitute appropriate values for these if you are trying this program on your own system.

2. Creates a database connection and registers the callback function declared in the CallBack class against the connection.

3. Uses the SYS_CONTEXT function to obtain the number of the instance to which the connection has been made.

4. Selects rows from the ALL_OBJECTS dictionary view, fetching them one row at a time and pausing for half a second between each row.

When the select statement has been running for a few seconds, shut down the instance on which the statement is running using SHUTDOWN ABORT:

```
[oracle@london1 oracle]$ sqlplus / as sysdba
SQL> SHUTDOWN ABORT
```

Alternatively, you can use SRVCTL to shut down the instance, for example:

```
[oracle@london1 oracle]$ srvctl stop instance -d RAC -i RAC2 -o abort
```

The program should pause for a few seconds and then resume returning rows from the point at which it stopped. The length of the interval depends on a number of factors, including the number of instances, the size of the buffer cache, and the latency of the interconnect.

If you are considering using TAF, you should remember that it is not suited to all applications. In fact, it only applies in very limited circumstances. While TAF works well for read-only applications, it presents some issues for applications that modify the database. In the event of a failure, any uncommitted transactions will be rolled back. Therefore, the application must be capable of detecting the failure and, if necessary, reapplying DML statements up to the point of failure. If this capability is a requirement, then the application must be capable of recording all statements issued in a transaction together with the values of any bind variables.

Note also that, while TAF can reauthorize a session, it does not restore the session to its previous state. Therefore, following an instance failure, you will need to restore any session variables, PL/SQL package variables, and instances of user-defined types. TAF will not restore these values automatically, so you will need to extend your applications to restore them manually.

For the reasons discussed previously, you may find that the areas within your applications that can take advantage of TAF are fairly limited. In Oracle 10.1 and above, there has been some de-emphasizing of the capabilities of TAF in favor of FAN and, specifically for JDBC applications, Fast Connection Failover (FCF). These are discussed in more detail in the next section.

Fast Application Notification

The Fast Application Notification (FAN) feature was introduced in Oracle 10.1. It enables automatic recovery of applications and workload rebalancing following changes to the cluster configuration. In order to use FAN events, applications must connect to the database using database services.

FAN has a number of advantages over previous solutions. It allows applications to balance workload across available nodes when database services start or stop. It avoids applications having to wait for TCP/IP timeouts when a node fails without closing its sockets. It prevents applications from attempting to connect to database services that are currently down and allows applications to reconnect when database services resume. It also prevents applications from processing data received from the database after the failure of the node, instance, or database service to which it is connected.

FAN can handle both UP and DOWN events. When an UP event occurs, new connections are created by the connection pool, so that the application can immediately use the new database services or instances. When a DOWN event occurs, connections to failed instances or nodes can be terminated. Uncommitted transactions can also be terminated, and the users can be immediately notified. Applications can then be redirected to the remaining instances. You can also implement server-side callouts, which can be configured to perform actions such as logging fault tickets or notifying the database administrator.

Whenever a state change occurs in the cluster, the RAC HA framework posts a FAN event immediately. Applications receive the FAN events and can react immediately to the event. With FAN, the application does not need to periodically poll the database to detect problems. In Oracle 10.1.03 and above, FAN events are also processed by the Oracle Net Services listeners and Connection Manager (CMAN).

You can use FAN events in the following three ways:

- On the database tier, you can implement FAN server-side callouts.

- Java applications can use FAN transparently using FCF, which was introduced in Oracle 10.1, by using the JDBC implicit connection cache on the application tier.

- Applications can use FAN programmatically using the Oracle Notification Service (ONS) API, which allows the application to subscribe to FAN events and execute event-handling actions.

FAN events are designed to require a minimal communication overhead, so they can be sent, queued, and received quickly. The application should receive FAN events more quickly than it can detect events itself using polling and/or time-outs.

The two categories of FAN events are as follows:

- **Service events**: Include application services and database services

- **Node events**: Include cluster membership states and node joining and leaving operations

Each FAN event consists of a header and a payload, which contains a set of name value parts. The payload has the following structure:

```
<event_type> VERSION=<n.n>
service=<service_name.db_domain_name>
[database=<db_unique_name> [instance=<instance_name>]]
[host=<hostname>]
status=<event_status> reason=<event_reason> [card=<n>]
timestamp=<event_date> <event_time>
```

where the following descriptions apply:

- **event_type**: Describes the type of FAN event.
- **service**: The name of the primary or preconnect application service.
- **database**: The name of the RAC database.
- **instance**: The name of the RAC instance.
- **host**: The name of the cluster node.
- **status**: Describes what event has occurred.
- **reason**: Describes why the event has occurred.
- **card**: Describes the server membership cardinality. This attribute indicates the number of service members that are currently online for a service and applies only to the UP event.
- **timestamp**: Contains the date and time the event was detected.

The event type field can take the values listed in Table 17-1.

Table 17-1. *FAN Event Types*

Event Type	Description
SERVICE	Primary application service event
SRV_PRECONNECT	Preconnect application service event (TAF)
SERVICEMEMBER	Application service on a specific instance event
DATABASE	Database event
INSTANCE	Instance event
ASM	ASM instance event
NODE	Cluster node event

Table 17-2 lists the values the status field can take.

Table 17-2. *FAN Status Field Values*

Status	Description
status=up	Managed resource comes up
status=down	Managed resource goes down
status=preconn_up	Preconnect application service comes up
status=preconn_down	Preconnect application service goes down
status=nodedown	Managed node goes down
status=not_restarting	Managed resource cannot failover to a remote node
status=unknown	Unrecognized status

The reason field can take the values listed in Table 17-3.

Table 17-3. *FAN Reason Field Values*

Reason	Type	Description
reason=user	Planned	User-initiated commands, such as srvctl and sqlplus
reason=failure	Unplanned	Managed resource polling checks detected a failure
reason=dependency	Unplanned	Dependency of another managed resource triggered a failure condition
reason=unknown	Unhandled	Unknown or internal application state when an event is triggered
reason=autostart	CRS boot	Initial cluster boot of a managed resource that has the profile attribute AUTO_START = 1 and that was offline before the last CRS shutdown
reason=boot	CRS boot	Initial cluster boot of a managed resource that was running before the last CRS shutdown

In Oracle 10.1, FAN events related to nodes are logged in the following directory:

```
$ORA_CRS_HOME/racg/dump
```

In Oracle 10.2, they are logged in

```
$ORA_CRS_HOME/log/<nodename>/racg
```

In Oracle 10.1, FAN events related to databases and services are written to the following directory:

```
$ORACLE_HOME/racg/dump
```

In Oracle 10.2, these events are written to

```
$ORACLE_HOME/log/<nodename>/racg
```

You can enable additional FAN diagnostics by setting the _USR_ORA_DEBUG parameter in $ORA_CRS_HOME/bin/racgwrap and $ORACLE_HOME/bin/racgwrap as follows:

```
export_USR_ORA_DEBUG =1
```

Oracle Notification Service

The Oracle Notification Service (ONS) is used by Oracle Clusterware to propagate FAN messages both within the RAC cluster and to clients and application-tier systems. ONS uses a simple publish and subscribe method to generate and deliver event messages to both local and remote consumers.

ONS is automatically installed as a node application on each node in the cluster. In Oracle 10.2, it is configured as part of the Oracle Clusterware installation process. ONS daemons run locally, sending and receiving messages from ONS daemons on other nodes in the cluster. The daemons are started automatically by Oracle Clusterware during the reboot process.

The ONS process is $ORA_CRS_HOME/opmn/bin/ons. Arguments include the following

- **-d**: Run in daemon mode
- **-a <command>**: Run administrative command, where <command> can be ping, shutdown, reload, or debug

You can check whether the ONS daemon is currently running using the SRVCTL command:

```
[oracle@london1 oracle]$ srvctl status nodeapps -n london1
VIP is running on node: london1
GSD is running on node: london1
Listener is running on node: london1
ONS daemon is running on node: london1
```

ONS can be configured in $ORA_CRS_HOME/opmn/conf/ons.config, which by default in Oracle 10.2 contains the following:

```
localport=6100
remoteport=6200
loglevel=3
useocr=on
```

The ONS configuration file can contain the following entries:

- **localport**: The port that ONS binds to, on the local interface, to talk to local clients.
- **remoteport**: The port that ONS binds to, on all interfaces, to talk to other ONS daemons.
- **nodes**: A list of other ONS daemons to communicate with, specified as either hostname | port or IP address | port.
- **loglevel**: The level of messages that should be logged by ONS. The range is 1 (minimum) to 9 (maximum) with a default level of 3.
- **logfile**: The file where log messages should be written. The default value is $ORA_CRS_HOME/opmn/logs/opmn.log.
- **useocr**: The location where node information should be stored. If the value is on, node information will be stored in the OCR; if the value is off, node information will be stored in the ONS configuration file. Do not specify useocr=on on the client side.

The ONS configuration file must contain entries for localport and remoteport. The remaining entries described previously are optional.

The nodes list should include all nodes in the RAC cluster and any other nodes where ONS is running to receive FAN events for applications, for example, the middle tier. Any ports specified in the nodes parameter should be remote. In the following example, the remote port is always 6200:

```
nodes=london1:6200,london2:6200,london7:6200,reading9:6200
```

By default, nodes configured in the OCR use port 4948. If useocr=off, the nodes and ports for the RAC cluster are taken from ons.config. If useocr=on, they are taken from the OCR. If useocr=on, then you must use the racgons utility to add ONS configuration to the OCR using the following syntax:

```
racgons add_config hostname:port [hostname:port] ...
```

For example, the following command adds nodes london1, london2, and reading9, all of which will use port 6200:

```
[oracle@london1 oracle]$ racgons add_config london1:6200 london2:6200 reading9:6200
```

You can subsequently delete nodes from the OCR ONS configuration. The syntax is

```
racgons remove_config hostname[:port] [hostname:port] ...
```

For example, the following command removes nodes london2 and reading9:

```
[oracle@london1 oracle]$ racgons remove_config london2:6200 reading9:6200
```

If no port is specified, all ports will be removed.

In Oracle 10.1.0.3, a bug caused nodes and ports defined in the OCR (useocr=on) to function incorrectly. In Oracle 10.1.0.3, therefore, nodes and ports should only be defined in ons.config.

ONSCTL

In Oracle 10.1 and 10.2, you cannot start and stop ONS independently of the other node applications using SRVCTL. You can, however, control ONS using the ONSCTL utility, which can start, stop, test, and debug ONS daemon. The ONSCTL utility should be run by the root user.

In Oracle 10.1 and above, you can check that ONS is running on all nodes using the onsctl ping command:

```
[oracle@london1 oracle]$ onsctl ping
ons is running...
```

If ONS is not running on the local node, you can restart it using

```
[oracle@london1 oracle]$ onsctl start
onsctl: ons started
```

You can stop the ONS daemon on the local node using

```
[oracle@london1 oracle]$ onsctl stop
onsctl: shutting down ons daemon ...
```

In Oracle 10.2 and above, you can instruct the ONS daemon to reread its configuration files without stopping and starting the ONS daemon using the following command:

```
[oracle@london1 oracle]$ onsctl reconfig
```

To determine the current configuration and status of the ONS daemon, use

```
[oracle@london1 oracle]$ onsctl debug
```

Finally, you can obtain a current list of ONSCTL commands using

```
[oracle@london1 oracle]$ onsctl help
```

or, for slightly more detailed information, you can use the following:

```
[oracle@london1 oracle]$ onsctl detailed
```

Server-Side Callouts

Server-side callouts provide a mechanism to program the HA framework to perform specific actions in response to FAN events. They can be simple scripts that can be deployed with minimum effort or compiled executables written in any programming language.

FAN events are generated in response to a state change, which can include the following:

- Starting or stopping the database
- Starting or stopping an instance
- Starting or stopping a service
- A node leaving the cluster

When a state change occurs, the RAC HA framework posts a FAN event to ONS immediately. When a node receives an event through ONS, it will asynchronously execute all executables in the server-side callouts directory, which is $ORA_CRS_HOME/racg/usrco. Server-side callouts must be stored in this directory; otherwise, they will not be executed.

If the $ORA_CRS_HOME/racg/usrco directory does not already exist, you should create it on every node in the cluster:

```
mkdir $ORA_CRS_HOME/racg/usrco
chown oracle:oinstall $ORA_CRS_HOME/racg/usrco
```

All callout programs should be created in this directory. In the following example, we will create a shell script called $ORA_CRS_HOME/racg/usrco/callout1, which contains the following:

```
#! /bin/ksh
logger "ONS:" $*
```

The first line of this script specifies the shell that should be used, in this case the Korn shell. The second line writes all arguments passed to the script to the system log, which is /var/log/messages by default.

You must set the owner and execute permission for the callout:

```
[root@london1 root]# chown oracle:oinstall $ORA_CRS_HOME/racg/usrco/callout1
[root@london1 root]# chmod 744 $ORA_CRS_HOME/racg/usrco/callout1
```

In addition, you must remember to copy the script to each node in the cluster. The script will automatically be executed whenever the HA framework generates a RAC event.

If you start the database using

```
[oracle@london1 oracle]$ srvctl start database -d RAC
```

you should see something similar to the following in the system log:

```
Aug 10 15:51:20 server3 logger: ONS:  ASM VERSION=1.0
service= database= instance=ASM1 host=server3 status=up
reason=boot timestamp=10-Aug-2005 15:51:16
Aug 10 15:52:10 server3 logger: ONS:  INSTANCE VERSION=1.0
service=RAC database=RAC instance=RAC1 host=server3 status=up
reason=boot timestamp=10-Aug-2005 15:52:09
Aug 10 15:52:35 server3 logger: ONS:  SERVICEMEMBER VERSION=1.0
service=SERVICE1 database=RAC instance=RAC1 host=server3 status=up
reason=user card=1 timestamp=10-Aug-2005 15:52:35
Aug 10 15:52:36 server3 logger: ONS:  DATABASE VERSION=1.0
service=RAC database=RAC instance= host=server3 status=up
reason=boot timestamp=10-Aug-2005 15:52:36
```

Fast Connection Failover

Fast Connection Failover (FCF) was introduced in Oracle 10.1 and builds on the infrastructure created by FAN events and ONS.

Most midtier applications use a connection pool. When multitier architectures were originally introduced, many stateless applications created a new connection to the Oracle database every time they needed to execute a statement, resulting in a highly inefficient process that severely limited scalability. More recent applications implement a connection pool, from which applications temporarily use existing connections, rather than creating new ones.

When an application utilizing a JDBC connection pool is configured to use FCF, it automatically subscribes to FAN events. It can react to UP and DOWN events from the database cluster. This enables the application to rapidly detect and clean up invalid cached connections in response to DOWN events communicated via ONS.

FCF also allows load balancing across available connections in response to UP events, allowing the workload to be distributed evenly across all available RAC instances. When an instance is restarted, an UP event is sent. New connections should then be directed to the new instance. The connection pool will attempt to rebalance connections by retiring some connections and creating new ones.

FCF has a number of prerequisites. The application must be written in Java, use the Oracle JDBC drivers, and enable the implicit connection cache. The application must also use service names to connect to the database, which must be Oracle 10.1.0.3 or above. ONS must be installed and configured on any client nodes. In other words, you must configure ONS on any application tier or other midtier servers that connect to the database.

In order to deploy FCF-enabled applications, you must first configure ONS on each RAC node. You must also install and configure ONS on each node in the application tier. The connection cache will not receive messages if the ONS daemon is not running on the local node.

Note that ONS was shipped in Oracle 10.1.0.2 and above. However, ONS was not shipped with the Oracle 10.1.0.2 client, so we recommend that you upgrade this client to Oracle 10.1.0.3 or above. If this is not possible, then you should obtain the patch for bug 3848905.

You can check whether the ONS daemon is active on the client:

```
[root@london1 root]# onsctl ping
```

On the middle tier, ONS is always configured in $ORACLE_HOME/opmn/conf/ons.config, which must contain values for the following parameters:

- **localport**: The port that ONS binds to, on the local interface, to communicate with local clients

- **remoteport**: The port that ONS binds to, on all interfaces, to communicate with other ONS daemons

- **nodes**: A list of other ONS daemons to communicate with specified as either hostname | port or IP address | port

The following is an example of an ONS configuration file for the middle tier:

```
localport=6100    # port ONS is writing to on this node
remote=6200       # port ONS is listening on this node
nodes=london1:6200,london2:6200,london7:6200,reading9:6200
```

The hostname of the local node can be included in the ons.config file, allowing the same file to be copied to every node in the configuration without change. The local node is discarded when the node list is read. You do not need to include all RAC nodes in the node list; at a minimum, each ONS client must be aware of at least one RAC node. However, unless you have an extremely large number of hosts, we recommend that you include all RAC nodes for increased resilience.

To use FAN and FCF with Oracle 10.1 and above, Java applications can receive FAN events using either thick or thin JDBC drivers. Applications must use the implicit connection cache, which can be enabled as follows:

```
OracleDataSource.setConnectionCachingEnabled (true);
```

When implicit caching is enabled, the first connection request to the OracleDataSource transparently creates a connection cache. In addition, the applications must also set the FastConnectionFailoverEnabled attribute to true. For example, the following code creates an FCF-enabled connection:

```
OracleDataSource ods = New OracleDataSource ();
ods.setUser ("USER1");
ods.setPassword ("USER1");
ods.setConnectionCachingEnabled (true);
ods.setFastConnectionFailoverEnabled (true);
ods.setConnectionCacheName ("MyCache");
```

```
ods.setConnectionCacheProperties (cp);
ods.setURL ("jdbc:oracle:thin:@(DESCRIPTION=
        (LOAD_BALANCE=on)
        (ADDRESS=(PROTOCOL=TCP)(HOST=london1-vip)(PORT=1521)
        (ADDRESS=(PROTOCOL=TCP)(HOST=london2-vip)(PORT=1521)
        (CONNECT_DATA=(SERVICE_NAME=SERVICE1)))");
```

Once enabled, the FastConnectionFailoverEnabled attribute cannot be disabled again during the lifetime of the cache.

When you start an FCF-enabled application, you must ensure that the CLASSPATH environment variable includes $ORACLE_HOME/opmn/lib/ons.jar.

In addition, you must also specify the following system property:

```
-Doracle.ons.oraclehome = <location of oracle home>
```

Alternatively, you can hard-code this property into your application, for example:

```
System.setProperty ("oracle.ons.oraclehome","/u01/app/oracle/product/10.2.0/db_1");
```

If you have enabled FCF and the node that you are connected to fails, the database will detect the error and roll back the transaction, while the FAN event is propagated to the JDBC application immediately. On receiving the FAN event, the cache manager will notify all connected sessions and clean up any other invalid connections. However, your session will not be automatically connected to another instance. Handling the error message and taking appropriate action within your application are your responsibilities.

When an application holding an invalid connection tries to use the connection again, it will receive the following Oracle error:

```
ORA-17008 Closed Connnection
```

When the application receives an ORA-17008 error, it should retry the connection request and repeat the transaction. The application need not roll back any uncommitted transactions at this point.

The real power of FCF can be demonstrated when a number of applications are connected to the same instance concurrently. If the instance fails, then all connections will be notified almost immediately of the failure and will fail with ORA-17008 the next time they attempt to execute an SQL statement. If FCF is not enabled, sessions may have to wait for TCP/IP timeouts before failing. Waits may be a considerable length of time, depending on the networking configuration.

We used the following program, called FCFDemo, to investigate FCF. This program should be executed in several concurrent shells on an ONS-enabled application server. The FCFDemo program queries the DBA_TABLES dictionary view and fetches the results back one row at a time, sleeping for five seconds between each fetch. If one instance on which the sessions are connected is killed, then all other sessions connected to that instance will receive an immediate notification. When the other sessions attempt to perform the next SQL statement, they will fail with ORA-17008.

```
public class FCFDemo
{
  public static void main (String[] args)
  {
    Connection connection = null;

    System.setProperty
    ("oracle.ons.oraclehome","/u01/app/oracle/product/10.2.0/db_1");
    try
    {
      // Create an OracleDataSource instance
      OracleDataSource ods = new OracleDataSource ();

      // Set the user name, password, driver type and network protocol
      ods.setUser ("US01");
      ods.setPassword ("US01");
      ods.setDriverType ("oci8");
      ods.setTNSEntryName ("SERVICE2");

      // enable implicit connection caching
      ods.setConnectionCachingEnabled (true);

      // enable fast connection failover
      ods.setFastConnectionFailoverEnabled (true);

      // create the connection (and transparently create the connection cache)
      connection = ods.getConnection ();

      // get the instance number of the current instance
      Statement statement = connection.createStatement ();
      ResultSet resultSet = statement.executeQuery
      ("SELECT SYS_CONTEXT ('USERENV','INSTANCE') FROM dual");
      while (resultSet.next ())
      {
        System.out.println (resultSet.getInt (1));
      }
      resultSet.close ();
      statement.close ();

      // select rows from a large table or view
      statement = connection.createStatement ();
      resultSet = statement.executeQuery
      ("SELECT object_id,object_name FROM dba_objects");

      // while there are still rows in the result set
      while (resultSet.next ())
      {
        // print one row
        System.out.println (resultSet.getInt (1) + " " + resultSet.getString(2));
        // sleep for 5 seconds
        try
        {
          Thread.sleep (5000);
        }
        catch (InterruptedException e) {}
      }
```

```
      resultSet.close ();
      statement.close ();
      connection.close ();
    }
    catch (SQLException e)
    {
      System.out.println ("SQLException");
      System.out.println (e.getMessage());
    }
  }
}
```

FCF is not compatible with TAF. In particular, you cannot use the same connection string. The differences between FCF and TAF follow:

- FCF supports application-level connection retries, enabling the application to determine whether to retry the connection or to throw an exception. TAF supports connection retries at the OCI/Net layer, which is less flexible.

- FCF is integrated with the implicit connection cache, which allows the connection cache manager to manage the cache for high availability. Failed connections can be invalidated in the cache. TAF works at the network level on a per-connection basis. Therefore, with TAF, the connection cache cannot be notified of failures.

- FCF is based on the RAC FAN mechanism, which is more efficient than TAF and can detect failures more quickly for both active and inactive connections. TAF is based on a network call mechanism, which is less efficient and potentially slower than FAN.

- FCF supports load balancing using UP events, allowing work to be distributed across active instances at runtime.

FCF may appear to be a retrograde step after TAF, and it is in some ways. In reality, the scope for using TAF is limited to read-only applications, as it rolls back uncommitted transactions before failing the connection over to another node. FCF, on the other hand, ultimately gives you more control over the behavior of your application, as you can handle any type of failure within your application code.

Oracle Clusterware High Availability Framework

In Oracle 10.2 and above, Oracle Clusterware includes an API that effectively allows you to configure your own applications to use the high availability features provided by Oracle Clusterware.

The OCR High Availability (HA) Framework allows you to protect your applications from failure. In the event of the failure of the node on which the application is running, Oracle Clusterware automatically fails over the application to another available node. Existing connections are lost, and for a short period during the failover, no connections are possible. However, within a few seconds the application should be available again on another node.

One obvious benefit of the OCR HA Framework is that it saves you from reinventing the wheel by developing your own clustering software. In addition, you can install Oracle Clusterware on as many nodes as you wish for free, as long as you have a full Oracle RAC license on at least one of the nodes within the same cluster.

On the minus side, you will need to write and maintain some additional code in order to use the HA Framework; the only restriction on the language you use is that it must be capable of returning an integer code on exit. Also, you should remember that your applications will be contributing to CPU consumption on nodes that have full RAC licenses, so in extreme situations, you may need to purchase additional cluster nodes or CPUs and licenses to maintain response times on your database cluster.

At the time of this writing, the OCR HA Framework was still very new technology, and few examples are in use. However, potential uses are for high availability monitoring software and real-time data feeds to and from other systems.

For an application to be compatible with Oracle Clusterware, it must have two basic properties:

- **Node independence**: The application must be capable of running on any node in the cluster. Therefore, application binaries should be available on all nodes in the cluster in local file systems or on shared storage. In addition, any other directories or files required by the application should be symmetrically available on all nodes.

- **Client connectivity**: Clients should be able to access the application on any node in the cluster. As the client does not initially know which node the application will be running on, Oracle uses application virtual IP addresses, which provide a method for consistently accessing the application from the network. If the node on which the application is running fails, both the application and the virtual IP address will fail over to another node. All clients should specify the virtual IP address, not the server address.

Oracle also provides a HA API, which is written in C and allows you to directly manipulate the OCR. See the Oracle documentation for further details.

The HA Framework provides the infrastructure to manage any application. Oracle Clusterware starts the application when the cluster is started. It monitors the application while it is running and restarts it if it fails. If the node on which the application is running fails, the Oracle Clusterware can be configured to restart the application on another node.

In order to use the HA Framework, you must perform the following actions:

1. Supply an action program that Oracle Clusterware will use to start, stop, and check the status of your application. This can be written in any appropriate language and is similar in concept to the service configuration scripts found in /etc/init.d.

2. Create an application VIP if the application will be accessed by external clients over the network.

3. Create an application profile, which is a text file describing the application and its protection attributes.

4. Register the application with Oracle Clusterware.

Example Application

The following example has been adapted from the Oracle white paper "Using Oracle Clusterware to Protect Third-Party Applications." That application returns the current time and date when it is queried by a telnet client. We have chosen to write our own client in C to allow us to use a structured IPC message to return the data, which is more common in production environments. The program includes the following files:

- HAFDemo.h: An include file containing constants and structures

- HAFDemoAction.c: An action program called by Oracle Clusterware

- HAFDemoServer.c: A server application program called by Oracle Clusterware

- HAFDemoClient.c: A client application program called by the end user

We describe these files in the sections that follow.

HAFDemo.h

The HAFDemo.h file contains the following:

```
// Define Application VIP address and port number as constants
#define VIP_ADDRESS    "147.43.1.200"
#define PORT           8888
#define SERVER_PROCESS "//tmp//HAFDemoServer &"

// HAFDemoServer Actions
#define QUERY          0
#define SHUTDOWN       1

// Define a message package to communicate between client and server
typedef struct ipc
{
  int action;           // QUERY or SHUTDOWN
  char timestamp[30];   // Set by QUERY action only
}
IPC;
```

We chose to hard-code the VIP address and port number for this application to reduce the complexity of the resulting code. These constants, together with the IPC message structure, are declared in haftest.h, which is included in each program file.

We copied the executables to the /tmp directory. The address of the HAFDemoServer program is also hard-coded in the include file.

HAFDemoAction.c

This program contains the interface between Oracle Clusterware and the application. The action program must accept three string parameters (start, stop, and check) and implement the following logic:

- **start**: If successful, return 0; otherwise, return 1.
- **stop**: If successful, return 0; otherwise, return 1.
- **check**: If the program is running, return 0; otherwise, return 1.

Note that the start option uses the system command to start the HAFDemoServer process, which is not particularly robust. If you implement this functionality in a production environment, you should use the fork or clone system call, together with appropriate error handling.

```
// HAFDemoAction
//
// Called by Oracle Clusterware
//
// Syntax is HAFDemoAction <command>
// where command in
//   start - start HAFDemoServer
//   stop  - stop HAFDemoServer
//   check - check HAFDemoServer is running
//
// Returns 0 for SUCCESS or 1 for FAILURE

#include <stdio.h>
#include <netinet/in.h>
#include "HAFDemo.h"
```

```
#define SUCCESS 0
#define FAILURE 1

int main (int argc, char **argv[])
{
  char command[128];
  int sockfd;
  int len;
  int res;
  struct sockaddr_in address;

  // get argument
  strcpy (command, (char *)argv[1]);

  // if argument is "start"
  if (strcasecmp (command, "start") == 0)
  {
    // start HAFDemoServer process (non-blocking)
    system (SERVER_PROCESS);
    return (SUCCESS);
  }

  // if argument is "stop"
  if (strcasecmp (command, "stop") == 0)
  {
    // create a socket
    sockfd = socket (PF_INET, SOCK_STREAM, 0);
    address.sin_family = AF_INET;
    address.sin_addr.s_addr = inet_addr ("127.0.0.1");
    address.sin_port = htons (PORT);

    // attempt to connect to HAFDemoServer
    res = connect (sockfd, (struct sockaddr *)&address, sizeof (address));

    // if connection was successful
    if (res != -1)
    {
      IPC ipc;

      // set action to shutdown
      ipc.action = SHUTDOWN;

      // send the message
      write (sockfd,&ipc,sizeof (ipc));
      close (sockfd);
    }
    return (SUCCESS);
  }

  // if argument is "check"
  if (strcasecmp (command, "check") == 0)
  {
    // create a socket
    sockfd = socket (PF_INET, SOCK_STREAM, 0);
    address.sin_family = AF_INET;
    address.sin_addr.s_addr = inet_addr ("127.0.0.1");
    address.sin_port = htons (PORT);
```

```
      // attempt to connect to HAFDemoServer
      res = connect (sockfd, (struct sockaddr *)&address, sizeof (address));

      // if connection was successful
      if (res != -1)
      {
        return (SUCCESS);
      }
    }

  return (FAILURE);
}
```

This program can be built using the following make command:

```
[oracle@london1 oracle]$ make HAFDemoAction
```

HAFDemoServer.c

The following program is the third-party server application:

```
// HAFDemoServer
//
// Called by HAFDemoServer
//
// Performs two actions
//    QUERY    : returns date and time
//    SHUTDOWN : shuts down

#include <netinet/in.h>       // Required for struct sockaddr_in
#include <time.h>             // Required for ctime
#include "HAFDemo.h"

int main ()
{
  int insock;
  int outsock;
  int addrlen;
  struct sockaddr_in inaddr;
  struct sockaddr_in from;
  time_t timeval;
  int allowreuse = 1;
  IPC ipc;

  // Create a socket - accept messages from any IP address
  insock = socket (PF_INET, SOCK_STREAM, 0);
  inaddr.sin_family = AF_INET;
  inaddr.sin_addr.s_addr = htonl (INADDR_ANY);
  inaddr.sin_port = htons (PORT);

  // Set option to allow reuse of address
  setsockopt
  (insock,SOL_SOCKET,SO_REUSEADDR,(char *)&allowreuse, sizeof (allowreuse));

  // bind socket to address
  bind (insock,(struct sockaddr *)&inaddr,sizeof (inaddr));
```

```
  // listen on socket
  listen (insock,5);

  while (1)
  {
    addrlen = sizeof (inaddr);

    // wait for a message
    outsock = accept (insock, (struct sockaddr *)&from, &addrlen);

    // read the message
    read (outsock,&ipc, sizeof (ipc));

    // if it is a shutdown message
    if (ipc.action == SHUTDOWN)
    {
      // close the sockets and exit
      close (insock);
      close (outsock);
      exit (0);
    }

    // get the date and time
    time (&timeval);

    // copy date and time into the IPC message
    strcpy ((char *)&ipc.timestamp,ctime(&timeval));

    // send the reply back to the client
    write (outsock,&ipc,sizeof (ipc));

    close (outsock);
  }
}
```

This program can be built using

```
[oracle@london1 oracle]$ make HAFDemoServer
```

HAFDemoClient.c

The following program is the third-party client application:

```
// HAFDemoClient
//
// Called by end-user
//
// No arguments

#include <stdio.h>
#include <netinet/in.h>

#include "HAFDemo.h"

#define FALSE (0==1)
#define TRUE (1==1)
```

```
int main ()
{
  struct sockaddr_in address;
  int sockfd;
  IPC ipc;
  int res;
  char *cptr;
  char s[128];

  while (TRUE)
  {
    printf ("Press NEWLINE to continue or q to quit: ");
    cptr = fgets (s,128,stdin);
    if ((*cptr == 'Q') || (*cptr == 'q'))
    {
      break;
    }

    // Create a socket
    sockfd = socket (PF_INET, SOCK_STREAM, 0);
    address.sin_family = AF_INET;
    address.sin_addr.s_addr = inet_addr (VIP_ADDRESS);
    address.sin_port = htons (PORT);

    // Attempt to connect to HAFDemoServer
    res = connect (sockfd, (struct sockaddr *)&address, sizeof (address));

    // If connection was successful
    if (res != -1)
    {
      // set action to query
      ipc.action = QUERY;

      // send message
      write (sockfd,&ipc,sizeof (ipc));

      // receive reply
      read (sockfd,&ipc,sizeof (ipc));

      printf ("Timestamp = %s",ipc.timestamp);

      close (sockfd);
    }
  }
}
```

This program can be built using

```
[oracle@london1 oracle]$ make HAFDemoClient
```

Implementing the HA Framework

Before placing the application under the protection of Oracle Clusterware, you must copy the programs to a known location. For example, copy all of the executables to the /tmp directory:

```
[oracle@london1 oracle]$ cp HAFDemoAction /tmp
[oracle@london1 oracle]$ cp HAFDemoServer /tmp
[oracle@london1 oracle]$ cp HAFDemoClient /tmp
```

Then perform the following steps:

1. Create an application VIP.

2. Create an application profile.

3. Register the application profile with Oracle Clusterware.

We describe these steps in detail in the following sections, and we also cover testing failover.

Create an Application VIP

The first step in implementing the HA Framework is to create an application VIP. The VIP is used by the client to locate the application, irrespective of the node it is currently running on.

In the following example, we will create an application VIP with the IP address 147.43.1.200 and the subnet mask of 255.255.0.0. You may wish to add an entry for hafdemovip to /etc/hosts or your DNS database.

As the oracle user, create a profile for the VIP:

```
[oracle@london1 oracle]$ $ORA_CRS_HOME/bin/crs_profile \
  -create hafdemovip \
  -t application
  -a $ORA_CRS_HOME/bin/usrvip \
  -o oi=eth0,ov=147.43.1.200,on=255.255.0.0
```

This command generates an application profile called hafdemovip.cap in the $ORA_CRS_HOME/crs/ public directory.

As the oracle user, register the VIP with Oracle Clusterware:

```
[oracle@london1 oracle]$ $ORA_CRS_HOME/bin/crs_register hafdemovip
```

You must configure the application VIP to run as the root user. Note that your own application can run as any user.

As the root user, set the owner of the application VIP to root:

```
[root@london1 root]# $ORA_CRS_HOME/bin/crs_setperm hafdemovip -o root
```

As the root user, grant the oracle user permission to run the script:

```
[root@london1 root]# $ORA_CRS_HOME/bin/crs_setperm hafdemovip -u user:oracle:r-x
```

As the oracle user, start the application VIP:

```
[oracle@london1 oracle]$ $ORA_CRS_HOME/bin/crs_start hafdemovip
```

Create an Application Profile

The next step is to generate an application profile, which is a text file containing a number of name value parameters. This file is generated by the crs_profile script. For example, the oracle user might use the following command to generate an application profile for the HAFDemo program:

```
[oracle@london1 oracle]$ $ORA_CRS_HOME/bin/crs_profile \
  -create hafdemo
  -t application
  -d "HAF Demo"
  -r hafdemovip
  -a /tmp/HAFDemoAction
  -o ci=5,ra=60
```

This command generates an application profile called hafdemo.cap in the $ORA_CRS_HOME/crs/ public directory. In this example, the description is "HAF Demo"; the required resource is the application VIP called hafdemovip; the action script is /tmp/HAFDemoAction; the check interval is five seconds; and in the event of failure, 60 restarts will be attempted.

Register the Application Profile with Oracle Clusterware

The next step is to register the application profile with Oracle Clusterware using the crs_register command. This command will register the contents of the application profile created by crs_profile in the OCR. This command succeeds silently, but it fails with an error message:

```
[oracle@london1 oracle]$ $ORA_CRS_HOME/bin/crs_register hafdemo
```

Finally, the application can be started using

```
[oracle@london1 oracle]$ $ORA_CRS_HOME/bin/crs_start hafdemo
```

At this point, you should be able to run the /tmp/HAFDemoClient program on the local node or on a remote node. This application will loop, requesting the date and time from the HAFDemoServer until you quit.

Testing Failover

If the node on which the application fails is shut down, Oracle should automatically fail over the application to another node. In this configuration, the /tmp/HAFDemoClient program may experience a delay while the failover is in progress. However, after a few seconds, the application VIP should have been moved to one of the remaining nodes, and the HAFDemoServer program should have been made available on that node.

HA Framework Commands

In Oracle 10.2, a number of existing commands have been enhanced to support the HA Framework. The executables can be found in the $ORA_CRS_HOME/bin directory and include the following:

- crs_profile
- crs_register
- crs_unregister
- crs_getperm
- crs_setperm
- crs_start
- crs_stop
- crs_stat
- crs_relocate

We describe these commands in more detail in the following sections.

crs_profile

The crs_profile command allows you to create and manipulate application profile files. It supports the following actions:

- create
- delete
- print
- template
- update
- validate

These actions are described in the following sections.

create

The first form of this command creates an application profile based on the arguments supplied. The syntax for this option follows:

```
crs_profile -create resource_name -t application
    [-dir directory_path] [-a action_script] [-B binary_pathname]
    [-d description] [-h hosting_members] [-r required_resources]
    [-l optional_resources] [-p placement_policy]
    [-o as=auto_start,ci=check_interval,ft=failure_threshold,
    fi=failure_interval,ra=restart_attempts,fd=failover_delay,
    st=script_timeout,ap=active_placement,bt=rebalance,
    ut=uptime_threshold,rt=start_timeout,pt=stop_timeout] [-f] [-q]
```

If this command is executed by the root user, the profile will be created in $ORA_CRS_HOME/crs/ profile directory; if the command is executed by any other user, the profile will be created in the $ORA_CRS_HOME/crs/public directory.

The -t argument specifies the type of resource. In this case, it is mandatory and must have the value application. The remaining arguments are optional and include the following:

- **-dir <directory path>**: Allows you to override the directory location.
- **-a <action_script>**: Specifies an action script or program (e.g., HAFDemoAction).
- **-B <binary pathname>**: Specifies the name of the application executable. crs_profile will generate an action script for this executable.
- **-d <description>**: Specifies a description (e.g., "HAFDemo").
- **-h <hosting nodes>**: Specifies a list of nodes in cluster on which application can be hosted.
- **-r <required resources>**: Specifies any required resources (e.g., hafdemovip).
- **-l <optional resources>**: Specifies any optional resources.
- **-p <placement policy>**: Specifies the policy Oracle uses to determine which node the application is initially started on. It can be PREFERRED or UNAVAILABLE.
- **-o <options>**: Specifies one or more options.

The options specified by -o correspond to parameters in the application profile. The options are listed in Table 17-4.

Table 17-4. *The crs_profile Optional Parameters*

Option	Parameter	Default Value
ap	ACTIVE_PLACEMENT	0
as	AUTO_START	restore
bt	PLACEMENT	balanced
ci	CHECK_INTERVAL	60
fd	FAILOVER_DELAY	0
fi	FAILURE_INTERVAL	0
ft	FAILURE_THRESHOLD	0
ra	RESTART_ATTEMPTS	1
st	SCRIPT_TIMEOUT	60
rt	START_TIMEOUT	0
pt	STOP_TIMEOUT	0
ut	UPTIME_THRESHOLD	7d

The purpose of each option is fairly self-explanatory. Further information can be found in the Oracle documentation. Now, consider the following example:

```
[oracle@london1 oracle]$ $ORA_CRS_HOME/bin/crs_profile \
   -create hafdemo
   -t application
   -d "HAF Demo"
   -r hafdemovip
   -a /tmp/HAFDemoAction
   -o ci=5,ra=60
```

In the preceding example, the description is "HAF Demo"; the required resource is the application VIP called hafdemovip; the action script is /tmp/HAFDemoAction; the check interval is five seconds; and in the event of failure, 60 restarts will be attempted.

The second form of this command creates an application profile based on a template file:

```
crs_profile -create resource_name -I template_file [-dir directory_path] [-f] [-q]
```

delete

The syntax for this option is

```
crs_profile -delete resource_name [-dir directory_path] [-q]
```

This command deletes an application profile, either from the default location or from the directory specified by the -dir option, for example:

```
[oracle@london1 oracle]$ crs_profile -delete hafdemo
```

When you are deleting resource profiles, make sure you are logged in as the user who created the resource; otherwise, the command will fail silently if it cannot find the file in the default location. If you are in doubt, specify the directory path explicitly using the -dir option.

print

This option prints all the parameters configured for the specified resource using the following syntax:

```
crs_profile -print [resource_name [...]] [-dir directory_path] [-q]
```

For example, the output of the -print option for the HAFDemo application is as follows:

```
[oracle@london1 oracle]$ crs_profile -print hafdemo
NAME=hafdemo
ACTION_SCRIPT=/tmp/HAFDemoServer
ACTIVE_PLACEMENT=0
AUTO_START=restore
CHECK_INTERVAL=5
DESCRIPTION=HAF Demo
FAILOVER_DELAY=0
FAILURE_INTERVAL=0
FAILURE_THRESHOLD=0
HOSTING_MEMBERS=
OPTIONAL_RESOURCES=
PLACEMENT=balanced
REQUIRED_RESOURCES=hafdemovip
RESTART_ATTEMPTS=60
SCRIPT_TIMEOUT=60
START_TIMEOUT=0
STOP_TIMEOUT=0
UPTIME_THRESHOLD=7d
USR_ORA_ALERT_NAME=
USR_ORA_CHECK_TIMEOUT=0
USR_ORA_CONNECT_STR=/ as sysdba
USR_ORA_DEBUG=0
USR_ORA_DISCONNECT=false
USR_ORA_FLAGS=
USR_ORA_IF=
USR_ORA_INST_NOT_SHUTDOWN=
USR_ORA_LANG=
USR_ORA_NETMASK=
USR_ORA_OPEN_MODE=
USR_ORA_OPI=false
USR_ORA_PFILE=
USR_ORA_PRECONNECT=none
USR_ORA_SRV=
USR_ORA_START_TIMEOUT=0
USR_ORA_STOP_MODE=immediate
USR_ORA_STOP_TIMEOUT=0
USR_ORA_VIP=
```

template

The template option allows you to create application profile templates from an existing resource or from a set of default values. This option has two variants. The first option variant allows you to create a template from an existing resource using

```
crs_profile -template resource_name [-dir directory_path] [-O template_file]
```

For example, to create a template called hafdemo_template from the HAFDemo application profile, use the following:

```
[oracle@london1 oracle]$ crs_profile -template hafdemo -O hafdemo_template.cap
```

If you do not specify a directory using the -dir option, the template will be created in the current working directory. If you do not specify a template file using the -O option, the template file will be called template.cap.

The second option variant creates a general application template using

```
crs_profile -template -t application [-O template_file]
```

For example, to create a general application template called general_template use the following:

```
[oracle@london1 oracle]$ crs_profile -template -t application \
-O general_template.cap
```

The template will be created in the current working directory. If you do not specify a template file using the -O option, the template file will be called template.cap.

update

The update option allows you to update the value of parameters in the application profile. You can update most of the parameters configurable in the create option. The syntax for this option is

```
crs_profile -update resource_name [-dir directory_path] [option ...]
    [-o option,...] [-q]
```

For example, use the following code to change the action script for the HAFDemo application to /tmp/HAFDemoAction2:

```
[oracle@london1 oracle]$ crs_profile -update hafdemo -a /tmp/HAFDemoAction2
```

validate

The validate option allows you to check the existence and content of the application profile. The syntax for this option follows:

```
crs_profile -validate resource_name [-dir directory_path] [-q]
```

To check the application profile for HAFDemo application, for example, use the following:

```
[oracle@london1 oracle]crs_profile -validate hafdemo
```

This command will check for the existence of the hafdemo.cap application profile in $ORA_CRS_HOME/crs/public. If the file exists, then the script checks that the NAME attribute matches the file name. The script also verifies the validity of all parameter names and that the appropriate values have been assigned.

The script terminates silently if no errors are found; otherwise, it reports any errors and aborts.

crs_register

The crs_register command reads the application profile and creates appropriate entries in the OCR using the following syntax:

```
crs_register resource_name [-dir directory_path] [...] [-u] [-f] [-q]
```

To register the HAFDemo application profile, for example, use

```
[oracle@london1 oracle]$ crs_register hafdemo
```

You may use the -dir option to specify a nondefault directory. You can also use the crs_register command to update entries in the OCR:

```
crs_register resource_name -update [option ...] [-o option,...] -q
```

For example, you can set the maximum number of restart attempts for the HAFDemo application to 30 in the OCR:

```
crs_register hafdemo -update -o ra=30
```

crs_unregister

This command can be used to remove the entries for an application profile from the OCR. The syntax for the `crs_unregister` command is

```
crs_unregister resource_name [...] [-q]
```

For example, to remove the entries for the HAFDemo application from the OCR, use the following:

```
[oracle@london1 oracle]$ crs_unregister hafdemo
```

crs_getperm

The `crs_getperm` command prints the current permissions for a resource. The syntax for this command is

```
crs_getperm resource_name [-u user|-g group] [-q]
```

To print all permissions for the resource, for example, use the following:

```
[oracle@london1 oracle]$ crs_getperm hafdemovip
Name: hafdemovip
owner:root:rwx,pgrp:oinstall:rwx:rwx,other::r--,:user:oracle:r-x,
```

and to print permissions for a specific user, use

```
[oracle@london1 oracle]$ crs_getperm hafdemovip -u oracle
Name: hafdemovip
r-x
```

Print permissions for a specific group as follows:

```
[oracle@london1 oracle]$ crs_getperm hafdemovip -g oinstall
Name: hafdemovip
rwx
```

crs_setperm

The `crs_setperm` command allows you to modify the permissions for a resource. You can assign permissions to the owner (user), users belonging to the primary group (group), and users belonging to other groups (other). Permissions include read (r), write (w), and execute (x).

The `crs_setperm` command has four options:

- Update permissions
- Delete permissions
- Change the owner of the resource
- Change the primary group of the resource

Update Permissions

This option allows you to set permissions for a resource. The syntax of this option is

```
crs_setperm resource_name -u aclstring [-q]
```

where `aclstring` is one of the following:

```
    user:<username>:<permission>
    group:<groupname>:<permission>
    other::<permission>
```

and `permission` is an ordered string containing `rwx` for read, write, and execute permissions if those permissions are granted or hyphens in the same positions if they are not granted:

```
[oracle@london1 oracle]$ crs_setperm hafdemo -u user:oracle:rwx
[oracle@london1 oracle]$ crs_setperm hafdemo -u group:oinstall:r-x
[oracle@london1 oracle]$ crs_setperm hafdemo -u other::r--
```

Delete Permissions

This option allows you to revoke permissions for a resource using the following syntax:

```
crs_setperm resource_name -x aclstring [-q]
```

See the preceding `create` option for the syntax of the `aclstring`. For example, to remove write and execute permissions from other users, use the following:

```
[oracle@london1 oracle]$ crs_setperm hafdemo -x other::-wx
```

Change the Owner of the Resource

The syntax for the command to change the resource's owner follows:

```
crs_setperm resource_name -o user_name [-q]
```

For example, to set the owner of the `HAFDemo` application to `root`, use

```
[oracle@london1 oracle]$ crs_setperm hafdemo -o root
```

Change Primary Group of Resource

The syntax for this command is

```
crs_setperm resource_name -g group_name [-q]
```

For example, to set the primary group of the `HAFDemo` application to `oinstall`, run

```
[oracle@london1 oracle]$ crs_setperm hafdemo -g oinstall
```

crs_start

The `crs_start` command can be used to start one or more applications. Its syntax is as follows:

```
crs_start resource_name [...] [-c cluster_member] [-f] [-q] ["attrib=value ..."]
crs_start -all [-q]
```

Start the `HAFDemo` application, for example, using

```
[oracle@london1 oracle]$ crs_start hafdemo
```

You can optionally specify a node on which to start the application. For example, to start the application on node `london1`, run the following:

```
[oracle@london1 oracle]$ crs_start hafdemo -c london1
```

You can also use this command to start all applications:

```
[oracle@london1 oracle]$ crs_start -all
```

crs_stop

The crs_stop command can be used to stop one or more applications using the syntax that follows:

```
crs_stop resource_name [...] [-f] [-q] ["attrib=value ..."]
crs_stop -c cluster_member [...] [-q] ["attrib=value ..."]
crs_stop -all [-q]
```

For example, you can stop the HAFDemo application as follows:

```
[oracle@london1 oracle]$ crs_stop hafdemo
Attempting to stop 'hafdemo' on member 'london1'
Stop of 'hafdemo' on member 'london1' succeeded
```

You can use this command to stop all applications currently running on a specific cluster member. For example, to stop the application on node london1, use the following:

```
[oracle@london1 oracle]$ crs_stop -c london1
```

You can also use this command to stop all applications on all nodes in the cluster:

```
[oracle@london1 oracle]$ crs_stop -all
```

Note that the -all and -c options will stop all node applications (GSD, VIP, listener, and ONS), as well as any database and ASM instances that are running on the node. Therefore, you should not use them as a shortcut when stopping your own applications.

You can force an application to stop by appending the -f option. This option is useful, particularly during development and testing, if the OCR has been left in an inconsistent state.

crs_stat

This crs_stat command can be used to check the current status of the application. The syntax for this command can take one of the following variants:

```
crs_stat [resource_name [...]] [-v] [-l] [-q] [-c cluster_member]
crs_stat [resource_name [...]] -t [-v] [-q] [-c cluster_member]
crs_stat -p [resource_name [...]] [-q]
crs_stat [-a] application -g
crs_stat [-a] application -r [-c cluster_member]
crs_stat -f [resource_name [...]] [-q] [-c cluster_member]
crs_stat -ls [resource_name [...]] [-q]
```

Without parameters, this command prints a summary the status of all resources registered in the OCR.

If you specify the name of your application, then crs_stat will return a four-line summary for that resource, for example:

```
[oracle@london1 oracle]$ crs_stat hafdemo
```

If the application is currently started, this command might return

```
NAME=hafdemo
TYPE=application
TARGET=ONLINE
STATE=ONLINE on london1
```

If the application is currently stopped, crs_stat might return   .

```
NAME=hafdemo
TYPE=application
TARGET=ONLINE
STATE=OFFLINE
```

The -v option prints slightly more verbose information, for example:

```
[oracle@london1 oracle]$ crs_stat hafdemo -v
NAME=hafdemo
TYPE=application
RESTART_ATTEMPTS=60
RESTART_COUNT=0
FAILURE_THRESHOLD=0
FAILURE_COUNT=0
TARGET=ONLINE
STATE=OFFLINE
```

The -t option prints a one-line summary for each resource:

```
[oracle@london1 oracle]$ crs_stat hafdemo -t
Name           Type          Target      State       Host
-------------- ------------- ----------- ----------- ----------
hafdemo        application   ONLINE      ONLINE      server3
```

If you append the -v option to the -t option, you get more verbose single-line output that includes the number of restart attempts and the number of failovers:

```
Name           Type          R/RA     F./FT    Target      State       Host
-------------- ------------- -------- -------- ----------- ----------- ----------
hafdemo        application   0/60     0/0      ONLINE      ONLINE      server3
```

If you use the -p option, crs_stat will print the values of all parameters for the application, for example:

```
[oracle@london1 oracle]$ crs_stat -p hafdemo
```

The output is similar to that generated by crs_profile -print. However, the input for crs_profile is the application profile *.cap file; the input for crs_stat is the OCR.

Finally, if you use the -ls option, crs_stat will list the application together with its permissions. For example, to list the HAFDemo application and its permissions, use the following:

```
[oracle@london1 oracle]$ crs_stat -ls hafdemo
Name           Owner         Primary PrivGrp      Permission
-------------- ------------- -------------------- ------------
hafdemo        oracle        oinstall             rwxrwxr--
```

crs_relocate

The crs_relocate command allows you to move a running application from one node to another. The syntax for this command is

```
crs_relocate resource_name [...] [-c cluster_member] [-f] [-q]["attrib=value ..."]
crs_relocate -s source_member [-c cluster_member] [-q]
```

Assuming that the HAFDemo application is currently running on london1, the following example relocates this application to london2:

```
[oracle@london1 oracle]$ crs_relocate hafdemo -c london2
```

You may need to append the -f option in order to force the application to be relocated to the new node:

```
[oracle@london1 oracle]$ crs_relocate hafdemo -c london2 -f
Attempting to stop 'hafdemo' on member 'london1'
Stop of 'hafdemo' on member 'london1' succeeded
Attempting to stop 'hafdemovip' on member 'london1'
Stop of 'hafdemovip' on member 'london1' succeeded
```

```
Attempting to start 'hafdemovip' on member 'london2'
Start of 'hafdemovip' on member 'london2' succeeded
Attempting to start 'hafdemo' on member 'london2'
Start of 'hafdemo' on member 'london2' succeeded
```

Note that the `crs_relocate` command resolves any dependencies. Therefore, in this case, it also automatically relocates the `hafdemovip` application to the new node.

Summary

This chapter examined a number of RAC-specific application programming techniques. If you develop software in-house or outsource bespoke development, we recommend that you review the contents of this chapter and, in light of the information contained within it, consider whether it would be beneficial to revise any of your existing standards or coding practices.

In our experience, Transparent Application Failover (TAF) is of little value to many sites, because uncommitted transactions are rolled back at the time of failover. However, we are beginning to see sites incorporate Fast Application Notification (FAN) into new, multitier Java applications, as the programming effort is minimal.

Though we envisage that the Oracle Clusterware High Availability (HA) Framework will take some time to become established, it does offer new ways to solve problems, such as single-instance database availability and sequence number generation. The HA Framework is one of the most exciting features currently offered within RAC, providing opportunities for designers and developers to devise truly innovative solutions.

CHAPTER 18
■ ■ ■

Using Administrative Tools

This chapter describes how to administer RAC databases using three tools: Enterprise Manager (EM), SRVCTL, and SQL*Plus. This chapter is not intended to be an in-depth examination of these tools, as each is worthy of a book in its own right. Rather, we aim to describe the capabilities of each tool and illustrate its use in various administrative tasks.

In a RAC database, you can start any number of the configured instances between one and the maximum available in any order. You can also stop any instance at any time.

Before you can start a RAC database, Oracle Clusterware must be running on at least one node in the cluster. In order to open the RAC database, a database instance must be started on at least one node in the cluster.

Shutting down a RAC instance does not directly interfere with the operation of any other instances, though there might be an impact on performance. You can shut down a RAC database completely by shutting down all instances that have the database open or mounted.

You can start up and shut down RAC instances using EM, SRVCTL, or SQL*Plus. You can start up and shut down all instances of a RAC database simultaneously using EM or SRVCTL.

Although EM has been vastly improved in Oracle 10g, it still does not handle start-up and shut-down very well. Therefore, unless you have a GUI-only policy, we recommend that you use SRVCTL to start and stop the database and/or instances and use EM for other administrative tasks.

Using EM

In Oracle 10.1 and above, EM is an HTML-based tool with RAC-specific administration and per-formance monitoring features. The EM Console provides a GUI-based central point of control for the entire Oracle environment

There are two versions of EM in Oracle 10.1 and above: Database Control and Grid Control. Database Control allows you to manage a single RAC database and its associated instances, listen-ers, and nodes. Grid Control allows you to manage multiple RAC databases and instances, listeners, nodes, application servers, HTTP servers, and web applications. It also allows you to create Data Guard standby databases.

If you use the Database Creation Assistant (DBCA) to create your database, EM Database Control will be automatically configured for your RAC database, and an EM Agent will be configured for each node in the cluster to perform database and instance discovery.

While Database Control is installed automatically by DBCA, Grid Control must be manually installed separately. Grid Control has a repository that can be stored in an existing database or a stand-alone database.

EM enables you to start, stop, and monitor databases, instances, and listeners. It also allows you to create and assign resource plans; administer storage, such as undo tablespaces and redo logs; manage archive logging; administer ASM; schedule backup and recovery jobs; modify parameters; set the alert threshold; and manage the database scheduler, schemas, security, and storage. EM can also be used to display the current host configuration, including memory, CPU, device I/O, network interfaces, and the operating system version. It can be used to apply Oracle patches as well.

EM Database Control uses the EM Agent to communicate with the database, instances, and other processes. You can check if the EM Agent is currently running using the following command:

```
[oracle@london1 oracle]$ emctl status dbconsole
```

If the Agent is running, this command will return output similar to the following:

```
Oracle EM 10g Database Control Release 10.2.0.1.0
Copyright (c) 1996, 2005 Oracle Corporation. All rights reserved.
http://london1:1158/em/console/aboutApplication
Oracle EM 10g is running.
------------------------------------------------------------
Logs are generated in directory
/u01/app/oracle/product/10.2.0/db_1/london1_RAC1/sysman/log
```

If the agent is not running, you can start it as follows:

```
[oracle@london1 oracle]$ emctl start dbconsole
```

The agent can be stopped again using the following:

```
[oracle@london1 oracle]$ emctl stop dbconsole
```

You can run EM for the RAC database in a browser using the URL returned by DBCA at the end of the database creation procedure, for example, http://london1:1158/em.

If the database is currently open, this URL causes the Login to Database page to be displayed, as shown in Figure 18-1.

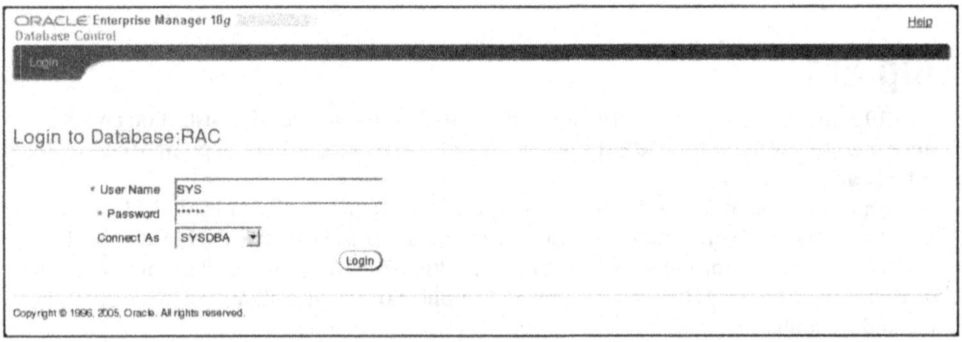

Figure 18-1. *The EM Login to Database page*

On the Login to Database page, you must enter your Oracle username and password. You must also enter your connection privilege, which defaults to Normal. You will need to change this to SYSOPER or SYSDBA if you intend to start and stop the database or instances or to perform various other administrative tasks. If you are running EM Database Control, the Cluster Database page will be displayed.

As EM Database Control uses a repository within the local database, you may wonder how EM behaves when the database is shut down. When you start EM, you may receive the message shown in Figure 18-2.

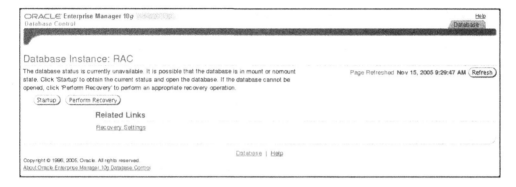

Figure 18-2. *The EM Database status unavailable message*

Receiving this message generally means that the database is not running. Click the Startup button to start the database or investigate any problem. You can also initiate recovery from this page.

Starting and Stopping Databases and Instances

To start up or shut down databases and instances, navigate to the Cluster Database page (Figure 18-3).

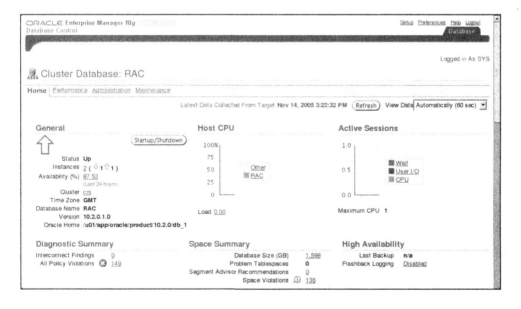

Figure 18-3. *The EM Cluster Database page*

On the Home tab of the Cluster Database page, click the Startup/Shutdown button. The Startup/Shutdown: Specify Credentials page will be displayed (Figure 18-4).

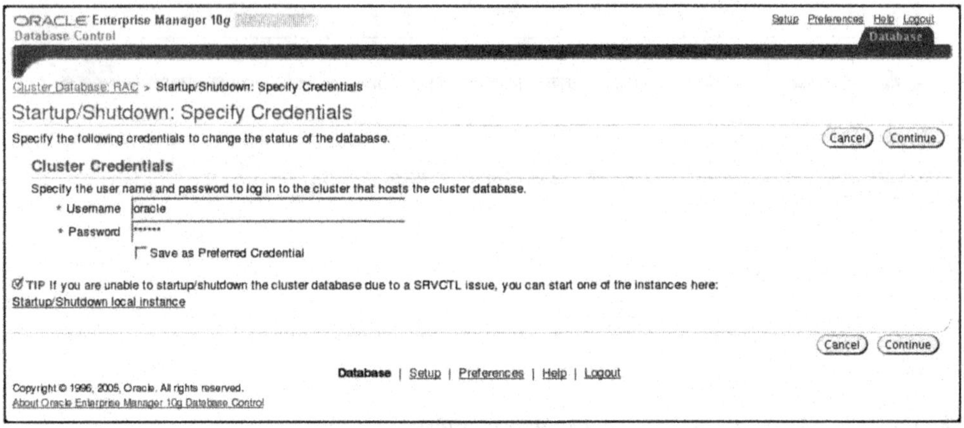

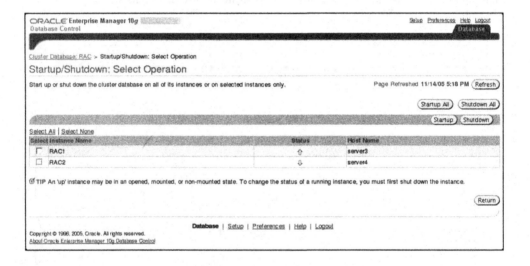

Figure 18-4. *The EM Startup/Shutdown: Specify Credentials page*

On the Specify Credentials page, enter your operating system username and password. The operating system user must be a member of the dba group. Next, the Startup/Shutdown: Select Operation page will be displayed (Figure 18-5).

Figure 18-5. *The EM Startup/Shutdown: Select Operation page*

On the Select Operation page, the status of each instance is indicated using a green up-arrow for instances that are currently running and a red down-arrow for instances that are currently stopped.

On this page, you can perform the following tasks:

- Start an individual instance by selecting the instance and clicking the Startup button
- Stop an individual instance by selecting the instance and clicking the Shutdown button
- Start all instances by clicking the Startup All button
- Shut down all instances by clicking the Shutdown All button

For all options, the Startup/Shutdown: Confirmation page will be displayed next (Figure 18-6).

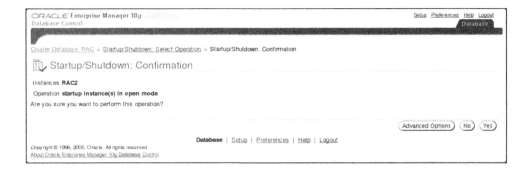

Figure 18-6. *The EM Startup/Shutdown: Confirmation page*

On the Confirmation page, you can specify the type of start-up or shutdown you require by clicking the Advanced Options button to open the Startup: Advanced Options page, as shown in Figure 18-7.

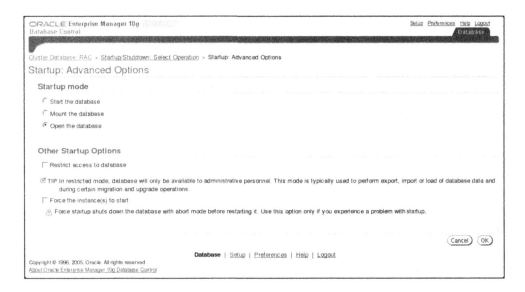

Figure 18-7. *The EM Startup: Advanced Options page*

The Startup: Advanced Options page allows you to specify the following start-up modes:

- Start the database (STARTUP NOMOUNT)
- Mount the database (STARTUP MOUNT)
- Open the database (default)

You can also specify whether you wish to start the database in restricted mode, in which case only administrators can log in. You can optionally specify the FORCE mode, in which case Oracle performs a SHUTDOWN ABORT followed by a STARTUP.

The Shutdown: Advanced Options page, shown in Figure 18-8, allows you to specify the following shutdown modes:

- **Normal**: Wait for all currently connected users to disconnect from their sessions.
- **Transactional**: Disconnect all connected users after transactions have completed.
- **Immediate**: Roll back active transactions and disconnect all connected users.
- **Abort**: Instantaneously shutdown by aborting the database instance.

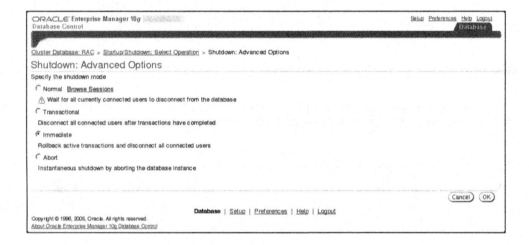

Figure 18-8. *The EM Shutdown: Advanced Options page*

Setting Parameters

On the Cluster Database page, click the Administration tab, and in the Database Configuration menu, select the Initialization Parameters option to display the Initialization Parameters page shown in Figure 18-9.

Alternatively, you can set parameters for an individual instance by selecting from the Instance list at the bottom of any tab on the Cluster Database page and selecting the Administration tab from the Database Instance page.

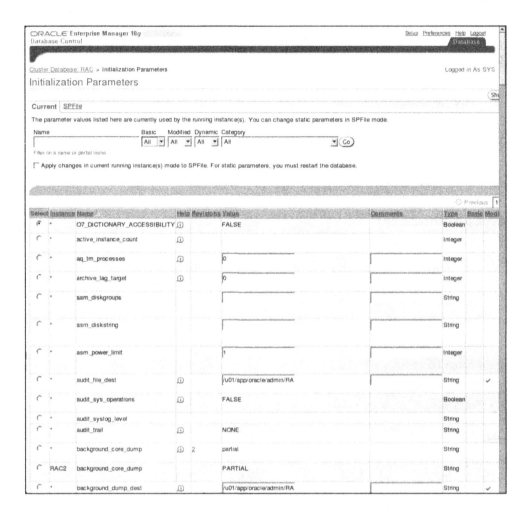

Figure 18-9. *The EM Initialization Parameters page*

The Initialization Parameters page contains two tabs: one for current (memory) parameters and the other for parameters set in the server parameter file (SPFILE). Both options display a list of available parameters that can be modified. All supported parameters and those unsupported parameters with nondefault parameters will be displayed over a number of pages.

You can filter parameters by name, by type (basic or advanced), or by category. You can also restrict the selection to parameters that are modifiable or parameters that are dynamic. On both tabs, you can optionally set parameters in both memory and the SPFILE.

Performance Options

In Oracle 10*g*, EM provides a wealth of performance information. In Oracle 10.2 in particular, this information has been enhanced for RAC users. We will discuss the performance information available in more detail in Chapter 24.

Administrative Options

EM administrative functionality can be accessed from the Administration tab on the Cluster Database page.

The Administration tab contains the following sections:

- Database Administration
- Schema
- Enterprise Management Administration

These sections' descriptions follow. Note that the content of this tab is generated dynamically. Therefore, the subsections and options may differ on your system.

Database Administration

The Database Administration section contains the following subsections, for which descriptions follow:

- Storage
- Database Configuration
- Database Scheduler
- Statistics Management
- Change Database
- Resource Manager
- Policies

Storage

The Storage subsection allows you to administer storage objects including control files, tablespaces, temporary tablespace groups, datafiles, rollback segments, redo log groups, and archived redo logs.

Database Configuration

In the Database Configuration subsection, you can administer initialization parameters, memory parameters, and undo management. You can also monitor and control database feature usage. This option gives a clear and concise view of which features have been used within the database, such as partitioning, Automatic Segment Space Management (ASSM), Automatic Undo Management, the Automatic Workload Repository (AWR), and the Recovery Manager (RMAN). In Oracle 10.2, this view reports 62 different features. High water marks for various objects are also reported, including the maximum numbers of concurrent sessions and CPUs. Depending on your license, you may wish to monitor these values to ensure that you are in compliance.

Database Scheduler

This subsection allows you to administer the database scheduler objects, including jobs, chains, schedules, programs, job classes, windows, window groups, and global attributes.

Statistics Management

The Statistics Management subsection allows you to manage optimizer statistics and configure statistics collection using the AWR.

Change Database

This subsection includes options to migrate the database to ASM and make dictionary-managed tablespaces into locally managed tablespaces. In a RAC environment, this subsection also allows you to add and delete instances.

Resource Manager

You can administer the Resource Manager with this subsection. It includes options to manage monitors, plans, consumer groups, and consumer group mappings.

Policies

This subsection allows you to administer the policy library and policy violations.

Schema

The Schema section contains the following subsections:

- Database Objects
- Programs
- XML Database
- Users and Privileges
- Materialized Views
- BI and OLAP
- User Defined Types

Database Objects

The Database Objects subsection allows you to administer schema objects, including tables, indexes, views, synonyms, sequences, database links, and directory objects. There is also an option to reorganize objects.

Programs

In the Programs subsection, you can administer PL/SQL and Java programs, including PL/SQL packages, headers and bodies, procedures, functions, and triggers; Java classes; and Java sources.

XML Database

This subsection allows you to administer XML support within the database, including configuration, resources, access control lists, XML schemas, XMLType Tables, and XMLType Views.

Users and Privileges

This subsection allows you to administer security features, including users, roles, profiles, and auditing.

Materialized Views

This subsection allows you to administer materialized views, materialized view logs, and refresh groups.

BI and OLAP

You can administer various data warehouse objects with the BI and OLAP subsection, including dimensions, cubes, OLAP dimensions, and measure folders.

User Defined Types

This subsection allows you to administer user-defined types, including abstract data types, VARRAYs, and nested tables.

Enterprise Manager Administration

The final section of the Administration tab allows you to administer EM itself, including options to manage administrators and to configure a notification schedule and blackout periods when the database will be unavailable.

Maintenance Options

EM allows you to perform a number of maintenance tasks, which can be accessed from the Maintenance Tab on the Cluster Database page.

The Maintenance Tab contains the following sections:

- High Availability
- Data Movement
- Software Deployments

High Availability

The High Availability section contains the following subsections:

- Backup/Recovery
- Backup/Recovery Settings
- Services

Backup/Recovery

This subsection contains options to schedule backups and perform recovery. It also allows you to manage current backups and restore points, which were introduced in Oracle 10.2, and to request backup reports.

Backup/Recovery Settings

The Backup/Recovery Settings subsection allows you to configure various RMAN parameters, including backup settings, recovery settings, and recovery catalog settings.

Services

In a RAC environment, this option allows you to configure database services.

Data Movement

The Data Movement section contains the following subsections:

- Move Row Data
- Move Database Files
- Streams

Move Row Data

The Move Row Data subsection allows you to manage export/import using the Data Pump. You cannot use this option if you have logged in using the SYSDBA role.

Move Database Files

This subsection allows you to manage transportable tablespaces.

Streams

You can set up and manage streams with this section.

Software Deployments

This section contains the following subsections:

- Installed Database Software
- Database Software Patching

Installed Database Software

The Installed Database Software subsection provides information about missing configuration information. By default, all nodes are automatically checked for this missing information on a daily basis.

Database Software Patching

This subsection allows you to view the patch cache and to apply patches. We recommend that you exercise extreme caution when using this option to patch RAC databases.

Using SRVCTL

The Server Control Utility (SRVCTL) is a command line tool that can perform many of the tasks that can be performed using EM. In Oracle 9.0.1 and 9.2, SRVCTL stored its information in the server management file (SRVM); in Oracle 10.1 and above, SRVCTL stores configuration and status information in the OCR. The information maintained by SRVCTL is used by several other Oracle tools, including EM. SRVCTL performs other operations, such as starting and stopping instances, by calling SQL*Plus on each node.

You can use SRVCTL to start, stop, and obtain the current status of the database, individual instances, and listener processes. It can be used to add and delete database and instance configuration information and to move instances from one node to another. Also, SRVCTL can set and unset environment variables at both the database and instance levels.

In Oracle 10.1 and 10.2, SRVCTL controls the following six types of objects:

- Database
- Instance
- Service
- Node applications
- ASM
- Listener

Node applications include the Global Services Daemon (GSD), the Oracle Notification Service (ONS), Virtual IP (VIP), and the Oracle Net Listener. The listener daemon can also be managed separately using the SRVCTL or LSNRCTL utilities.

The following sections describe the use of SRVCTL to manage

- Databases
- Instances
- Node applications
- Listeners

The SRVCTL utility can also be used to manage ASM instances and Services. This functionality is described in the following chapters:

- Storage management using ASM (Chapter 9)
- Workload management and services (Chapter 19)

SRVCTL Syntax

To get an overview of the syntax of SRVCTL, enter any invalid option, for example:

```
[oracle@london1 oracle]$ srvctl -help
```

This option will list a summary of valid commands:

```
Usage: srvctl <command> <object> [<options>]
    command:enable|disable|start|stop|relocate|status|add|remove|modify|getenv|
setenv|unsetenv|config
    objects: database|instance|service|nodeapps|asm|listener
For detailed help on each command and object and its options use:
    srvctl <command> <object> -h
```

In order to execute a SRVCTL command, you must specify both a command (action) and an object. You can list the syntax for all valid commands as follows:

```
[oracle@london1 oracle]$ srvctl -h
```

In Oracle 10.2, this command lists the syntax for over 60 commands. Some of these will be discussed in the following sections. You can obtain additional details about a particular option using the following syntax:

```
srvctl <command> <option> -h
```

For example, the following command prints help for the SRVCTL start database option:

```
[oracle@london1 oracle]$ srvctl start database -h
Usage: srvctl start database -d <name> [-o <start_options>] [-c <connect_str> | -q]
    -d <name>            Unique name for the database
    -o <start_options>   Options to startup command (e.g. open, mount, or nomount)
    -c <connstr>         Connect string (default: / as sysdba)
    -q                   Query connect string from standard input
    -h                   Print usage
```

You can check the current version of SRVCTL using the -V option, for example:

```
[oracle@london1 oracle]$ srvctl -V
srvctl version: 10.2.0.0.0
```

Administering Databases

You can use SRVCTL to perform the following database management tasks:

- Starting a database
- Stopping a database
- Checking the configuration of a database
- Checking the status of a database
- Adding a new database configuration
- Modifying an existing database configuration
- Removing an existing database configuration
- Disabling a database
- Enabling a database

Starting a Database

To start a database, use the following:

```
srvctl start database -d <name> [-o <start_options>] [-c <connect_str> | -q]
```

where start_options include open (the default), mount, and nomount. For example, to start a database named RAC, use

```
[oracle@london1 oracle]$ srvctl start database -d RAC
```

This command attempts to start all enabled instances for the database.

For both the start and stop commands, the connect string parameter specifies the connect string to be used to log in to the database. The connect string parameter defaults to "/ AS SYSDBA". Alternatively, you can specify the -q option, in which case SRVCTL will prompt for a connect string.

Stopping a Database

Stop a database as follows:

```
srvctl stop database -d <name> [-o <stop_options>] [-c <connect_str> | -q]
```

where stop_options include normal, transactional, immediate (the default), and abort. For example, to shut down a database named RAC, use the following:

```
srvctl stop database -d RAC
```

This command will stop all currently started instances for the database.

Checking the Configuration of a Database

Without arguments, config database returns the names of all databases configured in the OCR, for example:

```
[oracle@london1 oracle]$ srvctl config database
RAC
TEST
```

You can check the current configuration of all instances using the following syntax:

```
srvctl config database -d <database_name>
```

For example, the following command outputs the configuration of a database called RAC:

```
[oracle@london1 oracle]$ srvctl config database -d RAC
london1 RAC1 /u01/app/oracle/product/10.2.0/db_1
london2 RAC1 /u01/app/oracle/product/10.2.0/db_1
```

In Oracle 10.2 and above, you can obtain more detailed information by specifying the -a option:

```
[oracle@london1 oracle]$ srvctl config database -d RAC -a
london1 RAC1 /u01/app/oracle/product/10.2.0/db_1
london2 RAC2 /u01/app/oracle/product/10.2.0/db_1
DB_NAME: RAC
ORACLE_HOME: /u01/app/oracle/product/10.2.0/db_1
SPFILE: +DISKGROUP1/RAC/spfileRAC.ora
DOMAIN: null
DB_ROLE: null
START_OPTIONS: null
POLICY:   AUTOMATIC
ENABLE FLAG: DB ENABLED
```

In Oracle 10.2, you can obtain example client-side TNS entries for the services configured in the database by specifying the -t option:

```
[oracle@london1 oracle]$ srvctl config database -d RAC -t
Example client-side TNS entry for service SERVICE1:
SERVICE1 = (DESCRIPTION=(ADDRESS=(PROTOCOL=TCP)(HOST=db_vip)(PORT=dedicated_port))
(CONNECT_DATA=(SERVICE_NAME=SERVICE1)))
Example client-side TNS entry for service SERVICE2:
SERVICE2 = (DESCRIPTION=(ADDRESS=(PROTOCOL=TCP)(HOST=db_vip)(PORT=dedicated_port))
(CONNECT_DATA=(SERVICE_NAME=SERVICE2)))
Example client-side TNS entry for service SERVICE3:
SERVICE3 = (DESCRIPTION=(ADDRESS=(PROTOCOL=TCP)(HOST=db_vip)(PORT=dedicated_port))
(CONNECT_DATA=(SERVICE_NAME=SERVICE3)))
```

Checking the Status of a Database

You can check the current status of all instances on a database as follows:

```
srvctl status database -d <database_name>
```

For example, the following command returns the status of a database called RAC:

```
[oracle@london1 oracle]$ srvctl status database -d RAC
Instance RAC1 is running on node london1
Instance RAC2 is not running on node london2
```

In Oracle 10.2, you can optionally include information about the services by specifying the -v option:

```
[oracle@london1 oracle]$ srvctl status database -d RAC -v SERVICE1
Instance RAC1 is running on node london1
Instance RAC2 is not running on node london2
```

Adding a New Database Configuration

We recommend that you use DBCA to add and remove databases. However, you may still wish to create and drop them manually, in which case you must use SRVCTL to add the database to the OCR. You can add a database configuration using the following syntax:

```
srvctl add database -d <name> -o <oracle_home> [-m <domain_name>] [-p <spfile>]
[-A <name|ip>/netmask] [-r {PRIMARY | PHYSICAL_STANDBY | LOGICAL_STANDBY}]
[-s <start_options>] [-n <db_name>] [-y {AUTOMATIC | MANUAL}]
```

where start_options include open (the default), mount, and nomount.

You must specify the database name and the location of the Oracle Home. The remaining parameters are optional, including -m for the domain name, -p for the location of the server parameter file, -A for the hostname or IP address and subnet mask, and -r for the database role, which can be PRIMARY, PHYSICAL_STANDBY, or LOGICAL_STANDBY. The -n option specifies the value of the DB_NAME parameter for the database if this is different from the database name, specified by the mandatory -d option. The -y option specifies whether the database management policy is manual or automatic.

For example, to add a database called TEST using the Oracle Home currently specified by the $ORACLE_HOME environment variable, use the following:

```
[oracle@london1 oracle]$ srvctl add database -d TEST -o $ORACLE_HOME
```

Modifying an Existing Database Configuration

You can update a database configuration in the OCR using the following:

```
srvctl modify database -d <name> [-n <db_name] [-o <ohome>] [-m <domain>]
[-p <spfile>]  [-r {PRIMARY | PHYSICAL_STANDBY | LOGICAL_STANDBY}]
[-s <start_options>] [-y {AUTOMATIC | MANUAL}]
```

For example, you might need to move the server parameter file to another shared storage location:

```
[london1 oracle]$ srvctl modify database -d name -p /u03/oradata/RAC/spfileRAC.ora
```

Removing an Existing Database Configuration

You can remove a database using the following syntax:

```
srvctl remove database -d <name> [-f]
```

The following command, for example, removes a database called TEST:

```
[oracle@london1 oracle]$ srvctl remove database -d TEST
Remove the database TEST? (y/[n]) y
```

By default, SRVCTL will prompt for confirmation. You can force removal of the database by spec-ifying the -f option.

Disabling a Database

You can disable a database, so that it will not be started automatically when the node is restarted, as follows:

```
srvctl disable database -d <name>
```

Use the following example to disable a database called RAC:

```
[oracle@london1 oracle]$ srvctl disable database -d RAC
```

Enabling a Database

You can also enable a database, so that it can be started automatically when the node is restarted, using the following:

```
srvctl enable database -d <name>
```

For example, to enable a database called RAC, use

```
[oracle@london1 oracle]$ srvctl enable database -d RAC
```

Administering Instances

You can use SRVCTL to perform the following instance management tasks:

- Starting an instance
- Stopping an instance
- Checking the status of an instance
- Adding a new instance configuration
- Modifying an existing instance configuration
- Removing an existing instance configuration
- Disabling an instance
- Enabling an instance

Starting an Instance

To start an instance, use the following syntax:

```
srvctl start instance -d <name> -i "<inst_name_list>" [-o <start_options>]
[-c <connect_str> | -q]
```

where start_options include the following:

- nomount
- mount
- open (the default)

For example, to start an instance named RAC1, use

```
[oracle@london1 oracle]$ srvctl start instance -d RAC -i RAC1
```

You can optionally specify a list of instances. These must be separated by commas and enclosed by double quotes, for example:

```
[oracle@london1 oracle]$ srvctl start instance -d RAC -i "RAC3,RAC4"
```

Note that you must specify both the database name and the instance name; this allows you to use the same instance name for multiple databases. Using the same instance name may be useful in a development or QA environment.

Stopping an Instance

To stop an instance, use the following syntax:

```
srvctl stop instance -d <name> -i "<inst_name_list>" [-o <stop_options>]
[-c <connect_str> | -q]
```

where stop_options include:

- normal
- transactional
- immediate (the default)
- abort

For example, to stop an instance named RAC3, use the following command:

```
[oracle@london1 oracle]$ srvctl stop instance -d RAC -i RAC3
```

You can optionally specify a list of instances. These must be separated by commas and enclosed by double quotes, for example:

```
[oracle@london1 oracle]$ srvctl stop instance -d RAC -i "RAC3,RAC4"
```

Checking the Status of an Instance

You cannot check the current configuration of an individual instance. However, you can check the current status of a specified instance using the following syntax:

```
srvctl status instance -d <name> -i "<inst_name_list>" [-f] [-v] [-S <level>]
```

The following example checks the status of an instance called RAC1 in a database called RAC:

```
[oracle@london1 oracle]$ srvctl status instance -d RAC -i RAC1
Instance RAC1 is running on node primary1
```

You can optionally specify a list of instances. These must be separated by commas and enclosed by double quotes, for example:

```
[oracle@london1 oracle]$ srvctl status instance -d RAC -i "RAC1,RAC2"
Instance RAC1 is running on node london1
Instance RAC2 is not running on node london2
```

You can obtain information about database services currently running on the instance by specifying the -v option, for example:

```
[oracle@london1 oracle]$ srvctl status instance -d RAC -i RAC1 -v
Instance RAC1 is running on node primary1 with online services SERVICE1 SERVICE2
```

Adding a New Instance Configuration

You can add an instance to a database using the following syntax:

```
srvctl add instance -d <name> -i <inst_name> -n <node_name>
```

You must specify a database name, an instance name, and a node name, for example:

```
[oracle@london1 oracle]$ srvctl add instance -d RAC -i RAC3 -n london3
```

The database and node must exist. You cannot add the same instance to more than one node. You can, however, add more than one instance to the same node, although this is not advisable.

Modifying an Existing Instance Configuration

You can move an instance to another node as follows:

```
srvctl modify instance -d <name> -i <inst_name> -n <node_name>
```

For example, if instance RAC3 is currently running on node london3, and you wish to move it to london4, use the following command:

```
[oracle@london1 oracle]$ srvctl modify instance -d RAC -i RAC3 -n london4
```

In Oracle 10.2 and above, you can modify an instance to have a dependency on an ASM instance using

```
srvctl modify instance -d <name> -i <inst_name> {-s <asm_inst_name> | -r}
```

This is useful if you decide to implement ASM after implementing your RAC database and instances. To create a dependency for instance RAC3 on ASM instance +ASM3, use the following:

```
[oracle@london1 oracle]$ srvctl modify instance -d RAC -i RAC3 -s +ASM3
```

Note that the ASM instance must be configured on the same node as the database instance in order to create a dependency.

The dependency can be removed again as follows:

```
[oracle@london1 oracle]$ srvctl modify instance -d RAC -i RAC3 -r
```

Removing an Existing Instance Configuration

You can remove an instance from a database using the following syntax:

```
srvctl remove instance -d <name> -i <inst_name> [-f]
```

You must specify a database name and an instance name, for example:

```
[oracle@london1 oracle]$ srvctl remove instance -d RAC -i RAC3
Remove instance RAC3 from the database RAC? (y/[n]) y
```

By default, SRVCTL will prompt for confirmation. You can force removal by specifying the -f option.

Disabling an Instance

You can disable an instance, so that it will not be started automatically when the node is restarted, using the following syntax:

```
srvctl disable instance -d <name> -i "<inst_name_list>"
```

For example, to disable instance RAC3 in a database called RAC, use

```
[oracle@london1 oracle]$ srvctl disable instance -d RAC -i RAC3
```

You can optionally specify a list of instances. These must be separated by commas and enclosed by double quotes, for example:

```
[oracle@london1 oracle]$ srvctl disable instance -d RAC -i "RAC3,RAC4"
```

Enabling an Instance

You can use the following command to enable an instance, so that it can be started automatically when the node is restarted:

```
srvctl enable instance -d <name> -i "<inst_name_list>"
```

The following example enables instance RAC3 in a database called RAC:

```
[oracle@london1 oracle]$ srvctl enable instance -d RAC -i RAC3
```

You can optionally specify a list of instances. These must be separated by commas and enclosed by double quotes, for example:

```
[oracle@london1 oracle]$ srvctl enable instance -d RAC -i "RAC3,RAC4"
```

Administering Node Applications

The four node applications in Oracle 10.1 and above are as follows:

- Global Services Daemon (GSD)
- Oracle Notification Service (ONS)
- Virtual IP (VIP)
- Listener

These applications are all configured in the OCR. You can use SRVCTL to perform the following node application management tasks:

- Starting node applications
- Stopping node applications
- Checking the configuration of node applications
- Checking the status of node applications
- Adding node applications
- Removing node applications

Starting Node Applications

You can start all node applications on a specified node as follows:

```
srvctl start nodeapps -n <node_name>
```

For example, you can start all the node applications on the london1 node:

```
[oracle@london1 oracle]$ srvctl start nodeapps -n london1
```

Individual node applications cannot be started using the start nodeapps command.

Stopping Node Applications

You can use the following command to stop all node applications on a specified node:

```
srvctl stop nodeapps -n <node_name>
```

For example, to stop all of the node applications currently running on the london1 node, use the following:

```
[oracle@london1 oracle]$ srvctl stop nodeapps -n london1
```

You cannot stop individual node applications using the start nodeapps command.

Checking the Configuration of Node Applications

You can check the configuration of all node applications on a specified node:

```
srvctl config nodeapps -n <node_name> [-a] [-g] [-o] [-s] [-l]
```

This returns the node name, instance name, and $ORACLE_HOME directory, for example:

```
[oracle@london1 oracle]$ srvctl config nodeapps -n london1
london1 RAC1 /u01/app/oracle/product/10.2.0/db_1
```

The config nodeapps command includes a number of options that allow you to display details about specific node applications. To display the VIP configuration, use the -a option. This checks if VIP has been configured for this node and, if so, displays the VIP hostname, IP address, network mask, and interface name, for example:

```
[oracle@london1 oracle]$ srvctl config nodeapps -n london1 -a
VIP exists.: /london1-vip/147.43.1.201/255.255.0.0/eth0
```

The -g option checks if GSD has been configured for this node:

```
[oracle@london1 oracle]$ srvctl config nodeapps -n london1 -g
GSD exists.
```

The -s option checks if the ONS daemon has been configured for this node:

```
[oracle@london1 oracle]$ srvctl config nodeapps -n london1 -s
ONS daemon exists.
```

The -l option checks if the listener has been configured for this node:

```
[oracle@london1 oracle]$ srvctl config nodeapps -n london1 -l
Listener exists.
```

Checking the Status of Node Applications

You can check the status of all node applications on a specified node as follows:

```
srvctl status nodeapps -n <node_name>
```

The following example checks which node applications are currently running on the london1 node:

```
[oracle@london1 oracle]$ srvctl status nodeapps -n london1
VIP is running on node: london1
GSD is running on node: london1
Listener is running on node: london1
ONS is running on node: london1
```

Adding Node Applications

Node applications are normally created automatically during the installation process. To add node applications manually to a specified node, use the following command:

```
srvctl add nodeapps -n <node_name> -o <oracle_home> \
-A <name|ip>/netmask[/if1[|if2|...]]
```

For example, to add node applications to london3, you might use

```
[oracle@london1 oracle]$ srvctl add nodeapps -n london3 -o $ORACLE_HOME \
-A london3-vip/255.255.0.0/eth0
```

Removing Node Applications

You should rarely need to remove node applications, except possibly when relocating the Oracle Home directory or modifying the VIP address. To remove node applications manually from a specified node, use the following:

```
srvctl remove nodeapps -n "<node_name_list>" [-f]
```

For example, remove all node applications from london3 as follows:

```
[oracle@london1 oracle]$ srvctl remove nodeapps -n london3
```

You can optionally append the -f option to force removal of the node applications.

Administering the Listener

The listener is unique among the node applications in having a separate set of SRVCTL commands. You can use SRVCTL to perform the following listener management tasks:

- Checking the configuration of the listener
- Starting the listener
- Stopping the listener

Checking the Configuration of the Listener

You can check the configuration of the listener on a specified node as follows:

```
srvctl config listener -n <node_name>
```

For example, to check the listener name on london1 use

```
[oracle@london1 oracle]$ srvctl config listener -n london1
london1 LISTENER_LONDON1
```

Note that in Oracle 10.1 and above, by default, DBCA creates listeners with names in the format LISTENER_<node name>, for example, LISTENER_LONDON1. If you wish to administer these listeners using the LSNRCTL utility, you need to specify the listener name as a parameter, for example:

```
lsnrctl status LISTENER_LONDON1
```

Starting the Listener

You can start the listener process on a specified node using the following:

```
srvctl start listener -n <node_name> [-l <lsnr_name_list>]
```

For example, you can start the listener on london1:

```
[oracle@london1 oracle]$ srvctl start listener -n london1
```

You can optionally specify one or more listeners using the -l option, for example:

```
[oracle@london1 oracle]$ srvctl start listener -n london1 -l LISTENER_LONDON1
```

Stopping the Listener

You can stop the listener process on a specified node using the following command:

```
srvctl stop listener -n <node_name> [-l <lsnr_name_list>]
```

For example, stop the listener on london1 as follows:

```
[oracle@london1 oracle]$ srvctl stop listener -n london1
```

You can optionally specify one or more listeners using the -l option, for example:

```
[oracle@london1 oracle]$ srvctl stop listener -n london1 -l LISTENER_LONDON1
```

Using SQL*Plus

SQL*Plus can be used to perform certain administrative tasks on a RAC database. Unlike EM and SRVCTL, the commands only operate on the current instance. This can either be the local default instance, as specified by the $ORACLE_SID environment variable, or it can be a remote instance, specified by a Net Service Name.

In order to start and stop an instance, you will need to log in with the SYSDBA or SYSOPER privilege.

Setting the SQL*Plus Prompt

You can change the SQL*Plus prompt to include the name of the current instance using the SET SQLPROMPT command, for example:

```
SQL> SET SQLPROMPT '_CONNECT_IDENTIFIER> '
```

The _CONNECT_IDENTIFIER user variable will be replaced by the current instance name for the duration of the current session.

You can set this prompt globally for all SQL*Plus sessions by adding the above command to the SQL*Plus global login script, which is $ORACLE_HOME/sqlplus/admin/glogin.sql. If you do not use a shared Oracle Home directory, you will need to modify this script on every node in the cluster.

Connecting to a RAC Instance Using SQL*Plus

There are a number of ways to connect to a RAC instance using SQL*Plus. The method you use will be partly determined by the value of the REMOTE_LOGIN_PASSWORDFILE initialization parameter file.

If REMOTE_LOGIN_PASSWORDFILE is set to NONE, Oracle ignores any password file and privileged users must be authenticated by the operating system. You can specify the target instance by setting the $ORACLE_SID environment variable and running SQL*Plus, for example:

```
[oracle@london1 oracle]$ export ORACLE_SID=RAC1
[oracle@london1 oracle]$ sqlplus /nolog
SQL> CONNECT / AS SYSDBA
```

Use the NOLOG option if you are concerned that other users may have access to the ps command at operating system level, in which case you may compromise security.

You can also start SQL*Plus from the command line, for example:

```
[oracle@london1 oracle]$ export ORACLE_SID=RAC1
[oracle@london1 oracle]$ sqlplus / AS SYSDBA
```

Alternatively, you can specify a Net Service Name; for example, to connect to the instance RAC1, you might use the following:

```
[oracle@london1 oracle]$ sqlplus /nolog
SQL> CONNECT /@RAC1 AS SYSDBA
```

or you might use the following at the command line:

```
[oracle@london1 oracle]$ sqlplus /@RAC1 AS SYSDBA
```

Note that in the preceding examples, the instance name is the same as the Net Service Name. However, this will not necessarily be the case, and the names will definitely differ if you use an Oracle domain name.

If the REMOTE_LOGIN_PASSWORDFILE initialization parameter is set to SHARED, the password file can be shared by more than one database. However, the only user recognized by the password file is SYS, for example:

```
[oracle@london1 oracle]$ sqlplus SYS/<password> AS SYSDBA
```

or, using a Net Service Name

```
[oracle@london1 oracle]$ sqlplus SYS/<password>@RAC1 AS SYSDBA
```

If the REMOTE_LOGIN_PASSWORDFILE initialization parameter is set to EXCLUSIVE, the password file can only be used by one database. It can, however, contain many user names, for example:

```
[oracle@london1 oracle]$ sqlplus <username>/<password> AS SYSDBA
```

or, using a Net Service Name

```
[oracle@london1 oracle]$ sqlplus <username>/<password>@RAC1 AS SYSDBA
```

You can reconnect to another instance at any time. SQL*Plus automatically disconnects you from the original instance when you connect to another instance.

Note that you will need to connect directly to SQL*Plus (i.e., by setting the $ORACLE_SID) in order to start and stop database instances.

Starting an Instance

In order to start a database instance, you must have a shell session on the same node. You must set the $ORACLE_SID environment variable before running SQL*Plus; you cannot connect using a Net Service Name. If you wish to start more than one instance, you must run SQL*Plus on each node.

To start up a database instance, use the following command:

```
SQL> STARTUP
```

If this is the first instance to be started, the database will also be mounted and opened.

To start up a database instance without mounting or opening the database, use

```
SQL> STARTUP NOMOUNT
```

Start up a database instance and mount but do not open the database as follows:

```
SQL> STARTUP MOUNT
```

To stop and start a currently running instance use the following command:

```
SQL> STARTUP FORCE
```

This performs a SHUTDOWN ABORT followed by a STARTUP command.

There are a number of other options for the start-up command, including RECOVER, UPGRADE, and DOWNGRADE.

Stopping an Instance

In order to shut down a database instance, you must have a shell session on the same node. You must set the $ORACLE_SID environment variable before running SQL*Plus; you cannot connect using a Net Service Name. If you wish to shut down more than one instance, you must run SQL*Plus on each node. Alternatively, we recommend that you use Server Control Utility (SRVCTL) for this purpose.

To shut down the database, use the following command:

```
SQL> SHUTDOWN
```

This is equivalent to the SHUTDOWN NORMAL command and will wait until all active users have disconnected.

To shut down the database immediately, use

```
SQL> SHUTDOWN IMMEDIATE
```

This will terminate all sessions and roll back all active transactions.

You can also shut down the database without rolling back active transactions:

```
SQL> SHUTDOWN ABORT
```

Following a SHUTDOWN ABORT, the database will require instance recovery when it is restarted.

You can initiate a shutdown on the database that waits for all active transactions to commit or roll back using the following:

```
SQL> SHUTDOWN TRANSACTIONAL
```

This will wait until all transactions in the database have completed.

To initiate a shutdown on the local instance that waits for all active transactions to commit or roll back use

```
SQL> SHUTDOWN TRANSACTIONAL LOCAL
```

This will wait until all active transactions in the local instance have completed.

Note that in Oracle 9.0.1 and Oracle 9.2 some incompatibilities existed between SQL*Plus and SRVCTL. Therefore, if you are still using these versions, we recommend that you standardize—use either SQL*Plus or SRVCTL but do not use a combination of the two utilities to start and stop the database.

Setting Parameters in an Initialization Parameter File (PFILE)

The initialization parameter file contains a series of name-value pairs, for example:

```
sql_trace = true
```

Values can be split over multiple lines to improve readability, for example:

```
control_files = \
        '/u02/oradata/RAC/control01.ctl',\
        '/u03/oradata/RAC/control02.ctl',\
        '/u04/oradata/RAC/control03.ctl'
```

Lines in the file can be commented out by prefixing them with a # character, for example:

```
# This is a comment
PGA_AGGREGATE_TARGET = 100M;    # This is another comment
```

If you are using an initialization parameter file, some parameters can be modified dynamically while the instance is running using the ALTER SYSTEM command:

```
SQL> ALTER SYSTEM SET pga_aggregate_target = 100M;
```

In this case, the parameter will apply immediately to all sessions attached to the instance. However, some parameter values are only inspected when a session is connected, so existing sessions may not use the modified value. The current parameter values for the instance are externalized in the V$SYSTEM_PARAMETER dynamic performance view.

Other parameters can be modified for individual sessions. The changes apply until the session terminates or the parameter is modified again, for example:

```
SQL> ALTER SESSION SET sql_trace = TRUE;
```

The parameter values for the current session are externalized in the V$PARAMETER dynamic performance view.

The ALTER SYSTEM statement can optionally include the DEFERRED keyword, which indicates that the value will not be used for existing sessions but will be used by newly connecting sessions. The DEFERRED keyword can only be used for parameters where the IS_SYSMODIFIABLE column of V$PARAMETER is either IMMEDIATE or DEFERRED.

In a RAC environment, parameters can be global, in which case they apply to all instances, or instance specific.

Global parameters can be unprefixed, or they can be prefixed by an asterisk, for example:

```
pga_aggregate_target = 200M
*.pga_aggregate_target = 200M
```

You will see the latter format if your initialization parameter file has been created from an SPFILE.

Instance-specific parameters include a prefix, which specifies the instance to which they apply, for example

```
RAC1.instance_number = 1
RAC2.instance_number = 2
```

In all RAC configurations, you must provide instance-specific values for the parameters instance_name, instance_number, and thread. If automatic undo management is configured, you also need to provide an instance-specific value for undo_tablespace.

You can specify instance-specific values for many other parameters, which may be desirable where there is an asymmetric workload. However, remember that one of the main benefits of RAC is availability, and availability could be compromised if instance-specific parameters are modified in a way that affects instance-failover functionality.

Setting Parameters in a Server Parameter File (SPFILE)

If you use DBCA to create your RAC database, DBCA may provide an inappropriate default location, such as $ORACLE_HOME/dbs, for the SPFILE. You must override this location with one on shared storage. This location can be an ASM disk group, cluster file system, or shared raw device.

If you manually create the database, you should create the SPFILE from a text PFILE.

After the SPFILE has been created, a PFILE is still required for each instance. This must contain a value for the spfile parameter that specifies the location of the SPFILE, for example:

```
spfile = /u02/oradata/RAC/spfile.ora
```

The server parameter file can be created from an initialization parameter file using the CREATE SPFILE statement:

```
SQL> CREATE SPFILE = '/u02/oradata/RAC/spfile.ora'
> FROM PFILE = '/u01/app/oracle/OraHome_2/dbs/initRAC.ora';
```

An initialization parameter file can subsequently be generated from the server parameter using the CREATE PFILE statement:

```
SQL> CREATE PFILE = '/u01/app/oracle/OraHome_2/dbs/initRAC.ora'
> FROM SPFILE = '/u02/oradata/RAC/spfile.ora';
```

Oracle recommends that the server parameter is regularly backed up to a text file using the preceding syntax. The server parameter file can also be backed up using RMAN.

The server parameter file can either be updated using EM or the ALTER SYSTEM statement. If you attempt to modify the SPFILE with a text editor, you will corrupt the file and need to recreate it from a backup or regenerate it from an existing PFILE.

The ALTER SYSTEM statement behaves differently depending on whether the instance has been started using a server parameter file or an initialization parameter file.

If the instance is using a server parameter file, the ALTER SYSTEM statement includes a SCOPE clause where the SCOPE can be MEMORY, SPFILE, or BOTH. For example, the following statement

```
SQL> ALTER SYSTEM SET pga_aggregate_target = 100M SCOPE = MEMORY;
```

will change the value of the parameter in the memory of the current instance, but it will not update the server parameter file.

The statement

```
SQL> ALTER SYSTEM SET pga_aggregate_target = 100M SCOPE = SPFILE;
```

will update the server parameter file, but it will not affect the memory of the current instance.

Finally, the statement

```
SQL> ALTER SYSTEM SET pga_aggregate_target = 100M SCOPE = BOTH;
```

will update both the parameter value in memory and in the server parameter file. If the SCOPE clause is not specified, this behavior is the default.

The ALTER SYSTEM statement may optionally specify the DEFERRED keyword indicating that the value should only be used for newly connecting sessions.

The current parameter values in the server parameter file are externalized in the V$SPPARAMETER dynamic performance view.

You can optionally include a comment on the parameter change, for example:

```
SQL> ALTER SYSTEM SET pga_aggregate_target = 100M
> COMMENT 'This is a comment' SCOPE = BOTH;
```

You can see the comments in an SPFILE by querying the V$SPPARAMETER dynamic performance view.

An SPFILE can contain both global and instance-specific parameters. Global parameters are identified by an asterisk (*), while instance-specific parameters are identified by their Oracle system identifier (SID). Most parameters can have different values on different instances. These parameters have a default value that is the same for all instances. You can change the value on one or more specific instances using the SID clause of the ALTER SYSTEM statement, for example:

```
SQL> ALTER SYSTEM SET pga_aggregate_target = 200M SID = 'RAC1';
```

The same parameter could be reset explicitly for all instances as follows:

```
SQL> ALTER SYSTEM SET pga_aggregate_target = 200M SID = '*';
```

This is the default behavior when the instance has been started with a server parameter file.

You can also reset parameters to their default values individually, for example:

```
SQL> ALTER SYSTEM RESET pga_aggregate_target SCOPE=SPFILE SID = 'RAC1';
```

The same parameter could be set explicitly for all instances using the following command:

```
SQL> ALTER SYSTEM RESET pga_aggregate_target SCOPE=SPFILE SID = '*';
```

We recommend that you do not modify the values for any self-tuning parameters in the server parameter file, as overriding these settings may adversely affect performance.

The server parameter file can be logically corrupted, in which case it may not be possible to restart the instance. In the event of a logical corruption, there are a number of possible solutions, including using the original initialization parameter file to restart the instance. When you manually create a database, we recommend retaining the initialization parameter file for this purpose. Alternatively, you can use a backup of the server parameter file to restart the instance. Finally, if you do not have a recent backup, you can run the operating system `strings` utility against the server parameter file, redirecting the output to a new initialization parameter file. The resulting file will require some editing to convert it back to a `PFILE`, but this process will at least recover the latest parameter settings.

Summary

In this chapter, we outlined the three tools generally used for Oracle RAC administration: EM, SRVCTL, and SQL*Plus. In Oracle 10.2 and above, these tools have a fair amount of functionality in common; therefore, which tool you use for a particular task is largely a matter of personal preference.

In general, we find that SRVCTL is the best tool for starting and stopping the database and its instances. While the commands can be difficult to remember initially, the syntax is fairly logical, and of course, they can always be added to a shell script.

EM is generally the tool of choice for other tasks, especially those performed infrequently. We definitely recommend that you use this tool when configuring recently introduced features, such as Oracle Streams, Data Guard logical standby, and the Scheduler, as the PL/SQL APIs that support these features are extremely complex.

In our experience, the selection of administrative tools at each site is largely determined by the experience and preferences of the DBAs. However, we do recommend that you familiarize yourself with the functionality provided by each tool to ensure that you are not missing out.

■ ■ ■

## CHAPTER 19

Workload Management

In this chapter, we discuss workload management for RAC databases. We first examine the available methods to distribute workloads across the different nodes of a cluster, and then we describe the use of database services to manage the workload across a RAC database. Database services provide a powerful mechanism with which you can visualize and control demand for resources across the entire cluster.

Workload Distribution

In a cluster consisting of two or more nodes, it is necessary to have a method for distributing the workload across the nodes to maximize scalability and throughput. Workload distribution is also desirable from an availability point of view, to minimize the effect of individual node failures on overall throughput.

In an ideal world, the workload would be distributed equally across all nodes. In reality, for a number of reasons, it is not possible to achieve a perfectly balanced system. However, an extremely unbalanced system may cause significant problems if you are hitting a resource bottleneck on a particular node.

It is not possible to balance a database workload across nodes in the same way that, for example, packets might be balanced across network switches. This is because, while network switches do not perform any intelligent processing, it is much more difficult to predict the resource consumption of a unit of database work.

Oracle performs workload distribution using *connection balancing*. In other words, all load balancing activity is performed before a session establishes a connection. Once the connection has been established to a specific instance, the session will communicate with the same instance until either the session or the instance terminates.

In order to distribute workloads evenly, it is necessary to understand how the application establishes and uses connections. Establishing a connection is a relatively expensive operation requiring significant CPU and system resources to start the server process, allocate memory structures, and establish the application context. Once the connection is established, little effort is required to maintain it.

Connection balancing can occur on either the client side or the server side. *Client-side connection balancing* involves the selection of a random instance by the client process. *Server-side connection balancing* involves the selection of an instance by the listener daemon on the server, based on metrics received by the listener from the database. We discuss both types of connection balancing in the sections that follow.

Client-Side Connection Balancing

As previously mentioned, client-side connection balancing involves the selection of a random instance by the client process. The following tnsnames.ora entry uses client-side connection balancing:

```
RAC =
  (DESCRIPTION =
    (ADDRESS = (PROTOCOL = TCP)(HOST = london1)(PORT = 1521))
    (ADDRESS = (PROTOCOL = TCP)(HOST = london2)(PORT = 1521))
    (LOAD_BALANCE = ON)
    (FAILOVER = ON)
  (CONNECT_DATA =
    (SERVICE_NAME = RAC)
    (FAILOVER_MODE = (TYPE = SELECT)(METHOD = BASIC))
  )
)
```

When the LOAD_BALANCE parameter is set to ON, Oracle Net will select a node at random from the list of addresses to establish a connection with the various listeners. No load metrics are used for distributing work.

Client-side connection balancing works well if all instances are registered. Prior to Oracle 10.1, client-side connection balancing did not detect blocked, failed, or hung instances, which could lead to skewed connection loads on each node. In Oracle 10.1, the combination of Virtual IP (VIP) and Fast Application Notification (FAN) can be used to detect failed instances, resulting in a much more even distribution of connections across the nodes.

There are, however, a number of problems with client-side connection balancing. For example, client-side connection balancing is unaware of the existing load on the nodes and therefore does not take account of how many other clients are currently connected to the node or of the current workload on the node.

Another issue with client-side connection balancing is that the random algorithm is based on time slices that are relatively long. Therefore, if a large number of clients are attempting to connect concurrently, they may all be directed to the same node. This issue is particularly prevalent during scalability testing, where care must be taken to design tests that ramp up over a suitably long time period to ensure a realistic distribution of connections across all nodes in the cluster. Consequently, client-side connection balancing may be unsuitable for applications that add connections in batches.

Server-Side Connection Balancing

Server-side connection balancing works differently in Oracle 10.1 and Oracle 10.2, as we discuss in the following sections. In both versions, server-side connection balancing is enabled when the LOAD_BALANCE parameter is set to OFF in the tnsnames.ora file.

Server-side connection balancing is generally preferable to client-side connection balancing, as the listener processes have information on blocked, failed, and hung instances, and they also have the current loading and session status for each instance.

Oracle 10.1 Server-Side Connection Balancing

In Oracle 10.1, server-side connection balancing is driven by metrics. Possible metrics are the workload per node (CPU / Run queue length) or the number of current connections.

In server-side connection balancing, the TNS listener process performs intelligent load balancing when establishing connections between clients and servers. The database registers and reports load for both dedicated servers and shared servers (MTS).

Well-designed applications should connect once and remain connected because of the high cost of establishing a connection. This behavior is typical of application designs that implement middle-tier connection pooling. However, many applications still in use connect, execute a single statement or transaction, and then disconnect again.

The metric used to assign connections to instances should not vary over the lifetime of the connection. If the connection is expected to persist for a relatively long time, the current workload on the node is not a good metric, as the workload could be highly variable over the lifetime of the connection. Therefore, the connections should be distributed evenly across all nodes.

If each connection is expected to be long, then distribute the workload across all available nodes by setting the PREFER_LEAST_LOADED_NODE parameter to OFF in $TNS_ADMIN/listener.ora. However, if each connection is expected to be relatively short, you can send it to the least loaded node by setting the PREFER_LEAST_LOADED_NODE parameter to ON, which is the default value.

Logon storms occur when large numbers of clients attempt to establish connections over a very short period of time. If a system is subject to logon storms, then connecting to the least loaded node is not appropriate, because an interval of time is required to assess system load and communicate it back to the listener process. During this interval, the state of the database may have changed due to newly connected sessions.

Database metrics are reported by the PMON background process, which sends updated SERVICE_REGISTER information to the listener including the load, maximum load, instance load, and maximum load for the instance. PMON inspects the database metrics once every three seconds; however, it posts the listener process only when there has been a significant change. If a listener is shut down or fails, PMON checks whether it has been restarted once per minute.

Because the PMON process can register with remote listeners, each listener process is always aware of all instances and dispatchers, irrespective of the node on which they are running. The listener uses the load information to determine which instance to establish a connection with and, in the case of shared servers (MTS), which dispatcher to assign to the client.

If a database service has multiple instances on multiple nodes, the listener selects the least loaded instance on the least loaded node. If a shared server is configured, then the least loaded dispatcher of the selected instance is chosen. In addition, if a shared server is configured, all dispatchers on each instance must be cross-registered with the other listeners on the other nodes using the LISTENER attribute of the DISPATCHERS parameter.

Oracle 10.2 Server-Side Connection Balancing

In Oracle 10.2 and above, server-side load balancing has been enhanced. As in Oracle 10.1, the listener process distributes connection requests among active instances based on the current workload of each node and instance in the cluster. However, the mechanism by which the listener process is informed of the current workload for each node has been improved.

In Oracle 10.2 and above, RAC includes a load balancing advisory which can supply information to OCI, ODP.NET, and JDBC connection pools. Third-party applications can subscribe to the load balancing advisory using the Oracle Notification Service (ONS). The load balancing advisory can be used in a number of standard architectures where work is allocated including connection load balancing, transaction processing monitors, application servers, connection concentrators, hardware and software load balancers, job schedulers, batch schedulers, and message queuing systems. Load balancing advisory events include the current service level that an instance is providing for a service and a recommendation of how much of the workload should be sent to that instance.

The load balancing advisory monitors the current workload for each service in the instance and creates FAN events, which are sent to the connection pools whenever there is a change of configuration or status of one of the instances providing the service. This allows the connection pools to select the most appropriate instance when creating new connections.

The load balancing advisory is configured by specifying a load balancing goal when creating or modifying a service using the DBMS_SERVICE package or in Enterprise Manager (EM). The load balancing goal can take the value of NONE, SERVICE_TIME, or THROUGHPUT. Constants for the load balancing goal are defined in the DBMS_SERVICE package, as shown in Table 19-1.

Table 19-1. *Load Balancing Goals*

Name	Description
GOAL_NONE	Disables the load balancing advisory
GOAL_SERVICE_TIME	Specifies that the load balancing advisory is based on elapsed time for work done by service plus available bandwidth to service
GOAL_THROUGHPUT	Specifies that the load balancing advisory is based on rate that work is completed in service plus available bandwidth to service

You can also specify a connection load balancing goal for each service. This goal should be based on the average duration of each connection and takes the value LONG (the default) or SHORT, as shown in Table 19-2.

Table 19-2. *Connection Load Balancing Goals*

Name	Description
CLB_GOAL_LONG	Balances the number of connections per instance using session count per service
CLB_GOAL_SHORT	Uses the load balancing advisory if GOAL_SERVICE_TIME or GOAL_THROUGHPUT

The LONG connection load balancing goal should be specified for applications with connections of a long duration. This would include connection pools and also most OLTP and batch applications. LONG is the default connection load balancing goal.

The SHORT connection load balancing goal should be specified for applications with connections of a short duration, such as web applications that do not use a connection pool.

You can set the load balancing goal and the connection load balancing goal in the CREATE_SERVICE and MODIFY SERVICE procedures in the DBMS_SERVICE package. When you create a database using Database Creation Assistant (DBCA), server-side load balancing is configured and enabled by default. Services created using DBCA have the default settings of GOAL=NONE and CLB_GOAL=CLB_GOAL_LONG. These are also the default values if you create the service manually using the DBMS_SERVICE package.

You can specify nondefault values when you create the service, for example:

```
SQL> EXECUTE dbms_service.create_service -
> (service_name => 'SERVICE1',network_name => 'SERVICE1', -
> goal=> DBMS_SERVICE.GOAL_SERVICE_TIME, -
> clb_goal => DBMS_SERVICE.CLB_GOAL_SHORT);
```

You can modify the connection load balancing goal for a service using the MODIFY_SERVICE procedure of the DBMS_SERVICE package, as follows:

```
SQL> EXECUTE dbms_service.modify_service -
> (service_name => 'SERVICE1', -
> goal=> DBMS_SERVICE.GOAL_SERVICE_TIME, -
> clb_goal => DBMS_SERVICE.CLB_GOAL_LONG);
```

You can verify the current value of the connection load balancing goal by querying the DBA_SERVICES table, for example:

```
SQL> SELECT name, goal, clb_goal FROM dba_services;
```

You can also verify the current load balancing goal settings for each service in the V$SERVICES and V$ACTIVE_SERVICES dynamic performance views.

Database Services

In Oracle 10.1 and above, it is possible to define database services which represent a logical subset of the workload of an application. Each database service is a group of sessions performing the same type of work or running the same application and assigned to a pool of possible database instances. Database services can be managed as separate entities, reducing the management overhead and providing the basis for high availability. Database services simplify system deployment, testing, disaster recovery, and administration.

Database services have been available in single-instance environments for many years. In Oracle 10.1 and above, they can be used in conjunction with Resource Manager to control resource usage. In a single-instance environment, database services can also provide additional levels of granularity for statistics aggregation and tracing.

However, you can fully realize the potential of database services in a RAC environment by controlling which instances are allocated to different database services at different times. Database services are available continuously with the workload shared across one or more instances. Additional instances can be made available dynamically in response to failures or changes in workload. This helps you reflect business priorities and needs in your management of the database.

A *database service* is a logical grouping of sessions analogous to other logical groupings within Oracle, such as tablespaces and roles. Users with similar service-level requirements should all be assigned to the same service. The database services you define should reflect the main groups of resource consumers within your workload. For example, you may decide to create database services on a departmental basis, such as Accounts Payable, Accounts Receivable, and Customer Relationship Management. Alternatively, you may define database services to reflect types of workload, for example, Online, Reports, and Batch. With database services, users connect to a database without regard for which instance executes the SQL session.

Database services are the basis for workload management in a RAC database. You can assign a database service to specific instances within the cluster and control the resource consumption of the database service using Resource Manager. In the event of a failure or planned outage, you can define how resources will be automatically reallocated. Prior to Oracle 10.1, it was necessary to either reallocate such resources manually at the time of failure or run with additional unused capacity to allow for a future failure. Each database service is associated with a Net Service Name that enables users to connect to the service.

Each database service is initially assigned to one or more instances known as the PREFERRED instances, and they will be used when they are available. You can also assign the database service to one or more secondary instances which can be used if one of the PREFERRED instances is unavailable. If a PREFERRED instance fails, then Oracle will automatically move the database service from the failed instance to a surviving secondary instance. Secondary instances are rather confusingly known as AVAILABLE instances.

If a database service is relocated to an AVAILABLE instance following the failure of a PREFERRED instance, and the PREFERRED instance is subsequently restarted, the database service will not necessarily be relocated back from the AVAILABLE to the PREFERRED instance; this avoids a second service outage. It is possible to override this behavior manually by configuring FAN callouts.

In Oracle 10.2 and above, each database service is associated with a goal, which specifies whether connections should be made to instances assigned to the service based on service quality (response time) or overall system throughput (completing jobs and long-running queries as efficiently as possible).

Each database service can also be associated with a load balancing method, which can be LONG or SHORT. Long connections are defined as sessions which connect to the database once and then remain connected while a potentially large number of statements are executed. Short connections are sessions which connect, execute a handful of statements, and then disconnect. As the cost of establishing a connection is relatively high in terms of resources, Oracle Corporation recommends that applications use LONG connections wherever possible.

A session can also have associated Transparent Application Failover (TAF) characteristics. These characteristics specify whether, following a node or instance failure, sessions can resume processing SELECT statements on another node, and also whether sessions should preconnect to any failover instances. It is also possible to specify the maximum number of retry attempts in the event of a failover and a time-out between attempts.

Database services can be assigned to Resource Manager consumer groups, allowing you to restrict resource usage by database service within each instance. When a user connects with a specific database service, that user will automatically be assigned to the associated Resource Manager consumer group.

You can monitor the performance of database services individually and, if necessary, change the resources that are allocated to them. This may help you to achieve any service level agreements (SLAs) to which you are subject.

In Oracle 10.1 and above, a number of other Oracle features are aware of database services and can use them to manage their workloads, including Parallel Execution, the Job Scheduler, Advanced Queuing (AQ), and Streams.

Clients and middle-tier applications make connection requests by specifying a global database service name. In the event that one or more of the preferred instances is unavailable, the connection will transparently be redirected to any available alternate instance.

For example, consider a four-instance cluster running two database services called SERVICE1 and SERVICE2. You might configure these as shown in Table 19-3.

Table 19-3. *Sample Database Service Configuration*

Service	Instance 1	Instance 2	Instance 3	Instance 4
SERVICE1	Preferred	Preferred	Available	Available
SERVICE2	Available	Available	Preferred	Preferred

SERVICE1 will normally run on instances 1 and 2. However, if either of these instances becomes unavailable, the service can run on alternate instances 3 and 4. Similarly, SERVICE2 will normally run on instances 3 and 4, but if these become unavailable, it can run on alternate instances 1 and 2.

Database service names are stored by Oracle in the SERVICE_NAMES initialization parameter, which has a maximum size of 4KB. The maximum length of the service names of all services assigned to an instance therefore cannot exceed 4KB. You should not attempt to modify the SERVICE_NAMES parameter manually.

In Oracle 10.1 and above, a maximum of 64 database services can be created. Oracle creates two default services; the remaining 62 database services can be user-defined. The two default services are as follows:

- **SYS$BACKGROUND**: Used by background processes only

- **SYS$USERS**: Default service for user sessions that are not associated with any other database services

These services are always available on every instance within the database unless the instance is running in restricted mode. You cannot modify these database services or their attributes, and you also cannot stop or disable them.

Implementing Database Services

In this section, we discuss a number of practical topics associated with implementing database services:

- Performance
- Resource Manager
- Scheduler
- Parallel Execution

Performance

In previous releases, Oracle recommended distributing workload uniformly across all available nodes. This practice was intended to maximize the resources available to process the workload, including CPU, memory, network, and storage paths. This arrangement is still acceptable in many environments, as it simplifies configuration and optimizes availability.

One of Oracle 9*i*'s marketing messages was that applications would run on RAC without modification, implying a uniformly distributed workload. For many users, this was a valid proposition. However, a number of users found that their overall throughput could be increased by partitioning their workload. In Oracle 9*i*, this is generally achieved by addressing instances directly using the TNS Net Service Name.

The introduction of database services in Oracle 10.1 provides a formal mechanism by which you can partition your workload. Database services have existed in the Oracle database since Oracle 8, but in Oracle 10.1, they have become a central part of the RAC configuration. It is still possible to ignore services completely and to implement uniform workload distribution. However, you can potentially benefit from implementing database services, even on a two-node cluster.

Database services allow you to manage resource consumption more effectively. Using database services, it is possible to ring-fence specific instances for high-priority tasks. For example, we know several sites which use database services to control report generation. All reports covered by SLAs are run using a database service on one node; ad hoc reports use a database service on a second node. If the resource consumption for ad hoc reports is high, they will take longer to generate, but they will not impact any daily reports or other processing.

A second performance justification for using database services is that in many applications, the data is naturally partitioned. Therefore, it may be possible to create database services such that each service affects only a subset of the data blocks. If the number of nodes on which these data blocks are accessed is restricted, the result is a higher probability that any given data block will be in the local cache, leading to lower I/O rates.

Resource Manager

Database services can be used in conjunction with Resource Manager to control resource usage within the database. When a session connects to a specific database service, it can also be assigned to a resource consumer group for which maximum resource consumption can be defined. This allows the workload to be prioritized within each instance.

Use of database services with Resource Manager also provides a compelling argument for database consolidation. For example, many sites have multiple databases in their cluster, each of which has an instance on each node. However, there is no easy way to manage resource allocation between the instances on each node. While the operating system can be used to influence the priorities of individual processes, it is not aware of the needs of individual processes, such as background processes or those holding latches. In a consolidated database, there will be only one instance on each node, and Resource Manager can manage process priorities more effectively than the operating system.

In Oracle 10.2 and above, Resource Manager is configured by default when the database is installed using DBCA. To add a database service to a Resource Manager consumer group, you must first create a temporary working area as follows:

```
SQL> EXECUTE DBMS_RESOURCE_MANAGER.CREATE_PENDING_AREA;
```

You can then create the consumer group:

```
SQL> EXECUTE DBMS_RESOURCE_MANAGER.CREATE_CONSUMER_GROUP -
> (consumer_group => 'HIGH', comment => 'High priority consumer group');
```

Next you add the database services to the consumer group. In this example, we will add SERVICE1:

```
SQL> EXECUTE DBMS_RESOURCE_MANAGER.SET_CONSUMER_GROUP_MAPPING -
> (attribute => DBMS_RESOURCE_MANAGER.SERVICE_NAME, value => 'SERVICE1');
```

When you have finished modifying the Resource Manager configuration, you can deploy the changes as follows:

```
SQL> EXECUTE DBMS_RESOURCE_MANAGER.SUBMIT_PENDING_AREA;
```

You must also grant permission to sessions connecting to the database service to switch to the new consumer group:

```
SQL> EXECUTE DBMS_RESOURCE_MANAGER_PRIVS.GRANT_SWITCH_CONSUMER_GROUP -
> (grantee_name=> 'PUBLIC', consumer_group => 'HIGH', grant_option=> FALSE);
```

When a user connects to the database service, he or she will automatically be assigned to the correct consumer group.

Scheduler

In Oracle 10.1 and above, batch jobs can be executed by the Scheduler. Although the DBMS_JOB package introduced in Oracle 7 is still available for backward compatibility, the Scheduler is significantly more versatile and robust.

The Scheduler is both RAC-aware and designed to work with database services. Scheduler jobs are controlled by a job coordinator background process (CJQ0) running in each instance in the cluster. The job coordinator controls the job slave processes running on the local instance. In addition, the job coordinators communicate with each other across the cluster to determine how to distribute workload and to ensure availability.

Each database service should be associated with a Scheduler class. This allows Scheduler jobs to have service affinity, providing high availability and also allowing load balancing. For example, the following statement creates a job class called 'BATCH_CLASS' for a service called 'BATCH_SERVICE':

```
SQL> EXECUTE DBMS_SCHEDULER.CREATE_JOB_CLASS ( -
> JOB_CLASS_NAME = 'BATCH_CLASS', -
> RESOURCE_CONSUMER_GROUP => NULL, -
> SERVICE => 'BATCH_SERVICE', -
> LOGGING_LEVEL => DBMS_SCHEDULER.LOGGING_RUNS, -
> LOG_HISTORY => 50, -
> COMMITS => 'Overnight batch');
```

When a job is created, it should be assigned to the job class, for example:

```
SQL> EXECUTE DBMS_SCHEDULER.CREATE_JOB ( -
> JOB_NAME => 'Batch Update', -
> JOB_TYPE => STORED_PROCEDURE', -
> JOB_ACTION => 'USER1.BATCH_UPDATE ();' -
```

```
> NUMBER_OF_ARGUMENTS => 4, -
> START_DATE => SYSDATE + 1, -
> REPEAT_INTERVAL => 'FREQ:DAILY', -
> END_DATE => SYSDATE + 30, -
> JOB_CLASS => 'BATCH_CLASS', -
> ENABLED => TRUE, -
> AUTO_DROP => FALSE);
```

The job class will be used to identify which database service should be used to run the job. This, in turn, will be used to determine on which instances the job should run. If a primary (PREFERRED) instance is not available, then the job will be run on a secondary (AVAILABLE) instance. If the service has been assigned to a resource consumer group, then Resource Manager will enforce the resource limits specified for that group.

Parallel Execution

Parallel Execution is aware of database services. When a parallel job coordinator process creates a job slave, that slave inherits the database service from the coordinator. However, depending on the workload, the job coordinator can execute slaves on any instance in the cluster. In other words, the slaves are not restricted to running on the set of PREFERRED or AVAILABLE instances. Therefore, if you choose to take advantage of Parallel Execution, you should be aware that the distribution of workload across the nodes in the cluster may be affected.

At first sight, the ability of the job coordinator to allocate nodes outside the set assigned to the database service may appear to be an error. However, without this mechanism, it would not be possible to query the global (GV$) dynamic performance views, as these views are implemented using Parallel Execution, where the parallel job coordinator executes a job slave on each instance in the cluster. A process querying the global dynamic performance view must be able to access all instances, irrespective of any database service to which it might be connected.

Administering Database Services

When you create a RAC database, you can also create database services and assign them to instances using either Database Creation Assistant (DBCA) or the Server Control (SRVCTL) utility. After the database is operational, you can use DBCA, Enterprise Manager, or the SRVCTL command line utility to administer database services. Administrative tasks include creating, modifying, deleting, starting and stopping, enabling and disabling, and relocating database services.

Note that it is not possible to create or delete services in Oracle 10.1 Enterprise Manager. This restriction has been lifted in Oracle 10.2 and above.

Administering Database Services Using DBCA

You can use the DBCA Service Management page to manage database service assignments, instance preferences, and TAF policies. You can use DBCA to modify database service configurations while the database is started and also when it is shut down.

To add or modify database services, create an X Window terminal session and start the DBCA tool at the command line:

```
london1$ dbca
```

Then follow these steps:

1. On the Welcome page, select the Oracle Real Application Clusters database option and click Next.

2. On the Operations page, select Services Management and click Next.

3. On the List of Databases page, select the cluster database you wish to configure and click Next.

4. On the Database Services page (see Figure 19-1), any database services that have already been assigned to the database will be displayed. Here you can select any database service and specify the preferred and available instances. You can also select the TAF policy for the instance.

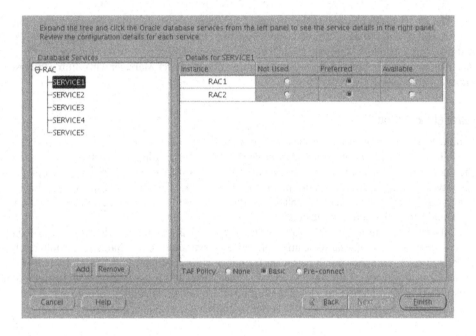

Figure 19-1. *DBCA Database Services configuration page*

To add a new database service, click the Add button. You will be prompted to enter a name for the new service. The new service will be added to the Database Services page. You can then set the instance and TAF details as just described.

You can also use this page to remove a database service by clicking the Remove button. The highlighted service will be removed.

5. Click the Finish button to display a summary message, and then click OK to apply the changes. A progress message is displayed while the database services are configured.

When you use DBCA to add database services, it adds them to the Oracle Cluster Registry (OCR), updates the Net Service entries for each service, and starts the services. When you use DBCA to remove database services, it stops the services, removes the Net Service entries, and deletes them from the OCR.

Administering Database Services Using Enterprise Manager

You can use EM to administer database services. In Oracle 10.1, the Enterprise Manager Database Service administration functionality is limited, so we recommend that you use DBCA instead. In Oracle 10.2, however, this functionality has been significantly enhanced, and we recommend using EM for all database service administration, including creation and deletion of services.

In Oracle 10.1 and above, you can use the Enterprise Manager Service Administration page to view the current database service configuration; enable, disable, start, stop, and relocate services; and for each database service, view the preferred instance, available instance, and TAF policy.

To access the Cluster Managed Database Services page from the Enterprise Manager Database Control home page, click the Administration tab. Under the High Availability options list, click Cluster Managed Database Services.

At this stage, you may be prompted for your operating system credentials, in which case enter your operating system username and password. The Cluster Managed Database Services page will be displayed, as shown in Figure 19-2. On this page, you can enable, disable, start, and stop services.

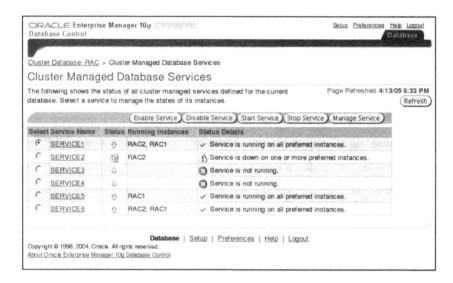

Figure 19-2. *Enterprise Manager Cluster Managed Database Services summary page*

If you click either the Service Name hyperlink or the Manage Service button, you will be taken to the service details page for the currently specified database service, as shown in Figure 19-3.

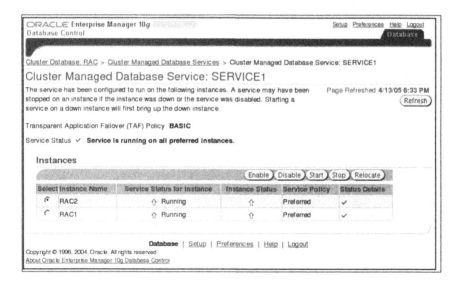

Figure 19-3. *Enterprise Manager Cluster Managed Database Service configuration page*

This service details page shows the allocation of instances for the specified database service. You can use this page to start, stop, and relocate database services on a specific instance.

You can use EM to administer database services after they have been created using DBCA or SRVCTL. In Oracle 10.1, you cannot use EM to create database services or to specify TAF policies.

In Oracle 10.2 and above, the Enterprise Manager Database Control has been enhanced to include the creation, configuration, and deletion of database services. In addition, the Cluster Managed Database Services page has moved. You can now access this page by selecting Maintenance ➤ Cluster Managed Database Services.

In Oracle 10.2, the Cluster Managed Database Services page includes buttons to start, stop, and test the connection to the selected database service. It also includes an Actions drop-down list which allows you to manage (the default), delete, enable, disable, and edit the properties of selected database services. Finally, a new Create Service button allows you to create a new service. If you click this button, you will be taken to the Create Service page (see Figure 19-4).

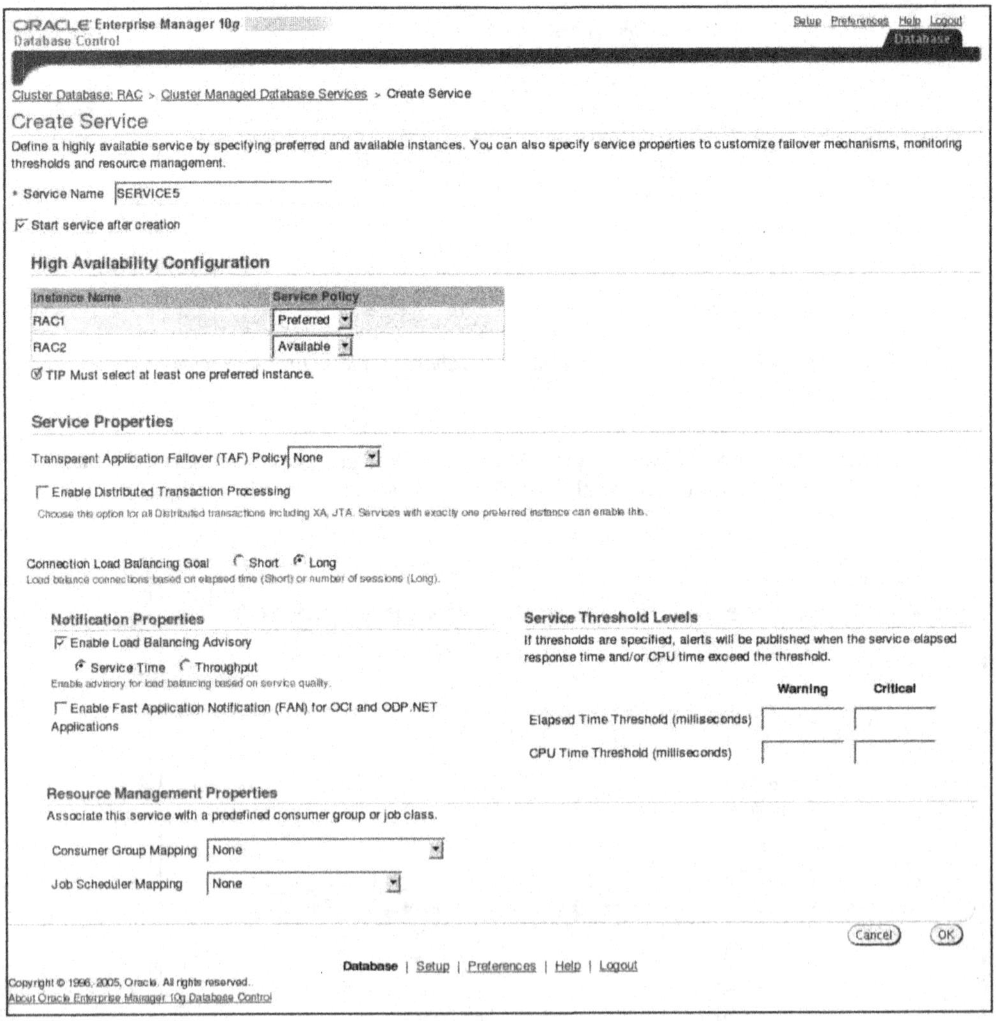

Figure 19-4. *Enterprise Manager Create Service page*

The Create Service page allows you to specify the following:

- A database service name
- A database service policy for each instance: Preferred (default), Available, or Not Used
- A TAF policy: None (default), Basic, or Preconnect
- A Connection Load Balancing Goal: Short (the default in EM, but not in the CREATE_SERVICE procedure of DBMS_SERVICE) or Long

You can also do the following:

- Enable the load balancing advisory, which is disabled by default, and specify the load balancing goal, which can be Service Time or Throughput.
- Enable Fast Application Notification (FAN) for connection pooling applications.
- Specify a consumer group mapping and a Job Scheduler mapping for Resource Manager.
- Specify warning and critical values for service threshold levels for elapsed time and CPU time. When these thresholds are exceeded, alerts will be published.

You can edit the same set of properties at any time by selecting an existing database service from the Cluster Managed Database Service page, selecting Edit Properties from the Action drop-down, and clicking Go.

Administering Database Services Using SRVCTL

You can add and remove database services using the SRVCTL utility. You can also manually stop or restart the service. In addition, you can disable the database service to prevent automatic restarts and subsequently re-enable it. Finally, you can relocate the database service to another node if necessary.

If you add, modify, or remove a service using SRVCTL, this action will update the OCR. However, it will not update the data dictionary or the listener configuration. You will also need to use the DBMS_SERVICE package to modify the service configuration in the data dictionary and update the tnsnames.ora file manually. Therefore, we recommend you use the DBCA utility to add, modify, or remove services in Oracle 10.1 and above, or EM in Oracle 10.2 and above.

Adding a Database Service

You can add database services as follows:

```
srvctl add service -d <database_name> -s <service_name> -r "<preferred list>"
    [-a "<available_list>"] [-P <TAF_policy]
```

You must specify a database name, service name, and at least one preferred server. You may optionally specify a comma-separated list of preferred instances and a similar list of available instances. The TAF policy can be NONE (which is the default value), BASIC, or PRECONNECT.

For example, to create SERVICE2 on database RAC with preferred instances RAC1 and RAC2, and available instances RAC3 and RAC4, use

```
london1$ srvctl add service -d RAC -s SERVICE2 -r "RAC1,RAC2" -a "RAC3,RAC4"
```

Starting a Database Service

Database services must be started before they can be used by a client connection to the instance. You can start a service as follows:

```
srvctl start service -d <database_name> [-s "<service_name_list>" [-i <inst_name>]]
[-o <start_options>] [-c <connect_str> | -q]
```

You must specify a database name. If you do not specify any other options, then all database services will be started. You can specify an individual service name or a comma-separated list of names. You can also optionally specify an instance name on which to start the database service. For example, you can start SERVICE1 and SERVICE2 on the RAC database as follows:

```
london1$ srvctl start service -d RAC -s "SERVICE1,SERVICE2"
```

Stopping a Database Service

You can stop database services using the following:

```
srvctl stop service -d <database_name> [-s "<service_name_list>" [-i <inst_name>]]
[-c <connect_str> | -q] [-f]
```

You must specify a database name. If you do not specify any other options, then all database services will be stopped. You can specify an individual service name or a comma-separated list of names. You can also optionally specify an instance name on which to stop the database service. Finally, you can specify the -f option to force the database service to disconnect all sessions during the stop operation.

For example, to force SERVICE2 and SERVICE3 to stop, use

```
london1$ srvctl stop service -d RAC -s "SERVICE2,SERVICE3" -f
```

If you shut down the database, Oracle will automatically stop all database services.

Checking the Current Database Service Configuration

You can check the current configuration of all database services as follows:

```
srvctl config service -d <database_name> [-s <service_name>] [-a] [-S <level>]
```

Here's an example:

```
london1$ srvctl config service -d RAC
SERVICE1 PREF: RAC2 RAC1 AVAIL:
SERVICE2 PREF: RAC1 AVAIL: RAC2
SERVICE3 PREF: RAC2 AVAIL: RAC1
SERVICE4 PREF: RAC1 RAC2 AVAIL:
SERVICE5 PREF: RAC1 AVAIL:
```

For each database service, this example shows the preferred (primary) and available (backup) instances. You can use the -s option to show the configuration of a specific database service. The -a option includes information about the configuration of TAF for the database service, for example:

```
london1$ srvctl config service -d RAC -a
SERVICE1 PREF: RAC2 RAC1 AVAIL:  TAF: basic
SERVICE2 PREF: RAC1 AVAIL: RAC2 TAF: NONE
SERVICE3 PREF: RAC2 AVAIL: RAC1 TAF: NONE
SERVICE4 PREF: RAC1 RAC2 AVAIL:  TAF: NONE
SERVICE5 PREF: RAC1 AVAIL:  TAF:NONE
```

The -S command specifies that additional information should be generated for EM.

Checking the Current Database Service Status

You can check the current status of one or more database services as follows:

```
srvctl status service -d <name> -s "<service_name_list>" [-f] [-v] [-S <level>]
```

Here's an example:

```
london1$ srvctl status service -d RAC -s "SERVICE1,SERVICE4"
Service SERVICE1 is running on instance(s) RAC2, RAC1
Service SERVICE2 is not running
```

The -f option includes disabled applications, and the -v option specifics verbose output.

Enabling and Disabling a Database Service

By default, all database services are enabled for automatic restart. However, for some administrative activities, you may wish to temporarily disable one or more database services to prevent automatic restart. You can disable and enable a database service on a specific node as follows:

```
srvctl disable service -d <database_name> -s "<service_name_list>" [-i <inst_name>]
srvctl enable service -d <database_name> -s "<service_name_list>" [-i <inst_name>]
```

For example, to disable and enable SERVICE2 on instance RAC4 of the RAC database, use the following:

```
london1$ srvctl disable service -d RAC -s SERVICE2 -i RAC4
london1$ srvctl enable service -d RAC -s SERVICE2 -i RAC4
```

Removing a Database Service

You can remove a database service using

```
srvctl remove service -d <database_name> -s <service_name> [ -i <inst_name>] [-f]
```

You must specify a database name and a service name. You can optionally specify an instance, and you can also specify the -f option to force the database service to disconnect all sessions. For example, to remove SERVICE4 from the RAC database, use the following:

```
london1$ srvctl remove service -d RAC -s SERVICE4
```

This command removes SERVICE4 from all instances.

Note that you cannot remove the default SYS$BACKGROUND and SYS$USERS database services, which are created by Oracle.

Relocating a Database Service

You may need to move a database service from one instance to another to rebalance workloads. You can relocate a database service as follows:

```
srvctl relocate service -d <database_name> -s <service_name>
-i <old_inst_name> -r <new_inst_name> [-f]
```

You must specify the database name, service name, and the old and new instance names. You can optionally specify the -f option, in which case all sessions will be disconnected during the relocation operation. For example, to relocate SERVICE3 from instance RAC2 to instance RAC4 on the RAC database, use

```
london1$ srvctl relocate service -d RAC -s SERVICE3 -i RAC2 -t RAC4
```

Administering Database Services Using the DBMS_SERVICE Package

When you create, modify, or delete database services using SRVCTL, the changes are recorded in the OCR only. It is also necessary to update the data dictionary using the DBMS_SERVICE package.

The DBMS_SERVICE package includes the following procedures:

- CREATE_SERVICE
- MODIFY_SERVICE
- DELETE_SERVICE
- START_SERVICE
- STOP_SERVICE
- DISCONNECT_SESSION

We describe these procedures in the following sections.

CREATE_SERVICE

This procedure creates a database service. It takes the following parameters:

- **SERVICE_NAME**: Associates the database service with a TNS Net Service name.
- **GOAL**: Specifies the load balancing goal. This parameter can take the following values:
  - DBMS_SERVICE.GOAL_NONE (default)
  - DBMS_SERVICE.GOAL_SERVICE_TIME
  - DBMS_SERVICE.GOAL_THROUGHPUT
- **CLB_GOAL**: Specifies the connection load balancing goal. This parameter can take the following values:
  - DBMS_SERVICE.CLB_GOAL_LONG (default)
  - DBMS_SERVICE.CLB_GOAL_SHORT
- **FAILOVER_METHOD**: Specifies the TAF failover method. This parameter can take the following values:
  - DBMS_SERVICE.FAILOVER_METHOD_NONE (default)
  - DBMS_SERVICE.FAILOVER_METHOD_BASIC

  Note that the PRECONNECT failover method is not supported for services.
- **FAILOVER_TYPE**: Specifies the TAF failover type. This parameter can take the following values:
  - DBMS_SERVICE.FAILOVER_TYPE_NONE (default)
  - DBMS_SERVICE.FAILOVER_TYPE_SESSION
- **FAILOVER_RETRIES**: Indicates the number of times to attempt to connect to failover instance following node or instance failure.
- **FAILOVER_DELAY**: Indicates the number of seconds to wait between each connection attempt.
- **DTP**: Specifies that the service can be used for distributed transactions.
- **AQ_HA_NOTIFICATIONS**: Specifies that high-availability events can be sent via AQ to OCI and ODP.NET clients that have registered to receive them.

You cannot specify the PREFERRED and AVAILABLE instances for a database service using this procedure. These are properties of the OCR and therefore must be specified using the SRVCTL utility.

If you choose to create a database service manually, you will also need to modify the tnsnames.ora network configuration file.

MODIFY_SERVICE

This procedure allows you to modify all of the parameters which can be set in CREATE_SERVICE, with the exception of the Net Service Name.

DELETE_SERVICE

This procedure allows you to delete a database service.

START_SERVICE

This procedure allows you to start a database service. You can optionally specify an instance on which to start the database service. If the instance name is NULL, then the database service will be started on the current instance. To start the database service on all instances, specify the constant DBMS_SERVICE.ALL_INSTANCES.

STOP_SERVICE

This procedure allows you to stop a database service. You can optionally specify an instance on which to stop the database service. If the instance name is NULL, then the database service will be stopped on the current instance. To stop the database service on all instances, specify the constant DBMS_SERVICE.ALL_INSTANCES.

DISCONNECT_SESSION

This procedure disconnects all sessions currently connected to the specified database service on the current instance.

Configuring Clients to Use Services

In addition to configuring database services on each instance, it is necessary to configure the Net Service Name for each client. You can do this in Oracle Names, in an LDAP directory, or using EZCONNECT. However, the simplest option is to add the service to the tnsnames.ora file, which resides in the $ORACLE_HOME/network/admin or the $TNS_ADMIN directory on each Oracle server and client.

For example, to configure SERVICE1 to run on hosts london1 and london2, use the following:

```
SERVICE1 =
  (DESCRIPTION =
    (LOAD_BALANCE = yes)
    (ADDRESS = (PROTOCOL = TCP)(HOST = london1-vip)(PORT = 1521))
    (ADDRESS = (PROTOCOL = TCP)(HOST = london2-vip)(PORT = 1521))
    (CONNECT_DATA =
      (SERVICE_NAME = SERVICE1)
    )
  )
```

Note that the HOST clause should specify the VIP addresses of the nodes, not their IP addresses. This allows the database service to be failed over automatically in the event of a node or instance failure.

You can include a database service name anywhere that you might use a Net Service Name, for example:

```
london1$ sqlplus USER1/PASSWORD1@SERVICE1

london1$sqlplus /NOLOG
SQL> CONNECT USER1/PASSWORD1@SERVICE1
```

You can also append a domain name to the database service name.

Troubleshooting Database Services

You can list which database services are currently available in the listener using the status option of the lsnrctl command, as follows:

```
london1 $ lsnrctl status
LSNRCTL for Linux: Version 10.2.0.1.0 - Production on 22-SEP-2005 21:07:09

Copyright (c) 1991, 2005 Oracle. All rights reserved.

Connecting to (ADDRESS=(PROTOCOL=tcp)(HOST=)(PORT=1521))
STATUS of the LISTENER
------------------------
Alias                     LISTENER_LONDON1
Version                   TNSLSNR for Linux: Version 10.2.0.1.0 - Production
Start Date                22-SEP-2005 09:48:12
Uptime                    9 days 11 hr. 18 min. 56 sec
Trace Level               off
Security                  ON: Local OS Authentication
SNMP                      OFF
Listener Parameter File   /u01/app/oracle/product/10.2.0/db_1/network/admin/
listener.ora
Listener Log File         /u01/app/oracle/product/10.2.0/db_1/network/admin/
listener_london1.log
Listening Endpoints Summary...
  (DESCRIPTION=(ADDRESS=(PROTOCOL=tcp)(HOST=147.43.1.201)(PORT=1521)))
  (DESCRIPTION=(ADDRESS=(PROTOCOL=tcp)(HOST=147.43.1.101)(PORT=1521)))
  (DESCRIPTION=(ADDRESS=(PROTOCOL=ipc)(KEY=EXTPROC)))
Services Summary...
Service "+ASM" has 1 instance(s).
  Instance "+ASM1", status BLOCKED, has 1 handler(s) for this service...
Service "+ASM_XPT" has 1 instance(s).
  Instance "+ASM1", status BLOCKED, has 1 handler(s) for this service...
Service "RAC" has 2 instance(s)
  Instance "RAC1", status BLOCKED, has 2 handler(s) for this service...
  Instance "RAC2", status BLOCKED, has 1 handler(s) for this service...
Service "RACXDB" has 2 instance(s)
  Instance "RAC1", status BLOCKED, has 1 handler(s) for this service...
  Instance "RAC2", status BLOCKED, has 1 handler(s) for this service...
Service "RAC_XPT" has 2 instance(s)
  Instance "RAC1", status BLOCKED, has 2 handler(s) for this service...
  Instance "RAC2", status BLOCKED, has 1 handler(s) for this service...
Service "SERVICE1" has 2 instance(s)
  Instance "RAC1", status BLOCKED, has 2 handler(s) for this service...
  Instance "RAC2", status BLOCKED, has 1 handler(s) for this service...
Service "SERVICE2" has 2 instance(s)
  Instance "RAC1", status BLOCKED, has 2 handler(s) for this service...
  Instance "RAC2", status BLOCKED, has 1 handler(s) for this service...
The command completed successfully.
```

You can obtain more detailed information using the services option of the lsnrctl command. For example, for SERVICE1, taking this action might return the following information:

```
london1$ lsnrctl services
Service "SERVICE1" has 2 instance(s)
  Instance "RAC1", status BLOCKED, has 2 handler(s) for this service...
    Handler(s):
      "DEDICATED" established:0 refused:0 state:ready
         REMOTE SERVER
         (ADDRESS=(PROTOCOL=TCP)(HOST=london1)(PORT=1521))
      "DEDICATED" established:1 refused:0 state:ready
         LOCAL SERVER
  Instance "RAC2", status BLOCKED, has 1 handler(s) for this service...
      "DEDICATED" established:1 refused:0 state:ready
         REMOTE SERVER
         (ADDRESS=(PROTOCOL=TCP)(HOST=london2)(PORT=1521))
```

You can obtain even more detail by enabling the verbose display mode in the LSNRCTL utility, for example:

```
london1$ lsnrctl
LSNRCTL> SET DISPLAYMODE VERBOSE
LSNRCTL> SERVICE
```

The output for this command includes all the environment variables that have been set for each service.

Monitoring Services

In this section, we discuss some of the views and features provided for monitoring services, including the following:

- Data dictionary views
- Dynamic performance views
- Metrics and thresholds
- Trace

Data Dictionary Views

The DBA_SERVICES data dictionary view provides information about currently configured database services. The DBA_SERVICES view contains the columns shown in Table 19-4.

Table 19-4. *DBA_SERVICES Data Dictionary View*

Column	Data Type	Notes
SERVICE_ID	NUMBER	
NAME	VARCHAR2(64)	
NAME_HASH	NUMBER	
NETWORK_NAME	VARCHAR2(512)	
CREATION_DATE	DATE	
CREATION_DATE_HASH	NUMBER	
FAILOVER_METHOD	VARCHAR2(64)	
FAILOVER_TYPE	VARCHAR2(64)	
FAILOVER_RETRIES	NUMBER(10)	

Continued

Table 19-4. *Continued*

Column	Data Type	Notes
FAILOVER_DELAY	NUMBER(10)	
MIN_CARDINALITY	NUMBER	
MAX_CARDINALITY	NUMBER	
GOAL	VARCHAR2(12)	Oracle 10.2 and above
DTP	VARCHAR2(1)	Oracle 10.2 and above
ENABLED	VARCHAR2(3)	Oracle 10.2 and above
AQ_HA_NOTIFICATION	VARCHAR2(3)	Oracle 10.2 and above
CLB_GOAL	VARCHAR2(5)	Oracle 10.2 and above

Dynamic Performance Views

In this section, we describe a number of dynamic performance views that support database services, including the following:

- GV$SERVICES
- GV$ACTIVE_SERVICES
- GV$SERVICEMETRIC
- GV$SERVICEMETRIC_HISTORY
- GV$SERVICE_WAIT_CLASS
- GV$SERVICE_EVENT
- GV$SERVICE_STATS
- GV$SERV_MOD_ACT_STATS

GV$SERVICES

You can check which database services are currently configured using the GV$SERVICES dynamic performance view. This view includes the columns shown in Table 19-5.

Table 19-5. *GV$SERVICES Dynamic Performance View*

Column	Data Type	Notes
INST_ID	NUMBER	
SERVICE_ID	NUMBER	
NAME	VARCHAR2(64)	
NAME_HASH	NUMBER	
NETWORK_NAME	VARCHAR2(512)	
CREATION_DATE	DATE	
CREATION_DATE_HASH	NUMBER	
GOAL	VARCHAR2(12)	Oracle 10.2 and above
DTP	VARCHAR2(1)	Oracle 10.2 and above
AQ_HA_NOTIFICATION	VARCHAR2(3)	Oracle 10.2 and above
CLB_GOAL	VARCHAR2(5)	Oracle 10.2 and above

GV$ACTIVE_SERVICES

You can check which database services are currently running using the GV$ACTIVE_SERVICES dynamic performance view. This view includes the columns shown in Table 19-6.

Table 19-6. *GV$ACTIVE_SERVICES Dynamic Performance View*

Column	Data Type	Notes
INST_ID	NUMBER	
SERVICE_ID	NUMBER	
NAME	VARCHAR2(64)	
NAME_HASH	NUMBER	
NETWORK_NAME	VARCHAR2(512)	
CREATION_DATE	DATE	
CREATION_DATE_HASH	NUMBER	
GOAL	VARCHAR2(12)	Oracle 10.2 and above
DTP	VARCHAR2(1)	Oracle 10.2 and above
BLOCKED	VARCHAR2(3)	Oracle 10.2 and above
AQ_HA_NOTIFICATION	VARCHAR2(3)	Oracle 10.2 and above
CLB_GOAL	VARCHAR2(5)	Oracle 10.2 and above

Note that database services will appear in this view once for each instance on which they are currently active, for example:

```
SQL> SELECT inst_id, service_id, name
> FROM gv$active_services
> WHERE name LIKE 'SERVICE%';
INST_ID SERVICE_ID NAME
------- ---------- ------------------------------------------------
      1          7 SERVICE1
      1          8 SERVICE2
      2          7 SERVICE1
      2          9 SERVICE3
```

In the example just shown, SERVICE1 is running on instances 1 and 2. SERVICE2 is only running on instance 1, and SERVICE3 is only running on instance 2.

GV$SERVICEMETRIC

You can check the value of a number of database service metrics using the GV$SERVICEMETRIC view. This view includes the columns shown in Table 19-7.

Table 19-7. *GV$SERVICEMETRIC Dynamic Performance View*

Column	Data Type	Notes
INST_ID	NUMBER	
BEGIN_TIME	DATE	
END_TIME	DATE	
INTSIZE_CSEC	NUMBER	
GROUP_ID	NUMBER	

Continued

Table 19-7. *Continued*

Column	Data Type	Notes
SERVICE_NAME_HASH	NUMBER	
SERVICE_NAME	VARCHAR2(64)	
CTMHASH	NUMBER	
ELAPSEDPERCALL	NUMBER	Deprecated in Oracle 10.2
CPUPERCALL	NUMBER	
DBTIMEPERCALL	NUMBER	Oracle 10.2 and above
CALLSPERSEC	NUMBER	Oracle 10.2 and above
DBTIMEPERSEC	NUMBER	Oracle 10.2 and above
GOODNESS	NUMBER	Oracle 10.2 and above
DELTA	NUMBER	Oracle 10.2 and above
FLAGS	NUMBER	Oracle 10.2 and above

This view returns two rows for each database service. The first row reports the metrics for the last five seconds (INTSIZE_CSEC = 500), and the second row reports the metrics for the last minute (INTSIZE_CSEC = 6,000).

In Oracle 10.1, this view only reports the elapsed time per call and the CPU time per call. In Oracle 10.2 and above, this view also reports the database time per call, the number of calls per second, and the database time per second.

In Oracle 10.2 and above, this view also reports GOODNESS, which indicates how attractive the instance is with respect to processing the workload presented to the database service. Lower numbers are preferred. If only one instance is available, then the GOODNESS value will be zero for all user-created database services. The number is internally calculated based on any goal (long or short) that was specified for that database service.

In Oracle 10.2 and above, the DELTA column predicts how much GOODNESS will increase for every additional session that connects to the instance. Remember that low values of GOODNESS are preferred, and therefore any increase implies a degradation of performance.

Finally, in Oracle 10.2 and above, the FLAGS column can contain the values shown in Table 19-8.

Table 19-8. *GV$SERVICEMETRIC FLAGS Column Values*

Value	Notes
0x01	Service is blocked from accepting new connections
0x02	Service is violating the threshold on one or more metrics
0x04	Value is unknown

GV$SERVICEMETRIC_HISTORY

The GV$SERVICEMETRIC_HISTORY view displays the recent history of metric values for each service. Table 19-9 lists the columns in this view.

Table 19-9. *GV$SERVICEMETRIC_HISTORY Dynamic Performance View*

Column	Data Type	Notes
INST_ID	NUMBER	
BEGIN_TIME	DATE	
END_TIME	DATE	

Column	Data Type	Notes
INTSIZE_CSEC	NUMBER	
GROUP_ID	NUMBER	
SERVICE_NAME_HASH	NUMBER	
SERVICE_NAME	VARCHAR2(64)	
CTMHASH	NUMBER	
ELAPSEDPERCALL	NUMBER	Deprecated in Oracle 10.2
CPUPERCALL	NUMBER	
DBTIMEPERCALL	NUMBER	Oracle 10.2 and above
CALLSPERSEC	NUMBER	Oracle 10.2 and above
DBTIMEPERSEC	NUMBER	Oracle 10.2 and above
GOODNESS	NUMBER	Oracle 10.2 and above
DELTA	NUMBER	Oracle 10.2 and above
FLAGS	NUMBER	Oracle 10.2 and above

This view contains 86 rows for each database service. By default, there are 25 5-second samples covering the last 2 minutes and 61 1-minute samples covering the last hour. The INTSIZE_CSEC column describes the interval size in centiseconds. For a 5-second sample, INTSIZE_CSEC takes the value of 500 or above; for a 60-second sample, INTSIZE_CSEC takes the value of 6,000 or above. Note that the sample length may vary slightly when the node is busy. Therefore, if you wish to include INTSIZE_CSEC in a WHERE clause, we recommend you use INTSIZE_CSEC < 6,000 for the short (5-second) interval and INTSIZE_CSEC >= 6,000 for the long (60-second) interval.

The metrics reported by this view are the same as those reported by GV$SERVICEMETRIC.

GV$SERVICE_WAIT_CLASS

The GV$SERVICE_WAIT_CLASS view was introduced in Oracle 10.1 and summarizes waits by wait class for each database service. Table 19-10 lists the columns in this view.

Table 19-10. *GV$SERVICE_WAIT_CLASS Dynamic Performance View*

Column	Data Type
INST_ID	NUMBER
SERVICE_NAME	VARCHAR2(64)
SERVICE_NAME_HASH	NUMBER
WAIT_CLASS_ID	NUMBER
WAIT_CLASS#	NUMBER
WAIT_CLASS	VARCHAR2(64)
TOTAL_WAITS	NUMBER
TIME_WAITED	NUMBER

In Oracle 10.1 and above, there are significantly more wait events than in previous releases. To facilitate drill down when investigating performance issues, waits are grouped into wait classes. In Oracle 10.2, there are ten wait classes:

- Application
- Cluster
- Commit
- Concurrency
- Configuration
- Idle
- Network
- Other
- System I/O
- User I/O

GV$SERVICE_EVENT

The GV$SERVICE_EVENT view was introduced in Oracle 10.1 and is enabled by default. The columns are as shown in Table 19-11.

Table 19-11. *GV$SERVICE_EVENT Dynamic Performance View*

Column	Data Type
INST_ID	NUMBER
SERVICE_NAME	VARCHAR2(64)
SERVICE_NAME_HASH	NUMBER
EVENT	VARCHAR2(64)
EVENT_ID	NUMBER
TOTAL_WAITS	NUMBER
TOTAL_TIMEOUTS	NUMBER
TIME_WAITED	NUMBER
AVERAGE_WAIT	NUMBER
MAX_WAIT	NUMBER
TIME_WAITED_MICRO	NUMBER

This view reports information similar to that reported by the GV$SYSTEM_EVENT and GV$SESSION_EVENT dynamic performance views. However, GV$SERVICE_EVENT aggregates wait event statistics by database service.

If you are experiencing wait events on a large system, you can use the GV$SERVICE_EVENT view as the next level of investigation to discover which database service is impacting performance. You can then proceed to investigate individual sessions within that database service.

GV$SERVICE_STATS

The GV$SERVICE_STATS view was introduced in Oracle 10.1. Table 19-12 lists the columns in this view.

Table 19-12. *GV$SERVICE_STATS Dynamic Performance View*

Column	Data Type
INST_ID	NUMBER
SERVICE_NAME_HASH	NUMBER

Column	Data Type
SERVICE_NAME	VARCHAR2(64)
STAT_ID	NUMBER
STAT_NAME	VARCHAR2(64)
VALUE	NUMBER

This view externalizes database service–level statistics. Only a limited subset of statistics is available. In Oracle 10.2, the statistics shown in Table 19-13 are recorded at the database service level.

Table 19-13. *Statistics Recorded at the Database Service Level*

Statistic Name	
DB CPU	DB time
application wait time	cluster wait time
concurrency wait time	db block changes
execute count	gc cr blocks receive time
gc cr blocks received	gc current block receive time
gc current blocks received	logons cumulative
opened cursors cumulative	parse count (total)
parse time elapsed	physical reads
physical writes	redo size
session cursor cache hits	session logical reads
sql execute elapsed time	user I/O wait time
user calls	user commits
user rollbacks	workarea executions - multipass
workarea executions - onepass	workarea executions - optimal

GV$SERV_MOD_ACT_STATS

The GV$SERV_MOD_ACT_STATS view was introduced in Oracle 10.1 and reports aggregate statistics for modules and actions for a specific database service. By default, this view is not populated; statistic collection must be enabled using the DBMS_MONITOR package. Table 19-14 lists this view's columns.

Table 19-14. *GV$SERV_MOD_ACT_STATS Dynamic Performance View*

Column	Data Type	Notes
INST_ID	NUMBER	
AGGREGATION_TYPE	VARCHAR2(21)	Oracle 10.2 and above
SERVICE_NAME	VARCHAR2(64)	
MODULE	VARCHAR2(49)	
ACTION	VARCHAR2(33)	
STAT_ID	NUMBER	
STAT_NAME	VARCHAR2(64)	
VALUE	NUMBER	

Statistics collection can be enabled for a database service either at the module level or for individual actions, for example:

```
SQL> EXEC DBMS_MONITOR.SERV_MOD_ACT_STAT_ENABLE ('SERVICE1','MODULE1');
SQL> EXEC DBMS_MONITOR.SERV_MOD_ACT_STAT_ENABLE ('SERVICE1','MODULE1','ACTION1');
```

In the first example, statistics collection is enabled for all actions within MODULE1. In the second example, statistics collection is enabled for ACTION1 only within MODULE1.

To disable statistics collection again, use

```
SQL> EXEC DBMS_MONITOR.SERV_MOD_ACT_STAT_DISABLE ('SERVICE1','MODULE1');
SQL> EXEC DBMS_MONITOR.SERV_MOD_ACT_STAT_DISABLE ('SERVICE1','MODULE1','ACTION1');
```

In Oracle 10.2, the AGGREGATION_TYPE column can return SERVICE_MODULE or SERVICE_MODULE_ACTION depending on the level of granularity requested for the statistics.

Metrics and Thresholds

In Oracle 10.1 and above, Oracle records metrics on database service usage. These are saved to the Automatic Workload Repository (AWR) at regular intervals and can be used subsequently by the Automatic Database Diagnostic Monitor (ADDM) and other advisors to generate recommendations.

It is possible to define thresholds for service-level metrics including the following:

- Elapsed time per call (Oracle 10.1 only)
- CPU time per call
- Database time per call (Oracle 10.2 and above)
- Calls per second (Oracle 10.2 and above)
- Database time per second (Oracle 10.2 and above)

Server-generated alerts can be triggered if the thresholds are violated. When an alert is generated, you can optionally perform a number of actions, including changing the priority of Scheduler jobs, relocating services to other available instances, or provisioning additional instances for the services.

In Oracle 10.1, you can identify the current values of CPU and elapsed time per call for each database service as follows:

```
SQL> SELECT service_name, elapsedpercall, cpupercall FROM v$servicemetric;
```

In Oracle 10.2 and above, the ELAPSEDPERCALL column has been deprecated in favor of the new DBTIMEPERCALL column:

```
SQL> SELECT service_name, dbtimepercall, cpupercall FROM v$servicemetric;
```

The following code sample sets a server alert threshold:

```
SQL> EXEC DBMS_SERVER_ALERT.SET_THRESHOLD ( -
> metrics_id => DBMS_SERVER_ALERT.ELAPSED_TIME_PER_CALL, -
> warning_operator => DBMS_SERVER_ALERT.OPERATOR_GE, -
> warning_value => 500000, -
> critical_operator => DBMS_SERVER_ALERT.OPERATOR_GE, -
> critical_value => 1000000, -
> observation_period => 15, -
> consecutive_occurrences => 3, -
> instance_name => 'RAC1', -
> object_type =>DBMS_SERVER.ALERT.OBJECT_TYPE_SERVICE, -
> object_name => 'SERVICE1');
```

The preceding code sets a threshold for the elapsed time per call metric for SERVICE1. An alert will be generated if a threshold is exceeded three times consecutively over a 15-minute period. A warning will be raised if the elapsed time per call exceeds half a second; a critical alert will be raised if the elapsed time per call exceeds one second.

Note that the server alert threshold must be set separately on each instance.

Trace

In Oracle 10.1 and above, it is possible to enable and disable trace for specific database services using the DBMS_MONITOR package. See Chapter 21 for further details.

Summary

In this chapter, we discussed workload management and database services. If your cluster does not run a symmetrical workload, then it is important to understand these concepts in order to maximize the use of resources across the cluster. The enhancements to workload management introduced in Oracle 10.2 allow you to formally specify the nature of your workload using well documented and supported mechanisms.

Database services provide a supported method of partitioning applications across the cluster. Correctly configured database services ensure that use of resources such as disk and CPU is maximized and also that traffic across the interconnect is minimized. In our opinion, database services provide one of the most effective tuning tools available to RAC developers and DBAs.

■ ■ ■

## CHAPTER 20

Adding and Deleting Nodes and Instances

To handle increasing workloads or seasonal peaks, you sometimes need to increase the number of instances in your cluster, which will normally require the addition of one or new nodes. In this chapter, we describe procedures for adding nodes and instances to and deleting them from your cluster.

Before you attempt to add or delete an instance on a production database, we strongly recommend that you test these procedures in a nonproduction environment. If you do not have sufficient hardware to add a node to your test cluster, you can try deleting an existing node and adding it again. Before attempting any of these procedures, ensure that you have backed up the OCR.

Adding or deleting multiple nodes in a single operation is possible. However, in our experience, most users will never wish to add or delete more than one node at a time. Therefore, in this chapter, we assume that only one node is being added or deleted. Our approach is always to research and test a limited number of reliable procedures rather than to develop a different strategy for every eventuality. While this approach is less important during initial deployment, it is much more efficient when you are developing and testing upgrade procedures.

Before you can increase the size of your cluster, you must ensure that the value of the CLUSTER_ DATABASE_INSTANCES parameter is set to an appropriate value. If you have built your database using DBCA, this parameter defaults to the number of instances in the cluster at the time of database creation. This parameter must have the same value on all nodes; therefore, to increase it you will need to restart all nodes. If you anticipate adding nodes to your cluster and cannot accept downtime, you may wish to set this parameter to an appropriate value. Increasing the CLUSTER_DATABASE_INSTANCES parameter will increase the amount of SGA memory required to support RAC on each node but should not have any other significant impact.

There are numerous variations on the procedures described in this chapter, depending on whether you are using ASM or a shared Oracle Home. These are well documented in Chapter 10 of the *Oracle Clusterware and Oracle Real Application Clusters Administration and Deployment Guide*.

Running GUI Tools

Many of the Oracle utilities are GUI-based and must be run within an X Window environment including the Oracle Universal Installer (OUI), the Database Configuration Assistant (DBCA), and the Network Configuration Assistant (NETCA). In addition, tools that perform actions on remote nodes require a shell that is configured to execute scp and ssh as the oracle user on the remote node silently.

If X Windows is not already running, log in as root and run the startx command:

```
[root@london1 root]# startx
```

Run the xhost command to allow all clients to connect to the X Windows host:

```
[root@london1 root]# xhost +
```

Change to the oracle user:

```
[root@london1 root]# su - oracle
```

Enable secure shell for scp copies and ssh execution on the new node:

```
[oracle@london1 oracle]$ ssh-agent $SHELL
[oracle@london1 oracle]$ ssh-add
```

Adding a Node

Adding a new instance to an existing RAC database requires a number of steps:

1. Plan the installation.
2. Install and configure the new hardware.
3. Configure the network.
4. Install the operating system.
5. Configure the storage.
6. Install Oracle Clusterware.
7. Install Oracle Database software.
8. Configure the listener.

We describe these steps in the sections that follow.

Plan the Installation

In this section, we assume that the new instance to be added will use identical hardware to the existing nodes in the cluster. While this is not mandatory, we recommend using similar hardware where possible to ensure more predictable performance across the cluster. In addition, using similar hardware will simplify fault-finding in the new node, as you will be able to compare it with existing ones.

Prior to ordering new hardware, check that you have physical space in your computer room for the new server. Also check that you have sufficient power and networking infrastructure capacity. Ensure that you specify all the correct components for the new server including CPUs, memory, local disks, network cards, and fiber channel cards, as appropriate.

Specify values for the following:

- IP address for the public network
- IP address for the private network (interconnect)
- Virtual IP (VIP address)
- Hostname
- Instance number
- Instance name
- ORACLE_SID

Identify current values for the following from one of the existing hosts:

- DNS domain name
- Oracle domain name
- Cluster name
- Database name
- Subnet mask
- DNS server addresses

Check the following on existing nodes:

- Disk partitioning
- Swap space

If you have planned for additional instances in advance, you may be able to add a new node without stopping the database. If you have not tested node addition prior to going live, we recommend that you stop all instances in the cluster while you are adding the node. As you may be reconfiguring storage and other shared resources, you may also wish to consider taking a database backup before adding the node.

Install and Configure the New Hardware

Install all CPUs, memory, local disks, network cards, and HBAs in the server. Install the server, and connect and test the power supply. Check that the BIOS layer has been correctly configured. In particular, on 32-bit Intel Xeon systems, check that Hyper-Threading (HT) has been enabled or disabled as appropriate.

Configure the Network

Configure the switches, routers, and any other network devices for the new server. Ensure that switches are configured for each network used by the new server, for example, the external network, interconnect network, and storage network. If necessary, add the public network IP and VIP addresses of the new server to DNS; otherwise, add the new server to the /etc/hosts files for all existing nodes in the cluster.

Install the Operating System

Install the operating system following the same procedure used for the original servers. If possible, use the same version of the operating system that was installed on the original servers. You may install a cloned image of the operating system from one of the existing servers, or you may choose to reinstall the operating system from CD-ROM or from a network server.

Create initial partitions on the local disk including root, swap, and any other custom partitions. The disk partitions do not have to be identical on each node. However, we recommend that the swap partition is at least the same size as those used on existing nodes.

Install any operating system patches drivers and other software packages that your standard installation requires. Either update the kernel parameters in /etc/sysctl.conf or copy this file from an existing node.

Create a home directory for the oracle user on the local disk. Create the dba group on the new node with the same group ID as allocated on the existing nodes. Also create an oracle user on the new node with the same user ID as assigned on the existing nodes. You can use the id utility to check the values on existing nodes.

Create a profile for the oracle user. For example, if you are using the bash shell, copy a .bash_profile file from the home directory of the oracle user on another node. Edit the .bash_profile file and modify any instance specific values, for example, the ORACLE_SID.

As the node will be added using the Oracle Universal Installer (OUI), you will need to configure ssh for the Oracle user on the new server, to enable files to be copied across the network and shell scripts to be executed remotely from the installation node. Verify that the Oracle user can run ssh and scp silently among all existing nodes on the cluster and the new node in both directions.

If you are not using DNS, add the IP addresses of all other nodes in the cluster to /etc/hosts, including the public and private network addresses and the VIP address. Check that you can communicate all existing nodes in the cluster using the ping utility. Remember to check both the external network and the interconnect network.

Configure the Storage

If you are using a Host Bus Adapter (HBA) to communicate with shared storage, then identify the World Wide Name (WWN) for the HBA on the server. On the Storage Area Network (SAN), associate each LUN used by the database with the WWN of each server.

Ensure that all HBA drivers or dual-pathing software has been installed on the new server. You may need to unload and reload the drivers using the modprobe utility or using rmmod and insmod in order for the server to see newly configured storage.

Run the fdisk utility on an existing node and the new node:

```
[root@london1 root]# fdisk -l
```

Try to replicate the order in which devices are configured on the other nodes. Although this operation is not essential, we recommend that you attempt to keep all systems as symmetrical as possible to reduce complexity and the potential for inadvertent errors.

If the logical drives are not being created in the same order, investigate the order that adapters appear in /etc/modules.conf. The order can vary according to the point during the installation process at which the HBAs were installed and when the LUNs were provisioned on the storage device.

If you are using raw devices, then configure /etc/system/rawdevices. You will need at least two new disk partitions to accommodate the redo logs on the new node. In addition, if you are using Automatic Undo Management, you will require an additional disk partition for the undo tablespace for the new node.

If you are using OCFS, download and install the appropriate RPM packages. Then configure /etc/ocfs.conf. If you copy this file from another host, ensure that you change the host name and IP address. Run ocfs_uid_gen to generate a new GUID for the node in /etc/ocfs.conf. Alternatively, generate a new /etc/ocfs.conf file using the ocfstool GUI tool.

Next, start the OCFS service as follows:

```
[root@london3 root]# /sbin/load_ocfs
```

Create a mount point for each file system. Add the OCFS file systems to /etc/fstab, and finally, mount the file systems:

```
[root@london3 root]# mount -a -t ocfs
```

Verify that the Oracle user on the new node has both read and write access to each of the new file systems.

Check that the Oracle user can read and write to each LUN. In addition to testing access privileges, we recommend that you test the performance of storage. If you are using a cluster file system, a simple test to use is the dd utility to create a large file on a local disk and then copy this file to and from the storage using the cp utility. If you are using raw devices, use the dd utility to copy the file to the storage instead of cp. This test is a quick way of verifying that the storage infrastructure has been correctly configured.

If you are using ASM, download and install the appropriate RPM packages. For the new node to access existing ASM disk groups, you must issue the following command:

```
[root@london3 root]# /etc/init.d/oracleasm scandisks
```

To extend an existing RAC database, you must configure storage on the new node to be the same as on existing nodes. Both the OCR and the voting disk must be accessible to the new node using the same pathname that is used on the existing nodes.

Install Oracle Clusterware

Oracle Clusterware is installed from one of the existing nodes using the OUI. Before installing Oracle Clusterware, ensure you have the correct hostname and domain name, as these are difficult to change after installation. Also check that the oracle user has permission to write to both the Oracle Clusterware home and the OUI directory on the new node. In this example, you will add new node london3 to existing nodes london1 and london2.

You must run the OUI as the oracle user from an X Window terminal shell on an existing node in the cluster. Start the OUI by running the addNode.sh script:

```
[oracle@london1 oracle] $ cd CRS_HOME/oui/bin
[oracle@london1 bin] $ ./addNode.sh
```

The addNode.sh script calls runInstaller with the -addNode option. The Welcome page will be displayed. Click Next to continue to the node specification page, which is shown in Figure 20-1.

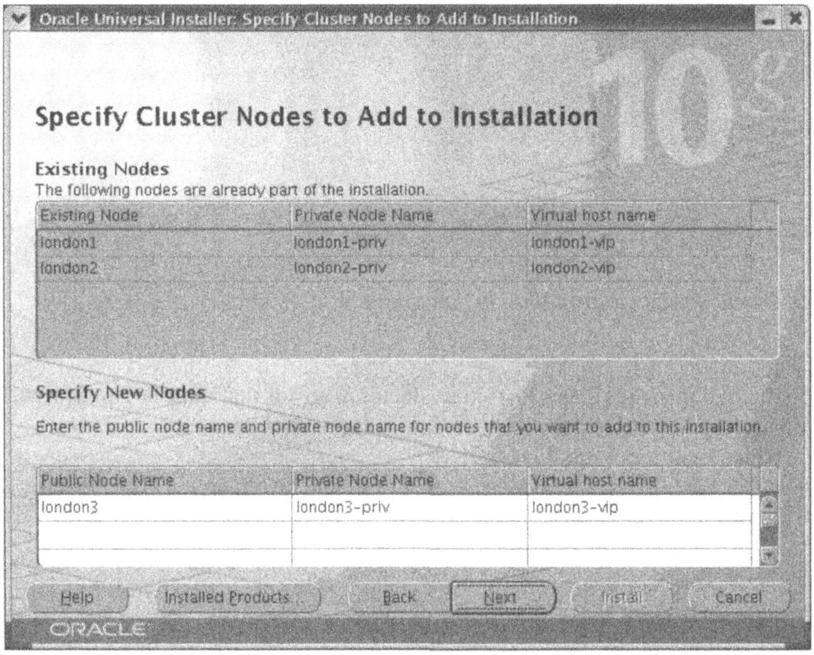

Figure 20-1. *The OUI Oracle Clusterware installation node specification page*

On the node specification page, enter the public and private node names and the virtual hostname for the new node in the lower panel. The new node names should already have been defined either in the /etc/hosts file on each node in the cluster or in DNS.

Click Next to proceed to the Cluster Node Addition Summary page, which displays a summary of the actions that will be performed. Click Install, and the Cluster Node Addition Progress page will be displayed, showing the current status of the cluster node addition process. The OUI performs the following actions:

- Creates scripts to be executed by the root user

- Copies the contents of the $CRS_HOME directory to the new node

- Updates the inventory

- Displays the Execute Configuration scripts dialog box shown in Figure 20-2

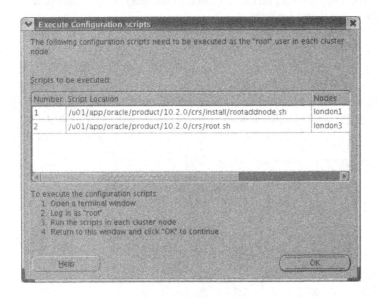

Figure 20-2. *The OUI Oracle Clusterware installation root configuration scripts*

The Execute Configuration scripts dialog box shows details of scripts that must be run with root privileges. Pay particular attention to the Nodes column on the right side of the table, which specifies the host on which each script should run.

The first script is $CRS_HOME/install/rootaddnode.sh and should be run on the existing node; in this example, we ran this script on london1:

```
[root@london1 root]# cd /u01/app/oracle/product/10.2.0/crs/install
[root@london1 install]# sh rootaddnode.sh
clscfg: EXISTING configuration version 3 detected.
clscfg: version 3 is 10G Release 2.
Attempting to add 1 new nodes to the configuration
Using ports: CSS=49895 CRS=49896 EVMC=49898 and EVMR=49897.
node <nodenumber>: <nodename> <private interconnect name> <hostname>
node 2: london3 london3-priv london3
Creating OCR keys for user 'root', privgrp 'root'..
Operation successful.
```

```
/u01/app/oracle/product/10.2.0/crs/bin/srvctl add nodeapps -n london3
 -A london3-vip/255.255.0.0/eth0 -o /u01/app/oracle/product/10.2.0/crs
```

The second script is $CRS_HOME/root.sh. This script should be run on the new node. In this case, we ran this script on london3:

```
[root@london3 root]# cd /u01/app/oracle/product/10.2.0/crs
[root@london3 crs]# sh root.sh
Checking to see if Oracle CRS stack is already configured
OCR LOCATIONS = /u02/oradata/RAC/OCRFile1,/u03/oradata/RAC/OCRFile2
OCR backup directory '/u01/app/oracle/product/10.2.0/crs/cdata/crs' does not exist.
Creating now
Setting the permissions on OCR backup directory
Setting up NS directories
Oracle Cluster Registry configuration upgraded successfully
clscfg: EXISTING configuration version 3 detected.
clscfg: version 3 is 10G Release 2.
assigning default hostname london1 for node 1.
assigning default hostname london2 for node 2.
assigning default hostname london3 for node 3.
Successfully accumulated necessary OCR keys.
Using ports: CSS=49895 CRS=49896 EVMC=49898 and EVMR=49897.
node <nodenumber>: <nodename> <private interconnect name> <hostname>
node 1: london1 london1-priv london1
node 2: london2 london2-priv london2
node 3: london3 london3-priv london3
clscfg: Arguments check out successfully.

NO KEYS WERE WRITTEN. Supply -force parameter to override.
-force is destructive and will destroy any previous cluster
configuration.
Oracle Cluster Registry for cluster has already been initialized
Startup will be queued to init within 90 seconds.
Adding daemons to inittab
Expecting the CRS daemons to be up within 600 seconds.
CSS is active on these nodes.
        london1
        london2
        london3
CSS is active on all nodes.
Waiting for the Oracle CRSD and EVMD to start
Waiting for the Oracle CRSD and EVMD to start
Oracle CRS stack installed and running under init(1M)
Running vipca(silent) for configuring nodeapps
IP address "london1-vip" has already been used. Enter an unused IP address.
IP address "london2-vip" has already been used. Enter an unused IP address.
```

The final two lines appear to be a bug in the node addition procedure. During Oracle Clusterware installation, the Virtual IP Configuration Assistant (VIPCA) is called by the root.sh script of the last node to be added to the cluster. It initializes the VIP addresses of all nodes in the cluster. However, in the case of node addition, the existing nodes should already have VIP addresses; therefore, the VIPCA command partially fails. However, it does appear to create a VIP address for the new node correctly.

When you have run both of the scripts successfully, click OK to display the End of Installation page and Exit to end the OUI session.

Add the Node-Specific Interface Configuration

The next step is to add the node-specific interface configuration. First, obtain the Oracle Notification Service (ONS) remote port number, which is specified in the file $CRS_HOME/opmn/conf/ons.config:

```
[oracle@london1 oracle]# cat $CRS_HOME/opmn/conf/ons.config
localport=6100
remoteport=6200
loglevel=3
useocr=on
```

In the preceding example, the remote port number is 6200.

Configure the Oracle Notification Services (ONS) port number by executing the racgons utility as the oracle user on one of the existing hosts. This utility has the following syntax:

```
    racgons add_config <new_node_name>:<remote_port>
```

The following example configures node london3 to use remote port number 6200:

```
[oracle@london1 root]$ cd $CRS_HOME/bin
[oracle@london1 bin]$ racgons add_config london3:6200
```

If successful, this command completes silently.

Verify Oracle Clusterware Installation Using CLUVFY

Before proceeding with the installation of the Oracle Database Software, it is recommended that you run the Cluster Verification Utility (CLUVFY) on each node in the cluster. Check the output carefully for errors and consult the documentation and/or the MetaLink web site if a problem is highlighted that cannot obviously be resolved.

On each node in the cluster, run the following commands to check the cluster manager and cluster components:

```
[oracle@london3 oracle]$ cluvfy comp clumgr -n all
[oracle@london3 oracle]$ cluvfy comp clu
```

On one node in the cluster, run the following command to confirm that Oracle Clusterware has successfully been installed and configured:

```
[oracle@london3 oracle]$ cluvfy stage -post crsinst -n all
```

Install Oracle Database Software

The next step is to install the Oracle Database software on the new node using the OUI. You must run the OUI as the oracle user from an X Window terminal shell on an existing node in the cluster:

```
[oracle@london1 oracle]$ cd $ORACLE_HOME/oui/bin
[oracle@london1 bin]$ ./addNode.sh
```

The OUI again displays the Welcome page. Click Next to continue to the Specify Cluster Nodes to Add to Installation page (Figure 20-3).

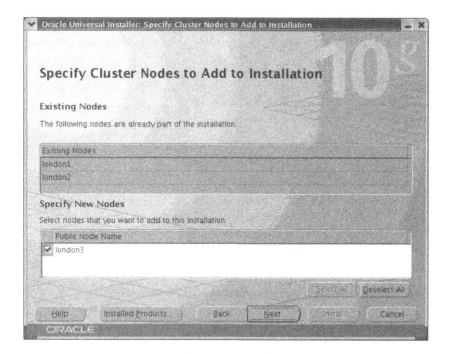

Figure 20-3. *The OUI Oracle Database Software installation node specification page*

On the node specification page, select the public node names for the new node from the lower panel. The OUI verifies that the new node is running and accessible over the network. It also checks that the Oracle user has write permission for the Oracle Home directory on the new node and the OUI inventory on all nodes.

Click Next to proceed to the Node Addition Summary page, which displays a summary of the actions that will be performed. Click Install to display the Cluster Node Addition Progress page, which shows the current status of the cluster node addition process. The OUI performs the following actions:

- Creates scripts to be executed by the root user
- Copies the contents of the $ORACLE_HOME directory to the new node
- Updates the inventory
- Displays the Execute Configuration scripts dialog box (Figure 20-4)

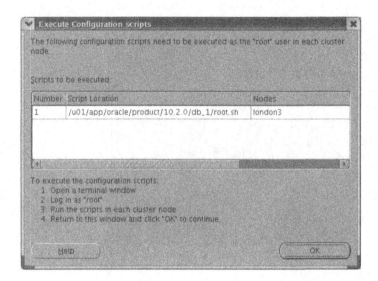

Figure 20-4. *OUI Oracle Database software Execute Configuration scripts dialog box*

The Execute Configuration scripts dialog box shows details of scripts that must be executed with root privileges. For Oracle database software installation, the only script is $CRS_HOME/root.sh, which should be run on the new node. In this case, we ran this script on london3:

```
[root@london3 root]# cd /u01/app/oracle/product/10.2.0/db_1
[root@london3 db_1]# sh root.sh
Running Oracle10 root.sh script...

The following environment variables are set as:
    ORACLE_OWNER= oracle
    ORACLE_HOME=  /u01/app/oracle/product/10.2.0/db_1

Enter the full pathname of the local bin directory: [/usr/local/bin]:
Creating /usr/local/bin directory...
    Copying dbhome to /usr/local/bin ...
    Copying oraenv to /usr/local/bin ...
    Copying coraenv to /usr/local/bin ...

Entries will be added to the /etc/oratab file as needed by
Database Configuration Assistant when a database is created
Finished running generic part of root.sh script.
Now product-specific root actions will be performed.
```

When you have run the script successfully, click OK on the Execute Configuration scripts dialog box to continue to the End of Installation page, and click Exit to end the OUI session.

Configure the Listener

On the new node in an X Window shell, create a listener process by running the Net Configuration Assistant (NETCA) as the oracle user, which opens the Configuration page shown in Figure 20-5.

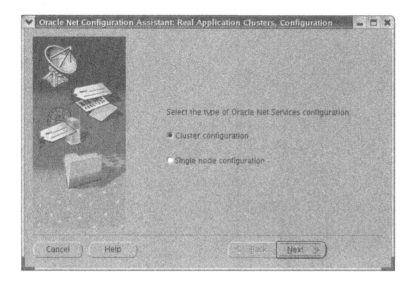

Figure 20-5. *The Net Configuration Assistant Configuration page*

On the Configuration page, select Cluster configuration and click Next to continue to the Active Nodes page (Figure 20-6).

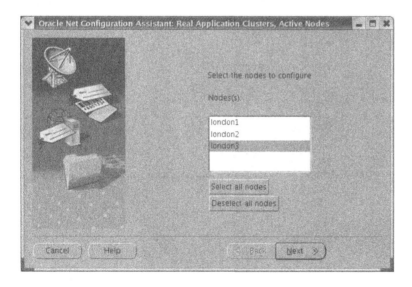

Figure 20-6. *The Net Configuration Assistant Active Nodes page*

On the Active Nodes page, select the node that you have added to the cluster. Click Next to continue to the Welcome page (Figure 20-7).

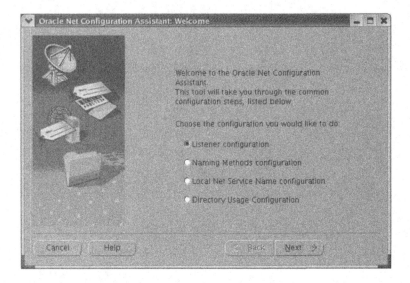

Figure 20-7. *The Net Configuration Assistant Welcome page*

On the Welcome page, select Listener configuration, and click Next to continue to the Listener page (Figure 20-8).

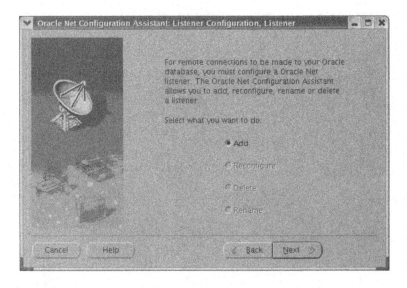

Figure 20-8. *The Net Configuration Assistant Listener page*

On the Listener page, select Add to add a new listener, and click Next to continue to the Listener Name page (Figure 20-9).

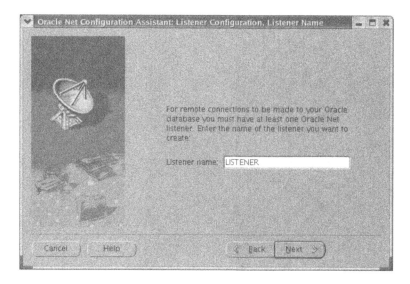

Figure 20-9. *The Net Configuration Assistant Listener Name page*

On the Listener Name page, specify a name for the listener. You should accept the default value unless you require a nonstandard network configuration. Click Next to continue to the Select Protocols page (Figure 20-10).

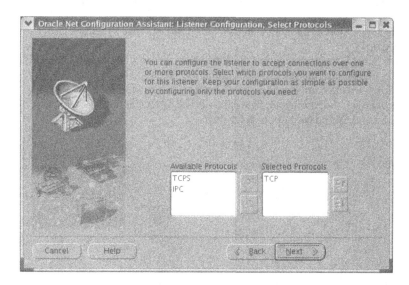

Figure 20-10. *The Net Configuration Assistant Select Protocols page*

On the Select Protocols page, the TCP protocol should be selected by default, which should be sufficient in most cases. Click Next to continue to the TCP/IP Protocol page (Figure 20-11).

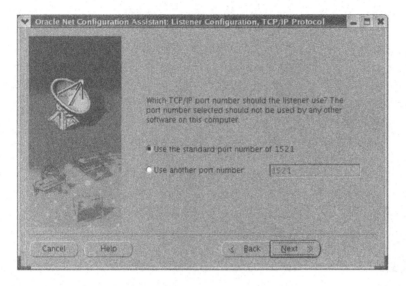

Figure 20-11. *The Net Configuration Assistant TCP/IP Protocol page*

On the TCP/IP Protocol page, specify the well-known IP port number on which the listener should listen for incoming TCP/IP messages. In Oracle, this port number traditionally defaults to 1521 for the first listener process on the node, which should be adequate for most systems. You may specify a different port number if necessary. You may wish to do so if, for example, you intend to run multiple versions of the Oracle Database software on the same cluster, for example, Oracle 9.2 and Oracle 10.1.

Click Next to continue to the More Listeners? page. Click Yes if you wish to configure another listener; click No otherwise.

Click Next to continue to the Listener Configuration Done page, and click Next again to return to the NETCA Welcome page. Click Finish on this page to terminate NETCA.

Terminating NETCA completes the configuration of the listener process. Unless the TNS_ADMIN environment variable has been set, the listener configuration file will be located in $ORACLE_HOME/network/admin/listener.ora and should contain the following:

```
SID_LIST_LISTENER_LONDON3 =
  (SID_LIST =
    (SID_DESC =
      (SID_NAME = PLSExtProc)
      (ORACLE_HOME = /u01/app/oracle/product/10.2.0/db_1)
      (PROGRAM = extproc)
    )
  )

LISTENER_LONDON3 =
  (DESCRIPTION_LIST =
    (DESCRIPTION =
      (ADDRESS = (PROTOCOL = TCP)(HOST = london3-vip)(PORT = 1521)(IP = FIRST))
      (ADDRESS = (PROTOCOL = TCP)(HOST = 147.43.1.103)(PORT = 1521)(IP = FIRST))
    )
  )
```

NETCA will also start the listener daemon. In this case, a listener will be started on node london3 with the name LISTENER_LONDON3.

Adding an Instance

The next step is to create an instance on the new node. In the following example, you will create a new instance RAC3 on london3. The existing database consists of instances RAC1 and RAC2 on nodes london1 and london2, respectively. In an X Window terminal window on an existing host, log in as the oracle user, and start the Database Configuration Assistant (DBCA):

```
[oracle@london1 oracle]$ cd $ORACLE_HOME/bin
[oracle@london1 bin]$ ./dbca
```

Once you log in, DBCA displays the Welcome page, which allows you to specify whether you wish to administer an Oracle Real Application Clusters database or a single instance database. Select Oracle Real Application Clusters database, and click Next to continue to the Operations page (Figure 20-12).

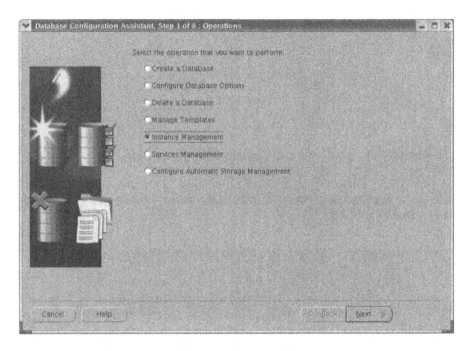

Figure 20-12. *The Database Configuration Assistant Operations page*

On the Operations page, select Instance Management, and click Next to continue to the Instance Management page (Figure 20-13).

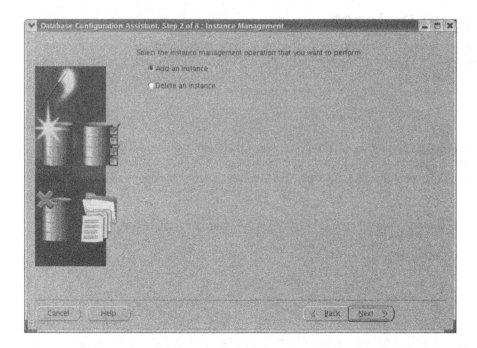

Figure 20-13. *The Database Configuration Assistant Instance Management page*

On the Instance Management page, select Add an instance, and click Next to display the List of cluster databases page (Figure 20-14).

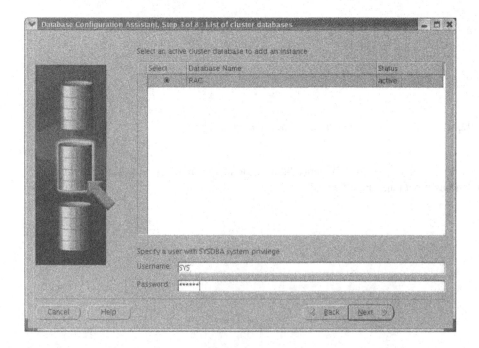

Figure 20-14. *The Database Configuration Assistant List of cluster databases page*

On the List of cluster databases page, select the database to which you wish to add the instance. If you are not using operating system authentication, you will be prompted for a user-name and password for a database user with SYSDBA privileges. Click Next to display the List of cluster database instances page for the selected database (Figure 20-15).

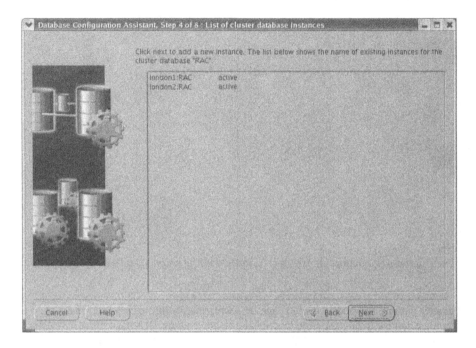

Figure 20-15. *The Database Configuration Assistant List of cluster database instances page*

The List of cluster database instances page shows you the nodes, names, and status of the existing instances in the cluster. You cannot modify any information on this page. Click Next to continue to the Instance naming and node selection page (Figure 20-16).

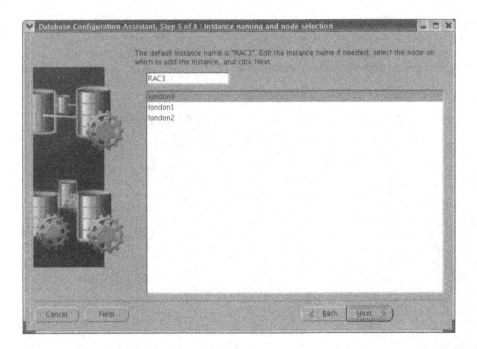

Figure 20-16. *The Database Configuration Assistant Instance naming and node selection page*

On the Instance naming and node selection page, DBCA will generate the next instance name in your current instance name sequence. You can override the instance name if it is not correct. Select the new node name from the list, and click Next to continue to the Database Services page (Figure 20-17).

On the Database Services page, specify for each service whether the new instance will be Preferred, Available, or Not Used. Click Next to continue to the Instance Storage page (Figure 20-18).

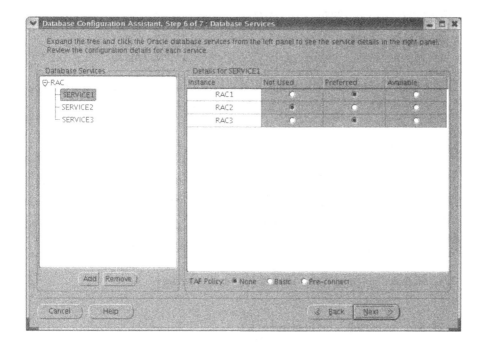

Figure 20-17. *The Database Configuration Assistant Database Services page*

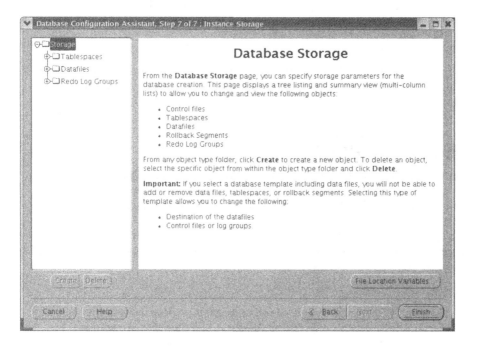

Figure 20-18. *The Database Configuration Assistant Instance Storage page*

On the Instance Storage page, you need to specify redo log files for the new instance. If you are using Automatic Undo Management, you also need to specify an undo tablespace; DBCA will suggest appropriate default values.

Click Finish to continue to the Summary page. When you have reviewed the summary, click OK to add the instance.

If you are using ASM on your cluster, DBCA will detect this usage and ask you to confirm that you wish to create an ASM instance on the new node (see Figure 20-19). Click Yes to continue.

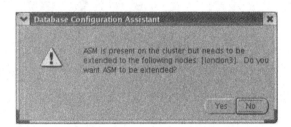

Figure 20-19. *The Database Configuration Assistant ASM extension message*

Next, DBCA will perform the following operations:

- Create and start an ASM instance on the new node if ASM was in use on existing instances
- Create the Oracle Net configuration
- Configure and start node applications for the listener and EM agent
- Create and start a database instance on the new node
- Create and start services on the new node

If the instance has been successfully added, DBCA will not inform you. It will, however, display a dialog asking if you want to perform another operation. Click Yes to return to the DBCA operations page or No to quit DBCA.

Deleting an Instance

This section describes the procedure for deleting a database instance using DBCA. DBCA deregisters the instance from all ONS listeners, deletes the instance from the node, removes the Oracle Net configuration, and deletes the Oracle Flexible Architecture (OFA) directory structure for the instance from the node.

You must run DBCA as the Oracle user from one of the nodes that you do not intend to delete. In the following example, DBCA is run on node london1 to delete the RAC3 instance RAC3, which is running on node london3:

```
[oracle@london1 oracle] $ dbca
```

DBCA displays the Welcome page that allows you to specify the type of database you wish to administer. Select Oracle Real Application Clusters database, and click Next to continue to the Operations page (Figure 20-20).

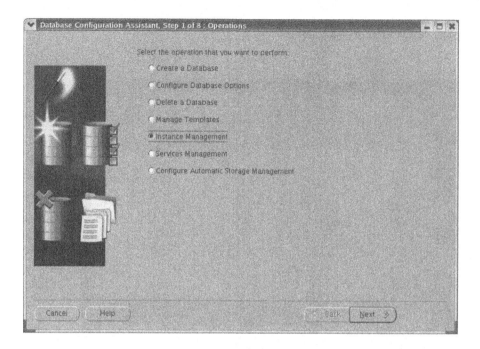

Figure 20-20. *The Database Configuration Assistant Operations page*

On the Operations page, select Instance Management, and click Next to display the Instance Management Page (Figure 20-21).

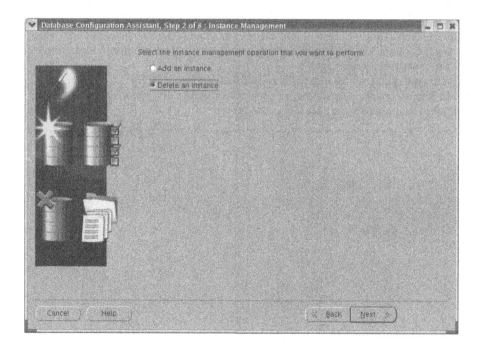

Figure 20-21. *The Database Configuration Assistant Instance Management page*

On the Instance Management page, select Delete an instance, and click Next to again display the List of cluster databases page (Figure 20-22).

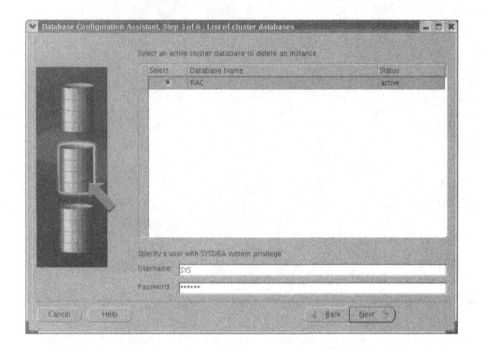

Figure 20-22. *The Database Configuration Assistant List of cluster databases page*

If you have more than one database in your cluster, you should select the database from which to delete the instance on the List of cluster databases page. Also, on this page, enter a username and password for a user with SYSDBA privileges.

Click Next to display a list of instances on this database (see Figure 20-23).

On the List of cluster database instance page, select the instance that you wish to delete. Click Next to display the Database Services page (Figure 20-24).

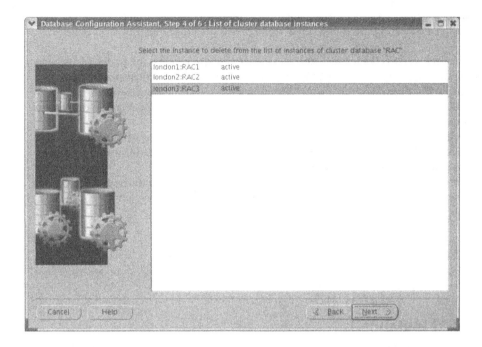

Figure 20-23. *The Database Configuration Assistant List of cluster database instances page*

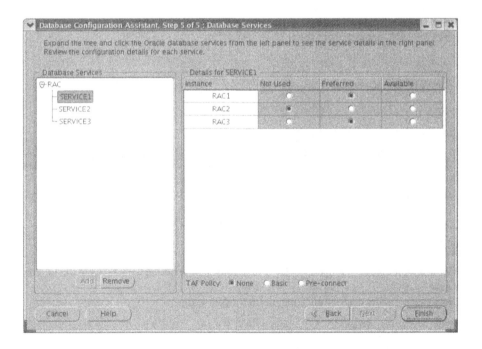

Figure 20-24. *The Database Configuration Assistant Database Services page*

The Database Services page shows you the services that are currently configured for the instance that you are deleting and allows you to reassign new preferred and available instances for each service.

DBCA will check whether the instance that you are intending to delete is the preferred instance for any currently configured services. If it finds any preferred instances, it will display a warning message. When you are satisfied with the service configuration, click Finish to display a summary page. Click OK to continue; a further confirmation message will appear. Click OK again to continue. A progress message is displayed while the instance is being deleted.

The specific instance and the Oracle Net configuration for that instance are removed by DBCA. When the deletion is complete, a dialog box appears asking if you want to perform another operation. Click Yes to return to the Operations page or No to exit DBCA.

If you are using ASM and have just deleted the last RDBMS instance on the node, the next step is to delete the ASM instance. This procedure is described in the following section.

Deleting a Node

To delete a node from an Oracle cluster, first delete all instances on that node. If you are using ASM, also delete the ASM instance from the node.

Delete ASM Instance

This section describes deleting an ASM instance from a specific node. We suggest that you back up the OCR before attempting this operation.

First, stop the ASM instance:

```
[oracle@london3 oracle]$ srvctl stop asm -n <node>
```

Then, delete the ASM instance from the OCR:

```
[oracle@london3 oracle]$ srvctl remove asm -n <node>
```

Remove the ASM instance log files:

```
[oracle@london3 oracle]$ rm -r $ORACLE_BASE/admin/+ASM
```

and remove the ASM database configuration files:

```
[oracle@london3 oracle]$ rm -r $ORACLE_HOME/dbs/*ASM*
```

Finally, remove all ASM entries from /etc/oratab. These entries have the prefix +ASM.

We recommend that you perform another backup of your OCR when you have completed this procedure.

Delete the Listener Process

You can delete the listener either using the NETCA or manually. This example uses NETCA to delete the listener on london3.

As the Oracle user, on any node in the cluster, run the following:

```
[oracle@london1 oracle]$ netca
```

This command will display the Configuration page shown in Figure 20-25.

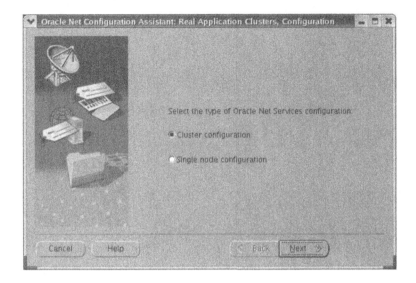

Figure 20-25. *The Net Configuration Assistant Configuration page*

On the Configuration page, select Cluster configuration, and click Next to open the Active Nodes page shown in Figure 20-26.

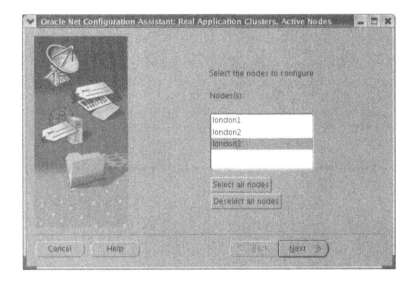

Figure 20-26. *The Net Configuration Assistant Active Nodes page*

On the Active Nodes page, select the node you wish to delete, and click Next to display the Welcome page shown in Figure 20-27.

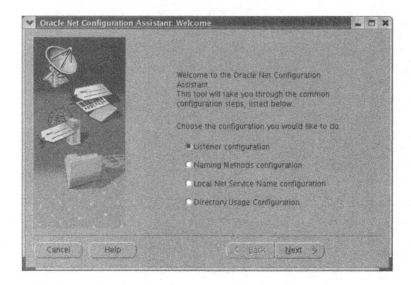

Figure 20-27. *The Net Configuration Assistant Welcome page*

On the Welcome page, select Listener configuration, and click Next to open the Listener page shown in Figure 20-28.

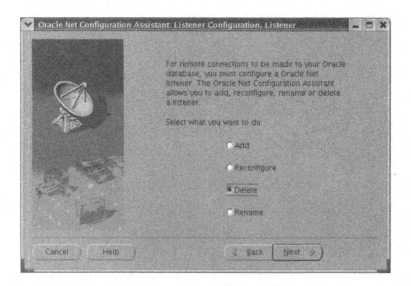

Figure 20-28. *The Net Configuration Assistant Listener page*

On the Listener page, this time select Delete, and click Next to open the Select Listener page shown in Figure 20-29.

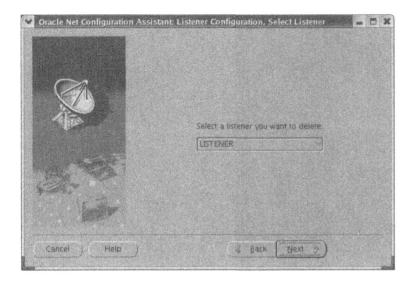

Figure 20-29. *The Net Configuration Assistant Select Listener page*

On the Select Listener page, specify the listener you want to delete. In most configurations, only one listener process will have been configured on each node; therefore, you will not be presented with a choice. Click Next to be prompted for confirmation. Click Yes to delete the listener.

The NETCA will stop the listener daemon and delete the contents of $TNS_ADMIN/listener.ora.

Delete the Oracle Database Software

The next step is to delete the Oracle Database software. On the node that you are deleting, in this case london3, as the oracle user in an X Window session, run the following command to update the local inventory:

```
[oracle@london3 oracle]$ cd $ORACLE_HOME/oui/bin
[oracle@london3 bin]$ ./runInstaller -updateNodeList ORACLE_HOME=$ORACLE_HOME \
CLUSTER_NODES="" -local
Starting Oracle Universal Installer...
No pre-requisite checks found in oraparam.ini, no system pre-requisite checks will
be executed
'UpdateNodeList' was successful
```

On the node that you are deleting, start the OUI and delete the Oracle Home:

```
[oracle@london3 oracle]$ cd $ORACLE_HOME/oui/bin
[oracle@london3 bin]$ ./runInstaller
```

The OUI Welcome page will be displayed again. Click Deinstall Products, and the Inventory dialog box will be displayed (see Figure 20-30).

Figure 20-30. *The OUI Oracle Database software deletion Inventory dialog box*

In the Inventory dialog box, select the check box for the Oracle Database Home, in this case OraDb10g_home1. Then click the Remove button.

A confirmation dialog box will be displayed. Click Yes to continue or No to exit. The Oracle Database software will be removed. When the operation is complete, the Inventory dialog box will be displayed again. Click Close to return to the OUI Welcome page and Cancel to exit the OUI session.

Note that if you are using an Oracle shared home, it is not necessary to delete the Oracle Home on the local node. However, you will need to run the following commands to detach the Oracle shared home from the local node:

```
[oracle@london3 oracle]$ cd $ORACLE_HOME/oui/bin
[oracle@london3 bin]$ ./runInstaller -detachhome -local ORACLE_HOME=$ORACLE_HOME
```

Update Inventories on Remaining Hosts

Your next step is to update the inventories on the remaining hosts. On one of the remaining nodes, in this case london1, as the oracle user in an X Window session, run the following command specifying the names of all remaining nodes for the CLUSTER_NODES parameter:

```
[oracle@london1 oracle]$ cd $ORACLE_HOME/oui/bin
[oracle@london1 bin]$ ./runInstaller -updateNodeList ORACLE_HOME=$ORACLE_HOME \
"CLUSTER_NODES=london1,london2"
Starting Oracle Universal Installer...
No pre-requisite checks found in oraparam.ini, no system pre-requisite checks will
be executed
'UpdateNodeList' was successful
```

Remove Node-Specific Interface Configuration

The next step is to remove the node-specific interface configuration. First, obtain the ONS remote port number, which is specified in the file $CRS_HOME/opmn/conf/ons.config, as follows:

```
[oracle@london1 oracle]$ cat $CRS_HOME/opmn/conf/ons.config
localport=6100
remoteport=6200
loglevel=3
useocr=on
```

In the preceding example, the remote port number is 6200. Remove the configuration by executing the `racgons` utility as the `oracle` user on one of the existing hosts. This utility has the following syntax:

```
racgons remove_config <new_node_name>:<remote_port>
```

For example, the following commands delete the node `london3`, which was configured to use remote port 6200:

```
[oracle@london1 oracle]$ cd $CRS_HOME/bin
[oracle@london1 bin]$ racgons remove_config london3:6200
racgons: Existing key value on london3 = 6200.
racgons: london3:6200 removed from OCR.
```

If you have created a local interface definition for the node that is being deleted, on an existing node, as the `oracle` user, delete the interface configuration for the node:

```
oifcfg delif -node <nodename>
```

For example, to delete the interface configuration for the node `london3`, use the following:

```
[oracle@london1 oracle]$ cd $CRS_HOME/bin
[oracle@london1 bin]$ oifcfg delif -node london3
```

Disable Oracle Clusterware Applications

Your next step is to disable any Oracle Clusterware applications that are running on the node to be deleted using the `$CRS_HOME/install/rootdelete.sh` command. This command takes the following syntax:

```
rootdelete.sh [local|remote] [sharedvar|nosharedvar] [sharedhome|nosharedhome]
```

This command should only be run once. If you are using a local file system, you must specify the `nosharedhome` argument. This option updates the permissions of local files, so that they can subsequently be removed by the `oracle` user.

If the OCR location file (`ocr.loc`) is on a shared file system, specify the `sharedvar` parameter. However, we recommend using the default location for this file, which is `/etc/ocr.loc`, in which case you should specify the `nosharedvar` parameter.

This step should be executed by the `root` user on the node that you are deleting, in this case, `london3`:

```
[root@london3 root]# cd $CRS_HOME/install
[root@london3 install]# sh rootdelete.sh remote nosharedvar nosharedhome
CRS-0210: Could not find resource 'ora.london3.LISTENER_LONDON3.lsnr'.
Shutting down Oracle Cluster Ready Services (CRS):
Stopping resources.
Successfully stopped CRS resources
Stopping CSSD.
Shutting down CSS daemon.
Shutdown request successfully issued.
Shutdown has begun. The daemons should exit soon.
Checking to see if Oracle CRS stack is down...
Oracle CRS stack is not running.
```

```
Oracle CRS stack is down now.
Removing script for Oracle Cluster Ready services
Updating ocr file for downgrade
Cleaning up SCR settings in '/etc/oracle/scls_scr'
```

This command shuts down the Oracle Clusterware daemons and deletes the Oracle Clusterware configuration files from the /etc/init.d and /etc/rc*.d directories. You can ignore the message about the listener process that was deleted in a previous step. If you are deleting multiple nodes, disable Oracle Clusterware on each node.

Delete the Node from the OCR

Next delete the node from the Oracle cluster and update the OCR using the $CRS_HOME/install/rootdeletenode.sh script. This script removes any remaining node applications and calls the delete option of the CLSCFG utility to update the OCR. The script should be run on one of the remaining nodes. Therefore, in this case, run the script on london1. The syntax for this script is

```
rootdeletenode.sh node1,node1-number,node2,node2-number,...
```

Note that the nodes and their numbers should be specified in a single, comma-separated list. You can obtain the node number for each node that you are deleting using the olsnodes -n utility, as in the following example:

```
[root@london1 root]# $CRS_HOME/bin/olsnodes -n
london1     1
london2     2
london3     3
```

For node london3, the node number is 3. Therefore, as the root user on node london1, we can run the following commands:

```
[root@london1 root]# cd $CRS_HOME/install
[root@london1 install]# ./rootdeletenode.sh london3,3
CRS nodeapps are deleted successfully
clscfg: EXISTING configuration version 3 detected.
clscfg: version 3 is 10G Release 2.
Node deletion operation successful.
'london3' deleted successfully
```

Delete the Oracle Clusterware Software

The next step is to delete the Oracle Clusterware software. As the oracle user on the node that you are deleting, in this case london3, run the following command in an X Window session to update the local inventory:

```
[oracle@london3 oracle]$ cd $CRS_HOME/oui/bin
[oracle@london3 bin]$ ./runInstaller -updateNodeList ORACLE_HOME=$CRS_HOME \
CLUSTER_NODES="" -local CRS=true
Starting Oracle Universal Installer...
No pre-requisite checks found in oraparam.ini, no system pre-requisite checks will
be executed
'UpdateNodeList' was successful
```

On the node that you are deleting, start the OUI, and delete the Oracle Home:

```
[oracle@london3 oracle]$ cd $CRS_HOME/oui/bin
[oralce@london3 bin]$ ./runInstaller
```

The OUI Welcome page will be displayed. Click Deinstall Products, and the Inventory dialog box will be displayed (see Figure 20-31).

Figure 20-31. *The OUI Oracle Clusterware deletion Inventory dialog box*

In the Inventory dialog box, select the check box for the Oracle Database Home, in this case OraCrs10g_home1. Then click Remove.

A confirmation dialog box will be displayed. Click Yes to continue or No to exit. A further dialog box will be displayed asking you to confirm deletion of the $CRS_HOME directory. Click Yes to delete this directory. The Oracle Clusterware software will be removed. When the operation is complete, the Inventory dialog box will be displayed again. Click Close to return to the OUI Welcome page and Cancel to exit the OUI session.

If you are using a shared Oracle Home, it is not necessary to delete the Oracle Home from the local node. However, you will need to run the following command:

```
[oracle@london3 oracle]$ cd $CRS_HOME/oui/bin
[oracle@london3 bin]$ ./runInstaller -detachhome -local ORACLE_HOME=$CRS_HOME
```

Update the Inventories on the Remaining Hosts

Next, update the inventories on the remaining hosts. On one of the remaining nodes, in this case london1, as the oracle user, in an X Window session, run the following command specifying the names of all remaining nodes for the CLUSTER_NODES parameter:

```
[oracle@london1 oracle]$ cd $CRS_HOME/oui/bin
[oracle@london1 bin]$ ./runInstaller -updateNodeList ORACLE_HOME=$CRS_HOME \
"CLUSTER_NODES=london1,london2"
Starting Oracle Universal Installer...
No pre-requisite checks found in oraparam.ini, no system pre-requisite checks will
be executed
'UpdateNodeList' was successful
```

Verify Node Deletion Using CLUVFY

The final step is to verify that the node has been successfully deleted and that it is no longer a member of the cluster by running the Cluster Verification Utility (CLUVFY) as the oracle user from any remaining node in the cluster. For example, on london1, run the following:

```
[oracle@london1 oracle]$ cluvfy comp crs -n all
```

The output from this command should not contain any references to the node that has just been deleted.

Summary

In this chapter, we described procedures for adding and deleting nodes and instances. We recommend that you become familiar with the node addition procedures, in case you need to add an instance to your database to increase throughput or to replace existing hardware. If you need to replace a server in your cluster, we recommend that you add the new node first and ensure that it is stable before removing the old node if possible.

If you are planning to build a support environment for your RAC database, you should plan to test these procedures regularly on each release of Oracle, as the software is still evolving rapidly.

If you do not have a support environment for your RAC database, ensure that you fully back up your RAC cluster, including the operating system, CRS home, OCR, voting disk, and database before attempting to add or delete nodes. Also, consult the current documentation and the MetaLink web site for changes in these procedures.

CHAPTER 21

■ ■ ■

Trace and Diagnostics

In this chapter, we will discuss methods for obtaining trace and diagnostic information from a RAC cluster. This chapter covers trace file locations, DBMS_MONITOR, and ORADEBUG.

DBMS_MONITOR is a package that was introduced in Oracle 10.1 that greatly simplifies and standardizes the commands required to enable and disable trace.

ORADEBUG is an undocumented utility, invoked from SQL*Plus, which allows users with the SYSDBA privilege to obtain a significant amount of additional trace and diagnostic information. A subset of this information is also available using the ALTER SESSION and ALTER SYSTEM commands.

Trace File Locations

In this section, we will discuss the locations where trace and diagnostic information is written by the Oracle database. Note that this is not an exhaustive list. For example, Oracle Clusterware trace information is written to locations within the $CRS_HOME directory as described in Chapter 16.

Alert Log

Each instance generates an alert log, which is written to the directory specified by the BACKGROUND_DUMP_DEST parameter. You can optionally locate this directory on shared storage, as all filenames include the instance name. The name of the alert log has the format alert_<SID>.log, for example, alert_RAC1.log.

The alert log contains a wealth of information about the database, including the following:

- Start-up and shutdown of instances
- Parameters and parameter changes
- DDL commands
- Failover and remastering details
- Archive logging information
- Online redo log switches
- Managed recovery operations
- Standby switchover and failover operations
- Process failures

The alert log should always be your first point of reference when you are investigating any database issues. It contains a complete history of all significant changes in the state of the database. If the BACKGROUND_DUMP_DEST parameter is not explicitly specified, the alert log will be written to the $ORACLE_HOME/dbs directory.

Trace Files

In an Oracle database, all processes optionally generate a trace file. In a single-instance database, trace files generated by background processes are written to the directory specified by the BACKGROUND_DUMP_DEST initialization parameter, and trace files generated by foreground processes are written to the directory specified by the USER_DUMP_DEST parameter.

The same initialization parameters are used in a RAC environment. If the directory specified is on shared storage, the trace directories can be shared by all instances. Each trace file name includes the instance name, so you will not experience any conflicts. If no suitable shared storage is available, the trace directory will be located on the local nodes.

In order to investigate performance issues in detail, you often need to enable additional trace functionality, which can be used to determine the actual execution plan used by a statement and to verify the bind variables used when parsing and executing a SQL statement. Trace can also be configured to include information about wait events occurring during the execution of a statement, which can be used to diagnose issues, such as contention and resource bottlenecks.

Trace files for server (foreground) processes are written to the directory specified by the USER_DUMP_DEST parameter. If you have used the default DBCA configuration to create your databases, USER_DUMP_DEST will be the $ORACLE_BASE/admin/<db_unique_name>/udump directory. Each server process trace file name has the following format:

```
<instance_name>_ora_<pid>.trc
```

where pid is the operating system process identifier.

Oracle also creates trace files for background processes. These are written to the directory specified by the BACKGROUND_DUMP_DEST parameter. The default DBCA location for this directory is $ORACLE_BASE/admin/<db_unique_name>/bdump. Each background process trace file name has the following format:

```
<instance_name>_<process_name>_<pid>.trc
```

where process_name is the four-character name of the background process, such as SMON, PMON, LGWR, and so on. There can be more than one instance of some background process, in which case, they are numbered sequentially starting at zero, for example, DBW0, DBW1, and so on. The maximum number of background processes of any type is hard-coded into the kernel but is subject to change from one release to the next.

A third type of trace file name is used for dynamically created background processes. These processes include dispatchers, shared servers, parallel execution slaves, and job queue slaves. The format of the trace file name for these processes is as follows:

```
<instance_name>_<process_name>_<pid>.trc
```

where process_name consists of a single character identifier for the process type and a three digit, zero-filled number. For example, dispatcher processes are named D000, D001, D002, and so on. Table 21-1 shows some of the alphanumeric process names.

Table 21-1. *Alphanumeric Process Names*

Process Type	Description	Examples
A	Streams Apply	A000, A001
C	Streams Capture	C000, C001
D	Dispatcher	D000, D001
S	Shared Server	S000, S001
J	Job Execution Slave	J000, J001
P	Parallel Execution Slave	P000, P001
Q	Advanced Queuing Slave	Q000, Q001

If you wish to identify a particular trace file, you can optionally specify a trace file identifier when the trace is enabled. This identifier will be appended to the trace file name, enabling you to identify the file quickly within the trace directory. For example, if the current trace file is called rac1_ora_12345.trc and if you specify the following:

```
SQL> ALTER SESSION SET tracefile_identifier = 'TEST';
```

all trace subsequently generated by the process will be written to rac1_ora_12345_test.trc until trace is disabled or a new trace file identifier is specified.

If you are attempting to trace a complex sequence of actions, you can specify a series of trace file identifiers to divide up a large trace file into more manageable pieces; for example, the following commands will generate a separate trace file for each step:

```
SQL> ALTER SESSION SET tracefile_identifier = 'STEP1';
...
SQL> ALTER SESSION SET tracefile_identifier = 'STEP2';
...
```

DBMS_MONITOR

Prior to Oracle 10.1, enabling trace was a complex process, mainly because about a dozen different methods were available, each of which was only applicable to limited situations. In Oracle 10.1 and above, the DBMS_MONITOR package provides a single API interface from which you can enable and disable trace for a specific session, module, action, or client identifier. In addition, DBMS_MONITOR provides other functionality to enable more granular collection of statistics for specified modules, actions, and client identifiers.

In order to enable trace in a specific session, you first need to identify the SID and, optionally, the serial number of the session. This information can be obtained from V$SESSION, for example:

```
SQL> SELECT sid, serial# FROM v$session WHERE username = 'USER1';
```

You may need to join V$SESSION to other dynamic performance views, such as V$SQL, in order to identify the session of interest.

To enable trace for a specific session, use the SESSION_TRACE_ENABLE procedure. For example, to enable trace for a session with a SID of 33, use the following:

```
SQL> EXECUTE dbms_monitor.session_trace_enable (session_id=>33);
```

This command will immediately enable trace for the specified session, which will be appended to the current trace file.

You can include bind variable information in the same trace file, for example:

```
SQL> EXECUTE dbms_monitor.session_trace_enable (session_id=>33,binds=>true);
```

By default wait information is included in the trace file. You can specify that wait events should be traced using:

```
SQL> EXECUTE dbms_monitor.session_trace_enable (session_id=>33,waits=>true);
```

You can also include both bind and wait information in the same trace file.

Trace can be disabled for the same session as follows:

```
SQL> EXECUTE dbms_monitor.session_trace_disable (session_id=>33);
```

In Oracle 10.2 and above, you can also enable trace for all sessions connected to the database or to a specific instance. Note that this will generate a very large amount of trace output very quickly. Make sure that the BACKGROUND_DUMP_DEST and USER_DUMP_DEST parameters do not specify a location in the root file system. Enabling trace globally will also slow down the database, so it is advisable not to enable it at instance level on a production system.

To enable trace for all sessions in the database, use the following:

```
SQL> EXECUTE dbms_monitor.database_trace_enable;
```

To enable trace for all sessions including bind variable values, use

```
SQL> EXECUTE dbms_monitor.database_trace_enable (binds=>true);
```

Trace can be enabled for all sessions including wait events as follows:

```
SQL> EXECUTE dbms_monitor.database_trace_enable (waits=>true);
```

You can also enable instance-wide trace for a specified instance, for example:

```
SQL> EXECUTE dbms_monitor.database_trace_enable (instance_name=>'RAC1');
```

Use the following to disable trace again:

```
SQL> EXECUTE dbms_monitor.database_trace_disable;
```

In the version we tested, using the DATABASE_TRACE_DISABLE procedure to disable instance-specific trace failed with the following error:

```
ORA-13870: Database-wide SQL tracing is not enabled
```

Therefore, we advise that you test enabling and disabling instance-specific trace in a nonproduction environment before attempting it at the instance level.

Tracing Applications

In Oracle 10.1 and above, you can enable database-wide trace for a specific database service, for example:

```
SQL> EXECUTE dbms_monitor.serv_mod_act_trace_enable (service_name=>'SERVICE1');
```

You can obtain a list of valid database services from EM, DBCA, or using the following command:

```
SQL> SELECT name FROM dba_services;
```

In Oracle 8.0 and above, you can divide applications in to modules and subdivide each module into a number of actions. You can include calls in your application to DBMS_APPLICATION_INFO to set the current module and action names. The first call must set both the module and action name, for example:

```
SQL> EXECUTE dbms_application_info.set_module -
> (module_name=>'MODULE1',action_name=>'ACTION1');
```

Subsequent calls can update the action name within the same module:

```
SQL> EXECUTE dbms_application_info.set_action (action_name=>'ACTION1');
```

You can verify the current module and action that a session is performing using the following:

```
SQL> SELECT module, action FROM v$session;
```

In Oracle 10.1 and above, you can enable trace based on a module or an action, for example:

```
SQL> EXECUTE dbms_monitor.serv_mod_act_trace_enable (service_name=>'SERVICE1');
```

▪**Note** You must specify a database service name. In our opinion, this requirement is an unfortunate limitation, since ser-vices are generally created by DBAs, while module and action names will be created by application developers. This limitation means that either service names must be known when the application is written, or the application must discover the current service name before enabling trace or statistics collection.

A session can detect the current database service using the following command:

```
SQL> SELECT SYS_CONTEXT ('USERENV','SERVICE_NAME') FROM DUAL;
```

If no database service has been specified, the SYS_CONTEXT function will return SYS$USERS.
To enable trace for all actions in an entire module, use the following:

```
SQL> EXECUTE dbms_monitor.serv_mod_act_trace_enable -
> (service_name=>'SERVICE1',module_name=>'MODULE1');
```

Enable trace for a specific action as follows:

```
SQL> EXECUTE dbms_monitor.serv_mod_act_trace_enable -
> (service_name=>'SERVICE1',module_name=>'MODULE1',action_name=>'ACTION1');
```

You can also enable tracing of binds and waits in the SERV_MOD_ACT_TRACE_ENABLE procedure.
To disable trace again, call the SERV_MOD_ACT_TRACE_DISABLE procedure with the same parameters, for example:

```
SQL> EXECUTE dbms_monitor.serv_mod_act_trace_disable -
(service_name=>'SERVICE1',module_name=>'MODULE1',action_name=>'ACTION1');
```

You can also use DBMS_MONITOR to enable collection of statistics for an application, as described in Chapter 19.

Tracing Multitier Applications

Most new applications now implement at least one application tier in addition to the database tier. This architecture is particularly prevalent in RAC environments, where customers frequently attempt to minimize the cost of Oracle licenses by moving as much non-Oracle processing as possible to other unlicensed servers.

Commonly, midtier applications log in to the Oracle database using a connection pool. It is equally common for such applications to log in to the database using a common username. However, the use of a common username makes monitoring individual sessions using tools such as EM more complicated, as differentiating between sessions is more difficult.

However, application developers can assign a client identifier to each session. The client identifier is a string with a maximum length of 64 bytes that identifies individual users, for example, their names, employee numbers, or customer numbers.

The client identifier is set using the SET_IDENTIFIER procedure in the DBMS_SESSION package, for example:

```
SQL> EXECUTE dbms_session.set_identifier ('CLIENT1');
```

The client identifier can subsequently be used to identify the session in V$SESSION, for example:

```
SQL> SELECT sid, serial# FROM v$session
> WHERE client_identifier = 'CLIENT1';
```

You can enable both trace and statistics collection based on a specified client identifier. To enable trace collection, use the following:

```
SQL> EXECUTE dbms_monitor.client_id_trace_enable (client_id=>'CLIENT1');
```

To disable trace collection again, use

```
SQL> EXECUTE dbms_monitor.client_id_trace_disable (client_id=>'CLIENT1');
```

You can also enable collection of statistics based on a specified client identifier:

```
SQL> EXECUTE dbms_monitor.client_id_stat_enable (client_id=>'CLIENT1');
```

Statistics collected for the session will be externalized in the V$CLIENT_STATS dynamic performance view, which was introduced in Oracle 10.1.

Disable collection of statistics again using the following:

```
SQL> EXECUTE dbms_monitor.client_id_stat_disable (client_id=>'CLIENT1');
```

DBA_ENABLED_TRACES

The DBA_ENABLED_TRACES view, which was introduced in Oracle 10.1, shows the current configuration of trace that has been enabled by DBMS_MONITOR. It does not show trace enabled by DBMS_MONITOR for individual sessions or trace enabled using other methods. The columns of the DBA_ENABLED_TRACES view are shown in Table 21-2.

Table 21-2. *The DBA_ENABLED_TRACES View*

Column Name	Data Type
TRACE_TYPE	VARCHAR2(21)
PRIMARY_ID	VARCHAR2(64)
QUALIFIER_ID1	VARCHAR2(48)
QUALIFIER_ID2	VARCHAR2(32)
WAITS	VARCHAR2(5)
BINDS	VARCHAR2(5)
INSTANCE_NAME	VARCHAR2(16)

The TRACE_TYPE column value can be one of the following:

- CLIENT_ID
- SERVICE
- SERVICE_MODULE
- SERVICE_MODULE_ACTION
- DATABASE

If the TRACE_TYPE is CLIENT_ID, the PRIMARY_ID column will contain the client identifier. If the TRACE_TYPE is SERVICE, SERVICE_MODULE, or SERVICE_MODULE_ACTION, the PRIMARY_ID column will contain the service name. If the TRACE_TYPE is SERVICE_MODULE, or SERVICE_MODULE_ACTION, the QUALIFIER_ID1 column will contain the module name. If the TRACE_TYPE is SERVICE_MODULE_ACTION, the QUALIFIER_ID2 column will contain the action name.

ORADEBUG

The ORADEBUG utility was originally a standalone program that could be optionally compiled on the VMS and Unix platforms. It was subsequently integrated into the SVRMGR utility. The SVRMGR utility was eventually deprecated and ORADEBUG is now incorporated in SQL*Plus.

To run ORADEBUG, you must be logged on with the SYSDBA privilege:

```
[oracle@london1 oracle]$ sqlplus /nolog
SQL> CONNECT / AS SYSDBA
```

You can obtain a list of the available ORADEBUG commands using the following:

```
SQL> ORADEBUG HELP
```

The list of available commands varies between releases but has become relatively consistent in Oracle 10.1 and above.

You should be aware that some ORADEBUG commands can be very dangerous and should only be used under supervision of Oracle Support. These include the POKE command, which can modify memory locations, and the SGA and CALL commands, which can execute functions in the kernel libraries. In addition, ORADEBUG is not officially supported, and you may find that commands that work on one platform fail on another. For instance, ORADEBUG is not aware of Microsoft Windows processes and memory structures, so you may have difficulty using it on that platform.

Before you can use most commands, you need to attach ORADEBUG to a process; otherwise, you will receive the following error:

```
ORA-00074: no process has been specified
```

There are three ways of attaching to a process. The simplest is to issue the following command:

```
SQL> ORADEBUG SETMYPID
```

This attaches ORADEBUG to the current SQL*Plus server process and is sufficient for most debug dumps. To use advanced functionality, you may need to attach to other processes. You can either specify the Oracle process ID or the operating system process ID.

The Oracle process ID can be found in the PID column of V$PROCESS. You can determine the PID of a server process by joining V$PROCESS with V$SESSION, for example:

```
SQL> SELECT p.pid
> FROM v$process p, v$session s
> WHERE p.addr = s.paddr
> AND s.username = 'USER1';
```

To attach ORADEBUG to a process using the Oracle process ID, use

```
SQL> ORADEBUG SETORAPID <pid>
```

You can also attach ORADEBUG using the operating system pid. You may have obtained this from an operating system utility, such as ps or top. Alternatively, it can be found in the SPID column of V$PROCESS.

To attach ORADEBUG to a process using the operating system process ID, use the following:

```
SQL> ORADEBUG SETOSPID <spid>
```

You can obtain a listing of the available dumps using the following command:

```
SQL> ORADEBUG DUMPLIST
```

The list of dumps changes with each release of Oracle, so you should run this command every time you install a new version. You should be aware that not all dump commands produce dump lists; some perform actions such as setting internal parameters or performing tests.

Each dump has one parameter, which normally specifies the level of detail included in the dump. Some dump commands have levels 1, 2, 3, and so on. Others use bit flags to control the amount of information dumped, for example, 1, 2, 4, 8, and so on. These can be combined together; for example, level 10 will contain level 2 and level 8 trace. Finally, some dumps use the level as a parameter to specify an object number.

Table 21-3 contains a list of useful general-purpose dumps.

Table 21-3. *Useful Named Dumps*

Command	Description
EVENTS	Dumps a list of currently enabled events in process
HANGANALYZE	Dumps state objects for all active processes
LATCHES	Dumps the current state of all latches
PROCESSSTATE	Dumps state objects for the current process
SYSTEMSTATE	Dumps state objects for all processes
HEAPDUMP	Dumps heap memory
HEAPDUMP_ADDR	Dumps subheap memory
GLOBAL_AREA	Dumps fixed memory
MODIFIED_PARAMETERS	Dumps a list of nondefault parameters for the current process
ERRORSTACK	Dumps the error stack for the current process
CALLSTACK	Dumps the call stack for the current process
BG_MESSAGES	Dumps background messages
ENQUEUES	Dumps the current state of all enqueues (locks)
GES_STATE	Dumps the Global Enqueue Service (GES) state
LOCKS	Dumps the current state of all locks
GC_ELEMENTS	Dumps the current state of global cache elements
FILE_HDRS	Dumps file headers
TREEDUMP	Dumps the index tree for specified index segment
ROW_CACHE	Dumps the dictionary (row) cache
LIBRARY_CACHE	Dumps the library cache
ASHDUMP	Dumps the Active Session History (ASH) buffer
CURSOR_STATS	Dumps statistics for all cursors in library cache

Of the dumps in Table 21-3, three are RAC-specific: GES_STATE, LOCKS, and GC_ELEMENTS.

GES_STATE

This dump contains a summary of the state of GES. It is also included in the SYSTEMSTATE dump. The first few lines of the dump contain a summary of the database resources currently required to support GES, for example:

```
KJC Communication Dump:
 state 0x5  flags 0x0  mode 0x0  inst 0  inc 4
 nrcv 2  nsp 2  nrcvbuf 1000
 reg_msg: sz 420  cur 38 (s:0 i:38) max 94  ini 1050
 big_msg: sz 4128  cur 17 (s:0 i:17) max 77  ini 964
 rsv_msg: sz 4128  cur 0 (s:0 i:0) max 0  tot 301
 rcvr: id 0  orapid 6  ospid 5181
 rcvr: id 1  orapid 7  ospid 5183
 send proxy: id 0  ndst 1 (1:0 )
 send proxy: id 1  ndst 1 (1:1 )
GES resource limits:
 ges resources: cur 0 max 0 ini 4161
 ges enqueues: cur 0 max 0 ini 6044
 ges cresources: cur 325 max 1070
 gcs resources: cur 5676 max 5676 ini 23774
  gcs shadows: cur 3660 max 3664 ini 23774
```

The dump also contains detailed information about message traffic for each destination on the local and remote instances. In the context of this report, a receiver is an LMD0 or an LMSn background process.

GC_ELEMENTS

The GC_ELEMENTS dump reports on the current state of all lock elements for the local instance, for example:

```
SQL> ORADEBUG SETMYPID
SQL> ORADEBUG DUMP GC_ELEMENTS 1
```

The output depends on whether the resource is locally or remotely mastered. For locally mastered blocks, the output has the following format:

```
GLOBAL CACHE ELEMENT DUMP (address: 0x233f3c78):
 id1: 0xbd21 id2: 0x10000 obj: 181 block: (1/48417)
 lock: SL rls: 0x0000 acq: 0x0000 latch: 0
 flags: 0x41 fair: 0 recovery: 0 fpin: 'kdswh05: kdsgrp'
 bscn: 0x0.3dd9a bctx: (nil) write: 0 scan: 0x0 xflg: 0 xid: 0x0.0.0
 GCS SHADOW 0x233f3cc0,1 sq[0x2efd5894,0x2ee6221c] resp[0x2ee62204,0xbd21.10000]
  pkey 181
  grant 1 cvt 0 mdrole 0x21 st 0x40 GRANTQ rl LOCAL
  master 0 owner 0 sid 0 remote[(nil),0] hist 0x119f
  history 0x1f.0x6.0x1.0x0.0x0.0x0. cflag 0x0 sender 0 flags 0x0 replay# 0
  disk: 0x0000.00000000 write request: 0x0000.00000000
  pi scn: 0x0000.00000000
  msgseq 0x0 updseq 0x0 reqids[1,0,0] infop 0x0
```

```
GCS RESOURCE 0x2ee62204 hashq [0x2ee2e634,0x2ff5a7b8] name[0xbd21.10000] pkey 181
  grant 0x233f3cc0 cvt (nil) send (nil),0 write (nil),0@65535
  flag 0x0 mdrole 0x1 mode 1 scan 0 role LOCAL
  disk: 0x0000.00000000 write: 0x0000.00000000 cnt 0x0 hist 0x0
        xid 0x0000.000.00000000 sid 0
  pkey 181
  hv 122 [stat 0x0, 0->0, wm 32767, RMno 0, reminc 0, dom 0]
  kjga st 0x4, step 0.0.0, cinc 4, rmno 4, flags 0x0
  lb 0, hb 0, myb 164, drmb 164, apifrz 0
  GCS SHADOW 0x233f3cc0,1 sq[0x2efd5894,0x2ee6221c] resp[0x2ee62204,0xbd21.10000]
    pkey 181
    grant 1 cvt 0 mdrole 0x21 st 0x40 GRANTQ rl LOCAL
    master 0 owner 0 sid 0 remote[(nil),0] hist 0x119f
    history 0x1f.0x6.0x1.0x0.0x0.0x0. cflag 0x0 sender 0 flags 0x0 replay# 0
    disk: 0x0000.00000000 write request: 0x0000.00000000
    pi scn: 0x0000.00000000
    msgseq 0x0 updseq 0x0 reqids[1,0,0] infop 0x0
  GCS SHADOW 0x2efd5894,1 sq[0x2ee6221c,0x233f3cc0] resp[0x2ee62204,0xbd21.10000]
    pkey 181
    grant 1 cvt 0 mdrole 0x21 st 0x40 GRANTQ rl LOCAL
    master 0 owner 1 sid 0 remote[0x21ff6760,1] hist 0x79
    history 0x39.0x1.0x0.0x0.0x0.0x0. cflag 0x0 sender 0 flags 0x0 replay# 0
    disk: 0x0000.00000000 write request: 0x0000.00000000
    pi scn: 0x0000.00000000
    msgseq 0x1 updseq 0x0 reqids[1,0,0] infop 0x0
```

In this example, dumped in instance 0, the master for the block is 0 (i.e., the block is locally mastered). The block has one lock element, one GCS resource structure, and two GCS shadow structures—one for each instance. The GCS shadow structure for the local instance is shown twice in the report. This duplication is an implementation feature of the report; this structure is only held once in memory.

If the block is mastered remotely, the output of this report is different, for example:

```
GLOBAL CACHE ELEMENT DUMP (address: 0x23bf02b8):
  id1: 0xef0e id2: 0x10000 obj: 573 block: (1/61198)
  lock: SL rls: 0x0000 acq: 0x0000 latch: 0
  flags: 0x41 fair: 0 recovery: 0 fpin: 'kdswh06: kdscgr'
  bscn: 0x0.2af32d bctx: (nil) write: 0 scan: 0x0 xflg: 0 xid: 0x0.0.0
  GCS CLIENT 0x23bf0300,1 sq[(nil),(nil)] resp[(nil),0xef0e.10000] pkey 573
    grant 1 cvt 0 mdrole 0x21 st 0x20 GRANTQ rl LOCAL
    master 1 owner 0 sid 0 remote[(nil),0] hist 0x7c
    history 0x3c.0x1.0x0.0x0.0x0.0x0. cflag 0x0 sender 2 flags 0x0 replay# 0
    disk: 0x0000.00000000 write request: 0x0000.00000000
    pi scn: 0x0000.00000000
    msgseq 0x1 updseq 0x0 reqids[1,0,0] infop 0x0
  pkey 573
  hv 94 [stat 0x0, 1->1, wm 32767, RMno 0, reminc 4, dom 0]
  kjga st 0x4, step 0.0.0, cinc 4, rmno 4, flags 0x0
  lb 0, hb 0, myb 225, drmb 225, apifrz 0
```

In this example, the block is mastered on another instance. The report contains detailed information about the lock element and the GCS client structure, which is embedded within the lock structure. If a GC_ELEMENTS dump is taken on the remote instance, the output will contain a lock element, GCS resource structure, and GCS shadow structures for the block shown in this example (1/61198).

The LOCKS dump produces identical output to the GC_ELEMENTS dump.

LKDEBUG

The LKDEBUG utility can be used to obtain information about the current state of GCS and GES structures in the instance. LKDEBUG is integrated into ORADEBUG. You must, therefore, be logged in with the SYSDBA privilege in order to use it.

You can display a list of available LKDEBUG options using the following command:

```
SQL> ORADEBUG LKDEBUG HELP
```

In Oracle 10.2, this command prints the following message:

```
Usage:lkdebug [options]
 -l [r|p] <enqueue pointer>    Enqueue Object
 -r <resource pointer>         Resource Object
 -b <gcs shadow pointer>       GCS shadow Object
 -p <process id>               client pid
 -P <process pointer>          Process Object
 -O <i1> <i2> <types>          Oracle Format resname
 -a <res/lock/proc>            all <res/lock/proc> pointers
 -A <res/lock/proc>            all <res/lock/proc> contexts
 -a <res> [<type>]             all <res> pointers by an optional type
 -a convlock                   all converting enqueue (pointers)
 -A convlock                   all converting enqueue contexts
 -a convres                    all res ptr with converting enqueues
 -A convres                    all res contexts with converting enqueues
 -a name                       list all resource names
 -a hashcount                  list all resource hash bucket counts
 -t                            Traffic controller info
 -s                            summary of all enqueue types
 -k                            GES SGA summary info
 -m pkey <objectno>            request for remastering this object at current
                               instance
 -m dpkey <objectno>           request for dissolving remastering of this object at
                               current instance
```

Most of the LKDEBUG commands write formatted dump information to trace files. The LKDEBUG output contains field descriptions, traverses pointers, and memory chains that cannot be accessed using fixed tables or dynamic performance views.

You do not need to attach ORADEBUG to a process using SETMYPID, SETORAPID, or SETOSPID in order to use LKDEBUG.

The LKDEBUG utility allows you to dump information about three types of objects: resources, enqueues, and processes. Some commands allow more granular choices, for example, to include GCS or GES structures only or to include a specific lock type.

Resources

A resource structure is allocated to every resource that is available globally. Resource structures are managed by GCS for blocks and GES for global locks. You can obtain a list of the addresses of all the global resources allocated for the current instance using the following command:

```
SQL> ORADEBUG LKDEBUG -a res
```

This command produces a list of resource pointers, for example:

```
resp 1 0x2d270bec
resp 2 0x2aee84c0
resp 3 0x2d1b0068
resp 4 0x2adfab58
resp 5 0x2acb19a0
etc
```

The GCS resource structure addresses can also be obtained from column KJBRRESP in X$KJBR, and the GES resource structure addresses can also be obtained from column KJIRFTRP in X$KJIRFT.

You can obtain more detailed information about each global resource structure as follows:

```
SQL> ORADEBUG LKDEBUG -A res
```

This command will output details of all GES resource structures followed by all GCS resource structures. The output for GCS includes resource, shadow/client, and lock elements. The output for a typical GES resource structure is as follows:

```
--------resource 0x2d270bec------------------
resname        : [0x7036b4fa][0x6e28d9a1],[LB]
Local node     : 0
dir_node       : 0
master_node    : 0
hv idx         : 103
hv last r.inc  : 0
current inc    : 4
hv status      : 0
hv master      : 0
open options   : dd
grant_bits     : KJUSERPR
grant mode     : KJUSERNL  KJUSERCR  KJUSERCW  KJUSERPR  KJUSERPW  KJUSEREX
count          : 0         0         0         1         0         0
val_state      : KJUSERVS_NOVALUE
valblk         : 0x00000000000000000000000000000000 .
access_node    : 0
vbreq_state    : 0
state          : x0
resp           : 0x2d270bec
On Scan_q?     : N
Total accesses: 100
Imm. accesses: 87
Granted_locks : 1
Cvting_locks  : 0
```

This example is for a global library cache object lock (LB).

The output for a typical GCS resource is as follows:

```
--------resource 0x2edf3b34------------------
GCS RESOURCE 0x2edf3b34 hashq [0x2ff5b858,0x2ee219e4] name[0x75c4.30000] pkey 8782
  grant 0x247eab00 cvt (nil) send (nil),0 write (nil),0@65535
  flag 0x0 mdrole 0x2 mode 2 scan 0 role LOCAL
  disk: 0x0000.00000000 write: 0x0000.00000000 cnt 0x0 hist 0x0
    xid 0x0000.000.00000000 sid 0
  pkey 8782
  hv 107 [stat 0x0, 0->0, wm 32767, RMno 0, reminc 0, dom 0]
  kjga st 0x4, step 0.0.0, cinc 4, rmno 4, flags 0x0
  lb 0, hb 0, myb 696, drmb 696, apifrz 0
  GCS SHADOW 0x247eab00,1 sq[0x2edf3b4c,0x2edf3b4c] resp[0x2edf3b34,0x75c4.30000]
```

```
  pkey 8782
  grant 2 cvt 0 mdrole 0x22 st 0x40 GRANTQ rl LOCAL
  master 0 owner 0 sid 0 remote[(nil),0] hist 0x106
  history 0x6.0x4.0x0.0x0.0x0.0x0. cflag 0x0 sender 0 flags 0x0 replay# 0
  disk: 0x0000.00000000 write request: 0x0000.00000000
  pi scn: 0x0000.00000000
  msgseq 0x0 updseq 0x0 reqids[1,0,0] infop 0x0
GLOBAL CACHE ELEMENT DUMP (address: 0x247eaab8):
  id1: 0x75c4 id2: 0x30000 obj: 8782 block: (3/30148)
  lock: XL rls: 0x0000 acq: 0x0000 latch: 2
  flags: 0x41 fair: 0 recovery: 0 fpin: 'kdiwh132: kdisdelete'
  bscn: 0x0.0 bctx: (nil) write: 0 scan: 0x0 xflg: 0 xid: 0x0.0.0
  lcp: (nil) lnk: [NULL] lch: [0x263dc9f4,0x263dc9f4]
  seq: 4 hist: 66 143:0 208 352
  LIST OF BUFFERS LINKED TO THIS GLOBAL CACHE ELEMENT:
    flg: 0x00042000 state: XCURRENT mode: NULL
      addr: 0x263dc944 obj: 8782 cls: PREWARM BLOCK bscn: 0x0.2d3338
```

The output for the GCS resource structure includes any related shadow structures. It also shows a list of lock elements that are currently using this resource and a list of associated buffers. Remember several buffers can have different consistent read versions of the same block.

You can print the same information for individual resources. For example, use the following command to print the preceding resource:

```
SQL> ORADEBUG LKDEBUG -r 0x2edf3b34
```

You can print individual shadow structures, for example:

```
SQL> ORADEBUG LKDEBUG -b 0x247eab00
```

This command, which uses the shadow address reported in the resource structure dump shown previously, returns output in the following format:

```
GCS SHADOW 0x247eab00,1 sq[0x2edf3b4c,0x2edf3b4c] resp[0x2edf3b34,0x75c4.30000]
  pkey 8782
  grant 2 cvt 0 mdrole 0x22 st 0x40 GRANTQ rl LOCAL
  master 0 owner 0 sid 0 remote[(nil),0] hist 0x106
  history 0x6.0x4.0x0.0x0.0x0.0x0. cflag 0x0 sender 0 flags 0x0 replay# 0
  disk: 0x0000.00000000 write request: 0x0000.00000000
  pi scn: 0x0000.00000000
  msgseq 0x0 updseq 0x0 reqids[1,0,0] infop 0x0
  pkey 8782
  hv 107 [stat 0x0, 0->0, wm 32767, RMno 0, reminc 0, dom 0]
  kjga st 0x4, step 0.0.0, cinc 4, rmno 4, flags 0x0
  lb 0, hb 0, myb 696, drmb 696, apifrz 0
GLOBAL CACHE ELEMENT DUMP (address: 0x247eaab8):
  id1: 0x75c4 id2: 0x30000 obj: 8782 block: (3/30148)
  lock: XL rls: 0x0000 acq: 0x0000 latch: 2
  flags: 0x41 fair: 0 recovery: 0 fpin: 'kdiwh132: kdisdelete'
  bscn: 0x0.0 bctx: (nil) write: 0 scan: 0x0 xflg: 0 xid: 0x0.0.0
  lcp: (nil) lnk: [NULL] lch: [0x263dc9f4,0x263dc9f4]
  seq: 4 hist: 66 143:0 208 352
  LIST OF BUFFERS LINKED TO THIS GLOBAL CACHE ELEMENT:
    flg: 0x00042000 state: XCURRENT mode: NULL
      addr: 0x263dc944 obj: 8782 cls: PREWARM BLOCK bscn: 0x0.2d3338
```

You can also obtain a list of valid GCS shadow objects from the KJBLLOCK column of the X$KJBL structure.

Locks

Lock structures (enqueues) are allocated to specific resources to indicate current ownership of that resource. Each resource can potentially have many lock structures. Each resource contains three double-linked lists of locks for holders, waiters, and converters. Locks on the holders queue are currently using the resource. Locks on the waiters queue wish to use the resource but are currently blocked by one or more holders. Locks on the converters list currently hold the resource but wish to hold the lock at a higher level. Converting locks generally get preference to reduce contention.

Locks for GES resources can be held at either the instance or process level, which implies that session state objects must be maintained for all GES locks, so that the LMON background process can clean up any currently held locks in the event of a process failure.

To list the addresses of all the lock structures in the instance, use the following:

```
SQL> ORADEBUG LKDEBUG -a lock
```

This command outputs a list of lock pointers, for example:

```
nlockp = 8270
lockp 0 0x2f520384
lockp 1 0x2fca9094
lockp 2 0x2fd138e0
lockp 3 0x2adf837c
lockp 4 0x2f56d994
lockp 5 0x2acb08a0
```

You can obtain additional information about the locks as follows:

```
SQL>ORADEBUG LKDEBUG -A lock
```

This command outputs detailed information for each lock, for example:

```
----------enqueue 0x2f520384------------------
lock version      : 5
Owner node        : 1
grant_level       : KJUSERPR
req_level         : KJUSERPR
bast_level        : KJUSERNL
notify_func       : 0x880f954
resp              : 0x2d270bec
procp             : 0x2f439150
pid               : 0
proc version      : 1
oprocp            : (nil)
opid              : 0
group lock owner  : (nil)
xid               : 0000-0000-00000000
dd_time           : 0.0 secs
dd_count          : 0
timeout           : 0.0 secs
On_timer_q?       : N
On_dd_q?          : N
lock_state        : GRANTED
Open Options      : KJUSERNO_XID
Convert options   : KJUSERGETVALUE
History           : 0x77d4977d
Msg_Seq           : 0x1
res_seq           : 6
valblk            : 0x00000000000000000000000000000000 .
```

You can also obtain information about a specific lock. For example, to dump detailed information about the lock shown in the preceding example, use the following:

```
SQL> ORADEBUG LKDEBUG -l r 0x2f520384
```

This output of this command will include the lock information shown previously and detailed information about the resource structure (as returned by the -A res command).

You can also print details about the LCK0 background process currently holding a specific lock and list the other locks that an individual process is holding. For example, for the lock address used in the previous section (0x2f620384) the following command:

```
SQL> ORADEBUG LKDEBUG -l p 0x2f520384
```

produces output in the following format:

```
-----------------proc----------------------
proc version     : 0
Local node       : 0
pid              : 5236
lkp_node         : 0
svr_mode         : 0
proc state       : KJP_NORMAL
Last drm hb acked : 0
Total accesses   : 43465
Imm. accesses    : 28963
Locks on ASTQ    : 0
Locks Pending AST : 0
Granted locks    : 5176
AST_Q:
PENDING_Q:
GRANTED_Q:
lp 0x2f4ad01c gl KJUSERPR rp 0x2d10dfc0 [0x6][0x2],[CI]
 master 0 pid 5236 bast 1 rseq 1 mseq 0 history 0x95
 open opt  KJUSERPROCESS_OWNED
lp 0x2f4ad1c4 gl KJUSERPR rp 0x2d10de48 [0x1a][0x2],[CI]
 master 0 pid 5236 bast 1 rseq 1 mseq 0 history 0x95
 open opt  KJUSERPROCESS_OWNED
lp 0x2f4ad36c gl KJUSERPR rp 0x2d10dcd0 [0x1d][0x2],[CI]
 master 1 pid 5236 bast 1 rseq 1 mseq 0 history 0x95
 open opt  KJUSERPROCESS_OWNED
etc
```

Processes

GES maintains locks for processes across all instances in the cluster. On each instance, it is necessary to maintain state information on both local and remote processes. This information is stored in GES process structures—one GES process structure is required for each process in each instance in the cluster.

You can list the addresses of all GES processes currently allocated in the local instance as follows:

```
SQL> ORADEBUG LKDEBUG -a proc
```

This command produces output in the following format:

```
nproc = 31
proc 0 0x2f435f50
proc 1 0x2f436270
proc 2 0x2f439dd0
proc 3 0x2f436590
proc 4 0x2f4368b0
proc 5 0x2f439790
proc 6 0x2f436bd0
```

You can also print detailed information about all GES process structures:

```
SQL>ORADEBUG LKDEBUG -A proc
```

This command produces output for each process in the following format:

```
--------procp 0x2f435f50------------------
proc version        : 0
Local node          : 0
pid                 : 5201
lkp_node            : 0
svr_mode            : 0
proc state          : KJP_NORMAL
Last drm hb acked   : 0
Total accesses      : 61949
Imm. accesses       : 61945
Locks on ASTQ       : 0
Locks Pending AST   : 0
Granted locks       : 0
```

You can obtain detailed information for a specific GES process structure. For example, to dump detailed information for the GES process structure shown previously, use the following command:

```
SQL> ORADEBUG LKDEBUG -P 0x2f435f50
```

Similar information can also be found in a system state dump. This can be obtained using the following command:

```
SQL> ORADEBUG DUMP SYSTEMSTATE 1
```

For the GES process structure shown previously, this dump included the following state object:

```
SO: 0x2f435f50, type: 19, owner: 0x3021aca0, flag: INIT/-/-/0x00
  GES MSG BUFFERS: st=emp chunk=0x(nil) hdr=0x(nil) lnk=0x(nil) flags=0x0 inc=4
    outq=0 sndq=0 opid=14 prmb=0x0
  mbg[i]=(1 1849) mbg[b]=(0 0) mbg[r]=(0 0)
  fmq[i]=(4 1) fmq[b]=(0 0) fmq[r]=(0 0)
  mop[s]=1850 mop[q]=0 pendq=0 zmbq=0
-----------process 0x0x2f435f50--------------------
proc version        : 0
Local node          : 0
pid                 : 5201
lkp_node            : 0
svr_mode            : 0
proc state          : KJP_NORMAL
Last drm hb acked   : 0
Total accesses      : 62311
Imm. accesses       : 62306
Locks on ASTQ       : 0
Locks Pending AST   : 0
```

```
Granted locks    : 0
AST_Q:
PENDING_Q:
 GRANTED_Q:
```

You can also dump the process information based on the operating system process ID, which can be obtained by searching backward in the system state dump. You also can obtain a list of valid Oracle process IDs from the SPID column of the V$PROCESS dynamic performance view; from various other dumps, including the system state object and hang analysis dumps; or from various operating system utilities, including ps and top. In the following example, the operating system PID is 5201:

```
SQL> ORADEBUG LKDEBUG -p 5201
```

This command produces output in the same format as the LKDEBUG -P option.

Resource Names

Oracle resource names consist of a two-character lock type and two integer identifiers. For a GCS resource, which will always be a block, the lock type is BL, and the identifiers represent the block number and the file number. For GES resources, the lock type can be any valid global lock type other than BL. The identifiers for GES resources are lock specific, and in Oracle 10.1 and above, they are described in the V$LOCK_TYPE dynamic performance view. For a number of GES lock types, Oracle combines the two identifiers together into a single hash value, which it uses to represent the underlying resource.

You can obtain a list of resource names from a number of sources, including the KJBRNAME column in X$KJBR, KJBLNAME in X$KJBL, KJIRFTRN in X$KJIRFT, and KJILKFTRN1/KJILKFTRN2 in X$KJILKFT. The resource names are externalized as a string, which you will need to manipulate in order to use it with LKDEBUG.

For example, if the KJBRNAME column of X$KJBR contains the following:

```
[0x849a][0x30000],[BL]
```

the lock type is BL, identifier1 is 0x849a, and identifier2 is 0x30000. The corresponding LKDEBUG dump command is as follows:

```
SQL> ORADEBUG LKDEBUG -O BL 0x849a 0x30000
```

If the resource is a block, this command will print the GCS resource, any associated GCS shadow or GCS client structures, and the lock element structure. If the resource is a lock, this command will print the GES resource and any associated lock structures on the granted or convert queues.

You can also obtain a list of GES resource names using the following command:

```
SQL> ORADEBUG LKDEBUG -a name
```

This command produces output in the following format:

```
#resname = 7145
LB-0x7036b4fa-0x6e28d9a1
IV-0xea4-0x1e140d05
QQ-0x3db15769-0x22bdb432
QQ-0xd8cfbb27-0x94f4f1b3
QC-0xba98c7ae-0x32f95f71
QL-0x6417aad7-0x24fb35e5
IV-0x238c-0x1e141532
QI-0xd1935e5a-0x4a3147aa
NB-0x3c7fb493-0xdf725888
QQ-0x4a356b88-0x74835668
QQ-0x232e0658-0xb194e373
```

Converting Locks

This report prints a list of pointers for all enqueues that are currently converting from one type to another, for example:

```
SQL> ORADEBUG LKDEBUG -a convlock
```

To include detailed information about each enqueue, use the following:

```
SQL> ORADEBUG LKDEBUG -A convlock
```

The detailed report shows the current lock held (grant_level) and the required lock level (req_level) for the enqueue. This information is also available in the V$GES_BLOCKING_ENQUEUE dynamic performance view.

Converting Resources

This report prints a list of pointers for all resources that have locks that are currently converting from one type to another, for example:

```
SQL> ORADEBUG LKDEBUG -a convres
```

Use the following command to include detailed information about each resource:

```
SQL> ORADEBUG LKDEBUG -A convres
```

The detailed report shows a summary of the number of enqueues holding each type of lock for the resource (grant_mode and count).

Resource Hash Buckets

GES resources are accessed through a hash array. By default, this array contains 1,024 buckets per instance. Each resource is protected by a ges resource hash list child latch. Each child latch protects a double-linked list of GES resources.

This report lists each block in the GES resource hash array and the number of GES resource structures in the list. To run this report, use the following:

```
SQL> ORADEBUG LKDEBUG -a hashcount
```

This command produces output in the following format:

```
Resource hash bucket     count
0                        4
1                        2
2                        3
3                        6
4                        6
5                        3
6                        0
7                        3
```

If the hash list becomes too long, you may need to increase the value of the _LM_RES_HASH_ bucket parameter.

Traffic Controller Information

This report lists traffic controller information for the current instance. The report contains the same information that is returned by the V$GES_TRAFFIC_CONTROLLER dynamic performance view. To run this report, use the following command:

```
SQL> ORADEBUG LKDEBUG -t
```

Enqueue Summary

This useful summary report describes the number of enqueues and resources currently in use for each type of lock, enabling you to obtain a quick overview of the lock types currently in use within GES. This summary report does not include GCS structures. For example, the following command:

```
SQL> ORADEBUG LKDEBUG -s
```

produces output in the following format:

```
TYPE            ENQUEUES        RESOURCES
----            --------        ---------
CF                     2                1
CI                   192              130
DF                    13                8
DM                     6                4
KK                     2                2
IR                     1                1
IV                   905              636
LB                   147              257
LE                     9               10
LF                     2                3
LK                     0               10
NB                   927              669
....
```

GES SGA Summary Information

This report prints a summary of information about RAC-specific structures in the SGA. This information is not directly available in any dynamic performance view.

A RAC-instance may have one or more LMSn background processes. Each LMSn process maintains a hash table to allow it to access the resources that it manages. By default, this table contains 512 buckets. This report provides a summary of the number of resources in each hash table bucket for each LMSn process and contains information about the current state of file and object affinity tables. For example, the following command:

```
SQL> ORADEBUG LKDEBUG -k
```

produces output in the following format:

```
node# 0, #nodes 2, state 4, msgver 4, rcvver 0 validver 4
valid domain 1
sync acks 0x00000000000000000000000000000000
Resource freelist #0 len 18098 lwm 18098 add 26430 rem 8332
LMS0:
Hash buckets log2(11)
Bucket# 0 #res 0
....
Bucket# 16 #res 8
```

```
Bucket# 17 #res 9
Bucket# 18 #res 7
Bucket# 19 #res 6
Bucket# 20 #res 4
Bucket# 21 #res 7
Bucket# 22 #res 7
Bucket# 23 #res 9
```

Object Remastering Request

The remaining LKDEBUG option is not a report but a command. This option allows you to force the remastering of a segment to the current instance. It takes one parameter—the data object ID of the object to be remastered. You can obtain the data object ID for any object using the DBA_OBJECTS dictionary view:

```
SQL> SELECT data_object_id FROM dba_objects
> WHERE owner = 'USER1'
> AND object_name = 'TABLE1'
> AND object_type = 'TABLE';
```

For example, assume a data object ID of 12345. The following command can be used to force the object to be remastered at the current instance:

```
SQL> ORADEBUG LKDEBUG -m pkey 12345
```

You can also revert to the default mastering distribution:

```
SQL> ORADEBUG LKDEBUG -m dpkey 12345
```

You can verify the current master of a specific segment in the GV$GCSPFMASTER_INFO dynamic performance view.

Events

You can also use ORADEBUG to enable and disable events. Events fall into a number of categories and can be used for many purposes, including enabling or disabling feature-specific trace, enabling or disabling functionality, and toggling switches such as compiler options.

Events are defined by error codes. They are generally undocumented, unsupported, and vary from one release to the next. No formal lists of events are available. However, you can discover which events may exist in your database by examining the $ORACLE_HOME/rdbms/mesg/oraus.msg file using a text editor or the strings utility in Linux and Unix. Note that the most recently added events for a given version of Oracle are not always documented in this file.

Each event has one or more levels. The level is an integer parameter, the behavior of which depends on the event. For example, for some events, the level determines the level of detail included in the trace file. For other events, the level may just be used as a flag to enable or disable the trace.

We recommend that you do not experiment with events, particularly on a live system, because you can corrupt the database. Only use events on a test or development system, where you can afford to lose the database. Some undocumented event levels can damage your database.

In addition to well-known events, such as 10046 (SQL trace) and 10053 (optimizer), there are a large number of RAC-specific events. We examine several of these events in the following section.

To enable an event using ORADEBUG, first attach the SQL*Plus session to the correct process using the SETMYPID, SETORAPID, or SETOSPID command; this process is described earlier in this chapter.

Next, you can specify an event together with a level, for example:

```
SQL> ORADEBUG EVENT 10046 trace name context forever, level 8
```

You can also enable events at session level, which may be necessary in a shared server environment, for example:

```
SQL> ORADEBUG SESSION_EVENT 10046 trace name context forever, level 8
```

To disable the event again, use the following:

```
SQL> ORADEBUG EVENT 10046 trace name context off
```

or use

```
SQL> ORADEBUG SESSION_EVENT 10046 trace name context off
```

You can also enable and disable events using the ALTER SESSION and ALTER SYSTEM commands. For example, enable trace, including wait events, at the session level as follows:

```
SQL> ALTER SESSION SET EVENTS '10046 trace name context forever, level 8'
```

To enable trace, including wait events, at system level, use the following command:

```
SQL> ALTER SYSTEM SET EVENTS '10046 trace name context forever, level 8'
```

To disable trace at the session level, use the following:

```
SQL> ALTER SESSION SET EVENTS '10046 trace name context off'
```

and to disable trace at the system level, use

```
SQL> ALTER SYSTEM SET EVENTS '10046 trace name context off'
```

RAC-Specific Events

There are a number of RAC-specific numeric events. Most of these events operate at level 1, though higher levels may generate additional levels of detail. Some useful RAC-specific events are shown in Table 21-4.

Table 21-4. *RAC-Specific Events*

Event Number	Description
10425	Trace global enqueue operations
10426	Trace GES/GCS reconfiguration
10427	Trace GES traffic controller
10428	Trace GES cached resource
10429	Trace GES IPC calls
10430	Trace GES/GCS dynamic remastering
10432	Trace GCS Cache Fusion calls (part 1)
10434	Trace GES multiple LMS*n*
10435	Trace GES deadlock detection
10439	Trace GCS Cache Fusion calls (part 2)
10706	Trace global enqueue manipulation
10708	Trace RAC buffer cache

For example, to enable tracing GCS Cache Fusion calls in the LMS0 process, first, identify the operating system process ID using the following:

```
[oracle@london1 oracle]$ ps -ef | grep lms0
```

or, alternatively, using the following SQL statement:

```
SQL> SELECT p.spid
> FROM v$process p, v$bgprocess b
> WHERE p.addr = b.paddr
> AND b.name = 'LMS0';
```

Set the operating system PID for the ORADEBUG session. For example, if the previous statement returned an operating system PID of 5183 then use:

```
SQL> ORADEBUG SETOSPID 5183
```

Enable the trace event. In this case, we are using level 65535, as this event appears to use a bit mask to enable various different trace functions:

```
SQL> ORADEBUG EVENT 10432 TRACE NAME CONTEXT FOREVER, LEVEL 65535;
```

Interpretation of the output of these events is beyond the scope of this book.

Summary

In this chapter, we discussed techniques for enabling trace and diagnostics within a RAC database. In our opinion, the DBMS_MONITOR package is a major step forward in terms of application instrumentation. If you have control over your development environment, we recommend that you consider implementing new standards to include calls to the DBMS_APPLICATION_INFO package to set the current module and action. If you use connection pooling within a multitier architecture, we also suggest that you use DBMS_SESSION to set the client identifier. Use of these features together with the configuration of services will allow you to drill down to performance problems in a much more granular and structured manner.

We have also examined the RAC-specific functionality of the ORADEBUG tool in some detail, including trace events and the LKDEBUG utility. The information provided by these tools, together with that reported by the fixed tables and dynamic performance views, is fundamental for those attempting to understand the internal mechanisms built into the Oracle kernel to support RAC.

## CHAPTER 22

RAC Internals

In this chapter, we will explore some of the internal mechanisms that are used to implement RAC databases. These mechanisms differentiate RAC from single-instance databases. It is important to understand the underlying behavior of RAC when you are designing high-capacity systems and addressing performance issues.

A RAC cluster consists of a single database and multiple instances. Each instance has a System Global Area (SGA) containing the same structures as a single-instance SGA, including the fixed and variable memory areas, buffer cache, and log buffer. Each instance has access to the shared database and can potentially read or update any block. Therefore, you need to coordinate block access between the instances in order to maintain consistency and data integrity. This process is known as *synchronization*, and it requires the preparation of consistent read and current versions of blocks, transmission of blocks between buffer caches, and intranode messaging.

In order to achieve synchronization between the instances of a cluster, two virtual services are implemented: the Global Enqueue Service (GES), which controls access to locks, and the Global Cache Service (GCS), which controls access to blocks.

The GES is a development of the Distributed Lock Manager (DLM), which was the mechanism used to manage both locks and blocks in Oracle Parallel Server (OPS). Within a clustered environment, you need to restrict access to database resources that are typically protected by latches or locks in a single-instance database. For example, objects in the dictionary cache are protected by implicit locks, and objects in the library cache must be protected by pins while they are being referenced. In a RAC cluster, these objects are represented by resources that are protected by global locks. GES is an integrated RAC component that coordinates global locks between the instances in the cluster. Each resource has a master instance that records its current status. In addition, the current status is recorded in all instances with an interest in that resource.

The GCS, which is another integrated RAC component, coordinates access to database blocks by the various instances. Block access and update are recorded in the Global Resource Directory (GRD), which is a virtual memory structure spanning across all instances. Each block has a master instance that maintains an entry in the GRD describing the current status of the block. GCS is the mechanism that Oracle uses to implement Cache Fusion.

The blocks and locks maintained by GCS and GES are known as *resources*. Access to these resources must be coordinated between all instances in the cluster. This coordination occurs at both instance level and database level. Instance-level resource coordination is known as *local resource coordination*; database-level coordination is known as *global resource coordination*. Local resource coordination in a RAC instance is identical to that in single-instance Oracle and includes block level access, space management, dictionary cache and library cache management, row-level locking, and System Change Number (SCN) generation. Global resource coordination is specific to RAC and uses additional SGA memory structures, algorithms, and background processes.

Both GCS and GES are designed to operate transparently to applications. In other words, you do not need to modify applications to run on a RAC cluster, as the same concurrency mechanisms are available in RAC as are found in single-instance Oracle databases.

The background processes that support GCS and GES use the interconnect network to communicate between instances. This network is also used by Oracle Clusterware and may optionally be used by the cluster file system (e.g., OCFS). GCS and GES operate independently of Oracle Clusterware. However, they do rely on it for information about the current status of each instance in the cluster. If information cannot be obtained from a particular instance, it will be shut down. This shutdown is required to ensure the integrity of the database, as each instance must be aware of all the others in order to coordinate access to the database.

Global Enqueue Services

In a RAC database, GES is responsible for interinstance resource coordination. GES manages all non–Cache Fusion intra-instance resource operations. It tracks the status of all Oracle enqueue mechanisms for resources that are accessed by more than one instance. Oracle uses GES enqueues to manage concurrency for resources operating on transactions, tables, and other structures within a RAC environment. GES is also responsible for deadlock detection.

GES controls all library cache locks and dictionary cache locks in the database. These resources are local in a single-instance database but global in a RAC database. Global locks are also used to protect the data structures used for transaction management. In general, transaction and table lock processing operate the same way in RAC as they do in single-instance Oracle databases.

All layers of Oracle use the same GES functions to acquire, convert, and release resources. The number of global enqueues is calculated automatically at start-up.

As with enqueues on single-instance Oracle, deadlocks may occur with global enqueues in a RAC cluster. For example, Instance 1 has an exclusive lock on Resource A, and Instance 2 has an exclusive lock on Resource B. Instance 2 requests an exclusive lock on Resource A, and Instance 1 requests an exclusive lock on Resource B. This deadlock situation will be detected by the LMD0 background process, which will write an error message to the alert log, for example:

```
Global Enqueue Services Deadlock detected. More info in file
 /u01/app/oracle/admin/RAC/bdump/rac1_lmd0_25084.trc.
```

Background Processes

GES performs most of its activities using the LMD0 and LCK0 background processes. In general, processes communicate with their local LMD0 background process to manipulate the global resources. The local LMD0 background process communicates with the LMD0 processes on other instances.

The LCK0 background process is used to obtain locks that are required by the entire instance. For example, LCK0 is responsible for maintaining dictionary (row) cache locks.

Server processes communicate with these background processes using messages known as Asynchronous Traps (AST). Asynchronous messages are used to avoid the background processes having to block while they are waiting for replies from instances on remote nodes. Background processes can also send Blocking Asynchronous Traps (BAST) to lock holding processes to request that they downgrade a currently held lock to a less restrictive mode.

Resources and Enqueues

A resource is a memory structure that represents some component of the database to which access must be restricted or serialized. In other words, the resource can only be accessed by one process or one instance concurrently. If the resource is currently in use, other processes or instances needing to access the resource must wait in a queue until the resource becomes available.

An enqueue is a memory structure that serializes access to a particular resource. If the resource is only required by the local instance, then the enqueue can be acquired locally, and no coordination is necessary. However, if the resource is required by a remote instance, then the local enqueue must become global.

Lock Types

Every lock has a type, which is a two character alphabetic identifier (e.g., BL, CU, SE, NB). The number of lock types varies with each release. Some lock types are only used in RDBMS instances, others in ASM instances, and the remainder are used in both.

Each lock type has two parameters, which are called *tags*. Each tag value is a 32-bit number. The tag values differ according to the lock type, but the name and the two tag values form a unique identifier for the lock. For example, for a library cache object LB lock, the parameters represent a portion of the hash value for the object, which is derived from the object name. On the other hand, for a TM lock, the first parameter contains the object number, and the second parameter describes whether the object is a table or a partition.

In Oracle 10.1 and above, the V$LOCK_TYPE dynamic performance view summarizes all implemented lock types.

Some lock types, for example, the TX transaction lock and the CU cursor lock, only affect the local instance; therefore, they can be managed locally. Other lock types, such as the TM table lock and the all library cache locks and pins, must be observed by all instances in the database; therefore, they must be managed globally.

The most common lock types seen in a RAC database are listed in Table 22-1.

Table 22-1. *Common Lock Types*

Type	Description
BL	Block (GCS)
CU	Cursor lock
HW	High water mark lock
L*	Library cache lock
N*	Library cache pin
Q*	Dictionary cache lock
SQ	Sequence cache
TM	Table lock
TS	Temporary segment
TT	Tablespace lock (for DDL)
TX	Transaction lock

The actual distribution of lock usage is application dependent.

Library Cache Locks

Each RAC instance has its own library cache. The library cache contains all statements and packages currently in use by the instance. In addition, the library cache contains all objects that are referenced by these statements and packages.

When a DML or DDL statement is parsed, all database objects that are referenced by that statement are locked using a library cache lock for the duration of the parse call. These objects include tables, indexes, views, packages, procedures, and functions. Referenced objects are also locked in the library cache during the compilation of all PL/SQL packages and Java classes.

When a statement is executed, all referenced objects are locked briefly to allow them to be pinned. Objects are pinned during statement execution to prevent modification of them by other processes, such as those executing DDL statements.

Namespaces

Every object in the library cache belongs to a namespace. The number of namespaces is release dependent; in Oracle 10.2, there can be a maximum of 64, although not all are used in that release. Within a namespace, each object name must be unique. For example, one of the namespaces is called TABL/PRCD/TYPE, which ensures that no table, procedure, or user-defined type can have the same name.

The namespace for each object is externalized as a NUMBER in the KGLHDNSP column of the X$KGLOB family of views.

You can obtain limited statistics for objects in the library cache, such as the number of gets and pins from the V$LIBRARYCACHE view. Note, however, that this view returns only a subset of namespaces from the X$KGLST base view.

Prior to Oracle 10g, you could also identify the namespace for each object from a library cache dump as follows:

```
SQL> ALTER SESSION SET EVENTS 'immediate trace name library_cache level 8';
```

In this dump, each object in the library cache has a namespace attribute. Unfortunately in Oracle 10.1 and 10.2, this attribute has become confused with the object type, which is externalized as KGLOBTYP in the X$KGLOB family of views. Although the namespace attribute is incorrect in the dump, you can still determine the true namespace by inspecting the instance lock types for the library cache locks and pins as described later in this section.

Hash Values

Every object in the library cache has a hash value. This is derived from a combination of the namespace and a name. In the case of stored objects, such as tables, the name is derived from the owner name, object name, and optionally, a remote link. In the case of transient objects, such as SQL statements, the name is derived from the text of the SQL statement.

Prior to Oracle 10.1, the hash value was represented by a 32-bit number, which is still calculated and externalized in the KGLNAHSH column of X$KGLOB. This 32-bit hash value was sufficient for most purposes, but could, on occasion, lead to collisions. Therefore, in Oracle 10.1 and above, a new hash value is calculated using a 128-bit value, which more or less guarantees uniqueness. This new value is externalized in the KGLNAHSV column of X$KGLOB.

Library Cache Lock Types

In a RAC environment, the names of library cache locks and pins that are set across all nodes in the cluster are determined by the namespace. Originally, the lock types for library cache locks were LA, LB, LC . . . LZ and library cache pins were NA, NB, NC . . . NZ, where the second letter corresponded to the number of the namespace. As these lock names were alphabetical, the sequence was exhausted after 26 namespaces. Therefore, two further sequences of lock type names were introduced to handle new namespaces. Library cache locks were allocated EA, EB, EC . . . EZ, and library cache pins were allocated GA, GB, GC . . .GZ. In recent versions, there are more than 52 namespaces, so a third series has been introduced with library cache locks types of VA, VB, VC . . . VZ and library cache pin types of YA, YB, YC . . .YZ.

Not all the lock types are used. For example, pipes that are created by the DBMS_PIPE object exist only on the local instance. Therefore, creating remote locks is not necessary. Consequently, the lock type LH, which corresponds to the PIPE namespace, is never used.

The parameters for the library cache locks and pins are the first and second 32-bit words from the 128-bit hash value (X$KGLOB.KGLNAHSV). Therefore, an object with the following hash value:

```
8b1d733608cd1ee696e689cc7fe2ae4b
```

will have the parameters 8b1d7336 and 08cd1ee6. The hash values for the lock and pin of a specific object will be identical.

Table 22-2 summarizes some of the more common namespaces and their associated lock types.

Table 22-2. *Common Namespaces and Their Associated Library Cache Lock and Pin Types*

	Namespace	Description	Lock	Pin
0	CRSR	Cursor	LA	NA
1	TABL/PRCD/TYPE	Table/procedure/type	LB	NB
2	BODY/TYBD	Package body/type body	LC	NC
3	TRGR	Trigger	LD	ND
4	INDX	Index	LE	NE
5	CLST	Cluster	LF	NF
9	DIR	Directory	LJ	NJ
10	QUEU	Queue	LK	NK
18	EVNT	Event	LS	NS
23	RULS	Ruleset	LX	NX
34	TRANS	Transaction	EI	GI
45	MVOBTBL	Materialized view table	ET	GT
48	MVOBIND	Materialized view index	EW	GW
51	JSGA	Java SGA	EZ	GZ

Note that the CRSR namespace, which contains all cursors, does not require any remote locks. Thus, the LA lock and NA pin are not used.

Invalidation Locks

In single-instance Oracle, library cache locks on objects that a statement references are retained in null mode after the statement has been parsed. In the event of another process wishing to modify one of the referenced objects, the null-mode library cache locks allow dependent objects in the library cache to be identified and invalidated.

In RAC, a more complex mechanism is required, because the object might be modified by a process in a different instance to the one holding the null lock. Therefore, in RAC, an invalidation (IV) instance lock is held on each instance by LCK0 for each database object currently in the cache. If a process needs to modify an object definition, it can take an exclusive mode lock on the resource, which forces the LCK0 processes to drop their shared lock and to implicitly invalidate all dependent objects.

The IV lock type has two parameters: the first is the object number, and the second is a time stamp issued with the lock was created.

Row Cache Locks

Each RAC instance has its own dictionary or row cache that is used to store elements of the data dictionary in the SGA in order to reduce the amount of physical I/O required when parsing statements. The data dictionary has the same structure in a RAC database as in a single-instance database. However, in a RAC database, the row caches are synchronized across all instances in the cluster.

In a single-instance database, access to dictionary cache objects is controlled using implicit locking; in a RAC instance, access is controlled using global locks.

Longtime Oracle users will remember that in Oracle 6.0 it was necessary to set initialization parameters that specified the size of each structure in the row cache. Since Oracle 7, these parameters have been managed automatically. However, the individual structures still exist and can be seen in the PARAMETER column of the V$ROWCACHE view. You can also see these structures in the output of a ROW_CACHE dump:

```
ALTER SESSION SET EVENTS 'immediate trace name row_cache level 10';
```

This dump shows the current contents of the row cache. The cache ID is listed on the first line of each entry, for example:

```
row cache parent object: address=0x29a0b9bc cid=8(dc_objects)
```

In the previous example, the row cache ID is 8, which is the cache containing object definitions.

Row cache lock types are based on the cache ID and are named QA, QB, QC, and so on. As Oracle software has developed, some row cache functionality has been replaced, and consequently, some row cache lock types have fallen into disuse. In Oracle 10.2, commonly used lock types include those shown in Table 22-3.

Table 22-3. *Commonly Used Row Caches and Their Associated Lock Types*

Cache ID	Cache Name	Lock
0	dc_tablespaces	QA
2	dc_segments	QC
3	dc_rollback_segments	QD
5	dc_tablespace_quotas	QF
8	dc_objects	QI
10	dc_usernames	QK
11	dc_object_ids	QL
13	dc_sequences	QN
14	dc_profiles	QO
16	dc_histogram_defs	QQ
17	dc_global_oids	QR
22	dc_awr_control	QW
24	outstanding_alerts	QY

Row cache locks are maintained globally by the LCK0 background process. If you perform a SYSTEMSTATE dump, you will discover that LCK0 is holding all the row cache locks for the instance. LCK0 also maintains Cross Instance (CI) locks and library cache pin locks (such as NB and NF) for stored objects that have been locked by recursive operations.

Tracing GES Activity

You can trace GES activity at several levels. You can include information about what enqueues are being set within the local instance by your current session as follows:

```
SQL> ALTER SESSION SET EVENTS '10704 trace name context forever, level 1';
```

You can obtain more detailed information by specifying level 2.
You can trace information about what enqueues are being set across all instances by GES:

```
SQL> ALTER SESSION SET EVENTS '10706 trace name context forever, level 1';
```

Finally, you can enable additional GES trace using event 10425, for example:

```
SQL> ALTER SESSION SET EVENTS '10425 trace name context forever, level 15';
```

Optimizing Global Enqueues

Global locking can significantly impact performance causing increased wait times and possibly even deadlocks. However, a few simple measures can greatly reduce the impact of global locking.

Much global locking is related to parsing activity. Therefore, you should avoid unnecessary parsing wherever possible. There are many ways to achieve this. In OLTP environments, literals should be replaced by bind variables. This replacement is best achieved by modifying the source code. However, if you do not have access to the source code, you might consider enabling cursor sharing, which achieves the same goal but incurs a slight overhead, as the text of every statement executed in the database must be scanned for literals before the statement is parsed.

PL/SQL contains a number of optimizations aimed at improving performance. For example, it does not close cursors when a statement completes. Instead, it effectively retains cursors in a pool in case they are needed again, which avoids the need to perform a soft parse if the cursor is executed again in the near future. If you develop your own applications in C or Java, you can copy this behavior and thereby reduce the amount of parsing required.

Another way to reduce parsing is simply to optimize the size of the library cache to reduce the number of cursors that are aged out of the cache and subsequently reloaded. You may also benefit from pinning commonly used packages and cursors in memory.

You should also attempt to remove unnecessary DDL statements from your application. The most common cause of these is the creation of temporary tables for intermediate steps in complex tasks, such as reports and batch processes. These tables can often be replaced by global temporary tables.

Finally, the impact of global enqueues can be reduced by simply executing fewer SQL statements, which can often be achieved by eliminating unnecessary statements. It can also be achieved by combining existing SQL statements, for example, using a UNION ALL. It is also worth examining your application logic to establish whether statements that are being executed procedurally (i.e., row by row) could be executed as a set operation. For example, you might be able to replace 100 single-row update statements with a single statement that updates all rows at the same time.

Global Cache Services

By default, a resource is allocated for each data block that is currently in the buffer cache of each instance. The resource remains allocated to the block until all copies of the block have been replaced in the buffer caches of all instances.

Global Resource Directory (GRD)

Information about resources is maintained in the GRD by the GCS and GES. The GRD is a memory structure that is distributed across all instances. The GRD is designed to provide enhanced runtime performance. Each instance is responsible for maintaining part of the GRD in its SGA; therefore, the overhead of maintaining the GRD is shared between all active instances. Information in the GRD is available to all instances, either directly if that information is maintained locally, or indirectly through communication with background processes on the remote node.

The GRD is also designed to provide fault tolerance. In the event of a node failure, the GRD is reconstructed by the remaining instances. As long as at least one active instance remains after recovery is completed, the shared database will still be accessible. GCS and GES are designed to be resilient in the event of multiple concurrent node failures.

The GRD is reconstructed whenever a node joins or leaves the cluster. The dynamic implementation of the GRD enables RAC instances to start and stop at any time and in any order. Every change in node membership results in a cluster reconfiguration.

Each resource is initially mapped onto an instance using a hashing algorithm. This instance is called the *resource master*. The master instance for a specific resource may change each time there is a cluster reconfiguration, which is known as *static resource mastering*.

In Oracle 10.1 and above, resources can also be remastered based on usage patterns to reduce network traffic and the consequent CPU resource consumption. This is known as *dynamic resource mastering*. In Oracle 10.1, GCS evaluates resource mastering periodically. If it detects a high level of affinity between a particular instance and blocks from a specific data file, then all blocks in the file may be remastered by that instance. In Oracle 10.2 and above, dynamic resource mastering is performed on a segment level, and GCS will initiate remastering if there is a high level of affinity between a particular instance and blocks from a specific segment.

Each instance maintains a portion of the GRD containing information about the current status of a subset of the global resources. This information, which is used during instance failure recovery and cluster reconfigurations, includes data block identifiers, the location of the current version of the data block, modes in which the data block is held by each instance, which can be null (N), shared (S), or exclusive (X), and the role in which each instance is holding the data block, which can be local or global.

When an instance requests a resource, such as a data block, it first contacts the resource master to ascertain the current status of the resource. If the resource is not currently in use, it can be acquired locally. If the resource is currently in use, then the resource master will request that the holding instance passes the resource to the requesting resource. If the resource is subsequently required for modification by one or more instances, the GRD will be modified to indicate that the resource is held globally.

If the local instance requires a read-consistent version of a block, it still contacts the resource master to ascertain if a version of the block that has the same or a more recent SCN exists in the buffer cache of any remote instance. If such a block exists, then the resource master will send a request to the relevant remote instance to forward a read-consistent version of the block to the local instance. If the remote instance is holding a version of the block at the requested SCN, it sends the block immediately. If the remote instance is holding a newer version of the block, it creates a copy of the block and applies undo to the copy to revert it to the correct SCN.

When a RAC instance requires a data block that is currently being updated on the local instance, the request is processed in exactly the same way that it would be in a single instance database. However, when a RAC instance requests a data block that is being updated on another instance, the block images are located, prepared, and transmitted by the GCS background processes (LMS*n*) on the remote instance.

Resource Modes

A data block can exist in multiple buffer caches. It can be held by multiple instances in different modes depending on whether the block is being read or updated by the instance. GCS uses the resource mode to determine whether the instance currently holding the block can modify it. There are three modes: null (N) mode, shared (S) mode, and exclusive (X) mode. These modes are summarized in Table 22-4.

Table 22-4. *Resource Modes*

Resource Mode	Identifier	Description
Null	N	No access rights.
Shared	S	Shared resources can be read by multiple instances but cannot be updated by any instance.
Exclusive	X	An instance holding a block in exclusive mode can modify the block. Only one instance can hold the instance in exclusive mode.

You can verify the current state of any buffer in the buffer cache of an instance by selecting the STATUS column from the V$BH dynamic performance view. The STATUS column can contain the values shown in Table 22-5.

Table 22-5. *V$BH Status Column Values*

Status	Resource Mode	Description
FREE		Buffer is not currently in use
CR	NULL	Consistent read (read only)
SCUR	S	Shared current block (read only)
XCUR	X	Exclusive current block (can be modified)
PI	NULL	Past image (read only)

The SCUR and PI states are RAC specific. The XCUR state must be assigned before the block can be modified. There can be only one copy of a block in the XCUR state in any buffer cache in the cluster database at any one time.

Resource Roles

A role is assigned to every resource held by an instance. This role can be either local or global. When a block is initially read into the buffer cache of an instance and no other instance has read the same block, the block can be locally managed. The GCS assigns a local role to the block. If the block has been modified by one instance and is transmitted to another instance, then it becomes globally managed, and the GCS assigns a global role to the block. When the block is transferred, the resource mode may remain exclusive, or it may be converted from exclusive to shared.

The GCS tracks the location, resource mode, and resource role of each block in the buffer cache of all instances. The GCS is used to ensure cache coherency when the current version of a data block is in the buffer cache of one instance and another requires the same block for update.

Cache Coherency

Cache coherency is an important concept in many computing technologies. In an Oracle RAC database, it is defined as the synchronization of data in multiple caches, so that reading a memory location through any cache will return the most recent data written to that location through any other cache. In other words, if a block is updated by any instance, then all other instances will be able to see that change the next time they access the block.

The GCS ensures cache coherency by requiring instances to acquire resources at a global level before modifying a database block. The GCS synchronizes global cache access, allowing only one instance to modify a block at a time.

Oracle uses a multiversioning architecture, in which there can be one current version of a block throughout all instances in the cluster. Only the current version of a block may be updated. There can also be any number of consistent read (CR) versions of the block. A consistent read version of a block represents a snapshot of the data in that block at a specific point in time. The time is represented by the SCN. Consistent read blocks cannot be modified, though they can be used as a starting point to construct earlier consistent blocks. The GCS manages both current and consistent read blocks.

If a local instance has modified a block and a remote instance requests it, the local instance creates a past image (PI) of the block before it transfers the block to the remote image. In the event of a node or instance failure, the PI can be used to reconstruct current and consistent read versions of the block.

Cache Fusion

Cache Fusion addresses several types of concurrency between different nodes:

- Concurrent reads
- Concurrent reads and writes
- Concurrent writes

Concurrent Reads

Concurrent reads on multiple nodes occur when two instances need to read the same block. In this case, no synchronization is required, as multiple instances can share data blocks for read access without any conflict.

Concurrent Reads and Writes

If one instance needs to read a block that was modified by another instance and has not yet been written to disk, this block can be transferred across the interconnect from the holding instance to the requesting instance. The block transfer is performed by the GCS background processes (LMS*n*) on the participating instances.

Concurrent Writes

When an instance updates a block in the buffer cache, the resulting block is called a *dirty buffer*. Only the current version of the block can be modified. The instance must acquire the current version of the block before it can modify it. If the current version of the block is not currently available, the instance must wait.

Before an instance can modify a block in the buffer cache, it must construct a redo record containing all the changes that will be applied to the block. When the redo record has been copied to the redo buffer, the changes it contains can be applied to the block(s) in the buffer cache. The dirty block will subsequently be written to disk by the DBWn background process. However, the dirty block cannot be written to disk until the change vector in the redo buffer has been flushed to the redo log file.

If the local instance needs to update a block, and it does not currently hold that block, it contacts the resource master to identify whether any other instance is currently holding the block. If a remote instance is holding a dirty version of the block, the remote instance will send the dirty block across the interconnect, so that the local instance can perform the updates on the most recent version of the block. The remote instance will retain a copy of the dirty block in its buffer cache until it receives a message confirming that the block has subsequently been written to disk. This copy is called a *past image* (PI). The GCS manages past images and uses them in failure recovery.

Note that a block does not have to be held by an instance in exclusive mode until the transaction has completed. Once a local instance has modified a row in current version of the block, the block can be passed to a remote instance where another transaction can modify a different row. However, the remote instance will not be able to modify the row changed by the local instance until the transaction on the local instance either commits or rolls back. In this respect, row locking behavior is identical to that on a single-instance Oracle database.

Prior to Oracle 8.1.5, if a local instance required a block that was currently dirty in the buffer cache of another instance, the remote instance would write the block back to the datafile and signal the local instance. The local instance would then read the block from disk into its buffer cache. This process is known as a *disk ping*. Disk pings are very resource intensive, as they require disk I/O and IPC communication between the instances.

In Oracle 8.1.5 and above, if the local instance required a block that was currently dirty in the buffer cache of another instance for a consistent read, the remote instance would construct a consistent image of the block at the required SCN and send the consistent block across the interconnect. This algorithm was known as Cache Fusion Phase I and was a significant step forward in cluster database technology.

In Oracle 9.0.1 and above, both consistent blocks and current blocks can be sent across the interconnect. The transfer of current blocks is made possible by the existence of past images (PI). This algorithm is known as Cache Fusion Phase II.

Although in a RAC database, Cache Fusion processing incurs overheads in the form of additional messaging, it does not necessarily increase the amount of I/O performed against the storage. When a local instance attempts to read a block that is not currently in the local buffer cache, it first contacts the resource master, which checks the current status of the block in the GRD. If a remote instance is currently holding the block, the resource master requests that the remote instance send the block to the local instance. For a consistent read, the remote instance will apply any undo necessary to restore the block to the appropriate SCN. Therefore, if the local instance attempts to read a block that is in the cache of any other instance, it will receive a copy of the block over the interconnect network. In this case, it is not necessary for the local instance to read the block from disk. While this mechanism requires the participation of two or three instances, consuming CPU and networking resources, these are generally less expensive than the cost of performing a single physical disk I/O.

When a local instance modifies a block, the changes are written immediately to the redo buffer and are flushed to the redo log by the log writer (LGWR) background process when the transaction is committed. However, the modified block is not written to disk by the database writer (DBWn) background process until a free buffer is required in the buffer cache for another block or a checkpoint occurs. If a remote instance requests the block for modification, the block will not be written to disk by the local instance. Instead, the block will be passed over the interconnect network to the remote instance for further modification. A past image (PI) block, which is a copy of the block at the time it was transferred, is retained in the buffer cache of the local instance until it receives confirmation that the remote instance has written the block to disk. As with reads, this mechanism requires the participation of two or three instances and is designed to avoid disk I/Os at the expense of additional CPU and networking resources.

The number of nodes involved in a read or write request that is satisfied by a block transfer across the interconnect depends on the location of the resource master. If the resource master is the same instance as the source instance for a read or the destination instance for a write, then only two instances will participate in the operation. If the resource master is on a different instance than the source or destination instance, three instances will participate in the operation. Obviously, there must be at least three active instances in the cluster for this situation to arise.

Cache Fusion Examples

The following section contains examples of the different types of behaviors of the Cache Fusion algorithm for block reads and updates. Each example will follow a single block as it is requested by various instances for both shared and exclusive access.

Example 1: Current Read with No Transfer

In the following examples, the database cluster consists of four instances, each of which has access to a database on shared disk. The block is initially only in the database on disk. It is currently at SCN 1318 (Figure 22-1).

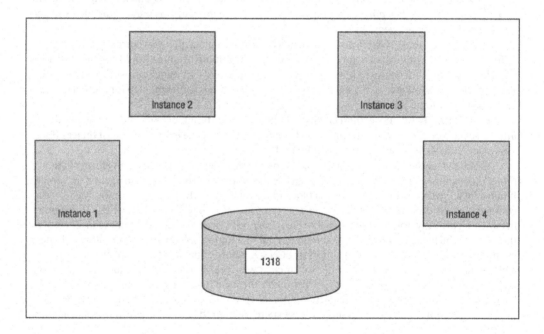

Figure 22-1. *Current read with no transfer initial state*

Instance 2 requests a current read of the block (Figure 22-2).

It first identifies the instance that is the resource master for the block by applying a hash function to the database block address (DBA) of the resource. In this case, the resource master instance is Instance 3. As Instance 2 only needs to perform a current read on the block, it sends a message to Instance 3 requesting shared access to the block.

Instance 3 checks in the GRD and discovers that the block is not currently being accessed by any instances. Therefore, Instance 3 immediately grants shared access on the block to Instance 2 (Figure 22-3).

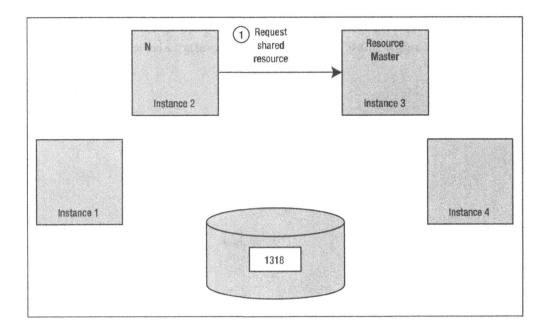

Figure 22-2. *Current read with no transfer step 1*

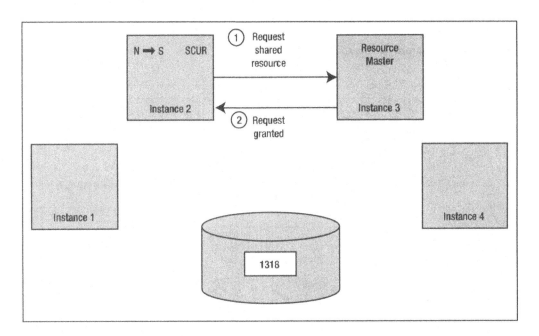

Figure 22-3. *Current read with no transfer step 2*

Instance 2 issues a system call to read the block directly from the database (Figure 22-4). The block is currently at SCN 1318.

The block is returned from disk and a current version is stored in the buffer cache (Figure 22-5). The SCN is still 1318.

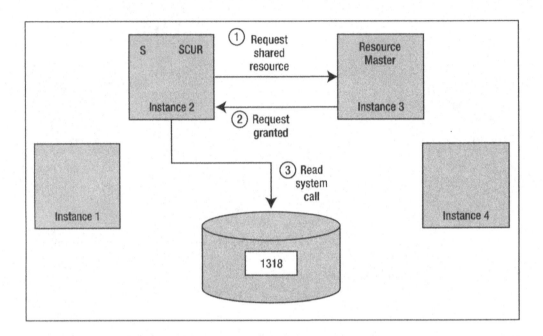

Figure 22-4. *Current read with no transfer step 3*

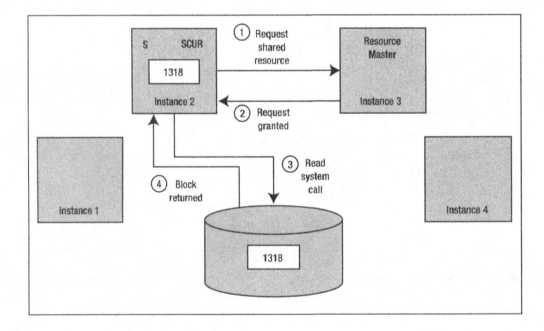

Figure 22-5. *Current read with no transfer step 4*

Example 2: Read-to-Write Transfer

This example shows how GCS satisfies a request by an instance to read a block for update where that block is already held read-only by another instance.

Instance 1 requests an exclusive read on the block. Initially, Instance 1 is not aware that the block is currently held by Instance 2. Instance 2 identifies the instance that is the resource master for the block applying a hash function to the database block address (DBA) of the resource. Instance 1 sends a message to Instance 3 requesting exclusive access to the block (Figure 22-6).

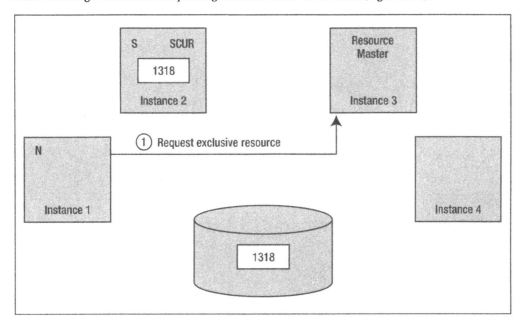

Figure 22-6. *Read-to-write transfer step 1*

Instance 3 checks in the GRD and discovers that the block is currently held by Instance 2 for shared (read) access. Instance 3 sends a message to Instance 2 requesting that it send the block to Instance 1 (Figure 22-7).

Instance 2 sends the block, still SCN 1318, to Instance 2 and downgrades the shared lock to a null lock (Figure 22-8).

Instance 1 receives the block and sends a message to Instance 3 to update the resource status by setting the lock mode on the block to exclusive (X) (Figure 22-9). Instance 3 updates the GRD. Instance 1 assumes an exclusive lock and updates the block at SCN 1320.

Note that RAC is designed to minimize the number of messages that pass across the interconnect network. Therefore, Instance 3 sends a message to Instance 2 requesting that it pass the block to Instance 1 and downgrades the shared lock to a null lock. However, Instance 2 does not reply directly back to Instance 3. Instead, it passes both the block and the resource status to Instance 1, which forwards the updated resource status back to Instance 3.

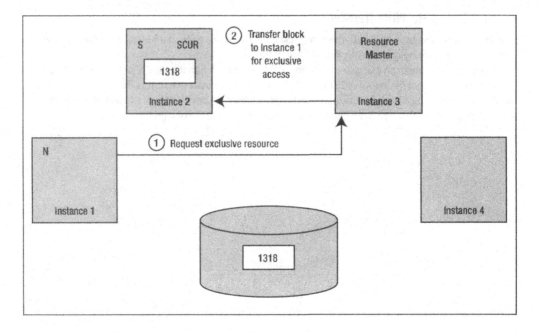

Figure 22-7. *Read-to-write transfer step 2*

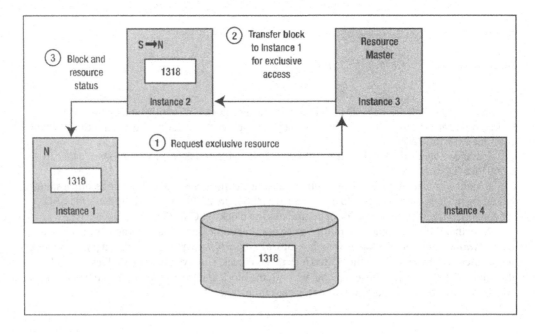

Figure 22-8. *Read-to-write transfer step 3*

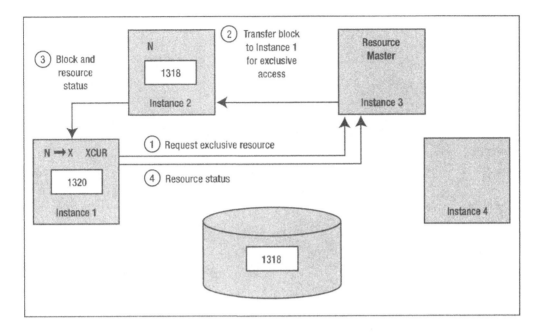

Figure 22-9. *Read-to-write transfer step 4*

Example 3: Write-to-Write Transfer

This example shows how GCS satisfies a request by an instance to read a block for update where that block is already held for update by another instance.

Instance 4 has also requested an exclusive read on the block. Initially, Instance 4 is not aware that the block is currently held by Instance 1. Instance 4 identifies that Instance 3 is the resource master instance for the block. Instance 4 sends a message to Instance 3 requesting exclusive access to the block (Figure 22-10).

Instance 3 checks in the GRD and discovers that the block is currently held by Instance 1 for exclusive (update) access. Instance 3 sends a message to Instance 1 requesting that it send the block to Instance 4 (Figure 22-11).

Instance 1 sends the block, still SCN 1320, to Instance 4 and downgrades the exclusive lock to a null lock (Figure 22-12).

Instance 4 receives the block and sends a message to Instance 3 to update the resource status, again setting the lock mode on the block to exclusive (Figure 22-13). Instance 3 updates the GRD. Instance 4 assumes an exclusive lock and updates the block at SCN 1323.

Note that Instance 1 will retain a past image (PI) copy of the block at SCN 1320 until the current version of the block (SCN 1323) is written to disk by Instance 4.

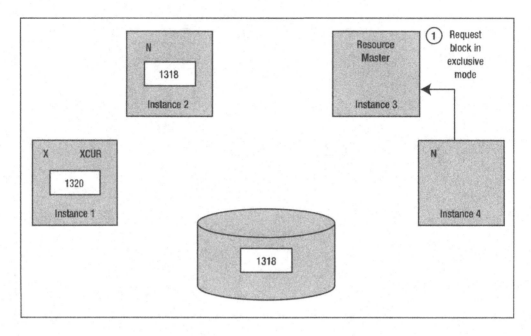

Figure 22-10. *Write-to-write transfer step 1*

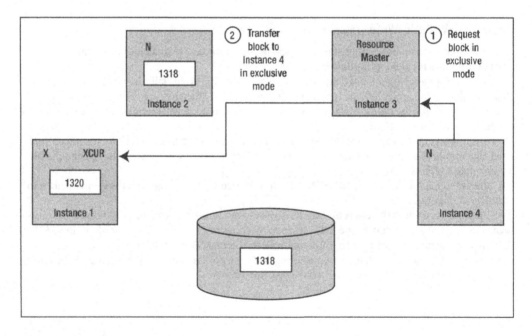

Figure 22-11. *Write-to-write transfer step 2*

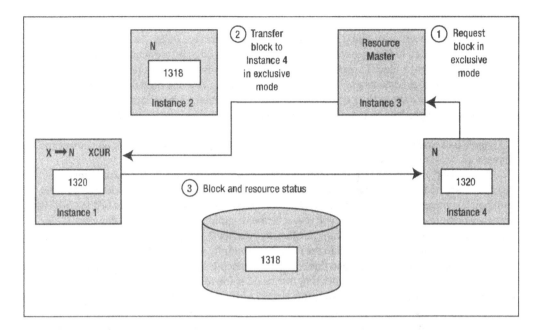

Figure 22-12. *Write-to-write transfer step 3*

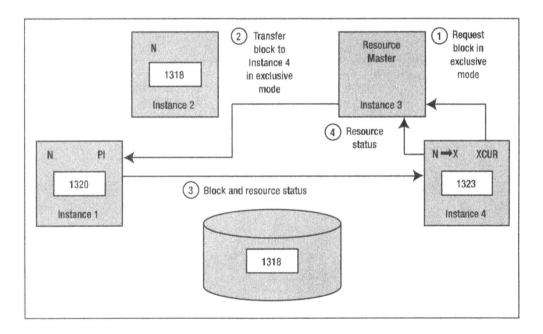

Figure 22-13. *Write-to-write transfer step 4*

Example 4: Write-to-Read Transfer

The behavior of the write-to-read transfer is determined by the _FAIRNESS_THRESHOLD parameter, which was introduced in Oracle 8.1.5 and defaults to 4. Prior to the introduction of this parameter, when Instance A held a block in exclusive mode and Instance B requested a read-only copy of that block, Instance A would downgrade its exclusive lock to a shared lock and send the block to Instance B, which would also set a shared lock on the block. However, if Instance A is performing frequent updates on the block, it will need to reacquire the block and set an exclusive lock again. If this process is repeated frequently, then Instance A will be continually interrupted, as it has to downgrade the exclusive lock to a shared lock and wait until Instance B has finished reading the block before it can convert the shared lock back into an exclusive lock.

The _FAIRNESS_THRESHOLD parameter modifies this behavior. When this parameter is set, Instance A will no longer downgrade the exclusive lock. Instead, it sends a null lock to Instance B, and then it can continue processing. However, if instance B requests the block _FAIRNESS_THRESHOLD times, by default 4, then Instance A will revert to the original behavior—it will downgrade the exclusive lock to a shared lock and ship the block to Instance B, which will also set a shared lock on the block. This behavior is explained in the following example.

Instance 2 requests a current read on the block. Instance 2 is not aware that the block is currently held by Instance 4. Instance 2 identifies that Instance 3 is the resource master instance for the block and sends a message to Instance 3 requesting shared access to the block (Figure 22-14).

Instance 3 checks in the GRD and discovers that the block is currently held by Instance 4 for exclusive (update) access. Instance 3 sends a message to Instance 4 requesting that it send the block to Instance 2 in shared mode (Figure 22-15).

Instance 4 sends the block to Instance 2 (Figure 22-16). Because the block has been requested less than _FAIRNESS_THRESHOLD times, Instance 4 retains the exclusive lock, and Instance 2 receives a null lock.

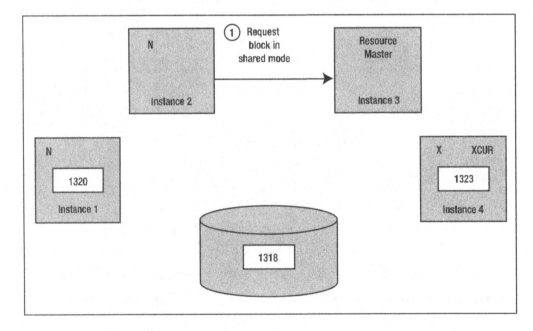

Figure 22-14. *Write-to-read transfer step 1*

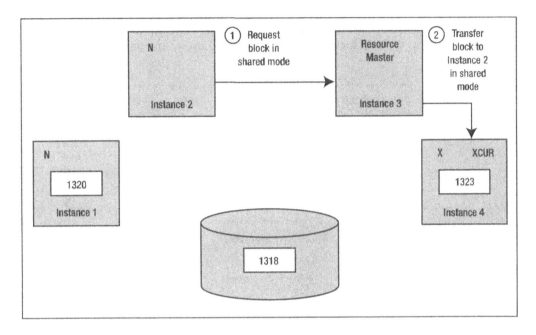

Figure 22-15. *Write-to-read transfer step 2*

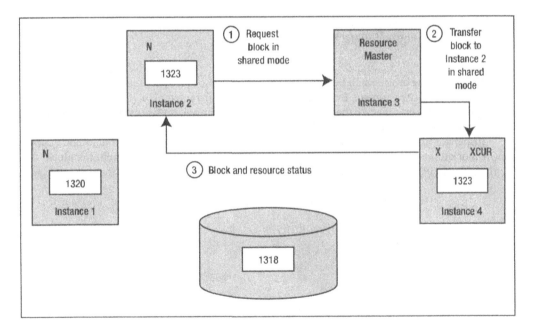

Figure 22-16. *Write-to-read transfer step 3*

Instance 2 receives the block and sends a message to Instance 3 to update the resource status (Figure 22-17). Instance 3 updates the GRD. Instance 2 assumes a null lock on the block and reads it. Instance 4 can update the block for which it continues to hold an exclusive process.

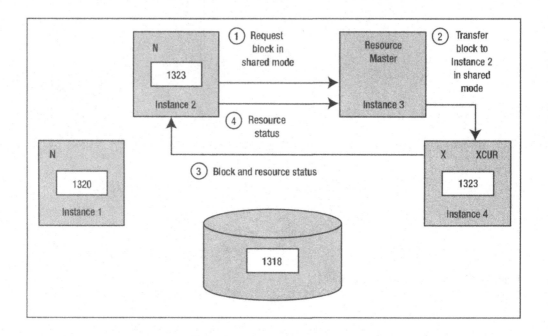

Figure 22-17. *Write-to-read transfer step 4*

The preceding process can be repeated the number of times specified by the _FAIRNESS_THRESHOLD parameter. By default, the value of this parameter is 4.

Instance 2 has now flushed the block from its buffer cache and needs to read it again. It sends a read request to the resource master, which is Instance 3 (Figure 22-18).

Instance 3 (the resource master) sends a message to Instance 4 requesting that it send a copy of the block to Instance 2 (Figure 22-19). Instance 4 notes that it has already sent the block _FAIRNESS_THRESHOLD times to Instance 2.

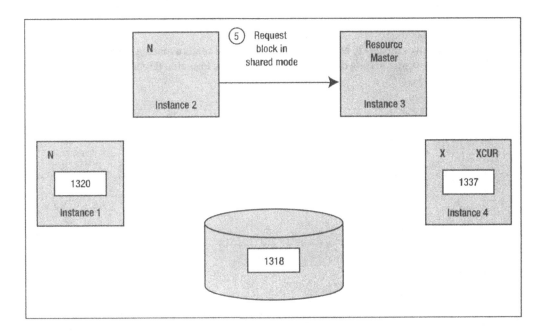

Figure 22-18. *Write-to-read transfer step 5*

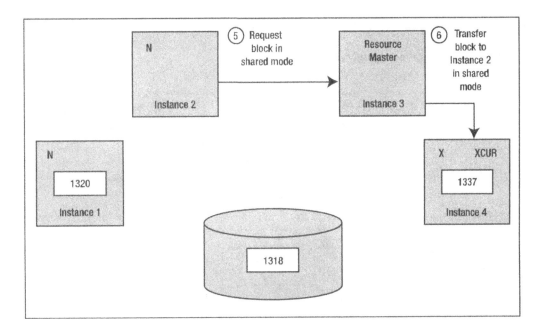

Figure 22-19. *Write-to-read transfer step 6*

Instance 4, therefore, downgrades the exclusive lock to a shared lock and sends the block to Instance 2 (Figure 22-20).

Instance 2 receives the block, assumes a shared lock, and sends a message to Instance 3 to update the resource status, setting the lock mode on the block to shared (Figure 22-21). Instance 3 updates the GRD.

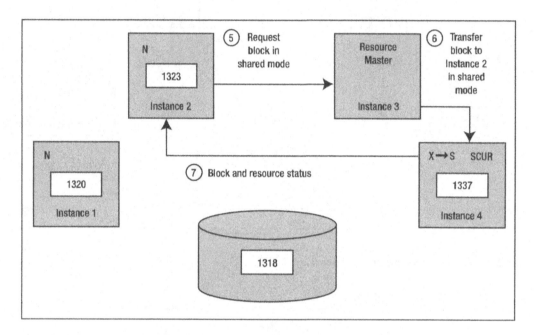

Figure 22-20. *Write-to-read transfer step 7*

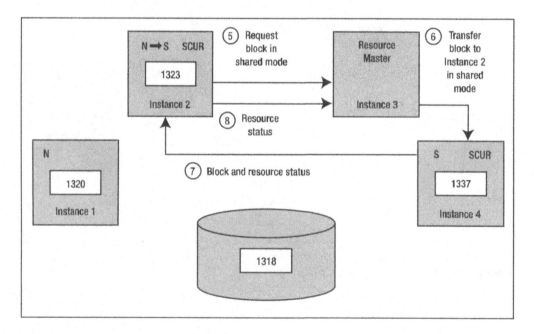

Figure 22-21. *Write-to-read transfer step 8*

Past Images

Recall that a past image is a copy of the block, including any changes, that is retained by the sending instance when a block is transferred to another instance. Past images are only created for write-write transfers, which occur when a block is modified by one instance and the same block then needs to be changed by another instance. Past images are retained for performance reasons, because in certain circumstances, they can reduce recovery time following an instance failure.

You saw in Example 3 that Instance 1 kept a past image copy of the block at SCN 1320 until the current version of the block (SCN 1323) was written back to disk by Instance 4. As all changes are recorded in the redo logs, you may be wondering why it is necessary to retain past images.

Consider the following scenario: Instance A reads a block into cache and then modifies it 1,000 times. Before the block has been written back to disk, Instance B requests the current version of the block to update it further. Instance A transfers the block and Instance B modifies it once. Instance B fails before the block is written back to disk.

If Instance A did not retain a past image copy of the block at the time of transfer to Instance B, then in order to perform recovery for Instance B, it would be necessary to read the block from disk and apply all 1,001 changes. However, if Instance A retained a past image, Instance A could be signaled to write the past image of the block back to disk, and only the redo for the single change made by Instance B would need to be applied.

Disk Writes

Dirty blocks in the buffer cache are written to disk when the instance requires additional buffers to satisfy free buffer requests or when it performs a checkpoint. Write requests can originate from any instance that has a current or past image of a block. The GCS ensures that only the current version of the block is written back to disk. In addition, it checks that any past image versions of the block are purged from the buffer caches of all other instances.

In the following example, the instance holding a past image buffer in null mode requests that Oracle write the buffer to disk.

In Figure 22-22, Instance 4 has an exclusive lock on the current version of the block at SCN 1323. The block is dirty. Instance 1 has a null lock on a past image of the block at SCN 1320. Instance 1 requires the buffer occupied by the past image of the block at SCN 1320. The shared disk currently contains the block at SCN 1318.

Instance 1 sends a message to Instance 3, which is the resource master instance for the block, requesting permission to flush the past image (Figure 22-23).

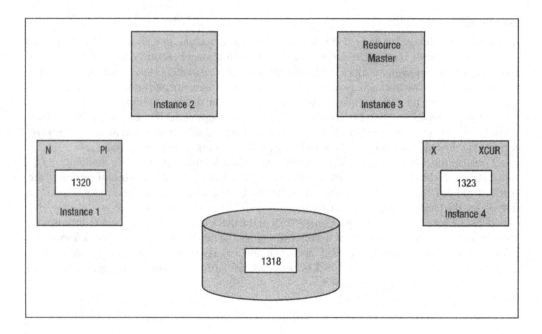

Figure 22-22. *Disk writes initial state*

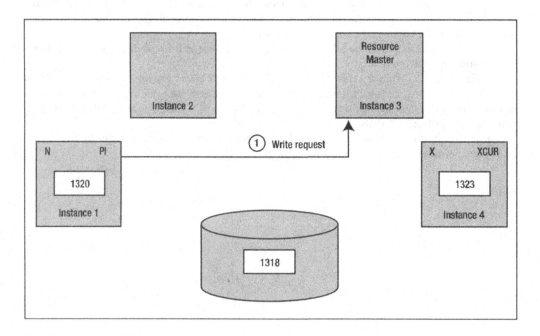

Figure 22-23. *Disk writes step 1*

Instance 3 sends a message to the Instance 4, which is holding the current version of the block, requesting that it write the block to disk (Figure 22-24).

Instance 4 writes the block to disk (Figure 22-25).

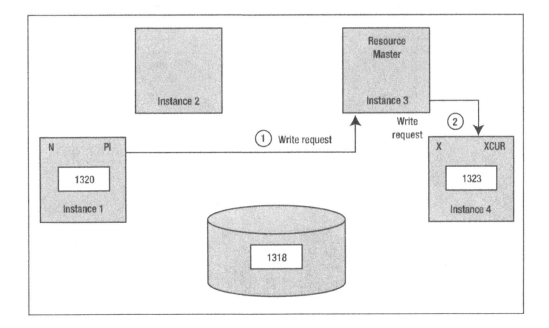

Figure 22-24. *Disk writes step 2*

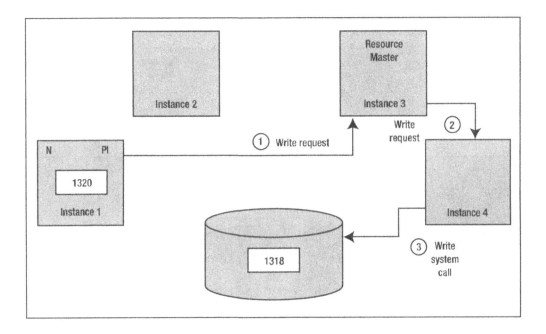

Figure 22-25. *Disk writes step 3*

Instance 4 notifies the resource master, which is Instance 3, that the block has been successfully written to disk (Figure 22-26). The resource role can now become local, as only Instance 1 is holding a copy of the block.

Instance 3 sends a message to Instance 1 requesting that it flush the past image for the block (Figure 22-27). Instance 1 frees the buffer used by the past image and releases the resource.

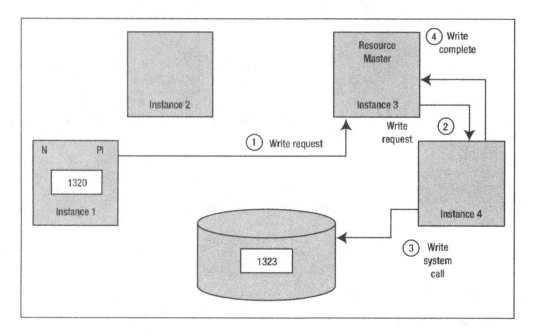

Figure 22-26. *Disk writes step 4*

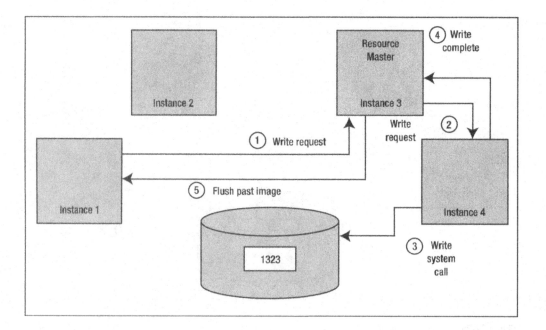

Figure 22-27. *Disk writes step 5*

At this point, if more than one instance was holding a past image of the block, the resource master would signal each instance requesting that the block was flushed.

System Change Numbers (SCNs)

In order to track changes to data blocks, Oracle assigns a numeric identifier to each version of the block. This identifier is effectively a logical time stamp and is known as an SCN. Oracle records the SCN in the redo record header for each set of changes in the redo log. It is also included in both the undo and data block changes.

When a session requests a consistent-read for a block, it specifies the block number and the SCN. If the current version of the block contains changes applied after the requested SCN (i.e., the current version of the block has a higher SCN), the current version will be cloned to a new buffer and undo will be applied to roll back the changes on the data block to the requested SCN.

The SCN is also sometimes called the System Commit Number, because on OLTP systems with short transactions, it appears that a new SCN is issued every time a transaction commits. However, this is not entirely correct; for a long-running transaction, several SCNs may be used during the lifetime of the transaction. In this case, changes written to the redo log for the same transaction will have different SCNs. Therefore, the name System Change Number is more appropriate.

Changes are written to the redo log in SCN order; therefore, if the database needs to be recovered, the redo log files can be scanned sequentially.

In a RAC environment, the SCN is used to order data block change events within each instance and across all instances. When a RAC database is recovered, the SCN is used to synchronize the application of changes recorded in each of the redo logs.

The generation of SCNs in a RAC database is more complex. Conceptually SCNs are generated by a single, central point similar to a sequence in a single-instance database. However, in reality, each instance generates SCNs independently of the other databases. As each instance can generate its own series of SCNs, a busy instance may generate more SCNs than a quiet instance. If this were allowed to happen, synchronizing the redo logs of the two instances during recovery processing would not be possible; SCNs must be regularly synchronized between instances to ensure that all instances are using the same SCN.

Therefore, Oracle maintains the SCN globally. On Linux, by default, the SCN is maintained by GCS using the Lamport SCN generation scheme. This scheme generates SCNs in parallel on all instances. These generated SCNs are piggybacked on all messages passed between instances. If a local instance receives an SCN from a remote instance that is higher than its current SCN, then the SCN of the remote instance is used instead. Therefore, multiple instances can generate SCNs in parallel without additional messaging between the instances.

Note that if the instances are idle, messages will still be exchanged between instances at regular intervals to coordinate the SCN. Each change to the SCN is recorded in the redo log. Therefore, an idle instance will always be performing a small amount of work and generating redo. Consequently, it is more difficult to perform controlled tests in a RAC environment than in single-instance Oracle.

Prior to Oracle 10.2, the Lamport SCN generation scheme was used when the value for the `MAX_COMMIT_PROPAGATION_DELAY` parameter was larger than the default value of 7 seconds. If this parameter was set to a value less than 7, Oracle would use the hardware clock for SCN generation.

In Oracle 10.2 and above, the broadcast on commit scheme is the default. You can verify which SCN generation scheme is in use by checking the alert log. For example, the alert log may contain the following:

```
Picked broadcast on commit scheme to generate SCNs
```

which indicates that the broadcast on commit SCN generation scheme is in use.

In Oracle 10.2 and above, Oracle recommends that the `MAX_COMMIT_PROPAGATION_DELAY` parameter is always set to 0.

Optimizing the Global Cache

In this section, you have seen that the amount of work performed by the cluster in support of the Global Cache Service is highly dependent on the usage of data blocks within the cluster. Although most applications will run on RAC without modification, you can reasonably expect to optimize their performance by partitioning them across the nodes. The benefit of application partitioning is that the aggregate size of the buffer cache across all instances is effectively increased, since fewer duplicate data blocks will be stored within it.

The partitioning option, which has been available since Oracle 8.0, allows you to physically partition tables. The introduction of database services in Oracle 10.1 provides a built-in mechanism that can be used to implement application partitioning. In particular, database services and the partitioning option can be used together to achieve node affinity for each physical partition. Finally, the introduction of dynamic resource remastering at object level allows Oracle to optimize the use of partitioned objects across the cluster by ensuring that they are locally mastered.

The key, therefore, to optimizing the global cache is to design your application in such a way that you minimize the number of blocks that are shared between instances, which will minimize the amount of interconnect traffic and the work performed by remote instances. Other ways to achieve this optimization might include implementing sequences, reverse key indexes, global temporary tables, or smaller block sizes or rebuilding tables with fewer rows per block.

Instance Recovery

In the final section of this chapter, we will briefly describe instance recovery. While it is important that your cluster can survive an instance failure and that the impact on throughput during instance recovery is acceptable to your business, understanding the concepts behind instance recovery is less important than understanding those underlying GCS or GES. This is because instance recovery only has a temporary performance impact, whereas the Global Services can affect your performance at all times.

In RAC, recovery is performed when an instance fails and another Oracle instance detects the failure. If more than one node fails at the same time, all instances will be recovered.

The amount of recovery processing required is proportional to the number of failed nodes and the amount of redo generated on those nodes since the last checkpoint. Following recovery, data blocks become available immediately.

When an instance detects that another instance has failed, the first phase of the recovery is the reconfiguration of the GES. Following this, the GCS resources can be reconfigured. During this phase, all GCS resource requests and write requests are suspended, and the GRD is frozen. However, instances can continue to modify data blocks as long as these blocks are in the local buffer cache and appropriate enqueues are already held.

In the next phase, the redo log file of the failed instance is read to identify all the blocks that may need to be recovered. In parallel, the GCS resources are remastered. This remastering involves redistributing the blocks in the buffer cache of the remaining instances to new resource masters. At the end of this phase, all blocks requiring recovery will have been identified.

In the third phase, buffer space is allocated for recovery and resources are created for all of the blocks requiring recovery. The buffer caches of all remaining instances are searched for past images of blocks that may have been in the buffer cache of the failed instance at the time of failure. If a PI buffer exists for any block, then this buffer is used as a starting point for the recovery of that block.

At this point, all resources and enqueues that will be required for the recovery process have been acquired. Therefore, the GRD can be unfrozen, allowing any data blocks that are not involved in the recovery process to be accessed. The system is now partially available.

In the next phase, each block that has been identified as needing recovery is reconstructed from a combination of the original block on disk, the most recent past image available, and the contents of the redo log of the failed instance. The recovered block is written back to disk, immediately after which the recovery resources are released, so that the block becomes available again. When all blocks have been recovered, the system is fully available again.

A block may be modified by the failed instance but not exist as a past image or a current block in any of the remaining instances. In this case, Oracle uses the redo log files of the failed instance to reconstruct the changes made to the block since the block was last written to disk. The buffer cache is flushed to disk by the database writer process when free buffers are required for new blocks. It is also flushed to disk whenever there is a database checkpoint, which occurs whenever there is a log file switch. Therefore, you only need to recover redo generated since the last log file switch. Consequently, the amount of redo and the amount of time required to apply the redo will be proportional to the size of the redo log file.

You can reduce the amount of time required for recovery by adjusting the mean time to recovery using the FAST_START_MTTR_TARGET parameter, which allows you to specify the maximum amount of time, in seconds, in which you wish the database to perform crash recovery. The FAST_START_MTTR_TARGET adjusts the frequency of checkpoints to limit potential recovery time. This parameter was introduced in Oracle 9.0.1 and replaces the FAST_START_IO_TARGET parameter, which specifies the target number of database blocks to be written in the event of a recovery, and the LOG_CHECKPOINT_INTERVAL parameter, which specifies the frequency of checkpoints in terms of 512-byte redo log blocks.

Summary

This chapter described some of the internal algorithms that are used within a RAC database. While understanding the exact implementation of each algorithm is not essential, having an appreciation of them when designing new systems is highly beneficial.

As you have seen, much of the performance of an Oracle RAC database depends on the application. Therefore, testing and benchmarking your application prior to going into production are vital to determine its effect on GCS and GES. By aiming to minimize the amount of interconnect traffic your application generates, you will maximize both performance and scalability.

CHAPTER 23

■■■

Benchmarking Tools: Hammerora and Swingbench

In Chapter 5 you reviewed the concepts of load testing and the interpretation of officially conducted benchmarks. In subsequent chapters you considered the stages required in installing and configuring all of the components for an optimal RAC on Linux configuration. In this chapter you will apply some of the previously learned concepts to test and verify your RAC installations.

There is a wide variety of commercial tools that can be used for testing Oracle environments. In this chapter we will focus on two tools that are in keeping with the Linux and open source philosophies, in that they are available without license cost and they run natively on the Linux platform.

Hammerora

Hammerora is an open source Oracle load-testing tool. It has been developed with Linux as the primary operating system environment since its inception and focuses on the Oracle database, as opposed to delivering general functionality across a wide number of database platforms.

Hammerora is designed around converting Oracle database trace files into a format that can be replayed against the database with multiple users enabling the construction of complex load-testing scenarios. Hammerora includes an implementation of the TPC-C benchmark specification for both schema creation and testing. This illustrates the type of application simulations that can be achieved. The concepts of the TPC-C benchmark are covered in Chapter 5.

An important requirement for any tool to create bespoke load tests is a powerful and easy-to-use language that enables the creation of custom programs. An additional requirement is an Oracle Call Interface (OCI) that can operate in a multithreaded environment to enable the efficient use of resources in creating multiple Oracle sessions. The use of the OCI means that any level of Oracle functionality can be implemented if desired. The ideal solution for a load-testing tool is the Tcl (Tool Command Language) coupled with the open source Oratcl interface, both available for download from http://www.tcl.tk and http://oratcl.sourceforge.net.

Tcl is a feature-rich interpretive language and therefore does not require you to compile load-testing programs before running them, thus enabling a rapid development turnaround. In addition, as Hammerora is based entirely on the Tcl programming model, it runs the load-test scripts natively without requiring an intermediate proprietary parse and execution engine, enabling a highly efficient solution. Tcl is a mature, robust, and scalable language that is documented extensively and therefore presents a simple yet extremely potent method for constructing the most demanding of load-testing environments. Because Tcl—and the OCI interface for Tcl; Oratcl—is built in the C programming language, it offers the highest level of performance available while maintaining the usability of a scripted interface.

The fact that Hammerora has been built entirely from Tcl can serve to demonstrate the language features available for designing and building load-test scripts. But in the unlikely event that a desired test environment cannot be generated solely from Tcl, you can add functionality using C if you desire, because the Tcl language is designed to be extensible.

A Hammerora installation on Linux is entirely open source—from the application itself to the Oratcl OCI interface, the Tcl/ Tk language, and the Linux operating system, all of which enable modification and customization at any level. The only additional requirement is the Oracle Instant Client to provide the Linux OCI libraries.

It is important to note that as well as being entirely open source, Hammerora is free software released under the GPL (General Public License). The Oracle Instant Client is also completely free of license cost. Both can be installed on freely available releases of Linux software. This presents the opportunity to construct an extensive load-testing infrastructure with no limit on the number of virtual users that can be simulated or the time for which they can be used and with no license fees at any level of the software implementation.

Installation

We advise installing Hammerora on one or more load-generation servers and not directly onto the Oracle database server itself, because, although the Hammerora client processes are extremely lightweight, running both the client and server software simultaneously on the same machine makes it more difficult to isolate and attribute the workloads accountable to each process. Using dedicated systems for each ensures that the server capacity for Oracle is accurately assessed.

When selecting a system for running Hammerora, we advise adopting a common-sense approach to sizing by choosing a server that could ordinarily be used for running the number of client sessions that you wish to simulate. This will depend on the application, workload, and target server capacity.

The Hammerora clients should be Linux-based systems with a thread environment of Native POSIX Thread Library for Linux (NPTL) introduced in 2002, as opposed to LinuxThreads. If using the freely available versions of Red Hat Linux, use version 9 and above or releases of the Fedora Project. For Red Hat Enterprise Linux use versions 3 and above. The client should be configured with an `oracle` user and `dba` group and the same operating system settings as the Oracle RAC database nodes. However, the required disk capacity is significantly lower than that of a database node, as Hammerora only requires a minimum installation of the Oracle Instant Client. If you have the full installation of the Oracle client, or server software such as Oracle Express Edition, you do not need the Instant Client and can proceed to setting the required environment variables.

To install the Instant Client, download the basic software package for Linux x86 from the Oracle Technology Network site at `http://www.oracle.com/technology/tech/oci/instantclient/index.html`. For Hammerora only the basic software is required, but the optional SQL*Plus package may also be desirable for independently testing network connectivity to target database systems.

On the client system, install the basic Instant Client package by unzipping the file into a directory such as `/home/oracle` and this will create a directory such as `instantclient_10_2`. Within this directory create an additional subdirectory called `lib` and move all of the Instant Client files into this subdirectory. Finally, check for the presence of the symbolic link `libclntsh.so` to the client code library. Although present in a standard client and server install, this link is not present in some Instant Client installations and therefore requires creating it manually. To do this, run the following command in the `lib` directory:

```
oracle@load1 lib]$ ln -s libclntsh.so.10.1 libclntsh.so
```

With the Instant Client or full client or server now installed, make sure that the oracle user's ORACLE_HOME and LD_LIBRARY_PATH environment variables are set to their appropriate values. For example

```
[oracle@load1 ~]$ export ORACLE_HOME=/home/oracle/instantclient_10_2
[oracle@load1 ~]$ export LD_LIBRARY_PATH=$ORACLE_HOME/lib
```

If using the Instant Client, it is necessary to configure the TNS_ADMIN environment variable to the full path of the local tnsnames.ora file to ensure successful network connectivity. We recommend setting this to the same directory as the Instant Client ORACLE_HOME. Alternatively, it is possible to locate the network configuration files under ORACLE_HOME/network/admin. If you installed the optional Instant Client SQL* Plus package, it will be possible to connect to the desired target databases at this stage.

If the environment variables are incorrectly set, the Oratcl libraries will fail to initialize, and, by default, Hammerora is configured to not start when this occurs. Oracle also advises that if you use LD_LIBRARY_PATH, the environment variable should contain the location of only one set of client libraries. For example, Oracle 10*g* should not simply be added to the same search path as an existing Oracle 9 client installation.

Once the Oracle client environment has been fully configured, as the oracle user, download the most recent release of the Hammerora software for Linux indicated by the -Linux-x86 extension from http://hammerora.sourceforge.net.

Ensure that the downloaded file has the correct file extension and make the file executable using the chmod command:

```
[oracle@load1 oracle]$ chmod u+x hammerora-Linux-x86
```

■**Note** The Hammerora software has a version-specific number in the executable file name and installed software that is not shown in this and subsequent examples.

Verify that the oracle user has write permissions on the intended installation directory. For this reason we recommend installing in the home directory of the oracle user or the Instant Client ORACLE_HOME directory. Hammerora is entirely self-contained within its installation directory, requiring no external files or libraries apart from the Oracle Instant Client itself, and therefore will not conflict with any system or custom installs of Tcl already present on the system.

The installer is graphical and therefore the oracle user must have permissions to open windows on the display configured in the DISPLAY environment variable. Initiate the install by running the executable hammerora-Linux-x86 as the oracle user.

```
[oracle@load1 oracle]$ ./hammerora-Linux-x86
```

The installer displays an initial confirmation window asking you whether you want to continue with the installation process. Click Yes to proceed to the welcome screen as shown in Figure 23-1.

Figure 23-1. *Hammerora installation welcome*

Click Next to continue past the welcome screen. On the license agreement page review the license information, select the acceptance check box, and click Yes. We strongly recommend that you be familiar with the conditions of the GNU Public License Agreement before proceeding. A copy of the license is included with the software after installation.

Review the Readme Information and click Next. This advises on the requirement of the installation of the Oracle Instant Client for Hammerora.

Select an installation directory and click Next or Browse for an alternative location. This destination should contain the full path and name of the directory to be created. Click Next, and the installer will proceed to extract and copy the installation files to the specified directory.

When the process is complete, click Finish, and optionally choose to start Hammerora immediately. You can also start Hammerora by running the executable `hammerora.tcl` script file in the installation directory:

```
[oracle@load1 hammerora]$ ./hammerora.tcl
```

Finally, if you wish to remove the software you can do so by running the `uninstall` command located in the install directory:

```
[oracle@load1 install]$ ./uninstall
```

At the confirmation select Yes. Hammerora will be completely removed from your system, including the installation directory. Click Finish.

Bespoke Application Load Tests

The power of Hammerora lies in its ability to easily and rapidly build script-based custom benchmarks to simulate a multiple-user scenario of any application that interacts with the Oracle database. In a RAC environment this proves particularly useful in establishing confidence by confirming that when migrating from a single instance environment to a RAC environment the application in question performs and scales as expected.

Hammerora converts Oracle trace files generated by enabling SQL trace event 10046 into the Oratcl format that can be replayed against the database. This event activates SQL statement tracing to include information at a greater level of detail than the standard SQL trace used as input to the TKPROF command-line utility for profiling Oracle sessions.

SQL trace is usually initiated with the command

```
SQL>ALTER SESSION SET SQL_TRACE = TRUE;
```

However, event 10046 can be set with a wide variety of commands, with package-based methods such as DBMS_SUPPORT.START_TRACE or DBMS_MONITOR.SESSION_TRACE_ENABLE, or with an ALTER SESSION command. We discussed trace and diagnostics in significantly greater depth in Chapter 21. In the context of this chapter it is important to note that the 10046 event can be set at levels 1, 4, 8, or 12. Level 1 gives identical functionality to SQL_TRACE, level 4 includes bind variable information, level 8 includes wait information, and level 12 gives binds and waits. For replaying session activity with Hammerora, level 4 is the most applicable setting. This can be enabled directly for a session with the following example:

```
SQL> ALTER SESSION SET EVENTS '10046 trace name context forever, level 4';
```

Once enabled the tracing can be disabled as follows:

```
SQL> ALTER SESSION SET EVENTS '10046 trace name context off';
```

It is important to note that with tracing there will always be an impact on performance, so tracing should only be enabled to capture session information and not during a performance test itself.

When the tracing activity is completed, the event results in the production of a trace file in the directory specified by the Oracle parameter USER_DUMP_DEST on the database server and not on the client. The file will be identifiable by the name ora_SPID.trc where SPID is the Linux process identifier of the client process. In a shared server environment the activities of a single user may be distributed across numerous trace files and it will therefore be necessary to use the trcsess command-line utility to extract the information from a single-client session into one raw trace file before using it as input to Hammerora.

As well as initiating a trace using DBMS_SUPPORT or DBMS_MONITOR and from within a session, for the purposes of testing you may also want to initiate a trace automatically from the point in time when a user connects to the database. The most appropriate method for doing this is to use a trigger, such as in the following example created as the SYS user with SYSDBA privileges to trace the activities of the SH user from the Oracle sample schemas:

```
create or replace trigger trace_trigger
after logon on database
begin
if ( user = 'SH' ) then
execute immediate
'alter session set events ''10046 trace name context forever, level 4''';
end if;
end;
/
```

The trigger can be enabled or disabled depending on the desire to generate trace information. To produce valid results it is important to remember to make sure that the trigger is disabled before running any multiple-user performance tests.

Creating a Trace File

To illustrate an application simulation scenario we will use an example based on the SH user of the default Oracle sample schemas. The most straightforward method to create the sample schemas is to select the check box on the Database Content page of a DBCA-based database creation.

For brevity we will focus the example on simulating a single data warehouse type query by the SH user using SQL*Plus. In practice, an application is most likely to demonstrate a greater level of complexity, and Hammerora is able to reproduce all DML and DDL operations from any application that interacts with the Oracle database. Examples of greater complexity are the stored procedures of the TPC-C type workload detailed later in this chapter.

The single SQL statement used is an example of the use of composite columns within a GROUP BY expression as part of a ROLLUP list. The statement is given a period of time available within the SALES table and a list of product names from the PRODUCTS table. It then returns multiple levels of subtotals for the sales channels and product IDs and a grand total for each. As a composite column, CHANNEL_ID and PROD_ID are treated as a single item for groupings.

```
SELECT time_id, channel_id, prod_id, ROUND (SUM(amount_sold)) AS TOTAL FROM SALES
WHERE time_id BETWEEN '01-JAN-98' AND '31-JAN-98'
AND prod_id IN
(SELECT prod_id FROM products WHERE prod_name IN
('5MP Telephoto Digital Camera','17" LCD w/built-in HDTV Tuner',➡
'Envoy 256MB - 40GB','Y Box','Mini DV Camcorder with 3.5" Swivel LCD'))
GROUP BY ROLLUP (time_id, (channel_id, prod_id));
```

As we are illustrating an application simulation we will use bind variables for the variables we want to change in the SQL statement and include the level 4 trace to generate the trace file for the SQL statement only. The following listing can be executed at the SQL*Plus prompt.

```
-- Listing hoex1.sql
variable t_id1 char(9);
execute :t_id1 := '01-JAN-98';
variable t_id2 char(9);
execute :t_id2 := '31-JAN-98';
variable pname1 varchar2(50);
execute :pname1 := '5MP Telephoto Digital Camera';
variable pname2 varchar2(50);
execute :pname2 := '17" LCD w/built-in HDTV Tuner';
variable pname3 varchar2(50);
execute :pname3 := 'Envoy 256MB - 40GB';
variable pname4 varchar2(50);
execute :pname4 := 'Y Box';
variable pname5 varchar2(50);
execute :pname5 := 'Mini DV Camcorder with 3.5" Swivel LCD';
ALTER SESSION SET EVENTS '10046 trace name context forever, level 4';
SELECT time_id, channel_id, prod_id, ROUND (SUM(amount_sold)) AS TOTAL FROM SALES
WHERE time_id BETWEEN TO_DATE(:t_id1) AND TO_DATE(:t_id2)
AND prod_id IN
(SELECT prod_id FROM products WHERE prod_name IN
(:pname1,:pname2,:pname3,:pname4,:pname5))
GROUP BY ROLLUP (time_id, (channel_id, prod_id));
ALTER SESSION SET EVENTS '10046 trace name context off';
```

Executing the script returns the following output:

```
SQL> @hoex1.sql

PL/SQL procedure successfully completed.

PL/SQL procedure successfully completed.

PL/SQL procedure successfully completed.

PL/SQL procedure successfully completed.

PL/SQL procedure successfully completed.
```

```
PL/SQL procedure successfully completed.

PL/SQL procedure successfully completed.

Session altered.

TIME_ID    CHANNEL_ID    PROD_ID       TOTAL
---------  -----------  ----------  ----------
02-JAN-98            3          15        2028
02-JAN-98            4          15        1014
02-JAN-98                                 3042
03-JAN-98            2          14        3374
03-JAN-98            2          15        2008
03-JAN-98            3          14        6654
03-JAN-98            3          15        4000
03-JAN-98            4          14        3327
03-JAN-98            4          15        3000
03-JAN-98                                22362
... (OUTPUT TRUNCATED)
31-JAN-98            3          13        2412
31-JAN-98                                 2412
                                        781918

120 rows selected.
```

This event produces the expected trace file in the USER_DUMP_DEST directory on the database server.

Converting the Trace File

Copy the trace file to the Hammerora client machine and load it into Hammerora by using the menu option File ➤ Open or the Open an Existing File Button.

The Open File dialog window has entries for the directory and a filter for the file type. By default the trace file extension is *.trc. Highlight the name of the recently created trace file and click OK to load the file.

The following is an excerpt from the generated trace file:

```
PARSING IN CURSOR #1 len=68 dep=0 uid=47 oct=42 lid=47 tim=1085788356279877
hv=3708311020 ad='556d8034'
ALTER SESSION SET EVENTS '10046 trace name context forever, level 4'
END OF STMT
EXEC #1:c=0,e=189,p=0,cr=0,cu=0,mis=0,r=0,dep=0,og=1,tim=1085788356279860
=====================
PARSING IN CURSOR #2 len=295 dep=0 uid=47 oct=3 lid=47
tim=1085788356317802 hv=3658952029 ad='556e4b88'
SELECT time_id, channel_id, prod_id, ROUND (SUM(amount_sold)) AS TOTAL FROM SALES
WHERE time_id BETWEEN TO_DATE(:t_id1) AND TO_DATE(:t_id2)
AND prod_id IN
(SELECT prod_id FROM products WHERE prod_name IN
(:pname1,:pname2,:pname3,:pname4,:pname5))
GROUP BY ROLLUP (time_id, (channel_id, prod_id))
END OF STMT
PARSE #2:c=0,e=186,p=0,cr=0,cu=0,mis=0,r=0,dep=0,og=1,tim=1085788356317788
BINDS #2:
 bind 0: dty=96 mxl=32(09) mal=00 scl=00 pre=00 oacflg=03 oacfl2=0010
size=704 offset=0
   bfp=40c13ef0 bln=32 avl=09 flg=05
    value="01-JAN-98"
```

```
bind 1: dty=96 mxl=32(09) mal=00 scl=00 pre=00 oacflg=03 oacfl2=0010
size=0 offset=32
   bfp=40c13f10 bln=32 avl=09 flg=01
   value="31-JAN-98"
 bind 2: dty=1 mxl=128(50) mal=00 scl=00 pre=00 oacflg=03 oacfl2=0010
size=0 offset=64
   bfp=40c13f30 bln=128 avl=28 flg=01
   value="5MP Telephoto Digital Camera"
```

Click the Convert Oracle Trace File to Oratcl button. The trace file is converted to Tcl that will replay the Oracle session as shown in the following example:

```
#!/usr/local/bin/tclsh8.4
package require Oratcl
####UPDATE THE CONNECT STRING BELOW###
#set connect user/password@rac1
set lda [oralogon $connect]
set curn1 [oraopen $lda ]
set sql1 "ALTER SESSION SET EVENTS '10046 trace name context forever, level 4' "
orasql $curn1 $sql1
set curn2 [oraopen $lda ]
set sql2 "SELECT time_id, channel_id, prod_id, ROUND➥
(SUM(amount_sold)) AS TOTAL FROM SALES WHERE time_id BETWEEN➥
TO_DATE(:t_id1) AND TO_DATE(:t_id2) AND prod_id IN ➥
(SELECT prod_id FROM products WHERE prod_name IN ➥
(:pname1,:pname2,:pname3,:pname4,:pname5)) ➥
GROUP BY ROLLUP (time_id, (channel_id, prod_id)) "
orasql $curn2 $sql2 -parseonly
orabindexec $curn2 :pname3 {Envoy 256MB - 40GB} :pname4 {Y Box} :t_id1➥
{01-JAN-98} :pname5 {Mini DV Camcorder with 3.5" Swivel LCD} :pname1➥
{5MP Telephoto Digital Camera} :t_id2 {31-JAN-98} :pname2 {17" LCD➥
w/built-in HDTV Tuner}
set row [orafetch $curn2 -datavariable output ]
while { [ oramsg  $curn2 ] == 0 } {
puts $output
set row [orafetch  $curn2 -datavariable output ]
}
oraclose $curn1
set curn1 [oraopen $lda ]
set sql1 "ALTER SESSION SET EVENTS '10046 trace name context off' "
orasql $curn1 $sql1
oraclose $curn1
oralogoff $lda
```

It is important to be aware that the trace file does not record the username or the password of the traced session, so this must be inserted manually before running the generated script.

At the line specifying the connect string, such as

```
#set connect user/password@rac1
```

remove the comment and enter the correct username and password. The instance name will be set to the instance name from where the trace file was taken.

Testing the Converted Trace File

To test the script, create and run a single virtual user with output. Select Virtual Users ➤ Vuser
Options from the menu to show the Virtual User Options window, shown in Figure 23-2.

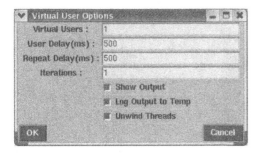

Figure 23-2. *Virtual User Options*

The first option is the number of virtual users to create. For testing, this should be left at the
default value of 1. When running a multiuser load test this value can be changed to any positive
numerical value. There is no set limit for the number of virtual users that can be created. However
you should consider the workload to be run and the number of Oracle users that would ordinarily be
expected to be run on the client simultaneously. In addition, Linux limits the stack size available to
an individual process. For example, on a standard Red Hat Linux installation, depending on the total
amount of memory available to the system, it limits the number of virtual users per Hammerora session to between 250 and 270. This soft limit can be increased with the command ulimit -s.

The User Delay(ms) value specifies the time in milliseconds between each user initiating the
script. The minimum value is 0.5 second (500 milliseconds). This value enables a variable and pro-
gressive ramping up of the workload, preventing a login storm where a large number of users are
attempting to connect to the target system at exactly the same time. The Repeat Delay(ms) is the
time for which each user will pause once a script is complete before reexecuting the next iteration of
the script. The Iterations value sets the total number of times the script is executed for each user.

The Show Output check box creates an output window with a grid displaying the most recent
five lines of output for each user. The window scrolls to display the output of all of the users configured. As with any scrolling text, displaying large volumes of output will have an impact on performance
compared to a non-output configuration.

If Show Output is selected, the option to Log Output to Temp also becomes available. This option
records all of the text written to the output window to a dedicated log file named hammerora.log
located in the directory specified by one of the environment variables $TMP, $TMPDIR, or $TEMP, or the
default directory /tmp. Every line written to the log file is prefixed by the thread ID of the writing virtual user, and the output is buffered in memory to reduce the impact on performance of continual
writes to disk. Finally, the Unwind Threads check box, which is selected by default, ensures that when
the threads are closed they are gracefully unwound as opposed to calling a direct thread exit call. In
both cases, if a thread is in a running state, and an unwind or exit command is received, it will not
be initiated until all of the previous commands in the script have completed.

Clicking OK will save the Virtual User Options selected. Clicking the Create Virtual Users button
creates the configured virtual users. The example shown in Figure 23-3 shows a single virtual user with
the thread ID and the idle status represented by a clock icon displayed in a table-based list in the
bottom pane. The Create button changes to Destroy Virtual Users, which will terminate the virtual
user threads by unwinding or exiting, depending on the configuration option selected. Attempting
to recreate the threads before the exit or unwind command has been received will fail until the previous running script has been completed.

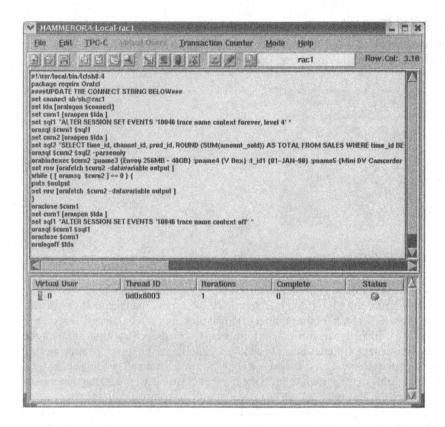

Figure 23-3. *A single virtual user*

Keep in mind that there is no way to interrupt a running Tcl thread before it has completed its current actions, and long-running scripts will run to completion.

After the virtual user threads have been created, the Virtual Users menu is grayed out, preventing the modification of any of the options without destroying and recreating them. At this point, with the virtual user thread created and sitting idle, clicking the hammer icon button, which is the Run Hammerora Loadtest button, asynchronously posts the Tcl script in the main window to the virtual user. It is configured with the status changed accordingly to illustrate the activity. A successful completion of the script is signified with a green tick in the status column. An error is signified by a red cross with the error message and corresponding thread ID detailed in the console window.

In the example, if the Log Output to Temp option has been selected, the Hammerora log file appears as follows:

```
Hammerora Log @ Sat Mar 26 14:51:30 GMT 2005
+-+-+-+-+-+-+-+-+-+-+-+-+-+-+-+-+-+-+-+-+-+-+-
tid0x8003:02-JAN-98 3 15 2028
tid0x8003:02-JAN-98 4 15 1014
tid0x8003:02-JAN-98 0 0 3042
tid0x8003:03-JAN-98 2 14 3374
tid0x8003:03-JAN-98 2 15 2008
tid0x8003:03-JAN-98 3 14 6654
tid0x8003:03-JAN-98 3 15 4000
tid0x8003:03-JAN-98 4 14 3327
tid0x8003:03-JAN-98 4 15 3000
tid0x8003:03-JAN-98 0 0 22362
```

The log file is useful for recording the output produced by all of the virtual users for analysis purposes.

The tested Tcl script is now in the simplest format for replaying a session with multiple users. Because this example is based on a SELECT statement you can replay the session simultaneously without error. However, it is important to be aware that when using DML, errors are most likely to result from replaying the unmodified output from a session. For example, when attempting to replay an identical INSERT or UPDATE statement, errors may occur due to constraint violations. This happens because you are attempting to insert or delete data that has already been inserted or deleted at the time that the session was traced.

Building a Load Test from a Converted Trace File

The most appropriate method for building a meaningful load-testing environment is to use the converted trace file as a base for enhancing the test with the Tcl language to generate a more complex script to vary the activities of the virtual users. Hammerora strictly adheres to the syntax of the Tcl language. Everything that can be used within a Tcl multithreaded environment can be used within Hammerora. For example, the opening and reading of the same file within the threads is entirely permissible; but writing to the same file is ill advised.

■ **Note** The Tcl command named puts has been redefined in Hammerora so that all output is redirected to the corresponding virtual user's output window. To write to a file opened by a virtual user, it is necessary to use the command _puts to which the original puts command has been renamed.

When building a load-testing script, the Test Tcl Code button illustrated by the monitor icon is useful for rapidly executing the script directly in a slave interpreter for syntax testing purposes. When the tested script has run to completion, the interpreter and window can be closed by clicking the same button, which is now called Stop Running Code. Due to the strict adherence to the standard Tcl syntax, it is also possible to run the script directly at the Tcl shell command line for testing purposes. While creating a load-testing script, the File ➤ Save menu option or Save Current File button can be used to save the Tcl script for reloading at a later point.

In this example, you want to measure the response time of the data warehousing query as you scale the number of users running the query against different time periods and different data sets by performing the following actions:

1. Take the query from the converted trace file and parse it.

2. Open a colon-separated file containing the input data to use for the query.

3. Read the data into a buffer and close the file.

The data is then iterated line-by-line and placed in the Tcl variables corresponding to bind variables to use in the query. The query is executed for every line of the input file using these bind variables, and the Tcl time command is used to record the time for execution in microseconds. The time is measured in elapsed time, not CPU time, and is saved for each iteration in the microsecs list. When all of the executions are complete, close the Oracle session, examine the execution times, and subsequently report on the maximum, total, and average user response times of the query. This example takes the form of the following listing:

```
#!/usr/local/bin/tclsh8.4
package require Oratcl
####UPDATE THE CONNECT STRING BELOW###
set connect sh/sh@rac
set lda [oralogon $connect]
```

```
set curn1 [oraopen $lda]
set sql1 "SELECT time_id, channel_id, prod_id, ROUND➥
(SUM(amount_sold)) AS TOTAL FROM SALES WHERE time_id BETWEEN➥
TO_DATE(:t_id1) AND TO_DATE(:t_id2) AND prod_id IN➥
(SELECT prod_id FROM products WHERE prod_name IN➥
(:pname1,:pname2,:pname3,:pname4,:pname5))➥
 GROUP BY ROLLUP (time_id, (channel_id, prod_id)) "
orasql $curn1 $sql1 -parseonly
set fd [ open /home/oracle/input1.txt r ]
set flbuff [read $fd]
close $fd
set filelist [split $flbuff "\n"]
unset flbuff
foreach line $filelist {
set params [ split [ regsub -all {(\ \ )} $line {} ] ":" ]
set startdate [ string trim [ lindex $params 0 ] ]
set enddate [ string trim [ lindex $params 1 ] ]
set pname1 [ string trim [ lindex $params 2] ]
set pname2 [ string trim [ lindex $params 3] ]
set pname3 [ string trim [ lindex $params 4 ] ]
set pname4 [ string trim [ lindex $params 5 ] ]
set pname5 [ string trim [ lindex $params 6 ] ]
set value [ time { orabindexec $curn1 :t_id1 $startdate :t_id2➥
$enddate :pname1 $pname1 :pname2 $pname2 :pname3 $pname3 :pname4➥
$pname4 :pname5 $pname5
set row [orafetch $curn1 -datavariable output ]
while { [ oramsg  $curn1 ] == 0 } {
set row [orafetch  $curn1 -datavariable output ] } } ]
regexp {([0-9]+)} $value all tim
lappend microsecs $tim
                        }
oraclose $curn1
oralogoff $lda
set max 0
foreach val $microsecs {
if { $val > $max } { set max $val } }
                        }
puts "Maximum user response time was $max microseconds"
set sum 0
foreach val $microsecs {
set sum [ expr { $sum+$val } ]
                        }
puts "Total user response time was $sum microseconds"
set N [ expr { [ llength $microsecs ] + 1 } ]
set average [ expr { $sum/$N } ]
puts "Average response time was $average microseconds"
```

A sample of the input data file for the year 2000 is as follows:

```
01-JAN-00:31-JAN-00:5MP Telephoto Digital Camera:17" LCD w/built-in
HDTV Tuner:Envoy 256MB - 40GB:Y Box:Mini DV Camcorder with 3.5" Swivel
LCD
01-FEB-00:29-FEB-00:Envoy Ambassador:Laptop carrying case:Home Theatre
Package with DVD-Audio/Video Play:18" Flat Panel Graphics
Monitor:Envoy External Keyboard
01-MAR-00:31-MAR-00:External 101-key keyboard:PCMCIA modem/fax 28800
baud:SIMM- 8MB PCMCIAII card:SIMM- 16MB PCMCIAII card:Multimedia
speakers- 3" cones
```

```
01-APR-00:30-APR-00:Unix/Windows 1-user pack:8.3 Minitower
Speaker:Mouse Pad:1.44MB External 3.5" Diskette:Multimedia speakers-
5" cones
01-MAY-00:31-MAY-00:PCMCIA modem/fax 19200 baud:External 6X CD-
ROM:External 8X CD-ROM:Envoy External 6X CD-ROM:Envoy External 8X CD-
ROM
01-JUN-00:30-JUN-00:Internal 6X CD-ROM:Internal 8X CD-ROM:O/S
Documentation Set - English:O/S Documentation Set - German:O/S
Documentation Set - French:O/S Documentation Set - Spanish
01-JUL-00:31-JUL-00:O/S Documentation Set - Italian:O/S Documentation
Set - Kanji:Standard Mouse:Deluxe Mouse:Keyboard Wrist Rest:CD-R Mini
Discs
01-AUG-00:31-AUG-00:Music CD-R:CD-RW, High Speed, Pack of 10:CD-RW,
High Speed Pack of 5:CD-R, Professional Grade, Pack of 10:OraMusic CD-
R, Pack of 10
```

It is now possible to conduct an initial load test by creating the desired number of users within the options defined in the Virtual User Options window, selecting the Show Output check box, and clicking the Run Hammerora Loadtest button. Each user logs into the target Oracle database and runs the script independently with output such as the following reported for every user:

```
Maximum user response time was 22551 microseconds
Total user response time was 208660 microseconds
Average response time was 14904 microseconds
```

This output can be seen in the Virtual User Output window shown in Figure 23-4.

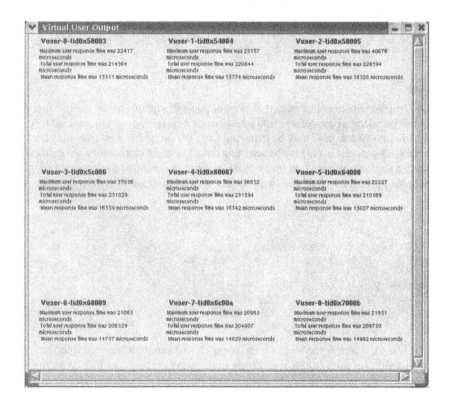

Figure 23-4. *Virtual User Output*

This framework can be used for conducting load-test scenarios, such as varying the number of users and observing the response times; comparing the results of the same application on different hardware; or analyzing the effects of modifying Oracle parameters for tuning. In total, it enables the simulation of how an application will be expected to behave once it is being run simultaneously by a production-level user base.

Randomized Workloads

For illustrative purposes the example is relatively simple with all of the users running the same queries sequentially. In practice, the use of standard techniques will often be used to ensure the most realistic workload. The most common of these is randomization of the workload where a simple random-number procedure, such as the following, can provide the foundation. This procedure accepts a positive minimum and maximum value up to 30,000 and returns a random value between these values inclusively.

```
proc RandomNumber { min max } {
    set maxFactor [expr [expr $max + 1] - $min]
    set value [expr int([expr rand() * 300000])]
    set value [expr [expr $value % $maxFactor] + $min]
return $value
}
```

This can then be used to vary the workload for each user, such as randomly selecting from a list of the query or stored procedure to run, or, in this example, randomly selecting the input data file from a list of files to ensure users have different working data sets.

```
set filelist [ list /home/oracle/input1.txt /home/oracle/input2.txt➥
/home/oracle/input3.txt /home/oracle/input4.txt /home/oracle/input5.txt ]
set choice [ RandomNumber 0 [ expr $ll - 1 ] ]
set fc [ lindex $filelist $choice ]
set fd [ open $fc r ]
```

Selective Workloads

There are times when instead of using randomized workloads you will want to specify the number of virtual users who will be taking a particular action by executing a certain portion of the load test script. For example, the first virtual user may be inserting data, the second virtual user may be deleting, while the remaining virtual users may be selecting data. The most straightforward method of implementing such a scenario is based on finding the position of the individual virtual user's thread identifier from the ordered list of all thread identifiers, which is accessible to all of the users, as in this example:

```
set mythread [thread::id]
set allthreads [split [thread::names]]
set totalvirtualusers [expr [llength $allthreads] - 1]
set myposition [expr $totalvirtualusers - [lsearch -exact $allthreads $mythread]]
switch $myposition {
1 { puts "I am the first virtual user, I'll be inserting" }
2 { puts "I am the second virtual user, I'll be deleting" }
default { puts "I am a default virtual user, I'll be selecting" }
}
```

An additional feature for selective workloads is the use of shared variables. For example, one virtual user may set the value of the variable warehouse in the array virtualuser to 10 with the tsv::set command:

```
tsv::set virtualuser warehouse 1
```

Another virtual user may then retrieve the value of this variable with the `tsv::get` command:

```
tsv::get  virtualuser warehouse
```

All commands on shared variables are atomic and therefore the variable remains locked until the command has completed in its entirety. If another thread attempts to access the shared variable while another command is in progress it will wait until the prior operation is complete. This implicit locking makes thread-shared variables exceptionally easy to use for communication between virtual users, compared to other languages where explicit mutex (mutual exclusion) locking is required in a multithreaded environment.

Script Execution Timings

It is important to remember that Hammerora has been built on the Tcl language primarily to leverage its functionality as a lightweight, interpretive command language for building load-testing scenarios, and therefore any commands within the Tcl language can be used within Hammerora. For example, it is possible to report the entire timed duration of a script using simple Tcl commands such as the following:

```
set start [ clock seconds ]
...
set end [ clock seconds ]
set wall [ expr $end - $start ]
puts "Wall time elapsed was $start to $end = $wall seconds"
```

The catch Command

One individual Tcl command that is particularly useful and merits attention is the `catch` command that can be used to catch any errors that occur within Oratcl and report the underlying Oracle error message. Wrapping an Oratcl command will take the following form where the `$curn1` variable represents the cursor under which the statement is running:

```
if {[ catch { ... } message] } {
puts $message
puts [ oramsg $curn1 all ]
}
```

The following shows the simplest example of the use of the `catch` command. The initial code shows the user SH opening a cursor and executing the command SELECT user FROM dual before closing the cursor and logging off. For brevity, the output of the command is not fetched. However, in this example, fetching the output would report back the username SH:

```
set connect sh/sh@rac1;
set lda [oralogon $connect]
set curn1 [oraopen $lda ]
set sql1 "SELECT user FROM dual"
orasql $curn1 $sql1
oraclose $curn1
oralogoff $lda
```

When running this script as expected, you get no errors and no output with the script running successfully to completion. However, consider the situation where there is a typing error in the SQL statement:

```
set sql1 "ELECT user FROM dual"
```

When this is run in a user thread, the thread execution fails and the console reports the following message:

```
Error in Thread tid0xc003 - orasql: SQL execution failed.
```

Adding a catch statement now takes the script to the following form:

```
set connect sh/sh@rac1
set lda [oralogon $connect]
set curn1 [oraopen $lda ]
set sql1 "ELECT user FROM dual"
if {[catch { orasql $curn1 $sql1 } message]} {
puts "SQL statement failed: $sql1 : $message"
puts [ oramsg $curn1 all ]
}
oraclose $curn1
oralogoff $lda
```

Rerunning the script results in a successful execution since the error is caught; the user sees the following output:

```
SQL statement failed: elect user from dual : orasql: SQL execution failed.
{900 ORA-00900: invalid SQL statement 0 0 0 0}
```

The fact that you now know that the error was due to an ORA-00900 makes diagnosis and resolution a great deal more straightforward. Even if you want the script to fail, when an error is encountered we recommend using the Tcl error command to manually raise the error with a customized error message.

The exit Command

An additional Tcl command briefly worth highlighting is the exit command. Hammerora is based on a Tcl-threads programming model that defines that the exit command called within any individual thread will exit the entire application, not just the individual thread in question. In Hammerora this means that any virtual user calling exit is requesting Hammerora to exit at the top level. This is unlikely to be the desired action and is therefore best avoided.

Since the programming constructs within Hammerora are standard Tcl, we will not elaborate further on the feature set of the language and, instead, for reference to developing Hammerora load tests, we advise consulting the documentation for Oratcl in conjunction with any guide to the Tcl programming language.

TPC-C Simulation

To illustrate the potential of Hammerora for designing and delivering load tests to custom specifications, look at the implementation of the database portion of the TPC-C benchmark specification built into Hammerora. It can be run in any Oracle database environment without the costly infrastructure or additional third-party software required for the officially sanctioned tests. This is possible since the TPC distributes its benchmark specifications to the public at no charge, and therefore presents a fully documented application that has been independently and scientifically designed from the ground up to create an accurate and repeatable workload on any database. The TPC-C benchmark has therefore not been designed to be particularly favorable or unfavorable to Oracle or an Oracle RAC environment. Instead it gives us a good, independent OLTP (online transaction processing) workload. The Hammerora implementation is based on "Appendix A: SAMPLE PROGRAMS" detailed in the TPC-C specification.

The repeatability aspect is the most crucial component in this form of generic benchmark. It signifies that the same workload can be run and re-run and be expected to achieve the same results and the same transaction profile. This is where the Hammerora implementation of TPC-C can prove particularly useful. It enables any Oracle DBA to quickly and easily generate a workload that can be used to compare and contrast the various hardware and software components within the stack for a generic transactional workload. Coupled with the ability to analyze the Oracle statistical data, to identify the bottleneck in performance, and ensure that the component being modified will actually have an impact on performance, it enables the DBA to answer questions such as

What processors and storage platforms deliver the best throughput at different levels of system load?

What are the measurable effects from setting different Oracle parameters or reorganizing tables?

How does RAC scale on my system when increasing the workload for a standard application compared to a single instance configuration?

It should always be remembered, however, that no generic application can ever fully indicate how a different application is expected to perform, and the ultimate test can only be done for an individual application using that application itself with its full dataset.

It is important to note that wherever possible the SQL for the TPC-C application has been copied directly from the TPC-C specification appendix and not optimized in any way. The reason for this is to achieve our aim of a repeatable workload that will produce consistent transaction levels. In contrast, the aim is explicitly not the self-defeating one of tuning the application to achieve the highest transaction rate possible. Instead, the application is taken as a given factor to assess the impact of modifying the components of the stack external to it. In addition, the TPC-C test is constructed from standard Oracle tables and indexes compatible with any version of Oracle. For this reason, when comparing the different releases of Oracle, you should always research whether the impact of new features within a release could make an appreciable difference. For example, within Oracle 10*g* the correct use of sorted hash clusters would considerably improve the performance of the application at the expense of rendering it incompatible with earlier releases of Oracle. The emphasis is therefore firmly on a generic usage.

The only modifications to the SQL derived from the example given in the TPC-C specification appendix were to enable compatibility with a PL/SQL implementation of the stored procedures and to correct the handful of discrepancies discovered in the sample programs. Wherever this has occurred, the textual specifications have prevailed.

Interpreting Transactions

It cannot be stressed strongly enough that the Hammerora implementation of the TPC-C benchmark sample programs is not a full implementation of a TPC-C benchmark. The Hammerora implementation is based upon the specification appendix examples that may not adhere to all of the requirements of the benchmark. In addition, within the examples it is clearly stated that only the basic functionality of the TPC-C transactions themselves is supplied. All the other mandatory components for an official TPC-C benchmark, such as terminal I/O operations and miscellaneous functions, have been omitted from the examples. On the other hand, using this database portion of the benchmark only provides an acceptable compromise for implementing an intelligently designed database workload without the overhead, complexity, and cost of putting into practice the additional components that would limit the ease in which the benchmark could be run in any Oracle environment.

For the reasons given previously, the transaction rates derived from a Hammerora load test can in no way whatsoever be compared with the tpmC rates derived from an official TPC-C benchmark. It is of vital importance that no confusion occurs in interpreting these transaction rates. As you have seen in Chapter 5 the official tpmC rates define the business transaction rate of the number of new orders recorded per minute while the application is also processing the other transactions. For Hammerora, you are recording the Oracle transaction rate as the total number of user commits and rollbacks per minute processed by every statement in the application. In a RAC environment this can be derived by executing the following statement and observing the delta value between subsequent executions:

```
SQL> SELECT SUM(value) FROM gv$sysstat WHERE name = 'user commits'➥
OR name = 'user rollbacks'
```

Note The view v$sysmetric also contains a precalculated transaction rate metric under the METRIC_NAME of User Transaction Per Sec.

Using this technique for observing the commit rate it should be clear that the values derived are valid for only comparing one run of the TPC-C application with another run of exactly the same unmodified application. It is extremely simple to modify the application to make it commit more frequently and artificially raise the recorded Oracle transaction rate. The ultimate result of this, however, would most likely be to reduce the business transaction rate of the overall number of new orders recorded. You can therefore only use the Oracle transaction rate as a guide to performance when the application remains unchanged. For the same reason, the transaction rates recorded can in no way be used comparatively with the performance of a non-Oracle database or with another application. The transaction rates you derive are valid only in comparing one run of the Hammerora TPC-C load test on Oracle with another run of exactly the same application.

Divulging Test Results

It is extremely important to note that when you purchased and agreed to your Oracle license or downloaded a development license it included the following clause:

You may not disclose results of any program benchmark tests without our prior consent.

In other words, any test results you derive from a Hammerora TPC-C load test are entirely for your own use and not for wider dissemination at the penalty of violating your Oracle license. This is an entirely sensible and practical standpoint. The Hammerora TPC-C tests are highly CPU-, memory-, and I/O-dependant, and it is unlikely, unless running with the highest specification hardware and a significantly large number of created warehouses, that you will achieve transaction rates remotely comparable to the officially sanctioned tests. Therefore, the only results that can be used as an indication of Oracle TPC-C results remain the officially published benchmarks on the TPC web site.

With the understanding of what you can infer from a Hammerora TPC-C test and, just as importantly, what you cannot, the following presents a step-by-step guide to preparing and running a Hammerora TPC-C load test scenario in a RAC environment.

TPC-C Test Hardware and Software Considerations

The first step is to decide on the hardware and software configuration for the test. As is the case when using a custom load test, for both a single instance and a RAC environment to achieve the most consistent result, it is advisable that you run your Oracle database on one set of servers and your Hammerora load-test clients from another, with an equal number of each as a starting point.

An ideal load-test client candidate is a server, such as a dual-processor class machine, driving a database such as a quad-processor database server. Again, common sense can provide the best guidance for assessing whether the load-test client would be expected to support the same number of real users in a production type scenario. The client does not have to be using the same Linux operating system release as the database server.

In addition to selecting the hardware configuration, it is necessary to decide on a testing strategy before software configuration begins. With the Hammerora TPC-C load test, this usually takes the form of a variation on one of two general scenarios. The first of these is to run the application in a form as close as possible to a genuine TPC-C test. This utilizes keying and thinking time for the virtual users and requires a significantly large number of virtual users to be created to drive the RAC server environment close to capacity.

This is the preferred scenario for mimicking the transaction profile of a real-world system with a large number of users making infrequent transactions with pauses for keying and thinking time in between transactions. This maintains a large number of connections and therefore tests the memory and process handling capability at a hardware and software level, similar to what would be experienced with a production system. The disadvantage of this approach is that, often in a testing environment, this requires significantly more load-test servers to be available than a one-to-one mapping with the database servers. Therefore this is a desirable but not necessarily achievable method for practical load testing.

A popular alternative is to step further away from the TPC-C specification and eliminate the keying and thinking time taken by the virtual users. When doing this it should not be underestimated how dramatically lower the number of virtual users required to drive the target RAC system to 100% CPU utilization will be when compared to a keying and thinking time configuration. A general guideline is to start with a number of virtual users between two to four times the number of CPU cores on the database servers. This second scenario is often used in making hardware comparisons for achieving maximum sustainable throughput.

On the Oracle RAC cluster, make sure there is an Oracle database configured to your specifications that you are going to install your TPC-C schema in and that you can connect to this through TNS from the Hammerora client. Also, make sure that the DBMS_RANDOM package has been installed in the database. This can be done manually by running the script $ORACLE_HOME/rdbms/admin/catoctk as the SYS user. In addition, the database requires a tablespace of sufficient size in which to install the TPC-C schema. For example

```
SQL> CREATE TABLESPACE TPCCTAB DATAFILE '/u01/oradata/TPCCTAB01.DBF' SIZE 2048M➡
EXTENT MANAGEMENT LOCAL SEGMENT SPACE MANAGEMENT AUTO;
```

When creating the tablespace allow for at least 100MB space consumption per warehouse to be created, plus additional growing room for conducting tests of 25% to 50%. It should be remembered that a genuine TPC-C test distributes an even number of users across all of the available warehouses and therefore the maximum throughput you will be able to achieve is dependent to some extent on the number of warehouses you create.

With a low number of warehouses, you may achieve the same levels of CPU utilization, but a greater proportion of the workload will be attributable to data contention. Therefore, the number of warehouses you choose to create is dependent on the scenario to test. To observe the operations of RAC with a high level of contention for data, plan for a small number of these warehouses, such as 10 or below. To observe the maximum level of throughput with minimal data contention, plan for a larger number of warehouses to create from 30 to 100. In Hammerora, the binding of virtual users to home warehouses is not as strict as the specification dictates, with all virtual users independently selecting a home warehouse at random from all of the warehouses available. It is therefore clear that the larger the number of warehouses available the less likely it will be that a number of virtual users select the same home warehouse.

With the target RAC database configured and a tablespace available for the TPC-C schema, the next step is to create and populate the TPC-C schema, which can be done from entirely within the Hammerora application.

Creating the TPC-C Schema

The first thing to do when creating the TPC-C schema is to start the Hammerora application at the command line:

```
[oracle@load1 hammerora]$ ./hammerora.tcl
```

From under the TPC-C menu, select TPC-C Schema Options. This displays the TPC-C Schema Options window, shown in Figure 23-5, with values that need to be modified according to the specific needs of your environment to create and populate the TPC-C schema.

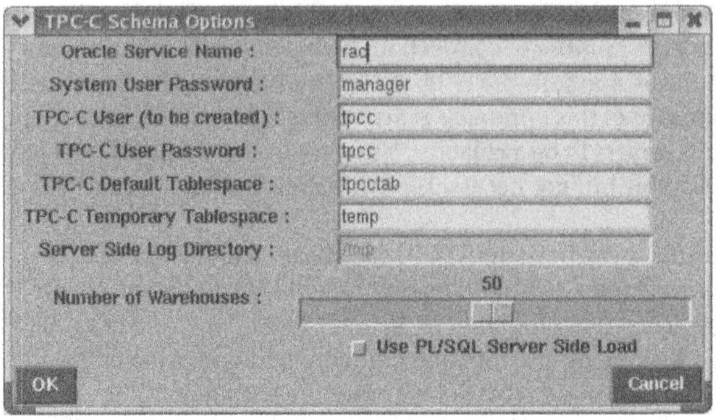

Figure 23-5. *TPC-C Schema Options*

Configure the values within the schema options according to the following requirements:

1. **Oracle Service Name**: The service name of the database that you created your TPC-C tablespace in and can connect to across the network.

2. **System User Password**: The password of the system user on your Oracle server so you could, for example, log in as system/manager@rac. The system user is used to create the owner of the TPC-C schema.

3. **TPC-C User** (to be created): The name of the user you want to own the TPC-C schema. This can be any name that is valid for an Oracle user and does not necessarily have to be tpcc.

4. **TPC-C User Password**: The password for the TPC-C user. Again, this can be anything you like that is valid as a password.

5. **TPC-C Default Tablespace**: The name of the tablespace you created on the server to store the TPC-C schema.

6. **TPC-C Temporary Tablespace**: The name of the temporary tablespace on your Oracle server for the TPC-C user.

7. **Server Side Log Directory**: The directory to use to record schema creation details when using a PL/SQL server-side load. This option will remain grayed out if the Use PL/SQL Server Side Load check box is not selected.

8. **Number of Warehouses**: The number of warehouses to be created within the schema. Move the slider to choose the amount.

9. **Use PL/SQL Server Side Load:** The PL/SQL version of the loader program on the server to be used instead of creating the data on the client. Ordinarily the Tcl data-creation process will complete more rapidly than the PL/SQL version, but this option may offer an advantage depending on the performance of the network between the Hammerora client and the Oracle database server by eliminating the network latency component.

Click OK to save the chosen values. When ready to proceed with the creation and population of the schema, click the Create TPC-C button to show a message box that confirms your settings. Click Yes. Hammerora will without intervention create the TPC-C user and tables and populate the tables with nonuniform random data created according to the rules detailed in the TPC-C specification. It will then create the required indexes and stored procedures and gather the schema statistics. Progress is indicated in the output written to the virtual User Output window, and completion is signified by a green tick displayed in the status of the virtual user running the creation, along with the message "TPCC SCHEMA COMPLETE" in the output window.

The creation and population process is in its entirety a single standard Tcl script with Oratcl commands that runs in the same manner as any script created for use in Hammerora. When the creation is complete you have a TPCC schema ready for receiving a load test. It is important to note that the TPC-C application has incorporated into its design the ability to run consecutive tests without an expected decline in the transaction rates. Due to this design it is not necessary to reset the database by recreating it back to a starting point before running consecutive tests.

The TPC-C user will now have the following tables and indexes created and populated, with statistics gathered. We recommend browsing the data within the tables and reviewing the stored procedures as a way to become familiar with the TPC-C application.

```
SQL> select tname, tabtype from tab;

TNAME                          TABTYPE
------------------------------ -------
CUSTOMER                       TABLE
DISTRICT                       TABLE
HISTORY                        TABLE
ITEM                           TABLE
NEW_ORDER                      TABLE
ORDERS                         TABLE
ORDER_LINE                     TABLE
STOCK                          TABLE
WAREHOUSE                      TABLE

SQL> select index_name, index_type from ind;

INDEX_NAME                     INDEX_TYPE
------------------------------ ----------
CUSTOMER_I1                    NORMAL
CUSTOMER_I2                    NORMAL
DISTRICT_I1                    NORMAL
INORD                          IOT - TOP
IORDL                          IOT - TOP
ITEM_I1                        NORMAL
ORDERS_I1                      NORMAL
ORDERS_I2                      NORMAL
STOCK_I1                       NORMAL
WAREHOUSE_I1                   NORMAL
```

Generating the TPC-C Workload

With the schema created and data populated the TPC-C workload is generated by another separate Tcl script. To utilize the script it needs to be loaded into the main Hammerora editor pane by selecting TPC-C Driver Script from under the TPC-C menu.

It is important to reiterate that the driver script, in common with the schema-creation script, is standard Tcl and Oratcl without modifications exclusive to Hammerora, which serves to illustrate the level of complexity available when creating bespoke application load tests.

The TPC-C driver script is entirely self-contained and requires no additional programming to be run directly against the target schema to generate a varied workload as accurately as possible according to the TPC-C specification.

Before doing so it is advisable to be familiar with the EDITABLEOPTIONS section of the script to understand and get the most from running the driver script. When the script is loaded this section appears at the very top:

```
#!/usr/local/bin/tclsh8.4
package require Oratcl
#EDITABLEOPTIONS##################################################
set total_iterations 1000 ;# Number of transactions before logging off
set RAISEERROR "false" ;# Exit script on Oracle error (true or false)
set KEYANDTHINK "true" ;# Time for user thinking and keying (true or false)
set connect tpcc/tpcc@oracle ;# Oracle connect string for tpc-c user
#EDITABLEOPTIONS##################################################
```

There are four options to consider:

- total_iterations
- RAISEERROR
- KEYANDTHINK
- connect

total_iterations

The total_iterations value is a value exclusive and internal to the TPC-C driver script and distinct from the Iterations value set in the Virtual User Options window. Whereas the general Hammerora Iterations value defines how many times that the entire script is repeated in its entirety, the total_iterations value determines the number of transactions from the driver script that the virtual user will complete after logging in with an Oracle session on the target database without logging off.

For example, the default value of 1,000 coupled with a general Hammerora Iterations value of 1 means that the virtual user will log in to the database, complete 1,000 transactions, log off, and complete the script. Increasing the Hammerora Iterations value to 2 means that after completion, the virtual user will log in again and complete another 1,000 transactions, making 2,000 transactions in total from two distinct Oracle sessions. Using both values in conjunction with each other enables a test scenario to be balanced between multiple session creations and a workload generated entirely from within a single session.

In a RAC environment the Hammerora Iterations value is particularly useful in testing load-balancing configuration between the instances within the cluster. This can be used with either client- or server-side load balancing to distribute the sessions from one instance of Hammerora across all of the nodes in the cluster. Alternatively, to ensure a precisely even distribution of connections across the cluster, you may want to run more than one instance of Hammerora in a master and slave configuration. The instances can be running on the same load server or different servers communicating by a network.

To do this, each instance of Hammerora can be linked with peer instances using sockets-based communication. The default mode of operation is in a local mode with no peers. To establish a link on the instance of Hammerora that is to act as the master, under the Mode menu, choose Select Mode, and in the dialog window select Master Mode.

This brings up the message "Switch from Local to Master Mode?" Answer Yes and a message box is shown detailing the socket ID and hostname on which the Hammerora is now listening. The Master Distribution button on the application also becomes active.

On one or more slave Hammerora instances, select Slave Options from the Mode menu and enter the hostname and ID of the master to connect to and click OK.

Navigate to the Select Mode dialog and select Slave Mode. If communication can be successfully established, all virtual user actions on the master, such as the creation and starting of virtual users, are now replicated onto the slave applications. Details of communication are reported in the respective consoles of the Hammerora application. The Master distribution button can be used to distribute the contents of the editor pane to the slave instances. Subsequently, modifying the connect string enables a fully automated test with the sessions targeted directly against the individual instances.

When performing load-balancing tests on RAC, the optional -failovercallback procname arguments to the Oratcl connect command can also prove useful in implementing transparent application failover within Oratcl to automatically reconnect to another RAC node when the connected node fails. This enables high-availability testing of the RAC environment. The procname argument is the name of a procedure to run after reconnection and is usually used for ALTER SESSION type statements.

The total_iterations value itself should be sized according to the desired duration of a virtual user session and the performance of the target database. The higher the sustained transaction rate of the target database, the proportionally shorter time it will take for the script to complete. Accordingly, there is no total_iterations value that benefits all load-testing scenarios and this value should be set within the context of each test environment.

It should also be noted that when setting the total_iterations value the user will complete the number of transactions defined before looking to see whether a thread termination signal has been posted. Therefore, setting a large value, initiating a load test, and then terminating the virtual users means that the virtual users will continue to run in the background until their allotted number of iterations is complete. It will not be possible to create any further virtual users until they have completed.

RAISEERROR

The RAISEERROR editable option can be set to the value of TRUE or FALSE. This determines whether Oracle errors caught by the driver script are simply displayed as output (if user output is selected) while the script continues to run, or whether on detection of an error, the error will be printed to the Hammerora console, and the virtual user will terminate immediately.

KEYANDTHINK

The KEYANDTHINK variable can also be set to the value of TRUE or FALSE and determines whether keying and thinking time is applied according to the requirements detailed by the TPC-C specification. As previously noted, setting this value to FALSE requires a significantly lower number of virtual users to achieve a high sustained level of throughput at the expense of generating an unrealistic workload that would not be experienced by a production type application.

connect

The connect option defines the connect string for the TPC-C schema owner. If the driver script is displayed directly after schema creation has completed, the connect string will include the username, the password, and the service name defined in the schema creation dialog.

Determining the Transaction Level

With the editable options set to the desired values, before proceeding directly into a measured load-test scenario, it is advisable to conduct a pretesting phase to ascertain the optimal test configuration to achieve the maximum sustainable throughput according to the number of user threads to configure. As the throughput will be determined by a wide variety of factors, one of which is the number of warehouses created, this can only be defined by running the tests with different numbers of users and observing the transaction rates achieved. Rerunning the tests with an increasing number of virtual users will raise the transaction rate to optimal point, beyond which increasing the number of virtual users will have decreasing returns on the throughput achieved.

To identify the Oracle transaction level during a load test, select the Counter Options menu option from the Transaction Counter menu. This displays the Transaction Count Options dialog box shown in Figure 23-6.

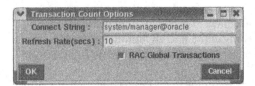

Figure 23-6. *Transaction Count Options dialog box*

Enter a Connect String with system-level privileges and a Refresh Rate in seconds for the transaction counter to refresh its display. Finally, in a RAC environment, select the RAC Global Transactions check box to ensure that the transaction level is recorded from every instance within the cluster, as opposed to only the instance where the transaction counter is logged in. Click OK to save the configured options to use when the transaction counter is started.

Create the desired number of users for the method described for bespoke application load tests. According to the strictest definition of the specification, this dictates ten virtual users per warehouse with the variable KEYANDTHINK set to TRUE. Click the Run Hammerora Loadtest button to begin the TPC-C simulation.

To observe the transactional activity, click the Transaction Counter button. This displays the Transactions per Minute window, shown in Figure 23-7.

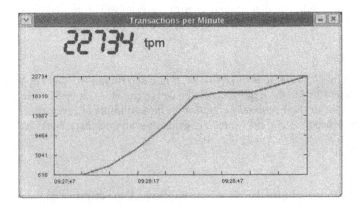

Figure 23-7. *Transactions per Minute*

Using this pretesting activity, it is possible to fine-tune the number of virtual users if attempting to achieve a level of maximum throughput and the number of total iterations required to achieve a test of the desired duration in time. When these values have been determined, they can be used as the input for a formal load-testing period, remembering that the application has been designed so that tests can be run back-to-back without having an impact on the expected transaction results.

Conducting the Test

When conducting a formal load test, the tests should be repeated a number of times over the same duration in time, with the average result taken across all of the tests. This serves to highlight and eliminate any statistical anomalies. In particular, the virtual users will select a home warehouse at random, which they maintain for the entire duration of the test. Therefore, depending on the number of virtual users and the number of warehouses, having two or more users select the same home warehouse may reduce the overall level of transactional throughput due to increased data contention.

When running a measured load test we advise you to measure and record performance data from the optimal source—the Oracle database itself. Hammerora has been designed so that the impact of the tool on the database itself is minimal. The only monitoring that occurs from the application is the periodic execution of a SELECT statement from a V$ view to determine the transaction rate, whereas extensive third-party monitoring during a load test can have a significant effect on the overall database throughput.

Leveraging the instrumentation available in Oracle to record load-test information at a minimal system cost is straightforward using the Automatic Workload Repository (AWR). We detail interacting with the AWR in Chapter 24; however, for testing purposes, a monitoring script is useful when operating in conjunction with the load test itself. The aim of the script is to run in parallel with the load test and wait for a predetermined period of time to enable the workload to ramp up to a sustainable level. The script then takes an AWR snapshot and waits for the duration of the test before taking another snapshot. The script should be run against every instance within the cluster.

An example monitoring script that can be run from within Hammerora is as follows. This script can be run independently against the target database, from a single chosen user thread as described previously in this chapter, or within a slave session of Hammerora to automate the capture of the Oracle performance statistics.

```
#!/usr/local/bin/tclsh8.4
package require Oratcl
#EDITABLEOPTIONS#############################################
set connect system/manager@rac1
set rampup 2;   #rampup time in minutes
set duration 10;  #duration in minutes
#EDITABLEOPTIONS#############################################
set ramptime 0
puts "Beginning rampup time of $rampup minutes"
set rampup [ expr $rampup*60000 ]
while {$ramptime != $rampup} {
after 60000
set ramptime [ expr $ramptime+60000 ]
puts "Rampup [ expr $ramptime / 60000 ] minutes complete ..."
}
puts "Rampup complete, Taking start AWR snapshot."
set lda [oralogon $connect]
oraautocom $lda on
set curn1 [oraopen $lda ]
set sql1 "BEGIN dbms_workload_repository.create_snapshot(); END;"
oraparse $curn1 $sql1
if {[catch {oraplexec $curn1 $sql1} message]}
{ error "Failed to create snapshot : $message" }
set sql2 "SELECT INSTANCE_NUMBER, INSTANCE_NAME, DB_NAME, DBID, SNAP_ID,⟿
TO_CHAR(END_INTERVAL_TIME,'DD MON YYYY HH24:MI') FROM⟿
( SELECT DI.INSTANCE_NUMBER, INSTANCE_NAME, DB_NAME, DI.DBID, SNAP_ID,⟿
END_INTERVAL_TIME FROM DBA_HIST_SNAPSHOT DS, DBA_HIST_DATABASE_INSTANCE DI⟿
ORDER BY SNAP_ID DESC ) WHERE ROWNUM = 1"
```

```
if {[catch {orasql $curn1 $sql2} message]} {
error "SQL statement failed: $sql2 : $message"
    } else {
orafetch  $curn1 -datavariable firstsnap
split  $firstsnap " "
puts "Start Snapshot [ lindex $firstsnap 4 ]
taken at [ lindex $firstsnap 5 ]
of instance [ lindex $firstsnap 1 ] ([lindex $firstsnap 0])
of database [ lindex $firstsnap 2 ] ([lindex $firstsnap 3])"
    }
puts "Timing test period of $duration in minutes"
set testtime 0
set duration [ expr $duration*60000 ]
while {$testtime != $duration} {
after 60000
set testtime [ expr $testtime+60000 ]
puts -nonewline "[ expr $testtime / 60000 ]  ...,"
    }
puts "Test complete, Taking end AWR snapshot."
oraparse $curn1 $sql1
if {[catch {oraplexec $curn1 $sql1} message]}
{ error "Failed to create snapshot : $message" }
if {[catch {orasql $curn1 $sql2} message]} {
error "SQL statement failed: $sql2 : $message"
    } else {
orafetch  $curn1 -datavariable endsnap
split  $endsnap " "
puts "End Snapshot [ lindex $endsnap 4 ]
taken at [ lindex $endsnap 5 ]
of instance [ lindex $endsnap 1 ] ([lindex $endsnap 0])
of database [ lindex $endsnap 2 ] ([lindex $endsnap 3])"
puts "Test complete: view report
from SNAPID [ lindex $firstsnap 4 ] to [ lindex $endsnap 4 ]"
    }
```

With the snapshots gathered, it is possible to view the performance results collected over the testing period using Oracle Enterprise Manager, or manually from the database server using the AWR reporting script specifying the snapshot IDs reported.

```
SQL>@?/rdbms/admin.awrrpt.sql
```

In addition to extensive performance information, you can use the report to determine the transaction rate observed by the database itself during the testing period. Within the "Load Profile" section, the report details the number of transactions per second observed by the instance:

```
Transactions:                854.84
```

It is simple to then add the values recorded on every instance within the cluster and multiply them by 60 to determine the overall transaction rate per minute observed for the test. This will coincide with the transaction rate observed within the Hammerora transaction counter.

The AWR report also contains a wealth of information that can be browsed at leisure after the test is complete. In Chapter 24, we present the guidelines for interpreting the RAC-related AWR report statistics. For example, if you are interested in a pseudo–tpmC-type number to obtain the number of business transactions, the "SQL Ordered by Elapsed Time" details the number of executions of each statement. Therefore, the total number of new orders processed across the entire cluster during the test period can easily be derived.

The "Operating System Statistics" section can also prove particularly useful if you wish to observe levels of processor performance for the application running on different systems. A great deal of information can be gathered and coupled with experience to provide valuable empirical evidence for generic Oracle OLTP performance observations.

Swingbench

Swingbench is a freely available tool designed for the load and stress testing of Oracle databases and can be downloaded from http://www.dominicgiles.com.

Swingbench is used extensively for visually demonstrating RAC functionality and can also be used to demonstrate additional Oracle features such as online table rebuilds, Data Guard, and online backup and recovery. Swingbench provides a comprehensive graphical toolset to observe system throughput and response times in a RAC environment.

By default, Swingbench includes two open source preconfigured benchmarks: Order Entry and Calling Circle. It also includes PL/SQL stubs to enable the development of a bespoke benchmark. Order Entry is based on a modified version of the oe sample schema included with the Oracle database so that the schema can be utilized independently. It is designed to demonstrate RAC functionality when there is a high level of contention on a small number of tables increasing the level of activity on the interconnect and memory.

Calling Circle implements an example OLTP online telecommunications application. Whereas Order Entry can be run continuously, Calling Circle requires the generation of input data files in advance. Both benchmarks induce a high level of CPU utilization, and it is recommended to use one processor per load generator for two processors per database server. Swingbench also offers an API for Java developers to create their own benchmarks by defining classes and parameters to be implemented by the Swingbench framework.

In a single-instance environment, Swingbench can be used exclusively to conduct a benchmark test. However, in a RAC environment, in addition to Swingbench, it is useful to configure two additional components (the coordinator and cluster overview) to implement an integrated RAC benchmark. The coordinator and cluster overview are already included with the standard Swingbench installation.

The following section will look in greater depth at the installation and configuration of Swingbench on two load-generation servers (load1 and load2) and the execution of an example Calling Circle benchmark.

Installation and Configuration

A prerequisite for running Swingbench on a load-generation server is a Java virtual machine (JVM). The actual JVM selected will depend on the client environment, but an example JVM for a Linux x86-based load generator is the Java 2 Platform, Standard Edition (J2SE) Java Runtime Environment (JRE).

This is available as a self-extracting compressed file that produces an RPM file and can be downloaded from the Sun Java software web site at http://java.sun.com.

Once the RPM file is extracted by running the .bin file, install the RPM file on all of the load-generation hosts with the following command:

```
[root@load1 root]# rpm -ivh j2re-*.rpm
```

It is also necessary to ensure that there is an installation of the Oracle client software on the load-generation servers. This can be an Instant Client installation or a full Oracle client install.

Once the JVM and Oracle client software are installed, uncompress the downloaded Swingbench file into a chosen directory as follows, the directory name should be the same on all of the load generation servers, such as /home/oracle.

```
[oracle@load1 oracle]$ unzip swingbench.zip
```

The naming convention for Swingbench uses the same convention as the Oracle software instal-lation, with the top-level directory referred to as SWINGHOME. In this top-level directory there is a file called swingbench.env that sets certain environment variables required by both Swingbench and the cluster overview component. It is necessary to modify the variables ORACLE_HOME, JAVAHOME, SWINGHOME, and LOADGENHOSTS in a RAC environment to reflect the locations of the installed software on the load-generation server as in this example:

```
#!/bin/bash
export ORACLE_HOME=/usr/lib/oracle/10.1.0.3/client
export JAVAHOME=/usr/java/j2re1.4.2_08
export SWINGHOME=/home/oracle/swingbench
export ANTHOME=$SWINGHOME/lib
export LD_LIBRARY_PATH=${LD_LIBRARY_PATH}:$ORACLE_HOME/lib
export LOADGENHOSTS='load1 load2'
export LOADGENUSER=oracle
export
CLASSPATH=$JAVAHOME/lib/rt.jar:$JAVAHOME/lib/tools.jar:
$ORACLE_HOME/jdbc/lib/ojdbc14.jar:$SWINGHOME/lib/mytransactions.jar:➥
${SWINGHOME}/lib/swingbench.jar:$ANTHOME/ant.jar
```

If using the Oracle Instant Client it is also important to modify one entry in the CLASSPATH envi-ronment variable from

```
$ORACLE_HOME/jdbc/lib/ojdbc14.jar
```

to

```
$ORACLE_HOME/lib/ojdbc14.jar
```

In addition, there is an XML file called swingconfig.xml in the SWINGHOME/bin directory that directs the configuration of Swingbench. By default, swingconfig.xml is configured to run the OrderEntry benchmark. If choosing to run this benchmark with an otherwise default configuration, it is neces-sary to modify only the parameter ConnectString to the value of your target database using a standard editor tool such as vi.

Swingbench can then be initiated from the SWINGHOME/bin directory by running the swingbench command:

```
[oracle@load1 bin]$ ./swingbench
```

The -h option displays the command-line parameters that can be specified at start-up. Simi-larly, the cluster overview can now be run from the same directory with the command

```
[oracle@load1 bin]$ ./clusteroverview
```

clusteroverview requires the coordinator process to be started and running on one of the load-generator hosts for it to successfully initialize. The configuration and interoperation of Swing-bench, the cluster overview, and the coordinator are best demonstrated with an example for which we will use the Calling Circle application.

Calling Circle

The Calling Circle application induces an intensive randomized database workload and is particularly relevant for measuring the throughput and response times of customer transactions and demonstrating the capabilities of RAC in failover and load-balancing scenarios.

The Calling Circle application is an example OLTP application that implements the customers of a telecommunications company registering, updating, and querying the details of its frequently dialed numbers to receive discount call rates.

The application was designed to present challenges to clustered Oracle solutions, such as sequence numbers and contention for right-growing indexes. The application also maintains change history for each simulated user's frequently called numbers, thereby proportionally increasing the volume of inserts and updates.

Before running Swingbench in a distributed manner against a RAC cluster, it is necessary to configure the coordinator and cluster overview processes. As opposed to operating Swingbench directly against the target database, the coordinator process communicates with one or more Swingbench load generators, synchronizing the starting and stopping of benchmarks and gathering statistics, which are then displayed centrally by the cluster overview.

Configuring Swingbench

Swingbench can be configured to operate the Calling Circle benchmark in one of two ways. Either the sample Calling Circle XML configuration file can be copied over the default `swingconfig.xml` file as follows:

```
[oracle@load1 bin]$ cp sample/ccconfig.xml swingconfig.xml
```

or the Calling Circle XML configuration file can be specified at start-up for `swingbench`:

```
[oracle@load1 bin]$ ./swingbench -c sample/ccconfig.xml
```

Using either method (we will use the copied configuration file here) ensures that the service name detailed in the XML file's `ConnectString` parameter is the correct one for your target cluster, such as the following on `load1`:

```
<ConnectString>london1:1521/RAC1</ConnectString>
```

and on `load2`:

```
<ConnectString>london2:1521/RAC2</ConnectString>
```

The `swingconfig.xml` file should be the same on all of the load-generation hosts. Select one of the load-generation hosts to also run the coordinator process and cluster-overview display. On this host only, in the `SWINGHOME/bin` directory, edit the `clusteroverview.xml` file to specify the location of the coordinator process running on one of the load-generation hosts such as the following:

```
<Coordinator>
  <Location>//load1/CoordinatorServer</Location>
</Coordinator>
```

In the `MonitoredDatabaseList` section, modify the details of the RAC instances to monitor. For example, the following section shows that the instance names RAC1 and RAC2 are shown, and the system user will log in to RAC1 on host london1 to monitor the activity of the CC user. The `ConnectString` must be of the form `<host>:<port>:<SID>` when using thin connections, or `tnsnames.ora` entry for OCI connections.

```
<MonitoredDatabaseList>
<MonitoredDatabase DisplayName="london1:1521:RAC1" Username="system"
Password="manager" DriverType="thin" ConnectString="london1:1521:RAC1"
 MonitoredUsers="CC" />
<MonitoredDatabase DisplayName=" london2:1521:RAC2"
Username="system" Password="manager" DriverType="thin"
ConnectString="london2:1521:RAC2" MonitoredUsers="CC" />
</MonitoredDatabaseList>
```

Creating the Schema

Before starting the coordinator, Swingbench, and cluster overview processes it is necessary to create the Calling Circle schema. The minimum size is 164MB, though the default is 1640MB. The schema can be created to any size up to 1,000% greater than the default installation. Creation is straightforward using the ccwizard process. The information required by the wizard can be provided manually in the wizard, or preconfigured by entering the information into the configuration file (ccwizard.xml) before running the tool as follows:

```
[oracle@load1 bin]$ ./ccwizard
```

When you see the Calling Circle Wizard welcome window, shown in Figure 23-8, click the Next button.

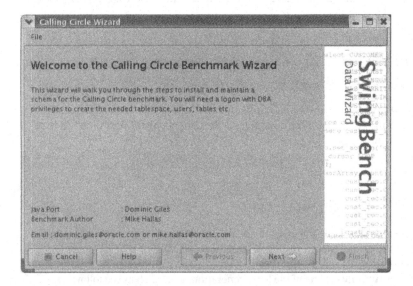

Figure 23-8. *Calling Circle Wizard welcome*

In the Select Task window, shown in Figure 23-9, select the Create the Calling Circle Schema button and click Next.

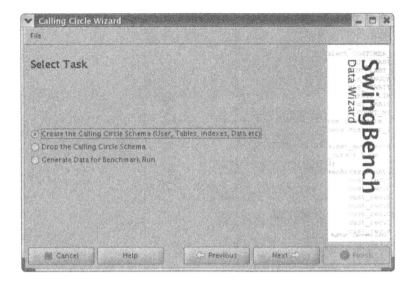

Figure 23-9. *Select Task*

In the Database Details window, shown in Figure 23-10, enter the details of the target database in which to create the schema and click Next.

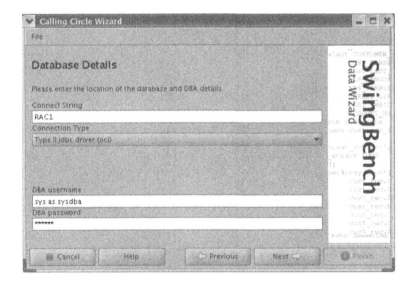

Figure 23-10. *Database Details*

Under Schema Details, shown in Figure 23-11, enter the username and password of the user, tablespaces, and datafiles to be created, and click Next.

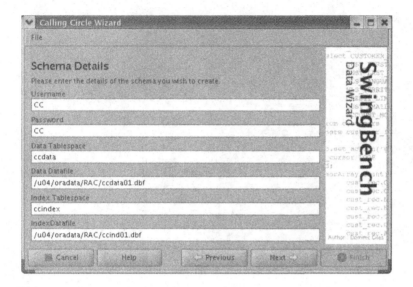

Figure 23-11. *Schema Details*

In the Schema Sizing window, shown in Figure 23-12, use the slider to select the schema size and click Next.

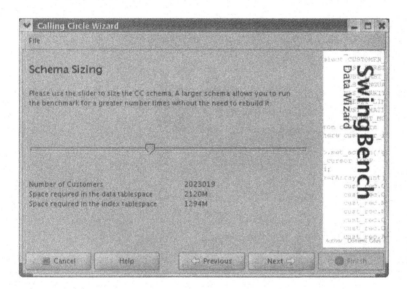

Figure 23-12. *Schema Sizing*

Click Finish, as shown in Figure 23-13, to complete the wizard and create the schema.

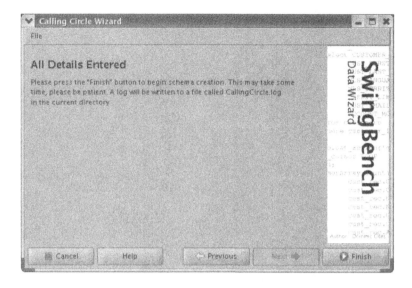

Figure 23-13. *All Details Entered*

Creating the Input Data

Before each run of the Calling Circle benchmark, it is necessary to create the input data for the benchmark run, using the ccwizard. In the Select Task window, shown in Figure 23-14, choose Generate Data for Benchmark Run and click Next.

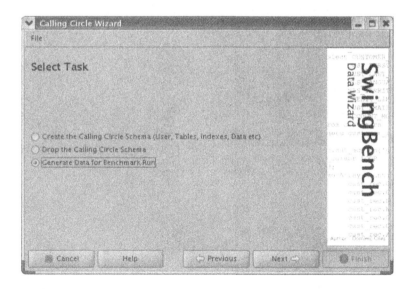

Figure 23-14. *Select Task*

In the Schema Details window, shown in Figure 23-15, enter the details for the configured schema and click Next.

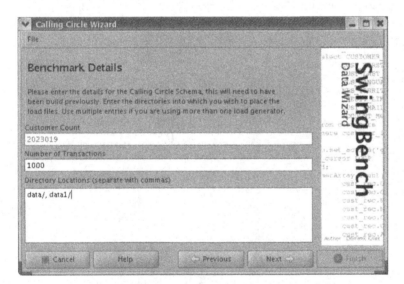

Figure 23-15. *Schema Details*

Before entering information in the Benchmark Details screen, shown in Figure 23-16, make sure that the same number of data directories exists for all of the load-generation hosts to be used in the benchmark. In this example, there are two hosts: load1 and load2. The data directory exists and therefore it is necessary to create an additional data1 directory owned by the oracle user in the SWINGHOME/bin directory before clicking Next.

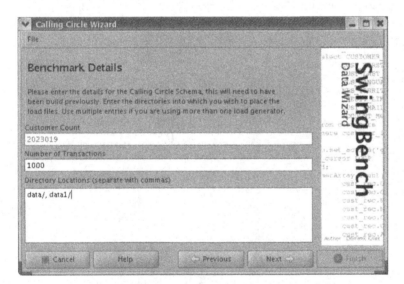

Figure 23-16. *Benchmark Details*

Press Finish, as shown in Figure 23-17, to create the benchmark data. When the process is finished, manually copy the generated data from the data1 and above directories to the SWINGHOME/bin/data directories on their corresponding hosts. In this example, the datafiles from data1 on load1 are copied to the SWINGHOME/bin/data directory on load2.

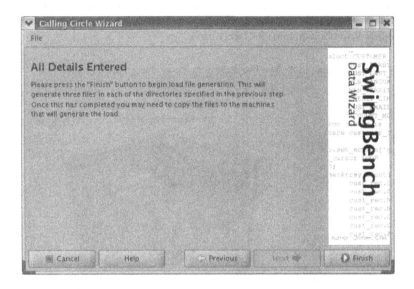

Figure 23-17. *All Details Entered*

Starting the Test

With the configuration files updated to the environment, the schema created, and the benchmark input data created and ready on all load-generation servers, start the coordinator process on the selected host with the following command:

```
[oracle@load1 bin]$ ./coordinator
Coordinator started Successfully
```

Then start Swingbench on all of the load generation servers, specifying the location of the coordinator process as a command-line option. Their controls will be disabled when running under a coordinator process.

```
[oracle@load1 bin]$ ./swingbench -co //load1/CoordinatorServer
```

The successful attachment to the coordinator will also be reported at the coordinator command line:

```
[oracle@load1 bin]$ ./coordinator
Coordinator started started Successfully
Added new client : id = 0 : connect string = london1:1521:RAC1
Current Connected clients = 1
Added new client : id = 0 : connect string = london1:1521:RAC1
Current connected clients = 2
```

Start the `clusteroverview` process on the configured host:

```
[oracle@load1 bin]$ ./clusteroverview
```

The cluster overview, shown in Figure 23-18, can now be used to control the load generators.

In the Cluster Overview screen, under the Databases tab, select the databases, and click the Start icon to commence monitoring of the databases. Under the Load Generators tab, highlight both load generators and click Start to commence the benchmark.

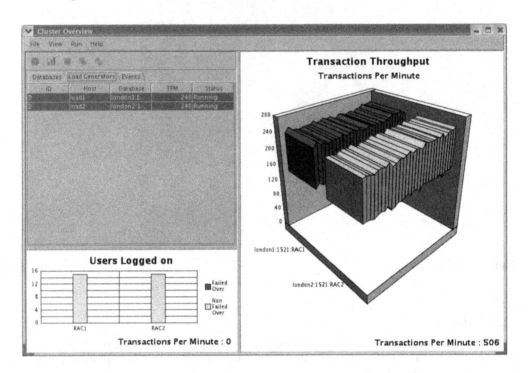

Figure 23-18. *Cluster Overview*

You can observe activity at a RAC level on the Cluster Overview screen with instance-level activity seen on the individual Swingbench generators, as shown in Figure 23-19.

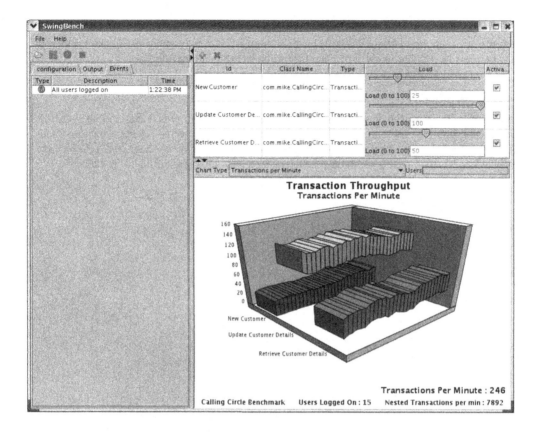

Figure 23-19. *Transaction throughput*

For advanced usage, Swingbench also includes clients with a reduced-graphical interface or a character-based interface, thereby enabling the use of multiple load-generation clients on the same server. For example, the following two commands implement the same functionality as Swingbench with different interfaces and, therefore, different levels of client-side graphical load.

```
[oracle@load1 bin]$ ./minibench -cs london1:1521:RAC1 -dt thin -uc 4 -max 0 -min 0
-r run1.dat -c sample/ccconfig.xml -D CC_DATA_DIR_LOC=data/
[oracle@load1 bin]$ ./charbench -cs london1:1521:RAC1 -dt thin -uc 4 -max 0 -min 0
-r run1.dat -c sample/ccconfig.xml -D CC_DATA_DIR_LOC=data/
```

The examples also illustrate how command-line arguments can be used to override the defaults given in the selected XML configuration file. This enables large numbers of minibench or charbench load generators to be created on a single client, each with differing configurations from the default, such as the use of multiple input data directories for the Calling Circle benchmark.

Developing Swingbench Benchmarks

There are two standard methods available for developing benchmarks within Swingbench, either by using preprovided PL/SQL stubs or by creating entirely new benchmarks in Java.

Using PL/SQL Stubs

Using the PL/SQL stubs is the most rapid method for developing customized benchmarks. To install the PL/SQL stubs, run the script storedprocedures.sql in the sql directory against a schema to be used for Swingbench development. The schema must be granted execute permissions on the DBMS_LOCK package to enable access to the Oracle Lock Management (OLM) services such as in the following dialog:

```
sqlplus sys/oracle@"rac1 as sysdba"
SQL*Plus: Release 10.1.0.3.0 - Production on Mon May 2 20:31:36 2005
Copyright (c) 1982, 2004, Oracle.  All rights reserved.
Connected to:
Oracle Database 10g Enterprise Edition Release 10.1.0.3.0 - Production
With the Partitioning, OLAP and Data Mining options
SQL> GRANT EXECUTE ON dbms_lock TO swingdev;
Grant succeeded.
SQL> connect swingdev/swingdev@tpcc
Connected.
SQL> @storedprocedures
Type created.
Package created.
Package body created.
SQL>
```

Under the chosen schema, create a type called integer_return_array and a package called swingbench that can be edited to create bespoke transactions. There are six predefined functions for new transactions, although this can be extended by modifying the code in the com.dom.benchmarking.swingbench.storedprocedures Java package.

The six functions available to modify are named storedprocedure1 to storedprocedure6, as follows:

```
function storedprocedure1(min_sleep integer, max_sleep integer) return
integer_return_array is
begin
init_dml_array();
sleep(min_sleep, max_sleep);
return dml_array;
end storedprocedure1;
```

As a stub, this can be modified to include the desired SQL operations or calls to additional procedures and, by default, includes a number of standard calls. For example, to select the number of customers from a customers table the code could be modified as follows:

```
function storedprocedure1(min_sleep integer, max_sleep integer) return
integer_return_array is
number_of_customers integer := 0;
begin
init_dml_array();
select count(1)
into number_of_customers
from customers;
increment_selects(1);
sleep(min_sleep, max_sleep);
return dml_array;
end storedprocedure1;
```

In the code, `init_dml()` resets the integer array that is returned from the function and that is used to record the number and type of DML operations performed in the bespoke code. `increment_selects()` updates the number of SELECT operations that have been performed. Similarly, there is an equivalent function to record the number of inserts, updates, deletes, commits, and rollbacks. It is always necessary to return `dml_array` at the end of each function. It is therefore relatively simple to create self-contained PL/SQL procedures to integrate into the Swingbench framework.

Defining Java-Based Tests

To create Java-based transactions, it is first necessary for developers to implement an interface such as the following:

```
public interface Task {
  public static final String JDBC_CONNECTION = "jdbcConnection";
  public static final String QUERY_TIMEOUT = "queryTimeOut";
  public void init(Map param) throws SwingBenchException;
  public void execute(Map param) throws SwingBenchException;
  public void close();
  public void addTaskListener(TaskListener transListener);
  public void removeTaskListener(TaskListener transListener);
  public void processTransactionEvent(boolean transactionSuccessful,
    long transactionPeriod, String id);
  public String getId();
  public void setId(String newProcessName);
  public void setThinkSleepTime(long newMinSleepTime, long newMaxSleepTime);
}
```

An abstract class, `JdbcTaskImpl`, implements all methods except for the `init()`, `execute()`, and `close()` methods. Tasks can therefore be created by enabling the developer to extend this class's functionality. For example, the following illustrates a Java-based stored procedure called `orderentry.browseandupdateorders`:

```
package com.dom.benchmarking.swingbench.plsqltransactions;

import com.dom.benchmarking.swingbench.event.JdbcTaskEvent;
import com.dom.benchmarking.swingbench.kernel.SwingBenchException;
import com.dom.benchmarking.swingbench.kernel.Task;
import com.dom.benchmarking.swingbench.utilities.RandomGenerator;

import com.protomatter.syslog.Syslog;

import java.sql.CallableStatement;
import java.sql.Connection;
import java.sql.SQLException;

import java.util.Map;

import oracle.jdbc.OracleTypes;
import oracle.sql.ARRAY;

public class BrowseAndUpdateOrders extends OrderEntryProcess {

  public BrowseAndUpdateOrders() {}

  public void close() {}
```

```java
public void init(Map params) {
  Connection connection = (Connection)params.get(Task.JDBC_CONNECTION);
  try {
    this.getMaxandMinCustID(connection);
  } catch (SQLException se) {
    Syslog.error(this, se);
  }
}

public void execute(Map params) throws SwingBenchException {
  Connection connection = (Connection)params.get(Task.JDBC_CONNECTION);
  int queryTimeOut = 60;
  if (params.get(Task.QUERY_TIMEOUT) != null)
    queryTimeOut = ((Integer)(params.get(Task.QUERY_TIMEOUT))).intValue();
  long executeStart = System.currentTimeMillis();
  int[] dmlArray = null;
  try {
    long start = System.currentTimeMillis();
    try {
      CallableStatement cs = connection.prepareCall(
        "{? = call orderentry.browseandupdateorders(?,?,?)}");
      cs.registerOutParameter(1, OracleTypes.ARRAY, "INTEGER_RETURN_ARRAY");
      cs.setInt(2, RandomGenerator.randomInteger(MIN_CUSTID, MAX_CUSTID));
      cs.setInt(3, (int) this.getMinSleepTime());
      cs.setInt(4, (int) this.getMaxSleepTime());
      cs.setQueryTimeout(queryTimeOut);
      cs.executeUpdate();
      dmlArray = (((ARRAY) cs.getArray(1)).getIntArray());
      cs.close();
    } catch (SQLException se) {
      throw new SwingBenchException(se.getMessage());
    }
  processTransactionEvent(new JdbcTaskEvent(this, getId(),
    (System.currentTimeMillis() - executeStart), true, dmlArray));
  } catch (SwingBenchException ex) {
    processTransactionEvent(new JdbcTaskEvent(this, getId(),
      (System.currentTimeMillis() - executeStart), false, dmlArray));
    throw new SwingBenchException(ex);
  }
}
}
```

First, the init() routine is called when the class loads, giving the class the chance to read in initial values from the file system or database. The execute() method executes the bespoke JDBC (Java Database Connectivity) operations and notifies the Swingbench framework of a successful or failed transaction by calling processTransactionEvent() and passing it a JdbcTaskEvent.

The execute() method is passed a hash map containing parameters for its execution. The JDBC transactions always contain two key pairs: the JDBC connection (JDBC_CONNECTION) and the query timeout (QUERY_TIMEOUT). Further values can also be passed by including them in the EnvironmentVariables element in the swingconfig.xml configuration file.

Examining the Source Code

The open source Java code in the SWINGHOME/source directory is provided along with a script (ant) for compilation. This compiles all of the Java under the source directory and creates a file called mytransaction.jar in the SWINGHOME/lib directory. This file contains the transactions in compiled form (class). The default configuration will use the transactions in mytransactions.jar before using the default preconfigured code.

To use the Java transactions, edit the default swingconfig.xml file to include the attribute SourceFile of the Transaction element such as in the following example:

```
<TransactionList>
<Transaction Id="HR Transaction : Add Employee"➥
SourceFile="com.daves.transaction.HR.addemployee"
Weight="100" Enabled="true" />
<Transaction Id="HR Transaction : Update Employee"➥
SourceFile="com.daves.transaction.HR.updemployee"
Weight="100" Enabled="true" />
</TransactionList>
```

It is now possible to use the developed Java code as a custom user-developed Swingbench benchmark.

Summary

In this chapter you have looked at the configuration and use of benchmarking tools applicable to testing within a RAC on Linux environment. In particular, you have considered two tools, Hammerora and Swingbench, which are both freely available and run natively within the Linux environment. You have then reviewed specific examples of building and conducting tests using these tools to verify the validity and performance of your RAC installations and applications.

■ ■ ■

## CHAPTER 24

Performance Monitoring

In this chapter, we consider some of the tools available for monitoring the performance of a RAC cluster. At both the Oracle RAC and Linux operating system levels, our focus is on capturing and interpreting the statistics generated by the tools incorporated in both environments. At the database level, we will concentrate on using Enterprise Manager (EM) and the Oracle performance monitoring tools based on the Automatic Workload Repository (AWR) and Active Session History (ASH). At the operating system level, we will pay particular attention to the command line tools available in all Linux environments, such as top, sar, and netstat, that supplement the findings from Oracle tools.

In the complex applications architectures implemented in modern systems, a performance bottleneck can occur anywhere, including in the application tiers, in the database, or at the operating system level. You should not necessarily assume that every performance problem is caused by the RAC cluster, and you should therefore attempt to implement end-to-end monitoring in your application so that you can quickly and accurately identify the application layer in which the problem is occurring.

Oracle Performance Monitoring

In Chapter 14, we introduced the Manageability Infrastructure and the integrated method in which the Oracle 10g database is instrumented. We discussed how the MMON and MMNL background processes automatically capture and store database statistics in the AWR and ASH. You also saw how the Advisory Framework provides tools to interpret these statistics. In Chapter 23, you saw an example of taking AWR snapshots and generating reports to measure benchmarking performance.

In this section, we provide an overview of RAC-specific EM performance views and detailed information on generating AWR reports and interpreting the RAC-specific information within them. We review the information stored in the ASH and how to use the Automatic Database Diagnostic Monitor (ADDM) to detect RAC-specific performance findings. We also cover performance tuning with the tool guaranteed to be available in every Oracle environment: SQL*Plus.

Performance Monitoring with Enterprise Manager

Chapter 14 covered how to install and configure EM, and Chapter 18 explored how to use EM to administer a RAC cluster. EM includes extensive capabilities for monitoring Oracle databases.

EM also includes functionality specifically to monitor RAC database performance, and we recommend that you become familiar with the RAC-specific pages of EM to gain a high-level overview of your RAC cluster's performance.

Figure 24-1 shows the Performance tab for a RAC database.

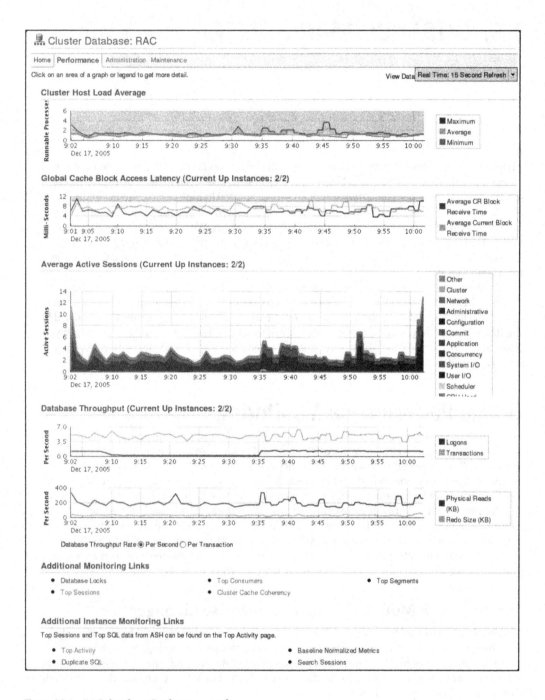

Figure 24-1. *RAC database Performance tab*

The first two graphs on the Performance tab show the Cluster Host Load Average and the Global Cache Block Access Latency. The third graph shows the number of Average Active Sessions throughout the reporting period. The final graph on the Performance tab shows the Database Throughput across all instances in terms of logons, transactions, physical reads, and redo size.

At the bottom of the Performance tab are five Additional Monitoring Links. The page you should use to monitor your interinstance communication is the Cluster Cache Coherency page, shown in Figure 24-2.

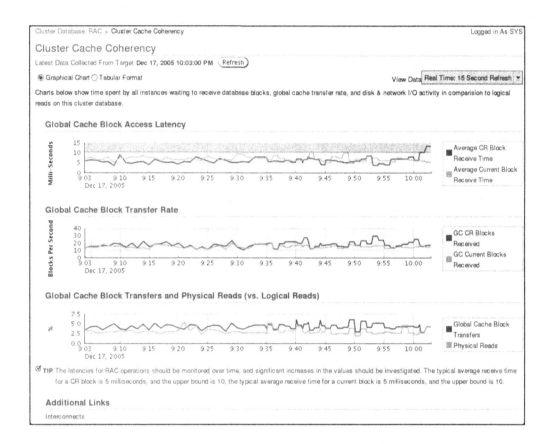

Figure 24-2. *Cluster Cache Coherency page*

The Cluster Cache Coherency page includes information on Global Cache Block Access Latency (this information also appears on the Performance tab), Global Cache Block Transfer Rate, and Global Cache Block Transfers and Physical Reads.

The metrics you will refer to most when reviewing your RAC's performance are observable within the Global Cache Block Transfer Rate view. In this view, you can observe the operation of Cache Fusion across the cluster. The constituent metrics are as follows:

- **GC CR Blocks Received**: This metric reflects the implementation of read consistency across the entire cluster. In other words, when a SELECT statement is in operation on one node in the cluster, if another session on any node in the cluster has changed those rows since the query started, the session will request the data block that contained the data when the query began. If the consistent read request cannot be satisfied from the local buffer cache, but it can be satisfied by shipping a data block from another instance in the cluster, then it is recorded in this metric.

- **GC Current Blocks Received**: This metric shows the interinstance transfer of data blocks that are in a current state. A data block is in a *current state* when it has been created or modified by an INSERT, UPDATE, or DELETE statement, and the most recent data reflecting this action resides in the buffer cache of an instance. If this current block is requested and successfully transferred directly to another instance in the cluster, it is recorded in this metric.

The Global Cache Block Transfers and Physical Reads graph compares the number of block transfers across the interconnect with the number of physical reads. Block transfers across the interconnect are usually more efficient than physical reads and are, therefore, favored by RAC where possible.

AWR Reports

In this section, we describe the AWR and show how to generate reports from its contents. AWR reports bear a close resemblance to those created by another Oracle tool called STATSPACK, which was introduced in Oracle 8.1.6. Both the AWR reporting tools and STATSPACK are available in Oracle 10*g* and allow you to save snapshots of the current values of various database statistics and then to compare the delta between two snapshots to determine the database workload during the intervening period.

We recommend that you use AWR reports instead of STATSPACK reports, if possible, for a number of reasons. First, AWR reports are based on the existing repository, which is located in the SYSAUX tablespace. In contrast, STATSPACK reports require a completely separate set of tables under the PERFSTAT schema. As the AWR runs by default, this may result in duplication of the diagnostic information being captured. The AWR automatically purges time-expired snapshots, whereas it is necessary to manually purge snapshots from the STATSPACK repository.

AWR reports contain more information than STATSPACK reports. In Oracle 10.1, this includes reports based on wait classes and metrics. In the future, any new features will be included in AWR reports. The information in the AWR also provides the foundation for tools such as ADDM operating under the Advisory Framework, whereas STATSPACK replicates the functionality of AWR reports only.

STATSPACK reports can be generated only in text format from SQL*Plus. AWR reports, however, can be generated in text or HTML format using either EM or SQL*Plus.

Finally, the generation of AWR snapshots is more efficient than that of STATSPACK snapshots. This is because AWR snapshots are generated by the MMON background process using non-SQL kernel calls, whereas STATSPACK snapshots are generated using SQL statements.

■Note Oracle recommends that you increase the size of the shared pool by 15%–20% to allow for the additional data structures used by the AWR infrastructure.

Generating AWR Reports

The AWR is created automatically if you have created the RAC database using DBCA, as detailed in Chapter 13. Alternatively, you can create the AWR manually using the script $ORACLE_HOME/rdbms/admin/catawr.sql.

A set of tables is created for the AWR under the SYS schema in the SYSAUX tablespace, and the AWR is implemented using three distinct sets of tables in the data dictionary. There are five control tables called WRM$_WR_CONTROL, WRM$_DATABASE_INSTANCE, WRM$_SNAPSHOT, WRM$SNAP_ERROR, and WRM$_BASELINE, with a DBA_HIST_% view for each of these tables.

In addition, there is a set of tables to hold the snapshots. These tables have the WRH$ prefix, for example, WRH$_SEG_STAT and WRH$_SQL_PLAN. There are approximately 60 of these tables. Each table has a DBA_HIST_% view with a similar name, for example, DBA_HIST_SEG_STAT and DBA_HIST_SQL_PLAN.

Baselines are held in a separate set of tables, each with the same name as the snapshot table with a _BL suffix. So, for example, for the snapshot table WRH$_LATCH, the baseline table is WRH$_LATCH_BL. There are no DBA_HIST_% views for the baseline tables.

At regular intervals, the MMON background processes triggers a snapshot of the current state of the database. The actual snapshot is performed by a MMON slave processes named M000. By default, snapshots are performed every 60 minutes and retained in the workload repository for seven days, after which they are automatically purged.

AWR snapshots are performed if the STATISTICS_LEVEL parameter is set to the default value of TYPICAL or to ALL. To disable AWR snapshots, you must set the STATISTICS_LEVEL parameter to BASIC; however, we do not recommended doing so, as it disables all other forms of statistics gathering.

You can check the current snapshot interval and retention time as follows:

```
SQL> SELECT snap_interval, retention FROM dba_hist_wr_control;
```

You can modify these values using the MODIFY_SNAPSHOT_SETTINGS procedure in DBMS_WORKLOAD_REPOSITORY. For example, to change the snapshot interval to 30 minutes and set the retention period to two weeks, use

```
SQL> EXECUTE dbms_workload_repository.modify_snapshot_settings -
> (interval => 30, retention => 20160);
```

Both the interval and retention parameters should be specified in minutes. If you specify an interval of 0, Oracle will set the snapshot interval to 1 year; if you specify a retention period of 0, Oracle will set the retention period to 100 years.

You can take a snapshot manually at any time for the particular instance you are connected to using the CREATE_SNAPSHOT procedure at the SQL*Plus prompt, for example:

```
SQL> EXECUTE dbms_workload_repository.create_snapshot;
```

This procedure can accept a single parameter specifying the flush level for the snapshot, which is either TYPICAL or ALL. You can also create snapshots from within EM; this functionality is available by navigating from the Administration page to the Workload Repository page and then to the Snapshots page.

When you have a stable workload, you can take a baseline, which records the difference between two snapshots. First, identify a suitable pair of snapshot IDs using the DBA_HIST_SNAPSHOT view:

```
SQL> SELECT snap_id, instance_number, startup_time,
> begin_interval_time,end_interval_time
> FROM dba_hist_snapshot;
```

Both snapshots must belong to the same instance and also have the same instance start-up time. For example, assuming that the start and end snapshots for the period of interest are 234 and 236, you can generate a baseline as follows:

```
SQL> EXECUTE dbms_workload_repository.create_baseline -
> ( -
>    start_snap_id => 234, -
>    end_snap_id => 236, -
>    baseline_name => 'Morning Peak' -
> );
```

You can check the current baselines in the DBA_HIST_BASELINE view. Unlike automatic snapshots, which will be purged at the end of the retention period, baselines will not be removed automatically. Baselines can be removed manually using the DROP_BASELINE procedure:

```
SQL> EXECUTE dbms_workload_repository.drop_baseline -
> ( -
>   baseline_name => 'Morning Peak' -
> );
```

You can extract reports from the AWR tables with the script $ORACLE_HOME/rdbms/admin/awrrpt.sql. As shown in the following listing, this script asks if you want the report output to be created in HTML or text format. It then asks you to specify the number of days of snapshots that you wish to view and, based on your response, it displays a list of the snapshots taken during this period. The script prompts you for the start and end snapshots for the report and also a file name in which to write the report. If no file name is specified, a default name based on the start and end snapshots will be used. Keep in mind that you cannot create valid reports for a period during which an instance shutdown has been performed.

```
SQL> @awrrpt

Current Instance
~~~~~~~~~~~~~~~~~

   DB Id    DB Name      Inst Num Instance
------------ ------------ -------- ------------
 2165634977 RAC                 1 RAC1

Specify the Report Type
~~~~~~~~~~~~~~~~~~~~~~~~~
Would you like an HTML report, or a plain text report?
Enter 'html' for an HTML report, or 'text' for plain text
Defaults to 'html'
Enter value for report_type: text

Type Specified:  text

EXT
----
.txt

Instances in this Workload Repository schema
~~~~~~~~~~~~~~~~~~~~~~~~~~~~~~~~~~~~~~~~~~~~~~

   DB Id     Inst Num DB Name      Instance     Host
------------ -------- ------------ ------------ ------------
* 2165634977        1 RAC          RAC1         london1
  2165634977        2 RAC          RAC2         london2

Using 2165634977 for database Id
Using           1 for instance number

Specify the number of days of snapshots to choose from
~~~~~~~~~~~~~~~~~~~~~~~~~~~~~~~~~~~~~~~~~~~~~~~~~~~~~~~~~

Entering the number of days (n) will result in the most recent
(n) days of snapshots being listed.  Pressing <return> without
specifying a number lists all completed snapshots.

Enter value for num_days: 1
```

```
Listing the last day's Completed Snapshots

                                                   Snap
Instance      DB Name        Snap Id   Snap Started     Level
----------    -----------    --------  ----------------  -----
RAC1          RAC              339 17 Apr 2006 09:17       1
                              340 17 Apr 2006 10:00       1
                              341 17 Apr 2006 11:00       1
                              342 17 Apr 2006 12:00       1
                              343 17 Apr 2006 13:00       1
                              344 17 Apr 2006 14:00       1
                              345 17 Apr 2006 15:00       1
                              346 17 Apr 2006 15:59       1
                              347 17 Apr 2006 16:59       1

Specify the Begin and End Snapshot Ids
~~~~~~~~~~~~~~~~~~~~~~~~~~~~~~~~~~~~~~~~~
Enter value for begin_snap: 346
Begin Snapshot Id specified: 346

Enter value for end_snap: 347
End   Snapshot Id specified: 347

Specify the Report Name
~~~~~~~~~~~~~~~~~~~~~~~~~
The default report file name is awrrpt_1_346_347.txt.  To use this name,
press <return> to continue, otherwise enter an alternative.

Enter value for report_name:

Using the report name awrrpt_1_346_347.txt
```

Interpreting the RAC Statistics of an AWR Report

You have now generated an AWR report to review the statistics captured across a period of time for an instance. If reviewing performance, you can and should generate reports for all instances within the cluster. The statistics contained within a report are for one instance only, and this instance will be recorded directly under the section heading WORKLOAD REPOSITORY report for, as shown here:

```
WORKLOAD REPOSITORY report for

DB Name      DB Id        Instance     Inst Num Release      RAC Host
-----------  -----------  -----------  -------- -----------  --- ------------
RAC          2165634977 RAC1               1 10.2.0.1.0  YES london1
```

Take time to examine the Load Profile section of this report. In particular, check that it covers the expected period and also that meaningful activity has taken place on the database during this period.

In the following sections, we concentrate on the differences between an AWR report for a single-instance database and a RAC database. Much of the content of an AWR report is identical for both.

Within an AWR report are two main sections containing RAC statistics. The first section appears immediately after the Top 5 Timed Events and includes Global Cache Load Profile, Global Cache Efficiency Percentages, Global Cache and Enqueue Services - Workload Characteristics, and Global Cache and Enqueue Services - Messaging Statistics. The second section appears at the end of the report and includes Global Enqueue Statistics, Global CR Served Stats, Global Current Served Stats, and Global Cache Transfer Stats.

Top 5 Timed Events

The Top 5 Timed Events will normally show the amount of CPU consumed and the top four wait events. For a given workload, this list of events should be relatively stable; you should investigate any significant variation. You will generally see CPU at the top of the list. However, CPU usage is not necessarily an indication of a healthy system, as the application may be CPU-bound. The most common wait events are db file sequential read, db file scattered read, db file parallel read, and log file sync.

For RAC databases, watch for wait events related to Global Cache Service (GCS), which are identified by the prefix gc or the Cluster wait. In a RAC environment, you should expect to see GCS events, but they should not be consuming the majority of the time on the system. The following example shows the Top 5 Timed Events from a reasonably healthy RAC system:

```
Top 5 Timed Events
~~~~~~~~~~~~~~~~~~~~~~~~                                  Avg      % Total
                                                         Wait     Call
Event                        Waits     Time (s)    (ms)    Time Wait Class
---------------------------  --------  ----------  ------  ----  ------------
CPU time                      1,242      33.82
log file sync               418,775     1,231        0    33.53 Commit
db file sequential read     172,766       388        0    10.57 User I/O
log file parallel write     560,263       234        0     6.38 System I/O
gc cr grant 2-way            73,315       161        0     4.38 Cluster
                            --------------------------------------------------
```

If your global cache events are prominent and, in particular, if they appear above CPU time in the report, this is an indication that you should drill down in the RAC statistics further in the report to identify if the amount of global cache traffic can be reduced.

Immediately after the Top 5 Timed Events, the first RAC-specific section summarizes the number of instances for the start and end snapshots, for example:

```
                        Begin   End
                        -----   -----
    Number of Instances:   2      2
```

Differing values indicate that an instance has been started or stopped during the snapshot period. If the number of instances is equal at the end of the period, this does not mean that one or more instances have joined or left the cluster during the snapshot period. Starting and stopping instances causes a higher than normal level of interinstance messaging, and the report should therefore be treated with caution.

Global Cache Load Profile

This section presents a summary of the traffic across the interconnect in terms of blocks exchanged by GCS and messages exchanged by both GCS and Global Enqueue Service (GES).

Consider this example:

```
Global Cache Load Profile
~~~~~~~~~~~~~~~~~~~~~~~~~~~~~~~~~~~~~~~~     Per Second     Per Transaction
                                            ----------     ---------------
    Global Cache blocks received:              16.72              7.61
     Global Cache blocks served:               16.83              7.66
        GCS/GES messages received:             49.74             22.64
           GCS/GES messages sent:              45.17             20.56
              DBWR Fusion writes:               2.18              0.99
Estd Interconnect traffic (KB):               286.94
```

Pay particular attention to the estimated interconnect traffic per second value at the end of this section. You should reference this value against the bandwidth of your network interconnect to ensure that your configuration has sufficient capacity for your requirements. As you can see in this example, two- to four-node clusters will rarely be expected to approach the bandwidth capacity of a Gigabit Ethernet interconnect.

Global Cache Efficiency Percentages

This section reports the percentage of blocks accessed from local cache, remote cache, and disk. In an optimum system, the percentage of local cache accesses should approach 100%, while the percentage of remote cache accesses and disk accesses should both approach 0%. The following example shows a level of efficiency percentages that you should expect to see:

```
Global Cache Efficiency Percentages (Target local+remote 100%)
~~~~~~~~~~~~~~~~~~~~~~~~~~~~~~~~~~~~~~~~~~~~~~~~~~~~~~~~~~~~~~~~~~~
Buffer access -  local cache %:    92.68
Buffer access - remote cache %:     4.26
Buffer access -         disk %:     3.06
```

Bear in mind that it takes significantly longer to read a block from disk than from a remote cache. You should therefore concentrate on reducing the amount of disk I/O before focusing on the global cache communication.

Global Cache and Enqueue Services - Workload Characteristics

This section describes the average times required to perform various GCS and GES tasks. Of these statistics, the most significant are the enqueue get time, which should ideally be below 1 ms, and the global cache cr and current block receive times.

```
Global Cache and Enqueue Services - Workload Characteristics
~~~~~~~~~~~~~~~~~~~~~~~~~~~~~~~~~~~~~~~~~~~~~~~~~~~~~~~~~~~~~~~~~~
                  Avg global enqueue get time (ms):     0.4

         Avg global cache cr block receive time (ms):   2.6
    Avg global cache current block receive time (ms):   2.1

           Avg global cache cr block build time (ms):   0.0
            Avg global cache cr block send time (ms):   0.0
           Avg global cache cr block flush time (ms):   87.9
      Global cache log flushes for cr blocks served %:   1.1

       Avg global cache current block pin time (ms):    0.0
      Avg global cache current block send time (ms):    0.0
     Avg global cache current block flush time (ms):   198.9
  Global cache log flushes for current blocks served %:  0.1
```

Global Cache and Enqueue Services - Messaging Statistics

This section describes average time to exchange different categories of interinstance messages.

```
Global Cache and Enqueue Services - Messaging Statistics
~~~~~~~~~~~~~~~~~~~~~~~~~~~~~~~~~~~~~~~~~~~~~~~~~~~~~~~~~~~~~
                 Avg message sent queue time (ms):     0.2
        Avg message sent queue time on ksxp (ms):     0.6
           Avg message received queue time (ms):     0.5
              Avg GCS message process time (ms):     0.1
              Avg GES message process time (ms):     0.0
```

```
                  % of direct sent messages:   64.71
                  % of indirect sent messages:  29.85
                  % of flow controlled messages: 5.43
```

SQL Statements

The AWR report contains a series of sections listing SQL statements in the library cache that exceed predefined thresholds. Of particular interest to RAC users is the SQL statements ordered By Cluster Wait Time section, which details the amount of time the statement was involved in waits for cluster resources. The cluster wait time is reported as a percentage of total elapsed time for the statement together with the elapsed time, CPU time, and number of executions.

For example, the following statement has experienced 65.9 seconds of cluster wait time over 3,414 executions. However, the cluster wait time represents only 3% of total elapsed time, which for most applications is acceptable.

```
SQL ordered by Cluster Wait Time  DB/Inst: RAC/RAC1  Snaps: 61-71

   Cluster      CWT % of    Elapsd        CPU                        Old
Wait Time (s) Elapsd Time  Time (s)    Time (s)    Executions   Hash Value
------------- ----------- ----------- ----------- ------------- ----------
      65.91         3.0    2,177.08       46.72        3,414 2369897509
Module: wish84t.exe
begin neword(:no_w_id,:no_max_w_id,:no_d_id,:no_c_id,:no_o_ol_cn
t,:no_c_discount,:no_c_last,:no_c_credit,:no_d_tax,:no_w_tax,:no
_d_next_o_id,TO_DATE(:timestamp,'YYYYMMDDHH24MISS')); END;
```

Dictionary Cache

The first subsection shows activity and hit rates for each object type within the dictionary cache. For RAC instances, a second subsection is included which reports the number of GES requests, conflicts, and releases for each object type. Look for excessive numbers of GES conflicts, especially for sequences.

Cache	GES Requests	GES Conflicts	GES Releases
dc_awr_control	2	2	0
dc_histogram_defs	29	0	0
dc_object_ids	4	0	0
dc_objects	28	1	0
dc_rollback_segments	22	0	0
dc_segments	50	9	0
dc_sequences	378	33	0
dc_tablespace_quotas	2	1	0
outstanding_alerts	178	64	0

Library Cache

This first subsection reports on activity in the library cache for each namespace. Oracle 10g can have up to 64 namespaces, but only the first 8 are reported in this section. For RAC databases, only the second subsection reports the number of GES lock requests, pin requests, pin releases, invalidation requests, and invalidations.

Namespace	GES Lock Requests	GES Pin Requests	GES Pin Releases	GES Inval Requests	GES Invali- dations
SQL AREA	0	0	0	0	0
TABLE/PROCEDURE	9,502	23	1	18	0
BODY	0	3	0	3	0
TRIGGER	0	0	0	0	0
INDEX	105	0	0	0	0
CLUSTER	125	0	0	0	0

Global Enqueue Statistics

In the event that any serious GES problems appear in the Top 5 Timed Events or in the Wait Events sections, this section can be used for further investigation.

```
Global Enqueue Stats  DB/Inst: RAC/RAC1  Snaps: 61-71

Statistic                               Total   per Second   per Trans
-----------------------------------   --------  ----------  ----------
acks for commit broadcast(actual)        6,287         1.7         0.8
acks for commit broadcast(logical        7,268         2.0         0.9
broadcast msgs on commit(actual)         5,917         1.6         0.7
broadcast msgs on commit(logical)        5,917         1.6         0.7
broadcast msgs on commit(wasted)             0         0.0         0.0
etc...
```

Global CR Server Statistics

This section contains the statistics for the number of blocks served by GCS. These statistics give an overview of GCS activity during the reporting period and are derived from the V$CR_BLOCK_SERVER dynamic performance view.

```
Global CR Served Stats  DB/Inst: RAC/RAC1  Snaps: 61-71

Statistic                      Total
----------------------------   --------------
CR Block Requests              32,526
CURRENT Block Requests            238
Data Block Requests            32,526
Undo Block Requests                 0
TX Block Requests                 238
```

Global Current Served Statistics

This section contains histograms of the GCS operations required to support current read requests, including block pinning, flushing redo to disk, and write operations, and is derived from the V$CURRENT_BLOCK_SERVER dynamic performance view. You should check this view if you believe that Cache Fusion is causing a bottleneck on systems with high levels of DML activity.

```
Global CURRENT Served Stats  DB/Inst: RAC/RAC1  Snaps: 61-71
-> Pins    = CURRENT Block Pin Operations
-> Flushes = Redo Flush before CURRENT Block Served Operations
-> Writes  = CURRENT Block Fusion Write Operations
```

```
Statistic         Total   % <1ms  % <10ms % <100ms   % <1s    % <10s

Pins             28,071   99.98     0.01     0.01     0.00     0.00
Flushes              35    2.86     8.57    31.43    54.29     2.86
Writes            7,814    1.96    41.73    31.81    22.06     2.43
```

Global Cache Transfer Statistics

This section was introduced in Oracle 10.2 and gives an overview of Global Cache transfer activity for each class of database buffer. This data is derived from the V$INSTANCE_CACHE_TRANSFER dynamic performance view and is especially useful in diagnosing whether cache transfer activity is affected by contention or a high level of system load.

```
Global Cache Transfer Stats  DB/Inst: RAC/RAC1  Snaps: 61-71
-> Immediate  (Immed) - Block Transfer NOT impacted by Remote Processing Delays
   Busy       (Busy)  - Block Transfer impacted by Remote Contention
   Congested (Congst) - Block Transfer impacted by Remote System Load
-> ordered by CR + Current Blocks Received desc


                   --------------- CR --------------  ----------- Current -----------
Inst Block          Blocks      %      %      %       Blocks      %      %      %
  No Class         Received  Immed   Busy Congst     Received  Immed   Busy Congst

   2 data blo       32,773   98.4    1.6     .0       27,199   99.4     .6     .0
   2 others            109   99.1     .9     .0          181  100.0     .0     .0
   2 undo hea          138   84.8   15.2     .0            6  100.0     .0     .0
```

Active Session History

Active Session History (ASH) was introduced in Oracle 10.1. It is a component of the AWR repository. ASH samples all sessions once per second and records information about those sessions that are currently waiting. This information is used by ADDM to classify any problems that have been identified.

For example, ADDM may be aware that a significant amount of time is being consumed waiting for I/O through waits for db file sequential read. ASH can identify specific files and blocks that are causing the waits. This data is used by ADDM to produce more accurate recommendations.

ASH acquires information directly by sampling the session state objects. The sampling default interval is 1,000 milliseconds (1 second).

ASH only records information about active sessions. It does not include information about recursive sessions or sessions waiting for idle events. This means that sessions waiting for SQL*Net message from client will not be included. ASH also excludes background processes waiting for their normal timer events or parallel slaves waiting for the PX_IDLE wait event.

The information collected by ASH is flushed to disk periodically. By default, only one out of every ten active session samples is flushed to disk. Information flushed from the ASH buffer to disk is written to the workload repository history table WRH$ACTIVE_SESSION_HISTORY, which is owned by SYS and stored in the SYSAUX tablespace.

The information collected by ASH is reported in EM. To view this information, from the Cluster Database Home Page in the Database Control, click the Performance tab. On the Cluster Database Performance Page, under the Additional Instance Monitoring Links heading, click the Top Activity link. The upper part of the Top Activity page shows a summary of CPU usage over the past hour. The lower part shows the Top SQL statements and the Top Sessions. You can run an ASH report from this page. When you click the Run ASH Report button, you will be prompted for start and end dates and times. If you click the Generate Report button, an HTML report will be generated immediately for the specified parameters. You can optionally save this report to file.

In Oracle 10.2 and above, a script is provided to report on the contents of the ASH repository. You can find this script in $ORACLE_HOME/rdbms/admin/ashrpt.sql. The script should be run in SQL*Plus, as follows:

```
sqlplus /nolog
SQL> connect / as sysdba
SQL> @$ORACLE_HOME/rdbms/admin/ashrpt.sql
```

The script will ask if you want the output to be generated in HTML or text format. It will then ask for a start time. You can specify this start time in terms of the current value of SYSDATE (e.g., -1 is one hour previously). You will then be prompted for the duration of the period covered by the report, specified in minutes. Finally, the report will prompt for an output file name. If you do not specify one, a default file name will be generated for you. For example, the file name ashrpt_1_0722_1331.txt was generated for a report created for instance 1 on July 22 at 1:31 pm.

Within the ASH report, the first section describes the environment in which the report was created, including the database, instance, release, node, and number of CPUs, and the sizes of the SGA, buffer cache, shared pool, and ASH buffer. The remainder of the report details the information specific to sessions active during the period of time for which the report was generated, and you should look for cluster-related activity within this session information.

Automatic Database Diagnostic Monitor

The ADDM was introduced in Oracle 10.1. It uses data captured in the AWR to diagnose database performance, identify any problems, and suggest potential solutions. ADDM is built directly into the kernel, minimizing any performance overhead.

ADDM analyzes database performance holistically. In other words, it considers all activity across the database before making recommendations about specific areas of the workload.

ADDM runs automatically after each AWR snapshot, and the results are saved in the database. If ADDM detects any issues, then alerts are generated which can be inspected in the EM tools.

You can also run an ADDM report manually using the following script:

```
$ORACLE_HOME/rdbms/admin/addmrpt.sql
```

This script is similar to those used to generate AWR reports. It prompts for a start and end snapshot, and also for the name of an output file. If no output file name is specified, then the report will be written to a file called

```
addmrpt_<instance>_<start_snapshot>_<stop_snapshot>.txt
```

for example:

```
addmrpt_1_511_512.txt
```

Although the procedure for running ADDM reports is similar to that used with AWR reports, the content of the report is significantly different.

The DBMS_ADVISOR package allows you to control ADDM. The simplest way to access this package is from EM, which shows a complete performance overview, including any recommendations, on a single page. The addmprt.sql script also calls the DBMS_ADVISOR package, allowing you to access ADDM manually. Finally, you can access the DBMS_ADVISOR API directly using PL/SQL calls.

ADDM stores information in a set of tables owned by SYS in the SYSAUX tablespace. The base tables have a prefix of WRI$%. These tables are accessible through a number of views with the prefix DBA_ADVISOR_%.

ADDM needs at least two snapshots in the AWR before it can perform any analysis. The ADDM report header describes the analysis period, database and instance names, hostname, and database version.

```
              DETAILED ADDM REPORT FOR TASK 'TASK_342' WITH ID 342
              ------------------------------------------------------

                  Analysis Period: 17-DEC-2005 from 21:00:16 to 22:00:19
              Database ID/Instance: 2165194178/1
          Database/Instance Names: RAC/RAC1
                        Host Name: london1
                 Database Version: 10.2.0.1.0
                   Snapshot Range: from 20 to 21
                    Database Time: 4426 seconds
            Average Database Load: 1.2 active sessions
```

The header specifies the Database Time, which in this case is 4,426 seconds. The ADDM report is based on this statistic. The report header also summarizes the average database load during the snapshot period, in terms of the average number of active sessions, providing a useful view of the level of activity on the database.

The report is divided up into findings, listed in descending order of their perceived impact on database time. Note that the order in which the findings are presented is dependent on the results of the analysis for that specific period.

The following is an example finding from an ADDM report. The finding highlights that RAC-based wait events are highlighted under the Cluster wait category, and in this case, the recommendation was to run the SQL Tuning Advisor on the statement in question.

```
FINDING 7: 4% impact (178 seconds)
-----------------------------------
SQL statements responsible for significant inter-instance messaging were found

   RECOMMENDATION 1: SQL Tuning, 38% benefit (1665 seconds)
      ACTION: Run SQL Tuning Advisor on the SQL statement with SQL_ID
         "8yvup05pk06ca".
         RELEVANT OBJECT: SQL statement with SQL_ID 8yvup05pk06ca and
         PLAN_HASH 3016086792
         SELECT S_QUANTITY, S_DATA, S_DIST_01, S_DIST_02, S_DIST_03,
         S_DIST_04, S_DIST_05, S_DIST_06, S_DIST_07, S_DIST_08, S_DIST_09,
         S_DIST_10 FROM STOCK WHERE S_I_ID = :B2 AND S_W_ID = :B1
      RATIONALE: SQL statement with SQL_ID "8yvup05pk06ca" was executed 33888
         times and had an average elapsed time of 0.048 seconds.
      RATIONALE: Average time spent in Cluster wait events per execution was
         0.0004 seconds.

   ...


   SYMPTOMS THAT LED TO THE FINDING:
   SYMPTOM: Wait class "Cluster" was consuming significant database time.
            (3.8% impact [170 seconds])
```

Performance Monitoring Using SQL*Plus

Since early versions of Oracle 7, the two main sources of information for performance tuning an Oracle database have been system statistics and wait events. Both have been extended with additional statistics and events in subsequent releases. There are a number of RAC-specific statistics and events.

In Oracle 9.2 and above, useful information could also be obtained from the segment statistics facility. In Oracle 10.1 and above, the kernel has been much more thoroughly instrumented, resulting in a large increase in the number of latches and wait events that are individually reported. Execution time information is also available in the form of time-based metrics.

In this section, we will examine some of performance tuning queries you can use to diagnose performance issues in a RAC environment.

GV$ Views

Before reviewing the SQL*Plus queries, we will briefly review the relationship between the X$ tables, GV$ views, and V$ views. All are compiled into the Oracle executable and exist for both single-instance and RAC databases.

X$ tables present instance or session memory structures as tables. Although they still exist, RAC-specific X$ tables are not populated for single-instance databases. X$ tables are defined in V$FIXED_TABLE.

GV$ views are also built into the Oracle executable. They therefore exist for all databases (including single-instance) and reference the X$ tables.

The standard V$ views are also built into the Oracle executable. In general, V$ views do not directly reference X$ tables; they generally use them indirectly via GV$ views using queries of the following form:

```
SELECT <column_list>
FROM gv$<view_name>
WHERE inst_id = USERENV ('INSTANCE');
```

Both the GV$ and V$ views are defined in V$FIXED_VIEW_DEFINITION.

In a RAC environment, a number of additional synonyms for GV$ and V$ views are created by the script $ORACLE_HOME/rdbms/admin/catclust.sql.

GV$ views include the instance number. When they are queried, the query is executed separately on all active instances using parallel execution. The results are merged on the instance initiating the query. In Oracle 10.1 and above, you will see parallel execution slaves called PZ99, PZ98, and so forth, which are used to execute these queries.

GV$ views are not meaningful in a few cases because the views are derived from the control files. As the control files are shared between all instances, the GV$ views return with duplicate sets of rows from each instance. For these views, we recommend using the local V$ dynamic performance views instead.

System Statistics

System statistics are maintained in each instance. They are reported in a number of dynamic performance views, including V$SYSSTAT, V$SESSTAT, and V$MYSTAT. In Oracle 10.2, a subset of 28 statistics is also reported at a session level in V$SERVICE_STATS.

Segment Statistics

Segment statistics were introduced in Oracle 9.2. They provide a powerful mechanism by which you can identify which objects are subject to I/O or contention. Prior to the introduction of segment statistics, this information could only be obtained using an event 10046 level 8 trace or by polling the V$SYSTEM_WAIT dynamic performance view. The level of granularity is the object, so you may still need to use the 10046 trace if you need to identify a specific block or set of blocks.

In Oracle 10.2, 12 segment statistics are maintained in all databases when the value of the STATISTICS_LEVEL parameter is TYPICAL or ALL. Three statistics report global cache activity at the object level, and you can use these to quickly pinpoint the segments in your database that are experiencing the highest levels of interinstance activity: gc cr blocks received, gc current blocks received, and gc buffer busy. You should be familiar with the first two statistics from the charts displayed in EM. The additional statistic, gc buffer busy, shows the segments experiencing levels of contention between instances.

The following example shows the global cache activity for the table segments of a schema named TPCC:

```
SQL> SELECT
>    table_name                 AS "Table Name",
>    gc_buffer_busy             AS "Buffer Busy",
>    gc_cr_blocks_received      AS "CR Blocks Received",
>    gc_current_blocks_received AS "Current Blocks Received"
> FROM
> (
>    SELECT table_name FROM dba_tables
>    WHERE owner = 'TPCC'
> ) t,
> (
>    SELECT object_name,value AS gc_buffer_busy
>    FROM v$segment_statistics
>    WHERE owner = 'TPCC'
>    AND object_type = 'TABLE'
>    AND statistic_name = 'gc buffer busy'
> ) ss1,
> (
>    SELECT object_name,value AS gc_cr_blocks_received
>    FROM v$segment_statistics
>    WHERE owner = 'TPCC'
>    AND object_type = 'TABLE'
>    AND statistic_name = 'gc cr blocks received'
> ) ss2,
> (
>    SELECT object_name,value AS gc_current_blocks_received
>    FROM v$segment_statistics
>    WHERE owner = 'TPCC'
>    AND object_type = 'TABLE'
>    AND statistic_name = 'gc current blocks received'
> ) ss3
> WHERE t.table_name = ss1.object_name
> AND t.table_name = ss2.object_name
> AND t.table_name = ss3.object_name;
```

For our example, this query returned the following output:

Table Name	Buffer Busy	CR Blocks Received	Current Blocks Received
CUSTOMER	0	54	434
DISTRICT	0	62	370
HISTORY	0	6	19
ITEM	0	0	637
ORDERS	1	250	574
STOCK	0	1193	531
WAREHOUSE	0	206	192

Pay particular attention to the buffer busy statistics to identify contention between instances.

If contention is high and there are a large number of rows per block, you may benefit from distributing the rows across a greater number of blocks by increasing the value of PCTFREE for the object in question.

Global Cache Services

You can investigate GCS activity in terms of consistent reads and current reads in greater detail using the statistics discussed in the following sections.

Consistent Reads

To monitor the performance of consistent reads, use this formula:

$$(\text{gc cr block receive time} \times 10) \,/\, (\text{gc cr blocks received})$$

which returns the average time for consistent read block requests for the instance in milliseconds and is the GC CR metric of the Global Cache Block Transfer Rate that you observe within the EM RAC performance views. This is the most important value for determining interconnect performance, as it usually reflects the largest constituent component of interconnect traffic.

Requests for global resources for data blocks originate in the buffer cache of the requesting instance. Before a request enters the GCS request queue, Oracle allocates data structures in the SGA to track the state of the request and collects statistics on these resource structures.

```
SQL> SELECT
>    gc_cr_block_receive_time AS "Receive Time",
>    gc_cr_blocks_received AS "Blocks Received",
>    (gc_cr_block_receive_time * 10) /
>      gc_cr_blocks_received AS "Average Latency (MS)"
> FROM
> (
>      SELECT value AS gc_cr_block_receive_time FROM v$sysstat
>      WHERE name = 'gc cr block receive time'
> ),
> (
>      SELECT value AS gc_cr_blocks_received FROM v$sysstat
>      WHERE name = 'gc cr blocks received'
> );
```

The following is an example of the output from this query:

```
Receive Time Blocks Received Average Latency (MS)
------------ --------------- --------------------
        5305            2179            24.3460303
```

The latency of a consistent block request is the time elapsed between the original request and the receipt of the consistent block image at the local instance. Using a Gigabit Ethernet interconnect, this value should normally be less than 5 ms and should not exceed 15 ms, although this can be affected by system configuration and volume. In this example, you see that the latency is 24 ms and therefore warrants further investigation You should first use the Linux operating system utilities, such as `netstat` detailed later in this chapter, to determine whether there are any network configuration issues, such as network packet send and receive errors. You should also use operating system utilities such as `top` and `sar` to measure the load on the nodes themselves.

If you have ensured that the interconnect is configured correctly and you are still experiencing high average latencies, consider reducing the value of `DB_FILE_MULTIBLOCK_READ_COUNT`. This parameter specifies the number of blocks a process will request in a single operation. The process will have to wait for all blocks to be returned; therefore, higher values may cause longer waits. Before you adjust this parameter, carefully assess the impact on the entire workload.

High average latencies may also be caused by a high number of incoming requests or multiple nodes dispatching requests to the LMS process. You can calculate the average LMS service time as follows:

```
average LMS service time = average latency
- average time to build consistent read block
- average time to wait for log flush
- average time to send completed block
```

Average latency is calculated as shown previously.

Average time to build a consistent read block is calculated as follows:

$$\text{gc cr block build time} / \text{gc cr blocks served}$$

Average time spent waiting for a redo log flush is calculated as follows:

$$\text{gc cr block flush time} / \text{gc cr blocks served}$$

Average time to send a completed block is calculated as follows:

$$\text{gc cr block send time} / \text{gc cr blocks served}$$

The following query can be used to calculate the average LMS service time for consistent block reads:

```
SQL> SELECT
>    average_latency AS "Average Latency",
>    average_build_time AS "Average Build Time",
>    average_flush_time AS "Average Flush Time",
>    average_send_time AS "Average Send Time",
>    average_latency - average_build_time - average_flush_time - average_send_time
>      AS "Average LMS Service Time"
> FROM
> (
>    SELECT
>    (gc_cr_block_receive_time * 10) / gc_cr_blocks_received AS average_latency,
>    (gc_cr_block_build_time * 10) / gc_cr_blocks_served AS average_build_time,
>    (gc_cr_block_flush_time * 10) / gc_cr_blocks_served AS average_flush_time,
>    (gc_cr_block_send_time * 10) / gc_cr_blocks_served AS average_send_time
>    FROM
>    (
>      SELECT value AS gc_cr_block_receive_time FROM v$sysstat
>      WHERE name = 'gc cr block receive time'
>    ),
>    (
>      SELECT value AS gc_cr_blocks_received FROM v$sysstat
>      WHERE name = 'gc cr blocks received'
>    ),
>    (
>      SELECT value AS gc_cr_block_build_time FROM v$sysstat
>      WHERE name = 'gc cr block build time'
>    ),
>    (
>      SELECT value AS gc_cr_block_flush_time FROM v$sysstat
>      WHERE name = 'gc cr block flush time'
>    ),
>    (
>      SELECT value AS gc_cr_block_send_time FROM v$sysstat
>      WHERE name = 'gc cr block send time'
>    ),
>    (
>      SELECT value AS gc_cr_blocks_served FROM v$sysstat
>      WHERE name = 'gc cr blocks served'
>    )
> );
```

The difference between the average latency time and the sum of the average build, flush, and send times represents the time spent in the LMS service and the time spent transmitting the messages across the interconnect. The following is example output from this query:

Average Latency	Average Build Time	Average Flush Time	Average Send Time	Average LMS Service Time
40.7488403	0.039572616	0.716264345	0.035615354	39.957388

In the example just shown, there is in fact a high LMS Service Time, and therefore the high latency should be addressed by improving the server node resources, such as processing power available. Further evidence for this diagnosis should be available from your operating system utilities.

Current Blocks

You can also use SQL*Plus to determine the current block activity, which is the GC Current metric of the Global Cache Block Transfer Rate from the EM RAC performance views. You can calculate the overall average latency involved in processing requests for current blocks using the following formula:

```
SQL> SELECT
>   gc_current_block_receive_time AS "Receive Time",
>   gc_current_blocks_received AS "Blocks Received",
>   (gc_current_block_receive_time * 10) / gc_current_blocks_received
>   AS "Average (MS)"
> FROM
> (
>   SELECT value AS gc_current_block_receive_time
>   FROM v$sysstat
>   WHERE name = 'gc current block receive time'
> ),
> (
>   SELECT value AS gc_current_blocks_received
>   FROM v$sysstat
>   WHERE name = 'gc current blocks received'
> );
```

Consider this example:

```
Receive Time Blocks Received Average (MS)
------------ --------------- ------------
       12279           14222   8.63380678
```

You can calculate the amount of overall latency that can be attributed to the LMS process using the following:

```
average LMS service time =
average latency
- average time to pin current blocks
- average time to wait for log flush
- average time to send completed block
```

The average latency is calculated as follows:

gc current block receive time / gc current blocks received

The average time to pin current blocks is calculated as follows:

gc current block pin time / gc current blocks served

The average time spent waiting for a redo log flush is calculated as follows:

gc current block flush time / gc current blocks served

And the average time to send a completed block is calculated as follows:

gc current block send time / gc current blocks served

You can use the following query to calculate the average LMS service time for current block reads:

```
SQL> SELECT
>    average_latency    AS "Average Latency",
>    average_pin_time   AS "Average Pin Time",
>    average_flush_time AS "Average Flush Time",
>    average_send_time  AS "Average Send Time",
>    average_latency - average_pin_time - average_flush_time - average_send_time
>    AS "Average LMS Service Time"
> FROM
> (
>   SELECT
>   (gc_current_block_receive_time * 10) / gc_current_blocks_received
>     AS average_latency,
>   (gc_current_block_pin_time * 10) / gc_current_blocks_served
>     AS average_pin_time,
>   (gc_current_block_flush_time * 10) / gc_current_blocks_served
>     AS average_flush_time,
>   (gc_current_block_send_time * 10) / gc_current_blocks_served
>     AS average_send_time
>   FROM
>   (
>     SELECT value AS gc_current_block_receive_time FROM v$sysstat
>     WHERE name = 'gc current block receive time'
>   ),
>   (
>     SELECT value AS gc_current_blocks_received FROM v$sysstat
>     WHERE name = 'gc current blocks received'
>   ),
>   (
>     SELECT value AS gc_current_block_pin_time FROM v$sysstat
>     WHERE name = 'gc current block pin time'
>   ),
>   (
>     SELECT value AS gc_current_block_flush_time FROM v$sysstat
>     WHERE name = 'gc current block flush time'
>   ),
>   (
>     SELECT value AS gc_current_block_send_time FROM v$sysstat
>     WHERE name = 'gc current block send time'
>   ),
>   (
>     SELECT value AS gc_current_blocks_served FROM v$sysstat
>     WHERE name = 'gc current blocks served'
>   )
> );
```

The following is an example of the output from this statement:

Average Latency	Average Build Time	Average Pin Time	Average Send Time	Average LMS Service Time
8.67584376	0.041137669	0.022696645	0.04397475	8.56803469

High latency values may indicate server or interconnect performance issues; however, you should reference your current block statistics against the possibility of contention for data between instances.

Global Enqueue Service

GES manages all the non–Cache Fusion intrainstance and interinstance resource operations. High GES workload request rates can adversely affect performance. To calculate the average global enqueue time in milliseconds, use the following statement:

```
SQL> SELECT
>    global_enqueue_get_time AS "Get Time",
>    global_enqueue_gets_sync AS "Synchronous Gets",
>    global_enqueue_gets_async AS "Asynchronous Gets",
>    (global_enqueue_get_time * 10) /
>    (global_enqueue_gets_sync + global_enqueue_gets_async)
>    AS "Average (MS)"
> FROM
> (
>    SELECT value AS global_enqueue_get_time
>    FROM v$sysstat
>    WHERE name = 'global enqueue get time'
> ),
> (
>    SELECT value AS global_enqueue_gets_sync
>    FROM v$sysstat
>    WHERE name = 'global enqueue gets sync'
> ),
> (
>    SELECT value AS global_enqueue_gets_async
>    FROM v$sysstat
>    WHERE name = 'global enqueue gets async'
> );
```

Get Time	Synchronous Gets	Asynchronous Gets	Average (MS)
159674	98861	10555	14.5932953

Synchronous gets are usually locking events, whereas asynchronous gets are usually caused by nonblocking interinstance process activity.

In the preceding example, the average global enqueue time is 14.6 ms, which is within an acceptable range. If this figure is greater than 20 ms, you should identify and rectify the cause within your application.

Library Cache

You can obtain further information about global enqueue activity caused by statement parsing and execution from the V$LIBRARYCACHE dynamic performance view. This view reports GES activity for locks, pins, and invalidations, for example:

```
SQL> SELECT
>    namespace                  AS "Namespace",
>    dlm_lock_requests          AS "Lock Requests",
>    dlm_pin_requests           AS "Pin Requests",
>    dlm_pin_releases           AS "Pin Releases",
>    dlm_invalidation_requests  AS "Invalidation Requests",
>    dlm_invalidations          AS "Invalidations"
> FROM v$librarycache;
```

Namespace	Lock Requests	Pin Requests	Pin Releases	Invalidation Requests	Invalidations
SQL AREA	0	0	0	0	0
TABLE/PROCEDURE	17725	3074	761	458	0
BODY	0	16	0	15	0
TRIGGER	0	6	0	6	0
INDEX	365	97	31	28	0
CLUSTER	581	14	0	8	0

If you see excessively high values in these columns, solutions include pinning packages in the shared pool using the KEEP procedure in the DBMS_SHARED_POOL package. Also investigate methods of keeping cursors open either within the application or by using the SESSION_CACHED_CURSORS parameter.

Dictionary Cache

You can obtain further information about global enqueue activity caused by statement pinning dictionary cache objects from the V$ROWCACHE dynamic performance view. This view reports GES lock requests, conflicts, and releases, for example:

```
SQL> SELECT
>    parameter      AS "Cache Name",
>    dlm_requests   AS "Requests",
>    dlm_conflicts  AS "Conflicts",
>    dlm_releases   AS "Releases"
> FROM v$rowcache;
```

Cache Name	Requests	Conflicts	Releases
dc_free_extents	0	0	0
dc_used_extents	0	0	0
dc_segments	557	8	197
dc_tablespaces	20	0	10
dc_tablespace_quotas	6	1	0
dc_files	0	0	0
dc_users	28	0	6
dc_rollback_segments	67	0	0
dc_objects	872	39	240
dc_global_oids	47	0	19
dc_constraints	0	0	0
dc_object_ids	886	0	287
dc_sequences	922	117	0
dc_usernames	12	0	6
dc_database_links	0	0	0
dc_histogram_defs	3422	0	901

Look for high values in the Conflicts column. In the preceding example, there have been 117 conflicts for sequences. Uncached sequences are one of the most common causes of performance issues in RAC.

Lock Conversions

In Oracle 10.1 and above, most of the statistics related to lock conversions can be obtained from V$GES_CONVERT_LOCAL and V$GES_CONVERT_REMOTE. These views show the number of lock conversions on the local system and on remote systems, respectively:

```
SQL> SELECT convert_type,average_convert_time, convert_count
SQ> FROM v$ges_convert_local;

CONVERT_TYPE    AVERAGE_CONVERT_TIME CONVERT_COUNT
--------------- -------------------- -------------
NULL -> SS                         0             0
NULL -> SX                         1             4
NULL -> S                          2          1798
NULL -> SSX                        2             2
NULL -> X                         87          1138
SS   -> SX                         0             0
SS   -> S                          0             0
SS   -> SSX                        0             0
SS   -> X                          0             0
SX   -> S                          0             0
SX   -> SSX                        0             0
SX   -> X                          0             0
S    -> SX                         0             0
S    -> SSX                        0             0
S    -> X                          1            50
SSX  -> X                          0             0
```

Lock conversions are essential to the efficient operation of a RAC database and are not necessarily harmful. However, it is important to check that lock conversions, like lock requests, are not being blocked by instances holding incompatible locks.

To check which instances are currently blocking other instances, use the following query:

```
SQL> SELECT
>   dl.inst_id,
>   s.sid,
>   p.spid,
>   dl.resource_name1,
>   decode (substr (dl.grant_level,1,8),
>     'KJUSERNL','Null',
>     'KJUSERCR','Row-S (SS)',
>     'KJUSERCW','Row-X (SX)',
>     'KJUSERPR','Share',
>     'KJUSERPW','S/Row-X (SSX)',
>     'KJUSEREX','Exclusive',
>   request_level) as grant_level,
>   decode(substr(dl.request_level,1,8),
>     'KJUSERNL','Null',
>     'KJUSERCR','Row-S (SS)',
>     'KJUSERCW','Row-X (SX)',
>     'KJUSERPR','Share',
>     'KJUSERPW','S/Row-X (SSX)',
>     'KJUSEREX','Exclusive',
```

```
>    request_level) as request_level,
>    decode(substr(dl.state,1,8),
>      'KJUSERGR','Granted','KJUSEROP','Opening',
>      'KJUSERCA','Cancelling',
>      'KJUSERCV','Converting'
>    ) as state,
>    sw.event,
>    sw.seconds_in_wait sec
> FROM
>    gv$ges_enqueue dl,
>    gv$process p,
>    gv$session s,
>    gv$session_wait sw
> WHERE blocker = 1
> AND (dl.inst_id = p.inst_id AND dl.pid = p.spid)
> AND (p.inst_id = s.inst_id AND p.addr = s.paddr)
> AND (s.inst_id = sw.inst_id AND s.sid = sw.sid)
> ORDER BY sw.seconds_in_wait DESC
```

To discover which sessions are currently being blocked, change the line

```
>    WHERE blocker = 1
```

to

```
>    WHERE blocked = 1
```

in the preceding query.

Linux Performance Monitoring

So far in this chapter, we have focused on Oracle performance monitoring tools. However, performance problems often occur outside the Oracle environment at the operating system, network, or storage level. It is therefore important to understand the information provided not only by the Oracle performance monitoring tools, but also by the standard operating system monitoring tools available on Linux. You can use the information provided by these tools to complement and support the findings from Oracle tools to fully diagnose RAC performance.

A number of GUI-based performance monitoring tools operate in the Linux environment, such as GKrellM. We recommend investigating GKrellM and other open source GUI programs when building of portfolio of operating system tools to complement EM. In keeping with our approach to Oracle performance monitoring, however, we believe that your level of expertise will benefit significantly from being familiar with the underlying statistics used by many of these tools. For this reason, our focus here is on the most commonly used command line operating system monitoring tools available with all Linux distributions.

ps

The command ps is one of the most basic, yet essential tools for analyzing performance on a Linux system. At its simplest, ps shows a list of processes, and if called without arguments, it displays the list of processes running under the current session, as shown here:

```
[oracle@london1 oracle]$ ps
  PID TTY          TIME CMD
 6923 ttyp1    00:00:00 bash
 6926 ttyp1    00:00:00 ps
```

Fortunately, ps can do a lot more than this and accepts a wealth of arguments to present process listings in almost every conceivable form. The arguments to ps can take three forms: standard System V Unix–type options that must be preceded by a dash, BSD-type options that are not preceded by a dash, and GNU long options that are preceded by two dashes. In effect, you may use different combinations of arguments to display similar forms of output. One combination of arguments that you will use most regularly is that of a full listing of all processes using the System V -ef arguments, of which the following are the first ten lines of output:

```
[oracle@london1 oracle]$ ps -ef
UID        PID  PPID  C STIME TTY          TIME CMD
root         1     0  0 Mar08 ?        00:00:09 init
root         2     0  0 Mar08 ?        00:00:00 [migration/0]
root         3     0  0 Mar08 ?        00:00:00 [migration/1]
root         4     0  0 Mar08 ?        00:00:00 [migration/2]
root         5     0  0 Mar08 ?        00:00:00 [migration/3]
root         6     0  0 Mar08 ?        00:00:00 [migration/4]
root         7     0  0 Mar08 ?        00:00:00 [migration/5]
root         8     0  0 Mar08 ?        00:00:00 [migration/6]
root         9     0  0 Mar08 ?        00:00:00 [migration/7]
```

For more details about each process, the -l argument gives a longer listing with the command ps -elf. You can pipe the output through grep to restrict the number of lines returned:

```
[oracle@london1 oracle]$ ps -elf | grep smon | grep -v grep
0 S oracle  14935   1  0  75   0 - 75913 semtim Mar08 ?  00:00:02  ora_smon_RAC1
```

However, instead of using ps with grep, pgrep can provide you with the same functionality in a single command. For example, the following extract uses the -flu arguments to display the processes owned by the user oracle:

```
[oracle@london1 oracle]$ pgrep -flu oracle
12343 /u01/app/oracle/product/10.2.0.1.0/bin/tnslsnr LISTENER_RAC1 -inherit
14922 ora_pmon_RAC1
14924 ora_psp0_RAC1
14926 ora_mman_RAC1
14928 ora_dbw0_RAC1
14931 ora_lgwr_RAC1
14933 ora_ckpt_RAC1
14935 ora_smon_RAC1
14938 ora_reco_RAC1
14940 ora_cjq0_RAC1
```

For identifying processes, another useful command is pidof, which can be used without arguments if you know the name of a process to quickly find its corresponding process identifier:

```
[oracle@london1 oracle]$ pidof ora_smon_RAC1
14935
```

free

The free command displays the status of your system's virtual memory at the current point in time. There are three rows of output: the Mem: row shows the utilization of the physical RAM installed in the machine, the -/+ buffers/cache: row shows the amount of memory assigned to system buffers and caches, and the Swap: row shows the amount of swap space used.

The following example shows a system with 8GB of RAM, and at first it may appear that this has nearly all been consumed, with only 25MB free. However, with free we can see that in fact the operating system assigns memory to buffers and cache if it is not being used for any other purpose; therefore, the actual figure representing free memory is over 7.2GB. If you are using any third-party system-monitoring tool that reports memory utilization to be high on a Linux system, you should always confirm this with free to ensure that the memory is not simply free in buffers and cache instead.

```
[root@london1 root]# cat free
             total        used        free      shared     buffers       cached
Mem:        7973792     7948236       25556           0      175140     7087124
-/+ buffers/cache:       685972     7287820
Swap:       8388600           0     8388600
```

This example also shows that the system is not using any of the configured swap space at this point in time. As we discussed in Chapter 10, unless you are creating a large number of processes on the system, swap space utilization should be minimal. If you monitor the memory utilization with free, and an increasing amount of swap space is being consumed, this will have a significantly negative performance impact.

By default, the values for free are expressed in kilobytes; however, you can specify the display in bytes, megabytes, or gigabytes to be used with the -b, -m, or -g flag, respectively. The -s flag can be used with an interval value to continually repeat the command according to the interval period. Alternatively, you can use the watch command to refresh the display in place, and by default running watch free will refresh in place every two seconds.

When working with Oracle, you should also be familiar with the output of /proc/meminfo, which is the location from which the information for free is derived. Within /proc/meminfo you can also see the amount of memory and swap that is free and used, and the amount of memory assigned to buffers and cache on an individual basis. In addition, /proc/meminfo includes the configuration of huge pages, the setting of which we discuss in Chapter 11.

This example of /proc/meminfo shows a system with a total of 128GB of RAM and 50 huge pages at 262MB each, which is a 12GB allocation in total. All of these huge pages are free, indicating that an Oracle SGA has not yet been allocated from this pool. You should also bear in mind when considering the output from all memory performance tools that an SGA allocated from huge pages will not be a candidate to be swapped to disk in any circumstance.

```
[root@london1 root]# cat /proc/meminfo
MemTotal:      128689536 kB
MemFree:        40052672 kB
Buffers:           10032 kB
Cached:         72412368 kB
SwapCached:            0 kB
Active:         70760704 kB
Inactive:        1730272 kB
HighTotal:             0 kB
HighFree:              0 kB
LowTotal:      128689536 kB
LowFree:        40052672 kB
SwapTotal:       2559968 kB
SwapFree:        2559936 kB
Dirty:                80 kB
Writeback:             0 kB
Mapped:           187392 kB
Slab:            2406240 kB
Committed_AS:     691712 kB
PageTables:         6144 kB
VmallocTotal: 137402172640 kB
VmallocUsed:      282688 kB
VmallocChunk: 137401889520 kB
HugePages_Total:      50
HugePages_Free:       50
Hugepagesize:     262144 kB
```

If you are interested in the cached objects in the kernel, you can view them in the output of /proc/slabinfo; however, you will most likely be interested only in specific entries, such as kiobuf related to asynchronous I/O activity. In addition, a utility called slabtop can display kernel slab information in real time. The form of the output of slabtop is similar to that of the more general-purpose top.

top

ps and free are very much static commands that return information about system processes and memory utilization within individual snapshots, but they are not designed to track usage over a longer period of time. The first tool we will consider with this monitoring capability is top.

If top is called without arguments, it will display output similar to the following while refreshing the screen by default every two seconds, without requiring watch to enable this functionality:

```
11:34:38  up 13 days,  5:29,  6 users,  load average: 1.61, 0.94, 0.42
342 processes: 339 sleeping, 3 running, 0 zombie, 0 stopped
CPU states:  cpu     user    nice  system    irq  softirq  iowait     idle
           total    13.2%    0.0%    6.3%   0.0%    0.6%   25.2%    54.4%
           cpu00    26.5%    0.0%    0.7%   0.0%    2.1%    4.5%    65.8%
           cpu01    11.1%    0.0%    1.9%   0.0%    0.0%    4.1%    82.7%
           cpu02    11.3%    0.0%    8.9%   0.0%    0.0%   32.5%    47.2%
           cpu03     3.7%    0.0%   12.9%   0.0%    0.0%   30.8%    52.4%
Mem:  7973792k av, 7956044k used,   17748k free,      0k shrd,  125008k buff
                   4946388k actv, 1331312k in_d,  128768k in_c
Swap: 8388600k av,       0k used, 8388600k free                7225316k cached

  PID USER     PRI  NI  SIZE   RSS SHARE STAT %CPU %MEM   TIME CPU COMMAND
 8788 oracle    23   0 20648  19M 18844 R    10.1  0.2   2:06   3 oracle
20195 oracle    16   0 44468  42M 41000 R     2.2  0.5   0:09   2 oracle
20137 oracle    15   0  8876 8400  6964 D     1.3  0.1   0:17   1 oracle
20147 oracle    16   0 11900  11M  6144 S     1.3  0.1   0:05   2 oracle
20135 oracle    16   0 13044  12M 11044 S     0.5  0.1   0:11   0 oracle
```

The top display is divided into two main sections. Within the top-level section, the most important information in monitoring an Oracle RAC node is the load average, CPU states, and memory and swap space. The load average shows the average number of processes in the queue waiting to be allocated CPU time over the previous 1, 5, and 15 minutes. During normal operations, the load averages should be maintained at low values. If these values consistently exceed the processor core count of the server, this is an indication that the system load is exceeding capacity. When this is the case, there is the potential that the GCS background processes (LMSn) could become starved of CPU time, resulting in a detrimental effect on the overall performance of the cluster.

The CPU states show the level of utilization of all of the CPUs installed on the system. The oracle user workload will be shown as user time; however, there will be additional levels of system time and iowait time related to Oracle activity. A high level of iowait time may indicate that investigation is required into disk performance as the CPUs are spending the majority of their time simply waiting for I/O requests to be processed. An overall indicator of CPU is the idle value showing spare capacity on the system. A consistently low idle time in conjunction with a high load average presents further evidence that the workload exceeds the ability of the system to process it.

The memory-related section displays information that bears a close resemblance to the output of free.

Within the bottom-level section are statistics related to the processes themselves running on the system. You can use this section to pinpoint which processes are using most of the CPU and memory on the system. In terms of memory as well as the total percentage utilization on the system, the SIZE field shows how much memory an individual process has allocated, and the RSS field (the Resident

Set Size) shows how much memory the process is using at the current time. For Oracle processes, these values should ordinarily be at similar levels.

From the example `top` output, we can see that the system is processing Oracle activity but is not under excessive workload at the present time.

`top` is very much an interactive tool and accepts single-letter commands to tailor the display. For example, you may use the u option to specify viewing processes solely for the `oracle` user by typing **u, oracle** or sort tasks by age by typing **A**. You should remember not to neglect monitoring system process tasks, however, as, for example, observing the `kswapd` process in `top` output on a regular basis would indicate a potential performance impact of utilizing swap space.

An important aspect of `top` is that in addition to displaying information, you may also interact with the processes themselves, such as altering their relative priorities or killing them altogether. Therefore, the help screen accessed by ? is a useful command for familiarizing yourself with the capabilities of the tool. You can terminate `top` by pressing the q key or Ctrl+C.

vmstat

The utility `vmstat`, as its name suggests, focuses on providing output about the usage of virtual memory. When called without arguments, `vmstat` will output information related to virtual memory utilization since the system was last booted. You are therefore most likely to call `vmstat` with two numerical arguments for the delay between sampling periods and the number of sampling periods in total. If you specify just one numerical argument, this will apply to the delay and the sampling will continue until the command is canceled with Ctrl+C. For example, the following will produce ten lines of output at three-second intervals:

```
[root@london1 root]# vmstat 3 10
procs                memory        swap       io       system        cpu
 r  b   swpd   free   buff  cache  si  so   bi   bo   in   cs us sy wa id
 0  0      0  27196 175956 7083064  0   0    0    1    4    3  0  0  0  3
 0  0      0  27120 175956 7083064  0   0    0   27  144  211  0  0  2 97
 0  0      0  28396 175992 7083048  0   0    0  213  176  408  1  2  2 95
 1  0      0  28380 176028 7083028  0   0    0  117  144  332  0  0  1 99
```

Within the output, the first two fields under `procs` show processes waiting for CPU runtime and processes that are in uninterruptible sleep state. A traditional implementation of `vmstat` on many UNIX systems and earlier Linux versions also showed a w field under this `procs` section to indicate processes that are swapped out; however, as entire processes are not swapped out under Linux, this w field is no longer included. As with `top`, the next four fields under the `memory` section should be familiar from the output of `free` showing the amount of swap space in use and the free and cached memory. The two fields under the `swap` section show the amount of memory being swapped in and out of disk per second. On an Oracle system, we would expect these values and the amount of swap in use to show a low or zero value. The fields under `io` show the blocks sent and received from block devices, and the fields under `system` show the level of interrupts and context switches. In a RAC environment, the levels of interrupts and context switches can be useful in evaluating the impact of the CPU servicing network-related activity such as interconnect traffic or the usage of Network Attached Storage.

Finally, the `cpu` section is similar to `top` in displaying the user, system, I/O wait, and idle CPU time, except in this case for all CPUs on the system.

In addition to the default output, `vmstat` also enables the display to be configured with a number of command line options. For example, -d displays disk statistics and -p the statistics for a particular disk partition specified at the command line. A summary of memory-related values can be given by the -s option.

netstat

You can use the netstat tool to display information related to the networking configuration and performance of your system, from routing tables to interface statistics and open ports. By default, netstat displays a list of all open sockets on the system, but a wide variety of command line options can be given to vary the details shown.

One form of output that you can produce with netstat is using the -i argument to display interface statistics. This output shows the statistics for a single Ethernet-based interface.

```
[root@london1 root]# netstat -i
Kernel Interface table
Iface     MTU Met   RX-OK RX-ERR RX-DRP RX-OVR   TX-OK TX-ERR TX-DRP TX-OVR Flg
eth0      1500   0    2462      0      0      0    2566      0      0      0 BMRU
lo       16436   0    2999      0      0      0    2999      0      0      0 LRU
```

This information can assist in diagnosing issues that you may suspect are resulting in poor network performance due to hardware errors, and you can observe continually updated values with the -c argument. Of the most importance, you should see values in the RX-OK and TX-OK fields increasing on all interfaces as network traffic is communicated, with no or low numbers in all of the other fields. In particular, increasing values in the RX-ERR and TX-ERR fields is an indication of a possible fault that requires further investigation.

For further diagnostic type information, running netstat with the -s argument produces a summary report on statistics for all protocols configured on the system. For Cache Fusion traffic on Linux, you should pay particular attention to the UDP protocol–related information on the packets sent and received and, most important, whether packet receive errors are evident.

The default output of netstat does not include listening sockets; these can be shown with the -l option. However, you will be more likely to prefer to display all established and listening socket-related information at the same time, which you can do with the -a argument. The output of netstat -a can be somewhat lengthy, and in particular all information under the section Active Unix domain sockets relates to interprocess communication on the local host and is not network related. To restrict the output to network activity you may also provide the additional --inet argument, for example:

```
[root@london1 root]# netstat --inet -a
Active Internet connections (servers and established)
Proto Recv-Q Send-Q Local Address              Foreign Address          State
tcp        0      0 *:32768                     *:*                      LISTEN
tcp        0      0 *:8001                      *:*                      LISTEN
tcp        0      0 localhost.localdomain:32769 *:*                      LISTEN
tcp        0      0 *:nfs                       *:*                      LISTEN
.....
udp        0      0 london1-priv:1278           *:*
udp        0      0 localhost.localdom:1535     *:*
udp        0      0 localhost.localdom:1279     *:*
```

This argument provides a significantly more readable display and a snapshot of all network-related activity on the system. Within the fields, Proto refers to the protocol, and therefore we can observe the RAC-related communication established under the UDP protocol. The Recv-Q and Send-Q fields, as their names suggest, relate to the receiving and send queues and should almost always be zero. If these values are increasing, in particular for the UDP protocol, then there is evidence that your interconnect cannot sustain your desired workload. The Local address field shows your hostname and port number, and similarly with the foreign address of the host to which you are connecting, this will be *:* until a connection is established. The State field will usually show LISTEN or ESTABLISHED for the TCP protocol; however, as UDP is a stateless protocol, these connections have no state entries. If you also provide the -n argument, no name lookups will be done, and IP addresses for all connections will be displayed.

To observe the network-related activity in real time, you can make use of the watch command again with watch "netstat --inet -a" to monitor the network connections being established on your system.

iostat

iostat is the first of a number of utilities we will discuss that is installed with the sysstat RPM package, along with mpstat and sar. The iostat utility also displays information related to CPU utilization, but it focuses upon providing detailed I/O statistics. As with vmstat, when iostat is run without any command line arguments, it reports statistics for average CPU utilization and disk devices since the most recent boot time.

```
[root@london1 root]# iostat
Linux 2.6.9-5.ELsmp (london1)     03/08/2005

avg-cpu:  %user   %nice   %sys %iowait   %idle
           2.14    0.00   2.15    0.04   95.72

Device:           tps   Blk_read/s   Blk_wrtn/s   Blk_read   Blk_wrtn
sda             16.37       294.99        86.41     133242      39030
```

The format of the CPU utilization contains the same fields we have seen with top and vmstat. The disk statistics show the device name, the number of I/O operations per second, the number of 512-byte blocks read and written per second, and the total number of 512-byte blocks read and written. iostat can also be supplied with one or two numerical arguments to represent the interval between sampling periods and the number of sampling periods in total. You may also specify statistics for a specific device using the -p argument, such as -p sda for device sda. If you only wish to view disk utilization information, you can use the -d option or alternatively -c for CPU only. The -k option displays disk information in kilobytes as opposed to blocks.

When using iostat to observe disk statistics in a RAC environment, you should be keenly aware of the infrastructure that lies between the operating system and the actual disk devices. As discussed in Chapter 7, the levels of abstraction can range from multipathing device drivers and host bus adapters to cache on the storage and a disk RAID configuration. Most important, because the disk devices of most interest to use are shared between all of the nodes in the cluster, any useful information that we can derive on any individual node is likely to be limited. iostat therefore may prove useful in providing a highly generalized overview of disk activity on the system, but there is no substitute for using the specialized storage analysis tools provided by the vendor of your chosen storage subsystem.

mpstat

The mpstat command by default shows a CPU utilization report similar to that produced by iostat for all statistics since boot time, with an additional field showing the number of interrupts per second. mpstat also accepts the same number and type of numeric arguments as vmstat and iostat to produce output at sampled intervals, for example:

```
[root@london1 root]# mpstat 3 10
Linux 2.6.9-5.ELsmp (london1)     03/08/2005

11:35:03    CPU   %user   %nice %system %iowait    %irq   %soft   %idle    intr/s
11:35:06    all    5.56    0.00    2.72    8.73    0.00    0.13   82.87    723.08
11:35:09    all   11.33    0.00    2.46   25.25    0.00    0.58   60.38   1630.33
11:35:12    all   11.46    0.00    5.54   24.71    0.00    0.46   57.83   1872.67
11:35:15    all   12.04    0.00    1.96   25.25    0.00    0.38   60.38   1623.67
11:35:18    all   10.71    0.00    2.54   25.54    0.00    0.38   60.83   1588.67
```

By default, mpstat reports CPU statistics averaged for all processors; however, the most significant difference with iostat is that the use of the -P argument given with either the CPU number starting at 0 or -P ALL displays output for all processors on an individual basis. When analyzing CPU performance with mpstat or other monitoring tools, remember that as discussed in Chapter 6, if you have a system equipped with dual or multicore CPUs, each CPU core will be presented to the monitoring tool as a distinct CPU, although the cores share some system resources. Similarly, Intel Hyper-Threaded CPUs will also present each CPU physically installed in the system as two CPUs for each physical core, enabling processes to be scheduled by the Linux operating system simultaneously to the same core.

sar

The system activity reporter (sar) is a powerful tool that can encompass virtually all of the performance information generated by the other performance tools discussed here. In fact, some of the statistics from sar may look familiar to users of Oracle EM, as sar underpins most of the host-based performance views, hence the requirement for the sysstat package to be installed on managed targets.

As its name suggests, sar is the front-end reporting tool and is accompanied by sadc, the system activity data collector. Reports can be generated by sar in an interactive manner or written to a file for longer-term data collection. When you install the sysstat package, it sets sadc to run periodically by configuring the sa1 script from the cron scheduled script /etc/cron.d/sysstat:

```
[root@london1 root]# cat /etc/cron.d/sysstat
# run system activity accounting tool every 10 minutes
*/10 * * * * root /usr/lib/sa/sa1 1 1
# generate a daily summary of process accounting at 23:53
53 23 * * * root /usr/lib/sa/sa2 -A
```

By default, this script is run every ten minutes, captures all system statistics for a one-second period, and appends the data to the current data file in the /var/log/sa directory, where the file is named sa with a suffix corresponding to the current date. Also within the same location as sa1 is the file sa2, which by default runs once per day. sa2 runs sar to generate a full report on all of the data captured in the previous day by sadc.

A sar report presents system performance data divided into 17 separate sections. Each section contains data related to a specific aspect of system performance ordered by time according to the ten-minute collection interval throughout a 24-hour period.

The standard statistics collection is useful for long-term performance monitoring and capacity planning trending activities; however, the one-second collection period at ten-minute intervals may not be sufficient for pinpointing specific performance issues. For this reason, you can also invoke sar directly to produce performance information on one or more of the specific performance-related areas to the screen. This interactive performance requires two numerical arguments: one for the interval between sampling periods and one for the number of sampling periods in total. Unlike the statistics commands such as vmstat that we have already seen, if you specify just the one numerical argument, sar will report statistics for the time interval specified by the argument once and exit. You may also provide arguments to specify the type of performance information to view. If you do not provide any arguments, you will by default be shown performance information for all CPUs. The following extract shows the first output of the CPU performance information for a three-second sampling period to be collected ten times:

```
[root@london1 root]# sar 3 10
Linux 2.6.9-5.ELsmp (london1)      06/20/2005

12:32:56        CPU     %user   %nice   %system %idle
12:32:59        0       40.33   0.00    20.00   39.67
12:32:59        1       37.67   0.00    18.00   44.33
```

12:32:59	2	54.33	0.00	20.33	25.33
12:32:59	3	60.00	0.00	16.33	23.67
12:32:59	4	38.00	0.00	19.33	42.67
12:32:59	5	37.00	0.00	28.00	35.00
12:32:59	6	50.33	0.00	24.33	25.33
12:32:59	7	50.00	0.00	24.33	25.67

To view additional or alternative performance information, you may provide other arguments, such as sar -n for network statistics or sar -b for I/O statistics, and the full range of options are detailed in the sar man page. To produce performance information on all sections interactively, you can call sar -A; however, be aware that the output is extensive. In conjunction with sar -A, you may also find the -o option useful in directing the output to a file. The default file location is the same as the regularly sampled sar data, and we therefore recommend that you specify a file name for detailed sar performance analysis work. For example, the following command collects all sar statistics at three-second intervals for a five-minute period into the file london1.sa:

```
[root@london1 root]# sar -A -o london1.sa 3 100
```

The file generated is in the sar binary format, and you will therefore also require sar to read the results file at a later point in time using the -f option, for example:

```
[root@london1 root]# sar -f london1.sa
```

As you would expect, the -f option is exclusive of the -o option, but it accepts the same command line arguments as when called in an interactive manner; therefore, this example shows the CPU information only. To display all of the information collected in the file, you will again need to specify the -A option:

```
[root@london1 root]# sar -A -f london1.sa
```

Although the text-based sar output provides you with all of the recorded performance information you require, simply browsing sar -A output for example may prove difficult in diagnosing any system performance issues that have occurred. Fortunately, the Interactive System Activity Grapher (isag) utility is available for graphing the data recorded in sar files. isag is no longer included automatically with the systtat RPM package, primarily due to its further dependence on the gnuplot package, but you can easily download and install the latest versions of isag and gnuplot to view your sar statistics. As you have collected your sar data in independent files, you do not need to install these packages on the nodes of the RAC cluster themselves—you may simply configure them on a stand-alone Linux client and transfer the sar files for analysis there. The isag utility is written in the TCL/TK language that is most likely installed by default on the Linux distribution installed on your client.

Once the necessary packages have been installed, you can call isag at the command line. By default, isag looks for sar data in the /var/log/sa directory; however, as you will have most likely downloaded all of the sar output from the nodes of your cluster to a central location, you will need to specify the arguments for this location and the mask used to select the files. In this example, the sar data has been downloaded to the oracle user's home directory, which we specify with the argument -p. As this is our present working directory, we provide the directory name of ".". All of the sar data files have been named to reflect the nodes from which they came, and therefore the mask argument -m with the file prefix london will load all data files beginning with london, such as london1.sa and london2.sa. If you wish to change the default height and width of the output, you may also use the -ght and -gwd arguments, respectively, although in this example we use the default settings.

```
[oracle@london1 oracle]$ ./isag -p . -m london
```

Once you have started isag, you will be able to select the input file under the data source tab. This tab offers a particularly useful way to compare the system performance of all of the nodes in the cluster. You can select a graph type, and then by changing between data sources, the graph type remains the same, enabling a visual comparison between the sar statistics from the different nodes in the cluster.

By selecting the graph type from the menu, isag enables you to view some of the most relevant data from your sar data, such as CPU Utilization, Memory Activities, and Network Statistics. Figure 24-3 illustrates the CPU Utilization viewed in isag.

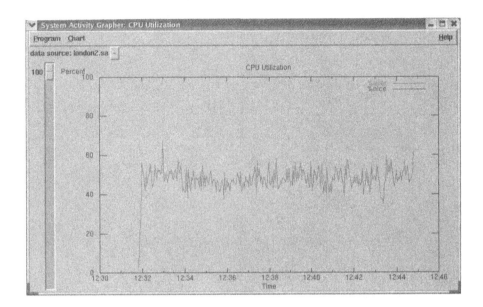

Figure 24-3. *isag CPU utilization*

As isag is open source, it is also possible to easily modify the code to graph any additional sar statistics not included by default. In particular, in a RAC environment, the statistics for the teamed network interconnect interface such as bond0 are worth including, and you can add these by duplicating and modifying the lines already in the isag program for the existing network statistics to create an additional view.

Summary

In this chapter, we described some of the tools and techniques available to you for monitoring the performance of your RAC cluster at both the Oracle and Linux levels. We considered the tools integrated within the Oracle 10g Manageability Infrastructure, such as EM and AWR reports. We also detailed the most common Linux command line tools so that you may confirm your Oracle findings in terms of server or interconnect performance with the statistics reported by the Linux operating system.

## CHAPTER 25

Backup and Recovery

In this chapter, we discuss some of the concepts and issues relating to backup and recovery of RAC databases. We will concentrate on Recovery Manager (RMAN), the standard backup and recovery package supplied with the database software. Even if you currently use third-party backup solutions for your single-instance database, we recommend that you seriously consider using the capabilities of RMAN in a RAC environment. RMAN is tightly integrated with the database and therefore generally provides the most efficient, supported, and widely available solution for backup and recovery. In addition, RMAN is RAC-aware and its price is already included as part of your Oracle license.

Backup and Recovery Strategy

Before you implement any backup solution, you must consider your backup strategy and, more important, your recovery strategy. There is no point in taking backups unless you are able to use them to recover from system failures.

For many sites, the backup and recovery strategy is determined by service level agreements (SLAs), which specify the maximum amount of acceptable downtime a site is willing to endure. This downtime is often expressed in terms of the mean time to recovery (MTTR), or the average time required to recover following a failure. For many sites, the starting point in developing a backup strategy is the recovery time.

When you are designing a backup and recovery strategy, you should consider the following issues:

- How long will it take to restore your database from tape?
- How long will it take to restore your database from image copies located on disk?
- How long will it take to recover your database using archived redo logs?

You should also consider the types of failure that may occur. The following list presents just a few of the many possibilities:

- Total database loss
- Loss of one or more tablespaces
- Loss of one or more datafiles
- Loss of control files
- Loss of online redo logs
- Loss of the server parameter file (init.ora)
- Loss of the text parameter file

- Loss of the password file
- Loss of database software
- Loss of Oracle Net configuration files
- Loss of the Enterprise Management (EM) agent
- Loss of operating system software
- Loss of operating system configuration files
- Corruption of individual disk data blocks

In a RAC environment you should also consider the following:

- Loss of OCR
- Loss of the voting disk
- Loss of Oracle Clusterware

Depending on the failure, you may need to restore back to the current point or to a historic point in time. Whenever possible, you should avoid performing a full system restore and perform, in order of preference, block media recovery, datafile recovery, or tablespace recovery. If you believe that your database will be susceptible to user errors, then you may wish to investigate flashback technology, which has been significantly enhanced in Oracle 10.1 and above.

Your recovery strategy should consider all the potential failures listed previously. It should also address any application-specific issues, such as data held in external files, and any third-party products in use in your servers, such as management or performance monitoring tools.

For each potential failure, you must ensure that you can recover within a period of time that is acceptable to your business. You should test and document the recovery process for each potential type of failure. As your database changes over time, you should retest your recovery procedures to verify that you can still meet your targets. Your documented procedures should allow time for problem investigation and high-level decision making.

The most effective to reduce recovery times is to stage backups to disk and subsequently write them to tape. In the event of a failure, you will still have a copy of the backup on disk. If you have sufficient disk space, then we recommend that you store a copy of the entire database online to avoid the need to restore backups from tape prior to running a recovery. If this is not possible for capacity or cost reasons, then we recommend that you store the most important database files on disk.

RMAN offers a number of techniques you can employ to reduce recovery times, including using incremental backups, image copies, and incrementally updated backups. If recovery times are a priority for your site, we recommend that you investigate these features in more detail.

Once you have determined your recovery strategy, you need to consider your backup strategy. Backup operations should have minimal performance impact on database operations. You may have a fixed time window in which you can perform backups. Alternatively, in a RAC environment, you may run backups on one or more nodes while processing continues on the remainder of the system. Your backup strategy must satisfy the requirements of your recovery strategy. If it does not, then you have a number of options:

- Modify the requirements of your recovery strategy.
- Increase the time window available for your backups, perhaps by reducing the duration of other system components such as batch processes.
- Increase the hardware resources available for your backups such as tape devices, disk space, and CPU.
- Offload backups to a dedicated backup server.

You can potentially reduce your backup times by staging your backup to disk and subsequently writing it to tape. Writing to disk is usually faster than writing to tape.

RMAN also offers a number of techniques to reduce backup times and resource usage, including incremental backups, parallelization, multiplexing, and block change tracking. If you wish to reduce your overall backup times, we recommend you investigate these features, which we discuss later in this chapter.

Recovery Manager (RMAN)

Recovery Manager (RMAN) was introduced in Oracle 8.0. RMAN provides a backup and recovery solution that is tightly integrated with the Oracle database.

You can run RMAN a stand-alone utility from the operating system command line in batch or interactive mode. You can also invoke RMAN using the Enterprise Manager Database Control or Grid Control. EM can configure backup settings, schedule and manage backups, configure recovery settings, and perform recovery.

RMAN allows you to back up either to disk or directly to tape. RMAN works with third-party products designed to support backup and recovery using offline storage media. It includes an API, known as the Media Management Layer (MML), which allows third-party vendors to integrate RMAN with their backup solution. The MML has intelligence about the hardware platform and can manipulate the tape drives, carousels, the tape library, and so forth. RMAN reads and writes the data and the MML manipulates the storage system, such as tape retrieval, tape switching, and so on. The storage vendor should provide an MML specific to the storage platform you have purchased.

RMAN manages the creation of database backups for the purpose of recovery. As mentioned previously, the database and archivelog files can be backed up either to disk or to tape. RMAN can back up the entire database, individual tablespaces, and individual datafiles, as well as archived redo logs, control files, and server parameter files. RMAN can also purge archived redo logs once they have been successfully written to the backup device.

In RMAN terminology, the database being backed up or restored is referred to as the *target database*. Backup files can be written either as backupsets or image copies. A *backupset* contains one or more files multiplexed together. It can contain one or more backup pieces. Backupsets are always used when writing to tape; they can be optionally used when writing to disk. RMAN only writes datafile blocks that have been initialized to the backupset.

Image copies are only written to disk. An image copy of a datafile consists of all blocks in that file including any uninitialized blocks. RMAN backups are typically smaller than image copies since RMAN only backs up initialized blocks that are needed for a recovery.

RMAN maintains status information in the database control file. You can also optionally create a *recovery catalog*, which is a set of tables, indexes, and packages stored in a secondary database known as the *catalog database*. The catalog database contains information about RMAN backups for all target databases in the enterprise. Use of the recovery catalog is mandatory for more complex configurations. The benefit of using a recovery catalog is that in a situation where you have lost all the copies of the control files for a database, RMAN can re-create the control files for you from the information contained in the recovery catalog. This process is more efficient than recovering an older copy of a control file and then performing a forward recovery to bring the control file up to date.

RMAN can be used to create duplicate or cloned databases, which are copies of existing databases. It can also be used to create standby databases. In both cases, the new database is known as the *auxiliary database*.

RMAN uses two PL/SQL packages in the target database: DBMS_RCVMAN and DBMS_BACKUP_RESTORE. The DBMS_RCVMAN package interfaces with the control file to obtain information about datafiles and archived redo logs. It also determines the workflow of the backup job. The DBMS_BACKUP_RESTORE package actually performs the backup job, which may be a backup or a restore operation.

When RMAN performs a backup, it reads blocks from the datafiles into a memory buffer. Blocks are verified in memory before they are written to the backup location. Therefore, RMAN provides early detection and some protection against block corruption. Corrupt blocks are reported and excluded from the backup.

RMAN backups are performed by channels which represent the interface between RMAN and the underlying operating system files. In early versions of RMAN, it was necessary to open and close all channels explicitly; in more recent versions, channels can be managed implicitly. Channels are assigned to physical backup devices such as tape drives. Typically, using more channels will allow your backup and recovery operations to complete faster.

RMAN can perform either full or incremental backups. With a full backup, all blocks are written to disk. With an incremental backup, RMAN inspects the block header to determine whether the block has been changed since the last time it was backed up and, if so, includes it in the incremental backup.

RMAN can perform backups more efficiently than most third-party tools, because it has access to the SGA and can therefore back up blocks that have been updated in the buffer cache but not necessarily written back to disk.

The basic RMAN recovery process generally involves two steps. The first step is to restore datafiles and archived redo logs from the backup device. This may be a backupset on tape or disk. One of the main benefits of RMAN is that, in conjunction with the MML, it can identify which tapes contain the disk blocks that need to be recovered, making the process more efficient and less prone to human error than a manual recovery. Alternatively, RMAN can be used to back up to disk, in which case the restore would probably be from the image copy on disk.

The second step is to perform media recovery to apply archived redo logs to the restored files. RMAN makes the recovery process very simple by identifying the object(s) that need recovery, retrieving the media that contains those objects, restoring only the required objects, and then automatically recovering the database.

RMAN Utility

RMAN includes a command line utility which runs as an Oracle client similar to EXP or SQL*Loader. It is created along with the other database utilities on every database at install time. As the RMAN utility communicates with the database using Oracle Net, the command line utility can also be installed on a remote client system such as a workstation.

The RMAN utility includes commands to run backups and restores, maintain the recovery catalog, maintain and execute scripts, and generate reports and lists. It also contains a command syntax interpreter that converts commands into remote procedure calls, which are passed to the target database where they are executed using PL/SQL packages.

Parameters

RMAN connects to the target database with the SYSDBA privilege using Oracle Net. It takes a number of parameters, the most important of which are as follows:

- TARGET <connect_string>: A mandatory connect string for the target database

- AUXILIARY <connect_string>: An optional connect string for the auxiliary database

- CATALOG <connect string>: An optional connect string for the catalog database

You can also specify the NOCATALOG option, which indicates that RMAN will store all information in the control file of the target database. In Oracle 9.0.1 and above, this is the default behavior, so it is no longer necessary to specify NOCATALOG explicitly, for example:

```
$ rman TARGET=SYS/ORACLE@RAC1 CATALOG=RMAN/RMAN@RMAN
$ rman TARGET=SYS/ORACLE@RAC1 NOCATALOG
```

Other useful options include CMDFILE, which allows you to specify the name of an input command file, and LOG, which allows you to specify an output message log file that can be optionally opened in append mode by specifying the APPEND keyword.

Spooling Output

You can spool the output of the RMAN utility to a log file using the SPOOL command. The syntax is slightly different from that used in SQL*Plus. To start spooling RMAN output to a file called rman.log, use the following command at the RMAN prompt:

```
RMAN> SPOOL LOG TO rman.log
```

```
RMAN> SPOOL LOG OFF
```

Scripts

You have two ways of running scripts in RMAN: text scripts and stored scripts. You can create a text script containing one or more commands in an operating system file. This file has no standard suffix. To execute the text script at the RMAN prompt, prefix the file name with the @ character. For example, to run a full backup of the database, use

```
RMAN> @FullBackup
```

where the file FullBackup might contain the following:

```
SPOOL LOG TO FullBackup.log;
BACKUP DATABASE;
SPOOL LOG OFF;
```

You can save backup and recovery scripts in the catalog database, protecting them from system failure. Scripts stored in the recovery catalog can be created, executed, deleted, or replaced. Stored scripts can be easier to administer than text scripts in environments where DBAs need to share scripts.

For example, you can create a stored script in the recovery catalog for the FullBackup script just shown as follows:

```
RMAN> CREATE SCRIPT fullbackup
> {
>   SPOOL LOG TO fullbackup.log;
>   BACKUP DATABASE;
>   SPOOL LOG OFF;
> };
```

You can execute, print, and delete this stored script using the following:

```
RMAN> EXECUTE SCRIPT fullbackup;
RMAN> PRINT SCRIPT fullbackup;
RMAN> DELETE SCRIPT fullbackup;
```

In Oracle 10.1 and above, you can create a stored script in the recovery catalog from a text script, for example:

```
RMAN> CREATE SCRIPT fullbackup FROM FILE '/home/oracle/scripts/FullBackup';
```

Also in Oracle 10.1 and above, you can create a text script from a stored script in the recovery catalog:

```
RMAN> PRINT SCRIPT fullbackup TO FILE '/home/oracle/scripts/FullBackup';
```

By default, all stored scripts are available only for the target database against which they were created. These are known as *local stored scripts*. In Oracle 10.1 and above, it is also possible to create *global stored scripts*, which can be shared by all databases in the recovery catalog. Global stored scripts are easier to administer and maintain, as you do not need to create new stored scripts when you add a new database. In addition, if you change the stored script, you only need to update it in one place.

For example, the FullBackup script discussed previously does not contain any database-specific information and is therefore a candidate for a global stored script:

```
RMAN> CREATE GLOBAL SCRIPT fullbackup
> {
>   SPOOL LOG TO fullbackup.log;
>   BACKUP DATABASE;
>   SPOOL LOG OFF;
> };
RMAN> EXECUTE GLOBAL SCRIPT fullbackup;
RMAN> PRINT GLOBAL SCRIPT fullbackup;
```

If the GLOBAL keyword is omitted, RMAN will first search for a local stored script called fullbackup. If one is not found, then the global stored script will be used.

Database Control Commands

In Oracle 8.1.5 and above, it is possible to start and stop the database from within the RMAN utility:

```
RMAN> STARTUP
RMAN> SHUTDOWN
```

These commands can also be embedded in backup scripts.

You can execute other SQL statements from the RMAN prompt using the SQL command, for example:

```
RMAN> SQL 'ALTER TABLESPACE ts2 BEGIN BACKUP';
```

RUN Commands

You can specify a sequential list of commands using the RUN command. The basic syntax of the RUN command is

```
RUN {
<command1>;
<command2>;
....
<commandN>;
}
```

In early versions of RMAN, RUN commands were commonly required because there were no default parameters. This meant, for example, that channels needed to be assigned for every command:

```
RMAN> RUN
> {
>   ALLOCATE CHANNEL channel1 TYPE SBT_TAPE;
>   BACKUP DATABASE PLUS ARCHIVELOG;
>   DELETE OBSOLETE;
>   RELEASE CHANNEL channel11;
> }
```

In Oracle 9.0.1 and above, it is possible to specify a default device type and also to set persistent channel parameters, so the use of RUN commands is now less common. However, RUN commands are still useful for the creation of recovery catalog scripts and also for grouping commands into logical units. In addition, RUN commands are useful for defining more complex operations. For example, the RESTORE operation uses the SET ARCHIVELOG DESTINATION command to specify a new location in which to restore archive redo logs:

```
RMAN> RUN
> {
>   SET ARCHIVELOG DESTINATION TO '/u03/oradata/RAC/temp';
>   RESTORE ARCHIVELOG ALL;
> }
```

In Oracle 9.0.1 and above, you can set default values for several RMAN parameters. RMAN can open and close channels implicitly, so it is often possible to execute a backup or restore operation without using a RUN command:

```
[oracle@london1 oracle]$ rman TARGET=/
RMAN> BACKUP DATABASE;
```

RMAN Repository

RMAN stores metadata about backups in the RMAN repository. RMAN metadata is always stored in the database control file. If you have configured a recovery catalog, then metadata will also be stored in the catalog schema. Use by RMAN of both the control file and the recovery catalog is discussed in the following sections.

Control File

In Oracle 8.0 and above, the control file structure has been enhanced to contain additional information to support RMAN. Some of this information is permanent; other information is transitory and is overwritten after a period of time.

RMAN uses the database control file for a number of purposes. The control file contains information about the number and size of datafiles. This information is used by RMAN to compile backup lists. The control file also contains information about archived redo logs, including their current status. This information allows RMAN to only back up completed archived redo logs and to determine when local archived redo log files can be deleted.

RMAN writes information about backups back to the control file, including details of which files have been backed up and the names of the backupsets, backup pieces, and image copies, along with checkpoint information.

To prevent the control file from becoming excessively large, you can use the CONTROL_FILE_RECORD_KEEP_TIME initialization parameter to specify the number of days to keep recyclable data. The default value is 7. If the value of this parameter is more than zero, and if additional space is required, the control file will expand as necessary. If the value of this parameter is zero, and extra space is required, existing data will be overwritten in order to maintain the control file at a constant size.

Recovery Catalog

You can optionally create a recovery catalog, which should be located in a separate database on a different server from the target database. The recovery catalog contains information about the physical structure of the target database, including the datafiles and archived redo logs. It also contains details of any backup and recovery operations performed by RMAN.

The recovery catalog is mandatory if you wish to use automated RMAN scripts for backup operations. It is also necessary if you wish to perform tablespace point-in-time recovery. You also need a recovery catalog to recover a database when the control file does not reflect the current database structure.

You must create the recovery catalog manually, but the same recovery catalog can be shared by multiple databases. In some RAC environments, where availability is a primary goal, the recovery catalog may even be stored in a RAC database. However, for most users, a single-instance database is sufficient. It is common practice to shut down the recovery catalog database once per day and to perform a cold backup of its contents. For most sites, this is a sufficient and cost-effective solution.

In Oracle 8.0, the recovery catalog was created by running the following script:

```
$ORACLE_HOME/rdbms/admin/catrman.sql
```

In Oracle 8.1.5 and above, the recovery catalog is created by executing the CREATE CATALOG command at the RMAN prompt. First, create a tablespace for the recovery catalog:

```
SQL> CREATE TABLESPACE rcvcat
> DATAFILE '/u02/oradata/RAC/rcvcat.dbf' SIZE 10M;
```

Next, create a user to own the recovery catalog schema:

```
SQL> CREATE USER rman IDENTIFIED BY rman
> DEFAULT TABLESPACE rcvcat
> TEMPORARY TABLESPACE temp
> QUOTA UNLIMITED ON rcvcat;
```

Grant the RECOVERY_CATALOG_OWNER permission to the new user:

```
SQL> GRANT RECOVERY_CATALOG_OWNER TO rman;
```

Then run the RMAN utility and create the catalog:

```
[oracle@london1 oracle]$ rman CATALOG=rman/rman@RAC1
RMAN> CREATE CATALOG TABLESPACE 'RCVCAT';
```

Note that the name of the tablespace must be enclosed in single or double quotes. This is because the tablespace name is case sensitive and must exactly match the name stored in the data dictionary.

You must initialize the recovery catalog with details of the target database before you can run RMAN. You must be connected to both databases at the same time through Oracle Net, for example:

```
[oracle@london1 oracle]$ rman TARGET / CATALOG rman/rman@RAC1
RMAN> REGISTER DATABASE;
```

In Oracle 10.1 and above, you can deregister the database again using the following command:

```
RMAN> UNREGISTER DATABASE;
```

The recovery catalog is not updated when a log switch occurs, when log files are archived, or when datafiles or redo logs are added. Therefore, from time to time you can manually resynchronize the recovery catalog using the command

```
RMAN> RESYNC CATALOG;
```

This command is executed automatically when the database is registered and also after every backup, restore, and recovery operation.

By default, the recovery catalog is resynchronized with the current control file. You can also resynchronize the recovery catalog with a backup control file, for example:

```
RMAN> RESYNC CATALOG FROM BACKUP CONTROLFILE '/u02/oradata/RAC/RAC_backupp.ctl';
```

Finally, if the database is opened with the RESETLOGS option, a new version or incarnation of the target database information must be created in the recovery catalog:

```
RMAN> RESET DATABASE;
```

This command must be executed before RMAN will allow further access to the recovery catalog. If you perform a point-in-time recovery, it may be necessary to reinstate the recovery catalog to a previous database incarnation. You can obtain details of the current and previous database incarnations from the V$DATABASE_INCARNATION dynamic performance view, for example:

```
RMAN> RESET DATABASE TO INCARNATION 2;
```

The recovery catalog contains approximately 30 views. Some of these correspond to dynamic performance views, which externalize sections of the control file. The remaining views are specific to the recovery catalog. All recovery catalog views are prefixed by RC_.

Table 25-1 shows recovery catalog views with their equivalent dynamic performance views.

Table 25-1. *Recovery Catalog Views and Their Equivalent Dynamic Performance Views*

Recovery Catalog View	Dynamic Performance View
RC_ARCHIVED_LOG	V$ARCHIVED_LOG
RC_BACKUP_CONTROLFILE	V$BACKUP_DATAFILE
RC_BACKUP_CORRUPTION	V$BACKUP_CORRUPTION
RC_BACKUP_DATAFILE	V$BACKUP_DATAFILE
RC_BACKUP_FILES	V$BACKUP_FILES
RC_BACKUP_PIECE	V$BACKUP_PIECE
RC_BACKUP_REDOLOG	V$BACKUP_REDOLOG
RC_BACKUP_SET	V$BACKUP_SET
RC_BACKUP_SPFILE	V$BACKUP_SPFILE
RC_CONTROLFILE_COPY	V$DATAFILE_COPY
RC_COPY_CORRUPTION	V$COPY_CORRUPTION
RC_DATABASE	V$DATABASE
RC_DATABASE_BLOCK_CORRUPTION	V$DATABASE_BLOCK_CORRUPTION
RC_DATABASE_INCARNATION	V$DATABASE_INCARNATION
RC_DATAFILE	V$DATAFILE
RC_DATAFILE_COPY	V$DATAFILE_COPY
RC_LOG_HISTORY	V$LOG_HISTORY
RC_OFFLINE_RANGE	V$OFFLINE_RANGE
RC_PROXY_ARCHIVEDLOG	V$PROXY_ARCHIVEDLOG
RC_PROXY_CONTROLFILE	V$PROXY_DATAFILE
RC_PROXY_DATAFILE	V$PROXY_DATAFILE
RC_REDO_LOG	V$LOG and V$LOGFILE
RC_REDO_THREAD	V$THREAD
RC_RMAN_CONFIGURATION	V$RM AN_CONFIGURATION
RC_RMAN_STATUS	V$RMAN_STATUS
RC_TABLESPACE	V$TABLESPACE

While there is a direct mapping between most of the recovery catalog views and their equivalent dynamic performance views, there are a few anomalies:

- V$BACKUP_DATAFILE contains information about datafiles and control files. In the recovery catalog, RC_BACKUP_DATAFILE contains datafile information only, and RC_BACKUP_CONTROLFILE contains control file information only.

- V$DATAFILE_COPY contains information about both datafiles and control files. In the recovery catalog, the equivalent RC_DATAFILE_COPY contains information about datafiles only, and RC_CONTROLFILE_COPY contains information about control files only.

- V$PROXY_DATAFILE contains information about both datafiles and control files. In the recovery catalog, the equivalent RC_PROXY_DATAFILE contains information about datafiles only, and RC_PROXY_CONTROLFILE contains information about control files only.

The remaining recovery catalog views do not have equivalent dynamic performance views:

- **RC_RESYNC**: Lists information about recovery catalog resynchronizations
- **RC_STORED_SCRIPT**: Lists information about scripts stored in the recovery catalog
- **RC_STORED_SCRIPT_LINE**: Lists individual lines of the scripts stored in the recovery catalog
- **RC_CHECKPOINT**: Has been deprecated and replaced by RC_RESYNC

Backup Sets

You can write your backups either to image copies or backup sets. An image copy can only be written to disk; it cannot be written to tape. There will be one image copy for each datafile backed up. The image copy will contain all blocks in the datafile, including uninitialized blocks.

In contrast, a backup set consists of one or more backup pieces. Each backup piece can contain blocks from one or more datafiles. The files can be multiplexed together so that more than one datafile can be included in the same backup piece. Multiplexed blocks are written to the backup piece in nonsequential order. However, only initialized datafile blocks are backed up, so the backupset can potentially be smaller than an image copy of the same datafile.

The two backupset types are datafile backupsets and archived redo log backupsets. Backupsets can be created from files in the target database, and they can also be created from image copies. Backupsets can be created for both full and incremental backups.

Backupsets can be written to disk or tape. They are often written to disk initially and then copied to tape in order to improve recovery times and to provide a greater utilization of tape drive resources. A backupset is the only format that RMAN writes to a tape device. RMAN automatically manages the staging of backupsets from disk to tape during backup, and from tape to disk during recovery.

Writing a backup to a backupset may be faster than writing a backup to an image copy. However, restoring from a backupset can be slower, especially if a large number of datafiles have been multiplexed together. Restore performance is less relevant if the backupset is being restored from tape.

You can control the number of datafiles backed up concurrently to the same backupset using the FILESPERSET parameter. If the value of this parameter is greater than 1, then datafiles will be multiplexed together. Multiplexed backupsets are more efficient during backups, but less efficient during restores. This is because in order to restore a multiplexed datafile, all blocks must be read from the backupset and blocks from other datafiles will be ignored. Therefore, the setting of the FILESPERSET parameter will depend on your backup strategy. If you wish to minimize backup times and the impact of backups on database performance, you should set a relatively high value for FILESPERSET; if you wish to minimize restore times and consequently minimize the mean time to recovery (MTTR) following a media failure, you should set a relatively low value for FILESPERSET.

If you need a compromise between the two objectives, then you should try to multiplex datafiles that will be recovered together (e.g., all the datafiles in the same tablespace).

Tags

RMAN allows you to specify a tag whenever you specify the name of a backupset or image copy. Tags are assigned during backup operations and referenced during restore operations. A tag is a user-defined identifier containing up to 30 alphanumeric characters. You can specify the same tag for more than one object, in which case RMAN will use the most recent appropriate version of the object.

Parameters

Prior to Oracle 9.0.1, RMAN had no concept of persistent parameters—all parameters had to be specified within each RUN command. In Oracle 9.0.1 and above, the persistent values for some parameters can be stored in the RMAN repository.

RMAN provides appropriate default values for most parameters. You can display the current values for all parameters using the SHOW ALL command, for example:

```
RMAN> SHOW ALL;
using target database controlfile instead of recovery catalog
RMAN configuration parameters are:
CONFIGURE RETENTION POLICY TO REDUNDANCY 1; #default
CONFIGURE BACKUP OPTIMIZATION OFF; #default
CONFIGURE DEFAULT DEVICE TYPE TO DISK; #default
CONFIGURE CONTROLFILE AUTOBACKUP OFF; #default
CONFIGURE CONTROLFILE AUTOBACKUP FORMAT FOR DEVICE TYPE DISK TO '%F'; #default
CONFIGURE DEVICE TYPE DISK PARALLELISM 1 BACKUP TYPE TO BACKUPSET; #default
CONFIGURE DATAFILE BACKUP COPIES FOR DEVICE TYPE DISK TO 1; #default
CONFIGURE ARCHIVELOG BACKUP COPIES FOR DEVICE TYPE DISK TO 1; #default
CONFIGURE MAXSETSIZE TO UNLIMITED; #default
CONFIGURE ARCHIVELOG DELETION POLICY TO NONE; #default
CONFIGURE SNAPSHOT CONTROLFILE NAME TO
'/u01/app/oracle/product/10.1.0/db/dbs/snapcf_RAC1.f'; #default
```

You can also show the value of an individual parameter using the SHOW command:

```
RMAN> SHOW RETENTION POLICY;
RMAN configuration parameters are:
CONFIGURE RETENTION POLICY TO REDUNDANCY 1; #default
```

You can permanently update a parameter value using the CONFIGURE command:

```
RMAN> CONFIGURE RETENTION POLICY TO RECOVERY WINDOW OF 7 DAYS;
new RMAN configuration parameters:
CONFIGURE RETENTION POLICY TO RECOVERY WINDOW OF 7 DAYS;
new RMAN configuration parameters are successfully stored
```

Finally, you can reset the value of any parameter back to its default value using the CLEAR keyword:

```
RMAN> CONFIGURE RETENTION POLICY CLEAR;
```

Nondefault RMAN parameter values are externalized in the V$RMAN_CONFIGURATION dynamic performance view in the target database.

We discuss these parameters in more detail in the following sections.

Retention Policy

Retention policies were introduced in Oracle 9.0.1 and define the rules that determine which backups are obsolete and eligible for deletion. There are two mutually exclusive types of retention policy: redundancy and the recovery window.

If you define a retention policy based on redundancy, then RMAN determines if a file is obsolete based on the number of times that file has been backed up, for example:

```
RMAN> CONFIGURE RETENTION POLICY TO REDUNDANCY 2;
```

The preceding policy specifies that each file must be backed up successfully twice before it can be deleted.

Alternatively, if you define a retention policy based on a recovery window, you can specify the time period for which all backups are retained, for example:

```
RMAN> CONFIGURE RETENTION POLICY TO RECOVERY WINDOW OF 7 DAYS;
```

The preceding policy specifies that backups must be retained for one week before they can be deleted.

Finally, you can specify the following:

```
RMAN> CONFIGURE RETENTION POLICY TO NONE;
```

where RMAN does not consider any backups or copies to be obsolete.

Your choice of retention policy is primarily determined by your backup and restore strategy. You also need to consider the availability of suitable storage. The default retention policy uses redundancy with a value of 1, so files are eligible for deletion after they have been backed up only once.

Following database creation or a change in retention policy, you may initially have obsolete backups. You can list obsolete backups using the following command:

```
RMAN> REPORT OBSOLETE;
```

You can delete obsolete backups using

```
RMAN> DELETE OBSOLETE;
```

By default, the DELETE OBSOLETE command will prompt for confirmation. You can force deletion of obsolete backups and copies using

```
RMAN> DELETE FORCE NOPROMPT OBSOLETE;
```

In Oracle 10.1 and above, configuring a Flashback Recovery Area will automatically age out old files based on the retention policy. If the Flashback Recovery Area is full and no files qualify for deletion, the current backup will fail. In addition, the ARCn process will hang, as archived redo logs cannot be written to the recovery area. In this situation, you have a number of alternatives to choose from, including backing up files in the recovery area to tape, increasing the size of your recovery area, or modifying your retention policy.

RMAN will not delete the only backup of a database before it has written a new one successfully. Therefore, irrespective of your retention policy, you should allocate sufficient space to your recovery area to contain two copies of your database.

Backup Optimization

In Oracle 9.0.1 and above, you can enable backup optimization as follows:

```
RMAN> CONFIGURE BACKUP OPTIMIZATION ON;
```

When backup optimization is enabled, RMAN skips files for which a backup already exists on the same device with the same header status. In other words, RMAN will not back up datafiles that have not been modified since the last backup.

Backup optimization is enabled only for the BACKUP DATABASE or BACKUP ARCHIVELOG command, when the ALL or LIKE options are specified. It is particularly useful for archivelog backups, as archived redo log files that have already been backed up can be skipped.

Default Device Type

In Oracle 9.0.1 and above, you can configure a default device type. Backups will be written to this device type unless explicitly overridden by the DEVICE TYPE clause in the BACKUP command.

The default device type is DISK. If you wish to change the default device type to tape, you can specify the following:

```
RMAN> CONFIGURE DEFAULT DEVICE TYPE TO SBT_TAPE;
```

Backup Type

If the device type is set to DISK, you can configure a default backup type, which can be either a backupset or an image copy:

```
RMAN> CONFIGURE DEVICE TYPE DISK BACKUP TYPE COPY;
RMAN> CONFIGURE DEVICE TYPE DISK BACKUP TYPE BACKUPSET;
```

The default backup type can be overridden in individual BACKUP commands, for example:

```
RMAN> BACKUP AS BACKUPSET DATABASE;
RMAN> BACKUP AS COPY DATABASE;
```

Channel Device Type

Prior to Oracle 9.0.1, channels had to be allocated and deallocated manually for every backup and restore operation. In Oracle 9.0.1 and above, it is possible to specify default values for the channel settings, which are persistent. RMAN uses these values implicitly unless they are overridden. As a result, it is rarely necessary to use a RUN command for RMAN operations.

If your default device type is disk, you can set the channel device type to include a FORMAT clause, which specifies that the backup will be written to a nondefault location. If you do not specify a format clause, the backup will be written to $ORACLE_HOME/dbs on the backup node. In a RAC environment, this is only acceptable if you are using a single node to perform all backup and restore operations. Therefore, we recommend that you modify the backup so that it is written to shared storage accessible to all nodes in the cluster, for example:

```
RMAN> CONFIGURE CHANNEL DEVICE TYPE DISK
> FORMAT '/u02/oradata/RAC/backup/RAC_%U';
```

You can specify format strings to customize the names of your backup files. If you do not specify a format string, then RMAN will use the %U string and create files in $ORACLE_HOME/dbs on the local host. The %U format string specifies a system-generated unique filename, which has different meanings for backup pieces and image copies. We recommend that you use this format unless you have more specific requirements.

The %U format string is converted into the strings described in Table 25-2.

Table 25-2. *%U Format String Values*

String	Description
%u_%p_%c	Backup piece
data-D-%d_id-%I_TS-%N_FNO-%f_%u	Image copy of datafile
arch-D_%d-id-%I_S-%e_T-%h_A-%a_%u	Image copy of archived redo log
cf-D_%d-id-%I_%u	Image copy of control file

where

- **%a**: Activation ID of database
- **%c**: Copy number of a backup piece within a set of duplexed backup pieces
- **%d**: Name of database
- **%e**: Archived log sequence number
- **%f**: Absolute file number (file#)
- **%h**: Archived redo log thread number
- **%I**: Database ID (DBID)
- **%N**: Tablespace name
- **%p**: Piece number within the backupset
- **%u**: Eight-character name generated from backup file number and creation time

A number of other format strings are available. See the *Oracle Database Recovery Manager Reference Guide* for further details.

If you are backing up to tape, you can set any permanent parameters for the tape device using the channel device type. For example, to specify a NetBackup tapeserver called tapeserver1, you might use the following:

```
RMAN> CONFIGURE CHANNEL DEVICE TYPE 'SBT_TAPE'
> PARMS 'ENV=(NB_ORA_SERV=tapeserver1)';
```

where the NB_ORA_SERV parameter is passed to the NetBackup Media Management Layer.

If you wish to test the SBT interface, but do not have a tape device connected to the system, Oracle provides a dummy library that simulates the behavior of a tape device, but writes the backup to disk. For example, you might use the following configuration:

```
RMAN> CONFIGURE CHANNEL DEVICE TYPE 'SBT_TAPE'
> PARMS 'SBT_LIBRARY=oracle.disksbt, ENV=(BACKUP_DIR=/u02/oradata/RAC/tape)';
```

Parallelization

Both backup and recovery operations may be run in parallel. If parallelization is configured, then two or more channels will be allocated for the operation, and RMAN breaks the backup workload into relatively equal workloads based on datafile size, disk affinity, and other factors.

In Oracle 9.0.1 and above, you can specify a default degree of parallelism for each backup device using the CONFIGURE command, for example:

```
RMAN> CONFIGURE DEVICE TYPE 'SBT_TAPE' PARALLELISM 4;
```

Using parallelization increases the resources required to perform a backup, but reduces the overall elapsed time to perform the backup.

It is recommended that you parallelize based on the number of available backup locations. Do not configure more than one channel per location. It is also recommended that you not implement parallelization if your backup location is a single disk or a single tape device. If two channels are allocated to one tape device, two backup sets will be interspersed together on the same tape. This will impact the performance of the restore operation, which will have to read more tape to access the files being recovered.

Control File Autobackup

The details of all backups are stored in the control file. Therefore, after completion of a database or archivelog backup, it is necessary to take a further backup of the control file. Prior to Oracle 9.2, it was necessary to manually back up the control file by specifying the INCLUDE CURRENT CONTROLFILE option.

In Oracle 9.2 and above, you can specify that the control file should be backed up automatically after every backup operation using the CONFIGURE command:

```
RMAN> CONFIGURE CONTROLFILE AUTOBACKUP ON;
```

By default, control file autobackups are disabled. The control file autobackup will always contain the most recent RMAN backup metadata. In the event that you lose your current control file, the control file autobackup can be used by RMAN to restore the database using the database ID (DBID).

If you are using a Flashback Recovery Area, the control file autobackup will be written to this location; if you are not using a Flashback Recovery Area, by default, the control file autobackup will be written to the $ORACLE_HOME/dbs directory if the default device type is disk, or to the tape device if the default device type is tape.

You can change the location for the control file autobackup using the CONFIGURE command:

```
RMAN> CONFIGURE CONTROLFILE AUTOBACKUP FORMAT = '/u02/oradata/RAC/cf_%F';
```

Note that the format string must include the %F format mask so that the backup can be identified by RMAN during restore operations.

In a RAC environment, if you are backing up from more than one node, the control file autobackup should be located on shared storage accessible to all nodes.

Snapshot Control File

RMAN needs a read-consistent view of the control file for long-running operations such as backups. However, the control file is extremely volatile, particularly in a RAC environment. In order to prevent RMAN from locking the current control file during long-running operations, thereby affecting database performance, RMAN uses snapshot control files.

A *snapshot control file* is a copy of the current control file. It is refreshed at the beginning of each backup operation to create a consistent view of the state of the database. The default location of the snapshot control file is in the $ORACLE_HOME/dbs directory, though it can, if necessary, be relocated. In a RAC environment, when backups are running on more than one node, the snapshot control file should be in a shared location, such as a clustered file system, so that any given node can have access to the file. Alternatively, if you choose to specify a local file system for the snapshot control file, the local destination must be identical on all nodes.

To show the current snapshot control file location, use the following:

```
RMAN> SHOW SNAPSHOT CONTROLFILE NAME;
```

To change the snapshot control file location, use the CONFIGURE command:

```
RMAN> CONFIGURE SNAPSHOT CONTROLFILE NAME TO '/u02/oradata/RAC/snap_RAC.scf';
```

Excluding Tablespaces

In Oracle 9.0.1 and above, tablespaces can be excluded from database backups using the CONFIGURE command, for example:

```
RMAN> CONFIGURE EXCLUDE FOR TABLESPACE ts1;
```

Tablespaces can be included in backups again by clearing the parameter:

```
RMAN> CONFIGURE EXCLUDE FOR TABLESPACE ts1 CLEAR;
```

It is not necessary to specify that read-only tablespaces should be excluded from the RMAN backup; Oracle already recognizes this fact.

Flashback Recovery Area

The Flashback Recovery Area was introduced in Oracle 10.1. It is a disk-based recovery area that can be used to store files for backup and recovery operations. If configured in a RAC environment, the Flashback Recovery Area must be shared between all instances. It can be located on an Automatic Storage Management (ASM) disk, a raw volume, a Cluster File System, or a shared directory that is mounted though NFS for each instance. A single Flashback Recovery Area can be shared by multiple Oracle databases. To use a shared area for multiple databases, each database must have a database name specified using the DB_NAME or DB_UNIQUE_NAME initialization parameter.

Within the Flashback Recovery Area, disk space is automatically managed by Oracle. Older backup files can be automatically deleted when they have been superseded or archived to offline storage devices.

The Flashback Recovery Area can be used to store all Oracle recovery files, which can be transient or permanent. Transient recovery files can be automatically deleted and include the following:

- Full datafile backups
- Incremental backups
- Datafile copies
- Control file (auto) backups
- Archived redo logs
- Block change tracking files
- Flashback logs

By default, Oracle also places mirrored copies of some database files in the Flashback Recovery Area. Permanent files such as the following should never be deleted:

- Mirrored copies of online redo logs
- Mirrored copies of the current control file

The Flashback Recovery Area is specified using the following two parameters:

- **DB_RECOVERY_FILE_DEST**: This parameter specifies a default location for the recovery area, which can be the name of a directory or ASM disk group. In a RAC environment, this location can also be an OCFS directory or a shared location on a cluster file system. This parameter has no default value, but it can be modified dynamically.

- **DB_RECOVERY_FILE_DEST_SIZE**: This parameter specifies the maximum size in bytes of the recovery area. The default value is 0, which specifies that there is no recovery area. This parameter can also be modified dynamically. You must set a value for this parameter before you can dynamically specify a value for DB_RECOVERY_FILE_DEST.

These parameters can be dynamically modified, allowing a newly specified Flashback Recovery Area to be available for immediate use without restarting the instances, for example:

```
SQL> ALTER SYSTEM SET db_recovery_file_dest_size = 1G SCOPE = BOTH;
SQL> ALTER SYSTEM SET db_recovery_file_dest = '/u02/oradata/RAC/fra' SCOPE = BOTH;
```

You can optionally use Oracle Managed Files (OMF) with the Flashback Recovery Area, in which case Oracle recommends that you set the DB_RECOVERY_FILE_DEST parameter to have the same value as either the DB_FILE_CREATE_DEST or DB_FILE_CREATE_ONLINE_LOG_DEST_n parameter.

The size of the Flashback Recovery Area is dependent on a number of factors, including the size and volatility of the database as well as the backup retention policy. Ideally, it should be large enough to contain a copy of all datafiles, all incremental backups since the last full backup, online redo logs, archived redo logs not yet written to tape, and control files.

When calculating the size of database copies, be aware that RMAN will not delete an existing backup until the next backup has been successfully created. Therefore, you will need to allocate sufficient space for at least two full backups in the Flashback Recovery Area in order to stage backups to disk before writing them to tape. If you do not wish to stage backups to disk, you can create a much smaller Flashback Recovery Area. At minimum, Oracle recommends that the Flashback Recovery Area contain sufficient space to store all archived redo logs not yet backed up to tape.

If you specify a Flashback Recovery Area, then the value of the LOG_ARCHIVE_DEST_10 parameter will be implicitly set to the value of DB_RECOVERY_FILE_DEST and archived redo logs will automatically be written to the flashback recovery location. You can still configure additional archived redo log locations using LOG_ARCHIVE_DEST_n parameters, for example, to copy archived redo logs to a standby database.

You can create the Flashback Recovery Area in one of three ways. You can specify it when the database is created using Database Creation Assistant (DBCA). You can create it dynamically without restarting the instance by setting the DB_RECOVERY_FILE_DEST and DB_RECOVERY_FILE_DEST_SIZE parameters. You can also create it using Enterprise Manager (EM).

In Oracle 10.1 and above, a new dynamic performance view called V$RECOVERY_FILE_DEST allows you to monitor the current status of the recovery area. This view includes the columns shown in Table 25-3.

Table 25-3. *V$RECOVERY_FILE_DEST Columns*

Column Name	Data Type	Description
NAME	VARCHAR2(513)	Pathname of recovery area
SPACE_LIMIT	NUMBER	Total space
SPACE_USED	NUMBER	Amount of space currently in use
SPACE_RECLAIMABLE	NUMBER	Amount of space that can be reclaimed
NUMBER_OF_FILES	NUMBER	Total number of files currently in the recovery area

You can stage the Flashback Recovery Area to tape at your convenience. Writing the Flashback Recovery Area to tape reduces the amount of housekeeping required and also decreases pressure on space, as transient files will be freed and aged out when additional space is required.

All backups on disk and tape are maintained according to the configured retention policy. You can back up the Flashback Recovery Area to tape using the following command:

```
RMAN> BACKUP RECOVERY AREA;
```

This command backs up the recovery area, including full backups, copies, incremental backups, control file autobackups, and archivelogs. It does not back up the block change tracking file, mirrored copes of the current control file, or online redo logs. Recovery files can only be written to tape (SBT channels).

If you are not using a Flashback Recovery Area, you can back up the same files using the following command:

```
RMAN> BACKUP RECOVERY FILES;
```

Performing Backups

To perform a backup, the target database must be in a mounted or an open state. In addition, if you are using a recovery catalog, the catalog database should also be mounted or open.

The backup command creates backupsets or image copies of datafiles, control files, archived redo logs, and the server parameter file. It does not back up password files or text parameter files. The number of backupsets created depends on several factors, including the number of files backed up, the number of tapes required, and the parallelism of the backup

All backups are created using the BACKUP command. As you would expect, this command has a large number of optional parameters. The basic syntax of the backup command is

```
BACKUP [<options>] <scope>
```

The options parameters describe how to perform the backup while the scope parameters define what to back up. If you do not specify any options, then Oracle will perform a full backup.

Options include the following:

- FULL: Performs a full backup (default).
- INCREMENTAL LEVEL <level>: Performs an incremental backup (this can be level 0 or 1).
- CUMULATIVE: For an incremental backup, includes all changes since the last level 0 backup.
- AS BACKUPSET: Creates a backupset (default).
- AS COMPRESSED BACKUPSET: Creates a compressed backupset.
- AS COPY: Creates an image copy.
- NOT BACKED UP [SINCE TIME <time>]: Only backs up files that have not been backed up since the last specified date and time.
- FORMAT <format>: Specifies storage location and filename format for a disk backup.
- TAG <tag>: Specifies a tag name for later identification of the backup.
- NOCHECKSUM: Disables checking for block corruption using a checksum algorithm.
- FILESPERSET <number>: Specifies the maximum number of datafiles that will be multiplexed into an individual backupset.
- MAXCORRUPT <number>: Specifies the maximum number of corrupt data blocks to back up before the backup is aborted.

- **SKIP <type>**: Skips the types of files specified during the backup. The types include OFFLINE, READONLY, and INACCESSIBLE.

- **CHANNEL <name>**: Specifies a nondefault channel.

- **DELETE INPUT**: Deletes input files after successful backup. This option applies only to archived redo log backups.

The scope of the backup can be defined using the following parameters:

- **DATABASE**: Backs up all datafiles and the control file.

- **TABLESPACE <tablespace_name>**: Backs up the specified tablespace.

- **DATAFILE <name> | <file#>**: Backs up the specified datafile. The file# can optionally be specified instead of the datafile name. The file# can be found in V$DATAFILE table.

- **ARCHIVELOG pattern | sequence range | time range**: Backs up the specified archivelogs.

- **CURRENT CONTROLFILE**: Backs up the current control file.

- **BACKUP CONTROLFILE**: Backs up a backup control file.

- **BACKUPSET <primary_key>**: Backs up the specified backupset on disk.

You can make a full backup of a database using the command

```
RMAN> BACKUP DATABASE;
```

This will write the database backup to a backupset. To back up a tablespace ts1 to a backupset, use the following:

```
RMAN> BACKUP TABLESPACE ts1;
```

To back up a datafile to a backupset, you can either specify the pathname or the file number. The file number can be found in the file# column of V$DATAFILE, for example:

```
RMAN> BACKUP DATAFILE '/u02/oradata/RAC/ts1_01.dbf';
RMAN> BACKUP DATAFILE 18;
```

By default, the backup will be written to the $ORACLE_HOME/dbs location. This is not appropriate in a RAC environment unless you are relying on a single node to perform all backup and restore operations. In this case, you have introduced a single point of failure. You should use an identical shared location for the backup on all nodes in the RAC cluster. You can specify the default location by specifying a format for the channel device type disk parameter using the CONFIGURE command. You can override this value using the FORMAT clause of the backup command, for example:

```
RMAN> BACKUP DATABASE FORMAT '/u02/oradata/RAC/backup/RAC_%U';
```

You can optionally specify the option AS BACKUPSET, which is the default:

```
RMAN> BACKUP AS BACKUPSET DATABASE;
```

In Oracle 10.1 and above, you can specify that the backupset's files should be compressed as it is backed up:

```
RMAN> BACKUP AS COMPRESSED BACKUPSET DATABASE;
```

Note You cannot compress an image copy. The compression option makes a significant difference in the size of the backupset. However, you should remember that compression will adversely impact restore times in the event of a media failure due to the fact that the files must be uncompressed as part of the recovery process.

You can also specify the AS COPY option to create an image copy. This option is covered in more detail in the following section.

In Oracle 9.0.1 and above, backups can be restarted using the NOT BACKED UP clause. This option will only back up files that have not been backed up since a specified date and time, for example:

```
RMAN> BACKUP DATABASE NOT BACKED UP SINCE TIME 'SYSDATE - 7';
```

You can use this clause to restart a backup operation if it fails after completing part of a previous backup. If the SINCE TIME clause is omitted, files that have never been backed up will be included in the backup job, for example:

```
RMAN> BACKUP DATABASE NOT BACKED UP;
```

In Oracle 9.0.1 and above, RMAN can back up the server parameter file (if one is configured). If you choose to use a text parameter file (PFILE), then you will need to back up this file independently of RMAN. In Oracle 9.2 and above, RMAN will automatically back up the current server parameter file, whenever it includes the current control file, in a backupset.

In Oracle 9.0.1 and above, you can use the PLUS ARCHIVELOG clause to specify that archived redo logs that have not previously been backed up should be included in the current backup, for example:

```
RMAN> BACKUP DATAFILE 7 PLUS ARCHIVELOG;
```

If you specify the PLUS ARCHIVELOG clause, RMAN will back up the online redo logs and all archived redo logs that have not yet been backed up.

You can also back up archived redo logs using the BACKUP ARCHIVELOG clause. For example, you can specify

```
RMAN> BACKUP ARCHIVELOG ALL DELETE INPUT;
```

This command backs up all archived redo logs and then deletes them if the backup operation completed successfully.

In Oracle 9.2 and above, you can specify the NOT BACKED UP n TIMES clause for the BACKUP ARCHIVELOG command to back up those logs that have not been backed up at least n number of times. This command enables multiple copies of each archivelog to be moved to tape, giving you an extra margin of safety in case of media failures with tape. RMAN only considers backups created on the same device type as the current backup. For example, this clause can be used to ensure that at least two copies of each archived redo log are written to tape:

```
RMAN> BACKUP ARCHIVELOG NOT BACKED UP 2 TIMES;
```

You can combine this command with a delete statement to back up every archived redo log twice, but then allow them to remain on disk in case they are needed for recovery. For example, to ensure that at least two copies of each archived redo log are written to tape and that the files remain on disk for a week before being deleted, use the following:

```
RMAN> BACKUP ARCHIVELOG NOT BACKED UP 2 TIMES;
RMAN> DELETE ARCHIVELOG COMPLETED BEFORE SYSDATE - 7;
```

RMAN does not back up temporary tablespaces if they are configured to use tempfiles. It will still attempt to back up temporary tablespaces if they are located in datafiles. Therefore, if you are using RMAN, you should use tempfiles for your temporary tablespaces wherever possible, particularly if your database was originally created in Oracle 8.0 or below and has been subsequently migrated.

In Oracle 10.1 and above, you can control and minimize the performance impact of the backup operation on other processes currently running in the database using the DURATION clause of the BACKUP command. The basic syntax is as follows:

```
DURATION <hours>:<minutes> [ PARTIAL ] [ MINIMIZE { TIME | LOAD }
```

If you specify a maximum duration in terms of hours and minutes, then the backup command will fail if this time is exceeded. You can use the PARTIAL keyword to specify that the backup should terminate without error at the end of the specified time period. In this case, you can continue with the backup at the next opportunity, for example:

```
RMAN> BACKUP DURATION 03:00 PARTIAL DATABASE;
```

You can specify that a backup should run as quickly as possible using the MINIMIZE TIME clause. This will cause the backup process to be prioritized over other database processes.

You can also specify that the backup should be run as slowly as possibly within the specified time period using the MINIMIZE LOAD clause. This will allow maximum resources to be dedicated to other processes in the database, for example:

```
RMAN> BACKUP DURATION 03:00 MINIMIZE LOAD DATABASE;
```

Image Copies

RMAN can make copies of Oracle datafiles known as *image copies*, which are block-for-block copies of the datafiles. As with backupset copies, RMAN uses memory buffers to make image copies and performs a corruption check on each block. However, for image copies, empty blocks are not eliminated.

Image copies can only be written to disk; they cannot be written directly to tape. You can make image copies of current datafiles, previously taken datafile copies, archived redo logs, and the current or backup control file. You can make only full copies of datafiles; it is not meaningful to create an incremental image copy of a datafile, as this is conceptually identical to performing an incremental backup to disk.

In the event of recovery being needed, the database can be switched to use the image copy of the database, and consequently no physical restore is necessary. Archived redo logs can be applied immediately to the image copy to recover committed transactions up to the time the failure occurred. Therefore, using image copies reduces the MTTR at the expense of using additional disk space. Therefore, if sufficient disk space is available, it is recommended that image copies are created for all datafiles. If insufficient space is available, then you should make image copies of the datafiles that would be most affected by a media failure and back up the remaining datafiles directly to tape.

Prior to Oracle 10.1, you should use the COPY command to create image copies, for example:

```
RMAN> COPY DATAFILE '/u02/oradata/RAC/ts02.dbf' TO '/u02/oradata/RAC/ts02_copy.dbf';
```

You must specify both the source and destination filenames. You can optionally specify a level of 0, in which case RMAN will create the image copy as a level 0 backup. Subsequent incremental backups will use this image copy as their baseline and will only back up blocks that have changed.

You can still use the COPY command in Oracle 10.1, but it has been deprecated in that release in favor of the BACKUP AS COPY command, for example:

```
RMAN> BACKUP AS COPY DATABASE;
RMAN> BACKUP AS COPY TABLESPACE users;
RMAN> BACKUP AS COPY DATAFILE '/u02/oradata/RAC/ts1.dbf';
RMAN> BACKUP AS COPY DATAFILE 9;
```

You do not need to specify a destination file name for this command, as RMAN will generate one automatically. By default, it will create the image copy in the Flashback Recovery Area if one is configured; otherwise, it will be created in the $ORACLE_HOME/dbs directory.

RMAN can also be used with non-RMAN image copies. The source of these copies could be mirrored datafiles on multiple disks or backups created using operating system utilities. These files must be manually added to the RMAN repository using the CATALOG command.

In this example, we will manually create an image copy for a datafile called /u02/oradata/RAC/ts1.dbf in a tablespace called ts1. First, put the tablespace in backup mode using

```
SQL> ALTER TABLESPACE ts1 BEGIN BACKUP;
```

Next, take an operating system copy using the cp utility:

```
cp /u02/oradata/RAC/ts1.dbf /u02/oradata/RAC/ts1_copy.dbf
```

Then take the tablespace out of backup mode:

```
SQL> ALTER TABLESPACE ts1 END BACKUP;
```

Catalog the new operating system file using the following:

```
RMAN> CATALOG DATAFILECOPY '/u02/oradata/RAC/ts1_copy.dbf'
```

You can check that the file has been successfully cataloged as follows:

```
RMAN> LIST DATAFILECOPY ALL;
```

Image copies can be backed up to backupsets on disk or tape using the BACKUP command with the COPY OF option, for example:

```
RMAN> BACKUP COPY OF DATABASE;
RMAN> BACKUP COPY OF TABLESPACE users;
RMAN> BACKUP COPY OF DATAFILE '/u02/oradata/RAC/ts1_1.dbf';
RMAN> BACKUP COPY OF DATAFILE 9;
```

Take care not to confuse BACKUP AS COPY, which creates an image copy, with BACKUP COPY OF, which backs up an image copy to a backupset.

Control file copies can also be backed up, but the syntax is slightly different:

```
RMAN> BACKUP CONTROLFILECOPY ALL;
```

If you need to subsequently recover the datafile, you can use the SWITCH command to convert the image copy into a current datafile. The SWITCH command switches the datafile names in the RMAN repository, after which the new datafile will require media recovery. This is equivalent to the behavior of the ALTER DATABASE RENAME DATAFILE command.

For example, assume you need to recover the datafile /u02/oradata/RAC/ts2.dbf. In order to switch to the copy, either the database must be mounted, but not open, or the datafile must be offline. In RMAN, you can refer to a datafile by its pathname or its file number. As RMAN generates long pathnames for copies, we recommend that you convert the pathname into a file number, for example:

```
SQL> SELECT file# FROM v$datafile
WHERE name = '/u02/oradata/RAC/ts2.dbf';

FILE#
   9
```

To take this datafile offline, use

```
RMAN> SQL 'ALTER DATABASE DATAFILE 9 OFFLINE';
```

You can then switch the datafile using

```
RMAN> SWITCH DATAFILE '/u02/oradata/RAC/ts2.dbf' TO COPY;
```

Finally, you will need to run media recovery on the datafile to apply any archived redo logs that have been created since the image copy was created.

```
RMAN> RECOVER DATAFILE 9;
```

In Oracle 10.1 and above, you can perform a fast recovery on the entire database using the `SWITCH` command:

```
RMAN> SWITCH DATABASE TO COPY;
```

`RMAN` will switch the names of the datafiles in the control file to point to image copies in the backup area. It converts the image copies into current datafiles and then runs recovery on them. This avoids the need to restore any backup files or image copies and is therefore much faster.

If you use the `SWITCH DATABASE` command, you should remember that you will no longer have an image copy backup. Therefore, you should create a new backup as quickly as possible. Alternatively, you may choose to create multiple image copies of your database so that you still have a backup after executing the `SWITCH DATABASE` command.

Incremental Backups

Backups can be full or incremental. If the backup destination is a backupset, then `RMAN` writes all initialized blocks in each datafile; if the backup destination is an image copy, then `RMAN` writes all blocks in each datafile, including uninitialized blocks. On the other hand, an incremental backup only writes those blocks, which have changed since the last backup was taken. This reduces the amount of time required to perform the backup. It also reduces the amount of storage required to store the backup. The downside to incremental backups is that more physical media (tapes or files) may be required to restore a consistent image of the file(s) you are recovering.

Recovery is more efficient using incremental backups than using archived redo logs, because physical blocks in an incremental backup can be written back to the database directly. On the other hand, in order to apply redo records from an archived redo log, each database block can potentially be read from the datafile, updated with the change vector, and then written back to the database. A single block may be subject to thousands of changes during the course of a day generating a similar number of redo log records. However, the corresponding incremental backup will contain only one copy of the block. Therefore, `RMAN` will always attempt to use incremental backups instead of archived redo logs.

By default, an incremental backup writes blocks that have changed since the last backup, which may have been a full backup or another incremental backup. For example, you might perform a full backup one day per week and an incremental backup on the other six days. However, if your database is subject to hot spots of activity, each incremental backup may contain roughly the same set of blocks. This will increase the duration of the restore process, which starts by restoring the last full backup and then applying successive incremental backups until all the changes have been recovered. You can optionally specify the `CUMULATIVE` option to consolidate information in several incremental backups. This will copy all changes since the last full backup. The resulting incremental backup may occupy more space, but recovery times will be reduced since the data you need will be on a smaller number of tapes, which will probably still be in your media racks.

Prior to Oracle 10.1, you could specify up to five levels of incremental backup (levels 0 to 4). These levels were considered too complicated to administer; therefore, in Oracle 10.1 and above, there are only two levels: level 0 and level 1.

A level 0 incremental backup performs a full backup of every block in the database. It also records the incremental SCN. You must take a level 0 incremental backup before you can take level 1 backup. However, you can subsequently take any number of level 1 backups.

It is recommended that you take full backups every day, if possible. If this is not possible, then it is recommended that you take a full backup at least once per week and then take incremental backups at frequent intervals during the intervening period.

In Oracle 10.1 and above, incremental backups can be applied to existing image copies, ensuring that a recent image is always available for fast media restore and recovery. Incrementally updated backups are described later in this chapter.

Block Change Tracking

While incremental backups write less data to disk or tape than full backups, it is still necessary to scan all blocks in the database in order to detect which blocks have changed since the last backup. Incremental backups require as many block reads as full backups. Therefore, if the database is not very volatile, then block scanning will probably represent the largest time component of the backup duration.

In Oracle 10.1 and above, it is possible to enable block change tracking to avoid scanning entire datafiles during incremental backups. When block change tracking is enabled, the amount of data scanned is proportional to the amount of data that has been changed. Block change tracking uses the Change Tracking Writer (CTWR) background process to record the physical locations of all database blocks changed since the last level 0 backup in a new recovery file called the *block change tracking file*. When an incremental level 1 backup is taken, the block change tracking file is referenced to determine which physical blocks should be included in the backup.

Block change tracking can be enabled when the database is either mounted or open. It is only really meaningful to enable block change tracking when the database is ARCHIVELOG mode. However, it can also be enabled when the database is in NOARCHIVELOG mode. In a RAC environment, all instances should use the same physical block change tracking file, which should be located on shared storage. Block change tracking is enabled using the ALTER DATABASE statement. Unlike other features, such as archive logging and standby protection modes, it is not necessary to shut down a RAC database and restart one instance in exclusive mode in order to enable block change tracking.

If you are using a Flashback Recovery Area, then the file name of the block change tracking file will be generated automatically using the following command:

```
SQL> ALTER DATABASE
> ENABLE BLOCK CHANGE TRACKING;
```

If you are not using a Flashback Recovery Area, then it is necessary to specify a name for the block change tracking file using this command:

```
SQL> ALTER DATABASE
> ENABLE BLOCK CHANGE TRACKING
> USING FILE '<filename>';
```

After you have enabled block change tracking, you should take a level 0 backup.

In a RAC environment, the file should be located on shared storage and should be physically accessible by all instances in the cluster. Oracle automatically determines the initial size of the block change tracking file based on factors such as the size of the database and the number of instances.

Block change tracking can subsequently be disabled using the following command:

```
SQL> ALTER DATABASE
> DISABLE BLOCK CHANGE TRACKING;
```

The current status of block change tracking function is externalized in the dynamic performance view V$BLOCK_CHANGE_TRACKING. This view includes the columns shown in Table 25-4.

Table 25-4. *V$BLOCK_CHANGE_TRACKING Columns*

Column Name	Data Type	Description
STATUS	VARCHAR2(10)	Status of block change tracking
FILE	VARCHAR2(513)	Pathname of block change tracking file
BYTES	NUMBER	Size in bytes of block change tracking file

While block change tracking has the potential to significantly improve performance, it comes at a cost of additional I/O required to maintain the block change tracking file. It also requires an extra background process that consumes additional CPU cycles. Consequently, as the number of block changes in the database increases, the effectiveness of block change tracking decreases. However, as it is possible to dynamically enable and disable this feature, you can easily evaluate its impact on throughput without adversely affecting database availability.

Incrementally Updated Backups

In Oracle 10.1 and above, it is possible to apply incremental backups to datafile copies. This means that datafile copies will be as recent as the last incremental backup. The benefit of this feature is that recovery times may be significantly reduced. In the event of a media failure, it will only be necessary switch to the datafile copy and then to apply redo that has been created since the last incremental backup, in order to recover the database.

Incremental backups can only be applied to a datafile copy created using a level 0 backup; they cannot be applied to a backupset. In addition, the incremental backup must be tagged, for example:

```
RMAN> BACKUP INCREMENTAL LEVEL 0 TAG 'TAG1' DATABASE;
```

You must specify the FOR RECOVERY OF COPY clause when taking the incremental backup:

```
RMAN> BACKUP INCREMENTAL LEVEL 1 FOR RECOVERY OF COPY
TAG 'TAG1' DATABASE;
```

This incremental backup can subsequently be applied to the datafile copies using

```
RMAN> RECOVER COPY OF DATABASE WITH TAG 'TAG1';
```

Recovery is faster with incrementally updated backups. Incremental backups can be applied to image copies before a media failure occurs. In the event of a failure, it is therefore only necessary to apply archived redo logs to the most recent incrementally updated image copies, thus minimizing recovery times.

Housekeeping

RMAN supports a number of housekeeping commands, including CROSSCHECK, LIST, REPORT, and DELETE. It is also necessary to perform additional maintenance whenever you use the DROP DATABASE command. These commands are discussed in the following sections.

CROSSCHECK Command

The CROSSCHECK command was introduced in Oracle 9.0.1. It allows you to compare the contents of the RMAN repository against disk or tape media. Objects will be marked EXPIRED, AVAILABLE, and UNAVAILABLE. The CROSSCHECK command only verifies the status of backups and image copies created on the current device type.

For example, if the device type is DISK (the default), you can cross-check all backup sets and image copies as follows:

```
RMAN> CROSSCHECK BACKUP;
```

Remember that the CROSSCHECK command will invoke a long-running media inventory operation that could affect ongoing or future backup and restore operations.

We recommend that you execute CROSSCHECK operations on a regular basis to verify that you have consistent backups and to determine the current location of your recovery media. The CROSSCHECK command will help you identify the current locations of media and will also audit that media to ensure you can perform a full recovery in the event of a catastrophic failure.

If you do not stage your backups to disk, we recommend that you create multiple tape copies. This will allow you to store one consistent backup set at a secure location offsite and to store a second backup set locally, from which backups can be restored if necessary. This will reduce the overall time required to perform a restore.

REPORT Command

You can use the REPORT command to generate reports from the RMAN repository. Reports can be generated listing files needing backup, files that are not currently recoverable, and backup files that can be deleted.

The basic syntax of the REPORT command is

```
REPORT <options> [<scope>]
```

Options for the REPORT command include the following:

- **NEED BACKUP**: Report all datafiles requiring backup
    - **INCREMENTAL <number>**: Report all datafiles requiring <number> or more incremental backups to be restored to the current state
    - **DAYS <number>**: Report datafiles not backed up for <number> or more days
    - **REDUNDANCY <number>**: Report datafiles requiring <number> of backups to fulfill the minimum number of redundant copies
    - **RECOVERY WINDOW OF <number> DAYS**: Report datafiles not backed up within the specified recovery window
- **OBSOLETE**: Report full backups, archived redo logs, and image copies that are no longer necessary and can be deleted
- **UNRECOVERABLE**: Report datafiles that are no longer recoverable from the currently available backups

Scope for the REPORT command includes the following:

- **DATABASE**: Report on all files in target database. You can optionally append a SKIP TABLESPACE clause to exclude a list of tablespaces from the report.
- **TABLESPACE <tablespace_name>**: Report on the specified tablespace.
- **DATAFILE <datafile>**: Report on the specified datafile.

If no scope is specified, then the default value is DATABASE.

For example, to report all datafiles in the target database, requiring the application of four or more incremental backups, to be recovered to the current state, use the following command:

```
RMAN> REPORT NEED BACKUP INCREMENTAL 4;
```

To report all datafiles in the target database that will need more than three days of archived redo logs, to be applied by the recovery process after the datafiles have been restored from the last full backup, use the following command:

```
RMAN> REPORT NEED BACKUP DAYS 3;
```

To report datafiles needing backup in order to maintain a recovery window of one week, use this command:

```
RMAN> REPORT NEED BACKUP RECOVERY WINDOW 7 DAYS;
```

To report all obsolete backups and image copies, use the following command:

```
RMAN> REPORT OBSOLETE;
```

To report obsolete backups and image that are not required to keep the database recoverable within a specified window of time (e.g., one week) use the following:

```
RMAN> REPORT OBSOLETE RECOVERY WINDOW 7 DAYS;
```

To report all datafiles in the target database that cannot be recovered from existing backups because redo may be missing because of NOLOGGING statements, use the following:

```
RMAN> REPORT UNRECOVERABLE;
```

LIST Command

You can use the LIST command to display information about backupsets and image copies in the RMAN repository. To list all backups currently in the repository, use this command:

```
RMAN> LIST BACKUP;
```

To list a summary of all backups currently in the repository, use the following:

```
RMAN> LIST BACKUP SUMMARY;
```

By default, the output of the LIST command is in backup order (BY BACKUP). In Oracle 9.0.1 and above, you can also specify that the output should be in file order (BY FILE). You can list all backups in the repository in file order as follows:

```
RMAN> LIST BACKUP BY FILE;
```

This command lists all datafile backups, archived log backups, control file backups, and server parameter file backups.

To list all backupsets, use

```
RMAN> LIST BACKUPSET ALL;
```

To list the contents of a specific backupset, use

```
RMAN> LIST BACKUPSET <key>;
```

where <key> is the primary key of the backupset.

To list all backups of a specific datafile, use

```
RMAN> LIST BACKUP OF DATAFILE <datafile>;
```

where <datafile> can be the pathname or the absolute file number (file#) of the datafile.

You can list all image copies of a specific tablespace, for example:

```
RMAN> LIST COPY OF TABLESPACE users;
```

Similarly, you can list all image copies of a specific datafile as follows:

```
RMAN> LIST COPY OF DATAFILE '/u02/oradata/RAC/users.dbf';
RMAN> LIST COPY OF DATAFILE 9;
```

Finally, to list all backups and image copies marked as expired by the CROSSCHECK command, use

```
RMAN> LIST EXPIRED;
```

DELETE Command

You can use the DELETE command to delete physical backups and copies and also to update records in the control file and remove records from the recovery catalog.

You can delete obsolete backups and image copies as follows:

```
RMAN> DELETE OBSOLETE;
```

Be default, the DELETE command displays a list of files to be deleted and prompts for confirmation. You can suppress the prompts and force deletion using

```
RMAN> DELETE FORCE NOPROMPT OBSOLETE;
```

The DELETE command can also be used to delete expired backups and image copies. The CROSSCHECK command marks backups and copies as being expired if the files are absent or inaccessible. To delete expired files, use

```
RMAN> DELETE EXPIRED;
```

DROP DATABASE Command

In Oracle 10.1 and above, you can use the DROP DATABASE command to delete an entire database, including all control files and datafiles. Clearly, this is a very powerful command, so you must be logged on with SYSDBA privilege to execute it. You can drop a database from either RMAN or SQL*Plus, for example:

```
RMAN> DROP DATABASE;
```

By default, the DROP DATABASE command will not delete any archived redo logs or image copies. In order to delete these files as well, use

```
RMAN> DROP DATABASE INCLUDING BACKUPS;
```

The DROP DATABASE command will not affect the recovery catalog. Therefore, you must remove the database manually using

```
RMAN> UNREGISTER DATABASE;
```

Performing a Restore

If you experience a media failure and need to recover your database, you must first either restore the datafiles and archived redo logs from a backupset, which may reside on disk or tape, or switch to image copies. The RESTORE command extracts files from backupsets for use in recovery.

By default, the RESTORE command overwrites the current versions of datafiles, control files, and archived redo logs. Alternatively, you can use the SET NEWNAME command to specify that the RESTORE command should write files to other locations.

In Oracle 10.1 and above, RMAN automatically identifies the correct backup to use for restore operations, which reduces the possibility of operator errors. Also in Oracle 10.1 and above, the restore process tolerates corrupt or missing backups. If the latest backup is not available, RMAN will automatically use an older backup for restore operations.

The basic syntax of the RESTORE command is

```
RESTORE <scope> [<options>]
```

Scope describes the objects to be restored and can include the following:

- **DATABASE**: Restore all datafiles in the target database, excluding any tablespaces specified by an optional SKIP clause.
- **TABLESPACE <tablespace_name>**: Restore all datafiles in the specified tablespace.
- **DATAFILE <name|file#>**: Restore the specified datafile by name or file number.
- **CONTROLFILE**: Restore the control file.
- **ARCHIVELOG <specifier>**: Restore the specified archived redo logs.
- **SPFILE**: Restore the server parameter file (Oracle 9.2 and above). You can optionally specify a text parameter file destination using the TO PFILE clause.

The RESTORE command has a number of useful options, including the following:

- **FORCE**: In Oracle 9.0.1 and above, RMAN restore does not overwrite existing files with backup files if the file headers are identical. You can override this functionality using the FORCE option.
- **FROM BACKUPSET**: Specifies that object should be restored from the most recent backupset.
- **FROM DATAFILECOPY**: Specifies that object should be restored from the most recent image copy.
- **PREVIEW [SUMMARY]**: Reports on the backups on disk or tape that will be used during the restore operation.
- **VALIDATE**: RMAN determines which backupsets, image copies, and archived redo logs are required for the restore operation, and scans them to verify their contents. No files are restored. You can use this option to verify the validity of existing backups and copies.

To restore the entire database, execute the following command:

```
RMAN> RESTORE DATABASE;
```

The database must be mounted using a current control file. Unlike the BACKUP DATABASE command, RESTORE DATABASE does not automatically include the control file and the server parameter files. These files must be restored explicitly using RESTORE CONTROLFILE and RESTORE SPFILE.

You can restore an individual tablespace, for example:

```
RMAN> RESTORE TABLESPACE users;
```

You can also restore a datafile specifying either the pathname or the absolute file number (file#):

```
RMAN> RESTORE DATAFILE '/u02/oradata/RAC/users.dbf';
RMAN> RESTORE DATAFILE 9;
```

You can restore all archived redo logs using the following:

```
RMAN> RESTORE ARCHIVELOG ALL;
```

Sometimes it may not be appropriate to restore all archived redo logs to the current archive log destination. For example, there may be a large number of files and insufficient space to store the logs.

In this case, you may wish to restore the files to a temporary directory. You can use the SET ARCHIVELOG DESTINATION command to specify a new destination:

```
RMAN> RUN
> {
>      SET ARCHIVELOG DESTINATION TO '/u03/oradata/RAC/temp';
>      RESTORE ARCHIVELOG ALL;
> }
```

To verify that the database can be restored from the current backups, use

```
RMAN> RESTORE DATABASE VALIDATE;
```

This command is particularly useful in a RAC environment, as it can help confirm that the archived log destinations have been configured correctly on all nodes.

If possible, RMAN will parallelize restoring datafiles and applying incremental backups. In this case, the number of channels that have been allocated in the configuration or the RMAN script determines the degree of parallelism that RMAN uses. RMAN will parallelize these operations across all available nodes.

Performing Recovery

Media or disk recovery is performed by the RECOVER command. This command can perform complete or incomplete database recovery. It can also perform complete recovery for specific tablespaces and datafiles.

The RECOVER command will apply incremental backups automatically if any exist. It will then apply archived redo logs to recover any remaining transactions.

If you are using a recovery catalog, then the catalog database should be available to support the RECOVER command. It must be available if you need to recover the current control file.

For database recovery, the target database must be mounted but not open. For tablespace and datafile recovery, the target database must be open, but all datafiles being recovered must be offline.

The basic syntax of the RECOVER command is

```
RECOVER <scope> [<options>]
```

Scope includes the following:

- **DATABASE**: Recover the entire database. If no UNTIL clause is specified, then a complete recovery will be performed; otherwise, incomplete recovery will be performed. You can specify a time, SCN, or redo log thread sequence number in the UNTIL clause. You can also exclude tablespaces from recovery using the SKIP clause.

- **TABLESPACE <tablespace_name>**: Recover the specified tablespace, which must be offline.

- **DATAFILE <pathname | file#>**: Recover the specified datafile, which must be offline.

Options include the following:

- **ALLOW <number> CORRUPTION**: This option tolerates a specified number of corrupt blocks before aborting the recovery operation.

- **DELETE ARCHIVELOG [MAXSIZE <size> K|M|G]**: This option deletes archived redo logs restored from backups or copies after they have been recovered. Archived redo logs that were on disk before the restore operation are not deleted. This feature is enabled by default if a Flashback Recovery Area is configured.

- **NOREDO**: This option only applies incremental backups. It is used for recovery of NOARCHIVELOG databases.

- **PARALLEL <degree>**: This option specifies the degree of parallelism. RMAN automatically calculates the optimum degree of recovery parallelism, so this option should only be necessary to control the impact of tablespace or datafile recovery on existing workload.

- **TEST**: In Oracle 9.0.1 and above, this option performs a trial recovery. Redo is applied as normal, but changes are not written to disk. Any errors encountered will be written to the alert log. This option be used in conjunction with a RESETLOGS operation.

To recover the entire database to the current point in time, use the following:

```
RMAN> RESTORE DATABASE;
RMAN> RECOVER DATABASE;
```

To recover the database to a previous point in time, you can specify a time, SCN, or log sequence number, for example:

```
> RMAN> RUN {
>       SET UNTIL TIME = '20-SEP-05 15:30:00';
>       RESTORE DATABASE;
>       RECOVER DATABASE;
> }
```

To recover a tablespace, you must first offline the tablespace:

```
> RMAN> RUN{
>       SQL 'ALTER TABLESPACE users OFFLINE IMMEDIATE';
>       RESTORE TABLESPACE users;
>       RECOVER TABLESPACE users;
>       SQL 'ALTER TABLESPACE users ONLINE';
> }
```

To recover a datafile, you can specify either the pathname or the absolute file number, which you can obtain from V$DATAFILE:

```
RMAN > RUN {
>       SQL 'ALTER DATABASE DATAFILE 9 OFFLINE';
>       RESTORE DATAFILE 9;
>       RECOVER DATAFILE 9;
>       SQL 'ALTER DATABASE DATAFILE 9 ONLINE';
> }
```

In Oracle 9.2 and above, you can use the DELETE ARCHIVELOG clause with the MAXSIZE option to control how much disk space is used during media recovery, for example:

```
RMAN> RECOVER TABLESPACE users DELETE ARCHIVELOG MAXSIZE 500M;
```

You can recover using an image copy as follows:

```
RMAN> RECOVER DATAFILECOPY '/u02/oradata/RAC/backup/users_copy.dbf';
```

You can use the same command to recover using an incrementally updated backup.

To perform a trial recovery, use the following:

```
RMAN> RECOVER DATABASE TEST;
```

RMAN automatically parallelizes recovery commands. It can also parallelize the application of archived redo logs. In this case, the number of parallel processes is determined by the RECOVERY_PARALLELISM parameter. RMAN will parallelize this operation by allocating multiple processes on a single node.

Block Media Recovery

In the default recovery method, known as Datafile Media Recovery, all blocks within a datafile are recovered. However, this is not always appropriate if only one or two blocks in the datafile have been corrupted.

In Oracle 9.0.1 and above, you can use Block Media Recovery (BMR) to recover individual data blocks. BMR enables specific blocks in a datafile to be restored from a backupset or image copy and then recovered using media recovery. Unlike in Datafile Media Recovery, in BMR the datafile remains available while the block is being recovered. In addition, the segment containing the blocks being recovered remains available. As such, BMR improves a database's availability, as the datafile and unaffected blocks in the segment remain unaffected. It also reduces MTTR, as it is necessary to apply redo only to the blocks being recovered.

Corrupt data blocks can be determined from trace files and the V$BLOCK_CORRUPTION and V$COPY_CORRUPTION dynamic performance views. Data block corruptions are reported by Oracle error ORA-1578, for example:

```
ORA-1578; ORACLE data block corrupted (file# 9, block# 4398)
```

Blocks can be recovered using the BLOCKRECOVER command. For example, to recover the block listed in the error message just shown, use the following:

```
RMAN> BLOCKRECOVER DATAFILE 9 BLOCK 4398;
```

You can also specify multiple blocks for the BLOCKRECOVER command, for example:

```
RMAN> BLOCKRECOVER DATAFILE 9 BLOCK 4398 DATAFILE 11 BLOCK 1436;
```

It is more efficient to recover all corrupt blocks at the same time, as it is necessary to sequentially read all archived redo logs since the last full backup in order to identify redo to be applied to the specific blocks.

BMR can only be used for the complete recovery of a data block. Corrupt data blocks will be made available to users when the data block has been fully recovered. BMR can be performed only from a full backup; it cannot use incremental backups.

RAC Considerations

Because RMAN is fully integrated with RAC, there are few differences between RMAN in a single-instance environment and in a multi-instance RAC environment. If you are considering a third-party solution, you should remember that most predate RAC (as, of course, does RMAN, which was introduced in Oracle 8.0). However, RMAN has some advantages in terms of the integration with the Oracle kernel and SGA, access to the control file, and integration with EM. In addition, if you have a license for your RAC database, then RMAN is free. If you do not already have a preferred backup product, we recommend that you investigate RMAN first.

If you already have a preferred backup solution supplied by a third-party vendor, then investigate it carefully to verify that RAC is fully supported. There is a difference between a product that is compatible with RAC (i.e., it doesn't crash) and a product that fully supports RAC.

If you intend to use a storage-based backup solution such as split mirroring or snapshots, then you need to be aware that any RMAN backup you take from the mirror or snapshot copy will update the control file on the mirror or snapshot. Therefore, if you need to perform a recovery on the production database, the control file may not be aware that the backup has been created. This problem is not insurmountable, but it may require some extra administrative effort to provide a robust and enduring solution.

Over the years, a number of RAC-specific enhancements have been applied to RMAN. In Oracle 8.1.5 and above, OPS environments, and in Oracle 9.0.1 and above RAC environments, RMAN can dynamically schedule the backup of datafiles via the node that demonstrates the best performance via disk affinity. Unfortunately, there is no easy way to verify this claim, but it may affect you if you intend to build a stretch cluster where some nodes experience longer response times from storage than others.

Prior to Oracle 9.2, it was necessary to use the SET AUTOLOCATE command to specify which nodes could access backup pieces or backup or restore operations. In Oracle 9.2 and above, RMAN automatically discovers this information for backup pieces, archived redo logs, datafile copies, and control file copies.

The RMAN utility connects to a single node in the cluster. All RMAN processes related to job building, control file access, and update are performed by that node.

RMAN uses Oracle Net Services to connect to the database. The connection must be dedicated (as opposed to shared) and not configured for failover or load balancing.

You can either use a single node for backup operations or distribute the workload across all nodes in the cluster. You can therefore allocate channels across all nodes in the cluster. For example, assume there is a tape device on each node:

```
RMAN> ALLOCATE CHANNEL channel1 TYPE SBT CONNECT SYS/ORACLE@RAC1;
RMAN> ALLOCATE CHANNEL channel2 TYPE SBT CONNECT SYS/ORACLE@RAC2;
```

Even if a single node is being used for backups, we recommend configuring a Media Management interface on each node in the cluster in case you need to perform a restore or recovery operation from a different node.

In a RAC cluster, a datafile restore can occur from any node in the cluster. You can distribute the workload across all nodes in the cluster by allocating one or more channels on each node.

In a RAC cluster, only one node can perform recovery operations. This node must have access to the archived redo logs from all nodes of the cluster.

Archived Redo Logs

In a RAC environment, each node generates a thread of archived redo logs. RMAN uses the V$ARCHIVE_LOG dynamic performance view, which externalizes the contents of the control file to determine which archived redo logs to backup. RMAN backs up all archive logs with a status of AVAILABLE. It does not back up archived redo logs with a status of DELETED or EXPIRED.

The status of archived redo logs in the control file can only be updated by RMAN. If you clean out archived redo logs manually using operating system commands, then subsequent archivelog backups will fail when they attempt to backup the nonexistent files. Therefore, if you implement RMAN, you should always use RMAN commands to delete archived redo logs.

The validity of any RMAN configuration is dependent on the configuration of archived redo log destinations.

Archived Redo Logs Written to the Flashback Recovery Area

The Flashback Recovery Area can be created on shared storage, including ASM, OCFS, NAS, and other cluster file systems. If all archived redo logs will be written to the Flashback Recovery Area, then any node can back up, restore, or recover the archived redo logs produced by every other node.

If you use a Flashback Recovery Area, you can distribute backups across all nodes. Alternatively, you can use a single-node backup strategy.

Archived Redo Logs Written to the Cluster File System

This can include OCFS, NAS, or a third-party cluster file systems. If all archived redo logs are written to shared storage accessible by all nodes, then any node can back up, restore, or recover the archived redo logs produced by every other node. You can use a single node to perform the backup operation or you can allocate a channel on each node to distribute the workload. This is the preferred solution for RAC databases without a Flashback Recovery Area.

Archived Redo Logs Available via NFS Mounts

If the archived redo logs are written from each node to every other node via NFS, then all archived redo logs can be backed up from any node. You can run the backup with all channels allocated to a single node. Alternatively, you can distribute channels across all available nodes to balance the workload. This is an acceptable solution, although it requires additional configuration.

Archived Redo Logs Written to Local Disk

If archived redo logs are written to a local disk on each node, RMAN will not be able find and read them from the other nodes and will fail to back up unreachable archived redo logs. RMAN connects to a single node and reads the current control file, which is shared by all nodes and lists all archived redo logs, but can't access archived redo logs on other nodes. This also introduces a single point of failure.

This configuration also has consequences for recovery, as in a RAC environment, recovery is performed by a single node. This node must have unambiguous access to the archived redo logs for all instances in the cluster.

If you wish to store archived redo logs on local disks, then you should attempt to copy every archive redo log, to at least one other node, in order to prevent the local disk from becoming a single point of failure. In addition, you should ensure that the LOG_ARCHIVE_DEST_n parameter for each instance specifies an instance specific location, which can be a shared filesystem or NFS mounted filesystem from any other node. You can use RMAN to back up the archived redo logs, because RMAN can restore them to any location so they can be used by the recovery session.

Summary

In this chapter, we discussed backup and recovery using Recovery Manager (RMAN), which is a fully RAC-aware solution. RMAN is unique among backup solutions for Oracle databases, because it is fully integrated into the database kernel and can read and update information in the control file. In addition, it is fully supported by Enterprise Manager (EM).

RMAN has evolved into a powerful and efficient backup solution, with advanced features such as block change tracking and incrementally updated backups. In our experience, the vast majority of RAC sites use RMAN for backup and recovery, and we therefore recommend that you thoroughly consider the capabilities of RMAN before investigating other Oracle backup solutions.

■ ■ ■

Disaster Recovery

Disaster recovery provides continuity of operations in the event of total loss of a site, which may be the result of a natural disaster, such as a hurricane, fire, or flood; terrorism; disruption to the power supply; an industrial dispute; or any other event that might affect the primary data center. A disaster recovery plan will therefore involve at least one secondary site that operations can be transferred to in the event of the loss of the primary site; this process is known as a failover.

The amount of data loss that might be acceptable and the time allowed to switch over to the standby site are business decisions that vary from site to site. For example, for a bank, no data loss is acceptable; therefore, every transaction must be applied to both the primary database and the standby database concurrently. At the other extreme, for a database providing data warehouse-type functionality, you may be able to reload any missing data onto the standby database after a failover has occurred; therefore, data loss is relatively unimportant.

The amount of time required to perform a failover is also usually determined by the business. Some sites have very high availability requirements and require very rapid failover performance. Other sites have less stringent requirements, and in our experience, failover targets can range from a few minutes up to 48 hours. The amount of data loss and the target failover time generally determine the ultimate cost of the disaster recovery solution.

A disaster recovery plan involves much more than just the configuration of a standby database. You must also provide adequate backup systems for your application tier, storage, networking, and any other components required to run your systems. In addition, you must remember that others may need to implement the disaster recovery plan, so it must be thoroughly tested and documented.

Most sites test their disaster recovery plans at least once a year—in many cases, more frequently. Regular testing ensures that the procedures are fully tested and that all staff members understand their roles in the event of a disaster.

In addition to planning for a disaster, you must also ensure that you can restore your primary site following a failover. In particular, you need to verify that you have the capability to transfer the data back from the standby site to reestablish the primary site. In some cases, transferring the entire database may be possible over the network; for larger databases, you may need to transfer the datafiles by tape or other physical media.

This chapter concentrates on the features provided by Oracle Data Guard, which is the Oracle disaster recovery solution for RAC databases. Many sites implement disaster recovery at the storage level, in which case changes are replicated at the SAN level between sites. This disaster recovery solution is not particularly efficient for Oracle databases, as each DML change will affect at least one data block, the undo block, and the redo log block, all of which must be transported across the network link. However, storage-level replication can still provide manageability economics of scale in environments where the SAN is also used to store data from non-Oracle applications, such as word processing or workflow management.

Oracle Data Guard

Oracle Data Guard was introduced on a limited number of platforms in Oracle 8*i* and became a mainstream product in Oracle 9*i*. It is effectively a marketing term describing the two main disaster recovery technologies currently available to Oracle users.

Disaster recovery with Data Guard involves creating a standby database, which is a snapshot of all or part of an existing or primary database. The standby database is periodically updated with changes that have been made to the primary database. In the event of the failure of the primary database, operations can be transferred to the standby database with, potentially, a minimal amount of downtime and with no or minimal data loss.

Oracle Data Guard supports two types of standby databases: physical standby and logical standby. In each case, the primary database ships redo logs to the standby database. Physical standby databases have been available since Oracle 7.3. In subsequent releases, their functionality has been significantly enhanced. They form the basis of Oracle Data Guard, which also includes logical standby databases, which were introduced in Oracle 9.2.

Oracle Data Guard can be managed within EM Grid Control or using SQL*Plus commands. While the EM GUI is more user-friendly and easier to use, in our experience, most users still prefer to manage their standby databases using SQL*Plus scripts. Therefore, we use SQL*Plus in the examples throughout the chapter.

A physical standby database is a copy of a primary database. The physical standby database is maintained by transporting redo over a network link from the primary database to the standby database and applying the contents of the redo logs to the standby database. The changes or *redo vectors* are applied directly to the blocks in the standby database. Thus, after application of the redo, the blocks in the primary and standby databases will be identical. Consequently, every row on the standby database will have the same ROWID as its counterpart on the primary.

Physical standby databases are normally deployed for disaster recovery. You can switch over or fail over to a physical standby database at any time. *Switchover* is a nondestructive operation in which the roles of the primary and standby databases are reversed. Following a switchover operation, a *switchback* operation can be performed to reverse the roles of the standby and primary database again.

Physical standby databases can also used for backups, reducing the load on the primary database. If recovery is temporarily suspended, physical standby databases can also be opened in read-only mode for reporting.

On the other hand, a logical standby database is a copy of a subset of tables in the primary database. As with a physical standby, redo is transported from the primary to the standby database. However, on a logical standby database, redo is converted back into SQL statements that are then applied to the database. As redo is applied using SQL statements, the primary and standby database can have the same logical structures, but different physical structures.

Logical standby databases are a distant relation of Oracle Streams, which was also introduced in Oracle 9.2. Both allow copies of a subset of tables in a primary database to be transported and applied to a secondary database while that database remains open to other users. The most significant difference is in the impact on the primary database. Oracle Streams collects its data directly by mining the redo logs on the primary database and storing the changes in a dedicated pool within the SGA for onward transmission to the secondary databases. On the other hand, logical standby databases receive transmitted redo and apply it to the local database. Therefore, Oracle Streams has a much greater potential impact on resource usage on the primary database than a logical standby database.

Logical standby databases are more flexible than physical standby databases, as they can be open while redo is being applied. DML can be applied to any object that is not currently in recovery. In addition, the logical standby database can support different indexes on objects being recovered, allowing the data to be used more efficiently for reporting.

Up to nine standby databases can be configured, which can be a mixture of physical and logical standbys. Multiple standby databases can be maintained in different locations, thus increasing the level of protection. You can also cascade redo from a physical standby database to another physical or logical standby. Some sites use cascaded standby databases to provide both disaster recovery and reporting facilities.

Despite its apparent advantages, logical standby database technology has not yet achieved widespread adoption in the Oracle user community. In our experience, physical standby databases are by far the most popular Oracle disaster recovery solution; therefore, they are the focus for the rest of this chapter.

Data Protection Modes

Physical standby databases operate in one of the following three data protection modes:

- Maximum performance
- Maximum availability
- Maximum protection

The three data protection modes differ mainly in their handling of errors, with the most rigorous treatment of error conditions implemented when the standby configuration is running in maximum protection mode.

Maximum Performance Mode

Maximum performance is the default mode and is required when configuring redo transport services to use the ARC*n* or LGWR background process with asynchronous network I/O.

While this option maximizes throughput, some data loss may be expected in the event of a failover.

Because of the more restrictive nature of the maximum availability and maximum protection options, we recommend that you configure and test redo transport services in maximum performance mode before enabling one of the other data protection modes.

Maximum Availability Mode

The maximum availability data protection mode is a compromise between performance and protection. It is generally used when redo transport services are configured to use the LGWR background process with synchronous I/O. While the possibility of data loss is reduced, a small amount of data may still be lost in the event of a failover.

This mode performs more rigorous error checking during start-up of the primary database. In particular, at least one log archive destination must have been configured to use the LGWR background process.

In the event of the last available standby database being shut down or failing for any reason, processing will continue on the primary database. When the standby database is restarted, any gaps in the archive log files can either be resolved manually or automatically using Fetch Archive Logging (FAL).

Maximum Protection Mode

This data protection mode is required for configurations where no data loss is acceptable. If this mode is specified, then redo transport services must be configured to use the LGWR background process with synchronous I/O and the AFFIRM attribute.

The main difference between this mode and the maximum availability mode is in the implementation of error handling. If the standby database is shut down or fails for any reason, the primary database will also be shut down immediately. The primary and standby databases are thus guaranteed to be identical, but the primary database may be shut down unexpectedly.

If this configuration is implemented and high availability is required, we recommend that you configure two or more physical standby databases in separate locations, in which case the primary database will only be shut down when the last remaining standby database becomes unavailable.

Setting the Data Protection Mode

The data protection mode must be set on the primary database and applies to the primary and standby databases. As the data protection mode is set using the ALTER DATABASE statement, you cannot set this mode directly in a cluster database. To set this mode, first set the CLUSTER_DATABASE parameter to FALSE:

```
SQL> ALTER SYSTEM SET cluster_database = FALSE SCOPE = FALSE;
```

Shut down the database, and start a single instance as follows:

```
[oracle@london1 oracle] $ srvctl stop database -d RAC
[oracle@london1 oracle] $ srvctl start instance -d RAC -i RAC1
```

Set the data protection mode using one of the following statements:

```
SQL> ALTER DATABASE SET STANDBY TO MAXIMIZE PERFORMANCE;
SQL> ALTER DATABASE SET STANDBY TO MAXIMIZE AVAILABILITY;
SQL> ALTER DATABASE SET STANDBY TO MAXIMIZE PROTECTION;
```

Set the CLUSTER_DATABASE parameter back to TRUE:

```
SQL> ALTER SYSTEM SET cluster_database = TRUE SCOPE = SPFILE;
```

Finally, stop the instance, and restart the database:

```
[oracle@london1 oracle] $ srvctl stop instance -d RAC -i RAC1
[oracle@london1 oracle] $ srvctl stop database -d RAC
```

Redo Transport Services

Physical standby databases require the transportation of redo log files from the primary to the standby database. When the redo is written to a remote node, it is received by the Remote File Server (RFS) background process at the destination. The RFS background process is started automatically when the standby database is mounted. The RFS process writes the redo to either a standby redo log file or an archived log file, depending on your configuration.

The bandwidth and latency of the network must be sufficiently high to handle the expected amount of redo. Latency is particularly important for zero and minimal data loss configurations, as redo must be transported successfully before a transaction completes. For all environments, the network must be sufficiently fast for redo to be transmitted and applied within an acceptable time frame. The required bandwidth and latency are dependent on the amount of redo generated and on the distribution of redo generation over time.

On the primary database, redo log files can be transported by either the ARCn or LGWR background process.

ARC*n* Background Process

In early versions of physical standby, redo logs were transported by the ARC*n* background process. Therefore, the redo logs could only be transported when a redo log switch occurred. Using this configuration, there was a very high probability of data loss in the event of a failure of the primary database.

Redo log transportation using the ARC*n* process is still available in Oracle 10.1 and above. Of the various methods available, this method has the least impact on performance and thus may still be relevant in environments such as data warehouses where failed jobs can be reexecuted. However, the ARC*n* background process should not be used in environments where zero or minimal data loss is a requirement.

LGWR Background Process

In Oracle 9.0.1 and above, physical standby has been enhanced, so that in addition to the ARC*n* background process, the LGWR background process can also transport redo to the standby database. Use of the LGWR background process allows zero or minimal data loss to be guaranteed. However, this level of availability may adversely affect performance.

The LGWR process can be configured to transport redo logs synchronously (SYNC mode) or asynchronously (ASYNC mode). If configured synchronously, redo is copied to all standby destinations at the same time that it is written to the online redo log files. If configured asynchronously, redo is buffered on the primary database and subsequently transported to the standby database by a separate background process. With synchronous mode, zero data loss can be guaranteed; with asynchronous mode, in the event of a failure of the primary database, the currently buffered redo can potentially be lost.

You can change between asynchronous and synchronous log transportation dynamically. However, any changes to the configuration parameters will not take effect until the next log switch operation on the primary database, which can be forced using either the following command:

```
SQL> ALTER SYSTEM SWITCH LOGFILE;
```

or the command

```
SQL> ALTER SYSTEM ARCHIVE LOG CURRENT;
```

Asynchronous Network I/O (ASYNC)

The implementation of asynchronous network I/O changed between Oracle 10.1 and 10.2. In Oracle 10.1 and previous versions, if the LGWR background process is configured to transport redo logs asynchronously, redo is written by the LGWR to a buffer in the SGA. The LGWR network server (LNS*n*) background process transports the redo from the buffer to the standby destination. In this configuration, some data can be lost in the event of a primary database failure. The amount of data lost is influenced by the size of the buffer, which is configurable. If the buffer is large, more data is likely to be lost, as this data cannot be subsequently transported to the standby. If the buffer is small, less data will be lost, but performance may be impacted, as the LNS*n* background process may not be able to transport redo as quickly as the LGWR background process can generate it. If this is the case, the LGWR process will hang while the LNS*n* process empties the buffer.

The maximum data transfer size using asynchronous network I/O is 10MB.

As long as the intermediate buffer is sufficiently large, the performance impact of using the LGWR background process in asynchronous mode is roughly equivalent to that of using the ARC*n* background process, but the probability of data loss is significantly reduced. For example, consider a database using 1GB redo logs. If redo transport services is configured to use the ARC*n* background process, a primary database failure will result in the loss of an average of around 500MB of redo data. However, if redo transport services is configured to use the LGWR background process with a buffer size of, for example, 20MB, then a primary database failure will result in the loss of an average of 10MB of redo.

In Oracle 10.2 and above, the LGWR process no longer writes redo to an intermediate buffer; instead, the LNSn background process reads directly from the redo log and transports the redo to the standby destination. Long-standing DBAs may initially find this counterintuitive, as disk contention could arise between the LNSn and LGWR background processes. However, almost without exception, RAC databases are implemented on storage devices that have local caches in which written blocks are initially cached and subsequently written to disk. If the LNSn process can read the redo from the write cache on the storage device before it is flushed out, then there should be negligible effect on LGWR performance. In addition, the LGWR no longer needs to make a write a copy of redo data to the SGA, which should slightly improve response times. At the time of this writing, we do not know any sites that implement this new feature.

We recommend that you configure the log archive destination on the primary database to use the LGWR background process with the ASYNC option for databases where some data loss is acceptable. Using this option, you can restrict the amount of data loss in the event of a primary database failure without significantly impacting performance. Using LGWR with the ASYNC option is particularly applicable if you have relatively high latency on the network link between the primary and the standby sites.

Synchronous Network I/O (SYNC)

If the LGWR background process is configured to transport redo logs synchronously, then redo must be copied to all standby destinations by the LGWR background process whenever it is written to the local online redo logs. Redo will be transferred every time a transaction commits, whenever the redo log buffer is more than one third full, at checkpoints, and at log switches. If automatic MTTR is configured, continuous checkpointing is enabled and writes may occur even more frequently.

The maximum data transfer size using synchronous network I/O is 1MB, though it is rarely achieved.

When the LGWR background process is configured to transport redo logs synchronously, you may specify whether an acknowledgement is sent by the RFS background process of the standby database. If the AFFIRM attribute is specified, an acknowledgement is sent by the RFS background process after the redo data has been written to disk. If the NOAFFIRM attribute is specified, then no acknowledgement is sent. As you would expect, the AFFIRM option has a slight impact on performance.

We recommend that you configure the log archive destination on the primary database to use the LGWR background process using the SYNC and AFFIRM options for zero and minimal data loss requirements. This configuration is unlikely to cause significant performance degradation on anything other that a highly write-intensive database.

If you configure synchronous network I/O, the latency of the network is critical. Every time a statement performs a commit on the primary database, it will have to wait until the redo write is acknowledged by the standby database. This delay can severely impact the performance of the primary database, so you need to consider the three-way trade-off among data loss, throughput, and cost.

Standby Redo Logs

In Oracle 9.0.1 and above, you can create standby redo logs, which are located on the standby database server and store the redo information transported from the primary database. They can only be used with physical (not logical) standby databases where the LGWR background process is used for log transmission. Every entry written to the online redo logs on the primary database is transferred to the standby destination and written to the standby redo log at the same time to minimize the possibility of data loss.

Standby redo logs are additional online redo logs and can be queried in the V$LOGFILE dynamic performance view. As such, they are restricted by the values of the MAXLOGFILES and MAXLOGMEMBERS parameters declared in the CREATE DATABASE statement. If the current values of these parameters are insufficient, you need to rebuild the control file before creating the standby redo logs.

Note that the size of the standby redo logs must be identical to the size of the existing online redo logs. If this condition is not met, the RFS background process will not be able to write to them.

If standby redo logs are configured, the RFS background process will write all transported redo into the standby redo log. When a log switch occurs, an ARCn background process on the standby database server will archive the standby redo log to an archived redo log, from which it will be subsequently applied to the standby database. In the event of a failover, information written to the standby redo logs will be available for recovery.

We recommend that you implement standby redo logs where possible. We also recommend that you configure standby redo logs symmetrically on the primary and standby databases. This minimizes the amount of reconfiguration necessary during a switchover or failover operation.

The number of standby redo log groups should be at least equal to the number of online redo log groups. We recommend that you use the following formula to determine the number of standby redo log groups in a RAC cluster:

Number of standby redo log groups = Number of online redo log groups + number of threads

Log Apply Services

Redo log application is performed by the Managed Recovery (MRP0) background process. Irrespective of the configuration of redo transport services, redo logs are only applied after a log file switch has occurred on the primary database. Therefore, the standby database will always lag behind the primary database. In Oracle 10.1 and above, you can configure the standby database to be updated synchronously, as redo is written to the standby redo log.

In the event of a failover, all remaining redo has to be applied to the standby database before it can be converted into a primary database. The amount of redo remaining to be applied will be related to the size of the redo logs. Therefore, we recommend that you take care when sizing redo logs in a RAC environment, so that you can achieve acceptable recovery times in the event of a failover.

Role Management

Within a disaster recovery configuration, each database has a specific role. *Role management* is the process of transitioning the database between one role and another.

Read-Only Mode

In Oracle 8.1.5 and above, you can cancel managed recovery on the standby database and open the database in read-only mode for reporting purposes. Managed recovery can subsequently be resumed. This feature works in a RAC environment for standby configurations using either the ARCn or LGWR background processes for log transportation.

Switchover

In Oracle 9.0.1 and above, you can perform a switchover operation such that the primary database becomes a new standby database, and the old standby database becomes the new primary database. A successful switchover operation should never result in any data loss, irrespective of the physical standby configuration.

Switchover works in a RAC environment for standby configurations using either the ARCn or LGWR background processes for log transportation.

Failover

Since Oracle 7.3, performing a failover operation from the primary database to the standby database has been possible. A failover operation may result in data loss, depending on the configuration of the log archive destinations on the primary database. The potential for data loss is determined by the configuration, as follows:

- `LGWR SYNC AFFIRM`: No redo data will be lost in the event of a failover.

- `LGWR SYNC NOAFFIRM`: The amount of redo data that will be lost in the event of a failover will be minimized. However, a small amount of data might be lost if the `RFS` background process fails to write currently buffered data back to disk following a failure of the primary database.

- `LGWR ASYNC`: Some redo data may be lost. The amount of data lost can be minimized, but not eliminated, by maximizing the size of the SGA buffer on the primary database.

- `ARCn`: Redo data will almost certainly be lost, because an open (not fully written) archived redo log file cannot be applied on the standby database.

RAC and Physical Standby

All physical standby database features work in a RAC environment; the combinations in Table 26-1 are all possible.

Table 26-1. *Possible Primary and Standby Database Combinations*

Primary Database	Standby Database
Single-instance	Single-instance
RAC	Single-instance
RAC	RAC
Single-instance	RAC

Although any combination is theoretically possible, licensing and hardware costs, along with technical constraints, limit the standby database architecture.

Within a RAC environment, each node in the primary database cluster is responsible for transporting its own redo to the standby database cluster. The standby database cluster can be configured so that each node receives redo from one or more of the primary nodes. However, only one node in the standby database cluster can apply the redo to the standby database. The remaining instances can participate in redo transport services, writing transmitted redo to standby or archived redo logs on shared storage. They cannot, however, provide log apply services, nor can they be open for read-only access while managed recovery is enabled on another node. Logs are transferred from the receiving instances to the recovery instance using *cross-instance archiving*, which is a service that is provided transparently to the standby database by the `ARCn` background process.

There are some very important implications for overall throughput here. Regardless of the number of nodes in a cluster configuration, redo generation on a RAC database with a physical standby will be constrained by the performance of a single node of the standby database when applying redo.

There are several ways to improve performance of log apply services in a RAC instance, including the following:

- Configure additional standby nodes to provide redo transport services.

- Reduce the size of the online redo logs to increase the frequency of log switches, which evens out the workload for the standby database.

- Use faster hardware on the standby node. Note that the operating system version and Oracle version must be identical on both the primary and the standby database. Therefore, you cannot use, for example, 32-bit processors for the primary and 64-bit processors for the standby.

- Reduce the amount of redo generated by the application.

RMAN

One of the benefits of using a physical standby database is that backups can be created directly from the standby database using the RMAN utility. Creating a standby database directly from an RMAN backup is beneficial for sites that have a limited backup window on their primary databases.

NOLOGGING Attribute

It is possible to specify the NOLOGGING attribute for a number of Oracle operations. If the NOLOGGING attribute is specified, no redo will be generated directly for that operation. Some redo may still be generated for recursive operations, such as data dictionary modifications. The NOLOGGING attribute can be specified for the following operations:

- Direct load (SQL*Loader)
- Direct load (INSERT)
- CREATE TABLE AS SELECT
- CREATE INDEX
- ALTER TABLE MOVE PARTITION
- ALTER TABLE SPLIT PARTITION
- ALTER INDEX SPLIT PARTITION
- ALTER INDEX REBUILD
- INSERT, UPDATE, and DELETE operations on out of line LOBs

The NOLOGGING attribute was originally introduced in Oracle 7.3, where it was known as the UNRECOVERABLE attribute; it was renamed in Oracle 8.0. NOLOGGING operations are unsuitable for use in standby database environments, as no redo information is generated on the primary database.

In Oracle 9.2 and above, you can specify FORCE LOGGING at database level and at tablespace level. For undo tablespaces, FORCE LOGGING is automatically specified. This attribute forces logging of all database changes, including those which explicitly specify the NOLOGGING attribute, which is a rare example within Oracle of an attribute that is specified at database or tablespace level overriding an attribute specified at object or statement level.

To force logging at database level, use the following:

```
SQL> ALTER DATABASE FORCE LOGGING;
```

Check if force logging is enabled as follows:

```
SQL> SELECT force_logging FROM v$database;
```

To disable force logging at database level, use

```
SQL> ALTER DATABASE NO FORCE LOGGING;
```

Note that this attribute appears to be stored in the control file only (i.e., not in the data dictionary) and may need to be reset again if the control file is rebuilt.

We recommend that you set this attribute globally on all databases that have either a physical or logical standby.

Archive Log Gaps

Gaps in archive log sequences are possible, particularly when testing new physical standby configurations. These gaps can often be identified using the GV$ARCHIVE_GAP dynamic performance view and are usually caused by the failure to transmit one or more redo logs to the standby database. The probability of an archive log gap occurring increases in a RAC environment, as there are more instances.

Archive log gaps can be resolved manually using operating system copy commands and the ALTER DATABASE REGISTER LOGFILE command.

Archive log gaps can also be resolved automatically using FAL, which minimizes the number of archive log gaps that require manual intervention. FAL is enabled by specifying appropriate values for the FAL_SERVER and FAL_CLIENT initialization parameters.

Initialization Parameters

We recommend that you use a Server Parameter File (SPFILE) on both the primary and standby databases, so that role transitions (switchover and failover) can be achieved with minimal reconfiguration. If the parameters are correctly configured, in Oracle 10.1 and above, no parameters need to be modified for a role transition, which minimizes the opportunity for human error when switching over or failing over the database. Prior to Oracle 10.1, it was necessary to modify the LOG_ARCHIVE_DEST_STATE_n parameter on both the primary and the standby databases.

The following sections describe the initialization parameters that affect standby databases.

LOG_ARCHIVE_DEST_n

This parameter defines the log transport destination. Up to ten destinations can be specified; although, in practice, it is rare to specify more than two.

Each parameter value can include a number of additional attributes. The most important attributes in Oracle 10.1 and above follow:

- **LOCATION**: Specifies the directory to which archived redo logs should be written.

- **SERVICE**: Specifies the Oracle Net service to which archived redo logs should be sent.

- **ARCH**: Uses the archiver process to collect redo data and transmit it to standby database. This process is the default unless the LGWR attribute is specified.

- **LGWR**: Uses the log writer process to transmit redo data to the standby database.

- **ASYNC**: Specifies that network I/O is to be performed asynchronously to the destination. This attribute is the default.

- **SYNC**: Specifies that network I/O is to be performed synchronously to the destination. In order words, the sender will wait until the network I/O has completed before continuing.

- **AFFIRM**: For SYNC only, indicates that the sender will wait for confirmation that I/O has been written to remote storage.

- **NOAFFIRM**: Indicates that the sender will not wait for I/O to be written to remote storage.

- **DB_UNIQUE_NAME**: Specifies the unique name of the destination database.

- **VALID_FOR**: Specifies when redo data can be transmitted to the destination. This attribute takes two parameters: a redo log type, which can be ONLINE_LOGFILES or STANDBY_LOGFILES, and a database role, which can be PRIMARY_ROLE or STANDBY_ROLE.

Typical values for the LOG_ARCHIVE_DEST_n parameters are as follows:

```
log_archive_dest_1 = 'LOCATION=<archive_log_directory>'
log_archive_dest_2 = 'SERVICE=<service_name>
```

The LOG_ARCHIVE_DEST_2 parameter generally specifies the standby destination. For example, if the service name is READING, then possible values for this parameter might include the following:

```
SERVICE=READING ARCH
SERVICE=READING LGWR ASYNC=2048
SERVICE=READING LGWR SYNC NOAFFIRM
SERVICE=READING LGWR SYNC AFFIRM
```

LOG_ARCHIVE_DEST_STATE_n

In Oracle 10.1 and above, this parameter has become effectively redundant, because of the introduction of the VALID_FOR attribute in the LOG_ARCHIVE_DEST_n parameter. However, you may still see this parameter in legacy standby configurations, in which case, it specifies whether the archive log destination is enabled or not. There are ten LOG_ARCHIVE_DEST_STATE_n parameters corresponding to the ten LOG_ARCHIVE_DEST_n parameters. Valid values are ENABLE and DEFER.

LOG_ARCHIVE_START

Prior to Oracle 10.1, this parameter enabled the ARC0 background process. In Oracle 10.1 and above, this parameter is set automatically when archive logging is enabled for the database as follows:

```
SQL> ALTER DATABASE ARCHIVELOG;
```

LOG_ARCHIVE_FORMAT

This parameter defines the archive log file name format. In a RAC environment, you need to differentiate among archive logs from different instances. Therefore, the template for the file name should include the thread number.

The variables shown in Table 26-2 can be used to specify the archive log file name format.

Table 26-2. *LOG_ARCHIVE_FORMAT Parameter Variables*

Variable	Description
%s	Log sequence number
%S	Log sequence number (zero filled)
%t	Thread number
%T	Thread number (zero filled)

In Oracle 10.1 and above, the default value is the following:

```
%t_%s_%r.dbf
```

DB_UNIQUE_NAME

This parameter, which was introduced in Oracle 10.1, specifies a globally unique name for the database. Both the primary and the standby database will have the same database name (DB_NAME) parameter, for example, RAC. The DB_UNIQUE_NAME is used to uniquely identify the databases, for example, LONDON and READING. We recommend that you use names that indicate the location of the database rather than its role. For example, assigning unique names like PRIMARY and STANDBY will lead to confusion following a switchover or failover operation.

LOG_ARCHIVE_CONFIG

The LOG_ARCHIVE_CONFIG parameter was introduced in Oracle 10.1 and can be used to enable or disable the transmission of redo logs to remote destinations and the receipt of remote redo logs. It also specifies the unique database names (DB_UNIQUE_NAME) for each database in the Data Guard configuration. The parameter value is a string that can contain the following values:

- **SEND**: Enables the sending of redo logs to remote destinations.
- **NOSEND**: Disables the sending of redo logs to remote destinations.
- **RECEIVE**: Enables the receipt of remotely archived redo logs.
- **NORECEIVE**: Disables the receipt of remotely archived redo logs.
- **DG_CONFIG**: Specifies a list of up to nine unique names for databases in the Data Guard configuration. This is basically a security feature.
- **NODG_CONFIG**: Specifies that any database can be part of the Data Guard configuration.

The default values for this parameter are SEND RECEIVE NODG_CONFIG, which should be sufficient in most simple configurations.

REMOTE_ARCHIVE_ENABLE

This Boolean parameter defines whether redo should be sent and/or received to and from remote archive destinations. In a simple physical standby RAC configuration, the REMOTE_ARCHIVE_ENABLE parameter should be set to TRUE on both databases.

This parameter is effectively deprecated in Oracle 10.1, where it should not be specified if you are setting a value for the LOG_ARCHIVE_CONFIG parameter, as the two parameters are mutually exclusive.

STANDBY_ARCHIVE_DEST

The STANDBY_ARCHIVE_DEST parameter defines the directory on the standby database to which archive log files should be written. If log transportation is configured to use the ARCn background process, archive log files will be written directly to this directory immediately as they are received by the RFS background process. If log transportation is configured to use the LGWR background process with standby redo logs, archive log files will only be written to this directory by the RFS background process when a log switch occurs on the primary database.

STANDBY_FILE_MANAGEMENT

This parameter specifies that datafiles will be automatically created on the standby database when they are created on the primary database. Possible values are AUTO or MANUAL.

We recommend setting this parameter to AUTO to reduce the amount of maintenance necessary when adding or extending datafiles.

FAL_CLIENT

Use the FAL_CLIENT parameter to specify the FAL client name that is used by the FAL service. On the primary database, it should be a service name referencing the primary database; on the standby database, it should be a service name referencing the standby database.

FAL_SERVER

This parameter specifies the FAL server name that is used by the FAL service. On the primary database, it should be a service name referencing the standby database, and on the standby database, it should be a service name referencing the primary database.

Creating a Physical Standby Database

This section describes creating a physical standby database. This example is based on a two-node RAC primary database on nodes london1 and london2, and a single-node RAC standby database on node reading1. For the examples in this section, DBCA is used create the two node primary database on OCFS, and default values are specified wherever possible.

We will configure the standby database in maximize performance mode using the ARCn background process. We have chosen this configuration, because in spite of the advanced functionality offered by Data Guard, in our experience, this is the configuration that customers most commonly choose to deploy.

The example uses a single node RAC standby database. The standby database does not need to include the RAC option. However, deploying the standby database with the RAC option configured will allow additional nodes to be added to the standby without any loss of service in the event of a disaster. In our opinion, this measure is prudent. If a disaster strikes and your primary site is unavailable for a significant amount of time, you will probably have more important issues to consider than the conversion of the standby database from single-instance to RAC. In addition, you may have lost your reference site.

The first step is to build the standby database servers. While you may wish to use identical hardware for the primary and standby servers, this is not essential as long as the architecture is the same (32-bit, x86-64, Itanium, etc.). Once the standby servers are built, perform the following actions on each server:

1. Install and patch the operating system.

2. Configure the operating system.

3. Install and configure shared storage.

4. Install Oracle Clusterware.

5. Install Oracle Database software.

6. Install management agents.

These actions are described in the following sections.

Install and Patch the Operating System

The operating system on the standby nodes should be identical to the one used on the primary nodes, although differences in hardware may require alternative drivers. Ensure that you install any patches or additional RPMs that you have deployed on your primary nodes.

Configure the Operating System

The operating system configuration on the standby nodes should also be as close as possible to that used on the primary nodes, including network (public and private interfaces), kernel, and storage configurations. You should also create an oracle user and group on each node and configure ssh for the oracle user as described in Chapter 11. Finally, ensure that you have created an $ORACLE_BASE directory of an adequate size on each node in the standby.

Install and Configure Shared Storage

You do not need to use the same type of shared storage on the standby server as the primary server, but it simplifies management of the standby configuration if you do. It does not make sense to mix ASM and non-ASM storage in the same standby configuration because of the difficulty of translating path names between the two types of storage.

Install Oracle Clusterware (CRS)

The version of Oracle Clusterware on the standby can be different from that used on the primary. This difference is important if you need to upgrade the Oracle Clusterware software, in which case, we recommend that you upgrade it on the standby nodes first.

Install Oracle Database Software

The Oracle Database software on the standby does have to be identical to that used on the primary. If you need to upgrade the RDBMS software, you will need to stop the standby database while you upgrade the primary database; then, upgrade the RDBMS software on the standby database before restarting the standby.

Install Management Agents

If you are using EM Grid Control, you should install the EM Agent on each node in the standby cluster as described in Chapter 14.

Enable Archiving on the Primary Database

If you wish to implement a standby database, archiving must be enabled on the primary database. You can check if archiving is enabled as follows:

```
SQL> ARCHIVE LOG LIST
Database log mode                No Archive Mode
Automatic Archival               Disabled
```

If archiving is not currently enabled, you need to allocate a directory for archive log files. In this example, the following directory is created on shared storage:

```
[oracle@london1 oracle] $ mkdir -p /u04/oradata/RAC/arch
```

If database log mode is No Archive Mode, archiving is currently disabled. In Oracle 10.1, you cannot directly enable archive logging in a RAC database. Instead, you must temporarily convert your RAC database to a single-instance database to issue the command.

First, change the CLUSTER_DATABASE parameter in the SPFILE to FALSE:

```
SQL> ALTER SYSTEM SET cluster_database = FALSE SCOPE = SPFILE;
```

The next time the database is stopped and started, it will be in single-instance mode. Stop the database:

```
[oracle@london1 oracle] $ srvctl stop database -d RAC
```

Start a single instance using the following:

```
[oracle@london1 oracle] $ srvctl start instance -d RAC -i RAC1 -o mount
```

Set and enable the log archive destination:

```
SQL> ALTER SYSTEM SET log_archive_dest_1 = 'LOCATION=/u04/oradata/RAC/arch';
```

Enable archiving as follows:

```
SQL> ALTER DATABASE ARCHIVELOG;
```

Change the CLUSTER_DATABASE parameter in the SPFILE back to TRUE:

```
SQL> ALTER SYSTEM SET cluster_database = TRUE SCOPE = SPFILE;
```

The next time the database is stopped and started, it will be a RAC database.

Use the following command to stop the instance:

```
[oracle@london1 oracle] $ srvctl stop instance -d RAC -i RAC1
```

Start the database:

```
[oracle@london1 oracle] $ srvctl start database -d RAC
```

In SQL*Plus, check that archiving is enabled:

```
SQL> ARCHIVE LOG LIST
Database log mode              Archive Mode
Automatic archival             Enabled
```

Verify that archiving is working correctly using the following command:

```
SQL> ALTER SYSTEM ARCHIVE LOG CURRENT;
```

This command should generate one archive log file in the archive destination for each instance, for example:

```
1_12_55659565.dbf
2_6_55659565.dbf
```

The first number indicates the redo thread that generated the archive log file. This number frequently, though not necessarily, corresponds to the instance number. In this example, the second number is the log sequence number and the third number is the database ID.

Create Password Files on Primary Nodes

To create a standby database, the primary database must use a password file. You can check whether a password file is in use by checking the value of the REMOTE_LOGIN_PASSWORDFILE initialization parameter, which should be set to EXCLUSIVE or SHARED. If this is not the case, you need to create a password file. Bear in mind that creating a password file may represent a significant change to your existing security procedures, so you may wish to discuss the matter with other DBAs.

If the REMOTE_LOGIN_PASSWORDFILE parameter is set to EXCLUSIVE, you need to create a separate password file for each database within your cluster. These files can be created by the Oracle user on shared storage or locally on each node. The password file is created by running the orapwd utility in the $ORACLE_HOME/dbs directory. The syntax follows:

```
[oracle@london1 oracle] $ orapwd file=orapw<SID> password=<password>
```

For example, if the SID is RAC1, enter the following command:

```
[oracle@london1 oracle] $ orapwd file=orapwRAC1 password=oracle
```

This command creates a password file called $ORACLE_HOME/dbs/orapwRAC1 with a SYS password of oracle. The command should be repeated on all nodes in the primary database cluster using the appropriate SID for each instance.

Force Logging on the Primary Database

You can set the NOLOGGING attribute for a number of operations to reduce the amount of redo generated. This attribute should not be used in standby database configurations, as it will prevent changes from being replicated to the standby.

We recommend that you force logging of all statements on the primary database using the following statement:

```
SQL> ALTER DATABASE FORCE LOGGING;
```

This attribute overrides any NOLOGGING attribute set at the statement level. This ALTER DATABASE option can be set while the database is open and the CLUSTER_DATABASE parameter is set to TRUE.

Back Up the Primary Database

The next step is to create a backup of the primary database. You can use an existing cold backup or RMAN backup:

```
[oracle@london1 oracle] $ mkdir -p /u04/oradata/RAC/backup
```

Start RMAN using the following command:

```
[oracle@london1 oracle] $ $ORACLE_HOME/bin/rman NOCATALOG TARGET <connect_string>
```

For example, the following command starts RMAN and connects to the RAC1 instance as the SYS user:

```
[oracle@london1 oracle] $ $ORACLE_HOME/bin/rman NOCATALOG TARGET sys/oracle@RAC1
```

Specify the full pathname for RMAN, as your operating system installation may also include a binary called rman, which is a reverse compiler for man pages.

Before creating the backup, we usually set a handful of configuration parameters, which are stored in the control file by RMAN:

```
RMAN> CONFIGURE CONTROLFILE AUTOBACKUP ON;
RMAN> CONFIGURE CONTROLFILE AUTOBACKUP FORMAT FOR DEVICE TYPE DISK TO
> '/u04/oradata/RAC/backup/%F';
RMAN> CONFIGURE CHANNEL 1 DEVICE TYPE DISK CONNECT 'sys/oracle@RAC1';
RMAN> CONFIGURE SNAPSHOT CONTROLFILE NAME TO '/u04/oradata/RAC/backup/snapcf_RAC.f';
```

You are now in a position to back up the database using a command such as the following:

```
RMAN> BACKUP
> FORMAT '/u04/oradata/RAC/backup/%d_D_%T_%u_s%s_p%p'
> DATABASE;
```

Back up the current control file, for example:

```
RMAN> BACKUP CURRENT CONTROLFILE FOR STANDBY
> FORMAT '/u04/oradata/RAC/backup/%d_C_%U';
```

Ensure that the most recent online redo logs have been archived. You can use the SQL prefix to run any SQL statement from within the RMAN utility. The SQL statement must be enclosed by double quotes as follows:

```
RMAN> SQL "ALTER SYSTEM ARCHIVE LOG CURRENT";
```

Finally, back up the archive log files:

```
RMAN> BACKUP
> FILESPERSET 10
> ARCHIVELOG ALL
> FORMAT '/u04/oradata/RAC/backup/%d_A_%T_%u_s%s_p%p';
```

Set Parameters on the Primary Database

At this point, a number of parameters can be set on the primary database:

```
SQL> ALTER SYSTEM SET db_unique_name = LONDON scope=spfile;
SQL> ALTER SYSTEM SET log_archive_dest_1 = 'LOCATION=/u04/oradata/RAC/arch';
SQL> ALTER SYSTEM SET log_archive_dest_2='SERVICE=READING
> VALID_FOR=(ONLINE_LOGFILES,PRIMARY_ROLE) DB_UNIQUE_NAME=READING' scope=spfile;
SQL> ALTER SYSTEM SET fal_client=LONDON scope=spfile;
SQL> ALTER SYSTEM SET fal_Server=READING scope=spfile;
SQL> ALTER SYSTEM SET standby_file_management=AUTO scope=spfile;
```

The primary database will be configured to archive redo logs locally, using LOG_ARCHIVE_DEST_1, and to a physical standby database in Reading, using LOG_ARCHIVE_DEST_2. In both cases, the ARCn background process will be used to transport the redo log files to the destination.

The VALID_FOR clause was introduced in Oracle 10.1 and allows you to specify the circumstances in which the log archive destination is valid. This clause effectively replaces the LOG_ARCHIVE_DEST_STATE_n parameter, which was previously used to enable and disable archive log destinations during role transitions.

The primary database must be stopped and restarted as follows for these parameter changes to take effect:

```
[oracle@london1 oracle] $ srvctl stop database -d RAC
[oracle@london1 oracle] $ srvctl start database -d RAC
```

Create Directories on Standby Nodes

Before the database can be restored, you need to create directories on the shared disks, for example:

```
[oracle@reading1 oracle] $ mkdir -p /u02/oradata/RAC
[oracle@reading1 oracle] $ mkdir -p /u03/oradata/RAC
[oracle@reading1 oracle] $ mkdir -p /u04/oradata/RAC
```

Also, create directories for the archived log files and backup:

```
[oracle@reading1 oracle] $ mkdir /u04/oradata/RAC/arch
[oracle@reading1 oracle] $ mkdir /u04/oradata/RAC/backup
```

All of the preceding directories should be owned by the oracle user.

In addition, on each node in the standby database, create a directory structure for the administrative files as the oracle user. Ideally, this directory structure should exactly mirror the same structure on the primary database to avoid requiring different BACKGROUND_DUMP_DEST and USER_DUMP_DEST parameters in the primary and standby databases. For example, for node reading1, create the following directories:

```
[oracle@reading1 oracle] $ mkdir $ORACLE_BASE/admin/RAC
[oracle@reading1 oracle] $ mkdir $ORACLE_BASE/admin/RAC/bdump
[oracle@reading1 oracle] $ mkdir $ORACLE_BASE/admin/RAC/cdump
[oracle@reading1 oracle] $ mkdir $ORACLE_BASE/admin/RAC/create
[oracle@reading1 oracle] $ mkdir $ORACLE_BASE/admin/RAC/hdump
[oracle@reading1 oracle] $ mkdir $ORACLE_BASE/admin/RAC/pfile
[oracle@reading1 oracle] $ mkdir $ORACLE_BASE/admin/RAC/udump
```

Create Password Files on Standby Nodes

A password file must be created on each standby node. You can copy the existing password file from a node on the primary database.

Alternatively, as the Oracle user, run the orapwd utility in the $ORACLE_HOME/dbs directory. If the REMOTE_LOGIN_PASSWORDFILE parameter is set to EXCLUSIVE, the syntax is as follows:

```
[oracle@reading1 oracle] $ orapwd file=orapw<SID> password=<password>
```

For example, create the password file for SID RAC1:

```
[oracle@reading1 oracle] $ orapwd file=orapwRAC1 password=oracle
```

This command creates a password file called $ORACLE_HOME/dbs/orapwRAC1 with a SYS password of oracle. Create a password on each of the remaining nodes in the standby cluster, specifying the appropriate value for the database SID.

Create Server Parameter File for Standby Database

As the primary database in this example uses an SPFILE, one should also be used for the standby database. You can copy the server parameter file from the primary to the standby database in two ways. You can copy the existing SPFILE directly from the primary to the standby. Alternatively, if you wish to modify the parameters, you can generate a PFILE from the SPFILE using SQL*Plus on the primary database, for example:

```
SQL > CREATE PFILE='/tmp/initRAC.ora' FROM SPFILE;
```

Copy this file across to the standby database:

```
[oracle@london1 oracle] $ scp /tmp/initRAC.ora reading1:/tmp/initRAC.ora
```

After making any necessary modifications to the PFILE for the standby database, create a new SPFILE from the PFILE:

```
SQL> CREATE SPFILE='/u02/oradata/RAC/spfileRAC.ora FROM PFILE='/tmp/initRAC.ora';
```

Note that the instance does not need to be running for SQL*Plus to create an SPFILE.

Create Initialization Parameter Files on Standby Nodes

Although this example uses an SPFILE for the standby database, you still need a PFILE on each node specifying the address of the SPFILE. The name of the PFILE may differ on each node, but the contents should be identical. For example, on reading1 where the SID is RAC1, the PFILE can be created using the following:

```
[oracle@reading1 oracle] $ cd $ORACLE_HOME/dbs
[oracle@reading1 dbs] $ echo "spfile=/u02/oradata/RAC/spfileRAC.ora" > initRAC1.ora
```

Copy the RMAN Backup from Primary to Standby

Copy the RMAN backup files from the primary database to the standby database. You can use a network copy utility, such as scp or ftp. In the following example, the files are copied from london1 to reading1:

```
[oracle@london1 oracle] $ scp london1:/u04/oradata/RAC/backup/* \
reading1:/u04/oradata/RAC/backup
```

In a production environment, you may need to consider this step carefully, because depending on the bandwidth and latency of your network, it can be very time-consuming. If the existing database is large enough, you may find transferring the datafiles to the standby destination by tape more efficient.

Whatever method you choose, remember that you may need to transfer a similar amount of data in the reverse direction if you need to rebuild the primary database after failing over to the standby. Your disaster recovery plan must account for this, particularly if you implement your standby database prior to going into production.

Update /etc/oratab on Standby Nodes

On each node, update /etc/oratab with details of the new database. In this example, the database name is RAC on both the primary and standby nodes, so the file can be updated using the following command:

```
[oracle@reading1 oracle] $ echo "RAC:${ORACLE_HOME}:N" >> /etc/oratab
```

Add the Standby Database to the OCR

The Oracle Cluster Registry (OCR) must be updated with details of the standby database and its instances.

First, add the standby database to the OCR:

```
[oracle@reading1 oracle] $ srvctl add database -d RAC \
> -o $ORACLE_HOME \
> -s /u02/oradata/RAC/spfileRAC.ora
```

Next, add each instance to the OCR:

```
[oracle@reading1 oracle] $ srvctl add instance -d RAC -i RAC1 -n reading1
```

Update the Listener Configuration Files on Standby Nodes

By default, the listener configuration file is $ORACLE_HOME/network/admin/listener.ora. If this is the first database on the standby nodes, the listener may not yet be configured. The following example is for the node called reading1:

```
LISTENER_READING1 =
  (DESCRIPTION_LIST =
    (DESCRIPTION =
      (ADDRESS_LIST =
```

```
        (ADDRESS = (PROTOCOL = TCP)(HOST = reading1-vip)(PORT = 1521))
      )
      (ADDRESS_LIST =
        (ADDRESS = (PROTOCOL = TCP)(HOST = reading1)(PORT = 1521))
      )
      (ADDRESS_LIST =
        (ADDRESS = (PROTOCOL = IPC)(KEY = EXTPROC))
      )
    )
  )

SID_LIST_LISTENER_READING1 =
  (SID_LIST =
    (SID_DESC =
      (ORACLE_HOME = /u01/app/oracle/product/10.2.0/db_1)
      (SID_NAME = RAC1)
    )
  )
)
```

Although the SID list is no longer required for default listener configurations in Oracle 10.1 and above, it is required for standby nodes on which you wish to clone or duplicate databases using RMAN. This example uses RMAN to create the standby database, so an SID list is included.

When you have updated listener.ora, restart the listener:

```
[oracle@reading1 oracle] $ lsnrctl reload LISTENER_READING1
```

Update the listener.ora file on each of the remaining nodes in the standby database, changing the node name in the listener name and host clauses and the SID name in the SID list.

Update Oracle Net Configuration Files on All Nodes

In this example, the Oracle Net configuration is defined in $ORACLE_HOME/network/admin/ tnsnames.ora. We recommend, if possible, that this file is identical on all nodes, including both the primary and standby clusters, to minimize the number of changes required in the event of a role transition. For example, the tnsnames.ora file might contain the following:

```
RAC1 =
  (DESCRIPTION =
    (ADDRESS = (PROTOCOL = TCP)(HOST = london1-vip)(PORT = 1521))
    (CONNECT_DATA =
      (SERVER = DEDICATED)
      (SERVICE_NAME = RAC)
      (INSTANCE_NAME = RAC1)
    )
  )

RAC2 =
  (DESCRIPTION =
    (ADDRESS = (PROTOCOL = TCP)(HOST = london2-vip)(PORT = 1521))
    (CONNECT_DATA =
      (SERVER = DEDICATED)
      (SERVICE_NAME = RAC)
      (INSTANCE_NAME = RAC2)
    )
  )
```

```
LONDON =
  (DESCRIPTION =
    (ADDRESS = (PROTOCOL = TCP)(HOST = london1-vip)(PORT = 1521))
    (ADDRESS = (PROTOCOL = TCP)(HOST = london2-vip)(PORT = 1521))
    (LOAD_BALANCE = yes)
    (CONNECT_DATA =
      (SERVER = DEDICATED)
      (SERVICE_NAME = RAC)
    )
  )

READING =
  (DESCRIPTION =
    (ADDRESS = (PROTOCOL = TCP)(HOST = reading1-vip)(PORT = 1521))
    (LOAD_BALANCE = yes)
    (CONNECT_DATA =
      (SERVER = DEDICATED)
      (SERVICE_NAME = RAC)
    )
  )
```

Set Parameters on the Standby Database

At this point, a number of parameters must be set on the standby database. The instance must be started, but not yet mounted, in order to update parameters in the server parameter file.

Start up an instance on the standby database:

```
[oracle@reading1 oracle] $ srvctl start instance -d RAC -i RAC1 -o nomount
```

Update the following parameters:

```
SQL> ALTER SYSTEM SET db_unique_name = READING scope=spfile;
SQL> ALTER SYSTEM SET log_archive_dest_1 = 'LOCATION=/u04/oradata/RAC/arch';
SQL> ALTER SYSTEM SET log_archive_dest_2='SERVICE=LONDON
> VALID_FOR=(ONLINE_LOGFILES,PRIMARY_ROLE) DB_UNIQUE_NAME=LONDON' scope=spfile;
SQL> ALTER SYSTEM SET fal_client=READING scope=spfile;
SQL> ALTER SYSTEM SET fal_Server=LONDON scope=spfile;
SQL> ALTER SYSTEM SET standby_file_management=AUTO scope=spfile;
```

Stop and restart the instance again for these parameter changes to take effect:

```
[oracle@reading1 oracle] $ srvctl stop instance -d RAC -i RAC1
[oracle@reading1 oracle] $ srvctl start instance -d RAC -i RAC1 -o nomount
```

Create Standby Database

A single instance has now been started, but not mounted, on the standby cluster; RMAN will connect to this instance to create the standby database.

You should run RMAN from a node in the primary cluster. The RMAN command line must specify both a TARGET, which is the primary instance, and an AUXILIARY, which is the standby instance, as in the following example:

```
[oracle@london1 oracle] $ $ORACLE_HOME/bin/rman NOCATALOG TARGET /
AUXILIARY sys/oracle@"(DESCRIPTION=(ADDRESS=(PROTOCOL=TCP)
(HOST=reading1)(PORT=1521))(CONNECT_DATA=(SID=RAC1)))"
```

This command should be typed in on a single line. The Oracle Net address for the standby database must include an SID. It cannot include a service name, and it must be a dedicated server connection (the default), rather than a shared server connection. The SID must be equivalent to the SID declared in the SID list in the `listener.ora` file on the standby node.

This example uses a full Oracle Net address instead of an alias, because this is the only place where this address is required. You can alternatively add this address to `tnsnames.ora` on the primary node and specify the TNS alias for that address at the command line.

At the RMAN prompt, run the following command to create a copy of the database at the standby location:

```
RMAN> DUPLICATE TARGET DATABASE FOR STANDBY DORECOVER NOFILENAMECHECK;
```

The amount of time this command takes to run is proportional to the size of your database. The DUPLICATE TARGET DATABASE FOR STANDBY command mounts the standby database before it restores the datafiles.

Enable Managed Recovery on the Standby Database

At this point, you have a mounted standby database. This standby location is available for redo transport services, but not yet for log apply services, for which you must enable managed recovery.

On the standby node (reading1), shut down and restart the database:

```
[oracle@reading1 oracle] $ srvctl stop database -d RAC -o immediate
[oracle@reading1 oracle] $ srvctl start instance -d RAC -i RAC1 -o nomount
```

In SQL*Plus, mount the standby database and start managed recovery:

```
SQL> ALTER DATABASE MOUNT STANDBY DATABASE;
SQL> ALTER DATABASE RECOVER MANAGED STANDBY DATABASE DISCONNECT FROM SESSION;
```

Check the Standby Configuration

You can quickly check that log files are being transported correctly across the network and applied to the standby database. On the standby node, tail the alert log file, for example:

```
[oracle@reading1 oracle] $ tail -f $ORACLE_BASE/admin/RAC/bdump/alert_RAC1.log
```

This command will display lines as they are appended to the alert log. On one of the primary instances, issue the following SQL statement:

```
SQL> ALTER SYSTEM ARCHIVE LOG CURRENT;
```

This command should cause a log file switch and archive the active redo log to the local and remote destinations. After a few seconds, you should see output in the standby alert log similar to the following:

```
Thu Apr 28 13:29:51 2006
RFS[1]: Archived Log: '/u04/oradata/RAC/arch/1_18_556731981.dbf'
Committing creation of archivelog '/u04/oradata/RAC/arch/1_18_556731981.dbf'
Thu Apr 28 13:29:53 2006
Media Recovery Log /u04/oradata/RAC/arch/1_18_556731981.dbf
Media Recovery Waiting for thread 2 sequence 11
```

Verify Log Transportation

If you are using the ARCn process to transport redo logs to the standby database, you can monitor progress using the GV$MANAGED_STANDBY dynamic performance view. On a primary node (london1), run the following:

```
SQL> SELECT inst_id, thread#, sequence#, block#
> FROM gv$managed_standby
> WHERE process = 'ARCH'
> AND client_process = 'RFS'
> ORDER BY inst_id;
```

On the standby node (reading1), run the following:

```
SQL> SELECT inst_id, thread#, sequence#, block#
> FROM gv$managed_standby
> WHERE process = 'RFS'
> AND client_process = 'ARCH'
> ORDER BY inst_id;
```

Compare the sequence numbers and the block numbers within each sequence to determine the amount of redo that remains to be transported between the primary and standby for each thread.

Role Management

In this section, we give examples of opening the physical standby database in read-only mode; switchover operations, which are nondestructive; and failover operations, which are normally destructive.

Read-Only Mode

The physical database can be opened in read-only mode to allow limited reporting access. While the physical database is opened for read access, redo cannot be applied. However, redo logs can still be transmitted from the primary database to the standby database. In this example, the standby database is reading1.

To open the standby database for read-only access, on the standby node (reading1) in SQL*Plus (with SYSDBA privilege), cancel managed recovery:

```
SQL> ALTER DATABASE RECOVER MANAGED STANDBY DATABASE CANCEL;
```

Open the standby database in read-only mode as follows:

```
SQL> ALTER DATABASE OPEN READ ONLY;
```

The database is now available to all users for read access only.
To resume managed recovery, execute the following command:

```
SQL> ALTER DATABASE RECOVER MANAGED STANDBY DATABASE
> DISCONNECT FROM SESSION;
```

Switchover

Prior to switching over in a RAC environment, only one instance can be running on the primary database and only one instance can be running on the standby. In this example, switchover is from london1 to reading1.

The first step is to shut down any additional instances. For example, on the primary run the following command:

```
[oracle@london1 oracle] $ srvctl stop instance -d RAC -i RAC2
```

Similarly, shut down any additional instances on the standby. Verify the database role and switchover status on both the primary and standby databases:

```
SQL> SELECT database_role,switchover_status FROM v$database;
```

On london1, the database role should be PRIMARY, and the switchover status should be TO STANDBY. On the standby database, the database role should be PHYSICAL STANDBY, and the switchover status can be either SESSIONS ACTIVE, NOT ALLOWED, or TO PRIMARY.

To switch over the database to the standby site, first convert the primary database to a standby database. On london1 in SQL*Plus, run the following command:

```
SQL> ALTER DATABASE COMMIT TO SWITCHOVER TO PHYSICAL STANDBY
> WITH SESSION SHUTDOWN;
```

On the old primary (london1), shut down the primary database, and start the new standby database:

```
[oracle@london1 oracle] $ srvctl stop database -d RAC -o normal
[oracle@london1 oracle] $ srvctl start instance -d RAC -i RAC1 -o nomount
```

On the new standby (london1), in SQL*Plus, mount the new standby database as follows:

```
SQL> ALTER DATABASE MOUNT STANDBY DATABASE;
```

At this point, you should have two standby databases. The database role in both databases should now be PHYSICAL STANDBY, and the switchover status should be TO_STANDBY.

Next, on the old standby (reading1), convert the database to a primary database:

```
SQL> ALTER DATABASE COMMIT TO SWITCHOVER TO PRIMARY
WITH SESSION SHUTDOWN;
```

The old standby (reading1) is now the new primary. Restart the new primary database on node reading1:

```
[oracle@reading1 oracle] $ srvctl stop database -d RAC -o immediate
[oracle@reading1 oracle] $ srvctl start database -d RAC
```

On the new primary (reading1), the database role should now be PRIMARY, and the switchover status should be TO STANDBY. On the new standby (london1), the database role should be PHYSICAL STANDBY, and the switchover status should be TO PRIMARY.

On the new primary (reading1), you can now resume managed recovery using the following command:

```
SQL> ALTER DATABASE RECOVER MANAGED STANDBY DATABASE
> DISCONNECT FROM SESSION;
```

You can switch the roles at any time before the standby database is activated. To switch back, follow the same procedure, reversing the roles of london1 and reading1.

Failover

There are two types of failover: graceful failover and forced failover. If you are using the ARC*n* background process to transport logs to the standby database, the only failover option available is forced failover.

Failover can be tested by aborting the primary database, as shown in the following example, in which failover is from london1 to reading1.

Before killing the primary database (london1), check that the standby database (reading1) is functioning correctly. Also, check the current status of the standby database using the following command:

```
SQL> SELECT database_role, switchover_status FROM v$database;
```

The database role should be PHYSICAL STANDBY, and the switchover status should be SESSIONS ACTIVE, NOT ALLOWED, or TO STANDBY.

In this example, abort the primary database (london1) using the following command:

```
[oracle@london1 oracle] $ srvctl stop database -d RAC -o abort
```

If you are testing physical standby with a view to using it in production, we recommend a more thorough test, such as switching off the main power or rebooting the servers as the root user as follows:

```
[root@london1 root] # init 0
```

On the standby (reading1), stop and restart the database:

```
[oracle@reading1 oracle] $ srvctl stop database -d RAC -o immediate
[oracle@reading1 oracle] $ srvctl start instance -d RAC -i RAC1 -o nomount
```

Next, on the standby (reading1), mount the standby database:

```
SQL> ALTER DATABASE MOUNT STANDBY DATABASE;
```

On the standby (reading1), activate the physical standby database:

```
SQL> ALTER DATABASE ACTIVATE PHYSICAL STANDBY DATABASE;
```

Enable any additional redo threads and restart any additional instances at this point. The new primary database (reading1) is now open and available for use. You still need to modify your network configuration to direct application servers and other clients at the new database.

In most circumstances, the primary database needs to be rebuilt following a failover. This rebuild can be achieved by building a standby database using the procedures discussed earlier in this chapter and performing a switchover operation.

Summary

This chapter discussed disaster recovery in a RAC environment, focusing on Oracle Data Guard, and gave an example of a simple Data Guard configuration using the ARC*n* background process. Space does not permit us to discuss all the possible configurations in this chapter. When implementing a disaster recovery solution, we recommend that you first familiarize yourself thoroughly with the available options in your version of Oracle.

When you implement your disaster recovery solution, make sure that you have planned all aspects. In particular, make sure that you have considered ways to reinstate your primary database following a failover to the standby database.

Remember to include all operating system changes, Oracle upgrades, patches, and any application changes in your standby environment when you update your production system.

And finally, of course, we recommend that you regularly test your disaster recovery solution to ensure that it still works. You should test you disaster recovery procedures to ensure that they have not been adversely affected by any operating system, Oracle, or application upgrade.

Third-Party Clustering Solutions

by Kevin Closson, PolyServe, Inc. Chief Architect

Ｉn this appendix, we will describe third-party clustering solutions and their relationships to Oracle RAC, with particular emphasis on PolyServe Matrix Server.

Clusterware

The term *clusterware* is used to describe a number of different technologies—so many, in fact, that the term is commonly misunderstood and thus misused. In the context of Oracle RAC, clusterware takes the form of two shared libraries that provide node membership services and internode communication functionality when dynamically linked with Oracle executables. The two types of clusterware for RAC follow:

- **Oracle Clusterware**: Also referred to as Oracle OSD Clusterware and Portable Clusterware in many MetaLink web site documents, this clusterware was licensed from Compaq initially. Oracle Clusterware became available for Oracle 9*i* on Windows and Linux as Oracle Cluster Management Services (OCMS) with the release of RAC in the summer of 2001. The Oracle10.1 counterpart of OCMS is Cluster Ready Services (CRS). In Oracle10.2, this product was renamed Oracle Clusterware.

- **Third-party clusterware**: In Oracle 9*i*, third-party clusterware was mandatory for RAC on all platforms except Linux and Windows, where OCMS was the supported clusterware. In Oracle 10.1 and above, it is optional, because Oracle Clusterware can run with or without it. Examples of supported third-party clusterware include Sun Cluster, HP Serviceguard and TruCluster, IBM High Availability Cluster Multiprocessing (HACMP) for AIX, Fujitsu PRIMECLUSTER, and Veritas Cluster Server.

Since the Oracle server mostly uses third-party clusterware packages for node membership services, integrating Oracle with third-party clusterware creates an unnecessary level of porting complexity. There is historical precedence for Oracle internalizing functionality that had otherwise been provided by the platform. Some may recall that the original Unix platforms supporting Oracle Parallel Server (OPS) (e.g., Sequent, and Pyramid Technologies) were responsible for providing node membership services and implemented a kernel distributed lock manager (DLM) that OPS integrated with.

Oracle 8 was the first release of the Oracle DLM, so OPS no longer needed kernel DLM services. If there are things that Oracle can do well without porting to underlying software, it makes perfect sense to do so—like internalizing node membership services (clusterware) through the licensing agreement made with Compaq.

The functionality provided to the Oracle server from vendor clusterware packages is extremely simple: message passing and node membership services. Much credit should be given to Oracle for identifying and eliminating unnecessary complexity by engineering a solution of its own.

In its simplest form, any software that performs any function on more than one interconnected computer system can be called clusterware. What functionality any given clusterware offers tends to determine the level of sophistication behind its implementation.

Several cluster architecture and implementation details set varying cluster technologies apart from each other. Some of the more important differences follow:

- **Processing mode**: Is the clusterware code implemented in user or kernel mode? Code that is not implemented in kernel mode has absolutely no guarantees of execution should a system become saturated and runs the risk of not being able to execute critical data integrity operations when they are most necessary. Generally, third-party clusterware is implemented in kernel mode, whereas Oracle Clusterware executes in user mode.

- **Fencing**: *Fencing* is a generic cluster term that relates to how a cluster handles nodes that should no longer have access to shared resources. It is a critical aspect of clustering from data integrity and application availability perspectives. The best clusterware imaginable is of little value if quality fencing is not implemented with a solid architectural approach. Fencing will be described in more detail later in this appendix.

- **Lock and metadata management architecture**: If clusterware includes a cluster file system, the implementation of cluster lock and file metadata management is crucial. A common shortcut approach to solving the problem is to have one master node in the cluster responsible for these activities. For obvious reasons, this approach can potentially result in a performance bottleneck and represents a single point of failure (consider what happens when the lock manager node dies). Conversely, sophisticated, high-quality cluster file systems are implemented with distributed and symmetric lock and metadata managers. While more difficult to implement, the distributed approach is fundamentally capable of better performance and availability, since there is no inherent single point of failure.

From a product-engineering standpoint, Oracle's decision to implement Oracle Clusterware makes a great deal of sense. With Oracle Clusterware, there is less porting activity for Oracle and, more important, no blame-shifting in critical support scenarios. When running RAC with Oracle Clusterware, customers are empowered by the fact that all RAC problems are entirely within the domain of Oracle's software, which is true even when Oracle Clusterware is executed alongside vendor clusterware.

Oracle currently offers no choice in clusterware for Oracle10g RAC on Linux—customers must run RAC with Oracle Clusterware. Although Oracle has stated that the future of RAC is to not integrate with third-party clusterware, that is certainly not the case today, even with Oracle 10.2. Oracle MetaLink's Certify web pages show support for both Oracle Clusterware and a variety of integrated third-party clusterware (e.g., HP MC/Serviceguard, IBM HACMP, Sun Cluster, and Veritas Cluster Server) on legacy Unix. On Linux, however, the nonintegrated approach is a reality today, so it is important to understand how the two coexist.

As an aside, third-party clusterware will not disappear just because RAC does not integrate it. There are many more purposes for clustering than those utilized by Oracle, so general-purpose clustering is here to stay. A great deal more digital content is stored as unstructured data than in databases, so technology that supports general-purpose data management is still an industry necessity. Also, many data centers wish to build and deploy clusters in a standard way that is optimized for Oracle and other cluster purposes, such as file serving.

Oracle RAC (and OPS before it) uses the following two clusterware libraries:

- `libskgxn.so`: This library contains the routines used by the Oracle server to maintain node membership services. These routines let Oracle know what nodes are in the cluster. Likewise, if Oracle wants to evict a node, it will call a routine in this library. Historically, this is the most widely implemented vendor-supplied clusterware.

- `libskgxp.so`: This library contains the Oracle server routines used for communication between instances (e.g., Cache Fusion, consistent-read sends, or lock conversions). This clusterware component has been implemented with varying degrees of success for integration with high-speed, low-latency interconnect protocols, such as InfiniBand, and products, such as HP Hyperfabric. Most production RAC implementations use the default `libskgxp.so` supplied by Oracle, which implements internode communication via UDP over Ethernet.

Third-Party Certification Programs

Ensuring that Oracle Clusterware and third-party clusterware are compatible is important. Therefore, in February 2006, Oracle Corporation launched a certification program whereby third-party vendors can obtain the following validations:

- Third-party Cluster File System (CFS) Validation
- Third-party Clusterware Compatibility

Further information about these programs is available on the Oracle web site (`http://www.oracle.com/technology/software/oce/oce_fact_sheet.htm`).

Third-Party Cluster File System Validation

The third-party CFS Validation is relatively straightforward. This certification consists of executing an extremely in-depth test suite produced by Oracle Corporation called the Oracle Certification Environment (OCE). The essence of the test suite is to successfully perform all RAC functionality against databases stored in the CFS.

Third-Party Clusterware Compatibility

Third-party clusterware compatibility is still sufficiently important to Oracle Corporation to warrant a separate program for testing.

PolyServe Matrix Server

PolyServe is one of the first vendor participants in the new third-party Cluster File System Verification and Clusterware Compatibility test programs to receive the Validated status. However, long before the test program existed, PolyServe supplied customers with an Oracle-optimized platform for deploying Oracle RAC.

The tests outlined in the new third-party Cluster File System Validation test suite have been used in PolyServe labs since 2001, when PolyServe was licensed to implement the Oracle Disk Manager Library (ODM). This testing, then, is nothing new, though the program for granting certification is. ODM will be discussed in more detail later in this appendix.

All RAC implementations on PolyServe Matrix Server exclusively use Oracle Clusterware. PolyServe recognized early on that the value brought to Oracle by custom implementations of `libskgxp.so` and `libskgxn.so` was minimal, so engineering effort was focused instead on producing a high-quality ODM library, sophisticated SAN management, industry-leading fencing options, and a general-purpose, database-optimized CFS.

Oracle databases have been deployed using file system tablespaces for many years. It is reasonable, therefore, to refer to file system–based deployments as the standard. With a base-configuration cluster (e.g., without value-add software such as PolyServe Matrix Server), DBAs are forced to think about raw disks. Whether simple raw partitions or ASM raw disk groups are used, there will be accompanying connectivity and provisioning headaches. Using raw disks may also incur operational overhead, requiring cross-organizational communications between the storage groups and the database administration group.

To system and storage administrators, ASM is a black box. Unless the sole use for storage in the data center is Oracle, and thus, storage administrators are relying entirely on Oracle space-utilization tools such as EM, administrators cannot even detect when ASM-managed space is approaching full capacity. A simple glance at df(1) or third-party systems management tools is no longer sufficient, so it becomes the responsibility of the DBA to monitor and plan use of storage and, if necessary, to request additional disk space from the storage administrator.

Compare this situation to the CFS storage model. The storage and system administrators have RAC storage utilization levels in plain sight using the same monitoring tools and methods they use for all the other applications they support. Oracle is a very important application, but storage and system administrators have a great deal more to think about. When RAC is deployed in Matrix Server, the storage and system administrators can add space to PolyServe dynamic volumes and grow the file systems without the database administration staff ever picking up the telephone. Action always yields better results than reaction.

Also, a lot of files that must go in shared disks cannot be placed into ASM. Some data centers strive for standardization. Clustered environments can be confusing enough, so changing both the fundamental way databases are stored and limiting the effectiveness of the storage group in one fell swoop can lead to disaster.

A number of new features were introduced in Oracle 10.1 to assist in configuring large databases, whether they are file-system based or ASM based. For instance, the Oracle 10*g* BIGFILE tablespace feature eliminates issues associated with large numbers of datafiles.

Since PolyServe dynamic volumes and CFS both support online resizing, you can create BIGFILE tablespaces that are able to grow as needed by the application to a limit of 16TB (in the current release).

So why use third-party clustering solutions? In the specific case of PolyServe, the motivating factors are cluster stability, cluster standardization, and simplicity through complete support for every Oracle file requirement. This is not to suggest that RAC itself is unstable. However, RAC can still be the victim of lower-level cluster instability. PolyServe makes clustering simple and stable.

Generally speaking, DBAs accustomed to deploying Oracle in a nonclustered environment are in for a bit of an awakening. Going from a non-RAC to a RAC environment means implementing shared storage. Without a high-quality CFS, standard deployment models cannot be used.

The PolyServe CFS supports asynchronous direct I/O for RAC on file system files. Furthermore, the file system and underlying volumes can be expanded online. Given these features, a RAC database doesn't seem that much different than a non-RAC database in a regular file system, such as ext3. PolyServe supports installing Oracle into a shared Oracle Home and Oracle E-Business Suite applications into a shared APPL_TOP directory.

Additionally, all Oracle files can be placed into the CFS. Without a general-purpose CFS, applications that use features such as External Tables, BFILEs, and UTL_FILEs will not function the same, or at all, with RAC. Using a CFS simplifies administration as well, since there is no need to navigate between servers to access ORACLE_BASE directories for logging, trace, scripts, and so forth. The idea behind a general-purpose CFS RAC deployment is to get a single-system feel, which is an important characteristic to a lot of data centers.

From a technology standpoint, PolyServe bundles several features that make RAC deployments simpler. The following sections will explore these features further.

Central Cluster Management Console

While Oracle provides EM for database-management features, a base-configuration deployment lacks a central GUI and CLI for the management and monitoring of the underlying cluster. The PolyServe central management console supports all aspects of configuring, monitoring, and event notification pertaining to the lower-level cluster.

SAN Management Layer

PolyServe includes global disk labeling, access protection, and multipath I/O. If the choice is made to deploy other multipath I/O solutions, PolyServe is integrated and tested to use them as well. This SAN management layer is essential in data assurance. Without a product like PolyServe, nothing prevents intentional or unintentional access from any node in the cluster to the raw disk, which contains important files, such as the OCR or system tablespace. PolyServe closes off access to the underlying raw disk interfaces for volumes that contain PolyServe file systems.

Sophisticated Fencing

As already discussed, fencing determines how a cluster handles nodes which should no longer be allowed access to shared resources. For example, if a node in the cluster has access to the shared disk, but has no functioning interconnects, it no longer belongs in the cluster. Fencing ensures that the node cannot make further modifications to the shared disks.

There are several different types of fencing. The most common type of fencing is known as STONITH (shoot the other node in the head). While STONITH is a common term, there is nothing common with how it is implemented from one vendor to the other. The general idea is that the healthy nodes in the cluster are empowered to determine that a node that should no longer be in the cluster. If such a determination is made, action is taken to power cycle the node, which can be done with network power switches for example. STONITH is a sound approach to fencing, because it is built on the notion that healthy nodes monitor and fence unhealthy nodes. This differs significantly from the fencing model implemented in Oracle Clusterware, which does not implement STONITH at all.

In Oracle Clusterware, nodes fence themselves by executing the reboot(8) command out of /etc/init.d/init.cssd. This is a very portable approach to fencing, but it raises the question, What happens if the node is so unhealthy that it cannot successfully execute the reboot(8) command? You may have encountered systems that were so despondent that commands no longer executed (e.g., complete virtual memory depletion). In a cluster, it is imperative that nodes get fenced when they should; otherwise, they can corrupt data. After all, there is a reason the node is being fenced.

Having a node with active I/O paths to shared storage after it is supposed to be fenced from the cluster is potentially dangerous. In those rare cases where Oracle's fencing mechanism is not able to perform its fencing operation, the underlying host clusterware will fence the node, as is the case with PolyServe Matrix Server. The criteria used by Oracle Clusterware to trigger fencing are the same criteria host clusterware use to take action. Oracle instituted the Clusterware Compatibility Test program to ensure that underlying clusterware is compatible with, and complimentary to, Oracle Clusterware.

STONITH is one form of fencing but far from the only one. PolyServe supports a form of STONITH in which the healthy nodes integrate with management interfaces, such as the HP Integrated Lights-Out (iLO) or Dell Remote Assistant Card (DRAC). Here again, the most important principle of clustering is implemented—healthy nodes take action to fence unhealthy nodes, which ensures the fencing will, in fact, occur. This form of STONITH is more sophisticated than the network power-switch approach, but in the end, they do the same thing—both approaches power cycle unhealthy nodes.

It is not always desirable to have an unhealthy server power cycled just for the sake of fencing, as there could be helpful state information available before the power reset. Losing that information may make cluster troubleshooting quite difficult. Also, if the condition that triggered the fencing persists across reboots, a reboot loop can occur. For this reason, PolyServe implements fabric fencing as an option for customers running RAC.

Fabric fencing is built on the PolyServe SAN management layer. PolyServe certifies a comprehensive list of Fibre Channel switches that are tested with the fabric-fencing code. All nodes in a PolyServe cluster have LAN connectivity to the Fibre Channel switch. With fabric fencing, healthy nodes make SNMP calls to the Fibre Channel switch to disable all SAN access from unhealthy nodes, so this form of fencing is built on the sound principle of having healthy servers fence unhealthy servers, leaving the fenced servers in an up state, but completely severed from shared disk access. Administrators can log in to the fenced server, view logs, and so on, but before the node can rejoin the cluster, it must be rebooted.

The most important aspect of host clusterware is that it is generally implemented in kernel mode. In the case of PolyServe, all aspects of SAN management, CFS, volume management, and so on are implemented in kernel mode. When fencing code is implemented in user mode, there is always the risk that the code will not get processor cycles to execute. Indeed, with clusters in general, overly saturated nodes can get fenced, because they are not responding to status requests by other nodes in the cluster. When nodes in the cluster become so saturated as to trigger fencing, having the fencing code execute in kernel mode provides a higher level of assurance that the fencing will take place successfully.

Dynamic Volume Manager

PolyServe implements a cluster volume manager that supports concatenation and striping of LUNs. The dynamic volume manager, in conjunction with the CFS, supports the ability to add space to file systems without interruption. Additionally, it provides support for very high-end scenarios, where data needs to be striped across multiple storage arrays. The volumes support online resizing operations, and in the current release, a volume can grow to 16TB.

CFS

Perhaps the most attractive component of PolyServe Matrix Server is the CFS. The PolyServe CFS is fully distributed and symmetric, which means there is no central lock manager or metadata server and thus no single point of failure. This architecture differentiates it from all other CFSs available on Linux. The file system is fully POSIX-compliant; moreover, it is optimized for Oracle, because it supports direct and asynchronous I/O.

The file system is where PolyServe implements Quality of Storage (QoS) features, such as online, dynamic data redistribution, and other features, such as snapshots. In the current release, file systems are limited to 16TB, but that limit is expected to increase in future releases. Such large file systems are important for the support of the Oracle10g BIGFILE tablespace feature. With BIGFILE tablespaces, a single datafile tablespace can grow to 32TB, dramatically reducing the number of files making up a very large Oracle database.

Matrix Server ODM

PolyServe Matrix Server provides an ODM implementation called MxODM to support the ODM interface. MxODM enables Oracle with asynchronous I/O on the direct I/O–mounted file systems, where Oracle stores datafiles and other database files, such as redo logs, control files, and archived redo logs. MxODM also offers a very rich I/O monitoring capability.

The MxODM I/O monitoring package provides the following basic performance information (referred to as the core reporting elements):

- Number of file read and write operations
- Read and write throughput per second, in kilobytes
- Count of synchronous and asynchronous I/O operations
- I/O service times

The core reporting elements can be provided at the following levels:

- **Clusterwide**: Provides aggregate information for all database instances on all nodes.
- **Database global level**: Limits information to a named database (e.g., PROD, DEV, FIN, or DSS).
- **Instance level**: Limits information to a named instance (e.g., PROD1, PROD8, DEV1, FIN4, or DSS6).
- **Node level**: Limits information to a named node (e.g., rhas1.acme.com or sles9-1.acme.com). This information is the aggregate of all instance activity on the named node. If a node hosts instances accessing different databases (e.g., $ORACLE_SID=PROD1 or $ORACLE_SID=DEV1), the core reporting elements will reflect the combined information for all instances on the named node.

Because MxODM understands Oracle file, process, and I/O types, the mxodmstat(8) command offers very specialized reporting capabilities. On complex clustered systems, it is nearly impossible to take a quick look at the clusterwide or per-instance activity for a given subsystem of the Oracle server. For instance, on an eight-node cluster with six PROD instances, two DEV instances, and Parallel Query slaves active only on nodes 1 through 4, a DBA will find it extremely difficult to ascertain clusterwide impact of the Parallel Query activity. Likewise, quickly determining the DBWn process activity for only the PROD instances on nodes 1 through 6 is nearly impossible without MxODM.

MxODM offers canned reporting that focuses on the following key Oracle subsystems:

- **Parallel Query**: This query returns the core reporting elements for only the Parallel Query slaves (e.g., ora_p000_PROD1, or ora_p001_PROD3). This is an extremely beneficial set of information, as it allows DBAs and system administrators to get a top-level view of the impact Parallel Query is having on the cluster, either as a whole or at the node level.
- **Log Writer**: This query focuses on only the LGWR processes and their activities at the cluster level, database level, or node level.
- **Database Writer**: This query is of the utmost value. It, too, can return all core reporting elements at all reporting levels; however, it can also limit reporting to only DBWn process activity. DBAs can glance at mxodmstat(8) output and easily determine the average DBWn I/O service times for all databases clusterwide, or they can focus on specific databases, nodes, or instances.

Though there is too much functionality in the mxodmstat package to describe in this appendix, the following examples illustrates the type of I/O monitoring this software package provides.

Consider what is involved in monitoring three databases that have instances spread across a 16-node cluster—a daunting task. A bird's-eye view can be obtained with mxodmstat, though. The following command shows aggregate top-level I/O activity for all databases broken down into reads and writes:

```
$ mxodmstat -i5 -a op
              Read                              Write
Sync  Async    KB/s  Ave ms    Sync  Async    KB/s  Ave ms
5018  6087   798799      14      16   2251   14933      15
2448  2743   361485      17       7    981    6298      14
1997  2114   279438      13       5    775    5067      12
2048  2123   281085      12       5    782    5046      16
1408  1786   233820      15       4    709    4802      17
```

The next command shows top-level I/O for all three databases. The following output is aggregate total I/O with breakouts for the counts of synchronous and asynchronous I/O as well as I/O service times:

```
$ mxodmstat -i5 -D
          dss                          dev                          prod
Sync Async   KB/s Ave ms    Sync Async   KB/s Ave ms    Sync Async   KB/s Ave ms
   9 5939 740196     10      10   341   5267    51      3957 1410  36687     15
   3 2160 269139     10       7   192   2635    60      1701  553  15682     17
   3 2151 268134     10       6   168   2222    44      1966  552  17877     13
   3 2093 260989     10       3   321   3495    65      1932  528  17481     14
   4 2081 259287     10       3   182   2468    46      1890  544  17133     12
   3 2154 268570     10       4    93   1737    43      1923  535  17441     16
   3 2116 263581     10       4   186   2663    47      1958  626  18427     13
```

The following mxodmstat output shows a flurry of DSS database activity:

```
$ mxodmstat -i 10 -D prod dss dev
         prod                          dss                          dev
Sync Async   KB/s Ave ms    Sync Async    KB/s Ave ms    Sync Async   KB/s Ave ms
3160 2714  34339     15       4  0.40     66     1        6    38   1624     4
2735 2775  33268     18       3  0.40     53     1        3    30   1364     5
2566 2301  29048     17       3  0.30     51     1        3   228   2917    53
2596 2119  27663     16       3  0.30     51     2        4   110   1808    53
2295 2110  25998     15       3  0.36     47     1        3   398   4200    59
2304 2085  25625     16       3  0.30     51     1        6    69   1469    38
1978 1932  21946     22       3  0.30     51     1        3    28   1212     5
2393 2541  29718     15       3   745  92698    12        4    28   1273     4
2584 2176  28052     16       3  2111 263050    10        4   224   2796    59
2604 2203  28431     16       3  2130 265467    10        3   142   2223    82
2490 2262  28155     16       6  2102 262051    10        4   436   4529    66
2537 2140  27485     16       3  2060 256738    10        6   117   1923    55
2658 2277  29227     16       3  1618 201924    10        3   148   2340    54
2581 2342  29259     15       3  0.40     48     1        4    82   5052    41
2596 2284  28791     15       3  0.40     51     1        4   118   4972    44
2565 2313  28975     16       3  0.20     54     1        3   404   4338    56
```

You can also use a drill-down command to see what processes are performing the I/O on the DSS database. The output shows that, throughout all of the DSS instances, the I/O is mostly performed by Parallel Query processes:

```
$ mxodmstat -i10 -D dss -s proc
                                          dss
  Background        DB Writer        Log Writer            PQO            Foreground
Sy As KB/s Ave   Sy As KB/s Ave   Sy As KB/s Ave   Sy As   KB/s Ave   Sy As KB/s Ave
 2  0   38   1    0  0    0   0    0  0 0.20   0    1  0      0   0     0  0    0   0
 3  0   51   2    0  0    0   0    0  0 0.30   0    8  0      0   0     0  0    0   0
 3  0   51   1    0  0    0   0    0  0 0.30   0    1  0      0   0     0  0    0   0
 3  0   50   5    0  0    0   0    0  0 0.40   0    6  0   1754 218683 10  0    0   0
 3  0   51   6    0  0    0   0    0  0 0.30   0    4  0   2113 263240 10  0    0   0
```

3	0	48	6	0	0	0	0	0	0.30	0	8	0	2114	263435	10	0	0	0	0
3	0	48	7	0	0	0	0	0	0.40	0	6	0	2132	265597	10	0	0	0	0
3	0	54	6	0	0	0	0	0	0.20	0	5	0	2124	264634	10	0	0	0	0
3	0	51	8	0	0	0	0	0	0.40	0	9	0	2106	262446	10	0	0	0	0
4	0	61	7	0	0	0	0	0	0.50	0	6	0	2118	263824	10	0	0	0	0
3	0	54	8	0	0	0	0	0	0.20	0	5	0	1726	215011	10	0	0	0	0
3	0	53	1	0	0	0	0	0	0.40	0	1	0	0	0	0	0	0	0	0
3	0	48	1	0	0	0	0	0	0.30	0	1	0	0	0	0	0	0	0	0

Finally, the following command shows monitoring of instances dss1 and dss2 only, broken down by reads and writes. Note that, after six lines of output (60 seconds), the I/O performed by dss1 and dss2 switched from 100 percent large, asynchronous reads by both instances to small, synchronous reads and just a few asynchronous writes performed by only dss1:

```
$ mxodmstat -i10 -I dss1 dss2 -a op
                    dss1                                      dss2
         Read            Write                    Read              Write
Syn Asy  KB/s Ave m Syn Asy  KB/s Ave m Syn Asy  KB/s Ave m Syn Asy  KB/s Ave m
  1 1233 153846  10   0   0     0     0   1 1240 154440  10   0   0     0     0
  1 1046 130483  10   0   0     0     0   1 1050 130728  10   0   0     0     0
  1 1060 132339  10   0   0     0     0   1 1058 131645  10   0   0     0     0
  1 1049 130899  10 0.30 0.10   5     6   1 1052 131013  10 0.30 0.20   5     6
  1 1043 130131  10 0.40 0.30   7     7   1 1050 130677  10 0.40 0.20   6     9
  8  321  40171  10 0.30  7    60     2  13  322  40291   9 0.30 0.10   5     2
529    0   8464   2 0.30  4   324     9   1    0    21     1 0.30 0.20   5     1
669    0  10698   1 0.30  2   517     6   1    0    16     1 0.30 0.20   5     3
720    0  11522   1 0.30  3   697     6   1    0    21     1 0.30 0.20   5     1
```

Summary

This appendix provided information about the Oracle third-party Cluster File System Validation and Clusterware Compatibility Test Program using PolyServe Matrix Server as a specific example of optional third-party software. Exploring important underlying concepts, such as fencing and processing modes for clusterware, shows that cluster platform choice is important. Additionally, we have shown that there is added value in some third-party clustering solutions, as in example of the PolyServe Matrix Server MxODM implementation, with its mxodmstat command for complex, clusterwide I/O monitoring and reporting.

Index

Special Characters

$CRS_HOME directory, 275, 317, 551, 553
$CRS_HOME/install/rootaddnode.sh script, 526
$CRS_HOME/install/rootdeletenode.sh script, 550
$CRS_HOME/install/rootdelete.sh command, 549
$CRS_HOME/opmn/conf/ons.config file, 528, 548
$CRS_HOME/root.sh script, 527, 530
$HISTSIZE environment variable, 390
$ORA_CRS_HOME/bin directory, 408, 454
$ORA_CRS_HOME/crs/profile directory, 455
$ORA_CRS_HOME/crs/public directory, 453–455
$ORA_CRS_HOME/racg/usrco directory, 442
$ORA_CRS_HOME/racg/usrco/callout1 shell script, 442
$ORA_CRS_HOME/racg/usrco directory, 442
$ORACLE_BASE directory, 730
$ORACLE_BASE/oraInventory directory, 306
$ORACLE_HOME directory, 483
$ORACLE_HOME environment variable, 479
$ORACLE_HOME/bin directory, 275, 328
$ORACLE_HOME/dbs directory, 210, 554, 695, 697, 701, 703, 732, 734
$ORACLE_HOME/lib environment variable, 434
$ORACLE_HOME/network/admin directory, 509
$ORACLE_HOME/network/admin/listener.ora file, 534
$ORACLE_HOME/network/admin/tnsnames.ora configuration, 736
$ORACLE_HOME/opmn/conf/ons.config, 443
$ORACLE_HOME/rdbms/admin/addmrpt.sql script, 661
$ORACLE_HOME/rdbms/admin/awrrpt.sql script, 654
$ORACLE_HOME/rdbms/admin/catclust.sql script, 663
$ORACLE_HOME/rdbms/admin/catxdbdbca.sql script, 224
$ORACLE_HOME/rdbms/lib directory, 103
$ORACLE_HOME/rdbms/mesg/oraus.msg file, 572
$ORACLE_SID environment variable, 485–487
$PATH environment variable, 328
$TNS_ADMIN directory, 509
$TNS_ADMIN environment variable, 431
$TNS_ADMIN/listener.ora file, 198, 547

_netdev, 178, 196
~/.bash_profile, 273, 277
~/.ssh directory, 279
+ (root) ASM directory, 229
+ASM default instance, 213–214
+ASM1 instance, 210
+ASM2 instance, 210

Numbers

10gR1 option, 321
32-bit mode, 107
32-bit processors, 101–104
64-bit mode, 107
64-bit processors, 101–104
802.3ad DYNAMIC mode, 123
10425 event, 573
10708 event, 573

A

Abort shutdown mode, 470
aclstring option, 459
actimeo parameter, NFS, 164
Active Nodes page, 531, 545
Active on Boot check box, 243
Active Session History (ASH), 18, 52, 364, 649, 660–661
Active Unix domain sockets section, 677
active-backup parameter, 288
Add a new node dialog box, 308
ADD ALIAS clause, 219
Add Initiator Groups page, 169
Add New Local User page, SUSE Linux Enterprise Server, 257
Add Node dialog box, 190
Add Partition dialog box, 241–242
addInstance command, 350
Additional Language Support page, 244
additional language support, Red Hat Enterprise Linux 4 AS, 244
Additional Management Agent option, 382
Additional Management Services, 369, 379
Additional Size Options, 242
ADDM (Automatic Database Diagnostic Monitor), 18, 52, 365, 518, 649, 660–662
addmrpt.sql script, 661
addNode option, 525
addNode.sh script, 525
Address Resolution Protocol (ARP), 271
administration, EM, 50–51
Administration tab, Enterprise Manager (EM), 223, 470, 472

Database Administration section, 472–473
overview, 472
Schema section, 473–474
administrative tools
CRSCTL, 51
Enterprise Manager (EM)
administrative options, 472–474
Database Control, 50
Grid Control, 50–51
maintenance options, 474–475
overview, 465–467
performance options, 471
setting parameters, 470–471
starting and stopping databases and
instances, 467–470
overview, 465
Server Control Utility (SRVCTL), 51
databases, 477–480
instances, 480–482
listener, 484–485
node applications, 482–484
overview, 475–476
syntax, 476
SQL*Plus, 51
connecting to RAC instance using
SQL*Plus, 486–487
overview, 485
setting parameters in initialization
parameter file (PFILE),
488–489
setting parameters in server parameter file
(SPFILE), 489–490
setting SQL*Plus prompt, 486
starting instance, 487
stopping instance, 487–488
Advanced Memory Buffer (AMB), 114
Advanced Networking Services (ANS), 287
Advanced Options page, 469–470
Advanced Queuing (AQ), 427–429
Advanced Server (AS), 237
Advisory Framework, 649
AFFIRM attribute, 719, 722, 727
Agent Configuration Assistant, 383–384
Agent Home, 384
AGENT_HOME directory, 374, 383
agent10g directory, 382
agent10g/install/unix/scripts/agentstup
directory, 383
agent10g/root.sh script, 378
agentca utility, 384
AgentDeploy application, 381
agentDownload script, 381
aggregates, 159–160
alert log, 553–554
ALERT_QUE parameter, 364
alias file names, 218–219
All Initialization Parameters button, 341
allocation unit, 215
Allowable Drives, 241
allroot.sh script, 377–378

ALTER DATABASE REGISTER LOGFILE
command, 726
ALTER DATABASE RENAME DATAFILE
command, 704
ALTER DATABASE statement, 706, 720, 732
ALTER DISKGROUP statement, 216, 218
ALTER SESSION FORCE PARALLEL command,
111
ALTER SESSION statement, 111, 573, 629
ALTER SYSTEM statement, 38, 488–490, 513, 573
ALTER_QUEUE_TABLE procedure, 429
AMB (Advanced Memory Buffer), 114
AMERICAN-AMERICA.UTF8 default value, 275
Anaconda installation, Red Hat Enterprise
Linux 4 AS, 238
ANALYZE statement, 73
ANS (Advanced Networking Services), 287
Apache/Apache/conf/httpd.conf file, 370
API (application programming interface), 17
apic=bigsmp parameter, 110
application design
bind variables, 70
overview, 70
sequences, 70–72
application development. See also Oracle
Clusterware High Availability (HA)
Framework
Fast Application Notification (FAN)
Fast Connection Failover (FCF), 442–446
Oracle Notification Service (ONS),
439–441
overview, 437–439
server-side callouts, 441–442
overview, 425
RAC-specific development considerations
instances and database services, 425–426
local and shared storage, 427–428
multiple SGAs, 426–427
node affinity, 428–430
overview, 425
Transparent Application Failover (TAF),
430–437
application I/O, 213
application programming interface (API), 17
application scalability, 5
apropos command, 389
AQ (Advanced Queuing), 427–429
AQ_HA_NOTIFICATIONS parameter, 508
AQ_TM_PROCESSES parameter, 45, 364, 372
ARBn background process, 48
ARC0 background process, 727
ARCH background process, 56
archive log gaps, 726
archived redo logs, 36, 68–69, 173
available via NFS mounts, 716
backupsets, 692
overview, 715
written to cluster file system, 715–716
written to Flashback Recovery Area, 715
written to local disk, 716

ARCHIVELOG mode, 44, 706
ARCHIVELOG option, 711
ARCHIVELOG pattern | sequence range | time
    range, 701
ARCHIVELOG template, 220
ARCn background process, 44–45, 126, 694, 719,
    721, 728–729, 733, 738, 740
ARCn configuration, 724
ARP (Address Resolution Protocol), 271
AS (Advanced Server), 237
AS BACKUPSET option, 700
AS COMPRESSED BACKUPSET option, 700
AS COPY option, 700, 702
ASH (Active Session History), 18, 52, 364, 649,
    660–661
ASHDUMP command, 560
Asianux, 29
ASM. See Automatic Storage Management
ASM storage option, 210
ASM_DISKGROUPS parameter, 215–216, 223
ASM_DISKSTRING parameter, 214–215, 223
ASM_POWER_LIMIT parameter, 214, 217,
    223
ASMB (Automated Storage Management)
    background process, 45, 214
ASMCMD. See Automated Storage Management
    Command Line Utility
    cd command, 225–226
    du command, 226
    find command, 226
    help command, 226–227
    ls command, 227–228
    lsct command, 228–229
    lsdg command, 229
    mkalias command, 229
    mkdir command, 229–230
    overview, 224–225
    pwd command, 230
    rm command, 230
    rmalias command, 230
ASSM (Automatic Segment Space
    Management), 13, 74–75, 472
AST (Asynchronous Traps), 576
ASYNC mode, 721, 722, 726
async_off option, 129
asynchronous I/O, 128–129, 173, 235, 249
asynchronous mirroring, 138
asynchronous network I/O (ASYNC), 721–722
Asynchronous Traps (AST), 576
ATTRIBUTES clause, 220
AUM (Automatic Undo Management), 17, 36,
    497, 524, 540
authorized_keys file, 280
AUTO value, 729
AUTOBACKUP template, 220
AUTOEXTEND parameter, 356
Automated Storage Management background
    process (ASMB), 214
Automated Storage Management Command
    Line (ASMCMD) utility, 220, 224, 228

Automatic Database Diagnostic Monitor
    (ADDM), 18, 52, 365, 518, 649, 660–662
Automatic Segment Space Management
    (ASSM), 13, 74–75, 472
Automatic Storage Management (ASM), 10, 18,
    65, 68, 93
    administration
        overview, 220
        using ASMCMD, 224–230
        using DBCA, 221
        using Enterprise Manager, 222–223
        using FTP, 223–224
        using SQL*Plus, 221
        using SRVCTL, 221–222
    ASM files
        file names, 217–219
        overview, 217
        templates, 219–220
    configuring, 329, 331–332
    disk, 698
    event type, 438
    file system, 32, 212
    installing
        configure option, 203–204
        createdisk option, 205
        deletedisk option, 205
        listdisks option, 205
        overview, 202–203
        querydisk option, 205
        scandisks option, 205
        start option, 204
        status option, 204
        stop option, 204
    instance
        adding manually, 210–211
        adding using DBCA, 206–208, 210
        background processes, 47–48,
            213–214
        creating disk group, 216
        deleting manually, 211–212
        deleting using DBCA, 211
        dropping disk group, 217
        failure groups, 215
        instance names, 213
        mirroring, 215
        modifying disk group, 216–217
        overview, 206, 213
        parameters, 214–215
        re-creating, 212
        redundancy, 216
        SGA, 213
        striping, 215
        using files instead of devices, 212
    monitoring
        dynamic performance views, 221, 231
        fixed views, 231–233
        overview, 231
    overview, 201–202
Automatic Storage Management (ASM) Disk
    Groups page, 208, 331, 336

Automatic Storage Management Instance page, Enterprise Manager, 222–223
Automatic Undo Management (AUM), 17, 36, 472, 524, 540
Automatic Workload Repository (AWR), 18, 52, 104, 472, 631, 649
Automatic Workload Repository (AWR) reports
  generating, 652–655
  interpreting RAC statistics of
    dictionary cache, 658
    global cache efficiency percentages, 657
    global cache (GCS) and enqueue services (GES), 657–658
    global cache load profile, 656–657
    global cache transfer statistics, 660
    global CR server statistics, 659
    global current served statistics, 659
    global enqueue statistics (GES), 659
    library cache, 658
    overview, 655
    SQL statements, 658
    Top 5 Timed Events, 656
  overview, 652
automounted disk groups (ASM_DISKGROUPS), 223
AUX_STAT$ table, 73
AUXILIARY <connect_string> parameter, 686
auxiliary database, 685
Available devices option, 194
AVAILABLE instance, 497, 501
AVG_BLOCKS_PER_KEY value, 89
AVG_BUSY_TICKS column, 111
AVG_IDLE_TICKS column, 111
AVG_IN_BYTES column, 111
AVG_OUT_BYTES column, 111
AWR. See Automatic Workload Repository

■ B

background processes, 576
  ASM instance background processes, 47–48
  overview, 42
  RDBMS instance background processes
    Data Guard-specific background processes, 47
    mandatory background processes, 42–44
    optional background processes, 44–45
    overview, 42
    RAC-specific background processes, 45–47
BACKGROUND_DUMP_DEST directory, 554
BACKGROUND_DUMP_DEST parameter, 47, 553, 554, 556
backing up OCR, 416–417
backup and recovery, 66–67
  OCFS1, 179
  overview, 55
  recovery manager (RMAN), 55
  storage-based, 55
BACKUP ARCHIVELOG command, 695, 702
BACKUP AS COPY command, 703–704

BACKUP command, 695, 700, 702, 704
BACKUP CONTROLFILE, 701
BACKUP COPY OF command, 704
BACKUP DATABASE command, 695, 711
backup node, 428
backup optimization, 694–695
backup sets, 692–693
backup software, 9
backup type, 695
backuploc option, OCRCONFIG, 416
BACKUPSET <primary_key>, 701
BACKUPSET template, 220
bandwidth, 720
bash shell, 273, 524
  command history, 390
  commands
    less, 393
    overview, 392
    printf, 392–393
  environment variables, 390–391
  for loops, 391–392
  overview, 389–390
  Tab completion, 390
.bash_profile command prompt, 291
.bash_profile file, 391, 524
basic input/output system (BIOS), 115
BAST (Blocking Asynchronous Traps), 576
BATCH_CLASS job class, 500
BATCH_SERVICE job class, 500
BCVs (SnapView Business Continuance Volumes), 147
BEA Tuxedo, 89
Benchmark Details screen, 640
benchmarking
  and load testing, 83–85
  overview, 83
  tools. See Hammerora; Swingbench
  TPC benchmarks
    overview, 86
    TPC-C benchmark, 86–91
    TPC-H benchmark, 91–98
Berkeley Software Distribution (BSD), 22
bespoke application load tests
  building load test from converted trace file
    catch command, 621–622
    exit command, 622
    overview, 617–620
    randomized workloads, 620
    script execution timings, 621
    selective workloads, 620–621
  converting trace file, 613–614
  creating trace file, 611–613
  overview, 610–611
  testing converted trace file, 615–617
BFILEs, 427
bg parameter, NFS, 164
BG_MESSAGES command, 560
BIGFILE keyword, 356
bin command, 224
bin directory, 320, 378

binary files, 224
Bind LUN operations, 155
bind variables, 70, 73
BIOS (basic input/output system), 115
BIOS layer, 237
BIOS-based systems, 239
bitmap blocks, 74
bitmap hierarchy, 75
Bitmap View tab, 181
BL lock, 577
block change tracking, 706–707
block I/O, 138
Block Media Recovery (BMR), 714
Block size option, 194
block sizes, 173
block-based storage, 143, 145
Blocking Asynchronous Traps (BAST), 576
BLOCKRECOVER command, 714
BMR (Block Media Recovery), 714
/boot (boot partition), 240, 252
Boot Loader Configuration page, 242
boot options, 250
boot partition (/boot), 240, 252
booting system
    bootloaders, 398–399
    initial ramdisk image, 399
    overview, 398
Bourne shell, 390
BSD (Berkeley Software Distribution), 22
BSD-type options, 673
B-trees, 78
buffer cache, 37, 43, 582, 588, 596, 604
business requirements, RAC design
    business constraints, 60–61
    overview, 59
    technical requirements, 59–60
    upgrade policy, 61–62
business transaction, 84
By Cluster Wait Time section, 658

■C
C++ compilers, 371
CACHE clause, 71
cache coherency, 108, 584
Cache Fusion, 13, 90, 105, 575
    concurrent reads, 584
    concurrent writes, 584–586
    examples
        current read with no transfer, 586–588
        overview, 586
        past images, 599
        read-to-write transfer, 589
        write-to-read transfer, 594–598
    intrainstance, 669
    overview, 584
    Phase I, 19, 585
    Phase II, 19, 585
    traffic, 89
cache hit, 108
cache line, 108

cache object lock (LB), 564
CALL command, 559
callbackFn method, 434
Calling Circle application
    configuring Swingbench, 635–636
    creating input data, 639–641
    creating schema, 636–639
    overview, 635
    starting test, 641–643
CALLSTACK command, 560
card description, 438
cat command, 394
CATALOG <connect string> parameter, 686
CATALOG command, 703
catalog database, 685
catch command, 621–622
CBO (cost-based optimizer), 60
ccwizard process, 636
cd command, 225–226
cdrecord utility, 237
CD-ROM file systems, 397
CD-ROM-based install, 237
CDSLs (Context Dependent Symbolic Links),
    172, 198–199
Certification Matrices page, 100
Change Tracking Writer (CTWR) background
    process, 706
CHANGETRACKING template, 220
CHANNEL <name> option, 701
channel device type, 695–696
character devices, 285
Character Sets tab, 341
charbench, 643
check string parameter, 448
checking state of Oracle Clusterware, 409
checkpoint (CKPT), 44, 127
CHECKPOINT_PROCESS parameter, 44
chkconfig command line utility, 116, 247, 261,
    286, 380, 387
chmod command, 321, 609
chown command, 278
CISC (complex instruction set computer)
    architecture, 105
CJQ0 (job coordinator background process),
    500
CKPT (checkpoint), 44, 127
CLARiiON cache, 153
CLARiiON CX storage, 152
class-C network address, 243
CLASSPATH environment variable, 276, 444,
    634
CLB_GOAL parameter, 508
CLB_GOAL_LONG, 496
CLB_GOAL_SHORT, 496
Clear All Data Blocks box, 184
CLEAR keyword, 693
Client connectivity property, 447
Client-side connection balancing, 493–494
client-side parameter file (PFILE), 34
Clock and Time Zone Configuration page, 255

clock rate, 105
clock speed, 105
CLSCFG utility, 550
cluster argument, 366
Cluster Cache Coherency page, 651
cluster configuration, 189
Cluster Database Instance page, 222
Cluster Database page, 467, 470, 536
Cluster Database Summary page, 222
cluster file system, 68, 171–172, 193, 715–716.
      See also Oracle Cluster File System
Cluster Host Load Average, 651
Cluster Installation Mode page, 382
cluster interconnect, 2
Cluster Managed Database Services, 503
Cluster Node Addition Progress page, 526,
      529
Cluster Node Addition Summary page, 526
Cluster Overview screen, 642
Cluster Ready Services Control (CRSCTL)
      command, 32
Cluster Ready Services (CRS), 17, 31, 401–402
Cluster Ready Services Daemon (CRSD), 17
Cluster Synchronization Services (CSS), 33, 402
Cluster Verification Utility (CLUVFY), 19, 32, 53,
      290, 295, 306, 315, 321, 404, 418, 419,
      528, 552
CLUSTER_DATABASE parameter, 40, 41, 121,
      214, 354, 361, 720, 731–732
CLUSTER_DATABASE_INSTANCES parameter,
      41, 521
CLUSTER_NAME environment variable, 382
CLUSTER_NODES parameter, 548, 551
clustered database concepts
    cluster terminology
       overview, 2
       shared-all clusters, 3–4
       shared-nothing clusters, 3
    disaster recovery, 7
    high availability, 4–5
    overview, 2
    scalability
       overview, 5–6
       scale-out, 6
       scale-up, 6
clustered file systems, 65
clusteroverview process, 642
clusteroverview.xml file, 635
Clusterware, 123
Clusterware Cluster Synchronization Services
      (CSS), 281
Clusterware High Availability Framework, 4
clusterware subdirectory, 306
CLUVFY (Cluster Verification Utility), 19, 32, 53,
      290, 295, 306, 315, 321, 404, 418, 419,
      528, 552
CMAN (Connection Manager), 437
CMDFILE option, 687
coarse striping, 215
color depth, 248

com.dom.benchmarking.swingbench.storedpr
      ocedures Java package, 644
comm_voting parameter, /etc/ocfs.conf
      configuration file, 175
command history, 390
command line utility, 686
Commit page, 163
compatibility mode, 107
complex instruction set computer (CISC)
      architecture, 105
components, Oracle Clusterware, 401–402
composite partitioned table, 79
Composite Query-per-Hour Performance
      Metric (QphH@Size), 86, 93
concurrent reads, 584
concurrent writes, 584–586
config database option, 477
config dbcontrol db command, 366
config nodeapps command, 483
Configuration Assistants page, 378
Configuration page, 530
Configuration tab, 223
Configure Automatic Storage Management
      option, 206, 221, 329, 332
CONFIGURE command, 693, 696–697, 701
Configure Database Options, 343
configure option, ASM, 203–204
configure option, /etc/init.d/oracleasm script,
      203
Configure Using DHCP check box, 243
configureASM command, 350
Configured Nodes tab, 181
configureDatabase command, 350
configuring
    OCFS Version 2 (OCFS2), 189, 191
    Oracle Cluster File System (OCFS), 175–176
    Oracle software. *See* installing and
      configuring Oracle software
    Swingbench, 633–634
configuring and verifying Linux, 285–287
    channel bonding, 287–290
    Cluster Verification (CVU or CLUVFY)
       component checks, 295–299
       Java Runtime Environment (JRE),
          291–292
       overview, 290
       stage checks, 292–295
       syntax, 292
    hangcheck-timer, 263–264
    hostnames and name resolution, 260–261
    kernel parameters
       example, 271–272
       network, 269–271
       open files, 271
       overview, 264–265
       semaphores, 268–269
       shared memory, 265–268
    Network Time Protocol (NTP), 261–262
    operating system and RPM package checks,
      259–260

Oracle user configuration
  creating dba and oinstall groups, 272
  creating Oracle software directories, 278
  creating oracle user, 272–273
  overview, 272
  setting environment variables, 273–277
  setting password for oracle user, 273
  setting security limits, 278–279
overview, 259
secure shell configuration, 279–281
shared storage configuration
  overview, 281
  partitioning, 281–284
connect command, 629
connect option, 629
Connect String, 630
CONNECT_IDENTIFIER user variable, 486
connection balancing, 493
connection load balancing, 48–49
Connection Manager (CMAN), 437
Connection Mode page, 344
connection pool, 557
ConnectString parameter, 634–635
consistent read (CR) versions, 584
consistent reads, global cache services (GCS),
       665–667
Contain process, 116
Context Dependent Symbolic Links (CDSLs),
       172, 198–199
contiguous space, 182
Continue process, 116
control file autobackup, 697
control files, 35, 689
CONTROL_FILE_RECORD_KEEP_TIME
       parameter, 689
CONTROL_FILES parameter, 35, 355
CONTROLFILE option, 711
CONTROLFILE template, 220
COPY command, 703
COPY OF option, 704
copyleft, 22
copy-on-write, 137
core frequency, 113
core processes, 241
coreutils project, Oracle, 188
cost-based optimizer (CBO), 60
Counter Options menu option, 630
cp utility, 524, 704
CPU cache, 108–110
CPU cost model, 73
CPU errors, 116
cpu section, 676
CPU time, 675
CPU utilization, 678
CPU_COUNT parameter, 110–111
cpuspeed command, 115
CR (consistent read) versions, 584
CR status column values, V$BH, 583
Create ASM Instance page, 207, 331
CREATE CATALOG command, 690

Create Custom Partition Setup, 251
Create Database operation, 210, 336
CREATE DATABASE statement, 39, 354–355, 722
Create Disk Group page, 331
CREATE DISKGROUP command, 216
CREATE PFILE statement, 489
CREATE SPFILE statement, 489
CREATE_JOB_CLASS procedure, 430
CREATE_QUEUE_TABLE procedure, 428
CREATE_SERVICE procedure, 496, 508
CREATE_SNAPSHOT procedure, 653
createCloneTemplate command, 350
CreateClustDBViews.sql, 358
createDatabase command, 350
CreateDBCatalog.sql script, 356–357
CreateDBFiles.sql, 355–356
CreateDB.sql, 354–355
createdisk option, 203, 205, 212, 304
createTemplateFromDB command, 350
CRM (customer relationship management), 12
CROSSCHECK command, 707–708, 710
cross-instance archiving, 724
CRS (Cluster Ready Services), 17, 31, 401–402
CRS (Oracle Clusterware), 298
CRS control (CRSCTL)
  checking state of Oracle Clusterware, 409
  debugging, 411–412
  enabling and disabling Oracle Clusterware,
       409
  listing CRS versions, 411
  managing voting disks, 410–411
  overview, 408
  setting CSS parameters, 410
  starting and stopping Oracle Clusterware,
       409
  state dumps, 413
crs option, 296–297
crs_getperm, 459
CRS_HOME environment variable, 275
crs_profile command, 453, 454–458
crs_register command, 454, 458
crs_relocate command, 462–463
crs_setperm command, 459–460
crs_start command, 460
CRS_STAT utility, 408, 413–415, 461–462
crs_stop command, 461
crs_unregister, 459
CRSCOMM module, 412
CRSCTL (Cluster Ready Services Control)
       command, 32
crsctl check crs, 409
CRSCTL utility, 51, 408, 412
CRSD (Cluster Ready Services Daemon), 17
crsd daemon, 402, 412–413, 416
crsd directory, 423
CRSR namespace, 579
CSS (Cluster Synchronization Services), 33, 281,
       402
cssd directory, 423
CSSD module, 412

CTWR (Change Tracking Writer) background process, 706
CU lock, 577
CUMULATIVE option, 700, 705
current blocks, global cache services (GCS), 667–669
CURRENT CONTROLFILE, 701
current read with no transfer, 586, 588
current state, 652
cursor sharing, 72, 581
CURSOR_STATS command, 560
Custom Database, 333
custom libraries, 66
Custom option, 318, 340
Custom Partitioning for Experts, 251
Custom Scripts tab, 339
customer relationship management (CRM), 12
CUSTOMER table record, 88
Customize the Set of Packages to Be Installed option, 245
CV_DESTLOC environment variable, 277
CV_JDKHOME environment variable, 277
cvuqdisk package, 296
CVUQDISK_GRP environment variable, 277

■D

DAPL (direct access programming library), 120
data blocks, 499, 582, 604
data center environment, 9
data dictionary, 74, 213
data dictionary views, 511–512
Data Guard, 16, 64
    logical standby, 56–57
    overview, 56
    physical standby, 56
Data Guard configuration, 728
Data Guard standby databases, 363
Data Guard-specific background processes, 47
Data Manipulation Language (DML) locks, 40
data protection modes
    maximum availability mode, 719
    maximum performance mode, 719
    maximum protection mode, 719–720
    overview, 719
    setting data protection mode, 720
Data Pump, 61, 475, 499
data redundancy, 215
data1 directory, 640
database backup, 66
database block address (DBA), 67, 586
database blocks, 67
Database buffer cache variable value, 102
Database Configuration Assistant (DBCA), 32, 54, 206, 327, 363, 365, 402, 465, 521, 535, 699
    adding ASM instance using, 206–208, 210
    ASM administration using, 221
    at command line, 350–351
    configuration, 554

deleting ASM instance using, 211
as GUI tool
    configuring Automatic Storage Management (ASM), 329–332
    creating database, 332–334, 336–344
    creating template, 345–348
    deleting database, 345
    managing instances, 349
    managing services, 349
    overview, 327–329
Database Content Page, 339, 343
Database Control, 50, 334, 363, 365–366, 465
database control commands, 688
database creation using scripts
    overview, 351
    primary node
        CreateClustDBViews.sql, 358
        CreateDBCatalog.sql, 356–357
        CreateDBFiles.sql, 355–356
        CreateDB.sql, 354–355
        emRepository.sql, 358
        interMedia.sql, 358
        JServer.sql, 357
        ordinst.sql, 358
        overview, 352
        PFILE, 353–354
        postDBCreation.sql, 359–360
        RAC1.sh, 352
        RAC1.sql, 352–353
        xdb_protocol.sql, 357
    running scripts, 361–362
    secondary nodes
        overview, 360
        RAC2.sh, 360
        RAC2.sql, 360–361
Database Credentials page, 334
database description, 438
Database Details window, 637
DATABASE event type, 438
Database File Locations page, 336, 342
database ID (DBID), 697
Database Identification page, 333
database instance, 213
database kernel, 213
database name (DB_NAME) parameter, 728
database option, 296–297
DATABASE option, 701, 708, 711
DATABASE scope, 712
database services
    administering
        configuring clients to use services, 509
        overview, 501
        using Database Creation Assistant (DBCA), 501–502
        using DBMS_SERVICE package, 507–509
        using Enterprise Manager (EM), 502–505
        using Server Control (SRVCTL), 505–507
    implementing
        overview, 499
        Parallel Execution, 501

performance, 499
Resource Manager, 499–500
Scheduler, 500–501
monitoring services
data dictionary views, 511–512
dynamic performance views, 512–518
metrics and thresholds, 518–519
overview, 511
trace, 519
overview, 497–498
troubleshooting, 510–511
Database Services page, 339, 349, 538, 542
Database Storage page, 341
Database Templates page, 332
Database Time, 662
Database Upgrade Assistant (DBUA), 54, 104
database writer (DBWn), 43, 125, 585
DATABASE_TRACE_DISABLE procedure, 556
DATABASE_TRACE_ENABLE procedure, 556
databases. *See also* database creation using
scripts; database services
administering using Server Control Utility
(SRVCTL)
checking configuration of database,
477–478
checking status of database, 478
configuration of database, adding new,
478–479
configuration of database, modifying
existing, 479
configuration of database, removing
existing, 479
disabling database, 479
enabling database, 479–480
overview, 477
starting database, 477
stopping database, 477
design
automatic segment space management
(ASSM), 74–75
cursor sharing, 72
dynamic sampling, 73
histograms, 73
locally managed tablespaces, 74
optimizer statistics, 72–73
overview, 72
partitioning, 76–81
reverse key indexes, 75–76
system statistics, 73
recovery, 66
replication, 7
scalability, 5
structure
archived logs, 36
control files, 35
datafiles, 34–35
online redo log files, 35
overview, 34
recovery area, 36
undo tablespaces, 36

DATAFILE <datafile> option, 708
DATAFILE <name|file#> option, 711
DATAFILE <name> | <file#>, 701
DATAFILE <pathname | file#>, 712
datafile backupsets, 692
datafile copies, 707
DATAFILE template, 220
datafiles, 34–35
DATAGUARDCONFIG template, 220
date and time, Red Hat Enterprise Linux 4 AS,
248
date command, 262
DAYS <number> option, 708
db file sequential read event, 126
DB_BLOCK_CHECKING parameter, 90
DB_BLOCK_CHECKSUM parameter, 90
DB_CACHE_SIZE parameter, 38
DB_FILE_CREATE_DEST parameter, 699
DB_FILE_CREATE_ONLINE_LOG_DEST_n
parameter, 699
DB_FILE_MULTIBLOCK_READ_COUNT
parameter, 126, 665
db_inst option, 299
DB_NAME (database name) parameter, 728
DB_NAME parameter, 41, 479, 698
DB_RECOVERY_FILE_DEST parameter, 699
DB_RECOVERY_FILE_DEST_SIZE parameter,
699
DB_UNIQUE_NAME (unique database names),
728
DB_UNIQUE_NAME parameter, 214, 698, 727,
728
DB_WRITER_PROCESSES parameter, 43, 130
DBA (database block address), 67, 586
dba group, 272–273, 298, 321
DBA_ALERT_HISTORY view, 365
DBA_ENABLED_TRACES, 558–559
DBA_HIST_ prefix, 364
DBA_HIST_%, 653
DBA_HIST_ACTIVE_SESS_HISTORY view, 364
DBA_HIST_BASELINE view, 654
DBA_HIST_SNAPSHOT view, 653
DBA_OBJECTS dictionary view, 572
DBA_OUTSTANDING_ALERTS view, 364
DBA_SERVICES data dictionary view, 511
DBA_TABLES dictionary, 444
DBCA. *See* Database Configuration Assistant
DBCA command, 485, 488
DBCA Service Management page, 501
DBCA tablespace, 652
DBCA template, 339
DBCA_RAW_CONFIG environment variable,
277
dbgen program, 94
dbhome volume, 160
DBID (database ID), 697
DBMS_ADVISOR package, 661
DBMS_ALERT package, 426
DBMS_APPLICATION_INFO, 427, 556
DBMS_AQADM package, 428, 429

DBMS_BACKUP_RESTORE package, 685
DBMS_JOB package, 19, 500
DBMS_LOCK package, 644
DBMS_MONITOR, 517, 553
   DBA_ENABLED_TRACES, 558–559
   overview, 555–556
   tracing applications, 556–557
   tracing multitier applications, 557–558
DBMS_PIPE object, 579
DBMS_PIPE package, 426–427
DBMS_RANDOM package, 625
DBMS_RCVMAN package, 685
DBMS_SCHEDULER package, 365, 429–430
DBMS_SERVER_ALERT package, 364
DBMS_SERVICE package, 495–496, 505
   CREATE_SERVICE, 508
   DELETE_SERVICE, 509
   DISCONNECT_SESSION, 509
   MODIFY_SERVICE, 509
   overview, 508
   START_SERVICE, 509
   STOP_SERVICE, 509
DBMS_SERVICE.ALL_INSTANCES constant, 509
DBMS_SESSION package, 558
DBMS_SHARED_POOL package, 372, 670
DBMS_STATS package, 73
DBS (demand-based switching), 115
DBSNMP parameter, 360
DBTIMEPERCALL column, 518
DBUA (Database Upgrade Assistant), 54, 104
DBWn background process, 43, 585
dd command, 188, 212, 286, 422, 524
DDL operations, 79
Deadline scheduler, 143
debugging, 186–187, 400, 411–412
debugocfs tool, 186
decision support system (DSS) benchmark, 86
Decode stage, 106
Dedicated Server mode, 341
default block size, 174
default cluster name, 190
default device type, 695
default listener configuration, 208
default rebalance power (ASM_POWER_LIMIT), 223
DEFERRED keyword, 488, 490
defragmentation, 61
degree of parallelism (DOP), 111
Deinstall Products, 324
deinstalling Oracle software, 324–325
DELAY attribute, 431
DELETE ARCHIVELOG clause, 712–713
DELETE command, 710
Delete Database option, 345
DELETE INPUT option, 701
DELETE OBSOLETE command, 694
DELETE_SERVICE, 509
deleteDatabase command, 350
deletedisk option, ASM, 205
deletedisk option, /etc/init.d/oracleasm script, 203

deleteInstance command, 350
deleting
   instances, 211–212, 540, 542, 544
   nodes
      deleting ASM instance, 544
      deleting listener process, 544–547
      deleting Oracle Clusterware software, 550–551
      deleting Oracle Database software, 547–548
      disabling Oracle Clusterware applications, 549–550
      from OCR, 550
      overview, 544
      removing node-specific interface configuration, 548–549
      updating inventories on remaining hosts, 548, 551
      verifying node deletion using Cluster Verification Utility (CLUVFY), 552
   OCR file, 420
delif option, 408
Demand-Based Power Management, 115
demand-based switching (DBS), 115
derived works, 24
destroking, 131
Destroy Virtual Users option, 615
/dev directory, 139
development and test systems, 62
device name slippage, 178
DEVICE TYPE clause, 695
devlabel command, 287
/dev/oracleasm device, 203
/dev/urandom pseudodevice, 176
df command, 397
DG_CONFIG parameter, 728
DHCP (Dynamic Host Configuration Protocol) protocol, 256
DIAG background process, 47
diagnostics. See trace and diagnostics
dictionary cache, 658, 670–671
dictionary managed tablespaces, 60
dir <directory path> argument, 455
dir option, 456, 458
direct access programming library (DAPL), 120
direct I/O, 129–130, 235
direct memory access (DMA), 108
DIRECTIO parameter, 129
directories, 218, 427
dirty blocks, 19, 599
dirty buffer, 584
disable option, /etc/init.d/oracleasm script, 203
DISABLE_HUGETLBFS environment variable, 276
disabling Oracle Clusterware, 409
disaster recovery, 7, 62–63
   archive log gaps, 726
   creating physical standby database
      adding standby database to Oracle Cluster Registry (OCR), 735

backing up primary database, 732–733

checking standby configuration, 738

configuring operating system, 730

copying RMAN backup from primary to standby, 735

creating directories on standby nodes, 733–734

creating initialization parameter files on standby nodes, 734

creating password files on primary nodes, 731–732

creating password files on standby nodes, 734

creating server parameter file for standby database, 734

creating standby database, 737–738

enabling archiving on primary database, 730–731

enabling managed recovery on standby database, 738

forcing logging on primary database, 732

installing and configuring shared storage, 730

installing and patching operating system, 730

installing management agents, 730

installing Oracle Clusterware (CRS), 730

installing Oracle Database software, 730

overview, 729

setting parameters on primary database, 733

setting parameters on standby database, 737

updating /etc/oratab on standby nodes, 735

updating listener configuration files on standby nodes, 735–736

updating Oracle Net configuration files on all nodes, 736–737

verifying log transportation, 738–739

Data Guard

logical standby, 56–57

overview, 56

physical standby, 56

data protection modes

maximum availability mode, 719

maximum performance mode, 719

maximum protection mode, 719–720

overview, 719

setting data protection mode, 720

hardware disaster recovery solutions, 57

initialization parameters

DB_UNIQUE_NAME, 728

FAL_CLIENT, 729

FAL_SERVER, 729

LOG_ARCHIVE_CONFIG, 728

LOG_ARCHIVE_DEST_n, 726–727

LOG_ARCHIVE_DEST_STATE_n, 727

LOG_ARCHIVE_FORMAT, 727–728

LOG_ARCHIVE_START, 727

overview, 726

REMOTE_ARCHIVE_ENABLE, 728

STANDBY_ARCHIVE_DEST, 728

STANDBY_FILE_MANAGEMENT, 729

log apply services, 723

NOLOGGING attribute, 725–726

Oracle Data Guard, 718–719

overview, 55, 717

RAC and physical standby, 724–725

redo transport services

ARCn background process, 721

asynchronous network I/O (ASYNC), 721–722

LGWR background process, 721

overview, 720

synchronous network I/O (SYNC), 722

RMAN, 725

role management

failover, 724, 740–741

overview, 723, 739

read-only mode, 723, 739

switchover, 723, 739–740

standby redo logs, 722–723

stretch clusters, 57

DISCONNECT_SESSION, 509

discrimination, 24

disk discovery path (ASM_DISKSTRING), 223

disk drive performance, 131

disk groups

creating, 216

dropping, 217

modifying, 216–217

Disk I/O statistics, 223

disk partitioning

Red Hat Enterprise Linux 4 AS, 239–242

SUSE Linux Enterprise Server, 251

disk partitions, 523

disk ping, 19, 585

Disk Setup page, 239

disk writes, 599, 601–603

DISK_ASYNCH_IO parameter, 130

disk-to-disk-to-tape method, 67

DISPATCHERS parameter, 495

display, Red Hat Enterprise Linux 4 AS, 248

DISPLAY environment variable, 179, 276, 305, 328, 609

distributed lock manager (DLM), 19, 575

DLM (distributed lock manager), 19, 575

DMA (direct memory access), 108

dmesg command, 290, 400

DML (Data Manipulation Language) locks, 40

DML_LOCKS parameter, 40

DMON operation, Data Guard, 47

DNS (Domain Name System) servers, 236

dollar sign ($) prefix, 390

Domain Name System (DNS) servers, 236

DOP (degree of parallelism), 111

DOWN event, 437, 442

downgrading OCR, 419–420

downtime, 61

DROP DATABASE command, 707, 710
DROP DISKGROUP statement, 217
DROP_BASELINE procedure, 654
dropping disk groups, 217
DSA version, 279
DSMn operation, Data Guard, 47
DSS (decision support system) benchmark, 86
DTP parameter, 508
du command, 226, 397
du -s command, Unix, 226
dual-processor class machine, 624
dual-pumped, 114
DUMPSET template, 220
DUPLICATE TARGET DATABASE FOR
        STANDBY command, 738
DURATION clause, 702
Dynamic Host Configuration Protocol (DHCP)
        protocol, 256
dynamic load balancing, 148
dynamic performance views, 52–53, 231
    GV$ACTIVE_SERVICES, 513
    GV$SERV_MOD_ACT_STATS, 517–518
    GV$SERVICE_EVENT, 516
    GV$SERVICE_STATS, 516–517
    GV$SERVICE_WAIT_CLASS, 515–516
    GV$SERVICEMETRIC, 513–514
    GV$SERVICEMETRIC_HISTORY, 514–515
    GV$SERVICES, 512
dynamic resource mastering, 582
dynamic sampling, 73

∎E
ECC (Error Correction Code), 115
echo command, 390, 394–395
Edit Runlevel menu, 387
EDITABLEOPTIONS section, 628
EFI (Extensible Firmware Interface), 238
ELAPSEDPERCALL column, 518
elevator option, 143
ELILO (Extended Linux Loader) boot loader,
        238, 398
EM. See Enterprise Manager
EM Agent, 365, 466, 494
EM Configuration Assistant, 360
EM Database Control, 360, 365
EM Grid Control Using a New Database
        installation, 376–377
EM Grid Control Using an Existing Database, 376
EM Management Agent, 381
EM_NODE argument, 366
EM_SID_LIST argument, 366
EMC CLARiiON, 147, 148, 152–158
EMC MirrorView, 147
EMC PowerPath software, 146
EMC SnapView, 147
emca -addInst db command, 366
emca command, 366
emca -deleteInst db command, 366
emca -displayConfig dbcontrol -cluster
        command, 366

emca -reconfig dbcontrol -cluster command,
        366
emctl command, 380, 383
emctl start agent command, 383
emctl start dbconsole command, 366
emctl start iasconsole command, 380
emctl start oms command, 380
emctl status agent command, 384
emctl status oms command, 380
emctl stop agent command, 383
emctl stop dbconsole command, 366
emctl stop oms command, 380
emctl upload command, 368, 384
emd.properties file, 367
emoms.properties file, 367–368
emRepository.sql, 358
Emulex LP9802 FC HBA, 150
emwd.pl watchdog script, 383
Enable Network Time Protocol check box, 248
Enable Read Cache check boxes, 155
Enable Write Cache check boxes, 155
enabling Oracle Clusterware, 409
ENQUEUES command, 560
Enterprise Edition installation, 318
Enterprise Manager Agent, 382
Enterprise Manager Console, 363
Enterprise Manager Database Control, 685
Enterprise Manager Database Control home
        page, 503
Enterprise Manager (EM), 17–18, 32, 52, 216,
        363, 649, 699
    administering database services using,
        502–505
    administrative options
        Database Administration section, 472–473
        Enterprise Manager (EM) administration,
        474
        overview, 472
        Schema section, 473–474
    ASM administration using
        Automatic Storage Management Instance
        page, 222–223
        Disk Group page, 223
        Member Disk Page, 223
        overview, 222
    Database Control, 50
    Grid Control, 50–51
    installing and configuring
        Database Control, 365–366
        Grid Control, 367–384
        Manageability Infrastructure, 364–365
        overview, 363–364
    maintenance options
        Data Movement section, 474–475
        High Availability section, 474
        overview, 474
        Software Deployments section, 475
    Oracle performance monitoring with, 649,
        651–652
    overview, 50, 465–467

performance options, 471
setting parameters, 470–471
starting and stopping databases and
instances, 467–470
Enterprise Manager Grid Control Using a New
Database installation, 374
Enterprise Manager Grid Control Using an
Existing Database, 375
Enterprise Manager XDB Configuration page,
224
enterprise resource planning (ERP), 12
Enterprise Server (ES) versions, 237
Enterprise-class applications, 101
entrypoint argument, 371
env command, 390
environment variables, 390–391, 475
setting
CLASSPATH, 276
CRS_HOME, 275
CV_DESTLOC, 277
CV_JDKHOME, 277
CVUQDISK_GRP, 277
DBCA_RAW_CONFIG, 277
DISABLE_HUGETLBFS, 276
DISPLAY, 276
example settings, 277
LD_ASSUME_KERNEL, 276
LD_LIBRARY_PATH, 275
NLS_LANG, 275
ORA_NLS10, 275
ORACLE_BASE, 274
ORACLE_HOME, 275
ORACLE_SID, 274
overview, 273–274
PATH, 275
SQLPATH, 276
SRVM_TRACE, 277
TEMP, 276
TMPDIR, 276
TNS_ADMIN, 275
EnvironmentVariables element, 646
EPIC (Explicitly Parallel Instruction Computing)
architecture, 105
ERP (enterprise resource planning), 12
Error Correction Code (ECC), 115
error-handling code, 240
ERRORSTACK command, 560
ES (Enterprise Server) versions, 237
/etc/fstab file, 103, 178
/etc/hosts file, 260, 406, 523, 526
/etc/init.d directory, 380, 383, 550
/etc/init.d/o2cb script, 189
/etc/init.d/ocfs script, 175
/etc/init.d/oracleasm script, 203, 205
/etc/init/o2cb script, 192
/etc/inittab file, 324, 325
/etc/modprobe.conf file, 150
/etc/ntp.conf file, 261–262
/etc/ntp/step-tickers file, 261, 262
/etc/ocfs2/cluster.conf file, 189, 191

/etc/ocfs.conf file, 175, 524
/etc/oracle directory, 378
/etc/oratab file, 211–212, 378, 735
/etc/passwd file, 272
/etc/rc*.d directory, 550
/etc/rc.d/init.d/firstboot script, 247
/etc/rc.d/rc.local file, 286
/etc/resolv.conf file, 261
/etc/sysconfig/firstboot file, 247
/etc/sysconfig/ntpd file, 262
/etc/sysconfig/oracleasm configuration,
204
/etc/sysctl.conf file, 271, 523
/etc/sysctl.conf parameter, 265
/etc/system/rawdevices file, 524
Ethernet, 119–120
Ethernet interconnects, fully redundant,
121–124
Ethernet-based interface, 677
Event Manager Daemon (EVMD), 17
Event Manager (EVM), 402
event_type description, 438
EVENTS command, 560
EVM (Event Manager), 402
EVMD (Event Manager Daemon), 17
evmd daemon, 402, 412
evmd directory, 423
EVMDCOMM module, 412
Ewing, Marc, 26
excluding tablespaces, 698
exclusive (update) access, 591
exclusive (X), 582–583
exclusive lock, 591
exclusive OR (XOR) operation, 134
Exclusive resource mode, 583
execute( ) method, 646
Execute Configuration scripts dialog box, 320,
526
Execute Configuration Scripts page, 383
Execute stage, 106
Existing Database option, 369
exit command, 622
Expert mode, 387
Expert Partitioner window, 252, 253
Explicitly Parallel Instruction Computing (EPIC)
architecture, 105
export option, OCRCONFIG, 416, 418
exporting OCR, 418–419
ext2 file system, 396
Ext2 fs (Linux Second Extended File System),
93
ext3 file system, 172
Extended Linux Loader (ELILO), 398
Extensible Firmware Interface (EFI), 238
External disk group, 210
external network, 523
external network configuration, 243
external redundancy, 216, 311
external scripts, 365
external tables, 427

■F

FAILGROUP clause, 216
failover, role management, 724, 740–741
FAILOVER MODE clause, 431
FAILOVER_DELAY parameter, 508
FAILOVER_METHOD parameter, 508
FAILOVER_RETRIES parameter, 508
FAILOVER_TYPE parameter, 508
failovercallback argument, 629
failure groups, 215
FAIRNESS_THRESHOLD parameter, 594
FAL (Fetch Archive Logging), 719
FAL_CLIENT parameter, 726, 729
FAL_SERVER parameter, 726, 729
FAN. *See* Fast Application Notification
Fast Application Notification (FAN), 18, 33, 425,
        494, 505
    event 444
    Fast Connection Failover (FCF), 442–446
    Oracle Notification Service (ONS), 439–441
    overview, 437–439
    server-side callouts, 441–442
Fast Connection Failover (FCF), 33–34, 437,
        442–446
FAST_START_MTTR_TARGET parameter, 127,
        605
FastConnectionFailoverEnabled attribute, 443
FB-DIMMs (Fully-Buffered Dual Inline Memory
        Modules), 114
FC (Fibre Channel), 118, 140–141
FC over TCP/IP (FCIP), 141
FC Protocol (FCP), 140
FCF (Fast Connection Failover), 33–34, 437,
        442–446
FCFDemo program, 444
FCIP (FC over TCP/IP), 141
FCP (FC Protocol), 140
fdisk command, 158, 282
fdisk -l command, 282
Fetch Archive Logging (FAL), 719
Fetch stage, 106
Fibre Channel (FC), 118, 140–141
Fibre Channel SAN, 141
Fibre Channel Storage Area Network (SAN), 138
Fibre Channel switch configuration, 151–152
FIFO (first in, first out) queue, 46
file entry structure, 187
file I/O, 138
File Listing tab, 180
file names, ASM, 217–219
file systems
    general, 396–397
    journaling, 188
    NFS, 397–398
File Transfer Protocol (FTP), ASM
        administration using, 223–224
FILE_HDRS command, 560
filename argument, 420
Filer - Use Command Line option, 161
Files tab, 223

FILESPERSET <number> option, 700
FILESPERSET parameter, 692
FILESYSTEMIO_OPTIONS parameter, 129,
        130
FileType, 218
find command, 226
fine striping, 215
Firewall Configuration page, 243
firewall configuration, Red Hat Enterprise Linux
        4 AS, 244
FireWire, 138
first in, first out (FIFO) queue, 46
Fixed Size, 241
fixed views, 231–233
FLARE LUN (FLU), 147
Flash Recovery Area, 18, 338
flashback recovery, 67, 694, 698–700, 715
FLASHBACK template, 220
Flexible Volume Parameters, 161
FLU (FLARE LUN), 147
flu arguments, 673
FO_ABORT failover, 433
FO_BEGIN failover, 433
FO_END failover, 433
FO_ERROR failover, 433
FO_NONE failover, 433
FO_REAUTH failover, 433
FO_RETRY failover, 433
FO_SELECT failover, 433
FO_SESSION failover, 433
for expression, 391–392
FOR RECOVERY OF COPY clause, 707
Force box, 184
FORCE LOGGING attribute, 725
force option, 410
FORCE option, 711
Force to Be a Primary Partition, 241
forced reads and writes, 128
FORMAT <format> option, 700
formatting
    OCFS partition, 177
    OCFS2 partition, 194–195
four-node RAC cluster, 62, 68
four-node stretch cluster, 63
free command, 673–675
free redistribution, 24
free software, 22–23
Free Software Foundation (FSF), 22
Free Space tab, 182
FREE status column values, V$BH, 583
freelist, 74
FROM BACKUPSET option, 711
FROM DATAFILECOPY option, 711
Front Side Bus (FSB), 114
FSB (Front Side Bus), 114
fsck.ocfs, 184
fsck.ocfs2, 197–198
FSF (Free Software Foundation), 22
fs.file-max kernel parameter, 278
fs.file-max parameter, 271

FTP (File Transfer Protocol), ASM administration using, 223–224
full backups, 686
FULL option, 700
FullBackup script, 687
fully qualified file names, 218
fully redundant Ethernet interconnects, 121–124
Fully-Buffered Dual Inline Memory Modules (FB-DIMMs), 114

G

GC CR Blocks Received metric, 652
GC CR metric, 665
GC Current Blocks Received, 652
GC Current metric, 667
gc prefix, 656
GC_ELEMENTS command, ORADEBUG utility, 560, 561–562
GC_ELEMENTS dump, 562
GC_FILES_TO_LOCKS parameter, 90
GCC (GNU C Compiler), 23
GCS. See Global Cache Services
GCS (current blocks, global cache services), 667–669
GCS background processes (LMSn), 582, 584
GCS resources, 562, 604
gcstartup script, 380, 383
gdb debugger, 400
General Public License (GPL), 22, 172, 608
general_template template, 457
Generate Data for Benchmark Run, 639
generateScripts command, 350
Generic Linux, 26
GES. See Global Enqueue Services
GES process structures, 567
ges resource hash list child latch, 570
GES_STATE command, ORADEBUG utility, 561
gid (group ID), 199, 321
Gigabit Ethernet, 89, 118, 119, 665
GKrellM environment, Linux, 672
global (GV$) dynamic performance views, 501
global block, 583
Global Cache Block Access Latency, 651
Global Cache Block Transfer Rate, 651, 665, 667
global cache efficiency percentages, 657
global cache events, 656
global cache (GCS) and enqueue services (GES), 657–658
global cache load profile, 656–657
Global Cache Services (GCS), 13, 37, 46, 575
    cache coherency, 584
    Cache Fusion
        concurrent reads, 584
        concurrent writes, 584–586
        examples, 586–598
        overview, 584
        past images, 599
    consistent reads, 665–667
    current blocks, 667–669

disk writes, 599–603
Global Resource Directory (GRD)
    overview, 582
    resource modes, 583
    resource roles, 583
optimizing global cache, 604
overview, 581, 664
system change numbers (SCNs), 603
global cache transfer statistics, 660
global current served statistics, 659
global enqueue activity, 669
Global Enqueue Service Daemon (LMD) processes, 46
Global Enqueue Service Monitor (LMON), 46
Global Enqueue Services (GES), 13, 37, 575, 656, 659, 669
    background processes, 576
    library cache locks
        hash values, 578
        invalidation locks, 579
        namespaces, 578
        overview, 577–578
        types of, 578–579
    lock types, 577
    optimizing global enqueues, 581
    overview, 576
    resources and enqueues, 576–577
    row cache locks, 580
    tracing GES activity, 581
global interface, 407
GLOBAL keyword, 688
global locking, 14, 581
global option, 407
global parameters, 40, 490
global resource coordination, 575
Global Resource Directory (GRD), 13, 37, 575
    overview, 582
    resource modes, 583
    resource roles, 583
Global Services Daemon Control Utility (GSDCTL), 34
Global Services Daemon (GSD), 34, 402, 476
global stored scripts, 688
GLOBAL_AREA command, 560
globalInitNLS error, 371
globally partitioned index, 78
Globally Unique Identifier (GUID), 156
Globally Unique Identifier (GUID) partition table (GPT) disk, 156
GMON background process, ASM, 48
GNU C, 371
GNU C Compiler (GCC), 23
GNU long options, 673
GNU Project, 22
GNU Public License Agreement, 610
GOAL parameter, 508
GOAL_NONE, 496
GOAL_SERVICE_TIME, 496
GOAL_THROUGHPUT, 496
GOODNESS value, 514

GPL (General Public License), 22, 172, 608
GPT (GUID partition table) format, 239, 242
Grand Unified Bootloader (GRUB), 398
graphical mode session, 386
graphical user interface (GUI), Oracle, 363
Graphics Card link, 258
GRD. *See* Global Resource Directory
grid architecture, 70
Grid Control, 50–51, 334, 363, 365, 685
    Management Agent installation, 381–384
    Management Service installation and
        configuration, 372–380
    overview, 366
    planning
        architecture and design, 369–370
        communication, 368–369
        Grid Control Console, 367
        Management Agent, 367
        Management Repository, 367
        Management Service, 367
        overview, 367
    preparing, 371
    starting and stopping Management Service,
        380–381
Grid Control Console, 367
Grid Control. Database Control, 465
Grid Control Management Agent, 365
Grid Control Management Service, 369
Grid Control super administrator password,
    376
GROUP BY expression, 612
group ID (gid), 199, 321
groupadd command, 272
groupmod command, 321
GRUB (Grand Unified Bootloader), 398
GRUB boot loader options, 243
GSD (Global Services Daemon), 34, 402, 476
GSDCTL (Global Services Daemon Control
    Utility), 34
GUI (graphical user interface), Oracle, 363
GUI mode, 405
GUI tools, running, 521–522
GUI-based performance monitoring tools, 672
GUID (Globally Unique Identifier), 156
guid parameter, /etc/ocfs.conf configuration
    file, 175
GUID partition table (GPT) format, 239, 242
GV$ views, 663
GV$ACTIVE_SERVICES, 513
GV$ARCHIVE_GAP dynamic performance view,
    726
GV$GCSPFMASTER_INFO dynamic
    performance view, 572
GV$MANAGED_STANDBY dynamic
    performance view, 738
GV$SERV_MOD_ACT_STATS, 517–518
GV$SERVICE_EVENT, 516
GV$SERVICE_STATS, 516–517
GV$SERVICE_WAIT_CLASS, 515–516
GV$SERVICEMETRIC, 513–514

GV$SERVICEMETRIC_HISTORY, 514–515
GV$SERVICES, 512
GV$SESSION_EVENT dynamic performance
    views, 516
GV$SYSTEM_EVENT dynamic performance
    views, 516

■H

HAFDemo application, 453, 457, 458, 461
hafdemo_template, 457
HAFDemoAction.c file, 447, 448–450
hafdemo.cap application profile, 454, 458
HAFDemoClient.c file, 447, 451–452
HAFDemo.h file, 447, 448
HAFDemoServer.c file, 447, 450–451
hafdemovip application VIP, 456
hafdemovip.cap application profile, 453
Hammerora
    bespoke application load tests
        building load test from converted trace
            file, 617–622
        converting trace file, 613–614
        creating trace file, 611–613
        overview, 610–611
        testing converted trace file, 615–617
    installing, 608–610
    overview, 607–608
    TPC-C simulation
        conducting test, 631–633
        creating schema, 625–627
        determining transaction level, 629–630
        divulging test results, 624
        generating workload, 627–629
        interpreting transactions, 623–624
        overview, 622–623
        test hardware and software
            considerations, 624–625
Hammerora TPC-C load test, 624
hammerora.tcl script file, 610
hang state, 263
HANGANALYZE command, 560
hangcheck_margin parameter, 263
hangcheck-delay module, 264
hangcheck-timer, 263–264
hangcheck-timer module, 263, 287
hard limit, 278
hard parameter, NFS, 164
hard parsing, 72
hardware. *See also* server architecture
    disaster recovery solutions, 57
    fully redundant Ethernet interconnects,
        121–124
    maintenance contracts, 65
    network I/O, 118–119
    Oracle availability, 100
    overview, 99
    private interconnect selection
        Ethernet, 119–120
        overview, 119
        RDMA, 120–121

requirements
    installing Linux, 236
    RAC design, 70
    scalability, 5
hash clustering, 79, 89
hash subpartitions, 80
hash values, 578
HBAs (host bus adapters), 9, 118, 131, 149–151, 399, 678
HEAPDUMP command, 560
HEAPDUMP_ADDR command, 560
help command, 226–227
help option, OCRCONFIG, 416
HHWM (high high water mark), 75
High (triple mirroring) disk group, 210
high high water mark (HHWM), 75
High Performance Computing (HPC), 102, 120
high redundancy, 216
high water mark (HWM), 75
histograms, 73
history of Linux
    free software, 22–23
    open source, 24–25
    overview, 21
    Unix, 21–22
home directory, 523
/home/oracle directory, 273
host bus adapters (HBAs), 9, 118, 131, 149–151, 399, 678
HOST clause, 509
host description, 438
hostnames and name resolution, 260–261
hot blocks, 75
hot pluggable, 118
Hot Spare, 155
housekeeping
    CROSSCHECK command, 707–708
    DELETE command, 710
    DROP DATABASE command, 710
    LIST command, 709–710
    overview, 707
    REPORT command, 708–709
HPC (High Performance Computing), 102, 120
HT (Hyper-Threading), 110, 523
HTTP protocol, 367–368
hugemem kernel, 104
hugetlb settings, 267
hugetlbfs file system, 268
HW lock, 577
HWM (high water mark), 75
hybrid workloads, 13
hyper pipelines, 106
Hyper-Threading (HT), 110, 523

IA64 EPIC architecture, 107
id command, 273
if statements, 391
ifcfg-bond0 file, 288
ifcfg-eth1 file, 288

ifcfg-eth2 file, 288
ifconfig command, 289
iFCP (Internet FC Protocol), 141
ILP (instruction-level parallelism), 106
image copies, 685, 703–705
Immediate shutdown mode, 470
imp utility, 61
import option, OCRCONFIG, 416, 418–419
importing OCR, 419
INCLUDE CURRENT CONTROLFILE option, 697
INCLUDING CONTENTS clause, 217
incomplete file names, 219
increment_selects( ) code, 645
INCREMENTAL <number>, 708
incremental backups, 686, 705–706
INCREMENTAL LEVEL <level> option, 700
incrementally updated backups, 707
index blocks, 76
index scans, 75
Index-Organized Tables (IOTs), 76, 89, 108
inet argument, 677
init( ) routine, 646
init command, 385, 398
init process, 387
init_dml( ) code, 645
initial ramdisk image, 399
initialization parameter file (PFILE), 38–39, 208, 331, 488–489
initialization parameters, 210
    DB_UNIQUE_NAME, 728
    FAL_CLIENT, 729
    FAL_SERVER, 729
    LOG_ARCHIVE_CONFIG, 728
    LOG_ARCHIVE_DEST_n, 726–727
    LOG_ARCHIVE_DEST_STATE_n, 727
    LOG_ARCHIVE_FORMAT, 727–728
    LOG_ARCHIVE_START, 727
    overview, 726
    REMOTE_ARCHIVE_ENABLE, 728
    STANDBY_ARCHIVE_DEST, 728
    STANDBY_FILE_MANAGEMENT, 729
Initialization Parameters page, 340–341, 470
initrd entry, 399
input file, 680
input/output (I/O) attributes, 118
insmod command, 176
INST_ID field, 426
install directory, 371
Installation Settings page, 253
installing
    Automatic Storage Management (ASM)
        configure option, 203–204
        createdisk option, 205
        deletedisk option, 205
        listdisks option, 205
        overview, 202–203
        querydisk option, 205
        scandisks option, 205
        start option, 204

status option, 204
stop option, 204
Hammerora, 608–610
Oracle Clusterware
   adding node-specific interface
      configuration, 528
   overview, 525–527
   verifying Oracle Clusterware installation
      using Cluster Verification Utility
      (CLUVFY), 528
Oracle Database software, 528–530
Swingbench, 633–634
installing and configuring Oracle software
configuration files
   /etc/inittab, 324
   inventory, 323
   OCR, 324
   overview, 323
deinstallation, 324–325
Oracle Clusterware
   overview, 303
   preinstallation tasks, 303–304
   running installer, 305–314
   verifying configuration, 304–305
   verifying installation, 314–315
Oracle Database software
   overview, 315
   running installer, 317–320
   verifying configuration, 315–317
overview, 301
preparing to install
   installation media, 302–303
   overview, 301–302
troubleshooting
   Cluster Verification Utility (CLUVFY), 321
   common problems, 321–322
   other information sources, 322–323
   overview, 320
installing Linux
hardware requirements, 236
networking requirements, 236–237
overview, 235–236
Red Hat Enterprise Linux 4 AS
   additional CDs, 249
   additional language support, 244
   Anaconda installation, 238
   Boot Loader Configuration page, 243
   date and time, 248
   disk partitioning, 239–242
   display, 248
   finishing setup, 249
   firewall configuration, 244
   installation complete, 247
   installation media check, 238
   installing packages, 247
   keyboard configuration, 238
   language selection, 238
   license agreement, 247
   manual package installation, 249–250
   Network Configuration page, 243

overview, 237
   package group selection, 245–247
   package installation defaults, 245
   reasons for registering, 249
   Red Hat Login, 249
   root password configuration, 245
   start installation, 247
   starting installation, 237–238
   system user, 249
   time zone selection, 244–245
   upgrade option, 238–239
   welcome, 247
SUSE Linux Enterprise Server
   Add New Local User page, 257
   Expert Partitioner window, 253
   installation settings, 251
   license agreement, 251
   network configuration, 256
   overview, 250
   partitioning, 251, 253
   preparing hard disk, 251–252
   previous installation, 251
   release notes, 258
   root password, 256
   selecting language, 251
   service configuration, 257
   Software Selection screen, 253–255
   starting installation, 250
   test Internet connection, 257
   time zone, 255–256
   user authentication method, 257
   Warning dialog box, 256
instance description, 438
instance enqueue (LCK0) background process, 47
INSTANCE event type, 438
Instance Management page, 535
Instance Storage page, 538
INSTANCE_GROUPS parameter, 111
INSTANCE_NAME parameter, 41
INSTANCE_NUMBER parameter, 41
INSTANCE_TYPE parameter, 213–214
instances
   adding, 535–538, 540
   administering using Server Control Utility
      (SRVCTL)
      checking status of instance, 481
      configuration of instance, adding new, 481
      configuration of instance, modifying
         existing, 481–482
      configuration of instance, removing
         existing, 482
      disabling instance, 482
      enabling instance, 482
      overview, 480
      starting, 480
      starting instance, 480
      stopping instance, 480–481
   administering using SQL*Plus
      starting instance, 487
      stopping instance, 487–488

ASM
    adding manually, 210–211
    adding using DBCA, 206–208, 210
    background processes, 213–214
    creating disk group, 216
    deleting manually, 211–212
    deleting using DBCA, 211
    dropping disk group, 217
    failure groups, 215
    instance names, 213
    mirroring, 215
    modifying disk group, 216–217
    overview, 206, 213
    parameters, 214–215
    re-creating, 212
    redundancy, 216
    SGA, 213
    striping, 215
    using files instead of devices, 212
and database services
    determining current instance, 425–426
    determining current service, 426
    overview, 425
deleting, 540, 542, 544
Global Cache Service (GCS), 37
Global Enqueue Service (GES), 37
overview, 36–37
instance-specific code, 15
instance-specific parameters, 40
Instant Client, 608, 633
instruction bundles, 107
instruction-level parallelism (ILP), 106
INSV operation, Data Guard, 47
Intel Hyper-Threaded CPUs, 679
Interactive System Activity Grapher (isag) utility, 680
interconnect configuration, 243
interconnect network, 523
interconnect traffic per second value, 657
interinstance resource operations, 669
interMedia.sql, 358
Internet connection, testing, 257
Internet FC Protocol (iFCP), 141
Internet Protocol Configuration Assistant (VIPCA), 404
Internet small computer system interface (iSCSI), 138, 141–142, 166–170
interval parameter, 653
Interval Time Counter (ITC) register, 263
INTSIZE_CSEC column, 515
invalidation (IV) instance lock, 579
invalidation locks, 579
inventory, 323
Inventory dialog box, 547, 551
I/O (input/output) attributes, 118
I/O operations per second (IOPS), 127
I/O option, 188
IOPS (I/O operations per second), 127
iostat utility, 678
IOTs (Index-Organized Tables), 76, 89, 108

iowait time, 675
IP address, 243
IP port number, 183
ip_address node section, 191
ip_address parameter, /etc/ocfs.conf
    configuration file, 175
ip_port node section, 191
ip_port parameter, /etc/ocfs.conf configuration
    file, 175
IS_SYSMODIFIABLE column, 488
isag (Interactive System Activity Grapher) utility,
    680
iSCSI (Internet small computer system
    interface), 138, 141–142, 166–170
iscsi nodename command, 167
iscsi start command, 167
iscsi-initiator-utils RPM package, 167
iscsi-ls command, 170
Issue/schedule stage, 106
Itanium-based systems, 100, 238, 240, 241, 242,
    250
ITC (Interval Time Counter) register, 263
ITEM table, 86
Iterations value, 615, 628
IV (invalidation) instance lock, 579

■J
Java 2 Platform, Standard Edition (J2SE), 633
Java Database Connectivity (JDBC), 34
Java Development Kit (JDK), 277
Java pool variable value, 102
Java Runtime Environment (JRE), 633
Java virtual machine (JVM), 633
Java-based daemon, 367
Java-Based tests, defining, 645–646
JBOD (Just a Bunch of Disks), 131
JDBC (Java Database Connectivity), 34
JDBC protocol, 368
JdbcTaskImpl abstract class, 645
JDK (Java Development Kit), 277
jitter, 139
Job Classes, 429
job coordinator background process (CJQ0),
    500
job Scheduler, 19
JOB_QUEUE_PROCESSES initialization
    parameter, 45
Jobs, 429
JRE (Java Runtime Environment), 633
JServer.sql, 357
Just a Bunch of Disks (JBOD), 131
JVM (Java virtual machine), 633

■K
Kerberos authentication, 224
kernel parameters, 164, 175, 188, 523
    example, 271–272
    network parameters
        net.core.rmem_default, 270
        net.core.rmem_max, 270

net.core.wmem_default, 270
net.core.wmem_max, 270
net.ipv4.conf.default.rp_filter, 270
net.ipv4.ip_forward, 270
net.ipv4.ip_local_port_range, 269
net.ipv4.tcp_keepalive_intvl, 271
net.ipv4.tcp_keepalive_probes, 271
net.ipv4.tcp_keepalive_time, 271
net.ipv4.tcp_retries2, 270–271
net.ipv4.tcp_rmem, 270
net.ipv4.tcp_syn_retries, 270–271
net.ipv4.tcp_wmem, 270
overview, 269
open files, 271
overview, 264–265
semaphores, 268–269
shared memory
kernel.shmall, 267
kernel.shmmax, 266
kernel.shmmni, 266
overview, 265–266
vm.nr_hugepages, 267–268
kernels, 23, 73, 662
KEYANDTHINK variable, 629–630
keyboard, video, mouse (KVM) switch, 248
keyboard configuration, Red Hat Enterprise
Linux 4 AS, 238
KGLNAHSH column, 578
kill script, 388
KJBLLOCK column, 565
KJBRNAME column, 569
KJBRRESP column, 564
Korn shell, 390
KVM (keyboard, video, mouse) switch, 248

■L
L* lock, 577
Lamport SCN generation scheme, 603
language selection
Red Hat Enterprise Linux 4 AS, 238
SUSE Linux Enterprise Server, 251
Language Selection page, 244
large object (LOB) structures, 427
Large pool variable value, 102
LARGE_POOL_SIZE parameter, 215
LaRoche, Florian, 28
LATCHES command, 560
latency, 130, 720
LB (cache object lock), 564
LB lock, 577
LCK0 (instance enqueue) background process,
47
LCK0 background process, 567, 576
LD_ASSUME_KERNEL environment variable,
276
LD_LIBRARY_PATH environment variable, 275,
434, 609
LDAP (Lightweight Directory Access Protocol)
servers, 236
least recently used (LRU) algorithm, 43

Least Recently Used (LRU) algorithm, 240
less command, 393
LGWR (log writer), 41, 125, 585
LGWR ASYNC configuration, 724
LGWR attribute, 726
LGWR background process, 43, 56, 126–127,
719, 721–722
LGWR network server (LNSn) background
process, 721
LGWR SYNC AFFIRM configuration, 724
LGWR SYNC NOAFFIRM configuration, 724
LHWM (low high water mark), 75
lib directory, 608
libaio packages, 250
library cache, 577, 658, 669–670
library cache locks
hash values, 578
invalidation locks, 579
namespaces, 578
overview, 577–578
types of, 578–579
LIBRARY_CACHE command, 560
license, 24–25
license agreement
Red Hat Enterprise Linux 4 AS, 247
SUSE Linux Enterprise Server, 251
Lightweight Directory Access Protocol (LDAP)
servers, 236
LILO (Linux Loader), 398
linear scalability, 6
LINEITEM table, 91, 92, 95, 97
link option, 177
link option, /etc/init.d/oracleasm script, 203
LINPACK Benchmark, 102
Linux. See also Linux administration
Asianux, 29
history of, 21–25
free software, 22–23
open source, 24–25
overview, 21
Unix, 21–22
overview, 21
performance monitoring
free command, 673–675
iostat command, 678
mpstat command, 678–679
netstat command, 677–678
overview, 672
ps command, 672–673
system activity reporter (sar), 679–681
top command, 675–676
vmstat command, 676
Red Hat Enterprise Linux, 26–27
SUSE Linux Enterprise Server, 27–28
Unbreakable Linux initiative, 25–26
Linux administration
bash shell
command history, 390
commands, 392–393
environment variables, 390–391

for loops, 391–392
overview, 389–390
Tab completion, 390
booting system
bootloaders, 398–399
initial ramdisk image, 399
overview, 398
debugging, 400
file systems
general file systems, 396–397
NFS, 397–398
kernel parameters, 394–395
log files, 400
manual pages, 388–389
overview, 385
packages, 393–394
run levels, 385–386
services, 387–388
swap space, 395–396
terminal sessions, 388
tracing, 400
Linux I/O scheduling, 143–144
Linux kernel, 235
Linux kernel parameter settings, 265
Linux Loader (LILO), 398
Linux Second Extended File System (Ext2 fs), 93
Linux SMP kernel, 103
Linux x86-64 server/processor architecture, 101
Linux-based RAC clusters, 236
LIST command, 709–710
list partitions, 80
listdisks option, 203, 205
listener, administering using Server Control
        Utility (SRVCTL), 484–485
LISTENER attribute, 495
Listener configuration, 546
listener process, 208, 544–547
listener.ora file, 172, 380, 736, 738
LKDEBUG utility
converting locks, 570
converting resources, 570
enqueue summary, 571
GES SGA summary information, 571
locks, 566–567
object remastering request, 572
overview, 563
processes, 567–569
resource hash buckets, 570
resource names, 569
resources, 563–565
traffic controller information, 571
LM_RES_HASH_ bucket parameter, 570
LMD0 background process, 576
LMDn background process, 46
LMON background process, 566
LMS process, 665
LMS0 process, 574
LMSn background process, 561
LMSn background processes, 571
ln -s command, 287

LNSn (LGWR network server) background
        process, 721
LNSn operation, Data Guard, 47
load balancing, 202
load balancing advisory, 505
load balancing advisory monitors, 495
Load Generators tab, 642
Load Profile section, 655
Load testing, 83
load testing and benchmarks, 83–85
LOAD_BALANCE parameter, 494
load_lineitem.log log file, 96
load-balancing hardware, 370
loader activity, 368
LOB (large object) structures, 427
Local address field, 677
local and shared storage
BFILEs, 427
custom features, 428
directories, 427
external tables, 427
overview, 427
UTL_FILE package, 428
local block, 583
local disk, archived redo logs written to, 716
local indexes, 78
local Oracle homes, 66
local resource coordination, 575
local stored scripts, 688
local time, 245
locally managed tablespaces, 74
localport entry, 440
localport parameter, 443
LOCATION attribute, 726
lock conversions, 671–672
lock mode, 589, 591
lock types, 577
locking events, 669
LOCKS command, 560
lockstep mode, 4
log apply services, 723
log file sync event, 127
log files, 400
Log Output to Temp option, 615–616
log writer (LGWR), 41, 125, 585
LOG_ARCHIVE_CONFIG parameter, 728
LOG_ARCHIVE_DEST_10 parameter, 699
LOG_ARCHIVE_DEST_n parameter, 716,
        726–727
LOG_ARCHIVE_DEST_STATE_n parameter,
        726–727
LOG_ARCHIVE_FORMAT parameter, 727–728
LOG_ARCHIVE_START parameter, 44, 727
LOG_CHECKPOINT_INTERVAL parameter, 127,
        605
LOG_CHECKPOINT_TIMEOUT parameter, 90,
        127
logfile entry, 440
logging, 423
logical design, 59

logical I/O, 73
logical standby, 56–57, 718
logical standby databases, 7, 62
logical unit numbers (LUNs), 93, 147, 154, 172
Logical Volume Managers (LVMs), 172, 201
login, Red Hat Enterprise Linux 4 AS, 249
Login to Database page, 466
loglevel entry, 440
Logon storms, 495
london1 nodes, 199, 299
london2 nodes, 199, 299
LONG connection load balancing, 496
long-lived connections, 49
loop devices, 212
losetup command, 212
low high water mark (LHWM), 75
lpfc driver, 150
LRU (least recently used) algorithm, 43, 240
ls command, 227–228, 388
ls -l command, 415
ls option, 415, 462
lsct command, 228–229
lsdg command, 229
lsmod command, 150
lsnrctl command, 510
LSNRCTL utility, 33, 476, 485
LSP0 operation, Data Guard, 47
LSP1 operation, Data Guard, 47
LSP2 operation, Data Guard, 47
lspci command, 288
LUNs (logical unit numbers), 93, 147, 154, 172
LVMs (Logical Volume Managers), 172, 201

■M

M000 slave process, MMON, 653
MAC (Media Access Control) address, 159
Machine Check Architectures, 116–117
machine name (mach), 199
Maintenance tab, Enterprise Manager (EM)
    Data Movement section, 474–475
    High Availability section, 474
    overview, 474
    Software Deployments section, 475
Makefile, 94
man command, 388
Manage Service button, 503
Manage Templates option, 345
Manageability Infrastructure, 364–365, 368, 649
Manageability Monitor Light (MMNL) process, 364
Manageability Monitor (MMON), 364
Managed Recovery (MRP0) background
    process, 723
Management Agent, 365, 367–368, 371, 384
Management Agent Home, 367, 368, 369, 378
Management Options page, 334
Management Repository, 363, 365, 366–368, 369, 372, 378, 384
Management Server, 367
Management Service, 363, 365, 367–369

Management Service Home (OMS Home), 367
Management Services, 366, 382
management software, 9
managing voting disks, 410–411
mandatory background processes, 42
    CKPT background process, 44
    DBWn background process, 43
    LGWR background process, 43
    MMAN background process, 44
    MMNL background process, 44
    MMON background process, 44
    PMON background process, 42–43
    SMON background process, 42
manual pages, 388–389
MANUAL value, 729
Manually Partition with Disk Druid option, 239
map command lists, 238
master boot record (MBR), 156, 239, 398
Master Mode, 628
MAX_COMMIT_PROPAGATION_DELAY
    parameter, 41, 603
MAX_JOB_SLAVE_PROCESSES parameter, 429
MAXCORRUPT <number> option, 700
maximum availability mode, 56, 719
maximum performance mode, 56, 719
maximum protection, 56
MAXIMUM PROTECTION mode, 39, 719–720
Maximum Transmission Unit (MTU), 123
MAXLOGFILES parameter, 722
MAXLOGMEMBERS parameter, 722
MB (modify the Size) option, 242
MBR (master boot record), 156, 239, 398
mean time between failures (MTBF), 142
mean time to recovery (MTTR), 66, 683, 692
Media Access Control (MAC) address, 159
Media Independent Interface (MII) link
    monitoring, 288
Media Management Layer (MML), 685
Member Disk Page, Enterprise Manager, 223
memory
    memory RAID, 114–115
    overview, 112
    physical memory, 112–114
    virtual memory, 112
memory addressability, 101
Memory Controller, 114
Memory Management Unit (MMU), 112
memory RAID, 114–115
memory section, 676
Memory tab, 340
MESI (Modified Exclusive Shared Invalid)
    protocol, 109
MetaLink, 375, 528
metaLUN, 147
METHOD attribute, 431
metrics and thresholds, 518–519
MGMT_METRICS_1DAY table, 367
MGMT_METRICS_1HOUR table, 367
MGMT_METRICS_RAW table, 367–368
MGMT_SEVERITY table, 369

MGMT_TABLESPACE tablespace, 367
MGMT_TABLESPACE_ECM_DEPOT_TS
    tablespace, 367
MII (Media Independent Interface) link
    monitoring, 288
minibench, 643
MINIMIZE LOAD clause, 703
minimize the mean time to recovery (MTTR),
    692
MINIMIZE TIME clause, 703
Minix operating system, 23
Miracle Linux, 29
MIRROR keyword, 220
mirrored (Normal) disk group, 210
mirroring, 137–138, 201, 215
misscount parameter, 263, 410
mission-critical application, 70
mkalias command, 229
mkdir command, 229–230
mkfs command, 396
mkfs.ocfs command, 178, 196
mkfs.ocfs2 command, 194
mkinitrd command, 151, 399
mkpart command, 284
mkswap command, 241
MMAN process, 44, 102
MML (Media Management Layer), 685
MMNL background process, 44, 364, 649
MMON background process, 44, 52, 364, 649
MMU (Memory Management Unit), 112
mode parameter, 288
Modified Exclusive Shared Invalid (MESI)
    protocol, 109
Modified Owned Exclusive Shared Invalid
    (MOESI) protocol, 109
Modified Shared Invalid (MSI) protocol, 109
MODIFIED_PARAMETERS command, 560
MODIFY SERVICE procedure, 496
modify the Size (MB) option, 242
MODIFY_SERVICE, 496, 509
modifying disk groups, 216–217
modprobe command, 151, 524
modprobe.conf file, 264
MOESI (Modified Owned Exclusive Shared
    Invalid) protocol, 109
MonitoredDatabaseList section, 635
monitoring
    Active Session History (ASH), 52
    Automatic Database Diagnostic Monitor
        (ADDM), 52
    Automatic Storage Management (ASM)
        dynamic performance views, 231
        fixed views, 231–233
        overview, 231
    Automatic Workload Repository (AWR), 52
    dynamic performance views, 52–53
    enterprise manager (EM), 52
    operating system utilities, 51
    overview, 51
    statistics, 53

monitoring database services
    data dictionary views, 511–512
    dynamic performance views, 512
        GV$ACTIVE_SERVICES, 513
        GV$SERV_MOD_ACT_STATS, 517–518
        GV$SERVICE_EVENT, 516
        GV$SERVICE_STATS, 516–517
        GV$SERVICE_WAIT_CLASS, 515–516
        GV$SERVICEMETRIC, 513–514
        GV$SERVICEMETRIC_HISTORY, 514–515
        GV$SERVICES, 512
    metrics and thresholds, 518–519
    overview, 511
    trace, 519
monitoring software, 9
more command, 393
mount command, 177, 195, 396, 398
Mount Point drop-down list, 241, 242, 252
mounted.ocfs, 185
mounted.ocfs2, 198
mounting
    OCFS file systems, 178–179
    OCFS2 file systems, 195–197
mpstat command, 678–679
MRP0 (Managed Recovery) background
    process, 47, 723
MS-DOS-based master boot record (MBR)
    format, 239
MSI (Modified Shared Invalid) protocol, 109
MTBF (mean time between failures), 142
MTTR (mean time to recovery), 66, 683, 692
MTU (Maximum Transmission Unit), 123
multi-drop-bus architecture, 113
multinode configuration, 71
multinode RAC database, 60
multipathing device drivers, 678
multipathing software, 9
multiple path support, 148
multiple SGAs
    DBMS_ALERT package, 426
    DBMS_PIPE package, 426–427
    overview, 426
    session variables package, 427
multiplexed blocks, 692
multitier applications, tracing, 557–558
multiuser load test, 615
mutual exclusion (mutex) locking, 621
mytransaction.jar directory, 646

N
N* lock, 577
na_admin graphical interface, 159
name cluster section, 191
NAME column, 84
name node section, 191
named-user licensing model, 10
namespaces, 578
NAS (Network Area Storage), 138, 144–146, 381
NAS-certified storage vendor, 381
Native POSIX Thread Library for Linux (NPTL), 608

Navisphere agent, 153
NB_ORA_SERV parameter, 696
NEED BACKUP option, REPORT command, 708
Net Service Name, 485
NetApp (Network Appliance) Filer model
    FAS920c, 158
NetApp Filer environment, 164
NetApp filer RAID configurations, 158–159
NetBackup Media Management Layer, 696
NetBackup tapeserver, 696
NETCA (Network Configuration Assistant),
    53–54, 208, 331, 521, 530
netdev keyword, 397
netstat command, 677–678
Network Address Setup page, 256
Network Appliance (NetApp) Filer model
    FAS920c, 158
Network Area Storage (NAS), 138, 144–146, 381
Network Cards Configuration page, 256
network configuration
    Red Hat Enterprise Linux 4 AS, 243
    SUSE Linux Enterprise Server, 256
Network Configuration Assistant (NETCA),
    53–54, 208, 331, 521, 530
Network Configuration page, 243
network connectivity, 321–322
Network File System (NFS), 144–145, 160–164,
    381, 397–398, 716
Network Information Service (NIS) servers, 236
network infrastructure, 9
Network Interface Cards (NICs), 9, 118, 142
Network Interfaces page, 405
network I/O
    overview, 118
    PCI, 118
    PCI-Express, 119
    PCI-X, 118–119
network parameters
    net.core.rmem_default, 270
    net.core.rmem_max, 270
    net.core.wmem_default, 270
    net.core.wmem_max, 270
    net.ipv4.conf.default.rp_filter, 270
    net.ipv4.ip_forward, 270
    net.ipv4.ip_local_port_range, 269
    net.ipv4.tcp_keepalive_intvl, 271
    net.ipv4.tcp_keepalive_probes, 271
    net.ipv4.tcp_keepalive_time, 271
    net.ipv4.tcp_retries2, 270–271
    net.ipv4.tcp_rmem, 270
    net.ipv4.tcp_syn_retries, 270–271
    net.ipv4.tcp_wmem, 270
    overview, 269
Network Time Protocol (NTP), 259, 261–262
Network Time Protocol tab, 248
networking requirements, installing Linux,
    236–237
NEXTVAL pseudocolumn, 71
NFS (Network File System), 144–145, 160–164,
    381, 397–398, 716

NFS Mounted Installation option, 381
nfs service, 397
nfslock service, 397
NFS-mounted file system, 370
NIC teaming software, 123
NICs (Network Interface Cards), 9, 118, 142
NIS (Network Information Service) servers, 236
NLS_LANG environment variable, 275
NOAFFIRM attribute, 722, 727
NOARCHIVELOG mode, 706, 731
NOCACHE clause, 72
NOCATALOG option, 686
NOCHECKSUM option, 700
noconfig option, 379
Node Addition Summary page, 529
node affinity
    Advanced Queuing (AQ), 428–429
    overview, 428
    scheduler, 429–430
node applications
    administering using Server Control Utility
        (SRVCTL)
        adding node applications, 484
        configuration of node applications,
            checking, 483–484
        overview, 482–483
        removing node applications, 484
        starting node applications, 483
        status of node applications, checking, 484
        stopping node applications, 483
    Global Services Daemon (GSD), 34
    listener, 33
    Oracle Notification Service (ONS)
        Fast Application Notification (FAN), 33
        Fast Connection Failover (FCF), 34
        overview, 33
    overview, 33
    virtual IP (VIP), 34
Node Configuration dialog box, 190
NODE event type, 438
Node events, 437
node failure, 60, 582
Node independence property, 447
node number (nodenum), 199
node option, 408
Node Selection page, 206, 329, 332, 537
node_count cluster section, 191
nodelist parameter, 406
nodereach check, 295
nodes, 14
    adding
        configuring listener, 530–534
        configuring network, 523
        configuring storage, 524–525
        installing and configuring new hardware,
            523
        installing operating system, 523–524
        installing Oracle Clusterware, 525–528
        installing Oracle Database software,
            528–530

overview, 522
  planning installation, 522–523
configuration, 186
deleting
  deleting ASM instance, 544
  deleting listener process, 544–547
  deleting Oracle Clusterware software,
    550–551
  deleting Oracle Database software,
    547–548
  disabling Oracle Clusterware applications,
    549–550
  from OCR, 550
  overview, 544
  removing node-specific interface
    configuration, 548–549
  updating inventories on remaining hosts,
    548, 551
  verifying node deletion using Cluster
    Verification Utility (CLUVFY), 552
  section, 191
nodes entry, 440
nodes parameter, 443
node-specific interface, 407
nodevips parameter, 406
NODG_CONFIG parameter, 728
nointr parameter, NFS, 164
NOLOG option, 486
NOLOGGING attribute, 725–726, 732
NOLOGGING statements, 709
nondefault passwords, 343
nonpartitioned index, 78
nonpartitioned object, 76
nontransactional system, 84
NonUniform Memory Access (NUMA), 236
nonvolatile RAM (NVRAM), 159
NORECEIVE parameter, 728
NOREDO options, 713
Normal (mirrored) disk group, 210
normal redundancy, 216, 311
Normal shutdown mode, 470
NOSEGMENT indexes, 76
NOSEND parameter, 728
nosharedhome argument, 549
nosharedvar parameter, 549
NOT BACKED UP [SINCE TIME <time>] option,
    700
NOT BACKED UP clause, 702
NOT BACKED UP n TIMES clause, 702
nowelcome argument, 371
NPTL (Native POSIX Thread Library for Linux),
    608
nr_requests parameter, 143
NSV0 operation, Data Guard, 47
NTP (Network Time Protocol), 259, 261–262
ntpdate command, 262
null (N), 582–583
null lock, 591
Null resource mode, 583
NUMA (NonUniform Memory Access), 236

number node section, 191
Number of node slots option, 194
numeric file names, 218
numeric value, 214
NVRAM (nonvolatile RAM), 159

▮O

o_direct flag, 196, 285
o_direct option, 188
O2CB driver, 192
o2cb service, 192–193
o2cb start command loads, 193
OBSOLETE option, REPORT command, 708
OC4J (Oracle Application Server Container for
    J2EE), 380
OCFS. See Oracle Cluster File System
OCFS format dialog box, 183
ocfs module, 176
OCFS partition, 173
OCFS Resize dialog box, 184
ocfs_support packages, 175
ocfs_uid_gen shell script, 176
ocfs_uid_gen utility, 183
OCFS2, 20
OCFS2 daemon processes, 189
ocfs2cdsl command, 199
ocfs2console GUI utility, 189
ocfs2console tool, 194–195, 197
ocfs2-tools package, 188
ocfsconsole package, 188
ocfsextfinder, 186
ocfslsnr daemon process, 177
ocfs-support package, 179
ocfstool, 179–184
ocfs-tools package, 179
OCI (Oracle Call Interface), 34, 433, 607
OCR. See Oracle Cluster Registry
OCR configuration tool (OCRCONFIG), 55, 408,
    417
  adding OCR file, 420
  backing up OCR, 416–417
  deleting OCR file, 420
  downgrading OCR, 419–420
  exporting OCR, 418–419
  importing OCR, 419
  moving OCR, 418
  overriding OCR mirroring, 421
  overview, 416
  repairing OCR configuration, 420–421
  replacing OCR file, 420
  restoring OCR, 417–418
  upgrading OCR, 419
OCR High Availability (HA) Framework, 446
OCR location file (ocr.loc), 549
OCR mirror file, 311
OCR mirror location, 403
OCRCHECK utility, 408, 417, 421
ocrcheck_<pid>.log file, 421
ocrcheck.log file, 421
ocrconfig_<pid>.log file, 416

ocrconfig_loc parameter, 418
ocrconfig.log file, 416, 418
OCRDUMP, 408, 422
ocrdump_<pid>.log file, 422
OCRDUMPFILE, 422
ocrdump.log file, 422
ocr.loc (OCR location file), 549
OCSSD (Oracle Cluster Synchronization
    Services Daemon), 17
ocssd daemon, 402, 412
OEM (Oracle Enterprise Manager), 50, 632
OFA (Oracle Flexible Architecture) directory,
    540
OIFCFG (Oracle Interface Configuration), 54,
    407–408
oinstall group, 272, 286, 298, 321
OLM (Oracle Lock Management) services, 644
olsnodes command, 315, 550
OLTP (online transaction processing), 6, 84, 622
OMF (Oracle Managed Files), 699
OMF-generated file name, 219
OMS Configuration stage, 378
OMS Home, 377
OMS Home (Management Service Home), 367
oms10g/install/unix/scripts/omsstup script,
    380
onboard RAID storage, 116
one-to-one mapping, 79, 217
online recovery, 148
online redo logs, 35, 174
online transaction processing (OLTP), 6, 84, 622
ONLINELOG template, 220
ONS. See Oracle Notification Service
ONS daemon, 443
ons.config file, 443
onsctl ping command, 441
ONSCTL utility, 441
Open Group, The, 22
OPEN option, 221
open software, 24–25
Open Software Foundation (OSF), 22
Open Source Support web site, 172
OPEN_CURSORS parameter, 372
operating system
    cache, 172
    and RPM package checks, 259–260
    scalability, 5
    software, 9
    utilities, 51
Operating System Statistics section, 633
Operations page, 328, 535
OPMN (Oracle Process Management and
    Notification) utility, 380
opmnctl command, 380
opmnctl startall command, 380
opmnctl startproc ias-component=WebCache
    command, 381
opmnctl status command, 380
opmnctl stopall command, 380
OPROCD (Process Monitor Daemon), 17

oprocd process monitor daemon, 263
OPS (Oracle Parallel Server), 1, 19, 128, 575
optimizer statistics, 72–73
optimizing global cache, 604
optimizing global enqueues, 581
optional background processes, 44–45
ORA_NLS10 environment variable, 275
ORA-17008 error, 444
Oracle 9i feature compared with Oracle 10g, 302
    Active Session History (ASH), 18
    Automatic Database Diagnostic Monitor
        (ADDM), 18
    Automatic Storage Management (ASM), 18
    Automatic Workload Repository (AWR), 18
    Cluster Verification Utility, 19
    database creation scripts, 351
    Enterprise Manager, 18
    Fast Application Notification (FAN), 18
    job Scheduler, 19
    Oracle Clusterware, 17
    Oracle services, 18
    overview, 17
    Virtual IP, 17–18
Oracle Application Server Container for J2EE
    (OC4J), 380
Oracle availability, 100
Oracle binaries, 66
Oracle Call Interface (OCI), 34, 433, 607
Oracle cluster, 261
Oracle Cluster File System (OCFS), 18
    cluster file systems, 171–172
    OCFS Version 2 (OCFS2)
        configuring, 189, 191
        formatting OCFS2 partition, 194–195
        mounting OCFS2 file systems, 195–197
        o2cb service, 192–193
        overview, 188
        tools and utilities, 197–199
        tuning OCFS2 partition, 197
    overview, 171
    Version 1 (OCFS)
        backup and recovery, 179
        configuring, 175–176
        debugging OCFS, 186–187
        design considerations, 173–174
        formatting OCFS partition, 177
        mounting OCFS file systems, 178–179
        operating system utilities, 188
        overview, 172–173
        starting OCFS service, 176–177
        tools and utilities, 179–186
        tracing OCFS, 187–188
Oracle Cluster Manager (oracm), 20, 31
Oracle Cluster Ready Services, 17, 303
Oracle Cluster Registry (OCR), 17, 20, 32, 122,
    172, 196, 281, 324, 402–403, 502
    adding standby database to, 735
    deleting nodes from, 550
Oracle Cluster Synchronization Services
    Daemon (OCSSD), 17

Oracle Clusterware, 17, 298, 327, 370
  administering
    CRS control (CRSCTL), 408–413
    CRS_STAT, 413–415
    OCRCHECK, 421
    OCRCONFIG, 416–421
    OCRDUMP, 422
    overview, 408
  administering voting disks, 422–423
  applications, disabling, 549–550
  components, 401–402
  deleting, 550–551
  files
    Oracle Cluster Registry (OCR), 402–403
    overview, 402
    voting disk, 403
  installation, 243, 439
  installing
    adding node-specific interface
      configuration, 528
    overview, 525–527
    verifying Oracle Clusterware installation
      using Cluster Verification Utility
      (CLUVFY), 528
  logging, 423
  Oracle Cluster Registry (OCR), 32
  Oracle Clusterware High Availability
    Framework, 403
  Oracle Interface Configuration (OIFCFG),
    407–408
  overview, 31–32, 303, 401
  partitions, 143
  preinstallation tasks, 303–304
  running installer, 305–306, 308–309, 311–314
  verifying configuration, 304–305
  verifying installation, 314–315
  Virtual Internet Protocol Configuration
    Assistant (VIPCA), 404–407
  voting disk, 33
Oracle Clusterware High Availability
    Framework, 403
Oracle Clusterware High Availability (HA)
    Framework, 425
  commands
    crs_getperm, 459
    crs_profile, 454–458
    crs_register, 458
    crs_relocate, 462–463
    crs_setperm, 459–460
    crs_start, 460
    crs_stat, 461–462
    crs_stop, 461
    crs_unregister, 459
    overview, 454
  example application
    HAFDemoAction.c, 448–450
    HAFDemoClient.c, 451–452
    HAFDemo.h, 448
    HAFDemoServer.c, 450–451
    overview, 447

  implementing
    create application profile, 453–454
    create application VIP, 453
    overview, 452–453
    register application profile with Oracle
      Clusterware, 454
    testing failover, 454
  overview, 446–447
Oracle Clusterware Home directory, 325
Oracle Data Guard, 62, 85, 243, 717–719
Oracle Database 10g, 201, 404
Oracle Database 10g RAC node, 244
Oracle database licenses, 10
Oracle Database Server software, 301, 303
Oracle database software, 327
Oracle Database software
  deleting, 547–548
  installing, 528–530
  overview, 315
  running installer, 317–320
  verifying configuration, 315–317
Oracle Enterprise Manager (OEM), 50, 632
Oracle executables, 202
Oracle Flexible Architecture (OFA) directory,
    540
Oracle home directory, 202, 208
Oracle Home directory, 484
Oracle Home naming approach, 374
Oracle Installer, 260
Oracle Interface Configuration (OIFCFG), 54,
    407–408
Oracle JDBC drivers, 443
Oracle Lock Management (OLM) services,
    644
Oracle Managed Files (OMF), 699
Oracle Net configuration, 544
Oracle Net Listener, 476
Oracle Net Services listeners, 437
Oracle Notification Service (ONS), 4, 402, 443,
    476, 500, 528
  Fast Application Notification (FAN), 33
  Fast Connection Failover (FCF), 34
  ONSCTL utility, 441
  overview, 33, 439–441
Oracle Notification Service (ONS) API, 437
Oracle Parallel Server (OPS), 1, 19, 128, 575
Oracle performance monitoring tools, 672
Oracle Process Management and Notification
    (OPMN) utility, 380
Oracle Real Application Clusters database, 328,
    535
Oracle Secure Backup, 55
Oracle Service Name, 626
Oracle services, 18
Oracle Storage Compatibility Program (OSCP),
    137
Oracle Streams, 718
Oracle system identifier (SID), 274
Oracle Technology Network (OTN) web site,
    302, 371

Oracle Universal Installer (OUI), 53, 272, 381, 521, 524, 547
ORACLE_BASE directory, 240, 242, 278, 374
ORACLE_BASE environment variable, 274, 306, 328, 371
ORACLE_HOME directory, 31, 273, 374, 380, 609
ORACLE_HOME environment variable, 274, 275, 305, 317, 328, 371, 609
ORACLE_HOME opmn/bin directory, 380
ORACLE_LOADER, 94, 96
ORACLE_SID environment variable, 221, 224, 274, 360, 371
oracleasm createdisk option, 215
oracleasm kernel module, 204
oracleasm script, 203, 212
OracleHomes subdirectory, 374
OracleOCIFailover interface, 433
oracle.sysman.eml.mntr.emdRepConnectDescr iptor field, 380
oracle.sysman.top.agent argument, 371
oracle.sysman.top.em_seed argument, 371
oracm (Oracle Cluster Manager), 20, 31
ORADEBUG utility
    events
        overview, 572–573
        RAC-specific events, 573–574
    GC_ELEMENTS command, 561–562
    GES_STATE command, 561
    LKDEBUG utility
        converting locks, 570
        converting resources, 570
        enqueue summary, 571
        GES SGA summary information, 571
        locks, 566–567
        object remastering request, 572
        overview, 563
        processes, 567–569
        resource hash buckets, 570
        resource names, 569
        resources, 563–565
        traffic controller information, 571
    overview, 559–561
orainstRoot.sh script, 377
oraInventory directory, 374, 378
orapwd command, 353
orarun RPM package, 260
Oratcl command, 621, 627
Oratcl libraries, 609
ORDER BY clause, 89
ORDER clause, 72
Order Entry benchmark, 633
ORDERDATE column, 77
orderentry.browseandupdateorders procedure, 645
ORDERS dimension table, 91
orders table, 80, 92
ordinst.sql, 358
OSCP (Oracle Storage Compatibility Program), 137
OSF (Open Software Foundation), 22

OTN (Oracle Technology Network) web site, 302, 371
OUI (Oracle Universal Installer), 53, 272, 381, 521, 524, 547
/oui/bin directory, 379
overriding OCR mirroring, 421
overscaling rule, 88
overwrite option, OCRCONFIG, 416

██P
package group selection, Red Hat Enterprise Linux 4 AS, 245–247
package installation defaults, Red Hat Enterprise Linux 4 AS, 245
PAE (Page Addressing Extensions), 103
page (pg) command, 393
Page Addressing Extensions (PAE), 103
PARALLEL <degree> options, 713
Parallel Cache Management (PCM), 19
Parallel Data Pump operations, 111
Parallel DML, 111
parallel execution, 61, 501
Parallel Query operation, 111
PARALLEL_AUTOMATIC_TUNING parameter, 111
PARALLEL_INSTANCE_GROUP parameter, 111
PARALLEL_MAX_SERVERS parameter, 111
PARALLEL_MIN_SERVERS parameter, 111
PARALLEL_THREADS_PER_CPU parameter, 111
parallelization, 61, 107, 696–697
PARAMETER column, 580
parameter file (PFILE), 208, 702
PARAMETERFILE template, 220
parameters. See also kernel parameters
    backup optimization, 694–695
    backup type, 695
    channel device type, 695–696
    control file autobackup, 697
    default device type, 695
    excluding tablespaces, 698
    global parameters, 40
    initialization parameter file (PFILE), 38–39
    instance-specific parameters, 40
    overview, 37–38, 693
    parallelization, 696–697
    RAC-specific parameters, 40–42
    RAM utility, 686–687
    retention policy, 694
    server parameter file (SPFILE), 39
    setting, 410
    snapshot control file, 697–698
parsing, 581
PART dimension table, 91
parted command, 283
PARTIAL keyword, 703
partition key, 76, 78–79
partitioning, 76–81
partitioning map, 242
partitioning option, 76, 604

partitioning pane, 242
PARTSUPP fact table, 91
passwd command, 273
Password Management button, 343
passwords, setting for user, 273
past image (PI), 128, 584–585, 591
PATH environment variable, 275
path failover, 148
Path page, 163
Payment transaction, 88
PCI (Peripheral Component Interconnect), 118
PCI-Express, 118–119
PCM (Parallel Cache Management), 19
PCTFREE attribute, 74
PCTUSED attribute, 74
pdksh package, 390
performance bottlenecks, 649
performance monitoring
    Linux
        free command, 673–675
        iostat command, 678
        mpstat command, 678–679
        netstat command, 677–678
        overview, 672
        ps command, 672–673
        system activity reporter (sar), 679–681
        top command, 675–676
        vmstat command, 676
    Oracle
        Active Session History (ASH), 660–661
        automatic database diagnostic monitor
            (ADDM), 661–662
        dictionary cache, 670–671
        with Enterprise Manager (EM), 649–652
        global cache services (GCS), 664–669
        global enqueue service (GES), 669
        GV$ views, 663
        library cache, 669–670
        lock conversions, 671–672
        overview, 649
        segment statistics, 663–664
        system statistics, 663
        using SQL*Plus, 662–663
    overview, 649
Performance tab, 223, 651
performance testing, 84
performing backups, 700–703
performing recovery
    Block Media Recovery (BMR), 714
    overview, 712–713
performing restore, 710–712
Peripheral Component Interconnect (PCI), 118
Perl scripts, 365, 384
persistent parameters, 693
PGA (program global area), 126
PGA_AGGREGATE_TARGET parameter, 90, 94,
    102, 266, 354, 372
physical design, 59
physical memory, 112–114
physical standby, 56, 718

PHYSICAL STANDBY command, 740
physical standby database creation
    adding standby database to Oracle Cluster
        Registry (OCR), 735
    backing up primary database, 732–733
    checking standby configuration, 738
    configuring operating system, 730
    copying RMAN backup from primary to
        standby, 735
    creating directories on standby nodes,
        733–734
    creating initialization parameter files on
        standby nodes, 734
    creating password files on primary nodes,
        731–732
    creating password files on standby nodes,
        734
    creating server parameter file for standby
        database, 734
    creating standby database, 737–738
    enabling archiving on primary database,
        730–731
    enabling managed recovery on standby
        database, 738
    forcing logging on primary database, 732
    installing and configuring shared storage,
        730
    installing and patching operating system, 730
    installing management agents, 730
    installing Oracle Clusterware (CRS), 730
    installing Oracle Database software, 730
    overview, 729
    setting parameters on primary database, 733
    setting parameters on standby database, 737
    updating /etc/oratab on standby nodes, 735
    updating listener configuration files on
        standby nodes, 735–736
    updating Oracle Net configuration files on all
        nodes, 736–737
    verifying log transportation, 738–739
PI (past image), 128, 584–585, 591
PI buffer, 604
PI status column values, V$BH, 583
pidof command, 673
ping utility, 321, 524
PIPE namespace, 579
pipeline, 106
Platform errors, 116
PL/SQL autonomous transaction, 71
PL/SQL packages, 437, 685
PL/SQL Server Side Load, 626
PL/SQL stubs, 644–645
PLUS ARCHIVELOG clause, 702
PMON (process monitor) background process,
    42–43, 495
point-in-time snapshots, 66
port numbers, 224
porting centers, 60
ports, 224
POSIX-compliant cluster file system, 188

POSIX-compliant file system, 172
postDBCreation.sql, 359–360
POWER clause, 217
power management, 115–116
PowerPath, 147–149
preconnect service, 432
prefer keyword, 262
PREFER_LEAST_LOADED_NODE parameter, 495
PREFER_LEAST_LOADED_NODE_LISTENER_ NAME parameter, 380
PREFERRED instance, 497, 501
preupgrade checks, 54
PREVIEW [SUMMARY] option, 711
Price/tpmC value, 88
primary database, 56
primary service, 432
primary_instance parameter, 429
print command, 284
print option, 457
printf command, 389–393
printf library call, 389
priv suffix, 308
private interconnect selection
   Ethernet, 119–120
   overview, 119
   RDMA, 120–121
Private interface type, 407
private IP addresses, 236
private network, 63
Pro*C application, 88
Process Monitor Daemon (OPROCD), 17
process monitor (PMON) background process, 42–43, 495
PROCESSES parameter, 102, 340
processors
   32-bit or 64-bit, 101–104
   architecture overview, 104–105
   CPU cache, 108–110
   IA64 EPIC, 107
   multicore processors, 110–111
   overview, 101
   x86 and x86-64, 105–107
PROCESSSTATE command, 560
processTransactionEvent( ) method, 646
/proc/meminfo command, 674
procname argument, 629
/proc/scsi/scsi command, 157
/proc/slabinfo command, 675
Product-Specific Prerequisite Checks page, 318, 374, 382
program global area (PGA), 126
proprietary kernel module, 26
Proxy Information, 375
ps command, 486, 672–673
PSP0 background process, ASM, 48
pstree command, 386
Public interface type, 407
public IP addresses, 236
public network, 63

put command, 224
pwd command, 230

■Q
Q process name, 555
Q* lock, 577
qa option, 286
qgen program, 92, 94, 97
QMNC (queue monitor coordinator) process, 45
QMNn (queue monitor) background processes, 45
QphH (queries per hour), 92
QphH@Size (Composite Query-per-Hour Performance Metric), 86, 93
quad-pumped, 114
queries per hour (QphH), 92
query set, 92
query streams, 93
querydisk option, 203, 205
queue monitor coordinator (QMNC) process, 45
queue monitor (QMNn) background processes, 45

■R
RAC (Real Application Clusters). *See also* RAC design; RAC internals; RAC statistics of AWR reports; RAC-specific background processes
   alternatives to
      Data Guard, 16
      overview, 15
      single instance databases, 16
      third-party clustering solutions, 16
   clustered database concepts
      cluster terminology, 2–4
      disaster recovery, 7
      high availability, 4–5
      overview, 2
      scalability, 5–6
   connecting to RAC instance SQL*Plus, 486–487
   differences between Oracle 9i and Oracle 10g
      Active Session History (ASH), 18
      Automatic Database Diagnostic Monitor (ADDM), 18
      Automatic Storage Management (ASM), 18
      Automatic Workload Repository (AWR), 18
      Cluster Verification Utility, 19
      Enterprise Manager, 18
      Fast Application Notification (FAN), 18
      Oracle Clusterware, 17
      Oracle services, 18
      overview, 17
      Scheduler, 19
      Virtual IP, 17–18
   differences between single-instance and RAC databases, 16–17

history of, 19–20
I/O characteristics
asynchronous I/O, 128–129
direct I/O, 129–130
forced reads and writes, 128
overview, 125
read activity, 125–126
write activity, 126–128
overview, 1–2
and physical standby, 724–725
reasons for deploying
cost of ownership advantages and
benefits, 8–10
high availability advantages and
disadvantages, 10–12
manageability advantages and
disadvantages, 14–15
overview, 7
scalability advantages and disadvantages,
12–14
transparency advantages and
disadvantages, 15
vs. SMP, 8
RAC clusters, 59, 649
RAC database, 465, 478
RAC database option, 206
RAC design
application design
bind variables, 70
overview, 70
sequences, 70–72
architecture
development and test systems, 62
disaster recovery, 62–63
overview, 62
reporting systems, 64
spare servers, 65
stretch clusters, 63–64
business requirements
business constraints, 60–61
overview, 59
technical requirements, 59–60
upgrade policy, 61–62
database design
automatic segment space management
(ASSM), 74–75
cursor sharing, 72
dynamic sampling, 73
histograms, 73
locally managed tablespaces, 74
optimizer statistics, 72–73
overview, 72
partitioning, 76–81
reverse key indexes, 75–76
system statistics, 73
hardware requirements, 70
overview, 59
storage requirements
archived redo logs, 68–69
ASM and cluster file systems, 65

backup and recovery, 66–67
overview, 65
shared Oracle homes vs. local Oracle
homes, 66
RAC instance, 16
RAC internals
Global Cache Services (GCS)
cache coherency, 584
Cache Fusion, 584–599
disk writes, 599–603
Global Resource Directory (GRD), 582–583
optimizing global cache, 604
overview, 581
system change numbers (SCNs), 603
Global Enqueue Services (GES)
background processes, 576
library cache locks, 577–579
lock types, 577
optimizing global enqueues, 581
overview, 576
resources and enqueues, 576–577
row cache locks, 580
tracing GES activity, 581
instance recovery, 604–605
overview, 575–576
RAC option, 201
RAC standby database, 729
RAC statistics of AWR reports, interpreting
dictionary cache, 658
global cache efficiency percentages, 657
global cache (GCS) and enqueue services
(GES), 657–658
global cache load profile, 656–657
global cache transfer statistics, 660
global CR server statistics, 659
global current served statistics, 659
global enqueue statistics (GES), 659
library cache, 658
overview, 655
SQL statements, 658
Top 5 Timed Events, 656
RAC Technologies Compatibility Matrix
(RTCM), 100
RAC-based Management Repository, 380
racg directory, 423
racgevt process, 402
racgons utility, 440, 528, 549
RAC-specific background processes, 45
DIAG, 47
LCK0, 47
LMDn, 46
LMON, 46
LMSn, 46
RAC-specific development considerations
instances and database services
determining current instance, 425–426
determining current service, 426
overview, 425
local and shared storage
BFILEs, 427

Find it faster at http://superindex.apress.com/

custom features, 428
directories, 427
external tables, 427
overview, 427
UTL_FILE package, 428
multiple SGAs
DBMS_ALERT package, 426
DBMS_PIPE package, 426–427
overview, 426
session variables package, 427
node affinity
Advanced Queuing (AQ), 428–429
overview, 428
scheduler, 429–430
overview, 425
RAC-specific parameters, 40–42
RAID, 131
RAID 0 striping, 131–132, 155
RAID 0+1 mirrored stripes, 133–134
RAID 1 mirroring, 132–133, 155
RAID 1/0, 155
RAID 10 striped mirrors, 133
RAID 5, 134–135, 155
RAID group, 154
RAID on motherboard (ROMB), 131
RAID storage, onboard, 116
RAID system, 201
RAID with Double Parity (RAID-DP), 159
RAID-DP (RAID with Double Parity), 159
RAISEERROR option, 629
RAM (DDR), 112
RAM (SDRAM), 112
RAM plus swap space, 240
random reads, 125
random-number procedure, 620
range partitioning, 77, 79, 80
range scan operations, 76
raw command, 286
raw devices, 171
rawdevices file, 286
RBAL (rebalance master background process),
ASM, 213
RBAL background process, 45, 48, 214
RC_CHECKPOINT recovery catalog views, 692
RC_RESYNC recovery catalog views, 692
RC_STORED_SCRIPT recovery catalog views,
692
RC_STORED_SCRIPT_LINE recovery catalog
views, 692
RDBMS default value, 214
RDBMS executables, 103
RDBMS instance, 213
RDBMS instance background processes
Data Guard-specific background processes,
47
mandatory background processes, 42
checkpoint (CKPT) background process,
44
database writer (DBWn) background
process, 43

LGWR background process, 43
MMAN background process, 44
MMNL background process, 44
MMON background process, 44
PMON background process, 42–43
SMON background process, 42
optional background processes, 44–45
overview, 42
RAC-specific background processes, 45–47
RDBMS libraries, 103
RDBMS software, 730
RDBMS value, 213
RDMA (remote direct memory access), 94, 119,
120–121
read activity, 125–126
read-only mode, 723, 739
read-to-write transfer, 589
Real Application Clusters. See RAC
reason description, 438
reason=autostart reason type, 439
reason=boot reason type, 439
reason=dependency reason type, 439
reason=failure reason type, 439
reason=unknown reason type, 439
reason=user reason type, 439
rebalance master background process (RBAL),
ASM, 213
rebalancing slave processes, ASM, 213
reboot command, 386, 398
RECEIVE parameter, 728
RECO background processes, 45
recompiled kernel, 26
RECOVER command, 712
Recover process, 116
recovery area, 36
recovery catalog, 685, 689–692
Recovery Configuration page, 338
Recovery Manager (RMAN), 35, 55, 217, 472,
683, 725
backup sets, 692–693
block change tracking, 706–707
copying RMAN backup from primary to
standby, 735
database control commands, 688
Flashback Recovery Area, 698–700
housekeeping, 707–710
image copies, 703–705
incremental backups, 705–706
incrementally updated backups, 707
overview, 685–686
parameters, 686–687, 693–698
performing backups, 700–703
performing recovery, 712–714
performing restore, 710–712
repository, 689–692
RMAN utility, 686–689
RUN commands, 688–689
scripts, 687–688
spooling output, 687
tags, 693

Recovery Point Objective (RPO), 66
recovery scripts, 687
RECOVERY WINDOW OF <number> DAYS
    option, 708
RECOVERY_CATALOG_OWNER permission,
    690
RECOVERY_PARALLELISM parameter, 713
re-creating ASM instance, 212
recursive sessions, 660
recv directory, 370
Recv-Q field, 677
Red Hat Certified Engineer (RHCE) program, 26
Red Hat Enterprise Linux 4 AS
    additional CDs, 249
    additional language support, 244
    Anaconda installation, 238
    Boot Loader Configuration page, 243
    date and time, 248
    disk partitioning, 239–242
    display, 248
    finishing setup, 249
    firewall configuration, 244
    installation media check, 238
    installing packages, 247
    keyboard configuration, 238
    language selection, 238
    license agreement, 247
    login, 249
    manual package installation, 249–250
    network configuration, 243
    overview, 237
    package group selection, 245–247
    package installation defaults, 245
    reasons for registering, 249
    root password configuration, 245
    start installation, 247
    starting installation
        on Itanium, 238
        overview, 237
        on x86 or x86-64, 237
    system user, 249
    time zone selection, 244–245
    upgrade option, 238–239
    Welcome screen, 247
Red Hat Enterprise Linux WS (Workstation), 27
Red Hat Login page, 249
Red Hat Network, 249
Red Hat Package Manager (RPM), 393
Redo log variable value, 102
redo logs, 35, 603, 689, 721
redo transport services
    ARCn background process, 721
    asynchronous network I/O (ASYNC),
        721–722
    LGWR background process, 721
    overview, 720
    synchronous network I/O (SYNC), 722
redo vectors, 718
redundancy, 215
REDUNDANCY <number> option, 708

redundancy level, 219
redundancy supported by ASM, 216
Redundant Array of Independent Disks. *See*
    RAID
registering Red Hat Enterprise Linux 4 AS, 249
Relational Database Management System. *See*
    RDBMS
release notes, SUSE Linux Enterprise Server, 258
remote direct memory access (RDMA), 94, 119,
    120–121
Remote File Server (RFS) background process,
    720, 722, 728
remote mirroring, 137
remote mirroring technologies, 137–138
remote server management, 117
REMOTE_ARCHIVE_ENABLE parameter, 728
REMOTE_LISTENER parameter, 354
REMOTE_LOGIN_PASSWORDFILE parameter,
    486, 731, 734
remoteport parameter, 440, 443
RENAME alias clause, 219
repair option, OCRCONFIG, 416, 420
repairing OCR configuration, 420–421
Repeat Delay(ms) value, 615
replace command, 420
replace option, OCRCONFIG, 416, 420
replacement server, 65
replacing OCR file, 420
REPORT command, 708–709
reporting systems, 64
Require Secure Communication, 376
Required Media dialog box, 247
RESETLOGS option, 691
Resident Set Size, 675
resize option, 184
resizeocfs, 185
Resource Manager, 497, 498, 499–500
Resource Manager subsection, of Database
    Administration section of
    Administration tab, Enterprise
    Manager (EM), 473
resource master, 582, 585
resource master instance, 599
restart argument, 286
restart command, 289
restart option, /etc/init.d/oracleasm script, 203
RESTORE <scope> [<options>] command, 711
RESTORE operation, 689, 710
restore option, OCRCONFIG, 416, 418–419
restoring OCR, 417–418
restrict line default, 262
retention parameter, 653
retention policy, 694
Retire stage, 106
RETRIES attribute, 431
REVERSE clause, 76
reverse key indexes, 75–76
RFS (Remote File Server) background process,
    720, 722, 728
RHCE (Red Hat Certified Engineer) program, 26

Ritchie, Dennis, 22
rm command, 199, 230
rmalias command, 230
RMAN. *See* Recovery Manager
RMAN >RESYNC CATALOG command, 690
RMAN backup, 732
RMAN command, 737
RMAN parameters, 474
RMAN template, 339
RMAN> BACKUP DATABASE command, 701
RMAN> BACKUP RECOVERY AREA command, 700
RMAN> DELETE FORCE NOPROMPT OBSOLETE command, 710
RMAN> DELETE OBSOLETE command, 710
RMAN> DROP DATABASE INCLUDING BACKUPS command, 710
RMAN> LIST BACKUP BY FILE command, 709
RMAN> LIST BACKUP command, 709
RMAN> LIST BACKUP SUMMARY command, 709
RMAN> LIST BACKUPSET ALL command, 709
RMAN> REPORT NEED BACKUP DAYS 3 command, 709
RMAN> REPORT NEED BACKUP INCREMENTAL 4 command, 708
RMAN> REPORT NEED BACKUP RECOVERY WINDOW 7 DAYS, 709
RMAN> REPORT OBSOLETE, 694, 709
RMAN> RESTORE DATABASE command, 711
rman.log file, 687
role management
    failover, 724, 740–741
    overview, 723, 739
    read-only mode, 723, 739
    switchover, 723, 739–740
ROMB (RAID on motherboard), 131
root (+) directory, 229
root partition (/), 240
root password
    Red Hat Enterprise Linux 4 AS, 245
    SUSE Linux Enterprise Server, 256
Root Password Configuration page, 245
root privileges, 530
root profile, 416
root user, 203, 312, 317, 320, 324, 327, 383, 453, 741
root.sh script, 263, 313, 320, 378, 383, 405, 527
rotations per minute (rpm), 130
Routing Configuration page, 256
row cache locks, 580
ROW_CACHE command, 560
RPM (Red Hat Package Manager), 393
rpm (rotations per minute), 130
rpm command, 250, 260
rpm suffix, 393
rpm utility, 394
RPO (Recovery Point Objective), 66
rsize/wsize parameter, NFS, 164
RSS field, 675

rstatd service, 387
RTCM (RAC Technologies Compatibility Matrix), 100
Run ASH Report button, 660
RUN command, 688–689, 695
Run Hammerora Loadtest button, 616, 619, 630
run levels, 385–386
runcluvfy.sh script, 292
runConfig.sh command, 379
runInstaller command, 371, 372, 382, 525
runlevel command, 386
Runlevel Editor, 387
rw parameter, NFS, 164
RX-ERR field, 677
RX-OK field, 677

■S

SAME (stripe-and-mirror-everything) methodology, 131
SAN. *See* storage area network
sar (system activity reporter), 679–681
sar binary format, 680
sar report, 679
SAS (Serial Attached SCSI), 140
S-ATA, 142–143
Save Current File button, 617
SaX2 utility, 258
/sbin/mkfs.ocfs utility, 177
SBT interface, 696
scalability
    overview, 5–6
    scale-out, 6
    scale-up, 6
    testing, 84
scandisks option, ASM, 205
scandisks option, /etc/init.d/oracleasm script, 203
scandisks procedure, 304
scattered read, 125
scatter/gather, 126
Scheduled Snapshots, 164
scheduler, 429–430, 500–501
Scheduler class, 500
Schedules, 429
Schema Details window, 637
Schema Sizing window, 637
SCN (system change number), 41, 127, 575, 603
SCOPE clause, 490
scp command, 280
scp utility, 322
screen resolution, 248
script-based database creation, 351
scripts, 687–688. *See also* database creation using scripts
SCSI (small computer system interface), 138, 139–140
scsi add-single-device command, 157
SCUR status column values, V$BH, 583
sd prefix, 139
SDK (Software Development Kit), 291

SDP (Sockets Direct Protocol), 120
seasonal peaks, 61
secondary_instance parameter, 429
secure shell, 322
secure shell (ssh), 32, 279
Security page, 163
seek time, 130
segment statistics, 663–664
Select Configuration Options page, 318
select failover, 431
Select Installation Type page, 318
Select Listener page, 546
Select Mode, 628
Select Operation page, 468
Select Protocols page, 533
SELECT statement, 49, 111, 431, 617, 631
Select Task window, 636
SELECT user FROM dual command, 621
self-tuning parameters, 490
semmni parameter, 269
semmns parameter, 269
semmsl parameter, 269
semop( ) system calls, 268
semopm parameter, 269
semopm semaphore, 271
SEND parameter, 728
Send-Q field, 677
SEQ$ data dictionary table, 71
sequence gaps, 72
sequences, 70–72
sequential numbers, 70
sequential reads, 125
Serial Attached SCSI (SAS), 140
SERV_MOD_ACT_TRACE_DISABLE procedure, 557
SERV_MOD_ACT_TRACE_ENABLE procedure, 557
server architecture
    additional platform features
        Machine Check Architectures, 116–117
        onboard RAID storage, 116
        overview, 115
        power management, 115–116
        remote server management, 117
        virtualization, 117
    memory
        memory RAID, 114–115
        overview, 112
        physical memory, 112–114
        virtual memory, 112
    overview, 101
    processors
        32-bit or 64-bit, 101–104
        architecture overview, 104–105
        CPU cache, 108–110
        IA64 EPIC, 107
        multicore processors, 110–111
        overview, 101
        x86 and x86-64, 105–107

Server Control Utility (SRVCTL), 17, 32, 33, 51, 221–222, 260, 402, 436, 475, 476, 487
    administering database services using
        adding database service, 505
        checking current database service configuration, 506
        checking current database service status, 506–507
        enabling and disabling database service, 507
        overview, 505
        relocating database service, 507
        removing database service, 507
        starting database service, 505–506
        stopping database service, 506
    commands, 484
    databases
        checking configuration of, 477–478
        checking status of, 478
        configuration, adding new, 478–479
        configuration, modifying existing, 479
        configuration, removing existing, 479
        disabling, 479
        enabling, 479–480
        overview, 477
        starting, 477
        stopping, 477
    instances
        checking status of, 481
        configuration, adding new, 481
        configuration, modifying existing, 481–482
        configuration, removing existing, 482
        disabling, 482
        enabling, 482
        overview, 480
        starting, 480
        stopping, 480–481
    listener
        configuration, checking, 485
        overview, 484–485
        starting, 485
        stopping, 485
    node applications
        adding, 484
        configuration, checking, 483–484
        overview, 482–483
        removing, 484
        starting, 483
        status of, checking, 484
        stopping, 483
    overview, 475–476
    syntax, 476
server management file (SRVM), 475
server parameter file (SPFILE), 34, 39, 208, 214–215, 331, 471, 489–490, 726
Server Side Log Directory, 626
ServerName parameter, 370
server-side callouts, 441–442
Server-side connection balancing, 493–497

SERVICE attribute, 726
service command, 324
service configuration, SUSE Linux Enterprise Server, 257
service definition file, 387
service description, 438
SERVICE event type, 438
Service events, 437
service level agreements (SLAs), 8, 60, 498, 683
Service Name hyperlink, 503
service rawdevices command, 286
SERVICE_NAME parameter, 508
SERVICE_NAMES parameter, 498
SERVICE_REGISTER parameter, 495
SERVICEMEMBER event type, 438
services, 48–49, 387–388
Services Management option, 349
services option, lsnrctl command, 510
session failover, 431
session variables package, 427
SESSION_CACHED_CURSORS parameter, 372, 670
SESSION_TRACE_ENABLE procedure, 555
SESSIONS ACTIVE, NOT ALLOWED command, 740
SET ARCHIVELOG DESTINATION command, 689, 712
SET ATTRIBUTE procedure, 430
SET AUTOLOCATE command, 715
SET NEWNAME command, 710
SET SQLPROMPT command, 486
SET_IDENTIFIER procedure, 558
SGA. See System Global Area
SGA command, 559
SGA_MAX_SIZE parameter, 102, 265–266
SGA_TARGET parameter, 44, 102, 265, 354, 372
SH user, 611
shared (S), 582–583
Shared Filesystem Loader, 370
shared memory parameters, 266
shared Oracle home, 66
Shared pool variable value, 102
Shared resource mode, 583
Shared Server mode, 341
shared storage. See local and shared storage
shared-all clusters, 3–4
shared-nothing clusters, 3
sharedvar parameter, 549
SHM_HUGETLB flag, 268
shmall parameter, 268
shmget( ) method, 265, 268
shmmax parameter, 266, 268
shmmax/system page, 267
shmmni parameter, 266
SHORT connection load balancing, 496
short-lived connections, 49
SHOW ALL command, 693
SHOW command, 693
show initiator command, 169
Show Output check box, 615, 619

Show Storage System Initiators check box, 153
showbackup option, 416, 417
SHUTDOWN ABORT option, 436, 470, 487–488
SHUTDOWN command, 221
SHUTDOWN NORMAL command, 487
SID (system identifier), 39, 490, 737
silent option, 406
Simple mode, 387
SINCE TIME clause, 702
single instance databases, 16
single point of failure (SPOF), 4
Single UNIX Specification, 22
single-instance environment, 16–17, 72, 213, 497
SIZE field, 675
Sizing tab, 340
SKIP <type> option, 701
slabtop utility, 675
SLAs (service level agreements), 8, 60, 498, 683
SLES8 (SuSE Enterprise Linux 8.0), 28
SLES9 (SUSE Linux Enterprise Server version 9), 28, 188, 250
small computer system interface (SCSI), 138, 139–140
SMALLFILE tablespaces, 356
SMON (system monitor) background process, 42
SMP (symmetric multiprocessing), 8
SMTP (specify a mail) server, 334
snapshot control file, 697–698
snapshot technologies, 137
SnapView Business Continuance Volumes (BCVs), 147
snooping protocol, 108
Sockets Direct Protocol (SDP), 120
soft limit, 278
Software Development Kit (SDK), 291
Software Selection screen, SUSE Linux Enterprise Server, 253–255
SORT_AREA_SIZE parameter, 90
source code, 24
source command, 391
Source Database page, 346
SourceFile attribute, 647
SP (speculative precomputation), 107
SPA (storage processor A), 146, 148
space allocation bitmap, 173
Spanning Tree Protocol (STP), 123
spare servers, 65
SPB (storage processor B), 148
SPB storage processor, 146
specify a mail (SMTP) server, 334
speculative precomputation (SP), 107
SPFILE (server parameter file), 34, 39, 208, 214–215, 331, 496, 514–516, 726, 734
SPFILE option, 711
SPFILE parameter, 42, 353, 360, 489
SPID column, 569
split brain syndrome, 57
split-brain scenario, 263

SPOF (single point of failure), 4
SPOOL command, 687
spooling output, 687
SQ lock, 577
SQL command, 688
SQL statement tracing, 610
SQL statements, 70, 658
SQL Tuning Advisor, 662
SQL*Plus, 51, 211–212, 224, 487, 512, 739
    ASM administration using, 221
    connecting to RAC instance SQL*Plus,
        486–487
    Oracle performance monitoring using,
        662–663
    overview, 485
    setting parameters in Initialization
        Parameter File (PFILE), 488–489
    setting parameters in Server Parameter File
        (SPFILE), 489–490
    setting SQL*Plus prompt, 486
    starting instance, 487
    stopping instance, 487–488
SQL*Plus package, 608, 611
SQL*Plus prompt, 653
SQL*Plus scripts, 718
SQLPATH environment variable, 276
SRV_PRECONNECT event type, 438
SRVCTL. See Server Control Utility
SRVM (server management file), 475
SRVM_TRACE environment variable, 277
ssh (secure shell), 32, 279–280
.ssh directory, 279
ssh utility, 322
ssh-add command, 305, 327
ssh-agent command, 305, 327
ssh-keygen command, 279
standard file system interface, 171
standby database, 56, 718
standby node, 739
standby redo logs, 722–723
STANDBY_ARCHIVE_DEST parameter, 728
STANDBY_FILE_MANAGEMENT parameter,
    729
start nodeapps command, 483
start option, 176, 448
start option, ASM, 204
start option, /etc/init.d/oracleasm script, 203
start string parameter, 448
start_options, 480, 505
START_SERVICE, 509
startall argument, 380
starting and stopping Oracle Clusterware, 409
startproc command, 381
STARTUP command, 221, 470, 487
STARTUP FORCE option, 221
STARTUP MOUNT option, 221
STARTUP NOMOUNT option, 221
STARTUP option, 495
STARTUP RESTRICT option, 221
Startup/Shutdown button, 468

startx command, 522
state dumps, 413
STATE field, 414, 677
stateful alerts, 364
Static Address Setup, 256
static commands, 675
static resource mastering, 582
statistics, 53
statistics collection, 518
STATISTICS_LEVEL parameter, 90, 653, 663
Statspack report, 104
STATSPACK tool, 18, 364, 652
STATUS column, 583
status description, 438
status option, 177
status option, ASM, 204
status option, /etc/init.d/oracleasm script, 203
status=down field value, 438
status=nodedown field value, 438
status=not_restarting field value, 438
status=preconn_down field value, 438
status=preconn_up field value, 438
status=unknown field value, 438
status=up field value, 438
stdout, 422
STOCK table, 90
STOCK table record, 88
stop option, ASM, 204
stop option, /etc/init.d/oracleasm script, 203
Stop Running Code button, 617
stop string parameter, 448
stop_options, 480
STOP_SERVICE, 509
stopall argument, 380
storage
    aggregates and volumes, 159–160
    disk drive performance, 130–131
    intelligent storage
        overview, 136–137
        remote mirroring technologies, 137–138
        snapshot technologies, 137
    iSCSI, 166–170
    NetApp filer RAID configurations, 158–159
    NFS, 160–164
    overview, 125
    RAC I/O characteristics
        asynchronous I/O, 128–129
        direct I/O, 129–130
        forced reads and writes, 128
        overview, 125
        read activity, 125–126
        write activity, 126–128
    RAID, 131
    RAID 0 striping, 131–132
    RAID 0+1 mirrored stripes, 133–134
    RAID 1 mirroring, 132–133
    RAID 10 striped mirrors, 133
    RAID 5, 134–135
    RAID summary, 136
    SAN storage example

EMC CLARiiON configuration, 152–158
Fibre Channel switch configuration, 151–152
HBA and driver configuration, 149–151
overview, 146–147
PowerPath, 147–149
snapshot backup and recovery, 164–166
storage cache, 135–136
storage protocols for Linux
 Fibre Channel, 140–141
 iSCSI, 141–142
 Linux I/O scheduling, 143–144
 NAS, 144–146
 overview, 138
 SAN, 144–146
 S-ATA, 142–143
 SCSI, 139–140
 using block-based storage, 143
storage, intelligent storage
 overview, 136–137
 remote mirroring technologies, 137–138
 snapshot technologies, 137
storage area network (SAN), 9, 55, 140, 145, 172
 compared with NAS, 144–146
 configuration, 239
 storage example
  EMC CLARiiON configuration, 152–158
  Fibre Channel switch configuration, 151–152
  HBA and driver configuration, 149–151
  overview, 146–147
  PowerPath, 147–149
storage infrastructure, 9
storage network, 63, 523
Storage Options page, 336
storage processor A (SPA), 146, 148
storage processor B (SPB), 148
storage requirements, RAC design
 archived redo logs, 68–69
 ASM and cluster file systems, 65
 backup and recovery, 66–67
 overview, 65
 shared Oracle homes vs. local Oracle homes, 66
storage scalability, 5
Storage subsection, of Database Administration section of Administration tab, Enterprise Manager (EM), 472
storage-based backup, 55, 66
storage-based recovery, 55, 66
storage-level replication mirrors, 7
storedprocedures.sql script, 644
STP (Spanning Tree Protocol), 123
strace command, 400
strace.txt file, 400
strategy, 683–685
stretch clusters, 7, 57, 63–64
strings utility, 490
stripe crossing, 136
stripe size, 217

stripe-and-mirror-everything (SAME) methodology, 131
striping, 201, 215, 219
stub-bus, 113
subdirectory, 224
subpartitions, 76
sum command, 302
Summary page, 377
super pipelines, 106
SUPPLIER imension table, 91
supported parameters, 37
SuSE Enterprise Linux 8.0 (SLES8), 28
SUSE Linux Enterprise Server, 27–28
 Add New Local User page, 257
 disk partitioning, 251
 Expert Partitioner window, 253
 installation settings, 251
 language selection, 251
 license agreement, 251
 network configuration, 256
 overview, 250
 preparing hard disk, 251–252
 previous installation, 251
 release notes, 258
 root password, 256
 service configuration, 257
 Software Selection screen, 253–255
 starting installation, 250
 test Internet connection, 257
 time zone, 255–256
 user authentication method, 257
 Warning dialog box, 256
SUSE Linux Enterprise Server version 9 (SLES9), 28, 188, 250
SUSE YaST installer, 251
SVRMGR utility, 559
swap partition, 240, 252
swap section, 676
swap space, 240, 395–396, 674
Swingbench
 Calling Circle application
  configuring Swingbench, 635–636
  creating input data, 639–641
  creating schema, 636–639
  overview, 635
  starting test, 641–643
 configuring, 633–634
 developing benchmarks
  defining Java-Based tests, 645–646
  examining source code, 646–647
  overview, 644
  using PL/SQL stubs, 644–645
 installing, 633–634
 overview, 633
swingbench command, 634
swingbench.env file, 634
swingconfig.xml configuration file, 646
swingconfig.xml directory, 634
SWINGHOME top-level directory, 634
SWINGHOME/bin directory, 634, 640

SWINGHOME/bin/data directories, 641
SWINGHOME/lib directory, 646
SWINGHOME/source directory, 646
SWITCH command, 704–705
SWITCH DATABASE command, 705
switch spanning, 123
switchback, 718
switchover, 718, 723, 739–740
symmetric multiprocessing (SMP), 8
symmetrical data structure, 68
SYNC (synchronous network I/O), 722
SYNC attribute, 726
SYNC mode, 721
synchronization, 575
synchronous network I/O (SYNC), 722
synchronous remote mirroring, 138
SYS schema, 73
SYS user password, 375
SYS$BACKGROUND default service, 498, 507
SYS$USERS default service, 498, 507
SYS$USERS dynamic performance view, 557
SYS_CONTEXT function, 425, 427, 557
/sys/asm directory, 224
SYSAUX tablespace, 52, 355, 365, 375, 652–653
sysctl -a command, 394
sysctl command, 394–395
sysctl -p command, 394
sysctl -w command, 395
SYSDBA privileges, 213, 224, 537, 542, 559, 563, 686
SYSMAN password, 376, 379
SYSMAN schema, 372
SYSMAN tablespace, 365
SYSMAN user, 384
sysman/admin/discover directory, 384
sysman/admin/emdrep/bin/RepManager utility, 372
sysman/config directory, 367–368
sysman/config/emoms.properties, 380
sysman/emd/targets.xml file, 384
sysman/end/upload directory, 368
sysman/recv directory, 368
SYSOPER privilege, 213
sysstat RPM package, 371, 678
system (sys), 199
system activity reporter (sar), 679–681
system alias, 218
system change number (SCN), 41, 127, 575, 603
System Clock Uses UTC, 245
system command, 448
System Commit Number, 603
System Global Area (SGA), 16, 18, 36, 213, 575
    multiple
        DBMS_ALERT package, 426
        DBMS_PIPE package, 426–427
        overview, 426
        session variables package, 427
system identifier (SID), 39, 490, 737
system monitor (SMON) background process, 42

System Settings, 238, 387
system statistics, 73, 663
system templates, 220
System User Password, 626
System V -ef arguments, 673
System V Unix-type options, 673
SYSTEMSTATE command, 560
SYSTEMSTATE dump, 561

■T

Tab completion, 390
table scans, 75
tablespace, 625
TABLESPACE <tablespace_name> option, 701, 708, 711, 712
TABL/PRCD/TYPE namespace, 578
TAF (Transparent Application Failover), 4, 48–50, 269, 340, 425, 430–437, 498
TAG <tag> option, 700
Tag tablespace name, 218
tags, 577, 693
tainted kernel, 26
Tanenbaum, Andrew, 23
tar command, 188
TARGET <connect_string> parameter, 686
target database, 685
TargetName string, 167
targets.xml file, 382, 384
Tcl (Tool Command Language), 607
Tcl commands, 621
Tcl language, 617
Tcl multithreaded environment, 617
Tcl programming model, 607
Tcl script, 627
Tcl shell command line, 617
Tcl time command, 617
Tcl-threads programming model, 622
TCO (total cost of ownership), 88
TCP (Transmission Control Protocol), 120, 141
tcp parameter, NFS, 164
tcp_keepalive_intvl parameter, 271
tcp_keepalive_probes parameter, 271
tcp_keepalive_time parameter, 271
tcp_retries2 parameter, 270
tcp_syn_retries parameter, 270
TCP/IP Offload Engines (TOEs), 120
TCP/IP Protocol page, 533
TCP/IP timeouts, 437
telinit command, 398
TEMP environment variable, 276
TEMPFILE template, 220
Template Management page, 345
Template Properties page, 346
template.cap file, 457
templates, ASM, 219–220
Templates tab, 223
terminal sessions, 388
TEST database, 479
TEST options, 713
Test Tcl Code button, 617

TEST/CONTROLFILE directory, 224
testing centers, 60
text parameter file (PFILE), 214–215
third-party clustering solutions, 16
third-party storage management products, 201
THREAD parameter, 42
throughput, 132
Time Model, 364
Time Stamp Counter (TSC) register, 263
time zone selection
    Red Hat Enterprise Linux 4 AS, 244–245
    SUSE Linux Enterprise Server, 255–256
timestamp description, 438
TLB (transaction look-aside buffer), 108, 112
TLB (Translation Lookaside Buffer) level, 267
TLB-based features, 235
TM lock, 577
/tmp directory, 391, 448, 452
TMPDIR environment variable, 276
/tmp/HAFDemoAction script, 456
/tmp/HAFDemoAction2 action script, 458
/tmp/HAFDemoClient program, 454
TNS listener process, 494
TNS_ADMIN environment variable, 275, 534
tnsnames.ora file, 431, 436, 494, 609, 736, 738
TO PRIMARY command, 740
TO STANDBY command, 740
TOEs (TCP/IP Offload Engines), 120
Tool Command Language (Tcl), 607
tools and utilities
    Cluster Verification Utility, 53
    database creation assistant (DBCA), 54
    Database Upgrade Assistant (DBUA), 54
    network configuration assistant (NetCA), 54
    OCR configuration tool (OCRCONFIG), 55
    Oracle interface configuration tool (OIFCFG), 54
    Oracle Universal Installer (OUI), 53
    overview, 53
    Virtual IP Configuration Assistant (VIPCA), 54
Top 5 Timed Events, 656, 659
Top Activity link, 660
top command, 675–676
top output, 676
TOP500 Supercomputers, 102
Torvalds, Linus, 23
total cost of ownership (TCO), 88
total_iterations value, 628–629
TPC (Transaction Processing Performance Council), 85
TPC benchmarks
    overview, 86
    TPC-C benchmark, 86–91
    TPC-H benchmark, 91–98
TPC-C Default Tablespace, 626
TPC-C Driver Script, 627
TPC-C Schema Options, 626
TPC-C simulation
    conducting test, 631–633

creating schema, 625–627
determining transaction level, 629–630
divulging test results, 624
generating workload
    connect, 629
    KEYANDTHINK, 629
    overview, 627–628
    RAISEERROR, 629
    total_iterations, 628–629
interpreting transactions, 623–624
overview, 622–623
test hardware and software considerations, 624–625
TPC-C Temporary Tablespace, 626
TPC-C User, 626
TPC-C User Password, 626
tpmC (transactions per minute), 86, 623
trace and diagnostics
    DBMS_MONITOR
        DBA_ENABLED_TRACES, 558–559
        overview, 555–556
        tracing applications, 556–557
        tracing multitier applications, 557–558
    ORADEBUG utility
        events, 572–574
        GC_ELEMENTS command, 561–562
        GES_STATE command, 561
        LKDEBUG utility, 563–572
        overview, 559–561
    overview, 553
    trace file locations, 553–555
trace directories, 554
trace file names, 554
trace files, 554
tracing, 187–188, 400
Transaction Count Options dialog box, 630
Transaction Counter button, 630
Transaction Counter menu, 630
Transaction element, 647
transaction look-aside buffer (TLB), 108, 112
Transaction Processing Performance Council. See TPC
Transactional shutdown mode, 470
transactions per minute (tpmC), 86, 623
Transactions per Minute window, 630
Translation Lookaside Buffer (TLB) level, 267
Transmission Control Protocol (TCP), 120, 141
Transparent Application Failover (TAF), 4, 48–50, 269, 340, 425, 430–437, 498
trcsess command line utility, 611
TREEDUMP command, 560
triple mirroring, 66
troubleshooting
    database services, 510–511
    Oracle software installation and configuration
        Cluster Verification Utility (CLUVFY), 321
        common problems, 321–322
        other information sources, 322–323
        overview, 320

TS lock, 577
TS1 tablespace, 219
TSC (Time Stamp Counter) register, 263
tsv::get command, 621
tsv::set command, 620
TT lock, 577
tunefs.ocfs2 command line utility, 197
tuneocfs utility, 184, 185–186
tuning OCFS2 partition, 197
TX lock, 577
TX transaction lock, 577
TX-ERR field, 677
TX-OK field, 677
TYPE attribute, 431

▉U

UDP (User Datagram Protocol), 120
uid (user IDs), 199, 321
ulimit command, 278, 279, 615
ULPs (Upper Layer Protocols), 140
umask command, 274
umount command, 396
uname -r command, 259, 268
unbounded partition, 77
Unbreakable Linux initiative, 25–26
Unbreakable Linux Partner Initiative, 235
undo tablespaces, 36
UNDO_RETENTION parameter, 90
UNDO_TABLESPACE parameter, 38, 42
unencoded bandwidth, 119
unique database names (DB_UNIQUE_NAME),
    728
UNIX operating systems, 21–22, 240
UNIX System Laboratories (USL), 22
UNRECOVERABLE attribute, 725
UNRECOVERABLE option, REPORT command,
    708
unset option, 410
unsupported parameters, 37
unzip command, 303
UP event, 437, 442
update (exclusive) access, 591
UPDATE GLOBAL INDEXES clause, 79
UPDATE statement, 109
Upgrade Examine page, 239
upgrading OCR, 419
Upper Layer Protocols (ULPs), 140
USE_INDIRECT_DATA_BUFFERS parameter,
    103
use_indirect_data_buffers=true parameter, 268
useocr entry, 440
user authentication method, SUSE Linux
    Enterprise Server, 257
user configuration
    creating dba and oinstall groups, 272
    creating Oracle software directories, 278
    creating oracle user, 272–273
    overview, 272
    setting environment variables
        CLASSPATH, 276

CRS_HOME, 275
CV_DESTLOC, 277
CV_JDKHOME, 277
CVUQDISK_GRP, 277
DBCA_RAW_CONFIG, 277
DISABLE_HUGETLBFS, 276
DISPLAY, 276
example settings, 277
LD_ASSUME_KERNEL, 276
LD_LIBRARY_PATH, 275
NLS_LANG, 275
ORA_NLS10, 275
ORACLE_BASE, 274
ORACLE_HOME, 275
ORACLE_SID, 274
overview, 273–274
PATH, 275
SQLPATH, 276
SRVM_TRACE, 277
TEMP and TMPDIR, 276
TNS_ADMIN, 275
    setting password for oracle user, 273
    setting security limits, 278–279
User Datagram Protocol (UDP), 120
User Delay(ms) value, 615
user IDs (uid), 199, 321
USER_CLUSTERS value, 89
USER_DUMP_DEST directory, 122
USER_DUMP_DEST parameter, 554, 556, 611
useradd command, 273
USERENV built-in function, 425
username, 224
USERS tablespace, 356
USERS user-defined alias, 230
USERS.272.563802217 file, 228
USL (UNIX System Laboratories), 22
/usr/local/bin directory, 378
UTC/GMT time, 245
utilities. See tools and utilities
UTL_FILE package, 428
UTL_FILE_DIR initialization parameter, 428

▉V

v option, 195, 414, 462, 476, 478, 481
V$ views, 663
V$ACTIVE_SERVICES dynamic performance
    view, 497
V$ACTIVE_SESSON_HISTORY view, 364
V$ARCHIVE_LOG dynamic performance view,
    715
V$ASM_ALIAS dynamic performance view, 231
V$ASM_CLIENT dynamic performance view,
    231
V$ASM_DISK dynamic performance view, 231
V$ASM_DISK_STAT dynamic performance
    view, 231
V$ASM_DISKGROUP dynamic performance
    view, 229, 231
V$ASM_DISKGROUP_STAT dynamic
    performance view, 231

V$ASM_FILE dynamic performance view, 231

V$ASM_OPERATION dynamic performance view, 231

V$ASM_TEMPLATE dynamic performance view, 231

V$BACKUP_DATAFILE dynamic performance view, 692

V$BH dynamic performance view, 583

V$BLOCK_CHANGE_TRACKING dynamic performance view, 706

V$BLOCK_CORRUPTION dynamic performance views, 714

V$CLIENT_STATS dynamic performance view, 558

V$COPY_CORRUPTION dynamic performance views, 714

V$CR_BLOCK_SERVER dynamic performance view, 659

V$CURRENT_BLOCK_SERVER dynamic performance view, 659

V$DATABASE_INCARNATION dynamic performance view, 691

V$DATAFILE_COPY dynamic performance view, 692

V$DB_CACHE_ADVICE view, 104

V$GES_BLOCKING_ENQUEUE dynamic performance view, 570

V$GES_CONVERT_LOCAL view, 671

V$GES_CONVERT_REMOTE view, 671

V$GES_TRAFFIC_CONTROLLER dynamic performance view, 571

V$INSTANCE dynamic performance view, 426

V$INSTANCE_CACHE_TRANSFER dynamic performance view, 660

V$LIBRARYCACHE dynamic performance view, 669

V$LIBRARYCACHE view, 578

V$LOCK_TYPE dynamic performance view, 569, 577

V$LOGFILE dynamic performance view, 722

V$OSSTAT performance view, 111

V$PARAMETER dynamic performance view, 488

V$PQ_SESSTAT table, 111

V$PQ_SYSSTAT table, 111

V$PROCESS dynamic performance view, 559, 569

V$PROXY_DATAFILE dynamic performance view, 692

V$RMAN_CONFIGURATION dynamic performance view, 693

V$ROWCACHE view, 580, 670

V$SERVICEMETRIC view, 364

V$SERVICES dynamic performance view, 497

V$SESSION dynamic performance view, 555, 558–559

V$SPPARAMETER dynamic performance view, 490

V$SQL dynamic performance view, 555

V$SYS_TIME_MODEL view, 365

V$SYSMETRIC view, 364

V$SYSSTAT view, 84

V$SYSTEM_PARAMETER dynamic performance view, 488

V$SYSTEM_WAIT dynamic performance view, 663

VALID_FOR clause, 727, 733

VALIDATE option, 711

VALUE column, 84

VALUES LESS THAN (MAXVALUE) clause, 78

variable warehouse, 620

/var/log/messages command, 157

/var/log/messages system log, 442

/var/log/messages utility, 187

/var/log/sa directory, 679–680

vendor-based support, 146

verbose option, 293

verifying Linux. *See* configuring and verifying Linux

vers parameter, NFS, 164

very large memory (VLM), 104

VFAT file system, 398

VIP (virtual IP), 34

VIP (Virtual IP), 476

VIP addresses, 236

vip suffix, 308

VIPCA (Virtual IP Configuration Assistant), 34, 54, 261, 276, 313, 404–407, 527

vipfile parameter, 407

Virtual IP, 17–18

Virtual IP Configuration Assistant (VIPCA), 34, 54, 261, 276, 313, 404–407, 527

virtual IP (VIP), 34, 476

Virtual IPs page, 405

virtual memory, 112, 235, 240

Virtual Network Computing (VNC), 276

Virtual User Options window, 615, 619

Virtual User Output window, 619

virtualization, 117

virtualuser array, 620

VLM (very large memory), 104

vm.disable_cap_mlock parameter, 268

vm.hugetlb_shm_group parameter, 268

vm.nr_hugepages parameter, 268

vmstat command, 676, 678

VNC (Virtual Network Computing), 276

Volume Add menu option, 160

volume header, 187

Volume label option, 194

volumes, 159–160

voting disk, 33, 403

voting sector, 187

■W

w option, 184, 283

WAFL (Write Anywhere File Layout) file system, 158

Wait Events section, 659

WAN (wide area network), 7

Warning dialog box, SUSE Linux Enterprise Server, 256

watch command, 129, 674
Web Cache, 368
Welcome page, 531
Welcome screen, Red Hat Enterprise Linux 4 AS,
        247
whatis database, 389
who -r command, 386
wide area network (WAN), 7
Window Groups, 429
workload management. *See also* database
        services
  connection load balancing, 49
  overview, 48, 493
  services, 48–49
  transparent application failover (TAF), 49–50
  workload distribution
    client-side connection balancing, 494
    overview, 493
    server-side connection balancing,
        494–497
WORKLOAD REPOSITORY report for section
        heading, 655
World Wide Name (WWN), 141, 151
WRH$ prefix, 653
WRH$ACTIVE_SESSION_HISTORY workload
        repository history table, 660
write activity, 126–128
Write Anywhere File Layout (WAFL) file system,
        158
write penalty, 134
write-back cache, 135
Write-back stage, 106
write-to-read transfer, 594, 596, 598
write-to-write transfer, 591
written to cluster file system, 715–716

written to Flashback Recovery Area, 715
written to local disk, 716
WWN (World Wide Name), 141, 151

■X
X lock (exclusive), 582–583
X Window environment, 246, 301, 327, 388
X$ tables, 663
X$KFALS fixed view, ASM, 232
X$KFDAT fixed view, ASM, 232
X$KFDSK fixed view, ASM, 232
X$KFFIL fixed view, ASM, 232
X$KFFXP fixed view, ASM, 232
X$KFGMG fixed view, ASM, 232
X$KFGRP fixed view, ASM, 232
X$KFKID fixed view, ASM, 232
X$KFMTA fixed view, ASM, 232
X$KFNCL fixed view, ASM, 232
X$KGLST base view, 578
X$KJBL structure, 565
X$KJBR column, 564
x86-64 architecture, 100
XCUR status column values, V$BH, 583
xdb_protocol.sql, 357
xhost command, 522
xntpd daemon, 262
XOR (exclusive OR) operation, 134
XTRANSPORT template, 220

■Y
y option, 198, 479
YaST (Yet Another Setup Tool), 250

■Z
z/LINUX architecture, 100

forums.apress.com

JOIN THE APRESS FORUMS AND BE PART OF OUR COMMUNITY. You'll find discussions that cover topics of interest to IT professionals, programmers, and enthusiasts just like you. If you post a query to one of our forums, you can expect that some of the best minds in the business—especially Apress authors, who all write with *The Expert's Voice™*—will chime in to help you. Why not aim to become one of our most valuable participants (MVPs) and win cool stuff? Here's a sampling of what you'll find:

DATABASES

Data drives everything.

Share information, exchange ideas, and discuss any database programming or administration issues.

INTERNET TECHNOLOGIES AND NETWORKING

Try living without plumbing (and eventually IPv6).

Talk about networking topics including protocols, design, administration, wireless, wired, storage, backup, certifications, trends, and new technologies.

JAVA

We've come a long way from the old Oak tree.

Hang out and discuss Java in whatever flavor you choose: J2SE, J2EE, J2ME, Jakarta, and so on.

MAC OS X

All about the Zen of OS X.

OS X is both the present and the future for Mac apps. Make suggestions, offer up ideas, or boast about your new hardware.

OPEN SOURCE

Source code is good; understanding (open) source is better.

Discuss open source technologies and related topics such as PHP, MySQL, Linux, Perl, Apache, Python, and more.

PROGRAMMING/BUSINESS

Unfortunately, it is.

Talk about the Apress line of books that cover software methodology, best practices, and how programmers interact with the "suits."

WEB DEVELOPMENT/DESIGN

Ugly doesn't cut it anymore, and CGI is absurd.

Help is in sight for your site. Find design solutions for your projects and get ideas for building an interactive Web site.

SECURITY

Lots of bad guys out there—the good guys need help.

Discuss computer and network security issues here. Just don't let anyone else know the answers!

TECHNOLOGY IN ACTION

Cool things. Fun things.

It's after hours. It's time to play. Whether you're into LEGO® MINDSTORMS™ or turning an old PC into a DVR, this is where technology turns into fun.

WINDOWS

No defenestration here.

Ask questions about all aspects of Windows programming, get help on Microsoft technologies covered in Apress books, or provide feedback on any Apress Windows book.

HOW TO PARTICIPATE:

Go to the Apress Forums site at **http://forums.apress.com/**.
Click the New User link.

You Need the Companion eBook

Your purchase of this book entitles you to buy the companion PDF-version eBook for only $10. Take the weightless companion with you anywhere.

We believe this Apress title will prove so indispensable that you'll want to carry it with you everywhere, which is why we are offering the companion eBook (in PDF format) for $10 to customers who purchase this book now. Convenient and fully searchable, the PDF version of any content-rich, page-heavy Apress book makes a valuable addition to your programming library. You can easily find and copy code—or perform examples by quickly toggling between instructions and the application. Even simultaneously tackling a donut, diet soda, and complex code becomes simplified with hands-free eBooks!

Once you purchase your book, getting the $10 companion eBook is simple:

➊ Visit **www.apress.com/promo/tendollars/**.

➋ Complete a basic registration form to receive a randomly generated question about this title.

➌ Answer the question correctly in 60 seconds, and you will receive a promotional code to redeem for the $10.00 eBook.

2560 Ninth Street • Suite 219 • Berkeley, CA 94710

eBookshop

THE EXPERT'S VOICE™

Offer valid through 02/07.